Timeline

The Story of Psychology: A Timeline

by Charles L. Brewer, Furman University

B.C.

387 — Plato, who believed in innate ideas, suggests that the brain is the seat of mental processes.

335 — Aristotle, who denied the existence of innate ideas, suggests that the heart is the seat of mental processes.

A.D.

1604 — Johannes Kepler describes inverted image on the retina.

1605 — Francis Bacon publishes *The Proficiency and Advancement of Learning*.

1636 — Harvard College is founded.

1637 — René Descartes, the French philosopher and mathematician who proposed mind-body interaction and the doctrine of innate ideas, publishes *A Discourse on Method*.

1690 — John Locke, the British philosopher who rejected Descartes' notion of innate ideas and insisted that the mind at birth is a "blank slate" (*tabula rasa*), publishes *An Essay Concerning Human Understanding*, which stresses empiricism over speculation.

1774 — Franz Mesmer, an Austrian physician, performs his first supposed cure using "animal magnetism" (later called Mesmerism and hypnosis). In **1777** he was expelled from the practice of medicine in Vienna.

1793 — Philippe Pinel releases the first mental patients from their chains at the Bicêtre Asylum in France and advocates more humane treatment of mental patients.

1802 — Thomas Young publishes *A Theory of Color Vision* in England. (His theory was later called the trichromatic theory.)

1808 — Franz Joseph Gall, a German physician, describes phrenology, the belief that the shape of a person's skull reveals mental faculties and character traits.

1834 — Ernst Heinrich Weber publishes *The Sense of Touch*, in which he discusses the just noticeable difference (*jnd*) and what we now call Weber's Law.

1848 — Phineas Gage suffers massive brain damage when a large iron rod accidentally pierces his brain, leaving his intellect and memory intact but altering his personality.

1859 — Charles Darwin publishes *On the Origin of Species by Means of Natural Selection*, synthesizing much previous work on the theory of evolution, including that of Herbert Spencer, who coined the phrase "survival of the fittest."

1861 — Paul Broca, a French physician, discovers an area in the left

1901 — Ten founders establish the British Psychological Society.

1905 — Mary Whiton Calkins becomes the first woman president of the APA.

Ivan Petrovich Pavlov begins publishing studies of conditioning in animals.

Alfred Binet and Théodore Simon produce the first intelligence test for assessing the abilities and academic progress of Parisian schoolchildren.

1913 — John B. Watson outlines the tenets of behaviorism in a *Psychological Review* article, "Psychology as the Behaviorist Views It."

1914 — During World War I, Robert Yerkes and his staff develop a group intelligence test for evaluating U.S. military personnel, which increases the U.S. public's acceptance of psychological testing.

1920 — Leta Stetter Hollingworth publishes *The Psychology of Subnormal Children*, an early classic. In **1921** she is cited in *American Men of Science* for her research on the psychology of women.

Francis Cecil Sumner receives a Ph.D. degree in psychology from Clark University, becoming the first African-American to earn a psychology doctorate.

John B. Watson and Rosalie Rayner report conditioning a fear reaction in a child called "Little Albert."

1921 — Hermann Rorschach, a Swiss psychiatrist, introduces the Rorschach inkblot test.

1923 — Developmental psychologist Jean Piaget publishes *The Language and Thought of the Child*.

1924 — Mary Cover Jones reports reconditioning a fear reaction in a child (Peter), a forerunner of systematic desensitization developed by Joseph Wolpe.

1927 — In *Introduction to the Technique of Child Analysis*, Anna Freud discusses psychoanalysis in the treatment of children.

1929 — Wolfgang Köhler publishes *Gestalt Psychology*, which criticizes behaviorism and outlines essential elements of the Gestalt position and approach.

1931 — Margaret Floy Washburn becomes the first female psychologist (and the second female scientist in any discipline) elected to the U.S. National Academy of Sciences.

1932 — In *The Wisdom of the Body*, Walter B. Cannon coins the term *homeostasis*, discusses the fight-or-flight response, and identifies hormonal changes associated with stress.

1869 — Francis Galton, Charles Darwin's cousin, publishes *Hereditary Genius*, in which he claims that intelligence is inherited. In **1876** he coins the expression "nature and nurture" to correspond with "heredity and environment."

1874 — Carl Wernicke, a German neurologist and psychiatrist, shows that damage to a specific area in the left temporal lobe (now called Wernicke's area) disrupts ability to comprehend or produce spoken or written language.

1879 — G. Stanley Hall receives from Harvard University's Department of Philosophy the first U.S. Ph.D. degree based on psychological research.

1878 — Wilhelm Wundt establishes at the University of Leipzig, Germany, the first psychology laboratory, which becomes a Mecca for psychology students from all over the world.

1883 — G. Stanley Hall, student of Wilhelm Wundt, establishes the first formal U.S. psychology laboratory at Johns Hopkins University.

1885 — Hermann Ebbinghaus publishes *On Memory*, summarizing his extensive research on learning and memory, including the "forgetting curve."

1886 — Joseph Jastrow receives from Johns Hopkins University the first Ph.D. degree in psychology awarded by a Department of Psychology in the United States.

1889 — Alfred Binet and Henri Beaunis establish the first psychology laboratory in France at the Sorbonne, and the first International Congress of Psychology meets in Paris.

1890 — William James, Harvard University philosopher and psychologist, publishes *The Principles of Psychology*, describing psychology as "the science of mental life."

1891 — James Mark Baldwin establishes the first psychology laboratory in the British Commonwealth at the University of Toronto.

1892 — G. Stanley Hall spearheads the founding of the American Psychological Association (APA) and becomes its first president.

1893 — Mary Whiton Calkins (pictured) and Christine Ladd-Franklin are the first women elected to membership in the APA.

1894 — Margaret Floy Washburn is the first woman to receive a Ph.D. degree in psychology (Cornell University).

1896 — Harvard University denies Mary Whiton Calkins admission to doctoral candidacy because of her gender, despite Hugo Münsterberg's claim that she was the best student he had ever had there.

1896 — John Dewey publishes "The Reflex Arc Concept in Psychology," helping to formalize the school of psychology called functionalism.

1898 — In "Animal Intelligence," Edward L. Thorndike, Columbia University, describes his learning experiments with cats in "puzzle boxes." In **1905**, he proposes the "law of effect."

1900 — Sigmund Freud publishes *The Interpretation of Dreams*,

1933 — Inez Beverly Prosser becomes the first African-American woman to receive a doctoral degree in psychology from a U.S. institution (Ph.D., University of Cincinnati).

1935 — Christiana Morgan and Henry Murray introduce the Thematic Apperception Test to elicit fantasies from people undergoing psychoanalysis.

1936 — Egas Moniz, Portuguese physician, publishes work on the first frontal lobotomies performed on humans.

1938 — B. F. Skinner publishes *The Behavior of Organisms*, which describes operant conditioning of animals.

1938 — Ugo Cerletti and Lucino Bini use electroshock treatment with a human patient.

1938 — In *Primary Mental Abilities*, Louis L. Thurstone proposes seven such abilities.

1939 — David Wechsler publishes the Wechsler-Bellevue intelligence test, forerunner of the Wechsler Intelligence Scale for Children (WISC) and the Wechsler Adult Intelligence Scale (WAIS).

1940 — Edward Alexander Bott helps to found the Canadian Psychological Association. He becomes its first president in **1940.**

1943 — Psychologist Starke Hathaway and physician J. Charnley McKinley publish the Minnesota Multiphasic Personality Inventory (MMPI).

1945 — World War II provides many opportunities for psychologists to enhance the popularity and influence of psychology, especially in applied areas.

1945 — Mamie Phipps Clark (pictured) receives a master's degree from Howard University. In collaboration with Kenneth B. Clark, she later extends her thesis, "The Development of Consciousness of Self in Negro Preschool Children," providing joint research cited in the U.S. Supreme Court's **1954** decision to end racial segregation in public schools.

1946 — Karen Horney, who criticized Freud's theory of female sexual development, publishes *Our Inner Conflicts*.

1946 — Benjamin Spock's first edition of *The Commonsense Book of Baby and Child Care* appears; the book will influence child rearing in North America for several decades.

1948 — Alfred Kinsey and his colleagues publish *Sexual Behavior in the Human Male*, and they publish *Sexual Behavior in the Human Female* in **1953.**

1948 — B. F. Skinner's novel, *Walden Two*, describes a Utopian community based on positive reinforcement, which becomes a clarion call for applying psychological principles in everyday living, especially communal living.

1948 — Ernest R. Hilgard publishes *Theories of Learning*, which was required reading for several generations of psychology students in North America.

1949 — Raymond B. Cattell publishes the Sixteen Personality Factor Questionnaire (16PF).

EXPLORING PSYCHOLOGY
Eighth Edition

David G. Myers
Hope College
Holland, Michigan

Custom Edition for Chattahoochee Technical College

Worth
Custom Publishing

ISBN-13: 978-1-4641-2891-2
ISBN-10: 1-4641-2891-X

© 2010 by Worth Publishers from *Exploring Psychology*, 8th Edition, by David G. Myers

Customized version © 2012
All rights reserved.

Printed in the United States of America

Worth Custom Publishing
Worth Publishers
41 Madison Avenue
New York, NY 10010

www.worthpublishers.com/custompub

A Guide to Thinking Critically

Cynthia Gray
Beloit College

Critical thinking: You have probably come across this term many times and have a pretty good sense of what it means. You are probably reasonably good at it—you wouldn't have made it this far in your academic career if you weren't. What is most certainly also true is that people—teachers, counselors, those rather anonymous others who write textbooks—keep telling you how important critical thinking is and that you should be learning to do it better. But how you are supposed to do that is often left unstated.

Critical thinking is a skill and, like any skill, your ability to execute it will improve with practice. The key is knowing what to practice and why. In this chapter, you will learn what critical thinking is and how it works. You will be given ample opportunities to practice it in the context of psychological inquiry. And although the skill of critical thinking applies to all fields of study, it has a special relationship to psychology. Why? As the science of cognition, emotion, and behavior, psychology teaches us about the processes of critical thinking and under what conditions this skill can be used effectively. Therefore, psychology gives us information about how to develop and understand the skills themselves. In addition to the material presented in this chapter, most of the chapters in your textbook also provide insight into the processes of critical thinking.

WHAT IS CRITICAL THINKING?

In this chapter, we are going to define critical thinking as the intentional application of reason and inquiry to make sense of new ideas and guide behavior. In addition to using terms very familiar to psychologists, like "reason," "inquiry," and "behavior," this definition allows us to highlight four key characteristics shared by most good definitions of critical thinking (see Figure 1 on the next page).

These principles are most easily illustrated with an example:

Caleb

> My seven-year old son, Caleb, and I were walking into the grocery store just before Easter when he asked, "Mommy, are you the one who puts the Easter candy in the basket?" After a moment of hesitation, I answered, "Yes. What made you think to ask me? Did you hear someone talking about it?" He said, "No. But I realized Mrs. Lemirande was the leprechaun, and so it just made sense." It took me a moment and a couple of questions, but I finally figured out his train of thought: We had just passed St. Patrick's Day, and his first-grade teacher (Mrs. Lemirande) had arranged a little party. In addition to some treats and crafts, the children came in to find a "leprechaun" had played some tricks on them—turning things upside down, putting chairs on top of desks, and mixing up supplies and materials. Caleb had put together a few facts: Chairs and desks are too heavy for children to lift; leprechauns are smaller than children; only teachers are allowed in the school before classes start; teachers generally clean up the rooms before the kids come in. He real-

ized that the only possible explanation was that his teacher was the leprechaun and that leprechauns must be make-believe. When he asked Mrs. Lemirande, she admitted it and explained that sometimes grown-ups like to make children feel special by surprising them, so they pretend something magical has happened. Fast-forward a few weeks, and the conversation turns to the Easter Bunny. Caleb puts together a new set of facts: Leprechauns are make-believe; grown-ups pretend to be magical creatures to surprise and please children; the Easter Bunny appears at night when parents are the only ones awake; and (in our case) Caleb never hears our bark-happy, bunny-chasing dog make a sound on the night the Easter Bunny visits. Realization: Mom and Dad must be the Easter Bunny. By the time we got out of the produce aisle, he had also figured out Santa Claus and the tooth fairy.

By putting together pieces of information, questioning conclusions, and looking for patterns that made sense in the world, Caleb was able to come closer to an accurate picture of how the world really works and put himself in a position to make better decisions. After all, as he pointed out to me during the same conversation, now that he KNOWS Mommy and Daddy are Santa Claus, he won't secretly write Santa to ask for anything he really wants; he'll come directly to us to make sure the message doesn't get lost. Critical thinking may occur naturally by way of instinct and curiosity. But this skill can be developed intentionally. In fact, that is the reason for this chapter: to provide some tools and resources to help you become better critical thinkers.

HOW DO YOU DEVELOP CRITICAL THINKING SKILLS?

I've already given the simple answer: practice. What do you practice? Well, that has a more complicated answer. As you read in the preceding section, there are several categories of skills at the core of critical thinking; most of these are associated with

FIGURE 1 Elements of Critical Thinking

Critical Thinking Is Active: It contrasts with more passive modes of thinking in which the thinker simply receives information as determined by others or the environment of which they are a part. Active thinking implies a user-driven interface with information; an individual seeks out data and manipulates it, asking questions and using the answers to seek out more information.

Critical Thinking Involves a Specific Set of Cognitive Skills or Habits: Broad terms for these skills include logic, reason, and inquiry and involve abilities like recognizing problems, figuring out how the problems might be solved, obtaining the most useful and usable information for solving the problems, and evaluating the effectiveness of both the thought process and any attempted solutions.

Critical Thinking Is Deliberate or Conscious: The purpose of this kind of thinking is to make sense of something; to intentionally apply a set of skills and habits to bring order and structure to ideas and information. Questions about the validity of information and its applicability to a given situation don't ask themselves: the thinker must create them.

Critical Thinking Guides Behavior: Drawing conclusions is only part of critical thinking; turning the conclusions into logical actions completes the picture. For someone to truly demonstrate critical thinking, both thoughts and actions need to align with the available information.

problem solving. In this section, we are going to focus on four broad, related skill sets: recognizing problems, recognizing potential solutions to problems, identifying and obtaining information relevant to the problem and/or its solutions, and evaluating the effectiveness of both the solution and the process.

Recognizing Problems

At its most basic level, recognizing problems requires realizing when there is a difference between what is *observed* and what is *expected*. Expectations are developed through experience: A baby learns about gravity by dropping a spoon from a high chair; a toddler learns about gravity by rolling a ball down a hill; a preschool-aged child learns about gravity by falling off a swing. Even very young children are surprised when they "drop" a balloon and it goes up instead of down; they already realize that is not the way things are supposed to behave.

Principles of psychology may be harder to conceptualize than the laws of physics. But throughout your lifetime, you are learning psychological principles with expectations about behavior, cognition, and emotion. As you study psychology, you learn the formal language for these expectations and discuss how the specifics of expectations related to behaviors, thoughts, and emotions do and do not depend upon the experiences of the individual. As your understanding of the formal language of psychology improves, so does your ability to accurately identify not only when *your* individual expectations do not match your observations but also when the expectations of the *discipline* do not match your observations. The former is interesting and valuable from the perspective of being self-aware and not making inaccurate or snap judgments about people and situations; the latter makes for good science.

Practice

The following exercise is based on similar exercises found in *The Critical Thinking Companion* (Halonen & Gray, 2001) and is designed to address two concepts essential to recognizing problems: pattern recognition and perspective-taking. Pattern recognition involves the careful and accurate observation of behavior and separation of the behavior itself from our interpretation of the behavior. Perspective-taking involves recognizing the degree to which our personal biases affect the way we observe and make judgments about what we observe. (To complete this exercise successfully, you will need to have completed or have access to materials from your textbook on neuroscience and behavior.)

Part I: Pattern Recognition: Figure 2 on the next page shows a human brain with labels for a number of structures and their functions. The brain image is accompanied by a table that has a list of brain areas corresponding to the image. For each brain area, list the primary function and how that area of the brain might be involved in the work of 1) a college student and 2) a stay-at-home parent of young children. (See "Medulla" in the table on the next page as a sample response.)

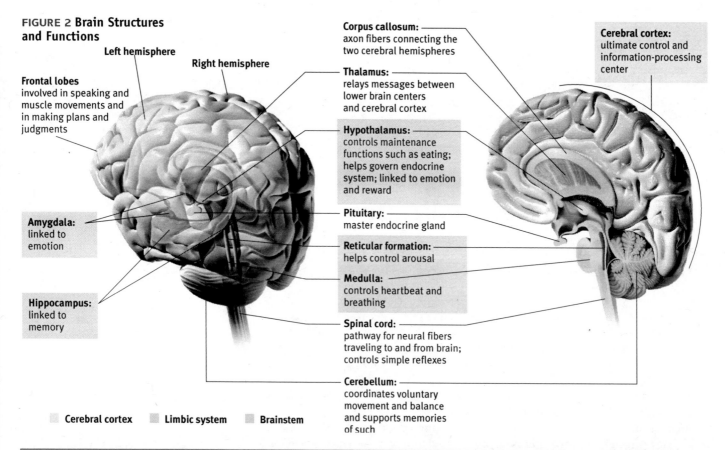

FIGURE 2 Brain Structures and Functions

Left hemisphere

Right hemisphere

Frontal lobes
involved in speaking and muscle movements and in making plans and judgments

Amygdala:
linked to emotion

Hippocampus:
linked to memory

Corpus callosum:
axon fibers connecting the two cerebral hemispheres

Thalamus:
relays messages between lower brain centers and cerebral cortex

Hypothalamus:
controls maintenance functions such as eating; helps govern endocrine system; linked to emotion and reward

Pituitary:
master endocrine gland

Reticular formation:
helps control arousal

Medulla:
controls heartbeat and breathing

Spinal cord:
pathway for neural fibers traveling to and from brain; controls simple reflexes

Cerebellum:
coordinates voluntary movement and balance and supports memories of such

Cerebral cortex:
ultimate control and information-processing center

▨ Cerebral cortex   ▨ Limbic system   ▨ Brainstem

Brain Area	Primary Function	How Involved in Work of College Student?	How Involved in Work of Stay-at-Home Parent?
Medulla	*Autonomic responses like breathing and heart rate*	*Keeping student alive; allowing appropriate physiological responses to stressful situations like tests, active situations like athletic competitions, and more relaxed moments with friends*	*Keeping parent alive; allowing appropriate physiological responses to stressful situations like crying or hurt children, active situations like games of tag, and relaxed moments during naptime*
Frontal lobe			
Cerebellum			
Hippocampus			
Amygdala			
Corpus callosum			
Hypothalamus			

Part II: Perspective Taking: You may have heard the story of Phineas Gage. In 1848, this young railroad worker was seriously injured when an iron rod used to set blast powder in rocks sparked, exploded, and then sent the 3-foot rod through Phineas' left cheek and out the top of his head (Figure 3). Within minutes of the accident, he was conscious and able to talk with the people around him, but Phineas wasn't the same man after that. The damage to his frontal lobes didn't affect his memory or physical abilities, but it did alter his judgment and ability to adhere to social conventions in speech and actions. He lost his job and became estranged from his family. (Additional information about Phineas's story is readily available; one website providing details about both available medical records and personal history is http://neurophilosophy.wordpress.com/2006/12/04/the-incredible-case-of-phineas-gage/)

FIGURE 3 **Phineas Gage Accident Reconstructed**

(A) Imagine for a minute that this type of injury affecting the frontal lobes had occurred for the two individuals in Part I. How might these individuals perceive the resulting changes? What might they and others perceive as problems? (Note your responses in the table below.)

	Likely Outcome of Damage	Person's Perception of Problems Resulting from Changes	Family's/Friends' Perceptions of Problems Resulting from Changes
College Student			
Stay-at-Home Parent			

(B) What if these individuals had instead experienced damage to the amygdala? How might their experiences and perceived problems be different? (Again, note your responses using the table on the next page.)

In addition to emphasizing the complex relationships between specific brain areas and an individual's actions and behaviors, completing this exercise will make it clear that the perception of a problem is closely tied to the inferences and assumptions of the individual making the observations. Simply, to perceive events of

	Likely Outcome of Damage	Person's Perception of Problems Resulting from Changes	Family's/Friends' Perceptions of Problems Resulting from Changes
College Student			
Stay-at-Home Parent			

any particular person, you need to step into that person's shoes. By doing so, you will see that the college student and the parent have very different observations of their friends and families. Sometimes identifying the problems we want to solve means looking at the world with a different set of biases and expectations.

SOMETHING TO CONSIDER

How might a social worker, psychologist, or case worker assigned to one of these individuals balance the "problems" of the individual with the brain injury with the "problems" of that individual's family?

Recognizing Potential Solutions

Once a problem has been identified, you can then begin to determine which potential solutions might work best. This actually takes two separate steps: (1) identifying what solutions would solve the problem, and then (2) figuring out which ones are workable in the given situation.

Recognizing Problems   Recognizing Potential Solutions

If the solution to your problem involves looking for the causes of something or the factors that influence something, you might be most interested in the *scientific problem-solving approach*. The focus here is often on answering the "why" questions: Why don't people help others in need? Why is nicotine so addictive? Why does my level of physical fatigue impact my mental performance?

If solving your problem involves overcoming obstacles or barriers, *practical problem solving* may be the most helpful approach to take. Examples of problems that may fall into this category are generally "how" questions: How do I get my dog to come when she's called? How can I give up smoking more easily? How can I more effectively remember people's names?

If you can't identify what it would take to solve your problem or if you are unable to turn your problem into "why" or "how" questions, perhaps you need to use creative problem-solving. "What if" questions often exemplify this approach: What if nothing changes the likelihood of a bystander offering to help in times of trouble? What if drugs weren't addictive? What if there were no long-term memory?

FIGURE 4 How to Think About Possible Solutions

While this probably sounds like a simple case of brainstorming and then using common sense to pick the best of the listed solutions, there is actually quite a bit more to it than that. There are multiple ways to approach solving problems, and each approach generates a different type of solution (Figure 4). Matching the approach and the type of solution it generates to the problem is sometimes the most complicated part of the critical-thinking process. Figure 4 presents some general rules of thumb you can use to begin thinking about possible solutions (adapted from Halonen & Gray, 2001).

Some of the questions in the first two categories are very similar, but they have different goals. In *scientific problem solving*, the goal is understanding the relationships; this approach tests specific predictions and assumptions to determine the relationships among the individual factors involved. (To review this process, re-read the section in your textbook on the scientific method.) In *practical problem solving*, the goal is using the relationships to make something happen. Here, the possible solutions come from an ability to generalize to other situations. *Creative problem solving* involves combining concepts and information in novel ways to create new realities and reshape the way we understand problems and issues; many advances in science come from such questions.

Let's consider a specific scenario. The first "why" question from the list on the right panel in Figure 4 arose in a very public forum in 1964, after the tragic case of Kitty Genovese—a young woman in New York who was killed in a public place after two visits from her attacker and within sight and earshot of many witnesses. Although later reports indicated that people were not as aware of her attack as originally assumed, the initial reports stated that over 30 people had heard the attack and ignored it, neither offering to help nor calling the police. Genovese's death sparked a whole line of research on what became known as the *bystander effect* and *altruism*, why people choose to help when someone else is in need. As this line of research developed, psychologists found that people are unlikely to come to someone's aid if there are other bystanders around, if the bystander doesn't identify with the victim (e.g., the victim is of a different race, background, or gender from the bystander), if the situation is ambiguous or the nature of the emergency unclear, if the bystander feels that offering assistance would be dangerous, or if the bystander doesn't feel qualified to offer aid. (To learn more about the bystander effect and altruism, consult the social psychology section of your textbook or another social psychology resource.)

Practice

Now, consider this situation: A middle-school math teacher in a large urban public school regularly teaches a diverse classroom population, with children from very different racial and ethnic groups, socioeconomic backgrounds, and with varying levels of academic performance. Recognizing the importance of the course content for her students' future success, she works hard to make sure the course is accessible to students at a variety of levels and has generally been rewarded with measurable student progress over the course of the year. With such diversity, however, comes a challenge: Many of her students have difficulty fully comprehending the course material, either because their family situations mean they miss class frequently or because the course materials aren't offered in their first language. She has suggested many times to the class that students consider working together, sharing notes, and translating materials; she has even created an on-line space where sharing of notes and materials is possible. Despite her efforts, students are not taking advantage of these opportunities. In fact, some students who have come to her for assistance have said other students have turned them down when they have asked if they could borrow notes.

Begin by identifying some of the potential problems. As you did in the previous (neuroscience and behavior) exercise, list at least a couple of problems from each of two different perspectives (using the table below).

Instructor's Perspective	Students' Perspective

Next, consider what kinds of problems these are. Rewrite the problems you've listed as questions (using the table below). What kind of question is each? (Is it a "why," "how," or "what if" question?)

Instructor's Perspective	Students' Perspective

There are so many different questions you could ask, I can't possibly guess one that matches exactly. But I'm willing to venture that at least one of those questions was a "why" question along the lines of either "Why won't the students work together?" (from the instructor's perspective) or "Why won't any of the other students in the class help me?" (from the student's perspective). In order to fully answer a "why" question, we have to identify a set of factors that might be involved in the relationship and generate a hypothesis about how those factors are involved. The next two steps will help you figure this out.

- Given what you have read about the bystander effect and other related social psychology concepts, generate a list of factors that might be involved in students' unwillingness to work together.

- Select two of these factors and generate a hypothesis about the class' cooperative behavior. (As a reminder, a hypothesis is a prediction about the cause of something.)

Review again the list of questions you generated and ask a "how" question. I can't guess exactly what questions you asked, but at least one was probably something like, "How do I encourage students to share their notes with each other?" (from the instructor's perspective) and "How do I get the notes and materials I need?" (from the students' perspective). As the next step in the process, do the following:

- Identify at least 3 concepts related to what we learned about the bystander effect that could apply to this situation. Using the table below, write each concept as a statement of what the student or instructor could do to change the behavior.

Concept	Statement

SOMETHING TO CONSIDER

Compare the output of the two different approaches. In what ways are they similar? In what ways are they different? Does one approach seem more appropriate for this situation, or are they both equally useful?

Finally, go through your list of questions a third time. Were there any "what if" questions? These are not as predictable, but such questions might take the following form: "What if cooperative behavior doesn't have anything to do with the students, but is more dependent on the structure of the class?" or even "What if working together isn't effective for learning?"

- If you did have any questions or problems more indicative of the creative problem-solving approach, what was your motivation? What in the scenario wasn't addressed by the other forms of problem solving?

- What new set of problems does this question (or set of questions) generate? Does this line of inquiry seem potentially productive?

Each of the three steps you went through in this exercise generated a statement that represents a "solution" to your problem. In the first, more scientific problem-solving approach, you could have generated at least as many hypotheses as you had related factors, and probably could have generated multiple hypotheses for some factors. In the approach best described as practical problem solving, you could have had multiple solutions for each barrier you identified. And, although you may not have had anything in the creative problem-solving category, such potential solutions become more likely the more you learn about a given area of study. The larger your knowledge base and the greater the depth of your understanding, the easier it becomes to make connections and see the common threads among things you previously perceived as different.

With all these potential solutions, you need to begin the second step of this stage in the process: determining which solutions are the most workable. Much of this kind of determination will happen when you actually begin to gather and look at relevant information, but some of it can occur as you look at the solutions and match them to your needs. Here are some questions you can ask yourself to narrow down your options.

- Does the solution relate directly to the problem? Would it meet my goal? If not, it's a good candidate for elimination.

- Is the solution within my sphere of influence? In other words, do I have some way of manipulating or changing the things that are a part of my proposed solution? If not, then it isn't a viable option.

- Can the solution be evaluated? Is there some way I can judge how effective it's been? If not, then it is probably not your best choice, either.

Once you've gone through these questions, the remaining solutions are good candidates for further consideration.

Obtaining Information

With a set of potential solutions in mind and a need to select the best among these solutions, it is time to refer to outside sources. Why? There are many reasons, but in summary: Using information outside our own personal experience and beliefs helps us recognize and avoid our personal biases, which actually may

| Recognizing Problems | Recognizing Potential Solutions | Obtaining Information |

have created or perpetuated the problem in the first place. Referencing outside sources doesn't necessarily mean going to the library (although that is not a bad start!), but it does mean looking for information relevant to our solution that is not just personally generated.

What kind of information will help determine the best solution? This should be the first question you ask yourself. If you have asked a "why" question and are interested in the relationship among specific factors, you will need information about how those factors influence or are influenced by your particular situation or setting. If your question is more of a "how" question, then the information you seek will probably focus on the particulars of your setting or situation itself. With "what if" questions, you may need either or both types of information, depending upon the question.

The next question you would want to ask is: "What is the best source of the information?" Again, this is going to be driven by your specific concern, although there are general principles. To understand relationships between and among specific factors and settings, you'll need to look for places where the factors interact and where that interaction can be controlled to varying degrees so that you can be sure that the relationship you observe is the one in which you are truly interested. To find ways to overcome obstacles you will often look to other places or people who operate within the same boundaries or with the same goals. With "what if" questions, you may very well find yourself looking to settings completely outside your immediate concern in order to establish whether or not your connections and ideas are possible.

Here are some examples and types of questions and possible sources of information:

- If a "why" question interested you in the relationship between group work and homework completion in middle school children, you would probably be best served by looking in schools and obtaining information from educators and others knowledgeable about children's cognitive and social development.

- If you were interested in "how" to get middle school children to complete more homework, you might look to fields where productivity is key, such as business.

- If you asked a "what if" question about designing an educational system that didn't have homework, you might search for information about other systems and cultures; perhaps sociological, anthropological, or literary publications would provide ideas and suggest approaches you could take.

Practice

Let's use a set of exercises (again, modified from Halonen & Gray, 2001) to practice identifying the type and sources of information we need to solve specific problems. These exercises will be easier to complete if you have recently read or reviewed material on learning in your textbook.

Scenario 1: In the table on the next page, you will find a list of situations many people would find trying. Read each scenario, decide on a problem it presents, and then state the problem. (If you like, state the problem as a question.) Identify at least one viable solution to the problem and then indicate both the type and source of information you need to make a decision about whether the solution is a good one.

Scenario 2: In this scenario, you are an industrial-organizational psychologist. (Corporations often hire I-O psychologists to help solve management and production problems.) Today, you are working with ROYAS-R-US to help them ensure that their workers make the most royas possible. Your employer wants to know how the method of paying people impacts their production; in particular, they want to

Scenario	Statement of Problem	Possible Solutions	Information Needed	Best Source of Information
Every time a toddler goes through the checkout line at the store, she screams until one of her parents buys her candy.				
In class, there is one student who always answers the teacher's questions and dominates the discussion, so the other students have stopped participating.				
Two siblings are always fighting. No matter how well they are playing while they are supervised, as soon as their parents leave the room, they start arguing again.				

know if paying people a weekly salary or for piecework would be more effective in raising the number of royas produced.

- Write a brief statement of the problem (phrased as a question if you would find it helpful).

- Briefly outline the process by which you would determine a solution or set of solutions.
- Identify the information necessary to select a solution.
- What is the best source of this information?

SOMETHING TO CONSIDER

In one sense, both of the above scenarios referenced practical problems; there is a situation-specific obstacle or barrier in each to overcome. In another way, however, they are different; the "Royas-R-Us" situation is very much one in which the goal is understanding the relationship between two factors: pay and production. How did your perception of these problems influence the type and source of the information you chose? In looking at your responses and those of your classmates, do you notice any patterns between the potential solutions and choice of information sources?

(Creative) Scenario 3: Just for fun, let's play with a more creative approach. First read the following nursery rhymes in the table:

Little Miss Muffett	Mary Had a Little Lamb	Jack & Jill	Old Mother Hubbard
Little Miss Muffet sat on her tuffet, eating her curds and whey. Along came a spider, who sat down beside her, and frightened Miss Muffet away.	Mary had a little lamb, whose fleece was white as snow, and everywhere that Mary went, the lamb was sure to go. It followed her to school one day, which was against the rules. It made the children laugh and play to see a lamb at school.	Jack and Jill went up the hill, to fetch a pail of water. Jack fell down, and broke his crown, and Jill came tumbling after.	Old Mother Hubbard went to the cupboard to fetch her poor dog a bone. But when she got there, the cupboard was bare, and so the poor dog had none.

Each of these nursery rhymes could be interpreted as the expression of a psychological problem. Maybe Miss Muffet is suffering from a phobia and Jack from a brain injury. Perhaps Mary needs to teach her lamb to stay, and Old Mother Hubbard has a memory problem that makes it difficult for her to manage her shopping or take care of her pet. Choose one nursery rhyme, decide what psychological problem it represents, and then write the solution in verse. I've provided an example to get you started:

The Old Woman Who Lived in a Shoe (ORIGINAL)	The Old Woman Who Lived in a Shoe (NEW)
There was an old woman who lived in a shoe; She had so many children, she didn't know what to do. So, she gave them their supper and gave them their bread, Then spanked them all soundly and sent them to bed.	There was an old woman who lived in a shoe; She had so many children, she didn't know what to do. Should she punish the bad or reinforce the good? Reinforcement works best, if only she would.

So, why would we consider this last exercise an exercise in critical thinking? First, it requires you to identify a problem. Second, you have to recognize what solutions show a shift in the usual perception of that problem, which is just a variation of identifying a workable solution. Third, you had to identify a source of information, even if it wasn't the commonly expected source. And finally, you had to decide if the solution you picked met the criteria of being different, funny, and in verse.

Evaluating Effectiveness

With information in hand, we can now choose a solution and evaluate our success. The choice of a specific solution should be logically determined, given the information gathered. If evidence suggests multiple solutions will be effective, choose among them. To do so, take into account the value of the evidence and the reliability of the source. Also, ask questions about the cost and availability of the resources needed to implement the solution in light of the potential gain.

Recognizing Problems	Recognizing Potential Solutions	Obtaining Information	Evaluating Effectiveness

With the solution selected and implemented, the question becomes: Did the application of a solution achieve the goal? Hopefully, the answer is "yes." If so, while we can't be absolutely certain our process was a good one, we can look for those places where what we did seemed particularly effective and helpful and build on those strategies next time. Identifying which components of a process will likely to be useful in the future and which were unlikely contributors to success is an important part of the critical thinking process.

When a solution doesn't work, or when you obtain results that weren't expected, it is vital NOT to think of this as a failure. Recognize it as additional information that can be used as a guide to finding a viable solution. Also, recognize it as an opportunity to understand where the process needs improvement. Asking and answering the following questions may be helpful:

- *Did the gathered information inform your choice of solution?* If you picked a solution without relying on the evidence gathered or when the evidence and the solution were in conflict, if you relied on gut feelings, common sense, or personal understanding of the situation, you might have missed a crucial connection or concept that would have guided your choice in another direction.

- *Was the source of information reliable?* While objectivity isn't always necessary, knowing the biases and agendas of your information sources are. Perhaps you were looking for information about how to quit smoking, and took information from the Internet without realizing that the sponsor of the web page was a tobacco company. Knowing the source had a vested interest in encouraging continued tobacco use would probably have changed the degree to which you relied on it as a source of useful information. In such cases, returning to your list of potential sources of information to see if this was the case and if other, less personally invested sources exist.

- *Did you consider alternative explanations?* There is always more than one way to look at a situation or to understand an issue. Could information have been interpreted another way that might have led to the choice of a different solution? Were there perhaps more potential solutions you didn't consider because you were focused on a particular perspective?

- *Were your assumptions clear?* This is perhaps the hardest question to answer; we often aren't even aware of our assumptions until someone points them out to us or we notice the different assumptions of others. Go back and try to look at your statement of the problem, your list of potential solutions, and your sources of information from the perspective of another. What things might someone else see, explain, or ask differently?

In many ways, having a process that DOESN'T work perfectly is more useful than having one that does, particularly at first. It makes it obvious there are flaws in the system and forces you to begin to look for those flaws and to strengthen them. When something works the first time, questions about what could be changed for the next time tend not to be asked until the next time—when something doesn't work.

SOMETHING TO CONSIDER

What would happen if you were always right? (And first consider that you wouldn't learn anything. Ever. Learning is what happens when we are wrong, when something doesn't turn out the way it should and we have to change what we do or how we do it.) Think of a time when you were wrong and what you changed because of it. Using the language of critical thinking, try to describe the process you went through to make that change. What were some of the barriers you faced?

SUMMARY

So, as we finish this chapter, it's reasonable to ask: Does critical thinking only apply to problems? Of course not, although that has been the focus of this chapter up until now. It is easier to talk about critical thinking in the context of problems or questions because that is when we naturally think about evidence and evaluation. If you look back at the work you've done in this chapter, you can see that everything you discussed and thought about was to help you develop the habits of clarity, accuracy, consistency, and open-mindedness (see Figure 5).

Here are four keys to success with critical thinking:

Clarity: Both "clearness of perception" and "freedom from ambiguity" are essential in the practice of critical thinking. Use language that can be understood by the people you want to communicate with. When there are misunderstandings in the things you write or say, don't just write them off to the other person's (or your own!) inattentiveness or lack of knowledge. Strive to express yourself in a different way, persisting until the thought is as clearly understood as you can make it. Being diligent about this will sharpen both your thought process and your use of language, as well as make you aware of the assumptions inherent in your own thinking.

Accuracy: The ability to be true, correct, or exact is what allows us to make judgments and evaluate outcomes. If we are inaccurate in identifying problems, we will ask the wrong questions, look for the wrong information, and probably change our behavior in ways that are not helpful or productive. Without precision in measurement or observation, the same event or experience will look different every time, and we will see randomness instead of predictability and pattern. Accuracy involves an active striving for a

CLARITY If you check most dictionaries, the definition of clarity will include references to "clearness of perception" and "freedom from ambiguity." Clarity allows for the clear formulation of thought, crisp articulation of ideas, and precise analysis of assumptions and inferences.

ACCURACY The quality of being, or ability to be, true, correct, or exact is what allows us to make judgments and evaluate outcomes. Accuracy involves an active striving for a match with "reality"; it improves when one's own judgments and interpretations are compared with others' and when practice leads to expertise in a given area.

CONSISTENCY Consistency is both the practice of applying critical thinking processes and principles to an examination of all questions and ideas and the agreement among the parts of a complex world view informed by such a process. No one is able to think critically about everything in every situation, but the habit of doing so regularly and across multiple settings allows for the possibility of a world view that is both internally consistent and externally valid.

OPEN-MINDEDNESS An adept critical thinker doesn't disbelieve everything but rather is willing to suspend belief until there is enough information to make a reasoned judgment. Aristotle called this the habit and practice of "entertaining thoughts without accepting them."

FIGURE 5 Four Keys to Critical Thinking

match with "reality"; it improves when one's own judgments and interpretations are compared with others' and when practice leads to expertise in a given area.

Consistency: When we regularly use the processes and techniques outlined in this unit to evaluate ideas and test assumptions, we become less subject to the agendas and potentially limited viewpoints of others. No one is able to think critically about everything in every situation. But making critical thinking a habit regularly and across multiple settings allows for the possibility of a world view that is both internally consistent (with the various parts operating in harmony and mutually compatible) and externally valid (aligning with the measurable and observable components of the real world).

When you first practice the skills outlined here, you will probably find yourself doing so most often in very structured settings, at the request of your teachers or mentors. As you become more adept, consider beginning to use them in settings outside the classroom, but where you know you have cause to question the assumptions and statements of others—for instance, situations of advertising and sales always provide excellent opportunities! As you become even more experienced and comfortable with the process, strive to apply your increasingly well-developed skills in ambiguous situations and to question personal assumptions.

Open-mindedness: This is a characteristic of critical thinking that often catches people by surprise, particularly if they associate the word "critical" with "disbelieving." In this context, critical is better described as "requiring evidence."

*NOTE: An adept critical thinker doesn't disbelieve everything, but rather is willing to suspend belief until there is enough information to make a reasoned judgment. Aristotle called this the habit and practice of "entertaining thoughts without accepting them." Ultimately, the best way to judge if we've been successful is to answer this question: Have we restructured our own beliefs and actions in accordance with the wider body of information we've now examined? If the answer is yes, we've been successful critical thinkers.

Resources

If you are interested in reading more about what critical thinking is and why it is so important, consider starting with some of these resources:

- "Critical Thinking" by QualiaSoup— http://www.youtube.com/watch?v=6OLPL5p0fMg
- "What is Critical Thinking" by the Critical Thinking Community: Foundation for Critical Thinking—http://www.criticalthinking.org/aboutCT/define_critical_thinking.cfm
- "What is Critical Thinking" by CriticalThinking.net (Robert H. Ennis)— http://www.criticalthinking.net/definition.html

If you would like to practice the skills of critical thinking within the context of psychology using exercises similar to some of those appearing in this supplement, consider working your way through the following handbook: Halonen, J., and Gray, C. (2001). *The critical thinking companion for introductory psychology*. New York: Worth Publishers.

If you would enjoying testing your critical thinking ability using a psychological case study, try: Tom Randall's *Halloween Party: A case study associated with "Critical Thinking, Thoughtful Writing: A Rhetoric with Readings" by Chaffee, J., McMahon, C., and Stout, B.* (new edition due out 2012)—http://college.cengage.com/english/chaffee/critical_thinking/3e/students/activity_randall/index.html

References

Halonen, J. and Gray, C. (2001). *The critical thinking companion for introductory psychology*. New York: Worth Publishers.

A Practical Guide to Study Skills

Amy Himsel
El Camino College

Learning How to Learn
   Let Go of What You Think You Know
   How Your Brain Really Works
   Getting Things into Your Head: Brain-Change Fundamentals

Crafting Your Mental Workout Plan
   Exercise Your Brain by Reading Before Class
   Go to Class and Train with an Expert
   Train Your Brain for Exams and Other Assessments

The Moment of Truth: Exam Day
   The First Thing to Do Is to Manage Your Stress
   Be Strategic in Completing the Exam

Actually Doing It
   Developing Habits of Self-Regulation and Self-Control

If At First You Don't Succeed

Like most of you, I had never been taught the best way to study. I am writing this chapter because I want studying to be less confusing and frustrating for you than it was for me, and I want you to know about study techniques that are effective and efficient. So, if you are ready for a change in your study habits, prepare to open your mind to some of the surprising findings from the science of studying. They reveal successful study strategies that will help you improve specific class and overall school performance. You'll discover that the brain has an incredible capacity to change when given the proper exercise—an ability you can apply to any area of your life.

Learning How to Learn

How do we learn? It's a simple question, but the answer is more complicated than you might expect.

Let Go of What You Think You Know

My study plan as a college freshman was straightforward: to memorize as many words as possible from my textbooks and professors' lectures. I was pretty good at this, furiously taking notes in class or as I read the course materials. I spent countless hours repeating the information in an effort to make it sink into my brain, and I earned a reputation for being one of the most studious (okay, obsessive) students in my dorm. So why wasn't I, master memorizer with a will of steel, earning straight As? Like many students, my assumptions about studying were guided more by "common sense" than by scientific reality. Unfortunately, then as now, "common-sense" notions are frequently incorrect (Stanovich, 2010).

It's easy to get tricked into thinking rote methods work because they *feel* so effective in the moment. During my marathon sessions of rote learning, I certainly *felt* like I was doing the right thing. But the proof is in the pudding, and my grades that first year did not match my feeling of mastery. Has this ever happened to you? If so, you are not alone. We are poor judges of how well we have learned something, and we chronically underestimate how much we know about a topic we have studied. Furthermore, the less we know about a topic, the less we realize we *don't* really know it (Kruger & Dunning, 1999). In the quest to become a better and more efficient learner, you must let go of what you think you know about studying and follow methods backed by science.

No matter what your grades were in the past or what your current habits or attitudes are, you can change for the better. Please don't underestimate the brain's potential for change. It is constantly changing due to experience, and you are capable of creating new experiences while you study. As you'll find out, if you learn how the brain works and give it proper attention and exercise, it can change to your benefit.

1

How Your Brain Really Works

Studying is about making memories, but memories are not made in a straightforward manner. We do not "place" information in one spot—like placing an item on a closet shelf, returning later to pick it up, dust it off, and then use it to answer a question on a test. Instead, we make memories when our brain's networks of connections are activated in patterns. Basically, here's what science tells us: Mental exercise creates and strengthens networks of connections in your brain similar to the way lifting weights strengthens your muscles (Medina, 2008). The more you "work" the information (for example, by explaining a concept in your own words), the more neural connections are made or strengthened and the stronger your memory becomes. As a result, you remember more when it's time to take a test.

But here's a surprising fact: Memories—including those formed while you study—are deeply personal, customized to fit your brain and nobody else's in exactly the same way. Why? Because learning is not like painting on a blank canvas. Rather, you start with a backdrop of networks that represent your current knowledge, preferences, and habits.

Simply put, you are your connections. You make long-lasting memories by weaving the new information into your unique brain cell connections. No two people will do this in exactly the same way. Likewise, there is no magic formula for studying well. With this in mind, start experimenting with the techniques described in this chapter to find out what works best for your brain. But please don't worry: You don't have to become an expert in neuroscience to learn how best to exercise your brain cell networks. Take a look at Figure 1, and then stay with me to learn the basics of brain change and how to apply that information to your everyday life as a student.

(a)

(a) Tom Barrick, Chris Clark, SGHMS/Photo Researchers

FIGURE 1 The Connectome These images are models created to represent the incredibly complex and unique networks of connections among brain cells. Nobody's connections are exactly the same as yours. Shown in (a) is a model of neuronal connections across different regions of the brain as a whole. The model in (b) shows a close-up of the complex connections that have formed between individual neurons.

(b)

(b) Image courtesy of Dr. Sebastian Seung: Neural "wiring" reconstructed from the retina V. Jain, J. Murray, S. Turaga, and S. Seung (MIT); K. Briggman, M. Helmstaedter, and W. Denk (MPG)

Getting Things into Your Head: Brain-Change Fundamentals

When you study, you start by bringing new information into your brain, a process referred to as encoding. Basically, when you pay attention to information, you encode it. Reading, listening to lectures, taking notes, and reviewing notes are all forms of encoding. But not all forms of encoding are equally helpful. Common study strategies—like rereading the text or notes, or trying to memorize definitions word for word—are rote methods that involve shallow processing, which results in very limited brain change. This kind of encoding produces only the weakest of neural connections, without generating enough raw material from which to later construct an accurate memory.

To study better, move beyond shallow encoding to process information at a deeper level. For example, relate the new information you are trying to learn to something that is already familiar to you. Let's say you need to learn the definition of the term *homeostasis* ("the maintenance of a steady internal state in the body"). That may seem very abstract until you think about your actual experiences with homeostasis—say, a time when you have felt hot and sweaty. That's your body trying to cool itself off, and that's a homeostatic experience. Ever felt dehydrated? That's your body signaling that more liquid is needed. Thinking in this way, you will find that homeostasis now seems far more familiar because you've connected it to knowledge and experiences that are already represented in your networks of brain cells. Even the simple act of putting things into your own words triggers deeper processing because you are converting the material into words that are more familiar to you. (See more about this in Table 1.)

Quality studying also requires practice in getting the learned information out again, a process referred to as *retrieval*. As a student, when I tried to remember the exact words of a definition, I was practicing retrieval—but only in a very shallow form. It is much better exercise for the brain when studying involves deeper methods of retrieval, like restating definitions in your own words (without peeking at your notes first!) or trying to explain the material to someone else.

TABLE 1 Rote Method Makeover

Common rote strategy	New and improved strategy
Reading	• Previewing each section before you read, and writing questions • Using questions to think while you read, and to test yourself after reading
Copying definitions	• Writing definitions in your own words
Memorizing definitions	• Stating definitions in your own words, as though you were trying to explain the terms to someone else
Copying notes	• Elaborating on your notes • Noting connections between your notes and your past knowledge or experience • Making connections between terms and concepts within the material
Rereading the text or your notes	• Processing your notes or the text in different ways • Self-testing with questions you wrote or those provided in the text • Testing yourself to see if you can repeat in your own words the material you have just read
Taking notes focused on the professor's words	• Writing down not only what is on the slide, board, or outline, but also supplementing with your own words • Marking spots of confusion and asking the professor for clarification later
Comparing your notes with a classmate to make sure you "got everything down"	• Discussing your notes with a classmate; explaining to each other the material in your notes • Filling in any gaps with your own words

The mental exercise involved in studying takes time to sink in and stabilize into lasting brain change. This is a process called *memory consolidation,* one that is similar to how your muscles need some rest after exercise in order to develop best. Memories settle into the fabric of the brain gradually, aided by time, sleep, and further mental exercise. Imagine what happens when you spend several hours drilling with rote methods and skimping on sleep in an effort to cram it all in: You actually make the task of learning harder on yourself by shortchanging your brain's memory consolidation process.

How do you apply these fundamentals to studying? What follows are some basic study tips to keep in mind.

Keep Things Challenging

Learning should not feel easy. To be more specific, creating strong, reliable memories—memories that are still there for you on the day of the exam—should not feel easy. Sorry, but that is true. Ignoring this fact is like expecting to housetrain your new puppy on day one. It's funny how this same advice is completely non-controversial when it comes to physical exercise. Who expects to develop impressive biceps by doing curls with only 1-pound weights? Challenging study stimulates deeper brain change, resulting in stronger memories that are more easily retrieved on demand. Scientists call this a "desirable difficulty" because the more you struggle to learn now, the stronger your neural networks become—and the less likely you are to forget the information later (Bjork & Bjork, 2011).

It all makes sense when you spell it out, but it's fascinating how quickly we forget and get tricked by our feelings in the moment. I used to parrot back all kinds of information and definitions in the midst of my marathon rote-method study sessions. It didn't feel difficult, especially after three hours of memorizing. I felt like I was really learning something, which made it all the more disappointing when my test scores showed otherwise. Sound familiar? If so, it's time once again to let go of what you think you know. When studying feels easy in the moment, that's exactly when you should doubt your mastery the most. In contrast, when you feel frustrated and unsure while studying, smile and pat yourself on the back—you are engaging in a vigorous mental workout. Those difficulties are desirable and will pay off big time later.

Space Out Your Study Sessions

I used to study for long stretches of time for each class. I figured the longer I kept at it, the better I would learn the material. Wrong. Contrary to common sense, it's much better exercise for your brain if you space out your study sessions for each class. Consider a weight-lifting analogy: If you wanted to tone up, would you expect your muscles to respond better to one five-hour workout a week than to five one-hour sessions a week? Of course not. Similarly, the brain responds best to short, focused study sessions spaced across several days.

Learning experts recommend you spend two to three hours studying for every hour spent at lectures. That's a lot of time, but it's much less overwhelming if you spread it out across several days. You'll see possible study schedules in the calendars in Figure 2.

Mix Things Up

Exercise your brain connections with some cross-training—that is, by varying the way you encode new information (see Figure 3 on page 6). Of course, it's a great idea to engage in traditional tasks like reading. But monitor your encoding: Are you just focused on memorizing words? If so, you are focused only on *visual encoding.* At that level, processing is shallow. So take another step and encode the information further. For example, the definition of a term will be most memorable if you focus on the meaning *(semantic encoding),* which is aided by putting the definition into your own words. Perhaps also try relating what you read to a body movement or gesture (Cook,

Marisol

2011	Sunday, Jul 17	Monday, Jul 18	Tuesday Jul 19	Wednesday, Jul 20	Thursday Jul 21	Friday, Jul 22	Saturday, Jul 23
11 AM						11:00 AM Study Psychology	11:00 AM Study English
Noon						12:00 PM Study Biology	12:00 PM Study Biology
1 PM	1:00 PM Study Chemistry			1:00 PM Study English			1:00 PM Study Chemistry
2 PM					2:00 PM Study Biology		
3 PM			3:00 PM Study English		3:00 PM Study English		
4 PM			4:00 PM Study Psychology		4:00 PM Study Psychology	4:00 PM Study Psychology	
5 PM			5:00 PM Study Chemistry	5:00 PM Study Chemistry		5:00 PM Study English	
6 PM		6:00 PM Study Psychology		6:00 PM Study Psychology		6:00 PM Study Chemistry	
7 PM		7:00 PM Study Chemistry		7:00 PM Study Biology			
8 PM		8:00 PM Study Biology	8:00 PM Study Biology				
9 PM		9:00 PM Study English					
10 PM							

Noah

2011	Sunday, Jul 17	Monday, Jul 18	Tuesday Jul 19	Wednesday, Jul 20	Thursday, Jul 21	Friday, Jul 22	Saturday, Jul 23
11 AM						11:00 AM Study Psychology	11:00 AM Study English
Noon						12:00 PM Study Biology	12:00 PM Study Biology
1 PM	1:00 PM Study Chemistry					1:00 PM Study English	1:00 PM Study Chemistry
2 PM	2:00 PM Study Psychology					2:00 PM Study Chemistry	2:00 PM Study Psychology
3 PM	3:00 PM Study Biology						
4 PM	4:00 PM Study English						
5 PM							
6 PM							
7 PM		7:00 PM Study Chemistry	7:00 PM Study Chemistry	7:00 PM Study Chemistry	7:00 PM Study Biology		
8 PM		8:00 PM Study Biology	8:00 PM Study English	8:00 PM Study English	8:00 PM Study English		
9 PM		9:00 PM Study Psychology	9:00 PM Study Biology	9:00 PM Study Psychology	9:00 PM Study Psychology		
10 PM							

FIGURE 2 Two Possible Study Calendars With this customized plan, both Marisol and Noah spend 2 to 3 hours studying for each hour of lecture. They space their studying out across the week in 1-hour blocks per subject—this practice allows rest between subjects for the brain connections they have exercised.

FIGURE 3 Levels of Processing
Processing a word deeply—by its meaning (semantic encoding)—produces better recognition of it at a later time than does shallow processing by attending to its appearance or sound. (From Craik & Tulving, 1975.)

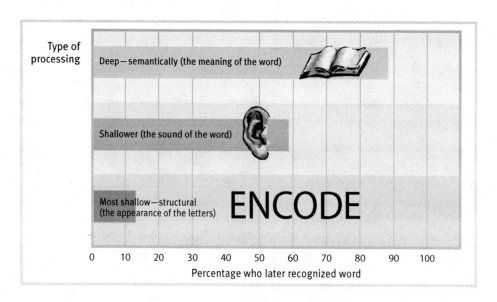

Mitchell, & Goldin-Meadow, 2008). For example, to remember that two variables move in opposite directions in a negative correlation, try moving your arms in different directions as you rehearse the material. You could also try linking the material with a catchy phrase or tune, anything to add an auditory component to the memory. Each encoding experience will present an opportunity to make connections; with more connections formed, more paths will lead to the memory. Remember to never turn down the opportunity to strengthen your memory with more connections!

Test Yourself, Early and Often

If just the mention of the word *test* increases your heart rate, then here's another opportunity to let go of what you think you know: Testing is your friend. Self-testing is one of the best ways to overcome the tendency to overestimate how much you know by providing a reality check of your actual knowledge (Rohrer & Pashler, 2010).

For everyone, self-testing not only reveals current competence but also provides another set of exercises to train the brain. Every time you test yourself, you engage the brain in an attempt to retrieve a memory. This act alone helps strengthen connections among your brain cells. Nevertheless, networks strengthened through study weaken over time. The fact that you once knew something provides no guarantee that you will know it when you are assessed. So test yourself repeatedly to ensure that those memories stay strong.

Combining self-testing with well-spaced study sessions is an even more useful strategy. Spread your self-testing out to create the best opportunity for a strenuous mental workout. When some time has elapsed, even just a day or two, some forgetting will inevitably occur. You would think that's bad, right? It's not. Experts are finding that forgetting helps us learn (Kornell, 2009). Basically, a little forgetting now provides you with a lot of desirable difficulties the next time you study the material. Think of it as one step backward that leads to two steps forward.

SECTION REVIEW

- Rote methods, like rereading the text or memorizing definitions, may *feel* like they work, but they are not very effective for long-term learning.
- The best way to study is to work the to-be-learned information into the unique set of connections that already exist among your brain cells.
- You exercise your brain (and learn best) when you keep study sessions challenging but brief, utilizing a variety of strategies and testing yourself often.

Test Yourself

Hint: Don't look back at the text until you have pulled out of your memory as much information as you can.

- What are rote methods, and why are they less effective than other study methods?
- Why is self-testing such a valuable study skill?

Try It

- Set a timer to go off at regular intervals (perhaps every 15 minutes) while you study. When the buzzer sounds, simply ask yourself: "Does this feel easy?" If so, evaluate your study methods and strive to create more desirable difficulties.
- Give yourself an exam reality check. After you take your next assessment in a class, predict the grade you earned and write it down in your notebook. When the assessment is returned, write your actual grade next to your prediction. Is there a discrepancy? If so, consider why.
- Create your own study calendar for the week ahead. Remember to allow 2 to 3 hours of study for each hour of lecture, and be sure to space out your study sessions for each class.

Crafting Your Mental Workout Plan

Let's get practical and discuss how to translate brain-change knowledge into your everyday life as a student before, during, and after classes.

Exercise Your Brain by Reading Before Class

Reading before class is one of the most overlooked ways to boost your learning in a college course. Think of how a warm-up prepares the body for a workout. Reading the material before class serves a similar function. If you first process this new information and get the neural networks primed, the result will be a much more productive time in class. Why? You will have an easier time figuring out which information is most important. What you hear in class will more easily connect with the networks in your brain because of the mental warm-up. So make the most of your reading by following these tips:

Invite Desirable Difficulties

Get a good workout while you read: If you feel your eyes skimming across the page, or if you reach the bottom and don't remember much (if anything) of what you just read, then you are barely processing the information at all. It happens to the best of us. The important thing is to catch yourself, shake the cobwebs out of your head, and start again with the goal of staying more engaged. Awareness is a step in the right direction. See Table 2 on the next page for specific tips on how to keep your brain active while reading.

Space It Out

If you have a 50-page chapter to read for Monday's class, break it down into smaller chunks (perhaps 15- to 20-page sections), and spread your reading out across a couple of days. Here's another reason to space things out: If you are zipping through a 50-page chapter in one sitting, I doubt that you are engaging desirable difficulties! Pace yourself. Course materials are often organized into sections with headers. Read one or two sections in one sitting, but no more than that. Remember, your brain needs breaks in order for memories to consolidate. Also, this will help you manage your attention better and help reading become more enjoyable.

TABLE 2 Desirable Difficulties While You Read

Here are two specific methods to trigger challenges that help you get the most out of your reading.

SQ3R: The Survey, Question, Read, Rehearse, and Review Strategy
One structured approach to reading for deep processing is SQ3R (Robinson, 1970). Here are the steps:

- Before you read, survey the section to get a general idea of what information you will encounter.
- Next, formulate a question to keep in mind as you read. Your text may already include learning objectives or preview questions that help with this step.
- Now you are ready to read, but you should read with your question in mind, actively considering what the answer might be. Take notes, putting things in your own words as much as you can.
- After you have finished reading a section, take time to rehearse: put the text material in your own words, then ask yourself the question again (but no peeking at the text or your notes until you have answered!).
- The last step is to review what you have learned, paying special attention to the notes in your own words.

3R: The Read-Recite-Review Strategy
The 3R approach (McDaniel, Howard, & Einstein, 2009) is another method to encourage deep processing while reading. You can use this technique repeatedly with your texts or your notes.

- Read a brief section or passage.
- Close your book or cover the text, then recite in your own words anything you can remember about what you have just read.
- Open the book and review the passage to check yourself.

Self-Test While You Read

As you read, think of questions you could ask yourself to test your learning. Write them down somewhere. When you reach the end of the section, use these questions as a self-test quiz. How much did you remember? Take note of the information that you left out, and go back to review that material.

Work the Information in Different Ways

First and foremost, make sure you are focused on the meaning of the words, not memorizing the author's words, which triggers only shallow encoding. How can you do this? Take notes while you read, but don't just copy from a book or screen. Instead, put things into your own words. Consider how this new information fits in with your uniquely wired brain. How does it link to your experiences? Does an image come to mind? If so, draw it. Does a silly thought occur to you? For example, I remember reading about the hippocampus, a brain structure involved with memory, and I immediately thought: "Hippos are similar to elephants, and elephants supposedly have good memories." It stuck. It worked for me, but it might not work for you. Remember, you are your connections, so make what you read stick in a way that makes sense to you!

Go to Class and Train with an Expert

Go to your classes—each and every one of them. These are golden opportunities your brain shouldn't miss. This is a chance to have a mental workout with an expert on the topic. At the very least, a missed class is a lost opportunity to find out what the professor thinks is most important (in other words, what material is most likely to appear on assessments).

Your professor will present the material in at least a slightly different way than it is presented in the readings, so that alone will provide some helpful cross-training to strengthen your neural networks. But it's ultimately up to you to make class worth your time. Just as simply moving your eyes across the page fails to result in much learning, sitting there and simply writing down whatever is on the board or slides only triggers the most shallow processing. So try the following procedures.

Create a Set of Complete and Personally Meaningful Notes

Notice that I said "create" instead of "take." This is an important distinction. When you "take" notes, you write down the exact words from the board or a slide, and that's it. Some students who are obsessive (as I was) attempt to write down as many words spoken by the professor as possible. In both cases, there is a misconception that the professor's words are magical: If you can just transfer them directly into your brain, you will be in good shape. It's simply not true. Research indicates that students who "create" comprehensive and elaborated notes tend to earn better grades (Peverly et al., 2007).

How do you do this? Of course you should write down the outline, terms, or key examples the professor has provided on the board or slides. And it's wise to jot down additional helpful details your professor may state, as long as you are not attempting to transcribe the words verbatim. What's most important is that you churn the information through your brain so it makes sense to you. You have to work with the information, and transform it in some way so it will become embedded within your neural networks. This strategy can range from simply putting things into your own words to jotting down a related example or a personal experience. It will build bridges that connect the professor's words with your brain.

Try some of these strategies to "create" your own notes:

- *Remind yourself to focus on the meaning, not just the words.* As much as possible, put things into your own words. Make your notes personally meaningful. If note taking seems quick and easy, view this as a warning sign. Keep desirable difficulties in mind.

- *Listen for organizational cues from your professor* (Kiewra, 2002). For example, a statement like "So we have just discussed X, and now I'd like to move to Y" is a clear signal that the lecture is shifting to a new topic. If the instructor tells you "There are four components of Z," use that as a signal to start a numbered list in your notes.

- *Develop a set of abbreviations and symbols.* Save time by abbreviating or using symbols whenever possible. Include those an individual professor uses and invent some of your own (see examples in Table 3). Just make sure the abbreviations and symbols help you make sense of the material.

- *Draw a representation of how concepts relate to each other.* Try venturing outside the standard outline structure. Consider using arrows, for example. Create drawings to represent the information.

- *Check yourself by noting spots where you got lost or confused.* I used to do this by writing a big question mark next to the spot where I got lost. After you mark the spot, shake out the mental cobwebs and then move on to keep up with the pace of the class. Stay after class to discuss the confusing part with the professor or a classmate. Do not wait.

- *As soon as possible after class, review your notes and jot down any additional information that comes to mind.* It's important to do this while the information is still fresh. Better yet, do this with a classmate. You may be able to fill in some blanks for each other. Kiewra (2002) calls this "the reconstruction strategy." But beware of shifting into rote mode! Don't just read and copy verbatim; actually discuss the notes, explain what they mean, and focus on which parts of the meaning either of you may have missed or misunderstood.

TABLE 3 Using Abbreviations in Your Notes

Allow your hands to keep up with the pace of class by using abbreviations in your notes. Here are just a few ideas to get you started, but the most important thing is to use symbols that make sense to your brain. What abbreviations could you add for some of the common words or phrases in your classes?

w/o	without
w/n	within
b/c	because
diffs	differences
beh	behavior
♂	male
♀	female
Ψ	psychology
?	ask professor
+	and
→	leads to, causes
≈	is similar to
≠	is not the same as

Train Your Brain for Exams and Other Assessments

Students often ask me how best to prepare for exams. It's a great question, but the problem is that most ask it less than a week before the exam. When should you start preparing for the exam? Today! But that doesn't mean you have to spend hours studying today. A little goes a long way, especially when you revisit the material several times a week. It's like going to the gym a few times a week instead of spending 10 hours there on Saturday to make up for a week of sloth. Here are some suggestions for how to proceed.

Process Your Notes Regularly

Research indicates that you will learn more from processing your notes than you learned while taking them (Kiewra, 2002; Knight & McKelvie, 1986). Rereading is not enough, and neither is copying notes verbatim. Oh, how I wish someone had told me this when I was a student! I wasted loads of time on this particular rote method. Of course, there is nothing wrong with rereading your notes the first time you revisit them. The problem is expecting that you will somehow be able to "write" the contents of your notes directly into your brain (Bjork & Bjork, 2011). This ignores the reality that each of us begins with a brain full of unique connections, where new information sticks best by being woven into the networks that already exist.

Use your notes as a springboard to organize and integrate the course material (see Figure 4). Consider how the different pieces of information connect to one another (*internal connections*), and then think about how the information relates to your prior knowledge and experiences (*external connections*) (Mayer, 1996). This is great exercise for the brain, helping to form and strengthen neural networks that can later consolidate into stronger memories.

- *Make internal links.* There are often numerous ways that the course material could be organized to show internal links, such as terms that can be grouped by some shared characteristic or terms that are notable for how they reveal opposite tendencies. Experiment with different ways to show internal links. You could construct a memory matrix, where you identify categories and appropriately place terms, concepts, or other information. Concept maps are another option; these are diagrams or figures you draw to show relationships among the various aspects of the material (see Figure 5).

- *Make external links.* You can relate the course material to information you currently know by forming mental representations. Depending on the way your mind works, this could come out in many different ways. The links could be visual. For example, I think of neural connections as colorful strands of yarn and of building strong memories as similar to knitting a blanket with that yarn. With further processing (strands/connections), the blanket (memory) becomes more and more resilient.

The links could also be verbal—for instance, analogies. Does a certain concept remind you of something else? If so, write in your notes: "It's like . . ." To understand how brain cells communicate, for example, you could note: "It's like a conversation." You could also imagine methods of linking the material to movements or sounds. Studies indicate that engaging the senses and motor skills when creating a memory yields additional cues that can help embed the new information more deeply into your brain (Glenberg, Brown, & Levin, 2007; Stevanoni & Salmon, 2005). The bottom line: You create stronger memories when you process the new information in a variety of ways.

FIGURE 4 Internal and External Links
While making notes, try to connect the new information with things you already know. This is one specific way to weave the material into your uniquely connected brain, as shown in blue. In addition, pay attention to the connections you see between the bits of new information you encounter, as shown in green. Both methods help you process the material deeply. (Illustration after Kiewra, 2002)

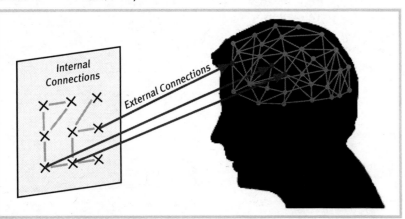

- *Simply ask "why"?* Doing so is a very effective and straightforward way to make external links. This method of triggering self-explanation has been shown to improve learning more than does simple summarizing or rereading of notes (Kiewra, 2002). Why does it work? It forces you to think about the meaning of the material instead of focusing on the memorization of words.

(a)

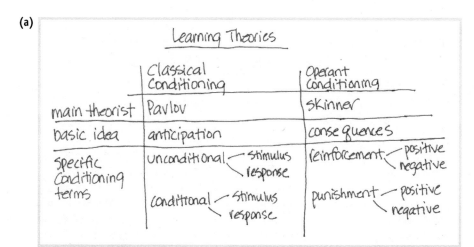

FIGURE 5 Memory Matrixes (a) and Concept Maps (b) **(a)** This memory matrix shows the distinctions a student made between two theories about learning. **(b)** This concept map shows how one student has organized her learning about energy and the natural laws governing it.

(b)

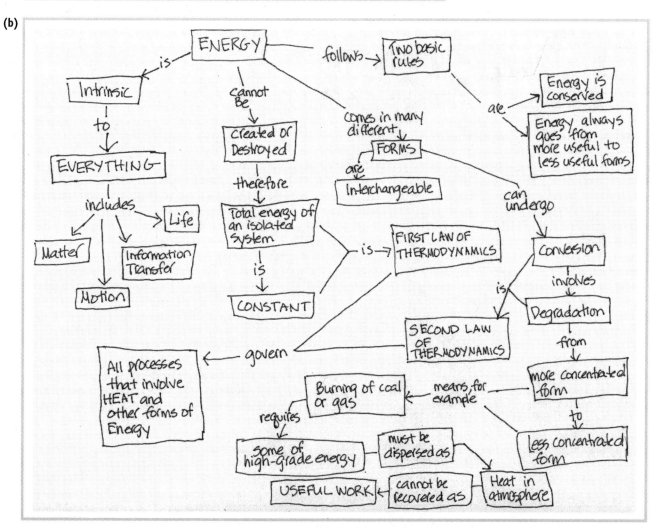

Check Your Learning Through Self-Testing—Repeatedly

How did you know that you could ride a bicycle? I remember the exhilarating feeling I had when the training wheels on my bike were removed and I rode down the driveway all on my own. It was scary at first, but eventually I brought the wobbles under control.

How do you know when you have really learned something? Most students rely on how familiar the material seems as they reread it or on how well they do on multiple-choice quizzes or test questions. Think about why that might be the case. Your notes, readings, and multiple-choice questions all contain the verbal equivalent of training wheels: words and organizational features that act as cues for your performance. The trouble is that, unlike training wheels on a bike, we don't realize how much our performance is assisted by these aids. The wheels come off for the exam—questions are in random order, unfamiliar wording is used, you're required to apply what you've learned—and suddenly your confidence is shaken. You feel wobbly. You discover that you really didn't know the material well.

Let's take the training wheels off for a moment, right now. Without looking back on the chapter, answer this question: How are memories formed in the brain?

Now look back to page 2 to check your answer. How much did you remember?

When you self-test like this, you get a more accurate view of how much you understand. This is especially true when you ask open-ended questions, like the one I used above—to answer, you are required to pull all of the information you can from the depths of your own brain. The real challenge is to put the course material away (for a few hours or a day) and then later see what you can still retrieve from the strands of information that were encoded. This strategy tests recall memory—a good countermeasure against that annoying human tendency to overestimate what you know.

There is another excellent reason to self-test: The act of trying to retrieve information helps us embed the information in the brain more deeply, which leads to stronger and more readily accessible memories. Remember, brain cell connections are strengthened by both encoding and retrieval. Making yourself come up with an answer (especially to an open-ended question) is one of the most effective exercises for your memory networks (Bjork & Bjork, 2011).

In short, self-testing is a great workout that will show you what you really do and don't know. Don't be surprised to find that there are some big gaps in your memory. Be happy you found them and can remedy the problem! Also, remember that if it's difficult while you're studying, it's more likely to be easier while you're being tested later. Self-testing creates desirable difficulties that strengthen your memories for long-term retention.

Here are some self-testing options you can try:

- *Use the tools the professor or text author gave you.* Many professors and texts provide lists of objectives, preview questions, or review questions. Just make sure to move beyond multiple-choice questions because, to begin with, they are easier. Focus on open-ended questions, like fill-in-the-blank or essay questions.

- *Make your own tests.* This is a lot easier than you might think. For example, go back to the questions you wrote in your notes while reading. Create flashcards and, on the back of each, write where in your notes the answer can be found. This will remind you not to try to rote-memorize "answers." You can also use the 3R method (look back at Table 2) as a simple and effective way to check your understanding while you study.

- *Mix up the order of questions.* This is a form of brain cross-training. If you always study everything in the same order, the order itself becomes a context cue that fools you into overestimating what you really know. Besides, many professors arrange their exam items in random order.

- *Try out a variety of study locations.* Even without our conscious awareness, cues from the places where we study help us form associations with the new material we are trying to learn (Smith, 2007; Smith & Vela, 2001). If we study in only one location, we create only one set of context cues to link to the material. Studying in many different locations gives you the chance to form multiple context cues. In other words, trying out different study locations can actually help you form more connections between brain cells relevant to the material. More connections equal stronger memories.

- *Sort items back into their categories.* Shuffle your flashcards and then sort them into piles by chapter or topic. Now you are forced to think about how the items are similar to or different from one another, which is excellent exercise for the mind. Even if this seems too hard, it can trigger deep learning because of the workout it gives your brain (Kornell, in press). Remember, difficulties help you learn!

- *Pretend it is your job to teach someone else this material, someone who really needs the information.* This makes you think about the meaning of the material instead of just focusing on the literal words. Actors often use this method (Noice & Noice, 2006). They are encouraged not to rote-memorize the script but to think of the motivations, goals, and reasons why the person would be saying these things. Even just talking to someone about the material—a classmate, friend, or family member—can serve as a self-test. The concepts that are hard for you to explain are those that need more attention.

- *It is never too early to self-test.* In fact, some research shows that it helps to start testing yourself even *before* you've read the text or attended a lecture on the topic, especially if you follow up by investigating the correct answer afterwards (Richland, Kornell, & Kao, 2009). Aren't you likely to answer incorrectly? Yes, but creating that initial challenge of retrieval for your brain cells prepares you for longer-term retention of the material over time. The answer is less important than the mental exercise the question triggers.

- *Self-test to keep memories strong.* Knowing something now doesn't mean you'll know it at test time. Why? Because your brain has undoubtedly changed, at least a little bit, since you first made that memory. Some students make the mistake of studying only the difficult material, assuming that they already know the easier material. But if brain cell pathways haven't been exercised, even if that material once felt "easy," you may fail to retrieve the information when it matters at a later date (like during an exam!). Remember, the brain responds like a muscle. Imagine that you have finally reached the point where your biceps are perfectly toned. Congratulations! But that doesn't mean you never have to work them again. The same is true of memory.

Remember: Self-test to study; test early and often. Don't wait until it's too late!

SECTION REVIEW
- Warm up your brain by taking a deep-processing approach to reading the assigned material before class.
- View each class as an opportunity to further exercise your brain. Create notes that go beyond the professor's words, and compare your notes with those of classmates afterwards.
- To find out what you have really learned, and to continue the workout of your brain cells, test yourself early and often.

Test Yourself
Hint: Don't look back at the text until you have pulled out of your memory as much information as you can.

- From the perspective of training your brain, what is the purpose of reading the assigned material before class?

- What is the difference between rereading your notes and processing your notes?
- How early and how often should you test yourself while studying?

Try It

- Flip back to a section of this chapter that you found challenging, and use the 3R method (look back at Table 2): Read the section, cover it, then recite anything at all that you remember from the passage. Be patient and give yourself enough time to truly drain the contents of your brain. Finally, uncover the section and review it to check your understanding. Remember, you can use this strategy anytime you read a text or process your notes.
- Ask another student to "reconstruct" lecture notes with you shortly after a class. Discuss the content of your notes to see if either of you missed any information. Resist the urge to simply copy missed information. Instead, explain the material to each other in your own words, focusing on the meaning.
- Examine a set of notes you have recently taken during class. "Re-create" these notes, putting the material in your own words and making internal or external linkages as much as possible. Then devise a plan for how to incorporate more note-creating techniques during the next class.
- Create a "cheat sheet" list of self-testing strategies to keep close at hand as a reminder while you study. During every session of studying on your calendar for the week ahead, strive to incorporate one or two of these strategies at regular intervals.

The Moment of Truth: Exam Day

I am a very anxious test-taker. I dealt with my anxiety by getting to class early on the day of a test and frantically scanning my notes to pack in as many last-minute bits of information as possible. I thought I was improving my chances of success. In reality, I was stressing myself out and making things worse. I was usually sleep-deprived as well, heaping another unnecessary burden on my maxed-out brain (see the feature Help Your Brain Help You: The Importance of Sleep).

The First Thing to Do Is to Manage Your Stress

Of course you are nervous: You feel motivated to do your best yet worried about the uncertainty inherent in testing. (What questions will be on the test? Will I know the answers?) The stress is even greater with past experiences of disappointment related to testing. Stress makes us feel threatened, and the body responds by increasing heart rate, generating sweat, and pumping stress hormones through the bloodstream. Unfortunately, those worries steal valuable brain energy and make it difficult for you to function at top capacity. Instead of worrying about your stress response, take action. Here are some ways to manage test-day stress:

Breathe Deeply to Reduce Your Stress Response

This advice is simple but absolutely true. You may not be able to prevent the stress reaction, but you can have an impact on how long it lasts and how intense it becomes. Your body is simply unable to sustain that intense fight-or-flight reaction forever. And you can hasten its decline by taking charge of the things you can control, like the rate of your breathing.

HELP YOUR BRAIN HELP YOU

The Importance of Sleep

Take care of yourself. This advice is obvious when it comes to physical health; for example, no runner in her right mind would suggest staying up all night before a marathon. Yet, like me, I bet many of you have treated your brain poorly in pursuit of better grades. Pressed for time, we assume we must skimp on sleep to learn the material. Let go of what you think you know, and let sleep improve your memory!

No, I'm not talking about sleeping with your book beneath your pillow. Getting a good night's sleep helps the brain form and keep memories. How? A well-rested brain is better at encoding (Walker, 2008). In other words, if you're chronically sleep deprived, your brain has a harder time processing new information. You make learning harder on yourself.

Sleep also helps us strengthen and maintain the networks of memories we have recently formed. While you sleep, the brain reactivates the memories you worked on during the day, a form of mental exercise that knits those memories more deeply into your network of connections (Rasch & Born, 2008). Even a short period of daytime sleep can trigger the consolidation process that helps stabilize new memories in the brain (Mednick, Cai, Kanady, & Drummond, 2008).

Why not just power through sleepiness with caffeine? That was my "solution." I thought that Diet Coke and coffee made up for the hours of sleep I regularly skipped. Nope. In fact, research suggests that a nap may benefit your brain more than a double-shot latte. One study found that a 60- to 90-minute nap boosted memory significantly more than a 200- to 300-mg dose of caffeine (Mednick et al., 2008). Sure, caffeine makes you feel more alert, but a nap actually helps you *strengthen* the memories you've studied so hard to create.

I'm sure it's obvious why all-nighters before an exam are an absolutely terrible idea: You harm your brain's natural ability to cement memories at the very time it's most critical that your brain be working at top capacity! But even skipping a couple of hours of sleep is enough to decrease your brain's potential. Of all the advice in this chapter, this is the piece I most desperately wish I had known back when I was in college. I could have studied less and slept more? That's right! And I probably would have earned the same, or even better, grades. It's too late for me, but not for you: Get plenty of sleep and help your brain help you learn!

Have a Stress-Reduction Plan for the Moments Before the Test Is Passed Out

Figure out what helps reduce your stress response, and take action. Are you a social person who relaxes by talking to others? If so, engage in conversation with another student. Or do you need to focus inward in order to calm yourself down? Does music help you relax? Recent research suggests that highly test-anxious students relax and perform better when they write out their test-related worries for 10 minutes before the exam (Ramirez & Beilock, 2011). Try some of these suggestions, and find out what works best for you.

Identify Factors That Influence Your Ability to Stay Focused During the Exam, and Ask About Possible Accommodations

For minor requests, ask your professor. For example, if you are easily distracted by noise, ask your professor if you can use earplugs (not earbuds) during the exam. If it is noisy in the hallway, ask if the professor could close the door. If you think you may have a disability that warrants more significant accommodations, make an appointment with the disabilities services department on campus well in advance of any exams. Typically, professors are unable to make significant accommodations without this kind of expertise involved.

Be Strategic in Completing the Exam

Try some of these tips to give your brain the best chance to perform.

Start by Skimming

Skim the exam from start to finish before starting to answer questions. Why? On a practical level, skimming lets you take stock of what is coming. It reminds you of how many items are on the exam. It allows you to check whether the exam is printed on both sides of the page, so you don't accidentally fail to answer any of the questions. But skimming is also an overlooked strategy for warming up your brain. As you quickly read each question, you are exposing yourself to a treasure-trove of cues that will spark activation of your neural networks. This may not happen immediately, and you may not be fully aware of it happening. But, when it helps, you will be happy you gave it a chance!

Write on the Exam (if permitted)

Your brain is very busy while you are taking an exam, so anything you can do to ease the cognitive strain can make a big difference. Circle important words (e.g., *not*, *all*, *except for*). Cross out answers you know are incorrect. Jot down notes, charts, figures—anything that comes to mind that could help you answer the question.

If You Are Uncertain, Mark the Question, Move On, and Return to It Later

As you work on other questions, the cues you encounter may begin to jostle connections and activate a pathway to the answer. When I was taking the statistics portion of my comprehensive exams in graduate school, I kept going back to the same question again and again. I just didn't know the answer. But eventually, after working on other parts of the test, the answer just popped into my head like a gift from the universe. I can't tell you how it happened, but obviously my work on the test shook up my neural networks and spread the activation to enough spots that allowed me to construct the memory. Sometimes you have to give your brain time to activate the proper networks. Remember, each memory may consist of thousands of connections, and any of these could serve as a lifeline to the information you need.

A Special Tip for Multiple-Choice Questions: Cover the Answer Choices, and Read Only the Stem of the Question First

Basically, treat a multiple-choice question like an open-ended question first, and try to recall the answer. Think of it as a strategy to warm up the relevant neural networks. Next, uncover the answer choices and make a decision. Why do this? Sometimes it's easy to overanalyze the answer choices, which can lead to confusion. Answer choices often contain a variety of cues that can lead you down the wrong neural pathways. Focus on the stem first, trigger those associations, and then consider the answer choices.

Don't Assume Your First Hunch Is Always Correct

Many of us have received the well-intentioned but misguided advice to trust our instincts and not change our initial answers. Let go of what you think you know! To the contrary, research indicates that students more often change from an incorrect to a correct answer than vice versa (Lilienfeld, Lynn, Ruscio, & Beyerstein, 2010). If you really don't know the answer, randomly making changes is not going to help improve your score. But if you are struck by compelling reasons that suggest your initial answer is incorrect, trust your reasoning.

A Special Tip for Essay Questions: Brainstorm and Outline First

You probably get more nervous about essay questions than multiple-choice ones, but don't let this fear freeze your brain. In the margins or on the back (if writing on the exam is permissible), sketch out any ideas that come to mind in response to the essay question. Try to organize these thoughts into some structure. This helps activate the relevant brain cell networks, basically warming up the brain. If the answer isn't coming to you, move on to other questions and come back to it later. Sometimes the act of answering other questions will remind you of other bits of relevant information. As that happens, write those ideas alongside the others. When you are ready to answer the essay question, make sure you provide the information that is requested. For example, compare/contrast questions require you not only to define concepts but also to show how they are similar to and different from one another. Application questions require that you not only provide definitions but also show how terms or concepts relate to a given example.

Don't Rush Through the Exam Just to "Get It Over With"

We all look forward to unpleasant experiences coming to an end. My dentist is a terrific person, but dental work is unpleasant, and I want appointments to be over as quickly as possible. It's only natural that you would feel the same way about exams. However, unlike being at the dentist, you decide how quickly to work on a test; within the overall testing-time framework, you decide when the ordeal is over. The anticipation is enticing: You look forward to the feeling of relief.

In my class, I often hear audible sighs as students walk out the door after taking a test. This desire for relief can lead you to work faster than you should, increasing your odds of misreading questions or making other careless mistakes. So take all the time you are given to show all of what you know on an exam.

SECTION REVIEW

- Manage your pre-exam stress so you can devote more of your brain's resources to demonstrating your mastery.
- Be strategic in completing the exam: Skim to get an overview, make notes to aid your memory, and allow the experience of taking the exam to activate the connections you made while studying.
- Do not rush. Take the time you are given to show what you really know!

Test Yourself
Hint: Don't look back at the text until you have pulled out of your memory as much information as you can.

- What impact does stress have on your brain?
- How can skimming the exam influence your memory?
- What should you do if you are having second thoughts about an answer you chose?

Try It

- Reflect on your typical pre-exam experience. What changes could you make to improve your brain's ability to do its best for you? Identify at least one strategy you could incorporate when you take your next exam.
- Evaluate the strategies you typically follow while taking exams, and plan out the changes you could make to improve your performance on the next one.
- The next time you take an exam, introduce a "mindful moment" whenever you feel overwhelmed. Try the S.T.O.P. method (Stahl & Goldstein, 2010): *Stop* (simply take a brief moment to pause). *Take* a deep breath. Without passing judgment, *Observe* what's going on in your mind and body (Is your heart rate elevated? Are anxious thoughts interfering with your reasoning?). Finally, *Proceed* (check the time, note how many more items you have to complete, and decide which test-taking strategies to use next). Remind yourself of this strategy by writing "STOP" at the top of your exam.

Actually Doing It

Consider this question: What are the observable behaviors that successful students engage in consistently? At this point, you should have all kinds of answers. That's the easy part. But consider a trickier question: Once successful, how do you prevent yourself from slipping back into old, ineffective patterns of study behavior, like cramming, depriving yourself of sleep, and rote memorizing? Unfortunately, "saying" is much easier than "doing." But take heart: Any pattern of behavior or thinking you engage in that is detrimental to your learning is still just a habit. Habits reflect well-worn pathways in the neural networks of the brain, like a map of our current default settings. Habits are not eliminated overnight, but they can be changed through awareness, persistence, and motivation (see the feature Help Your Brain Help You: The Trouble with Multitasking to learn about a common habit that makes learning more difficult).

Developing Habits of Self-Regulation and Self-Control

Changing habits requires plenty of self-regulation, something that is challenging for most of us. If you've ever known what you needed to do but had trouble actually doing it, you know what this is like. We need to exercise self-control, putting off something very interesting right now in order to do something else that is less interesting but will pay off big time later. Luckily, we can build self-control over time; it's another mental muscle that responds to training (Muraven, 2010). The benefits extend well beyond studying, too; our strengthened self-control helps us modify any habit or learn any new skill—from quitting smoking to learning a new job.

HELP YOUR BRAIN HELP YOU

The Trouble with Multitasking

Are you easily bored? I am. I get bored while I'm cleaning or doing laundry, so I often listen to a podcast or audiobook. It makes the time pass more quickly. As long as one of the tasks is virtually mindless (like folding laundry), multitasking can work just fine. But when you try to do two cognitively complex tasks at once—like studying while texting or IMing—the brain protests. Why? The brain cannot simultaneously engage in two tasks requiring complex cognition. Instead, it shifts back and forth between tasks. When you study, you exercise one set of networks in the brain. When you read and answer a text message, you switch to a completely different network. All of this switching puts a lot of stress on your brain. It's like requiring one conductor to switch back and forth between two different orchestras performing different pieces. Your brain is designed to do its best work when focused on one task (Rubenstein, Myer, & Evans, 2001). When you try to multitask while studying, you activate a less flexible and more basic area of the brain capable of only the most shallow processing (Foerde, Knowlton, & Poldrack, 2006).

You may feel like multitasking is necessary in order to keep you from feeling so bored. Maybe it seems like you're able to study longer while watching TV, using Facebook, or talking to friends. If this is the case, I need you to let go of what you think you know. Yes, time may seem to pass more quickly, but you are making things much harder on your brain by providing it with a very weak form of exercise. By eliminating distractions, you make your studying more efficient and effective. In short, multitasking wastes time; performing one task at a time saves time.

What if you are a chronic multitasker? Can you train your brain to switch between tasks without any declines in brain performance? The scientific evidence suggests the answer is no: Practice does not make perfect. In fact, those who multitask most often tend to show the steepest declines in their cognitive performance while multitasking (Ophir, Nass, & Wagner, 2009)!

If you are easily bored while studying, evaluate your study habits. Spending several hours memorizing definitions or rereading notes? That's boring. Instead of pulling out your cell phone or turning on the TV, use the strategies discussed in this chapter. Remember, studying that feels challenging now pays off the most later, and it also happens to be much less boring than memorizing flashcards. So try something different. Spend shorter periods of time on each subject, and alternate between subjects. Make a concept map. Create some open-ended questions and test yourself. Pretend you are teaching the material to someone else. Focus on having a high-quality mental workout, and your urge to multitask won't be so strong.

Procrastination is one of the biggest self-control challenges we face. It feels good in the moment because we have avoided an aversive task. In regard to studying, students procrastinate for many reasons. Some are afraid of failure, and some believe they do their best work under the pressure of the last minute. Whatever the reason, procrastination gives us an escape from an unpleasant feeling. But it always catches up with us in the end. One study found that students who procrastinated reported more health problems near the end of the term, perhaps because of the stress of all of that cramming. On top of that, their grades suffered as well (Tice & Baumeister, 1997). Here are some strategies you can use to strengthen your self-control.

Start with a Short Burst

If you are having trouble getting started with a task, make it very easy at first. Work on the dreaded task for only 10 minutes, and then take a 2-minute break to do something more interesting. Go back for another 10-minute work session, and then take another 2-minute break. Repeat as necessary! I do this to kick-start my grading, which at first leaves me feeling overwhelmed. But when I think about only spending 10 minutes on grading, it's no longer a big deal. What usually happens next is that the simple act of getting started breaks the spell of procrastination. I find that after a few 10-minute bursts, I can work longer.

Make Sure You Are Spacing Out Your Studying

Remember, it's better for your brain if your study sessions are short and frequent. This helps with procrastination as well, because a 1-hour study session seems far less dreadful than a 5-hour marathon.

Capitalize on Your Strengths and Interests

Fuse something that provides immediate rewards with something that advances you toward your long-term goal (Steel, 2007). For example, if you are a very social person who loves meeting new people, form a study group early in the semester and start meeting regularly. If you love nature, incorporate a short session of reading into your next hike. In other words, find ways to link studying with some of the things you love.

Make Small Changes in Your Environment to Stay Focused on Your Goals

People striving to meet health-related goals do this by eliminating unhealthy foods from their pantry at home. You can do something similar to advance your academic goals. Reduce distractions by turning off any indicators of new texts or e-mails. Better yet, put your cell phone in a different room. Is the Internet a constant temptation? Temporarily disable your online access. Do you have trouble staying focused in class? Sit where you are not able to see the clock, or put your watch or cell phone away so you can't see the time. Why? The more we check the time, the more slowly time seems to pass (Sackett, Meyvis, Nelson, Converse, & Sackett, 2010). Try sitting in the front row, where the professor is more likely to notice your behavior. That way, you're less likely to feel tempted to give into your urge to text, sleep, or daydream.

Act "As If"

Have you ever felt your attitude needed an adjustment? Try changing your behavior first. Do you think this is the most boring class in the world? Act "as if" you are interested: Get to class early, sit near the front, listen intently with an expression of interest, and create great notes. Quite literally, play the role of "interested student." Do this to boost your studying outside class (if necessary) as well. Obviously, this will feel very strange at first, but research indicates that our attitudes often shift to line up with our behaviors (Festinger, 1957). This may not become your favorite class, but acting "as if" is likely to help improve your attitude and motivation. As a result, you have more energy to apply effective study strategies!

SECTION REVIEW

- Habits are behaviors learned over time. As such, habits can be unlearned through persistence and patience.
- Self-control and self-regulation habits are central to long-term, effective studying.
- You should focus on making small changes first.

Test Yourself

Hint: Don't look back at the text until you have pulled out of your memory as much information as you can.

- How is practicing self-control like engaging a muscle?
- Why can it be beneficial to your studying to act "as if" you are more interested and motivated than you sometimes really feel?

Try It

- Think back to a time when you successfully changed a habit. How did you do it? Adapt elements of that experience to change your least effective study habits.
- If you tend to put things off, choose one procrastination-reduction method to apply in the week ahead.
- Identify the biggest distractions you face while studying, and make changes to your environment to minimize these distractions the next time you study.

If At First You Don't Succeed . . .

Effective habits for studying and self-regulation come from the same place: the well-trained brain. Imagine your brain cells lifting weights, getting stronger and building more connections every day. It will take time to figure out which strategies work best for you, so be prepared to experiment. Remember, your brain is wired uniquely; the strategies that work best for you may be different from those that work best for others. You may also find that different classes require different strategies, so prepare to modify your approach accordingly.

Allow yourself to be human. You will probably lapse back into ineffective strategies or habits occasionally. What matters most is what you do next. Take a lesson from a recent study on procrastination (Wohl, Pychyl, & Bennet, 2010). Students who forgave themselves for procrastinating before Exam 1 were much less likely to procrastinate before Exam 2. Self-forgiveness prevented them from spiraling into apathy, like a dieter who slips up with one cookie and decides he might as well eat the whole box. The self-forgivers acknowledged their slip-up and took the next opportunity to get back on track again. So with these findings in mind, keep persisting!

Whether your future plans include academics or not, I hope the practical advice offered in this chapter will help you make long-lasting changes in the way you approach any type of learning experience.

References

Bjork, E., & Bjork, R. (2011). Making things hard on yourself, but in a good way: Creating desirable difficulties to enhance learning. In M. A. Gernsbacher, R. W. Pew, L. W. Hough, & J. R. Pomerantz (Eds.), *Psychology and the real world: Essays illustrating fundamental contributions to society* (pp. 56–64). New York: Worth Publishers.

Cook, S. W., Mitchell, Z., & Goldin-Meadow, S. (2008). Gesturing makes learning last. *Cognition, 106* (2), 1047–1058. doi:10.1016/j.cognition.2007.04.010

Craik, F. I. M., & Tulving, E. (1975). Depth of processing and the retention of words in episodic memory. *Journal of Experimental Psychology: General, 104*, 268-294.

Festinger, L. (1957). *A theory of cognitive dissonance.* Evanston, IL: Row, Peterson.

Foerde, K., Knowlton, B. J., & Poldrack, R. A. (2006). Modulation of competing memory systems by distraction. *Proceedings of the National Academy of Sciences, 103*(31), 11778–11783. doi:10.1073/pnas.0602659103

Glenberg, A., Brown, M., & Levin, J. (2007). Enhancing comprehension in small reading groups using a manipulation strategy. *Contemporary Educational Psychology, 32*(3), 389–399. doi:10.1016/j.cedpsych.2006.03.001

Karpicke, J. D., & Blunt, J. R. (2011). Retrieval practice produces more learning than elaborative studying with concept mapping. *Science, 331*(6018), 772–775. doi:10.1126/science.1199327

Kiewra, K. A. (2002). How classroom teachers can help students learn and teach them how to learn. *Theory into Practice, 41*(2), 71–80.

Knight, L. J., & McKelvie, S. J. (1986). Effects of attendance, note-taking, and review on memory for a lecture: Encoding vs. external storage functions of notes. *Canadian Journal of Behavioural Science/Revue canadienne des sciences du comportement, 18*(1), 52–61. doi:10.1037/h0079957

Kornell, N. (in press). Discrimination learning: Training methods. In H. Pashler (Ed.), *Encyclopedia of the mind.* Thousand Oaks: Sage Reference.

Kornell, N. (2009). Optimising learning using flashcards: Spacing is more effective than cramming. *Applied Cognitive Psychology, 23*(9), 1297–1317. doi:10.1002/acp.1537

Kruger, J., & Dunning, D. (1999). Unskilled and unaware of it: How difficulties in recognizing one's own incompetence lead to inflated self-assessments. *Journal of Personality and Social Psychology, 77*(6), 1121–1134. doi:10.1037/0022-3514.77.6.1121

Lilienfeld, S. O., Lynn, S. J., Ruscio, J., & Beyerstein, B. L. (2010). *50 great myths of popular psychology: Shattering widespread misconceptions about human behavior.* Malden, MA: Wiley-Blackwell.

Mayer, R. E. (1996). Learning strategies for making sense out of expository text: The SOI model for guiding three cognitive processes in knowledge construction. *Educational Psychology Review, 8*(4), 357–371. doi:10.1007/BF01463939

McDaniel, M. A., Howard, D. C., & Einstein, G. O. (2009). The Read-Recite-Review study strategy: Effective and portable. *Psychological Science, 20*(4), 516–522. doi:10.1111/j.1467-9280.2009.02325.x

Medina, J. (2008). *Brain rules: 12 principles for surviving and thriving at work, home, and school.* Seattle, WA: Pear Press.

Mednick, S., Cai, D., Kanady, J., & Drummond, S. (2008). Comparing the benefits of caffeine, naps and placebo on verbal, motor and perceptual memory. *Behavioural Brain Research, 193*(1), 79–86. doi:10.1016/j.bbr.2008.04.028

Muraven, M. (2010). Practicing self-control lowers the risk of smoking lapse. *Psychology of Addictive Behaviors, 24*(3), 446–452. doi:10.1037/a0018545

Noice, H., & Noice, T. (2006). What studies of actors and acting can tell us about memory and cognitive functioning. *Current Directions in Psychological Science, 15*(1), 14–18.

Ophir, E., Nass, C., & Wagner, A. D. (2009). From the cover: Cognitive control in media multitaskers. *Proceedings of the National Academy of Sciences, 106*(37), 15583–15587. doi:10.1073/pnas.0903620106

Peverly, S. T., Ramaswamy, V., Brown, C., Sumowski, J., Alidoost, M., & Garner, J. (2007). What predicts skill in lecture note taking? *Journal of Educational Psychology, 99*(1), 167–180. doi:10.1037/0022-0663.99.1.167

Ramirez, G., & Beilock, S. L. (2011). Writing about testing worries boosts exam performance in the classroom. *Science, 331*(6014), 211–213. doi:10.1126/science.1199427

Rasch, B., & Born, J. (2008). Reactivation and consolidation of memory during sleep. *Current Directions in Psychological Science, 17*(3), 188–192.

Richland, L. E., Kornell, N., & Kao, L. S. (2009). The pretesting effect: Do unsuccessful retrieval attempts enhance learning? *Journal of Experimental Psychology: Applied, 15*(3), 243–257. doi:10.1037/a0016496

Robinson, F. P. (1970). *Effective study.* New York: HarperCollins.

Rohrer, D., & Pashler, H. (2010). Recent research on human learning challenges conventional instructional strategies. *Educational Researcher, 39*(5), 406–412. doi:10.3102/0013189X10374770

Rubinstein, J. S., Meyer, D. E., & Evans, J. E. (2001). Executive control of cognitive processes in task switching. *Journal of Experimental Psychology: Human Perception and Performance, 27*(4), 763–797. doi:10.1037//0096-1523.27.4.763

Sackett, A. M., Meyvis, T., Nelson, L. D., Converse, B. A., & Sackett, A. L. (2010). You're having fun when time flies: The hedonic consequences of subjective time progression. *Psychological Science, 21*(1), 111–117. doi:10.1177/0956797609354832

Smith, S. M. (2007). Context and human memory. In H. L. Roediger, Y. Dudai, & S. M. Fitzpatrick (Eds.), *Science of memory: Concepts* (pp. 111–114). Oxford: Oxford University Press.

Smith, S. M., & Vela, E. (2001). Environmental context dependent memory: A review and meta analysis. *Psychonomic Bulletin and Review, 8,* 203–220.

Stahl, B., & Goldstein, E. (2010). *A mindfulness-based stress reduction workbook.* Oakland, CA: New Harbinger Publications.

Stanovich, K. (2010). *How to think straight about psychology* (9th ed.). Boston: Allyn & Bacon.

Stanovich, K. E. (2010). *Rationality and the reflective mind.* New York: Oxford University Press.

Steel, P. (2007). The nature of procrastination: A meta-analytic and theoretical review of quintessential self-regulatory failure. *Psychological Bulletin, 133*(1), 65–94. doi:10.1037/0033-2909.133.1.65

Stevanoni, E., & Salmon, K. (2005). Giving memory a hand: Instructing children to gesture enhances their event recall. *Journal of Nonverbal Behavior, 29*(4), 217–233. doi:10.1007/s10919-005-7721-y

Tice, D. M., & Baumeister, R. F. (1997). Longitudinal study of procrastination, performance, stress, and health: The costs and benefits of dawdling. *Psychological Science, 8*(6), 454–458. doi:10.1111/j.1467-9280.1997.tb00460.x

Walker, M. P. (2008). Sleep-dependent memory processing. *Harvard Review of Psychiatry, 16*(5), 287–298. doi:10.1080/10673220802432517

Wohl, M. J., Pychyl, T. A., & Bennett, S. H. (2010). I forgive myself, now I can study: How self-forgiveness for procrastinating can reduce future procrastination. *Personality and Individual Differences, 48*(7), 803–808. doi:10.1016/j.paid.2010.01.029

For Frank Vattano,
master teacher, mentor to teachers,
wellspring of creative resources, and
encouraging friend

DAVID MYERS

received his psychology Ph.D. from the University of Iowa. He has spent his career at Hope College, Michigan, where he has taught dozens of introductory psychology sections. Hope College students have invited him to be their commencement speaker and voted him "outstanding professor."

Myers' scientific articles have, with support from National Science Foundation grants, appeared in more than two dozen scientific periodicals, including *Science, American Scientist, Psychological Science,* and the *American Psychologist.* In addition to his scholarly writing and his textbooks for introductory and social psychology, he also digests psychological science for the general public. His writings have appeared in three dozen magazines, from *Today's Education* to *Scientific American.* He also has authored five general audience books, including *The Pursuit of Happiness* and *Intuition: Its Powers and Perils.*

David Myers has chaired his city's Human Relations Commission, helped found a thriving assistance center for families in poverty, and spoken to hundreds of college and community groups. Drawing on his experience, he also has written articles and a book *(A Quiet World)* about hearing loss, and he is advocating a transformation in American assistive listening technology (see hearingloop.org).

He bikes to work year-round and plays daily pick-up basketball. David and Carol Myers have raised two sons and a daughter.

BRIEF CONTENTS

Preface...xv

CHAPTER 1 Thinking Critically With Psychological Science 1

CHAPTER 2 The Biology of Mind...35

CHAPTER 3 Consciousness and the Two–Track Mind.......................65

CHAPTER 4 Nature, Nurture, and Human Diversity 105

CHAPTER 5 Developing Through the Life Span 137

CHAPTER 6 Sensation and Perception..179

CHAPTER 7 Learning 225

CHAPTER 8 Memory..257

CHAPTER 9 Thinking, Language, and Intelligence 291

CHAPTER 10 Motivation..339

CHAPTER 11 Emotions, Stress, and Health....................................375

CHAPTER 12 Personality..419

CHAPTER 13 Psychological Disorders 453

CHAPTER 14 Therapy...493

CHAPTER 15 Social Psychology 525

APPENDIX A Statistical Reasoning in Everyday Life A-1

APPENDIX B Psychology at Work B-1

APPENDIX C Careers in Psychology...C-1

APPENDIX D Answers to *Test for Success: Critical Thinking Exercises*......D-1

Glossary G-1

References...R-1

Name Index NI-1

Subject Index SI-1

CONTENTS

Preface xv

1

CHAPTER 1

Thinking Critically With Psychological Science

What Is Psychology?...................................2
   Psychology's Roots 2
   Contemporary Psychology 5

Why Do Psychology? 9
   What About Intuition and Common Sense? 10
   The Scientific Attitude 11
   Critical Thinking 13

How Do Psychologists Ask and Answer Questions? ...14
   The Scientific Method 14
   Description 15
   Correlation 18
   Experimentation 21

Frequently Asked Questions About Psychology 25

Tips for Studying Psychology 29

35

CHAPTER 2

The Biology of Mind

Neural Communication 35
   Neurons 35
   How Neurons Communicate 36
   How Neurotransmitters Influence Us 38

The Nervous System................................39
   The Peripheral Nervous System 39
   The Central Nervous System 40

The Endocrine System..............................42

The Brain 44
   Older Brain Structures 44
   CLOSE-UP: The Tools of Discovery—Having Our Head
     Examined 45
   The Cerebral Cortex 50
   Our Divided Brain 57
   Right-Left Differences in the Intact Brain 60

65

CHAPTER 3

Consciousness and the Two-Track Mind

The Brain and Consciousness 66
   Dual Processing 66
   Selective Attention 68

Sleep and Dreams.................................70
   Biological Rhythms and Sleep 70
   Why Do We Sleep? 75
   Sleep Disorders 78
   Dreams 80

Hypnosis..84
   Facts and Falsehoods 84
   Explaining the Hypnotized State 86

Drugs and Consciousness..........................88
   Dependence and Addiction 88
   Psychoactive Drugs 89
   Influences on Drug Use 97

105

CHAPTER 4
Nature, Nurture, and Human Diversity

Behavior Genetics: Predicting Individual Differences 105
  Genes: Our Codes for Life 106
  Twin and Adoption Studies 106
  Temperament, Personality, and Heredity 110
  Gene-Environment Interactions 111

Evolutionary Psychology:
Understanding Human Nature 113
  Natural Selection and Adaptation 113
  Evolutionary Success Helps Explain Similarities 114
  An Evolutionary Explanation of Human Sexuality 115
  THINKING CRITICALLY ABOUT: The Evolutionary Perspective
    on Human Sexuality 117

Parents and Peers 117
  Parents and Early Experiences 118
  Peer Influence 120

Cultural Influences 121
  Variation Across Cultures 122
  Variation Over Time 123
  Culture and the Self 123
  Culture and Child-Rearing 125
  Developmental Similarities Across Groups 125

Gender Development 126
  Gender Similarities and Differences 126
  The Nature of Gender 129
  The Nurture of Gender 130

Reflections on Nature and Nurture 131

137

CHAPTER 5
Developing Through the Life Span

Prenatal Development and the Newborn 137
  Conception 137
  Prenatal Development 138
  The Competent Newborn 139

Infancy and Childhood 140
  Physical Development 140
  Cognitive Development 142
  CLOSE-UP: Autism and "Mind-Blindness" 146
  Social Development 149

Adolescence 154
  Physical Development 155
  Cognitive Development 157
  Social Development 159
  Emerging Adulthood 162

Adulthood 163
  Physical Development 163
  Cognitive Development 166
  Social Development 168

Reflections on Two Major Developmental Issues 173
  Continuity and Stages 173
  Stability and Change 174

179

CHAPTER 6
Sensation and Perception

Sensing the World: Some Basic Principles 180
   Thresholds **181**
   Sensory Adaptation **183**

Vision 185
   The Stimulus Input: Light Energy **185**
   The Eye **186**
   Visual Information Processing **188**
   Color Vision **191**

Other Important Senses 193
   Hearing **193**
   Touch **196**
   Pain **198**
   Taste **201**
   Smell **202**

Perceptual Organization 205
   Form Perception **205**
   Depth Perception **207**
   Perceptual Constancy **210**

Perceptual Interpretation 213
   Sensory Deprivation and Restored Vision **213**
   Perceptual Adaptation **214**
   Perceptual Set **215**
   THINKING CRITICALLY ABOUT: Extrasensory Perception **218**

225

CHAPTER 7
Learning

How Do We Learn? 225

Classical Conditioning 227
   Pavlov's Experiments **228**
   Extending Pavlov's Understanding **232**
   Pavlov's Legacy **234**

Operant Conditioning 236
   Skinner's Experiments **236**
   Extending Skinner's Understanding **243**
   Skinner's Legacy **244**
   CLOSE-UP: Training Our Mates **246**
   Contrasting Classical and Operant Conditioning **246**

Learning by Observation 248
   Mirrors in the Brain **248**
   Bandura's Experiments **249**
   Applications of Observational Learning **250**

257

CHAPTER 8
Memory

The Phenomenon of Memory 257

Studying Memory: Information-Processing Models . . .258

Encoding: Getting Information In 259
   How We Encode: Levels of Processing **259**
   What We Encode **262**

Storage: Retaining Information 265
Sensory Memory 265
Working/Short-Term Memory 266
Long-Term Memory 267
Storing Information in the Brain 267

Retrieval: Getting Information Out 273
Retrieval Cues 273

Forgetting 276
Encoding Failure 277
Storage Decay 277
Retrieval Failure 278
CLOSE-UP: Retrieving Passwords 280

Memory Construction 281
Misinformation and Imagination Effects 282
Source Amnesia 283
Children's Eyewitness Recall 284
Repressed or Constructed Memories of Abuse? 285

Improving Memory 287

291
CHAPTER 9
Thinking, Language, and Intelligence

Thinking 291
Concepts 291
Solving Problems 292
Making Decisions and Forming Judgments 294
THINKING CRITICALLY ABOUT: The Fear Factor—Do We Fear the Right Things? 298

Language 302
Language Development 302
Thinking and Language 306
Animal Thinking and Language 309

Intelligence 313
What Is Intelligence? 313

Assessing Intelligence 319
CLOSE-UP: Extremes of Intelligence 322
Genetic and Environmental Influences on Intelligence 324
Group Differences in Intelligence Test Scores 328

339
CHAPTER 10
Motivation

Motivational Concepts 340
Instincts and Evolutionary Psychology 340
Drives and Incentives 340
Optimum Arousal 341
A Hierarchy of Motives 342

Hunger 343
The Physiology of Hunger 344
The Psychology of Hunger 346
Obesity and Weight Control 347
CLOSE-UP: Eating Disorders 348
CLOSE-UP: Waist Management 356

Sexual Motivation 357
The Physiology of Sex 357
The Psychology of Sex 359
Adolescent Sexuality 361
Sexual Orientation 363
Sex and Human Values 368

The Need to Belong 369

375

CHAPTER 11
Emotions, Stress, and Health

420

CHAPTER 12
Personality

Theories of Emotion 376

Embodied Emotion 378
  Emotions and the Autonomic Nervous System 378
  Brain and Other Physiological Indicators of Emotions 379
  Cognition and Emotion 379
  THINKING CRITICALLY ABOUT: Lie Detection 380

Expressed Emotion 383
  Detecting Emotion 383
  Gender, Emotion, and Nonverbal Behavior 385
  Culture and Emotional Expression 386
  The Effects of Facial Expressions 388

Experienced Emotion 389
  Anger 389
  Happiness 391
  CLOSE-UP: How to Be Happier 397

Stress and Health 398
  Stress and Illness 398
  Stress and the Heart 402
  Stress and Susceptibility to Disease 403
  THINKING CRITICALLY ABOUT: Complementary and
    Alternative Medicine 406

Promoting Health 408
  Coping With Stress 408
  CLOSE-UP: Pets Are Friends, Too 410
  Managing Stress 411
  CLOSE-UP: The Relaxation Response 413

The Psychoanalytic Perspective 420
  Exploring the Unconscious 420
  The Neo-Freudian and Psychodynamic Theorists 423
  Assessing Unconscious Processes 424
  Evaluating the Psychoanalytic Perspective 426

The Humanistic Perspective 429
  Abraham Maslow's Self-Actualizing Person 429
  Carl Rogers' Person-Centered Perspective 430
  Assessing the Self 431
  Evaluating the Humanistic Perspective 431

The Trait Perspective 432
  Exploring Traits 432
  Assessing Traits 433
  THINKING CRITICALLY ABOUT: How to Be a "Successful"
    Astrologer or Palm Reader 434
  The Big Five Factors 436
  Evaluating the Trait Perspective 437

The Social-Cognitive Perspective 439
  Reciprocal Influences 439
  Personal Control 440
  CLOSE-UP: Toward a More Positive Psychology 443
  Assessing Behavior in Situations 445
  Evaluating the Social-Cognitive Perspective 445

Exploring the Self 446
  The Benefits of Self-Esteem 447
  Self-Serving Bias 447

453

CHAPTER 13
Psychological Disorders

Perspectives on Psychological Disorders 454

Defining Psychological Disorders 454

THINKING CRITICALLY ABOUT: ADHD—Normal High Energy or Genuine Disorder? 455

Understanding Psychological Disorders 455

Classifying Psychological Disorders 457

CLOSE-UP: The "un-DSM": A Diagnostic Manual of Human Strengths 459

Labeling Psychological Disorders 459

THINKING CRITICALLY ABOUT: Insanity and Responsibility 461

Anxiety Disorders 461

Generalized Anxiety Disorder 462

Panic Disorder 462

Phobias 462

Obsessive-Compulsive Disorder 463

Post-Traumatic Stress Disorder 464

Understanding Anxiety Disorders 465

Somatoform Disorders 468

Dissociative Disorders 468

Dissociative Identity Disorder 469

Understanding Dissociative Identity Disorder 469

Mood Disorders 470

Major Depressive Disorder 470

Bipolar Disorder 471

Understanding Mood Disorders 472

CLOSE-UP: Suicide 474

Schizophrenia 480

Symptoms of Schizophrenia 480

Onset and Development of Schizophrenia 481

Understanding Schizophrenia 482

Personality Disorders 486

Antisocial Personality Disorder 486

Understanding Antisocial Personality Disorder 487

Rates of Psychological Disorders 488

493

CHAPTER 14
Therapy

The Psychological Therapies 494

Psychoanalysis 494

Humanistic Therapies 495

Behavior Therapies 497

Cognitive Therapies 501

Group and Family Therapies 503

Evaluating Psychotherapies 504

Is Psychotherapy Effective? 505

The Relative Effectiveness of Different Therapies 506

Evaluating Alternative Therapies 507

Commonalities Among Psychotherapies 509

Culture and Values in Psychotherapy 511

CLOSE-UP: A Consumer's Guide to Psychotherapists 512

The Biomedical Therapies 512

Drug Therapies 513

Brain Stimulation 516

Psychosurgery 519

Preventing Psychological Disorders 520

525

CHAPTER 15

Social
Psychology

Social Thinking 525
Attributing Behavior to Persons or to Situations **525**
Attitudes and Actions **527**
CLOSE-UP: Abu Ghraib Prison: An "Atrocity-Producing Situation"? **530**

Social Influence 531
Conformity and Obedience **532**
Group Influence **537**
The Power of Individuals **541**

Social Relations 542
Prejudice **542**
CLOSE-UP: Automatic Prejudice **543**
Aggression **548**
THINKING CRITICALLY ABOUT: Do Video Games Teach, or Release, Violence? **552**
CLOSE-UP: Online Matchmaking **555**
Attraction **555**
Altruism **561**
Conflict and Peacemaking **563**

Appendix A: Statistical Reasoning in Everyday Life

Describing Data A-1
Measures of Central Tendency **A-1**
Measures of Variation **A-3**
Correlation: A Measure of Relationships **A-4**

Making Inferences A-6
When Is an Observed Difference Reliable? **A-6**
CLOSE-UP: Cross-Sectional and Longitudinal Studies **A-7**
When Is a Difference Significant? **A-7**

Appendix B: Psychology at Work
CLOSE-UP: I/O Psychology at Work **B-2**

Personnel Psychology B-3
Harnessing Strengths **B-3**
CLOSE-UP: Discovering Your Strengths **B-3**
Appraising Performance **B-5**

Organizational Psychology B-7
Satisfaction and Engagement **B-7**
CLOSE-UP: Doing Well While Doing Good: "The Great Experiment" **B-8**
Managing Well **B-9**

Human Factors Psychology B-12

Appendix C: Careers in Psychology

Preparing for a Career in Psychology C-1
The Bachelor's Degree **C-1**
Postgraduate Degrees **C-3**
The Master's Degree **C-4**
Doctoral Degrees **C-4**

Subfields of Psychology C-4

Preparing Early for Graduate Study in Psychology C-9

For More Information C-10

Appendix D: Answers to Test for Success: Critical Thinking Exercises D-1

Glossary G-1

References R-1

Name Index NI-1

Subject Index SI-1

With each new edition, I've found myself traveling a familiar path. When it is first published, I am relieved after many months of intense effort, and I am thrilled—sure that it is my best effort yet. Shortly thereafter, as new research comes out elaborating on concepts that the current edition teaches, and as thoughtful instructors and students begin writing with suggestions for improvement, and then when commissioned reviews and survey results start coming in, I have second thoughts about the current edition's seeming perfection. As my chapter-by-chapter storage cubbies begin fattening with new material, my eagerness for the next edition grows. By the time the new edition is ready to come out, I grimace when reminded of people using the old edition, which once seemed so perfect!

This eighth edition of *Exploring Psychology* is no exception. This is now my best effort ever, much improved over the previous work! Among the many changes I am delighted to offer are

- hundreds of *new research citations* representing the most exciting and important new discoveries in our field.
- *organizational changes* based on changes in the field. For example, the heavily revised consciousness chapter now follows the neuroscience chapter and is titled Consciousness and the Two-Track Mind to reflect the dual-processing and cognitive neuroscience themes.
- *fine-tuned writing* with countless small and large improvements in the way concepts are presented, supported by the input and creative ideas of hundreds of contributing instructors, students, and friends.
- a sharp *new art program* that teaches more effectively.
- continually improving coverage of *cultural and gender diversity issues.*

I find myself fascinated by today's psychology, with its studies of the neuroscience of our moods and memories, the reach of our adaptive unconscious, and the shaping power of the social and cultural context. Psychological science is increasingly attuned to the relative effects of nature and nurture, to gender and cultural diversity, to our conscious and unconscious information processing, and to the biology underlying our behavior. (See **TABLES 1** and **2** on the next page.) I am grateful for the privilege of assisting with the teaching of this mind-expanding discipline to so many students. To be entrusted with discerning and communicating psychology's insights is both an exciting honor and a great responsibility.

The thousands of instructors and millions of students who have worked with this book have contributed immensely to its development. Much of this has occurred spontaneously, through correspondence and conversations. For this edition, we also formally involved over 300 researchers and teaching psychologists, along with many students, in our efforts to gather accurate and up-to-date information about the field of psychology and the content, pedagogy, and supplements needs of instructors and students in the introductory course. We look forward to continuing feedback as we strive, over future editions, to create an ever-better book and supplements.

What Continues?

Throughout its eight editions, my vision for *Exploring Psychology* has not wavered: *to merge rigorous science with a broad human perspective in a book that engages both mind and heart.* My aim has been to create a state-of-the-art introduction to psychology,

TABLE 1 Evolutionary Psychology and Behavior Genetics

*In addition to the coverage found in Chapter 4, the **evolutionary perspective** is covered on the following pages:*

Anxiety disorders, pp. 466–467
Attraction, p. 556
Biological predispositions
  in learning, pp. 232–234
  in operant conditioning, pp. 243–244
Brainstem, p. 44
Consciousness, p. 65
Depression, p. 520
  and light exposure therapy, p. 509
Emotional expression, p. 387
  effects of facial expressions, p. 388
Emotion-detecting ability, pp. 328–329
Evolutionary perspective, defined, p. 7
Exercise, p. 412
Fear, pp. 298–299
Feature detection, pp. 188–189
Hearing, p. 193
Hunger and taste preference, pp. 346–347

Instincts, p. 340
Intelligence, pp. 314, 319, 331–332
Language, pp. 302, 304
Love, p. 169
Math and spatial ability, pp. 329–330
Mating preferences, pp. 116–117
Menopause, p. 164
Need to belong, p. 370
Obesity, p. 347
Overconfidence, p. 297
Perceptual adaptation, pp. 214–215
Puberty, onset of, p. 162
Sensation, p. 180
Sensory adaptation, pp. 183–184
Sexual orientation, p. 366
Sexuality, pp. 116–117, 357
Sleep, pp. 71, 77
Smell, p. 204
Taste, p. 201

*In addition to the coverage found in Chapter 4, **behavior genetics** is covered on the following pages:*

Abuse, intergenerational transmission of, p. 251
Aggression, p. 548
Depth perception, p. 207
Drives and incentives, pp. 340–341
Drug dependence, p. 98
Drug use, pp. 97–98
Eating disorders, p. 348
Happiness, pp. 396–397
Hunger and taste preference, pp. 346–347
Intelligence, pp. 324–325
  Down syndrome, pp. 322–323
Language, p. 304
Learning, pp. 232–234, 243–244
Memory, pp. 272, 273
Motor development, p. 141
Obesity and weight control, p. 353
Perception, p. 213
Personality traits, pp. 433–436

Psychological disorders:
  ADHD, p. 455
  anxiety disorders, pp. 466–467
  biopsychosocial approach, pp. 456–457
  mood disorders, pp. 474–476
  personality disorders, pp. 487–488
  schizophrenia, pp. 484–485
Romantic love, p. 169
Sexual orientation, p. 366
Sexuality, p. 357
Smell, pp. 202–204
Stress:
  AIDS, p. 405
  cancer, p. 405
  personality and illness, pp. 402–404
  psychoneuroimmunology, p. 404
Traits, pp. 433, 436

TABLE 2 Neuroscience

*In addition to the coverage found in Chapter 2, **neuroscience** can be found on the following pages:*

ADHD and the brain, p. 455
Aggression, pp. 548–549
Aging: physical exercise and the brain, p. 166
Antisocial personality disorder, p. 487
Autism, pp. 146–147
Brain activity and:
  aging, pp. 165–166, 271
  dementia and Alzheimer's, pp. 167–168, 268
  dreams, pp. 80–83
  emotion, pp. 156, 268–269, 379, 381–382, 386
  sleep, pp. 70–74
Brain development:
  adolescence, pp. 156–157
  experience and, pp. 118–119
  infancy and childhood, p. 140
  sexual differentiation in utero, p. 129
Cognitive neuroscience, pp. 4, 66
Drug dependence, p. 98
Emotion and cognition, pp. 381–382
Emotional intelligence and brain damage, p. 318
ESP and fMRI testing, p. 220
Fear-learning, p. 467
Fetal alcohol syndrome and brain abnormalities, p. 138
Hallucinations and:
  hallucinogens, pp. 95–97

near-death experiences, pp. 95–96
sleep, p. 82
Hormones and:
  abuse, p. 153
  development, pp. 129, 155–157
  emotion, pp. 376–377
  gender, p. 129
  memory, pp. 268–269
  sex, p. 164
  sexual behavior, pp. 358–359
  stress, pp. 378, 399, 403–404, 409
  weight control, pp. 344–346
Hunger, pp. 344–346
Hypnotized brain, pp. 86–87
Insight, p. 293
Intelligence and:
  creativity, p. 317
  twins, p. 325
Language, pp. 304–305
  and statistical learning, pp. 304–305
  and thinking in images, pp. 307–309
Light exposure therapy:
  brain scans, p. 509
Meditation, p. 412
Memory:
  and physical storage of, pp. 267–268
  and implicit/explicit memories, pp. 269–272
  and sleep, pp. 77, 82

Mirror neurons, pp. 248–249
Neuroscience perspective, defined, p. 7
Neurostimulation therapy and:
  deep-brain stimulation, p. 518
  magnetic stimulation, pp. 517–519
Neurotransmitters and:
  anxiety disorders, pp. 467, 514
  biomedical therapy and:
    depression, pp. 476, 514–515
    ECT, pp. 516–517
    schizophrenia, pp. 482, 514
  child abuse, p. 153
  cognitive-behavior therapy for obsessive-compulsive disorder, p. 503
  curare, p. 39
  depression, p. 476
  drugs, pp. 88, 89–95
  exercise, pp. 411–412
  schizophrenia, pp. 482–483, 485
Optimum arousal: rewards, p. 341
Orgasm, p. 357
Pain, pp. 198–199
  phantom limb pain, p. 199
Parallel vs. serial processing, p. 190
Perception:
  brain damage and, pp. 188–189, 190
  color vision, pp. 191–192

feature detection, pp. 188–189
transduction, p. 185
visual information processing, pp. 185, 186–191
Perceptual organization, pp. 205–212
Personality and brain-imaging, p. 433
PET scans and obsessive-compulsive disorder, p. 519
Post-traumatic stress disorder and the limbic system, pp. 464–465
Prejudice (automatic) and the amygdala, p. 544
Psychosurgery: lobotomy, p. 519
Schizophrenia and brain abnormalities, pp. 483, 485
Sensation:
  body position and movement, p. 197
  hearing, pp. 193–195
  sensory adaptation, p. 184
  smell, pp. 202–204
  taste, pp. 201–202
  touch, p. 197
Sexual orientation, pp. 366–367
Sleep:
  memory and, p. 77
  recuperation during, p. 77
Smell and emotion, p. 204
Unconscious mind, p. 427

written with sensitivity to students' needs and interests. I aspire to help students understand and appreciate the wonder of important phenomena of their lives. I also want to convey the inquisitive spirit with which psychologists *do* psychology. The study of psychology, I believe, enhances our abilities to restrain intuition with critical thinking, judgmentalism with compassion, and illusion with understanding.

Believing with Henry David Thoreau that "Anything living is easily and naturally expressed in popular language," I seek to communicate psychology's scholarship with crisp narrative and vivid storytelling. Writing as a solo author, I hope to tell psychology's story in a way that is warmly personal as well as rigorously scientific. I love to reflect on connections between psychology and other realms, such as literature, philosophy, history, sports, religion, politics, and popular culture. And I love to provoke thought, to play with words, and to laugh.

Successful SQ3R Study Aids

1: *Exploring Psychology's* **complete system of learning aids includes numbered Preview Questions, which appear in this format throughout the book.**

Exploring Psychology has retained its popular system of study aids, integrated into an SQ3R structure that augments the narrative without disrupting it. Each chapter opens with a chapter outline that enables students to quickly *survey* its major topics. Numbered Preview *Questions* at the start of new major topics define the learning objectives that will guide students as they *read*. *Rehearse* It! quizzes at the end of major sections will stimulate students to rehearse what they have learned. These test items offer students an opportunity to review key ideas and to practice the multiple-choice test format. All **key terms** are defined in the margins for ready reference while students are being introduced to the new term in the narrative (see sample at right). Periodic Thinking Critically About and Close-Up boxes encourage development of critical thinking skills as well as application of the new concepts. The chapter-ending *Review* is structured as a set of answers to the numbered Preview Questions. Test for Success: Critical Thinking Exercises at the end of each chapter challenge students to think scientifically while reviewing the key concepts of the chapter. The Tips for Studying Psychology section at the end of Chapter 1 explains the SQ3R-based system of study aids, suggesting how students can *survey, question, read, rehearse,* and *review* the material for maximum retention.

----

key terms Look for complete definitions of important terms in the margin near their introduction in the narrative.

In the margins of this book, students will find interesting and informative review notes, and quotes from researchers and others that will encourage them to be active learners and apply what they are learning.

Goals for the Eighth Edition

Although supplemented by added story telling, this new edition retains its predecessor's voice and much of its content and organization. It also retains the goals— the guiding principles—that have animated the previous seven editions:

1. ***To exemplify the process of inquiry*** I strive to show students not just the outcome of research, but how the research process works. Throughout, the book tries to excite the reader's curiosity. It invites readers to imagine themselves as participants in classic experiments. Several chapters introduce research stories as mysteries that progressively unravel as one clue after another falls into place. (Chapter 2, for example, outlines the historical story of research on the brain's processing of language.)

2. ***To teach critical thinking*** By presenting research as intellectual detective work, I exemplify an inquiring, analytical mind-set. Whether students are studying development, cognition, or statistics, they will become involved in, and see the rewards of, critical reasoning. Moreover, they will discover how an empirical approach can help them evaluate competing ideas and claims for highly publicized phenomena—ranging from subliminal persuasion, ESP, and hypnosis to astrology, alternative therapies, and repressed and recovered memories.

3. ***To put facts in the service of concepts*** My intention is not to fill students' intellectual file drawers with facts, but to reveal psychology's major concepts— to teach students how to think, and to offer psychological ideas worth thinking about. In each chapter I place emphasis on those concepts I hope students will carry with them long after they complete the course. Always, I try to follow Albert Einstein's dictum that "everything should be made as simple as possible, but not simpler."

4. ***To be as up to date as possible*** Few things dampen students' interest as quickly as the sense that they are reading stale news. While retaining psychology's classic studies and concepts, I also present the discipline's most important recent developments. Nearly 482 references in this edition are dated 2007 or later.

5. ***To integrate principles and applications*** Throughout—by means of anecdotes, case histories, and the posing of hypothetical situations—I relate the findings of basic research to their applications and implications. Where psychology can illuminate pressing human issues—be they racism and sexism, health and happiness, or violence and war—I have not hesitated to shine its light.

6. ***To enhance comprehension by providing continuity*** Many chapters have a significant issue or theme that links subtopics, forming a thread that ties the chapter together. The Learning chapter conveys the idea that bold thinkers can serve as intellectual pioneers. The Thinking, Language, and Intelligence chapter raises the issue of human rationality and irrationality. The Psychological Disorders chapter conveys empathy for, and understanding of, troubled lives. "The uniformity of a work," observed Edward Gibbon, "denotes the hand of a single artist." Because the book has a single author, other threads, such as behavior genetics and cultural diversity, weave throughout the whole book, and students hear a consistent voice.

7. ***To reinforce learning at every step*** Everyday examples and rhetorical questions encourage students to process the material actively. Concepts presented earlier are frequently applied, and thereby reinforced, in later chapters. For instance, in Chapter 3, students learn that much of our information processing occurs *outside* of our conscious awareness. Ensuing chapters reinforce this concept. The SQ3R system of pedagogical aids augments learning without interrupting the text narrative. A marginal glossary helps students master important terminology. Major sections begin with numbered Preview Questions and end with Rehearse It sections for self-testing on key concepts. End-of-chapter reviews repeat the Preview Questions and answer them. And the end-of-chapter Test for Success: Critical Thinking Exercises invite students to review and apply key concepts in thought-provoking ways.

8. ***To convey respect for human unity and diversity*** Especially in Chapter 4, Nature, Nurture, and Human Diversity, but also throughout the book, readers will see evidence of our human kinship—our shared biological heritage, our common mechanisms of seeing and learning, hungering and feeling, loving and hating. They will also better understand the dimensions of our diversity—our *individual* diversity in development and aptitudes, temperament and personality, and disorders and health; and our *cultural* diversity in attitudes and expressive styles, child-rearing and care for the elderly, and life priorities.

What's New?

Despite the overarching continuity, there is change and updating on every page. I have introduced the following major changes to *Exploring Psychology,* Eighth Edition:

Increased Coverage of Cultural and Gender Diversity

This edition presents an even more thoroughly cross-cultural perspective on psychology (**TABLE 3**)—reflected in research findings and in text and photo examples. Coverage of the psychology of women and men is thoroughly integrated (see **TABLE 4** on the next page). In addition, I am working to offer a world-based psychology for our worldwide student readership. Thus, I continually search the world for research findings and text and photo examples, conscious that readers may be in Melbourne, Sheffield, Vancouver, or Nairobi. North American and European examples come easily, given that I reside in the United States, maintain contact with friends and colleagues in Canada, subscribe to several European periodicals, and live periodically in the U.K. This edition, for example, offers many dozens of Canadian, British, and Australian and New Zealand examples. We are all citizens of a shrinking world, thanks to increased migration and the growing global economy. Thus, American students, too, benefit from information and examples that internationalize their world-consciousness. And if psychology seeks to explain *human* behavior (not just American or Canadian or Australian behavior), the broader the scope of studies presented, the more accurate is our picture

TABLE 3   Culture and Multicultural Experience

*From Chapter 1 to Chapter 15, coverage of **culture and multicultural experience** can be found on the following pages:*

Aggression, p. 551
AIDS, pp. 300, 404–405
Anger, p. 390
Animal research ethics, pp. 26–27
Attraction:
  love and marriage, p. 560
  speed-dating, p. 555
Attractiveness, p. 116
Attribution, political effects of, p. 527
Body ideal, p. 348
Complementary/alternative medicine, p. 406
Conformity, pp. 532, 534
Corporal punishment practices, p. 242
Cultural norms, pp. 122, 130, 132
Culture:
  context effects, p. 217
  definition, p. 121
  and the self, pp. 123–124
  shock, pp. 122, 401
Deaf culture, pp. 56, 60, 303, 304–305, 311
Development:
  adolescence, p. 155
  attachment, pp. 151–152
  child-rearing, p. 125
  cognitive development, p. 148
  moral development, p. 158
  similarities, pp. 125–126
  social development, p. 152
Drugs:
  psychological effects of, p. 88
  use of, p. 99

Emotion:
  emotion-detecting ability, pp. 383–384
  experiencing, p. 390
  expressing, pp. 385, 386–388
Enemy perceptions, p. 565
Fear, p. 299
Flynn effect, p. 323
Fundamental attribution error, p. 526
Gender:
  roles, p. 130
  social power, p. 127
Grief, expressing, p. 172
Happiness, pp. 395–396
Hindsight bias, p. 10
History of psychology, pp. 1–4
Homosexuality, views on, p. 16
Human diversity/kinship, pp. 25–26, 121–123
Identity, forming a social, p. 159
Individualism/collectivism, pp. 123–124
Intelligence, pp. 313, 329–330, 331–332
  bias, pp. 333–334
  nutrition and, pp. 331–332
Language, pp. 121, 302, 303, 306–307
  monolingual/bilingual, p. 307
Leaving the nest, p. 162
Life satisfaction, pp. 393–395
Life-span and well-being, pp. 170–171

Marriage, p. 169
Mating preferences, p. 116
Meditation, pp. 412–413
Memory encoding, p. 264
Mental illness rate, pp. 488–489
Motivation: hierarchy of needs, p. 342
Need to belong, pp. 369–371
Neurotransmitters: curare, p. 39
Obesity, pp. 347–350, 353–354
Obesity guidance/counseling, p. 350
Observational learning: television and aggression, p. 251
Optimism and health, p. 409
Organ donation, p. 301
Pace of life, pp. 17, 122
Pain, perception of, p. 200
Parapsychology, p. 218
Parent and peer relationships, pp. 160–161
Peacemaking and:
  conciliation, pp. 566–567
  contact, p. 565
  cooperation, p. 566
Peer influence, p. 120
Personal space, p. 122
Personality, p. 440
Prejudice, pp. 23, 28, 542–547
Psychological disorders:
  antisocial personality disorder, p. 488
  cultural norms, p. 454
  depression, pp. 473, 478

  dissociative personality disorder, p. 469
  eating disorders, pp. 348, 456
  rates of, p. 453
  schizophrenia, pp. 456, 483–484
  somatoform, p. 468
  suicide, p. 474
  susto, p. 456
  taijin-kyofusho, p. 456
Psychotherapy:
  culture and values in, p. 511
  EMDR training, p. 508
Puberty and adult independence, p. 162
Self-esteem, p. 396
Self-serving bias, p. 448
Sex drive, p. 115
Sexual orientation, pp. 363–364
Similarities, pp. 114–115
Social clock, pp. 168–169
Social-cultural perspective, p. 7
Social loafing, p. 538
Spirituality: Israeli kibbutz communities, pp. 414–415
Stress:
  adjusting to a new culture, p. 401
  racism and, p. 401
Taste preferences, pp. 346–347
Teen sexuality, pp. 361–362
Testing bias, pp. 333–334

See also Chapter 15, Social Psychology, pp. 525–570

TABLE 4 The Psychology of Men and Women

*Coverage of the **psychology of men and women** can be found on the following pages:*

ADHD, p. 455

Adulthood: physical changes, pp. 164–166

Aggression, pp. 549–553
  and pornography, pp. 551–553
  and rape, pp. 552–553
  and spousal abuse, pp. 549–550

Alcohol:
  addiction and, p. 90
  sexual aggression and, p. 91
  use, pp. 90–91

Antisocial personality disorder, p. 486

Attraction, pp. 555–558

Autism, p. 146

Behavioral effects of gender, p. 26

Biological predispositions, and the color red, p. 234

Biological sex/gender, p. 129

Bipolar disorder, p. 472

Body image, p. 349

Color vision, p. 191

Conformity: obedience, p. 535

Dating, p. 555

Depression, pp. 470–471, 472–473, 477

Dream content, p. 80

Drug use:
  biological influences, p. 98
  psychological/social-cultural influences, p. 99

Eating disorders, pp. 348–349

Emotion-detecting ability, pp. 328–329, 385–386

Empty nest, p. 170

Father care, pp. 151–152, 362

Freud's views:
  evaluating, p. 426
  identification/gender identity, p. 422
  Oedipus/Electra complexes, p. 422
  penis envy, p. 424

Gender:
  and anxiety, p. 462
  and child-rearing, pp. 131, 348
  development, pp. 126–131
  prejudice, pp. 542–543
  roles, p. 130
  similarities/differences, pp. 126–128

Gendered brain, pp. 129, 360, 368

Generic pronoun "he", p. 307

Grief, p. 172

Group polarization, p. 539

Happiness, p. 397

Hormones and:
  aggression, p. 549
  sexual behavior, pp. 358–359
  sexual development, pp. 129, 155–157

testosterone-replacement therapy, p. 359

Intelligence, pp. 328–331
  bias, p. 333
  low extreme, p. 322

Life expectancy, pp. 126–127

Losing weight, p. 355

Marriage, pp. 169–170, 409–410

Maturation, pp. 155–157

Menarche, p. 155

Menopause, p. 164

Midlife crisis, p. 168

Obesity and:
  genetic factors, p. 353
  guidance/counseling, p. 350
  health risks, p. 350
  ingested calories, p. 354
  weight discrimination, pp. 350–351

Observational learning:
  sexually violent media, p. 253
  TV's influence, p. 251

Pornography, p. 360

Post-traumatic stress disorder: development of, p. 465

Prejudice, pp. 542–545

Psychological disorders, rates of, p. 489

Religious involvement and: life expectancy, p. 414

REM sleep, arousal in, p. 74

Romantic love, pp. 559–560

Savant syndrome, p. 315

Schizophrenia, pp. 481–482

Sexual abuse, p. 115

Sexual attraction, pp. 115–117

Sexual disorders, p. 358

Sexual fantasies, p. 360

Sexual orientation, pp. 363–368

Sexuality, pp. 357–362
  adolescent, pp. 361–362
  evolutionary explanation, pp. 115–117
  external stimuli, p. 360

Sleep, p. 75

Stereotyping, p. 217

Stress:
  and depression, p. 403
  and heart disease, p. 402
  and HIV, p. 405
  and the immune system, p. 403
  response, p. 399

Suicide, p. 474

Women in psychology, pp. 2–3

See also Chapter 15, Social Psychology, pp. 525–570

of this world's people. My aim is to expose all students to the world beyond their own culture. Thus, I continue to welcome input and suggestions from all readers. *Chapter 4, Nature, Nurture, and Human Diversity,* encourages students to appreciate cultural and gender differences and commonalities, and to consider the interplay of nature and nurture.

Many new photos showcase the diversity of cultures within North America, as well as across the globe. In addition to significant cross-cultural examples and research presented within the narrative, these new photos and their informative captions freshen each chapter and broaden students' perspectives in applying psychological science to their own world and to the worlds across the globe.

Emphasis on the Biological-Psychological-Social/Cultural Levels of Analysis Approach in Psychology

This edition systematically includes coverage of the biological, psychological, and social-cultural influences on our behavior. A significant section in Chapter 1 introduces the levels-of-analysis approach, setting the stage for future chapters, and levels-of-analysis figures in many chapters help students understand concepts in the biopsychosocial context.

Greater Sensitivity to the Clinical Perspective

With helpful guidance from clinical psychologist colleagues, I have become more mindful of the clinical angle on various concepts within psychology, which has sensitized and improved the Personality, Psychological Disorders, and Therapy chapters, among others. For example, the Emotions, Stress, and Health chapter now covers problem-focused and emotion-focused coping strategies, and the Thinking, Language, and Intelligence chapter describes some possible uses of intelligence-test results in clinical settings.

New Teaching and Learning Resources

Our supplements and media have been celebrated for their quality, abundance, and accuracy. The package available for *Exploring Psychology*, Eighth Edition, raises the bar even higher with PsychPortal, which includes an interactive eBook, a suite of interactive components, the powerful Online Study Center, the Video Tool Kit for Introductory Psychology, and the *Scientific American* News Feed. PsychPortal also enables instructors to monitor their students' engagement with its learning tools. See page xxii for details.

Enhanced Critical Thinking Coverage

I aim to introduce students to critical thinking in a natural way throughout the book, with even more in the narrative that encourages active learning of psychology's key concepts. The eighth edition includes the following opportunities for students to learn or practice their critical thinking skills.

- *NEW Test for Success: Critical Thinking Exercises,* contributed by Amy Himsel (El Camino College) and appearing at the end of each chapter, offer students an excellent opportunity to check their understanding of key concepts in the chapter, while learning and practicing critical thinking.
- *Chapter 1 takes a unique, critical thinking approach to introducing students to psychology's research methods,* emphasizing the fallacies of our everyday intuition and common sense and, thus, the need for psychological science. *Critical thinking* is introduced as a key term in this chapter.
- *"Thinking Critically About . . ." boxes* are found throughout the book, modeling for students a critical approach to some key issues in psychology. Chapter 11, for example, has an updated box, Thinking Critically About: The Fear Factor—Do We Fear the Right Things?
- *Detective-style stories* throughout the narrative get students thinking critically about psychology's key research questions.
- *"Apply this"* and *"Think about it"* style discussions keep students active in their study of each chapter.
- *Critical examinations of pop psychology* spark interest and provide important lessons in thinking critically about everyday topics.
- **Appendix A: Statistical Reasoning in Everyday Life** encourages students to focus on thinking smarter by applying simple statistical principles to everyday reasoning.

See **TABLE 5** for a complete list of this text's coverage of critical thinking topics and Thinking Critically About boxes.

APA Learning Goals and Outcomes for Psychology Majors

In March 2002, an American Psychological Association (APA) Task Force created a set of Learning Goals and Outcomes for students graduating with psychology majors from four-year schools (www.apa.org/ed/pcue/reports.html). Psychology departments in many schools have since used these goals and outcomes to help them establish their own benchmarks. Some instructors are eager to know whether a given text for the introductory course helps students get a good start at achieving these goals. *Exploring Psychology*, Eighth Edition, will work nicely to help you begin to address these goals in your department. See www.worthpublishers.com/myers for a detailed guide to how *Exploring Psychology*, Eighth Edition, corresponds to the APA Learning Goals and Outcomes.

TABLE 5	Critical Thinking and Research Emphasis

Critical thinking coverage, and in-depth stories of psychology's *scientific research* process, can be found on the following pages:

Thinking Critically About . . . **boxes:**

The Fear Factor—Do We Fear the Right Things?, pp. 298–299

Lie Detection, p. 380

Complementary and Alternative Medicine, p. 406

How to Be a "Successful" Astrologer or Palm Reader, pp. 434–435

ADHD—Normal High Energy or Genuine Disorder?, p. 455

Insanity and Responsibility, p. 461

Critical Examinations of Pop Psychology:

Why do psychology?, pp. 9–13

Perceiving order in random events, pp. 20–21

Do we use only 10 percent of our brains?, p. 53

Can hypnosis enhance recall? Coerce action? Be therapeutic? Alleviate pain?, pp. 84–86

Has the concept of "addiction" been stretched too far?, pp. 88–89

Near–death experiences, pp. 95–96

Critiquing the evolutionary perspective, p. 117

How much credit (or blame) do parents deserve?, pp. 119–120

Is there extrasensory perception?, pp. 218–220

How valid is the Rorschach test?, pp. 425–426

Is repression a myth?, pp. 426–427

Is Freud credible?, pp. 426–428

Is psychotherapy effective?, pp. 505–507

Evaluating alternative therapies, pp. 507–509

Do video games teach or release violence?, p. 552

Thinking Critically With Psychological Science:

The limits of intuition and common sense, pp. 10–11

The scientific attitude, pp. 11–13

"Critical thinking" introduced as a key term, p. 13

The scientific method, pp. 14–15

Correlation and causation, pp. 18–19

Illusory correlation, pp. 19–20

Exploring cause and effect, pp. 21–22

Random assignment, pp. 22–23

Independent and dependent variables, pp. 23–24

Statistical reasoning, Appendix A, pp. A-1–A-7

Describing data, pp. A-1–A-6

Making inferences, pp. A-6–A-7

Scientific Detective Stories:

Is breast milk better than formula?, pp. 21–23

Our divided brains, pp. 57–60

Why do we sleep?, pp. 75–78

Why do we dream?, pp. 81–83

Is hypnosis an extension of normal consciousness or an altered state?, pp. 86–87

Twin and adoption studies, pp. 106–110

How a child's mind develops, pp. 142–148

Aging and intelligence, pp. 167–168

Parallel processing, pp. 190–191

How do we see in color?, pp. 191–192

How do we store memories in our brains?, pp. 267–272

How are memories constructed?, pp. 281–286

Do animals exhibit language?, pp. 311–313

Why do we feel hunger?, pp. 344–346

What determines sexual orientation?, pp. 364–368

The pursuit of happiness: Who is happy, and why?, pp. 391–397

Why—and in whom—does stress contribute to heart disease?, pp. 402–403

How and why is social support linked with health?, pp. 409–410

Self-esteem versus self-serving bias, pp. 447–449

What causes mood disorders?, pp. 472–480

Do prenatal viral infections increase risk of schizophrenia?, pp. 483–484

Is psychotherapy effective?, pp. 505–506

Why do people fail to help in emergencies?, pp. 561–563

Innovative Multimedia Supplements Package

Exploring Psychology boasts impressive electronic and print supplements titles. For more information about any of these titles, visit Worth Publishers' online catalog at worthpublishers.com.

PsychPortal

Integrating the best online material that Worth has to offer, PsychPortal is an innovative learning space that combines a powerful quizzing engine with unparalleled media resources (see **FIGURE 1**). PsychPortal conveniently offers all the functionality you need to support your online or hybrid course. Yet it is flexible, customizable, and simple enough to enhance your traditional course—and it enables you to track your students' engagement. The following interactive learning materials contained within PsychPortal make it truly unique:

- ***An interactive eBook*** allows students to highlight, bookmark, and make their own notes just as they would with a printed textbook.
- Tom Ludwig's (Hope College) suite of interactive media—**PsychSim 5.0** and the new **Concepts in Action**—bring key concepts to life.
- ***The Online Study Center*** combines PsychPortal's powerful assessment engine with Worth's unparalleled collection of interactive study resources. Based on their quiz results, students receive Personalized Study Plans directing them to sections in the book and also to simulations, animations, links, and tutorials that will help them succeed in mastering the concepts. Instructors can access reports indicating their students' strengths and weaknesses (based on

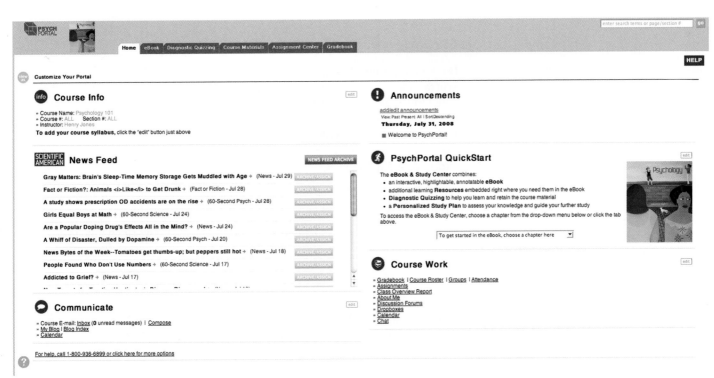

FIGURE 1
PsychPortal opening page

class quiz results) and browse suggestions for helpful presentation materials (from Worth's renowned videos and demonstrations) to focus their teaching efforts accordingly.

- *Video Tool Kit* includes more than 100 engaging video modules that instructors can easily assign, assess, and customize for their students (**FIGURE 2**). Videos cover classic experiments, current news footage, and cutting-edge research, all of which are sure to spark discussion and encourage critical thinking.
- **Scientific American** *News Feed* highlights current behavioral research.

FIGURE 2
Sample from our Video Tool Kit

Creating False Memories A Laboratory Study

1. After a week of being asked about the false photo, what percent of students recalled having had a hot-air balloon ride?

- a. 15
- b. 35
- c. 50
- d. 75

Additional Student Media

- Book Companion Site
- Worth eBook for *Exploring Psychology*
- The Online Study Center
- 60-Second Psych (*Scientific American* podcasts)
- Psych2Go (audio downloads for study and review)
- PsychSim 5.0 (on CD-ROM)
- Video Tool Kit (online)

Course Management

- Enhanced Course Management Solutions for users of WebCT, Blackboard, Desire2Learn, and Angel.

Assessment

- Printed Test Bank, Volumes 1 and 2
- Diploma Computerized Test Bank
- i•Clicker Radio Frequency Classroom Response System

Presentation

- ActivePsych: Classroom Activities Project and Video Teaching Modules (including Worth's *Digital Media Archive,* Second Edition, and *Scientific American Frontiers* Video Collection, Third Edition)
- Instructor's Resources CD-ROM
- Worth's Image and Lecture Gallery at worthpublishers.com/ilg

Video Resources

- Instructor's Video Tool Kit
- Moving Images: Exploring Psychology Through Film
- Worth *Digital Media Archive*
- *Psychology: The Human Experience* Teaching Modules
- *The Many Faces of Psychology* Video
- *Scientific American Frontiers* Video Collection, Second Edition
- *The Mind* Video Teaching Modules, Second Edition
- *The Brain* Video Teaching Modules, Second Edition

Print Resources

- Instructor's Resources and Lecture Guides
- Instructor's Media Guide for Introductory Psychology
- Study Guide
- *Pursuing Human Strengths: A Positive Psychology Guide*
- *Critical Thinking Companion,* Second Edition

Scientific American Resources

- *Scientific American Mind*
- *Scientific American Reader to Accompany Myers*
- *Improving the Mind and Brain: A Scientific American Special Issue*
- *Scientific American Explores the Hidden Mind: A Collector's Edition*

In Appreciation

If it is true that "whoever walks with the wise becomes wise" then I am wiser for all the wisdom and advice received from expert colleagues. Aided by nearly a thousand consultants and reviewers over the last two decades, this has become a better, more accurate book than one author alone (this author, at least) could write. As my editors and I keep reminding ourselves, all of us together are smarter than any one of us.

My indebtedness continues to each of the teacher-scholars whose influence I acknowledged in the seven previous editions, and also to the innumerable researchers who have been so willing to share their time and talent to help me accurately report their research.

My gratitude extends to the colleagues who contributed criticism, corrections, and creative ideas related to the content, pedagogy, and format of this new edition and its supplements package. For their expertise and encouragement, and the gifts of their time to the teaching of psychology, I thank

Kerm Almos,
Capital University

Grace Austin,
Sacramento City College

Cynthia Bane,
Wartburg College

Arthur L. Beaman,
University of Kentucky

Rochelle Bergstrom,
Minnesota State University, Moorhead

Joan Warmbold Boggs,
Oakton Community College

Megan E. Bradley,
Frostburg State University

Gregory Braswell,
Illinois State University

Ray Brogan,
Northern Virginia Community College

Kelly Charlton,
University of North Carolina at Pembroke

Kathy Coiner,
Scott Community College

Perry Collins,
Wayland Baptist University

Daniel Collison,
Muskegon Community College

Verne C. Cox,
University of Texas, Arlington

Damien Cronin,
Lake Superior College

Patricia Crowe,
Hawkeye Community College

Alice Davidson,
Rollins College

Mark W. Davis,
Northwestern Oklahoma State University

Jessica Michelle Dennis,
California State University, Los Angeles

Anne Duran,
California State University, Bakersfield

Andrea Ericksen,
San Juan College

Kim D. Felsenthal,
Berkeley College

Jan L. Fertig,
Milwaukee School of Engineering

Lisa Fozio-Thielk,
Waubonsee Community College

Patricia A. Giacomini,
Springfield College/Benedictine University

Jay Green,
Tarrant County College, NW Campus

C. Dominik Guess,
University of North Florida

Diane M. Hall,
Bay Path College

Toni Harris,
Virginia State University

Sarah E. Henseler,
St. Edward's University

Charles J. Huffman,
James Madison University

Matthew I. Isaak,
University of Louisiana at Lafayette

Jerwen Jou,
University of Texas, Pan American

Min Ju,
SUNY New Paltz

Franz Klutschkowski,
North Central Texas College

Melinda A. Leonard,
University of Louisville

Bernard H. Levin,
Blue Ridge Community College

Miriam Liss,
University of Mary Washington

Peter Marcus,
Borough of Manhattan Community College, CUNY

J. Trevor Milliron,
Lee University

Fabian Novello,
Clark State Community College

Fawn Oates,
Red Rocks Community College

Susan L. O'Donnell,
George Fox University

Roberta Paley,
Fashion Institute of Technology

Jeanne A. Phelps,
Missouri State University

John Pierce,
Philadelphia University

Matthew A. Poinsett,
Eastern Michigan University

Jim Previte,
Victor Valley College

Mark Prokosch,
Elon University

Christopher K. Randall,
Kennesaw State University

Randall Russac,
University of North Florida

Patricia Santoro,
Frostburg State University

Aubrey Shoemaker,
Walters State Community College

Christopher L. Smith,
Tyler Junior College

Roy H. Smith,
University of Mary Washington

Nancy Smuckler,
University of Wisconsin, Milwaukee

Gail Stewart,
Pierce College, Puyallup

Kevin W. Sumrall,
Lone Star College, Montgomery

Jean Twenge,
San Diego State University

Michael A. Vandehey,
Midwestern State University

Gail Vivian,
Holyoke Community College

Katrina L. Walker,
Virginia State University

Teresa Watters,
Mount Ida College/Queens University

At Worth Publishers a host of people played key roles in creating this eighth edition.

Although the information gathering is never-ending, the formal planning began as the author-publisher team gathered for a two-day retreat in June 2007. This happy and creative gathering included John Brink, Martin Bolt, Thomas Ludwig, Richard Straub, and me from the author team, along with my assistants Kathryn Brownson and Sara Neevel. We were joined by Worth Publishers executives Tom Scotty, Elizabeth Widdicombe, and Catherine Woods; editors Christine Brune, Kevin Feyen, Nancy Fleming, Tracey Kuehn, Betty Probert, and Peter Twickler; artistic director Babs Reingold; and sales and marketing colleagues Kate Nurre, Tom Kling, Guy Geraghty, Sandy Manly, Amy Shefferd, Rich Rosenlof, and Brendan Baruth. The input and brainstorming during this meeting of minds gave birth, among other things, to the thoroughly revised Chapter 3, Consciousness and the Two-Track Mind.

Christine Brune, chief editor, is a wonder worker. She offers just the right mix of encouragement, gentle admonition, attention to detail, and passion for excellence. An author could not ask for more.

Development editor Nancy Fleming is one of those rare editors who is gifted both at "thinking big" about a chapter while also applying her sensitive, graceful, line-by-line touches. Senior Psychology Acquisitions Editor Kevin Feyen has become a valued team leader, thanks to his dedication, creativity, and sensitivity. Publisher Catherine Woods helped construct and execute the plan for this text and its supplements. Sharon Prevost and Andrea Musick coordinated production of the huge supplements package for this edition. Betty Probert efficiently edited and produced the print supplements and, in the process, also helped fine-tune the whole

What Is Psychology?

1: What are some important milestones in the development of the science of psychology?[1]

Psychology's Roots

Once upon a time, on a planet in this neighborhood of the universe, there came to be people. Soon thereafter, these creatures became intensely interested in themselves and in one another: "Who are we? What produces our thoughts? Our feelings? Our actions? And how are we to understand and manage those around us?"

Psychological Science Is Born

To be human is to be curious about ourselves and the world around us. Before 300 B.C.E., the Greek naturalist and philosopher Aristotle (384–322 B.C.E.) theorized about learning and memory, motivation and emotion, perception and personality. Today we chuckle at some of his guesses, like his suggestion that a meal makes us sleepy by causing gas and heat to collect around the source of our personality, the heart. But credit Aristotle with asking the right questions.

Philosophers' thinking about thinking continued until the birth of psychology as we know it, on a December day in 1879, in a small, third-floor room at Germany's University of Leipzig. There, two young men were helping an austere, middle-aged professor, Wilhelm Wundt, create an experimental apparatus. Their machine measured the time lag between people's hearing a ball hit a platform and their pressing a telegraph key (Hunt, 1993). Curiously, people responded in about one-tenth of a second when asked to press the key as soon as the sound occurred—and in about two-tenths of a second when asked to press the key as soon as they were consciously aware of perceiving the sound. (To be aware of one's awareness takes a little longer.) Wundt was seeking to measure "atoms of the mind"—the fastest and simplest mental processes. Thus began what many consider psychology's first experiment, launching the first psychological laboratory, staffed by Wundt and psychology's first graduate students.

This young science of psychology developed from the more established fields of philosophy and biology. Wundt was both a philosopher and a physiologist. Ivan Pavlov, who pioneered the study of learning, was a Russian physiologist. Sigmund Freud, who developed an influential theory of personality, was an Austrian physician. Jean Piaget, the last century's most influential observer of children, was a Swiss biologist. William James, author of an important 1890 textbook, was an American philosopher. This list of pioneering psychologists—"Magellans of the mind," as Morton Hunt (1993) has called them—illustrates psychology's origins in many disciplines and countries.

As these names illustrate, the early pioneers of most fields, including psychology, were predominantly men. When James' student Mary Calkins completed all the requirements for a Harvard Ph.D., outscoring all the male students on their exams, Harvard denied her the degree she had earned, offering her instead a degree from Radcliffe College, its undergraduate sister school for women. Although Calkins resisted the unequal treatment and refused the degree, she went on to become the American Psychological Association's (APA's) first female president in 1905. Margaret Floy Washburn became the first woman to receive a psychology Ph.D. and, in 1921, the second to be elected an APA president.

Information sources are cited in parentheses, with name and date. Every citation can be found in the end-of-book References, with complete documentation that follows American Psychological Association style.

[1] A Preview Question appears at the beginning of major chapter sections. Search actively for the answer to the question as you read through the section. Later, you can check your understanding by taking a Rehearse It! quiz and by reading the numbered Chapter Review at the end of the chapter.

Hoping to satisfy their curiosity about people and to remedy their own woes, millions turn to "psychology." They listen to talk-radio counseling, read articles on psychic powers, and attend stop-smoking hypnosis seminars. Searching for the meaning of dreams, the path to ecstatic love, and the roots of personal happiness, they consult self-help Web sites, popular books, magazines, and TV.

Others, intrigued by claims of psychological truth, wonder: Do mothers and infants bond in the first hours after birth? Should we trust childhood sexual abuse memories that get "recovered" in adulthood—and prosecute the alleged predators? Are first-born children more driven to achieve? Does psychotherapy heal?

For many people, psychologists are folks who analyze personality, offer counseling, and dispense child-rearing advice. Do they? Yes, and much more. Consider some of psychology's questions that from time to time you may wonder about:

A smile is a smile the world around Throughout this book, you will see examples not only of our cultural and gender diversity but also of the similarities that define our shared human nature. People in different cultures vary in when and how often they smile, but a naturally happy smile *means* the same thing anywhere in the world.

- Have you ever found yourself reacting to something as one of your biological parents would—perhaps in a way you vowed you never would—and then wondered how much of your personality you inherited? *To what extent are person-to-person differences in personality predisposed by our genes? To what extent by our home and community environments?*
- Have you ever worried about how to act among people of a different culture, race, or gender? *In what ways are we alike as members of the human family? How do we differ?*
- Have you ever awakened from a nightmare and, with a wave of relief, wondered why you had such a crazy dream? *How often, and why, do we dream?*
- Have you ever played peekaboo with a 6-month-old and wondered why the baby finds the game so delightful? The infant reacts as though, when you momentarily move behind a door, you actually disappear—only to reappear later out of thin air. *What do babies actually perceive and think?*
- Have you ever wondered what leads to school and work success? Are some people just born smarter? *Does sheer intelligence explain why some people get richer, think more creatively, or relate more sensitively?*
- Have you ever become depressed or anxious, perhaps over a lost job during the recent economic crash, and wondered whether you'll ever feel "normal"? *What triggers our bad moods—and our good ones?*

Such questions provide grist for psychology's mill, because psychology is a science that seeks to answer all sorts of questions about us all—how and why we think, feel, and act as we do.

"I have made a ceaseless effort not to ridicule, not to bewail, not to scorn human actions, but to understand them."

—Benedict Spinoza,
A Political Treatise, 1677

Chapter Outline

- **What Is Psychology?**
  Psychology's Roots
  Contemporary Psychology

- **Why Do Psychology?**
  What About Intuition and
    Common Sense?
  The Scientific Attitude
  Critical Thinking

- **How Do Psychologists Ask
  and Answer Questions?**
  The Scientific Method
  Description
  Correlation
  Experimentation

- **Frequently Asked
  Questions About
  Psychology**

- **Tips for Studying
  Psychology**

book. Lorraine Klimowich, with help from Greg Bennetts, provided invaluable support in commissioning and organizing the multitude of reviews, mailing information to professors, and handling numerous other daily tasks related to the book's development and production. Lee Ann McKevitt and Paul Lacy did a splendid job of laying out each page. Bianca Moscatelli and Donna Ranieri worked together to locate the myriad photos.

Associate Managing Editor Tracey Kuehn displayed tireless tenacity, commitment, and impressive organization in leading Worth's gifted artistic production team and coordinating editorial input throughout the production process. Project Editor Leigh Renhard and Production Manager Sarah Segal masterfully kept the book to its tight schedule, and Babs Reingold skillfully directed creation of the beautiful new design and art program. Production Manager Stacey Alexander, along with supplements production editor Jenny Chiu, did their usual excellent work of producing the many supplements.

To achieve our goal of supporting the teaching of psychology, this teaching package not only must be authored, reviewed, edited, and produced, but also made available to teachers of psychology. For their exceptional success in doing that, our author team is grateful to Worth Publishers' professional sales and marketing team. We are especially grateful to Executive Marketing Manager Kate Nurre, Marketing Manager Amy Shefferd, and National Psychology and Economics Consultant Tom Kling both for their tireless efforts to inform our teaching colleagues of our efforts to assist their teaching, and for the joy of working with them.

At Hope College, the supporting team members for this edition included Kathryn Brownson, who researched countless bits of information, proofed hundreds of pages, and updated all the cross-reference tables in this Preface. Kathryn has become a knowledgeable and sensitive adviser on many matters, and Sara Neevel has become our high-tech manuscript developer, *par excellence*.

Again, I gratefully acknowledge the influence and editing assistance of my writing coach, poet Jack Ridl, whose influence resides in the voice you will be hearing in the pages that follow. He, more than anyone, cultivated my delight in dancing with the language, and taught me to approach writing as a craft that shades into art.

After hearing countless dozens of people say that this book's supplements have taken their teaching to a new level, I reflect on how fortunate I am to be a part of a team in which everyone has produced on-time work marked by the highest professional standards. For their remarkable talents, their long-term dedication, and their friendship, I thank Martin Bolt (Instructor's Resources), John Brink (Test Bank), Thomas Ludwig (PsychPortal, etc.), and Richard Straub (Study Guide).

Finally, my gratitude extends to the many students and instructors who have written to offer suggestions, or just an encouraging word. It is for them, and those about to begin their study of psychology, that I have done my best to introduce the field I love.

The day this book went to press was the day I started gathering information and ideas for the ninth edition. Your input will again influence how this book continues to evolve. So, please, do share your thoughts.

David Myers

Hope College
Holland, Michigan 49422-9000 USA
davidmyers.org

Wilhelm Wundt Wundt (far left) established the first psychology laboratory at the University of Leipzig, Germany.

Sigmund Freud The controversial ideas of this famed personality theorist and therapist have influenced many people's self-understanding.

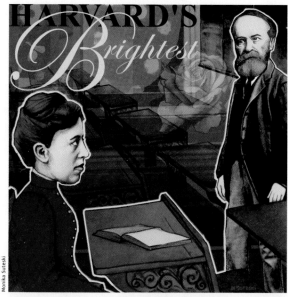

William James and Mary Whiton Calkins James, legendary teacher-writer, mentored Calkins, who became a pioneering memory researcher and the first woman to be president of the American Psychological Association.

Margaret Floy Washburn The first woman to receive a psychology Ph.D., Washburn synthesized animal behavior research in *The Animal Mind*.

The rest of the story of psychology—the subject of this book—develops at many levels. With activities ranging from the study of nerve cell activity to the study of international conflicts, *psychology* is not easily defined.

In psychology's early days, *introspection*—focusing on inner sensations, images, and feelings—was common. Wundt used this approach, as did James in his examination of the stream of consciousness and of emotion. Freud emphasized the ways emotional responses to childhood experiences and our unconscious thought processes affect our behavior. Thus, until the 1920s, *psychology* was defined as "the science of mental life."

Throughout the text, important concepts are **boldfaced.** *As you study, you can find these terms with their definitions in a nearby margin and in the Glossary at the end of the book.*

behaviorism the view that psychology (1) should be an objective science that (2) studies behavior without reference to mental processes. Most research psychologists today agree with (1) but not with (2).

humanistic psychology historically significant perspective that emphasized the growth potential of healthy people and the individual's potential for personal growth.

cognitive neuroscience the interdisciplinary study of the brain activity linked with cognition (including perception, thinking, memory, and language).

psychology the science of behavior and mental processes.

nature-nurture issue the longstanding controversy over the relative contributions that genes and experience make to the development of psychological traits and behaviors. Today's science sees traits and behaviors arising from the interaction of nature and nurture.

From the 1920s into the 1960s, American psychologists, initially led by flamboyant and provocative John B. Watson and later by the equally provocative B. F. Skinner, dismissed introspection and redefined *psychology* as "the scientific study of observable behavior." After all, said these **behaviorists,** science is rooted in observation. You cannot observe a sensation, a feeling, or a thought, but you *can* observe and record people's *behavior* as they respond to different situations.

Humanistic psychology rebelled against both behaviorism and Freudian psychology. Pioneers Carl Rogers and Abraham Maslow found behaviorism's focus on learned behaviors too mechanic. And rather than focusing on the meaning of early childhood memories, as a psychoanalyst might, the humanistic psychologists emphasized the importance of current environmental influences on our growth potential, and the importance of having our needs for love and acceptance satisfied.

In the 1960s, another movement emerged as psychology began to recapture its initial interest in mental processes. This *cognitive revolution* supported ideas developed by earlier psychologists, such as the importance of how our mind processes and retains information. Cognitive psychology and more recently **cognitive neuroscience** (the study of brain activity linked with mental activity) have also suggested new ways to understand and treat psychological disorders.

To encompass psychology's concern with observable behavior *and* with inner thoughts and feelings, today we define **psychology** as the *science of behavior and mental processes.*

Let's unpack this definition. *Behavior* is anything an organism *does*—any action we can observe and record. Yelling, smiling, blinking, sweating, talking, and questionnaire marking are all observable behaviors. *Mental processes* are subjective experiences: sensations, perceptions, dreams, thoughts, beliefs, and feelings.

The key word in psychology's definition is *science.* Psychology, as I will emphasize throughout this book, is less a set of findings than a way of asking and answering questions. My aim, then, is not merely to report results but also to show you how psychologists play their game. You will see how researchers evaluate conflicting opinions and ideas. And you will learn how all of us, whether scientists or simply curious people, can think smarter when describing and explaining the events of our lives.

John B. Watson and Rosalie Rayner Working with Rayner, Watson championed psychology as the science of behavior. Together, they demonstrated conditioned responses on a baby who became famous as "Little Albert."

B. F. Skinner A leading behaviorist, Skinner rejected introspection and studied how consequences shape behavior.

Contemporary Psychology

Like its pioneers, today's psychologists are citizens of many lands. The International Union of Psychological Science has 69 member nations, from Albania to Zimbabwe. Across the world, psychologists have wrestled with many issues, viewing behavior from the differing perspectives offered by the subfields in which they teach, work, and do research.

Psychology's Biggest Question

2: What is psychology's historic big issue?

Psychology's biggest and most persistent issue (and the focus of Chapter 3) has been the **nature-nurture issue**—*the controversy over the relative contributions of biology and experience to the development of our traits and behaviors:* Do our human traits develop through experience, or are we born with them?

The nature-nurture debate weaves a thread from the ancient Greeks' time to our own. Philosopher Plato (428–348 B.C.E.) assumed that character and intelligence are largely inherited and that certain ideas are inborn. Aristotle countered that there is nothing in the mind that does not first come in from the external world through the senses. Today's psychologists explore the issue by asking, for example:

- Are gender differences (the characteristics people associate with male and female) biologically predisposed or socially constructed?
- Is children's grammar mostly innate or formed by experience?
- How are differences in intelligence and personality influenced by heredity and by environment?
- Are sexual behaviors more "pushed" by inner biology or "pulled" by external incentives?
- Should we treat psychological disorders—depression, for example—as disorders of the brain, disorders of thought, or both?

Such debates continue. Yet over and over again we will see that in contemporary science the nature-nurture tension dissolves: *Nurture works on what nature endows.* Our species is biologically endowed with an enormous capacity to learn and adapt. Moreover, every psychological event (every thought, every emotion) is simultaneously a biological event. Thus, depression can be both a brain disorder and a thought disorder.

Global psychology Psychology is growing and it is globalizing. Today's psychologists are citizens of many lands—69 lands, according to the International Union of Psychological Science. Their number is mushrooming. In China, for example, 5 universities had psychology departments in 1985; by the last century's end, there were 40 (Zhang & Xu, 2006). And worldwide, ideas are working their way across borders now more than ever, as happened in 2007 at this international psychology conference in India. "We are moving rapidly toward a single world of psychological science," reported Robert Bjork (2000).

For more of the important developments in psychology's history, see the Timeline inside the front and back covers.

A nature-made nature-nurture experiment Identical twins *(left)* share the same genes and, usually, the same environment. Fraternal twins *(right)* usually share the same environment but not the same genes. These differences make twins ideal participants in studies of hereditary and environmental influences on intelligence, personality, and other traits. Twin studies provide a rich array of findings—described in later chapters—that underscore the importance of both nature and nurture.

levels of analysis the differing complementary views, from biological to psychological to social-cultural, for analyzing any given phenomenon.

biopsychosocial approach an integrated approach that incorporates biological, psychological, and social-cultural levels of analysis.

Views of anger How would each of psychology's levels of analysis explain what's going on here?

Psychology's Three Main Levels of Analysis

3: **What are psychology's levels of analysis and related perspectives?**

Each of us is a complex system that is part of a larger social system. But each of us is also composed of smaller systems, such as our nervous system and body organs, which are composed of still smaller systems—cells, molecules, and atoms.

These tiered systems suggest different **levels of analysis,** which offer complementary outlooks. It's like explaining why grizzly bears hibernate. Is it because hibernation helped their ancestors to survive and reproduce? Because their inner physiology drives them to do so? Because cold environments hinder food gathering during winter? Such perspectives are complementary because "everything is related to everything else" (Brewer, 1996). Together, different levels of analysis form an integrated **biopsychosocial approach,** which considers the influences of biological, psychological, and social-cultural factors (**FIGURE 1.1**).

Each level provides a valuable vantage point for looking at behavior, yet each by itself is incomplete. Like different academic disciplines, psychology's varied perspectives ask different questions and have their own limits. One perspective may stress the biological, psychological, or social-cultural level more than another, but the different perspectives described in **TABLE 1.1** complement one another. Consider, for example, how they shed light on anger.

- Someone working from a *neuroscience perspective* might study brain circuits that cause us to be "red in the face" and "hot under the collar."
- Someone working from the *evolutionary perspective* might analyze how anger facilitated the survival of our ancestors' genes.
- Someone working from the *behavior genetics perspective* might study how heredity and experience influence our individual differences in temperament.
- Someone working from the *psychodynamic perspective* might view an outburst as an outlet for unconscious hostility.
- Someone working from the *behavioral perspective* might attempt to determine which external stimuli trigger angry responses or aggressive acts.
- Someone working from the *cognitive perspective* might study how our interpretation of a situation affects our anger and how our anger affects our thinking.
- Someone working from the *social-cultural perspective* might explore how expressions of anger vary across cultural contexts.

FIGURE 1.1 Biopsychosocial approach This integrated viewpoint incorporates various levels of analysis and offers a more complete picture of any given behavior or mental process.

Biological influences:
- natural selection of adaptive traits
- genetic predispositions responding to environment
- brain mechanisms
- hormonal influences

Psychological influences:
- learned fears and other learned expectations
- emotional responses
- cognitive processing and perceptual interpretations

Behavior or mental process

Social-cultural influences:
- presence of others
- cultural, societal, and family expectations
- peer and other group influences
- compelling models (such as in the media)

TABLE 1.1 Psychology's Current Perspectives

Perspective	Focus	Sample Questions
Neuroscience	How the body and brain enable emotions, memories, and sensory experiences	How are messages transmitted within the body? How is blood chemistry linked with moods and motives?
Evolutionary	How the natural selection of traits promoted the survival of genes	How does evolution influence behavior tendencies?
Behavior genetics	How much our genes and our environment influence our individual differences	To what extent are psychological traits such as intelligence, personality, sexual orientation, and vulnerability to depression attributable to our genes? To our environment?
Psychodynamic	How behavior springs from unconscious drives and conflicts	How can someone's personality traits and disorders be explained in terms of sexual and aggressive drives or as the disguised effects of unfulfilled wishes and childhood traumas?
Behavioral	How we learn observable responses	How do we learn to fear particular objects or situations? What is the most effective way to alter our behavior, say, to lose weight or stop smoking?
Cognitive	How we encode, process, store, and retrieve information	How do we use information in remembering? Reasoning? Solving problems?
Social-cultural	How behavior and thinking vary across situations and cultures	How are we humans alike as members of one human family? As products of different environmental contexts, how do we differ?

The point to remember: Like two-dimensional views of a three-dimensional object, each of psychology's perspectives is helpful. But each by itself fails to reveal the whole picture.

So bear in mind psychology's limits. Don't expect it to answer the ultimate questions, such as those posed by Russian novelist Leo Tolstoy (1904): "Why should I live? Why should I do anything? Is there in life any purpose which the inevitable death that awaits me does not undo and destroy?" Instead, expect that psychology will help you understand why people think, feel, and act as they do. Then you should find the study of psychology fascinating and useful.

Psychology's Subfields

4: **What are some of psychology's subfields?**

Picturing a chemist at work, you probably envision a white-coated scientist surrounded by glassware and high-tech equipment. Picture a psychologist at work and you would be right to envision

- a white-coated scientist probing a rat's brain.
- an intelligence researcher measuring how quickly an infant shows boredom by looking away from a familiar picture.
- an executive evaluating a new "healthy life-styles" training program for employees.
- someone at a computer keyboard analyzing data on whether adopted teens' temperaments more closely resemble those of their adoptive parents or their biological parents.
- a therapist listening carefully to a client's depressed thoughts.
- a traveler visiting another culture and collecting data on variations in human values and behaviors.
- a teacher or writer sharing the joy of psychology with others.

The cluster of subfields we call psychology is a meeting ground for different disciplines. Thus, it's a perfect home for those with wide-ranging interests. In their diverse activities, from biological experimentation to cultural comparisons, the tribe of psychology is united by a common quest: describing and explaining behavior and the mind underlying it.

"I'm a social scientist, Michael. That means I can't explain electricity or anything like that, but if you ever want to know about people I'm your man."

I see you! A biological psychologist might view this child's delighted response as evidence of brain maturation. A cognitive psychologist might see it as a demonstration of the baby's growing knowledge of his surroundings. For a cross-cultural psychologist, the role of grandparents in different societies might be the issue of interest. As you will see throughout this book, these and other perspectives offer complementary views of behavior.

Some psychologists conduct **basic research** that builds psychology's knowledge base. In the pages that follow we will meet a wide variety of such researchers, including *biological psychologists* exploring the links between brain and mind; *developmental psychologists* studying our changing abilities from womb to tomb; *cognitive psychologists* experimenting with how we perceive, think, and solve problems; and *social psychologists* exploring how we view and affect one another.

These and other psychologists also may conduct **applied research** that tackles practical problems. *Industrial-organizational psychologists,* for example, use psychology's concepts and methods in the workplace to help organizations and companies select and train employees, boost morale and productivity, design products, and implement systems.

Although most psychology textbooks focus on psychological science, psychology is also a helping profession devoted to such practical issues as how to have a happy marriage, how to overcome anxiety or depression, and how to raise thriving children. As a science, psychology at its best bases such interventions on *evidence of effectiveness.* **Counseling psychologists** help people to cope with challenges and crises (including academic, vocational, and marital issues) and to improve their personal and social functioning. **Clinical psychologists** assess and treat mental, emotional, and behavior disorders (APA, 2003). Both counseling and clinical psychologists administer and interpret tests, provide counseling and therapy, and sometimes conduct basic and applied research. By contrast, **psychiatrists,** who also often provide psychotherapy, are medical doctors licensed to prescribe drugs and otherwise treat physical causes of psychological disorders. (Some clinical psychologists have lobbied for a similar right to prescribe mental-health–related drugs, and in 2002 and 2004 New Mexico and Louisiana became the first states to grant that right to specially trained and licensed psychologists.)

basic research pure science that aims to increase the scientific knowledge base.

applied research scientific study that aims to solve practical problems.

counseling psychology a branch of psychology that assists people with problems in living (often related to school, work, or marriage) and in achieving greater well-being.

clinical psychology a branch of psychology that studies, assesses, and treats people with psychological disorders.

psychiatry a branch of medicine dealing with psychological disorders; practiced by physicians who sometimes provide medical (for example, drug) treatments as well as psychological therapy.

Psychology: A science and a profession Psychologists experiment with, observe, test, and treat behavior. Here we see psychologists testing a child, measuring emotion-related physiology, and doing face-to-face therapy.

With perspectives ranging from the biological to the social, and with settings from the laboratory to the clinic, psychologists teach in medical schools, law schools, and theological seminaries, and they work in hospitals, factories, and corporate offices. They engage in interdisciplinary studies, such as psychohistory (the psychological analysis of historical characters), psycholinguistics (the study of language and thinking), and psychoceramics (the study of crackpots).[2]

Psychology also influences modern culture. Knowledge transforms us. Learning about the solar system and the germ theory of disease alters the way people think and act. Learning psychology's findings also changes people: They less often judge psychological disorders as moral failings, treatable by punishment and ostracism. They less often regard and treat women as men's mental inferiors. They less often view and rear children as ignorant, willful beasts in need of taming. "In each case," noted Morton Hunt (1990, p. 206), "knowledge has modified attitudes, and, through them, behavior." Once aware of psychology's well-researched ideas—about how body and mind connect, how a child's mind grows, how we construct our perceptions, how we remember (and misremember) our experiences, how people across the world differ (and are alike)—your mind may never again be quite the same.

Want to learn more? See Appendix C, Careers in Psychology, at the end of this book for more information about psychology's subfields and to learn about the many interesting options available to those with bachelor's, master's, and doctoral degrees in psychology.

"Once expanded to the dimensions of a larger idea, [the mind] never returns to its original size."

—Oliver Wendell Holmes, 1809–1894

REHEARSE IT!

1. In 1879, in psychology's first experiment, _____ and his students measured the time lag between hearing a ball hit a platform and pressing a key.
   a. Jean Piaget
   b. William James
   c. Sigmund Freud
   d. Wilhelm Wundt

2. A prominent psychology text was published in 1890. Its author was
   a. Wilhelm Wundt.
   b. Mary Whiton Calkins.
   c. Carl Rogers.
   d. William James.

3. In the early twentieth century, _____ redefined *psychology* as "the science of observable behavior."
   a. John B. Watson
   b. Abraham Maslow
   c. William James
   d. Sigmund Freud

4. The perspective in psychology that focuses on how behavior and thought differ from situation to situation and from culture to culture is the
   a. cognitive perspective.
   b. behavioral perspective.
   c. social-cultural perspective.
   d. neuroscience perspective.

5. In the history of psychology, a major topic has been the relative influence of nature and nurture. Nature is to nurture as
   a. personality is to intelligence.
   b. biology is to experience.
   c. intelligence is to biology.
   d. psychological traits are to behaviors.

6. A psychologist using the behavioral perspective would be most likely to study
   a. the effect of school uniforms on classroom behaviors.
   b. the hidden meaning in children's themes and drawings.
   c. the age at which children can learn algebra.
   d. whether certain mathematical abilities appear to be inherited.

7. A psychologist treating emotionally troubled adolescents at a local mental health agency is most likely to be a(n)
   a. research psychologist.
   b. psychiatrist.
   c. industrial-organizational psychologist.
   d. clinical psychologist.

8. A psychologist conducting basic research to expand psychology's knowledge base would be most likely to
   a. design a computer screen with limited glare and assess the effect on computer operators' eyes after a day's work.
   b. treat older people who are overcome by depression.
   c. observe 3- and 6-year-olds solving puzzles and analyze differences in their abilities.
   d. interview children with behavioral problems and suggest treatments.

Answers: 1. d, 2. d, 3. a, 4. c, 5. b, 6. a, 7. d, 8. c.

Why Do Psychology?

Although in some ways we outsmart the smartest computers, our intuition often goes awry. To err is human. Enter psychological science. With its procedures for gathering and sifting evidence, science restrains error. As we familiarize ourselves with its strategies and incorporate its underlying principles into our daily thinking, we can think smarter. Psychologists use the science of behavior and mental processes to better understand why people think, feel, and act as they do.

[2] Confession: I wrote the last part of this sentence on April Fools' Day.

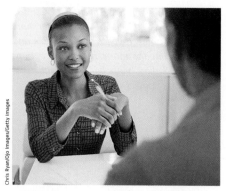

The limits of intuition Personnel interviewers tend to be overconfident of their gut feelings about job applicants. Their confidence stems partly from their recalling cases where their favorable impression proved right, and partly from their ignorance about rejected applicants who succeeded elsewhere.

"He who trusts in his own heart is a fool."

—Proverbs 28:26

"Life is lived forward, but understood backward."

—Philosopher Søren Kierkegaard, 1813–1855

"Anything seems commonplace, once explained."

—Dr. Watson to Sherlock Holmes

hindsight bias the tendency to believe, after learning an outcome, that we would have foreseen it. (Also known as the *I-knew-it-all-along phenomenon.*)

What About Intuition and Common Sense?

5: Why are the answers that flow from the scientific approach more reliable than those based on intuition and common sense?

Some people suppose that psychology merely documents and dresses in jargon what people already know: "So what else is new—you get paid for using fancy methods to prove what my grandmother knew?"

Others place their faith in human intuition. Former President George W. Bush described the feeling to Bob Woodward (2002) in explaining his decision to launch the Iraq war: "I'm a gut player. I rely on my instincts." Today's psychological science does document a vast intuitive mind. As we will see throughout this text, our thinking, memory, and attitudes operate on two levels—conscious and unconscious—with the larger part operating automatically, off-screen. Like jumbo jets, we fly mostly on autopilot. So, should we, like former President Bush, listen to the whispers of our inner wisdom and trust "the force within"? Or should we more often be subjecting our intuitive hunches to skeptical scrutiny?

This much seems certain. Intuition is important, but we often underestimate its perils. My geographical intuition tells me that Reno is east of Los Angeles, that Rome is south of New York, that Atlanta is east of Detroit. But I am wrong, wrong, and wrong. As Madeleine L'Engle observed, "The naked intellect is an extraordinarily inaccurate instrument" (1973). Two phenomena—*hindsight bias* and *judgmental overconfidence*—illustrate why we cannot rely solely on intuition and common sense.

Did We Know It All Along? Hindsight Bias

How easy it is to seem astute when drawing the bull's eye after the arrow has struck. After the U.S. occupation of Iraq led to a bloody civil war rather than a peaceful democracy, commentators saw the result as inevitable. *Before* the invasion was launched, these results seemed anything but obvious: In voting to allow the Iraq invasion, most U.S. senators did not anticipate the chaos that would seem so predictable in hindsight. Finding that something has happened makes it seem inevitable, a tendency we call **hindsight bias** (also known as the *I-knew-it-all-along phenomenon*). Hindsight bias is widespread. Some 100 studies have observed it in various countries and among both children and adults (Balmut et al., 2007).

The phenomenon is easy to demonstrate: Give half the members of a group some purported psychological finding, and give the other half an opposite result. Tell the first group, "Psychologists have found that separation weakens romantic attraction. As the saying goes, 'Out of sight, out of mind.'" Ask them to imagine why this might be true. Most people can, and nearly all will then regard this true finding as unsurprising.

Tell the second group the opposite, "Psychologists have found that separation strengthens romantic attraction. As the saying goes, 'Absence makes the heart grow fonder.'" People given this untrue result can also easily imagine it, and they overwhelmingly see it as unsurprising common sense. Obviously, when both a supposed finding and its opposite seem like common sense, there is a problem.

Such errors in our recollections and explanations show why we need psychological research. Just asking people how and why they felt or acted as they did can sometimes be misleading—*not* because common sense is usually wrong, but because common sense more easily describes what *has* happened than what *will* happen. As physicist Neils Bohr reportedly said, "Prediction is very difficult, especially about the future."

Nevertheless, Grandma's intuition is often right. As Yogi Berra once said, "You can observe a lot by watching." (We have Berra to thank for other gems, such as "Nobody ever comes here—it's too crowded.") Because we're all behavior watchers, it would be surprising if many of psychology's findings had *not* been foreseen.

Indeed, note Daniel Gilbert, Brett Pelham, and Douglas Krull (2003), "good ideas in psychology usually have an oddly familiar quality, and the moment we encounter them we feel certain that we once came close to thinking the same thing ourselves and simply failed to write it down." Good ideas are like good inventions; once created, they seem obvious. (Why did it take so long for someone to invent suitcases on wheels and Post-it Notes?)

But sometimes Grandma's intuition, informed by countless casual observations, has it wrong. In later chapters we will see how research has overturned popular ideas—that familiarity breeds contempt, that dreams predict the future, and that most of use only 10 percent of our brain. We will also see how it has surprised us with discoveries about how the brain's chemical messengers control our moods and memories, about other animals' abilities, and about the effects of stress on our capacity to fight disease.

Hindsight bias *After the 2007 Virginia Tech massacre of 32 people, it seemed obvious that school officials should have locked down the school (despite its having the population of a small city) after the first two people were murdered. With 20/20 hindsight, everything seems obvious.*

Overconfidence

We humans tend to think we know more than we do. Asked how sure we are of our answers to factual questions (Is Boston north or south of Paris?), we tend to be more confident than correct.[3] Or consider these three anagrams, which Richard Goranson (1978) asked people to unscramble:

WREAT → WATER
ETRYN → ENTRY
GRABE → BARGE

About how many seconds do you think it would have taken you to unscramble each of these? Did hindsight influence you? Knowing the answers tends to make us overconfident—surely the solution would take only 10 seconds or so. In reality, the average problem solver spends 3 minutes, as you also might, given a similar anagram without a solution: OCHSA. (See the solution below, in the margin.)

Are we any better at predicting our social behavior? To find out, Robert Vallone and his associates (1990) had students predict at the beginning of the school year whether they would drop a course, vote in an upcoming election, call their parents more than twice a month, and so forth. On average, the students felt 84 percent confident in making these self-predictions. Later quizzes about their actual behavior showed their predictions were only 71 percent correct. Even when students were 100 percent sure of themselves, their self-predictions erred 15 percent of the time.

The point to remember: Hindsight bias and overconfidence often lead us to overestimate our intuition. But scientific inquiry can help us sift reality from illusion.

Fun anagram solutions from Wordsmith.org:
Elvis = lives
Dormitory = dirty room
Slot machines = cash lost in 'em

"We don't like their sound. Groups of guitars are on their way out."

—Decca Records, in turning down a recording contract with the Beatles in 1962

"They couldn't hit an elephant at this distance."

—General John Sedgwick just before being killed during a U.S. Civil War battle, 1864

Solution to anagram on previous page:
CHAOS.

The Scientific Attitude

6: **What attitudes characterize scientific inquiry, and what does it mean to think critically?**

Underlying all science is, first, a hard-headed *curiosity,* a passion to explore and understand without misleading or being misled. Some questions *(Is there life after death?)* are beyond science. To answer them in any way requires a leap of faith. With many other ideas *(Can some people demonstrate ESP?),* the proof is in the pudding. No matter how sensible or crazy an idea sounds, scientists ask, *"Does it work?"* When put to the test, can its predictions be confirmed?

"The scientist . . . must be free to ask any question, to doubt any assertion, to seek for any evidence, to correct any errors."

—Physicist J. Robert Oppenheimer, *Life,* October 10, 1949

[3] Boston is south of Paris.

The Amazing Randi The magician James Randi exemplifies skepticism. He has tested and debunked a variety of psychic phenomena.

"A skeptic is one who is willing to question any truth claim, asking for clarity in definition, consistency in logic, and adequacy of evidence."

—Philosopher Paul Kurtz,
  The Skeptical Inquirer, 1994

"My deeply held belief is that if a god anything like the traditional sort exists, our curiosity and intelligence are provided by such a god. We would be unappreciative of those gifts . . . if we suppressed our passion to explore the universe and ourselves."

—Carl Sagan, *Broca's Brain,* 1979

This scientific approach has a long history. As ancient a figure as Moses used such an approach. How do you evaluate a self-proclaimed prophet? His answer: Put the prophet to the test. If the predicted event "does not take place or prove true," then so much the worse for the prophet (*Deuteronomy* 18:22). By letting the facts speak for themselves, Moses was using what we now call an *empirical approach.* Magician James Randi uses this approach when testing those claiming to see auras around people's bodies:

> **Randi:** *Do you see an aura around my head?*
> **Aura-seer:** *Yes, indeed.*
> **Randi:** *Can you still see the aura if I put this magazine in front of my face?*
> **Aura-seer:** *Of course.*
> **Randi:** *Then if I were to step behind a wall barely taller than I am, you could determine my location from the aura visible above my head, right?*

Randi once told me that no aura-seer he asked would agree to take this simple test.

When subjected to such scrutiny, crazy-sounding ideas sometimes find support. More often, science becomes society's garbage disposal by sending crazy-sounding ideas to the waste heap, atop previous claims of perpetual motion machines, miracle cancer cures, and out-of-body travels into centuries past. Today's presumed "truths" sometimes become tomorrow's fallacies. To sift reality from fantasy, sense from nonsense, therefore requires a scientific attitude: being skeptical but not cynical, open but not gullible.

"To believe with certainty," says a Polish proverb, "we must begin by doubting." As scientists, psychologists approach the world of behavior with a *curious skepticism,* persistently asking two questions: *What do you mean? How do you know?*

Putting a scientific attitude into practice requires not only curiosity and skepticism but also *humility*—an awareness of our own vulnerability to error and an openness to surprises and new perspectives. In the last analysis, what matters is not my opinion or yours, but the truths nature reveals in response to our questioning. If people or other animals don't behave as our ideas predict, then so much the worse for our ideas. This humble attitude was expressed in one of psychology's early mottos: "The rat is always right."

Historians of science tell us that these three attitudes—curiosity, skepticism, and humility—helped make modern science possible. Many of its founders, including Copernicus and Newton, were people whose religious convictions made them humble before nature and skeptical of mere human authority (Hooykaas, 1972; Merton, 1938). Some deeply religious people today may view science, including psychological science, as a threat. Yet, notes sociologist Rodney Stark (2003a,b), the scientific revolution was led mostly by deeply religious people acting on the idea that "in

Non Sequitur

order to love and honor God, it is necessary to fully appreciate the wonders of his handiwork."

Of course, scientists, like anyone else, can have big egos and may cling to their preconceptions. We all view nature through the spectacles of our preconceived ideas. Nevertheless, the ideal that unifies psychologists with all scientists is the curious, skeptical, humble scrutiny of competing ideas. As a community, scientists check and recheck one another's findings and conclusions.

Critical Thinking

The scientific attitude prepares us to think smarter. Smart thinking, called **critical thinking,** examines assumptions, discerns hidden values, evaluates evidence, and assesses conclusions. Whether reading a news report or listening to a conversation, critical thinkers ask questions. They wonder, How do they know that? What is this person's agenda? Is the conclusion based on anecdote and gut feelings, or on evidence? Does the evidence justify a cause-effect conclusion? What alternative explanations are possible?

Has psychology's critical inquiry been open to surprising findings? The answer, as ensuing chapters illustrate, is plainly *yes.* Believe it or not . . .

- massive losses of brain tissue early in life may have minimal long-term effects (see Chapter 2).
- within days, newborns can recognize their mother's odor and voice (see Chapter 5).
- brain damage can leave a person able to learn new skills yet unaware of such learning (see Chapter 8).
- electroconvulsive therapy (delivering an electric shock to the brain) is often a very effective treatment for severe depression (see Chapter 14).

And has critical inquiry convincingly debunked popular presumptions? The answer, as ensuing chapters also illustrate, is again *yes.* The evidence indicates that . . .

- sleepwalkers are *not* acting out their dreams (see Chapter 3).
- our past experiences are *not* all recorded verbatim in our brains (see Chapter 8).
- most people do *not* suffer from unrealistically low self-esteem, and high self-esteem is not all good (see Chapter 12).
- opposites do *not* generally attract (see Chapter 15).

In each of these instances and more, what has been learned is not what is widely believed.

"The real purpose of the scientific method is to make sure Nature hasn't misled you into thinking you know something you don't actually know."

—Robert M. Pirsig, *Zen and the Art of Motorcycle Maintenance,* 1974

----

critical thinking thinking that does not blindly accept arguments and conclusions. Rather, it examines assumptions, discerns hidden values, evaluates evidence, and assesses conclusions.

REHEARSE IT!

9. *Hindsight bias* refers to our tendency to
a. perceive events as obvious or inevitable after the fact.
b. be more confident than correct in estimating distances.
c. overestimate our ability to predict the future.
d. make judgments that fly in the face of common sense.

10. As scientists, psychologists view theories with curiosity, skepticism, and humility. This means that they
a. approach research with a negative cynicism.
b. assume that an article published in a reputable journal must be true.
c. believe that every important human question can be studied scientifically.
d. are willing to ask questions and to reject claims that cannot be verified by research.

11. A newspaper article describes how a "cure for cancer has been found." A critical thinker probably will
a. dismiss the article as untrue.
b. accept the information as a wonderful breakthrough.
c. question the article, evaluate the evidence, and assess the conclusions.
d. question the article but quickly accept it as true if the author has an excellent reputation.

Answers: 9. a, 10. d, 11. c.

theory an explanation using an integrated set of principles that organizes observations and predicts behaviors or events.

hypothesis a testable prediction, often implied by a theory.

operational definition a statement of the procedures (operations) used to define research variables. For example, *human intelligence* may be operationally defined as "what an intelligence test measures."

replication repeating the essence of a research study, usually with different participants in different situations, to see whether the basic finding extends to other participants and circumstances.

case study an observation technique in which one person is studied in depth in the hope of revealing universal principles.

How Do Psychologists Ask and Answer Questions?

Psychologists arm their scientific attitude with the scientific method. In its attempt to describe and explain human nature, psychological science welcomes competing ideas and plausible-sounding theories. And it puts them to the test, with careful observation and rigorous analysis. If a theory works—if the data support its predictions—so much the better for that theory. If the predictions fail, the theory will be revised or rejected.

The Scientific Method

7: **How do psychologists use the scientific method to construct theories?**

In everyday conversation, we often use *theory* to mean "mere hunch." In science, however, *theory* is linked with *observation*. A scientific **theory** *explains* through an integrated set of principles that *organizes* observations and *predicts* behaviors or events. By organizing isolated facts, a theory simplifies. There are too many facts about behavior to remember them all. By linking facts and bridging them to deeper principles, a theory offers a useful summary. As we connect the observed dots, a coherent picture emerges.

A good theory of depression, for example, helps us organize countless depression-related observations into a short list of principles. Imagine that we observe over and over that people with depression describe their past, present, and future in gloomy terms. We might therefore theorize that at the heart of depression lies low self-esteem. So far so good: Our self-esteem principle neatly summarizes a long list of facts about people with depression.

Yet no matter how reasonable a theory may sound—and low self-esteem seems a reasonable explanation of depression—we must put it to the test. A good theory produces testable predictions, called **hypotheses.** By enabling us to test and to reject or revise the theory, such predictions give direction to research. They specify what results would support the theory and what results would disconfirm it. To test our self-esteem theory of depression, we might assess people's self-esteem by having them respond to statements such as "I have good ideas" and "I am fun to be with." Then we could see whether, as we hypothesized, people who report poorer self-images also score higher on a depression scale (**FIGURE 1.2**).

In testing our theory, we should be aware that it can bias our observations: We may see what we expect. Having theorized that depression springs from low self-esteem, we may perceive depressed people's neutral comments as self-disparaging. The

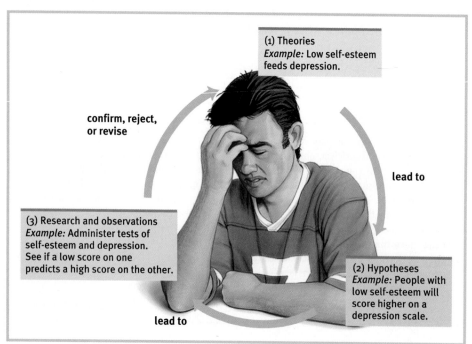

(1) Theories
Example: Low self-esteem feeds depression.

confirm, reject, or revise

lead to

(3) Research and observations
Example: Administer tests of self-esteem and depression. See if a low score on one predicts a high score on the other.

(2) Hypotheses
Example: People with low self-esteem will score higher on a depression scale.

lead to

FIGURE 1.2 The scientific method A self-correcting process for asking questions and observing nature's answers.

urge to see what we expect is an ever-present temptation, in the laboratory and outside of it. According to the bipartisan U.S. Senate Select Committee on Intelligence (2004), preconceived expectations that Iraq had weapons of mass destruction led intelligence analysts to wrongly interpret ambiguous observations as confirming that theory, and this theory-driven conclusion then led to the preemptive U.S. invasion of Iraq.

As a check on their biases, psychologists report their research with precise **operational definitions** of procedures and concepts. *Hunger,* for example, might be defined as "hours without eating," *generosity* as "money contributed." Using these carefully worded statements, other researchers can **replicate** (repeat) the original observations with different participants, materials, and circumstances. If they get similar results, confidence in the finding's reliability grows. The first study of hindsight bias aroused psychologists' curiosity. Now, after many successful replications with differing people and questions, we feel sure of the phenomenon's power.

In the end, our theory will be useful if it (1) effectively *organizes* a range of self-reports and observations, and (2) implies clear *predictions* that anyone can use to check the theory or to derive practical applications. (If we boost people's self-esteem, will their depression lift?) Eventually, our research will probably lead to a revised theory (such as the one in Chapter 13) that better organizes and predicts what we know about depression.

As we will see next, we can test our hypotheses and refine our theories using *descriptive* methods (which describe behaviors, often using case studies, surveys, or naturalistic observations), *correlational* methods (which associate different factors), and *experimental* methods (which manipulate factors to discover their effects). To think critically about popular psychology claims, we need to recognize these methods and know what conclusions they allow.

Good theories explain by
1. organizing and linking observed facts.
2. implying hypotheses that offer testable predictions and, sometimes, practical applications.

Description

8 : **How do psychologists observe and describe behavior?**

The starting point of any science is description. In everyday life, all of us observe and describe people, often drawing conclusions about why they behave as they do. Professional psychologists do much the same, though more objectively and systematically.

The Case Study

Among the oldest research methods, the **case study** examines one individual in depth in the hope of revealing things true of us all. Much of our early knowledge about the brain, for example, came from case studies of individuals who suffered a particular impairment after damage to a certain brain region. Intensive case studies can be very revealing. They show us what *can* happen, and they often suggest directions for further study.

But sometimes individual cases may mislead us. If the individual being studied is atypical, the unrepresentative information can lead to mistaken judgments and false conclusions. Indeed, anytime a researcher mentions a finding ("Smokers die younger: 95 percent of men over 85 are nonsmokers") someone is sure to offer a contradictory anecdote ("Well, I have an uncle who smoked two packs a day and lived to be 89"). Dramatic stories and personal experiences (even psychological case examples) command our attention, and they are easily remembered. Which of the following do you find more memorable? (1) "In one study of 1300 dream reports concerning a kidnapped child, only 5 percent correctly envisioned the child as dead (Murray & Wheeler, 1937)." (2) "My friend dreamed his sister was in a car accident, and two days later she died in a head-on collision!" Numbers can be numbing, but the plural of *anecdote* is not *evidence*.

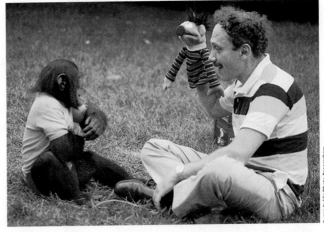

The case of the conversational chimpanzee In case studies of chimpanzees, psychologists have asked whether language is uniquely human. Here Nim Chimpsky signs *hug* as his trainer, psychologist Herbert Terrace, shows him the puppet Ernie. But is Nim really using language? We'll explore that issue in Chapter 9.

"Given a thimbleful of [dramatic] facts we rush to make generalizations as large as a tub."

—Psychologist Gordon Allport,
The Nature of Prejudice, 1954

survey a technique for ascertaining the self-reported attitudes or behaviors of a particular group, usually by questioning a representative, random sample of the group.

population all the cases in a group being studied, from which samples may be drawn. (*Note:* Except for national studies, this does *not* refer to a country's whole population.)

random sample a sample that fairly represents a population because each member has an equal chance of inclusion.

naturalistic observation observing and recording behavior in naturally occurring situations without trying to manipulate and control the situation.

Drawing by D. Fradon; © 1969 The New Yorker Magazine, Inc.

"How would you like me to answer that question? As a member of my ethnic group, educational class, income group, or religious category?"

With very large samples, estimates become quite reliable. E is estimated to represent 12.7 percent of the letters in written English. E, in fact, is 12.3 percent of the 925,141 letters in Melville's Moby Dick, *12.4 percent of the 586,747 letters in Dickens'* A Tale of Two Cities, *and 12.1 percent of the 3,901,021 letters in 12 of Mark Twain's works* (Chance News, *1997*).

The point to remember: Individual cases can suggest fruitful ideas. What's true of all of us can be glimpsed in any one of us. But to discern the general truths that cover individual cases, we must answer questions with other research methods.

The Survey

The **survey** method looks at many cases in less depth. A survey asks people to report their behavior or opinions. Questions about everything from sexual practices to political opinions are put to the public. Harris and Gallup polls have revealed that 89 percent of Americans favor equal job opportunities for homosexual people, that 96 percent would like to change something about their appearance, and in late 2008, that 80 percent said the faltering economy was a significant source of stress. In Britain, seven in ten 18- to 29-year-olds support gay marriage; among those over 50, about the same percentage oppose it (a generation gap found in many Western countries). But asking questions is tricky, and the answers often depend on the ways questions are worded and respondents are chosen.

WORDING EFFECTS Even subtle changes in the order or wording of questions can have major effects. Should cigarette ads or pornography be allowed on television? People are much more likely to approve "not allowing" such things than "forbidding" or "censoring" them. In one national survey, only 27 percent of Americans approved of "government censorship" of media sex and violence, though 66 percent approved of "more restrictions on what is shown on television" (Lacayo, 1995).

People are similarly much more approving of "affirmative action" than "preferential treatment," and of "revenue enhancers" than of "taxes." Because wording is such a delicate matter, critical thinkers will reflect on how the phrasing of a question might affect people's expressed opinions.

RANDOM SAMPLING In everyday thinking, the temptation to generalize from a few memorable anecdotes or unrepresentative personal experiences is nearly irresistible. Given (a) a statistical summary of a professor's student evaluations and (b) the vivid comments of two irate students, an administrator's impression of the professor may be influenced as much by the two unhappy students as by the many favorable evaluations in the statistical summary.

The point to remember: For an accurate picture of a whole population's attitudes and experience, there's only one game in town—a *representative sample.*

But it's not always possible to survey everyone in a group. So how do you obtain a representative sample—say, of the students at your college or university? How could you choose a smaller group that would represent the total student **population,** the whole group you want to study and describe? Usually, you would choose a **random sample,** in which every person in the entire group has an equal chance of participating. You might number the names in the general student listing and then use a random number generator to pick the participants for your survey. Large representative samples are better than small ones, but a small representative sample of 100 is better than an unrepresentative sample of 500.

Political pollsters sample voters in national election surveys just this way. Using only 1500 randomly sampled people, drawn from all areas of a country, they can provide a remarkably accurate snapshot of the nation's opinions. Without random sampling, large samples—including call-in phone samples and TV or Web site polls—often merely give misleading results.

The point to remember: Before accepting survey findings, think critically: Consider the sample. You cannot compensate for an unrepresentative sample by simply adding more people.

Naturalistic Observation

A third descriptive method records behavior in natural environments. These **naturalistic observations** range from watching chimpanzee societies in the jungle, to unobtrusively videotaping (and later systematically analyzing) parent-child interactions in different cultures, to recording racial differences in self-seating patterns in a student lunchroom.

Like case studies and surveys, naturalistic observation does not *explain* behavior. It *describes* it. Nevertheless, descriptions can be revealing. We once thought, for example, that only humans use tools. Then naturalistic observation revealed that chimpanzees sometimes insert a stick in a termite mound and withdraw it, eating the stick's load of termites. Such unobtrusive naturalistic observations paved the way for later studies of animal thinking, language, and emotion, which further expanded our understanding of our fellow animals. "Observations, made in the natural habitat, helped to show that the societies and behavior of animals are far more complex than previously supposed," noted chimpanzee observer Jane Goodall (1998). For example, chimpanzees and baboons have been observed using deception. Psychologists Andrew Whiten and Richard Byrne (1988) repeatedly saw one young baboon pretending to have been attacked by another as a tactic to get its mother to drive the other baboon away from its food. The more developed a primate species' brain, the more likely it is that the animals will display deceptive behaviors (Byrne & Corp, 2004).

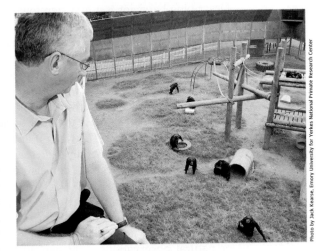

A natural observer
Chimpanzee researcher Frans de Waal (2005) reports that "I am a born observer. . . . When picking a seat in a restaurant I want to face as many tables as possible. I enjoy following the social dynamics—love, tension, boredom, antipathy— around me based on body language, which I consider more informative than the spoken word. Since keeping track of others is something I do automatically, becoming a fly on the wall of an ape colony came naturally to me."

Photo by Jack Kearse, Emory University for Yerkes National Primate Research Center

Naturalistic observations also illuminate human behavior. Here are three you might enjoy.

- *A funny finding.* We humans laugh 30 times more often in social situations than in solitary situations. (Have you noticed how seldom you laugh when alone?) As we laugh, 17 muscles contort our mouth and squeeze our eyes, and we emit a series of 75-millisecond vowel-like sounds that are spaced about one-fifth of a second apart (Provine, 2001).
- *Sounding out students.* What, really, are introductory psychology students saying and doing during their everyday lives? To find out, Matthias Mehl and James Pennebaker (2003) equipped 52 such students from the University of Texas with belt-worn Electronically Activated Recorders (EARs). For up to four days, the EARs captured 30 seconds of the students' waking hours every 12.5 minutes, thus enabling the researchers to eavesdrop on more than 10,000 half-minute life slices by the end of the study. On what percentage of the slices do you suppose they found the students talking with someone? What percentage captured the students at a computer keyboard? The answers: 28 and 9 percent. (What percentage of *your* waking hours are spent in these activities?)
- *Culture, climate, and the pace of life.* Naturalistic observation also enabled Robert Levine and Ara Norenzayan (1999) to compare the pace of life in 31 countries. (Their operational definition of *pace of life* included walking speed, the speed with which postal clerks completed a simple request, and the accuracy of public clocks.) Their conclusion: Life is fastest paced in Japan and Western Europe, and slower paced in economically less-developed countries. People in colder climates also tend to live at a faster pace (and are more prone to die from heart disease).

Naturalistic observation offers interesting snapshots of everyday life, but it does so without controlling for all the factors that may influence behavior. It's one thing

An EAR for natural observation
Psychologists Matthias Mehl and James Pennebaker have used Electronically Activated Recorders (EARs) to sample naturally occurring slices of daily life.

Courtesy of Matthias Mehl

correlation the extent to which two factors vary together, and thus of how well either factor predicts the other. The *correlation coefficient* is the mathematical expression of the relationship, ranging from −1 to +1.

illusory correlation the perception of a relationship where none exists.

to observe the pace of life in various places, but another to explain why some people walk faster than others. Yet naturalistic observation, like surveys, can provide data for correlational research.

Correlation

9: What are positive and negative correlations, and why do they enable prediction but not cause-effect explanation?

Describing behavior is a first step toward predicting it. Surveys and naturalistic observations often show us that one trait or behavior is related to another. In such cases, we say the two **correlate.** A statistical measure (the *correlation coefficient*) helps us figure how closely two things vary together, and thus how well either one *predicts* the other. Knowing how much aptitude test scores *correlate* with school success tells us how well the scores *predict* school success.

A *positive correlation* (between 0 and +1.00) indicates a *direct* relationship, meaning that two things increase together or decrease together.

A *negative correlation* (between 0 and −1.00) indicates an *inverse* relationship: As one thing increases, the other decreases. Our earlier findings on self-esteem and depression illustrate a negative correlation: People who score *low* on self-esteem tend to score *high* on depression. Negative correlations could go as low as −1.00, which means that, like people on the opposite ends of a teeter-totter, one set of scores goes down precisely as the other goes up.

Here are four news reports of correlational research, some derived from surveys or natural observations. Can you spot which are reporting positive correlations, which negative? (See the margin on the next page to check your answers.)

1. The more young children watch TV, the less they read (Kaiser, 2003).
2. The more sexual content teens see on TV, the more likely they are to have sex (Collins et al., 2004).
3. The longer children are breast-fed, the greater their later academic achievement (Horwood & Fergusson, 1998).
4. The more often adolescents eat breakfast, the lower their body mass index (Timlin et al., 2008).

Though informative, psychology's correlations usually leave most of the variation among individuals unpredicted. As we will see, there is a positive correlation between parents' abusiveness and their children's later abusiveness when they become parents. But this does not mean that most abused children become abusive. The correlation simply indicates a statistical relationship: Most abused children do not grow into abusers, but nonabused children are even less likely to become abusive.

The point to remember: A correlation coefficient helps us see the world more clearly by revealing the extent to which two things relate.

Correlation and Causation

Correlations point us toward predictions, but usually imperfect ones. Low self-esteem correlates with (and therefore predicts) depression. (This correlation might be indicated by a correlation coefficient, or just by a finding that people who score on the lower half of a self-esteem scale have an elevated depression rate.) So, does low self-esteem *cause* de-

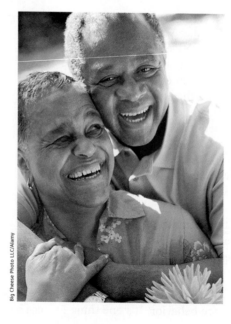

Correlation need not mean causation Length of marriage correlates positively with hair loss in men. Does this mean that marriage causes men to lose their hair (or that balding men make better husbands)? In this case, as in many others, a third factor obviously explains the correlation: Golden anniversaries and baldness both accompany aging.

Big Cheese Photo LLC/Alamy

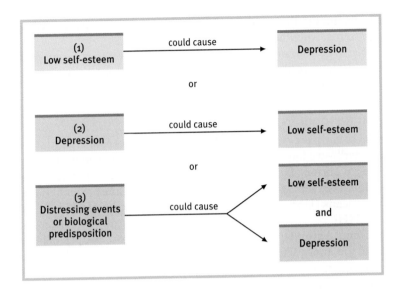

FIGURE 1.3 Three possible cause-effect relationships People low in self-esteem are more likely to report depression than are those high in self-esteem. One possible explanation of this negative correlation is that a bad self-image causes depressed feelings. But, as the diagram indicates, other cause-effect relationships are possible.

pression? If, based on the correlational evidence, you assume that it does, you have much company. A nearly irresistible thinking error is assuming that an association proves causation. But no matter how strong the relationship, it does not *prove* anything!

As options 2 and 3 in **FIGURE 1.3** show, we'd get the same negative correlation between low self-esteem and depression if depression caused people to be down on themselves, or if some third factor—such as heredity or brain chemistry—caused both low self-esteem and depression.

This point is so important—so basic to thinking smarter with psychology—that it merits one more example. A survey of over 12,000 adolescents found that the more teens feel loved by their parents, the less likely they are to behave in unhealthy ways—having early sex, smoking, abusing alcohol and drugs, exhibiting violence (Resnick et al., 1997). "Adults have a powerful effect on their children's behavior right through the high school years," gushed an Associated Press (AP) story reporting the finding. But this correlation comes with no built-in cause-effect arrow. Said differently (turn the volume up here), *association does not prove causation.* Thus, the AP could as well have reported, "Well-behaved teens feel their parents' love and approval; out-of-bounds teens more often think their parents are disapproving jerks."

The point to remember: Correlation indicates the *possibility* of a cause-effect relationship, *but it does not prove causation.* Knowing that two events are associated need not tell us anything about causation. Remember this principle and you will be wiser as you read and hear news of scientific studies.

Illusory Correlations

Correlation coefficients make visible the relationships we might otherwise miss. They also restrain our "seeing" relationships that actually do not exist. A perceived but nonexistent correlation is an **illusory correlation.** When we *believe* there is a relationship between two things, we are likely to *notice* and *recall* instances that confirm our belief (Trolier & Hamilton, 1986). We are especially likely to notice and remember the occurrence of two dramatic or unusual events in sequence—say, a premonition of an unlikely phone call followed by the call. When the call does not follow the premonition, we are less likely to note and remember the nonevent.

Illusory correlations help explain many superstitious beliefs, such as the presumption that infertile couples who adopt become more likely to conceive (Gilovich, 1991). Illusory thinking also helps explain why so many people believe that sugar makes children hyperactive, that getting chilled and wet causes us to

A New York Times *writer reported a massive survey showing that "adolescents whose parents smoked were 50 percent more likely than children of nonsmokers to report having had sex." He concluded (would you agree?) that the survey indicated a causal effect— that "to reduce the chances that their children will become sexually active at an early age" parents might "quit smoking" (O'Neil, 2002).*

Answers to correlation questions: 1. negative, 2. positive, 3. positive, 4. negative.

catch a cold, and that changes in the weather trigger arthritis pain. We are, it seems, prone to perceiving patterns, whether they're there or not.

The point to remember: When we notice random coincidences, we may forget that they are random and instead see them as correlated. Thus, we can easily deceive ourselves by seeing what is not there.

Perceiving Order in Random Events

In our natural eagerness to make sense of our world—what poet Wallace Stevens called our "rage for order"—we look for order even in random data. And we usually find it, because—here's a curious fact of life—*random sequences often don't look random.* Consider a random coin flip: If someone flipped a coin six times, which of the following sequences of heads (H) and tails (T) would be most likely: HHHTTT or HTTHTH or HHHHHH?

Daniel Kahneman and Amos Tversky (1972) found that most people believe HTTHTH would be the most likely random sequence. Actually, all three are equally likely (or, you might say, equally unlikely). A bridge or poker hand of 10 through ace, all of hearts, would seem extraordinary; actually, it would be no more or less likely than any other specific hand of cards (**FIGURE 1.4**).

Bizarre-looking, perhaps. But actually no more unlikely than any other number sequence.

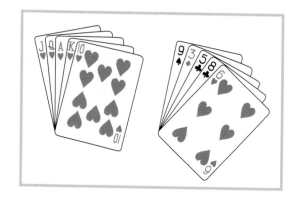

FIGURE 1.4 Two random sequences Your chances of being dealt either of these hands are precisely the same: 1 in 2,598,960.

Given enough random events, something weird will happen Angelo and Maria Gallina were the beneficiaries of one of those extraordinary chance events when they won two California lottery games on the same day.

In actual random sequences, patterns and streaks (such as repeating digits) occur more often than people expect. To demonstrate this phenomenon for myself (as you can do), I flipped a coin 51 times, with these results:

1. H	11. T	21. T	31. T	41. H	51. T
2. T	12. H	22. T	32. T	42. H	
3. T	13. H	23. H	33. T	43. H	
4. T	14. T	24. T	34. T	44. H	
5. H	15. T	25. T	35. T	45. T	
6. H	16. H	26. T	36. H	46. H	
7. H	17. T	27. H	37. T	47. H	
8. T	18. T	28. T	38. T	48. T	
9. T	19. H	29. H	39. H	49. T	
10. T	20. H	30. T	40. T	50. T	

Looking over the sequence, patterns jump out: Tosses 10 to 22 provided an almost perfect pattern of pairs of tails followed by pairs of heads. On tosses 30 to 38 I had a "cold hand," with only one head in eight tosses. But my fortunes immediately reversed with a "hot hand"—seven heads out of the next nine tosses. Similar patterns and streaks happen in basketball shooting, baseball hitting, and mutual fund stock pickers' selections (Gilovich et al., 1985; Malkiel, 1989, 1995; Myers, 2002). These sequences often don't look random and so are overinterpreted ("When you're hot, you're hot!").

What explains these streaky patterns? Was I exercising some sort of paranormal control over my coin? Did I snap out of my tails funk and get in a heads groove? No such explanations are needed, for these are the sorts of streaks found in any random data. Comparing each toss to the next, 24 of the 50 comparisons yielded a changed result—just the sort of near 50-50 result we expect from coin tossing. Despite seeming patterns, the outcome of one toss gives no clue to the outcome of the next.

However, some happenings seem so extraordinary that, mystified, we struggle to conceive an ordinary, chance-related explanation. Statisticians are less mystified. When Evelyn Marie Adams won the New Jersey lottery *twice*, newspapers reported the odds of her feat as 1 in 17 trillion. Bizarre? Actually, 1 in 17 trillion are indeed the odds that a given person who buys a single ticket for two New Jersey lotteries will win both times. And given the millions of people who buy U.S. state lottery tickets, reported statisticians Stephen Samuels and George McCabe (1989), it was "practically a sure thing" that someday, somewhere, someone would hit a state jackpot twice. Indeed, said fellow statisticians Persi Diaconis and Frederick Mosteller (1989), "with a large enough sample, any outrageous thing is likely to happen." An event that happens to but 1 in 1 billion people every day occurs about six times a day, 2000 times a year.

On March 11, 1998, Utah's Ernie and Lynn Carey gained three new grandchildren when three of their daughters gave birth—on the same day (Los Angeles Times, 1998).

"The really unusual day would be one where nothing unusual happens."
—Statistician Persi Diaconis (2002)

REHEARSE IT!

12. The predictions implied by a theory are called
a. operational definitions.
b. correlations.
c. hypotheses.
d. replications.

13. Which of the following is NOT one of the techniques psychologists use to observe and describe behavior?
a. A case study
b. Naturalistic observation
c. Correlational research
d. A phone survey

14. You wish to take an accurate poll in a certain country by questioning people who truly represent the country's adult population. Therefore, you need to ensure that you question
a. at least 50 percent males and 50 percent females.
b. a small but intelligent sample of the population.
c. a very large sample of the population.
d. a random sample of the population.

15. A study finds that the more childbirth training classes women attend, the less pain medication they require during childbirth. This finding can be stated as a(n)
a. positive correlation.
b. negative correlation.
c. cause-effect relationship.
d. illusory correlation.

16. Knowing that two events are correlated provides
a. a basis for prediction.
b. an explanation of why the events are related.
c. proof that as one increases, the other also increases.
d. an indication that an underlying third factor is at work.

17. Some people wrongly perceive that their dreams predict future events. This is an example of a(n) _____ correlation.
a. negative
b. positive
c. illusory
d. naturalistic

Answers: 12. c, 13. c, 14. d, 15. b, 16. a, 17. c.

Experimentation

10: How do experiments, powered by random assignment, clarify cause and effect?

Happy are they, remarked the Roman poet Virgil, "who have been able to perceive the causes of things." To isolate cause and effect, psychologists can eliminate (or screen out) the influence of other factors that may account for the results they observe. For example, researchers have found that breast-fed infants grow up with somewhat higher intelligence scores than do infants bottle-fed with cow's milk (Angelsen et al., 2001; Mortensen et al., 2002; Quinn et al., 2001). They have also found that breast-fed British babies have been more likely than their bottle-fed counterparts to eventually move into a higher social class (Martin et al., 2007). But the "breast is best" intelligence effect shrinks when researchers compare breast-fed and bottle-fed children from the same families (Der et al., 2006).

experiment a research method in which an investigator manipulates one or more factors (independent variables) to observe the effect on some behavior or mental process (the dependent variable). By *random assignment* of participants, the experimenter aims to control other relevant factors.

random assignment assigning participants to experimental and control groups by chance, thus minimizing preexisting differences between those assigned to the different groups.

experimental group in an experiment, the group that is exposed to the treatment, that is, to one version of the independent variable.

control group in an experiment, the group that is *not* exposed to the treatment; contrasts with the experimental group and serves as a comparison for evaluating the effect of the treatment.

double-blind procedure an experimental procedure in which both the research participants and the research staff are ignorant (blind) about whether the research participants have received the treatment or a placebo. Commonly used in drug-evaluation studies.

placebo [pluh-SEE-bo; Latin for "I shall please"] **effect** experimental results caused by expectations alone; any effect on behavior caused by the administration of an inert substance or condition, which the recipient assumes is an active agent.

So, does this mean that smarter mothers (who in modern countries more often breast-feed) have smarter children? Or, as some researchers believe, do the nutrients of mother's milk contribute to brain development? To help answer this question, researchers have *controlled for* (statistically removed differences in) certain other factors, such as maternal age, education, and income. And they have found that in infant nutrition, mother's milk correlates modestly but positively with later intelligence.

Correlational research cannot control for all possible influences on a result. But researchers can isolate cause and effect with an **experiment.** Experiments enable a researcher to focus on the possible effects of one or more factors by (1) *manipulating the factors of interest* and (2) *holding constant (controlling) other factors.* With parental permission, a British research team randomly assigned 424 hospital preterm infants either to standard infant formula feedings or to donated breast-milk feedings (Lucas et al., 1992). On intelligence tests taken at age 8, the children nourished with breast milk had significantly higher intelligence scores than their formula-fed counterparts.

Random Assignment

No single experiment is conclusive, of course. But by **randomly assigning** infants to one feeding group or the other, researchers were able to hold constant all factors except nutrition. This eliminated alternative explanations and supported the conclusion that breast is indeed best for developing intelligence (at least for preterm infants). If a behavior (such as test performance) changes when we vary an experimental factor (such as infant nutrition), then we infer that the factor is having an effect.

The point to remember: Unlike correlational studies, which uncover naturally occurring relationships, an experiment manipulates a factor to determine its effect.

Consider, then, how we might use this method to assess a therapeutic intervention. Our tendency to seek new remedies when we are ill or emotionally down can produce misleading testimonies. If three days into a cold we start taking vitamin C tablets and find our cold symptoms lessening, we may credit the pills rather than the cold naturally subsiding. Similarly, in the 1700s, blood-letting *seemed* effective: People sometimes improved after the treatment. When they didn't, the practitioner inferred the disease was just too advanced to be reversed. (We, of course, now know that usually blood-letting is a *bad* treatment.) Whether a remedy is truly effective or not, enthusiastic users will probably endorse it. To find out whether it actually *is* effective, we must experiment.

And that is precisely how investigators evaluate new drug treatments and new methods of psychological therapy (Chapter 14). Participants in these studies are randomly assigned to research groups. One group, the **experimental group,** receives a treatment (such as medication or other therapy). The other group, the **control group,** receives a pseudotreatment—an inert *placebo* (perhaps a pill with no drug in it).

Participants are often *blind* (uninformed) about what treatment, if any, they are receiving. If the study is using a **double-blind procedure,** neither the participants nor the research assistants collecting the data will know which group is receiving the treatment. Researchers take these measures because, to know how effective a therapy really is, they must control for a possible **placebo effect**—results created by the participants' belief in a treatment's healing powers or the staff's enthusiasm for its potential. The placebo effect is well documented in reducing pain, depression, and anxiety (Kirsch & Sapirstein, 1998). Just *thinking* you are getting a treatment can boost your spirits, relax your body, and relieve your symptoms. And the more expensive the placebo, the more "real" it seems: A fake pill that costs U.S.$2.50 works better than one costing 10 cents (Waber et al., 2008).

"If I don't think it's going to work, will it still work?"

By randomly assigning people to the experimental and control conditions, researchers can be fairly certain the two groups are otherwise identical. Random assignment roughly equalizes the two groups in age, attitudes, and every other characteristic. With random assignment, as occurred with the infants in the breast-milk experiment, we also can conclude that any later differences between people in the experimental and control groups will usually be the result of the treatment.

Independent and Dependent Variables

11: **What are independent and dependent variables, and how do they differ?**

Here is an even more potent example of a double-blind experiment: The drug Viagra was approved for use after 21 clinical trials. One trial was an experiment in which researchers randomly assigned 329 men with erectile dysfunction to either an experimental group (Viagra takers) or a control group (placebo takers). In this double-blind procedure, neither the men nor the person who gave them the pills knew which drug they were receiving. The result: At peak doses, 69 percent of Viagra-assisted attempts at intercourse were successful, compared with 22 percent for men receiving the placebo (Goldstein et al., 1998). Viagra worked.

This simple experiment manipulated just one factor: the drug dosage (none versus peak dose). We call this experimental factor the **independent variable** because we can vary it *independently* of other factors, such as the men's age, weight, and personality (which random assignment should control). Experiments examine the effect of one or more independent variables on some measurable behavior, called the **dependent variable** because it can vary *depending* on what takes place during the experiment. Both variables are given precise *operational definitions,* which specify the procedures that manipulate the independent variable (the precise drug dosage and timing in this study) or measure the dependent variable (the questions that assessed the men's responses). These definitions answer the "What do you mean?" question with a level of precision that enables others to repeat the study.

Let's pause to check your understanding using a simple psychology experiment: To test the effect of perceived ethnicity on the availability of a rental house, Adrian Carpusor and William Loges (2006) sent identically worded e-mail inquiries to 1115 Los Angeles-area landlords. The researchers varied the ethnic connotation of the sender's name and tracked the percentage of positive replies (invitations to view the apartment in person). "Patrick McDougall," "Said Al-Rahman," and "Tyrell Jackson" received, respectively, 89 percent, 66 percent, and 56 percent invitations.

In this experiment, what was the independent variable? The dependent variable? (See the answers in margin to the right)

Experiments can also help us evaluate social programs. Do early childhood education programs boost impoverished children's chances for success? What are the effects of different anti-smoking campaigns? Do school sex-education programs reduce teen pregnancies? To answer such questions, we can experiment: If an intervention is welcomed but resources are scarce, we could use a lottery to randomly assign some people (or regions) to experience the new program and others to a control group. If later the two groups differ, the intervention's effect will be confirmed (Passell, 1993). Sometimes, however, experiments are not feasible or ethical. For example, we cannot randomly assign children to be raised by spanking or non-spanking parents. Instead, we correlate parental spanking amounts with children's behavior.

Let's recap. A *variable* is anything that can vary (infant nutrition, intelligence, TV exposure—anything within the bounds of what is feasible and ethical). Experiments aim to *manipulate* an *independent* variable, *measure changes* in the *dependent* variable, and *control* (minimize the possible effects of) all other variables. An experiment has at least two different groups: an *experimental group* and a *comparison* or *control group.*

Note the distinction between random sampling in surveys (discussed earlier) and random assignment in experiments (depicted in Figure 1.5 on the next page). Random sampling *helps us generalize to a larger population.* Random assignment *controls extraneous influences, which helps us infer cause and effect.*

The independent variable, which the researchers manipulated, was the ethnicity-related names. The dependent variable, which they measured, was the positive response rate.

---

independent variable the experimental factor that is manipulated; the variable whose effect is being studied.

---

dependent variable the outcome factor; the variable that may change in response to manipulations of the independent variable.

Random assignment works to equate the groups before any treatment effects. (**FIGURE 1.5** illustrates the breast-milk experiment's design.) In this way, an experiment tests the effect of at least one *independent variable* (what we manipulate) on at least one *dependent variable* (the outcome we measure). **TABLE 1.2** compares the features of psychology's research methods.

FIGURE 1.5 Experimentation To discern causation, psychologists may randomly assign some participants to an experimental group, others to a control group. Measuring the dependent variable (intelligence score in later childhood) will determine the effect of the independent variable (type of milk).

TABLE 1.2 Comparing Research Methods

Research Method	Basic Purpose	How Conducted	What Is Manipulated	Weaknesses
Descriptive	To observe and record behavior	Do case studies, surveys, or naturalistic observations	Nothing	No control of variables; single cases may be misleading
Correlational	To detect naturally occurring relationships; to assess how well one variable predicts another	Compute statistical association, sometimes among survey responses	Nothing	Does not specify cause and effect
Experimental	To explore cause and effect	Manipulate one or more factors; use random assignment	The independent variable(s)	Sometimes not feasible; results may not generalize to other contexts; not ethical to manipulate certain variables

REHEARSE IT!

18. Descriptive and correlational studies describe behavior, detect relationships, and predict behavior. But to explain behaviors, psychologists use
a. naturalistic observation.
b. experiments.
c. surveys.
d. case studies.

19. To test the effect of a new drug on depression, we randomly assign people to control and experimental groups. Those in the experimental group take a pink pill containing the new medication; those in the control group take a pink pill that contains no medication. Which statement is true?
a. The medication is the dependent variable.

b. Depression is the independent variable.
c. Participants in the control group take a placebo.
d. Participants in the experimental group take a placebo.

20. A double-blind procedure is often used to prevent researchers' biases from influencing the outcome of an experiment. In this procedure,
a. only the participants know whether they are in the control group or the experimental group.
b. experimental and control group members will be carefully matched for age, sex, income, and education level.
c. neither the participants nor the researchers know who is in the experimental group or control group.

d. someone separate from the researcher will ask people to volunteer for the experimental group or the control group.

21. A researcher wants to determine whether noise level affects the blood pressure of elderly people. In one group she varies the level of noise in the environment and records participants' blood pressure. In this experiment, the level of noise is the
a. control condition.
b. placebo.
c. dependent variable.
d. independent variable.

Answers: 18. b, 19. c, 20. c, 21. d.

Frequently Asked Questions About Psychology

culture the enduring behaviors, ideas, attitudes, and traditions shared by a group of people and transmitted from one generation to the next.

We have reflected on how a scientific approach can restrain biases. We have seen how case studies, surveys, and naturalistic observations help us describe behavior. We have also noted that correlational studies assess the association between two factors, which indicates how well one thing predicts another. We have examined the logic that underlies experiments, which use control conditions and random assignment of participants to isolate the effects of an independent variable on a dependent variable.

Yet, even knowing this much, you may still be approaching psychology with a mixture of curiosity and apprehension. So before we plunge in, let's entertain some frequently asked questions.

12: Can laboratory experiments illuminate everyday life?

When you see or hear about psychological research, do you ever wonder whether people's behavior in the lab will predict their behavior in real life? For example, does detecting the blink of a faint red light in a dark room have anything useful to say about flying a plane at night? After viewing a violent, sexually explicit film, does an aroused man's increased willingness to push buttons that he thinks will electrically shock a woman really say anything about whether violent pornography makes a man more likely to abuse a woman?

Before you answer, consider: The experimenter *intends* the laboratory environment to be a simplified reality—one that simulates and controls important features of everyday life. Just as a wind tunnel lets airplane designers re-create airflow forces under controlled conditions, a laboratory experiment lets psychologists re-create psychological forces under controlled conditions.

An experiment's purpose is not to re-create the exact behaviors of everyday life but to test *theoretical principles* (Mook, 1983). In aggression studies, deciding whether to push a button that delivers a shock may not be the same as slapping someone in the face, but the principle is the same. *It is the resulting principles—not the specific findings—that help explain everyday behaviors.*

When psychologists apply laboratory research on aggression to actual violence, they are applying theoretical principles of aggressive behavior, principles they have refined through many experiments. Similarly, it is the principles of the visual system, developed from experiments in artificial settings (such as looking at red lights in the dark), that we apply to more complex behaviors such as night flying. And many investigations show that principles derived in the laboratory do typically generalize to the everyday world (Anderson et al., 1999).

The point to remember: Psychologists' concerns lie less with particular behaviors than with the general principles that help explain many behaviors.

A cultured greeting Because culture shapes people's understanding of social behavior, actions that seem ordinary to us may seem quite odd to visitors from far away. Yet underlying these differences are powerful similarities. Supporters of newly elected leaders everywhere typically greet them with pleased deference, though not necessarily with bows and folded hands, as in India. Here influential and popular politician Sonia Gandhi greeted some of her constituents shortly after her election.

13: Does behavior depend on one's culture and gender?

What can psychological studies done in one time and place, often with White Europeans or North Americans, really tell us about people in general? As we will see time and again, **culture**—shared ideas and behaviors that one generation passes on to the next—matters. Our culture shapes our behavior. It influences our standards of promptness and frankness, our attitudes toward premarital sex and varying body shapes, our tendency to be casual or formal, our willingness to make eye contact, our conversational distance, and much, much more. Being aware of such differences, we can restrain our assumptions that others will think and act as we do. Given the growing mixing and clashing of cultures, our need for such awareness is urgent.

It is also true, however, that our shared biological heritage unites us as a universal human family. The same underlying processes guide people everywhere:

- People diagnosed with dyslexia, a reading disorder, exhibit the same brain malfunction whether they are Italian, French, or British (Paulesu et al., 2001).
- Variation in languages may impede communication across cultures. Yet all languages share deep principles of grammar, and people from opposite hemispheres can communicate with a smile or a frown.
- People in different cultures vary in feelings of loneliness. But across cultures, loneliness is magnified by shyness, low self-esteem, and being unmarried (Jones et al., 1985; Rokach et al., 2002).

We are each in certain respects like all others, like some others, and like no other. Studying people of all races and cultures helps us discern our similarities and our differences, our human kinship and our diversity.

You will see throughout this book that *gender* matters, too. Researchers report gender differences in what we dream, in how we express and detect emotions, and in our risk for alcohol dependence, depression, and eating disorders. Gender differences fascinate us, and studying them is potentially beneficial. For example, many researchers believe that women carry on conversations more readily to build relationships, and that men talk more to give information and advice (Tannen, 1990). Knowing this difference can help us prevent conflicts and misunderstandings in everyday relationships.

But again, psychologically as well as biologically, women and men are overwhelmingly similar. Whether female or male, we learn to walk at about the same age. We experience the same sensations of light and sound. We feel the same pangs of hunger, desire, and fear. We exhibit similar overall intelligence and well-being.

The point to remember: Even when specific attitudes and behaviors vary by gender or across cultures, as they often do, the underlying processes are much the same.

14: Why do psychologists study animals, and is it ethical to experiment on animals?

Many psychologists study animals because they find them fascinating. They want to understand how different species learn, think, and behave. Psychologists also study animals to learn about people, by doing experiments permissible only with animals. We humans are not *like* animals; we *are* animals and our physiology resembles that of many other species. Animal experiments have therefore led to treatments for human diseases—insulin for diabetes, vaccines to prevent polio and rabies, transplants to replace defective organs.

Humans are complex, but the same processes by which we learn are present in rats, monkeys, and even sea slugs. The simplicity of the sea slug's nervous system is precisely what makes it so revealing of the neural mechanisms of learning.

If we share important similarities with other animals, then should we not respect them? "We cannot defend our scientific work with animals on the basis of the similarities between them and ourselves and then defend it morally on the basis of differences," noted Roger Ulrich (1991). The animal protection movement protests the use of animals in psychological, biological, and medical research. But researchers remind us that the animals used worldwide each year in research are but a fraction of 1 percent of the billions of animals killed annually for food. And yearly, for every dog or cat used in an experiment and cared for under humane regulations, 50 others are killed in humane animal shelters (Goodwin & Morrison, 1999).

Some animal protection organizations want to replace experiments on animals with naturalistic observation. Many animal researchers respond that this is not a question of good versus evil but of compassion for animals versus compassion for people.

"All people are the same; only their habits differ."

—Confucius, 551–479 B.C.E.

"Rats are very similar to humans except that they are not stupid enough to purchase lottery tickets."

—Dave Barry, July 2, 2002

"I believe that to prevent, cripple, or needlessly complicate the research that can relieve animal and human suffering is profoundly inhuman, cruel, and immoral."

—Psychologist Neal Miller, 1983

Out of this heated debate, two issues emerge. The basic one is whether it is right to place the well-being of humans above that of animals. In experiments on stress and cancer, is it right that mice get tumors in the hope that people might not? Should some monkeys be exposed to an HIV-like virus in the search for an AIDS vaccine? Is our use and consumption of other animals as natural as the behavior of carnivorous hawks, cats, and whales? The answers to such questions vary by culture. In Gallup surveys in Canada and the United States, about 60 percent of adults deem medical testing on animals "morally acceptable." In Britain, only 37 percent do (Mason, 2003).

If we give human life first priority, the second issue is, What safeguards should protect the well-being of animals in research? One survey of animal researchers gave an answer, with 98 percent or more in favor of government regulations protecting primates, dogs, and cats, and 74 percent in favor of regulations providing for the humane care of rats and mice (Plous & Herzog, 2000). Many professional associations and funding agencies already have such guidelines. For example, British Psychological Society guidelines call for housing animals under reasonably natural living conditions, with companions for social animals (Lea, 2000). American Psychological Association (2002) guidelines mandate ensuring the "comfort, health, and humane treatment" of animals and minimizing "infection, illness, and pain." Humane care also leads to more effective science, because pain and stress would distort the animals' behavior during experiments.

Animals have themselves benefited from animal research. One famous example was Louis Pasteur's experiments with rabies, which caused some dogs to suffer but led to a vaccine that spared not only millions of people but also millions of dogs from an agonizing death. More recently, by measuring stress hormone levels in samples of millions of dogs brought each year to animal shelters, researchers devised handling and stroking methods that reduce stress and ease the dogs' transition to adoptive homes (Tuber et al., 1999). Other studies have helped improve care and management in animals' natural habitats. By revealing our behavioral kinship with animals and the remarkable intelligence of chimpanzees, gorillas, and other animals, experiments have also led to increased empathy and protection for them. At its best, a psychology concerned for humans and sensitive to animals serves the welfare of both.

15 : Is it ethical to experiment on people?

If the image of researchers delivering supposed electric shocks troubles you, you may be relieved to know that in most psychological studies, especially those with human participants, blinking lights, flashing words, and pleasant social interactions are more common.

Occasionally, though, researchers do temporarily stress or deceive people, but only when they believe it is essential to a justifiable end, such as understanding and controlling violent behavior or studying mood swings. Such experiments wouldn't work if the participants knew all there was to know about the experiment beforehand. Wanting to be helpful, the participants might try to confirm the researcher's predictions.

The American Psychological Association (1992), the British Psychological Society (1993), and psychologists internationally (Pettifor, 2004) have developed ethical principles to guide investigators. They include (1) obtaining potential participants' informed consent, (2) protecting participants from harm and discomfort, (3) keeping information about individual participants confidential, and (4) fully explaining the research afterward. Moreover, most universities today screen research proposals through an ethics committee that safeguards the well-being of every participant.

"Please do not forget those of us who suffer from incurable diseases or disabilities who hope for a cure through research that requires the use of animals."

—Psychologist Dennis Feeney (1987)

"The righteous know the needs of their animals."

—Proverbs 12:10

"The greatness of a nation can be judged by the way its animals are treated."

—Mahatma Gandhi, 1869–1948

Animal research benefiting animals
Thanks partly to research on the benefits of novelty, control, and stimulation, these gorillas are enjoying an improved quality of life in New York's Bronx Zoo. As they would in the wild, they now work for their supper (Stewart, 2002).

The ideal is for a researcher to be sufficiently informative *and* considerate that participants will leave feeling at least as good about themselves as when they came in. Better yet, they should be repaid by having learned something. If treated respectfully, most participants enjoy or accept their engagement (Epley & Huff, 1998; Kimmel, 1998). Indeed, say psychology's defenders, professors provoke much greater anxiety by giving and returning course exams than do researchers in the typical experiment.

16: Is psychology free of value judgments?

Psychology is definitely not value-free. Values affect what we study, how we study it, and how we interpret results. Researchers' values influence their choice of topics. Should we study worker productivity or worker morale? Sex discrimination or gender differences? Conformity or independence? Values can also color "the facts." As we noted earlier, what we want or expect to see can bias our observations and interpretations (**FIGURE 1.6**).

FIGURE 1.6 What do you see? People interpret ambiguous information to fit their preconceptions. Did you see a duck or a rabbit? Before showing some friends this image, ask them if they can see the duck lying on its back (or the bunny in the grass). (From Shepard, 1990.)

Even the words we use to describe something can reflect our values. Are the sex acts we do not practice "perversions" or "sexual variations"? In psychology or in everyday speech, labels describe and labels evaluate. One person's *rigidity* is another's *consistency*. One person's *faith* is another's *fanaticism*. Our labeling someone as *firm* or *stubborn, careful* or *picky, discreet* or *secretive* reveals our feelings.

"It is doubtless impossible to approach any human problem with a mind free from bias."

—Simone de Beauvoir, *The Second Sex*, 1953

Popular applications of psychology also contain hidden values. If you defer to "professional" guidance about how to live—how to raise children, how to achieve self-fulfillment, what to do with sexual feelings, how to get ahead at work—you are accepting value-laden advice. A science of behavior and mental processes can certainly help us reach our goals, but it cannot decide what those goals should be.

Psychology is value-laden. Is it also dangerously powerful, as some people worry? Is it an accident that astronomy is the oldest science and psychology the youngest? To some people, exploring the external universe seems far safer than exploring our own inner universe. Might psychology, they ask, be used to manipulate people?

Knowledge, like all power, can be used for good or evil. Nuclear power has been used to light up cities—and to demolish them. Persuasive power has been used to educate people—and to deceive them. Although psychology does indeed have the power to deceive, its purpose is to enlighten. Every day, psychologists are exploring ways to enhance learning, creativity, and compassion. Psychology speaks to many of our world's great problems—war, overpopulation, prejudice, family crises, crime—all of which involve attitudes and behaviors. Psychology also speaks to our deepest longings—for nourishment, for love, for happiness. And as you will see, one of the newer developments in this field—*positive psychology*—has as its goal exploring and promoting human strengths. Psychology cannot address all of life's great questions, but it speaks to some mighty important ones.

Psychology speaks In making its historic 1954 school desegregation decision, the U.S. Supreme Court cited the expert testimony and research of psychologists Kenneth Clark and Mamie Phipps Clark (1947). The Clarks reported that, when given a choice between Black and White dolls, most African-American children chose the White doll, which seemingly indicated internalized anti-Black prejudice.

REHEARSE IT!

22. The laboratory environment is designed to
    a. exactly re-create the events of every-day life.
    b. re-create psychological forces under controlled conditions.
    c. create opportunities for naturalistic observation.
    d. minimize the use of animals and humans in psychological research.

23. Which of the following is true regarding gender differences and similarities?

    a. Differences between the genders outweigh any similarities.
    b. Despite some gender differences, the underlying processes of human behavior are the same.
    c. Both similarities and differences between the genders depend more on biology than on environment.
    d. Gender differences are so numerous, it is difficult to make meaningful comparisons.

24. In defending their experimental research with animals, psychologists have noted that
    a. animals' physiology and behavior can tell us much about our own.
    b. animal experimentation sometimes helps animals as well as humans.
    c. advancing the well-being of humans justifies animal experimentation.
    d. all of these statements are correct.

Answers : 22. b, 23. b, 24. d

Tips for Studying Psychology

17: How can psychological principles help you as a student?

The investment you are making in studying psychology should enrich your life and enlarge your vision. Although many of life's significant questions are beyond psychology, some very important ones are illuminated by even a first psychology course. Through painstaking research, psychologists have gained insights into brain and mind, dreams and memories, depression and joy. Even the unanswered questions can enrich us, by renewing our sense of mystery about "things too wonderful" for us yet to understand. Your study of psychology can also help teach you *how to ask and answer important questions*—how to think critically as you evaluate competing ideas and claims.

Having your life enriched and your vision enlarged (and getting a decent grade) requires effective study. As you will see in Chapter 8, to master information you must *actively process it*. Your mind is not like your stomach, something to be filled passively; it is more like a muscle that grows stronger with exercise. Countless experiments reveal that people learn and remember best when they put material in their own words, rehearse it, and then review and rehearse it again.

The **SQ3R** study method incorporates these principles (Robinson, 1970). SQ3R is an acronym for its five steps: *Survey, Question, Read, Rehearse, Review*.

- To study a chapter, first *survey*, taking a bird's-eye view. Scan the headings, and notice how the chapter is organized.
- As you prepare to read each section, use its heading or numbered Preview Question to form your own *question* to answer as you read. For this section, you might have asked, "How can I most effectively and efficiently master the information in this book?"
- Then *read*, actively searching for the answer to your question. At each sitting, read only as much of the chapter (usually a single main section) as you can absorb without tiring. Read actively and critically. Ask questions. Take notes. Consider implications: How does what you've read relate to your own life? Does it support or challenge your assumptions? How convincing is the evidence?
- Having read a section, *rehearse* in your own words what you have read. Test yourself by trying to answer your question, rehearsing what you can recall, then glancing back over what you can't recall.
- Finally, *review:* Read over any notes you have taken, again with an eye on the chapter's organization, and quickly review the whole chapter.

Survey, question, read, rehearse, review. I have organized this book's chapters to facilitate your use of the SQ3R study system. Each chapter begins with a chapter

SQ3R a study method incorporating five steps: *Survey, Question, Read, Rehearse, Review*.

outline that aids your *survey*. Headings and numbered Preview *Questions* suggest issues and concepts you should consider as you *read*. The material is organized into sections of readable length. At the end of main sections, there are *Rehearse It* questions that help you test and *rehearse* what you've learned before moving on, and more *Test for Success* exercises follow at the chapter's end. The answers to the Preview Questions help you *review* the chapter's essentials, and the list of key terms helps you check your mastery of important concepts. Survey, question, read . . .

Five additional study tips may further boost your learning:

Distribute your study time. One of psychology's oldest findings is that *spaced practice*—perhaps one hour a day, six days a week—promotes better retention than *massed practice*—cramming it into one long study blitz. For example, rather than trying to read an entire chapter in a single sitting, read just one main section and then turn to something else.

Spacing your study sessions requires a disciplined approach to managing your time. (Richard O. Straub explains time management in the helpful *Study Guide* that accompanies this text.)

Learn to think critically. Whether you are reading or in class, note people's *assumptions* and *values*. What perspective or bias underlies an argument? *Evaluate evidence.* Is it anecdotal? Correlational? Experimental? *Assess conclusions.* Are there alternative explanations? (Use the Test for Success: Critical Thinking Exercises at the end of each chapter to build your critical thinking skills as you check your understanding of the chapter's main concepts.)

In class, listen actively. Listen for the main ideas and subideas of a lecture. *Write them down.* Ask questions during and after class. In class, as in your private study, process the information actively and you will understand and retain it better. As psychologist William James urged a century ago, *"No reception without reaction, no impression without . . . expression."*

Overlearn. We are prone to overestimating how much we know. You may understand a chapter as you read it, but by devoting extra study time to testing yourself and reviewing what you think you know, you will retain your new knowledge long into the future.

Be a smart test-taker. If a test contains both multiple-choice questions and an essay question, turn first to the essay. Read the question carefully, noting exactly what the instructor is asking. On the back of a page, pencil in a list of points you'd like to make and then organize them. Before writing, put aside the essay and work through the multiple-choice questions. (As you do so, your mind may continue to mull over the essay question. Sometimes the objective questions will bring pertinent thoughts to mind.) Then reread the essay question, rethink your answer, and start writing. When you finish, proofread your answer to eliminate spelling and grammatical errors that make you look less competent than you are. When reading multiple-choice questions, don't confuse yourself by trying to imagine how each choice might be the right one. Instead, try to answer each question as if it were a fill-in-the-blank question. First cover the answers and form a sentence in your mind, recalling what you know to complete the sentence. Then read the answers on the test and find the alternative that best matches your own answer.

While exploring psychology, you will learn much more than effective study techniques. Psychology deepens our appreciation for how we humans perceive, think, feel, and act. By so doing it can indeed enrich our lives and enlarge our vision. Through this book I hope to help guide you toward that end. As educator Charles Eliot said a century ago: "Books are the quietest and most constant of friends, and the most patient of teachers."

Thinking Critically With Psychological Science

What Is Psychology?

1 What are some important milestones in the development of the science of psychology?

Psychological science's first laboratory appeared in 1879, launched by Wilhelm Wundt and his students. The field's early scholars came from several disciplines and many countries.

Psychology began as a "science of mental life." In the 1920s, under the influence of the *behaviorists*, it evolved into the "scientific study of observable behavior." After the cognitive revolution in the 1960s, *psychology* has been widely defined as the "science of behavior and mental processes."

2 What is psychology's historic big issue?

Psychology's biggest and most enduring concern has been the *nature-nurture issue*, the controversy over the relative contributions of the influences of genes and experience. Today's science emphasizes the interaction of genes and experiences in specific environments.

3 What are psychology's levels of analysis and related perspectives?

The *biopsychosocial approach* integrates information from the biological, psychological, and social-cultural *levels of analysis*. Psychologists study human behaviors and mental processes from many different perspectives (including the neuroscience, evolutionary, behavior genetics, psychodynamic, behavioral, cognitive, and social-cultural).

4 What are some of psychology's subfields?

Some psychologists specialize in *basic research* (often in the subfields of biological, developmental, cognitive, personality, and social psychology). Others, for example, industrial-organizational psychologists, do *applied research. Counseling psychologists* and *clinical psychologists* practice psychology as a helping profession. Clinical psychologists study, assess, and treat (with psychotherapy) people with psychological disorders. *Psychiatrists* also study, assess, and treat people with disorders, but as medical doctors, they may prescribe drugs in addition to psychotherapy.

Why Do Psychology?

5 Why are the answers that flow from the scientific approach more reliable than those based on intuition and common sense?

Common sense often serves us well, but we are prone to *hindsight bias* (the "I-knew-it-all-along phenomenon"), a tendency to believe, after learning an outcome, that we would have foreseen it. We also are routinely overconfident of our judgments, thanks partly to our bias to seek information that confirms them. Although limited by the testable questions it can address, scientific inquiry can help us sift reality from illusion and restrain the biases of our unaided intuition.

6 What attitudes characterize scientific inquiry, and what does it mean to think critically?

The three components of the scientific attitude are (1) a curious eagerness to (2) skeptically scrutinize competing ideas and (3) an open-minded humility before nature. This attitude carries into everyday life as *critical thinking*, which examines assumptions, discerns hidden values, evaluates evidence, and assesses outcomes. Putting ideas, even crazy-sounding ideas, to the test helps us winnow sense from nonsense.

How Do Psychologists Ask and Answer Questions?

7 How do psychologists use the scientific method to construct theories?

Psychological *theories* organize observations and imply predictive *hypotheses*. After constructing precise *operational definitions* of their procedures, researchers test their hypotheses, validate and refine the theory, and, sometimes, suggest practical applications. If other researchers obtain similar results by *replicating* the study with different participants and conditions, we can then place greater confidence in the conclusion.

8 How do psychologists observe and describe behavior?

Psychologists observe and describe behavior using individual *case studies, surveys* among *random samples* of a *population*, and *naturalistic observations*. In generalizing from observations, representative samples are a better guide than vivid anecdotes.

9 What are positive and negative correlations, and why do they enable prediction but not cause-effect explanation?

A positive *correlation* (ranging from 0 to +1.00) indicates a direct relationship: Two factors rise or decrease together. A negative correlation (ranging from 0 to −1.00), indicates an inverse relationship: As one item increases, the other decreases. An association (sometimes stated as a correlation coefficient) indicates the possibility of a cause-effect relationship, but it does not prove the direction of the influence, or whether an underlying third factor may explain the correlation. *Illusory correlations* are random events that we notice and falsely assume are related. Patterns or sequences occur naturally in sets of random data. Our tendency to interpret these patterns as meaningful connections may be an attempt to make sense of the world around us.

10 How do experiments, powered by random assignment, clarify cause and effect?

To discover cause-effect relationships, psychologists conduct *experiments*, manipulating one or more factors of interest and controlling other factors. *Random assignment* minimizes preexisting differences between the *experimental group* (exposed to the treatment) and the *control group* (given a placebo or different version of the treatment). Studies may use a *double-blind procedure* to avoid a *placebo effect* and researchers' bias.

11 **What are independent and dependent variables, and how do they differ?**

An *independent variable* is the factor you manipulate to study its effect. A *dependent variable* is the factor you measure to discover any changes that occur in response to these manipulations.

Frequently Asked Questions About Psychology

12 **Can laboratory experiments illuminate everyday life?**

By intentionally creating a controlled, artificial environment in the lab, researchers aim to test theoretical principles. These general principles help explain everyday behaviors.

13 **Does behavior depend on one's culture and gender?**

Attitudes and behaviors vary across *cultures,* but the underlying principles vary much less because of our human kinship. Although gender differences tend to capture attention, it is important to remember our greater gender similarities.

14 **Why do psychologists study animals, and is it ethical to experiment on animals?**

Some psychologists are primarily interested in animal behavior. Others study animals to better understand the physiological and psychological processes shared by humans. Under ethical and legal guidelines, animals used in experiments rarely experience pain. Nevertheless, animal rights groups raise an important issue: Even if it leads to the relief of human suffering, is an animal's temporary suffering justified?

15 **Is it ethical to experiment on people?**

Researchers may temporarily stress or deceive people in order to learn something important. Professional ethical standards provide guidelines concerning the treatment of both human and animal participants.

16 **Is psychology free of value judgments?**

Psychologists' values influence their choice of research topics, their theories and observations, their labels for behavior, and their professional advice. Applications of psychology's principles have been used mainly in the service of humanity.

Tips for Studying Psychology

17 **How can psychological principles help you as a student?**

Research has shown that learning and memory are enhanced by active study. The *SQ3R* study method—survey, question, read, rehearse, and review—applies the principles derived from this research.

Terms and Concepts to Remember

behaviorism, p. 4
humanistic psychology, p. 4
cognitive neuroscience, p. 4
psychology, p. 4
nature-nurture issue, p. 5
levels of analysis, p. 6
biopsychosocial approach, p. 6
basic research, p. 8
applied research, p. 8
counseling psychology, p. 8
clinical psychology, p. 8
psychiatry, p. 8

hindsight bias, p. 10
critical thinking, p. 13
theory, p. 14
hypothesis, p. 14
operational definition, p. 15
replication, p. 15
case study, p. 15
survey, p. 16
population, p. 16
random sample, p. 16
naturalistic observation, p. 17
correlation, p. 18

illusory correlation, p. 19
experiment, p. 22
random assignment, p. 22
experimental group, p. 22
control group, p. 22
double-blind procedure, p. 22
placebo effect, p. 22
independent variable, p. 22
dependent variable, p. 23
culture, p. 25
SQ3R, p. 29

Test for Success: Critical Thinking Exercises
By Amy Himsel, El Camino College

1. "Nurture works on what nature endows." Describe what this means, using your own words.

2. How can you use your knowledge of the scientific attitude to help you evaluate claims in the media, even if you're not a scientific expert on the issue?

3. Here are some recently reported correlations, with interpretations drawn by journalists. Further research, often including experiments, has clarified cause and effect in each case. Knowing just these correlations, can you come up with other possible explanations for each of these?
   a. Alcohol use is associated with violence. (One interpretation: Drinking triggers or unleashes aggressive behavior.)

b. Educated people live longer, on average, than less-educated people. (One interpretation: Education lengthens life and enhances health.)

c. Teens engaged in team sports are less likely to use drugs, smoke, have sex, carry weapons, and eat junk food than are teens who do not engage in team sports. (One interpretation: Team sports encourage healthy living.)

d. Adolescents who frequently see smoking in movies are more likely to smoke. (One interpretation: Movie stars' behavior influences impressionable teens.)

4. As you watch an Orlando Magic basketball game with your friend, he says that Dwight Howard really has a hot hand right now and the other players should give him the ball as soon as possible. Based on your knowledge of our tendency toward illusory thinking, how should you respond?

5. Foot pads purported to draw toxins out of the body during sleep have become popular lately. Testimonials suggest that foot pads remove toxins from the body and also help alleviate a variety of health problems, including fatigue and backaches. How can we determine whether foot pads are actually effective?

The Test for Success exercises offer you a chance to apply your critical thinking skills to aspects of the material you have just read. Suggestions for answering these questions can be found in Appendix D at the back of the book.

 Multiple-choice self-tests and more may be found at www.worthpublishers.com/myers.

Chapter Outline

- **Neural Communication**
  Neurons
  How Neurons Communicate
  How Neurotransmitters
   Influence Us

- **The Nervous System**
  The Peripheral Nervous System
  The Central Nervous System

- **The Endocrine System**

- **The Brain**
  Older Brain Structures
  CLOSE-UP: The Tools of
   Discovery—Having Our Head
   Examined
  The Cerebral Cortex
  Our Divided Brain
  Right-Left Differences in the
   Intact Brain

2: The Biology of Mind

Imagine that just moments before your death, someone removed your brain from your body and kept it alive by floating it in a tank of fluid while feeding it enriched blood. Would you still be in there? Further imagine that your still-living brain has been transplanted into the body of a person whose own brain was severely damaged. To whose home should the recovered patient return?

If you answered that the patient should return to your home, you illustrated what most of us believe—that we reside in our head. An acquaintance of mine received a new heart donated by a woman who in turn had received a matching heart-lung transplant. When the two chanced to meet in their hospital ward, the donor introduced herself: "I think you have my heart." But only her heart; her self, she assumed, still resided in her skull.

In this chapter, we explore the biology of the mind—the links between our brain and our behavior. No principle is more central to today's psychology, or to this book, than this: *Everything psychological—every idea, every mood, every urge—is simultaneously biological.* We may talk separately of biological and psychological influences, but to think, feel, or act without a body would be like running without legs.

Biological psychologists study the links between our biology and our behavior. In this chapter we start small and build from the bottom up—from nerve cells up to the brain.

"You're certainly a lot less fun since the operation."

Neural Communication

The human body is complexity built from simplicity. Part of this complexity is our amazing internal communication system, which makes the Internet look simple. Across the world, researchers are unlocking the mysteries of how our brain uses electrical and chemical processes to take in, organize, interpret, store, and use information. The story begins with the system's basic building block, the *neuron,* or nerve cell. We'll look first at its structure, and then at how neurons work together.

Neurons

1: **What are neurons, and how do they transmit information?**

Neurons differ, but all are variations on the same theme. Each consists of a *cell body* and its branching fibers. The bushy **dendrite** fibers receive information and conduct it toward the cell body. From there, the cell's **axon** (sometimes covered with a *myelin sheath*) passes the message along to other neurons or to muscles or glands. Axons speak. Dendrites listen.

Unlike the short dendrites, axons can be very long, projecting several feet through the body. A neuron carrying orders to a leg muscle, for example, has a cell body and axon roughly on the scale of a basketball attached to a rope 4 miles long.

biological psychology the scientific study of the links between biological (genetic, neural, hormonal) and psychological processes. (Some biological psychologists call themselves *behavioral neuroscientists, neuropsychologists, behavior geneticists, physiological psychologists,* or *biopsychologists.*)

neuron a nerve cell; the basic building block of the nervous system.

dendrite the neuron's bushy, branching extensions that receive messages and conduct impulses toward the cell body.

axon the neuron's extension that passes messages through its branching terminal fibers that form junctions with other neurons, muscles, or glands.

35

action potential a neural impulse; a brief electrical charge that travels down an axon.

threshold the level of stimulation required to trigger a neural impulse.

synapse [SIN-aps] the junction between the axon tip of the sending neuron and the dendrite or cell body of the receiving neuron. The tiny gap at this junction is called the *synaptic gap* or *synaptic cleft*.

neurotransmitters chemical messengers that cross the synaptic gaps between neurons. When released by the sending neuron, neurotransmitters travel across the synapse and bind to receptor sites on the receiving neuron, thereby influencing whether that neuron will generate a neural impulse.

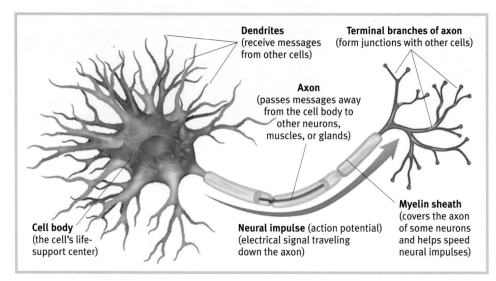

Dendrites (receive messages from other cells)

Terminal branches of axon (form junctions with other cells)

Axon (passes messages away from the cell body to other neurons, muscles, or glands)

Cell body (the cell's life-support center)

Neural impulse (action potential) (electrical signal traveling down the axon)

Myelin sheath (covers the axon of some neurons and helps speed neural impulses)

FIGURE 2.1 **A motor neuron**

Neurons transmit messages when stimulated by signals from our senses or when triggered by chemical signals from neighboring neurons. At such times, a neuron fires an impulse, called the **action potential**—a brief electrical charge that travels down its axon (**FIGURE 2.1**).

Depending on the type of fiber, a neural impulse travels at speeds ranging from a sluggish 2 miles per hour to a breakneck 200 or more miles per hour. But even this top speed is 3 million times slower than that of electricity through a wire. We measure brain activity in milliseconds (thousandths of a second) and computer activity in nanoseconds (billionths of a second). Thus, unlike the nearly instantaneous reactions of a high-speed computer, your reaction to a sudden event, such as a child darting in front of your car, may take a quarter-second or more. Your brain is vastly more complex than a computer, but slower at executing simple responses.

Each neuron is a miniature decision-making device performing complex calculations as it receives signals from hundreds, even thousands, of other neurons. Most of these signals are *excitatory,* somewhat like pushing a neuron's accelerator. Others are *inhibitory,* more like pushing its brake. If excitatory signals minus inhibitory signals exceed a minimum level of stimulation, or **threshold,** the combined signals trigger an action potential. (Think of it this way: If the excitatory party animals outvote the inhibitory party poopers, the party's on.) The action potential then travels down the axon, which branches into junctions with hundreds or thousands of other neurons and with the body's muscles and glands.

Increasing the level of stimulation above the threshold will not increase the neural impulse's intensity. The neuron's reaction is an *all-or-none response:* Like guns, neurons either fire or they don't. How, then, do we detect the intensity of a stimulus? How do we distinguish a gentle touch from a big hug? A strong stimulus—a slap rather than a tap—can trigger *more* neurons to fire, and to fire more often. But it does not affect the action potential's strength or speed. Squeezing a trigger harder won't make a bullet go faster.

"What one neuron tells another neuron is simply how much it is excited."

—Francis Crick, *The Astonishing Hypothesis,* 1994

"The body is made up of millions and millions of crumbs."

How Neurons Communicate

2: How do nerve cells communicate with other nerve cells?

Neurons interweave so intricately that even with a microscope you would have trouble seeing where one neuron ends and another begins. Scientists once believed that the axon of one cell fused with the dendrites of another in an uninterrupted fabric.

Then British physiologist Sir Charles Sherrington (1857–1952) noticed that neural impulses were taking an unexpectedly long time to travel a neural pathway. Inferring that there must be a brief interruption in the transmission, Sherrington called the meeting point between neurons a **synapse.**

We now know that the axon terminal of one neuron is in fact separated from the receiving neuron by a *synaptic gap* (or *synaptic cleft*) less than a millionth of an inch wide. Spanish anatomist Santiago Ramon y Cajal (1852–1934) marveled at these near-unions of neurons, calling them "protoplasmic kisses." "Like elegant ladies air-kissing so as not to muss their makeup, dendrites and axons don't quite touch," notes poet Diane Ackerman (2004). How do the neurons execute this protoplasmic kiss, sending information across the tiny synaptic gap? The answer is one of the important scientific discoveries of our age.

When an action potential reaches the knoblike terminals at an axon's end, it triggers the release of chemical messengers called **neurotransmitters** (**FIGURE 2.2**). Within 1/10,000th of a second, the neurotransmitter molecules cross the synaptic gap and bind to receptor sites on the receiving neuron—as precisely as a key fits a lock. For an instant, the neurotransmitter unlocks tiny channels at the receiving site, and electrically charged atoms flow in, exciting or inhibiting the receiving neuron's readiness to fire. Then, in a process called *reuptake*, the sending neuron reabsorbs the excess neurotransmitters.

> "All information processing in the brain involves neurons 'talking to' each other at synapses."
>
> —Neuroscientist Solomon H. Snyder (1984)

FIGURE 2.2 **How neurons communicate**

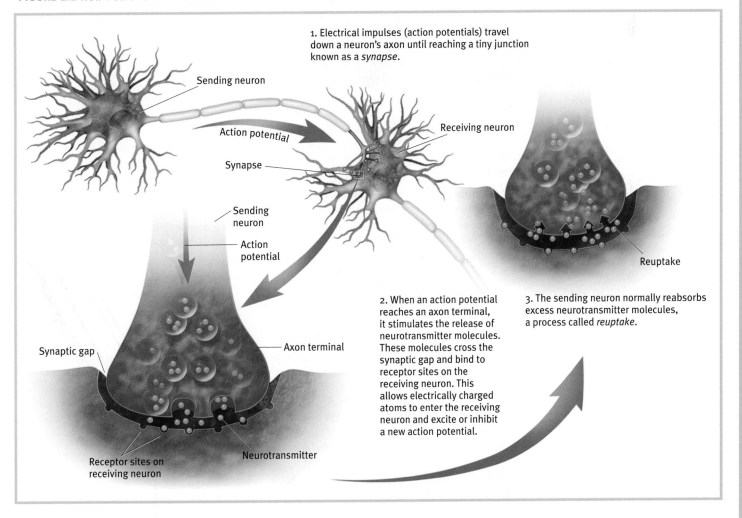

1. Electrical impulses (action potentials) travel down a neuron's axon until reaching a tiny junction known as a *synapse*.

Sending neuron

Action potential

Receiving neuron

Synapse

Sending neuron

Action potential

Axon terminal

Synaptic gap

Receptor sites on receiving neuron

Neurotransmitter

Reuptake

2. When an action potential reaches an axon terminal, it stimulates the release of neurotransmitter molecules. These molecules cross the synaptic gap and bind to receptor sites on the receiving neuron. This allows electrically charged atoms to enter the receiving neuron and excite or inhibit a new action potential.

3. The sending neuron normally reabsorbs excess neurotransmitter molecules, a process called *reuptake*.

endorphins [en-DOR-fins] "morphine within"—natural, opiatelike neurotransmitters linked to pain control and to pleasure.

"When it comes to the brain, if you want to see the action, follow the neurotransmitters."

—Neuroscientist Floyd Bloom (1993)

How Neurotransmitters Influence Us

3: How do neurotransmitters influence behavior?

In their quest to understand neural communication, researchers have discovered dozens of different neurotransmitters and raised new questions: Are certain neurotransmitters found only in specific places? How do they affect our moods, memories, and mental abilities? Can we boost or diminish these effects through drugs or diet?

Later chapters explore neurotransmitter influences on hunger and thinking, depression and euphoria, addictions and therapy. For now, let's glimpse how neurotransmitters influence our motions and our emotions. A particular pathway in the brain may use only one or two neurotransmitters (**FIGURE 2.3**), and particular neurotransmitters may have particular effects on behavior and emotions (**TABLE 2.1** offers examples). Acetylcholine (ACh) is one of the best-understood neurotransmitters. In addition to its role in learning and memory, ACh is the messenger at every junction between a motor neuron (which carries information from the brain and spinal cord to the body's tissues) and skeletal muscles. When ACh is released to our muscle cell receptors, the muscle contracts. If ACh transmission is blocked, as happens during some kinds of anesthesia, the muscles cannot contract and we are paralyzed.

Candace Pert and Solomon Snyder (1973) made an exciting discovery about neurotransmitters when they attached a radioactive tracer to morphine, showing where it was taken up in an animal's brain. The morphine, an opiate drug that elevates mood and eases pain, bound to receptors in areas linked with mood and pain sensations. But why would the brain have these "opiate receptors"? Why would it have a chemical lock, unless it also had a natural key to open it?

Researchers soon confirmed that the brain does indeed produce its own naturally occurring opiates. Our body releases several types of neurotransmitter molecules similar to morphine in response to pain and vigorous exercise. These **endorphins** (short for *end*ogenous [produced within] m*orphine*), as we now call them, help explain good feelings such as the "runner's high," the painkilling effects of acupuncture, and the indifference to pain in some severely injured people.

Seratonin pathways

Dopamine pathways

FIGURE 2.3 Neurotransmitter pathways
Each of the brain's differing chemical messengers has designated pathways where it operates. Shown here are the pathways for serotonin and dopamine (Carter, 1998).

Both photos from Mapping the Mind, Rita Carter, © 1989 University of California Press

TABLE 2.1 **Some Neurotransmitters and Their Functions**

Neurotransmitter	Function	Examples of Malfunctions
Acetylcholine (ACh)	Enables muscle action, learning, and memory	With Alzheimer's disease, ACh-producing neurons deteriorate.
Dopamine	Influences movement, learning, attention, and emotion	Excess dopamine receptor activity is linked to schizophrenia. Starved of dopamine, the brain produces the tremors and decreased mobility of Parkinson's disease.
Serotonin	Affects mood, hunger, sleep, and arousal	Undersupply is linked to depression. Prozac and some other antidepressant drugs raise serotonin levels.
Norepinephrine	Helps control alertness and arousal	Undersupply can depress mood.
Endorphins	Lessen pain and boost mood	If flooded with articifial opiates, the brain may stop producing endorphins, causing intense discomfort.

Drugs and other chemicals affect brain chemistry at synapses, often by either exciting or inhibiting neurons' firing. *Agonist* molecules may be similar enough to a neurotransmitter to bind to its receptor and mimic its effects. Some opiate drugs are agonists and produce a temporary "high" by amplifying normal sensations of arousal or pleasure. *Antagonists* also bind to receptors but their effect is instead to block a neurotransmitter's functioning. They may occupy sites on the receiving neuron and block the neurotransmitter's effects. Curare, a poison some South American Indians have applied to hunting-dart tips, occupies and blocks ACh receptor sites on muscles, producing paralysis in animals struck by the dart.

> Physician Lewis Thomas, on the endorphins: "There it is, a biologically universal act of mercy. I cannot explain it, except to say that I would have put it in had I been around at the very beginning, sitting as a member of a planning committee."
>
> —*The Youngest Science*, 1983

REHEARSE IT!

1. The neuron fiber that carries messages to other neurons is the
   a. dendrite.
   b. axon.
   c. cell body.
   d. myelin.

2. The tiny space between the axon of a sending neuron and the dendrite or cell body of a receiving neuron is called the
   a. axon terminal.
   b. branching fiber.
   c. synaptic gap.
   d. threshold.

3. The neuron's response to stimulation is an all-or-none response, meaning that the intensity of the stimulus determines
   a. whether or not an impulse is generated.
   b. how fast an impulse is transmitted.
   c. how intense an impulse will be.
   d. whether the stimulus is excitatory or inhibitory.

4. When an action potential reaches the axon terminal of a neuron, it triggers the release of chemical messengers called
   a. dendrites.
   b. synapses.
   c. neural impulses.
   d. neurotransmitters.

5. Endorphins are released in the brain in response to
   a. morphine or heroin.
   b. pain or vigorous exercise.
   c. the all-or-none response.
   d. all of these answers are correct.

Answers: 1. b, 2. c, 3. a, 4. d, 5. b.

The Nervous System

4: What are the functional divisions of the nervous system?

To live is to take in information from the world and the body's tissues, to make decisions, and to send back information and orders to the body's tissues. All this happens thanks to our body's **nervous system.** The brain and spinal cord form the **central nervous system (CNS),** the body's decision maker. The **peripheral nervous system (PNS)** is responsible for gathering information and for transmitting CNS decisions to other body parts. **Nerves,** electrical cables formed of bundles of axons, link the CNS with the body's sensory receptors, muscles, and glands. The optic nerve, for example, bundles a million axons into a single cable carrying the messages each eye sends to the brain (Mason & Kandel, 1991).

Information travels in the nervous system through three types of neurons. **Sensory neurons** carry messages from the body's tissues and sensory receptors inward to the brain and spinal cord, for processing. The central nervous system then sends instructions out to the body's tissues via the **motor neurons.** In between the sensory input and motor output, **interneurons** process information within the CNS. Our complexity resides mostly in our interneuron systems. Our nervous system has a few million sensory neurons, a few million motor neurons, and billions and billions of interneurons.

The Peripheral Nervous System

Our peripheral nervous system has two components—somatic and autonomic. Our **somatic nervous system** enables voluntary control of our skeletal muscles. As you now reach the bottom of this page, your somatic nervous system will report to your

nervous system the body's speedy, electrochemical communication network, consisting of all the nerve cells of the peripheral and central nervous systems.

central nervous system (CNS) the brain and spinal cord.

peripheral nervous system (PNS) the sensory and motor neurons that connect the central nervous system (CNS) to the rest of the body.

nerves bundled axons that form neural "cables" connecting the central nervous system with muscles, glands, and sense organs.

sensory neurons neurons that carry incoming information from the sensory receptors to the brain and spinal cord.

motor neurons neurons that carry outgoing information from the brain and spinal cord to the muscles and glands.

interneurons neurons within the brain and spinal cord that communicate internally and intervene between the sensory inputs and motor outputs.

somatic nervous system the division of the peripheral nervous system that controls the body's skeletal muscles. Also called the *skeletal nervous system.*

FIGURE 2.4 The functional divisions of the human nervous system

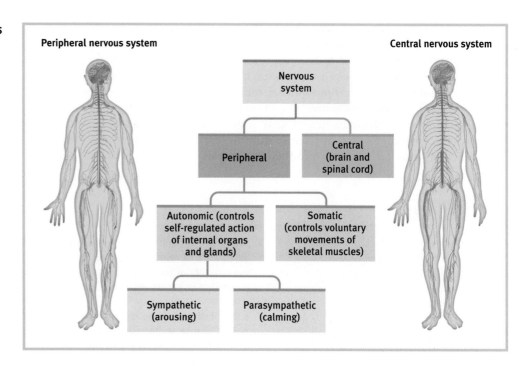

brain the current state of your skeletal muscles and carry instructions back, triggering your hand to turn the page.

Our **autonomic nervous system** controls our glands and the muscles of our internal organs, influencing such functions as glandular activity, heartbeat, and digestion. Like an automatic pilot, this system may be consciously overridden, but usually it operates on its own (autonomously). **FIGURE 2.4** outlines the nervous system.

The autonomic nervous system serves two important, basic functions (**FIGURE 2.5**). The **sympathetic nervous system** arouses and expends energy. If something alarms, enrages, or challenges you, your sympathetic system will accelerate your heartbeat, raise your blood pressure, slow your digestion, raise your blood sugar, and cool you with perspiration, making you alert and ready for action. When the stress subsides, your **parasympathetic nervous system** produces opposite effects. It conserves energy as it calms you by decreasing your heartbeat, lowering your blood sugar, and so forth. In everyday situations, the sympathetic and parasympathetic nervous systems work together to keep you in a steady internal state.

The Central Nervous System

From the simplicity of neurons "talking" to other neurons arises the complexity of the central nervous system's brain and spinal cord.

It is the brain that enables our humanity—our thinking, feeling, and acting. Tens of billions of neurons, each communicating with thousands of other neurons, yield an ever-changing wiring diagram that dwarfs a powerful computer. With some 40 billion neurons, each having roughly 10,000 contacts with other neurons, we end up with perhaps 400 trillion synapses—places where neurons meet and greet their neighbors (de Courten-Myers, 2005). A grain-of-sand–sized speck of your brain contains some 100,000 neurons and one billion "talking" synapses (Ramachandran & Blakeslee, 1998).

The brain's neurons cluster into work groups called *neural networks.* To understand why, Stephen Kosslyn and Olivier Koenig (1992, p. 12) have invited us to "think about why cities exist; why don't people distribute themselves more evenly across the countryside?" Like people networking with people, neurons network with nearby neurons with which they can have short, fast connections.

Stephen Colbert: "How does the brain work? Five words or less."
Steven Pinker: "Brain cells fire in patterns."

—*The Colbert Report,* February 8, 2007

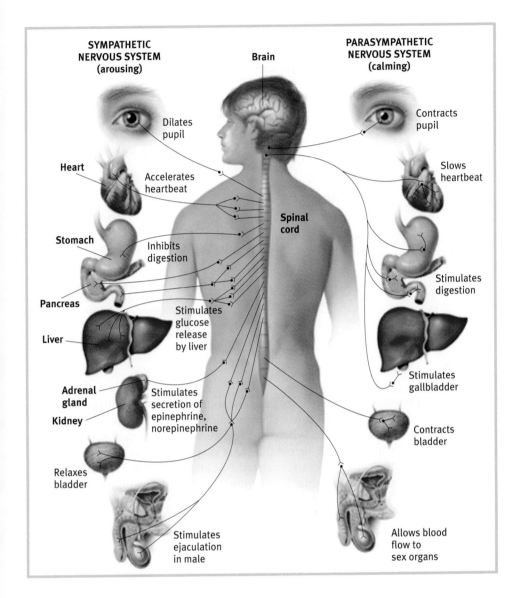

SYMPATHETIC NERVOUS SYSTEM (arousing)

Brain

PARASYMPATHETIC NERVOUS SYSTEM (calming)

Dilates pupil

Contracts pupil

Heart

Accelerates heartbeat

Spinal cord

Slows heartbeat

Stomach

Inhibits digestion

Stimulates digestion

Pancreas

Liver

Stimulates glucose release by liver

Stimulates gallbladder

Adrenal gland

Kidney

Stimulates secretion of epinephrine, norepinephrine

Contracts bladder

Relaxes bladder

Stimulates ejaculation in male

Allows blood flow to sex organs

FIGURE 2.5 The dual functions of the autonomic nervous system The autonomic nervous system controls the more autonomous (or self-regulating) internal functions. Its *sympathetic division* arouses and expends energy. Its *parasympathetic division* calms and conserves energy, allowing routine maintenance activity. For example, sympathetic stimulation accelerates heartbeat, whereas parasympathetic stimulation slows it.

The *spinal cord* is an information highway connecting the peripheral nervous system to the brain. Ascending neural fibers send up sensory information, and descending fibers send back motor-control information. The neural pathways governing our **reflexes,** our automatic responses to stimuli, illustrate the spinal cord's work. A simple spinal reflex pathway is composed of a single sensory neuron and a single motor neuron. These often communicate through an interneuron. The knee-jerk response, for example, involves one such simple pathway. A headless warm body could do it.

Another such pathway enables the pain reflex (see **FIGURE 2.6** on the next page). When your finger touches a flame, neural activity excited by the heat travels via sensory neurons to interneurons in your spinal cord. These interneurons respond by activating motor neurons leading to the muscles in your arm. Because the simple pain reflex pathway runs through the spinal cord and right back out, your hand jerks from the candle's flame *before* your brain receives and responds to the information that causes you to feel pain. That's why it feels as if your hand jerks away not by your choice, but on its own.

Information travels to and from the brain by way of the spinal cord. Were the top of your spinal cord severed, you would not feel pain from your body below. Nor would you feel pleasure. With your brain literally out of touch with your body, you

autonomic [aw-tuh-NAHM-ik] **nervous system** the part of the peripheral nervous system that controls the glands and the muscles of the internal organs (such as the heart). Its sympathetic division arouses; its parasympathetic division calms.

sympathetic nervous system the division of the autonomic nervous system that arouses the body, mobilizing its energy in stressful situations.

parasympathetic nervous system the division of the autonomic nervous system that calms the body, conserving its energy.

reflex a simple, automatic response to a sensory stimulus, such as the knee-jerk response.

1. In this simple hand-withdrawal reflex, information is carried from skin receptors along a sensory neuron to the spinal cord (shown by the red arrow). From here it is passed via interneurons to motor neurons that lead to muscles in the hand and arm (blue arrow).

Sensory neuron (incoming information)

Brain

Interneuron

Spinal cord

Motor neuron (outgoing information)

Muscle

Skin receptors

2. Because this reflex involves only the spinal cord, the hand jerks away from the candle flame even before information about the event has reached the brain, causing the experience of pain.

FIGURE 2.6 A simple reflex

would lose all sensation and voluntary movement in body regions with sensory and motor connections to the spinal cord below its point of injury. You would exhibit the knee-jerk without feeling the tap. When the brain center keeping the brakes on erections is severed, men paralyzed below the waist may be capable of an erection (a simple reflex) if their genitals are stimulated (Goldstein, 2000). Women similarly paralyzed may respond with vaginal lubrication. But, depending on where and how completely the spinal cord is severed, they may be genitally unresponsive to erotic images and have no genital feeling (Kennedy & Over, 1990; Sipski & Alexander, 1999). To produce bodily pain or pleasure, the sensory information must reach the brain.

REHEARSE IT!

6. The autonomic nervous system controls internal functions, such as heart rate and glandular activity. The word *autonomic* means
   a. calming.
   b. voluntary.
   c. self-regulating.
   d. arousing.

7. The sympathetic nervous system arouses us for action and the parasympathetic nervous system calms us down. Together, the two systems make up the
   a. autonomic nervous system.
   b. somatic nervous system.
   c. central nervous system.
   d. peripheral nervous system.

8. The neurons of the spinal cord are part of the
   a. somatic nervous system.
   b. central nervous system.
   c. autonomic nervous system.
   d. peripheral nervous system.

Answers: 6. c, 7. a, 8. b.

The Endocrine System

5: **How does the endocrine system—the body's slower information system—transmit its messages?**

endocrine [EN-duh-krin] **system** the body's "slow" chemical communication system; a set of glands that secrete hormones into the bloodstream.

hormones chemical messengers that are manufactured by the endocrine glands, travel through the bloodstream, and affect other tissues.

So far we have focused on the body's speedy electrochemical information system. Interconnected with the nervous system is a second communication system, the **endocrine system.** The endocrine system's glands secrete another form of chemical messengers, **hormones,** which travel through the bloodstream and affect other tissues, including the brain. When they act on the brain, they influence our interest in sex, food, and aggression. **FIGURE 2.7** illustrates the locations and functions of glands in the endocrine system.

Some hormones are chemically identical to neurotransmitters (those chemical messengers that diffuse across a synapse and excite or inhibit an adjacent neuron). The endocrine system and nervous system are therefore close relatives: Both produce molecules that act on receptors elsewhere. Like many relatives, they also differ. The speedy nervous system zips messages from eyes to brain to hand in a fraction of a second. Endocrine messages trudge along in the bloodstream, taking several seconds or more to travel from the gland to the target tissue. If the nervous system's communication delivers messages rather like e-mail, the endocrine system is the body's snail mail. But slow and steady sometimes wins the race. Endocrine messages tend to outlast the effects of neural messages. That helps explain why upset feelings may linger, sometimes beyond our thinking about what upset us. In a moment of danger, for example, the autonomic nervous system orders the **adrenal glands** on top of the kidneys to release *epinephrine* and *norepinephrine*

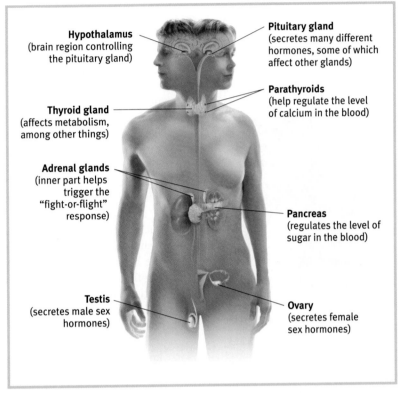

Hypothalamus (brain region controlling the pituitary gland)

Thyroid gland (affects metabolism, among other things)

Adrenal glands (inner part helps trigger the "fight-or-flight" response)

Testis (secretes male sex hormones)

Pituitary gland (secretes many different hormones, some of which affect other glands)

Parathyroids (help regulate the level of calcium in the blood)

Pancreas (regulates the level of sugar in the blood)

Ovary (secretes female sex hormones)

FIGURE 2.7 **The endocrine system**

(also called *adrenaline* and *noradrenaline*). These hormones increase heart rate, blood pressure, and blood sugar, providing us with a surge of energy. When the emergency passes, the hormones—and the feelings of excitement—linger a while. The endocrine system's hormones influence many aspects of our lives—growth, reproduction, metabolism, mood—and work with our nervous system to keep everything in balance while we respond to stress, exertion, and our own thoughts.

The most influential endocrine gland is the **pituitary gland,** a pea-sized structure located in the core of the brain, where it is controlled by an adjacent brain area, the *hypothalamus* (which you will hear more about shortly). The pituitary releases hormones that influence growth. Its secretions also influence the release of hormones by other endocrine glands. The pituitary, then, is a sort of master gland (whose own master is the hypothalamus). For example, under the brain's influence, the pituitary triggers your sex glands to release sex hormones. These in turn influence your brain and behavior.

This feedback system (brain → pituitary → other glands → hormones → brain) reveals the intimate connection of the nervous and endocrine systems. The nervous system directs endocrine secretions, which then affect the nervous system. Conducting and coordinating this whole electrochemical orchestra is that maestro we call the brain.

adrenal [ah-DREEN-el] **glands** a pair of endocrine glands that sit just above the kidneys and secrete hormones (epinephrine and norepinephrine) that help arouse the body in times of stress.

pituitary gland the endocrine system's most influential gland. Under the influence of the hypothalamus, the pituitary regulates growth and controls other endocrine glands.

REHEARSE IT!

9. The most influential endocrine gland, known as the master gland, is the
a. pituitary.
b. hypothalamus.
c. kidney.
d. adrenal.

10. _____ secrete(s) epinephrine and norepinephrine, helping to arouse the body during times of stress.
a. Adrenal glands
b. The pituitary gland
c. The hypothalamus
d. Neurotransmitters

Answers: 9. a, 10. a.

The Brain

6: **How do neuroscientists study the brain's connections to behavior and mind?**

When you think *about* your brain, you're thinking *with* your brain—sending billions of neurotransmitter molecules across countless millions of synapses. Indeed, say neuroscientists, *the mind is what the brain does.*

Even in a motionless body, the brain—and mind—may, in some cases, be active. One 23-year-old woman showed no outward signs of conscious awareness after a traffic accident. Nevertheless, when researchers asked her to imagine playing tennis or moving around her home, brain scans revealed activity like that of healthy volunteers (Owen et al., 2006). As she imagined playing tennis, for example, an area of her brain controlling arm and leg movements became active.

A century ago, scientists had no tools high-powered yet gentle enough to reveal such activity in a living human brain. Clinical observations had unveiled some brain-mind connections. Physicians noted, for example, that damage to one side of the brain often caused numbness or paralysis on the body's opposite side, suggesting that the body's right side is wired to the brain's left side, and vice versa. Others noticed that damage to the back of the brain disrupted vision, and that damage to the left-front part of the brain produced speech difficulties. Gradually, these early explorers were mapping the brain.

Now, within a lifetime, the whole brain-mapping process has changed. The known universe's most amazing organ is being probed and mapped by a new generation of neural mapmakers. Whether in the interests of science or medicine, they can selectively **lesion** (destroy) tiny clusters of normal or defective brain cells, leaving the surrounding tissue unharmed. Today's scientists can snoop on the messages of individual neurons, using modern microelectrodes with tips so small they can detect the electrical pulse in a single neuron. For example, we can now detect exactly where the information goes in a cat's brain when someone strokes its whisker. They can also electrically, chemically, or magnetically stimulate various parts of the brain and note the effects; eavesdrop on the chatter of billions of neurons; and see color representations of the brain's energy-consuming activity.

These techniques for peering into the thinking, feeling brain are doing for psychology what the microscope did for biology and the telescope did for astronomy. Close-Up: The Tools of Discovery—Having Our Head Examined looks at some of the techniques that enable neuroscientists to study the working brain.

Older Brain Structures

7: **What are the functions of important lower-level brain structures?**

Indicators of an animal's capacities come from its brain structures. In primitive animals, such as sharks, a not-so-complex brain primarily regulates basic survival functions: breathing, resting, and feeding. In lower mammals, such as rodents, a more complex brain enables emotion and greater memory. In advanced mammals, such as humans, a brain that processes more information enables foresight as well.

This increasing complexity arises from new brain systems built on top of the old, much as the Earth's landscape covers the old with the new. Digging down, one discovers the fossil remnants of the past—brainstem components performing for us much as they did for our distant ancestors. Let's start with the brain's basement and work up to the newer systems.

The Brainstem

The brain's oldest and innermost region is the **brainstem.** It begins where the spinal cord swells slightly after entering the skull. This slight swelling is the

Banking brains Francine Benes, director of McLean Hospital's Brain Bank, sees the collection as a valuable database.

Tom Landers/Boston Globe

---

lesion [LEE-zhuhn] tissue destruction. A brain lesion is a naturally or experimentally caused destruction of brain tissue.

---

brainstem the oldest part and central core of the brain, beginning where the spinal cord swells as it enters the skull; the brainstem is responsible for automatic survival functions.

---

electroencephalogram (EEG) an amplified recording of the waves of electrical activity that sweep across the brain's surface. These waves are measured by electrodes placed on the scalp.

PET (positron emission tomography) scan a visual display of brain activity that detects where a radioactive form of glucose goes while the brain performs a given task.

MRI (magnetic resonance imaging) a technique that uses magnetic fields and radio waves to produce computer-generated images of soft tissue. MRI scans show brain anatomy.

---

fMRI (functional MRI) a technique for revealing bloodflow and, therefore, brain activity by comparing successive MRI scans. fMRI scans show brain function.

---

medulla [muh-DUL-uh] the base of the brainstem; controls heartbeat and breathing.

Close-Up:

The Tools of Discovery—Having Our Head Examined

Right now, your mental activity is giving off telltale electrical, metabolic, and magnetic signals that neuroscientists could trap to observe your brain at work. For example, electrical activity in your brain's billions of neurons sweeps in regular waves across its surface. An **electroencephalogram (EEG)** will give an amplified read-out of such waves (**FIGURE 2.8**).

"You must look into people, as well as at them," advised Lord Chesterfield in a 1746 letter to his son. Newer windows into the brain give us that Supermanlike ability to see inside a living brain. One such tool, the **PET (positron emission tomography) scan** (**FIGURE 2.9**), depicts brain activity by showing each brain area's consumption of its chemical fuel, the sugar glucose. Active neurons are glucose hogs, and after a person receives temporarily radioactive glucose, the PET scan can track the gamma rays released by this "food for thought" as the person performs a given task. Rather like weather radar showing rain activity, PET scan "hot spots" show which brain areas are most active as the person does mathematical calculations, looks at images of faces, or daydreams.

FIGURE 2.9 **The PET Scan** To obtain a PET scan, researchers inject volunteers with a low and harmless dose of a short-lived radioactive sugar. Detectors around the person's head pick up the release of gamma rays from the sugar, which has concentrated in active brain areas. A computer then processes and translates these signals into a map of the brain at work.

MRI (magnetic resonance imaging) can also be used to scan the brain or other body parts. In MRI brain scans, the person's head is put in a strong magnetic field, which aligns the spinning atoms of brain molecules. Then a radio wave pulse momentarily disorients the atoms. When the atoms return to their normal spin, they release signals that provide a detailed picture of the brain's soft tissues. MRI scans have revealed a larger-than-average neural area in the left hemisphere of musicians who display perfect pitch (Schlaug et al., 1995). They have also revealed enlarged *ventricles*—fluid-filled brain areas (marked by the red arrows in **FIGURE 2.10**)—in some patients with schizophrenia, a disabling psychological disorder.

A special application of MRI—**fMRI (functional MRI)**—can reveal the brain's functioning as well as its structure. Where the brain is especially active, blood goes. By comparing MRI scans taken less than a second apart, researchers can watch the brain "light up" (with increased oxygen-laden bloodflow) as a person performs different mental functions. As the person looks at a scene, for example, the fMRI machine detects blood rushing to the back of the brain, which processes visual information (see Figure 2.21, in the discussion of cortex functions). Such snapshots of the brain's changing activity are providing new insights into how the brain divides its labor.

To be learning about the neurosciences now is like studying world geography while Magellan was exploring the seas. This truly is the golden age of brain science.

FIGURE 2.8 **An electroencephalograph providing amplified tracings of waves of electrical activity in the brain** Here it is displaying the brain activity of this 4-year-old who has epilepsy.

FIGURE 2.10 **MRI scan of a healthy individual (left) and a person with schizophrenia (right)** Note the enlarged ventricle, the fluid-filled brain region at the tip of the arrow in the image on the right.

medulla. Here lie the controls for your heartbeat and breathing. Just above the medulla sits the *pons,* which helps coordinate movements. If a cat's brainstem is severed from the rest of the brain above it, the animal will still breathe and live—and even run, climb, and groom (Klemm, 1990). But cut off from the brain's higher regions, it won't purposefully run or climb to get food.

FIGURE 2.11 The brainstem and thalamus The brainstem, including the pons and medulla, is an extension of the spinal cord. The thalamus is attached to the top of the brainstem. The reticular formation passes through both structures.

The brainstem is a crossover point, where most nerves to and from each side of the brain connect with the body's opposite side. This peculiar cross-wiring is but one of the brain's many surprises.

The Thalamus

Sitting at the top of the brainstem is the **thalamus** (**FIGURE 2.11**). This joined pair of egg-shaped structures acts as the brain's sensory switchboard. It receives information from all the senses except smell and routes it to the higher brain regions that deal with seeing, hearing, tasting, and touching. Think of the thalamus as being to sensory input what London is to England's trains: a hub through which traffic passes en route to various destinations. The thalamus also receives some of the higher brain's replies, which it then directs to the medulla and to the cerebellum.

The Reticular Formation

Inside the brainstem, between your ears, lies the **reticular** ("netlike") **formation,** a finger-shaped network of neurons that extends from the spinal cord right up through the thalamus. As the spinal cord's sensory input travels up to the thalamus, some of it travels through the reticular formation, which filters incoming stimuli and relays important information to other areas of the brain.

In 1949, Giuseppe Moruzzi and Horace Magoun discovered that electrically stimulating the reticular formation of a sleeping cat almost instantly produced an awake, alert animal. When Magoun *severed* a cat's reticular formation from higher brain regions, without damaging the nearby sensory pathways, the effect was equally dramatic: The cat lapsed into a coma from which it never awakened. The reticular formation affects arousal.

The Cerebellum

Extending from the rear of the brainstem is the baseball-sized **cerebellum,** meaning "little brain," which is what its two wrinkled halves resemble (**FIGURE 2.12**). As you will see in Chapter 8, the cerebellum enables one type of nonverbal learning and memory. It helps us judge time, modulate our emotions, and discriminate sounds and textures (Bower & Parsons, 2003). It also coordinates voluntary movement.

thalamus [THAL-uh-muss] the brain's sensory switchboard, located on top of the brainstem; it directs messages to the sensory receiving areas in the cortex and transmits replies to the cerebellum and medulla.

reticular formation a nerve network in the brainstem that plays an important role in controlling arousal.

cerebellum [sehr-uh-BELL-um] the "little brain" at the rear of the brainstem; functions include some nonverbal learning, processing sensory input, and coordinating movement output and balance.

limbic system neural system (including the *hippocampus, amygdala,* and *hypothalamus*) located below the cerebral hemispheres; associated with emotions and drives.

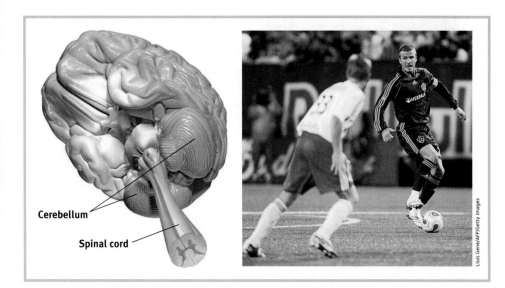

Lluis Gene/AFP/Getty Images

FIGURE 2.12 The brain's organ of agility Hanging at the back of the brain, the cerebellum coordinates our voluntary movements, as when David Beckham directs the ball precisely.

Cerebellum

Spinal cord

When soccer great David Beckham fires the ball into the net with a perfectly timed kick, give his cerebellum some credit. If you injured your cerebellum, you would have difficulty walking, keeping your balance, or shaking hands. Your movements would be jerky and exaggerated. Under alcohol's influence on the cerebellum, walking may lack coordination, as many a driver has learned after being pulled over and given a roadside test.

Note: These older brain functions all occur without any conscious effort. This illustrates another of our recurring themes: *Our brain processes most information outside of our awareness.* We are aware of the *results* of our brain's labor (say, our current visual experience) but not of *how* we construct the visual image. Likewise, whether we are asleep or awake, our brainstem manages its life-sustaining functions, freeing our newer brain regions to think, talk, dream, or savor a memory.

> "Consciousness is a small part of what the brain does."
>
> —Neuroscientist Joseph LeDoux, in "Mastery of Emotions," 2006

REHEARSE IT!

11. The brainstem is the oldest and innermost region of the brain. The part of the brainstem that controls heartbeat and breathing is the
    a. cerebellum.
    b. medulla.
    c. cortex.
    d. thalamus.

12. The thalamus receives information from the sensory neurons and routes it to the higher brain regions that control the senses. The thalamus functions like a
    a. memory bank.
    b. balance center.
    c. breathing regulator.
    d. switchboard.

13. The lower brain structure that governs arousal is the
    a. spinal cord.
    b. cerebellum.
    c. reticular formation.
    d. medulla.

14. The part of the brain that coordinates voluntary movement is the
    a. cerebellum.
    b. medulla.
    c. thalamus.
    d. reticular formation.

Answers: 11. b, 12. d, 13. c, 14. a.

The Limbic System

At the border ("limbus") between the brain's older parts and the *cerebral hemispheres*—the two halves of the brain—is the **limbic system** (FIGURE 2.13 on the next page). We will see in Chapter 8 how one limbic system component, the *hippocampus,* processes memory. (If animals or humans lose their hippocampus to surgery or injury, they become unable to process new memories of facts and episodes.) For now, let's look at the limbic system's links to emotions (such as fear and anger) and to basic motives (such as those for food and sex).

FIGURE 2.13 **The limbic system** This neural system sits between the brain's older parts and its cerebral hemispheres. The limbic system's hypothalamus controls the nearby pituitary gland.

FIGURE 2.15 **Aggression as a brain state** Back arched and fur fluffed, this fierce cat is ready to attack. Electrical stimulation of a cat's amygdala provokes reactions such as the one shown here, suggesting its role in emotions like rage. Which division of the autonomic nervous system is activated by such stimulation?

The cat would be aroused via its sympathetic nervous system.

FIGURE 2.16 **The hypothalamus** This small but important structure, colored yellow/orange in this MRI scan photograph, helps keep the body's internal environment in a steady state.

FIGURE 2.14 **The amygdala**

THE AMYGDALA In the limbic system, two lima-bean–sized neural clusters, the **amygdala,** influence aggression and fear (**FIGURE 2.14**). In 1939, psychologist Heinrich Klüver and neurosurgeon Paul Bucy surgically lesioned the part of a rhesus monkey's brain that included the amygdala. The result? The formerly ill-tempered monkey turned into the most mellow of creatures. Poke it, pinch it, do virtually anything that normally would trigger a ferocious response, and still the animal remained placid. What then might happen if we electrically stimulated the amygdala in a normally placid domestic animal, such as a cat? Do so in one spot and the cat prepares to attack, hissing with its back arched, its pupils dilated, its hair on end (**FIGURE 2.15**). Move the electrode only slightly within the amygdala, cage the cat with a small mouse, and now it cowers in terror.

These experiments confirm the amygdala's role in rage and fear, including the perception of these emotions and the processing of emotional memories (Anderson & Phelps, 2000; Poremba & Gabriel, 2001). Still, we must be careful. The brain is not neatly organized into structures that correspond to our categories of behavior. Aggressive and fearful behavior involves neural activity in many brain levels. Even within the limbic system, stimulating structures other than the amygdala can evoke such behavior. If you charge your car's dead battery, you can activate the engine. Yet the battery is merely one link in an integrated system that makes a car go.

THE HYPOTHALAMUS Just below *(hypo)* the thalamus is the **hypothalamus** (**FIGURE 2.16**), an important link in the chain of command governing bodily maintenance. Some neural clusters in the hypothalamus influence hunger; others regulate thirst, body temperature, and sexual behavior.

The hypothalamus both monitors blood chemistry and takes orders from other parts of the brain. For example, thinking about sex (in your brain's cerebral cortex) can stimulate your hypothalamus to secrete hormones. These hormones in turn trigger the adjacent "master gland," the pituitary (see Figure 2.13), to influence hormones released by other glands. (Once again, we see the interplay between the nervous and endocrine systems: The brain influences the endocrine system, which in turn influences the brain.)

A remarkable discovery about the hypothalamus illustrates how progress in science often occurs—when curious, open-minded investigators make an unexpected observation. Two young McGill University neuropsychologists, James Olds and Peter Milner (1954), were trying to implant an electrode in a rat's reticular formation when they made a magnificent mistake: They incorrectly placed the electrode in what they later discovered was a region of the rat's hypothalamus (Olds, 1975). Curiously, as if seeking more stimulation, the rat kept returning to the location where it had been stimulated by this misplaced electrode. On discovering their mistake, Olds and Milner alertly realized they had stumbled upon a brain center that provides a pleasurable reward.

In a meticulous series of experiments, Olds (1958) went on to locate other "pleasure centers," as he called them. (What the rats actually experience only they know, and they aren't telling. Rather than attribute human feelings to rats, today's scientists refer to *reward centers,* not "pleasure centers.") When allowed to press pedals to trigger their own stimulation in these areas, rats

would sometimes do so at a feverish pace—up to 7000 times per hour—until they dropped from exhaustion. Moreover, to get this stimulation, they would even cross an electrified floor that a starving rat would not cross to reach food (**FIGURE 2.17**).

Reward centers in nearby brain areas were later discovered in many other species, including goldfish, dolphins, and monkeys. In fact, animal research has revealed both a general reward system that triggers the release of the neurotransmitter dopamine, and distributed specific centers associated with the pleasures of eating, drinking, and sex. Animals, it seems, come equipped with built-in systems that reward activities essential to survival.

Do we humans also have brain centers for pleasure? Indeed we do. To calm violent patients, one neurosurgeon implanted electrodes in such areas. Stimulated patients reported mild pleasure; however, unlike Olds' rats, they were not driven to a frenzy (Deutsch, 1972; Hooper & Teresi, 1986). Some researchers believe that addictive disorders, such as alcohol dependence, substance abuse, and binge eating, may stem from a *reward deficiency syndrome*—a genetically disposed deficiency in the natural brain systems for pleasure and well-being that leads people to crave whatever provides that missing pleasure or relieves negative feelings (Blum et al., 1996).

FIGURE 2.18 locates the brain areas discussed in this chapter, including the cerebral cortex, our next topic.

FIGURE 2.17 Rat with an implanted electrode With an electrode implanted in a reward center of its hypothalamus, the rat readily crosses an electrified grid, accepting the painful shocks, to press a pedal that sends electrical impulses to that center.

Stimulation pedal   Electrified grid

amygdala [uh-MIG-duh-la] two lima-bean–sized neural clusters in the limbic system; linked to emotion.

hypothalamus [hi-po-THAL-uh-muss] a neural structure lying below (*hypo*) the thalamus; it directs several maintenance activities (eating, drinking, body temperature), helps govern the endocrine system via the pituitary gland, and is linked to emotion and reward.

"If you were designing a robot vehicle to walk into the future and survive, . . . you'd wire it up so that behavior that ensured the survival of the self or the species—like sex and eating—would be naturally reinforcing."

—Candace Pert (1986)

FIGURE 2.18 Brain structures and their functions

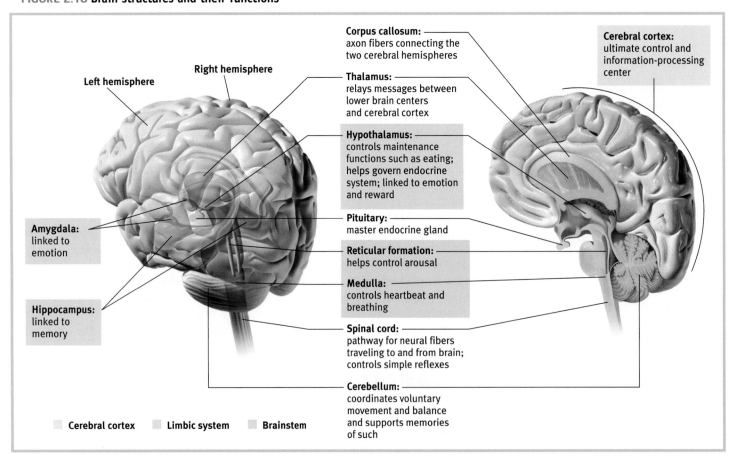

Corpus callosum: axon fibers connecting the two cerebral hemispheres

Left hemisphere

Right hemisphere

Thalamus: relays messages between lower brain centers and cerebral cortex

Cerebral cortex: ultimate control and information-processing center

Hypothalamus: controls maintenance functions such as eating; helps govern endocrine system; linked to emotion and reward

Amygdala: linked to emotion

Pituitary: master endocrine gland

Reticular formation: helps control arousal

Medulla: controls heartbeat and breathing

Hippocampus: linked to memory

Spinal cord: pathway for neural fibers traveling to and from brain; controls simple reflexes

Cerebellum: coordinates voluntary movement and balance and supports memories of such

Cerebral cortex   Limbic system   Brainstem

15. The limbic system, a doughnut-shaped structure at the border of the brain's older parts and the cerebral hemispheres, is associated with basic motives, emotions, and memory functions. Two parts of the limbic system are the amygdala and the
    a. cerebral hemispheres.
    b. hippocampus.
    c. thalamus.
    d. pituitary.

16. A cat's ferocious response to electrical brain stimulation would lead you to suppose the electrode had touched the
    a. hippocampus.
    b. pituitary.
    c. hypothalamus.
    d. amygdala.

17. The neural structure that most directly regulates eating, drinking, and body temperature is the

    a. endocrine system.
    b. hypothalamus.
    c. hippocampus.
    d. amygdala.

18. The initial reward center discovered by Olds and Milner was located in the
    a. hippocampus.
    b. brainstem.
    c. hypothalamus.
    d. spinal cord.

Answers: 15. b, 16. d, 17. b, 18. c.

The Cerebral Cortex

The people who first dissected and labeled the brain used the language of scholars—Latin and Greek. Their words are actually attempts at graphic description: For example, cortex means "bark," cerebellum is "little brain," and thalamus is "inner chamber."

Older brain networks sustain basic life functions and enable memory, emotions, and basic drives. Newer neural networks within the *cerebrum*—the two large hemispheres that contribute 85 percent of the brain's weight—form specialized work teams that enable our perceiving, thinking, and speaking. Covering those hemispheres, like bark on a tree, is the **cerebral cortex,** a thin surface layer of interconnected neural cells. It is your brain's thinking crown, your body's ultimate control and information-processing center.

As we move up the ladder of animal life, the cerebral cortex expands, tight genetic controls relax, and the organism's adaptability increases. Frogs and other amphibians with a small cortex operate extensively on preprogrammed genetic instructions. The larger cortex of mammals offers increased capacities for learning and thinking, enabling them to be more adaptable.

Structure of the Cortex

 How is the cerebral cortex organized?

If you opened a human skull, exposing the brain, you would see a wrinkled organ, shaped somewhat like the meat of an oversized walnut. Without these wrinkles, a flattened cerebral cortex would require triple the area—roughly that of a very large pizza. The brain's ballooning left and right hemispheres are filled mainly with axons connecting the cortex to the brain's other regions. The cerebral cortex—that thin surface layer—contains some 20 to 23 billion nerve cells and 300 trillion synaptic connections (de Courten-Myers, 2005). Being human takes a lot of nerve.

Stepping back to consider the whole cortex, you would see that each hemisphere is divided into four *lobes*, geographic subdivisions separated by prominent *fissures*, or folds (**FIGURE 2.19**). Starting at the front of your brain and moving over the top, there are the **frontal lobes** (behind your forehead), the **parietal lobes** (at the top and to the rear), and the **occipital lobes** (at the back of your head). Reversing direction and moving forward, just above your ears, you find the **temporal lobes.** Each of the four lobes carries out many functions, and many functions require the interplay of several lobes.

Functions of the Cortex

 What are the functions of the cerebral cortex?

More than a century ago, autopsies of people who had been partially paralyzed or speechless revealed damaged cortical areas. But this rather crude evidence did not

cerebral [seh-REE-bruhl] **cortex** the intricate fabric of interconnected neural cells covering the cerebral hemispheres; the body's ultimate control and information-processing center.

frontal lobes portion of the cerebral cortex lying just behind the forehead; involved in speaking and muscle movements and in making plans and judgments.

parietal [puh-RYE-uh-tuhl] **lobes** portion of the cerebral cortex lying at the top of the head and toward the rear; receives sensory input for touch and body position.

occipital [ahk-SIP-uh-tuhl] **lobes** portion of the cerebral cortex lying at the back of the head; includes areas that receive information from the visual fields.

temporal lobes portion of the cerebral cortex lying roughly above the ears; includes the auditory areas, each receiving information primarily from the opposite ear.

motor cortex an area at the rear of the frontal lobes that controls voluntary movements.

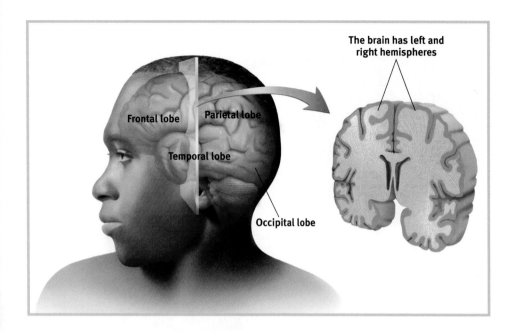

FIGURE 2.19 **The cortex and its basic subdivisions**

convince researchers that specific parts of the cortex perform specific complex functions. After all, if control of speech and movement were diffused across the cortex, damage to almost any area might produce the same effect. A television with its power cord cut would go dead, but we would be fooling ourselves if we thought we had "localized" the picture in the cord.

MOTOR FUNCTIONS Scientists had better luck in localizing simpler brain functions. For example, in 1870, when German physicians Gustav Fritsch and Eduard Hitzig applied mild electrical stimulation to parts of a dog's cortex, they made an important discovery: They could make parts of its body move. The effects were selective: Stimulation caused movement only when applied to an arch-shaped region at the back of the frontal lobes, running roughly ear-to-ear across the top of the brain. Moreover, stimulating parts of this region in the left or right hemisphere caused movements of specific body parts on the *opposite* side of the body. Fritsch and Hitzig had discovered what is now called the **motor cortex.**

MAPPING THE MOTOR CORTEX Luckily for brain surgeons and their patients, the brain has no sensory receptors. Knowing this, Otfrid Foerster and Wilder Penfield in the 1930s were able to map the motor cortex in hundreds of wide-awake patients by stimulating different cortical areas and observing the body's responses. They discovered that body areas requiring precise control, such as the fingers and mouth, occupied the greatest amount of cortical space.

Spanish neuroscientist José Delgado repeatedly demonstrated the mechanics of motor behavior. In one human patient, he stimulated a spot on the left motor cortex that triggered the right hand to make a fist. Asked to keep the fingers open during the next stimulation, the patient, whose fingers closed despite his best efforts, remarked, "I guess, Doctor, that your electricity is stronger than my will" (Delgado, 1969, p. 114).

More recently, scientists have been able to predict a monkey's arm motion a tenth of a second before it moves—by repeatedly measuring motor cortex activity preceding specific arm movements (Gibbs, 1996). Such findings have opened the door to a new generation of *prosthetics* (artificial body part replacements).

SENSORY FUNCTIONS If the motor cortex sends messages out to the body, where does the cortex receive the incoming messages? Penfield also identified the cortical

Demonstration: *Try moving your right hand in a circular motion, as if polishing a table. Now start your right foot doing the same motion synchronized with the hand. Now reverse the foot motion (but not the hand). Tough, huh? But easier if you try moving the* left *foot opposite to the right hand. The left and right limbs are controlled by opposite sides of the brain, so their opposed activities interfere less with each other.*

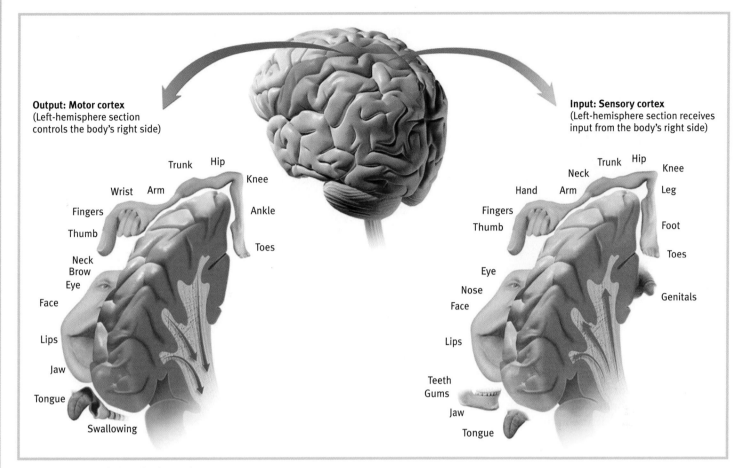

Output: Motor cortex
(Left-hemisphere section controls the body's right side)

Input: Sensory cortex
(Left-hemisphere section receives input from the body's right side)

FIGURE 2.20 Left-hemisphere tissue devoted to each body part in the motor cortex and the sensory cortex As you can see from this classic though inexact representation, the amount of cortex devoted to a body part is not proportional to that part's size. Rather, the brain devotes more tissue to sensitive areas and to areas requiring precise control. Thus, the fingers have a greater representation in the cortex than does the upper arm.

area that specializes in receiving information from the skin senses and from the movement of body parts. This area at the front of the parietal lobes, parallel to and just behind the motor cortex, we now call the **sensory cortex.** (**FIGURE 2.20** outlines both the motor cortex and the sensory cortex.) Stimulate a point on the top of this band of tissue and a person may report being touched on the shoulder; stimulate some point on the side and the person may feel something on the face.

The more sensitive the body region, the larger the sensory cortex area devoted to it. Your supersensitive lips project to a larger brain area than do your toes, which is one reason we kiss with our lips rather than touch toes. Rats have a large brain area devoted to their whisker sensations, and owls to their hearing sensations.

Scientists have identified additional areas where the cortex receives input from senses other than touch. At this moment, you are receiving visual information in the visual cortex in your occipital lobes, at the very back of your brain (**FIGURES 2.21** and **2.22**). A bad enough bash there would make you blind. Stimulated there, you might see flashes of light or dashes of color. (In a sense, we *do* have eyes in the back of our head!) From your occipital lobes, visual information goes to other areas that specialize in tasks such as identifying words, detecting emotions, and recognizing faces.

Any sound you now hear is processed by your auditory cortex in your temporal lobes

FIGURE 2.21 New technology shows the brain in action This fMRI (functional MRI) scan shows the visual cortex in the occipital lobes activated (color representation of increased bloodflow) as a research participant looks at a photo. When the person stops looking, the region instantly calms down.

(Figure 2.22). (If you think of your clenched fist as your brain, and hold it in front of you, your thumb would roughly correspond to one of your temporal lobes.) Most of this auditory information travels a circuitous route from one ear to the auditory receiving area above your opposite ear. If stimulated there, you might hear a sound. MRI scans of people with schizophrenia reveal active auditory areas in the temporal lobes during auditory hallucinations (Lennox et al., 1999). Even the phantom ringing sound experienced by people with hearing loss is—if heard in one ear—associated with activity in the temporal lobe on the brain's opposite side (Muhlnickel, 1998).

ASSOCIATION AREAS So far, we have pointed out small areas of the cortex that either receive sensory input or direct muscular output. In humans, that leaves a full three-fourths of the thin, wrinkled layer, the cerebral cortex, uncommitted to sensory or motor activity. What, then, goes on in this vast region of the brain? Neurons in these **association areas** (the peach-colored areas in **FIGURE 2.23**) integrate information. They link sensory inputs with stored memories—a very important part of thinking.

Electrically probing the association areas doesn't trigger any observable response. So, unlike the sensory and motor areas, association area functions cannot be neatly mapped. Their silence has led to what Donald McBurney (1996, p. 44) called "one of the hardiest weeds in the garden of psychology": the claim that we ordinarily use only 10 percent of our brains. (If true, wouldn't this imply a 90 percent chance that a bullet to your brain would land in an unused area?) Surgically lesioned animals and brain-damaged humans bear witness that association areas are not dormant. Rather, these areas interpret, integrate, and act on information processed by the sensory areas.

Association areas are found in all four lobes. In the frontal lobes, they enable judgment, planning, and processing of new memories. People with damaged frontal lobes may have intact memories, high scores on intelligence tests, and great cake-baking skills. Yet they would not be able to plan ahead to *begin* baking a cake for a birthday party (Huey et al., 2006).

Frontal lobe damage also can alter personality, removing a person's inhibitions. Consider the classic case of railroad worker Phineas Gage. One afternoon in 1848, Gage, then 25 years old, was packing gunpowder into a rock with a tamping iron. A spark ignited the gunpowder, shooting the rod up through his left cheek and out the top of his skull, leaving his frontal lobes massively damaged (**FIGURE 2.24** on the next page). To everyone's amazement, he was immediately able to sit up and speak, and after the wound healed he returned to work. But the affable, soft-spoken Phineas Gage was now irritable, profane, and dishonest. Although his mental abilities and memories were intact, his personality was not. This person, said his friends, was "no longer Gage." He eventually lost his job and ended up earning his living as a fairground exhibit.

FIGURE 2.22 The visual cortex and auditory cortex The visual cortex of the occipital lobes at the rear of your brain receives input from your eyes. The auditory cortex, in your temporal lobes—above your ears—receives information from your ears.

sensory cortex area at the front of the parietal lobes that registers and processes body touch and movement sensations.

association areas areas of the cerebral cortex that are not involved in primary motor or sensory functions; rather, they are involved in higher mental functions such as learning, remembering, thinking, speaking, and integrating information.

FIGURE 2.23 Areas of the cortex in four mammals More intelligent animals have increased "uncommitted" or association areas of the cortex. These vast areas of the brain are responsible for integrating and acting on information received and processed by sensory areas.

FIGURE 2.24 Phineas Gage reconsidered
Using measurements of his skull (which was kept as a medical record) and modern neuroimaging techniques, researcher Hanna Damasio and her colleagues (1994) reconstructed the probable path of the rod through Gage's brain.

With his frontal lobes ruptured, Gage's moral compass had disconnected from his behavior. Similar impairments to moral judgment have appeared in more recent studies of people with damaged frontal lobes. Not only may they become less inhibited (without the frontal lobe brakes on their impulses), but their moral judgments seem unrestrained by normal emotions. Would you advocate pushing someone in front of a runaway boxcar to save five others? Most people do not, but those with damage to a brain area behind the eyes often do (Koenigs et al., 2007).

Association areas also perform other mental functions. In the parietal lobes, parts of which were large and unusually shaped in Albert Einstein's normal-weight brain, they enable mathematical and spatial reasoning (Witelson et al., 1999). An area on the underside of the right temporal lobe enables us to recognize faces. If a stroke or head injury destroyed this area of your brain, you would still be able to describe facial features and to recognize someone's gender and approximate age, yet be strangely unable to identify the person as, say, Jack Black, or even your grandmother.

LANGUAGE: SPECIALIZATION AND INTEGRATION We think of speaking and reading, or writing and reading, or singing and speaking as merely different examples of the same general ability—language. But consider this curious finding: **Aphasia,** an impaired use of language, can result from damage to any one of several cortical areas. Even more curious, some people with aphasia can speak fluently but cannot read (despite good vision), while others can comprehend what they read but cannot speak. Still others can write but not read, read but not write, read numbers but not letters, or sing but not speak. What does this tell us about the mystery of how we use language, and how did researchers solve this mystery?

Clue 1 In 1865, French physician Paul Broca reported that after damage to a specific area of the left frontal lobe (later called **Broca's area**) a person would struggle to speak words while still being able to sing familiar songs and comprehend speech. Damage to Broca's area disrupts speaking.

Clue 2 In 1874, German investigator Carl Wernicke discovered that after damage to a specific area of the left temporal lobe (**Wernicke's area**) people could speak only meaningless words. Asked to describe a picture that showed two boys stealing cookies behind a woman's back, one patient responded: "Mother is away her working her work to get her better, but when she's looking the two boys looking the other part. She's working another time" (Geschwind, 1979). Damage to Wernicke's area also disrupts understanding.

Clue 3 A third brain area, the *angular gyrus,* is involved in reading aloud. It receives visual information from the visual area and recodes it into an auditory form, which Wernicke's area uses to derive its meaning. Damage to the angular gyrus leaves a person able to speak and understand, but unable to read.

Clue 4 Nerve fibers interconnect these brain areas.

Almost a century after Broca's and Wernicke's findings, Norman Geschwind assembled these and other clues into an explanation of how distinct neural networks in our brain enable language (**FIGURES 2.25** and **2.26**). When you read aloud, the words (1) register in the visual area, (2) are relayed to the angular gyrus, which transforms the words into an auditory code that (3) is received and understood in the nearby Wernicke's area, and (4) is sent to Broca's area, which (5) controls the

---

aphasia impairment of language, usually caused by left-hemisphere damage either to Broca's area (impairing speaking) or to Wernicke's area (impairing understanding).

Broca's area controls language expression; an area of the frontal lobe, usually in the left hemisphere, that directs the muscle movements involved in speech.

Wernicke's area controls language reception; a brain area, usually in the left temporal lobe, that is involved in language comprehension and expression.

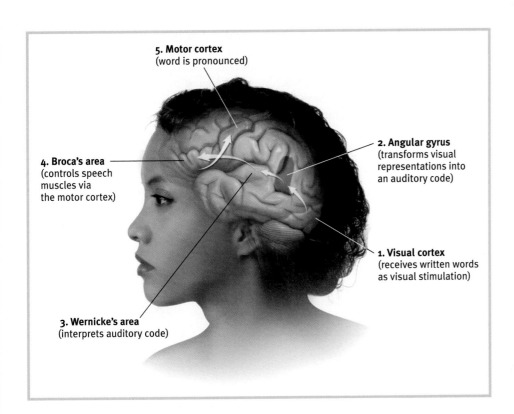

FIGURE 2.25 A simplified model of brain areas involved in language processing

motor cortex as it creates the pronounced word. Depending on which link in this chain is damaged, a different form of aphasia occurs.

The big point to remember is this: *In processing language, as in other forms of information processing, the brain operates by dividing its mental functions—speaking, perceiving, thinking, remembering—into subfunctions.* Your conscious experience of reading this page *seems* indivisible, but your brain is computing each word's form, sound, and meaning using different neural networks (Posner & Carr, 1992). We will see this division of labor again in Chapter 6, in the discussion of vision.

These specialized networks help explain a funny finding. Functional MRI scans show that we process jokes playing on meaning ("Why don't sharks bite lawyers? . . . Professional courtesy") in a different brain area than jokes playing on words ("What kind of lights did Noah use on the ark? . . . Flood lights") (Goel & Dolan, 2001). Think about it: *What you experience as a continuous, indivisible stream of experience is actually but the visible tip of a subdivided information-processing iceberg, most of which lies beneath the surface of your awareness.*

(a)
Hearing words
(auditory cortex and Wernicke's area)

(b)
Seeing words
(visual cortex and angular gyrus)

(c)
Speaking words
(Broca's area and the motor cortex)

FIGURE 2.26 Brain activity when hearing, seeing, and speaking words PET scans such as these detect the activity of different areas of the brain.

"It is the way systems interact and have a dynamic interdependence that is—unless one has lost all sense of wonder—quite awe-inspiring."

—Simon Conway Morris,
"The Boyle Lecture," 2005

To sum up, the mind's subsystems are localized in particular brain regions, yet the brain acts as a unified whole. Moving your hand, recognizing faces, perceiving scenes, comprehending language—all depend on specific neural networks. Yet complex functions such as listening, learning, and loving involve the coordination of many brain areas. Together, these two principles—specialization and integration—describe the brain's functioning.

REHEARSE IT!

19. If a neurosurgeon stimulated your right motor cortex, you would most likely
    a. see light.
    b. hear a sound.
    c. feel a touch on the right arm.
    d. move your left leg.

20. Which of the following body regions has the greatest representation in the sensory cortex?

    a. Knee
    b. Toes
    c. Forehead
    d. Thumb

21. The "uncommitted" areas that make up about three-fourths of the cerebral cortex are called
    a. occipital lobes.
    b. fissures.
    c. association areas.
    d. Wernicke's area.

22. Judging and planning are enabled by the _____ lobes.
    a. occipital
    b. parietal
    c. frontal
    d. temporal

Answers: 19. d, 20. d, 21. c, 22. c.

The Brain's Plasticity

10: To what extent can a damaged brain reorganize itself?

Our brains are sculpted not only by our genes but also by our experiences. In Chapter 4, we'll focus more on how experience molds the brain, but for now, let's turn to evidence from studies of the brain's **plasticity,** its ability to modify itself after some types of damage.

Unlike cut skin, severed neurons usually do not regenerate (if your spinal cord were severed, you would probably be permanently paralyzed). And some very specific brain functions seem preassigned to particular areas. One newborn who suffered damage to the facial recognition areas on both temporal lobes never regained a normal ability to recognize faces (Farah et al., 2000). But there is good news: Some neural tissue can *reorganize* in response to damage. It happens within all of us, as the brain repairs itself after little mishaps.

Our brains are most plastic when we are young children (Kolb, 1989; see also **FIGURE 2.27**). The brain's plasticity is good news for those blind or deaf. Blindness or deafness makes unused brain areas available for other uses (Amedi et al., 2005). If a blind person uses one finger to read Braille, the brain area dedicated to that finger expands as the sense of touch invades the visual cortex that normally helps people see (Barinaga, 1992a; Sadato et al., 1996). Temporarily "knock out" the visual cortex with magnetic stimulation, and a lifelong-blind person will make more errors on a *language* task (Amedi et al., 2004). Similarly, in people whose native language is signed, not spoken, the area of the temporal lobe normally dedicated to hearing waits in vain for stimulation. Finally, it looks for other signals to process, such as those from the visual system. That helps explain the finding that many deaf people have enhanced peripheral vision (Bosworth & Dobkins, 1999).

FIGURE 2.27 Brain plasticity If surgery or an injury destroys one part of a child's brain or, as in the case of this 6-year-old, even an entire *hemisphere* (removed to eliminate seizures), the brain will compensate by putting other areas to work. One Johns Hopkins medical team reflected on the child hemispherectomies they had performed. Although use of the opposite hand is compromised, they reported being "awed" by how well children retain their memory, personality, and humor after removal of either brain hemisphere (Vining et al., 1997). The younger the child, the greater the chance that the remaining hemisphere can take over the functions of the one that was surgically removed (Choi, 2008).

Joe McNally/Joe McNally Photography

Plasticity is especially evident after serious damage. If a slow-growing tumor in the left hemisphere disrupts language, the right hemisphere may compensate (Thiel et al., 2006). Lose a finger and the sensory cortex that received its input will begin to receive input from the adjacent fingers, which then become more sensitive (Fox, 1984). Lost fingers also feature in another mysterious phenomenon. As Figure 2.20 shows, the hand is between the sensory cortex's face and arm regions. When stroking the arm of someone whose hand had been amputated, V. S. Ramachandran found that the person felt the sensations not only on the area stroked but also on the nonexistent ("phantom") fingers. Sensory fibers that terminate on adjacent areas had invaded the brain area vacated by the hand.

Note, too, that the toes region is adjacent to the genitals. So what do you suppose was the sexual intercourse experience of another Ramachandran patient whose lower leg had been amputated? "I actually experience my orgasm in my foot. And there it's much bigger than it used to be because it's no longer just confined to my genitals" (Ramachandran & Blakeslee, 1998, p. 36).

Although brain modification often takes the form of reorganization, evidence suggests that, contrary to long-held belief, adult mice and humans can also generate new brain cells (Jessberger et al., 2008). Monkey brains illustrate **neurogenesis** by forming thousands of new neurons each day. These baby neurons originate deep in the brain and may then migrate elsewhere and form connections with neighboring neurons (Gould, 2007). Master stem cells that can develop into any type of brain cell have also been discovered in the human embryo. If mass-produced in a lab and injected into a damaged brain, might neural stem cells turn themselves into replacements for lost brain cells? Might we someday be able to rebuild damaged brains, much as we reseed damaged lawns? Might new drugs spur the production of new nerve cells? Stay tuned. Today's biotech companies are hard at work on such possibilities (Gage, 2003). In the meantime, we can all benefit from other natural promoters of neurogenesis, such as exercise, sleep, and nonstressful but stimulating environments (Iso et al., 2007; Pereira et al., 2007; Stranahan et al., 2006).

Our Divided Brain

11: What do split brains reveal about the functions of our two brain hemispheres?

For more than a century, clinical evidence has shown that the brain's two sides serve differing functions. This hemispheric specialization (or *lateralization*) is apparent after brain damage. Accidents, strokes, and tumors in the left hemisphere can impair reading, writing, speaking, arithmetic reasoning, and understanding. Similar lesions in the right hemisphere seldom have such dramatic effects.

By 1960, many interpreted these differences as evidence that the left hemisphere is the "dominant" or "major" hemisphere, and its silent companion to the right is the "subordinate" or "minor" hemisphere. Then researchers found that the "minor" right hemisphere was not so limited after all. The story of this discovery is a fascinating chapter in psychology's history.

Splitting the Brain

In 1961, two Los Angeles neurosurgeons, Philip Vogel and Joseph Bogen, speculated that major epileptic seizures were caused by an amplification of abnormal brain activity bouncing back and forth between the two cerebral hemispheres. If so, they wondered, could they put an end to this biological tennis game by severing the **corpus callosum** (see **FIGURE 2.28** on the next page), the wide band of axon fibers connecting the two hemispheres and carrying messages between them?

Vogel and Bogen knew that psychologists Roger Sperry, Ronald Myers, and Michael Gazzaniga had divided the brains of cats and monkeys in this manner, with

plasticity the brain's ability to change, especially during childhood, by reorganizing after damage or by building new pathways based on experience.

neurogenesis the formation of new neurons.

corpus callosum [KOR-pus kah-LOW-sum] the large band of neural fibers connecting the two brain hemispheres and carrying messages between them.

FIGURE 2.28 The corpus callosum This large band of neural fibers connects the two brain hemispheres. To photograph the half brain shown at left, a surgeon separated the hemispheres by cutting through the corpus callosum and lower brain regions. In the view on the right, brain tissue has been cut back to expose the corpus callosum and bundles of fibers coming out from it.

Corpus callosum

Martin M. Rother

Courtesy of Terence Williams, University of Iowa

split brain a condition resulting from surgery that isolates the brain's two hemispheres by cutting the fibers (mainly those of the corpus callosum) connecting them.

no serious ill effects. So the surgeons operated. The result? The seizures were all but eliminated. Moreover, the patients with these **split brains** were surprisingly normal, their personality and intellect hardly affected. Waking from surgery, one even joked that he had a "splitting headache" (Gazzaniga, 1967).

Sperry and Gazzaniga's studies of people with split brains provide a key to understanding the two hemispheres' complementary functions. As **FIGURE 2.29** explains, the peculiar nature of our visual wiring enabled the researchers to send information to a patient's left or right hemisphere. As the person stared at a spot, they flashed a stimulus to its right or left. They could do this with you, too, but in your intact brain, the hemisphere receiving the information would instantly pass the news to its partner across the valley. Not so in patients who had undergone split-brain surgery. Their corpus callosum—the phone cables responsible for transmitting messages from one hemisphere to the other—had been severed. This enabled the researchers to quiz each hemisphere separately.

In an early experiment, Gazzaniga (1967) asked these patients to stare at a dot as he flashed HE·ART on a screen (**FIGURE 2.30**). Thus, HE appeared in their left visual field (which transmits to the right hemisphere) and ART in the right field (which transmits to the left hemisphere). When he then asked what they had seen, the patients *said* they had seen ART. But when asked to *point* to the word, they were startled when their left hand (controlled by the right hemisphere) pointed to HE. Given an opportunity to express itself, each hemisphere reported what it had seen. The right hemisphere (controlling the left hand) intuitively knew what it could not verbally report.

FIGURE 2.29 The information highway from eye to brain Information from the left half of your field of vision goes to your right hemisphere, and information from the right half of your visual field goes to your left hemisphere, which usually controls speech. (Note, however, that each eye receives sensory information from both the right and left visual fields.) Data received by either hemisphere are quickly transmitted to the other across the corpus callosum. In a person with a severed corpus callosum, this information sharing does not take place.

Left visual field

Right visual field

Optic nerves

Optic chiasm

Speech

Visual area of left hemisphere

Corpus callosum

Visual area of right hemisphere

"Look at the dot."

(a)

Two words separated by a dot
are momentarily projected.

(b)

"What word did you see?"   or   "Point with your left hand
to the word you saw."

(c)

FIGURE 2.30 **Testing the divided brain**
When an experimenter flashes the word HEART across the visual field, a woman with a split brain reports seeing the portion of the word transmitted to her left hemisphere. However, if asked to indicate with her left hand what she saw, she points to the portion of the word transmitted to her right hemisphere. (From Gazzaniga, 1983.)

"Do not let your left hand know
what your right hand is doing."

—Matthew 6:3

FIGURE 2.31 **Try this!** Joe, who has had split-brain surgery, can simultaneously draw two different shapes.

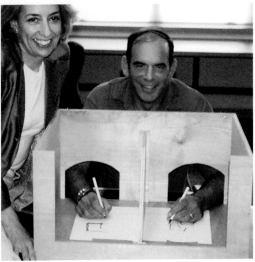

When a picture of a spoon was flashed to their right hemisphere, the patients could not *say* what they had viewed. But when asked to *identify* what they had viewed by feeling an assortment of hidden objects with their left hand, they readily selected the spoon. If the experimenter said, "Right!" the patient might reply, "What? Right? How could I possibly pick out the right object when I don't know what I saw?" It is, of course, the left hemisphere doing the talking here, bewildered by what the nonverbal right hemisphere knows.

A few people who have had split-brain surgery have been for a time bothered by the unruly independence of their left hand, which might unbutton a shirt while the right hand buttoned it, or put grocery store items back on the shelf after the right hand put them in the cart. It was as if each hemisphere was thinking "I've half a mind to wear my green (blue) shirt today." Indeed, said Sperry (1964), split-brain surgery leaves people "with two separate minds." With a split brain, both hemispheres can comprehend and follow an instruction to copy—*simultaneously*—different figures with the left and right hands (Franz et al., 2000; see also **FIGURE 2.31**). (Reading these reports, I fantasize a person enjoying a solitary game of "rock, paper, scissors"—left versus right hand.)

When the "two minds" are at odds, the left hemisphere does mental gymnastics to rationalize reactions it does not understand. If a patient follows an order sent to the right hemisphere ("Walk"), a strange thing happens. Unaware of the order, the left hemisphere doesn't know why the patient begins walking. Yet, when asked why, the patient doesn't say "I don't know." Instead,

Question: *If we flashed a red light to the right hemisphere of a person with a split brain and flashed a green light to the left hemisphere, would each observe its own color? Would the person be aware that the colors differ? What would the person verbally report seeing?*

Answers: Yes, No, Green.

the interpretive left hemisphere improvises—"I'm going into the house to get a Coke." Thus, Gazzaniga (1988), who considers these patients "The most fascinating people on earth," concluded that the conscious left hemisphere is an "interpreter" or press agent that instantly constructs theories to explain our behavior.

Right-Left Differences in the Intact Brain

So, what about the 99.99+ percent of us with undivided brains? Does each of *our* hemispheres also perform distinct functions? Several different types of studies indicate they do.

When a person performs a *perceptual* task, for example, brain waves, bloodflow, and glucose consumption reveal increased activity in the *right* hemisphere. When the person speaks or calculates, activity increases in the *left* hemisphere.

A dramatic demonstration of hemispheric specialization happens before some types of brain surgery. To check the location of language centers, the surgeon injects a sedative into the neck artery feeding blood to the left hemisphere. Before the injection, the patient is lying down, arms in the air, chatting with the doctor. Can you predict what happens when the drug flows into the artery going to the left hemisphere? Within seconds, the person's right arm falls limp. The patient also usually becomes speechless until the drug wears off. When the drug enters the artery to the right hemisphere, the *left* arm falls limp, but the person can still speak.

Which hemisphere would you suppose enables sign language among deaf people? The right, because of its visual-spatial superiority? Or the left, because it typically processes language? Studies reveal that, just as hearing people usually use the left hemisphere to process speech, deaf people use the left hemisphere to process sign language (Corina et al., 1992; Hickok et al., 2001). A stroke in the left hemisphere will disrupt a deaf person's signing, much as it would disrupt a hearing person's speaking. The same brain area is similarly involved in both spoken and signed speech production (Corina, 1998). To the brain, language is language, whether spoken or signed.

Although the left hemisphere is adept at making quick, literal interpretations of language, the right hemisphere excels in making inferences (Beeman & Chiarello, 1998; Bowden & Beeman, 1998; Mason & Just, 2004). Primed with the flashed word *foot,* the left hemisphere will be especially quick to recognize the closely associated word *heel.* But if primed with *foot, cry,* and *glass,* the right hemisphere will more quickly recognize another word distantly related to all three *(cut).* And if given an insightlike problem—"What word goes with *boot, summer,* and *ground?*"—the right hemisphere more quickly than the left recognizes the solution *(camp).* As one patient explained after a right-hemisphere stroke, "I understand words, but I'm missing the subtleties."

The right hemisphere performs other tasks as well. It helps us modulate our speech to make meaning clear, as when we ask "What's that in the road ahead?" instead of "What's that in the road, a head?" (Heller, 1990).

The right hemisphere also helps orchestrate our sense of self. People who suffer partial paralysis will sometimes obstinately deny their impairment—strangely claiming they can move a paralyzed limb—if the damage is to the right hemisphere (Berti et al., 2005). With right-brain damage, some patients have difficulty perceiving who other people are in relation to themselves, as in the case of a man who saw medical caretakers as family (Feinberg & Keenan, 2005). Others fail to recognize themselves in a mirror, or they assign ownership of a limb to someone else ("that's my husband's arm"). The power of the right brain appeared in an experiment in which people with normal brains viewed a series of images that progressively morphed from the face of a co-worker into their own face. As people recognized themselves, parts of their right brain displayed sudden activity. But when magnetic stimulation disrupted their normal right-brain activity, they had difficulty recognizing themselves in the morphed photos (Uddin et al., 2005, 2006).

Simply looking at the two hemispheres, so alike to the naked eye, who would suppose they contribute uniquely to the harmony of the whole? Yet a variety of observations—of people with split brains and people with normal brains—converge beautifully, leaving little doubt that we have unified brains with specialized parts.

The mind seeking to understand the brain—that is indeed among the ultimate scientific challenges. And so it will always be. To paraphrase cosmologist John Barrow, a brain simple enough to be understood is too simple to produce a mind able to understand it.

REHEARSE IT!

23. Plasticity—the brain's ability to reorganize itself after damage—is especially evident in the brains of
a. split-brain patients.
b. young adults.
c. young children.
d. right-handed people.

24. An experimenter flashes the word HERON across the visual field of a man whose corpus callosum has been severed. HER is transmitted to his right hemisphere and ON to his left hemisphere. When asked to indicate what he saw, the man
a. says he saw HER but points to ON.
b. says he saw ON but points to HER.
c. says he saw HERON but points to HER.
d. says he saw HERON but points to ON.

25. Studies of people with split brains and brain scans of those with undivided brains indicate that the left hemisphere excels in
a. processing language.
b. visual perceptions.
c. making inferences.
d. neurogenesis.

26. Damage to the brain's right hemisphere is most likely to reduce a person's ability to
a. recite the alphabet rapidly.
b. make inferences.
c. understand verbal instructions.
d. solve arithmetic problems.

Answers: 23. c, 24. b, 25. a, 26. b.

CHAPTER REVIEW

The Biology of Mind

Neural Communication

1 What are neurons, and how do they transmit information?

Neurons are the elementary components of the nervous system, the body's speedy electrochemical information system. A neuron sends signals through its *axons*, and receives signals through its branching *dendrites*. If the combined signals are strong enough, the neuron fires, transmitting an electrical impulse (the *action potential*) down its axon by means of a chemistry-to-electricity process. The neuron's reaction is an all-or-none process.

2 How do nerve cells communicate with other nerve cells?

When action potentials reach the end of an axon (the axon terminals), they stimulate the release of *neurotransmitters*. These chemical messengers carry a message from the sending neuron across a *synapse* to receptor sites on a receiving neuron. The sending neuron, in a process called reuptake, then normally reabsorbs the excess neurotransmitter molecules in the synaptic gap. The receiving neuron, if the signals from that neuron and others are strong enough, generates its own action potential and relays the message to other cells.

3 How do neurotransmitters influence behavior?

Each neurotransmitter travels a designated path in the brain and has a particular effect on behavior and emotions. Acetylcholine affects muscle action, learning, and memory. *Endorphins* are natural opiates released in response to pain and exercise.

The Nervous System

4 What are the functional divisions of the nervous system?

The *nervous system* is divided into the *central nervous system (CNS—the brain and spinal cord)* and the *peripheral nervous system (PNS)*, which connects the CNS to the rest of the body by means of *nerves*. The PNS has two main divisions. The *somatic nervous system* enables voluntary control of the skeletal muscles. The *autonomic nervous system*, through its *sympathetic* and *parasympathetic* divisions, controls involuntary muscles and glands. Neurons are the basic building blocks of the nervous system. *Sensory neurons* carry incoming information from sense receptors to the brain and spinal cord, and *motor neurons* carry information from the brain and spinal cord out to the muscles and glands. *Interneurons* communicate within the brain and spinal cord and between sensory and motor neurons. Neurons cluster into working neural networks.

The Endocrine System

5 How does the endocrine system—the body's slower information system—transmit its messages?

The *endocrine system* is a set of glands that secrete *hormones* into the bloodstream, where they travel through the body and affect other tissues, including the brain. In an intricate feedback system, the brain's hypothalamus influences the *pituitary gland* (the endocrine system's master gland) which influences other glands (such as the *adrenals*) to release hormones, which in turn influence the brain.

The Brain

6 How do neuroscientists study the brain's connections to behavior and mind?

Clinical observations and *lesioning* have revealed the general effects of brain damage. *MRI* scans now reveal brain structures, and *EEG, PET,* and *fMRI (functional MRI)* recordings reveal brain activity.

7 What are the functions of important lower-level brain structures?

The *brainstem,* the oldest part of the brain, is responsible for automatic survival functions. Its components are the *medulla* (which controls heartbeat and breathing), the pons (which helps coordinate movements), and the *reticular formation* (which affects arousal). The *thalamus,* the brain's sensory switchboard, sits above the brainstem. The *cerebellum,* attached to the rear of the brainstem, enables some types of nonverbal learning and memory; coordinates muscle movement; and helps process sensory information.

The *limbic system's* neural centers include the hippocampus (which processes memories of facts and episodes), the *amygdala* (involved in emotions such as aggression and fear), and the *hypothalamus* (involved in various drives, maintenance functions, and pleasurable rewards). The hypothalamus also controls the pituitary, which influences other glands to release hormones.

8 How is the cerebral cortex organized?

The *cerebral cortex* is the thin layer of interconnected neurons covering the brain's hemispheres. Prominent folds divide each hemisphere into four lobes—the *frontal, parietal, occipital,* and *temporal.*

9 What are the functions of the cerebral cortex?

Some brain regions serve specific functions. The *motor cortex* (at the rear of the frontal lobes) controls muscle movement. The *sensory cortex* (at the front of the parietal lobes) receives information from our senses. Most of the cortex is devoted to uncommitted *association areas,* which integrate information involved in learning, remembering, thinking, and other higher-level functions. Language depends on a chain of events in several brain regions, particularly *Broca's area, Wernicke's area,* and the angular gyrus. Damage to any of these regions may cause one of several types of *aphasia.*

10 To what extent can a damaged brain reorganize itself?

If one hemisphere is damaged early in life, the other will pick up many of its functions. This *plasticity* diminishes later in life. Some brain areas are capable of *neurogenesis* (forming new neurons).

11 What do split brains reveal about the functions of our two brain hemispheres?

Split-brain research (experiments on people with a severed *corpus callosum*) has confirmed that in most people, the left hemisphere is the more verbal, and that the right hemisphere excels in visual perception and making inferences. Studies of healthy people with intact brains confirm that each hemisphere makes unique contributions to the integrated functioning of the brain.

Terms and Concepts to Remember

biological psychology, p. 35

neuron, p. 35

dendrite, p. 35

axon, p. 35

action potential, p. 36

threshold, p. 36

synapse [SIN-aps], p. 37

neurotransmitters, p. 37

endorphins [en-DOR-fins], p. 38

nervous system, p. 39

central nervous system (CNS), p. 39

peripheral nervous system (PNS), p. 39

nerves, p. 39

sensory neurons, p. 39

motor neurons, p. 39

interneurons, p. 39

somatic nervous system, p. 39

autonomic [aw-tuh-NAHM-ik] nervous system, p. 40

sympathetic nervous system, p. 40

parasympathetic nervous system, p. 40

reflex, p. 41

endocrine [EN-duh-krin] system, p. 42

hormones, p. 42

adrenal [ah-DREEN-el] glands, p. 43

pituitary gland, p. 43

lesion [LEE-zhuhn], p. 44

brainstem, p. 44

electroencephalogram (EEG), p. 45

PET (positron emission tomography) scan, p. 45

MRI (magnetic resonance imaging), p. 45

fMRI (functional magnetic resonance imaging), p. 45

medulla [muh-DUL-uh], p. 45

thalamus [THAL-uh-muss], p. 46

reticular formation, p. 46

cerebellum [sehr-uh-BELL-um], p. 46

limbic system, p. 47

amygdala [uh-MIG-duh-la], p. 48

hypothalamus [hi-po-THAL-uh-muss], p. 48

cerebral [seh-REE-bruhl] cortex, p. 50

frontal lobes, p. 50

parietal [puh-RYE-uh-tuhl] lobes, p. 50

occipital [ahk-SIP-uh-tuhl] lobes, p. 50

temporal lobes, p. 50

motor cortex, p. 51

sensory cortex, p. 52

association areas, p. 53

aphasia, p. 54

Broca's area, p. 54

Wernicke's area, p. 54

plasticity, p. 56

neurogenesis, p. 57

corpus callosum [KOR-pus kah-LOW-sum], p. 57

split brain, p. 58

Test for Success: Critical Thinking Exercises
By Amy Himsel, El Camino College

1. In *The Astonishing Hypothesis* (1994, p. 49), Sir Francis Crick noted, "What one neuron tells another neuron is simply how much it is excited." Using terms from this chapter, compare the neural communication when we are (a) tapped gently on the arm, and (b) slapped across the face.

2. Which area of the human brain is most similar to that of primitive animals? Which part of the human brain distinguishes us the most from primitive animals?

3. We are not conscious of many brain processes that help create our experiences. To appreciate how much is going on outside of our awareness, we can imagine functioning without certain brain areas. For example, what would it be like to talk on the phone with your mother if you didn't have temporal lobe association areas? What would you hear? What would you understand?

4. Neurons bunch together in networks, just as people tend to congregate in cities—in each case, shorter distances enable efficient communication. Yet your brain somehow integrates information transmitted from distant regions. How do different neural networks communicate with one another to let you, for example, respond when a friend greets you at a party?

5. In what brain region would damage be most likely to disrupt your ability to skip rope? Your ability to sense tastes and sounds? In what brain region would damage perhaps leave you in a coma? Without the very breath and heartbeat of life?

The Test for Success exercises offer you a chance to apply your critical thinking skills to aspects of the material you have just read. Suggestions for answering these questions can be found in Appendix D at the back of the book.

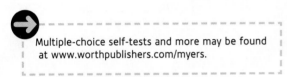

Multiple-choice self-tests and more may be found at www.worthpublishers.com/myers.

Chapter Outline

● **The Brain and Consciousness**
Dual Processing
Selective Attention

● **Sleep and Dreams**
Biological Rhythms and Sleep
Why Do We Sleep?
Sleep Disorders
Dreams

● **Hypnosis**
Facts and Falsehoods
Explaining the Hypnotized State

● **Drugs and Consciousness**
Dependence and Addiction
Psychoactive Drugs
Influences on Drug Use

Consciousness and the Two-Track Mind

Consciousness can be a funny thing. It offers us weird experiences, as when entering sleep or leaving a dream, and sometimes it leaves us wondering who is really in control. After putting me under the influence of nitrous oxide, my dentist tells me to turn my head to the left. My conscious mind resists: "No way," I silently say. "You can't boss me around!" Whereupon my robotic head, ignoring my conscious mind, turns obligingly under the dentist's control.

And then there are those times when consciousness seems to split. Reading *Green Eggs and Ham* to my preschooler for the umpteenth time, my obliging mouth could say the words while my mind wandered elsewhere. That wandering half-mind helps me again if someone drops by my office while I'm typing this sentence. It's not a problem; my fingers can complete it as I strike up a conversation.

Was my drug-induced dental experience akin to people's experiences with other *psychoactive drugs* (mood- and perception-altering substances)? Was my automatic obedience to my dentist like people's responses to a hypnotist? Or does a split in consciousness, like those that we have when our mind goes elsewhere while reading or typing, explain people's behavior while under hypnosis? And during sleep, when and why do those weird dream experiences occur?

But first questions first: What is consciousness? Every science has concepts so fundamental they are nearly impossible to define. Biologists agree on what is alive but not on precisely what *life* is. In physics, *matter* and *energy* elude simple definition. To psychologists, *consciousness* is similarly a fundamental yet slippery concept.

The difficulty of scientifically studying consciousness is apparent in psychology's history. At its beginning, *psychology* was "the description and explanation of states of consciousness" (Ladd, 1887). But during the first half of the twentieth century, many psychologists—including those in the emerging school of *behaviorism* (Chapter 7)—turned instead to direct observations of behavior. By the 1960s, psychology had nearly lost consciousness and was defining itself as "the science of behavior." Consciousness was likened to a car's speedometer: "It doesn't make the car go, it just reflects what's happening" (Seligman, 1991, p. 24).

After 1960, mental concepts began to reemerge. Advances in neuroscience made it possible to relate brain activity to sleeping, dreaming, and other mental states. Psychologists of all persuasions were affirming the importance of *cognition*, or mental processes. Psychology was regaining consciousness. For most psychologists today, **consciousness** is our awareness of ourselves and our environment. Over the course of a day, a week, a month, we flit between various states of consciousness, including sleeping, waking, and various altered states (see **FIGURE 3.1** on the next page).

consciousness our awareness of ourselves and our environment.

FIGURE 3.1 States of consciousness In addition to normal, waking awareness, consciousness comes to us in altered states, including daydreaming, sleeping, meditating, and drug-induced hallucinating.

Some states occur spontaneously	Daydreaming	Drowsiness	Dreaming
Some are physiologically induced	Hallucinations	Orgasm	Food or oxygen starvation
Some are psychologically induced	Sensory deprivation	Hypnosis	Meditation

The Brain and Consciousness

1: What is the "dual processing" being revealed by today's cognitive neuroscience?

In today's science, one of the most hotly pursued research quests is to understand the biology of consciousness. Scientists now assume, in the words of neuroscientist Marvin Minsky (1986, p. 287), that "the mind is what the brain does."

Some psychologists speculate that consciousness must offer an evolutionary advantage (Barash, 2006). Perhaps consciousness helps us act in our long-term interests (by considering consequences and helping us read others' intentions). Even so, that leaves us with the so-called "hard problem": How do brain cells jabbering to one another create our awareness of the taste of a taco, the pain of a toothache, the feeling of fright?

Such questions are at the heart of *cognitive neuroscience*—the interdisciplinary study of brain activity linked with our mental processes—that is today relating specific brain states to conscious experiences. Based on your brain-activation patterns, neuroscientists can now, in some limited ways, read your mind. They can, for example, tell which of 10 similar objects (hammer, drill, and so forth) you are viewing (Shinkareva et al., 2008).

Discovering which brain region becomes active with a particular conscious experience strikes many people as interesting but not mind-blowing. (If everything psychological is simultaneously biological, then our ideas, emotions, and spirituality must all, somehow, be embodied.) What *is* mind-blowing to many of us is the growing evidence that we have, so to speak, two minds, each supported by its own neural equipment.

Dual Processing

At any moment, you and I are aware of little more than what's on the screen of our consciousness. But one of the grand ideas of recent cognitive neuroscience is that much of our brain work occurs off stage, out of sight. We saw this in Chapter 2's discussion of the conscious "left brain" and more intuitive "right brain" revealed by studies of people following split-brain surgery. Later chapters will explore our hidden mind at work in research on unconscious *priming,* on conscious *(explicit)* and unconscious *(implicit)* memories, on conscious versus automatic prejudices, and on the out-of-sight processing that enables sudden insights and creative moments. Perception, memory, thinking, language, and attitudes all operate on two levels—a conscious, deliberate "high road" and an unconscious, automatic "low road." Today's researchers call this **dual processing.** We know more than we know we know.

dual processing the principle that information is often simultaneously processed on separate conscious and unconscious tracks.

The Two-Track Mind

A scientific story illustrates the mind's two levels. Sometimes, as this story illustrates, science is stranger than science fiction.

During my sojourns at Scotland's University of St. Andrews, I came to know cognitive neuroscientists Melvyn Goodale and David Milner (2004, 2006). A local woman, whom they call D. F., was overcome by carbon monoxide one day while showering. The resulting brain damage left her unable to recognize and discriminate objects visually. Yet she was only partly blind, for she would act as if she could see. Asked to slip a postcard into a vertical or horizontal mail slot, she could do so without error. Although unable to report the width of a block in front of her, she could grasp it with the correct finger-thumb distance.

How could this be? Don't we have one visual system? Goodale and Milner knew from animal research that the eye sends information simultaneously to different brain areas, which have different tasks. Sure enough, a scan of D. F.'s brain activity revealed normal activity in the area concerned with reaching for and grasping objects, but damage in the area concerned with consciously recognizing objects.

How strangely intricate is this thing we call vision, concluded Goodale and Milner in their aptly titled book, *Sight Unseen.* We may think of our vision as one system that controls our visually guided actions, but it is actually a dual-processing system. A *visual perception track* enables us "to create the mental furniture that allows us to think about the world"—to recognize things and to plan future actions. A *visual action track* guides our moment-to-moment actions.

On rare occasions, the two conflict. Shown the *hollow face illusion* (**FIGURE 3.2**), people will mistakenly perceive the inside of a mask as a protruding face. Yet they will unhesitatingly and accurately reach into the inverted mask to flick off a buglike target stuck on the face. What their mind doesn't know, their hand does.

This big idea—that much of our everyday thinking, feeling, and acting operates outside our conscious awareness—"is a difficult one for people to accept," observed New York University psychologists John Bargh and Tanya Chartrand (1999). We are understandably biased to believe that our own intentions and deliberate choices rule our lives. And, indeed, consciousness enables us to exert voluntary control and to communicate our mental states to others. But in the mind's downstairs, there is much, much more to being human. Beneath the surface, unconscious information processing occurs simultaneously on many parallel tracks.

Unconscious parallel processing frees your conscious mind to deal with new challenges. Traveling by car on a familiar route, your hands and feet do the driving while your mind rehearses your upcoming day. Running on automatic pilot allows your consciousness—your mind's CEO—to monitor the whole system and react to problems, while many assistants automatically take care of routine business.

Serial conscious processing, though slower than parallel processing, is skilled at solving new problems, which require our focused attention. Try this: If you are right-handed, you can move your right foot in a smooth counterclockwise circle, and you can write the number 3 repeatedly with your right hand—but probably not at the same time. (If you are musically inclined, try something equally difficult: Tap a steady beat three times with your left hand while tapping four times with your right hand.) Both tasks require attention, which can be in only one place at a time. If time is nature's way of keeping everything from happening at once, then consciousness is nature's way of keeping us from thinking and doing everything at once.

FIGURE 3.2 The hollow face illusion
What you see (an illusory protruding face from a reverse mask, as in the box at upper right) may differ from what you do (reach for a speck on the face inside the mask).

selective attention the focusing of conscious awareness on a particular stimulus.

Selective Attention

2: How much information do we consciously attend to at once?

Through **selective attention,** your conscious awareness focuses, like a flashlight beam, on only a very limited aspect of all that you experience. By one estimate, your five senses take in 11,000,000 bits of information per second, of which you consciously process about 40 (Wilson, 2002). Yet your mind's unconscious track intuitively makes great use of the other 10,999,960 bits. Until reading this sentence, for example, you have been unaware that your shoes are pressing against your feet or that your nose is in your line of vision. Now, suddenly, your attentional spotlight shifts. Your feet feel encased, your nose stubbornly intrudes on the page before you. While attending to these words, you've also been blocking from awareness information coming from your peripheral vision. But you can change that. As you stare at the X below, notice what surrounds the book (the edges of the page, your desktop, and so forth).

X

Another example of selective attention, the *cocktail party effect,* is your ability to attend to only one voice among many. (Let another voice speak your name and your cognitive radar, operating on the mind's other track, will instantly bring that voice into consciousness.) This focused listening comes at a cost. Imagine hearing two conversations over a headset, one in each ear, and being asked to repeat the message in your left ear while it is spoken. When paying attention to what is being said in your left ear, you won't perceive what is said in your right. Asked later what language your right ear heard, you may draw a blank (though you could report the speaker's gender and loudness).

SELECTIVE ATTENTION AND ACCIDENTS Trying to talk on the phone while driving requires your selective attention to shift back and forth from the road to the phone. When a demanding situation requires your full attention, you'll probably stop talking. But this process of switching attentional gears, especially when shifting to complex tasks, can entail a slight and sometimes fatal delay in coping (Rubenstein et al., 2001). The U.S. National Highway Traffic Safety Board (2006) estimates that almost 80 percent of vehicle crashes involve driver distraction. In University of Utah driving-simulation experiments, students conversing on cell phones were slower to detect and respond to traffic signals, billboards, and other cars (Strayer & Johnston, 2001; Strayer et al., 2003).

Because attention is selective, attending to a phone call (or a GPS navigation system or a DVD player) causes inattention to other things. Thus, when University of Sydney researchers (McEvoy et al., 2005, 2007) analyzed phone records for the moments before a car crash, they found that cell-phone users (even with hands-free sets) were four times more at risk. Having a passenger increased risk only 1.6 times. This difference in risk also appeared in an experiment that asked drivers to pull off at a freeway rest stop 8 miles ahead. Of drivers conversing with a passenger, 88 percent pulled off. Of those talking on a cell phone, 50 percent drove on by (Strayer & Drews, 2007). Even hands-free cell-phone talking is more distracting than a conversation with passengers, who can see the driving demands and pause the conversation.

Walking while talking can also pose dangers, as one naturalistic observation of Ohio State University pedestrians found (Nasar et al., 2008). Half the people on cell phones and only a quarter without this distraction exhibited unsafe road-crossing behavior, such as by crossing when a car was approaching.

Cell-phone inattention Just before this 2008 Los Angeles train crashed, killing 25 people, the train engineer reportedly was receiving and sending text messages.

Alex Koester/The New York Times

SELECTIVE INATTENTION At the level of conscious awareness, we are "blind" to all but a tiny sliver of the immense array of visual stimuli constantly before us. Researchers (Becklen & Cervone, 1983; Neisser, 1979) have demonstrated this dramatically by showing people a one-minute video in which images of three black-shirted men tossing a basketball were superimposed over the images of three white-shirted players. The viewers' supposed task was to press a key every time a black-shirted player passed the ball. Most focused their attention so completely on the game that they failed to notice a young woman carrying an umbrella saunter across the screen midway through the video. Seeing a replay of the video, viewers were astonished at their **inattentional blindness** (Mack & Rock, 2000). In a repeat of the experiment, smart-aleck researchers Daniel Simons and Christopher Chabris (1999) sent a gorilla-suited assistant through the swirl of players (**FIGURE 3.3**). During its 5- to 9-second cameo appearance, the gorilla paused to thump its chest. Still, half the conscientious pass-counting participants failed to see it.

inattentional blindness failing to see visible objects when our attention is directed elsewhere.

change blindness failing to notice changes in the environment.

FIGURE 3.3 **Gorillas in our midst** When attending to one task (counting basketball passes by one of the three-person teams) about half the viewers displayed inattentional blindness by failing to notice a clearly visible gorilla passing through.

Magicians exploit our change blindness by selectively riveting our attention on one hand's dramatic act with inattention to the change accomplished by the other hand.

In other experiments, people have also exhibited a blindness to change. After a brief visual interruption, a big Coke bottle may disappear, a railing may rise, clothing color may change, but, more often than not, viewers won't notice (Resnick et al., 1997; Simons, 1996; Simons & Ambinder, 2005). This form of inattentional blindness, called **change blindness**, occurred among people giving directions to a construction worker. Most people failed to notice that the worker had been replaced by someone else (**FIGURE 3.4**). Out of sight, out of mind.

FIGURE 3.4 **Change blindness** While a man (white hair) provides directions to a construction worker, two experimenters rudely pass between them carrying a door. During this interruption, the original worker switches places with another person wearing different colored clothing. Most people, focused on their direction giving, do not notice the switch.

FIGURE 3.5 The pop-out phenomenon

Some stimuli, however, are so powerful, so strikingly distinct, that we experience *pop-out*, as with the only smiling face in **FIGURE 3.5**. We don't choose to attend to these stimuli; they draw our eye and demand our attention.

Our selective attention extends even into our sleep, as we will see next.

Sleep and Dreams

"I love to sleep. Do you? Isn't it great? It really is the best of both worlds. You get to be alive and unconscious."

—Comedian Rita Rudner, 1993

Sleep—the irresistible tempter to whom we inevitably succumb. Sleep—the equalizer of presidents and peasants. Sleep—sweet, renewing, mysterious sleep.

While sleeping, you may feel "dead to the world," but you are not. Even when you are deeply asleep, your perceptual window is not completely shut. You move around on your bed, but you manage not to fall out. The occasional roar of passing vehicles may leave your deep sleep undisturbed, but a cry from a baby's nursery quickly interrupts it. So does the sound of your name. EEG recordings confirm that the brain's auditory cortex responds to sound stimuli even during sleep (Kutas, 1990). And when you are asleep, as when you are awake, you process most information outside your conscious awareness.

Dolphins, porpoises, and whales sleep with one side of their brain asleep at a time (Miller et al., 2008).

Many of sleep's mysteries are now being solved as some people sleep, attached to recording devices, while others observe. By recording brain waves and muscle movements, and by observing and occasionally waking sleepers, researchers are glimpsing things that a thousand years of common sense never told us. Perhaps you can anticipate some of their discoveries. Are the following statements true or false?

1. When most people dream of performing some activity, their limbs often move in concert with the dream.
2. Older adults sleep more than young adults.
3. Sleepwalkers are acting out their dreams.
4. Sleep experts recommend treating insomnia with an occasional sleeping pill.
5. Some people dream every night; others seldom dream.

All these statements (adapted from Palladino & Carducci, 1983) are false. To see why, read on.

Biological Rhythms and Sleep

3: How do our biological rhythms influence our daily functioning and our sleep and dreams?

Like the ocean, life has its rhythmic tides. Over varying time periods, our bodies fluctuate, and with them, our minds. Let's look more closely at two of those biological rhythms—our 24-hour biological clock and our 90-minute sleep cycle.

Circadian Rhythm

The rhythm of the day parallels the rhythm of life—from our waking at a new day's birth to our nightly return to what Shakespeare called "death's counterfeit." Our bodies roughly synchronize with the 24-hour cycle of day and night through a biological clock called the **circadian rhythm** (from the Latin *circa,* "about," and *diem,* "day"). Body temperature rises as morning approaches, peaks during the day, dips for a time in early afternoon (when many people take siestas), and then begins to drop again before we go to sleep. Thinking is sharpest and memory most accurate when we are at our daily peak in circadian arousal. Pulling an all-nighter, we may feel groggiest about 4:00 A.M., and then we get a second wind after our normal wake-up time arrives.

Bright light in the morning tweaks the circadian clock by activating light-sensitive retinal proteins. These proteins control the circadian clock by triggering signals to the brain's *suprachiasmatic nucleus (SCN)*—a pair of grain-of-rice-sized, 20,000-cell clusters in the hypothalamus (Foster, 2004). The SCN does its job in part by causing the brain's pineal gland to decrease its production of the sleep-inducing hormone *melatonin* in the morning or increase it in the evening (**FIGURE 3.6**).

circadian [ser-KAY-dee-an] **rhythm** the biological clock; regular bodily rhythms (for example, of temperature and wakefulness) that occur on a 24-hour cycle.

At about age 20 (slightly earlier for women), we begin to shift from being evening-energized "owls" to being morning-loving "larks" (Roenneberg et al., 2004). Most 20-year-olds are owls, with performance improving across the day (May & Hasher, 1998). Most older adults are larks, with performance declining as the day wears on. Retirement homes are typically quiet by mid-evening; in university dorms, the day is far from over.

FIGURE 3.6 The biological clock Light striking the retina signals the suprachiasmatic nucleus (SCN) to suppress the pineal gland's production of the sleep hormone melatonin. At night, the SCN quiets down, allowing the pineal gland to release melatonin into the bloodstream.

Bright light at night helps delay sleep, thus resetting our biological clock when we stay up late and sleep in on weekends (Oren & Terman, 1998). Sleep often eludes those who sleep till noon on Sunday and then go to bed just 11 hours later in preparation for the new workweek. They are like New Yorkers whose biology is on California time. But what about North Americans who fly to Europe, and who need to be up when their circadian rhythm cries "Sleep!"? Studies in the laboratory and with shift workers have found that bright light—spending the next day outdoors—helps reset the biological clock (Czeisler et al., 1986, 1989; Eastman et al., 1995).

Curiously—given that our ancestors' body clocks were attuned to the rising and setting sun of the 24-hour day—many of today's young adults adopt something closer to a 25-hour day, by staying up too late to get 8 hours of sleep. For this, we can thank (or blame) Thomas Edison, inventor of the light bulb. Being bathed in light disrupts our 24-hour biological clock (Czeisler et al., 1999; Dement, 1999). This helps explain why, until our later years, we must discipline ourselves to go to bed and force ourselves to get up. Most animals, too, when placed under unnatural constant illumination will exceed a 24-hour day. Artificial light delays sleep.

If our natural circadian rhythm were attuned to a 23-hour cycle, would we instead need to discipline ourselves to stay up later at night and sleep in longer in the morning?

Sleep Stages

4: **What is the biological rhythm of our sleep?**

As sleep overtakes us and different parts of our brain's cortex stop communicating, consciousness fades (Massimini et al., 2005). But our still-active sleeping brain does not then emit a constant dial tone, because sleep has its own biological rhythm. About every 90 minutes, we pass through a cycle of five distinct sleep

REM sleep rapid eye movement sleep; a recurring sleep stage during which vivid dreams commonly occur. Also known as *paradoxical sleep*, because the muscles are relaxed (except for minor twitches) but other body systems are active.

alpha waves the relatively slow brain waves of a relaxed, awake state.

sleep periodic, natural loss of consciousness—as distinct from unconsciousness resulting from a coma, general anesthesia, or hibernation. (Adapted from Dement, 1999.)

hallucinations false sensory experiences, such as seeing something in the absence of an external visual stimulus.

delta waves the large, slow brain waves associated with deep sleep.

stages. This elementary fact apparently was unknown until 8-year-old Armond Aserinsky went to bed one night in 1952. His father, Eugene, a University of Chicago graduate student, needed to test an electroencephalograph he had been repairing that day (Aserinsky, 1988; Seligman & Yellen, 1987). Placing electrodes near Armond's eyes to record the rolling eye movements then believed to occur during sleep, Aserinsky watched the machine go wild, tracing deep zigzags on the graph paper. Could the machine still be broken? As the night proceeded and the activity periodically recurred, Aserinsky finally realized that the fast, jerky eye movements were accompanied by energetic brain activity. Awakened during one such episode, Armond reported having a dream. Aserinsky had discovered what we now know as **REM sleep** (*r*apid *e*ye *m*ovement sleep).

To find out if similar cycles occur during adult sleep, Nathaniel Kleitman (1960) and Aserinsky pioneered procedures that have now been used with thousands of volunteers. To appreciate their methods and findings, imagine yourself in their lab. As the hour grows late, you feel sleepy and you yawn in response to reduced brain metabolism. (Yawning, which can be socially contagious, stretches your neck muscles and increases your heart rate, which increases your alertness [Moorcroft, 2003]). When you are ready for bed, the researcher tapes electrodes just outside the corners of your eyes (to detect eye movements), to your scalp (to detect your brain waves), and on your chin (to detect muscle tension) (**FIGURE 3.7**). Other devices allow the researcher to record your heart rate, your respiration rate, and your genital arousal.

When you are in bed with your eyes closed, the researcher in the next room sees on the EEG the relatively slow **alpha waves** of your awake but relaxed state (**FIGURE 3.8**). As you adapt to all this equipment, you grow tired and, in an unremembered moment, slip into **sleep.** The transition is marked by the slowed breathing and the irregular brain waves of Stage 1 (**FIGURE 3.9**).

In one of his 15,000 research participants, William Dement (1999) observed the moment the brain's perceptual window to the outside world slammed shut. Dement asked this sleep-deprived young man, lying on his back with eyelids taped open, to press a button every time a strobe light flashed in his eyes (about every 6 seconds). After a few minutes the young man missed one. Asked why, he said, "Because there was no flash." But there was a flash. He missed it because (as his brain activity revealed) he had fallen asleep for 2 seconds. Unaware that he had done so, he had missed not only the flash 6 inches from his nose but also the abrupt moment of his entry into sleep.

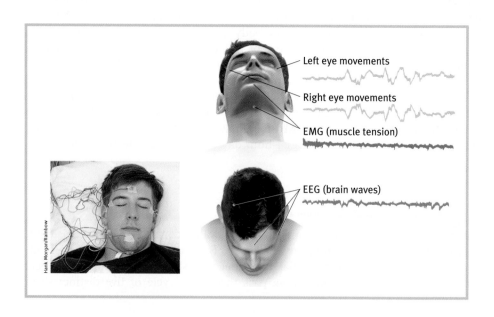

FIGURE 3.7 Measuring sleep activity
Sleep researchers measure brain-wave activity, eye movements, and muscle tension by electrodes that pick up weak electrical signals from the brain, eye, and facial muscles. (From Dement, 1978.)

Left eye movements

Right eye movements

EMG (muscle tension)

EEG (brain waves)

Hank Morgan/Rainbow

FIGURE 3.8 **Brain waves and sleep stages** The regular alpha waves of an awake, relaxed state are quite different from the slower, larger delta waves of deep Stage 4 sleep. Although the saw-toothed REM sleep waves resemble the near-waking Stage 1 sleep waves, the body is more aroused during REM sleep than during Stage 1 sleep. (From Dement, 1978.)

FIGURE 3.9 **The moment of sleep** We seem unaware of the moment we fall into sleep, but someone eavesdropping on our brain waves could tell. (From Dement, 1999.)

During this brief Stage 1 sleep you may experience fantastic images, resembling **hallucinations**—sensory experiences that occur without a sensory stimulus. You may have a sensation of falling (at which moment your body may suddenly jerk) or of floating weightlessly. Such *hypnagogic* sensations may later be incorporated into memories. People who claim to have been abducted by aliens—often shortly after getting into bed—commonly recall being floated off or pinned down on their beds (Clancy, 2005).

You next relax more deeply and begin about 20 minutes of Stage 2 sleep, characterized by the periodic appearance of *sleep spindles*—bursts of rapid, rhythmic brain-wave activity (see Figure 3.8). Although you could still be awakened without too much difficulty, you are now clearly asleep.

For the next few minutes, you go through the transitional Stage 3 to the deep sleep of Stage 4. First in Stage 3, and increasingly in Stage 4, your brain emits large, slow **delta waves.** These two slow-wave stages last for about 30 minutes, during which you would be hard to awaken. Curiously, it is at the end of the deep sleep of Stage 4 that children may wet the bed or begin sleepwalking. About 20 percent of 3- to 12-year-olds have at least one episode of sleepwalking, usually lasting 2 to 10 minutes; some 5 percent have repeated episodes (Giles et al., 1994).

REM Sleep

About an hour after you first fall asleep, a strange thing happens. Rather than continuing in deep slumber, you ascend from your initial sleep dive. Returning through Stage 3 and Stage 2 (where you spend about half your night), you enter the most intriguing sleep phase—REM sleep. For about 10 minutes, your brain waves become rapid and saw-toothed, more like those of the nearly awake Stage 1 sleep. But unlike Stage 1 sleep, during REM sleep your heart rate rises, your breathing becomes rapid and irregular, and every half-minute or so your eyes dart around in momentary bursts of activity behind closed lids. Because anyone watching a sleeper's eyes

To catch your own hypnagogic experiences after going to bed, you might have a "Snooze" alarm awaken you every five minutes.

"Boy are my eyes tired! I had REM sleep all night long."

can notice these REM bursts, it is amazing that science was ignorant of REM sleep until 1952. The stages in a typical night's sleep are summarized in **FIGURE 3.10.**

Except during very scary dreams, your genitals become aroused during REM sleep, and you have an erection or increased vaginal lubrication and clitoral engorgement, regardless of whether the dream's content is sexual (Karacan et al., 1966). Men's common "morning erection" stems from the night's last REM period, often just before waking. In young men, sleep-related erections outlast REM periods, lasting 30 to 45 minutes on average (Karacan et al., 1983; Schiavi & Schreiner-Engel, 1988). A typical 25-year-old man therefore has an erection during nearly half his night's sleep, a 65-year-old man for one-quarter. Many men troubled by *erectile dysfunction* (impotence) have sleep-related erections, suggesting the problem is not between their legs.

Although your brain's motor cortex is active during REM sleep, your brainstem blocks its messages, leaving muscles relaxed—so relaxed that, except for an occasional finger, toe, or facial twitch, you are essentially paralyzed. Moreover, you cannot easily be awakened. Thus, REM sleep is sometimes called *paradoxical* sleep, with the body internally aroused and externally calm.

More intriguing than the paradoxical nature of REM sleep is what the rapid eye movements announce: the beginning of a dream. Even those who claim they never dream will, more than 80 percent of the time, recall a dream after being awakened during REM sleep. Unlike the fleeting images of Stage 1 sleep ("I was thinking about my exam today," or "I was trying to borrow something from someone"), REM sleep dreams are often emotional, usually storylike, and more richly hallucinatory.

The sleep cycle repeats itself about every 90 minutes. As the night wears on, deep Stage 4 sleep gets progressively briefer and then disappears. The REM and Stage 2 sleep periods get longer (see Figure 3.10b). By morning, 20 to 25 percent of our average night's sleep—some 100 minutes—has been REM sleep. Thirty-seven percent of people report rarely or never having dreams "that you can remember the next morning" (Moore, 2004). Unknown to those people, they spend about 600 hours a year experiencing some 1500 dreams, or more than 100,000 dreams over a typical lifetime—dreams swallowed by the night but never acted out, thanks to REM's protective paralysis.

Horses, which spend 92 percent of each day standing and can sleep standing, must lie down for REM sleep (Morrison, 2003).

People rarely snore during dreams. When REM starts, snoring stops.

FIGURE 3.10 The stages in a typical night's sleep Most people pass through the five-stage sleep cycle (graph a) several times, with the periods of Stage 4 sleep and then Stage 3 sleep diminishing and REM sleep periods increasing in duration. Graph b plots this increasing REM sleep and decreasing deep sleep based on data from 30 young adults. (From Cartwright, 1978; Webb, 1992.)

Why Do We Sleep?

The idea that "everyone needs 8 hours of sleep" is untrue. Newborns spend nearly two-thirds of their day asleep, most adults no more than one-third. Age-related differences in average sleeping time are rivaled by the differences among individuals at any age. Some people thrive with fewer than 6 hours per night; others regularly rack up 9 hours or more. Such sleep patterns may be genetically influenced. In studies of the pattern and duration of sleep among fraternal and identical twins, only the identical twins were strikingly similar (Webb & Campbell, 1983).

Sleep patterns are also culturally influenced. In the United States and Canada, for example, adults average just over 8 hours per night (Hurst, 2008; Robinson & Martin, 2007). (The weeknight sleep of many students and workers falls short of this average [NSF, 2008].) North Americans are nevertheless sleeping less than their counterparts a century ago. Thanks to modern light bulbs, shift work, and social diversions, those who would have gone to bed at 9:00 P.M. are now up until 11:00 P.M. or later. Thomas Edison (1948) was pleased to accept credit for this, believing that less sleep meant more productive time and greater opportunities.

Allowed to sleep unhindered, most adults will sleep at least 9 hours a night (Coren, 1996). With that much sleep, we awake refreshed, sustain better moods, and perform more efficient and accurate work. Compare that with a succession of 5-hour nights, when we accumulate a sleep debt that cannot be paid off by one long marathon sleep. "The brain keeps an accurate count of sleep debt for at least two weeks," observed sleep researcher William Dement (1999, p. 64). With our body yearning for sleep, we will begin to feel terrible. Trying to stay awake, we will eventually lose. In the tiredness battle, sleep always wins.

Obviously, then, we need sleep. Sleep commands roughly one-third of our lives—some 25 years, on average. But why? It seems an easy question to answer: Just keep people awake for several days and note how they deteriorate. If you were a volunteer in such an experiment, how do you think it would affect your body and mind? You would, of course, become terribly drowsy—especially during the hours when your biological clock programs you to sleep. But could the lack of sleep physically damage you? Would it noticeably alter your biochemistry or body organs? Would you become emotionally disturbed? Mentally disoriented?

Some sleep deeply, some not The fluctuating sleep cycle enables safe sleep for these firefighters battling California wildfires. One benefit of communal sleeping is that someone will probably be awake or easily roused in the event of a threat.

The Effects of Sleep Loss

5: How does sleep loss affect us?

Good news! Psychologists have discovered a treatment that strengthens memory, increases concentration, boosts mood, moderates hunger and obesity, fortifies the disease-fighting immune system, and lessens the risk of fatal accidents. Even better news: The treatment feels good, it can be self-administered, the supplies are limitless, and it's available free! If you are a typical university-age student, often going to bed near 2:00 A.M. and dragged out of bed six hours later by the dreaded alarm, the treatment is simple: Each night, just add an hour to your sleep.

The U.S. Navy and the National Institutes of Health have demonstrated the benefits of unrestricted sleep in experiments in which volunteers spent 14 hours daily in bed for at least a week. For the first few days, the volunteers averaged 12 hours or more sleep each day, apparently paying off a sleep debt that averaged 25 to 30 hours. That accomplished, they then settled back to 7.5 to 9 hours nightly and, with no sleep debt, felt energized and happier (Dement, 1999). In one Gallup survey (Mason, 2005), 63 percent of adults who reported getting the sleep they need also reported being "very satisfied" with their personal life (as did only 36 percent of those needing more sleep).

Unfortunately, many of us are suffering from patterns that not only leave us sleepy but also thwart our having an energized feeling of well-being. Teens who

In a 2001 Gallup poll, 61 percent of men, but only 47 percent of women, said they got enough sleep.

typically need 8 or 9 hours of sleep now average less than 7 hours—nearly 2 hours less each night than did their counterparts of 80 years ago (Holden, 1993; Maas, 1999). In one survey, 28 percent of high school students acknowledged falling asleep in class at least once a week (Sleep Foundation, 2006). When the going gets boring, the students start snoring.

Even when awake, students often function below their peak. And they know it: Four in five American teens and three in five 18- to 29-year-olds wish they could get more sleep on weekdays (Mason, 2003, 2005). Yet that teen who staggers glumly out of bed in response to an unwelcome alarm, yawns through morning classes, and feels half-depressed much of the day may be energized at 11 P.M. and mindless of the next day's looming sleepiness (Carskadon, 2002).

At Stanford University, 80 percent of students are "dangerously sleep deprived." Dement (1997) said, "Sleep deprivation [entails] difficulty studying, diminished productivity, tendency to make mistakes, irritability, fatigue." A large sleep debt "makes you stupid," he noted (1999, p. 231).

It can also make you fatter. Sleep deprivation increases ghrelin, a hunger-arousing hormone, and decreases its hunger-suppressing partner, leptin (more on these in Chapter 10). Sleep deprivation also increases cortisol, a stress hormone that stimulates the body to make fat. Sure enough, children and adults who sleep less than normal are fatter than those who sleep more (Chen et al., 2008; Knutson et al., 2007; Schoenborn & Adams, 2008). And experimental sleep deprivation of adults increases appetite and eating (Nixon et al., 2008; Patel et al., 2006; Spiegel et al., 2004; Van Cauter et al., 2007). This may help explain the common weight gain among sleep-deprived students (although a review of 11 studies reveals that the mythical "freshman 15" is, on average, closer to a "first-year 4" [Hull et al., 2007]).

In addition to making us more vulnerable to obesity, sleep deprivation can suppress immune cells that fight off viral infections and cancer (Motivala & Irwin, 2007). This may help explain why people who sleep 7 to 8 hours a night tend to outlive those who are chronically sleep deprived, and why older adults who have no difficulty falling or staying asleep tend to live longer than their sleep-deprived age-mates (Dement, 1999; Dew et al., 2003). When infections do set in, we typically sleep more, boosting our immune cells.

Chronic sleep debt also alters metabolic and hormonal functioning in ways that mimic aging and are conducive to hypertension and memory impairment (Spiegel et al., 1999; Taheri, 2004). Other effects include irritability, slowed performance, and impaired creativity, concentration, and communication (Harrison & Horne, 2000). Reaction times slow and errors increase on visual tasks similar to those involved in screening airport baggage, performing surgery, and reading X-rays (Horowitz et al., 2003).

Sleep deprivation can be devastating for driving, piloting, and equipment operating. Driver fatigue contributes to an estimated 20 percent of American traffic accidents (Brody, 2002) and to some 30 percent of Australian highway deaths (Maas, 1999). Consider the timing of the 1989 *Exxon Valdez* oil spill; Union Carbide's 1984 Bhopal, India, disaster; and the 1979 Three Mile Island and 1986 Chernobyl nuclear accidents—all occurred after midnight, when operators in charge were likely to be drowsiest and unresponsive to signals that require an alert response. When sleepy frontal lobes confront an unexpected situation, misfortune often results.

Stanley Coren capitalized on what is, for many North Americans, a semi-annual sleep-manipulation experiment—the "spring forward" to "daylight savings" time and "fall backward" to "standard" time. Searching millions of records, Coren found that in both Canada and the United States, accidents increased immediately after the time change that shortens sleep (**FIGURE 3.11**).

But let's put all this positively: To manage your life with enough sleep to awaken naturally and well rested is to be more alert, productive, happy, healthy, and safe.

"Tiger Woods said that one of the best things about his choice to leave Stanford for the professional golf circuit was that he could now get enough sleep."

—Stanford sleep researcher William Dement, 1997

Jose Luis Pelaez, Inc/Corbis

Sleepless and suffering This fatigued, sleep-deprived person may also experience a depressed immune system, impaired concentration, and a greater vulnerability to accidents.

In 1989, Michael Doucette was named America's Safest Driving Teen. In 1990, while driving home from college, he fell asleep at the wheel and collided with an oncoming car, killing both himself and the other driver. Michael's driving instructor later acknowledged never having mentioned sleep deprivation and drowsy driving (Dement, 1999).

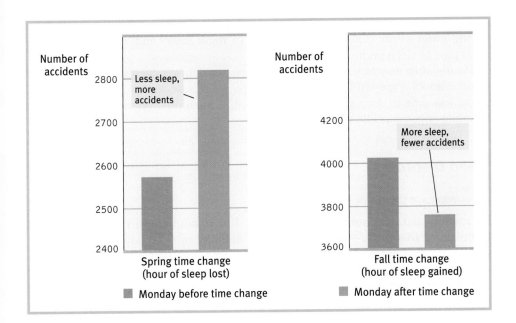

FIGURE 3.11 Canadian traffic accidents
On the Monday after the spring time change, when people lose one hour of sleep, accidents increased as compared with the Monday before. In the fall, traffic accidents normally increase because of greater snow, ice, and darkness, but they diminished after the time change. (Adapted from Coren, 1996.)

Sleep Theories

6: Why do we sleep?

So, nature charges us for our sleep debt. But why do we have this need for sleep?

We have very few answers, but sleep may have evolved for five reasons: First, *sleep protects*. When darkness precluded our distant ancestors' hunting and food gathering and made travel treacherous, they were better off asleep in a cave, out of harm's way. Those who didn't try to navigate around rocks and cliffs at night were more likely to leave descendants. This fits a broader principle: A species' sleep pattern tends to suit its ecological niche. Animals with the most need to graze and the least ability to hide tend to sleep less. Elephants and horses sleep 3 to 4 hours a day, gorillas 12 hours, and cats 14 hours. For bats and eastern chipmunks, both of which sleep 20 hours, to live is hardly more than to eat and to sleep (Moorcroft, 2003). (Would you rather be like a giraffe and sleep 2 hours a day, or a bat and sleep 20?)

Second, *sleep helps us recuperate*. It helps restore and repair brain tissue. Animals with high waking metabolism (such as bats) burn a lot of calories, producing a lot of *free radicals*, molecules that are toxic to neurons. Sleeping a lot gives resting neurons time to repair themselves, while allowing unused connections to weaken (Siegel, 2003; Vyazovskiy et al., 2008). Think of it this way: When consciousness leaves your house, brain construction workers come in for a makeover.

But sleep is not just for keeping us safe and for repairing our brain. New research reveals that *sleep is for making memories*—for restoring and rebuilding our fading memories of the day's experiences. People trained to perform tasks recall them better after a night's sleep, or even after a short nap, than after several hours awake (Walker & Stickgold, 2006). And in both humans and rats, neural activity during slow-wave sleep reenacts and promotes recall of prior novel experiences (Peigneux et al., 2004; Ribeiro et al., 2004).

Sleep also feeds creative thinking. On occasion, dreams have inspired noteworthy literary, artistic, and scientific achievements. It was, for example, a dream that clued chemist August Kekulé to the structure of benzene (Ross, 2006). More commonplace is the boost that a complete night's sleep gives to our thinking and learning. People who work on a task, then sleep on it, solve problems more insightfully than do those who stay awake (Wagner et al., 2004). They can also, after sleep, better discern connections among different novel pieces of information (Ellenbogen et al.,

"Sleep faster, we need the pillows."

—Yiddish proverb

2007). Even 15-month-olds, if retested after a nap, better recall relationships among novel words (Gómez et al., 2006). To think smart and see connections, it often pays to sleep on it.

Finally, *sleep may play a role in the growth process.* During deep sleep, the pituitary gland releases a growth hormone. As we age, we release less of this hormone and spend less time in deep sleep (Pekkanen, 1982). Such discoveries are beginning to solve the ongoing riddle of sleep.

Sleep Disorders

7: **What are the major sleep disorders?**

No matter what their normal need for sleep, 1 in 10 adults, and 1 in 4 older adults, complain of **insomnia**—not an occasional inability to sleep when anxious or excited, but persistent problems in falling or staying asleep (Irwin et al., 2006).

From middle age on, sleep is seldom uninterrupted. Being occasionally awakened becomes the norm, not something to fret over or treat with medication. And some people do fret unnecessarily about their sleep (Coren, 1996). In laboratory studies, insomnia complainers do sleep less than others, but they typically overestimate—by about double—how long it takes them to fall asleep. They also underestimate by nearly half how long they actually have slept. Even if we have been awake only an hour or two, we may *think* we have had very little sleep because it's the waking part we remember.

The most common quick fixes for true insomnia—sleeping pills and alcohol—can aggravate the problem, reducing REM sleep and leaving the person with next-day blahs. Nevertheless, sales of sleeping pills soared 60 percent from 2000 to 2006 (Saul, 2007). Those who rely on them may need increasing doses to get an effect; then, when the drug is discontinued, the insomnia can worsen.

Scientists are searching for natural chemicals that are abundant during sleep, hoping they might be synthesized as a sleep aid without side effects. In the meantime, sleep experts offer other natural alternatives:

- Exercise regularly but not in the late evening. (Late afternoon is best.)
- Avoid all caffeine after early afternoon, and avoid rich foods before bedtime. Instead, try a glass of milk, which provides raw materials for the manufacture of serotonin, a neurotransmitter that facilitates sleep.
- Relax before bedtime, using dimmer light.
- Sleep on a regular schedule (rise at the same time even after a restless night) and avoid naps. Sticking to a schedule boosts daytime alertness, too, as shown in an experiment in which University of Arizona students averaged 7.5 hours of sleep a night on either a varying or consistent schedule (Manber et al., 1996).
- Hide the clock face so you aren't tempted to check it repeatedly.
- Reassure yourself that a temporary loss of sleep causes no great harm.
- Realize that for any stressed organism, being vigilant is natural and adaptive. A personal conflict during the day often means a fitful sleep that night (Åkerstedt et al., 2007; Brisette & Cohen, 2002). Managing your stress levels will enable more restful sleeping. (See Chapter 11 for more on stress.)
- If all else fails, settle for less sleep, either going to bed later or getting up earlier.

Rarer but also more troublesome than insomnia are the sleep disorders *narcolepsy, sleep apnea, night terrors,* and *sleepwalking.*

Narcolepsy (from *narco,* "numbness," and *lepsy,* "seizure") sufferers experience periodic, overwhelming sleepiness. Attacks usually last less than 5 minutes but sometimes occur at the most inopportune times, perhaps just after taking a terrific swing at a softball or when laughing loudly, shouting angrily, or having sex (Dement, 1978, 1999). In severe cases, the person may collapse directly into a brief period of REM sleep, with an accompanying loss of muscular tension. People with narcolepsy—1 in

"The lion and the lamb shall lie down together, but the lamb will not be very sleepy."

—Woody Allen, in the movie
Love and Death, 1975

"Sleep is like love or happiness. If you pursue it too ardently it will elude you."

—Wilse Webb, *Sleep: The Gentle Tyrant,* 1992

"In 1757 Benjamin Franklin gave us the axiom, 'Early to bed, early to rise, makes a man healthy, wealthy, and wise.' It would be more accurate to say 'consistently to bed and consistently to rise . . .' "

—James B. Maas, *Power Sleep,* 1999

off the mark.com   by Mark Parisi

LET ME GET THIS STRAIGHT, IT'S BEEN TWO CONSECUTIVE HOURS SINCE YOU'VE SLEPT?

WHEN CATS EXPERIENCE INSOMNIA

Economic-recession stress can rob sleep
A National Sleep Foundation (2009) survey found 27 percent of people reporting sleeplessness related to the economy and their personal finances and employment. Higher stress levels, and more restless sleep, may plague those standing in unemployment lines such as this one.

2000 of us, estimates the Stanford University Center for Narcolepsy (2002)—must therefore live with extra caution. As a traffic menace, "snoozing is second only to boozing," says the American Sleep Disorders Association, and those with narcolepsy are especially at risk (Aldrich, 1989).

Sleep apnea also puts millions of people at increased risk of traffic accidents (Teran-Santos et al., 1999). Although 1 in 20 of us has this disorder, it was unknown before modern sleep research. *Apnea* means "with no breath," and people with this condition intermittently stop breathing during sleep. After an airless minute or so, decreased blood oxygen arouses them and they wake up enough to snort in air for a few seconds, in a process that repeats hundreds of times each night, depriving them of slow-wave sleep. Apart from complaints of sleepiness and fatigue, and irritability or depression during the day—and their mate's complaints about their loud "snoring"—apnea sufferers often have no recall of these episodes (Peppard et al., 2006).

Sleep apnea is associated with obesity, and as the number of obese Americans has increased, so has this disorder, particularly among overweight men, including some football players (Keller, 2007). Anyone who snores at night, feels tired during the day, and possibly has high blood pressure as well (increasing the risk of a stroke or heart attack) should be checked for apnea (Dement, 1999). A physician may prescribe a masklike device with an air pump that keeps the sleeper's airway open and breathing regular. If one doesn't mind looking a little goofy in the dark (imagine a snorkeler at a slumber party), the treatment can effectively treat both the apnea and associated depressed energy and mood.

Unlike sleep apnea, **night terrors** target mostly children, who may sit up or walk around, talk incoherently, experience a doubling of heart and breathing rates, and appear terrified (Hartmann, 1981). They seldom wake up fully during an episode and recall little or nothing the next morning—at most, a fleeting, frightening image. Night terrors are not nightmares (which, like other dreams, typically occur during early morning REM sleep); night terrors usually occur during the first few hours of Stage 4.

Children also are most prone to *sleepwalking*—another Stage 4 sleep disorder—and to *sleeptalking*, conditions that run in families. (Sleeptalking—usually garbled or nonsensical—can occur during Stage 2 or any other sleep stage [Mahowald & Ettinger, 1990].) Occasional childhood sleepwalking occurs for about one-third of those with a sleepwalking fraternal twin and half of those with a sleepwalking identical twin. The same is true for sleeptalking (Hublin et al., 1997, 1998). Sleepwalking is usually harmless and unrecalled the next morning. Sleepwalkers typically return to bed on their own or are guided there by a family member. Young children, who have the deepest and lengthiest Stage 4 sleep, are the most likely to experience both night terrors and sleepwalking. As we grow older and deep Stage 4 sleep diminishes, so do night terrors and sleepwalking. After being sleep deprived, people sleep more deeply, which increases any tendency to sleepwalk (Zadra et al., 2008).

Imagine observing a person with narcolepsy in medieval times. Might such symptoms (especially the instant dreams from dropping into REM sleep) have seemed like demon possession?

Did Brahms need his own lullabies?
Cranky, overweight, and nap-prone, Johannes Brahms exhibited common symptoms of sleep apnea (Margolis, 2000).

insomnia recurring problems in falling or staying asleep.

narcolepsy a sleep disorder characterized by uncontrollable sleep attacks. The sufferer may lapse directly into REM sleep, often at inopportune times.

sleep apnea a sleep disorder characterized by temporary cessations of breathing during sleep and repeated momentary awakenings.

night terrors a sleep disorder characterized by high arousal and an appearance of being terrified; unlike nightmares, night terrors occur during Stage 4 sleep, within two or three hours of falling asleep, and are seldom remembered.

REHEARSE IT!

3. Our body temperature tends to rise and fall in sync with a biological clock, which is referred to as
   a. the circadian rhythm.
   b. narcolepsy.
   c. REM sleep.
   d. hypnagogic sensations.

4. During Stage 1 light sleep, a person is most likely to experience
   a. sleep spindles.
   b. hallucinations.
   c. night terrors or nightmares.
   d. rapid eye movements.

5. The brain emits large, slow delta waves during the deepest stage of sleep, called
   a. Stage 2.
   b. Stage 4.
   c. REM sleep.
   d. paradoxical sleep.

6. During sleep we pass through a cycle of five stages, each with characteristic brain waves. As the night progresses, the REM stage
   a. gradually disappears.
   b. becomes briefer and briefer.
   c. remains about the same.
   d. becomes progressively longer.

7. Which of the following is NOT one of the theories that have been proposed to explain why we need sleep?
   a. Sleep has survival value.
   b. Sleep helps us recuperate.
   c. Sleep rests the eyes.
   d. Sleep plays a role in the growth process.

8. Two sleep disorders are narcolepsy and sleep apnea. With narcolepsy, the person _____; with sleep apnea, the person _____.
   a. has persistent problems falling sleep; experiences a doubling of heart and breathing rates
   b. experiences a doubling of heart and breathing rates; has persistent problems falling asleep
   c. intermittently stops breathing; suffers periodic, overwhelming sleepiness
   d. suffers periodic, overwhelming sleepiness; intermittently stops breathing

Answers: 3. a, 4. b, 5. b, 6. d, 7. c, 8. d.

Dreams

8:

What do we dream?

Now playing at an inner theater near you: the premiere showing of a sleeping person's vivid dream. This never-before-seen mental movie features captivating characters wrapped in a plot so original and unlikely, yet so intricate and so seemingly real, that the viewer later marvels at its creation.

Waking from a troubling dream, wrenched by its emotions, who among us has not wondered about this weird state of consciousness? How can our brain so creatively, colorfully, and completely construct this alternative, conscious world? In the shadowland between our dreaming and waking consciousness, we may even wonder for a moment which is real.

Discovering the link between REM sleep and dreaming opened a new era in dream research. Instead of relying on someone's hazy recall hours or days after having a dream, researchers could catch dreams as they happened. They could awaken people during or within 3 minutes after a REM sleep period and hear a vivid account.

What We Dream

Daydreams tend to involve the familiar details of our life—perhaps picturing ourselves explaining to an instructor why a paper will be late, or replaying in our minds personal encounters we relish or regret. REM **dreams**—"hallucinations of the sleeping mind" (Loftus & Ketcham, 1994, p. 67)—are vivid, emotional, and bizarre—so vivid that we may confuse them with reality. Awakening from a nightmare, a 4-year-old may be sure there is a bear in the house.

We spend six years of our life in dreams, many of which are anything but sweet. For both women and men, 8 in 10 dreams are marked by at least one negative event or emotion (Domhoff, 2007). People commonly dream of repeatedly failing in an attempt to do something; of being attacked, pursued, or rejected; or of experiencing misfortune (Hall et al., 1982). Dreams with sexual imagery occur less often than you might think. In one study, only 1 dream in 10 among young men and 1 in 30 among young women had sexual overtones (Domhoff, 1996). More commonly, the story line of our dreams incorporates traces of previous days' nonsexual experiences and preoccupations (De Koninck, 2000):

"I do not believe that I am now dreaming, but I cannot prove that I am not."

—Philosopher Bertrand Russell (1872–1970)

Would you suppose that people dream if blind from birth? Studies of blind people in France, Hungary, Egypt, and the United States all found them dreaming of using their nonvisual senses—hearing, touching, smelling, tasting (Buquet, 1988; Taha, 1972; Vekassy, 1977).

- After suffering a trauma, people commonly report nightmares (Levin & Nielsen, 2007). One sample of Americans who were recording their dreams during September 2001 reported an increase in threatening dreams following the 9/11 attack (Propper et al., 2007).
- After playing the computer game "Tetris" for seven hours and then being awakened repeatedly during their first hour of sleep, 3 in 4 people reported experiencing images of the game's falling blocks (Stickgold et al., 2000).
- People in hunter-gatherer societies often dream of animals; urban Japanese rarely do (Mestel, 1997).
- Compared with nonmusicians, musicians report twice as many dreams of music (Uga et al., 2006).

Sensory stimuli in our sleeping environment may also intrude. A particular odor or the telephone's ringing may be instantly and ingeniously woven into the dream story. In a classic experiment, William Dement and Edward Wolpert (1958) lightly sprayed cold water on dreamers' faces. Compared with sleepers who did not get the cold-water treatment, these people were more likely to dream about a waterfall, a leaky roof, or even about being sprayed by someone. Even while in REM sleep, focused on internal stimuli, we maintain some awareness of changes in our external environment.

> "For what one has dwelt on by day, these things are seen in visions of the night."
>
> —Menander of Athens (342–292 B.C.E.), *Fragments*

A popular sleep myth: If you dream you are falling and hit the ground (or if you dream of dying), you die. (Unfortunately, those who could confirm these ideas are not around to do so. Some people, however, have had such dreams and are alive to report them.)

MAXINE

So, could we learn a foreign language by hearing it played while we sleep? If only it were so easy. While sleeping we can learn to associate a sound with a mild electric shock (and to react to the sound accordingly). But we do not remember recorded information played while we are soundly asleep (Eich, 1990; Wyatt & Bootzin, 1994). In fact, anything that happens during the 5 minutes just before we fall asleep is typically lost from memory (Roth et al., 1988). This explains why sleep apnea patients, who repeatedly awaken with a gasp and then immediately fall back to sleep, do not recall the episodes. It also explains why dreams that momentarily awaken us are mostly forgotten by morning. To remember a dream, get up and stay awake for a few minutes.

> "Follow your dreams, except for that one where you're naked at work."
>
> —Attributed to Henny Youngman

Why We Dream

9: Why do we dream?

Dream theorists have proposed several explanations of why we dream, including these:

To satisfy our own wishes. In 1900, in his landmark book *The Interpretation of Dreams*, Freud offered what he thought was "the most valuable of all the discoveries it has been my good fortune to make": Dreams provide a psychic safety valve that discharges otherwise unacceptable feelings. According to Freud, a dream's **manifest content** (the remembered story line) is a censored, symbolic version of its **latent content,** which consists of unconscious drives and wishes that would be

dream a sequence of images, emotions, and thoughts passing through a sleeping person's mind. Dreams are notable for their hallucinatory imagery, discontinuities, and incongruities, and for the dreamer's delusional acceptance of the content and later difficulties remembering it.

manifest content according to Freud, the remembered story line of a dream (as distinct from its latent, or hidden, content).

latent content according to Freud, the underlying meaning of a dream (as distinct from its manifest content).

"When people interpret [a dream] as if it were meaningful and then sell those interpretations, it's quackery."

—Sleep researcher J. Allan Hobson (1995)

Rapid eye movements also stir the liquid behind the cornea; this delivers fresh oxygen to corneal cells, preventing their suffocation.

threatening if expressed directly. Although most dreams have no overt sexual imagery, Freud nevertheless believed that most adult dreams can be "traced back by analysis to erotic wishes." Thus, a cylindrical object such as a gun might be a disguised representation of a penis.

Freud considered dreams the key to understanding our inner conflicts. However, his critics say it is time to wake up from Freud's dream theory, which is a scientific nightmare. Based on the accumulated science, "there is no reason to believe any of Freud's specific claims about dreams and their purposes," notes dream researcher William Domhoff (2003). Some contend that even if dreams are symbolic, they could be interpreted any way one wished. Others maintain that dreams hide nothing. A dream about a gun is a dream about a gun. Legend has it that even Freud, who loved to smoke cigars, acknowledged that "sometimes, a cigar is just a cigar." Freud's wish-fulfillment theory of dreams has in large part given way to other theories.

To *file away* memories. Researchers who see dreams as *information processing* believe that dreams may help sift, sort, and fix the day's experiences in our memory. As we noted earlier, people tested the next day generally improve on a learned task after a night of memory consolidation. Even after two nights of recovery sleep, those who have been deprived of both slow-wave and REM sleep don't do as well as those who sleep undisturbed on their new learning (Stickgold et al., 2000, 2001). People who hear unusual phrases or learn to find hidden visual images before bedtime remember less the next morning if awakened every time they begin REM sleep than they do if awakened during other sleep stages (Empson & Clarke, 1970; Karni & Sagi, 1994).

Brain scans confirm the link between REM sleep and memory. The brain regions that buzz as rats learn to navigate a maze, or as people learn to perform a visual-discrimination task, buzz again during later REM sleep (Louie & Wilson, 2001; Maquet, 2001). So precise are these activity patterns that scientists can tell where in the maze the rat would be if awake. Others, unpersuaded by such studies, note that memory consolidation may occur during non-REM sleep (Siegel, 2001; Vertes & Siegel, 2005). This much seems true: A night of solid sleep (and dreaming) has an important place in our lives. To sleep, perchance to remember. This is important news for students, many of whom, observed researcher Robert Stickgold (2000), suffer from a kind of sleep bulimia—binge-sleeping on the weekend. "If you don't get good sleep and enough sleep after you learn new stuff, you won't integrate it effectively into your memories," he warned. That helps explain why secondary students with high grades have averaged 25 minutes more sleep a night and have gone to bed 40 minutes earlier than their lower-achieving classmates (Wolfson & Carskadon, 1998).

To *develop and preserve neural pathways.* Some researchers speculate that dreams may also serve a *physiological* function. Perhaps the brain activity associated with REM sleep provides the sleeping brain with periodic stimulation. This theory makes developmental sense. As you will see in Chapter 4, stimulating experiences develop and preserve the brain's neural pathways. Infants, whose neural networks are fast developing, spend much of their abundant sleep time in REM sleep.

To *make sense of neural static.* Other theories propose that dreams erupt from neural activity spreading upward from the brainstem (Antrobus, 1991; Hobson, 2003, 2004). According to one version—the *activation-synthesis* theory—this neural activity is random, and dreams are the brain's attempt to make sense of it. Much as a neurosurgeon can produce hallucinations by stimulating different parts of a patient's cortex, so can stimulation originating within the brain. These internal stimuli activate brain areas that process visual images, but not the visual cortex area, which receives raw input from the eyes.

PET scans of sleeping people also reveal increased activity during REM sleep in the amygdala, in the emotion-related limbic system. In contrast, frontal lobe regions responsible for inhibition and logical thinking seem to idle, which may explain why our dreams are less inhibited than we are when awake (Maquet et al., 1996). Add the limbic system's emotional tone to the brain's visual bursts and—Voila!—we

TABLE 3.1 Dream Theories

Theory	Explanation	Critical Considerations
Freud's wish-fulfillment	Dreams provide a "psychic safety valve"—expressing otherwise unacceptable feelings; contain manifest (remembered) content and a deeper layer of latent content—a hidden meaning.	Lacks any scientific support; dreams may be interpreted in many different ways.
Information-processing	Dreams help us sort out the day's events and consolidate our memories.	But why do we sometimes dream about things we have not experienced?
Physiological function	Regular brain stimulation from REM sleep may help develop and preserve neural pathways.	This may be true, but it does not explain why we experience *meaningful* dreams.
Activation-synthesis	REM sleep triggers neural activity that evokes random visual memories, which our sleeping brain weaves into stories.	The individual's brain is weaving the stories, which still tells us something about the dreamer.
Cognitive development	Dream content reflects dreamers' cognitive development—their knowledge and understanding.	Does not address the neuroscience of dreams.

dream. Damage either the limbic system or the visual centers active during dreaming, and dreaming itself may be impaired (Domhoff, 2003).

To reflect cognitive development. Some dream researchers dispute both the Freudian and activation-synthesis theories, preferring instead to see dreams as part of brain maturation and cognitive development (Domhoff, 2003; Foulkes, 1999). For example, prior to age 9, children's dreams seem more like a slide show and less like an active story in which the dreamer is an actor. Dreams overlap with waking cognition and feature coherent speech. They draw on our concepts and knowledge.

TABLE 3.1 compares major dream theories. Although sleep researchers debate dreams' function—and some are skeptical that dreams serve any function—there is one thing they agree on: We need REM sleep. Deprived of it by repeatedly being awakened, people return more and more quickly to the REM stage after falling back to sleep. When finally allowed to sleep undisturbed, they literally sleep like babies—with increased REM sleep, a phenomenon called **REM rebound.** Withdrawing REM-suppressing sleeping medications also increases REM sleep, but with accompanying nightmares.

Most other mammals also experience REM rebound, suggesting that the causes and functions of REM sleep are deeply biological. That REM sleep occurs in mammals—and not in animals such as fish, whose behavior is less influenced by learning—also fits the information-processing theory of dreams.

So does this mean that because dreams serve physiological functions and extend normal cognition, they are psychologically meaningless? Not necessarily. Every psychologically meaningful experience involves an active brain. We are once again reminded of a basic principle: *Biological and psychological explanations of behavior are partners, not competitors.* Dreams may be akin to abstract art—open to more than one meaningful interpretation.

Dreams are a fascinating altered state of consciousness. But other influences—hypnosis, drugs, and even near-death experiences—can also alter conscious awareness.

Question: *Does eating spicy foods cause one to dream more?*
Answer: *Any food that causes you to awaken more increases your chance of recalling a dream (Moorcroft, 2003).*

REM rebound the tendency for REM sleep to increase following REM sleep deprivation (created by repeated awakenings during REM sleep).

REHEARSE IT!

9. In interpreting dreams, Freud was most interested in their
   a. information-processing function.
   b. physiological function.
   c. manifest content, or story line.
   d. latent content, or hidden meaning.

10. The activation-synthesis theory suggests that dreams

   a. are the brain's attempt to make sense of random neural activity.
   b. provide a rest period for overworked brains.
   c. serve as a safety valve for unfulfilled desires.
   d. reflect the dreamer's level of cognitive development.

11. The tendency for REM sleep to increase following REM sleep deprivation is referred to as
   a. paradoxical sleep.
   b. deep sleep.
   c. REM rebound.
   d. slow-wave sleep.

Answers: 9. d, 10. a, 11. c.

Hypnosis

10: **What is hypnosis, and what powers does a hypnotist have over a hypnotized subject?**

Imagine you are about to be hypnotized. The hypnotist invites you to sit back, fix your gaze on a spot high on the wall, and relax. In a quiet voice the hypnotist suggests, "Your eyes are growing tired. . . . Your eyelids are becoming heavy . . . now heavier and heavier. . . . They are beginning to close. . . . You are becoming more deeply relaxed. . . . Your breathing is now deep and regular. . . . Your muscles are becoming more and more relaxed. Your whole body is beginning to feel like lead."

After a few minutes of this *hypnotic induction,* you may experience **hypnosis.** When the hypnotist suggests, "Your eyelids are shutting so tight that you cannot open them even if you try," it may indeed seem beyond your control to open your eyelids. Told to forget the number 6, you may be puzzled when you count 11 fingers on your hands. Invited to smell a sensuous perfume that is actually ammonia, you may linger delightedly over its pungent odor. Told that you cannot see a certain object, such as a chair, you may indeed report that it is not there, although you manage to avoid the chair when walking around (illustrating once again that two-track mind of yours).

But is hypnosis really an *altered* state of consciousness? Let's start with some agreed-upon facts and falsehoods.

Facts and Falsehoods

Those who study hypnosis have agreed that its power resides not in the hypnotist but in the subject's openness to suggestion (Bowers, 1984). Hypnotists have no magical mind-control power; they merely engage people's ability to focus on certain images or behaviors. But how open to suggestions are we?

Can Anyone Experience Hypnosis?

To some extent, we are all open to suggestion. When people stand upright with their eyes closed and are told that they are swaying back and forth, most will indeed sway a little. In fact, *postural sway* is one of the items assessed on the Stanford Hypnotic Susceptibility Scale. People who respond to such suggestions without hypnosis are the same people who respond with hypnosis (Kirsch & Braffman, 2001).

After giving a brief hypnotic induction, a hypnotist suggests a series of experiences ranging from easy (your outstretched arms will move together) to difficult (with eyes open, you will see a nonexistent person). Highly hypnotizable people—say, the 20 percent who can carry out a suggestion not to smell or react to a bottle of ammonia held under their nose—are those who easily become deeply absorbed in imaginative activities (Barnier & McConkey, 2004; Silva & Kirsch, 1992). Typically, they have rich fantasy lives and become totally engaged in the imaginary events of a novel or movie. (Perhaps you can recall being riveted by a movie into a trancelike state, oblivious to the people or noise surrounding you.) Many researchers refer to hypnotic "susceptibility" as hypnotic *ability*—the ability to focus attention totally on a task, to become imaginatively absorbed in it, to entertain fanciful possibilities.

Can Hypnosis Enhance Recall of Forgotten Events?

Can hypnotic procedures enable people to recall kindergarten classmates? To retrieve forgotten or suppressed details of a crime? Should testimony obtained under hypnosis be admissible in court?

Most people believe (wrongly, as Chapter 8 will explain) that our experiences are all "in there," recorded in our brain and available for recall if only we can break through our own defenses (Loftus, 1980). In one community survey, 3 in 4 people agreed with the inaccurate statement that hypnosis enables people to "recover accurate memories as far back as birth" (Johnson & Hauck, 1999). But 60 years of research disputes such claims. "Hypnotically refreshed" memories combine fact with fiction. Without either person being aware of what is going on, a hypnotist's hints— "Did you hear loud noises?"—can plant ideas that become the subject's pseudomemory. Thus, American, Australian, and British courts generally ban testimony from witnesses who have been hypnotized (Druckman & Bjork, 1994; Gibson, 1995; McConkey, 1995).

Other striking examples of memories created under hypnosis come from the thousands of people who since 1980 have reported being abducted by UFOs. Most such reports have come from people who are predisposed to believe in aliens, are highly hypnotizable, and have undergone hypnosis (Newman & Baumeister, 1996; Nickell, 1996).

Can Hypnosis Force People to Act Against Their Will?

Researchers have induced hypnotized people to perform an apparently dangerous act: plunging one hand briefly into fuming "acid," then throwing the "acid" in a researcher's face (Orne & Evans, 1965). Interviewed a day later, these people exhibited no memory of their acts and emphatically denied they would ever follow such orders.

Had hypnosis given the hypnotist a special power to control others against their will? To find out, researchers Martin Orne and Frederich Evans unleashed that enemy of so many illusory beliefs—the control group. Orne asked other individuals to *pretend* they were hypnotized. Laboratory assistants, unaware that those in the experiment's control group had not been hypnotized, treated both groups the same. The result? All the *un*hypnotized participants (perhaps believing that the laboratory context assured safety) performed the same acts as those who were hypnotized.

Such studies illustrate a principle that Chapter 15 emphasizes: *An authoritative person in a legitimate context can induce people—hypnotized or not—to perform some unlikely acts.* Hypnosis researcher Nicholas Spanos (1982) put it directly: "The overt behaviors of hypnotic subjects are well within normal limits."

Can Hypnosis Be Therapeutic?

Hypnotherapists try to help patients harness their own healing powers (Baker, 1987). **Posthypnotic suggestions** have helped alleviate headaches, asthma, and stress-related skin disorders. One woman, who for more than 20 years suffered from open sores all over her body, was asked to imagine herself swimming in shimmering, sun-lit liquids that would cleanse her skin, and to experience her skin as smooth and unblemished. Within three months her sores had disappeared (Bowers, 1984).

In one statistical digest of 18 studies, the average client whose therapy was supplemented with hypnosis showed greater improvement than 70 percent of other therapy patients (Kirsch et al., 1995, 1996). Hypnosis seemed especially helpful for treatment of obesity. However, drug, alcohol, and smoking addictions have not responded well to hypnosis (Nash, 2001). In controlled studies, hypnosis speeds the disappearance of warts, but so do the same positive suggestions given without hypnosis (Spanos, 1991, 1996).

Can Hypnosis Alleviate Pain?

Yes, hypnosis *can* relieve pain (Druckman & Bjork, 1994; Patterson, 2004). When unhypnotized people put their arm in an ice bath, they feel intense pain within 25 seconds. When hypnotized people do the same after being given suggestions to feel no pain, they indeed report feeling little pain. As some dentists know, even light hypnosis can reduce fear, thus reducing hypersensitivity to pain.

Nearly 10 percent of us can become so deeply hypnotized that we can even undergo major surgery without anesthesia. Half of us can gain at least some pain relief

---

"Hypnosis is not a psychological truth serum and to regard it as such has been a source of considerable mischief."

—Researcher Kenneth Bowers (1987)

See Chapter 8 for a more detailed discussion of how people may construct false memories.

"It wasn't what I expected. But facts are facts, and if one is proved to be wrong, one must just be humble about it and start again."

—Agatha Christie's Miss Marple

hypnosis a social interaction in which one person (the hypnotist) suggests to another (the subject) that certain perceptions, feelings, thoughts, or behaviors will spontaneously occur.

posthypnotic suggestion a suggestion, made during a hypnosis session, to be carried out after the subject is no longer hypnotized; used by some clinicians to help control undesired symptoms and behaviors.

from hypnosis. In surgical experiments, hypnotized patients have required less medication, recovered sooner, and left the hospital earlier than unhypnotized people in control groups, thanks to the inhibition of pain-related brain activity (Askay & Patterson, 2007; Spiegel, 2007). The surgical use of hypnosis has flourished in Europe, where one Belgian medical team has performed more than 5000 surgeries with a combination of hypnosis, local anesthesia, and a mild sedative (Song, 2006).

Explaining the Hypnotized State

11: Is hypnosis an extension of normal consciousness or an altered state?

We have seen that hypnosis involves heightened suggestibility. We have also seen that hypnotic procedures do not endow the hypnotist with special powers. But they can sometimes help people overcome stress-related ailments and cope with pain. So, just what *is* hypnosis?

Hypnosis as a Social Phenomenon

Some researchers believe that hypnotic phenomena reflect the workings of normal consciousness and the power of social influence (Lynn et al., 1990; Spanos & Coe, 1992). They point out how powerfully our interpretations and attentional spotlight influence our ordinary perceptions.

Does this mean that people are consciously faking hypnosis? No—like actors caught up in their roles, subjects begin to feel and behave in ways appropriate for "good hypnotic subjects." The more they like and trust the hypnotist, the more they allow that person to direct their attention and fantasies (Gfeller et al., 1987). "The hypnotist's ideas become the subject's thoughts," explained Theodore Barber (2000), "and the subject's thoughts produce the hypnotic experiences and behaviors." If told to scratch their ear later when they hear the word *psychology,* subjects will likely do so only if they think the experiment is still under way (and scratching is therefore expected). If an experimenter eliminates their motivation for acting hypnotized—by stating that hypnosis reveals their "gullibility"—subjects become unresponsive.

Based on such findings, advocates of the *social influence theory* contend that hypnotic phenomena—like the behaviors associated with other supposed altered states, such as dissociative identity disorder (discussed in Chapter 13) and spirit or demon possession—are an extension of everyday social behavior, not something unique to hypnosis (Spanos, 1994, 1996).

Hypnosis as Divided Consciousness

Most hypnosis researchers grant that normal social and cognitive processes play a part in hypnosis, but they nevertheless believe hypnosis is more than inducing someone to play the role of "good subject." For one thing, hypnotized subjects will sometimes carry out suggested behaviors on cue, even when they believe no one is watching (Perugini et al., 1998). Moreover, distinctive brain activity accompanies hypnosis. When deeply hypnotized people in one experiment were asked to imagine a color, areas of their brain lit up as if they were really seeing the color. Mere imagination had become—to the hypnotized person's brain—a compelling hallucination (Kosslyn et al., 2000).

These results would not have surprised famed researcher Ernest Hilgard (1986, 1992), who believed hypnosis involves not only social influence but also a special dual-processing state of **dissociation**—a split between different levels of consciousness. Hilgard viewed hypnotic dissociation as a vivid form of everyday mind splits—similar to doodling while listening to a lecture or typing the end of a sentence while starting a conversation. Hilgard felt that when, for example, hypnotized people lower

dissociation a split in consciousness, which allows some thoughts and behaviors to occur simultaneously with others.

Attention is diverted from a painful ice bath. How?

Divided-consciousness theory:

Hypnosis has caused a split in awareness.

Social influence theory:

The subject is so caught up in the hypnotized role that she ignores the cold.

Courtesy of News and Publications Service, Stanford University

FIGURE 3.12 Dissociation or role-playing? This hypnotized woman tested by Ernest Hilgard exhibited no pain when her arm was placed in an ice bath. But asked to press a key if some part of her felt the pain, she did so. To Hilgard, this was evidence of dissociation, or divided consciousness. Proponents of social influence theory, however, maintain that people responding this way are caught up in playing the role of "good subject."

their arm into an ice bath, as in **FIGURE 3.12**, that hypnosis dissociates the sensation of the pain stimulus (of which the subjects are still aware) from the emotional suffering that defines their experience of pain. The ice water therefore feels cold—very cold—but not painful.

Hypnotic pain relief may also result from another form of dual processing we've discussed—*selective attention*—as when an injured athlete, caught up in the competition, feels little or no pain until the game ends. Support for this view comes from PET scans showing that hypnosis reduces brain activity in a region that processes painful stimuli, but not in the sensory cortex, which receives the raw sensory input (Rainville et al., 1997). Hypnosis does not block sensory input, but it may block our *attention* to those stimuli.

Although the divided-consciousness theory of hypnosis is controversial, this much seems clear: There is, without doubt, much more to thinking and acting than we are conscious of. Our information processing, which starts with selective attention, is divided into simultaneous conscious and nonconscious realms. In hypnosis as in life, *much of our behavior occurs on autopilot.* We have two-track minds.

Yet, there is also little doubt that social influences do play an important role in hypnosis. So, might the two views—social influence and divided consciousness—be bridged? Researchers John Kihlstrom and Kevin McConkey (1990) have argued that there is no contradiction between the two approaches, which are converging toward a *unified account of hypnosis:* Thus, hypnosis can be an extension *both* of normal principles of social influence and of everyday dissociations between our conscious awareness and our automatic behaviors. Hypnosis researchers are moving beyond the "hypnosis is social influence" *versus* "hypnosis is divided consciousness" debate (Killeen & Nash, 2003; Woody & McConkey, 2003). They are instead exploring how brain activity, attention, and social influences interact to affect hypnotic phenomena.

"The total possible consciousness may be split into parts which co-exist but mutually ignore each other."

—William James,
Principles of Psychology, 1890

REHEARSE IT!

12. People who are hypnotizable and will carry out a hypnotic suggestion typically
a. have rich fantasy lives.
b. have low self-esteem.
c. are subject to hallucinations.
d. are faking their actions.

13. Most experts agree that hypnosis can be effectively used to
a. elicit testimony about a "forgotten" event.
b. re-create childhood experiences.
c. relieve pain.
d. block sensory input.

14. Hilgard believed that hypnosis involves dissociation, or
a. an extension of social pressure.
b. heightened suggestibility.
c. a state of divided consciousness.
d. conscious enactment of a hypnotic role.

Answers: 12. a, 13. c, 14. c.

"Just tell me where you kids got the idea to take so many drugs."

Drugs and Consciousness

There is controversy about whether hypnosis uniquely alters consciousness, but there is little dispute that some drugs do. **Psychoactive drugs** are chemicals that change perceptions and moods through their actions at the neural synapses (see Chapter 2). Let's imagine a day in the life of a legal-drug user. It begins with a wake-up latte. By midday, several cigarettes have calmed frazzled nerves before an appointment at the plastic surgeon's office for wrinkle-smoothing Botox injections. A diet pill before dinner helps stem the appetite, and its stimulating effects can later be partially offset with a glass of wine and two Tylenol PMs. And if performance needs enhancing, there are beta blockers for onstage performers, Viagra for middle-aged men, hormone-delivering "libido patches" for middle-aged women, and Adderall for students hoping to focus their concentration. Before drifting off into REM-depressed sleep, our hypothetical drug user is dismayed by news reports of pill-sharing, pill-popping college students and of celebrity deaths attributed to accidental overdoses of lethal drug combinations.

Dependence and Addiction

12: What are tolerance, dependence, and addiction, and what are some common misconceptions about addiction?

Why might a person who rarely drinks alcohol get tipsy on one can of beer, but an experienced drinker show few effects until the second six-pack? Continued use of alcohol and other psychoactive drugs produces **tolerance.** As the user's brain adapts its chemistry to offset the drug effect (a process called *neuroadaptation*), the user requires larger and larger doses to experience the same effect (**FIGURE 3.13**). Despite the connotations of alcohol "tolerance," the person's brain, heart, and liver suffer damage from the chronic, excessive amounts of alcohol being "tolerated."

Users who stop taking psychoactive drugs may experience the undesirable side effects of **withdrawal.** As the body responds to the drug's absence, the user may feel physical pain and intense cravings, indicating **physical dependence.** People can also develop **psychological dependence,** particularly for stress-relieving drugs. Such drugs, although not physically addictive, can become an important part of the user's life, often as a way of relieving negative emotions. With either physical or psychological dependence, the user's primary focus may be obtaining and using the drug.

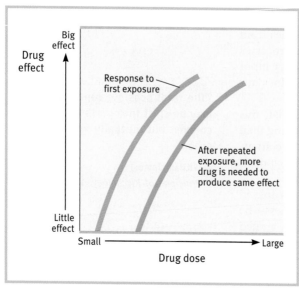

FIGURE 3.13 Drug tolerance With repeated exposure to a psychoactive drug, the drug's effect lessens. Thus, it takes bigger doses to get the desired effect.

The odds of getting hooked after trying various drugs:

Marijuana: 9 percent
Alcohol: 15 percent
Heroin: 23 percent
Tobacco: 32 percent

Source: *National Academy of Science, Institute of Medicine (Brody, 2003).*

Misconceptions About Addiction

An **addiction** is a compulsive craving for a substance despite adverse consequences and often with physical symptoms such as aches, nausea, and distress following sudden withdrawal. Worldwide, reports the World Health Organization (2008), 90 million people suffer from such problems related to alcohol and other drugs.

In recent pop psychology, the supposedly irresistible seduction of addiction has been extended to cover many behaviors formerly considered bad habits or even sins. Has the concept been stretched too far? Are addictions as irresistible as commonly believed? Let's consider three big questions.

1. Do addictive drugs quickly corrupt? For example, morphine taken to control pain is powerfully addictive. Does it often lead to heroin abuse? People given morphine to control pain rarely develop the cravings of the addict who uses morphine as a mood-altering drug (Melzack, 1990). But some people—perhaps 10 percent—do indeed have a hard time using a psychoactive drug in moderation or stopping altogether. Even so, controlled, occasional users of drugs such as alcohol and marijuana far outnumber those addicted to these substances (Gazzaniga, 1988; Siegel, 1990). "Even for a very addictive drug like cocaine, only 15 to 16 percent of people become addicted within 10 years of first use," report Terry Robinson and Kent Berridge (2003). Much the same is true for rats, only some of which become compulsively addicted to cocaine (Deroche-Garmonet et al., 2004).

2. Can addictions be overcome voluntarily, without therapy? Helpful as therapy or group support may be, people often recover on their own. True, addictions can be powerful, and some addicts do benefit from treatment programs. Alcoholics Anonymous, for example, has supported many people in overcoming their alcohol dependence. But the recovery rates of treated and untreated groups differ less than one might suppose.

Moreover, viewing addiction as a disease, as diabetes is a disease, can undermine self-confidence and the will to change cravings that, without treatment, "one cannot fight." And that, critics say, would be unfortunate, for many people do voluntarily stop using addictive drugs, without any treatment. Most of America's 41 million ex-smokers kicked the habit on their own, usually after prior failed efforts or treatments.

3. Can we extend the concept of addiction to cover not just drug dependencies, but a whole spectrum of repetitive, pleasure-seeking behaviors? We can, and we have, but should we? The addiction-as-disease-needing-treatment idea has been suggested for a host of driven behaviors, including too much eating, shopping, exercise, sex, gambling, and work. Initially, we may use the term metaphorically ("I'm a science fiction addict"), but if we begin taking the metaphor as reality, addiction can become an all-purpose excuse. Those who embezzle to feed their "gambling addiction," surf the Web half the night to satisfy their "Internet addiction," or abuse or betray to indulge their "sex addiction" can then explain away their behavior as an illness.

Sometimes, though, behaviors such as gambling, playing video games, or surfing the Internet do become compulsive and dysfunctional, much like abusive drug taking (Griffiths, 2001; Hoeft et al., 2008). Some Internet users, for example, do display an apparent inability to resist logging on, and staying on, even when this excessive use impairs their work and relationships (Ko et al., 2005). So, there may be justification for stretching the addiction concept to cover certain social behaviors. Debates over the addiction-as-disease model continue.

Psychoactive Drugs

The three major categories of psychoactive drugs—*depressants*, *stimulants*, and *hallucinogens*—all do their work at the brain's synapses. They stimulate, inhibit, or mimic the activity of the brain's own chemical messengers, the neurotransmitters. Our culturally influenced expectations also play a role in the way drugs affect us (Ward, 1994). If one culture assumes that a particular drug produces euphoria (or aggression or sexual arousal) and another does not, each culture may find its expectations fulfilled.

Depressants

13: What are depressants, and what are their effects?

Depressants are drugs such as alcohol, barbiturates (tranquilizers), and opiates that calm neural activity and slow body functions.

ALCOHOL True or false? In large amounts, alcohol is a depressant; in small amounts, it is a stimulant. *False.* Low doses of alcohol may, indeed, enliven a drinker, but they do so by slowing brain activity that controls judgment and inhibitions. Alcohol

---

psychoactive drug a chemical substance that alters perceptions and moods.

tolerance the diminishing effect with regular use of the same dose of a drug, requiring the user to take larger and larger doses before experiencing the drug's effect.

withdrawal the discomfort and distress that follow discontinuing the use of an addictive drug.

physical dependence a physiological need for a drug, marked by unpleasant withdrawal symptoms when the drug is discontinued.

psychological dependence a psychological need to use a drug, such as to relieve negative emotions.

addiction compulsive drug craving and use, despite adverse consequences.

depressants drugs (such as alcohol, barbiturates, and opiates) that reduce neural activity and slow body functions.

"About 70 percent of Americans have tried illicit drugs, but . . . only a few percent have done so in the last month. . . . Past age 35, the casual use of illegal drugs virtually ceases." Having sampled the pleasures and their aftereffects, "most people eventually walk away."

—Neuropsychologist Michael Gazzaniga (1997)

"That is not one of the seven habits of highly effective people."

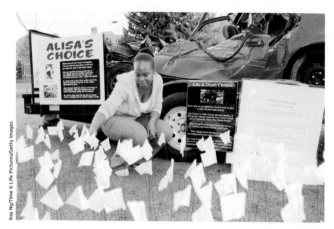

Dangerous disinhibition Alcohol consumption leads to feelings of invincibility, which become especially dangerous behind the wheel of a car, such as this one totaled by a teenage drunk driver. This Colorado University Alcohol Awareness Week exhibit prompted many students to post their own anti-drinking pledges (white flags).

Scan of woman with alcohol dependence | Scan of woman without alcohol dependence

FIGURE 3.14 Alcohol dependence shrinks the brain MRI scans show brain shrinkage in women with alcohol dependence (left) compared with women in a control group (right).

A University of Illinois campus survey showed that before sexual assaults, 80 percent of the male assailants and 70 percent of the female victims had been drinking (Camper, 1990). Another survey of 89,874 American collegians found alcohol or drugs involved in 79 percent of unwanted sexual intercourse experiences (Presley et al., 1997).

lowers our inhibitions, slows neural processing, disrupts memory formation, and reduces self-awareness.

DISINHIBITION Alcohol is an equal-opportunity drug: It increases harmful tendencies—as when angered people become aggressive after drinking. And it increases helpful tendencies—as when tipsy restaurant patrons leave extravagant tips (M. Lynn, 1988). *The urges you would feel if sober are the ones you will more likely act upon when intoxicated.*

SLOWED NEURAL PROCESSING Low doses of alcohol relax the drinker by slowing sympathetic nervous system activity. In larger doses, alcohol can become a staggering problem: Reactions slow, speech slurs, skilled performance deteriorates. Paired with sleep deprivation, alcohol is a potent sedative. (Although either sleep deprivation or drinking can put a driver at risk, their combination is deadlier yet.) These physical effects, combined with lowered inhibitions, contribute to alcohol's worst consequences—several hundred thousand lives claimed worldwide each year in alcohol-related accidents and violent crime. Car accidents occur despite most drinkers' belief (when sober) that driving under the influence of alcohol is wrong and despite their insisting that they would not do so. Yet, as blood-alcohol levels rise and moral judgments falter, people's qualms about drinking and driving lessen. Virtually all will drive home from a bar, even if given a breathalyzer test and told they are intoxicated (Denton & Krebs, 1990; MacDonald et al., 1995).

MEMORY DISRUPTION Alcohol disrupts the processing of recent experiences into long-term memories. Thus, heavy drinkers may not recall people they met the night before or what they said or did while intoxicated. These blackouts result partly from the way alcohol suppresses REM sleep, which helps fix the day's experiences into permanent memories.

The effects of heavy drinking on the brain and cognition can be long-term. In rats, at a developmental period corresponding to human adolescence, binge-drinking diminishes the genesis of nerve cells, impairs the growth of synaptic connections, and contributes to nerve cell death (Crews et al., 2006, 2007). MRI scans show another way prolonged and excessive drinking can affect cognition (**FIGURE 3.14**). It can shrink the brain, especially in women, who have less of a stomach enzyme that digests alcohol (Wuethrich, 2001). Girls and young women can also become addicted to alcohol more quickly than boys and young men do, and they are at risk for lung, brain, and liver damage at lower consumption levels (CASA, 2003).

REDUCED SELF-AWARENESS AND SELF-CONTROL Alcohol also reduces self-awareness (Hull et al., 1986). This may help explain why people who want to suppress their awareness of failures or shortcomings are more likely to drink than are those who feel good about themselves. Losing a business deal, a game, or a romantic partner sometimes elicits a drinking binge. By focusing attention on the immediate situation and away from any future consequences, alcohol also lessens impulse control (Steele & Josephs, 1990). In surveys of rapists, more than half acknowledge drinking before committing their offense (Seto & Barbaree, 1995).

EXPECTANCY EFFECTS As with other psychoactive drugs, alcohol's behavioral effects stem not only from its alteration of brain chemistry but also from the user's expectations. When people believe that alcohol affects social behavior in certain ways, and believe, rightly or wrongly, that they have been drinking alcohol, they will behave accordingly (Leigh, 1989). In a now-classic experiment, researchers (Abrams & Wilson, 1983) gave Rutgers University men who volunteered for a study on "alcohol and sexual stimulation" either an alcoholic or a nonalcoholic drink. (Both had strong tastes that masked any alcohol.) In each group, half the participants thought they were drinking alcohol and half thought they were not. After watching an erotic movie clip, the men who *thought* they had consumed alcohol were more likely to report having strong sexual fantasies and feeling guilt-free. Being able to *attribute* their sexual responses to alcohol released their inhibitions— whether they actually had drunk alcohol or not. Alcohol's effect lies partly in that powerful sex organ, the mind.

ALCOHOL + SEX = THE PERFECT STORM Alcohol's effects on self-control and social expectations often converge in sexual situations. More than 600 studies have explored the link between drinking and risky sex, with "the overwhelming majority" finding the two correlated (Cooper, 2006).

BARBITURATES The **barbiturate** drugs, or *tranquilizers,* mimic the effects of alcohol. Because they depress nervous system activity, barbiturates such as Nembutal, Seconal, and Amytal are sometimes prescribed to induce sleep or reduce anxiety. In larger doses, they can lead to impaired memory and judgment or even death. If combined with alcohol—as sometimes happens when people take a sleeping pill after an evening of heavy drinking—the total depressive effect on body functions can be lethal.

OPIATES The **opiates**—opium and its derivatives, morphine and heroin—also depress neural functioning. Pupils constrict, breathing slows, and lethargy sets in as blissful pleasure replaces pain and anxiety. But for this short-term pleasure the user may pay a long-term price: a gnawing craving for another fix, a need for progressively larger doses, and the extreme discomfort of withdrawal. When repeatedly flooded with an artificial opiate, the brain eventually stops producing its own opiates, the *endorphins.* If the artificial opiate is then withdrawn, the brain lacks the normal level of these painkilling neurotransmitters. Those who cannot or choose not to tolerate this state may pay an ultimate price—death by overdose.

Stimulants

14: What are stimulants, and what are their effects?

Stimulants such as caffeine and nicotine temporarily excite neural activity and arouse body functions. People use these substances to stay awake, lose weight, or boost mood or athletic performance. This category of drugs also includes **amphetamines,** and the even more powerful cocaine, Ecstasy, and *methamphetamine* ("speed"). All strong stimulants increase heart and breathing rates and cause pupils to dilate, appetite to diminish (because blood sugar increases), and energy and self-confidence to rise. And, as with other drugs, the benefits of stimulants come with a price. These substances can be addictive and may induce an aftermath crash into fatigue, headaches, irritability, and depression (Silverman et al., 1992).

METHAMPHETAMINE **Methamphetamine** is chemically related to its parent drug, *amphetamine* (NIDA, 2002, 2005) but has even greater effects. Methamphetamine triggers the release of the neurotransmitter dopamine, which stimulates brain cells that enhance energy and mood. The result can include eight hours or so of heightened energy and euphoria.

Over time, methamphetamine may reduce baseline dopamine levels, leaving the user with permanently depressed functioning. Methamphetamine's possible aftereffects include irritability, insomnia, hypertension, seizures, social isolation, depression, and occasional violent outbursts

barbiturates drugs that depress the activity of the central nervous system, reducing anxiety but impairing memory and judgment.

opiates opium and its derivatives, such as morphine and heroin; they depress neural activity, temporarily lessening pain and anxiety.

stimulants drugs (such as caffeine, nicotine, amphetamines, and the even more powerful cocaine, Ecstasy, and methamphetamine) that excite neural activity and speed up body functions.

amphetamines drugs that stimulate neural activity, causing speeded-up body functions and associated energy and mood changes.

methamphetamine a powerfully addictive drug that stimulates the central nervous system, with speeded-up body functions and associated energy and mood changes; over time, appears to reduce baseline dopamine levels.

Dramatic drug-induced decline This woman's methamphetamine addiction led to obvious physical changes. Her decline is evident in these two photos, taken at age 36 (left) and, after four years of addiction, at age 40 (right).

National Pictures/Topham/The Image Works

(Homer et al., 2008). The British government now classifies *crystal meth*, the highly addictive crystalized form of methamphetamine, alongside cocaine and heroin as one of the most dangerous drugs (BBC, 2006).

CAFFEINE Caffeine, the world's most widely consumed psychoactive substance, can now be found not only in coffee, tea, and soda but also in fruit juices, mints, energy drinks, bars, and gels—and even in soap. Coffees and teas vary in their caffeine content, with a cup of drip coffee surprisingly having more caffeine than a shot of espresso, and teas having less. A mild dose of caffeine typically lasts three or four hours, which—if taken in the evening—may be long enough to impair sleep. Like other drugs, caffeine used regularly and in heavy doses produces tolerance: Its stimulating effects lessen. And discontinuing heavy caffeine intake often produces withdrawal symptoms, including fatigue and headache.

NICOTINE Imagine that cigarettes were harmless—except, once in every 25,000 packs, an occasional innocent-looking one is filled with dynamite instead of tobacco. Not such a bad risk of having your head blown off. But with 250 million packs a day consumed worldwide, we could expect more than 10,000 gruesome daily deaths (more than three times the 9/11 fatalities each and every day)—surely enough to have cigarettes banned everywhere.[1]

The lost lives from these dynamite-loaded cigarettes approximate those from today's actual cigarettes. Each year throughout the world, tobacco kills nearly 5.4 million of its 1.3 billion customers, reports the World Health Organization (WHO). (Imagine the outrage if terrorists took down an equivalent of 25 loaded jumbo jets today, let alone tomorrow and every day thereafter.) And by 2030, annual deaths will increase to 8 million, according to WHO predictions. That means that *1 billion* twenty-first-century people may be killed by tobacco (WHO, 2008).

A teen-to-the-grave smoker has a 50 percent chance of dying from the habit, and the death is often agonizing and premature. Eliminating smoking would increase life expectancy more than any other preventive measure. Why, then, do so many people smoke?

Smoking usually begins during early adolescence. (If you are in college or university, and if by now the cigarette manufacturers haven't attracted your business, they almost surely never will.) Adolescents, self-conscious and often thinking the world is watching their every move, are vulnerable to smoking's allure. They may first light up to imitate glamorous celebrities, or to project a mature image, or to get the social reward of being accepted by other smokers (Cin et al., 2007; Tickle et al., 2006). Mindful of these tendencies, cigarette companies have effectively modeled smoking with themes that appeal to youths: sophistication, independence, adventure-seeking, social approval. Typically, teens who start smoking also have friends who smoke, who suggest its pleasures, and who offer them cigarettes (Eiser, 1985; Evans et al., 1988; Rose et al., 1999). Among teens whose parents and best friends are nonsmokers, the smoking rate is close to zero (Moss et al., 1992; also see FIGURE 3.15).

Those addicted to nicotine find it very hard to quit because tobacco products are as powerfully and quickly addictive as heroin and cocaine. As with other addictions, a smoker becomes dependent; each year fewer than one of every seven smokers who want to quit will do so. Smokers also develop tolerance, eventually needing larger and larger doses to get the same effect. Quitting causes nicotine-withdrawal symptoms, including craving, insomnia, anxiety, and irritability. Even attempts to quit within the first weeks of smoking often fail as nicotine cravings set in (DiFranza, 2008). And all it takes to relieve this aversive state is a cigarette—a portable nicotine dispenser.

"There is an overwhelming medical and scientific consensus that cigarette smoking causes lung cancer, heart disease, emphysema, and other serious diseases in smokers. Smokers are far more likely to develop serious diseases, like lung cancer, than nonsmokers."

—Philip Morris Companies Inc., 1999

Smoke a cigarette and nature will charge you 12 minutes—ironically, just about the length of time you spend smoking it (Discover, 1996).

Humorist Dave Barry (1995) recalling why he smoked his first cigarette the summer he turned 15: "Arguments against smoking: 'It's a repulsive addiction that slowly but surely turns you into a gasping, gray-skinned, tumor-ridden invalid, hacking up brownish gobs of toxic waste from your one remaining lung.' Arguments for smoking: 'Other teenagers are doing it.' Case closed! Let's light up!"

"To cease smoking is the easiest thing I ever did; I ought to know because I've done it a thousand times."

—Mark Twain, 1835–1910

Asked "If you had to do it all over again, would you start smoking?" more than 85 percent of adult smokers answer No *(Slovic et al., 2002).*

---

[1]This analogy, adapted here with world-based numbers, was suggested by mathematician Sam Saunders, as reported by K. C. Cole (1998).

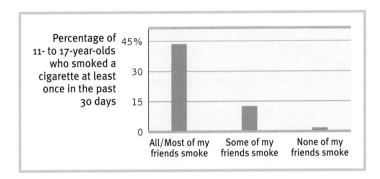

Percentage of 11- to 17-year-olds who smoked a cigarette at least once in the past 30 days

45%
30
15
0

All/Most of my friends smoke · Some of my friends smoke · None of my friends smoke

FIGURE 3.15 Peer influence Kids don't smoke if their friends don't (Philip Morris, 2003). A correlation-causation question: Does the close link between teen smoking and friends' smoking reflect peer influence? Teens seeking similar friends? Or both?

Nicotine, like other addictive drugs, is not only mood-altering, it is also reinforcing. Smoking delivers its hit of nicotine within 7 seconds, triggering the release of epinephrine and norepinephrine, which in turn diminish appetite and boost alertness and mental efficiency (**FIGURE 3.16**). At the same time, nicotine stimulates the central nervous system to release other neurotransmitters that calm anxiety and reduce sensitivity to pain. For example, nicotine stimulates the release of dopamine and (like heroin and morphine) natural opioids (Nowak, 1994; Scott et al., 2004). These rewards keep people smoking even when they wish they could stop—indeed, even when they know they are committing slow-motion suicide (Saad, 2002).

Nevertheless, half of all Americans who have ever smoked have quit, and 81 percent of those who haven't yet quit wish to (Jones, 2007). For those who endure, the acute craving and withdrawal symptoms gradually dissipate over the ensuing six months (Ward et al., 1997). These nonsmokers may live not only healthier but also happier lives. Smoking correlates with higher rates of depression, chronic disabilities, and divorce (Doherty & Doherty, 1998; Vita et al., 1998). Healthy living seems to add both years to life and life to years.

Nic-A-Teen Aware that virtually all smokers start as teenagers—and that sales would plummet if no teens were enticed to smoke—cigarette companies target teens. They have portrayed tough, appealing, socially adept smokers in the hopes that teens will imitate. Teen smoking went up in the 1990s (Brody, 2001), coinciding with an increased number of appealing smokers in popular films, including a younger Johnny Depp in this film, *The Source.*

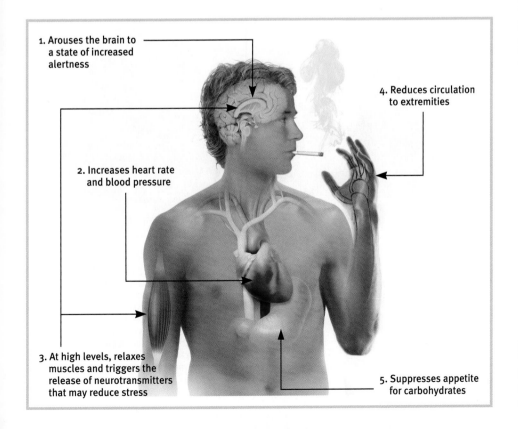

1. Arouses the brain to a state of increased alertness

4. Reduces circulation to extremities

2. Increases heart rate and blood pressure

3. At high levels, relaxes muscles and triggers the release of neurotransmitters that may reduce stress

5. Suppresses appetite for carbohydrates

FIGURE 3.16 Where there's smoke . . . : The physiological effects of nicotine Nicotine reaches the brain within 7 seconds, twice as fast as intravenous heroin. Within minutes, the amount in the blood soars.

COCAINE Cocaine use offers a fast track from euphoria to crash. When sniffed ("snorted"), and especially when injected or smoked ("free-based"), cocaine enters the bloodstream quickly. The result: a "rush" of euphoria that depletes the brain's supply of the neurotransmitters dopamine, serotonin, and norepinephrine (**FIGURE 3.17**). Within 15 to 30 minutes, a crash of agitated depression follows as the drug's effect wears off.

In national surveys, 5 percent of U.S. high school seniors and 5 percent of British 18- to 24-year-olds reported having tried cocaine during the past year (Home Office, 2003; Johnston et al., 2008). Nearly half of the drug-using seniors had smoked *crack*, a crystallized form of cocaine. This faster-working, potent form of the drug produces a briefer but more intense high, a more intense crash, and a craving for more, which wanes after several hours only to return several days later (Gawin, 1991).

Cocaine-addicted monkeys have pressed levers more than 12,000 times to gain one cocaine injection (Siegel, 1990). Many regular cocaine users—animal and human—do become addicted. In situations that trigger aggression, ingesting cocaine may heighten reactions. Caged rats fight when given foot shocks, and they fight even more when given cocaine *and* foot shocks. Likewise, humans ingesting high doses of cocaine in laboratory experiments impose higher shock levels on a presumed opponent than do those receiving a placebo (Licata et al., 1993). Cocaine use may also lead to emotional disturbances, suspiciousness, convulsions, cardiac arrest, or respiratory failure.

As with all psychoactive drugs, cocaine's psychological effects depend not only on the dosage and form consumed but also on the situation and the user's expectations and personality. Given a placebo, cocaine users who *think* they are taking cocaine often have a cocainelike experience (Van Dyke & Byck, 1982).

"Cocaine makes you a new man. And the first thing that new man wants is more cocaine."

—Comedian George Carlin (1937–2008

The recipe for Coca-Cola originally included an extract of the coca plant, creating a cocaine tonic for tired elderly people. Between 1896 and 1905, Coke was indeed "the real thing."

FIGURE 3.17 **Cocaine euphoria and crash**

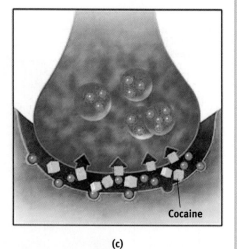

(a) Neurotransmitters carry a message from a sending neuron across a synapse to receptor sites on a receiving neuron.

(b) The sending neuron normally reabsorbs excess neurotransmitter molecules, a process called reuptake.

(c) By binding to the sites that normally reabsorb neurotransmitter molecules, cocaine blocks reuptake of dopamine, serotonin, and norepinephrine (Ray & Ksir, 1990). The extra neurotransmitter molecules therefore remain in the synapse, intensifying their normal mood-altering effects and producing a euphoric rush. When the cocaine level drops, the absence of these neurotransmitters produces a crash.

ECSTASY **Ecstasy,** a street name for **MDMA** (methylene-dioxymethamphetamine), is both a stimulant and a mild hallucinogen. As an amphetamine derivative, it triggers dopamine release. But its major effect is releasing stored serotonin and blocking its reabsorption, thus prolonging serotonin's feel-good flood (Braun, 2001). About a half-hour after taking an Ecstasy pill, users enter a three- to four-hour period of feelings of emotional elevation and, given a social context, connectedness with those around them ("I love everyone").

During the late 1990s, Ecstasy's popularity soared as a "club drug" taken at night clubs and all-night raves (Landry, 2002). There are, however, reasons not to be ecstatic about Ecstasy. One is its dehydrating effect, which—when combined with prolonged dancing—can lead to severe overheating, increased blood pressure, and death. Another is that long-term, repeated leaching of brain serotonin can damage serotonin-producing neurons, leading to decreased output and increased risk of permanently depressed mood (Croft et al., 2001; McCann et al., 2001; Roiser et al., 2005). Ecstasy also suppresses the disease-fighting immune system, impairs memory, slows thought, and disrupts sleep by interfering with serotonin's control of the circadian clock (Laws & Kokkalis, 2007; Pacifici et al., 2001; Schilt et al., 2007). Ecstasy delights for the night but dispirits the morrow.

The hug drug MDMA, known as Ecstasy, produces a euphoric high and feelings of intimacy. But repeated use destroys serotonin-producing neurons and may permanently deflate mood and impair memory.

Hallucinogens

15: What are hallucinogens, and what are their effects?

Hallucinogens distort perceptions and evoke sensory images in the absence of sensory input (which is why these drugs are also called *psychedelics,* meaning "mind-manifesting"). Some, such as LSD and MDMA (Ecstasy), are synthetic. Others, including the mild hallucinogen marijuana, are natural substances.

LSD In 1943, Albert Hofmann reported perceiving "an uninterrupted stream of fantastic pictures, extraordinary shapes with intense, kaleidoscopic play of colors" (Siegel, 1984). Hofmann, a chemist, had created—and on one Friday afternoon in April 1943 accidentally ingested—**LSD** (lysergic acid diethylamide). The result reminded him of a childhood mystical experience that had left him longing for another glimpse of "a miraculous, powerful, unfathomable reality" (Smith, 2006).

LSD and other powerful hallucinogens are chemically similar to (and therefore block the actions of) a subtype of the neurotransmitter serotonin (Jacobs, 1987). The emotions of an LSD trip vary from euphoria to detachment to panic. The user's current mood and expectations color the emotional experience, but the perceptual distortions and hallucinations have some commonalities. Psychologist Ronald Siegel (1982) reported that whether you provoke your brain to hallucinate by drugs, loss of oxygen, or extreme sensory deprivation, "it will hallucinate in basically the same way." The experience typically begins with simple geometric forms, such as a lattice, a cobweb, or a spiral. The next phase consists of more meaningful images; some may be superimposed on a tunnel or funnel, others may be replays of past emotional experiences. As the hallucination peaks, people frequently feel separated from their body and experience dreamlike scenes so real that they may become panic-stricken or harm themselves.

These sensations are strikingly similar to the **near-death experience,** an altered state of consciousness reported by about one-third of those who survive a brush with death, as when revived from cardiac arrest (Moody, 1976; Ring, 1980; Schnaper, 1980). Many experience bright lights or beings of light, a replay of old

Ecstasy (MDMA) a synthetic stimulant and mild hallucinogen. Produces euphoria and social intimacy, but with short-term health risks and longer-term harm to serotonin-producing neurons and to mood and cognition.

hallucinogens psychedelic ("mind-manifesting") drugs, such as LSD, that distort perceptions and evoke sensory images in the absence of sensory input.

LSD a powerful hallucinogenic drug; also known as acid *(lysergic acid diethylamide).*

near-death experience an altered state of consciousness reported after a close brush with death (such as through cardiac arrest); often similar to drug-induced hallucinations.

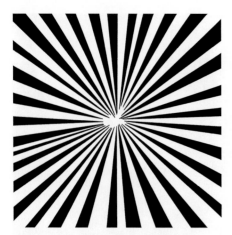

FIGURE 3.18 Near-death vision or hallucination? Psychologist Ronald Siegel (1977) reported that people under the influence of hallucinogenic drugs often see "a bright light in the center of the field of vision. . . . The location of this point of light create[s] a tunnel-like perspective."

memories, visions of tunnels (**FIGURE 3.18**), and out-of-body sensations (Siegel, 1980). Given that oxygen deprivation and other insults to the brain are known to produce hallucinations, it is difficult to resist wondering whether a brain under stress manufactures the near-death experiences. Patients who have experienced temporal lobe seizures have reported similarly profound mystical experiences, as have solitary sailors and polar explorers while enduring monotony, isolation, and cold (Suedfeld & Mocellin, 1987).

MARIJUANA Marijuana consists of the leaves and flowers of the hemp plant, which for 5000 years has been cultivated for its fiber. Whether smoked or eaten, marijuana's major active ingredient, **THC** (delta-9-tetrahydrocannabinol), produces a mix of effects. (Smoking marijuana gets the drug into the brain in about 7 seconds, producing a greater effect than does eating the drug, which causes its peak concentration to be reached at a slower, unpredictable rate.) Like alcohol, marijuana relaxes, disinhibits, and may produce a euphoric high. But marijuana is also a mild hallucinogen, amplifying sensitivity to colors, sounds, tastes, and smells. And unlike alcohol, which the body eliminates within hours, THC and its by-products linger in the body for a month or more. Thus, contrary to the usual tolerance phenomenon, regular users may achieve a high with smaller amounts of the drug than occasional users would need to get the same effect.

A user's experience can vary with the situation. If the person feels anxious or depressed, using marijuana may intensify these feelings. And studies controlling for other drug use and personal traits have found that the more one uses marijuana, the greater one's risk of anxiety, depression, or possibly schizophrenia (Hall, 2006; Murray et al., 2007; Patton et al., 2002). Daily use bodes a worse outcome than infrequent use.

The National Academy of Sciences (1982, 1999) and National Institute on Drug Abuse (2004) have identified other marijuana consequences. Like alcohol, marijuana impairs the motor coordination, perceptual skills, and reaction time necessary for safely operating an automobile or other machine. "THC causes animals to misjudge events," reported Ronald Siegel (1990, p. 163). "Pigeons wait too long to respond to buzzers or lights that tell them food is available for brief periods; and rats turn the wrong way in mazes." Marijuana also disrupts memory formation and interferes with immediate recall of information learned only a few minutes before. Such cognitive effects outlast the period of smoking (Messinis et al., 2007). Prenatal exposure through maternal marijuana use also impairs brain development (Berghuis et al., 2007; Huizink & Mulder, 2006). Heavy adult use for over 20 years is associated with a shrinkage of brain areas that process memories and emotions (Yücel et al., 2008).

Scientists have shed light on marijuana's cognitive, mood, and motor effects with the discovery of concentrations of THC-sensitive receptors in the brain's frontal lobes, limbic system, and motor cortex (Iversen, 2000). As the 1970s discovery of receptors for morphine put researchers on the trail of morphinelike neurotransmitters (the endorphins), so the more recent discovery of *cannabinoid receptors* has led to a successful hunt for naturally occurring THC-like molecules that bind with cannabinoid receptors. These molecules may naturally control pain. If so, this would help explain why marijuana can be therapeutic for those who suffer the pain, nausea, and severe weight loss associated with AIDS (Watson et al., 2000). Such uses have motivated legislation in some states to make the drug legally available for medical purposes. To avoid the toxicity of marijuana smoke—which, like cigarette smoke, can cause cancer, lung damage, and pregnancy complications—the Institute of Medicine recommends medical inhalers to deliver the THC.

* * *

THC the major active ingredient in marijuana; triggers a variety of effects, including mild hallucinations.

Despite their differences, the psychoactive drugs summarized in **TABLE 3.2** share a common feature: They trigger negative aftereffects that offset their immediate positive

TABLE 3.2 A Guide to Selected Psychoactive Drugs

Drug	Type	Pleasurable Effects	Adverse Effects
Alcohol	Depressant	Initial high followed by relaxation and disinhibition	Depression, memory loss, organ damage, impaired reactions
Heroin	Depressant	Rush of euphoria, relief from pain	Depressed physiology, agonizing withdrawal
Caffeine	Stimulant	Increased alertness and wakefulness	Anxiety, restlessness, and insomnia in high doses; uncomfortable withdrawal
Methamphet-amine	Stimulant	Euphoria, alertness, energy	Irritability, insomnia, hypertension, seizures
Cocaine	Stimulant	Rush of euphoria, confidence, energy	Cardiovascular stress, suspiciousness, depressive crash
Nicotine	Stimulant	Arousal and relaxation, sense of well-being	Heart disease, cancer
Ecstasy (MDMA)	Stimulant; mild hallucinogen	Emotional elevation, disinhibition	Dehydration, overheating, depressed mood, impaired cognitive and immune functioning
Marijuana	Mild hallucinogen	Enhanced sensation, relief of pain, distortion of time, relaxation	Impaired learning and memory, increased risk of psychological disorders, lung damage from smoke

effects and grow stronger with repetition. And that helps explain both tolerance and withdrawal. As the opposing, negative aftereffects grow stronger, it takes larger and larger doses to produce the desired high (tolerance), causing the aftereffects to worsen in the drug's absence (withdrawal). This in turn creates a need to switch off the withdrawal symptoms by taking yet more of the drug.

Influences on Drug Use

16: **Why do some people become regular users of consciousness-altering drugs?**

Drug use by North American youth increased during the 1970s. Then, with increased drug education and a more realistic and deglamorized media depiction of taking drugs, drug use declined sharply. After the early 1990s, the cultural antidrug voice softened, and drugs for a time were again glamorized in some music and films. Consider these marijuana-related trends:

- In the University of Michigan's annual survey of 15,000 U.S. high school seniors, the proportion who believe there is "great risk" in regular marijuana use rose from 35 percent in 1978 to 79 percent in 1991, then retreated to 55 percent in 2007 (Johnston et al., 2008).
- After peaking in 1978, marijuana use by U.S. high school seniors declined through 1992, then rose, but has recently been tapering off (see **FIGURE 3.19** on the next page). Among Canadian 15- to 24-year-olds, 23 percent report using marijuana monthly, weekly, or daily (Health Canada, 2007).

For some adolescents, occasional drug use represents thrill seeking. Why, though, do others become regular drug users? In search of answers, researchers have engaged biological, psychological, and social-cultural levels of analysis.

Biological Influences

Some people may be biologically vulnerable to particular drugs. For example, evidence accumulates that heredity influences some aspects of alcohol abuse problems, especially those appearing by early adulthood (Crabbe, 2002):

- Adopted individuals are more susceptible to alcohol dependence if one or both biological parents have a history of it.

"How strange would appear to be this thing that men call pleasure! And how curiously it is related to what is thought to be its opposite, pain! . . . Wherever the one is found, the other follows up behind."

—Plato, *Phaedo,* fourth century B.C.E.

In the real world, alcohol accounts for one-sixth or less of beverage use. In TV land, drinking alcohol occurs more often than the combined drinking of coffee, tea, soft drinks, and water (Gerbner, 1990).

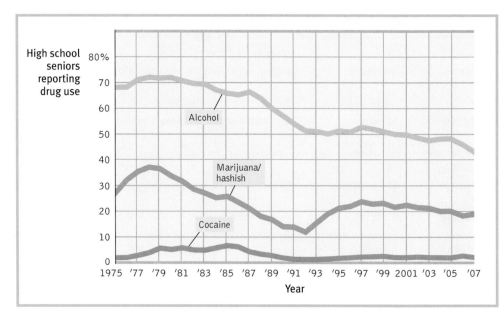

FIGURE 3.19 Trends in drug use The percentage of U.S. high school seniors who report having used alcohol, marijuana, or cocaine during the past 30 days declined from the late 1970s to 1992, when it partially rebounded for a few years. (From Johnston et al., 2009.)

- Having an identical rather than fraternal twin with alcohol dependence puts one at increased risk for alcohol problems (Kendler et al., 2002). (In marijuana use also, identical twins more closely resemble each other than do fraternal twins.)
- Boys who at age 6 are excitable, impulsive, and fearless (genetically influenced traits) are more likely as teens to smoke, drink, and use other drugs (Masse & Tremblay, 1997).
- Researchers have bred rats and mice that prefer alcoholic drinks to water. One such strain has reduced levels of the brain chemical NPY. Mice engineered to *overproduce* NPY are very sensitive to alcohol's sedating effect and drink little (Thiele et al., 1998).
- Researchers have identified genes that are more common among people and animals predisposed to alcohol dependence, and they are seeking genes that contribute to tobacco addiction (NIH, 2006; Nurnberger & Bierut, 2007). These culprit genes seemingly produce deficiencies in the brain's natural dopamine reward system, which is impacted by addictive drugs. With repeated use, the drugs disrupt normal dopamine balance while triggering temporary dopamine-produced pleasure. Studies of how drugs reprogram the brain's reward systems raise hopes for anti-addiction drugs that might block or blunt the effects of alcohol and other drugs (Miller, 2008; Wilson & Kuhn, 2005).

Psychological and Social-Cultural Influences

Psychological and social-cultural influences also contribute to drug use (**FIGURE 3.20**). One psychological factor that has appeared in studies of youth and young adults (Newcomb & Harlow, 1986) is the feeling that life is meaningless and directionless, a common feeling among school dropouts who subsist without job skills, without privilege, and with little hope.

Heavy users of alcohol, marijuana, and cocaine often display other psychological influences. Many have experienced significant stress or failure and are depressed. Females with a history of depression, eating disorders, or sexual or physical abuse are at risk for substance addiction, as are those undergoing school or neighborhood transitions (CASA, 2003; Logan et al., 2002). Monkeys, too, develop a taste for alcohol when stressed by permanent separation from their mother at birth (Small, 2002). By temporarily dulling the pain of self-awareness, alcohol may offer a way to

Warning signs of alcohol dependence
- *Drinking binges*
- *Regretting things done or said when drunk*
- *Feeling low or guilty after drinking*
- *Failing to honor a resolve to drink less*
- *Drinking to alleviate depression or anxiety*
- *Avoiding family or friends when drinking*

Biological influences:
- genetic predispositions
- variations in neurotransmitter systems

Psychological influences:
- lacking sense of purpose
- significant stress
- psychological disorders, such as depression

Drug use

Social-cultural influences:
- urban environment
- cultural attitude toward drug use
- peer influences

FIGURE 3.20 Levels of analysis for drug use The biopsychosocial approach enables researchers to investigate drug use from complementary perspectives.

avoid coping with depression, anger, anxiety, or insomnia. As Chapter 7 explains, behavior is often controlled more by its immediate consequences than by its later ones.

Drug use also has social roots. When young unmarried adults leave home, alcohol and other drug use increases; when they marry and have children, it decreases (Bachman et al., 1997). Among teenagers, most drinking is done for social reasons, not as a way to cope with problems (Kuntsche et al., 2005). Social influence also appears in the differing rates of drug use across cultural and ethnic groups. For example, a 2003 survey of 100,000 teens in 35 European countries found that marijuana use in the prior 30 days ranged from zero to 1 percent in Romania and Sweden to 20 to 22 percent in Britain, Switzerland, and France (ESPAD, 2003). Independent U.S. government studies of drug use in households nationwide and among high schoolers in all regions reveal that African-American teens have sharply lower rates of drinking, smoking, and cocaine use (Johnston et al., 2007). Alcohol and other drug addiction rates have also been extremely low in the United States among Orthodox Jews, Mormons, the Amish, and Mennonites (Trimble, 1994). Relatively drug-free small towns and rural areas tend to constrain any genetic predisposition to drug use, report Lisa Legrand and her colleagues (2005). For those whose genetic predispositions nudge them toward substance use, "cities offer more opportunities" and less supervision.

Whether in cities or rural areas, peers influence attitudes about drugs. They also throw the parties and provide the drugs. If an adolescent's friends use drugs, the odds are that he or she will, too. If the friends do not, the opportunity may not even arise. Teens who come from happy families, who do not begin drinking before age 14, and who do well in school tend not to use drugs, largely because they rarely associate with those who do (Bachman et al., 2007; Hingson et al., 2006; Oetting & Beauvais, 1987, 1990).

Peer influence, however, is not just a matter of what friends do and say but also of what adolescents *believe* friends are doing and favoring. In one survey of sixth graders in 22 U.S. states, 14 percent believed their friends had smoked marijuana, though only 4 percent acknowledged doing so (Wren, 1999). University students are not immune to such misperceptions: Drinking dominates social occasions partly because students overestimate their fellow students' enthusiasm for alcohol and underestimate their views of its risks (Prentice & Miller, 1993; Self, 1994) **(TABLE 3.3)**.

Culture and Alcohol
Percentage drinking weekly or more:

United States	30%
Canada	40%
Britain	58%

(Gallup poll, from Moore, 2006)

TABLE 3.3 Facts About "Higher" Education

College and university students drink more alcohol than their nonstudent peers and exhibit 2.5 times the general population's rate of substance abuse.

Fraternity and sorority members report nearly twice the binge-drinking rate of nonmembers.

Since 1993, campus smoking rates have declined, alcohol use has been steady, and abuse of prescription opioids, stimulants, tranquilizers, and sedatives has increased, as has marijuana use.

Source: NCASA, 2007.

SNAPSHOTS

Once upon a time, peer pressure caused Bob to start smoking.

Twenty years later, it forces him to quit.

(c) Love A141

© Jason Love

People whose beginning use of drugs was influenced by their peers are more likely to stop using when friends stop or the social network changes (Kandel & Raveis, 1989). One study that followed 12,000 adults over 32 years found that smokers tend to quit in clusters (Christakis & Fowler, 2008). Within a social network, the odds of a person's quitting increased when a spouse, friend, or co-worker stopped smoking. Similarly, most soldiers who became drug-addicted while in Vietnam ceased their drug use after returning home (Robins et al., 1974).

As always with correlations, the traffic between friends' drug use and our own may be two-way: Our friends influence us. Social networks matter. But we also select as friends those who share our likes and dislikes.

What do the findings on drug use suggest for drug prevention and treatment programs? Three channels of influence seem possible:

- Educate young people about the long-term costs of a drug's temporary pleasures.
- Help young people find other ways to boost their self-esteem and purpose in life.
- Attempt to modify peer associations or to "inoculate" youths against peer pressures by training them in refusal skills.

People rarely abuse drugs if they understand the physical and psychological costs, feel good about themselves and the direction their lives are taking, and are in a peer group that disapproves of using drugs. These educational, psychological, and social-cultural factors may help explain why 42 percent of U.S. high school dropouts, but only 15 percent of college graduates, have reported smoking (Ladd, 1998).

REHEARSE IT!

15. Continued use of a psychoactive drug produces tolerance. This usually means that the user will
    a. feel physical pain and intense craving.
    b. be irreversibly addicted to the substance.
    c. need to take larger doses to get the desired effect.
    d. be able to take smaller doses to get the desired effect.

16. The depressants include alcohol, barbiturates,
    a. and opiates.
    b. cocaine, and morphine.
    c. caffeine, nicotine, and marijuana.
    d. and amphetamines.

17. Because alcohol _____, it may make a person more helpful or more aggressive.
    a. causes alcoholic blackouts
    b. destroys REM sleep

    c. produces hallucinations
    d. lowers inhibitions

18. Nicotine and cocaine stimulate neural activity, speed up body functions, and
    a. induce sensory hallucinations.
    b. interfere with memory.
    c. induce a temporary sense of well-being.
    d. lead to heroin use.

19. Long-term use of Ecstasy can
    a. depress sympathetic nervous system activity.
    b. deplete the brain's supply of epinephrine.
    c. deplete the brain's supply of dopamine.
    d. damage serotonin-producing neurons.

20. Near-death experiences are strikingly similar to the hallucinations evoked by
    a. heroin.

    b. cocaine.
    c. LSD.
    d. alcohol.

21. Use of marijuana
    a. impairs motor coordination, perception, reaction time, and memory.
    b. inhibits people's emotions.
    c. leads to dehydration and overheating.
    d. stimulates brain cell development.

22. Social-cultural explanations for drug use often focus on the effect of peer influence. An important *psychological* contributor to drug use is
    a. inflated self-esteem.
    b. the feeling that life is meaningless and directionless.
    c. genetic predispositions.
    d. overprotective parents.

Answers: 15. c, 16. a, 17. d, 18. c, 19. d, 20. c, 21. a, 22. b.

Consciousness and the Two-Track Mind

The Brain and Consciousness

1 What is the "dual processing" being revealed by today's cognitive neuroscience?

Cognitive neuroscientists and others studying the brain mechanisms underlying *consciousness* and cognition have discovered a two-track human mind, each with its own neural processing. This *dual processing* affects our perception, memory, and attitudes at an explicit, conscious level and at an implicit, unconscious level.

2 How much information do we consciously attend to at once?

We *selectively attend* to, and process, a very limited aspect of incoming information. We even display *inattentional blindness,* blocking out events and changes in our visual world. Shifting the spotlight of our attention from one thing to another contributes to car and pedestrian accidents.

Sleep and Dreams

3 How do our biological rhythms influence our daily functioning and our sleep and dreams?

Our internal biological rhythms create periodic physiological fluctuations. The *circadian rhythm's* 24-hour cycle regulates our daily schedule of sleeping and waking, in part in response to light on the retina. Shifts in schedules can reset our biological clock.

4 What is the biological rhythm of our sleep?

We cycle through five *sleep* stages in about 90 minutes. Leaving the *alpha waves* of the awake, relaxed stage, we descend into transitional Stage 1 sleep, often with the sensation of falling or floating. Stage 2 sleep (in which we spend the most time) follows about 20 minutes later, with its characteristic sleep spindles. Then follow Stages 3 and 4, together lasting about 30 minutes, with large, slow *delta waves.* Reversing course, we retrace our path, but with one difference: We experience periods of *REM (rapid eye movement) sleep.* Most dreaming occurs in this fifth stage (also known as paradoxical sleep) of internal arousal but outward paralysis. During a normal night's sleep, periods of Stages 3 and 4 sleep shorten and REM sleep lengthens.

5 How does sleep loss affect us?

Sleep deprivation causes fatigue and impairs concentration, creativity, and communication. It also can lead to obesity, hypertension, a suppressed immune system, irritability, and slowed performance (with greater vulnerability to accidents).

6 Why do we sleep?

Sleep (1) may have played a protective role in human evolution by keeping people safe during potentially dangerous periods; gives the brain time to (2) restore and repair damaged neurons and (3) store and rebuild memories of the day's experiences. Sleep also (4) promotes creative problem solving the next day, and (5) encourages growth (the pituitary gland secretes a growth hormone in Stage 4 sleep).

7 What are the major sleep disorders?

The major disorders of sleep include *insomnia* (recurring wakefulness), *narcolepsy* (sudden uncontrollable sleepiness or lapsing into REM sleep), *sleep apnea* (the stopping of breathing while asleep), *night terrors* (high arousal and the appearance of being terrified), sleepwalking, and sleeptalking. Sleep apnea mainly targets older overweight men. Children are most prone to night terrors, sleepwalking, and sleeptalking.

8 What do we dream?

We usually *dream* of ordinary events and everyday experiences, most involving some anxiety or misfortune. Fewer than 10 percent (and less among women) of dreams have any sexual content. Most dreams occur during REM sleep; those that happen during non-REM sleep tend to be vague fleeting images.

9 Why do we dream?

There are five major views of the function of dreams. (1) Freudian: to provide a safety valve, with *manifest content* (or story line) acting as a censored version of *latent content* (a hidden meaning that gratifies our unconscious wishes). (2) Information-processing: to sort out the day's experiences and fix them in memory. (3) Brain stimulation: to preserve neural pathways in the brain. (4) Activation-synthesis: to make sense of the brain's neural static by weaving it into a story line. (5) Cognitive-development: Dream content represents the dreamer's level of development, knowledge, and understanding. The belief that REM sleep and its associated dreams serve an important function is supported by *REM rebound,* which occurs following REM deprivation.

Hypnosis

10 What is hypnosis, and what powers does a hypnotist have over a hypnotized subject?

Hypnosis is a social interaction in which one person suggests to another that certain perceptions, feelings, thoughts, or behaviors will spontaneously occur. Hypnotized people, like unhypnotized people, may perform unlikely acts when told to do so by an authoritative person. *Posthypnotic suggestions* have helped people harness their own healing powers but have not been very effective in treating addiction. Hypnosis can help relieve pain, but it does not enhance recall of forgotten events (it may even evoke false memories).

11 Is hypnosis an extension of normal consciousness or an altered state?

Many psychologists believe that hypnosis is a form of normal social influence and that hypnotized people act out the role of "good subject." Other psychologists view hypnosis as a *dissociation,* an instance of the dual-track mind in which normal sensations and conscious awareness are split. A unified account of hypnosis melds these two views and studies how brain activity, attention, and social influences interact in hypnosis.

Drugs and Consciousness

12 **What are tolerance, dependence, and addiction, and what are some common misconceptions about addiction?**

Psychoactive drugs alter perceptions and moods. Their continued use produces *tolerance* (requiring larger doses to achieve the same effect) and may lead to *physical* or *psychological dependence*. *Addiction* is compulsive drug craving and use. Despite popular beliefs, addictive drugs do not usually quickly corrupt, and therapy is not always required to overcome addiction. Debate continues over whether the concept of addiction can meaningfully be extended to other behaviors in addition to chemical dependence.

13 **What are depressants, and what are their effects?**

Depressants, such as alcohol, *barbiturates,* and the *opiates,* dampen neural activity and slow body functions. Alcohol disinhibits—it increases the likelihood that we will act on our impulses, whether harmful or helpful. Alcohol also slows nervous system activity and impairs judgment, disrupts memory processes by suppressing REM sleep, and reduces self-awareness. User expectations strongly influence alcohol's behavioral effects.

14 **What are stimulants, and what are their effects?**

Stimulants—caffeine, nicotine, the *amphetamines,* cocaine, *Ecstasy,* and *methamphetamine*—excite neural activity and speed up body functions. All are highly addictive. Continued use of methamphetamine may permanently reduce dopamine production. Nicotine's effects make smoking a difficult habit to kick, but the percentage of Americans who smoke is nevertheless decreasing. Cocaine gives users a 15- to 30-minute high, followed by a crash. Its risks include suspiciousness and cardiovascular stress. Ecstasy, a combined stimulant and mild hallucinogen, produces a euphoric high and feelings of intimacy. Its users risk immune system suppression, permanent damage to mood and memory, and (if taken during physical activity) dehydration and escalating body temperatures.

15 **What are hallucinogens, and what are their effects?**

Hallucinogens—such as *LSD* and marijuana—distort perceptions and evoke *hallucinations*—sensory images in the absence of sensory input. Mood and expectations influence LSD's effects, but hallucinations and emotions varying from euphoria to panic are common. Patients who report a *near-death experience* often describe profound mystical feelings that may resemble drug-induced hallucinations. Marijuana's main ingredient, *THC,* may trigger feelings of disinhibition, euphoria, relaxation, relief from pain, and intense sensitivity to sensory stimuli. It may also increase feelings of depression or anxiety, impair motor coordination and reaction time, disrupt memory formation, and damage lung tissue (because of the inhaled smoke).

16 **Why do some people become regular users of consciousness-altering drugs?**

Some people may be biologically more likely to become dependent on drugs such as alcohol. Psychological factors (such as stress, depression, and hopelessness) and social factors (such as peer pressure) combine to lead many people to experiment with—and sometimes become dependent on—drugs. Cultural and ethnic groups have differing rates of drug use. Each type of influence—biological, psychological, and social-cultural—offers a possible path for drug prevention and treatment programs.

Terms and Concepts to Remember

consciousness, p. 65

dual processing, p. 67

selective attention, p. 68

inattentional blindness, p. 69

change blindness, p. 69

circadian [ser-KAY-dee-an] rhythm, p. 71

REM sleep, p. 72

alpha waves, p. 72

sleep, p. 72

hallucinations, p. 72

delta waves, p. 73

insomnia, p. 78

narcolepsy, p. 78

sleep apnea, p. 79

night terrors, p. 79

dream, p. 80

manifest content, p. 81

latent content, p. 81

REM rebound, p. 83

hypnosis, p. 84

posthypnotic suggestion, p. 85

dissociation, p. 86

psychoactive drug, p. 88

tolerance, p. 88

withdrawal, p. 88

physical dependence, p. 88

psychological dependence, p. 88

addiction, p. 88

depressants, p. 89

barbiturates, p. 91

opiates, p. 91

stimulants, p. 91

amphetamines, p. 91

metamphetamine, p. 91

Ecstasy (MDMA), p. 95

hallucinogens, p. 95

LSD, p. 95

near-death experience, p. 95

THC, p. 96

Test for Success: Critical Thinking Exercises
By Amy Himsel, El Camino College

1. Research on the two-track mind shows that we know more than we know we know. Might we function better if we were completely conscious of all of our thought processes?

2. In the discussion of sleep stages, a man in a cartoon states, "Boy, are my eyes tired! I had REM sleep all night long!" In reality, how tiring is REM sleep, and how much time do we spend in it?

3. Sleep researcher William Dement said that a large sleep debt "makes you stupid" (1999, p. 231). What are some of the ways sleep deprivation can affect cognitive performance?

4. "For what one has dwelt on by day, these things are seen in visions of the night" (Menander of Athens [342–292 B.C.E.], *Fragments*). Consider this quote from the wish-fulfillment, in-formation-processing, and activation-synthesis perspectives on dreaming.

5. Fourth-century-B.C.E. philosopher Plato observed, "How strange would appear to be this thing that men call pleasure! And how curiously it is related to what is thought to be its opposite, pain! . . . Wherever the one is found, the other follows up behind." Explain how this pleasure-pain description applies to the neurotransmitter activity underlying repeated use of heroin.

The Test for Success questions offer you a chance to apply your critical thinking skills to aspects of the material you have just read. Suggestions for answering these questions can be found in Appendix D at the back of the book.

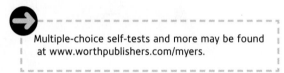

Multiple-choice self-tests and more may be found at www.worthpublishers.com/myers.

Chapter Outline

● **Behavior Genetics: Predicting Individual Differences**
  Genes: Our Codes for Life
  Twin and Adoption Studies
  Temperament, Heredity, and Personality
  Gene-Environment Interactions

● **Evolutionary Psychology: Understanding Human Nature**
  Natural Selection and Adaptation
  Evolutionary Success Helps Explain Similarities
  An Evolutionary Explanation of Human Sexuality
  THINKING CRITICALLY ABOUT: The Evolutionary Perspective on Human Sexuality

● **Parents and Peers**
  Parents and Early Experiences
  Peer Influence

● **Cultural Influences**
  Variation Across Cultures
  Variation Over Time
  Culture and the Self
  Culture and Child-Rearing
  Developmental Similarities Across Groups

● **Gender Development**
  Gender Similarities and Differences
  The Nature of Gender
  The Nurture of Gender

● **Reflections on Nature and Nurture**

4: Nature, Nurture, and Human Diversity

What makes you you? In important ways, we are each unique. We look different. We sound different. We have varying personalities, interests, and cultural and family backgrounds.

We are also the leaves of one tree. Our human family shares not only a common biological heritage—cut us and we bleed—but also common behavioral tendencies. Our shared brain architecture predisposes us to sense the world, develop language, and feel hunger through identical mechanisms. Whether we live in the Arctic or the tropics, we prefer sweet tastes to sour. We divide the color spectrum into similar colors. And we feel drawn to behaviors that produce and protect offspring.

Our kinship appears in our social behaviors as well. Whether named Wong, Nkomo, Smith, or Gonzales, we start fearing strangers at about eight months, and as adults we prefer the company of those with attitudes and attributes similar to our own. Coming from different parts of the globe, we know how to read one another's smiles and frowns. As members of one species, we affiliate, conform, return favors, punish offenses, organize hierarchies of status, and grieve a child's death. A visitor from outer space could drop in anywhere and find humans dancing and feasting, singing and worshiping, playing sports and games, laughing and crying, living in families and forming groups. Taken together, such universal behaviors define our human nature.

What causes our striking diversity, and also our shared human nature? How much are human differences shaped by our differing genes? And how much by our **environment**—by every external influence, from maternal nutrition while in the womb to social support while nearing the tomb? To what extent are we formed by our upbringing? By our culture? By our current circumstances? By people's reactions to our genetic dispositions? This chapter begins to tell the complex story of how our genes *(nature)* and environments *(nurture)* define us.

environment every nongenetic influence, from prenatal nutrition to the people and things around us.

behavior genetics the study of the relative power and limits of genetic and environmental influences on behavior.

The nurture of nature Parents everywhere wonder: Will my baby grow up to be peaceful or aggressive? Homely or attractive? Successful or struggling at every step? What comes built in, and what is nurtured—and how? Research reveals that nature and nurture together shape our development—every step of the way.

Behavior Genetics: Predicting Individual Differences

If Jaden Agassi, son of tennis stars Andre Agassi and Stephanie Graf, grows up to be a tennis star, should we attribute his superior talent to his Grand Slam genes? To his growing up in a tennis-rich environment? To high expectations? Such questions intrigue **behavior geneticists,** who study our differences and weigh the effects and interplay of heredity and environment.

"Thanks for almost everything, Dad."

Genes: Our Codes for Life

1: Our genes predispose our biology. Does this mean they determine our behavior?

Behind the story of our body and of our brain—surely the most awesome thing on our little planet—is the heredity that interacts with our experience to create both our universal human nature and our individual and social diversity. Barely more than a century ago, few would have guessed that every cell nucleus in your body contains the genetic master code for your entire body. It's as if every room in the Empire State Building had a book containing the architect's plans for the entire structure. The plans for your own book of life run to 46 chapters—23 donated by your mother (from her egg) and 23 by your father (from his sperm). Each of these 46 chapters, called a **chromosome,** is composed of a coiled chain of the molecule **DNA** *(deoxyribonucleic acid)* (**FIGURE 4.1**). **Genes,** small segments of the giant DNA molecules, form the words of those chapters. All told, you have 30,000 or so gene words. Genes can be either active *(expressed)* or inactive. Environmental events "turn on" genes, rather like hot water enabling a tea bag to express its flavor. When turned on, genes provide the code for creating *protein molecules,* the building blocks of physical development.

Geneticists and psychologists are interested in the occasional variations found at particular gene sites in human DNA. Slight person-to-person variations from the common pattern give clues to our uniqueness—why one person has a disease that another does not, why one person is short and another tall, why one is outgoing and another shy. For example, you may recall from Chapter 1 that research indicates that breast-feeding boosts later intelligence. This turns out to be true only for the 90 percent of infants with a gene that assists in breaking down fatty acids present in human milk (Caspi et al., 2007). Studies of 1037 New Zealand adults and 2232 English 12- and 13-year olds found no breast-feeding boost among those not carrying the gene.

Most of our traits are influenced by many genes. How tall you are, for example, reflects the size of your face, vertebrae, leg bones, and so forth—each of which may be influenced by different genes interacting with your environment. Complex traits such as intelligence, happiness, and aggressiveness are similarly influenced by groups of genes. Thus our genetic predispositions—our genetically influenced traits—help explain both our shared human nature and our human diversity.

> "Your DNA and mine are 99.9 percent the same. . . . At the DNA level, we are clearly all part of one big worldwide family."
>
> —Francis Collins, Human Genome Project director, 2007

> "We share half our genes with the banana."
>
> —Evolutionary biologist Robert May, president of Britain's Royal Society, 2001

FIGURE 4.1 The human building blocks: The nucleus of every human cell contains chromosomes, each of which is made up of two strands of DNA connected in a double helix.

Chromosome

Cell

Gene

Nucleus

DNA

Twin and Adoption Studies

2: How do twin and adoption studies help us understand the relative influences of environment and heredity?

To tease apart the influences of environment and heredity, behavior geneticists would need to design two types of scientific experiments. The first would control the home environment while varying heredity. The second would control heredity while varying the home environment. Such experiments with human infants would be unethical, but happily for our purposes, nature has done this work for us.

Identical Versus Fraternal Twins

Identical twins develop from a single *(monozygotic)* fertilized egg. Thus they are *genetically* identical—nature's own human clones (**FIGURE 4.2**). Indeed, they are clones who share not only the same genes but the same conception, uterus, birth date, and usually the same cultural history.

Identical twins | Fraternal twins

Same sex only | Same or opposite sex

FIGURE 4.2 **Same fertilized egg, same genes; different eggs, different genes**
Identical twins develop from a single fertilized egg, fraternal twins from two.

chromosomes threadlike structures made of DNA molecules that contain the genes.

DNA (deoxyribonucleic acid) a complex molecule containing the genetic information that makes up the chromosomes.

genes the biochemical units of heredity that make up the chromosomes; a segment of DNA capable of synthesizing a protein.

identical twins twins who develop from a single fertilized egg that splits in two, creating two genetically identical organisms.

fraternal twins twins who develop from separate fertilized eggs. They are genetically no closer than brothers and sisters, but they share a fetal environment.

Fraternal twins develop from separate *(dizygotic)* fertilized eggs. They share a fetal environment, but they are genetically no more similar than ordinary brothers and sisters.

Shared genes can translate into shared experiences. A person whose identical twin has Alzheimer's disease, for example, has a 60 percent risk of getting the disease. If the affected twin is fraternal, the risk is only 30 percent (Plomin et al., 1997).

Are identical twins, being genetic clones of each other, also behaviorally more similar than fraternal twins? Studies of thousands of twin pairs in Sweden, Finland, and Australia provide a consistent answer: On both extraversion (outgoingness) and neuroticism (emotional instability), identical twins are much more similar than fraternal twins.

When John Loehlin and Robert Nichols (1976) gave a battery of questionnaires to 850 U.S. twin pairs, identical twins, more than fraternal twins, also reported being treated alike. So, did their experience rather than their genes account for their similarity? *No*, said Loehlin and Nichols; identical twins whose parents treated them alike were not psychologically more alike than identical twins who were treated less similarly. In explaining individual differences, genes matter.

Fraternal twins These siblings share a birthday, but not identical genes. Having formed from two separate eggs, they share no more genes than does any other sibling pair.

More twins Curiously, twinning rates vary by race. The rate among Caucasians is roughly twice that of Asians and half that of Africans. In Africa and Asia, most twins are identical. In Western countries, most twins are fraternal, and fraternal twins are increasing with the use of fertility drugs (Hall, 2003; Steinhauer, 1999).

Separated Twins

Imagine the following science fiction experiment: A mad scientist decides to separate identical twins at birth, then rear them in differing environments. Better yet, consider a *true* story:

On a chilly February morning in 1979, some time after divorcing his first wife, Linda, Jim Lewis awoke in his modest home next to his second wife, Betty. Determined that this marriage would work, Jim had a habit of leaving love notes to Betty around the house. As he lay in bed he thought about others he had loved, including his son, James Alan, and his faithful dog, Toy.

Jim was looking forward to spending part of the day in his basement woodworking shop, where he had put in many happy hours building furniture, picture frames, and other items, including a white bench now circling a tree in his front yard. Jim also liked to spend free time driving his Chevy, watching stock-car racing, and drinking Miller Lite beer.

Jim was basically healthy, except for occasional half-day migraine headaches and blood pressure that was a little high, perhaps related to his chain-smoking habit. He had become overweight a while back but had shed some of the pounds. Having undergone a vasectomy, he was done having children.

What was extraordinary about Jim Lewis, however, was that at that same moment (I am not making this up) there existed another man—also named Jim—for whom all these things (right down to the dog's name) were also true.[1] This other Jim—Jim Springer—just happened, 38 years earlier, to have been his womb-mate. Thirty-seven days after their birth, these genetically identical twins were separated, adopted by blue-collar families, and reared with no contact or knowledge of each other's whereabouts until the day Jim Lewis received a call from his genetic clone (who, having been told he had a twin, set out to find him).

One month later, the brothers became the first twin pair tested by University of Minnesota psychologist Thomas Bouchard and his colleagues (1998), beginning a study of separated twins that extends to the present. Given tests measuring their personality, intelligence, heart rate, and brain waves, the Jim twins—despite 38 years of separation—were virtually as alike as the same person tested twice. Their voice intonations and inflections were so similar that, hearing a playback of an earlier interview, Jim Springer guessed "That's me." Wrong—it was his brother.

Identical twins Oskar Stohr and Jack Yufe presented equally striking similarities. One was raised by his grandmother in Germany as a Catholic and a Nazi, while the other was raised by his father in the Caribbean as a Jew. Nevertheless, they shared

---

[1] Actually, this description of the two Jims errs in one respect: Jim Lewis named his son James Alan. Jim Springer named his James Allan.

Sweden has the world's largest national twin registry—140,000 living and dead twin pairs—which forms part of a massive registry of 600,000 twins currently being sampled in the world's largest twin study (Wheelwright, 2004; www.genomeutwin.org).

Bouchard's famous twin research was, appropriately enough, conducted in Minneapolis, the "Twin City" (with St. Paul), and home to the Minnesota Twins baseball team.

"In some domains it looks as though our identical twins reared apart are . . . just as similar as identical twins reared together. Now that's an amazing finding and I can assure you none of us would have expected that degree of similarity."

—Thomas Bouchard (1981)

Identical twins are people two Identical twins Jim Lewis and Jim Springer were separated shortly after birth and raised in different homes without awareness of each other. Research has shown remarkable similarities in the life choices of separated identical twins, lending support to the idea that genes influence personality.

traits and habits galore. They liked spicy foods and sweet liqueurs, fell asleep in front of the television, flushed the toilet before using it, stored rubber bands on their wrists, and dipped buttered toast in their coffee. Stohr was domineering toward women and yelled at his wife, as did Yufe before he and his wife separated. Both married women named Dorothy Jane Scheckelburger. Okay, the last item is a joke. But as Judith Rich Harris (2006) notes, it is hardly weirder than some other reported similarities.

Aided by publicity in magazine and newspaper stories, Bouchard and his colleagues (1990; DiLalla et al., 1996; Segal, 1999) located and studied 80 pairs of identical twins reared apart. They continued to find similarities not only of tastes and physical attributes but also of personality (characteristic patterns of thinking, feeling, and acting), abilities, attitudes, interests, and even fears.

In Sweden, Nancy Pedersen and her co-workers (1988) identified 99 separated identical twin pairs and more than 200 separated fraternal twin pairs. Compared with equivalent samples of identical twins reared together, the separated identical twins had somewhat less identical personalities. Still, separated twins were more alike if genetically identical than if fraternal. And separation shortly after birth (rather than, say, at age 8) did not amplify their personality differences.

Stories of startling twin similarities do not impress Bouchard's critics, who remind us that "the plural of *anecdote* is not *data*." They contend that if any two strangers were to spend hours comparing their behaviors and life histories, they would probably discover many coincidental similarities. If researchers created a control group of biologically unrelated pairs of the same age, sex, and ethnicity, who had not grown up together but who were as similar to one another in economic and cultural background as are many of the separated twin pairs, wouldn't these pairs also exhibit striking similarities (Joseph, 2001)? Bouchard replies that separated fraternal twins do not exhibit similarities comparable to those of separated identical twins. Twin researcher Nancy Segal (2000) has noted that *virtual twins*—same-age, biologically unrelated siblings—are also much more dissimilar.

Even the more impressive data from personality assessments are clouded by the reunion of many of the separated twins some years before they were tested. Moreover, identical twins share an appearance, and the responses it evokes, and adoption agencies tend to place separated twins in similar homes. Despite these criticisms, the striking twin-study results helped shift scientific thinking toward a greater appreciation of genetic influences.

If genetic influences help explain individual differences, do they also help explain group differences between men and women, or between people of different races? Not necessarily. Individual differences in height and weight, for example, are highly heritable; yet nutritional rather than genetic influences explain why, as a group, today's adults are taller and heavier than those of a century ago. The two groups differ, but not because human genes have changed in a mere century's eyeblink of time. Ditto aggressiveness, a genetically influenced trait. Today's peaceful Scandinavians differ from their more aggressive Viking ancestors, despite carrying many of the same genes.

Biological Versus Adoptive Relatives

For behavior geneticists, nature's second type of real-life experiment—adoption—creates two groups: *genetic relatives* (biological parents and siblings) and *environmental relatives* (adoptive parents and siblings). For any given trait, we can therefore ask whether adopted children are more like their biological parents, who contributed their genes, or their adoptive parents, who contribute a home environment. While sharing that home environment, do adopted siblings also come to share traits?

The stunning finding from studies of hundreds of adoptive families is that people who grow up together, whether biologically related or not, do not much resemble one another in personality (McGue & Bouchard, 1998; Plomin et al., 1998; Rowe,

Twins Lorraine and Levinia Christmas, driving to deliver Christmas presents to each other near Flitcham, England, collided (Shepherd, 1997).

Coincidences are not unique to twins. Patricia Kern of Colorado was born March 13, 1941, and named Patricia Ann Campbell. Patricia DiBiasi of Oregon also was born March 13, 1941, and named Patricia Ann Campbell. Both had fathers named Robert, worked as bookkeepers, and at the time of this comparison had children ages 21 and 19. Both studied cosmetology, enjoyed oil painting as a hobby, and married military men, within 11 days of each other. They are not genetically related. (From an AP report, May 2, 1983.)

"We carry to our graves the essence of the zygote that was first us."

—Mary Pipher, *Seeking Peace: Chronicles of the Worst Buddhist in the World,* 2009

Nature or nurture or both? When talent runs in families, as with the Williams sisters, how do heredity and environment together do their work?

Sean Garnsworthy/Getty Images

"Mom may be holding a full house while Dad has a straight flush, yet when Junior gets a random half of each of their cards his poker hand may be a loser."

—David Lykken (2001)

The greater uniformity of adoptive homes—mostly healthy, nurturing homes—helps explain the lack of striking differences when comparing child outcomes of different adoptive homes (Stoolmiller, 1999).

1990). In traits such as extraversion and agreeableness, adoptees are more similar to their biological parents than to their caregiving adoptive parents.

The finding is important enough to bear repeating: The environment shared by a family's children has virtually no discernible impact on their personalities. Two adopted children reared in the same home are no more likely to share personality traits with each other than with the child down the block. Heredity shapes other primates' personalities, too. Macaque monkeys raised by foster mothers exhibit social behaviors that resemble their biological, rather than foster, mothers (Maestripieri, 2003). Add all this to the similarity of identical twins, whether they grow up together or apart, and the effect of a shared rearing environment seems shockingly modest.

What we have here is perhaps "the most important puzzle in the history of psychology," contends Steven Pinker (2002): Why are children in the same family so different? Why does shared family environment have so little effect on children's personalities? Is it because each sibling experiences unique peer influences and life events? Because sibling relationships ricochet off each other, amplifying their differences? Because siblings—despite sharing half their genes—have very different combinations of genes and may evoke very different kinds of parenting? Such questions fuel behavior geneticists' curiosity.

The minimal shared-environment effect does not mean that adoptive parenting is a fruitless venture. The genetic leash may limit the family environment's influence on personality, but parents do influence their children's attitudes, values, manners, faith, and politics (Reifman & Cleveland, 2007). A pair of adopted children or identical twins *will*, especially during adolescence, have more similar religious beliefs if reared together (Kelley & De Graaf, 1997; Koenig et al., 2005; Rohan & Zanna, 1996). Parenting matters!

Moreover, in adoptive homes, child neglect and abuse and even parental divorce are rare. (Adoptive parents are carefully screened; natural parents are not.) So it is not surprising that, despite a somewhat greater risk of psychological disorder, most adopted children thrive, especially when adopted as infants (Loehlin et al., 2007; van IJzendoorn & Juffer, 2006; Wierzbicki, 1993). Seven in eight report feeling strongly attached to one or both adoptive parents. As children of self-giving parents, they grow up to be more self-giving and altruistic than average (Sharma et al., 1998). Many score higher than their biological parents on intelligence tests, and most grow into happier and more stable adults. In one Swedish study, infant adoptees grew up with fewer problems than were experienced by children whose biological mothers had initially registered them for adoption but then decided to raise the children themselves (Bohman & Sigvardsson, 1990). Regardless of personality differences between parents and their adoptees, children benefit from adoption.

Temperament, Heredity, and Personality

3: **What is the relationship between temperament and personality?**

As most parents will tell you after having their second child, babies differ even before gulping their first breath. Heredity predisposes one quickly apparent aspect of personality—**temperament,** or emotional excitability (Rothbart, 2007). From their first weeks of life, some infants are reactive, intense, and fidgety. Others are easygoing, quiet, and placid. *Difficult* babies are more irritable, intense, and unpredictable. *Easy* babies are cheerful, relaxed, and predictable in feeding and sleeping.

temperament a person's characteristic emotional reactivity and intensity.

interaction the interplay that occurs when the effect of one factor (such as environment) depends on another factor (such as heredity).

Slow-to-warm-up infants tend to resist or withdraw from new people and situations (Chess & Thomas, 1987; Thomas & Chess, 1977).

Compared with fraternal twins, genetically identical twins have more similar temperaments. The genetic effect appears in one's physiology. Anxious, inhibited infants have high and variable heart rates and a reactive nervous system; when facing new or strange situations they become more physiologically aroused (Kagan & Snidman, 2004). Such temperament differences tend to persist. Consider:

- The most emotionally reactive newborns tend also to be the most reactive 9-month-olds (Wilson & Matheny, 1986; Worobey & Blajda, 1989).
- Exceptionally inhibited and fearful 2-year-olds often are still relatively shy as 8-year-olds; about half will become introverted adolescents (Kagan et al., 1992, 1994).
- The most emotionally intense preschoolers tend to be relatively intense young adults (Larsen & Diener, 1987). In one study of more than 900 New Zealanders, emotionally reactive and impulsive 3-year-olds developed into somewhat more impulsive, aggressive, and conflict-prone 21-year-olds (Caspi, 2000).

Such evidence adds to the emerging conclusion that our biologically rooted temperament provides building blocks for our enduring personality (McCrae et al., 2000, 2007; Rothbart et al., 2000).

"Oh, he's cute, all right, but he's got the temperament of a car alarm."

Gene-Environment Interactions

4: **How do genes and environments interact?**

Can we then assume that our personality is merely a product of our genes? No, because genes and environment—nature and nurture—work together like two hands clapping.

Among our similarities, the most important—the behavioral hallmark of our species—is our enormous adaptive capacity. Some human traits, such as having two eyes, develop the same in virtually every environment. But other traits are expressed only in particular environments. Go barefoot for a summer and you will develop toughened, callused feet—a biological adaptation to friction. Meanwhile, your shod neighbor will remain a tenderfoot. The difference between the two of you is, of course, an effect of environment. But it is also the product of a biological mechanism—adaptation. Our shared biology enables our developed diversity (Buss, 1991).

Genes are *self-regulating.* Rather than acting as blueprints that lead to the same result no matter the context, genes react. An African butterfly that is green in summer turns brown in fall, thanks to a temperature-controlled genetic switch. The genes that produce brown in one situation produce green in another. So, too, people with identical genes but differing experiences will have similar but not identical minds. One twin may fall in love with someone quite different from the co-twin's love.

Asking whether our personality is more a product of our genes or our environment is like asking whether the area of a field is more the result of its length or its width. We could, however, ask whether the differing areas of various fields are more the result of *differences* in their length or their width, and also whether person-to-person personality differences are influenced more by nature or nurture.

To say that genes and experience are *both* important is true. But more precisely, they **interact.** Imagine two babies, one genetically predisposed to be easy-going, sociable, and attractive, the other less so. Assume further that the first baby elicits more affectionate and stimulating care than the second and so develops into a warmer and more outgoing person. As the two children grow older, the more naturally outgoing child more often seeks activities and friends that encourage further social confidence.

"Men's natures are alike; it is their habits that carry them far apart."

—Confucius, *Analects,* 500 B.C.E.

"The title of my science project is 'My Little Brother: Nature or Nurture.'"

Gene-environment interaction People respond differently to a Will Ferrell (shown at left) than to fellow actor Zac Efron, (right).

"Heredity deals the cards; environment plays the hand."

—Psychologist Charles L. Brewer (1990)

"I thought that sperm-bank donors remained anonymous."

What has caused their resulting personality differences? Neither heredity nor experience dances alone. Environments trigger gene activity. (Scientists are now exploring environmental influences on when particular genes generate proteins.) Our genetically influenced traits—the other partner in the dance—also *evoke* significant responses in others. Thus, a child's impulsivity and aggression may evoke an angry response from a teacher who otherwise reacts warmly to the child's model classmates. Parents, too, may treat their own children differently; one child elicits punishment, another does not. In such cases, the child's nature and the parents' nurture interact. Neither operates apart from the other. Gene and scene dance together.

Evocative interactions may help explain why identical twins reared in different families recall their parents' warmth as remarkably similar—almost as similar as if they had had the same parents (Plomin et al., 1988, 1991, 1994). Fraternal twins have more differing recollections of their early family life—even if reared in the same family! "Children experience us as different parents, depending on their own qualities," noted Sandra Scarr (1990). Moreover, a *selection effect* may be at work. As we grow older we select environments well suited to our natures.

So, from conception onward, we are the product of a cascade of interactions between our genetic predispositions and our surrounding environments. Depending on our traits, we actively select certain environments. And we evoke reactions from our environments. Thus, our genes affect how people react to and influence us. Biological traits have social consequences. So, forget nature *versus* nurture; think nature *via* nurture.

REHEARSE IT!

1. The threadlike structures made largely of DNA molecules are called
   a. gene complexes.
   b. nuclei.
   c. chromosomes.
   d. cells.

2. When the mother's egg and the father's sperm unite, each contributes
   a. one chromosome pair.
   b. 23 chromosomes.
   c. 23 chromosome pairs.
   d. 30,000 chromosomes.

3. Fraternal twins result when
   a. a single egg is fertilized by a single sperm and then splits.

   b. a single egg is fertilized by two sperm and then splits.
   c. two eggs are fertilized by two sperm.
   d. two eggs are fertilized by a single sperm.

4. Adoption studies seek to understand genetic influences on personality. They do this mainly by
   a. comparing adopted children with nonadopted children.
   b. evaluating whether adopted children's personalities more closely resemble those of their adoptive parents or their biological parents.
   c. studying the effect of prior neglect on adopted children.

   d. studying the effect of children's age at adoption.

5. Personality tends to be stable over time. For example,
   a. temperament is a product of learning and can therefore be unlearned.
   b. temperament seems to be biologically based and tends to remain stable throughout life.
   c. temperament changes significantly during adolescence.
   d. fraternal twins tend to have more similar temperaments than do identical twins.

Answers: 1. c, 2. b, 3. c, 4. b, 5. b.

Evolutionary Psychology: Understanding Human Nature

5: How do evolutionary psychologists use natural selection to explain behavior tendencies?

Behavior geneticists explore the genetic and environmental roots of human differences. **Evolutionary psychologists** instead focus mostly on what makes us so much alike as humans. They use Charles Darwin's principle of **natural selection** to understand the roots of behavior and mental processes. Richard Dawkins (2007) calls natural selection "arguably the most momentous idea ever to occur to a human mind." The idea, simplified, is this:

- Organisms' varied offspring compete for survival.
- Certain biological and behavioral variations increase their reproductive and survival chances in their environment.
- Offspring that survive are more likely to pass their genes to ensuing generations.
- Thus, over time, population characteristics may change.

To see these principles at work, let's consider a straightforward example in foxes.

Natural Selection and Adaptation

A fox is a wild and wary animal. If you capture a fox and try to befriend it, be careful. Stick your hand in the cage and, if the timid fox cannot flee, it may make a snack of your fingers. Dmitry Belyaev, of the Russian Academy of Science's Institute of Cytology and Genetics, wondered how our human ancestors had domesticated dogs from their equally wild wolf forebears. Might he, within a comparatively short stretch of time, accomplish a similar feat by transforming the fearful fox into a friendly fox?

To find out, Belyaev set to work with 30 male and 100 female foxes. From their offspring he selected and mated the tamest 5 percent of males and 20 percent of females. (He measured tameness by the foxes' responses to attempts to feed, handle, and stroke them.) Over more than 30 generations of foxes, Belyaev and his successor, Lyudmila Trut, repeated that simple procedure. Forty years and 45,000 foxes later, they had a new breed of foxes that, in Trut's (1999) words, are "docile, eager to please, and unmistakably domesticated. . . . Before our eyes, 'the Beast' has turned into 'beauty,' as the aggressive behavior of our herd's wild [ancestors] entirely disappeared." So friendly and eager for human contact are they, so inclined to whimper to attract attention and to lick people like affectionate dogs, that the cash-strapped institute seized on a way to raise funds—marketing its foxes to people as house pets.

When certain traits are *selected*—by conferring a reproductive advantage to an individual or a species—those traits, over time, will prevail. Dog breeders, as Robert Plomin and his colleagues (1997) remind us, have given us sheepdogs that herd, retrievers that retrieve, trackers that track, and pointers that point. Psychologists, too, have bred dogs, mice, and rats whose genes predispose them to be serene or reactive, quick learners or slow.

Does natural selection also explain our human tendencies? Nature has indeed selected advantageous variations from among the new gene combinations produced at each human conception and the **mutations** (random errors in gene replication) that sometimes result. But the tight genetic leash that predisposes a dog's retrieving, a cat's pouncing, or an ant's nest building is looser on humans. The genes selected during our ancestral history provide more than a long leash; they endow us with a great capacity to learn and therefore to *adapt* to life in varied environments, from the tundra to the jungle. Genes and experience together wire the brain. Our adaptive flexibility in responding to different environments contributes to our *fitness*—our ability to survive and reproduce.

evolutionary psychology the study of the roots of behavior and mental processes, using the principles of natural selection.

natural selection the principle that, among the range of inherited trait variations, those that lead to increased reproduction and survival will most likely be passed on to succeeding generations.

mutation a random error in gene replication that leads to a change.

From wary to winsome More than 40 years into the fox-breeding experiment, most of the offspring are devoted, affectionate, and capable of forming strong bonds with people.

L. N. Trut, American Scientist (1999) 87: 160–169

Evolutionary Success Helps Explain Similarities

Although human differences grab our attention, our deep similarities also demand explanation. And in the big picture, our lives are remarkably alike. Visit the international arrivals area at Amsterdam's Schipol Airport, a world hub where arriving passengers meet their excited loved ones. There you will see the same delighted joy in the faces of Indonesian grandmothers, Chinese children, and homecoming Dutch. Evolutionary psychologist Steven Pinker (2002, p. 73) believes it is no wonder that our emotions, drives, and reasoning "have a common logic across cultures." Our shared human traits "were shaped by natural selection acting over the course of human evolution."

Our Genetic Legacy

Our behavioral and biological similarities arise from our shared human *genome,* our common genetic profile. No more than 5 percent of the genetic differences among humans arise from population group differences. Some 95 percent of genetic variation exists *within* populations (Rosenberg et al., 2002). The typical genetic difference between two Icelandic villagers or between two Kenyans is much greater than the *average* difference between the two groups. Thus, noted geneticist Richard Lewontin (1982), if after a worldwide catastrophe only Icelanders or Kenyans survived, the human species would suffer only "a trivial reduction" in its genetic diversity.

Despite high infant mortality and rampant disease in past millennia, not one of your countless ancestors died childless.

And how did we develop this shared human genome? At the dawn of human history, our ancestors faced certain questions: Who is my ally, who my foe? What food should I eat? With whom should I mate? Some individuals answered those questions more successfully than others. For example, women who experienced nausea in the critical first three months of pregnancy were predisposed to avoid certain bitter, strongly flavored, and novel foods. Avoiding such foods has survival value, since they are the very foods most often toxic to embryonic development (Schmitt & Pilcher, 2004). Early humans disposed to eat nourishing rather than poisonous foods survived to contribute their genes to later generations. Those who deemed leopards "nice to pet" often did not.

Similarly successful were those whose mating helped them produce and nurture offspring. Over generations, the genes of individuals not so disposed tended to be lost from the human gene pool. As genes contributing to success continued to be selected, behavioral tendencies and thinking and learning capacities emerged that prepared our Stone Age ancestors to survive, reproduce, and send their genes into the future.

As inheritors of this prehistoric genetic legacy, we are predisposed to behave in ways that promoted our ancestors' surviving and reproducing. We love the taste of sweets and fats, which once were hard to come by but which prepared our ancestors to survive famines. With famine now rare in Western cultures, and sweets and fats beckoning us from store shelves, fast-food outlets, and vending machines, obesity has become a growing problem. Our natural dispositions, rooted deep in history, are mismatched with today's junk-food environment (Colarelli & Dettman, 2003). We are, in some ways, biologically prepared for a world that no longer exists.

Evolutionary Psychology Today

Those who are troubled by an apparent conflict between scientific and religious accounts of human origins may find it helpful to recall (Chapter 1) that different perspectives of life can be complementary. For example, the scientific account attempts to tell us when and how; religious creation stories usually aim to tell about an ultimate who and why. As Galileo explained to the Grand Duchess Christina, "The Bible teaches how to go to heaven, not how the heavens go."

Darwin's theory of evolution has been an organizing principle for biology for a long time. As Jared Diamond (2001) noted, "Virtually no contemporary scientists believe that Darwin was basically wrong." Today, Darwin's theory lives on in the *second Darwinian revolution*: the application of evolutionary principles to psychology. In concluding *On the Origin of Species*, Darwin (1859, p. 346) anticipated this revolution, foreseeing "open fields for far more important researches. Psychology will be based on a new foundation."

Evolutionary psychologists have addressed questions such as these:

- Why do infants start to fear strangers about the time they become mobile?
- Why are biological fathers so much less likely than unrelated boyfriends to abuse and murder the children with whom they share a home?
- Why do so many more people have phobias about spiders, snakes, and heights than about more dangerous threats, such as guns and electricity?
- Why do humans share some universal moral ideas?
- How are men and women alike? How and why do men's and women's sexuality differ?

We will consider such questions in later chapters. To see how evolutionary psychologists think and reason, let's pause now to explore that last question.

gender in psychology, the biologically and socially influenced characteristics by which people define *male* and *female*.

An Evolutionary Explanation of Human Sexuality

6: **How might an evolutionary psychologist explain gender differences in mating preferences?**

Having faced many similar challenges throughout history, men and women have adapted in similar ways. Whether male or female, we eat the same foods, avoid the same predators, and perceive, learn, and remember similarly. It is only in those domains where we have faced differing adaptive challenges—most obviously in behaviors related to reproduction—that we differ, say evolutionary psychologists.

Gender Differences in Sexuality

And differ we do. Psychologists Roy Baumeister, Kathleen Catanese, and Kathleen Vohs (2001) invite us to consider who desires more frequent sex, thinks more about sex, masturbates more often, initiates more sex, and sacrifices more to gain sex? The answers, they report, are *men, men, men, men,* and *men.* No surprise, then, that in one BBC survey of more than 200,000 people in 53 nations, men everywhere more strongly agreed that "I have a strong sex drive" and "It doesn't take much to get me sexually excited" (Lippa, 2008).

Indeed, "with few exceptions anywhere in the world," reported cross-cultural psychologist Marshall Segall and his colleagues (1990, p. 244), "males are more likely than females to initiate sexual activity." This is among the largest of **gender** differences in sexuality (Regan & Atkins, 2007). Consider:

- In a survey of 289,452 entering U.S. college students, 58 percent of men but only 34 percent of women agreed that "if two people really like each other, it's all right for them to have sex even if they've known each other for a very short time" (Pryor et al., 2005). "I can imagine myself being comfortable and enjoying 'casual' sex with different partners," agreed 48 percent of men and 12 percent of women in a survey of 4901 Australians (Bailey et al., 2000).
- In another survey of 3432 U.S. 18- to 59-year-olds, 48 percent of the women but only 25 percent of the men cited affection as a reason for first intercourse. And how often do they think about sex? "Every day" or "Several times a day," acknowledged 19 percent of the women and 54 percent of the men (Laumann et al., 1994). Ditto for the sexual thoughts of Canadians: "Several times a day," agreed 11 percent of women and 46 percent of men (Fischtein et al., 2007).
- In surveys, gay men (like straight men) report more interest in uncommitted sex, more responsiveness to visual sexual stimuli, and more concern with their partner's physical attractiveness than do lesbian women (Bailey et al., 1994; Doyle, 2005; Schmitt, 2007).

"Not tonight, hon, I have a concussion."

"It's not that gay men are oversexed; they are simply men whose male desires bounce off other male desires rather than off female desires."

—Steven Pinker, *How the Mind Works,* 1997

Natural Selection and Mating Preferences

Evolutionary psychologists use natural selection to explain why—worldwide—women's approach to sex is usually more relational, and men's more recreational (Schmitt, 2005, 2007). Their explanation goes like this: While a woman usually incubates and nurses one infant at a time, a man can spread his genes through other females. Our natural yearnings are our genes' way of reproducing themselves. In our ancestral history, women most often sent their genes into the future by pairing wisely, men by pairing widely. "Humans are living fossils—collections of mechanisms produced by prior selection pressures," said evolutionary psychologist David Buss (1995).

And what do heterosexual men and women find attractive in a mate? Some desired traits, such as a woman's youthful appearance (**FIGURE 4.3**), cross place and time (Buss, 1994). Evolutionary psychologists say that men who were drawn to healthy, fertile-appearing women—women with smooth skin and a youthful shape suggesting many childbearing years to come—stood a better chance of sending their genes into the future. Moreover, men are most attracted to women who, in the ancestral past (when ovulation began later than today), were at ages associated with peak fertility (Kenrick et al., in press). Thus, teen boys are most excited by a woman several years older than themselves. Mid-twenties men prefer women around their own age. And older men prefer younger women. This pattern consistently appears across European singles ads, Indian marital ads, and marriage records from North and South America, Africa, and the Philippines (Singh, 1993; Singh & Randall, 2007).

Women, in turn, prefer stick-around dads over likely cads. They are attracted to men who seem mature, dominant, bold, and affluent, with a potential for long-term mating and investment in their joint offspring (Gangestad & Simpson, 2000; Singh, 1995). From an evolutionary perspective, such attributes connote a capacity to support and protect (Buss, 1996, 2000; Geary, 1998).

There is a principle at work here, say evolutionary psychologists: Nature selects behaviors that increase the likelihood of sending one's genes into the future. As mobile gene machines, we are designed to prefer whatever worked for our ancestors in their environments. They were predisposed to act in ways that would leave grandchildren—had they not been, we wouldn't be here. And as carriers of their genetic legacy, we are similarly predisposed.

Without disputing nature's selection of traits that enhance gene survival, critics see problems with this explanation of human sexuality. They believe that the evolutionary perspective overlooks some important influences on human sexuality (see Thinking Critically About: The Evolutionary Perspective on Human Sexuality).

"What about you, Walter—how do you feel about same-age marriage?"

"I had a nice time, Steve. Would you like to come in, settle down, and raise a family?"

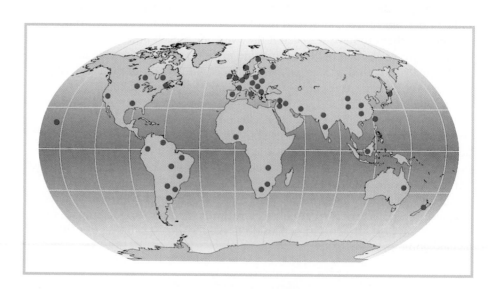

FIGURE 4.3 Worldwide mating preferences In a wide range of cultures studied (indicated by the red dots), men more than women preferred physical features suggesting youth and health—and reproductive potential. Women more than men preferred mates with resources and social status. Researchers credit (or blame) natural selection (Buss, 1994).

Thinking Critically About:

The Evolutionary Perspective on Human Sexuality

7: What are the key criticisms of the evolutionary perspective on human sexuality?

Evolutionary psychology, say some critics, starts with an effect (such as the gender sexuality difference) and works backward to propose an explanation. They invite us to imagine a different result and reason backward. If men were uniformly loyal to their mates, might we not reason that the children of these committed, supportive fathers would more often survive to perpetuate their genes? Might not men also be better off bonded to one woman—both to increase their odds of impregnation and to keep her from the advances of competing men? Might not a ritualized bond—a marriage—also spare women from chronic male harassment? Such suggestions are, in fact, evolutionary explanations for why humans tend to pair off monogamously. One can hardly lose at hindsight explanation, which is, said paleontologist Stephen Jay Gould (1997), mere "speculation [and] guesswork in the cocktail party mode."

Some also worry about the social consequences of evolutionary psychology. Does it suggest a genetic determinism that strikes at the heart of progressive efforts to remake society (Rose, 1999)? Does it undercut moral responsibility? Could it be used to rationalize "high-status men marrying a series of young, fertile women" (Looy, 2001)?

Others argue that evolutionary explanations blur the line between genetic legacy and social-cultural traditions relating to mate preferences. Show Wendy Wood and Alice Eagly (2002, 2007) a culture with gender inequality—where men are providers and women are homemakers—and they will show you a culture where men strongly desire youth and domestic skill in their potential mates, and where women seek status and earning potential in their mates. Show Wood and Eagly a culture with gender equality, and they will show you a culture with smaller gender differences in mate preferences.

Much of who we are is not hard-wired, agree evolutionary psychologists. They reassure us that men and women, having faced similar adaptive problems, are far

more alike than different, and that humans have a great capacity for learning and social progress. (We come equipped to adapt and survive, whether living in igloos or tree houses.) Further, they agree that what's considered attractive does vary somewhat with time and place. The voluptuous Marilyn Monroe ideal of the 1950s has been replaced by a leaner (yet still curvy) athletic image in the twenty-first-century. Cultural expectations can bend the genders. If socialized to value lifelong commitment, men may sexually bond with one partner; if socialized to accept casual sex, women may willingly have sex with many partners.

Even granting all that, the evolutionary psychologists point to the coherence and explanatory power of evolutionary principles, especially those offering testable predictions (for example, that we will favor others to the extent that they share our genes or can later reciprocate our favors). Moreover, they remind us that the study of how we came to be need not dictate how we ought to be. Understanding our propensities sometimes helps us overcome them.

REHEARSE IT!

6. Evolutionary psychologists are most likely to focus on
   a. how we differ from one another.
   b. the links between social expectations and behavior.
   c. natural selection of the fittest adaptations.
   d. random assignment of genes over several generations.

Answer: 6. c.

Parents and Peers

8: To what extent are our lives shaped by early stimulation, by parents, and by peers?

We have seen how our genes, as expressed in specific environments, influence our developmental differences. We are not "blank slates," note Douglas Kenrick and his colleagues (in press). We are more like coloring books, with certain lines predisposed and experience filling in our picture. We are formed by nature and nurture. But what are the most influential components of our nurture? How do our early experiences, our family and peer relationships, and all our other experiences guide our development and contribute to our diversity?

Parents and Early Experiences

The formative nurture that conspires with nature begins at conception, with the prenatal environment in the womb, as embryos receive differing nutrition and varying levels of exposure to toxic agents (more on this in Chapter 5). Nurture then continues outside the womb, where our early experiences foster brain development.

Experience and Brain Development

Our genes dictate our overall brain architecture, but experience fills in the details, developing neural connections and preparing our brain for thought and language and other later experiences. So how do early experiences leave their "marks" in the brain? Mark Rosenzweig and David Krech opened a window on that process when they raised some young rats in solitary confinement and others in a communal playground. When they later analyzed the rats' brains, those who died with the most toys had won. The rats living in the enriched environment, which simulated a natural environment, usually developed a heavier and thicker brain cortex (**FIGURE 4.4**).

Rosenzweig was so surprised by this discovery that he repeated the experiment several times before publishing his findings (Renner & Rosenzweig, 1987; Rosenzweig, 1984). So great are the effects that, shown brief video clips of rats, you could tell from their activity and curiosity whether their environment had been impoverished or enriched (Renner & Renner, 1993). Bryan Kolb and Ian Whishaw (1998) noted extraordinary changes after 60 days in the enriched environment; the rats' brain weights increased 7 to 10 percent and the number of synapses mushroomed by about 20 percent.

Such results have motivated improvements in environments for laboratory, farm, and zoo animals—and for children in institutions. Stimulation by touch or massage also benefits infant rats and premature babies (Field et al., 2007). "Handled" infants of both species develop faster neurologically and gain weight more rapidly. By giving preemies massage therapy, neonatal intensive care units now help them to go home sooner (Field et al., 2006).

Both nature and nurture sculpt our synapses. After brain maturation provides us with an abundance of neural connections, our experiences trigger a *pruning process*. Sights and smells, touches and tugs activate connections and strengthen them. Unused neural pathways weaken and degenerate. Similar to pathways through a forest, popular paths are broadened and less-traveled paths gradually disappear. The result by puberty is a massive loss of unemployed connections.

Here at the juncture of nurture and nature is the biological reality of early childhood learning. During early childhood—while excess connections are still on call—youngsters can most easily master such skills as the grammar and accent of another language. Lacking any exposure to language before adolescence, a person will never master any language (see Chapter 9).

Stringing the circuits young String musicians who started playing before age 12 have larger and more complex neural circuits controlling the note-making left-hand fingers than do string musicians whose training started later (Elbert et al., 1995).

FIGURE 4.4 Experience affects brain development Mark Rosenzweig and David Krech raised rats either alone in an environment without playthings, or with other rats in an environment enriched with playthings changed daily. In 14 of 16 repetitions of this basic experiment, rats in the enriched environment developed significantly more cerebral cortex (relative to the rest of the brain's tissue) than did those in the impoverished environment.

Impoverished environment | Impoverished rat brain cell | Enriched environment | Enriched rat brain cell

FIGURE 4.5 A trained brain A well-learned finger-tapping task activates more motor cortex neurons (orange area, right) than were active in the same brain before training (left). (From Karni et al., 1998.)

Likewise, lacking visual experience during the early years, people whose vision is later restored by cataract removal never achieve normal perceptions (see Chapter 6). The brain cells normally assigned to vision have died or been diverted to other uses. The brain's rule: Use it or lose it.

Although normal stimulation during the early years is critical, our brain's development does not end with childhood. As we saw in Chapter 2's discussion of brain plasticity, our neural tissue is ever changing. If a monkey is trained to push a lever with a finger several thousand times a day, the brain tissue controlling that finger will change to reflect the experience. Human brains work similarly (**FIGURE 4.5**). Whether learning to keyboard or skateboard, we perform with increasing skill as our brain incorporates the learning.

How Much Credit (or Blame) Do Parents Deserve?

In procreation, a woman and a man shuffle their gene decks and deal a life-forming hand to their child-to-be, who is then subjected to countless influences beyond their control. Parents, nonetheless, feel enormous satisfaction in their children's successes, and feel guilt or shame over their failures. They beam over the child who wins an award. They wonder where they went wrong with the child who is repeatedly called into the principal's office. Freudian psychiatry and psychology have been among the sources of such ideas, by blaming problems from asthma to schizophrenia on "bad mothering." Society reinforces such parent-blaming: Believing that parents shape their offspring as a potter molds clay, people readily praise parents for their children's virtues and blame them for their children's vices. Popular culture endlessly proclaims the psychological harm toxic parenting inflicts on fragile children. No wonder having and raising children can seem so risky.

But do parents really produce future adults with an inner wounded child by being (take your pick from the toxic-parenting lists) overbearing—or uninvolved? Pushy—or ineffectual? Overprotective—or distant? Are children really so easily wounded? If so, should we then blame our parents for our failings, and ourselves for our children's failings? Or does all the talk of wounding fragile children through normal parental mistakes trivialize the brutality of real abuse?

Parents do matter. The power of parenting to shape our differences is clearest at the extremes. Chapter 5 will provide the sharpest examples—the abused who become abusive, the neglected who become neglectful, the loved but firmly handled children who become self-confident and socially competent. And, as we saw earlier in the discussion of adoptive parenting, the power of the family environment frequently shows up in children's political attitudes, religious beliefs, and personal manners. It appears in the remarkable academic and vocational successes of children of the refugee "boat people" fleeing Vietnam and Cambodia—successes attributed to close-knit, supportive, even demanding families (Caplan et al., 1992).

"Genes and experiences are just two ways of doing the same thing— wiring synapses."

—Joseph LeDoux, *The Synaptic Self,* 2002

Even among chimpanzees, when one infant is hurt by another, the victim's mother will often attack the offender's mother (Goodall, 1968).

"So I blame you for everything— whose fault is that?"

Yet in personality measures, shared environmental influences—including, as we have seen, the home influences siblings share—typically account for less than 10 percent of children's differences. In the words of behavior geneticists Robert Plomin and Denise Daniels (1987), "Two children in the same family [are on average] as different from one another as are pairs of children selected randomly from the population." To developmental psychologist Sandra Scarr (1993), this implied that "parents should be given less credit for kids who turn out great and blamed less for kids who don't." Knowing children are not easily sculpted by parental nurture, perhaps parents can relax a bit more and love their children for who they are.

Peer Influence

As children mature, what other experiences do the work of nurturing? At all ages, but especially during childhood and adolescence, we seek to fit in with groups and are subject to group influences.

Consider the power of peers (Harris, 1998, 2000):

- Preschoolers who disdain a certain food often will eat that food if put at a table with a group of children who like it.
- Children who hear English spoken with one accent at home and another in the neighborhood and at school will invariably adopt the accent of their peers, not their parents. Accents (and slang) reflect culture, "and children get their culture from their peers," notes Judith Rich Harris (2007).
- Teens who start smoking typically have friends who model smoking, suggest its pleasures, and offer cigarettes (Rose et al., 1999, 2003). Part of this peer similarity may result from a selection effect, as kids seek out peers with similar attitudes and interests. Those who smoke (or don't) may select as friends those who also smoke (or don't).

Howard Gardner (1998) has concluded that parents and peers are complementary:

> Parents are more important when it comes to education, discipline, responsibility, orderliness, charitableness, and ways of interacting with authority figures. Peers are more important for learning cooperation, for finding the road to popularity, for inventing styles of interaction among people of the same age. Youngsters may find their peers more interesting, but they will look to their parents when contemplating their own futures. Moreover, parents [often] choose the neighborhoods and schools that supply the peers.

As Gardner points out, parents can influence the culture that shapes the peer group, by helping to select their children's neighborhood and schools. And because

> "If you want to blame your parents for your own adult problems, you are entitled to blame the genes they gave you, but you are not entitled— by any facts I know—to blame the way they treated you. . . . We are not prisoners of our past."
>
> —Martin Seligman, *What You Can Change and What You Can't,* 1994

> "Men resemble the times more than they resemble their fathers."
>
> —Ancient Arab proverb

Peer power As we develop, we play, mate, and partner with peers. No wonder children and youths are so sensitive and responsive to peer influences.

neighborhood influences matter, parents may want to become involved in youth intervention programs aiming at a whole school or neighborhood. If the vapors of a toxic climate are seeping into a child's life, that climate—not just the child—needs reforming. Even so, peers are but one medium of cultural influence.

> "It takes a village to raise a child."
>
> —African proverb

REHEARSE IT!

7. Normal levels of stimulation are important during infancy and early childhood because during these years,
   a. a rich environment can override a child's genetic limits.
   b. experience stimulates the growth of billions of new brain cells.
   c. experience activates and preserves neural connections that might otherwise die from disuse.
   d. experience triggers the rapid development and production of human growth hormones.

8. Children and youth are particularly responsive to influences of their
   a. peers.
   b. fathers.
   c. teachers and caretakers.
   d. mothers.

Answers: 7. c, 8. a.

Cultural Influences

9: **How do cultural norms affect our behavior?**

Compared with the narrow path taken by flies, fish, and foxes, the road along which environment drives us is wider. The mark of our species—nature's great gift to us—is our ability to learn and adapt. We come equipped with a huge cerebral hard drive ready to receive many gigabytes of cultural software.

Culture is the behaviors, ideas, attitudes, values, and traditions shared by a group of people and transmitted from one generation to the next (Brislin, 1988). Human nature, notes Roy Baumeister (2005), seems designed for culture. We are social animals, but more. Wolves are social animals; they live and hunt in packs. Ants are incessantly social, never alone. But "culture is a better way of being social," notes Baumeister. Wolves function pretty much as they did 10,000 years ago. You and I enjoy things unknown to most of our century-ago ancestors, including electricity, indoor plumbing, antibiotics, and the Internet. Culture works.

As we will see in Chapter 9, primates exhibit the rudiments of culture, with local customs of tool use, grooming, and courtship. Younger chimpanzees and macaque monkeys sometimes invent local customs (potato washing, in one famous example) and pass them on to their peers and offspring. But human culture does more. It supports our species' survival and reproduction by enabling social, educational, and economic systems that give us an edge. Having learned economic lessons from the 1930s Great Depression, governments worked to avoid another in 2009.

Thanks to our mastery of language, we humans enjoy the *preservation of innovation*. Within the span of this day, I have, thanks to my culture, made good use of Post-it Notes, Google, and a single-shot skinny latte. On a grander scale, we have culture's accumulated knowledge to thank for the last century's 30-year extension of the average life expectancy in most countries where this book is being read. Moreover, culture enables an efficient *division of labor*. Although one lucky person gets his name on this book's cover, the product actually results from the coordination and commitment of a team of women and men, no one of whom could produce it alone.

Across cultures, we differ in our language, our monetary systems, our sports, which fork—if any—we eat with, even which side of the road we drive on. But beneath these differences is our great similarity—our capacity for culture. Culture provides the shared and transmitted customs and beliefs that enable us to communicate, to exchange money for things, to play, to eat, and to drive with agreed-upon

culture the enduring behaviors, ideas, attitudes, values, and traditions shared by a group of people and transmitted from one generation to the next.

rules and without crashing into one another. This shared capacity for culture enables our striking group differences. Human nature manifests human diversity.

If we all lived in homogeneous ethnic groups in separate regions of the world, as some people still do, cultural diversity would be less relevant. In Japan, almost 99 percent of the country's 127 million people are of Japanese descent. Internal cultural differences are therefore minimal compared with those found in Los Angeles, where the public schools recently taught 82 different languages, or in Toronto or Vancouver, where minorities are one-third of the population and many are immigrants (as are 13.4 percent of all Canadians and 23 percent of Australians) (Axiss, 2007; Statistics Canada, 2002). I am ever mindful that the readers of this book are culturally diverse. You and your ancestors reach from Australia to Africa and from Singapore to Sweden.

Variation Across Cultures

We see our adaptability in cultural variations among our beliefs and our values, in how we raise our children and bury our dead, and in what we wear (or whether we wear anything at all). Riding along with a unified culture is like biking with the wind: As it carries us along, we hardly notice it is there. When we try riding *against* the wind we feel its force. Face to face with a different culture, we become aware of the cultural winds. Visiting Europe, most North Americans notice the smaller cars, the left-handed use of the fork, the uninhibited attire on the beaches. Stationed in Iraq, Afghanistan, and Kuwait, American and European soldiers alike realized how liberal their home cultures were. Arriving in North America, visitors from Japan and India struggle to understand why so many people wear their dirty *street* shoes in the house.

Each cultural group evolves its own **norms**—rules for accepted and expected behavior. Many South Asians have a norm for eating only with the right hand's fingers. The British have a norm for orderly waiting in line. Sometimes social expectations seem oppressive: "Why should it matter how I dress?" Yet, norms grease the social machinery and free us from self-preoccupation. Knowing when to clap or bow, which fork to pick up first at a dinner party, and what sorts of gestures and compliments are appropriate—whether to greet people by shaking hands or kissing each cheek, for example—we can relax and enjoy one another without fear of embarrassment or insult.

When cultures collide, their differing norms often befuddle. For example, if someone invades our **personal space**—the portable buffer zone we like to maintain around our bodies—we feel uncomfortable. Scandinavians, North Americans, and the British have traditionally preferred more personal space than do Latin Americans, Arabs, and the French (Sommer, 1969). At a social gathering, a Mexican seeking a comfortable conversation distance may end up walking around a room with a backpedaling Canadian. (You can experience this at a party by playing Space Invader as you talk with someone.) To the Canadian, the Mexican may seem intrusive; to the Mexican, the Canadian may seem standoffish.

Cultures also vary in their expressiveness. Those with roots in northern European culture have perceived people from Mediterranean cultures as warm and charming but inefficient. The Mediterraneans, in turn, have seen northern Europeans as efficient but cold and preoccupied with punctuality (Triandis, 1981).

Cultures vary in their pace of life, too. People from time-conscious Japan—where bank clocks keep exact time, pedestrians walk briskly, and postal clerks fill requests speedily—may find themselves growing impatient when visiting Indonesia, where clocks keep less accurate time and the pace of life is more leisurely (Levine & Norenzayan, 1999). In adjusting to their host countries, the first wave of U.S. Peace Corps volunteers reported that two of their greatest culture shocks, after the language differences, were the differing pace of life and the people's differing sense of punctuality (Spradley & Phillips, 1972).

Cultures differ Behavior seen as appropriate in one culture may violate the norms of another group. In Arab societies, but not in Western cultures, heterosexual men often greet one another with a kiss.

Annie Griffiths Belt/Corbis

Variation Over Time

Consider, too, how rapidly cultures may change over time. English poet Geoffrey Chaucer (1342–1400) is separated from a modern Briton by only 20 generations, but the two would converse with great difficulty. In the thin slice of history since 1960, most Western cultures have changed with remarkable speed. Middle-class people fly to places they once only read about, work in air-conditioned comfort where they once sweltered, and enjoy the convenience of anywhere-anytime electronic communication with those they once snail-mailed. With greater economic independence, today's women are more likely to marry for love and less likely to endure abusive relationships out of economic need.

But some changes seem not so wonderfully positive. Had you fallen asleep in the United States in 1960 and awakened today, you would open your eyes to a culture with more divorce, delinquency, and depression. You would also find North Americans—like their counterparts in Britain, Australia, and New Zealand—spending more hours at work, fewer hours sleeping, and fewer hours with friends and family (Frank, 1999; Putnam, 2000).

Whether we love or loathe these changes, we cannot fail to be impressed by their breathtaking speed. And we cannot explain them by changes in the human gene pool, which evolves far too slowly to account for high-speed cultural transformations. Cultures vary. Cultures change. And cultures shape our lives.

Culture and the Self

10: How do individualist and collectivist cultural influences affect people?

Cultures vary in the extent to which they give priority to the nurturing and expression of personal identity or group identity. To grasp the difference, imagine that someone were to rip away your social connections, making you a solitary refugee in a foreign land. How much of your identity would remain intact?

If as our solitary traveler you pride yourself on your **individualism,** a great deal of your identity would remain intact—the very core of your being, the sense of "me," the awareness of your personal convictions and values. Individualists (often people from North America, Western Europe, Australia, or New Zealand) give relatively greater priority to personal goals and define their identity mostly in terms of personal attributes (Schimmack et al., 2005). They strive for personal control and individual achievement. In American culture, with its relatively big "I" and small "we," 85 percent of people say it is possible "to pretty much be who you want to be" (Sampson, 2000).

Individualists share the human need to belong. They join groups, but they are less focused on group harmony and doing their duty to the group (Brewer & Chen, 2007). And being more self-contained, they more easily move in and out of groups. They feel relatively free to switch places of worship, leave one job for another, or even leave their extended families and migrate to a new place. Marriage is often for as long as they both shall love.

If set adrift in a foreign land as a **collectivist,** you might experience a greater loss of identity. Cut off from family, groups, and loyal friends, you would lose the connections that have defined who you are. In a collectivist culture, group identifications provide a sense of belonging, a set of values, a network of caring individuals, an assurance of security. In return, collectivists have deeper, more stable attachments to their groups, often their family, clan, or company. In South Korea, for example, people place less value on expressing a consistent, unique self-concept, and more on tradition and shared practices (Choi & Choi, 2002).

Valuing communal solidarity, people in collectivist cultures place a premium on preserving group spirit and making sure others never lose face. What people say

norm an understood rule for accepted and expected behavior. Norms prescribe "proper" behavior.

personal space the buffer zone we like to maintain around our bodies.

individualism giving priority to one's own goals over group goals and defining one's identity in terms of personal attributes rather than group identifications.

collectivism giving priority to group goals (often those of the extended family or work group) and defining one's identity accordingly.

reflects not only what they feel (their inner attitudes) but what they presume others feel (Kashima et al., 1992). Avoiding direct confrontation, blunt honesty, and uncomfortable topics, people often defer to others' wishes and display a polite, self-effacing humility (Markus & Kitayama, 1991). Elders and superiors receive respect, and duty to family may trump personal career preferences. In new groups, collectivists may be shy and more easily embarrassed than are individualist Westerners (Singelis et al., 1995, 1999). People in Japanese and Chinese cultures, for example, exhibit greater shyness toward strangers and greater concern for social harmony and loyalty (Bond, 1988; Cheek & Melchior, 1990; Triandis, 1994). When the priority is "we," not "me," that individualized latte—"decaf, single shot, skinny, extra hot"—that feels so good to a North American in a coffee shop might sound more like a selfish demand in Seoul (Kim & Markus, 1999).

To be sure, there is diversity within cultures. Even in the most individualistic countries, some people manifest collectivist values. But in general, people (especially men) in competitive, individualist cultures have more personal freedom, are less geographically bound to their families, enjoy more privacy, and take more pride in personal achievements (**TABLE 4.1**). During the 2000 and 2002 Olympic games, U.S. gold medal winners and the U.S. media covering them attributed the achievements mostly to the athletes themselves (Markus et al., 2006). "I think I just stayed focused," explained swimming gold medalist Misty Hyman. "It was time to show the world what I could do. I am just glad I was able to do it." Japan's gold medalist in the women's marathon, Naoko Takahashi, had a different explanation: "Here is the best coach in the world, the best manager in the world, and all of the people who support me—all of these things were getting together and became a gold medal." Even in describing friends, Westerners tend to use trait-describing adjectives ("she is helpful"), whereas East Asians more often use verbs that describe behaviors in context ("she helps her friends") (Maass et al., 2006).

Individualism's benefits can come at the cost of more loneliness, more divorce, more homicide, and more stress-related disease (Popenoe, 1993; Triandis et al., 1988). Demands for more romance and personal fulfillment in marriage can subject relationships to more pressure (Dion & Dion, 1993). In one survey, "keeping romance alive" was rated as important to a good marriage by 78 percent of U.S. women but only 29 percent of Japanese women (*American Enterprise*, 1992). In China, love songs often express enduring commitment and friendship (Rothbaum & Tsang, 1998). As one song put it, "We will be together from now on. . . . I will never change from now to forever."

> "One needs to cultivate the spirit of sacrificing the *little me* to achieve the benefits of the *big me.*"
>
> —Chinese saying

Uniform requirements People in individualist Western cultures sometimes see traditional Japanese culture as confining. But from the Japanese perspective, the same tradition may express a "serenity that comes to people who know exactly what to expect from each other" (Weisz et al., 1984).

TABLE 4.1 **Value Contrasts Between Individualism and Collectivism**

Concept	Individualism	Collectivism
Self	Independent (identity from individual traits)	Interdependent (identity from belonging)
Life task	Discover and express one's uniqueness	Maintain connections, fit in, perform role
What matters	Me—personal achievement and fulfillment; rights and liberties; self-esteem	Us—group goals and solidarity; social responsibilities and relationships; family duty
Coping method	Change reality	Accommodate to reality
Morality	Defined by individuals (self-based)	Defined by social networks (duty-based)
Relationships	Many, often temporary or casual; confrontation acceptable	Few, close and enduring; harmony valued
Attributing behavior	Behavior reflects one's personality and attitudes	Behavior reflects social norms and roles

Sources: Adapted from Thomas Schoeneman (1994) and Harry Triandis (1994).

Culture and Child-Rearing

Child-rearing practices reflect cultural values that vary across time and place. Do you prefer children who are independent or children who comply? If you live in a Westernized culture, the odds are you prefer independence. "You are responsible for yourself," Western families and schools tell their children. "Follow your conscience. Be true to yourself. Discover your gifts. Think through your personal needs." A half-century and more ago, Western cultural values placed greater priority on obedience, respect, and sensitivity to others (Alwin, 1990; Remley, 1988). "Be true to your traditions," parents then taught their children. "Be loyal to your heritage and country. Show respect toward your parents and other superiors." Cultures can change.

Many Asians and Africans live in cultures that value emotional closeness. Rather than being given their own bedrooms and entrusted to day care, infants and toddlers may sleep with their mothers and spend their days close to a family member (Morelli et al., 1992; Whiting & Edwards, 1988). These cultures encourage a strong sense of *family self*—a feeling that what shames the child shames the family, and what brings honor to the family brings honor to the self.

Children across place and time have thrived under various child-rearing systems. Upper-class British parents traditionally handed off routine caregiving to nannies, then sent their children off to boarding school at about age 10. These children and their boarding-school peers generally grew up to be pillars of British society, as had their parents before them. In the African Gusii society, babies nurse freely but spend most of the day on their mother's back—with lots of body contact but little face-to-face and language interaction. When the mother becomes pregnant, the toddler is weaned and handed over to someone else, often an older sibling. Westerners may wonder about the negative effects of this lack of verbal interaction, but then the African Gusii would in turn wonder about Western mothers pushing their babies around in strollers and leaving them in playpens and car seats (Small, 1997). Such diversity in child-rearing cautions us against presuming that our culture's way is the only way to rear children successfully.

Developmental Similarities Across Groups

Mindful of how others differ from us, we often fail to notice the similarities predisposed by our shared biology. One 49-country study revealed that nation-to-nation differences in personality traits such as conscientiousness and extraversion are smaller than most people suppose (Terracciano et al., 2005). Australians see themselves as outgoing, German-speaking Swiss see themselves as conscientious, and Canadians see themselves as agreeable. Actually, these national stereotypes exaggerate differences that, although real, are modest. Compared with the person-to-person differences within groups, the differences between groups are small. Regardless of our culture, we humans are more alike than different. We share the same life cycle. We speak to our infants in similar ways and respond similarly to their coos and cries (Bornstein et al., 1992a,b). All over the world, the children of warm and supportive parents feel better about themselves and are less hostile than are the children of punitive and rejecting parents (Rohner, 1986; Scott et al., 1991).

Even differences *within* a culture, such as those sometimes attributed to race, are often easily explained by an interaction between our biology and our culture. David Rowe and his colleagues (1994, 1995) illustrated this with an analogy: Black men tend to have higher blood pressure than White men. Suppose that (1) in both groups salt consumption correlates with blood pressure, and (2) salt consumption is higher among Black men than among White men. The blood pressure "race difference" might then actually be, at least partly, a *diet* difference—a cultural preference for certain foods.

Cultures vary In Scotland's Orkney Islands' town of Stromness, social trust has enabled parents to park their toddlers outside of shops.

Parental involvement promotes development Parents in every culture facilitate their children's discovery of their world, but cultures differ in what they deem important. Asian cultures place more emphasis on school and hard work than do North American cultures. This may help explain why Japanese and Taiwanese children get higher scores on mathematics achievement tests.

"When [someone] has discovered why men in Bond Street wear black hats he will at the same moment have discovered why men in Timbuctoo wear red feathers."

—G. K. Chesterton, *Heretics,* 1905

And that, said Rowe and his colleagues, parallels psychological findings. Although Latino, Asian, Black, White, and Native Americans differ in school achievement and delinquency, the differences are "no more than skin deep." To the extent that family structure, peer influences, and parental education predict behavior in one of these ethnic groups, they do so for the others as well.

So, as members of different ethnic and cultural groups, we may differ in surface ways, but as members of one species we seem subject to the same psychological forces. Our languages vary, yet they reflect universal principles of grammar (Chapter 9). Our tastes vary, yet they reflect common principles of hunger (Chapter 10). Our social behaviors vary, yet they reflect pervasive principles of human influence (Chapter 15). Cross-cultural research can help us appreciate both our cultural diversity *and* our human likeness.

REHEARSE IT!

9. *Personal space,* the portable buffer zone people like to maintain around their bodies, differs from culture to culture. These differences are examples of
a. genetic variation.
b. individual influences.
c. cultural norms.
d. collectivist influences.

10. Individualist cultures tend to value _____; collectivist cultures tend to value _____.
a. interdependence; independence
b. independence; interdependence
c. group solidarity; uniqueness
d. duty to family; personal fulfillment

11. Human developmental processes tend to _____ from one group to another because we are members of _____.
a. be the same; the same ethnic group
b. be the same; the same species
c. differ; different species
d. differ; different ethnic groups

Answers: 9. c, 10. b, 11. b.

Gender Development

As we will see in Chapter 9, we humans share an irresistible urge to organize our worlds into simple categories. Among the ways we classify people—as tall or short, fat or slim, smart or dull—one stands out: At your birth, everyone wanted to know, "Boy or girl?" Our biological sex in turn helps define our *gender,* the biological and social characteristics by which people define *male* or *female.* In considering how nature and nurture together create social diversity, gender is the prime case example. Earlier we considered one significant gender difference—in sexual interests and behaviors. Let's recap this chapter's theme—that nature and nurture together create our differences and commonalities—by considering other gender variations.

Gender Similarities and Differences

11: **What are some ways in which males and females tend to be alike and to differ?**

Having faced similar adaptive challenges, we are in most ways alike. Men and women are not from different planets—Mars and Venus—but from the same planet Earth. Tell me whether you are male or female and you give me virtually no clues to your vocabulary, intelligence, and happiness, or to the mechanisms by which you see, hear, learn, and remember. Your "opposite" sex is, in reality, your very similar sex. And should we be surprised? Among your 46 chromosomes, 45 are unisex.

But males and females also differ, and differences command attention. Some much talked-about differences are actually quite modest, as Janet Hyde (2005) illustrated by graphically representing the gender difference in self-esteem scores, across many studies (**FIGURE 4.6**). Some differences are more striking. Compared with the average man, the average woman enters puberty two years sooner, lives five years longer, carries 70 percent more fat, has 40 percent less muscle, and is 5 inches shorter. Other gender differences appear throughout this book. Women can become sexually re-aroused immediately after orgasm. They smell fainter odors, express emotions more freely, and are offered help more often. They are doubly vulnerable to depression and anxiety, and their risk of developing eating disorders is 10 times greater. But, then, men are some four times more likely to commit suicide or suffer alcohol dependence. They are far more often diagnosed with autism, color-blindness, attention-deficit hyperactivity disorder (as children), and antisocial personality disorder (as adults). Choose your gender and pick your vulnerability.

How much does biology bend the genders? What portion of our differences are socially constructed—by the gender roles our culture assigns us, and by how we are socialized as children? To answer those questions, let's look more closely at some average gender differences in aggression, social power, and social connectedness.

Gender and Aggression

In surveys, men admit to more **aggression** than do women, and experiments confirm that men tend to behave more aggressively, such as by administering what they believe are more painful electric shocks (Bettencourt & Kernahan, 1997). The aggression gender gap pertains to *physical* aggression (such as hitting) rather than *relational* aggression (such as excluding someone). The gender gap in physical aggression appears in everyday life at various ages and in various cultures, especially those with gender inequality (Archer, 2004, 2006). Violent crime rates most strikingly illustrate the gender difference. The male-to-female arrest ratio for murder, for example, is 10 to 1 in the United States and almost 7 to 1 in Canada (FBI, 2007; Statistics Canada, 2007).

Around the world, hunting, fighting, and warring are primarily men's activities (Wood & Eagly, 2002, 2007). Men also express more support for war. The Iraq war, for example, has consistently been supported more by American men than by American women (Newport et al., 2007).

Gender and Social Power

From Nigeria to New Zealand, people worldwide have perceived men as more dominant, forceful, and independent, women as more deferential, nurturant, and affiliative (Williams & Best, 1990). Indeed, in most societies men *are* socially dominant, and they place more importance on power and achievement (Schwartz & Rubel, 2005). When groups form, whether as juries or companies, leadership tends to go to males (Colarelli et al., 2006). As leaders, men tend to be more directive, even autocratic; women tend to be more democratic, more welcoming of subordinates' participation in decision making (Eagly & Carli, 2007; van Engen & Willemsen, 2004). When people interact, men are more likely to utter opinions, women to express support (Aries, 1987; Wood, 1987). These differences carry into everyday behavior, where men are more likely to act as powerful people often do—talking assertively, interrupting, initiating touches, staring more, and smiling less (Hall, 1987; Leaper & Ayres, 2007; Major et al., 1990).

Such behaviors help sustain social power inequities. When political leaders are elected, they usually are men, who held 82 percent of the seats in the world's governing parliaments in 2009 (IPU, 2009). When salaries are paid, those in traditionally male occupations receive more.

FIGURE 4.6 **Much ado about a small difference** Janet Hyde (2005) shows us two normal distributions that differ by the approximate magnitude of the gender difference in self-esteem, averaged over all available samples. Moreover, though we can identify gender differences, the variation among individual women and among individual men greatly exceeds the difference between the average woman and man.

aggression physical or verbal behavior intended to hurt someone.

Women's 2009 representations in national parliaments ranged from 10 percent in the Arab States to 41 percent in Scandinavia, with 17 percent in the United States and 22 percent in Canada (IPU, 2009).

Every man for himself, or tend and befriend? Gender differences in the way we interact with others begin to appear at a very young age.

"In the long years liker must they grow; The man be more of woman, she of man."

—Alfred Lord Tennyson, *The Princess,* 1847

Gender and Social Connectedness

To Carol Gilligan and her colleagues (1982, 1990), the "normal" struggle to create a separate identity describes Western individualist males more than relationship-oriented females. Gilligan believes females tend to differ from males both in being less concerned with viewing themselves as separate individuals and in being more concerned with "making connections."

These gender differences in connectedness surface early in children's play, and they continue with age. Boys typically play in large groups with an activity focus and little intimate discussion (Rose & Rudolph, 2006). Girls usually play in smaller groups, often with one friend. Their play tends to be less competitive than boys' and more imitative of social relationships. Both in play and other settings, females are more open and responsive to feedback than are males (Maccoby, 1990; Roberts, 1991).

Females tend to be more *interdependent* than males. As teens, girls spend more time with friends and less time alone (Wong & Csikszentmihalyi, 1991). As late adolescents, they spend more time on social-networking Internet sites (Pryor et al., 2007). As adults, women take more pleasure in talking face-to-face, and they tend to use conversation more to explore relationships. Men enjoy doing activities side-by-side, and they tend to use conversation to communicate solutions (Tannen, 1990; Wright, 1989). The communication difference is apparent even in student e-mails, from which people in one New Zealand study could correctly guess the author's gender two-thirds of the time (Thomson & Murachver, 2001).

These gender differences are sometimes reflected in patterns of phone communication. In France, women make 63 percent of phone calls and, when talking to a woman, stay connected longer (7.2 minutes) than men do when talking to other men (4.6 minutes) (Smoreda & Licoppe, 2000). So, does this confirm the idea that women are just more talkative? When researchers (Mehl et al., 2007) counted the number of words 396 college students spoke in an average day, they found that talkativeness varied enormously—by 45,000 words between their most and least talkative participants. (How many words would you guess you speak each day?) Contrary to stereotypes of jabbering women, both men and women averaged about 16,000 words daily.

Women worldwide orient their interests and vocations more to people and less to things (Lippa, 2005, 2006, 2008). In the workplace, they are less often driven by money and status and more apt to opt for reduced work hours (Pinker, 2008). In the home, they provide most of the care to the very young and the very old. In the greeting card aisles, they make 85 percent of the purchases (*Time,* 1997). Women's emphasis on caring helps explain another interesting finding: Although 69 percent of people have said they have a close relationship with their father, 90 percent said they feel close to their mother (Hugick, 1989). When wanting understanding and someone with whom to share worries and hurts, both men and women usually turn to women, and both have reported their friendships with women to be more intimate, enjoyable, and nurturing (Rubin, 1985; Sapadin, 1988). And when they themselves must cope with stress, women more than men turn to others for support—they *tend and befriend* (Tamres et al., 2002; Taylor, 2002).

Gender differences in power, connectedness, and other traits peak in late adolescence and early adulthood—the very years most commonly studied (also the years of dating and mating). As teenagers, girls become progressively less assertive and more flirtatious; boys become more domineering and unexpressive. But by age 50, these differences have diminished. Men become more empathic and less domineering and women, especially if working, become more assertive and self-confident (Kasen et al., 2006; Maccoby, 1998).

The Nature of Gender

12: How do nature and nurture together form our gender?

What explains our gender diversity? Is biology destiny? Are we shaped by our cultures? A biopsychosocial view suggests it is both, thanks to the interplay among our biological dispositions, our developmental experiences, and our current situations (Wood & Eagly, 2002, 2007).

In domains where men and women have faced similar challenges—regulating heat with sweat, developing tastes that nourish, growing calluses where the skin meets friction—the sexes are similar. Even when describing the ideal mate, both men and women put traits such as "kind," "honest," and "intelligent" at the top of their lists. But in domains pertinent to mating, evolutionary psychologists contend, guys act like guys whether they are elephants or elephant seals, rural peasants or corporate presidents. Such gender differences may be influenced genetically, by our differing *sex chromosomes* and, physiologically, from our differing concentrations of *sex hormones.*

Males and females are variations on a single form. Seven weeks after conception, you were anatomically indistinguishable from someone of the other sex. Then your genes activated your biological sex, which was determined by your twenty-third pair of chromosomes, the two sex chromosomes. From your mother, you received an **X chromosome.** From your father, you received the one chromosome out of 46 that is not unisex—either another X chromosome, making you a girl, or a **Y chromosome,** making you a boy. The Y chromosome includes a single gene that throws a master switch triggering the testes to develop and produce the principal male hormone, **testosterone.** Females also have testosterone, but less of it. The male's greater testosterone output starts the development of external male sex organs at about the seventh week.

Another key period for sexual differentiation falls during the fourth and fifth prenatal months, when sex hormones bathe the fetal brain and influence its wiring. Different patterns for males and females develop under the influence of the male's greater testosterone and the female's ovarian hormones (Hines, 2004; Udry, 2000). Recent research confirms male-female differences during development in brain areas with abundant sex hormone receptors (Cahill, 2005).

In adulthood, parts of the frontal lobes, an area involved in verbal fluency, are reportedly thicker in women. Part of the parietal cortex, a key area for space perception, is thicker in men. Gender differences also appear in the hippocampus, the amygdala, and the volume of brain *gray matter* (the neural bodies) versus *white matter* (the axons and dendrites).

Further evidence of biology's influence on gender development comes from studies of genetic males who, despite normal male hormones and testes, are born without penises or with very small ones. A study of 14 boys who had undergone early sex-reassignment surgery (which is now controversial) and were raised as girls found that 6 later declared themselves as males, 5 were living as females, and 3 had an unclear sexual identity (Reiner & Gearhart, 2004). In one famous case, the parents of a Canadian boy who lost his penis to a botched circumcision followed advice to raise him as a girl rather than as a damaged boy. Alas, "Brenda" Reimer was not like most other girls. "She" didn't like dolls. She tore her dresses with rough-and-tumble play. At puberty she wanted no part of kissing boys. Finally, Brenda's parents explained what had happened, whereupon this young person immediately rejected the assigned female identity, got a haircut, and chose a male name, David. He ended up marrying a woman, becoming a stepfather, and, sadly, later committing suicide (Colapinto, 2000).

"Sex matters," concludes the National Academy of Sciences (2001). In combination with the environment, sex-related genes and physiology "result in behavioral and cognitive differences between males and females."

X chromosome the sex chromosome found in both men and women. Females have two X chromosomes; males have one. An X chromosome from each parent produces a female child.

Y chromosome the sex chromosome found only in males. When paired with an X chromosome from the mother, it produces a male child.

testosterone the most important of the male sex hormones. Both males and females have it, but the additional testosterone in males stimulates the growth of the male sex organs in the fetus and the development of the male sex characteristics during puberty.

Courtesy of Nick Downes.

The Nurture of Gender

Although biologically influenced, gender is also socially constructed. What biology initiates, culture accentuates.

Gender Roles

Sex indeed matters. But from a biopsychosocial perspective, culture and the immediate situation matter, too. *Culture,* as we noted earlier, is everything shared by a group and transmitted across generations. We can see culture's shaping power in the social expectations that guide men's and women's behavior. In psychology, as in the theater, a **role** refers to a cluster of prescribed actions—the behaviors we expect of those who occupy a particular social position. One set of norms defines our culture's **gender roles**—our expectations about the way men and women should behave. In the United States 30 years ago, it was standard for men to initiate dates, drive the car, and pick up the check, and for women to decorate the home, buy and care for the children's clothes, and select the wedding gifts.

Gender roles exist outside the home, too. Compared with employed women, employed men in the United States spend about an hour and a half more on the job each day and about one hour less on household activities and caregiving (Amato et al., 2007; Bureau of Labor Statistics, 2004; Fisher et al., 2006). I do not have to tell you which parent, about 90 percent of the time in two-parent U.S. families, has stayed home with a sick child, arranged for the baby-sitter, or called the doctor (Maccoby, 1995). In Australia, women devote 54 percent more time to unpaid household work and 71 percent more time to child care than do men (Trewin, 2001).

Gender roles can smooth social relations, saving awkward decisions about who does the laundry this week and who mows the lawn. But they often do so at a cost: If we deviate from such conventions, we may feel anxious.

Do gender roles reflect what is biologically natural for men and women? Or do cultures construct them? Gender-role diversity over time and space indicates that culture has a big influence. Nomadic societies of food-gathering people have only a minimal division of labor by sex. Boys and girls receive much the same upbringing. In agricultural societies, where women work in the fields close to home, and men roam more freely herding livestock, children typically socialize into more distinct gender roles (Segall et al., 1990; Van Leeuwen, 1978).

Among industrialized countries, gender roles and attitudes vary widely (UNICEF, 2006). Australia and the Scandinavian countries offer the greatest gender equity, Middle Eastern and North African countries the least (Social Watch, 2006). And consider: Would you say life is more satisfying when both spouses work for pay and share child care? If so, you would agree with most people in 41 of 44 countries, according to a Pew Global Attitudes survey (2003). Even so, the culture-to-culture differences were huge, ranging from Egypt, where people disagreed 2 to 1, to Vietnam, where people agreed 11 to 1.

Attitudes about gender roles also vary over time. In the late 1960s and early 1970s, with the flick of an apron, the number of U.S. college women hoping to be full-time homemakers had plunged. In the three decades after 1976, the percentage of women in medical, law, and psychology programs roughly doubled.

Gender ideas vary not only across cultures and over time, but also across generations. When families emigrate from Asia to Canada and the United States, their children tend to grow up with peers from a new culture. Many immigrant children, especially girls, feel torn between the competing sets of gender-role norms presented by peers and parents (Dion & Dion, 2001).

"Sex brought us together, but gender drove us apart."

"Genes, by themselves, are like seeds dropped onto pavement: powerless to produce anything."

—Primatologist Frans B. M. de Waal (1999)

The gendered tsunami In Sri Lanka, Indonesia, and India, the gendered division of labor helped explain the excess of female deaths from the 2004 tsunami. In some villages, 80 percent of those killed were women, who were mostly at home while the men were more likely to be at sea fishing or doing out-of-the-home chores (Oxfam, 2005).

Gender and Child-Rearing

As society assigns each of us to a gender, the social category of male or female, the inevitable result is our strong **gender identity,** our sense of *being* male or female. To varying extents, we also become **gender typed.** That is, some boys more than others exhibit traditionally masculine traits and interests, and some girls more than others become distinctly feminine.

Social learning theory assumes that children learn gender-linked behaviors by observing and imitating and by being rewarded or punished. "Nicole, you're such a good mommy to your dolls"; "Big boys don't cry, Alex." But parental modeling and rewarding of male-female differences aren't enough to explain gender typing (Lytton & Romney, 1991). In fact, even when their families discourage traditional gender typing, children usually organize themselves into "boy worlds" and "girl worlds," each guided by rules for what boys and girls do.

Cognition (thinking) also matters. In your own childhood, as you struggled to comprehend the world, you—like other children—formed *schemas,* or concepts that helped you make sense of your world. One of these was a schema for your own gender (Bem, 1987, 1993). Your *gender schema* then became a lens through which you viewed your experiences. Social learning shapes gender schemas. Before age 1, children begin to discriminate male and female voices and faces (Martin et al., 2002). After age 2, language forces children to begin organizing their worlds on the basis of gender. English, for example, uses the pronouns *he* and *she;* other languages classify objects as masculine ("*le* train") or feminine ("*la* table").

Young children are "gender detectives," explain Carol Lynn Martin and Diane Ruble (2004). Once they grasp that two sorts of people exist—and that they are of one sort—they search for clues about gender, and they find them in language, dress, toys, and songs. Girls, they may decide, are the ones with long hair. Having divided the human world in half, 3-year-olds will then like their own sex better and seek out their own kind for play. And having compared themselves with their concept of gender, they will adjust their behavior accordingly ("I am male—thus, masculine, strong, aggressive," or "I am female—therefore, feminine, sweet, and helpful"). The rigidity of boy-girl stereotypes peaks at about age 5 or 6. If the new neighbor is a boy, a 6-year-old girl may just assume he cannot share her interests. For young children, gender looms large.

role a set of expectations (norms) about a social position, defining how those in the position ought to behave.

gender role a set of expected behaviors for males or for females.

gender identity our sense of being male or female.

gender typing the acquisition of a traditional masculine or feminine role.

social learning theory the theory that we learn social behavior by observing and imitating and by being rewarded or punished.

REHEARSE IT!

12. A fertilized egg will develop into a boy if it receives
   a. an X chromosome from its mother.
   b. an X chromosome from its father.
   c. a Y chromosome from its mother.
   d. a Y chromosome from its father.

13. "Gender role" refers to our
   a. sense of being male or female.

   b. expectations about the way males and females should behave.
   c. biological sex.
   d. hormonally influenced differences in brain development.

14. As a consequence of the gender assigned to us by society, we develop a gender identity, which means that we

   a. exhibit traditional masculine or feminine roles.
   b. are socially categorized as male or female.
   c. have a sense of being male or female.
   d. have an ambiguous biological sex.

Answers: 12. d, 13. b, 14. c.

Reflections on Nature and Nurture

"There are trivial truths and great truths," reflected the physicist Niels Bohr on some of the paradoxes of modern science. "The opposite of a trivial truth is plainly false. The opposite of a great truth is also true." It appears true that our ancestral history helped form us as a species. Where there is variation, natural selection, and heredity, there will be evolution. The unique gene combination created when our mother's egg engulfed our father's sperm predisposed both our shared humanity and our individual differences. This is a great truth about human nature. Genes form us.

But it also is true that our experiences form us. In our families and in our peer relationships, we learn ways of thinking and acting. Differences initiated by our nature may be amplified by our nurture. If their genes and hormones predispose males to be more physically aggressive than females, culture may magnify this gender difference through norms that encourage males to be macho and females to be the kinder, gentler sex. If men are encouraged toward roles that demand physical power, and women toward more nurturing roles, each may then exhibit the actions expected of them and find themselves shaped accordingly. Roles remake their players. Presidents in time become more presidential, servants more servile. Gender roles similarly shape us.

But gender roles are converging. Brute strength has become increasingly irrelevant to power and status (think Bill Gates and Oprah Winfrey). Thus both women and men are now seen as "fully capable of effectively carrying out organizational roles at all levels," note Wendy Wood and Alice Eagly (2002). And as women's employment in formerly male occupations has increased, gender differences in traditional masculinity or femininity and in what one seeks in a mate have diminished (Twenge, 1997). As the roles we play change over time, we change with them.

* * * * *

If nature and nurture jointly form us, are we "nothing but" the product of nature and nurture? Are we rigidly determined?

We *are* the product of nature and nurture (**FIGURE 4.7**), but we are also an open system. Genes are all-pervasive but not all-powerful; people may defy their genetic bent to reproduce, by electing celibacy. Culture, too, is all-pervasive but not all-powerful; people may defy peer pressures and do the opposite of the expected. To excuse our failings by blaming our nature and nurture is what philosopher-novelist Jean-Paul Sartre called "bad faith"—attributing responsibility for one's fate to bad genes or bad influences.

In reality, we are both the creatures and the creators of our worlds. We are—it is a great truth—the products of our genes and environments. Nevertheless (another great truth) the stream of causation that shapes the future runs through our present choices. Our decisions today design our environments tomorrow. Mind matters. The human environment is not like the weather—something that just happens. We are its architects. Our hopes, goals, and expectations influence our future. And that is what enables cultures to vary and to change so quickly.

* * * * *

I know from my mail and from public opinion surveys that some readers feel troubled by the naturalism and evolutionism of contemporary science. Readers from other nations bear with me, but in the United States there is a wide gulf between scientific and lay thinking about evolution. "The idea that human minds are the product of evolution is . . . unassailable fact," declared a 2007 editorial in *Nature*, a leading science magazine. That sentiment concurs with a 2006 statement of "evidence-based facts" about evolution jointly issued by the national science academies of 66 nations (IAP, 2006). In *The Language of God,* Human Genome Project

FIGURE 4.7 **The biopsychosocial approach to development**

Biological influences:
• Shared human genome
• Individual genetic variations
• Prenatal environment
• Sex-related genes, hormones, and physiology

Psychological influences:
• Gene-environment interactions
• Neurological effect of early experiences
• Responses evoked by our own temperament, gender, etc.
• Beliefs, feelings, and expectations

Individual development

Social-cultural influences:
• Parental influences
• Peer influences
• Cultural norms

"Let's hope that it's not true; but if it is true, let's hope that it doesn't become widely known."

—Lady Ashley, commenting on Darwin's theory

director Francis Collins (2006, pp. 141, 146), a self-described evangelical Christian, compiles the "utterly compelling" evidence that leads him to conclude that Darwin's big idea is "unquestionably correct." Yet a Gallup poll reports that half of U.S. adults do not believe in evolution's role in "how human beings came to exist on Earth" (Newport, 2007). Many of those who dispute the scientific story worry that a science of behavior (and evolutionary science in particular) will destroy our sense of the beauty, mystery, and spiritual significance of the human creature. For those concerned, I offer some reassuring thoughts.

When Isaac Newton explained the rainbow in terms of light of differing wavelengths, the poet Keats feared that Newton had destroyed the rainbow's mysterious beauty. Yet, noted Richard Dawkins (1998) in *Unweaving the Rainbow,* Newton's analysis led to an even deeper mystery—Einstein's theory of special relativity. Moreover, nothing about Newton's optics need diminish our appreciation for the dramatic elegance of a rainbow arching across a brightening sky.

When Galileo assembled evidence that the Earth revolved around the Sun, not vice versa, he did not offer irrefutable proof for his theory. Rather, he offered a coherent explanation for a variety of observations, such as the changing shadows cast by the Moon's mountains. His explanation eventually won the day because it described and explained things in a way that made sense, that hung together. Darwin's theory of evolution likewise is a coherent view of natural history. It offers an organizing principle that unifies various observations.

Collins is not the only person of faith to find the scientific idea of human origins congenial with his spirituality. In the fifth century, St. Augustine (quoted by Wilford, 1999) wrote, "The universe was brought into being in a less than fully formed state, but was gifted with the capacity to transform itself from unformed matter into a truly marvelous array of structures and life forms." Some 1600 years later, Pope John Paul II in 1996 welcomed a science-religion dialogue, finding it noteworthy that evolutionary theory "has been progressively accepted by researchers, following a series of discoveries in various fields of knowledge."

Meanwhile, many people of science are awestruck at the emerging understanding of the universe and the human creature. It boggles the mind—the entire universe popping out of a point some 14 billion years ago, and instantly inflating to cosmological size. Had the energy of this Big Bang been the tiniest bit less, the universe would have collapsed back on itself. Had it been the tiniest bit more, the result would have been a soup too thin to support life. Astronomer Sir Martin Rees has described *Just Six Numbers* (1999), any one of which, if changed ever so slightly, would produce a cosmos in which life could not exist. Had gravity been a tad bit stronger or weaker, or had the weight of a carbon proton been a wee bit different, our universe just wouldn't have worked.

What caused this almost-too-good-to-be-true, finely tuned universe? Why is there something rather than nothing? How did it come to be, in the words of Harvard-Smithsonian astrophysicist Owen Gingerich (1999), "so extraordinarily right, that it seemed the universe had been expressly designed to produce intelligent, sentient beings"? Is there a benevolent superintelligence behind it all? Have there instead been an infinite number of universes born and we just happen to be the lucky inhabitants of one that, by chance, was exquisitely fine-tuned to give birth to us? Or does that idea violate *Occam's razor,* the principle that we should prefer the simplest of competing explanations? On such matters, a humble, awed, scientific silence is appropriate, suggested philosopher Ludwig Wittgenstein: "Whereof one cannot speak, thereof one must be silent."

Rather than fearing science, we can welcome its enlarging our understanding and awakening our sense of awe. In *The Fragile Species,* Lewis Thomas (1992) described his utter amazement that the Earth in time gave rise to bacteria and eventually to Bach's Mass in B-Minor. In a short 4 billion years, life on Earth has come from nothing to structures as complex as a 6-billion-unit strand of DNA and the incomprehensible intricacy of the human brain. Atoms no different from those in a

"Is it not stirring to understand how the world actually works—that white light is made of colors, that color measures light waves, that transparent air reflects light . . . ? It does no harm to the romance of the sunset to know a little about it."

—Carl Sagan, *Skies of Other Worlds,* 1988

"The causes of life's history [cannot] resolve the riddle of life's meaning."

—Stephen Jay Gould, *Rocks of Ages: Science and Religion in the Fullness of Life,* 1999 rock somehow formed dynamic entities that became conscious. Nature, says cosmologist Paul Davies (2007), seems cunningly and ingeniously devised to produce extraordinary, self-replicating, information-processing systems—us. Although we appear to have been created from dust, over eons of time, the end result is a priceless creature, one rich with potential beyond our imagining.

CHAPTER REVIEW

Nature, Nurture, and Human Diversity

Behavior Genetics: Predicting Individual Differences

1 Our genes predispose our biology. Does this mean they determine our behavior?

Our heredity and our experiences interact to create our individual and social differences. *Behavior geneticists* seek to quantify genetic and *environmental* influences on our traits. *Chromosomes* are coils of *DNA* containing *gene* segments that, when "turned on" (expressed), code for the proteins that form our body's building blocks. Most human traits are influenced by many genes acting together.

2 How do twin and adoption studies help us understand the relative influences of environment and heredity?

Studies of *identical twins, fraternal twins,* and adoptive families help clarify the influence of genetic nature and of environmental nurture.

3 What is the relationship between temperament and personality?

Temperament, or emotional reactivity, is one aspect of personality (characteristic patterns of thinking, feeling, and acting).

4 How do genes and environments interact?

The stability of temperament suggests a genetic predisposition. To say that genes and environments *interact* means that our genes influence our abilities and the ways others react to us, but our environments also trigger gene activity.

Evolutionary Psychology: Understanding Human Nature

5 How do evolutionary psychologists use natural selection to explain behavior tendencies?

Evolutionary psychologists seek to understand how *natural selection* has shaped our traits and behavior tendencies. The principle of natural selection states that variations increasing the odds of reproducing and surviving are most likely to be passed on to future generations. Some variations arise from new gene combinations at conception, others from *mutations* (random errors in gene replication). Charles Darwin, whose theory of evolution has for a long time been an organizing principle in biology, anticipated the contemporary application of evolutionary principles in psychology.

6 How might an evolutionary psychologist explain gender differences in mating preferences?

Applying principles of natural selection, evolutionary psychologists reason that men's attraction to multiple healthy, fertile-appearing partners increases their chances of spreading their genes widely. Women usually incubate and nurse one baby at a time. They can increase their own and their children's chances of survival by searching for mates with a long-term capacity to support and protect their joint offspring.

7 What are the key criticisms of the evolutionary perspective on human sexuality?

Critics argue that the evolutionary perspective on human sexuality (1) starts with an effect and works backward to an explanation, (2) underemphasizes social influences, and (3) could absolve people from taking responsibility for their sexual behavior. Evolutionary psychologists cite the value of testable predictions based on evolutionary principles, as well as the coherence and explanatory power of those principles. They also remind us that understanding our predispositions can help us overcome them.

Parents and Peers

8 To what extent are our lives shaped by early stimulation, by parents, and by peers?

A developing child's brain changes as neural connections increase in areas associated with stimulating activity, and unused synapses degenerate. Parents influence their children in areas such as manners and political and religious beliefs, but not in other areas, such as personality. Language and other behaviors are shaped by peer groups, as children adjust to fit in. Parents' decisions about children's neighborhoods and schools can moderate the influence of peer group culture.

Cultural Influences

9 How do cultural norms affect our behavior?

Cultural *norms* are rules for accepted and expected behaviors. Across places and over time *cultures* differ in their behaviors, attitudes, ideas, values, and traditions. Despite cultural variations, many common forces influence human behavior.

10 How do individualist and collectivist cultural influences affect people?

Individualist cultures (mostly Western) value personal independence and individual achievement and define identity in terms of self-esteem, personal goals and attributes, and personal rights and liberties. *Collectivist* cultures, like those of many parts of Asia and Africa, value interdependence, tradition, and harmony, and they define identity in terms of group goals, memberships, and commit-

ments. Within any culture, the degree of individualism or collectivism varies from person to person.

Gender Development

11 What are some ways in which males and females tend to be alike and to differ?

Human males and females are more alike than different, thanks to their similar genetic inheritance and physical abilities. Males and females do differ in body fat, muscle, height, age of onset of puberty, and life expectancy. They also vary in their vulnerability to certain disorders, and in such areas as *aggression,* social power, and social connectedness.

12 How do nature and nurture together form our gender?

Biological sex is determined by the twenty-third pair of chromosomes. The mother always contributes an *X chromosome;* the father gives either an X (producing a female) or a *Y chromosome* (which triggers additional *testosterone* release and male sex organs). *Gender* is the set of biological and social characteristics by which people define male and female. Sex-related genes and hormones interact with developmental experiences to produce gender differences in behavior. *Gender roles,* expected behaviors for males and females, vary with culture, across place and time. *Social learning theory* proposes that we learn *gender identity* as we learn other things—through reinforcement, punishment, and observation.

Terms and Concepts to Remember

environment, p. 105

behavior genetics, p. 105

chromosomes, p. 106

DNA (deoxyribonucleic acid), p. 106

genes, p. 106

identical twins, p. 107

fraternal twins, p. 107

temperament, p. 110

interaction, p. 111

evolutionary psychology, p. 113

natural selection, p. 113

mutation, p. 113

gender, p. 115

culture, p. 121

norm, p. 122

personal space, p. 122

individualism, p. 123

collectivism, p. 123

aggression, p. 127

X chromosome, p. 129

Y chromosome, p. 129

testosterone, p. 129

role, p. 130

gender role, p. 130

gender identity, p. 131

gender typing, p. 131

social learning theory, p. 131

Test for Success: Critical Thinking Exercises
By Amy Himsel, El Camino College

1. If heredity is a primary influence on personality, how can we explain why some siblings, who have different combinations of their parents' genes, have very similar personalities?

2. "Use it or lose it" is a phrase often used when discussing strategies to stave off brain aging and decline in adulthood. In reality, this rule is just as critical during infancy. Explain why.

3. It's been said that our female ancestors most often sent their genes into the future by pairing wisely, and our male ancestors by pairing widely. How does the evolutionary psychology perspective explain why these adaptive patterns are still seen in the behaviors and priorities of contemporary men and women who have more choices about when and whether they will have children?

4. Primatologist Frans B. M. de Waal (1999) observed that "genes, by themselves, are like seeds dropped onto pavement: powerless to produce anything." Explain what this means, in terms of our human characteristics.

5. Consider the Chinese saying, "One needs to cultivate the spirit of sacrificing the *little me* to achieve the benefits of the *big me.*" What is the *little me?* The *big me?* How might a staunch individualist react to this saying?

The Test for Success exercises offer you a chance to apply your critical thinking skills to aspects of the material you have just read. Suggestions for answering these questions can be found in Appendix D at the back of the book.

 Multiple-choice self-tests and more may be found at www.worthpublishers.com/myers.

Chapter Outline

- **Prenatal Development and the Newborn**
  Conception
  Prenatal Development
  The Competent Newborn

- **Infancy and Childhood**
  Physical Development
  Cognitive Development
  CLOSE-UP: Autism and "Mind-Blindness"
  Social Development

- **Adolescence**
  Physical Development
  Cognitive Development
  Social Development
  Emerging Adulthood

- **Adulthood**
  Physical Development
  Cognitive Development
  Social Development

- **Reflections on Two Major Developmental Issues**
  Continuity and Stages
  Stability and Change

5 : Developing Through the Life Span

As we journey through life—from womb to tomb—when and how do we develop? Virtually all of us began walking around age 1 and talking by age 2. As children, we engaged in social play in preparation for life's work. As adults, we all smile and cry, love and loathe, and occasionally ponder the fact that someday we will die. **Developmental psychology** examines how people are continually developing—physically, cognitively, and socially—from infancy through old age. Much of its research centers on three major issues:

1. *Nature/nurture:* How do genetic inheritance *(our nature)* and experience *(the nurture we receive)* influence our development?
2. *Continuity/stages:* Is development a gradual, continuous process like riding an escalator, or does it proceed through a sequence of separate stages, like climbing rungs on a ladder?
3. *Stability/change:* Do our early personality traits persist through life, or do we become different persons as we age?

In Chapter 4, we engaged the nature/nurture issue. At this chapter's end, we will reflect on the continuity and stability issues.

> **developmental psychology** a branch of psychology that studies physical, cognitive, and social change throughout the life span.

> "Nature is all that a man brings with him into the world; nurture is every influence that affects him after his birth."
>
> —Francis Galton,
> *English Men of Science,* 1874

Prenatal Development and the Newborn

1 : How does life develop before birth?

Conception

Nothing is more natural than a species reproducing itself. Yet nothing is more wondrous. With humans, the process starts when a woman's ovary releases a mature egg—a cell roughly the size of the period at the end of this sentence. Like space voyagers approaching a huge planet, the 200 million or more deposited sperm begin their race upstream, approaching a cell 85,000 times their own size. The relatively few reaching the egg release digestive enzymes that eat away its protective coating (**FIGURE 5.1**). As soon as one sperm begins to penetrate and is welcomed in, the egg's surface blocks out the others. Before half a day elapses, the egg nucleus and the sperm nucleus fuse. The two have become one. Consider it your most fortunate of moments. Among 200 million sperm, the one needed to make you, in combination with that one particular egg, won the race.

FIGURE 5.1 Life is sexually transmitted (a) Sperm cells surround an ovum. (b) As one sperm penetrates the egg's jellylike outer coating, a series of chemical events begins that will cause sperm and egg to fuse into a single cell. If all goes well, that cell will subdivide again and again to emerge 9 months later as a 100-trillion-cell human being.

Both photos Lennart Nilsson/Albert Bonniers Publishing Company

(a)

(b)

137

First known photo of Olympic swimming champion, Michael Phelps
If the playful cartoonist were to convey literal truth, a second arrow would also point to the egg that contributed the other half of Michael Phelps' genes.

Prenatal development

zygote:	*conception to 2 weeks*
embryo:	*2 weeks through 8 weeks*
fetus:	*9 weeks to birth*

"You shall conceive and bear a son. So then drink no wine or strong drink."

—Judges 13:7

Prenatal Development

Fewer than half of all fertilized eggs, called **zygotes,** survive beyond the first 2 weeks (Grobstein, 1979; Hall, 2004). But for you and me, good fortune prevailed. One cell became 2, then 4—each just like the first—until this cell division produced a zygote of some 100 cells within the first week. Then the cells began to differentiate—to specialize in structure and function. How identical cells do this—as if one decides "I'll become a brain, you become intestines!"—is a puzzle that scientists are just beginning to solve.

About 10 days after conception, the zygote attaches to the mother's uterine wall, beginning approximately 37 weeks of the closest human relationship. The zygote's inner cells become the **embryo** (**FIGURE 5.2a**). Over the next 6 weeks, organs begin to form and function. The heart begins to beat.

By 9 weeks after conception, the embryo looks unmistakably human (**FIGURE 5.2b**). It is now a **fetus** (Latin for "offspring" or "young one"). During the sixth month, organs such as the stomach have developed enough to allow a prematurely born fetus a chance of survival.

At each prenatal stage, genetic and environmental factors affect our development. The *placenta*, which formed as the zygote's outer cells attached to the uterine wall, transfers nutrients and oxygen from mother to fetus. The placenta also screens out many potentially harmful substances. But some substances slip by, including **teratogens,** which are harmful agents such as viruses and drugs. If the mother carries the HIV virus, her baby may also. If she is a heroin addict, her baby will be born a heroin addict. If she smokes, she will not smoke alone; both she and her fetus will experience reduced blood oxygen and a shot of nicotine. If she is a heavy smoker, her fetus may receive fewer nutrients and be born underweight and at risk for various problems (Pringle et al., 2005).

There is no known safe amount of alcohol during pregnancy. Alcohol enters the woman's bloodstream—and her fetus'—and depresses activity in both their central nervous systems. A pregnant mother's alcohol use may prime her offspring to like alcohol. In experiments, when pregnant rats drink alcohol, their young offspring later display a liking for alcohol's odor (Youngentob et al., 2007). Teens whose mothers drank when pregnant are at risk for heavy drinking and alcohol dependence. Even light drinking can affect the fetal brain (Braun, 1996; Ikonomidou et al., 2000), and persistent heavy drinking will put the fetus at risk for birth defects and later intellectual or developmental disabilities. For 1 in about 800 infants, the effects are visible as **fetal alcohol syndrome (FAS),** marked by a small, misproportioned head and lifelong brain abnormalities (May & Gossage, 2001).

FIGURE 5.2 Prenatal development (a) The embryo grows and develops rapidly. At 40 days, the spine is visible and the arms and legs are beginning to grow. (b) By the end of the second month, when the fetal period begins, facial features, hands, and feet have formed. (c) As the fetus enters the fourth month, its 3 ounces could fit in the palm of your hand.

(a)

(b)

(c)

Images courtesy of Lennart Nilsson/Albert Bonniers Publishing Company

The Competent Newborn

2: **What are some newborn abilities?**

Having survived prenatal hazards, we as newborns came equipped with automatic responses ideally suited for our survival. We withdrew our limbs to escape pain. If a cloth over our face interfered with our breathing, we turned our head from side to side and swiped at it.

New parents are often in awe of the coordinated sequence of *reflexes* by which their baby gets food. When something touches their cheek, babies turn toward that touch, open their mouth, and vigorously *root* for a nipple. Finding one, they automatically close on it and begin sucking—which itself requires a coordinated sequence of reflexive *tonguing*, *swallowing*, and *breathing*. Failing to find satisfaction, the hungry baby may cry—a behavior parents find highly unpleasant and very rewarding to relieve.

"I felt like a man trapped in a woman's body. Then I was born."
—Comedian Chris Bliss

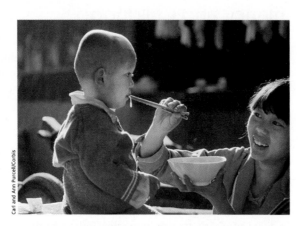

Prepared to feed and eat Animals are predisposed to respond to their offsprings' cries for nourishment.

Moreover, psychologists have discovered that we are born preferring sights and sounds that facilitate social responsiveness. As newborns, we turn our heads in the direction of human voices. We gaze longer at a drawing of a facelike image (**FIGURE 5.3**) than at a bull's-eye pattern; yet we gaze more at a bull's-eye pattern—which has contrasts much like those of the human eye—than at a solid disk (Fantz, 1961). We prefer to look at objects 8 to 12 inches away. Wonder of wonders, that just happens to be the approximate distance between a nursing infant's eyes and its mother's (Maurer & Maurer, 1988).

Within days after birth, our brain's neural networks were stamped with the smell of our mother's body. Thus, a week-old nursing baby, placed between a gauze pad from its mother's bra and one from another nursing mother, will usually turn toward the smell of its own mother's pad (MacFarlane, 1978). At 3 weeks, if given a pacifier that sometimes turns on recordings of its mother's voice and sometimes that of a female stranger's, an infant will suck more vigorously when it hears its now-familiar mother's voice (Mills & Melhuish, 1974). So not only could we as young infants see what we needed to see, and smell and hear well, we were already using our sensory equipment to learn.

zygote the fertilized egg; it enters a 2-week period of rapid cell division and develops into an embryo.

embryo the developing human organism from about 2 weeks after fertilization through the second month.

fetus the developing human organism from 9 weeks after conception to birth.

teratogens agents, such as chemicals and viruses, that can reach the embryo or fetus during prenatal development and cause harm.

fetal alcohol syndrome (FAS) physical and cognitive abnormalities in children caused by a pregnant woman's heavy drinking. In severe cases, symptoms include noticeable facial misproportions.

FIGURE 5.3 **Newborns' preference for faces** When shown these two stimuli with the same elements, Italian newborns spent nearly twice as many seconds looking at the facelike image (Johnson & Morton, 1991). Canadian newborns—average age 53 minutes in one study—displayed the same apparently inborn preference to look toward faces (Mondloch et al., 1999).

REHEARSE IT!

1. Which of the following is NOT one of the three major issues that interest developmental psychologists?
   a. Nature/nurture
   b. Reflexes/unlearned behaviors
   c. Stability/change
   d. Continuity/stages

2. Body organs first begin to form and function during the period of the _____; within 6 months, during the period of the _____, the organs are sufficiently functional to allow a chance of survival.
   a. zygote; embryo
   b. zygote; fetus
   c. embryo; fetus
   d. placenta; fetus

3. Teratogens are chemicals that pass through the placenta's screen and may harm an embryo or fetus. Which of the following is NOT a teratogen?
   a. Oxygen
   b. Heroin
   c. Alcohol
   d. Nicotine

4. Stroke a newborn's cheek and the infant will root for a nipple. This illustrates
   a. a reflex.
   b. nurture.
   c. differentiation.
   d. continuity.

Answers: 1. b, 2. c, 3. a, 4. a.

Infancy and Childhood

> "It is a rare privilege to watch the birth, growth, and first feeble struggles of a living human mind."
>
> —Annie Sullivan, in Helen Keller's *The Story of My Life,* 1903

During infancy, a baby grows from newborn to toddler, and during childhood from toddler to teenager. We all traveled this path, developing physically, cognitively, and socially. From infancy on, brain and mind—neural hardware and cognitive software—develop together.

Physical Development

3: During infancy and childhood, how do the brain and motor skills develop?

Brain Development

In your mother's womb, your developing brain formed nerve cells at the explosive rate of nearly one-quarter million per minute. On the day you were born, you had most of the brain cells you would ever have. However, your nervous system was immature: After birth, the branching neural networks that eventually enabled you to walk, talk, and remember had a wild growth spurt (**FIGURE 5.4**). From ages 3 to 6, the most rapid growth was in your frontal lobes, which enable rational planning. This helps explain why preschoolers display a rapidly developing ability to control their attention and behavior (Garon et al., 2008).

The association areas—those linked with thinking, memory, and language—are the last cortical areas to develop. As they do, mental abilities surge (Chugani & Phelps, 1986; Thatcher et al., 1987). Fiber pathways supporting language and agility proliferate into puberty, after which a pruning process shuts down excess connections and strengthens others (Paus et al., 1999; Thompson et al., 2000).

As a flower unfolds in accord with its genetic instructions, so do we, in the orderly sequence of biological growth processes called **maturation.** Maturation decrees many of our commonalities—from standing before walking, to using nouns before adjectives. Severe deprivation or abuse can retard development, and ample experiences of talking and reading with parents will help sculpt neural connections. Yet the genetic growth tendencies are inborn. Maturation sets the basic course of development; experience adjusts it.

FIGURE 5.4 Drawings of human cerebral cortex sections In humans, the brain is immature at birth. As the child matures, the neural networks grow increasingly more complex.

At birth   3 months   15 months

FIGURE 5.5 Triumphant toddlers Sit, crawl, walk, run—the sequence of these motor development milestones is the same the world around, though babies reach them at varying ages.

Motor Development

The developing brain enables physical coordination. As an infant's muscles and nervous system mature, more complicated skills emerge. With occasional exceptions, the sequence of physical (motor) development is universal. Babies roll over before they sit unsupported, and they usually creep on all fours before they walk (**FIGURE 5.5**). These behaviors reflect not imitation but a maturing nervous system; blind children, too, crawl before they walk.

There are, however, individual differences in timing. In the United States, for example, 25 percent of all babies walk by age 11 months, 50 percent within a week after their first birthday, and 90 percent by age 15 months (Frankenburg et al., 1992). The recommended infant *back-to-sleep position* (putting babies to sleep on their back to reduce the risk of a smothering crib death) has been associated with somewhat later crawling but not with later walking (Davis et al., 1998; Lipsitt, 2003).

Genes play a major role in motor development. Identical twins typically begin sitting up and walking on nearly the same day (Wilson, 1979). Maturation—including the rapid development of the cerebellum at the back of the brain—creates our readiness to learn walking at about age 1. Experience before that time has a limited effect. This is true for other physical skills, including bowel and bladder control. Before necessary muscular and neural maturation, neither pleading nor punishment will produce successful toilet training.

Maturation and Infant Memory

Our earliest memories seldom predate our third birthday. We see this *infantile amnesia* in the memories of some preschoolers who experienced an emergency fire evacuation caused by a burning popcorn maker. Seven years later, they were able to recall the alarm and what caused it—*if* they were 4 to 5 years old at the time. Those experiencing the event as 3-year-olds could not remember the cause and usually misrecalled being already outside when the alarm sounded (Pillemer, 1995). Other studies confirm that the average age of earliest conscious memory is 3.5 years (Bauer, 2002). By 4 to 5 years, childhood amnesia is giving way to remembered experiences (Bruce et al., 2000). But even into adolescence, the brain areas underlying memory continue to mature (Bauer, 2007).

Although we *consciously* recall little from before age 4, our memory was processing information during those early years. In 1965, while finishing her doctoral work, Carolyn Rovee-Collier observed an infant memory. She was also a new mom, whose colicky 2-month-old, Benjamin, could be calmed by moving a crib mobile. Weary of bonking the mobile, she strung a cloth ribbon connecting the mobile to Benjamin's foot. Soon, he was kicking his foot to move the mobile. Thinking about her unintended home experiment, Rovee-Collier realized that, contrary to popular

In the eight years following the 1994 launch of a U.S. "Back to Sleep" educational campaign, the number of infants sleeping on their stomach dropped from 70 to 11 percent—and SIDS (Sudden Infant Death Syndrome) deaths fell by half (Braiker, 2005).

"This is the path to adulthood. You're here."

Can you recall your first day of preschool (or your third birthday party)?

---

maturation biological growth processes that enable orderly changes in behavior, relatively uninfluenced by experience.

FIGURE 5.6 **Infant at work** Babies only 3 months old can learn that kicking moves a mobile, and they can retain that learning for a month. (From Rovee-Collier, 1989, 1997.)

"Who knows the thoughts of a child?"

—Poet Nora Perry

"Childhood has its own way of seeing, thinking, and feeling, and there is nothing more foolish than the attempt to put ours in its place."

—Philosopher Jean-Jacques Rousseau, 1798

opinion at that time, babies are capable of learning. To know for sure that little Benjamin wasn't just a whiz kid, Rovee-Collier had to repeat the experiment with other infants (Rovee-Collier, 1989, 1999). Sure enough, they, too, soon kicked more when linked to a mobile, both on the day of the experiment and the day after. They had learned the link between moving legs and moving mobile. If, however, she hitched them to a different mobile the next day, the infants showed no learning. Their actions indicated that they remembered the original mobile and recognized the difference. Moreover, if tethered to the familiar mobile a month later, they remembered the association and again began kicking (**FIGURE 5.6**).

Evidence of early processing also appeared in a study in which 10-year-olds were shown photos of preschoolers and asked to spot their former classmates. Although they consciously recognized only 1 in 5 of their onetime compatriots, their physiological responses (measured as skin perspiration) were greater to their former classmates whether or not they consciously recognized them (Newcombe et al., 2000). What the conscious mind does not know and cannot express in words, the nervous system somehow remembers.

Cognitive Development

4: **From the perspectives of Piaget and of today's researchers, how does a child's mind develop?**

Cognition refers to all the mental activities associated with thinking, knowing, remembering, and communicating. Somewhere on your life journey you became conscious. When was that, and how did your mind unfold from there? Developmental psychologist Jean Piaget (pronounced Pee-ah-ZHAY) spent his life searching for the answers to such questions. His interest began in 1920, when he was in Paris developing questions for children's intelligence tests. While administering the tests, Piaget became intrigued by children's *wrong* answers, which, he noted, were often strikingly similar among children of a given age. Where others saw childish mistakes, Piaget saw intelligence at work.

A half-century spent with children convinced Piaget that a child's mind is not a miniature model of an adult's. Thanks partly to his work, we now understand that children reason *differently*, in "wildly illogical ways about problems whose solutions are self-evident to adults" (Brainerd, 1996).

Piaget's studies led him to believe that a child's mind develops through a series of stages, in an upward march from the newborn's simple reflexes to the adult's abstract reasoning power. Thus, an 8-year-old can comprehend things a toddler cannot, such as the analogy that "getting an idea is like having a light turn on in your head," or that a miniature slide is too small for sliding, and a miniature car is much too small to get into (**FIGURE 5.7**). But our adult minds likewise engage in reasoning uncomprehended by 8-year-olds.

FIGURE 5.7 **Scale errors** Psychologists Judy DeLoache, David Uttal, and Karl Rosengren (2004) report that 18- to 30-month-old children may fail to take the size of an object into account when trying to perform impossible actions with it. At left, a 21-month-old attempts to slide down a miniature slide. At right, a 24-month-old opens the door to a miniature car and tries to step inside.

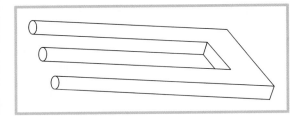

FIGURE 5.8 An impossible object
Look carefully at the "devil's tuning fork" (left). Now look away—no, better first study it some more—and then look away and draw it. . . . Not so easy, is it? Because this tuning fork is an impossible object, you have no schema for such an image.

cognition all the mental activities associated with thinking, knowing, remembering, and communicating.

schema a concept or framework that organizes and interprets information.

assimilation interpreting our new experiences in terms of our existing schemas.

accommodation adapting our current understandings (schemas) to incorporate new information.

Piaget's core idea is that the driving force behind our intellectual progression is an unceasing struggle to make sense of our experiences: "Children are active thinkers, constantly trying to construct more advanced understandings of the world" (Siegler & Ellis, 1996). To this end, the maturing brain builds **schemas,** concepts or mental molds into which we pour our experiences (**FIGURE 5.8**). In Chapter 4, we explored the idea of how children form a *gender schema*. By adulthood we have built countless schemas, ranging from *cats* and *dogs* to our concept of *love*.

To explain how we use and adjust our schemas, Piaget proposed two more concepts. First, we **assimilate** new experiences—we interpret them in terms of our current understandings (schemas). Having a simple schema for *cow*, for example, a toddler may call all four-legged animals *cows*. But as we interact with the world, we also adjust, or **accommodate,** our schemas to incorporate information provided by new experiences. Thus, the child soon learns that the original *cow* schema is too broad and accommodates by refining the category.

Piaget believed that as children construct their understandings, they experience spurts of change, followed by greater stability as they move from one cognitive plateau to the next. Let's consider these stages, as Piaget viewed them, in the light of current thinking.

Piaget's Theory and Current Thinking

Piaget proposed that children progress through four stages of cognitive development, each with distinctive characteristics that permit specific kinds of thinking (**TABLE 5.1**).

Jean Piaget (1896–1980) "If we examine the intellectual development of the individual or of the whole of humanity, we shall find that the human spirit goes through a certain number of stages, each different from the other" (1930).

TABLE 5.1 Piaget's Stages of Cognitive Development

Typical Age Range	Description of Stage	Developmental Phenomena
Birth to nearly 2 years	*Sensorimotor* Experiencing the world through senses and actions (looking, hearing, touching, mouthing, and grasping)	• Object permanence • Stranger anxiety
2 to about 6 or 7 years	*Preoperational* Representing things with words and images; using intuitive rather than logical reasoning	• Pretend play • Egocentrism
About 7 to 11 years	*Concrete operational* Thinking logically about concrete events; grasping concrete analogies and performing arithmetical operations	• Conservation • Mathematical transformations
About 12 through adulthood	*Formal operational* Abstract reasoning	• Abstract logic • Potential for mature moral reasoning

FIGURE 5.9 Object permanence Infants younger than 6 months seldom understand that things continue to exist when they are out of sight. But for this infant, out of sight is definitely not out of mind.

sensorimotor stage in Piaget's theory, the stage (from birth to about 2 years of age) during which infants know the world mostly in terms of their sensory impressions and motor activities.

object permanence the awareness that things continue to exist even when not perceived.

preoperational stage in Piaget's theory, the stage (from about 2 to 6 or 7 years of age) during which a child learns to use language but does not yet comprehend the mental operations of concrete logic.

conservation the principle (which Piaget believed to be a part of concrete operational reasoning) that properties such as mass, volume, and number remain the same despite changes in the forms of objects.

egocentrism in Piaget's theory, the preoperational child's difficulty taking another's point of view.

theory of mind people's ideas about their own and others' mental states—about their feelings, perceptions, and thoughts, and the behaviors these might predict.

Question: If most 2½-year-olds do not understand how miniature toys can symbolize real objects, should anatomically correct dolls be used when questioning such children about alleged physical or sexual abuse? Judy DeLoache (1995) reports that "very young children do not find it natural or easy to use a doll as a representation of themselves."

SENSORIMOTOR STAGE In the **sensorimotor stage,** from birth to nearly age 2, babies take in the world through their senses and actions—through looking, hearing, touching, mouthing, and grasping.

Very young babies seem to live in the present: Out of sight is out of mind. In one test, Piaget showed an infant an appealing toy and then flopped his beret over it. Before the age of 6 months, the infant acted as if the toy ceased to exist. Young infants lack **object permanence**—the awareness that objects continue to exist when not perceived. By 8 months, infants begin exhibiting memory for things no longer seen. If you hide a toy, the infant will momentarily look for it (**FIGURE 5.9**). Within another month or two, the infant will look for it even after being restrained for several seconds.

But does object permanence in fact blossom at 8 months, much as tulips blossom in spring? Today's researchers see development as more continuous than Piaget did, and they believe object permanence unfolds gradually. Even young infants will at least momentarily look for a toy where they saw it hidden a second before (Moore & Meltzoff, 2008; Wang et al., 2004).

Researchers also believe Piaget and his followers underestimated young children's competence. Like adults staring in disbelief at a magic trick (the "Whoa!" look), infants look longer at an unexpected and unfamiliar scene of a car seeming to pass through a solid object, a ball stopping in midair, or an object violating object permanence by magically disappearing (Baillargeon, 1995, 2008; Wellman & Gelman, 1992). Babies, it seems, have a more intuitive grasp of simple laws of physics than Piaget realized.

PREOPERATIONAL STAGE Piaget believed that until about age 6 or 7, children are in a **preoperational stage**—too young to perform mental operations. For a 5-year-old, the milk that seems "too much" in a tall, narrow glass may become an acceptable amount if poured into a short, wide glass. Focusing only on the height dimension, this child cannot perform the operation of mentally pouring the milk back, because she lacks the concept of **conservation**—the principle that quantity remains the same despite changes in shape (**FIGURE 5.10**).

Piaget did not view the stage transitions as abrupt. Even so, symbolic thinking appears at an earlier age than he supposed. Judy DeLoache (1987) discovered this when she showed children a model of a room and hid a model toy in it (a miniature stuffed dog behind a miniature couch). The 2½-year-olds easily remembered where to find the miniature toy, but they could not use the model to locate an actual stuffed dog behind a couch in a real room. Three-year-olds—only 6 months older—usually went right to the actual stuffed animal in the real room, showing they *could* think of the model as a symbol for the room. Piaget probably would have been surprised.

FIGURE 5.10 Piaget's test of conservation This preoperational child does not yet understand the principle of conservation of substance. When the milk is poured into a tall, narrow glass, it suddenly seems like "more" than when it was in the shorter, wider glass. In another year or so, she will understand that the volume stays the same.

EGOCENTRISM Piaget contended that preschool children are **egocentric:** They have difficulty perceiving things from another's point of view. Asked to "show Mommy your picture," 2-year-old Gabriella holds the picture up facing her own eyes. Three-year-old Gray makes himself "invisible" by putting his hands over his eyes, assuming that if he can't see his grandparents, they can't see him. Children's conversations also reveal their egocentrism, as one young boy demonstrated (Phillips, 1969, p. 61):

"Do you have a brother?"
"Yes."
"What's his name?"
"Jim."
"Does Jim have a brother?"
"No."

Like Gabriella, TV-watching preschoolers who block your view of the TV assume that you see what they see. They simply have not yet developed the ability to take another's viewpoint. Even as adults, we often overestimate the extent to which others share our opinions and perspectives, as when we assume that something will be clear to others if it is clear to us, or that e-mail recipients will "hear" our "just kidding" intent (Epley et al., 2004; Kruger et al., 2005). Children, however, are even more susceptible to this *curse of knowledge.*

THEORY OF MIND When Little Red Riding Hood realizes her "grandmother" is really a wolf, she swiftly revises her ideas about the creature's intentions and races away. Preschoolers, although still egocentric, develop this ability to infer others' mental states when they begin forming a **theory of mind** (a term first coined by psychologists David Premack and Guy Woodruff, to describe chimpanzees' seeming ability to read intentions). As research with Chinese preschoolers illustrates, talking about others enhances a child's developing ability to infer their states of mind (Lu et al., 2008).

As children's ability to take another's perspective develops, they seek to understand what made a playmate angry, when a sibling will share, and what might make a parent buy a toy. And they begin to tease, empathize, and persuade. Between about 3½ and 4½, children worldwide come to realize that others may hold false beliefs (Callaghan et al., 2005; Sabbagh et al., 2006). Jennifer Jenkins and Janet Astington (1996) showed Toronto children a Band-Aids box and asked them what was inside. Expecting Band-Aids, the children were surprised to discover that the box actually contained pencils. Asked what a child who had never seen the box would think was inside, 3-year-olds typically answered "pencils." By age 4 to 5, the children's theory of mind had leapt forward, and they anticipated their friends' false belief that the box would hold Band-Aids. Children with autism (see Close-Up: Autism and "Mind-Blindness") have difficulty understanding that another's state of mind differs from their own.

"It's too late, Roger—they've seen us."

Roger has not outgrown his early childhood egocentrism.

Use your finger to trace a capital E on your forehead. When Adam Galinsky and his colleagues (2006) invited people to do that, they were more egocentric—less likely to draw it from the perspective of someone looking at them—if they were first made to feel powerful. Other studies confirm that feeling powerful reduces people's sensitivity to how others see, think, and feel.

Family Circus ® Bil Keane

TELL ME, JEFFY, WHAT WAS THIS FUN DREAM ABOUT LAST NIGHT?

"Don't you remember, Grandma? You were in it with me."

Close-Up:

Autism and "Mind-Blindness"

Diagnoses of **autism,** a disorder marked by communication and social deficiencies and repetitive behaviors, have been increasing. Once believed to affect 1 in 2500 children, autism or a related disorder will now afflict 1 in 150 American children and, in Britain's London area, 1 in 86 children (Baird et al., 2006; CDC, 2007; Lilienfeld & Arkowitz, 2007). The increase in autism diagnoses may reflect a relabeling of children's disorders (Gernsbacher et al., 2005; Grinker, 2007; Shattuck, 2006). As autism diagnoses have increased, the number of children considered "cognitively disabled" or "learning disabled" has decreased.

The underlying source of autism's symptoms seems to be poor communication among brain regions that normally work together to let us take another's viewpoint. People with autism are therefore said to have an *impaired theory of mind* (Rajendran & Mitchell, 2007). They have difficulty inferring others' thoughts and feelings. They do not appreciate that playmates and parents might view things differently. Mindreading that most find intuitive *(Is that face conveying a happy smile, a self-satisfied smirk, or a contemptuous sneer?)* is difficult for those with autism. Most children learn that another child's pouting mouth signals sadness, and that twinkling eyes mean happiness or mischief. A child with autism fails to understand these signals (Frith & Frith, 2001).

autism a disorder that appears in childhood and is marked by deficient communication, social interaction, and understanding of others' states of mind.

Autism This speech-language pathologist is helping a boy with autism learn to form sounds and words. Autism, which afflicts four boys for every girl, is marked by deficient social and communication skills and difficulty in grasping others' states of mind.

To encompass the variations in autism, today's researchers refer to *autism spectrum disorder.* One variation in this spectrum is *Asperger syndrome,* a "high-functioning" form of autism. Asperger syndrome is marked by normal intelligence, often accompanied by exceptional skill or talent in a specific area, but deficient social and communication skills (and thus an inability to form normal peer relationships).

Psychologist Simon Baron-Cohen (2008) proposes that autism, which afflicts four boys for every girl, represents an "extreme male brain." Girls are naturally predisposed to be "empathizers," he contends. They are better at reading facial expressions and gestures—a challenging task for those with autism. And, although the sexes overlap, boys are, he believes, better "systemizers"—understanding things according to rules or laws, as in mathematical and mechanical systems. "If two 'systemizers' have a child, this will increase the risk of the child having autism," Baron-Cohen theorizes. And

because of *assortative mating*—people's tendency to seek spouses who share their interests—two systemizers will indeed often mate. "I do not discount environmental factors," he notes. "I'm just saying, don't forget about biology."

Sibling and twin studies provide some evidence of biology's influence. A younger sibling of a child with autism is at a heightened risk of 15 percent or so (Sutcliffe, 2008). In identical twins, if one twin is diagnosed with autism, the chances are 70 percent that the co-twin also will have autism (Sebat et al., 2007). Random genetic mutations in sperm-producing cells may play a role. As men age, these mutations become more frequent, which may help explain why an over-40 man has a much higher risk of fathering a child with autism than does a man under 30 (Reichenberg et al., 2007). Genetic influences appear to do their damage by altering brain synapses (Crawley, 2007; Garber, 2007).

Biology's role in autism also appears in brain-function studies. People without

---

concrete operational stage in Piaget's theory, the stage of cognitive development (from about 6 or 7 to 11 years of age) during which children gain the mental operations that enable them to think logically about concrete events.

CONCRETE OPERATIONAL STAGE By about 6 or 7 years of age, said Piaget, children enter the **concrete operational stage.** Given concrete materials, they begin to grasp conservation. Understanding that change in form does not mean change in quantity, they can mentally pour milk back and forth between glasses of different shapes. They also enjoy jokes that allow them to use this new understanding:

autism often yawn after seeing others yawn. And as they view and imitate another's smiling or frowning, they feel something of what the other is feeling, thanks to their brain's *mirror neurons* (more on this in Chapter 7). Not so among those with autism, who are less imitative and show much less activity in brain areas involved in mirroring others' actions (Dapretto et al., 2006; Perra et al., 2008; Senju et al., 2007). When people with autism watch another person's hand movements, for example, their brain displays less than normal mirroring activity (Oberman & Ramachandran, 2007; Théoret et al., 2005).

Such discoveries have launched explorations of treatments that might alleviate some of autism's symptoms by triggering mirror neuron activity (Ramachandran & Oberman, 2006). For example, seeking to "systemize empathy," Baron-Cohen and his Cambridge University colleagues (2007; Golan et al., 2007) collaborated with Britain's National Autistic Society and a film production company. Knowing that television shows with vehicles have been most popular for kids with autism, they created a series of animations that grafted emotion-conveying faces onto toy tram,

train, and tractor characters in a pretend boy's bedroom (**FIGURE 5.11**). After the boy leaves for school, the characters come to life and have experiences that lead them to display various emotions (which I predict you would enjoy viewing at www.thetransporters.com). The children expressed a surprising ability to generalize what they had learned to a new, real context. By the end of the intervention, their previously deficient ability to recognize emotions on real faces equaled that of children without autism.

"The neighbor's dog has bitten people before. He is barking at Louise."

FIGURE 5.11 Transported into a world of emotion (a) A research team at Cambridge University's Autism Research Centre introduced children with autism to emotions experienced and displayed by toy vehicles. (b) After four weeks of viewing animations, the children displayed a markedly increased ability to recognize emotions in human as well as the toy faces.

Point to the face that shows how Louise is feeling.

Accuracy scores

After intervention, children with autism become better able to identify which facial emotion matches the context.

■ Typical control (no training) ■ Faces intervention

(a) Emotion-conveying faces grafted onto toy trains

(b) Matching new scenes and faces (and data for two trials)

© Crown copyright, MMVI, www.thetransporters.com, courtesy Changing Media Development

Mr. Jones went into a restaurant and ordered a whole pizza for his dinner. When the waiter asked if he wanted it cut into 6 or 8 pieces, Mr. Jones said, "Oh, you'd better make it 6, I could never eat 8 pieces!" (McGhee, 1976).

Piaget believed that during the concrete operational stage, children fully gain the mental ability to comprehend mathematical transformations and conservation. When my daughter Laura was 6, I was astonished at her inability to reverse simple

formal operational stage in Piaget's theory, the stage of cognitive development (normally beginning about age 12) during which people begin to think logically about abstract concepts

arithmetic. Asked, "What is 8 plus 4?" she required 5 seconds to compute "12," and another 5 seconds to then compute 12 minus 4. By age 8, she could answer a reversed question instantly.

FORMAL OPERATIONAL STAGE By age 12, our reasoning expands from the purely concrete (involving actual experience) to encompass abstract thinking (involving imagined realities and symbols). As children approach adolescence, said Piaget, many become capable of solving hypothetical propositions and deducing consequences: *If* this, *then* that. Systematic reasoning, what Piaget called **formal operational** thinking, is now within their grasp.

Although full-blown logic and reasoning await adolescence, the rudiments of formal operational thinking begin earlier than Piaget realized. Consider this simple problem:

If John is in school, then Mary is in school. John is in school. What can you say about Mary?

Formal operational thinkers have no trouble answering correctly. But neither do most 7-year-olds (Suppes, 1982).

Reflecting on Piaget's Theory

"Assessing the impact of Piaget on developmental psychology is like assessing the impact of Shakespeare on English literature."

—Developmental psychologist
Harry Beilin (1992)

What remains of Piaget's ideas about the child's mind? Plenty—enough to merit his being singled out by *Time* magazine as one of the twentieth century's 20 most influential scientists and thinkers and rated in a survey of British psychologists as the greatest psychologist of that century (*Psychologist*, 2003). Piaget identified significant cognitive milestones and stimulated worldwide interest in how the mind develops. His emphasis was less on the ages at which children typically reach specific milestones than on their sequence. Studies around the globe, from aboriginal Australia to Algeria to North America, have confirmed that human cognition unfolds basically in the sequence Piaget described (Lourenco & Machado, 1996; Segall et al., 1990).

However, today's researchers see development as more continuous than did Piaget. By detecting the beginnings of each type of thinking at earlier ages, they have revealed conceptual abilities Piaget missed. Moreover, they see formal logic as a smaller part of cognition than he did. Piaget would not be surprised that today, as part of our own cognitive development, we are adapting his ideas to accommodate new findings.

Piaget's emphasis on how the child's mind grows through interaction with the physical environment is complemented by the Russian psychologist Lev Vygotsky's emphasis on how the child's mind grows through interaction with the *social* environment. If Piaget's child was a young scientist, Vygotsky's was a young apprentice. By mentoring children and giving them new words, parents and others provide a temporary *scaffold* from which children can step to higher levels of thinking (Renninger & Granott, 2005). Language, an important ingredient of social mentoring, provides the building blocks for thinking, noted Vygotsky (who was born the same year as Piaget, but died prematurely of tuberculosis).

Lev Vygotsky (1895–1934) Vygotsky, a Russian developmental psychologist, pictured here with his daughter, studied how a child's mind feeds on the language of social interaction.

James V. Wertsch/Washington University

IMPLICATIONS FOR PARENTS AND TEACHERS Future parents and teachers remember: Young children are incapable of adult logic. Preschoolers who stand in the way when others are trying to watch TV simply have not learned to take another's viewpoint. What seems simple and obvious to us—getting off a teeter-totter will cause a friend on the other end to crash—may be incomprehensible to a 3-year-old. Also remember that children are not passive receptacles waiting to be filled with knowledge. Better to build on what they already know, engaging them in concrete demonstrations and stimulating them to think for themselves. And, finally, accept children's cognitive immaturity as adaptive. It is nature's strategy for keeping children close to protective adults and providing time for learning and socialization (Bjorklund & Green, 1992).

REHEARSE IT!

5. Maturation, the orderly sequence of biological growth, explains why
  a. children with autism have difficulty inferring others' thoughts and feelings.
  b. most children have begun walking by about 12 months.
  c. early experiences have no effect on brain tissue.
  d. object permanence is present at birth.

6. Between ages 3 and 6, the human brain experiences the greatest growth in the _____ lobes, which we use for rational planning, and which continue developing at least into adolescence.
  a. parietal
  b. temporal
  c. frontal
  d. occipital

7. Which of the following is true of motor-skill development?
  a. It is determined solely by genetic factors.
  b. The sequence, but not the timing, is universal.
  c. The timing, but not the sequence, is universal.
  d. It is determined solely by environmental factors.

8. During the preoperational stage, a young child's thinking is
  a. abstract.
  b. negative.
  c. conservative.
  d. egocentric.

9. Children acquire the mental operations necessary to understand conservation during the

  a. sensorimotor stage.
  b. preoperational stage.
  c. concrete operational stage.
  d. formal operational stage.

10. Although Piaget's stage theory continues to inform our understanding of children's thinking, many researchers believe that
  a. Piaget's "stages" begin earlier and development is more continuous than he realized.
  b. children do not progress as rapidly as Piaget predicted.
  c. few children really progress to the concrete operational stage.
  d. there is no way of testing much of Piaget's theoretical work.

Answers: 5. b, 6. c, 7. b, 8. d, 9. c, 10. a.

Social Development

5: How do parent-infant attachment bonds form?

From birth, babies in all cultures are social creatures, developing an intense bond with their caregivers. Infants come to prefer familiar faces and voices, then to coo and gurgle when given a parent's attention. At about 8 months, soon after object permanence emerges and children become mobile, a curious thing happens: They develop **stranger anxiety.** They may greet strangers by crying and reaching for familiar caregivers. "No! Don't leave me!" their distress seems to say. Children this age have schemas for familiar faces; when they cannot assimilate the new face into these remembered schemas, they become distressed (Kagan, 1984). Once again, we see an important principle: *The brain, mind, and social-emotional behavior develop together.*

Origins of Attachment

One-year-olds typically cling tightly to a parent when they are frightened or expect separation. Reunited after being separated, they shower the parent with smiles and hugs. No social behavior is more striking than this intense and mutual infant-parent bond. This **attachment** bond is a powerful survival impulse that keeps infants close to their caregivers. Infants become attached to those—typically their parents—who are comfortable and familiar. For many years, developmental psychologists reasoned that infants became attached to those who satisfied their need for nourishment. It made sense. But an accidental finding overturned this explanation.

BODY CONTACT During the 1950s, University of Wisconsin psychologists Harry Harlow and Margaret Harlow bred monkeys for their learning studies. To equalize experiences and to isolate any disease, they separated the infant monkeys from their mothers shortly after birth and raised them in sanitary individual cages, which included a cheesecloth baby blanket (Harlow et al., 1971). Then came a surprise: When their blankets were taken to be laundered, the monkeys became distressed.

Christina Kennedy/Alamy

Stranger anxiety A newly emerging ability to evaluate people as unfamiliar and possibly threatening helps protect babies 8 months and older.

stranger anxiety the fear of strangers that infants commonly display, beginning by about 8 months of age.

attachment an emotional tie with another person; shown in young children by their seeking closeness to the caregiver and showing distress on separation.

FIGURE 5.12 **The Harlows' mothers** Psychologists Harry Harlow and Margaret Harlow raised monkeys with two artificial mothers—one a bare wire cylinder with a wooden head and an attached feeding bottle, the other a cylinder with no bottle but covered with foam rubber and wrapped with terry cloth. The Harlows' discovery surprised many psychologists: The infants much preferred contact with the comfortable cloth mother, even while feeding from the nourishing mother.

Lee Kirkpatrick (1999) reports that for some people a perceived relationship with God functions as do other attachments, by providing a secure base for exploration and a safe haven when threatened.

Attachment When French pilot Christian Moullec took off in his microlight plane, his imprinted geese, which he had raised since their hatching, followed closely. The same imprinting procedure has been used to guide endangered whooping cranes to their winter nesting grounds (Mooallem, 2009).

The Harlows recognized that this intense attachment to the blanket contradicted the idea that attachment derives from an association with nourishment. But how could they show this more convincingly? To pit the drawing power of a food source against the contact comfort of the blanket, they created two artificial mothers. One was a bare wire cylinder with a wooden head and an attached feeding bottle, the other a cylinder wrapped with terry cloth.

When raised with both, the monkeys overwhelmingly preferred the comfy cloth mother (**FIGURE 5.12**). Like human infants clinging to their mothers, the monkeys would cling to their cloth mothers when anxious. When venturing into the environment, they used her as a secure base, as if attached to her by an invisible elastic band that stretched only so far before pulling them back. Researchers soon learned that other qualities—rocking, warmth, and feeding—made the cloth mother even more appealing.

Human infants, too, become attached to parents who are soft and warm and who rock, feed, and pat. Much parent-infant emotional communication occurs via touch (Hertenstein et al., 2006), which can be either soothing (snuggles) or arousing (tickles). Human attachment also consists of one person providing another with a secure base from which to explore and a safe haven when distressed. As we mature, our secure base and safe haven shift—from parents to peers and partners (Cassidy & Shaver, 1999). But at all ages we are social creatures. We gain strength when someone offers, by words and actions, a safe haven: "I will be here. I am interested in you. Come what may, I will actively support you" (Crowell & Waters, 1994).

FAMILIARITY Contact is one key to attachment. Another is familiarity. In many animals, attachments based on familiarity likewise form during a **critical period**—an optimal period when certain events must take place to facilitate proper development (Bornstein, 1989). For goslings, ducklings, or chicks, that period falls in the hours shortly after hatching, when the first moving object they see is normally their mother. From then on, the young fowl follow her, and her alone.

Konrad Lorenz (1937) explored this rigid attachment process, called **imprinting.** He wondered: What would ducklings do if he was the first moving creature they observed? What they did was follow him around: Everywhere that Konrad went, the ducks were sure to go. Further tests revealed that although baby birds imprint best to their own species, they also will imprint to a variety of moving objects—an animal of another species, a box on wheels, a bouncing ball (Colombo, 1982; Johnson, 1992). And, once formed, this attachment is difficult to reverse.

Children—unlike ducklings—do not imprint. However, they do become attached to what they've known. *Mere exposure* to people and things fosters fondness (see Chapter 15). Children like to reread the same books, rewatch the same movies, reenact family traditions. They prefer to eat familiar foods, live in the same familiar neighborhood, attend school with the same old friends. Familiarity is a safety signal. Familiarity breeds content.

Attachment Differences

6 : How have psychologists studied children's differing attachments, and what have they learned?

What accounts for children's attachment differences? Placed in a *strange situation* (usually a laboratory playroom), about 60 percent of infants display *secure attachment*. In their mother's presence they play comfortably, happily exploring their new environment. When she leaves, they are distressed; when she returns, they seek contact with her. Other infants avoid attachment or show *insecure attachment*. They are less likely to explore their surroundings; they may even cling to their mother. When she leaves, they either cry loudly and remain upset or seem indifferent to her departure and return (Ainsworth, 1973, 1989; Kagan, 1995; van IJzendoorn & Kroonenberg, 1988).

Mary Ainsworth (1979), who designed the strange situation experiments, studied attachment differences by observing mother-infant pairs at home during their first six months. Later she observed the 1-year-old infants in a strange situation without their mothers. Sensitive, responsive mothers—those who noticed what their babies were doing and responded appropriately—had infants who exhibited secure attachment. Insensitive, unresponsive mothers—mothers who attended to their babies when they felt like doing so but ignored them at other times—had infants who often became insecurely attached. The Harlows' monkey studies, with unresponsive artificial mothers, produced even more striking effects. When put in strange situations without their artificial mothers, the deprived infants were terrified (**FIGURE 5.13**).

But is attachment style the *result* of parenting? Or is attachment style the result of genetically influenced *temperament*—a person's characteristic emotional reactivity and intensity? Shortly after birth, some babies are noticeably *difficult*—irritable, intense, and unpredictable. Others are *easy*—cheerful, relaxed, and feeding and sleeping on predictable schedules (Chess & Thomas, 1987). By neglecting such inborn differences, the parenting studies, Judith Harris (1998) noted, are like "comparing foxhounds reared in kennels with poodles reared in apartments." To separate nature and nurture, Dutch researcher Dymphna van den Boom (1990, 1995) varied parenting while controlling temperament. (Pause and think: If you were the researcher, how might you have done this?)

Van den Boom's solution was to randomly assign one hundred 6- to 9-month-old temperamentally difficult infants to either an experimental group, in which mothers received personal training in sensitive responding, or to a control group, in which they did not. At 12 months of age, 68 percent of the infants in the experimental group were rated securely attached, as were only 28 percent of those in the control group. Other studies have also found that intervention programs can increase parental sensitivity and, to a lesser extent, infant attachment security (Bakermans-Kranenburg et al., 2003; Van Zeijl et al., 2006).

As these examples indicate, researchers have more often studied mother care than father care. Infants who lack a caring mother are said to suffer "maternal deprivation"; those lacking a father's care merely experience "father absence."

critical period an optimal period shortly after birth when an organism's exposure to certain stimuli or experiences produces proper development.

imprinting the process by which certain animals form attachments during a critical period very early in life.

FIGURE 5.13 Social deprivation and fear Monkeys raised with artificial mothers were terror-stricken when placed in strange situations without their surrogate mothers. (Today's climate of greater respect for animal welfare prevents such primate studies.)

"We need fathers to realize that responsibility does not end at conception. We need them to realize that what makes you a man is not the ability to have a child—it's the courage to raise one."

—Barack Obama,
Father's Day sermon, 2008

Fantastic father Among the Aka people of Central Africa, fathers form an especially close bond with their infants, even suckling the babies with their own nipples when hunger makes the child impatient for Mother's return. According to anthropologist Barry Hewlett (1991), fathers in this culture are holding or within reach of their babies 47 percent of the time.

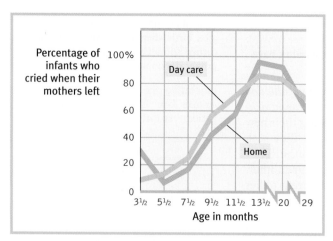

FIGURE 5.14 Infants' distress over separation from parents In an experiment, groups of infants were left by their mothers in an unfamiliar room. In both groups, the percentage who cried when the mother left peaked at about 13 months. Whether the infant had experienced day care made little difference. (From Kagan, 1976.)

"Out of the conflict between trust and mistrust, the infant develops hope, which is the earliest form of what gradually becomes faith in adults."

—Erik Erikson, 1983

"What is learned in the cradle, lasts to the grave."

—French proverb

basic trust according to Erik Erikson, a sense that the world is predictable and trustworthy; said to be formed during infancy by appropriate experiences with responsive caregivers.

This reflects a wider attitude in which "fathering a child" has meant impregnating, and "mothering" has meant nurturing. But fathers are more than just mobile sperm banks. Across nearly 100 studies worldwide, a father's love and acceptance have been comparable to a mother's love in predicting their offspring's health and well-being (Rohner & Veneziano, 2001). In one mammoth British study following 7259 children from birth to adulthood, those whose fathers were most involved in parenting (through outings, reading to them, and taking an interest in their education) tended to achieve more in school, even after controlling for many other factors, such as parental education and family wealth (Flouri & Buchanan, 2004).

Whether children live with one parent or two, are cared for at home or in a day-care center, live in North America, Guatemala, or the Kalahari Desert, their anxiety over separation from parents peaks at around 13 months, then gradually declines (**FIGURE 5.14**). Does this mean our need for and love of others also fades away? Hardly. Our capacity for love grows, and our pleasure in touching and holding those we love never ceases. The power of early attachment does nonetheless gradually relax, allowing us to move out into a wider range of situations, communicate with strangers more freely, and stay emotionally attached to loved ones despite distance.

ATTACHMENT AND ADULT RELATIONSHIPS Developmental theorist Erik Erikson (1902–1994), working in collaboration with his wife, Joan Erikson, said that securely attached children approach life with a sense of **basic trust**—a sense that the world is predictable and reliable. He attributed basic trust not to environment or inborn temperament, but to early parenting. He theorized that infants blessed with sensitive, loving caregivers form a lifelong attitude of trust rather than fear.

Although debate continues, many researchers now believe that our early attachments form the foundation for our adult relationships and our comfort with affection and intimacy (Birnbaum et al., 2006; Fraley, 2002). Adult styles of romantic love do tend to exhibit secure, trusting attachment; insecure, anxious attachment; or the avoidance of attachment (Feeney & Noller, 1990; Rholes & Simpson, 2004; Shaver & Mikulincer, 2007). Moreover, these adult attachment styles in turn affect relationships with our children, as avoidant people find parenting more stressful and unsatisfying (Rholes et al., 2006).

DEPRIVATION OF ATTACHMENT If secure attachment nurtures social competence, what happens when circumstances prevent a child from forming attachments? In all of psychology, there is no sadder research literature. Babies reared in institutions without the stimulation and attention of a regular caregiver, or locked away at home under conditions of abuse or extreme neglect, are often withdrawn, frightened, even speechless. Those abandoned in Romanian orphanages during the 1980s looked "frighteningly like [the Harlows'] monkeys" (Carlson, 1995). If institutionalized more than eight months, they often bore lasting emotional scars (Chisholm, 1998; Malinosky-Rummell & Hansen, 1993; Rutter et al., 1998).

The Harlows' monkeys bore similar scars if reared in total isolation, without even an artificial mother. As adults, when placed with other monkeys their age, they either cowered in fright or lashed out in aggression. When they reached sexual maturity, most were incapable of mating. If artificially impregnated, females often were neglectful, abusive, even murderous toward their first-born. A recent experiment with primates confirms the abuse-breeds-abuse phenomenon. Whether reared by biological or adoptive mothers, 9 of 16 females who were abused by their mothers became abusive parents, as did no female reared by a nonabusive mother (Maestripieri, 2005).

In humans, too, the unloved sometimes become the unloving. Most abusive parents—and many condemned murderers—report having been neglected or battered as children (Kempe & Kempe, 1978; Lewis et al., 1988). But does this mean that today's victim is predictably tomorrow's victimizer? No. Though most abusers were indeed abused, most abused children do *not* later become violent criminals or abusive parents. Most children growing up under adversity (as did the surviving children of the Holocaust) are *resilient;* they become normal adults (Helmreich, 1992; Masten, 2001).

But others, especially those who experience no sharp break from their abusive past, don't bounce back so readily. Some 30 percent of people who have been abused do abuse their children—a rate lower than that found in the primate study, but four times the U.S. national rate of child abuse (Dumont et al., 2007; Kaufman & Zigler, 1987; Widom, 1989a,b).

Extreme early trauma seems to leave footprints on the brain. If repeatedly threatened and attacked while young, normally placid golden hamsters grow up to be cowards when caged with same-sized hamsters, or bullies when caged with weaker ones (Ferris, 1996). Such animals show changes in the brain's serotonin system, a neurotransmitter that calms aggressive impulses. A similarly sluggish serotonin response has been found in abused children who become aggressive teens and adults. "Stress can set off a ripple of hormonal changes that permanently wire a child's brain to cope with a malevolent world," concludes abuse researcher Martin Teicher (2002).

Such findings help explain why young children terrorized through physical abuse or wartime atrocities (being beaten, witnessing torture, and living in constant fear) may suffer other lasting wounds—often nightmares, depression, and an adolescence troubled by substance abuse, binge eating, or aggression (Kendall-Tackett et al., 1993, 2004; Polusny & Follette, 1995; Trickett & McBride-Chang, 1995). Child sexual abuse, especially if severe and prolonged, places children at increased risk for health problems, psychological disorders, substance abuse, and criminality (Freyd et al., 2005; Tyler, 2002). Abuse victims are at considerable risk for depression *if* they carry a gene variation that spurs stress-hormone production (Bradley et al., 2008). As we will see again and again, behavior and emotion arise from a particular environment interacting with particular genes.

Parenting Styles

7: **What are the three primary parenting styles, and what outcomes are associated with them?**

Some parents spank, some reason. Some are strict, some are lax. Some show little affection, some liberally hug and kiss. Do such differences in parenting styles affect children?

The most heavily researched aspect of parenting has been how, and to what extent, parents seek to control their children. Investigators have identified three parenting styles:

1. *Authoritarian* parents impose rules and expect obedience: "Don't interrupt." "Keep your room clean." "Don't stay out late or you'll be grounded." "Why? Because I said so."
2. *Permissive* parents submit to their children's desires. They make few demands and use little punishment.
3. *Authoritative* parents are both demanding and responsive. They exert control by setting rules and enforcing them, but they also explain the reasons for rules. And, especially with older children, they encourage open discussion and allow some exceptions to rules.

Too hard, too soft, and just right, these styles have been called. Research indicates that children with the highest self-esteem, self-reliance, and social competence usually have warm, concerned, *authoritative* parents (Baumrind, 1996; Buri et al., 1988; Coopersmith, 1967). Those with authoritarian parents tend to have less social skill and self-esteem, and those with permissive parents tend to be more aggressive and immature. The participants in most studies have been middle-class White families, and some critics suggest that effective parenting may vary by culture. Yet studies with families of other races and in more than 200 cultures worldwide confirm the social and academic correlates of loving and authoritative parenting (Rohner & Veneziano, 2001; Sorkhabi, 2005; Steinberg & Morris, 2001).

A word of caution: The association between certain parenting styles (being firm but open) and certain childhood outcomes (social competence) is correlational. As Chapter 1 emphasized, *correlation is not causation*. (Perhaps you can imagine possible explanations for this parenting-competence link.)

Parents struggling with conflicting advice and with the stresses of child-rearing should remember that *all advice reflects the advice giver's values*. For those who prize unquestioning obedience from a child, an authoritarian style may have the desired effect. For those who value children's sociability and self-reliance, authoritative firm-but-open parenting is advisable.

The investment in raising a child buys many years not only of joy and love but of worry and irritation. Yet for most people who become parents, a child is one's biological and social legacy—one's personal investment in the human future. Remind young adults of their mortality and they will express increased desire for children (Wisman & Goldenberg, 2005). To paraphrase psychiatrist Carl Jung, we reach backward into our parents and forward into our children, and through their children into a future we will never see, but about which we must therefore care.

"You are the bows from which your children as living arrows are sent forth."

—Kahlil Gibran, *The Prophet,* 1923

REHEARSE IT!

11. Faced with a new babysitter, an 8-month-old infant often shows distress, a behavior referred to as
    a. conservation.
    b. stranger anxiety.
    c. imprinting.
    d. maturation.

12. In a series of experiments, the Harlows found that monkeys raised with artificial mothers tended, when afraid, to cling to

    a. the wire mother.
    b. the cloth mother.
    c. whichever mother held the feeding bottle.
    d. other infant monkeys.

13. From the very first weeks of life, infants differ in their characteristic emotional reactions, with some infants being intense and anxious, while others are easygoing and relaxed. These differences are usually explained as differences in
    a. attachment.
    b. imprinting.
    c. temperament.
    d. parental responsiveness.

Answers: 11. b, 12. b, 13. c.

Adolescence

Many psychologists once believed that childhood sets our traits. Today's developmental psychologists see development as lifelong. At a five-year high school reunion, former best friends may be surprised at their divergence; a decade later, they may have trouble sustaining a conversation.

As the *life-span perspective* emerged, psychologists began to look at how maturation and experience shape us not only in infancy and childhood, but also in adolescence and beyond. **Adolescence**—the years spent morphing from child to adult—starts with the physical beginnings of sexual maturity and ends with the social achievement of independent adult status (which means that in some cultures, where teens are self-supporting, adolescence hardly exists).

G. Stanley Hall (1904), one of the first psychologists to describe adolescence, believed that the tension between biological maturity and social dependence creates a period of "storm and stress." Indeed, after age 30, many who grow up in independence-fostering Western cultures look back on their teenage years as a time they

How will you look back on your life 10 years from now? Are you making choices that someday you will recollect with satisfaction?

would not want to relive, a time when their peers' social approval was imperative, their sense of direction in life was in flux, and their feeling of alienation from their parents was deepest (Arnett, 1999; Macfarlane, 1964).

But for many, adolescence is a time of vitality without the cares of adulthood, a time of rewarding friendships, heightened idealism, and a growing sense of life's exciting possibilities.

Physical Development

8: What physical changes mark adolescence?

Adolescence begins with **puberty,** the time when we mature sexually. Puberty follows a surge of hormones, which may intensify moods and which trigger a two-year period of rapid physical development, usually beginning at about age 11 in girls and at about age 13 in boys. About the time of puberty, boys' growth propels them to greater height than their female counterparts (**FIGURE 5.15**). During this growth spurt, the **primary sex characteristics**—the reproductive organs and external genitalia—develop dramatically. So do **secondary sex characteristics,** the nonreproductive traits such as breasts and hips in girls, facial hair and deepened voice in boys, pubic and underarm hair in both sexes (see **FIGURE 5.16** on the next page). A year or two before puberty, however, boys and girls often feel the first stirrings of attraction toward those of the other (or their own) sex (McClintock & Herdt, 1996).

In girls, puberty starts with breast development, which now often begins by age 10 (Brody, 1999). But puberty's landmarks are the first ejaculation in boys *(spermarche),* usually by about age 14, and the first menstrual period in girls (**menarche**—meh-NAR-key), usually within a year of age 12½ (Anderson et al., 2003). Nearly all adult women recall their first menstrual period and remember experiencing a mixture of pride, excitement, embarrassment, and apprehension (Greif & Ulman, 1982; Woods et al., 1983). Girls who have been prepared for menarche usually experience it as a positive life transition. Most men similarly recall their first ejaculation, which usually occurs as a nocturnal emission (Fuller & Downs, 1990).

Just as in the earlier life stages, the *sequence* of physical changes in puberty (for example, breast buds and visible pubic hair before menarche) is far more predictable

adolescence the transition period from childhood to adulthood, extending from puberty to independence.

puberty the period of sexual maturation, during which a person becomes capable of reproducing.

primary sex characteristics the body structures (ovaries, testes, and external genitalia) that make sexual reproduction possible.

secondary sex characteristics nonreproductive sexual characteristics, such as female breasts and hips, male voice quality, and body hair.

menarche [meh-NAR-key] the first menstrual period.

Menarche appears to occur a few months earlier, on average, for girls who have experienced stresses related to father absence or sexual abuse (Vigil et al., 2005; Zabin et al., 2005).

FIGURE 5.15 Height differences Throughout childhood, boys and girls are similar in height. At puberty, girls surge ahead briefly, but then boys overtake them at about age 14. (Data from Tanner, 1978.) Sexual development and growth spurts are now beginning somewhat earlier than was the case a half-century ago (Herman-Giddens et al., 2001).

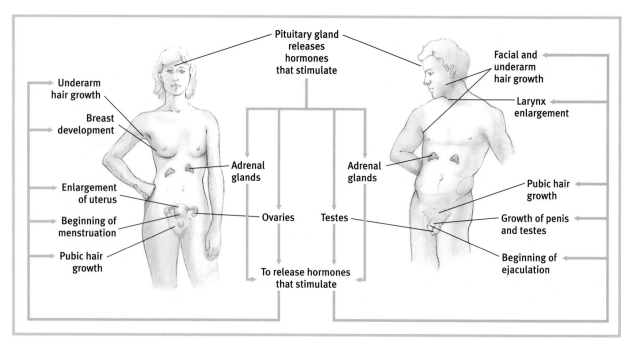

FIGURE 5.16 Body changes at puberty
At about age 11 in girls and age 13 in boys, a surge of hormones triggers a variety of physical changes.

than their *timing*. Some girls start their growth spurt at 9, some boys as late as age 16. Though such variations have little effect on height at maturity, they may have psychological consequences. For boys, early maturation pays dividends: Being stronger and more athletic during their early teen years, they tend to be more popular, self-assured, and independent, though also more at risk for alcohol use, delinquency, and premature sexual activity (Lynne et al., 2007; Steinberg & Morris, 2001). For girls, early maturation can be stressful (Mendle et al., 2007). If a young girl's body is out of sync with her own emotional maturity and her friends' physical development and experiences, she may begin associating with older adolescents or may suffer teasing or sexual harassment. It is not only when we mature that counts, but how people react to our genetically influenced physical development. Remember: *Heredity and environment interact.*

An adolescent's brain is also a work in progress. As teens mature, their frontal lobes continue to develop. The growth of *myelin,* the fatty tissue that forms around axons and speeds neurotransmission, enables better communication with other brain regions (Kuhn, 2006; Silveri et al., 2006). These developments bring improved judgment, impulse control, and the ability to plan for the long term.

Frontal lobe maturation lags the emotional limbic system. Puberty's hormonal surge and limbic system development help explain teens' occasional impulsiveness, risky behaviors, emotional storms—slamming doors and turning up the music (Casey et al., 2008). No wonder younger teens (whose unfinished frontal lobes aren't yet fully equipped for making long-term plans and curbing impulses) so often succumb to the lure of smoking, which most adult smokers could tell them they will later regret. Teens actually don't underestimate the risks of smoking—or fast driving or unprotected sex—they just, when reasoning from their gut, weigh the benefits more heavily (Reyna & Farley, 2006; Steinberg, 2007).

So, when Junior drives recklessly and academically self-destructs, should his parents reassure themselves that "he can't help it; his frontal cortex isn't yet fully grown"? They can at least take hope: The brain with which Junior begins his teens differs from the brain with which he will end his teens. Unless he slows his brain development with heavy drinking—leaving him prone to impulsivity and addiction—his frontal lobes will continue maturing until about age 25 (Beckman, 2004; Crews et al., 2007).

"Young man, go to your room and stay there until your cerebral cortex matures."

In 2004, the American Psychological Association joined seven other medical and mental health associations in filing U.S. Supreme Court briefs, arguing against the death penalty for 16- and 17-years-olds. The briefs documented the teen brain's immaturity "in areas that bear upon adolescent decision-making." Teens are "less guilty by reason of adolescence," suggested psychologist Laurence Steinberg and law professor Elizabeth Scott (2003). In 2005, by a 5-to-4 margin, the Court concurred, declaring juvenile death penalties unconstitutional.

> "If a gun is put in the control of the prefrontal cortex of a hurt and vengeful 15-year-old, and it is pointed at a human target, it will very likely go off."
>
> —National Institutes of Health brain scientist Daniel R. Weinberger, "A Brain Too Young for Good Judgment," 2001

Cognitive Development

9: **How did Piaget and Kohlberg describe adolescent cognitive and moral development?**

As young teenagers become capable of thinking about their thinking, and of thinking about other people's thinking, they begin imagining what other people are thinking about *them*. (Adolescents might worry less if they understood their peers' similar preoccupation.) As their cognitive abilities mature, many begin to think about what is ideally possible and compare that with the imperfect reality of their society, their parents, and even themselves.

> "When the pilot told us to brace and grab our ankles, the first thing that went through my mind was that we must all look pretty stupid."
>
> —Jeremiah Rawlings, age 12, after a 1989 DC-10 crash in Sioux City, Iowa

Developing Reasoning Power

During the early teen years, reasoning is often self-focused. Adolescents may think their private experiences are unique, something parents just could not understand: "But, Mom, *you* don't really know how it feels to be in love" (Elkind, 1978).

Gradually, though, most achieve the intellectual summit Piaget called *formal operations,* and they become more capable of abstract reasoning. Adolescents ponder and debate human nature, good and evil, truth and justice. Having left behind the concrete images of early childhood, they may now seek a deeper conception of God and existence (Elkind, 1970; Worthington, 1989). The ability to reason hypothetically and deduce consequences also enables them to detect inconsistencies in others' reasoning and to spot hypocrisy. This can lead to heated debates with parents and silent vows never to lose sight of their own ideals (Peterson et al., 1986).

"Ben is in his first year of high school, and he's questioning all the right things."

Developing Morality

Two crucial tasks of childhood and adolescence are discerning right from wrong and developing character—the psychological muscles for controlling impulses. Much of our morality is rooted in gut-level reactions, for which the mind seeks rationalization (Haidt, 2006). Often, reason justifies passions such as disgust or liking. Yet to be a moral person is to *think* morally and *act* accordingly.

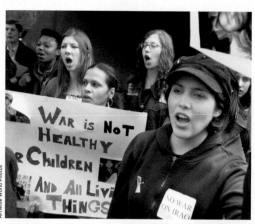

Demonstrating their reasoning ability
Although on opposite sides of the Iraq war debate, these teens are demonstrating their ability to think logically about abstract topics. According to Piaget, they are in the final cognitive stage, formal operations.

Moral reasoning New Orleans Hurricane Katrina victims were faced with a moral dilemma: Should they help themselves to household necessities? Their reasoning likely reflected different levels of moral thinking, even if they behaved similarly.

Piaget (1932) believed that children's moral judgments build on their cognitive development. Agreeing with Piaget, Lawrence Kohlberg (1981, 1984) sought to describe the development of *moral reasoning,* the thinking that occurs as we consider right and wrong. Kohlberg posed moral dilemmas (for example, whether a person should steal medicine to save a loved one's life) and asked children, adolescents, and adults if the action was right or wrong. He then analyzed their answers for evidence of stages of moral thinking.

His findings led him to believe that as we develop intellectually, we pass through three basic levels of moral thinking:

- *Preconventional morality* Before age 9, most children's morality focuses on self-interest: They obey rules either to avoid punishment or to gain concrete rewards.
- *Conventional morality* By early adolescence, morality focuses on caring for others and on upholding laws and social rules, simply because they are the laws and rules.
- *Postconventional morality* With the abstract reasoning of formal operational thought, people may reach a third moral level. Actions are judged "right" because they flow from people's rights or from self-defined, basic ethical principles.

Kohlberg claimed these levels form a moral ladder. As with all stage theories, the sequence is unvarying. We begin on the bottom rung and ascend to varying heights.

Research confirms that children in various cultures progress from Kohlberg's preconventional level into his conventional level (Gibbs et al., 2007). The postconventional level is more controversial. It appears mostly in the European and North American educated middle class, which prizes *individualism*—giving priority to one's own goals rather than to group goals (Eckensberger, 1994; Miller & Bersoff, 1995). Critics have therefore contended that Kohlberg's theory is biased against the moral reasoning of members of collectivist societies such as China and India. Moreover, people's thinking about real-world moral choices also engages their emotions, and moral feelings don't easily fit into Kohlberg's neat stages (Krebs & Denton, 2005).

Many character-education programs therefore tend to focus both on thinking about moral issues but also on *doing* the right thing. They teach children *empathy* for others' feelings and also the self-discipline needed to restrain one's own impulses—to delay small gratifications now to enable bigger rewards later. Those who do learn to *delay gratification* become more socially responsible, academically successful, and productive (Funder & Block, 1989; Mischel et al., 1988, 1989). In service-learning programs, teens tutor, clean up their neighborhoods, and assist the elderly, and their sense of competence and desire to serve increase at the same time that their school absenteeism and drop-out rates diminish (Andersen, 1998; Piliavin, 2003). Moral action feeds moral attitudes.

"I am a bit suspicious of any theory that says that the highest moral stage is one in which people talk like college professors."

—James Q. Wilson, *The Moral Sense,* 1993

"It is a delightful harmony when doing and saying go together."

—Michel Eyquem de Montaigne (1533–1592)

Social Development

10:

What are the social tasks and challenges of adolescence?

Theorist Erik Erikson (1963) contended that each stage of life has its own *psychosocial* task, a crisis that needs resolution. Young children wrestle with issues of *trust*, then *autonomy* (independence), then *initiative* (**TABLE 5.2**). School-age children strive for *competence*, feeling able and productive. The adolescent's task, said Erikson, is to synthesize past, present, and future possibilities into a clearer sense of self. Adolescents wonder, "Who am I as an individual? What do I want to do with my life? What values should I live by? What do I believe in?" Erikson called this quest the adolescent's *search for identity.*

Forming an Identity

To refine their sense of identity, adolescents in individualistic cultures usually try out different "selves" in different situations. They may act out one self at home, another with friends, and still another at school or on Facebook. If two situations overlap—as when a teenager brings home friends—the discomfort can be considerable. The teen asks, "Which self should I be? Which is the real me?" The resolution is a self-definition that unifies the various selves into a consistent and comfortable sense of who one is—an **identity.**

For both adolescents and adults, group identities often form around how we differ from those around us. When living in Britain, I became conscious of my Americanness. When spending time with my daughter in South Africa, I become conscious of my minority (White) race. When surrounded by women, I am mindful of my gender identity. For international students, for people with a disability, for those on a team, a **social identity** often forms around their distinctiveness.

identity our sense of self; according to Erikson, the adolescent's task is to solidify a sense of self by testing and integrating various roles.

social identity the "we" aspect of our self-concept; the part of our answer to "Who am I?" that comes from our group memberships.

> "Self-consciousness, the recognition of a creature by itself as a 'self,' [cannot] exist except in contrast with an 'other,' a something which is not the self."
>
> —C. S. Lewis, *The Problem of Pain*, 1940

TABLE 5.2 Erikson's Stages of Psychosocial Development

Stage (approximate age)	Issue	Description of Task
Infancy (to 1 year)	Trust vs. mistrust	If needs are dependably met, infants develop a sense of basic trust.
Toddlerhood (1 to 3 years)	Autonomy vs. shame and doubt	Toddlers learn to exercise their will and do things for themselves, or they doubt their abilities.
Preschool (3 to 6 years)	Initiative vs. guilt	Preschoolers learn to initiate tasks and carry out plans, or they feel guilty about their efforts to be independent.
Elementary school (6 years to puberty)	Industry vs. inferiority	Children learn the pleasure of applying themselves to tasks, or they feel inferior.
Adolescence (teen years into 20s)	Identity vs. role confusion	Teenagers work at refining a sense of self by testing roles and then integrating them to form a single identity, or they become confused about who they are.
Young adulthood (20s to early 40s)	Intimacy vs. isolation	Young adults struggle to form close relationships and to gain the capacity for intimate love, or they feel socially isolated.
Middle adulthood (40s to 60s)	Generativity vs. stagnation	In middle age, people discover a sense of contributing to the world, usually through family and work, or they may feel a lack of purpose.
Late adulthood (late 60s and up)	Integrity vs. despair	Reflecting on his or her life, an older adult may feel a sense of satisfaction or failure.

Competence vs. inferiority

Intimacy vs. isolation

intimacy in Erikson's theory, the ability to form close, loving relationships; a primary developmental task in late adolescence and early adulthood.

Who shall I be today? By varying the way they look, adolescents try out different "selves." Although we eventually form a consistent and stable sense of identity, the self we present may change with the situation.

But not always. Erikson noticed that some adolescents forge their identity early, simply by adopting their parents' values and expectations. (Traditional, less individualistic cultures inform adolescents about who they are, rather than encouraging them to decide on their own.) Other adolescents may adopt an identity defined in opposition to parents but in conformity with a particular peer group—jocks, preps, geeks, goths.

Most young people do develop a sense of contentment with their lives. When American teens were asked whether a series of statements described them, 81 percent said *yes* to "I would choose my life the way it is right now." But others never quite seem to find themselves: The other 19 percent agreed with "I wish I were somebody else." In response to another question, 28 percent agreed that "I often wonder why I exist" (Lyons, 2004). Reflecting on their existence, 75 percent of American collegians say they "discuss religion/spirituality" with friends, "pray," and agree that "we are all spiritual beings" and "search for meaning/purpose in life" (Astin et al., 2004; Bryant & Astin, 2007). This would not surprise Stanford psychologist William Damon and his colleagues (2003), who contend that a key task of adolescent development is to achieve a purpose—a desire to accomplish something personally meaningful that makes a difference to the world beyond oneself.

The late teen years, when many people in industrialized countries begin attending college or working full time, provide new opportunities for trying out possible roles. Many college seniors have achieved a clearer identity and a more positive self-concept than they had as first-year students (Waterman, 1988). In several nationwide studies, researchers have given young Americans tests of self-esteem. (Sample item: "I am able to do things as well as most other people.") During the early to mid-teen years, self-esteem falls and, for girls, depression scores often increase, but then self-image rebounds during the late teens and twenties (Robins et al., 2002; Twenge & Campbell, 2001; Twenge & Nolen-Hoeksema, 2002).

Erikson contended that the adolescent identity stage is followed in young adulthood by a developing capacity for **intimacy.** With a clear and comfortable sense of who you are, said Erikson, you are ready to form emotionally close relationships. Such relationships are, for most of us, a source of great pleasure. When Mihaly Csikszentmihalyi (pronounced chick-SENT-me-hi) and Jeremy Hunter (2003) used a beeper to sample the daily experiences of American teens, they found them unhappiest when alone and happiest when with friends. As Aristotle long ago recognized, we humans are "the social animal."

Parent and Peer Relationships

As adolescents in Western cultures seek to form their own identities, they begin to pull away from their parents (Shanahan et al., 2007). The preschooler who can't be close enough to her mother, who loves to touch and cling to her, becomes the 14-year-old who wouldn't be caught dead holding hands with Mom. The transition occurs gradually (**FIGURE 5.17**). By adolescence, arguments occur more often, usually over mundane

"She says she's someone from your past who gave birth to you, and raised you, and sacrificed everything so you could have whatever you wanted."

things—household chores, bedtime, homework (Tesser et al., 1989). Parent-child conflict during the transition to adolescence tends to be greater with first-born than with second-born children (Shanahan et al., 2007).

For a minority of parents and their adolescents, differences lead to real splits and great stress (Steinberg & Morris, 2001). But most disagreements are at the level of harmless bickering. And most adolescents—6000 of them in 10 countries, from Australia to Bangladesh to Turkey—have said that they like their parents (Offer et al., 1988). "We usually get along but . . . ," adolescents often report (Galambos, 1992; Steinberg, 1987).

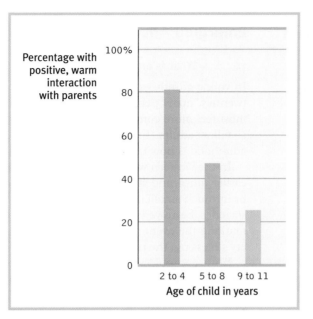

FIGURE 5.17 The changing parent-child relationship Interviews from a large, national study of Canadian families reveal that the typically close, warm relationships between parents and preschoolers loosen as children become older. (Data from Statistics Canada, 1999.)

Positive parent-teen relations and positive peer relations often go hand-in-hand. High school girls who have the most affectionate relationships with their mothers tend also to enjoy the most intimate friendships with girlfriends (Gold & Yanof, 1985). And teens who feel close to their parents tend to be healthy and happy and to do well in school (Resnick et al., 1997). Of course, we can state this correlation the other way: Misbehaving teens are more likely to have tense relationships with parents and other adults.

Adolescence is typically a time of diminishing parental influence and growing peer influence. Asked in a survey if they had "ever had a serious talk" with their child about illegal drugs, 85 percent of American parents answered *yes*. But if the parents had indeed given this earnest advice, many teens apparently had tuned it out: Only 45 percent could recall such a talk (Morin & Brossard, 1997).

As we noted in Chapter 4, heredity does much of the heavy lifting in forming individual personality differences, and parent and peer influences do much of the rest. Most teens are herd animals. They talk, dress, and act more like their peers than their parents. In 2008, according to a Nielsen study, the average American 13- to 17-year old sent or received more than 1700 text messages a month (Steinhauer & Holson, 2008). Many adolescents become absorbed by Internet social networking through sites such as chat rooms, Facebook, and MySpace. For better or for worse—and sometimes with a compulsive use that produces "Facebook fatigue"—online communication stimulates intimate self-disclosure (Subrahmanyam & Greenfield, 2008; Valkenburg & Peter, 2009). What their friends are, they often become, and what "everybody's doing," they often do. In teen calls to hotline counseling services, peer relationships are the most discussed topic (Boehm et al., 1999).

For those who feel excluded, the pain is acute. "The social atmosphere in most high schools is poisonously clique-driven and exclusionary," observed social psychologist Elliot Aronson (2001). Most excluded "students suffer in silence. . . . A small number act out in violent ways against their classmates." They are also are vulnerable to loneliness, low self-esteem, and depression (Steinberg & Morris, 2001). Most children and youth, however, benefit from their friendships (Berndt & Murphy, 2002). A positive academic reputation among their peers helps boost their academic self-concept and performance (Gest et al., 2008). In ways both bad and good, peer approval matters.

Teens see their parents as having more influence in other areas—for example, in shaping their religious faith and in thinking about college and career choices (*Emerging Trends,* 1997). A Gallup Youth Survey reveals that most share their parent's political views (Lyons, 2005).

"I love u guys."

—Emily Keyes' final text message to her parents before dying in a Colorado school shooting, 2006

"How was my day? How was my day? Must you micromanage my life?"

emerging adulthood for some people in modern cultures, a period from the late teens to mid-twenties, bridging the gap between adolescent dependence and full independence and responsible adulthood.

Emerging Adulthood

11: What is emerging adulthood?

In young adulthood, emotional ties with parents loosen further. During their early twenties, many people still lean heavily on their parents. But by the late twenties, most feel more comfortably independent and better able to empathize with parents as fellow adults (Frank, 1988; White, 1983). This graduation from adolescence to adulthood is now taking longer in some cultures.

In the Western world, adolescence now roughly corresponds to the teen years. At earlier times, and still today in other parts of the world, this slice of the life span has been much smaller (Baumeister & Tice, 1986). Shortly after sexual maturity, such societies bestowed adult responsibilities and status on the young person, often marking the event with an elaborate initiation—a public *rite of passage*. With society's blessing, the new adult would then work, marry, and have children.

With compulsory schooling, independence has been occurring later in many Western industrialized countries. From Europe to Australia, adolescents now take more time to finish college, leave the nest, and establish careers. In the United States, for example, the average age at first marriage varies by ethnic group but has increased more than four years since 1960 (to 27 for men, 25 for women).

While cultural traditions were changing, Western adolescents were also beginning to develop earlier. Today's earlier sexual maturity is related both to increased body fat (which can support pregnancy and nursing) and to weakened parent-child bonds, including absent fathers (Ellis, 2004). Together, delayed independence and earlier sexual maturity have widened the once-brief interlude between biological maturity and social independence (**FIGURE 5.18**).

Especially for those still in school, the time from 18 to the mid-twenties is an increasingly not-yet-settled phase of life, which some now call **emerging adulthood** (Arnett, 2006, 2007; Reitzle, 2006). Unlike some other cultures with an abrupt transition to adulthood, Westerners typically ease their way into their new status. Those who leave home for college, for example, are separated from parents and, more than ever before, managing their time and priorities. Yet they may remain dependent on their parents' financial and emotional support and may return home for holidays. For many others, their parents' home may be the only affordable place to live. No longer adolescents, these emerging adults have not yet assumed full adult responsibilities and independence, and they feel "in between." But adulthood emerges gradually, and often with diminishing bouts of depression or anger and increased self-esteem (Galambos et al., 2006).

"When I was your age, I was an adult."

FIGURE 5.18 The transition to adulthood is being stretched from both ends In the 1890s, the average interval between a woman's first menstrual period and marriage, which typically marked a transition to adulthood, was about 7 years; in industrialized countries today it is about 12 years (Guttmacher, 1994, 2000). Although many adults are unmarried, later marriage combines with prolonged education and earlier menarche to help stretch out the transition to adulthood.

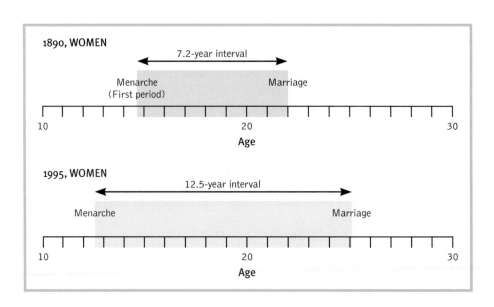

REHEARSE IT!

14. Adolescence is marked by the onset of
    a. an identity crisis.
    b. puberty.
    c. separation anxiety.
    d. parent-child conflict.

15. Primary sex characteristics relate to
    _____; secondary sex characteristics
    refer to _____.
    a. ejaculation; menarche
    b. breasts and facial hair; ovaries and
       testes
    c. emotional maturity; hormone surges
    d. reproductive organs; nonreproductive
       traits

16. According to Piaget, the ability to think
    logically about abstractions indicates
    a. concrete operational thought.
    b. egocentrism.
    c. formal operational thought.
    d. conservation.

17. According to Kohlberg, preconventional
    morality focuses on _____; conven-
    tional morality is more concerned with
    _____.
    a. upholding laws and social rules;
       self-interest
    b. self-interest; basic ethical principles
    c. upholding laws and social rules;
       basic ethical principles
    d. self-interest; upholding laws and
       social rules

18. In Erikson's stages, the primary task dur-
    ing adolescence is
    a. attaining formal operations.
    b. forging an identity.
    c. developing a sense of intimacy with
       another person.
    d. living independent of parents.

19. Some developmental psychologists now
    refer to the period from age 18 to the
    mid-twenties and beyond (up to the
    time of social independence) as
    a. emerging adulthood.
    b. adolescence.
    c. formal operations.
    d. true maturity.

Answers: 14. b, 15. d, 16. c, 17. d, 18. b, 19. a.

Adulthood

At one time, psychologists viewed the center-of-life years between adolescence and old age as one long plateau. No longer. Those who follow the unfolding of people's adult lives now believe our development continues.

It is more difficult to generalize about adulthood stages than about life's early years. If you know that James is a 1-year-old and Jamal is a 10-year-old, you could say a great deal about each child. Not so with adults who differ by a similar number of years. The boss may be 30 or 60; the marathon runner may be 20 or 50; the 19-year-old may be a parent who supports a child or a child who receives an allowance. Yet our life courses are in some ways similar. Physically, cognitively, and especially socially, we are at age 50 different from our 25-year-old selves. In the discussion that follows, we recognize these differences and use three terms: *early adulthood* (roughly twenties and thirties), *middle adulthood* (to age 65), and *late adulthood* (the years after 65). Remember, though, that within each of these stages, people vary widely in physical, psychological, and social development.

"I am still learning."
—Michelangelo, 1560, at age 85

Adult abilities vary widely Eighty-seven-year-olds: Don't try this. In 2002, George Blair became the world's oldest barefoot water skier, 18 days after his eighty-seventh birthday.

How old does a person have to be before you think of him or her as old? The average 18- to 29-year-old says 67. The average person 60 and over says 76 (Yankelovich, 1995).

Physical Development

12: What physical changes occur during middle and late adulthood?

Our physical abilities—muscular strength, reaction time, sensory keenness, and cardiac output—all crest by the mid-twenties. Like the declining daylight after the summer solstice, the decline of physical prowess begins imperceptibly. Athletes are often the first to notice. World-class sprinters and swimmers peak by their early twenties. Women—who mature earlier than men—also peak earlier. But most of us—especially those of us whose daily lives do not require top physical performance—hardly perceive the early signs of decline.

"Happy fortieth. I'll take the muscle tone in your upper arms, the girlish timbre of your voice, your amazing tolerance for caffeine, and your ability to digest french fries. The rest of you can stay."

FIGURE 5.19
Gradually accelerating decline An analysis of aging and batting averages of all twentieth-century major league baseball players revealed a gradual but accelerating decline in players' later years (Schall & Smith, 2000).

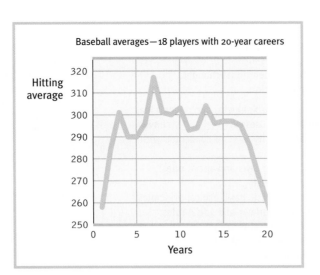

Baseball averages—18 players with 20-year careers

Physical Changes in Middle Adulthood

Middle-aged athletes know all too well that physical decline gradually accelerates (**FIGURE 5.19**). As a 66-year-old who plays basketball, I now find myself occasionally wondering whether my team really needs me to run for that loose ball. But even diminished vigor is sufficient for normal activities. Moreover, during early and middle adulthood, physical vigor has less to do with age than with a person's health and exercise habits. Many of today's physically fit 50-year-olds run four miles with ease, while sedentary 25-year-olds find themselves huffing and puffing up two flights of stairs.

Aging also brings a gradual decline in fertility. For a 35- to 39-year-old woman, the chances of getting pregnant after a single act of intercourse are only half those of a woman 19 to 26 (Dunson et al., 2002). A woman's foremost biological sign of aging, the onset of **menopause,** ends her menstrual cycles, usually within a few years of age 50. Will she see it as a sign that she is losing her femininity and growing old? Or will she view it as liberation from menstrual periods and fears of pregnancy? As in so many areas, her expectations and attitudes will influence the emotional impact of this event.

Men experience no equivalent to menopause—no cessation of fertility, no sharp drop in sex hormones. They do experience a gradual decline in sperm count, testosterone level, and speed of erection and ejaculation. Some may also experience distress related to their perception of declining virility and physical capacities. But most age without such problems.

In a national survey of Canadians ages 40 to 64, only 3 in 10 rated their sex life as less enjoyable than during their twenties (Wright, 2006). After middle age, most men and women remain capable of satisfying sexual activity. In another survey by the National Council on Aging, 39 percent of people over 60 expressed satisfaction with the amount of sex they were having and 39 percent said they wished for sex more frequently (Leary, 1998). And in an American Association of Retired Persons sexuality survey, it was not until age 75 or older that most women and nearly half of men reported little sexual desire (DeLamater & Sill, 2005).

Physical Changes in Later Life

Is old age "more to be feared than death" (Juvenal, *Satires*)? Or is life "most delightful when it is on the downward slope" (Seneca, *Epistulae ad Lucilium*)? What is it like to grow old?

SENSORY ABILITIES Although physical decline begins in early adulthood, we are not usually acutely aware of it until later life, when the stairs get steeper, the print gets smaller, and other people seem to mumble more. Visual sharpness diminishes, and distance perception and adaptation to changes in light level are less acute. Muscle strength, reaction time, and stamina also diminish noticeably, as do vision, the sense of smell, and hearing (**FIGURE 5.20**). In Wales, teens' loitering around a convenience store has been discouraged by a device that emits an aversive high-pitched sound that almost no one over 30 can hear (Lyall, 2005). Some students have also used that pitch to their advantage with cell-phone ring tones that their instructors cannot hear (Vitello, 2006).

With age, the eye's pupil shrinks and its lens becomes less transparent, reducing the amount of light reaching the retina. In fact, a 65-year-old retina receives only about one-third as much light as its 20-year-old counterpart (Kline & Schieber, 1985). Thus, to see as well as a 20-year-old when reading or driving, a 65-year-old

"If the truth were known, we'd have to diagnose [older women] as having P.M.F.—Post-Menstrual Freedom."

—Social psychologist Jacqueline Goodchilds (1987)

"The things that stop you having sex with age are exactly the same as those that stop you riding a bicycle (bad health, thinking it looks silly, no bicycle)."

—Alex Comfort, *The Joy of Sex,* 2002

"For some reason, possibly to save ink, the restaurants had started printing their menus in letters the height of bacteria."

—Dave Barry, *Dave Barry Turns Fifty,* 1998

Most stairway falls taken by older people occur on the top step, precisely where the person typically descends from a window-lit hallway into the darker stairwell (Fozard & Popkin, 1978). Our knowledge of aging could be used to design environments that would reduce such accidents (National Research Council, 1990).

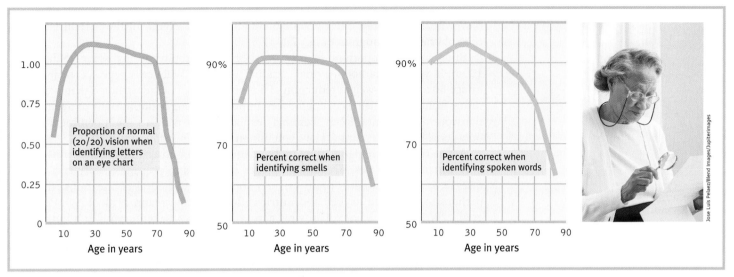

FIGURE 5.20 **The aging senses** Sight, smell, and hearing all are less acute among those over age 70. (From Doty et al., 1984.)

needs three times as much light—a reason for buying cars with untinted windshields. This also explains why older people sometimes ask younger people, "Don't you need better light for reading?"

HEALTH For those growing older, there is both bad and good news about health. The bad news: The body's disease-fighting immune system weakens, making older people more susceptible to life-threatening ailments such as cancer and pneumonia. The good news: Thanks partly to a lifetime's accumulation of antibodies, people over 65 suffer fewer short-term ailments, such as common flu and cold viruses. They are, for example, half as likely as 20-year-olds and one-fifth as likely as preschoolers to suffer upper respiratory flu each year (National Center for Health Statistics, 1990).

Aging levies a tax on the brain by slowing our neural processing. Up to the teen years, we process information with greater and greater speed (Fry & Hale, 1996; Kail, 1991). But compared with teens and young adults, older people take a bit more time to react, to solve perceptual puzzles, even to remember names (Bashore et al., 1997; Verhaeghen & Salthouse, 1997). The lag is greatest on complex tasks (Cerella, 1985; Poon, 1987). At video games, most 70-year-olds are no match for a 20-year-old. And, as **FIGURE 5.21** indicates, fatal accident rates per mile driven increase sharply after age 75. By age 85, they exceed the 16-year-old level.

menopause the time of natural cessation of menstruation; also refers to the biological changes a woman experiences as her ability to reproduce declines.

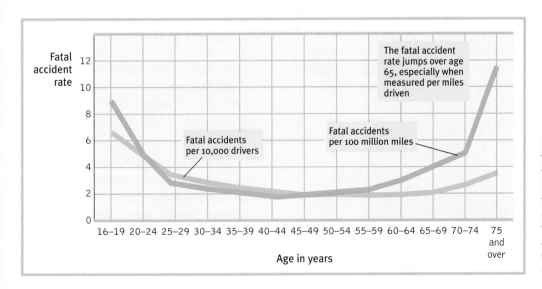

FIGURE 5.21 **Age and driver fatalities** Slowing reactions contribute to increased accident risks among those 75 and older, and their greater fragility increases their risk of death when accidents happen (NHTSA, 2000). Would you favor driver exams based on performance, not age, to screen out those whose slow reactions or sensory impairments indicate accident risk?

Nevertheless, because older people drive less, they account for fewer than 10 percent of crashes (Coughlin et al., 2004).

Brain regions important to memory begin to atrophy during aging (Schacter, 1996). In young adulthood, a small, gradual net loss of brain cells begins, contributing by age 80 to a brain-weight reduction of 5 percent or so. Earlier, we noted that late-maturing frontal lobes help account for teen impulsivity. Late in life, atrophy of the inhibition-controlling frontal lobes seemingly explains older people's frank comments and occasional blunt questions ("Have you put on weight?") (von Hippel, 2007).

Active older adults tend to be mentally quick older adults. Physical exercise not only enhances muscles, bones, and energy and helps to prevent obesity and heart disease, it also stimulates brain cell development and neural connections, thanks perhaps to increased oxygen and nutrient flow (Kempermann et al., 1998; Pereira et al., 2007). That may explain why, across 20 studies, sedentary older adults randomly assigned to aerobic exercise programs have exhibited enhanced memory and sharpened judgment (Colcombe & Kramer, 2003; Colcombe et al., 2004; Weuve et al., 2004). Exercise also promotes neurogenesis (the birth of new nerve cells) in the hippocampus, a brain region important for memory (Pereira et al., 2007). We are more likely to rust from disuse than to wear out from overuse.

Cognitive Development

13: How do memory and intelligence change with age?

Among the most intriguing developmental psychology questions is whether adult cognitive abilities, such as memory, intelligence, and creativity, parallel the gradually accelerating decline of physical abilities.

Aging and Memory

If you are within five years of 20, what experiences from your last year will you likely never forget? (This is the time of your life you may best remember when you are 50.)

As we age, we remember some things well. Looking back in later life, people asked to recall the one or two most important events over the last half-century tend to name events from their teens or twenties (Conway et al., 2005; Rubin et al., 1998). Whatever people experience around this time of life—the Iraq war, the events of 9/11, the civil rights movement, World War II—becomes pivotal (Pillemer, 1998; Schuman & Scott, 1989). Our teens and twenties are a time of many memorable "firsts"—first date, first job, first going to college or university, first meeting your parents-in-law.

Early adulthood is indeed a peak time for some types of learning and remembering. In one experiment, Thomas Crook and Robin West (1990) invited 1205 people to learn some names. Fourteen videotaped people said their names, using a common format: "Hi, I'm Larry." Then the same individuals reappeared and said, for example, "I'm from Philadelphia"—thus providing visual *and* voice cues for remembering their name. As **FIGURE 5.22** shows, everyone remembered more names after a second and third replay of the introductions, but younger adults consistently surpassed older adults. Perhaps it is not surprising, then, that nearly two-thirds of people over age 40 say their memory is worse than it was 10 years ago (KRC, 2001).

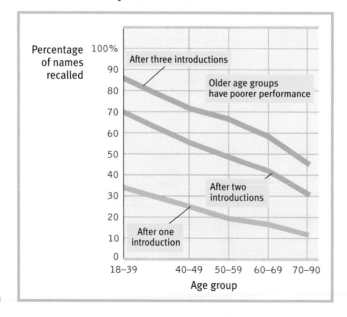

FIGURE 5.22 Tests of recall Recalling new names introduced once, twice, or three times is easier for younger adults than for older ones. (Data from Crook & West, 1990.)

But consider another experiment (Schonfield & Robertson, 1966), in which adults of various ages learned a list of 24 words. Without giving any clues, the researchers then asked some to *recall* as many words as they could from the list, and others simply to *recognize* words, using multiple-choice questions. Although younger adults had better recall, no age-related memory decline appeared on the recognition tests (**FIGURE 5.23**). So, how well older people remember depends: Are they being asked simply to *recognize* what they have tried to memorize (minimal decline) or to *recall* it without clues (greater decline)?

No matter how quick or slow we are, remembering seems also to depend on the type of information we are trying to retrieve. If the information is meaningless—nonsense syllables or unimportant events—then the older we are, the more errors we are likely to make. If the information is *meaningful,* older people's rich web of existing knowledge will help them to catch it, though they may take longer than younger adults to *produce* the words and things they know (Burke & Shafto, 2004). (Quick-thinking game show winners are usually younger to middle-aged adults.) Older people's capacity to learn and remember *skills* also declines less than their verbal recall (Graf, 1990; Labouvie-Vief & Schell, 1982; Perlmutter, 1983).

Aging and Intelligence

What happens to our broader intellectual powers as we age? Do they gradually decline, as does our ability to recall new material? Or do they remain constant, as does our ability to recognize meaningful material?

Whether intelligence increases or decreases with age depends on the type of intellectual performance we measure. **Crystallized intelligence**—our accumulated knowledge as reflected in vocabulary and analogies tests—*increases* up to old age. **Fluid intelligence**—our ability to reason speedily and abstractly, as when solving novel logic problems—*decreases* slowly up to age 75 or so, then more rapidly, especially after age 85 (Cattell, 1963; Horn, 1982). We can see this pattern in the intelligence scores of a national sample of adults (Kaufman et al., 1989). After adjustments for education, verbal scores (which reflect crystallized intelligence) held relatively steady from ages 20 to 74. Nonverbal, puzzle-solving intelligence declined.

So, with age, we lose and we win. We lose recall memory and processing speed, but we gain vocabulary and knowledge (Park et al., 2002). Our decisions also become less distorted by negative emotions such as anxiety, depression, and anger (Blanchard-Fields, 2007; Carstensen & Mikels, 2005). These cognitive differences help explain why mathematicians and scientists produce much of their most creative work during their late twenties or early thirties, whereas those in literature, history, and philosophy tend to produce their best work in their forties, fifties, and beyond, after accumulating more knowledge (Simonton, 1988, 1990). For example, poets (who depend on fluid intelligence) reach their peak output earlier than prose authors (who need a deeper knowledge reservoir), a finding observed in every major literary tradition, for both living and dead languages.

Recently, psychologists who study the aging mind have been debating whether "brain-fitness" computer training programs can stave off cognitive decline. Given what we know about the brain's plasticity, can using our brains—with memory, visual speed, and problem-solving exercises—avert losing our minds? "At every point in life, the brain's natural plasticity gives us the ability to improve how our brains function," says neuroscientist-entrepreneur Michael Merzenich (2007). With support from the National Institutes of Health and the National Institute on Aging, researchers are exploring possible benefits of cognitive training (Mahncke et al., 2006). One five-year study of nearly 3000 people in six cities found that 10 one-hour cognitive training sessions, with follow-up booster sessions a year (and more) later, led to improved cognitive scores on tests related to their training (Boron et al.,

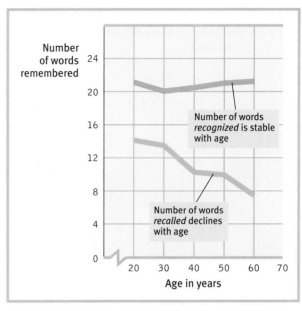

FIGURE 5.23 Recall and recognition in adulthood In this experiment, the ability to *recall* new information declined during early and middle adulthood, but the ability to *recognize* new information did not. (From Schonfield & Robertson, 1966.)

"In youth we learn, in age we understand."

—Marie Von Ebner-Eschenbach, *Aphorisms,* 1883

- -

crystallized intelligence our accumulated knowledge and verbal skills; tends to increase with age.

- -

fluid intelligence our ability to reason speedily and abstractly; tends to decrease during late adulthood.

social clock the culturally preferred timing of social events such as marriage, parenthood, and retirement.

2007; Willis et al., 2006). Based on such findings, some computer game makers are marketing daily brain-exercise programs for the elderly. But Timothy Salthouse (2006, 2007), a veteran researcher of cognitive aging, advises caution. The available evidence, he contends, does not indicate that the benefits of brain-mind exercise programs generalize to other tasks.

Despite age-related cognitive changes, studies in several countries indicate that age is only a modest predictor of abilities such as memory and intelligence. Mental ability more strongly correlates with proximity to death. Tell me whether someone is 70, 80, or 90, and you haven't told me much about the person's mental sharpness. But if you tell me whether someone is 8 months or 8 years from death, regardless of age, you'll give me a better clue to the person's mental ability. Especially in the last three or four years of life, cognitive decline typically accelerates (Wilson et al., 2007). Researchers call this near-death drop *terminal decline* (Backman & MacDonald, 2006).

Social Development

14: What themes and influences mark our social journey from early adulthood to death?

Many differences between younger and older adults are created by significant life events. A new job means new relationships, new expectations, and new demands. Marriage brings the joy of intimacy and the stress of merging your life with another's. The birth of a child introduces responsibilities and alters your life focus. The death of a loved one creates an irreplaceable loss. Do these adult life events shape a sequence of life changes?

Adulthood's Ages and Stages

As people enter their forties, they undergo a transition to middle adulthood, a time when they realize that life will soon be mostly behind instead of ahead of them. Some psychologists have argued that for many the *midlife transition* is a crisis, a time of great struggle, regret, or even feeling struck down by life. The popular image of the midlife crisis is an early-forties man who forsakes his family for a younger girlfriend and a hot sports car. But the fact—reported by large samples of people—is that unhappiness, job dissatisfaction, marital dissatisfaction, divorce, anxiety, and suicide do *not* surge during the early forties (Hunter & Sundel, 1989; Mroczek & Kolarz, 1998). Divorce, for example, is most common among those in their twenties, suicide among those in their seventies and eighties. One study of emotional instability in nearly 10,000 men and women found "not the slightest evidence" that distress peaks anywhere in the midlife age range (**FIGURE 5.24**).

For the 1 in 4 adults who do report experiencing a life crisis, the trigger is not age, but a major event, such as illness, divorce, or job loss (Lachman, 2004). Some middle-aged adults describe themselves as a "sandwich generation," as they simultaneously support both their aging parents and their emerging adult children or grandchildren (Riley & Bowen, 2005).

Life events trigger transitions to new life stages at varying ages. The **social clock**—the definition of "the right time" to leave home, get a job, marry, have children, and retire—varies from era to era and culture to culture. In Western Europe, fewer than 10 percent of men over 65 remain in the work force, as do 16 percent in the United States, 36 percent in Japan, and 69 percent in Mexico (Davies et al., 1991). And the once-rigid sequence for

> "Midway in the journey of our life I found myself in a dark wood, for the straight way was lost."
>
> —Dante, *The Divine Comedy*, 1314

> "The important events of a person's life are the products of chains of highly improbable occurrences."
>
> —Joseph Traub, "Traub's Law," 2003

FIGURE 5.24 Early forties midlife crises? Among 10,000 people responding to a national health survey, there was no early forties increase in emotional instability ("neuroticism") scores. (From McCrae & Costa, 1990.)

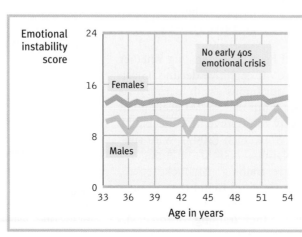

many Western women—of student to worker to wife to at-home mom to worker again—has loosened. Contemporary women occupy these roles in any order or all at once. The social clock still ticks, but people feel freer about being out of sync with it.

Adulthood's Commitments

Two basic aspects of our lives dominate adulthood. Erik Erikson called them *intimacy* (forming close relationships) and *generativity* (being productive and supporting future generations). Researchers have chosen various terms—*affiliation* and *achievement, attachment* and *productivity, commitment* and *competence.* Sigmund Freud (1935) put it most simply: The healthy adult, he said, is one who can *love* and *work.*

LOVE We typically flirt, fall in love, and commit—one person at a time. "Pair-bonding is a trademark of the human animal," observed anthropologist Helen Fisher (1993). From an evolutionary perspective, relatively monogamous pairing makes sense: Parents who cooperated to nurture their children to maturity were more likely to have their genes passed along to posterity than were parents who didn't.

Adult bonds of love are most satisfying and enduring when marked by a similarity of interests and values, a sharing of emotional and material support, and intimate self-disclosure (see Chapter 15). Couples who seal their love with commitment—via, in one Vermont study, marriage for heterosexual couples and civil unions for homosexual couples—more often endure (Balsam et al., 2008). Marriage bonds are especially likely to last when couples marry after age 20 and are well educated. Compared with their counterparts of 40 years ago, people in Western countries *are* better educated and marrying later. Yet, ironically, they are nearly twice as likely to divorce. (Both Canada and the United States now have about one divorce for every two marriages [Bureau of the Census, 2007], and in Europe, divorce is only slightly less common.) The divorce rate partly reflects women's lessened economic dependence on men, and men and women's rising expectations. We now hope not only for an enduring bond, but also for a mate who is a wage earner, caregiver, intimate friend, and warm and responsive lover.

Might test-driving life together in a "trial marriage" minimize divorce risk? In a 2001 Gallup survey of American twenty-somethings, 62 percent thought it would (Whitehead & Popenoe, 2001). In reality, in Europe, Canada, and the United States, those who cohabit before marriage have had *higher* rates of divorce and marital dysfunction than those who did not cohabit (Dush et al., 2003; Popenoe & Whitehead, 2002). The risk appears greatest for cohabiting prior to engagement (Kline et al., 2004).

American children born to cohabiting parents are about five times more likely to experience their parents' separation than are children born to married parents (Osborne et al., 2007). Two factors contribute. First, cohabiters tend to be initially less committed to the ideal of enduring marriage. Second, they become even less marriage-supporting while cohabiting.

Nonetheless, the institution of marriage endures. Worldwide, reports the United Nations, 9 in 10 heterosexual adults marry. And marriage is a predictor of happiness, health, sexual satisfaction, and income. National Opinion Research Center surveys of more than 40,000 Americans since 1972 reveal that 40 percent of married adults, though only 23 percent of unmarried adults, have reported being "very happy." Lesbian couples, too, report greater well-being than those who are alone (Peplau & Fingerhut, 2007; Wayment & Peplau, 1995). Moreover, neighborhoods with high marriage rates typically have low rates of social pathologies such as crime, delinquency, and emotional disorders among children (Myers & Scanzoni, 2005).

Often, love bears children. For most people, this most enduring of life changes is a happy event. "I feel an overwhelming love for my children unlike anything I feel for anyone else," said 93 percent of American mothers in a national survey (Erickson & Aird, 2005). Many fathers feel the same. A few weeks after the birth of my first child I was suddenly struck by a realization: "So *this* is how my parents felt about me!"

"One can live magnificently in this world if one knows how to work and how to love."

—Leo Tolstoy, 1856

Love Intimacy, attachment, commitment—love by whatever name—is central to healthy and happy adulthood.

What do you think? Does marriage correlate with happiness because marital support and intimacy breed happiness, because happy people more often marry and stay married, or both?

When children begin to absorb time, money, and emotional energy, satisfaction with the marriage itself may decline. This is especially likely among employed women who, more than they expected, carry the traditional burden of doing the chores at home. Putting effort into creating an equitable relationship can thus pay double dividends: a more satisfying marriage, which breeds better parent-child relations (Erel & Burman, 1995).

Although love bears children, children eventually leave home. This departure is a significant and sometimes difficult event. For most people, however, an empty nest is a happy place (Adelmann et al., 1989; Glenn, 1975). Many parents experience a "postlaunch honeymoon," especially if they maintain close relationships with their children (White & Edwards, 1990). As Daniel Gilbert (2006) has said, "The only known symptom of 'empty nest syndrome' is increased smiling."

If you have left home, did your parents suffer the "empty nest syndrome"—a demoralized loss of purpose? Did they mourn the lost joy of listening for you in the wee hours of Saturday morning? Or did they discover a new freedom and (if still married) renewed satisfaction with their own relationship?

WORK For many adults, the answer to "Who are you?" depends a great deal on the answer to "What do you do?" For women and men, choosing a career path is difficult, especially during bad economic times. Even in the best of times, few students in their first two years of college or university can predict their later careers. Most shift from their initially intended major, many find their postcollege employment in a field not directly related to their major, and most will change careers (Rothstein, 1980).

In the end, happiness is about having work that fits your interests and provides you with a sense of competence and accomplishment. It is having a close, supportive companion who cheers your accomplishments (Gable et al., 2006). And for some, it includes having children who love you and whom you love and feel proud of.

Job satisfaction and life satisfaction
Work can provide us with a sense of identity and competence and opportunities for accomplishment. Perhaps this is why challenging and interesting occupations enhance people's happiness.

"I hope I die before I get old," sang rock star Pete Townshend—when he was 20.

Well-Being Across the Life Span

To live is to grow older. This moment marks the oldest you have ever been and the youngest you will henceforth be. That means we all can look back with satisfaction or regret, and forward with hope or dread. When asked what they would have done differently if they could relive their lives, people's most common answer is "Taken my education more seriously and worked harder at it" (Kinnier & Metha, 1989; Roese & Summerville, 2005). Other regrets—"I should have told my father I loved him," "I regret that I never went to Europe"—also focus less on mistakes made than on the things one *failed* to do (Gilovich & Medvec, 1995).

From the teens to midlife, people typically experience a strengthening sense of identity, confidence, and self-esteem (Miner-Rubino et al., 2004; Robins & Trzesniewski, 2005). In later life, challenges arise: Income shrinks, work is often taken away, the body deteriorates, recall fades, energy wanes, family members and friends die or move away, and the great enemy, death, looms ever closer. Small wonder that most presume that happiness declines in later life (Lacey et al., 2006). But the over-65 years are not notably unhappy, as Ronald Inglehart (1990) discovered when he amassed interviews conducted during the 1980s with representative samples of nearly 170,000 people in 16 nations (**FIGURE 5.25**). Newer surveys of some 2 million people worldwide confirm that happiness is slightly higher among both young and older adults than among those middle-aged.

If anything, positive feelings grow after midlife and negative feelings subside (Charles et al., 2001; Mroczek, 2001). National studies in both Britain and Australia

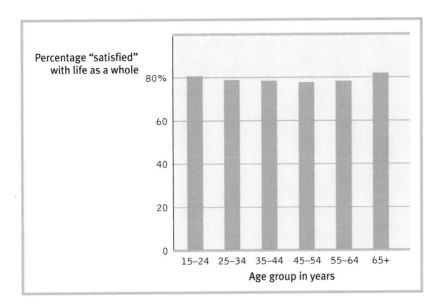

reveal that the risk of depression tapers off in later life (Blanchflower & Oswald, 2008; Troller et al., 2007). Consider:

- Older adults increasingly use words that convey positive emotions (Pennebaker & Stone, 2003).
- Older adults attend less and less to negative information. For example, they are slower than younger adults to perceive negative faces (Carstensen & Mikels, 2005).
- The amygdala, a neural processing center for emotions, shows diminishing activity in older adults in response to negative events, but it maintains its responsiveness to positive events (Mather et al., 2004; Williams et al., 2006).
- Brain-wave reactions to negative images diminish with age (Kisley et al., 2007).

Moreover, at all ages, the bad feelings we associate with negative events fade faster than do the good feelings we associate with positive events (Walker et al., 2003). This contributes to most older people's sense that life, on balance, has been mostly good. Given that growing older is an outcome of living (an outcome most prefer to early dying), the positivity of later life is comforting. More and more people flourish into later life, thanks to biological, psychological, and social-cultural influences (**FIGURE 5.26**).

> At twenty we worry about what others think of us. At forty we don't care what others think of us. At sixty we discover they haven't been thinking about us at all.
>
> —Anonymous

> "The best thing about being 100 is *no peer pressure.*"
>
> —Lewis W. Kuester, 2005, on turning 100

Biological influences:
- no genetic predisposition to dementia or other diseases
- appropriate nutrition

Psychological influences:
- optimistic outlook
- physically and mentally active life-style

Successful aging

Social-cultural influences:
- support from family and friends
- meaningful activities
- cultural respect for aging
- safe living conditions

FIGURE 5.26 Biopsychosocial influences on successful aging Biological, psychological, and social-cultural factors affect the way we age. With the right genes, we have a good chance of aging successfully if we maintain a positive outlook, stay mentally and physically active, and remain connected to family and friends.

"Love—why, I'll tell you what love is: It's you at 75 and her at 71, each of you listening for the other's step in the next room, each afraid that a sudden silence, a sudden cry, could mean a lifetime's talk is over."

—Brian Moore,
The Luck of Ginger Coffey, 1960

FIGURE 5.27 Life satisfaction before, during the year of, and after a spouse's death Richard Lucas and his collaborators (2003) examined data collected from repeated annual surveys of more than 30,000 Germans. They identified 513 married people who had experienced a spouse's death and had not remarried. In this group, life satisfaction began to dip during the prewidowhood year, dropped significantly during the year of the spouse's death, and then eventually rebounded to nearly the earlier level. (*Source:* Richard Lucas.)

Death and Dying

Most of us will suffer and cope with the deaths of relatives and friends. Usually, the most difficult separation is from a spouse—a loss suffered by five times more women than men. When, as usually happens, death comes at an expected late-life time, the grieving may be relatively short-lived. (**FIGURE 5.27** shows the typical emotional path before and after a spouse's death.) But even 20 years after losing a spouse, people still talk about the long-lost partner once a month on average (Carnelley et al., 2006).

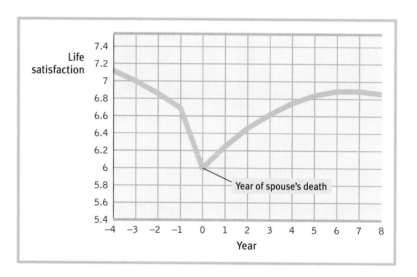

Grief is especially severe when a loved one's death comes suddenly and before its expected time on the social clock. The sudden illness that claims a 45-year-old life partner or the accidental death of a child may trigger a year or more of memory-laden mourning that eventually subsides to a mild depression (Lehman et al., 1987).

For some, however, the loss is unbearable. One Danish long-term study of more than 1 million people found that about 17,000 of them had suffered the death of a child under 18. In the five years following that death, 3 percent of them had a first psychiatric hospitalization. This rate was 67 percent higher than the rate recorded for parents who had not lost a child (Li et al., 2005).

Even so, reactions to a loved one's death range more widely than most suppose. Some cultures encourage public weeping and wailing; others hide grief. Within any culture, individuals differ. Given similar losses, some people grieve hard and long, others are more resilient (Ott et al., 2007). Contrary to popular misconceptions, however,

- terminally ill and bereaved people do not go through identical predictable stages, such as denial before anger (Nolen-Hoeksema & Larson, 1999). A Yale study following 233 bereaved individuals through time did, however, find that yearning for the loved one reached a high point four months after the loss, with anger peaking, on average, about a month later (Maciejewski et al., 2007).
- those who express the strongest grief immediately do not purge their grief more quickly (Bonanno & Kaltman, 1999; Wortman & Silver, 1989).
- bereavement therapy and self-help groups offer support, but there is similar healing power in the passing of time, the support of friends, and the act of giving support and help to others (Brown et al., 2008). Grieving spouses who talk often with others or receive grief counseling adjust about as well as those who grieve more privately (Bonanno, 2001, 2004; Genevro, 2003; Stroebe et al., 2001, 2002, 2005).

"Donald is such a fatalist—he's convinced he's going to grow old and die."

We can be grateful for the waning of death-denying attitudes. Facing death with dignity and openness helps people complete the life cycle with a sense of life's meaningfulness and unity—the sense that their existence has been good and that life and death are parts of an ongoing cycle. Although death may be unwelcome, life itself can be affirmed even at death. This is especially so for people who review their lives not with despair but with what Erik Erikson called a sense of *integrity*—a feeling that one's life has been meaningful and worthwhile.

> "Consider, friend, as you pass by, as you are now, so once was I. As I am now, you too shall be. Prepare, therefore, to follow me."
>
> —Scottish tombstone epitaph

REHEARSE IT!

20. By age 65, a person would be most likely to experience a cognitive decline in the ability to
   a. recall and list all the important terms and concepts in a chapter.
   b. select the correct definition in a multiple-choice question.
   c. evaluate whether a statement is true or false.
   d. exercise sound judgment in answering an essay question.

21. Freud defined the healthy adult as one who is able to love and work. Erikson agreed, observing that the adult struggles to attain intimacy and
   a. affiliation.
   b. identity.
   c. competence.
   d. generativity.

22. Contrary to what many people assume,
   a. older people are much happier than adolescents.
   b. men in their forties express much greater dissatisfaction with life than do women of the same age.
   c. people of all ages report similar levels of happiness.
   d. those whose children have recently left home—the empty nesters—have the lowest level of happiness of all groups.

Answers: 20. a, 21. d, 22. c.

Reflections on Two Major Developmental Issues

We began our survey of developmental psychology by identifying three pervasive issues: (1) how development is steered by genes and by experience, (2) whether development is a gradual, continuous process or a series of discrete stages, and (3) whether development is characterized more by stability over time or by change. We considered the first issue in Chapter 4. It is time to reflect on the second and third issues.

Continuity and Stages

Do adults differ from infants as a giant redwood differs from its seedling—a difference created by gradual, cumulative growth? Or do they differ as a butterfly differs from a caterpillar—a difference of distinct stages?

Generally speaking, researchers who emphasize experience and learning see development as a slow, continuous shaping process. Those who emphasize biological maturation tend to see development as a sequence of genetically predisposed stages or steps: Although progress through the various stages may be quick or slow, everyone passes through the stages in the same order.

Are there clear-cut stages of psychological development, as there are physical stages such as walking before running? We have considered the stage theories of Jean Piaget on cognitive development, Lawrence Kohlberg on moral development, and Erik Erikson on psychosocial development (summarized in **FIGURE 5.28** on the next page). And we have seen their stage theories criticized: Young children have some abilities Piaget attributed to later stages. Kohlberg's work reflected a worldview characteristic of educated people in individualistic cultures and emphasized thinking over acting. Adult life does not progress through the fixed, predictable series of steps Erikson envisioned.

TOO MUCH COFFEE MAN BY SHANNON WHEELER

LIFE:

PLAY, SCHOOL, PLAY, SCHOOL, PLAY, SCHOOL, PLAY, SCHOOL, FIRST LOVE, BRIEF HAPPINESS, BREAK UP, REGRET, SCHOOL, SCHOOL, SCHOOL, SCHOOL, SCHOOL, SCHOOL, SCHOOL, SCHOOL, SCHOOL, SCHOOL, SCHOOL, SCHOOL, SCHOOL, SCHOOL, SCHOOL, SCHOOL, PLAY, WORK, PLAY, WORK, PLAY, WORK, PLAY, WORK, IDEALISM, EFFORT, REJECTION, FAILURE, WORK, EFFORT, FAILURE, COMPROMISE, WORK, WORK, WORK, WORK, WORK, WORK, PLAY, COMMITMENT, WORK, WORK, WORK, WORK, WORK, WORK, PLAY, WORK, WORK, WORK, WORK, WORK, WORK, WORK, WORK, PLAY, WORK, WORK, WORK, WORK, WORK, WORK, WORK, WORK, PLAY, WORK, WORK, WORK, WORK, WORK, WORK, WORK, WORK, PLAY, WORK, WORK, WORK, WORK, WORK, WORK, WORK, WORK, PLAY, WORK, WORK, WORK, WORK, WORK, WORK, WORK, WORK, PLAY, WORK, WORK, WORK, WORK, WORK, WORK, WORK, WORK, PLAY, WORK, WORK, WORK, WORK, WORK, WORK, WORK, WORK, PLAY, WORK, WORK, WORK, WORK, WORK, WORK, WORK, WORK, PLAY, WORK, WORK, WORK, WORK, WORK, WORK, WORK, WORK, PLAY, WORK, WORK, WORK, WORK, WORK, WORK, WORK, WORK, PLAY, WORK, WORK, WORK, WORK, WORK, WORK, WORK, WORK, PLAY, WORK, WORK, WORK, WORK, WORK, WORK, WORK, WORK, PLAY, WORK, WORK, WORK, WORK, WORK, WORK, WORK, WORK, PLAY, RETIRE, PLAY, DIE.

Stages of the life cycle

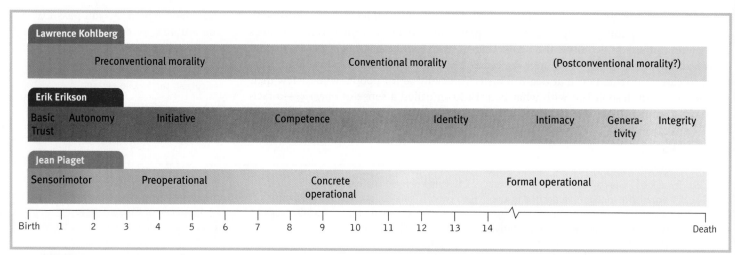

FIGURE 5.28
Comparing the stage theories

Although research casts doubt on the idea that life proceeds through neatly defined, age-linked stages, the concept of *stage* remains useful. The human brain does experience growth spurts during childhood and puberty that correspond roughly to Piaget's stages (Thatcher et al., 1987). And stage theories contribute a developmental perspective on the whole life span, by suggesting how people of one age think and act differently when they arrive at a later age.

Stability and Change

This leads us to the final question: Over time, are people's personalities consistent, or do they change? If reunited with a long-lost grade school friend, would you instantly recognize that "it's the same old Andy"? Or does a person befriended during one period of life seem like a different person at a later period? (That was the experience of a friend of mine who failed to recognize his former classmate at their 40–year college reunion. The aghast "unknown" classmate was his long-ago ex-wife.)

Researchers who have followed lives through time have found evidence for both stability and change. There is continuity to personality and yet, happily for troubled children and adolescents, life is a process of becoming: The struggles of the present may be laying a foundation for a happier tomorrow. More specifically, researchers generally agree on the following points:

1. The first two years of life provide a poor basis for predicting a person's eventual traits (Kagan et al., 1978, 1998). Older children and adolescents also change. Although delinquent children have elevated rates of later work problems, substance abuse, and crime, many confused and troubled children have blossomed into mature, successful adults (Moffitt et al., 2002; Roberts et al., 2001; Thomas & Chess, 1986).

2. As people grow older, personality gradually stabilizes (Hampson & Goldberg, 2006; Johnson et al., 2005; Terracciano et al., 2006). Some characteristics, such as temperament, are more stable than others, such as social attitudes (Moss & Susman, 1980). When a research team led by Avshalom Caspi (2003) studied 1000 New Zealanders from age 3 to 26, they were struck by the consistency of temperament and emotionality across time.

3. In some ways, we all change with age. Most shy, fearful toddlers begin opening up by age 4, and most people become more self-disciplined, stable, agreeable, and self-confident in the years after adolescence (McCrae & Costa, 1994; Roberts et al., 2003, 2006, 2008). Many irresponsible 18-year-olds have

As adults grow older, there is continuity of self.

"As at 7, so at 70."

—Jewish proverb

matured into 40-year-old business or cultural leaders. (If you are the former, you aren't done yet.) Such changes can occur without changing a person's position *relative to others* of the same age. The hard-driving young adult may mellow by later life, yet still be a relatively hard-driving senior citizen.

Finally, we should remember that life requires *both* stability and change. Stability enables us to depend on others, provides our identity, and motivates our concern for the healthy development of children. Change motivates our concern about present influences, sustains our hope for a brighter future, and lets us adapt and grow with experience.

> "At 70, I would say the advantage is that you take life more calmly. You know that 'this, too, shall pass'!"
>
> —Eleanor Roosevelt, 1954

REHEARSE IT!

23. Developmental researchers who emphasize learning and experience tend to believe in _____; those who emphasize biological maturation tend to believe in _____.
   a. nature; nurture
   b. continuity; stages

c. stability; change
d. randomness; predictability

24. Although development is lifelong, there is stability of personality over time. For example,
   a. most personality traits emerge in infancy and persist throughout life.

b. temperament tends to remain stable throughout life.
c. few people change significantly after adolescence.
d. people tend to undergo greater personality changes as they age.

Answers: 23. b, 24. b.

CHAPTER REVIEW

Developing Through the Life Span

Prenatal Development and the Newborn

1 How does life develop before birth?

Developmental psychologists study physical, cognitive, and social changes throughout the life span. At conception, one sperm cell unites with an egg to form a *zygote*. During weeks 2 through 8, the developing *embryo's* body organs begin to form and function. By 9 weeks, the *fetus* is recognizably human. *Teratogens*, potentially harmful agents, can pass through the placental screen and harm the developing embryo or fetus, as happens with *fetal alcohol syndrome*.

2 What are some newborn abilities?

Newborns are born with sensory equipment and reflexes that facilitate their survival and their social interactions with adults. For example, they quickly learn to discriminate their mother's smell and sound.

Infancy and Childhood

3 During infancy and childhood, how do the brain and motor skills develop?

Both heredity and experience sculpt the brain's nerve cells; their interconnections multiply rapidly after birth. Our complex motor skills—sitting, crawling, walking, running—develop in a predictable sequence, though timing is a function of individual *maturation* and culture. We have no conscious memories of events we experience before about age 3½, but physiological responses show that very young children have processed information they cannot verbally express.

4 From the perspectives of Piaget and of today's researchers, how does a child's mind develop?

Piaget proposed that children actively construct and modify their understanding of the world while interacting with the world. They form *schemas* that help them organize their experiences. Progressing from the simplicity of the *sensorimotor stage* of the first two years, in which they develop *object permanence*, children move to more complex ways of thinking. In the *preoperational stage* they develop a *theory of mind* (absent in children with *autism*), but they are *egocentric* and unable to perform simple logical operations. At about age 6 or 7, children enter the *concrete operational stage* and can perform concrete operations, such as those required to comprehend the principle of *conservation* of substance. By about age 12, many enter the *formal operational stage* and can think logically about abstract ideas. Research supports the sequence Piaget proposed for human *cognition*. But young children's abilities develop earlier and more continuously than Piaget believed. The child's mind also grows through social interaction, as Lev Vygotsky emphasized.

5 How do parent-infant attachment bonds form?

At about 8 months, infants begin to display *stranger anxiety*. *Attachments* form not simply because parents gratify biological needs but, more important, because they are comfortable, familiar, and responsive. Humans do not experience the rigid attachment process, called *imprinting*, that occurs in ducks and other animals during a *critical period*.

6 **How have psychologists studied children's differing attachments, and what have they learned?**

Strange situation experiments show that some children are securely attached and others are insecurely attached. Sensitive, responsive parents tend to have securely attached children. The attachment styles of early childhood may reappear in later relationships with loved ones. This lends support to Erikson's idea that *basic trust* is formed in infancy by our experiences with responsive caregivers. Children are very resilient. But those who are severely neglected by their parents and caregivers may be at risk for attachment problems.

7 **What are the three primary parenting styles, and what outcomes are associated with them?**

Authoritarian parenting has been linked with lower social skills and self-esteem. Permissive parenting has been linked with aggressive and immature behaviors in children. Authoritative parenting is associated with high self-esteem, self-reliance, and social competence. But these findings are correlational and may reflect social and ethical differences rather than cause-effect.

Adolescence

8 **What physical changes mark adolescence?**

Adolescence is the transition period between *puberty* and social independence. During puberty, both *primary* and *secondary sex characteristics* develop dramatically. Boys seem to benefit from early maturation, girls from late maturation. During adolescence, the growth of myelin speeds neurotransmission and the brain's frontal lobes continue to develop, enabling improved judgment, impulse control, and long-term planning.

9 **How did Piaget and Kohlberg describe adolescent cognitive and moral development?**

Piaget theorized that adolescents develop a capacity for formal operations and that this development is the foundation for moral judgment. Kohlberg proposed a three-stage theory of moral reasoning, from a preconventional morality of self-interest, to a conventional morality concerned with upholding laws and social rules, to (in some people) a postconventional morality of universal ethical principles. Kohlberg's critics argue that his theory represents morality from the perspective of middle-class individualists, and that it also fails to account for moral actions and emotions.

10 **What are the social tasks and challenges of adolescence?**

Erikson theorized that the psychosocial task of adolescence is solidifying a sense of self—an *identity*. This often means "trying on" a number of different selves. During adolescence, parental influence diminishes and peer influence increases.

11 **What is emerging adulthood?**

The transition from adolescence to adulthood is now taking longer. *Emerging adulthood* is the period from age 18 to the mid-twenties, when many young people are not yet fully independent. Critics note that this stage is found mostly in today's Western cultures.

Adulthood

12 **What physical changes occur during middle and late adulthood?**

Decline of muscular strength, reaction time, sensory abilities, and cardiac output begins in the late twenties and continues throughout middle and late adulthood. Around age 50, *menopause* ends women's period of fertility but usually does not trigger psychological problems or interfere with a satisfying sex life. Men do not undergo a similar sharp drop in hormone levels or fertility. The immune system weakens in later life, increasing the risk of life-threatening illnesses, but accumulated antibodies protect older people from many short-term ailments. In late adulthood, neural processing slows, and some brain regions atrophy.

13 **How do memory and intelligence change with age?**

As the years pass, recall begins to decline, especially for meaningless information, but recognition memory remains strong. *Fluid intelligence* declines in later life but *crystallized intelligence* does not. Mental ability correlates more strongly with nearness to death than with absolute age.

14 **What themes and influences mark our social journey from early adulthood to death?**

Adults do not progress through an orderly sequence of age-related social stages. Transitions are more often triggered by life events. The strict dictates of the *social clock*—the culturally preferred timing of social events—have loosened. The dominant themes of adulthood are love and work, which Erikson called *intimacy* and generativity. Life satisfaction tends to remain high across the life span. Expressions of grief vary from person to person and from culture to culture.

Terms and Concepts to Remember

developmental psychology, p. 137
zygote, p. 138
embryo, p. 138
fetus, p. 138
teratogens, p. 138
fetal alcohol syndrome (FAS), p. 139
maturation, p. 140

cognition, p. 142
schema, p. 143
assimilation, p. 143
accommodation, p. 143
sensorimotor stage, p. 144
object permanence, p. 144
preoperational stage, p. 144

conservation, p. 144
egocentrism, p. 145
theory of mind, p. 145
concrete operational stage, p. 146
autism, p. 146
formal operational stage, p. 148
stranger anxiety, p. 149

attachment, p. 149

critical period, p. 150

imprinting, p. 150

basic trust, p. 152

adolescence, p. 154

puberty, p. 155

primary sex characteristics, p. 155

secondary sex characteristics, p. 155

menarche [meh-NAR-key], p. 155

identity, p. 159

social identity, p. 159

intimacy, p. 160

emerging adulthood, p. 162

menopause, p. 164

crystallized intelligence, p. 167

fluid intelligence, p. 167

social clock, p. 168

Test for Success: Critical Thinking Exercises

By Amy Himsel, El Camino College

1. "Nature is all that a man brings with him into the world; nurture is every influence that affects him after his birth," Francis Galton (*English Men of Science,* 1874). What part of this quote would need to be updated to reflect current research?

2. We all learned to walk as infants, and we retain that learning as adults. Yet we would be unable to consciously recall just how we achieved this feat. Why can't we reconstruct those memories?

3. A counselor has advised a teenager's frustrated parents that his behavior may improve when his brain matures. What evidence supports the counselor's suggestion?

4. "I hope I die before I get old," sang rock star Peter Townshend—when he was 20. What could you tell other 20-year-olds to make them feel more optimistic about aging?

5. Research has shown that living together before marriage predicts an increased likelihood of future divorce. Can you imagine two possible explanations for this correlation?

The Test for Success exercises offer you a chance to apply your critical thinking skills to aspects of the material you have just read. Suggestions for answering these questions can be found in Appendix D at the back of the book.

Multiple-choice self-tests and more may be found at www.worthpublishers.com/myers.

Chapter Outline

● **Sensing the World:**
  Some Basic Principles
  Thresholds
  Sensory Adaptation

● **Vision**
  The Stimulus Input: Light Energy
  The Eye
  Visual Information Processing
  Color Vision

● **Other Important Senses**
  Hearing
  Touch
  Pain
  Taste
  Smell

● **Perceptual Organization**
  Form Perception
  Depth Perception
  Perceptual Constancy

● **Perceptual Interpretation**
  Sensory Deprivation and
    Restored Vision
  Perceptual Adaptation
  Perceptual Set
  THINKING CRITICALLY ABOUT:
    Extrasensory Perception

6: Sensation and Perception

"I have perfect vision," explains my colleague, Heather Sellers, an acclaimed writer and writing teacher. Her vision may be fine, but there is a problem with her perception. She cannot recognize faces.

In her memoir, *Face First,* Sellers (2010) tells of awkward moments resulting from her lifelong *prosopagnosia*—face blindness.

> In college, on a date at the Spaghetti Station, I returned from the bathroom and plunked myself down in the wrong booth, facing the wrong man. I remained unaware he was not my date even as my date (a stranger to me) accosted Wrong Booth Guy, and then stormed out of the Station. I can't distinguish actors in movies and on television. I do not recognize myself in photos or video. I can't recognize my stepsons in the soccer pick-up line; I failed to determine which husband was mine at a party, in the mall, at the market.

Her inability to recognize acquaintances means that people sometimes perceive her as snobby or aloof. "Why did you walk past me?" someone might later ask. Similar to those of us with hearing loss who fake hearing during trite social conversation, Sellers sometimes fakes recognition. She often smiles at people she passes, in case she knows them. Or she pretends to know the person with whom she is talking. (To avoid the stress associated with such perception failures, people with serious hearing loss or with prosopagnosia often shy away from busy social situations.) But there is an upside: When encountering someone who previously irritated her, she typically won't feel ill will, because she doesn't recognize the person.

This curious mix of "perfect vision" and face blindness illustrates the distinction between sensation and perception. When Sellers looks at a friend, her *sensation* is normal: Her sensory receptors detect the same information yours would, and they transmit that information to her brain. And her *perception*—the organization and interpretation of sensory information that enables her to consciously recognize objects—is almost normal. Thus, she may recognize people from their hair, their gait, their voice, or their particular physique, just not their face. She can see the elements of their face—the nose, the eyes, the chin—and yet, at a party, "[I introduce myself] to my colleague Gloria THREE TIMES." Her experience is much like the struggle you or I would have trying to recognize a specific penguin in a group of waddling penguins.

Thanks to an area on the underside of your brain's right hemisphere, you can recognize a human face (but not a penguin's) in one-seventh of a second. As soon as you detect a face, you recognize it (Jacques & Rossion, 2006).

How do you do it? Twenty-four hours a day, all kinds of stimuli from the outside world bombard your body. Meanwhile, in a silent, cushioned, inner world, your brain floats in utter darkness. By itself, it sees nothing. It hears nothing. It feels nothing. *So, how does the world out there get in?*

To modernize the question: How do we construct our representations of the external world? How do a campfire's flicker, crackle, and smoky scent activate neural

sensation the process by which our sensory receptors and nervous system receive and represent stimulus energies from our environment.

perception the process of organizing and interpreting sensory information, enabling us to recognize meaningful objects and events.

bottom-up processing analysis that begins with the sensory receptors and works up to the brain's integration of sensory information.

top-down processing information processing guided by higher-level mental processes, as when we construct perceptions drawing on our experience and expectations.

psychophysics the study of relationships between the physical characteristics of stimuli, such as their intensity, and our psychological experience of them.

absolute threshold the minimum stimulation needed to detect a particular stimulus 50 percent of the time.

subliminal below one's absolute threshold for conscious awareness.

connections? And how, from this living neurochemistry, do we create our conscious experience of the fire's motion and temperature, its aroma and beauty? In search of answers to such questions, let's look more closely at what psychologists have learned about how we sense and perceive the world around us.

Sensing the World: Some Basic Principles

1: **What do we mean by *bottom-up processing* and *top-down processing?***

In our everyday experiences, **sensation** and **perception** blend into one continuous process. In this chapter, we slow down that process to study its parts.

We start with the sensory receptors and work up to higher levels of processing. Psychologists refer to sensory analysis that starts at the entry level as **bottom-up processing.** But our minds also *interpret* what our senses *detect*. We construct perceptions drawing both on sensations coming bottom-up to the brain and on our experience and expectations, which psychologists call **top-down processing.** For example, as our brain deciphers the information in **FIGURE 6.1**, bottom-up processing enables our sensory systems to detect the lines, angles, and colors that form the horses, rider, and surroundings. Using top-down processing, we consider the painting's title, notice the apprehensive expressions, and then direct our attention to aspects of the painting that will give those observations meaning.

For humans as for other species, nature's sensory gifts suit the recipients' needs, enabling organisms to obtain information essential to their survival. Consider:

- A frog, which feeds on flying insects, has eyes with receptor cells that fire only in response to small, dark, moving objects. A frog could starve to death knee-deep in motionless flies. But let one zoom by and the frog's "bug detector" cells snap awake.
- A male silkworm moth has receptors so sensitive to the female sex-attractant odor that a single female need release only a billionth of an ounce per second to attract every male silkworm moth within a mile. That is why there continue to be silkworms.

FIGURE 6.1 What's going on here? Our sensory and perceptual processes work together to help us sort out the complex images, including the hidden faces, in this Bev Doolittle painting, "The Forest Has Eyes."

Detail, *The Forest Has Eyes* by Bev Doolittle © The Greenwich Workshop, Inc., Trumbull, CT.

We are similarly equipped to detect the important features of our environment. Our ears are most sensitive to sound frequencies that include human voice consonants and a baby's cry.

We begin our exploration of our sensory gifts with a question that cuts across all our sensory systems: What stimuli cross our threshold for conscious awareness?

Thresholds

2: **What are absolute and difference thresholds, and do stimuli below the absolute threshold have any influence?**

We exist in a sea of energy. At this moment, you and I are being struck by X-rays and radio waves, ultraviolet and infrared light, and sound waves of very high and very low frequencies. To all of these we are blind and deaf. Other animals detect a world that lies beyond human experience (Hughes, 1999). Migrating birds stay on course aided by an internal magnetic compass. Bats and dolphins locate prey with sonar (bouncing echoing sound off objects). On a cloudy day, bees navigate by detecting polarized light from an invisible (to us) sun.

The shades on our own senses are open just a crack, allowing us only a restricted awareness of this vast sea of energy. Let's see what **psychophysics** has discovered about the physical energy we can detect and its effect on our psychological experience.

Absolute Thresholds

To some kinds of stimuli we are exquisitely sensitive. Standing atop a mountain on an utterly dark, clear night, most of us could see a candle flame atop another mountain 30 miles away. We could feel the wing of a bee falling on our cheek. We could smell a single drop of perfume in a three-room apartment (Galanter, 1962).

Our awareness of these faint stimuli illustrates our **absolute thresholds**—the minimum stimulation necessary to detect a particular light, sound, pressure, taste, or odor 50 percent of the time. To test your absolute threshold for sounds, a hearing specialist would expose each of your ears to varying sound levels. For each tone, the test would define where half the time you correctly detect the sound and half the time you do not. For each of your senses, that 50-50 recognition point defines your absolute threshold.

Subliminal Stimulation

Hoping to penetrate our unconscious, entrepreneurs offer recordings that supposedly speak directly to our brains to help us lose weight, stop smoking, or improve our memories. Masked by soothing ocean sounds, unheard messages ("I am thin," "Smoke tastes bad," or "I do well on tests. I have total recall of information") will, they say, influence our behavior. Such claims make two assumptions: (1) We can unconsciously sense **subliminal** (literally, "below threshold") stimuli, and (2) without our awareness, these stimuli have extraordinary suggestive powers. Can we? Do they?

Can we sense stimuli below our absolute thresholds? In one sense, the answer is clearly *yes*. Remember that an "absolute" threshold is merely the point at which we detect a stimulus *half the time* (**FIGURE 6.2**). At or slightly below this threshold, we will still detect the stimulus some of the time.

FIGURE 6.2 Absolute threshold Can I detect this sound? An *absolute threshold* is the intensity at which a person can detect a stimulus half the time. Hearing tests locate these thresholds for various frequency levels.

Can we be affected by stimuli so weak as to be unnoticed? Under certain conditions, the answer is *yes*. An invisible image or word can briefly **prime** your response to a later question. In a typical experiment, the image or word is quickly flashed, then replaced by a *masking stimulus* that interrupts the brain's processing before conscious perception. For example, one experiment subliminally flashed either emotionally positive scenes (kittens, a romantic couple) or negative scenes (a werewolf, a dead body) an instant before participants viewed slides of people (Krosnick et al., 1992). The participants consciously perceived either scene as only a flash of light. Yet the people somehow looked nicer if their image immediately followed unperceived kittens rather than an unperceived werewolf.

This experiment illustrates an intriguing phenomenon: Sometimes we *feel* what we do not know and cannot describe. An imperceptibly brief stimulus often triggers a weak response that *can* be detected by brain scanning (Blankenburg et al., 2003; Haynes & Rees, 2005, 2006). The conclusion (turn up the volume here): *Much of our information processing occurs automatically, out of sight, off the radar screen of our conscious mind.*

But does the fact of subliminal *sensation* verify entrepreneurial claims of subliminal *persuasion?* Can advertisers really manipulate us with "hidden persuasion"? The near-consensus among researchers is *no*. Their verdict is similar to that of astronomers who say of astrologers, *yes,* they are right that stars and planets are out there; but *no,* the celestial bodies don't directly affect us. The laboratory research reveals a *subtle, fleeting* effect. Priming thirsty people with the subliminal word *thirst* might therefore, for a brief interval, make a thirst-quenching beverage ad more persuasive (Strahan et al., 2002). Likewise, priming thirsty people with Lipton Ice Tea may increase their choosing the primed brand (Karremans et al., 2006). But the subliminal-message hucksters claim something different: a *powerful, enduring* effect on behavior.

When Anthony Greenwald and his colleagues (1991, 1992) tested that claim in 16 experiments evaluating subliminal self-help tapes, their results were uniform: None had any therapeutic effect beyond that of a placebo (the effect of one's belief in them). Their conclusion: "Subliminal procedures offer little or nothing of value to the marketing practitioner" (Pratkanis & Greenwald, 1988).

Difference Thresholds

To function effectively, we need absolute thresholds low enough to allow us to detect important sights, sounds, textures, tastes, and smells. We also need to detect small differences among stimuli. A musician must detect minute discrepancies in an instrument's tuning. Parents must detect the sound of their own child's voice amid other children's voices. Even after living two years in Scotland, sheep *baa's* all sound alike to my ears. But not to those of ewes, which I have observed streaking, after shearing, directly to the *baa* of their lamb amid the chorus of other distressed lambs.

The **difference threshold,** also called the *just noticeable difference (jnd),* is the minimum difference a person (or sheep) can detect between any two stimuli half the time. That detectable difference increases with the size of the stimulus. Thus, if you add 1 ounce to a 10-ounce weight, you will detect the difference; add 1 ounce to a 100-ounce weight and you probably will not.

More than a century ago, Ernst Weber noted something so simple and so widely applicable that people today still refer to it

> "The heart has its reasons which reason does not know."
>
> —Pascal, *Pensées*, 1670

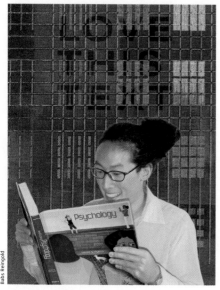

Babs Reingold

Subliminal persuasion? Although subliminally presented stimuli *can* subtly influence people, experiments discount attempts at subliminal advertising and self-improvement. (The playful message here is not actually subliminal —because you can easily perceive it.)

The difference threshold In this computer-generated copy of the Twenty-third Psalm, each line of the typeface changes imperceptibly. How many lines are required for you to experience a just noticeable difference?

The LORD is my shepherd;
I shall not want.
He maketh me to lie down
in green pastures:
he leadeth me
beside the still waters.
He restoreth my soul:
he leadeth me
in the paths of righteousness
for his name's sake.
Yea, though I walk through the valley
of the shadow of death,
I will fear no evil:
for thou art with me;
thy rod and thy staff
they comfort me.
Thou preparest a table before me
in the presence of mine enemies:
thou anointest my head with oil,
my cup runneth over.
Surely goodness and mercy
shall follow me
all the days of my life:
and I will dwell
in the house of the LORD
for ever.

as **Weber's law:** For their difference to be perceptible, two stimuli must differ by a constant *proportion*—not a constant amount. The exact proportion varies, depending on the stimulus. For the average person to perceive their differences, two lights must differ in intensity by 8 percent. Two objects must differ in weight by 2 percent. And two tones must differ in frequency by only 0.3 percent (Teghtsoonian, 1971).

Sensory Adaptation

3: What is the function of sensory adaptation?

Entering your neighbors' living room, you smell a musty odor. You wonder how they can stand it, but within minutes you no longer notice it. **Sensory adaptation**—our diminishing sensitivity to an unchanging stimulus—has come to your rescue. (To experience this phenomenon, move your watch up your wrist an inch: You will feel it—but only for a few moments.) After constant exposure to a stimulus, our nerve cells fire less frequently.

Why, then, if we stare at an object without flinching, does it not vanish from sight? Because, unnoticed by us, our eyes are always moving, flitting from one spot to another enough to guarantee that stimulation on the eyes' receptors continually changes (**FIGURE 6.3**).

What if we actually could stop our eyes from moving? Would sights seem to vanish, as odors do? To find out, psychologists have devised ingenious instruments for maintaining a constant image on the eye's inner surface. Imagine that we have fitted a volunteer, Mary, with one of these instruments—a miniature projector mounted on a contact lens. When Mary's eye moves, the image from the projector moves as well. So everywhere that Mary looks, the scene is sure to go.

> "We need above all to know about changes; no one wants or needs to be reminded 16 hours a day that his shoes are on."
>
> —Neuroscientist David Hubel (1979)

For 9 in 10 people—but for only 1 in 3 of those with schizophrenia—this eye flutter turns off when the eye is following a moving target (Holzman & Matthyss, 1990).

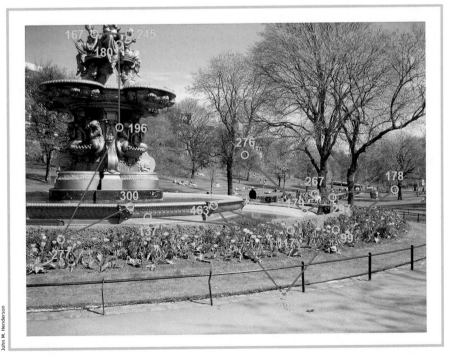

John M. Henderson

FIGURE 6.3 The jumpy eye University of Edinburgh psychologist John Henderson (2007) illustrates how a person's gaze jumps from one spot to another every third of a second or so. Eye-tracking equipment shows how a typical person views a photograph of Edinburgh's Princes Street Gardens. Circles represent fixations, and the numbers indicate the time of fixation in milliseconds (300 milliseconds = three-tenths of a second).

priming the activation, often unconsciously, of certain associations, thus predisposing one's perception, memory, or response.

difference threshold the minimum difference between two stimuli required for detection 50 percent of the time. We experience the difference threshold as a *just noticeable difference* (or *jnd*).

Weber's law the principle that, to be perceived as different, two stimuli must differ by a constant minimum percentage (rather than a constant amount).

sensory adaptation diminished sensitivity as a consequence of constant stimulation.

FIGURE 6.4 Sensory adaptation: now you see it, now you don't! (a) A projector mounted on a contact lens makes the projected image move with the eye. (b) Initially, the person sees the stabilized image, but soon she sees fragments fading and reappearing. (From "Stabilized images on the retina," by R. M. Pritchard. Copyright © 1961 Scientific American, Inc. All rights reserved.)

(a)   (b)

"My suspicion is that the universe is not only queerer than we suppose, but queerer than we can suppose."

—J. B. S. Haldane, *Possible Worlds,* 1927

If we project the profile of a face through such an instrument, what will Mary see? At first, she will see the complete profile. But within a few seconds, as her sensory system begins to fatigue, things will get weird. Bit by bit, the image will vanish, only later to reappear and then disappear—in recognizable fragments or as a whole (**FIGURE 6.4**).

Although sensory adaptation reduces our sensitivity, it offers an important benefit: freedom to focus on *informative* changes in our environment without being distracted by the constant chatter of uninformative background stimulation. Our sensory receptors are alert to novelty; bore them with repetition and they free our attention for more important things. Stinky or heavily perfumed people don't notice their odor because, like you and me, they adapt to what's constant and only detect change. This reinforces a fundamental lesson: *We perceive the world not exactly as it is, but as it is useful for us to perceive it.*

Our sensitivity to changing stimulation helps explain television's attention-grabbing power. Cuts, edits, zooms, pans, sudden noises—all demand attention, even from TV researchers: During interesting conversations, notes Percy Tannenbaum (2002), "I cannot for the life of me stop from periodically glancing over to the screen."

Sensory thresholds and adaptation are only two of the commonalities shared by the senses. All our senses receive sensory stimulation, transform it into neural information, and deliver that information to the brain. How do the senses work? How do we see? Hear? Smell? Taste? Feel pain? Keep our balance?

REHEARSE IT!

1. Sensation is to _____ as perception is to _____.
   a. absolute threshold; difference threshold
   b. bottom-up processing; top-down processing
   c. interpretation; detection
   d. conscious awareness; persuasion

2. To construct meaning from our external environment, we organize and interpret sensory information. This is the process of
   a. sensation.
   b. priming.
   c. bottom-up processing.
   d. perception.

3. Subliminal stimuli, such as undetectably faint sights or sounds, are
   a. too weak to be processed by the brain in any way.
   b. consciously perceived more than 50 percent of the time.
   c. always strong enough to affect our behavior.
   d. below the absolute threshold for conscious awareness.

4. Another term for the difference threshold is
   a. just noticeable difference.
   b. sensory adaptation.
   c. absolute threshold.
   d. subliminal stimulation.

5. Weber's law states that for a difference to be perceived, two stimuli must differ by
   a. a fixed unchanging amount.
   b. a constant minimum percentage.
   c. a constantly changing amount.
   d. more than 7 percent.

6. Sensory adaptation has survival benefits because it helps us focus on
   a. visual stimuli.
   b. auditory stimuli.
   c. constant features of the environment.
   d. important changes in the environment.

Answers: 1. b, 2. d, 3. d, 4. a, 5. b, 6. d.

Vision

4: What is the energy that we see as visible light?

One of nature's great wonders is neither bizarre nor remote, but commonplace: How does our material body construct our conscious visual experience? How do we transform particles of light energy into colorful sights?

Part of this genius is our ability to convert one sort of energy to another. Our eyes, for example, receive light energy and transform it into neural messages that our brain then processes into what we consciously see. How does such a taken-for-granted yet remarkable thing happen?

The Stimulus Input: Light Energy

Scientifically speaking, what strikes our eyes is not color but pulses of energy that our visual system perceives as color. What we see as visible light (**FIGURE 6.5**) is but a thin slice of the whole spectrum of *electromagnetic energy* ranging from the imperceptibly short waves of gamma rays to the long waves of radio transmission. Other organisms are sensitive to differing portions of this spectrum. Bees, for instance, cannot see red but can see ultraviolet light.

Two physical characteristics of light help determine our sensory experience of them. Light's **wavelength**—the distance from one wave peak to the next—influences our perception of its **hue** (the color we experience, such as blue or green). **Intensity,** the amount of energy in a light wave (as determined by the wave's amplitude, or

wavelength the distance from the peak of one light or sound wave to the peak of the next. Electromagnetic wavelengths vary from the short blips of cosmic rays to the long pulses of radio transmission.

hue the dimension of color that is determined by the wavelength of light; what we know as the color names *blue*, *green*, and so forth.

intensity the amount of energy in a light or sound wave, which we perceive as brightness or loudness, as determined by the wave's amplitude.

FIGURE 6.5 The spectrum of electromagnetic energy This spectrum ranges from gamma rays as short as the diameter of an atom to radio waves over a mile long. The narrow band of wavelengths visible to the human eye (shown enlarged) extends from the shorter waves of blue-violet light to the longer waves of red light.

FIGURE 6.6 The physical properties of waves (a) Waves vary in *wavelength* (the distance between successive peaks). *Frequency,* the number of complete wavelengths that can pass a point in a given time, depends on the wavelength. The shorter the wavelength, the higher the frequency. (b) Waves also vary in *amplitude* (the height from peak to trough). Wave amplitude determines the intensity of colors.

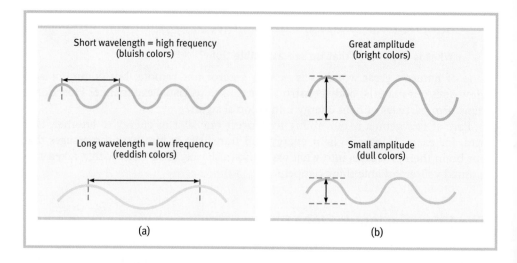

Short wavelength = high frequency
(bluish colors)

Long wavelength = low frequency
(reddish colors)

(a)

Great amplitude
(bright colors)

Small amplitude
(dull colors)

(b)

height), influences our perception of its brightness (**FIGURE 6.6**). To understand how we transform physical energy into color and meaning, we first need to understand vision's window, the eye.

The Eye

5: **How does the eye transform light energy into neural messages?**

Light enters the eye through the *cornea,* which protects the eye and bends light to provide focus (**FIGURE 6.7**). The light then passes through the *pupil,* a small adjustable opening surrounded by the *iris,* a colored muscle that adjusts light intake. The iris dilates or constricts in response to light intensity and even to inner emotions. (When we're feeling amorous, our telltale dilated pupils and dark eyes subtly signal our interest.) Each iris is so distinctive that an iris-scanning machine could confirm your identity.

Behind the pupil is a *lens* that focuses incoming light rays into an image on the **retina,** a multilayered tissue on the eyeball's sensitive inner surface. The lens focuses the rays by changing its curvature in a process called **accommodation.**

For centuries, scientists knew that when an image of a candle passes through a small opening, it casts an inverted mirror image on a dark wall behind. If the retina receives this sort of upside-down image, as in Figure 6.7, how can we see the world right side up? Eventually, the answer became clear: The retina doesn't "see" a whole image. Rather, its millions of receptor cells convert particles of light energy into neural impulses and forward those to the brain. There, the impulses are reassembled into a perceived, upright-seeming image.

Lens
Pupil
Iris
Cornea

Retina
Fovea (point of central focus)
Optic nerve to brain's visual cortex
Blind spot

FIGURE 6.7 The eye Light rays reflected from the candle pass through the cornea, pupil, and lens. The curvature and thickness of the lens change to bring either nearby or distant objects into focus on the retina. Rays from the top of the candle strike the bottom of the retina and those from the left side of the candle strike the right side of the retina. The candle's retinal image is thus upside-down and reversed.

The Retina

If you could follow a single light-energy particle into your eye, you would first make your way through the retina's outer layer of cells to its buried receptor cells, the **rods** and **cones** (**FIGURE 6.8**). There, you would see the light energy trigger chemical changes that would spark a neural impulse, activating neighboring *bipolar cells.* The

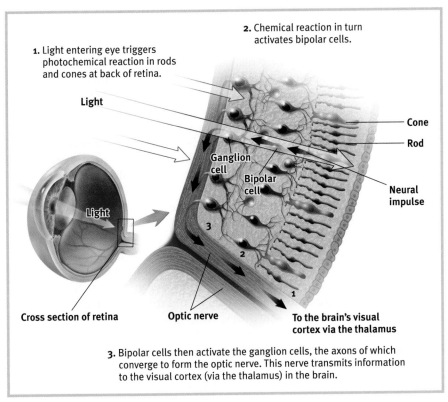

1. Light entering eye triggers photochemical reaction in rods and cones at back of retina.

2. Chemical reaction in turn activates bipolar cells.

Light

Cone

Rod

Ganglion cell

Bipolar cell

Neural impulse

Light

Cross section of retina

Optic nerve

To the brain's visual cortex via the thalamus

3. Bipolar cells then activate the ganglion cells, the axons of which converge to form the optic nerve. This nerve transmits information to the visual cortex (via the thalamus) in the brain.

FIGURE 6.8 **The retina's reaction to light**

retina the light-sensitive inner surface of the eye, containing the receptor rods and cones plus layers of neurons that begin the processing of visual information.

accommodation the process by which the eye's lens changes shape to focus near or far objects on the retina.

rods retinal receptors that detect black, white, and gray; necessary for peripheral and twilight vision, when cones don't respond.

cones retinal receptor cells that are concentrated near the center of the retina and that function in daylight or in well-lit conditions. The cones detect fine detail and give rise to color sensations.

optic nerve the nerve that carries neural impulses from the eye to the brain.

blind spot the point at which the optic nerve leaves the eye, creating a "blind" spot because no receptor cells are located there.

bipolar cells in turn would activate the neighboring *ganglion cells.* Following the particle's path, you would see axons from this network of ganglion cells converging, like the strands of a rope, to form the **optic nerve** that carries information to your brain (where the thalamus will receive and distribute the information). The optic nerve can send nearly 1 million messages at once through its nearly 1 million ganglion fibers. (The auditory nerve, which enables hearing, carries much less information through its mere 30,000 fibers.)

Where the optic nerve leaves the eye there are no receptor cells—creating a **blind spot** (**FIGURE 6.9**), which you normally don't notice because your two eyes work together to send information to your brain. But even if you close one eye, you won't see a black hole on your TV screen. Without seeking your approval, your brain will fill in the hole.

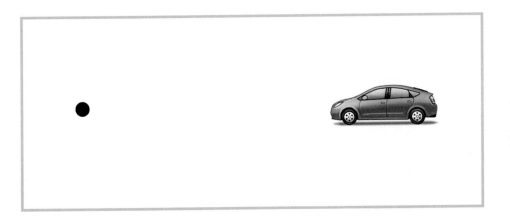

FIGURE 6.9 **The blind spot** There are no receptor cells where the optic nerve leaves the eye (see Figure 6.8). This creates a blind spot in your vision. To demonstrate, close your left eye, look at the black dot, and hold the page about a foot from your face, at which point the car will disappear. The blind spot does not normally impair your vision, because your eyes are moving and because one eye catches what the other misses.

TABLE 6.1 **Receptors in the Human Eye: Rod-Shaped Rods and Cone-Shaped Cones**

	Cones	Rods
Number	6 million	120 million
Location in retina	Center	Periphery
Sensitivity in dim light	Low	High
Color sensitivity	High	Low
Detail sensitivity	High	Low

Rods and cones differ in their geography and in the tasks they handle (**TABLE 6.1**). Cones cluster in and around the **fovea,** the retina's area of central focus (see Figure 6.7). Many cones have their own hotline to the brain—bipolar cells that help relay the cone's individual message to the visual cortex, which devotes a large area to input from the fovea. These direct connections preserve the cones' precise information, making them better able to detect fine detail. Rods have no such hotline; they share bipolar cells with other rods, sending combined messages. To experience this difference in sensitivity to details, pick a word in this sentence and stare directly at it, focusing its image on the cones in your fovea. Notice that words a few inches off to the side appear blurred? Their image strikes the more peripheral region of your retina, where rods predominate. The next time you are driving or biking, note, too, that you can detect a car in your peripheral vision well before perceiving its details.

Cones also enable you to perceive color. In dim light they become ineffectual, so you see no colors. Rods, which enable black-and-white vision, remain sensitive in dim light, and several rods will funnel their faint energy output onto a single bipolar cell. Thus, cones and rods each provide a special sensitivity—cones to detail and color, and rods to faint light.

When you enter a darkened theater or turn off the light at night, your pupils dilate to allow more light to reach your retina. It typically takes 20 minutes or more before your eyes fully adapt. You can demonstrate dark adaptation by closing or covering one eye for up to 20 minutes. Then make the light in the room not quite bright enough to read this book with your open eye. Now open the dark-adapted eye and read (easily). This period of dark adaptation parallels the average natural twilight transition between the sun's setting and darkness.

Visual Information Processing

6: How does the brain process visual information?

Visual information percolates through progressively more abstract levels. At the entry level, the retina processes information before routing it via the thalamus to the brain's cortex. The retina's neural layers—which are actually brain tissue that migrates to the eye during early fetal development—don't just pass along electrical impulses; they also help encode and analyze the sensory information. The third neural layer in a frog's eye, for example, contains the "bug detector" cells that fire only in response to moving flylike stimuli.

After processing by your retina's nearly 130 million receptor rods and cones, information travels to your bipolar cells, then to your million or so ganglion cells, through their axons making up the optic nerve, to your brain. Any given retinal area relays its information to a corresponding location in the visual cortex, in the occipital lobe at the back of your brain (**FIGURE 6.10**).

Feature Detection

Nobel Prize winners David Hubel and Torsten Wiesel (1979) demonstrated that neurons in the occipital lobe's visual cortex receive information from individual ganglion cells in the retina. These **feature detector** cells derive their name from their ability to respond to a scene's specific features—to particular edges, lines, angles, and movements.

Feature detectors in the visual cortex pass such information to other cortical areas where teams of cells (*supercell clusters*) respond to more complex patterns. One temporal lobe area just behind your right ear, for example, enables you to perceive faces. If this region were damaged, you might recognize other forms and objects,

fovea the central focal point in the retina, around which the eye's cones cluster.

feature detectors nerve cells in the brain that respond to specific features of a stimulus, such as shape, angle, or movement.

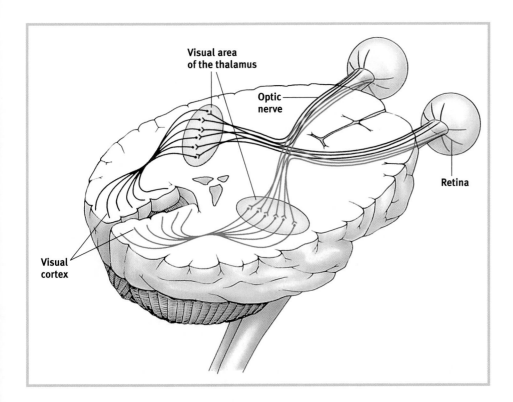

FIGURE 6.10 Pathway from the eyes to the visual cortex Ganglion axons forming the optic nerve run to the thalamus, where they synapse with neurons that run to the visual cortex.

but, like Heather Sellers, not familiar faces. Functional MRI (fMRI) scans show other brain areas lighting up when people view other object categories (Downing et al., 2001). Amazingly specific combinations of activity may appear (**FIGURE 6.11**). "We can tell if a person is looking at a shoe, a chair, or a face, based on the pattern of their brain activity," notes researcher James Haxby (2001).

Psychologist David Perrett and his colleagues (1988, 1992, 1994) reported that for biologically important objects and events, monkey brains (and surely ours as well) have a "vast visual encyclopedia" distributed as cells that specialize in responding to one type of stimulus—such as a specific gaze, head angle, posture, or body movement. Other supercell clusters integrate this information and fire only when the cues collectively indicate the direction of someone's attention and approach. This instant analysis, which aided our ancestors' survival, also helps a soccer goalie anticipate the direction of an impending kick, and a driver anticipate a pedestrian's next movement.

■ Faces	■ Chairs
■ Houses	■ Houses and chairs

FIGURE 6.11 The telltale brain Looking at faces, houses, and chairs activates different brain areas in this right-facing brain.

Well-developed supercells In this 2007 World Cup match, Brazil's Marta instantly processed visual information about the positions and movements of Australia's defenders and goalie (Melissa Barbieri) and somehow managed to get the ball around them all and into the net.

parallel processing the processing of many aspects of a problem simultaneously; the brain's natural mode of information processing for many functions, including vision. Contrasts with the step-by-step (serial) processing of most computers and of conscious problem solving.

Parallel Processing

Unlike most computers, which do step-by-step *serial processing*, our brain engages in **parallel processing:** doing many things at once. The brain divides a visual scene into subdimensions, such as color, movement, form, and depth (**FIGURE 6.12**), and works on each aspect simultaneously (Livingstone & Hubel, 1988). We then construct our perceptions by integrating the separate but parallel work of these different visual teams.

FIGURE 6.12 Parallel processing Studies of patients with brain damage suggest that the brain delegates the work of processing color, movement, form, and depth to different areas. After taking a scene apart, how does the brain integrate these subdimensions into the perceived image? The answer to this question is the ultimate quest of vision research.

Destroying or disabling the neural workstation for other visual subtasks produces different peculiar results, as happened to "Mrs. M." (Hoffman, 1998). Since a stroke damaged areas near the rear of both sides of her brain, she can no longer perceive movement. People in a room seem "suddenly here or there but I have not seen them moving." Pouring tea into a cup is a challenge because the fluid appears frozen—she cannot perceive it rising in the cup.

Others with stroke or surgery damage to their brain's visual cortex have experienced *blindsight,* a localized area of blindness in part of their field of vision (Weiskrantz, 1986; see also Chapter 2). Shown a series of sticks in the blind field, they report seeing nothing. Yet when asked to guess whether the sticks are vertical or horizontal, their visual intuition typically offers the correct response. When told, "You got them all right," they are astounded. There is, it seems, a second "mind"— a parallel processing system—operating unseen.

A scientific understanding of visual information processing leaves many neuropsychologists awestruck. As Roger Sperry (1985) observed, the "insights of science give added, not lessened, reasons for awe, respect, and reverence." Think about it: As you look at someone, visual information is transformed into millions of neural impulses, sent to your brain, constructed into component features, and finally, in some as-yet mysterious way, composed into a meaningful image, which you compare with previously stored images and recognize: "That's Sara!" Likewise, as you read this page, the printed squiggles are transmitted by reflected light rays onto your retina, which triggers a process that sends formless nerve impulses to several areas of your brain, which integrates the information and decodes meaning, thus completing the transfer of information across time and space from my mind to your mind. The whole process (**FIGURE 6.13**) is more complex than taking apart a car,

FIGURE 6.13 A simplified summary of visual information processing

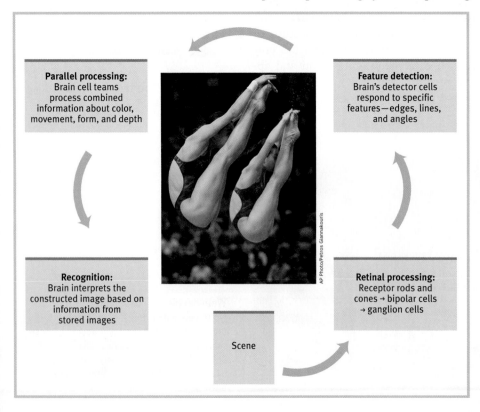

Parallel processing: Brain cell teams process combined information about color, movement, form, and depth

Feature detection: Brain's detector cells respond to specific features—edges, lines, and angles

Recognition: Brain interprets the constructed image based on information from stored images

Retinal processing: Receptor rods and cones → bipolar cells → ganglion cells

Scene

AP Photo/Petros Giannakouris

piece by piece, transporting it to a different location, then having specialized workers reconstruct it. That all of this happens instantly, effortlessly, and continuously is indeed awesome.

> "I am . . . wonderfully made."
>
> —King David, Psalm 139:14

Color Vision

7: What theories help us understand color vision?

We talk as though objects possess color: "A tomato is red." Perhaps you have pondered the old question, "If a tree falls in the forest and no one hears it, does it make a sound?" We can ask the same of color: If no one sees the tomato, is it red?

The answer is *no*. First, the tomato is everything *but* red, because it *rejects* (reflects) the long wavelengths of red. Second, the tomato's color is our mental construction. As Isaac Newton (1704) noted, "The [light] rays are not colored." Color, like all aspects of vision, resides not in the object but in the theater of our brains, as evidenced by our dreaming in color.

In the study of vision, one of the most basic and intriguing mysteries is how we see the world in color. How, from the light energy striking the retina, does the brain manufacture our experience of color—and of such a multitude of colors? Our difference threshold for colors is so low that we can discriminate some 7 million different color variations (Geldard, 1972).

At least most of us can. For about 1 person in 50, vision is color deficient—and that person is usually male, because the defect is genetically sex-linked. To understand why some people's vision is color deficient, it will help to first understand how normal color vision works.

Modern detective work on the mystery of color vision began in the nineteenth century when Hermann von Helmholtz built on the insights of an English physicist, Thomas Young. Knowing that any color can be created by combining the light waves of three primary colors—red, green, and blue—Young and von Helmholtz inferred that the eye must have three corresponding types of color receptors. Years later, researchers measured the response of various cones to different color stimuli and confirmed the **Young-Helmholtz trichromatic (three-color) theory.** Indeed, the retina has three types of color receptors, each especially sensitive to one of three colors. And those colors are, in fact, red, green, and blue. When we stimulate combinations of these cones, we see other colors. For example, there are no receptors especially sensitive to yellow. Yet when both red-sensitive and green-sensitive cones are stimulated, we see yellow.

> "Only mind has sight and hearing; all things else are deaf and blind."
>
> —Epicharmus, *Fragments*, 550 B.C.E.

Young-Helmholtz trichromatic (three-color) theory the theory that the retina contains three different color receptors—one most sensitive to red, one to green, one to blue—which, when stimulated in combination, can produce the perception of any color.

Most people with color-deficient vision are not actually "colorblind." They simply lack functioning red- or green-sensitive cones, or sometimes both. Their vision—perhaps unknown to them, because their lifelong vision *seems* normal—is monochromatic (one-color) or dichromatic (two-color) instead of trichromatic, making it impossible to distinguish the red and green in **FIGURE 6.14** (Boynton, 1979). Dogs, too, lack receptors for the wavelengths of red, giving them only limited, dichromatic color vision (Neitz et al., 1989).

But trichromatic theory cannot solve all parts of the color vision mystery, as Ewald Hering soon noted. For example, we see yellow when mixing red and green light. But how is it that those blind to red and green can often still see yellow? And why does yellow appear to be a pure color and not a mixture of red and green, the way purple is of red and blue?

FIGURE 6.14 Color-deficient vision People who suffer red-green deficiency have trouble perceiving the number within the design.

FIGURE 6.15 Afterimage effect
Stare at the center of the flag for a minute and then shift your eyes to the dot in the white space beside it. What do you see? (After tiring your neural response to black, green, and yellow, you should see their opponent colors.) Stare at a white wall and note how the size of the flag grows with the projection distance!

Hering, a physiologist, found a clue in the well-known occurrence of *afterimages*. When you stare at a green square for a while and then look at a white sheet of paper, you see red, green's *opponent color*. Stare at a yellow square and you will later see its opponent color, blue, on the white paper (as in the flag demonstration in **FIGURE 6.15**). Hering surmised that there must be two additional color processes, one responsible for red-versus-green perception, and one for blue-versus-yellow.

A century later, researchers confirmed Hering's **opponent-process theory.** As visual information leaves the receptor cells, we analyze it in terms of three sets of opponent colors: *red-green, yellow-blue,* and *white-black*. In the retina and in the thalamus (where impulses from the retina are relayed en route to the visual cortex), some neurons are turned "on" by red but turned "off" by green. Others are turned on by green but off by red (DeValois & DeValois, 1975).

Opponent processes explain afterimages, such as in the flag demonstration, in which we tire our green response by staring at green. When we then stare at white (which contains all colors, including red), only the red part of the green-red pairing will fire normally.

The present solution to the mystery of color vision is therefore roughly this: Color processing occurs in two stages. The retina's cones for red, green, and blue respond in varying degrees to different color stimuli, as the Young-Helmholtz trichromatic theory suggested. The cones' signals are then processed by the nervous system's opponent-process cells, en route to the visual cortex.

opponent-process theory the theory that opposing retinal processes (red-green, yellow-blue, white-black) enable color vision. For example, some cells are stimulated by green and inhibited by red; others are stimulated by red and inhibited by green.

REHEARSE IT!

7. The physical characteristic of light that determines the color we experience, such as blue or green, is
   a. intensity.
   b. wavelength.
   c. amplitude.
   d. hue.

8. The blind spot in your retina is located in an area where
   a. there are rods but no cones.
   b. there are cones but no rods.
   c. the optic nerve leaves the eye.
   d. the bipolar cells meet the ganglion cells.

9. Cones are the eye's receptor cells that are especially sensitive to _____ light and are responsible for our _____ vision.

   a. bright; black-and-white
   b. dim; color
   c. bright; color
   d. dim; black-and-white

10. The brain cells that respond maximally to certain bars, edges, and angles are called
    a. rods and cones.
    b. feature detectors.
    c. bipolar cells.
    d. ganglion cells.

11. The brain's ability to process many aspects of an object or problem simultaneously is called
    a. parallel processing.
    b. serial processing.

    c. opponent processing.
    d. accommodation.

12. Two theories together account for color vision. The Young-Helmholtz theory shows that the eye contains _____, and the Hering theory accounts for the nervous system's having _____.
    a. opposing retinal processes; three pairs of color receptors
    b. opponent-process cells; three types of color receptors
    c. three pairs of color receptors; opposing retinal processes
    d. three types of color receptors; opponent-process cells

Answers: 7. b, 8. c, 9. c, 10. b, 11. a, 12. d.

Other Important Senses

For humans, vision is the major sense. More of our brain cortex is devoted to vision than to any other sense. Yet without our senses of hearing, touch, body position and movement, taste, and smell, our capacities for experiencing the world would be vastly diminished.

Hearing

Like our other senses, our **audition,** or hearing, is highly adaptive. We hear a wide range of sounds, but we hear best those sounds with frequencies in a range corresponding to that of the human voice. We also are acutely sensitive to faint sounds, an obvious boon for our ancestors' survival when hunting or being hunted, or for detecting a child's whimper. (If our ears were much more sensitive, we would hear a constant hiss from the movement of air molecules.)

We are also remarkably attuned to variations in sounds. We easily detect differences among thousands of human voices: Answering the phone, we recognize a friend calling from the moment she says "Hi." A fraction of a second after such events stimulate receptors in the ear, millions of neurons have simultaneously coordinated in extracting the essential features, comparing them with past experience, and identifying the stimulus (Freeman, 1991). For hearing as for seeing, we will consider the fundamental question: How do we do it?

The Stimulus Input: Sound Waves

8: What are the characteristics of air pressure waves that we hear as sound?

Draw a bow across a violin, and the resulting stimulus energy is sound waves—jostling molecules of air, each bumping into the next, like a shove transmitted through a concert hall's crowded exit tunnel. Those waves of compressed and expanded air are like the ripples on a pond circling out from where a stone has been tossed. As we swim in our ocean of moving air molecules, our ears detect these brief air pressure changes. Exposed to a loud, low bass sound—perhaps from a bass guitar or a cello—we can also *feel* the vibration, and we hear by both air and bone conduction.

The ears then transform the vibrating air into nerve impulses, which our brain decodes as sounds. The strength, or *amplitude,* of sound waves (recall Figure 6.6, which illustrated amplitude in relation to vision) determines their *loudness.* Waves also vary in length, and therefore in **frequency.** Their frequency determines the **pitch** we experience: Long waves have low frequency—and low pitch. Short waves have high frequency—and high pitch. A violin produces much shorter, faster sound waves than does a cello.

We measure sounds in decibels. The absolute threshold for hearing is arbitrarily defined as zero decibels. Every 10 decibels correspond to a tenfold increase in sound intensity. Thus, normal conversation (60 decibels) is 10,000 times more intense than a 20-decibel whisper. And a temporarily tolerable 100-decibel passing subway train is 10 billion times more intense than the faintest detectable sound.

The Ear

9: How does the ear transform sound energy into neural messages?

To hear, we must somehow convert sound waves into neural activity. The human ear accomplishes this feat through an intricate mechanical chain reaction. First, the visible *outer ear* channels the sound waves through the auditory canal to the *eardrum,* a

audition the sense or act of hearing.

frequency the number of complete wavelengths that pass a point in a given time (for example, per second).

pitch a tone's experienced highness or lowness; depends on frequency.

The sounds of music A violin's short, fast waves create a high pitch, a cello's longer, slower waves a lower pitch. Differences in the waves' height, or amplitude, also create differing degrees of loudness.

(a)

OUTER EAR   MIDDLE EAR   INNER EAR

Semicircular canals

Bones of the middle ear

Bone

Auditory nerve

Cochlea

Sound waves

Eardrum

Oval window (where stirrup attaches)

Auditory canal

Auditory cortex of temporal lobe

(b)

Enlargement of middle ear and inner ear, showing cochlea partially uncoiled for clarity

Hammer   Anvil   Cochlea, partially uncoiled

Sound waves

Auditory nerve

Nerve fibers to auditory nerve

Protruding hair cells

Eardrum   Stirrup   Oval window   Motion of fluid in the cochlea

FIGURE 6.16 Hear here: How we transform sound waves into nerve impulses that our brain interprets (a) The outer ear funnels sound waves to the eardrum. The bones of the middle ear amplify and relay the eardrum's vibrations through the oval window into the fluid-filled cochlea. (b) As shown in this detail of the middle and inner ear, the resulting pressure changes in the cochlear fluid cause the basilar membrane to ripple, bending the hair cells on the surface. Hair cell movements trigger impulses at the base of the nerve cells, whose fibers converge to form the auditory nerve, which sends neural messages to the thalamus and on to the auditory cortex.

tight membrane that vibrates with the waves. The **middle ear** then transmits the eardrum's vibrations through a piston made of three tiny bones (the *hammer, anvil,* and *stirrup*) to the **cochlea,** a snail-shaped tube in the **inner ear (FIGURE 6.16a).** The incoming vibrations cause the cochlea's membrane (the *oval window*) to vibrate, jostling the fluid that fills the tube (Figure 6.16b). This motion causes ripples in the *basilar membrane,* bending the *hair cells* lining its surface, not unlike the wind bending a wheat field. Hair cell movement triggers impulses in the adjacent nerve cells, whose axons converge to form the *auditory nerve,* which sends neural messages (via the thalamus) to the temporal lobe's *auditory cortex.* From vibrating air to moving piston to fluid waves to electrical impulses to the brain: Voila! We hear.

My vote for the most intriguing part of the hearing process is the hair cells. A Howard Hughes Medical Institute (2008) report on these "quivering bundles that let us hear" marvels at their "extreme sensitivity and extreme speed." A cochlea has 16,000 of them, which sounds like a lot until we compare that with an eye's 130 million or so receptor rods and cones. But consider their responsiveness. Deflect the tiny bundles of cilia on the tip of a hair cell by the width of an atom—the equivalent of displacing the top of the Eiffel Tower by half an inch—and the alert hair cell, thanks to a special protein at its tip, triggers a neural response (Corey et al., 2004).

Dr. Fred Hossler/Visuals Unlimited

Be kind to your inner ear's hair cells
When vibrating in response to sound, the hair cells shown here lining the cochlea produce an electrical signal.

Decibels

140	Rock band (amplified) at close range
130	
120	Loud thunder
110	Jet plane at 500 feet
100	Subway train at 20 feet
90	
80	Busy street corner
70	
60	Normal conversation
50	
40	
30	
20	Whisper
10	
0	Threshold of hearing

Prolonged exposure above 85 decibels produces hearing loss

Richard Kaylin/Stone/Getty Images

FIGURE 6.17 The intensity of some common sounds At close range, the thunder that follows lightning has 120-decibel intensity.

Damage to hair cells accounts for most hearing loss. They have been likened to shag carpet fibers. Walk around on them and they will spring back with a quick vacuuming. But leave a heavy piece of furniture on them for a long time and they may never rebound. As a general rule, if we cannot talk over a noise, it is potentially harmful, especially if prolonged and repeated (Roesser, 1998). Such experiences are common when sound exceeds 100 decibels, as happens in venues from frenzied sports arenas to bagpipe bands to iPods playing near maximum volume (**FIGURE 6.17**). Ringing of the ears after exposure to loud machinery or music indicates that we have been bad to our unhappy hair cells. As pain alerts us to possible bodily harm, ringing of the ears alerts us to possible hearing damage. It is hearing's equivalent of bleeding.

Teen boys more than teen girls or adults blast themselves with loud volumes for long periods (Zogby, 2006). Males' greater noise exposure may help explain why men's hearing tends to be less acute than women's. But male or female, those who spend many hours in a loud nightclub, behind a power mower, or above a jackhammer should wear earplugs. "Condoms or, safer yet, abstinence," say sex educators. "Earplugs or walk away," say hearing educators.

Perceiving Loudness

So, how do we detect loudness? It is not, as I would have guessed, from the intensity of a hair cell's response. Rather, a soft, pure tone activates only the few hair cells attuned to its frequency. Given louder sounds, neighboring hair cells also respond. Thus, the brain can interpret loudness from the *number* of activated hair cells.

If a hair cell loses sensitivity to soft sounds, it may still respond to loud sounds. This helps explain another surprise: Really loud sounds may seem loud both to people with hearing loss and to those with normal hearing. As a person with hearing loss, I used to wonder what really loud music must sound like to people with normal hearing. Now I realize it can sound much the same; where we differ is in our sensation of soft sounds.

middle ear the chamber between the eardrum and cochlea containing three tiny bones (hammer, anvil, and stirrup) that concentrate the vibrations of the eardrum on the cochlea's oval window.

cochlea [KOHK-lee-uh] a coiled, bony, fluid-filled tube in the inner ear through which sound waves trigger nerve impulses.

inner ear the innermost part of the ear, containing the cochlea, semicircular canals, and vestibular sacs.

kinesthesis [kin-ehs-THEE-sehs] the system for sensing the position and movement of individual body parts.

vestibular sense the sense of body movement and position, including the sense of balance.

Locating Sounds

10: How do we locate sounds?

Why don't we have one big ear—perhaps above our one nose? The better to hear you, as the wolf said to Red Riding Hood. As the placement of our eyes allows us to sense visual depth, so the placement of our two ears allows us to enjoy stereophonic ("three-dimensional") hearing.

FIGURE 6.18 How we locate sounds Sound waves strike one ear sooner and more intensely than the other. From this information, our nimble brain computes the sound's location. As you might therefore expect, people who lose all hearing in one ear often have difficulty locating sounds.

Two ears are better than one for at least two reasons: If a car to the right honks, your right ear receives a more *intense* sound, and it receives sound slightly *sooner* than your left ear (**FIGURE 6.18**). Because sound travels 750 miles per hour and our ears are but 6 inches apart, the intensity difference and the time lag are extremely small. However, our supersensitive auditory system can detect such minute differences (Brown & Deffenbacher, 1979; Middlebrooks & Green, 1991). A just noticeable difference in the direction of two sound sources corresponds to a time difference of just 0.000027 seconds!

So how well do you suppose we do at locating a sound that is equidistant from our two ears, such as those that come from directly ahead, behind, overhead, or beneath us? Not very well. Why? Because such sounds strike the two ears simultaneously. Sit with closed eyes while a friend snaps fingers around your head. You will easily point to the sound when it comes from either side, but you will likely make some mistakes when it comes from directly ahead, behind, above, or below. That is why, when trying to pinpoint a sound, you cock your head, so that your two ears will receive slightly different messages.

Touch

11: How do we sense touch and sense our body's position and movement? How do we experience pain?

Although it may not be the first sense to come to mind, touch is vital. Right from the start, touch is essential to our development. Infant rats deprived of their mother's grooming produce less growth hormone and have a lower metabolic rate—a good way to keep alive until the mother returns, but a reaction that stunts growth if prolonged. Infant monkeys allowed to see, hear, and smell—but not touch—their mother become desperately unhappy; those separated by a screen with holes that allow touching are much less miserable. As we noted in Chapter 4, premature human babies gain weight faster and go home sooner if they are stimulated by hand massage. As lovers, we yearn to touch—to kiss, to stroke, to snuggle. And even strangers, touching only their forearms and separated by a curtain, can communicate anger, fear, disgust, love, gratitude, and sympathy at levels well above chance (Hertenstein et al., 2006).

Humorist Dave Barry may be right to jest that your skin "keeps people from seeing the inside of your body, which is repulsive, and it prevents your organs from falling onto the ground." But skin does much more. Our

The precious sense of touch As William James wrote in his *Principles of Psychology* (1890), "Touch is both the alpha and omega of affection."

"sense of touch" is actually a mix of distinct senses, with different types of specialized nerve endings within the skin. Touching various spots on the skin with a soft hair, a warm or cool wire, and the point of a pin reveals that some spots are especially sensitive to pressure, others to warmth, others to cold, still others to pain.

Surprisingly, there is no simple relationship between what we feel at a given spot and the type of specialized nerve ending found there. Only pressure has identifiable receptors. Other skin sensations are variations of the basic four (*pressure, warmth, cold,* and *pain*):

- Stroking adjacent pressure spots creates a tickle.
- Repeated gentle stroking of a pain spot creates an itching sensation.
- Touching adjacent cold and pressure spots triggers a sense of wetness, which you can experience by touching dry, cold metal.

Touch sensations involve more than tactile stimulation, however. A self-produced tickle produces less somatosensory cortex activation than the same tickle would from something or someone else (Blakemore et al., 1998). (The brain is wise enough to be most sensitive to unexpected stimulation.) This top-down influence on touch sensation also appears in the *rubber-hand illusion.* Imagine yourself looking at a realistic rubber hand while your own hand is hidden (**FIGURE 6.19**). If an experimenter simultaneously touches your fake and real hands, you likely will perceive the rubber hand as your own and sense it being touched. Even just "stroking" the fake hand with a laser light produces, for most people, an illusory sensation of warmth or touch in their unseen real hand (Durgin et al., 2007). Touch is not only a bottom-up property of your senses but also a top-down product of your brain and your expectations.

Important sensors in your joints, tendons, bones, and ears, as well as your skin sensors enable your **kinesthesis**—your sense of the position and movement of your body parts. By closing your eyes or plugging your ears you can momentarily imagine being without sight or sound. But what would it be like to live without touch or kinesthesis—without, therefore, being able to sense the positions of your limbs when you wake during the night? Ian Waterman of Hampshire, England, knows. In 1972, at age 19, Waterman contracted a rare viral infection that destroyed the nerves enabling his sense of light touch and of body position and movement. People with this condition report feeling disembodied, as though their body is dead, not real, not theirs (Sacks, 1985). With prolonged practice, Waterman has learned to walk and eat—by visually focusing on his limbs and directing them accordingly. But if the lights go out, he crumples to the floor (Azar, 1998). Even for the rest of us, vision interacts with kinesthesis. Stand with your right heel in front of your left toes. Easy. Now close your eyes and you will probably wobble.

A companion **vestibular sense** monitors your head's (and thus your body's) position and movement. The biological gyroscopes for this sense of equilibrium are in your inner ear. The *semicircular canals,* which look like a three-dimensional pretzel (Figure 6.16a), and the *vestibular sacs,* which connect the canals with the cochlea, contain fluid that moves when your head rotates or tilts. This movement stimulates hairlike receptors, which send messages to the cerebellum at the back of the brain, thus enabling you to sense your body position and to maintain your balance.

If you twirl around and then come to an abrupt halt, neither the fluid in your semicircular canals nor your kinesthetic receptors will immediately return to their neutral state. The dizzy aftereffect fools your brain with the sensation that you're still spinning. This illustrates a principle that underlies perceptual illusions: Mechanisms that normally give us an accurate experience of the world can, under special conditions, fool us. Understanding how we get fooled provides clues to how our perceptual system works.

FIGURE 6.19 The rubber-hand illusion When a researcher simultaneously touches a volunteer's real and fake hands, the volunteer feels as though the seen fake hand is her own (MacLachlan et al. 2003).

The intricate vestibular sense These Cirque du Soleil performers can thank their inner ears for the information that enables their brains to monitor their bodies' position so expertly.

A pain-free, problematic life Ashlyn Blocker (right), shown here with her mother and sister, has a rare genetic disorder. She feels neither pain nor extreme hot and cold. She must frequently be checked for accidentally self-inflicted injuries that she herself cannot feel. "Some people would say [that feeling no pain is] a good thing," says her mother. "But no, it's not. Pain's there for a reason. It lets your body know something's wrong and it needs to be fixed. I'd give anything for her to feel pain" (quoted by Bynum, 2004).

Pain

Be thankful for occasional pain. Pain is your body's way of telling you something has gone wrong. Drawing your attention to a burn, a break, or a sprain, pain orders you to change your behavior—"Stay off that turned ankle!" The rare people born without the ability to feel pain may experience severe injury or even die before early adulthood. Without the discomfort that makes us occasionally shift position, their joints fail from excess strain, and without the warnings of pain, the effects of unchecked infections and injuries accumulate (Neese, 1991).

More numerous are those who live with chronic pain, which is rather like an alarm that won't shut off. The suffering of such people, and of those with persistent or recurring backaches, arthritis, headaches, and cancer-related pain, prompts two questions: What is pain? How might we control it?

Understanding Pain

Our pain experiences vary widely, depending on our physiology, our experiences and attention, and our surrounding culture (Gatchel et al., 2007). Thus, our feelings of pain combine both bottom-up sensations and top-down processes.

BIOLOGICAL INFLUENCES There is no one type of stimulus that triggers pain (as light triggers vision). Instead, there are different *nociceptors*—sensory receptors that detect hurtful temperatures, pressure, or chemicals (**FIGURE 6.20**).

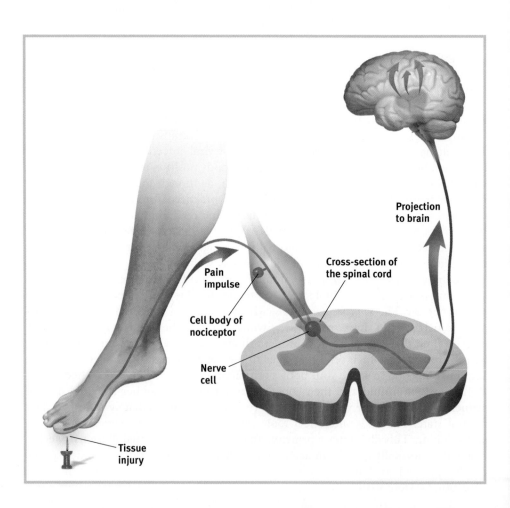

FIGURE 6.20 The pain circuit Sensory receptors (nociceptors) respond to potentially damaging stimuli by sending an impulse to the spinal cord, which passes the message to the brain, which interprets the signal as pain.

Projection to brain

Cross-section of the spinal cord

Pain impulse

Cell body of nociceptor

Nerve cell

Tissue injury

Although no theory of pain explains all available findings, psychologist Ronald Melzack and biologist Patrick Wall's (1965, 1983) classic **gate-control theory** provides a useful model. The spinal cord contains small nerve fibers that conduct most pain signals, and larger fibers that conduct most other sensory signals. Melzack and Wall theorized that the spinal cord contains a neurological "gate." When tissue is injured, the small fibers activate and open the gate, and you feel pain. Large-fiber activity closes the gate, blocking pain signals and preventing them from reaching the brain. Thus, one way to treat chronic pain is to stimulate (by massage, by electric stimulation, or by acupuncture) "gate-closing" activity in the large neural fibers (Wall, 2000). Rubbing the area around your stubbed toe will create competing stimulation that will block some pain messages.

But pain is not merely a physical phenomenon of injured nerves sending impulses to the brain—like pulling on a rope to ring a bell. Melzack and Wall noted that brain-to-spinal-cord messages can also close the gate, helping to explain some striking influences on pain. When we are distracted from pain (a psychological influence) and soothed by the release of *endorphins,* our natural painkillers (a biological influence), our experience of pain may be greatly diminished. Sports injuries may go unnoticed until the after-game shower. People who carry a gene that boosts the availability of endorphins are less bothered by pain, and their brain is less responsive to pain (Zubieta et al., 2003). Others, who carry a mutated gene that disrupts pain circuit neurotransmission, may be unable to experience pain (Cox et al., 2006). Such discoveries may point the way toward new pain medications that mimic these genetic effects.

The brain can also create pain, as it does in people's experiences of *phantom limb sensations,* when it misinterprets the spontaneous central nervous system activity that occurs in the absence of normal sensory input. As the dreamer may see with eyes closed, so some 7 in 10 amputees may feel pain or movement in nonexistent limbs (Melzack, 1992, 2005). (An amputee may also try to step off a bed onto a phantom limb or to lift a cup with a phantom hand.) Even those born without a limb sometimes perceive sensations from the absent arm or leg. The brain, Melzack (1998) surmises, comes prepared to anticipate "that it will be getting information from a body that has limbs."

A similar phenomenon occurs with other senses. People with hearing loss often experience the sound of silence: phantom sounds—a ringing-in-the-ears sensation known as *tinnitus.* Those who lose vision to glaucoma, cataracts, diabetes, or macular degeneration may experience phantom sights—nonthreatening hallucinations (Ramachandran & Blakeslee, 1998). Some with nerve damage have had taste phantoms, such as ice water seeming sickeningly sweet (Goode, 1999). Others have experienced phantom smells, such as nonexistent rotten food. The point to remember: *We feel, see, hear, taste, and smell with our brain,* which can sense even without functioning senses.

PSYCHOLOGICAL INFLUENCES The psychological effects of distraction are clear in the stories of athletes who, focused on winning, play through the pain. Carrie Armel and Vilayanur Ramachandran (2003) cleverly illustrated psychological influences on pain with another version of the rubber-hand illusion. They bent a finger slightly backward on the unseen hands of 16 volunteers, while simultaneously "hurting" (severely bending) a finger on a visible fake rubber hand. The volunteers felt as if their real finger were being bent, and they responded with increased skin perspiration.

We also seem to edit our *memories* of pain, which often differ from the pain we actually experienced. In experiments, and after medical procedures, people overlook a pain's duration. Their memory snapshots instead record two factors: First, people tend

gate-control theory the theory that the spinal cord contains a neurological "gate" that blocks pain signals or allows them to pass on to the brain. The "gate" is opened by the activity of pain signals traveling up small nerve fibers and is closed by activity in larger fibers or by information coming from the brain.

"When belly with bad pains doth swell, It matters naught what else goes well."

—Sadi, *The Gulistan,* 1258

"Pain is increased by attending to it."

—Charles Darwin, *Expression of Emotions in Man and Animals,* 1872

Playing with pain In a 2008 NBA championship series game, Boston Celtics star Paul Pierce screamed in pain after an opposing player stepped on his right foot, causing his knee to twist and pop. After being carried off the court, he came back and played through the pain, which reclaimed his attention after the game's end.

to record pain's *peak* moment, which can lead them to recall variable pain, with peaks, as worse (Stone et al., 2005). Second, they register how much pain they felt at the *end,* as Daniel Kahneman and his co-researchers (1993) discovered when they asked people to immerse one hand in painfully cold water for 60 seconds, and then the other hand in the same painfully cold water for 60 seconds followed by a slightly less painful 30 seconds more. Which of these experiences would you expect to recall as most painful?

Curiously, when asked which trial they would prefer to repeat, most preferred the longer trial, with more net pain—but less pain at the end. A physician used this principle with patients undergoing colon exams—lengthening the discomfort by a minute, but lessening its intensity (Kahneman, 1999). Although the extended milder discomfort added to their net pain experience, patients who received this taper-down treatment later recalled the exam as less painful than did those whose pain ended abruptly.

SOCIAL-CULTURAL INFLUENCES Our perception of pain also varies with our social situation and our cultural traditions. We tend to perceive more pain when others also seem to be experiencing pain (Symbaluk et al., 1997). This may help explain other apparent social aspects of pain, as when pockets of Australian keyboard operators during the mid-1980s suffered outbreaks of severe pain during typing or other repetitive work—without any discernible physical abnormalities (Gawande, 1998). Sometimes the pain in sprain is mainly in the brain—literally. When feeling empathy for another's pain, a person's own brain activity may partly mirror that of the other's brain in pain (Singer et al, 2004).

Thus, our perception of pain is a biopsychosocial phenomenon (**FIGURE 6.21**). Viewing pain this way can help us better understand how to cope with pain and treat it.

FIGURE 6.21 **Biopsychosocial approach to pain** Our experience of pain is much more than neural messages sent to the brain.

Controlling Pain

If pain is where body meets mind—if it is both a physical and a psychological phenomenon—then it should be treatable both physically and psychologically. Depending on the type of symptoms, pain control clinics select one or more therapies from a list that includes drugs, surgery, acupuncture, electrical stimulation, massage, exercise, hypnosis, relaxation training, and thought distraction.

Even an inert placebo can help. After being injected in the jaw with a stinging saltwater solution, men in one experiment were given a placebo that was said to relieve pain. They immediately felt better, a result associated with activity in a brain area that releases natural pain-killing opiates (Scott et al., 2007; Zubieta et al., 2005). Being given fake pain-killing chemicals caused the brain to dispense real ones. "Believing becomes reality," noted one commentator (Thernstrom, 2006), as "the mind unites with the body."

Another experiment pitted two placebos—fake pills and pretend acupuncture—against each other (Kaptchuk et al., 2006). People with persistent arm pain (270 of them) received either sham acupuncture (with trick needles that retracted without puncturing the skin) or blue cornstarch pills that looked like pills often prescribed for strain injury. A fourth of those receiving the nonexistent needle pricks and 31

No distraction   Distraction

percent of those receiving the pills complained of side effects, such as painful skin or dry mouth and fatigue. After two months, both groups were reporting less pain, with the fake acupuncture group reporting the greater pain drop.

Distracting people with pleasant images ("Think of a warm, comfortable environment") or drawing their attention away from the painful stimulation ("Count backward by 3's") is an especially effective way to increase pain tolerance (Fernandez & Turk, 1989; McCaul & Malott, 1984). A well-trained nurse may distract needle-shy patients by chatting with them and asking them to look away when inserting the needle. For burn victims receiving excruciating wound care, an even more effective distraction comes from immersion in a computer-generated 3-D world, like the snow scene in **FIGURE 6.22**. Functional MRI (fMRI) scans reveal that playing in the virtual reality reduces the brain's pain-related activity (Hoffman, 2004). Because pain is in the brain, diverting the brain's attention may bring relief.

FIGURE 6.22 Virtual-reality pain control For burn victims undergoing painful skin repair, an escape into virtual reality can powerfully distract attention, thus reducing pain and the brain's response to painful stimulation. The fMRI scans (above right) illustrate a lowered pain response when the patient is distracted.

Taste

12: How do we experience taste?

Like touch, our sense of taste involves several basic sensations. Taste's sensations were once thought to be sweet, sour, salty, and bitter, with all others stemming from mixtures of these four (McBurney & Gent, 1979). Then, as investigators searched for specialized nerve fibers for the four taste sensations, they encountered a receptor for what we now know is a fifth—the savory meaty taste of *umami*, best experienced as the flavor enhancer monosodium glutamate.

Tastes exist for more than our pleasure (see **TABLE 6.2**). Pleasureful tastes attracted our ancestors to energy- or protein-rich foods that enabled their survival. Aversive tastes deterred them from new foods that might be toxic. We see the inheritance of this biological wisdom in today's 2- to 6-year-olds, who are typically fussy eaters, especially when offered new meats or bitter-tasting vegetables, such as spinach and Brussels sprouts (Cooke et al., 2003). Meat and plant toxins were both potentially dangerous sources of food poisoning for our ancestors, especially for children. Given repeated small tastes of disliked new foods, children will, however, typically begin to accept them (Wardle et al., 2003).

Taste is a chemical sense. Inside each little bump on the top and sides of your tongue are 200 or more taste buds, each containing a pore that catches food chemicals. Into each taste bud pore, 50 to 100 taste receptor cells project antennalike hairs that sense food molecules. Some receptors respond mostly to sweet-tasting molecules, others to salty-, sour-, bitter-, or unami-tasting ones. It doesn't take much to trigger a response that alerts your brain's temporal lobe. If a stream of water is pumped across your tongue, the addition of a concentrated salty or sweet

TABLE 6.2

The Survival Functions of Basic Tastes

Taste	Indicates
Sweet	Energy source
Salty	Sodium essential to physiological processes
Sour	Potentially toxic acid
Bitter	Potential poisons
Umami	Proteins to grow and repair tissue

(Adapted from Cowart, 2005.)

sensory interaction the principle that one sense may influence another, as when the smell of food influences its taste.

taste for but one-tenth of a second will get your attention (Kelling & Halpern, 1983). When a friend asks for "just a taste" of your soft drink, you can squeeze off the straw after a mere fraction of a second.

Taste receptors reproduce themselves every week or two, so if you burn your tongue with hot food it hardly matters. However, as you grow older, the number of taste buds decreases, as does taste sensitivity (Cowart, 1981). (No wonder adults enjoy strong-tasting foods that children resist.) Smoking and alcohol use accelerate these declines. Those who lose their sense of taste report that food tastes like "straw" and is hard to swallow (Cowart, 2005).

Essential as taste buds are, there's more to taste than meets the tongue. As with other senses, your expectations influence your brain's response. Being told that a wine costs $90 rather than its real $10 price makes an inexpensive wine taste better and triggers more activity in a brain area that responds to pleasant experiences (Plassmann et al., 2008). As happens with the pain placebo effect, the brain's thinking frontal lobes offer information that other brain regions act upon.

Sensory Interaction

Taste also illustrates another curious phenomenon. Hold your nose, close your eyes, and have someone feed you various foods. A slice of apple may be indistinguishable from a chunk of raw potato. A piece of steak may taste like cardboard. Without their smells, a cup of cold coffee may be hard to distinguish from a glass of red wine. To savor a taste, we normally breathe the aroma through our nose—which is why eating is not much fun when you have a bad cold. Smell can also change our perception of taste: A drink's strawberry odor enhances our perception of its sweetness. This is **sensory interaction** at work—the principle that one sense may influence another. Smell plus texture plus taste equals flavor.

Sensory interaction similarly influences what we hear. If I (as a person with hearing loss) watch a video with simultaneous captioning, I have no trouble hearing the words I am seeing (and may therefore think I don't need the captioning). If I then turn off the captioning, I suddenly realize I need it (**FIGURE 6.23**). But what do you suppose happens if we *see* a speaker saying one syllable while we *hear* another? Surprise: We may perceive a third syllable that blends both inputs. Seeing the mouth movements for *ga* while hearing *ba*, we may perceive *da*—a phenomenon known as the *McGurk effect*, after its discoverers, psychologist Harry McGurk and his assistant John MacDonald (1976).

Sensory interaction can also affect vision and touch. A weak flicker of light that we have trouble perceiving becomes more visible when accompanied by a short burst of sound (Kayser, 2007). In detecting events, the brain can combine simultaneous visual and touch signals, thanks to neurons projecting from the somatosensory cortex back to the visual cortex (Macaluso et al., 2000).

Courtesy of RNID www.rnid.org.uk

FIGURE 6.23 Sensory interaction When a hard-of-hearing listener sees an animated face forming the words being spoken at the other end of a phone line, the words become easier to understand (Knight, 2004).

Smell

13: How do we experience smell?

Inhale, exhale. Inhale, exhale. Breaths come in pairs—except at two moments: birth and death. Between those two moments, you will daily inhale and exhale nearly 20,000 breaths of life-sustaining air, bathing your nostrils in a stream of scent-laden molecules. The resulting experiences of smell *(olfaction)* are strikingly intimate: You inhale something of whatever or whoever it is you smell.

Like taste, smell is a chemical sense. We smell something when molecules of a substance carried in the air reach a tiny cluster of 5 million or more receptor cells at

Impress your friends with your new word for the day: People unable to see are said to experience blindness. People unable to hear experience deafness. People unable to smell experience anosmia.

the top of each nasal cavity (**FIGURE 6**.24). These olfactory receptor cells, waving like sea plants on a reef, respond selectively—to the aroma of a cake baking, to a wisp of smoke, to a friend's fragrance. Instantly, they alert the brain through their axon fibers.

Even nursing infants and their mothers have a literal chemistry to their relationship. They quickly learn to recognize each other's scents (McCarthy, 1986). Aided by smell, a mother fur seal returning to a beach crowded with pups will find her own. Our own sense of smell is less impressive than the acuteness of our seeing and hearing. Looking out across a garden, we see its forms and colors in exquisite detail and hear a variety of birds singing, yet we smell little of it without sticking our nose into the blossoms.

Odor molecules come in many shapes and sizes—so many, in fact, that it takes many different receptors to detect them. A large family of genes designs the 350 or so receptor proteins that recognize particular odor molecules (Miller, 2004). Richard Axel and Linda Buck (1991) discovered (in work for which they received a 2004 Nobel Prize) that these receptor proteins are embedded on the surface of nasal cavity neurons. As a key slips into a lock, so odor molecules slip into these receptors. Yet we don't seem to have a distinct receptor for each detectable odor. This suggests that some odors trigger a combination of receptors, in patterns that are interpreted by the olfactory cortex. As the English alphabet's 26 letters can combine to form many words, so odor molecules bind to different receptor arrays, producing the 10,000 odors we can detect (Malnic et al., 1999). It is the combinations of

Humans have 10 to 20 million olfactory receptors. A bloodhound has some 200 million (Herz, 2001).

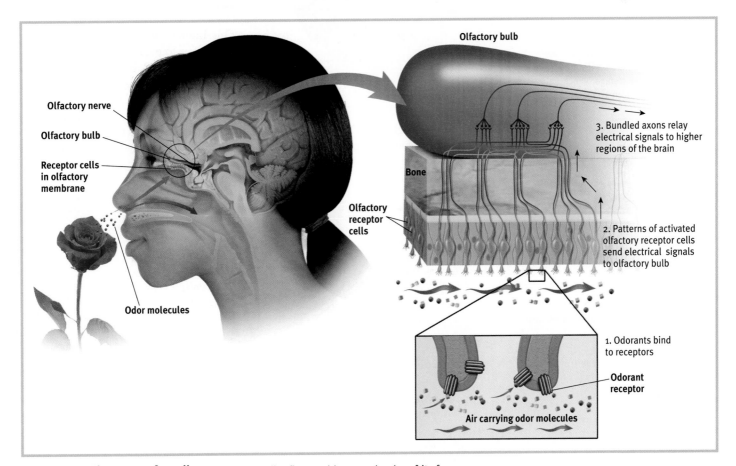

Olfactory bulb

Olfactory nerve

Olfactory bulb

Receptor cells in olfactory membrane

Bone

Olfactory receptor cells

Odor molecules

3. Bundled axons relay electrical signals to higher regions of the brain

2. Patterns of activated olfactory receptor cells send electrical signals to olfactory bulb

1. Odorants bind to receptors

Odorant receptor

Air carrying odor molecules

FIGURE 6.24 The sense of smell If you are to smell a flower, airborne molecules of its fragrance must reach receptors at the top of your nose. Sniffing swirls air up to the receptors, enhancing the aroma. The receptor cells send messages to the brain's olfactory bulb, and then onward to the temporal lobe's primary smell cortex and to the parts of the limbic system involved in memory and emotion.

"The smell and taste of things bears unfaltering, in the tiny and almost impalpable drop of their essence, the vast structure of recollection."

—French novelist Marcel Proust, in *Remembrance of Things Past* (1913), describing how the aroma and flavor of a bit of cake soaked in tea resurrected long-forgotten memories of the old family house.

olfactory receptors, which activate different neuron patterns, that allow us to distinguish between the aromas of fresh-brewed and hours-old coffee (Buck et al., 2006).

For humans, the attractiveness of smells depends on learned associations (Herz, 2001). Babies are not born with a built-in preference for the smell of their mother's breast; as they nurse, their preference builds. After a good experience becomes associated with a particular scent, people come to like that scent, which helps explain why people in the United States tend to like the smell of wintergreen (which they associate with candy and gum) more than do those in Great Britain (where it often is associated with medicine). In another example of odors evoking unpleasant emotions, Rachel Herz and her colleagues (2004) frustrated Brown University students with a rigged computer game in a scented room. Later, if exposed to the same odor while working on a verbal task, the students' frustration was rekindled and they gave up sooner than others exposed to a different odor or no odor.

Though it's difficult to recall odors by name, we have a remarkable capacity to recognize long-forgotten odors and their associated memories (Engen, 1987; Schab, 1991). The smell of the sea, the scent of a perfume, the aroma of a favorite relative's kitchen can bring to mind a happy time. It's a phenomenon understood by the British travel agent chain Lunn Poly. To evoke memories of lounging on sunny, warm beaches, the company once piped the aroma of coconut suntan oil into its shops (Fracassini, 2000).

Our brain's circuitry helps explain an odor's power to evoke feelings and memories (**FIGURE 6.25**). A hotline runs between the brain area receiving information from the nose and the brain's ancient limbic centers associated with memory and emotion. Smell is primitive. Eons before the elaborate analytical areas of our cerebral cortex had fully evolved, our mammalian ancestors sniffed for food—and for predators.

Processes smell (near memory area)

Processes taste

FIGURE 6.25 The olfactory brain
Information from the taste buds (yellow arrow) travels to an area of the temporal lobe not far from where the brain receives olfactory information, which interacts with taste. The brain's circuitry for smell (red arrow) also connects with areas involved in memory storage, which helps explain why a smell can trigger a memory explosion.

REHEARSE IT!

13. The amplitude of a sound wave determines our perception of
a. loudness.
b. pitch.
c. audition.
d. frequency.

14. The frequency of sound waves determines their pitch. The _____ the waves are, the lower their frequency is and the _____ their pitch.
a. shorter; higher
b. longer; lower
c. lower; longer
d. higher; shorter

15. The snail-shaped tube in the inner ear, where sound waves are converted into neural activity, is called the

a. anvil.
b. basilar membrane.
c. cochlea.
d. oval window.

16. Of all the skin senses, only _____ has its own identifiable receptor cells.
a. pressure
b. warmth
c. cold
d. pain

17. The vestibular sense monitors the body's position and movement. Vestibular sense receptors are located in the
a. skin.
b. brain.
c. inner ear.
d. skeletal muscles.

18. The gate-control theory of pain proposes that
a. special pain receptors send signals directly to the brain.
b. pain is a property of the senses, not of the brain.
c. small spinal cord nerve fibers conduct most pain signals.
d. the stimuli that produce pain are unrelated to other sensations.

19. A food's smell or aroma can greatly enhance its taste. This is an example of
a. sensory adaptation.
b. the placebo effect.
c. gate-control theory.
d. sensory interaction.

Answers: 13. a, 14. b, 15. c, 16. a, 17. c, 18. c, 19. d.

Perceptual Organization

14: How did the Gestalt psychologists understand perceptual organization, and how do figure-ground and grouping principles contribute to our perceptions?

We have examined the processes by which we sense sights and sounds, touch and movement, tastes and smells. Now our central question is, How do we see not just shapes and colors, but a rose in bloom, a loved one's face, a beautiful sunset? How do we hear not just a mix of pitches and rhythms, but a child's cry of pain, the hum of distant traffic, a symphony? In short, how do we organize and interpret our sensations so that they become meaningful perceptions?

Early in the twentieth century, a group of German psychologists noticed that when given a cluster of sensations, people tend to organize them into a **gestalt**, a German word meaning a "form" or a "whole." For example, look at **FIGURE 6.26**. Note that the individual elements of this figure are really nothing but eight blue circles, each containing three converging white lines. Yet when we view them all together, we see a *whole*, a form that psychologists call a *Necker cube*.

Over the years, the Gestalt psychologists provided compelling demonstrations and described principles by which we organize our sensations into perceptions. As you read further about these principles, keep in mind the fundamental truth they illustrate: *Our brain does more than register information about the world.* Perception is not just opening a shutter and letting a picture print itself on the brain. We constantly filter sensory information and infer perceptions in ways that make sense to us. Mind matters.

gestalt an organized whole. Gestalt psychologists emphasized our tendency to integrate pieces of information into meaningful wholes.

figure-ground the organization of the visual field into objects (the *figures*) that stand out from their surroundings (the *ground*).

FIGURE 6.26 A Necker cube What do you see: circles with white lines, or a cube? If you stare at the cube, you may notice that it reverses location, moving the tiny X in the center from the front edge to the back. At times, the cube may seem to float in front of the page, with circles behind it; other times the circles may become holes in the page through which the cube appears, as though it were floating behind the page. There is far more to perception than meets the eye. (From Bradley et al., 1976.)

Form Perception

Imagine designing a video/computer system that, like your eye/brain system, can recognize faces at a glance. What abilities would it need?

Figure and Ground

To start with, the system would need to recognize faces as distinct from their backgrounds. Likewise, our first perceptual task is to perceive any object (the figure) as distinct from its surroundings (the ground). Among the voices you hear at a party, the one you attend to becomes the figure; all others, part of the ground. As you read, the words are the figure; the white paper, the ground. In **FIGURE 6.27**, the **figure-ground** relationship continually reverses—but always we organize the stimulus into a figure seen against a ground. Such reversible figure-and-ground illustrations demonstrate again that the same stimulus can trigger more than one perception.

Grouping

Having discriminated figure from ground, we (and our video/computer system) now have to organize the figure into a meaningful form. Some basic features of a scene—such as color, movement, and light/dark contrast—we process instantly and automatically (Treisman, 1987). To bring order and form to these basic sensations,

FIGURE 6.27
Reversible figure and ground

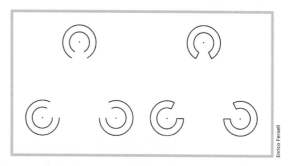

| Proximity | Similarity |
| Continuity | Connectedness |

FIGURE 6.28 Organizing stimuli into groups We could perceive the stimuli shown here in many ways, yet people everywhere see them similarly. The Gestalt psychologists believed this shows that the brain follows rules to order sensory information into wholes.

our minds follow certain rules for **grouping** stimuli together. These rules, identified by the Gestalt psychologists and applied even by infants, illustrate the idea that the perceived whole differs from the sum of its parts (Quinn et al., 2002; Rock & Palmer, 1990):

Proximity We group nearby figures together, as in **FIGURE 6.28**. We see three sets of two lines, not six separate lines.

Similarity We group similar figures together. We see the triangles and circles as vertical columns of similar shapes, not as horizontal rows of dissimilar shapes.

Continuity We perceive smooth, continuous patterns rather than discontinuous ones. The pattern in the lower-left corner of Figure 6.28 could be a series of alternating semicircles, but we perceive it as two continuous lines—one wavy, one straight.

Connectedness Because they are uniform and linked, we perceive each set of two dots and the line between them as a single unit.

Closure We fill in gaps to create a complete, whole object. Thus we assume that the circles (below left) are complete but partially blocked by the (illusory) triangle. Add nothing more than little line segments that close off the circles (below right) and now your brain stops constructing a triangle.

Such principles usually help us construct reality. Sometimes, however, they lead us astray, as when we look at the doghouse in **FIGURE 6.29**.

FIGURE 6.29 Grouping principles What's the secret to this impossible doghouse? You probably perceive this doghouse as a gestalt—a whole (though impossible) structure. Actually, your brain imposes this sense of wholeness on the picture. As Figure 6.34 shows, Gestalt grouping principles such as closure and continuity are at work here.

Depth Perception

15: **How do we see the world in three dimensions?**

From the two-dimensional images falling on our retinas, we somehow organize three-dimensional perceptions. **Depth perception,** seeing objects in three dimensions, enables us to estimate their distance from us. At a glance, we estimate the distance of an oncoming car or the height of a house. This ability is partly innate. Eleanor Gibson and Richard Walk (1960) discovered this using a miniature cliff with a drop-off covered by sturdy glass. Gibson's inspiration for these experiments occurred while she was picnicking on the rim of the Grand Canyon. She wondered: Would a toddler peering over the rim perceive the dangerous drop-off and draw back?

Back in their Cornell University laboratory, Gibson and Walk placed 6- to 14-month-old infants on the edge of a safe canyon—a **visual cliff** (FIGURE 6.30). When the infants' mothers then coaxed them to crawl out onto the glass, most refused to do so, indicating that they could perceive depth. Crawling infants come to the lab after lots of learning. Yet newborn animals with virtually no visual experience—including young kittens, a day-old goat, and newly hatched chicks—respond similarly. To Gibson and Walk, this suggested that mobile newborn animals come prepared to perceive depth.

FIGURE 6.30 **Visual cliff** Eleanor Gibson and Richard Walk devised this miniature cliff with a glass-covered drop-off to determine whether crawling infants and newborn animals can perceive depth. Even when coaxed, infants are reluctant to venture onto the glass over the cliff.

Each species, by the time it is mobile, has the perceptual abilities it needs. But if biological maturation predisposes our wariness of heights, experience amplifies it. Infants' wariness increases with their experiences of crawling, no matter when they begin to crawl (Campos et al., 1992).

How do we do it? How do we transform two differing two-dimensional retinal images into a single three-dimensional perception? The process begins with *depth cues,* some that depend on the use of two eyes, and others that are available to each eye separately.

Binocular Cues

Try this: With both eyes open, hold two pens or pencils in front of you and touch their tips together. Now do so with one eye closed. With one eye, the task becomes noticeably more difficult, demonstrating the importance of **binocular cues** in judging the distance of nearby objects. For carnivores catching prey, and humans catching a ball, two eyes are better than one.

Because our eyes are about 2½ inches apart, our retinas receive slightly different images of the world. When the brain compares these two images, the difference between them—their **retinal disparity**—provides one important binocular cue to the relative distance of different objects. When you hold your finger directly in front of

grouping the perceptual tendency to organize stimuli into coherent groups.

depth perception the ability to see objects in three dimensions although the images that strike the retina are two-dimensional; allows us to judge distance.

visual cliff a laboratory device for testing depth perception in infants and young animals.

binocular cues depth cues, such as retinal disparity, that depend on the use of two eyes.

retinal disparity a binocular cue for perceiving depth: By comparing images from the retinas in the two eyes, the brain computes distance—the greater the disparity (difference) between the two images, the closer the object.

FIGURE 6.31 The floating finger sausage Hold your two index fingers about 5 inches in front of your eyes, with their tips a half-inch apart. Now look beyond them and note the weird result. Move your fingers out farther and the retinal disparity—and the finger sausage—will shrink.

your nose, your retinas receive quite different views. (You can see this if you close one eye and then the other, or create a finger sausage as in **FIGURE 6.31**.) At a greater distance—say, when you hold your finger at arm's length—the disparity is smaller.

The creators of three-dimensional (3-D) movies simulate or exaggerate retinal disparity by photographing a scene with two cameras placed a few inches apart (a feature we might want to build into our seeing computer). When we view the movie through spectacles that allow the left eye to see the image from the left camera and the right eye the image from the right camera, the 3-D effect mimics or exaggerates normal retinal disparity. Similarly, twin cameras in airplanes can take photos of terrain for integration into 3-D maps.

Monocular Cues

monocular cues depth cues, such as interposition and linear perspective, available to either eye alone.

How do we judge whether a person is 10 or 100 meters away? In both cases, retinal disparity while looking straight ahead is slight. At such distances, we depend on **monocular cues** (available to each eye separately). Monocular cues also influence our everyday perceptions. Is the St. Louis Gateway Arch (**FIGURE 6.32**)—the world's largest human-made illusion—taller than it is wide? Or wider than it is tall? To most

of us, it appears taller. Actually, its height and width are equal, and this famous arch is an example of the unexplained *horizontal-vertical illusion*—our perceiving vertical dimensions as longer than identical horizontal dimensions. No wonder people (even experienced bartenders) pour less juice when given a tall, thin glass rather than a short, wide glass (Wansink & van Ittersum, 2003, 2005).

Relative height is a possible contributor to the horizontal-vertical illusion. **FIGURE 6.33** illustrates this and other monocular cues.

FIGURE 6.32 The St. Louis gateway arch Which is greater: its height or width?

FIGURE 6.33 Monocular depth cues

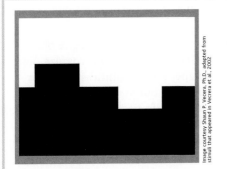

Relative height We perceive objects higher in our field of vision as farther away. Because we perceive the lower part of a figure-ground illustration as closer, we perceive it as figure (Vecera et al., 2002). Invert the illustration above and the black becomes ground, like a night sky.

Relative size If we assume two objects are similar in size, *most* people perceive the one that casts the smaller retinal image as farther away.

Interposition If one object partially blocks our view of another, we perceive it as closer. The depth cues provided by interposition make this an impossible scene.

Linear perspective Parallel lines, such as railroad tracks, appear to converge with distance. The more they converge, the greater their perceived distance.

Light and shadow Nearby objects reflect more light to our eyes. Thus, given two identical objects, the dimmer one seems farther away. Shading, too, produces a sense of depth consistent with our assumption that light comes from above. Invert the illustration below and the hollow in the bottom row will become a hill.

Direction of passenger's motion ⟶

Relative motion As we move, objects that are actually stable may appear to move. If while riding on a bus you fix your gaze on some object—say, a house—the objects beyond the fixation point appear to move with you; objects in front of the fixation point appear to move backward. The farther those objects are from the fixation point, the faster they seem to move.

perceptual constancy perceiving objects as unchanging (having consistent shapes, size, lightness, and color) even as illumination and retinal images change.

FIGURE 6.34 The solution Another view of the impossible doghouse in Figure 6.29 reveals the secrets of this illusion. From the photo angle in Figure 6.29, the grouping principle of closure leads us to perceive the boards as continuous.

Perceptual Constancy

16: How do perceptual constancies help us organize our sensations into meaningful perceptions?

So far, we have noted that our video/computer system must first perceive objects as we do—as having a distinct form and location. Its next task is to recognize objects without being deceived by changes in their shape, size, brightness, or color—an ability we call **perceptual constancy.** Regardless of our viewing angle, distance, and illumination, this top-down process lets us identify people and things in less time than it takes to draw a breath. This human perceptual feat, which has intrigued researchers for decades, provides a monumental challenge for our perceiving computer.

Shape and Size Constancies

Sometimes an object whose actual shape cannot change *seems* to change shape with the angle of our view (**FIGURE 6.35**). More often, thanks to *shape constancy,* we perceive the form of familiar objects, such as the door in **FIGURE 6.36**, as constant even while our retinal image of it changes.

Thanks to *size constancy,* we perceive objects as having a constant size, even while our distance from them varies. We assume a car is large enough to carry people, even when we see its tiny image from two blocks away.

Perceived distance and perceived size are so closely and effortlessly connected that we speak of the *size-distance relationship.* Given an object's perceived distance and the size of its image on our retinas, we instantly and unconsciously infer the object's size. Although the monsters in **FIGURE 6.37a** cast the same retinal images, the linear perspective tells our brain that the monster in pursuit is farther away. We therefore perceive it as larger.

This interplay between perceived size and perceived distance helps explain several well-known illusions. For example, can you imagine why the Moon looks up to 50 percent larger when near the horizon than when high in the sky? For at least 22 centuries, scholars have debated this question (Hershenson, 1989). One reason for the *Moon illusion* is that cues to objects' distances make the horizon Moon—like the distant monster in Figure 6.37a and the distant bar in the *Ponzo illusion* in Figure 6.37b—appear farther away and therefore larger than the Moon high in the night sky (Kaufman & Kaufman, 2000). Take away these distance cues—by looking at the

FIGURE 6.35 Perceiving shape Do the tops of these tables have different dimensions? They appear to. But—believe it or not—they are identical. (Measure and see.) With both tables, we adjust our perceptions relative to our viewing angle.

FIGURE 6.36 Shape constancy A door casts an increasingly trapezoidal image on our retinas as it opens, yet we still perceive it as rectangular.

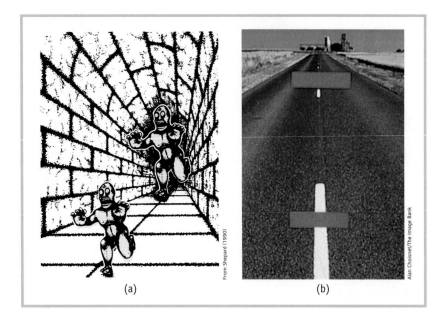

(a)

(b)

FIGURE 6.37 **The interplay between perceived size and distance** (a) The monocular cues for distance (such as linear perspective and relative height) make the pursuing monster look larger than the pursued. It isn't. (b) This visual trick, called the Ponzo illusion, is based on the same principle as the fleeing monsters. The two red bars cast identical-size images on our retinas. But experience tells us that a more distant object can create the same-size image as a nearer one only if it is actually larger. As a result, we perceive the bar that seems farther away as larger.

horizon Moon (or each monster or each bar) through a paper tube—and the object immediately shrinks.

Size-distance relationships also explain why the two same-age girls seem so different in size in the *Ames illusion* (**FIGURE 6.38**). As the diagram reveals, the girls are actually about the same size, but the room is distorted. Viewed with one eye through a peephole, its trapezoidal walls produce the same images as those of a normal rectangular room viewed with both eyes. Presented with the camera's one-eyed view, the brain makes the reasonable assumption that the room *is* normal and each girl is therefore the same distance from us. And given the different sizes of their images on the retina, our brain ends up calculating that the girls are very different in size.

Our occasional misperceptions reveal the workings of our normally effective perceptual processes. The perceived relationship between distance and size is usually valid. But under special circumstances it can lead us astray—as when helping to create the Moon illusion and the Ames illusion.

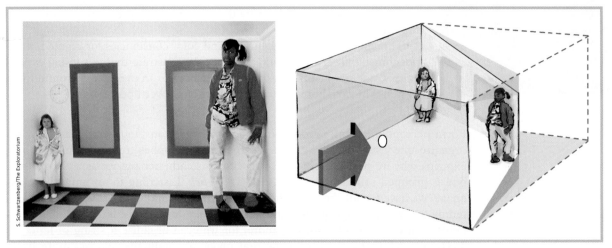

FIGURE 6.38 **The illusion of the shrinking and growing girls** This distorted room, designed by Adelbert Ames, appears to have a normal rectangular shape when viewed through a peephole with one eye. The girl in the right corner appears disproportionately large because we judge her size based on the false assumption that she is the same distance away as the girl in the far corner.

FIGURE 6.39 Relative luminance Squares A and B are identical in color, believe it or not. (If you don't believe me, photocopy the illustration, cut out the squares, and compare.) But we perceive B as lighter, thanks to its surrounding context.

Courtesy Edward Adelson

Lightness Constancy

White paper reflects 90 percent of the light falling on it; black paper, only 10 percent. A black paper in sunlight may reflect 100 times more light than a white paper viewed indoors, but it still looks black (McBurney & Collings, 1984). This illustrates *lightness constancy* (also called *brightness constancy*); we perceive an object as having a constant lightness even while its illumination varies.

Perceived lightness depends on *relative luminance*—the amount of light an object reflects relative to its surroundings (**FIGURE 6.39**). If you view sunlit black paper through a narrow tube so nothing else is visible, it may look gray, because in bright sunshine it reflects a fair amount of light. View it without the tube and it is again black, because it reflects much less light than the objects around it.

Color Constancy

Color constancy operates in a similar way. As light changes, a red apple in a fruit bowl retains its redness. Recall that our experience of color depends on the wavelength information received by the cones in our retina. But it also depends on the surrounding *context*. If you view only part of that apple through a narrow tube, its color will seem to change as the light changes. But if you see the whole apple in context, as one item in a bowl of fresh fruit, its red color will remain roughly constant as the lighting and wavelengths shift. You and I see color thanks to our brain's computations of the light reflected by any object *relative to its surrounding objects*. But only if we grew up with normal light, it seems. Monkeys raised under a restricted range of wavelengths later have great difficulty recognizing the same color when illumination varies (Sugita, 2004).

In a context that does not vary, we maintain color constancy. But what if we change the context? If you guessed that the perceived color would change, you're right, as is dramatically apparent in **FIGURE 6.40**. This principle—that the brain computes the color of objects not in isolation but relative to their context—matters to artists, interior decorators, and clothing designers. Our perception of the color of a wall or of a streak of paint on a canvas is determined not just by the paint in the can but by the surrounding colors.

Though we take size, brightness, and color constancies for granted, these phenomena are truly remarkable. They demonstrate that our visual experiences come not just from isolated objects but from everything around them as well. The take-home lesson: Comparisons govern perceptions.

color constancy perceiving familiar objects as having consistent color, even if changing illumination alters the wavelengths reflected by the object.

R. Beau Lotto at University College, London

FIGURE 6.40 Color depends on context Believe it or not, these three blue disks are identical in color.

"From there to here, from here to there, funny things are everywhere."

—Dr. Seuss, *One Fish, Two Fish, Red Fish, Blue Fish*, 1960

* * *

Form perception, depth perception, and perceptual constancy illuminate how we organize our visual world. Perceptual organization applies to other senses, too. It explains why we perceive a grandfather clock's steady ticking not as a *tick-tick-tick* but as grouped sounds, say, *TICK-tick, TICK-tick*. Listening to an unfamiliar language, we have trouble hearing where one word stops and the next one begins. Listening to our own language, we automatically hear distinct words. This, too, reflects perceptual organization. But it is more, for we even organize a string of letters—THEDOGATEMEAT—into words that make an intelligible phrase, more likely "The dog ate meat" than "The do gate me at" (McBurney & Collings, 1984). This process involves not only the organization we've been discussing, but also interpretation—discerning meaning in what we perceive—the topic we turn to next.

REHEARSE IT!

20. In listening to a concert, you follow the lead singer and perceive the other musicians as accompaniment; this illustrates the organizing principle of
a. figure-ground.
b. shape constancy.
c. grouping.
d. depth or distance perception.

21. Our tendencies to fill in the gaps and to perceive a pattern as continuous are two different examples of the organizing principle called
a. the Ames illusion.
b. depth perception.
c. shape constancy.
d. grouping.

22. Visual cliff experiments on depth perception suggest that
a. infants have not yet developed depth perception.
b. crawling infants perceive depth.
c. we have no way of knowing whether infants can perceive depth.
d. humans are the only animals that can perceive depth in infancy.

23. Depth perception underlies our ability to
a. group similar items in a gestalt.
b. perceive objects as having a constant shape or form.
c. judge distances.
d. fill in the gaps in a figure.

24. Examples of monocular cues, which are available to either eye alone, include interposition and
a. closure.
b. retinal disparity.
c. linear perspective.
d. brightness contrast.

25. Perceiving tomatoes as consistently red, despite shifting illumination, is an example of
a. form perception.
b. perceptual constancy.
c. retinal disparity.
d. grouping.

Answers: 20, a, 21, d, 22, b, 23, c, 24, c, 25, b.

Perceptual Interpretation

Philosophers have debated whether our perceptual abilities should be credited to our nature or our nurture. To what extent do we learn to perceive? German philosopher Immanuel Kant (1724–1804) maintained that knowledge comes from our inborn ways of organizing sensory experiences. Indeed, we come equipped to process sensory information. But British philosopher John Locke (1632–1704) argued that through our experiences we also learn to perceive the world. Indeed, we learn to link an object's distance with its size. So, just how important is experience? How radically does it shape our perceptual interpretations?

"Let us then suppose the mind to be, as we say, white paper void of all characters, without any ideas: How comes it to be furnished? . . . To this I answer, in one word, from EXPERIENCE."

—John Locke, *An Essay Concerning Human Understanding,* 1690

Sensory Deprivation and Restored Vision

17: What does research on sensory restriction and restored vision reveal about the effects of experience?

Writing to John Locke, William Molyneux wondered whether "a man *born* blind, and now adult, taught by his *touch* to distinguish between a cube and a sphere" could, if made to see, visually distinguish the two. Locke's answer was *no,* because the man would never have *learned* to see the difference.

Molyneux' hypothetical case has since been put to the test with a few dozen adults who, though blind from birth, have gained sight (Gregory, 1978; von Senden, 1932). Most had been born with cataracts—clouded lenses that allowed them to see only diffused light, rather as you or I might see a diffuse fog through a Ping-Pong ball sliced in half. After cataract surgery, the patients could distinguish figure from ground and could sense colors—suggesting that these aspects of perception are innate. But

Mike May, Allison Allano Photography

Learning to see At age 3, Mike May lost his vision in an explosion. On March 7, 2000, after a new cornea restored vision to his right eye, he got his first look at his wife and children. Alas, although signals were reaching his long dormant visual cortex, it lacked the experience to interpret them. Faces, apart from features such as hair, were not recognizable. Expressions eluded him. Yet he could see an object in motion and has been gradually learning to navigate his world and to marvel at such things as dust floating in sunlight (Abrams, 2002).

FIGURE 6.41 Perceiving composite faces To most people, the top halves of these two faces, created by Richard Le Grand and his colleagues (2004), look different. Actually, they are the same, though paired with two different lower face halves. People deprived of visual experience early in life have more difficulty perceiving whole faces, which ironically enables their superiority at recognizing that the top halves of these faces are identical.

much as Locke supposed, they often could not visually recognize objects that were familiar by touch.

Experience also influences our perception of faces. You and I perceive and recognize individual faces as a whole. Show us the same top half of a face paired with two different bottom halves (as in **FIGURE 6.41**), and the identical top halves will seem different. People deprived of visual experience during childhood surpass the rest of us at recognizing that the top halves are the same, because they didn't learn to process faces as a whole (Le Grand et al., 2004). One 43-year-old man whose sight was restored after 40 years of blindness could associate people with distinct features ("Mary's the one with red hair"). But he could not instantly recognize a face. He also lacked perceptual constancy: As people walked away from him they seemed to be shrinking in size (Bower, 2003). Vision, such cases make clear, is partly an acquired sense.

Seeking to gain more control than is provided by clinical cases, researchers have conducted Molyneux' imaginary experiment with infant kittens and monkeys. In one experiment, they outfitted them with goggles through which the animals could see only diffuse, unpatterned light (Wiesel, 1982). After infancy, when their goggles were removed, these animals exhibited perceptual limitations much like those of humans born with cataracts. They could distinguish color and brightness, but not the form of a circle from that of a square. Their eyes had not degenerated; their retinas still relayed signals to their visual cortex. But lacking stimulation, the cortical cells had not developed normal connections. Thus, the animals remained functionally blind to shape. Experience guides, sustains, and maintains the brain's neural organization.

In both humans and animals, a similar period of sensory restriction does no permanent harm if it occurs later in life. Cover the eye of an animal for several months during adulthood, and its vision will be unaffected after the eye patch is removed. Remove cataracts that developed after early childhood, and a human, too, will enjoy normal vision.

The effects of visual experiences during infancy in cats, monkeys, and humans suggest there is a *critical period* (Chapter 5) for normal sensory and perceptual development. So, too, with some auditory experiences. Cochlear implants given to congenitally deaf kittens and human infants seem to trigger an "awakening" of the pertinent brain area (Klinke et al., 1999; Sirenteanu, 1999). Nurture sculpts what nature has endowed.

Perceptual Adaptation

18: **How adaptable is our ability to perceive?**

Given a new pair of glasses, we may feel slightly disoriented, even dizzy. Within a day or two, we adjust to the changed visual input. **Perceptual adaptation** has made the world seem normal again. But imagine a far more dramatic new pair of glasses—one that shifts the apparent location of objects 40 degrees to the left. When you first put them on and toss a ball to a friend, it sails off to the left. Walking forward to shake hands with the person, you veer to the left.

Could you adapt to this distorted world? Chicks cannot. When fitted with such lenses, they have continued to peck where food grains *seemed* to be (Hess, 1956; Rossi, 1968). But we humans adapt to distorting lenses quickly. Within a few minutes your throws would again be accurate, your stride on target. Remove the lenses and you would experience an aftereffect: At first your throws would err in the *opposite* direction, sailing off to the right; but again, within minutes you would readapt.

Indeed, given an even more radical pair of glasses—one that literally turns the world upside down—you could still adapt. Psychologist George Stratton (1896)

Perceptual adaptation "Oops, missed," thinks researcher Hubert Dolezal as he views the world through inverting goggles. Yet, believe it or not, kittens, monkeys, and humans can adapt to an inverted world.

experienced this when he invented, and for eight days wore, optical headgear that flipped left to right *and* up to down, making him the first person to experience a right-side-up retinal image while standing upright. The ground was up, the sky was down.

At first, Stratton felt disoriented. When he wanted to walk, he found himself searching for his feet, which were now "up." Eating was nearly impossible. He became nauseated and depressed. But Stratton persisted, and by the eighth day he could comfortably reach for an object in the right direction and walk without bumping into things. When he finally removed the headgear, he readapted quickly.

Later experiments replicated Stratton's experience (Dolezal, 1982; Kohler, 1962). After a period of adjustment, people wearing the optical gear have even been able to ride a motorcycle, ski the Alps, and fly an airplane. Did they adjust by perceptually converting their strange worlds to "normal" views? No. Actually, the world around them still seemed above their heads or on the wrong side. But by actively moving about in these topsy-turvy worlds, they adapted to the context and learned to coordinate their movements.

Perceptual Set

19: **How do our expectations, contexts, and emotions influence our perceptions?**

As everyone knows, to see is to believe. As we less fully appreciate, to believe is to see. Our experiences, assumptions, and expectations may give us a **perceptual set,** or mental predisposition, that greatly influences (top-down) what we perceive. People perceive an adult-child pair as looking more alike when told they are parent and child (Bressan & Dal Martello, 2002). And consider: Is the image in the center picture of **FIGURE 6.42** a man playing a saxophone or a woman's face? What we see in such a drawing can be influenced by first looking at either of the two unambiguous versions (Boring, 1930).

Once we have formed a wrong idea about reality, we have more difficulty seeing the truth. Everyday examples of perceptual set abound. In 1972, a British newspaper published genuine, unretouched photographs of a "monster" in Scotland's Loch Ness—"the most amazing pictures ever taken," stated the paper. If this information creates in you the same perceptual set it did in most of the paper's readers, you, too, will see the monster in the photo reproduced in **FIGURE 6.43a** (on the next page). But when Steuart Campbell (1986) approached the photos with a different perceptual set, he saw a curved tree trunk—as had others the day the photo was shot. With this different perceptual set, you may now notice that the object is floating motionless, without any rippling water or wake around it—hardly what we would expect of a lively monster.

When shown the phrase:
  Mary had a
  a little lamb
many people perceive what they expect, and miss the repeated word. Did you?

FIGURE 6.42 Perceptual set Show a friend either the left or right image. Then show the center image and ask, "What do you see?" Whether your friend reports seeing a saxophonist or a woman's face will likely depend on which of the other two drawings was viewed first. In each of those images, the meaning is clear, and it will establish perceptual expectations.
(Sara Nadar, © 1990 Roger N. Shepard)

FIGURE 6.43 Believing is seeing What do you perceive in these photos? (a) Is this Nessie, the Loch Ness monster, or a log? (b) Are these flying saucers or clouds? We often perceive what we expect to see.

(a)   (b)

Perceptual set can similarly influence what we hear. Consider the kindly airline pilot who, on a takeoff run, looked over at his depressed co-pilot and said, "Cheer up." The co-pilot heard the usual "Gear up" and promptly raised the wheels—before they left the ground (Reason & Mycielska, 1982). Perceptual set also influences young children's taste preferences. By a 6-to-1 margin in one experiment, they judged french fries as tasting better when served in a McDonald's bag rather than a plain white bag (Robinson et al., 2007). Clearly, much of what we perceive comes not just from the world "out there" but also from what's behind our eyes and between our ears.

What determines our perceptual set? Through experience we form concepts, or *schemas*, that organize and interpret unfamiliar information (see Chapter 5). Our preexisting schemas for male saxophonists and women's faces, for monsters and tree trunks, for clouds and UFOs, all influence how we interpret ambiguous sensations with top-down processing.

"The temptation to form premature theories upon insufficient data is the bane of our profession."

—Sherlock Holmes, in Arthur Conan Doyle's *The Valley of Fear*, 1914

Context Effects

Context, as we saw earlier, guides our perception of lightness and color. Context shapes perception in other ways, too. A given stimulus may trigger radically different perceptions, partly because of our differing perceptual sets, but also because of the immediate context. Some examples:

- Imagine hearing a noise interrupted by the words "eel is on the wagon." Likely, you would actually perceive the first word as *wheel*. Given "eel is on the orange," you would hear *peel*. This curious phenomenon, discovered by Richard Warren, suggests that the brain can work backward in time to allow a later stimulus to determine how we perceive an earlier one. The context creates an expectation that, top-down, influences our perception as we match our bottom-up signal against it (Grossberg, 1995).
- Did the pursuing monster in Figure 6.37a look aggressive? Did the identical pursued one seem frightened? If so, you experienced a context effect.
- Is the "magician's cabinet" in **FIGURE 6.44** sitting on the floor or hanging from the ceiling? How we perceive it depends on the context defined by the rabbits.

FIGURE 6.44 Context effects: the magician's cabinet Is the box in the far left frame lying on the floor or hanging from the ceiling? What about the one on the far right? In each case, the context defined by the inquisitive rabbits guides our perceptions. (From Shepard, 1990.)

Even hearing sad rather than happy music can predispose people to perceive a sad meaning in spoken homophonic words—*mourning* rather than *morning, die* rather than *dye, pain* rather than *pane* (Halberstadt et al., 1995). To experience the context effect yourself, answer this question: How tall is the shorter player in **FIGURE 6.45**? The "little guy" in that photo is actually a 6′9″ former Hope College basketball center who towers over me. But he seemed like a short player when matched in a semi-pro game against the world's tallest basketball player, 7′9″ Sun Ming Ming from China.

The effects of perceptual set and context show how experience helps us construct perception. In everyday life, our stereotypes (another instance of perceptual set) can color our perceptions. Without the obvious gender cues of pink or blue, people will struggle over whether to call the new baby "he" or "she." But told an infant is "David," people (especially children) may perceive "him" as bigger and stronger than if the same infant is called "Diana" (Stern & Karraker, 1989). Some differences, it seems, exist merely in the eyes of their beholders.

To return to the question "Is perception innate or learned?" we can answer: It's both. The river of perception is fed by sensation, cognition, and emotion. And that is why we need multiple levels of analysis (**FIGURE 6.46**). "Simple" perceptions are the brain's creative products.

If we accept the statement that perception is the product of sensation and cognition, what can we say about extrasensory perception (ESP), which claims that perception can occur apart from sensory input? For more on that question, see Thinking Critically About: Extrasensory Perception (on the next page).

* * *

To feel awe and to gain a deep reverence for life, we need look no further than our own perceptual system and its capacity for organizing formless nerve impulses into colorful sights, vivid sounds, and evocative smells. As Shakespeare's Hamlet recognized, "There are more things in Heaven and Earth, Horatio, than are dreamt of in your philosophy." Within our ordinary sensory and perceptual experiences lies much that is truly extraordinary—surely much more than has so far been dreamt of in our psychology.

FIGURE 6.45 Big and "little"

"We hear and apprehend only what we already half know."

—Henry David Thoreau, *Journal,* 1860

"So, how does the mind work? I don't know. You don't know. Pinker doesn't know. And, I rather suspect, that if God were to tell us, we wouldn't understand."

—Jerry Fodor,
"Reply to Steven Pinker," 2005

Culture and context effects What is above the woman's head? In one study, nearly all the East Africans who were questioned said the woman was balancing a metal box or can on her head and that the family was sitting under a tree. Westerners, for whom corners and boxlike architecture are more common, were more likely to perceive the family as being indoors, with the woman sitting under a window. (Adapted from Gregory & Gombrich, 1973.)

Biological influences:
• sensory analysis
• unlearned sensory abilities
• critical period for sensory development

Psychological influences:
• Gestalt principles
• learned schemas
• context effects
• perceptual set

Perception: Our version of reality

Social-cultural influences:
• cultural assumptions and expectations

FIGURE 6.46 Perception is a biopsychosocial phenomenon Psychologists study how we perceive with different levels of analysis, from the biological to the social-cultural.

Thinking Critically About:

Extrasensory Perception

20: What are the claims of ESP, and what have most research psychologists concluded after putting these claims to the test?

Can we perceive only what we sense? Or, as nearly half of Americans believe, are we capable of **extrasensory perception (ESP)** without sensory input (AP, 2007; Moore, 2005)?

Are there indeed people—any people—who can read minds, see through walls, or foretell the future? Several universities—five in Great Britain and one each in Sweden, The Netherlands, and Australia—either have **parapsychology** units or have added faculty chairs or research units for parapsychology (Turpin, 2005). Parapsychologists in such places do experiments that search for possible ESP and other paranormal phenomena.

But other research psychologists and scientists—including 96 percent of the scientists in the U.S. National Academy of Sciences—are skeptical that such phenomena exist (McConnell, 1991). If ESP is real, we would need to overturn the scientific understanding that we are creatures whose minds are tied to our physical brains and whose perceptual experiences of the world are built of sensations. Sometimes new evidence does overturn our scientific preconceptions. Science, as we will see throughout this book, offers us various surprises—about the extent of the unconscious mind, about the effects of emotions on health, about what heals and what doesn't, and much more. Before we evaluate claims of ESP, let's review them.

---

extrasensory perception (ESP) the controversial claim that perception can occur apart from sensory input; includes telepathy, clairvoyance, and precognition.

---

parapsychology the study of paranormal phenomena, including ESP and psychokinesis.

SNAPSHOTS

Thank you for calling the Psychic Hotline. How can I help you?

You tell *me...*

(c) Love 650

© Jason Love

Claims of ESP

Claims of paranormal phenomena *(psi)* include astrological predictions, psychic healing, communication with the dead, and out-of-body experiences. But the most testable and (for a perception discussion) most relevant claims are for three varieties of ESP:

- *Telepathy,* or mind-to-mind communication: one person sending thoughts to another or perceiving another's thoughts.
- *Clairvoyance,* or perceiving remote events, such as sensing that a friend's house is on fire.
- *Precognition,* or perceiving future events, such as a political leader's death or a sporting event's outcome.

Closely linked with these are claims of *psychokinesis (PK),* or "mind over matter," such as levitating a table or influencing the roll of a die. (The claim is illustrated by the wry request, "Will all those who believe in psychokinesis please raise my hand?")

Premonitions or Pretensions?

Can psychics see into the future? Although one might wish for a psychic stock forecaster, the tallied forecasts of "leading psychics" reveal meager accuracy.

During the 1990s, the tabloid psychics were all wrong in predicting surprising events. (Madonna did not become a gospel singer, the Statue of Liberty did not lose both its arms in a terrorist blast, Queen Elizabeth did not abdicate her throne to enter a convent.) And the new-century psychics missed the big-news events. Where were the psychics on 9/10 when we needed them? Why, despite a $50 million reward offered, could none of them help locate Osama bin Laden after 9/11 or step forward to predict the impending stock market crashes in 2008? Gene Emery (2004), who has tracked annual psychic forecasts for 26 years, reports that almost never have unusual predictions come true, and virtually never have psychics anticipated any of the year's headline events.

Analyses of psychic visions offered to police departments have revealed that these, too, are no more accurate than guesses made by others (Reiser, 1982). Most police departments are wise to all this. When Jane Ayers Sweat and Mark Durm (1993) asked the police departments of America's 50 largest cities whether they ever used psychics, 65 percent said they never had. Of those that had, not one had found it helpful.

Psychics working with the police do, however, generate hundreds of predictions. This increases the odds of an occasional correct guess, which psychics can then report to the media. Moreover, vague predictions can later be interpreted ("retrofitted") to match events that provide a perceptual set for "understanding" them. Nostradamus, a sixteenth-century French psychic, explained in an unguarded moment that his ambiguous prophecies "could not possibly be understood till they were interpreted after the event and by it."

Dreams are also often interpreted after the event, as we recall or reconstruct

"A person who talks a lot is sometimes right."

—Spanish proverb

those that appear to have come true. Two Harvard psychologists (Murray & Wheeler, 1937) tested the prophetic power of dreams after aviator Charles Lindbergh's baby son was kidnapped and murdered in 1932, but before the body was discovered. When the researchers invited the public to report their dreams about the child, 1300 visionaries submitted dream reports. How many accurately envisioned the child dead? Five percent. How many also correctly anticipated the body's location—buried among trees? Only 4 of the 1300. Although this number was surely no better than chance, to those 4 dreamers the accuracy of their apparent precognitions must have seemed uncanny.

Throughout the day, each of us imagines many events. Given the billions of events in the world each day, and given enough days, some stunning coincidences are sure to occur. By one careful estimate, chance alone would predict that more than a thousand times a day someone on Earth will think of someone and then within the ensuing five minutes will learn of the person's death (Charpak & Broch, 2004). With enough time and people, the improbable becomes inevitable.

That was the experience of comics writer John Byrne (2003). Six months after his Spider-Man story about a New York blackout appeared, New York suffered a massive blackout. A subsequent Spider-Man storyline involved a major earthquake in Japan. "And again," he recalled, "the real thing happened in the month the issue hit the stands." Later, when working on a Superman comic book, he "had the Man of Steel fly to the rescue when disaster beset the NASA space shuttle. The *Challenger* tragedy happened almost immediately thereafter" (with time for the issue to be redrawn). "Most recently, and chilling, came when I was writing and drawing Wonder Woman and did a story in which the title character was killed as a prelude to her becoming a goddess." The issue cover "was done as a newspaper front page, with the headline 'Princess Diana Dies.' (Diana is Wonder Woman's real name.) That issue went on

sale on a Thursday. The following Saturday . . . I don't have to tell you, do I?"

Putting ESP to Experimental Test

In the past, there have been all kinds of strange ideas—that bumps on the head reveal character traits, that bloodletting is a cure-all, that each sperm cell contains a miniature person. Faced with such claims—or with claims of mind-reading or out-of-body travel or communication with the dead—how can we separate bizarre ideas from those that sound bizarre but are true? At the heart of science is a simple answer: *Test them to see if they work.* If they do, so much the better for the ideas. If they don't, so much the better for our skepticism.

> "At the heart of science is an essential tension between two seemingly contradictory attitudes—an openness to new ideas, no matter how bizarre or counterintuitive they may be, and the most ruthless skeptical scrutiny of all ideas, old and new."
>
> Carl Sagan (1987)

This scientific attitude has led both believers and skeptics to agree that what parapsychology needs is a reproducible

phenomenon and a theory to explain it. Parapsychologist Rhea White (1998) spoke for many in saying that "the image of parapsychology that comes to my mind, based on nearly 44 years in the field, is that of a small airplane [that] has been perpetually taxiing down the runway of the Empirical Science Airport since 1882 . . . its movement punctuated occasionally by lifting a few feet off the ground only to bump back down on the tarmac once again. It has never taken off for any sustained flight."

Seeking a reproducible phenomenon, how might we test ESP claims in a controlled experiment? An experiment differs from a staged demonstration. In the laboratory, the experimenter controls what the "psychic" sees and hears. On stage, the psychic controls what the audience sees and hears. Time and again, skeptics note, so-called psychics have exploited unquestioning audiences with mind-blowing performances in which they *appeared* to communicate with the spirits of the dead, read minds, or levitate objects—only to have it revealed that their acts were nothing more than the illusions of stage magicians.

One set of experiments has invited "senders" to telepathically transmit one of four visual images to "receivers"

Testing psychic powers in the British population
Hertfordshire University psychologist Richard Wiseman created a "mind machine" to see if people can influence or predict a coin toss. Using a touch-sensitive screen, visitors to festivals around the country were given four attempts to call heads or tails. Using a random-number generator, a computer then decided the outcome. When the experiment concluded in January 2000, nearly 28,000 people had predicted 110,972 tosses—with 49.8 percent correct.

Continued on next page

deprived of sensation in a nearby chamber (Bem & Honorton, 1994). The result? A reported 32 percent accurate response rate, surpassing the chance rate of 25 percent. But follow-up studies have (depending on who was summarizing the results) failed to replicate the phenomenon or produced mixed results (Bem et al., 2001; Milton & Wiseman, 2002; Storm, 2000, 2003).

BIZARRO
By DAN PIRARO

HEY! WE WERE JUST *THINKING* ABOUT CALLING OUT FOR PIZZA!

I KNOW!

PSYCHIC PIZZA DELIVERED 15 MINUTES *BEFORE* YOU ORDER OR IT'S *FREE!*

Which supposed psychic ability does Psychic Pizza claim?

Answer: Telepathy

If ESP nevertheless exists, might it subtly register in the brain? To find out, Harvard researchers Samuel Moulton and Stephen Kosslyn (2008) had a sender try to send one of two pictures telepathically to a receiver lying in an fMRI machine. In these pairs (mostly couples, friends, or twins), the receivers guessed the picture's content correctly at the level of chance (50.0 percent). Moreover, their brains responded no differently when later viewing the actual pictures "sent" by ESP. "These findings," concluded the researchers, "are the strongest evidence yet obtained against the existence of paranormal mental phenomena."

"A psychic is an actor playing the role of a psychic."

Psychologist-magician Daryl Bem (1984)

From 1998 to 2010, one skeptic, magician James Randi, offered $1 million "to anyone who proves a genuine psychic power under proper observing conditions" (Randi, 1999, 2008). French, Australian, and Indian groups have made parallel offers of up to 200,000 euros to anyone with demonstrable paranormal abilities (CFI, 2003). Large as these sums are, the scientific seal of approval would be worth far more to anyone whose claims could be authenticated. To refute those who say there is no ESP, one need only produce a

And, as you already know, the Lakers will win tomorrow 98-93. Stay tuned for next week's scores, even though you already know those, too, right HERE on ESP-N, the Psychic Sports Channel!

single person who can demonstrate a single, reproducible ESP phenomenon. (To refute those who say pigs can't talk would take but one talking pig.) So far, no such person has emerged. Randi's offer was well-publicized, and dozens of people were tested, sometimes under the scrutiny of an independent panel of judges. Still, nothing.

"People's desire to believe in the paranormal is stronger than all the evidence that it does not exist."

—Susan Blackmore, "Blackmore's first law," 2004

REHEARSE IT!

26. After surgery to restore vision, patients who had been blind from birth had difficulty
    a. recognizing objects by touch.
    b. recognizing objects by sight.
    c. distinguishing figure from ground.
    d. distinguishing between bright and dim light.

27. Experiments in which volunteers wear glasses that displace or invert their visual fields show that, after a period of disorientation, people learn to function quite well. This ability is called
    a. context effect.
    b. perceptual set.
    c. sensory interaction.
    d. perceptual adaptation.

28. Our perceptual set influences what we perceive. This mental predisposition reflects our
    a. experiences, assumptions, and expectations.
    b. perceptual adaptation.
    c. skill at extrasensory perception.
    d. perceptual constancy.

Answers: 26. b, 27. d, 28. a.

CHAPTER REVIEW

Sensation and Perception

Sensing the World: Some Basic Principles

1 **What do we mean by *bottom-up processing* and *top-down processing*?**

Bottom-up processing is sensory analysis that begins at the entry level, with information flowing from the sensory receptors to the brain. *Top-down processing* is analysis that begins with the brain and flows down, filtering information through our experience and expectations to produce perceptions.

2 **What are absolute and difference thresholds, and do stimuli below the absolute threshold have any influence?**

Our *absolute threshold* for any stimulus is the minimum stimulation needed to be consciously aware of it 50 percent of the time. Our *difference threshold* (also called just noticeable difference, or jnd) is the barely noticeable difference we discern between two stimuli 50 percent of the time. *Priming* shows that we can process some information from *subliminal* stimuli—those below our absolute threshold for conscious awareness. But the effect is not powerful or enduring. *Weber's law* states that, to be perceived as different, two stimuli must differ by a constant minimum proportion.

3 **What is the function of sensory adaptation?**

By diminishing our sensitivity to constant or routine stimuli, *sensory adaptation* focuses our attention on informative changes in our environment.

Vision

4 **What is the energy that we see as visible light?**

Each sense receives stimulation, transforms it into neural signals, and sends these neural messages to the brain. In vision, the signals consist of light-energy particles from a thin slice of the broad spectrum of electromagnetic energy. The *hue* we perceive in a light depends on its *wavelength*, and its brightness depends on its *intensity*.

5 **How does the eye transform light energy into neural messages?**

Light-energy particles enter the eye, are focused by a lens, and then strike the eye's inner surface, the *retina*. The retina's light-sensitive *rods* and color-sensitive *cones* convert the light energy into neural impulses which, after processing by bipolar and ganglion cells, travel through the *optic nerve* to the brain.

6 **How does the brain process visual information?**

Impulses travel along the optic nerve, to the thalamus, and on to the visual cortex. In the visual cortex, *feature detectors* respond to specific features of the visual stimulus and pass information to higher-level supercells in other cortical areas. *Parallel processing* by separate neural teams in the brain enables the simultaneous processing of many aspects of visual information. Other neural teams integrate the results and compare them with stored information, enabling perceptions.

7 **What theories help us understand color vision?**

The *Young-Helmholtz trichromatic (three-color) theory* proposed that the retina contains three types of color receptors. Research has confirmed that we have three types of cones, each especially sensitive to the wavelengths of red, green, or blue. Hering's *opponent-process theory* proposed three additional color processes (red-versus-green, blue-versus-yellow, black-versus-white). Research has also confirmed that, en route to the brain, neurons in the retina and the thalamus code the color-related information from the cones into pairs of opponent colors. Thus, color processing occurs in two stages.

Other Important Senses

8 **What are the characteristics of air pressure waves that we hear as sound?**

Sound waves are bands of compressed and expanded air. Our ears detect these air pressure changes and transform them into neural impulses for decoding in the brain. Sound waves vary in *frequency*, which we experience as differing *pitch*, and amplitude, which we perceive as differing loudness.

9 **How does the ear transform sound energy into neural messages?**

The visible outer ear channels sound waves through the auditory canal, causing tiny vibrations in the eardrum. The bones of the *middle ear* amplify the vibrations and relay them to the fluid-filled *cochlea* in the *inner ear*. Pressure changes in the cochlear fluid cause the basilar membrane to ripple, bending tiny hair cells that send neural messages (via the thalamus) to the auditory cortex in the brain.

10 **How do we locate sounds?**

Sound waves strike one ear sooner and more intensely than the other. The brain analyzes these minute differences between the two ears' messages and computes the sound's source.

11 **How do we sense touch and sense our body's position and movement? How do we experience pain?**

Touch is actually several senses—pressure, warmth, cold, and pain. Only pressure has identifiable receptors. Through *kinesthesis*, we sense the position and movement of body parts. We monitor the body's position and maintain our balance with our *vestibular sense*. The *gate-control theory* of pain proposes a "gate" in the spinal cord that either opens to permit pain signals traveling up small nerve fibers to reach the brain, or closes to prevent their passage. Three sets of influences—biological, psychological, and social-cultural— contribute to our experience of pain and can be used in treatments to control pain.

12 **How do we experience taste?**

Taste, a chemical sense, is a composite of five basic sensations— sweet, sour, salty, bitter, and umami. Smells, as well as our expectations, can influence our perception of taste. This is an example of *sensory interaction*, which can affect other senses, too.

13 How do we experience smell?

Some 10 million olfactory receptor cells, with their approximately 350 different receptor proteins, contribute to the chemical sense of smell. The proteins recognize individual odor molecules. Combinations of receptors send patterns of messages to the brain's olfactory bulb, then to the temporal lobe and to parts of the limbic system. Odors can spontaneously evoke memories and feelings, due in part to the close connections between brain areas that process smell and memory.

Perceptual Organization

14 How did the Gestalt psychologists understand perceptual organization, and how do figure-ground and grouping principles contribute to our perceptions?

Gestalt psychologists described principles by which the brain organizes fragments of sensory data into *gestalts*, or meaningful forms. To recognize an object, we must first perceive it (see it as a *figure*) as distinct from its surroundings (the *ground*). We bring order and form to stimuli by organizing them into meaningful *groups*, following the rules of proximity, similarity, continuity, connectedness, and closure.

15 How do we see the world in three dimensions?

Depth perception is our ability to see objects in three dimensions, which lets us judge distance. The *visual cliff* and other research demonstrates that many species perceive the world in three dimensions at, or very soon after, birth. *Binocular cues,* such as *retinal disparity,* are depth cues that rely on information from both eyes. *Monocular cues* (such as relative size, interposition, relative height, relative motion, linear perspective, and light and shadow) let us judge depth using information transmitted by only one eye.

16 How do perceptual constancies help us organize our sensations into meaningful perceptions?

Perceptual constancy enables us to perceive objects as stable despite the changing image they cast on our retinas. Through shape and size constancies, we perceive familiar objects as unchanging in shape or size despite their changing retinal images. Knowing an object's size gives us clues to its distance; knowing its distance gives clues about its size. Through lightness (or brightness) constancy we perceive an object as having a constant lightness even when the light cast upon it changes, because the brain perceives lightness relative to surrounding objects. *Color constancy* is our ability to perceive consistent color in objects, even though the lighting and wavelengths shift. Our brain constructs our experience of the color of an object through comparisons with surrounding objects.

Perceptual Interpretation

17 What does research on sensory restriction and restored vision reveal about the effects of experience?

Both lines of research show there is a critical period for some aspects of sensory and perceptual development. After surgery to restore sight, people who were born blind cannot recognize shapes, forms, and complete faces. After experiencing severely restricted visual input, animals suffer enduring visual handicaps when their visual exposure is returned to normal. Without early stimulation, the brain's neural organization does not develop normally.

18 How adaptable is our ability to perceive?

Perceptual adaptation is evident when people wear glasses that shift the world slightly to the left or right, or even upside-down. Initially disoriented, they manage to adapt to their new context.

19 How do our expectations, contexts, and emotions influence our perceptions?

Perceptual set is a mental predisposition that functions as a lens through which we perceive the world. Our learned concepts (schemas) prime us to organize and interpret ambiguous stimuli in certain ways. The context surrounding a stimulus creates expectations that guide our perceptions.

20 What are the claims of ESP, and what have most research psychologists concluded after putting these claims to the test?

The three most testable forms of *extrasensory perception (ESP)* are telepathy (mind-to-mind communication), clairvoyance (perceiving remote events), and precognition (perceiving future events). Most research psychologists' skepticism focuses on two points. First, to believe in ESP, you must believe the brain is capable of perceiving without sensory input. Second, psychologists and *parapsychologists* have been unable to replicate (reproduce) ESP phenomena under controlled conditions.

Terms and Concepts to Remember

sensation, p. 180
perception, p. 180
bottom-up processing, p. 180
top-down processing, p. 180
psychophysics, p. 181
absolute threshold, p. 181
subliminal, p. 181

priming, p. 182
difference threshold, p. 182
Weber's law, p. 183
sensory adaptation, p. 183
wavelength, p. 185
hue, p. 185
intensity, p. 185

retina, p. 186
accommodation, p. 186
rods, p. 186
cones, p. 186
optic nerve, p. 187
blind spot, p. 187
fovea, p. 188

feature detectors, p. 188

parallel processing, p. 190

Young-Helmholtz trichromatic (three-color) theory, p. 191

opponent-process theory, p. 192

audition, p. 193

frequency, p. 193

pitch, p. 193

middle ear, p. 194

cochlea [KOHK-lee-uh], p. 194

inner ear, p. 194

kinesthesis [kin-ehs-THEE-sehs], p. 197

vestibular sense, p. 197

gate-control theory, p. 199

sensory interaction, p. 202

gestalt, p. 205

figure-ground, p. 205

grouping, p. 206

depth perception, p. 207

visual cliff, p. 207

binocular cues, p. 207

retinal disparity, p. 207

monocular cues, p. 208

perceptual constancy, p. 210

color constancy, p. 212

perceptual adaptation, p. 214

perceptual set, p. 215

extrasensory perception (ESP), p. 218

parapsychology, p. 218

Test for Success: Critical Thinking Exercises
By Amy Himsel, El Camino College

1. Before reading this question, you probably didn't notice the sensation of your shoes touching your feet. Yet it's likely you notice them now. Why?

2. Why do you feel a little dizzy immediately after a roller coaster ride?

3. Why might it be helpful for people with chronic pain to meditate or exercise?

4. What mental processes allow you to perceive a lemon as yellow?

The Test for Success exercises offer you a chance to apply your critical thinking skills to aspects of the material you have just read. Suggestions for answering these questions can be found in Appendix D at the back of the book.

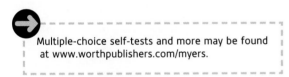

Multiple-choice self-tests and more may be found at www.worthpublishers.com/myers.

Chapter Outline

- **How Do We Learn?**

- **Classical Conditioning**
  Pavlov's Experiments
  Extending Pavlov's
  Understanding
  Pavlov's Legacy

- **Operant Conditioning**
  Skinner's Experiments
  Extending Skinner's
  Understanding
  Skinner's Legacy
  Contrasting Classical and
  Operant Conditioning
  CLOSE-UP: Training Our
  Partners

- **Learning by Observation**
  Mirrors in the Brain
  Bandura's Experiments
  Applications of Observational
  Learning

7: Learning

When a chinook salmon first emerges from its egg in a stream's gravel bed, its genes provide most of the behavioral instructions it needs for life. It knows instinctively how and where to swim, what to eat, and how to protect itself. Following a built-in plan, the young salmon soon begins its trek to the sea. After some four years in the ocean, the mature salmon returns to its birthplace. It navigates hundreds of miles to the mouth of its home river and then, guided by the scent of its home stream, begins an upstream odyssey to its ancestral spawning ground. Once there, the salmon seeks out the best temperature, gravel, and water flow for breeding. It then mates and, its life mission accomplished, dies.

Unlike salmon, we are not born with a genetic plan for life. Much of what we do we learn from experience. Although we struggle to find the life direction a salmon is born with, our learning gives us more flexibility. We can learn how to build grass huts or snow shelters, submarines or space stations, and thereby adjust to almost any environment. Indeed, nature's most important gift to us may be our *adaptability*—our capacity to learn new behaviors that help us cope with changing circumstances.

Learning breeds hope. What is learnable we can potentially teach—a fact that encourages parents, educators, coaches, and animal trainers. What has been learned we can potentially change by new learning—an assumption that underlies counseling, psychotherapy, and rehabilitation programs. No matter how unhappy, unsuccessful, or unloving we are, that need not be the end of our story.

No topic is closer to the heart of psychology than **learning,** a *relatively permanent behavior change due to experience.* In earlier chapters we considered the learning of a drug's expected effect, of gender roles, and of visual perceptions. In later chapters we will see how learning shapes our thought and language, our motivations and emotions, our personalities and attitudes. This chapter examines three types of learning: *classical conditioning, operant conditioning,* and *observational learning.*

"Actually, sex just isn't that important to me."

"Learning is the eye of the mind."
—Thomas Drake, *Bibliotheca Scholastica Instructissima,* 1633

How Do We Learn?

1: **What distinguishes the basic forms of learning?**

More than 200 years ago, philosophers such as John Locke and David Hume echoed Aristotle's conclusion from 2000 years earlier: We learn by association. Our minds naturally connect events that occur in sequence. Suppose you see and smell freshly baked bread, eat some, and find it satisfying. The next time you see and smell fresh bread, that experience will lead you to expect that eating it will once again be satisfying. So, too, with sounds. If you associate a sound with a frightening consequence, hearing the sound alone may trigger your fear. As one 4-year-old exclaimed after watching a TV character get mugged, "If I had heard that music, I wouldn't have gone around the corner!" (Wells, 1981).

learning a relatively permanent change in an organism's behavior due to experience.

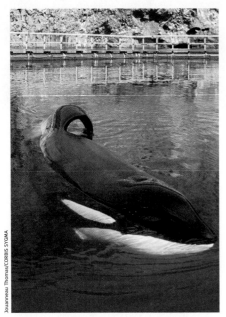

Nature without appropriate nurture
Keiko—the killer whale of *Free Willy* fame—
had all the right genes for being dropped right
back into his Icelandic home waters. But lacking life experience, he required caregivers to
his life's end in a Norwegian fjord.

*Most of us would be unable to name the order
of the songs on our favorite CD or playlist.
Yet, hearing the end of one piece cues (by
association) an anticipation of the next.
Likewise, when singing your national
anthem, you associate the end of each line
with the beginning of the next. (Pick a line
out of the middle and notice how much harder it is to recall the* previous *line.)*

Learned associations also feed our habitual behaviors (Wood & Neal, 2007). As
we repeat behaviors in a given context—sleeping in a certain posture in bed, walking the same route on campus, eating popcorn in a movie theater—the behaviors
become associated with the contexts. Our next experience of the context then automatically triggers our habitual response. Such associations can make it hard to kick
a smoking habit; when back in the smoking context, the urge to light up can be
powerful (Siegel, 2005).

Other animals also learn by association. Disturbed by a squirt of water, the sea
slug *Aplysia* protectively withdraws its gill. If the squirts continue, as happens naturally in choppy water, the withdrawal response diminishes. (The slug's response
habituates.) But if the sea slug repeatedly receives an electric shock just after being
squirted, its withdrawal response to the squirt instead grows stronger. The animal
relates the squirt to the impending shock. Complex animals can learn to relate
their own behavior to its outcomes. Seals in an aquarium will repeat behaviors,
such as slapping and barking, that prompt people to toss them a herring.

By linking two events that occur close together, both the sea slug and the seals
exhibit **associative learning.** The sea slug associates the squirt with an impending
shock; the seal associates slapping and barking with a herring treat. Each animal has
learned something important to its survival: predicting the immediate future.

The significance of an animal's learning is illustrated by the challenges captive-
bred animals face when introduced to the wild. After being bred and raised in captiv-
ity, 11 Mexican gray wolves—extinct in the United States since 1977—were released
in Arizona's Apache National Forest in 1998. Eight months later, a lone survivor was
recaptured. The pen-reared wolves had learned how to hunt—and to move 100 feet
away from people—but had not learned to run from a human with a gun. Their story
is not unusual. Twentieth-century records document 145 reintroductions of 115
species. Of those, only 11 percent produced self-sustaining populations in the wild.
Successful adaptation requires both nature (the needed genetic predispositions) and
nurture (a history of appropriate learning).

Conditioning is the process of learning associations. In *classical conditioning,* we
learn to associate two stimuli and thus to anticipate events. We learn that a flash of
lightning signals an impending crack of thunder, so when lightning flashes nearby,
we start to brace ourselves (**FIGURE 7.1**).

In *operant conditioning,* we learn to associate a response (our behavior) and its
consequence and thus to repeat acts followed by good results (**FIGURE 7.2**) and avoid
acts followed by bad results.

FIGURE 7.1 Classical conditioning

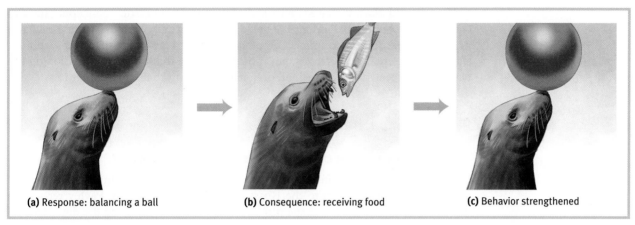

(a) Response: balancing a ball   (b) Consequence: receiving food   (c) Behavior strengthened

FIGURE 7.2 **Operant conditioning**

To simplify, we will explore these two types of associative learning separately. Often they occur together, as on one Japanese cattle ranch, where the clever rancher outfitted his herd with electronic pagers, which he calls from his cell phone. After a week of training, the animals learn to associate two stimuli—the beep on their pager and the arrival of food (classical conditioning). But they also learn to associate their hustling to the food trough with the pleasure of eating (operant conditioning).

The concept of association by conditioning provokes questions: What principles influence the learning and the loss of associations? How can these principles be applied? And what really are the associations: Does the beep on a steer's pager evoke a mental representation of food, to which the steer responds by coming to the trough? Or does it make little sense to explain conditioned associations in terms of cognition? (In Chapter 8, Memory, we will see how the brain stores and retrieves learning.)

Conditioning is not the only form of learning. Through *observational learning,* we learn from others' experiences. Chimpanzees, too, may learn behaviors merely by watching others perform them. If one sees another solve a puzzle and gain a food reward, the observer may perform the trick more quickly.

By conditioning and by observation we humans learn and adapt to our environments. We learn to expect and prepare for significant events such as food or pain *(classical conditioning).* We also learn to repeat acts that bring good results and to avoid acts that bring bad results *(operant conditioning).* By watching others we learn new behaviors *(observational learning).* And through language, we also learn things we have neither experienced nor observed.

Classical Conditioning

For many people, the name Ivan Pavlov (1849–1936) rings a bell. His early-twentieth-century experiments—now psychology's most famous research—are classics, and the phenomenon he explored we justly call **classical conditioning.**

Pavlov's work also laid the foundation for many of psychologist John B. Watson's ideas, which influenced North American psychology during the first half of the twentieth century, in a movement called **behaviorism.** In searching for laws underlying learning, Watson (1913) urged his colleagues to discard reference to inner thoughts, feelings, and motives. The science of psychology should instead study how organisms respond to stimuli in their environments, said Watson: "Its theoretical goal is the prediction and control of behavior. Introspection forms no essential part of its methods." Simply said, psychology should be an objective science based on observable behavior.

associative learning learning that certain events occur together. The events may be two stimuli (as in classical conditioning) or a response and its consequences (as in operant conditioning).

classical conditioning a type of learning in which one learns to link two or more stimuli and anticipate events.

behaviorism the view that psychology (1) should be an objective science that (2) studies behavior without reference to mental processes. Most research psychologists today agree with (1) but not with (2).

Watson and Pavlov shared both a disdain for "mentalistic" concepts (such as consciousness) and a belief that the basic laws of learning were the same for all animals, whether dogs or humans. Few researchers today propose that psychology should ignore mental processes, but most now agree that classical conditioning is a basic form of learning by which all organisms adapt to their environment.

Pavlov's Experiments

2: **How does a neutral stimulus become a conditioned stimulus?**

Pavlov was driven by a lifelong passion for research. After setting aside his initial plan to follow his father into the Russian Orthodox priesthood, Pavlov received a medical degree at age 33 and spent the next two decades studying the digestive system. This work earned him Russia's first Nobel Prize in 1904. But it was his novel experiments on learning, to which he devoted the last three decades of his life, that earned this feisty scientist his place in history.

Ivan Pavlov "Experimental investigation . . . should lay a solid foundation for a future true science of psychology" (1927).

Pavlov's new direction came when his creative mind seized on an incidental observation. Without fail, putting food in a dog's mouth caused the animal to salivate. Moreover, the dog began salivating not only to the taste of the food, but also to the mere sight of the food, or the food dish, or the person delivering the food, or even the sound of that person's approaching footsteps. At first, Pavlov considered these "psychic secretions" an annoyance—until he realized they pointed to a simple but important form of learning.

Pavlov and his assistants tried to imagine what the dog was thinking and feeling as it drooled in anticipation of the food. This only led them into fruitless debates. So, to explore the phenomenon more objectively, they experimented. To eliminate other possible influences, they isolated the dog in a small room, secured it in a harness, and attached a device to divert its saliva to a measuring instrument. From the next room, they presented food—first by sliding in a food bowl, later by blowing meat powder into the dog's mouth at a precise moment. They then paired various **neutral stimuli (NS)**—events the dog could see or hear but didn't associate with food—with food in the dog's mouth. If a sight or sound regularly signaled the arrival of food, would the dog learn the link? If so, would it begin salivating in anticipation of the food?

The answers proved to be *yes* and *yes.* Just before placing food in the dog's mouth to produce salivation, Pavlov sounded a tone. After several pairings of tone and food, the dog, anticipating the meat powder, began salivating to the tone alone. In later experiments, a buzzer, a light, a touch on the leg, even the sight of a circle set off the drooling.[1] (This procedure works with people, too. When hungry young Londoners viewed abstract figures before smelling peanut butter or vanilla, their brain soon responded in anticipation to the abstract images alone [Gottfried et al., 2003]).

Because salivation in response to food in the mouth was unlearned, Pavlov called it an **unconditioned response (UR).** Food in the mouth automatically, *unconditionally,* triggers a dog's salivary reflex (**FIGURE 7.3**). Thus, Pavlov called the food stimulus an **unconditioned stimulus (US).**

neutral stimulus (NS) in classical conditioning, a stimulus that elicits no response before conditioning.

unconditioned response (UR) in classical conditioning, the unlearned, naturally occurring response to the unconditioned stimulus (US), such as salivation when food is in the mouth.

unconditioned stimulus (US) in classical conditioning, a stimulus that unconditionally—naturally and automatically—triggers a response.

conditioned response (CR) in classical conditioning, the learned response to a previously neutral (but now conditioned) stimulus (CS).

conditioned stimulus (CS) in classical conditioning, a previously neutral stimulus that, after association with an unconditioned stimulus (US), comes to trigger a conditioned response.

[1]The "buzzer" (English translation) was perhaps Pavlov's supposed bell—a small electric bell (Tully, 2003).

BEFORE CONDITIONING

An unconditioned stimulus (US) produces an unconditioned response (UR).

A neutral stimulus (NS) produces no salivation response.

DURING CONDITIONING

AFTER CONDITIONING

The unconditioned stimulus is repeatedly presented just after the neutral stimulus. The unconditioned stimulus continues to produce an unconditioned response.

The previously neutral stimulus alone now produces a conditioned response (CR), thereby becoming a conditioned stimulus (CS).

FIGURE 7.3 Pavlov's classic experiment
During conditioning, Pavlov presented a neutral stimulus (a tone) just before an unconditioned stimulus (food in mouth). The neutral stimulus then became a conditioned stimulus, producing a conditioned response.

Salivation in response to the tone was conditional upon the dog's learning the association between the tone and the food. Today we call this learned response the **conditioned response (CR).** The previously neutral (in this context) tone stimulus that now triggered the conditional salivation we call the **conditioned stimulus (CS).** Distinguishing these two kinds of stimuli and responses is easy: Conditioned = learned; *un*conditioned = *un*learned.

Let's check your understanding with a second example. An experimenter sounds a tone just before delivering an air puff to your blinking eye. After several repetitions, you blink to the tone alone. What is the NS? The US? The UR? The CS? The CR?[2]

If Pavlov's demonstration of associative learning was so simple, what did he do for the next three decades? What discoveries did his research factory publish in his 532 papers on salivary conditioning (Windholz, 1997)? He and his associates explored five major conditioning processes: *acquisition, extinction, spontaneous recovery, generalization,* and *discrimination.*

PEANUTS

[2]NS = tone before procedure; US = air puff; UR = blink to air puff; CS = tone after procedure; CR = blink to tone

Acquisition

3: In classical conditioning, what are the processes of acquisition, extinction, spontaneous recovery, generalization, and discrimination?

To understand the **acquisition,** or initial learning, of the stimulus-response relationship, Pavlov and his associates had to confront the question of timing: How much time should elapse between presenting the neutral stimulus (the tone, the light, the touch) and the unconditioned stimulus? In most cases, not much—half a second usually works well.

What do you suppose would happen if the food (US) appeared before the tone (NS) rather than after? Would conditioning occur?

Not likely. With but a few exceptions, conditioning doesn't happen when the NS follows the US. Remember, classical conditioning is biologically adaptive because it helps humans and other animals *prepare* for good or bad events. To Pavlov's dogs, the originally neutral tone (NS) becomes a (CS) after signaling an important biological event—the arrival of food (US). To deer in the forest, the snapping of a twig (CS) may signal a predator's approach (US). If the good or bad event had already occurred, the stimulus would not likely signal anything significant.

Michael Domjan (1992, 1994, 2005) showed how a CS can signal another important biological event, by conditioning the sexual arousal of male Japanese quail. Just before presenting an approachable female, the researchers turned on a red light. Over time, as the red light continued to herald the female's arrival, the light caused the male quail to become excited. They developed a preference for their cage's red-light district, and when a female appeared, they mated with her more quickly and released more semen and sperm (Matthews et al., 2007). All in all, the quail's capacity for classical conditioning gives it a reproductive edge. Again we see the larger lesson: *Conditioning helps an animal survive and reproduce—by responding to cues that help it gain food, avoid dangers, locate mates, and produce offspring* (Hollis, 1997).

In humans, too, objects, smells, and sights associated with sexual pleasure—even a geometric figure in one experiment—can become conditioned stimuli for sexual arousal (Byrne, 1982). Psychologist Michael Tirrell (1990) recalled: "My first girlfriend loved onions, so I came to associate onion breath with kissing. Before long, onion breath sent tingles up and down my spine. Oh what a feeling!" (**FIGURE 7.4**).

Through **higher-order conditioning,** a new neutral stimulus can become a new conditioned stimulus. All that's required is for it to become associated with a

Check yourself: If the aroma of cake baking sets your mouth to watering, what is the US? The CS? The CR? See inverted answer below.

Remember:
US = *Unconditioned **S**timulus*
UR = *Unconditioned **R**esponse*
CS = *Conditioned **S**timulus*
CR = *Conditioned **R**esponse*

The cake (and its taste) are the US. The associated aroma is the CS. Salivation to the associated aroma is the CR.

acquisition in classical conditioning, the initial stage, when one links a neutral stimulus and an unconditioned stimulus so that the neutral stimulus begins triggering the conditioned response. In operant conditioning, the strengthening of a reinforced response.

higher-order conditioning a procedure in which the conditioned stimulus in one conditioning experience is paired with a new neutral stimulus, creating a second (often weaker) conditioned stimulus. For example, an animal that has learned that a tone predicts food might then learn that a light predicts the tone and begin responding to the light alone. (Also called *second-order conditioning.*)

extinction the diminishing of a conditioned response; occurs in classical conditioning when an unconditioned stimulus (US) does not follow a conditioned stimulus (CS); occurs in operant conditioning when a response is no longer reinforced.

spontaneous recovery the reappearance, after a pause, of an extinguished conditioned response.

generalization the tendency, once a response has been conditioned, for stimuli similar to the conditioned stimulus to elicit similar responses.

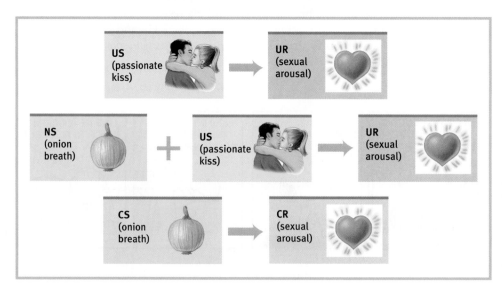

FIGURE 7.4 An unexpected CS Onion breath does not usually produce sexual arousal. But when repeatedly paired with a passionate kiss, it can become a CS and do just that.

previously conditioned stimulus. If a tone regularly signals food and produces salivation, then a light that becomes associated with the tone may also begin to trigger salivation. Although this higher-order conditioning (also called *second-order conditioning*) tends to be weaker than first-stage conditioning, it influences our everyday lives. Imagine that something makes us very afraid (perhaps a guard dog associated with a previous dog bite). If something else, such as the sound of a barking dog, brings to mind that guard dog, the bark alone may make us feel a little afraid.

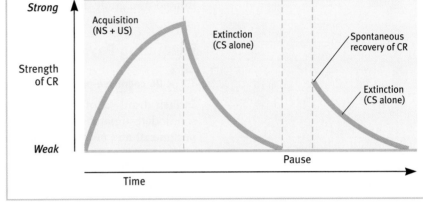

Extinction and Spontaneous Recovery

After conditioning, what happens if the CS occurs repeatedly without the US? Will the CS continue to elicit the CR? Pavlov discovered that when he sounded the tone again and again without presenting food, the dogs salivated less and less. Their declining salivation illustrates **extinction,** the diminished responding that occurs when the CS (tone) no longer signals an impending US (food).

Pavlov found, however, that if he allowed several hours to elapse before sounding the tone again, the salivation to the tone would reappear spontaneously (**FIGURE 7.5**). This **spontaneous recovery**—the reappearance of a (weakened) CR after a pause—suggested to Pavlov that extinction was suppressing the CR rather than eliminating it.

After breaking up with his fire-breathing heartthrob, Tirrell also experienced extinction and spontaneous recovery. He recalls that "the smell of onion breath (CS), no longer paired with the kissing (US), lost its ability to shiver my timbers. Occasionally, though, after not sensing the aroma for a long while, smelling onion breath awakens a small version of the emotional response I once felt."

Generalization

Pavlov and his students noticed that a dog conditioned to the sound of one tone also responded somewhat to the sound of a different tone that had never been paired with food. Likewise, a dog conditioned to salivate when rubbed would also drool a bit when scratched (Windholz, 1989) or when touched on a different body part. This tendency to respond to stimuli similar to the CS is called **generalization.**

Generalization can be adaptive, as when toddlers taught to fear moving cars also become afraid of moving trucks and motorcycles. So automatic is generalization that one Argentine writer who underwent torture still recoils with fear when he sees black shoes—his first glimpse of his torturers as they approached his cell. Generalization of anxiety reactions has been demonstrated in laboratory studies comparing abused with nonabused children (**FIGURE 7.6**). Shown an angry face on a computer screen, abused children's brain-wave responses are dramatically stronger and longer lasting (Pollak et al., 1998).

Because of generalization, stimuli similar to naturally disgusting or appealing objects will, by association, evoke some disgust or liking. Normally desirable foods, such as fudge, are unappealing when shaped to resemble dog feces (Rozin et al., 1986). Adults with childlike facial features (round face, large forehead, small chin, large eyes) are perceived as having childlike warmth, submissiveness, and naiveté (Berry & McArthur, 1986). In both cases, people's emotional reactions to one stimulus generalize to similar stimuli.

FIGURE 7.5 Idealized curve of acquisition, extinction, and spontaneous recovery The rising curve shows that the CR rapidly grows stronger as the NS and US are repeatedly paired *(acquisition)*, then weakens as the CS is presented alone *(extinction)*. After a pause, the CR reappears *(spontaneous recovery)*.

Stimulus generalization

"I don't care if she's a tape dispenser. I love her."

FIGURE 7.6 Child abuse leaves tracks in the brain Seth Pollak (University of Wisconsin–Madison) reports that abused children's sensitized brains react more strongly to angry faces. This generalized anxiety response may help explain why child abuse puts children at greater risk of psychological disorder.

discrimination in classical conditioning, the learned ability to distinguish between a conditioned stimulus and stimuli that do not signal an unconditioned stimulus.

"All brains are, in essence, anticipation machines."

—Daniel C. Dennett,
Consciousness Explained, 1991

Discrimination

Pavlov's dogs also learned to respond to the sound of a particular tone and *not* to other tones. **Discrimination** is the learned ability to *distinguish* between a conditioned stimulus (which predicts the US) and other irrelevant stimuli. Being able to recognize differences is adaptive. Slightly different stimuli can be followed by vastly different consequences. Confronted by a guard dog, your heart may race; confronted by a guide dog, it probably will not.

Extending Pavlov's Understanding

4: Do cognitive processes and biological constraints affect classical conditioning?

In their dismissal of "mentalistic" concepts such as consciousness, Pavlov and Watson underestimated the importance of *cognitive processes* (thoughts, perceptions, expectations) and *biological constraints* on an organism's learning capacity.

Cognitive Processes

The early behaviorists believed that rats' and dogs' learned behaviors could be reduced to mindless mechanisms, so there was no need to consider cognition. But Robert Rescorla and Allan Wagner (1972) explained why an animal can learn the *predictability* of an event. If a shock always is preceded by a tone, and then may also be preceded by a light that accompanies the tone, a rat will react with fear to the tone but not to the light. The tone is a better predictor, and the more predictable the association, the stronger the conditioned response. It's as if the animal learns an *expectancy*, an awareness of how likely it is that the US will occur.

Such experiments help explain why classical conditioning treatments that ignore cognition often have limited success. For example, people receiving therapy for alcohol dependency may be given alcohol spiked with a nauseating drug. Will they then associate alcohol with sickness? If classical conditioning were merely a matter of "stamping in" stimulus associations, we might hope so, and to some extent this does occur (as we will see in Chapter 14). However, the awareness that the nausea is induced by the drug, not the alcohol, often weakens the association between drinking alcohol and feeling sick. So, even in classical conditioning, it is (especially with humans) not simply the CS–US association but also the thought that counts.

Biological Predispositions

Ever since Charles Darwin, scientists have assumed that all animals share a common evolutionary history and thus commonalities in their makeup and functioning. Pavlov and Watson, for example, believed that the basic laws of learning were essentially similar in all animals. So it should make little difference whether one studied pigeons or people. Moreover, it seemed that any natural response could be conditioned to any neutral stimulus. As learning researcher Gregory Kimble proclaimed in 1956, "Just about any activity of which the organism is capable can be conditioned and . . . these responses can be conditioned to any stimulus that the organism can perceive" (p. 195).

Twenty-five years later, Kimble (1981) humbly acknowledged that "half a thousand" scientific reports had proven him wrong. More than the early behaviorists realized, an animal's capacity for conditioning is constrained by its biology. Each species' predispositions prepare it to learn the associations that enhance its survival. Environments are not the whole story.

John Garcia was among those who challenged the prevailing idea that all associations can be learned equally well. While researching the effects of radiation on laboratory animals, Garcia and Robert Koelling (1966) noticed that rats began to avoid drinking water from the plastic bottles in radiation chambers. Could classical conditioning be the culprit? Might the rats have linked the plastic-tasting water (a CS) to the sickness (UR) triggered by the radiation (US)?

To test their hunch, Garcia and Koelling gave the rats a particular taste, sight, or sound and later also gave them radiation or drugs (US) that led to nausea and vomiting (UR). Two startling findings emerged: First, even if sickened as late as several hours after tasting a particular novel flavor, the rats thereafter avoided that flavor. This appeared to violate the notion that for conditioning to occur, the US must immediately follow the CS.

Second, the sickened rats developed aversions to tastes but not to sights or sounds. This contradicted the behaviorists' idea that any perceivable stimulus could serve as a CS. But it made adaptive sense, because for rats the easiest way to identify tainted food is to taste it. (If sickened after sampling a new food, they thereafter avoid the food—which makes it difficult to eradicate a population of "bait-shy" rats by poisoning.)

Humans, too, seem biologically prepared to learn some associations rather than others. If you become violently ill four hours after eating contaminated mussels, you will probably develop an aversion to the taste of mussels but not to the sight of the associated restaurant, its plates, the people you were with, or the music you heard there. In contrast, birds, which hunt by sight, appear biologically primed to develop aversions to the *sight* of tainted food (Nicolaus et al., 1983). Organisms are predisposed to learn associations that help them adapt.

Garcia and Koelling's taste-aversion research is but one instance in which psychological experiments that began with the discomfort of some laboratory animals ended by enhancing the welfare of many others. In one well-known conditioned taste-aversion study, coyotes and wolves that were tempted into eating sheep carcasses laced with a sickening poison developed an aversion to sheep meat (Gustavson et al., 1974, 1976). Two wolves later penned with a live sheep seemed actually to fear it. The study not only saved the sheep from their predators, but also saved the sheep-shunning coyotes and wolves from angry ranchers and farmers who had wanted to destroy them. Later applications of Garcia and Koelling's findings have prevented baboons from raiding African gardens, raccoons from attacking chickens, and ravens and crows from feeding on crane eggs—all while preserving predators who occupy an important ecological niche (Garcia & Gustavson, 1997).

All these cases support Darwin's principle that natural selection favors traits that aid survival. Our ancestors who readily learned taste aversions were unlikely to eat the same toxic food again and were more likely to survive and leave descendants. Nausea, like anxiety, pain, and other bad feelings, serves a good purpose. Like a low-oil warning on a car dashboard, each alerts the body to a threat (Neese, 1991).

The discovery of biological constraints affirms the value of the biopsychosocial approach, which considers different perspectives, including biological and cognitive influences (see **FIGURE 7.7** on the next page), in seeking to understand phenomena such as learning. Responding to stimuli that announce significant events, such as food or pain, is adaptive. So is a genetic predisposition to associate a CS with a US

John Garcia As the laboring son of California farmworkers, Garcia attended school only in the off-season during his early childhood years. After entering junior college in his late twenties, and earning his Ph.D. in his late forties, he received the American Psychological Association's Distinguished Scientific Contribution Award "for his highly original, pioneering research in conditioning and learning." He was also elected to the National Academy of Sciences.

Taste aversion If you became violently ill after eating mussels, you probably would have a hard time eating them again. Their smell and taste would have become a CS for nausea. This learning occurs readily because our biology prepares us to learn taste aversions to toxic foods.

"Once bitten, twice shy."
—G. F. Northall, *Folk-Phrases,* 1894

"All animals are on a voyage through time, navigating toward futures that promote their survival and away from futures that threaten it. Pleasure and pain are the stars by which they steer."
—Psychologists Daniel T. Gilbert and Timothy D. Wilson, "Prospection: Experiencing the Future," 2007

FIGURE 7.7 Biopsychosocial influences on learning Today's learning theorists recognize that our learning results not only from environmental experiences, but also from cognitive and biological influences.

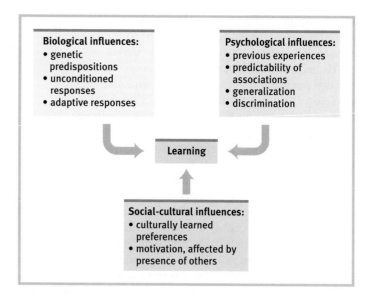

Biological influences:
- genetic predispositions
- unconditioned responses
- adaptive responses

Psychological influences:
- previous experiences
- predictability of associations
- generalization
- discrimination

Learning

Social-cultural influences:
- culturally learned preferences
- motivation, affected by presence of others

Courtesy of Kathryn Brownson, Hope College

FIGURE 7.8 Romantic red In a series of experiments that controlled for other factors (such as the brightness of the image), men (but not women) found women more attractive and sexually desirable when framed in red (Elliot & Niesta, 2008).

that follows predictably and immediately: Causes often immediately precede effects. So once again, we see an important principle at work: *Learning enables organisms to adapt to their environment.*

This may help explain why we humans seem to be naturally disposed to learn associations between the color red and women's sexuality, note Andrew Elliot and Daniela Niesta (2008). Female primates display red when nearing ovulation. In human females, enhanced bloodflow produces the red blush of flirtation and sexual excitation. Does the frequent pairing of red and sex—with Valentine's hearts, red-light districts, and red lipstick—naturally enhance men's attraction to women? Elliot and Niesta's experiments consistently suggest that, without men's awareness, it does (**FIGURE 7.8**).

Pavlov's Legacy

5: Why is Pavlov's work important?

What remains of Pavlov's ideas? A great deal. Most psychologists agree that classical conditioning is a basic form of learning. Judged by today's knowledge of cognitive processes and biological predispositions, Pavlov's ideas were incomplete. But if we see further than Pavlov did, it is because we stand on his shoulders.

Why does Pavlov's work remain so important? If he had merely taught us that old dogs can learn new tricks, his experiments would long ago have been forgotten. Why should we care that dogs can be conditioned to salivate at the sound of a tone? The importance lies first in this finding: *Many other responses to many other stimuli can be classically conditioned in many other organisms*—in fact, in every species tested, from earthworms to fish to dogs to monkeys to people (Schwartz, 1984). Thus, classical conditioning is one way that virtually all organisms learn to adapt to their environment.

Second, *Pavlov showed us how a process such as learning can be studied objectively.* He was proud that his methods involved virtually no subjective judgments or guesses about what went on in a dog's mind. The salivary response is a behavior measurable in cubic centimeters of saliva. Pavlov's success therefore suggested a scientific model for how the young discipline of psychology might proceed—by isolating the basic building blocks of complex behaviors and studying them with objective laboratory procedures.

Applications of Classical Conditioning

6: **What have been some applications of classical conditioning?**

Other chapters in this text—on consciousness, motivation, emotion, health, psychological disorders, and therapy—show how Pavlov's principles of classical conditioning apply to human health and well-being. Two examples:

- Former drug users often feel a craving when they are again in the drug-using context—with people or in places they associate with previous highs. Thus, drug counselors advise addicts to steer clear of people and settings that may trigger these cravings (Siegel, 2005).
- Classical conditioning even works on the body's disease-fighting immune system. When a particular taste accompanies a drug that influences immune responses, the taste by itself may come to produce an immune response (Ader & Cohen, 1985).

Pavlov's work also provided a basis for John Watson's (1913) idea that human emotions and behaviors, though biologically influenced, are mainly a bundle of conditioned responses. Working with an 11-month-old named Albert, Watson and Rosalie Rayner (1920; Harris, 1979) showed how specific fears might be conditioned. Like most infants, "Little Albert" feared loud noises but not white rats. Watson and Rayner presented a white rat and, as Little Albert reached to touch it, struck a hammer against a steel bar just behind his head. After seven repeats of seeing the rat and hearing the frightening noise, Albert burst into tears at the mere sight of the rat (an ethically troublesome study by today's standards). What is more, five days later Albert showed generalization of his conditioned response by reacting with fear to a rabbit, a dog, and a sealskin coat, but not to dissimilar objects such as toys.

Although Little Albert's fate is unknown, Watson's is not. After losing his professorship at Johns Hopkins University over an affair with Rayner (whom he later married), he became the J. Walter Thompson advertising agency's resident psychologist. There he used his knowledge of associative learning to conceive many successful campaigns, including one for Maxwell House that helped make the "coffee break" an American custom (Hunt, 1993).

Some psychologists, noting that Albert's fear wasn't learned quickly, had difficulty repeating Watson and Rayner's findings with other children. Nevertheless, Little Albert's case has had legendary significance for many psychologists. Some have wondered if each of us might not be a walking repository of conditioned emotions. Might extinction procedures or even new conditioning help us change our unwanted responses to emotion-arousing stimuli? One patient, who for 30 years had feared going into an elevator alone, did just that. Following his therapist's advice, he forced himself to enter 20 elevators a day. Within 10 days, his fear had nearly vanished (Ellis & Becker, 1982). In Chapters 13 and 14 we will see more examples of how psychologists use behavioral techniques to treat emotional disorders and promote personal growth.

"[Psychology's] factual and theoretical developments in this century—which have changed the study of mind and behavior as radically as genetics changed the study of heredity—have all been the product of objective analysis—that is to say, behavioristic analysis."

—Psychologist Donald Hebb (1980)

In Watson and Rayner's experiment, what was the US? The UR? The NS? The CS? The CR? See inverted answer below.

The US was the loud noise; the UR was the startled fear response; the NS was the rat before it was paired with the loud noise; the CS was the rat after being paired with the noise; the CR was fear.

John B. Watson Watson (1924) admitted to "going beyond my facts" when offering his famous boast: "Give me a dozen healthy infants, well-formed, and my own specified world to bring them up in and I'll guarantee to take any one at random and train him to become any type of specialist I might select—doctor, lawyer, artist, merchant-chief, and, yes, even beggar-man and thief, regardless of his talents, penchants, tendencies, abilities, vocations, and race of his ancestors."

REHEARSE IT!

1. *Learning* is defined as "a relatively permanent change in an organism's behavior due to
   a. instinct."
   b. mental processes."
   c. experience."
   d. formal education."

2. Two forms of associative learning are classical conditioning, in which the organism associates _____, and operant conditioning, in which the organism associates _____.
   a. two responses; a response and a consequence
   b. two stimuli; two responses
   c. two stimuli; a response and a consequence
   d. two responses; two stimuli

3. In Pavlov's experiments, dogs learned to salivate in response to a tone. The tone is therefore a(an)
   a. conditioned stimulus.
   b. unconditioned stimulus.
   c. neutral stimulus.
   d. unconditioned response.

4. Dogs can learn to respond (by salivating, for example) to one kind of stimulus (a circle, for example) and not to another (a square). This process is an example of
   a. generalization.
   b. discrimination.
   c. acquisition.
   d. spontaneous recovery.

5. Early behaviorists believed that for conditioning to occur, the unconditioned stimulus (US) must immediately follow the neutral stimulus (NS). _____ demonstrated this was not always so.
   a. The Little Albert experiment
   b. Pavlov's experiments with dogs
   c. Watson's behaviorism theory
   d. Garcia and Koelling's taste-aversion studies

6. Taste-aversion research has shown that animals develop aversions to certain tastes but not to sights or sounds. This finding supports
   a. Pavlov's demonstration of generalization.
   b. Darwin's principle that natural selection favors traits that aid survival.
   c. Watson's view that study should be limited to observable behavior.
   d. the early behaviorists' view that organisms can be conditioned to any stimulus.

7. After Watson and Rayner classically conditioned a small child named Albert to fear a white rat, the child later showed fear in response to a rabbit, a dog, and a sealskin coat. Little Albert's fear of objects resembling the rat illustrates
   a. extinction.
   b. generalization.
   c. spontaneous recovery.
   d. discrimination between two stimuli.

Answers: 1. c, 2. c, 3. a, 4. b, 5. d, 6. b, 7. b.

Operant Conditioning

7: What is operant conditioning, and how does it differ from classical conditioning?

It's one thing to classically condition a dog to salivate at the sound of a tone, or a child to fear moving cars. To teach an elephant to walk on its hind legs or a child to say *please*, we must turn to another type of learning—operant conditioning.

Classical conditioning and operant conditioning are both forms of associative learning, yet their difference is straightforward:

- *Classical conditioning* forms associations between stimuli (a CS and the US it signals). It also involves **respondent behavior**—actions that are automatic responses to a stimulus (such as salivating in response to meat powder and later in response to a tone).
- In **operant conditioning,** organisms associate their own actions with consequences. Actions followed by reinforcers increase; those followed by punishers decrease. Behavior that *operates* on the environment to *produce* rewarding or punishing stimuli is called **operant behavior.**

We can therefore distinguish classical from operant conditioning by asking: *Is the organism learning associations between events it does not control* (classical conditioning)? *Or is it learning associations between its behavior and resulting events* (operant conditioning)?

Skinner's Experiments

B. F. Skinner (1904–1990) was a college English major and an aspiring writer who, seeking a new direction, entered graduate school in psychology. He went on to become modern behaviorism's most influential and controversial figure. Skinner's

---

respondent behavior behavior that occurs as an automatic response to some stimulus.

operant conditioning a type of learning in which behavior is strengthened if followed by a reinforcer or diminished if followed by a punisher.

operant behavior behavior that operates on the environment, producing consequences.

law of effect Thorndike's principle that behaviors followed by favorable consequences become more likely.

operant chamber in operant conditioning research, a chamber (also known as a *Skinner box*) containing a bar or key that an animal can manipulate to obtain a food or water reinforcer; attached devices record the animal's rate of bar pressing or key pecking.

shaping an operant conditioning procedure in which reinforcers guide behavior toward closer and closer approximations of the desired behavior.

FIGURE 7.9 Cat in a puzzle box Thorndike (1898) used a fish reward to entice cats to find their way out of a puzzle box (right) through a series of maneuvers. The cats' performance tended to improve with successive trials (left), illustrating Thorndike's *law of effect*. (Adapted from Thorndike, 1898.)

work elaborated what psychologist Edward L. Thorndike (1874–1949) called the **law of effect:** Rewarded behavior is likely to recur (**FIGURE 7.9**). Using Thorndike's law of effect as a starting point, Skinner developed a *behavioral technology* that revealed principles of *behavior control*. These principles also enabled him to teach pigeons such unpigeonlike behaviors as walking in a figure 8, playing Ping-Pong, and keeping a missile on course by pecking at a screen target.

For his pioneering studies, Skinner designed an **operant chamber,** popularly known as a *Skinner box* (**FIGURE 7.10**). The box has a bar (a lever) that an animal presses—or a key (a disc) that an animal pecks—to release a reward of food or water, and a device that records these responses. Operant conditioning experiments have done far more than teach us how to pull habits out of a rat. They have explored the precise conditions that foster efficient and enduring learning.

FIGURE 7.10 A Skinner box Inside the box, the rat presses a bar for a food reward. Outside, a measuring device (not shown here) records the animal's accumulated responses.

Shaping Behavior

In his experiments, Skinner used **shaping,** a procedure in which *reinforcers,* such as food, gradually guide an animal's actions toward a desired behavior. Imagine that you wanted to condition a hungry rat to press a bar. First, you would watch how the animal naturally behaves, so that you could build on its existing behaviors. You might give the rat a food reward each time it approaches the bar. Once the rat is approaching regularly, you would require it to move closer before rewarding it, then closer still. Finally, you would require it to touch the bar before you gave it the food. With this method of *successive approximations,* you reward responses that are ever-closer to the final desired behavior, and you ignore all other responses. By making rewards contingent on desired behaviors, researchers and animal trainers gradually shape complex behaviors.

Shaping can also help us understand what nonverbal organisms perceive. Can a dog distinguish red and green? Can a baby hear the difference between lower- and higher-pitched tones?

Shaping rats to save lives A Gambian giant pouched rat, having been shaped to sniff out land mines, receives a bite of banana after successfully locating a mine during training in Mozambique.

A discriminating creature University of Windsor psychologist Dale Woodyard uses a food reward to train this manatee to discriminate between objects of different shapes, colors, and sizes. Manatees remember such responses for a year or more.

If we can shape them to respond to one stimulus and not to another, then we know they can perceive the difference. Such experiments have even shown that some animals can form concepts. If an experimenter reinforces a pigeon for pecking after seeing a human face, but not after seeing other images, the pigeon learns to recognize human faces (Herrnstein & Loveland, 1964). In this experiment, a face is a *discriminative stimulus;* like a green traffic light, it signals that a response will be reinforced. After being trained to discriminate among flowers, people, cars, and chairs, pigeons can usually identify the category in which a new pictured object belongs (Bhatt et al., 1988; Wasserman, 1993). They have even been trained to discriminate between Bach's music and Stravinsky's (Porter & Neuringer, 1984).

In everyday life, we continually reward and shape others' behavior, said Skinner, but we often do so unintentionally. Billy's whining, for example, annoys his mystified parents, but look how they typically deal with Billy:

> **Billy:** *Could you tie my shoes?*
> **Father:** (Continues reading paper.)
> **Billy:** *Dad, I need my shoes tied.*
> **Father:** *Uh, yeah, just a minute.*
> **Billy:** *DAAAAD! TIE MY SHOES!*
> **Father:** *How many times have I told you not to whine? Now, which shoe do we do first?*

Billy's whining is reinforced, because he gets something desirable—his dad's attention. Dad's response is reinforced because it gets rid of something aversive—Billy's whining.

Or consider a teacher who pastes gold stars on a wall chart after the names of children scoring 100 percent on spelling tests. As everyone can then see, some children consistently do perfect work. The others, who take the same test and may have worked harder than the academic all-stars, get no rewards. The teacher would be better advised to apply the principles of operant conditioning—to reinforce all spellers for gradual improvements (successive approximations toward perfect spelling of words they find challenging).

HI AND LOIS

Types of Reinforcers

8: **What are the basic types of reinforcers?**

People often refer rather loosely to the power of "rewards." This idea gains a more precise meaning in Skinner's concept of a **reinforcer:** any event that strengthens (increases the frequency of) a preceding response. A reinforcer may be a tangible reward, such as food or money. It may be praise or attention—even being yelled at, for a child hungry for attention. Or it may be an activity—borrowing the family car after doing the dishes, or taking a break after an hour of study.

Although anything that serves to increase behavior is a reinforcer, reinforcers vary with circumstances. What's reinforcing to one person (rock concert tickets) may not be to another. What's reinforcing in one situation (food when hungry) may not be in another.

reinforcer in operant conditioning, any event that *strengthens* the behavior it follows.

positive reinforcement increasing behaviors by presenting positive stimuli, such as food. A positive reinforcer is any stimulus that, when *presented* after a response, strengthens the response.

negative reinforcement increasing behaviors by stopping or reducing negative stimuli. A negative reinforcer is any stimulus that, when *removed* after a response, strengthens the response. (Note: negative reinforcement is not punishment.)

primary reinforcer an innately reinforcing stimulus, such as one that satisfies a biological need.

conditioned reinforcer a stimulus that gains its reinforcing power through its association with a primary reinforcer; also known as a *secondary reinforcer.*

TABLE 7.1 **Ways to Increase Behavior**

Operant Conditioning Term	Description	Examples
Positive reinforcement	Add a desirable stimulus	Getting a hug; receiving a paycheck
Negative reinforcement	Remove an aversive stimulus	Fastening seatbelt to turn off beeping

Positive reinforcement A heat lamp positively reinforces this Taronga Zoo meerkat's behavior during a cold snap in Sydney, Australia.

Up to now, we've really been discussing **positive reinforcement,** which strengthens a response by *presenting* a typically pleasurable stimulus after a response. But there are *two* basic kinds of reinforcement (**TABLE 7.1**). **Negative reinforcement** *strengthens* a response by *reducing* or *removing* something undesirable or unpleasant, as when an organism escapes an aversive situation. Taking aspirin may relieve your headache, and pushing the snooze button will silence your annoying alarm. These welcome results (end of pain, end of alarm) provide negative reinforcement and increase the odds that you will repeat these behaviors. For drug addicts, the negative reinforcement of ending withdrawal pangs can be a compelling reason to resume using (Baker et al., 2004).

Note that contrary to popular usage, *negative reinforcement is not punishment.* (*Advice:* Repeat the last five words in your mind, because this is one of psychology's most often misunderstood concepts.) Rather, negative reinforcement *removes* a punishing (aversive) event.

Sometimes negative and positive reinforcement coincide. Imagine a worried student who, after goofing off and getting a bad exam grade, studies harder for the next exam. This increased effort may be negatively reinforced by reducing anxiety, and positively reinforced by receiving a better grade. Whether it works by reducing something aversive, or by giving something desirable, *reinforcement is any consequence that strengthens behavior.*

Remember whining Billy? In that example, whose behavior was positively reinforced and whose was negatively reinforced? See inverted answer below.

Billy's whining was positively reinforced, because Billy got something desirable—his father's attention. His dad's response to the whining (doing what Billy wanted) was negatively reinforced, because it got rid of Billy's annoying whining.

PRIMARY AND CONDITIONED REINFORCERS **Primary reinforcers**—getting food when hungry or having a painful headache go away—are unlearned. They are innately satisfying. **Conditioned reinforcers,** also called *secondary reinforcers,* get their power through learned association with primary reinforcers. If a rat in a Skinner box learns that a light reliably signals that food is coming, the rat will work to turn on the light. The light has become a conditioned reinforcer associated with food. Our lives are filled with conditioned reinforcers—money, good grades, a pleasant tone of voice—each of which has been linked with more basic rewards. If money is a conditioned reinforcer—if people's desire for money is derived from their desire for food—then hunger should also make people more money-hungry, reasoned one European research team (Briers et al., 2006). Indeed, in their experiments, people were less likely to donate to charity when food deprived, and less likely to share money with fellow participants when in a room with hunger-arousing aromas.

IMMEDIATE AND DELAYED REINFORCERS Let's return to the imaginary shaping experiment in which you were conditioning a rat to press a bar. Before performing this "wanted" behavior, the hungry rat will engage in a sequence of "unwanted" behaviors—scratching, sniffing, and moving around. If you present food immediately after any one of these behaviors, the rat will likely repeat that rewarded behavior. But what if the rat presses the bar while you are distracted, and you delay giving the reinforcer? If the delay lasts longer than 30 seconds, the rat will not learn to press the bar. You will have reinforced other incidental behaviors—more sniffing and moving—that intervened after the bar press.

Unlike rats, humans do respond to delayed reinforcers: the paycheck at the end of the week, the good grade at the end of the semester, the trophy at the end of the season. Indeed, to function effectively we must learn to delay gratification. In laboratory

"Oh, not bad. The light comes on, I press the bar, they write me a check. How about you?"

continuous reinforcement reinforcing the desired response every time it occurs.

partial (intermittent) reinforcement reinforcing a response only part of the time; results in slower acquisition of a response but much greater resistance to extinction than does continuous reinforcement.

fixed-ratio schedule in operant conditioning, a reinforcement schedule that reinforces a response only after a specified number of responses.

variable-ratio schedule in operant conditioning, a reinforcement schedule that reinforces a response after an unpredictable number of responses.

fixed-interval schedule in operant conditioning, a reinforcement schedule that reinforces a response only after a specified time has elapsed.

variable-interval schedule in operant conditioning, a reinforcement schedule that reinforces a response at unpredictable time intervals.

"The charm of fishing is that it is the pursuit of what is elusive but attainable, a perpetual series of occasions for hope."

—Scottish author John Buchan (1875–1940)

testing, some 4-year-olds show this ability. In choosing a candy, they prefer having a big reward tomorrow to munching on a small one right now. Learning to control our impulses in order to achieve more valued rewards is a big step toward maturity (Logue, 1998a,b). No wonder children who make such choices have tended to become socially competent and high-achieving adults (Mischel et al., 1989).

But to our detriment, small but immediate consequences (the enjoyment of watching late-night TV, for example) are sometimes more alluring than big but delayed consequences (feeling alert tomorrow). For many teens, the immediate gratification of risky, unprotected sex in passionate moments prevails over the delayed gratifications of safe sex or saved sex (Loewenstein & Furstenberg, 1991). And for too many of us, the immediate rewards of today's gas-guzzling vehicles, air travel, and air conditioning have prevailed over the bigger future consequences of global climate change, rising seas, and extreme weather.

Reinforcement Schedules

9: **How do different reinforcement schedules affect behavior?**

So far, most of our examples have assumed **continuous reinforcement:** Reinforcing the desired response every time it occurs. Under such conditions, learning occurs rapidly, which makes continuous reinforcement preferable until a behavior is mastered. But extinction also occurs rapidly. When reinforcement stops—when we stop delivering food after the rat presses the bar—the behavior soon stops. If a normally dependable candy machine fails to deliver a chocolate bar twice in a row, we stop putting money into it (although a week later we may exhibit spontaneous recovery by trying again).

Real life rarely provides continuous reinforcement. Salespeople do not make a sale with every pitch, nor do anglers get a bite with every cast. But they persist because their efforts are occasionally rewarded. This persistence is typical with **partial (intermittent) reinforcement** schedules, in which responses are sometimes reinforced, sometimes not. Although initial learning is slower, intermittent reinforcement produces greater *resistance to extinction* than is found with continuous reinforcement. Imagine a pigeon that has learned to peck a key to obtain food. When the experimenter gradually phases out the delivery of food until it occurs only rarely and unpredictably, pigeons may peck 150,000 times without a reward (Skinner, 1953). Slot machines reward gamblers in much the same way—occasionally and unpredictably. And like pigeons, slot players keep trying, time and time again. With intermittent reinforcement, hope springs eternal.

Lesson for parents: Partial reinforcement also works with children. *Occasionally* giving in to children's tantrums for the sake of peace and quiet intermittently reinforces the tantrums. This is the very best procedure for making a behavior persist.

Skinner (1961) and his collaborators compared four schedules of partial reinforcement. Some are rigidly fixed, some unpredictably variable.

Fixed-ratio schedules reinforce behavior after a set number of responses. Just as coffee shops reward us with a free drink after every 10 purchased, laboratory animals may be reinforced on a fixed ratio of, say, one reinforcer for every 30 responses. Once conditioned, the animal will pause only briefly after a reinforcer and will then return to a high rate of responding (**FIGURE 7.11**).

Variable-ratio schedules provide reinforcers after an unpredictable number of responses. This is what slot-machine players and fly-casting anglers experience— unpredictable reinforcement—and what makes gambling and fly fishing so hard to extinguish even when both are getting nothing for something. Like the fixed-ratio schedule, the variable-ratio schedule produces high rates of responding, because reinforcers increase as the number of responses increases.

Fixed-interval schedules reinforce the first response after a fixed time period. Like people checking more frequently for the mail as the delivery time approaches,

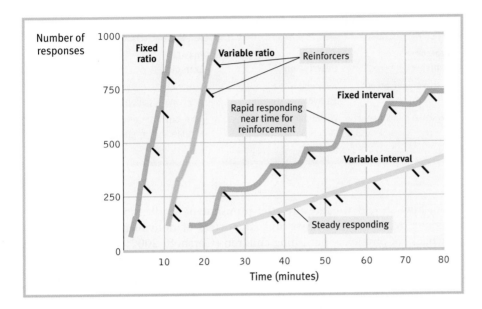

FIGURE 7.11 Intermittent reinforcement schedules Skinner's laboratory pigeons produced these response patterns to each of four reinforcement schedules. (Reinforcers are indicated by diagonal marks.) For people, as for pigeons, reinforcement linked to number of responses (a *ratio schedule*) produces a higher response rate than reinforcement linked to amount of time elapsed (an *interval schedule*). But the predictability of the reward also matters. An unpredictable (*variable*) schedule produces more consistent responding than does a predictable (*fixed*) schedule.

or checking to see if the Jell-O has set, pigeons on a fixed-interval schedule peck a key more frequently as the anticipated time for reward draws near, producing a choppy stop-start pattern (see Figure 7.11) rather than a steady rate of response.

Variable-interval schedules reinforce the first response after *varying* time intervals. Like the "You've got mail" that finally rewards persistence in rechecking for e-mail, variable-interval schedules tend to produce slow, steady responding. This makes sense, because there is no knowing when the waiting will be over (**TABLE 7.2**).

Animal behaviors differ, yet Skinner (1956) contended that the reinforcement principles of operant conditioning are universal. It matters little, he said, what response, what reinforcer, or what species you use. The effect of a given reinforcement schedule is pretty much the same: "Pigeon, rat, monkey, which is which? It doesn't matter. . . . Behavior shows astonishingly similar properties."

Door-to-door salespeople are reinforced by which schedule? People checking the oven every 2 minutes to see if the cookies are done are on which schedule? Frequent-flyer programs offering a free flight after every 25,000 travel miles are using which reinforcement schedule? See inverted answers below.

Door-to-door salespeople are reinforced on a variable-ratio schedule (after varying numbers of rings). Cookie checkers are reinforced on a fixed-interval schedule. Frequent-flyer programs use a fixed-ratio schedule.

TABLE 7.2 Schedules of Reinforcement

	Fixed	Variable
Ratio	*Every so many:* reinforcement after every *nth* behavior, such as buy 10 coffees, get 1 free, or pay per product unit produced	*After an unpredictable number:* reinforcement after a random number of behaviors, as when playing slot machines or fly-casting
Interval	*Every so often:* reinforcement for behavior after a fixed time, such as Tuesday discount prices	*Unpredictably often:* reinforcement for behavior after a random amount of time, as in checking for e-mail

Punishment

10: How does punishment affect behavior?

Reinforcement increases a behavior; **punishment** does the opposite. A *punisher* is any consequence that *decreases* the frequency of a preceding behavior (see **TABLE 7.3** on the next page).

Swift and sure punishers can powerfully restrain unwanted behavior. The rat that is shocked after touching a forbidden object and the child who loses a treat after running into the street will learn not to repeat the behavior. Some punishments, though unintentional, are nevertheless quite effective: A dog that has learned to come running at the sound of an electric can opener will stop coming if its owner starts running the machine to attract the dog and banish it to the basement.

punishment an event that *decreases* the behavior it follows.

TABLE 7.3 **Ways to Decrease Behavior**

Type of Punisher	Description	Possible Examples
Positive punishment	Administer an aversive stimulus	Spanking; receiving a parking ticket
Negative punishment	Withdraw a desirable stimulus	Time-out from privileges (such as time with friends); revoked driver's license

So, how should we interpret the punishment studies in relation to parenting practices? Many psychologists and supporters of nonviolent parenting note four drawbacks of physically punishing children (Gershoff, 2002; Marshall, 2002).

1. *Punished behavior is suppressed, not forgotten.* This suppression, though temporary, may (negatively) reinforce parents' punishing behavior. The child swears, the parent swats, the parent hears no more swearing and feels the punishment successfully stopped the behavior. No wonder spanking is a hit with so many U.S. parents of 3- and 4-year-olds—more than 9 in 10 of whom have acknowledged spanking their children (Kazdin & Benjet, 2003).

2. *Punishment teaches discrimination.* Was the punishment effective in putting an end to the swearing? Or did the child simply learn that it's not okay to swear around the house, but it is okay to swear elsewhere?

3. *Punishment can teach fear.* The child may generalize what has been learned, associating fear not only with the undesirable behavior but also with the person delivering the punishment or the place it occurred. Thus, children may learn to fear a punishing teacher and try to avoid school. For such reasons, most European countries have banned hitting children in schools and child-care institutions (Leach, 1993, 1994). Eleven countries, including those in Scandinavia, have further outlawed hitting by parents, giving children the same legal protection given to spouses (EPOCH, 2000).

4. *Physical punishment may increase aggressiveness by modeling aggression as a way to cope with problems.* Many aggressive delinquents and abusive parents come from abusive families (Straus & Gelles, 1980; Straus et al., 1997). Some researchers dispute this drawback. They agree that spanked children are at increased risk for aggression. Likewise, they say, people who have undergone psychotherapy are more likely to suffer depression—because they had preexisting problems that triggered the treatments (Larzelere, 2000, 2004). Which is the chicken and which is the egg? The correlations don't hand us an answer.

If one adjusts for preexisting antisocial behavior, then an occasional single swat or two to misbehaving 2- to 6-year-olds looks more effective (Baumrind et al., 2002; Larzelere & Kuhn, 2005). That is especially so if the swat is used only as a backup when milder disciplinary tactics (such as a *time-out*, removing them from reinforcing surroundings) fail, and when the swat is combined with a generous dose of reasoning and reinforcing. Remember: *Punishment tells you what not to do; reinforcement tells you what to do.* This dual approach can be effective. When children with self-destructive behaviors bite themselves or bang their heads, they may be mildly punished (say, with a squirt of water in the face), but they may also be rewarded (with positive attention and food) when they behave well. In high school classrooms, teachers can give feedback on papers by saying, "No, but try this . . ." and "Yes, that's it!" Such responses reduce unwanted behavior while reinforcing more desirable alternatives.

Parents of delinquent youth are often unaware of how to achieve desirable behaviors without screaming or hitting their children (Patterson et al., 1982, 2005).

In operant conditioning, discrimination occurs when an organism learns that certain responses, but not others, will be reinforced.

In operant conditioning, generalization occurs when an organism's response to similar stimuli is also reinforced.

Children see, children do? Children who often experience physical punishment tend to display more aggression.

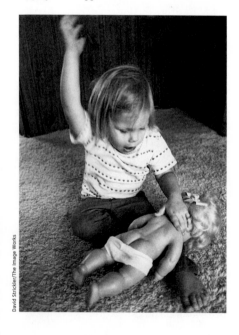

David Strickler/The Image Works

Training programs can help reframe contingencies from dire threats to positive incentives—turning "You clean up your room this minute or no dinner!" to "You're welcome at the dinner table after you get your room cleaned up." When you stop to think about it, many threats of punishment are just as forceful, and perhaps more effective, if rephrased positively. Thus, "If you don't get your homework done, there'll be no car" would better be phrased as . . .

What punishment often teaches, said Skinner, is how to avoid it. Most psychologists now favor an emphasis on reinforcement: Notice people doing something right and affirm them for it.

Extending Skinner's Understanding

11: Do cognitive processes and biological constraints affect operant conditioning?

Skinner granted the existence of private thought processes and the biological underpinnings of behavior. Nevertheless, many psychologists criticized him for discounting the importance of these influences.

Cognition and Operant Conditioning

A mere eight days before dying of leukemia, Skinner (1990) stood before the American Psychological Association convention for one final critique of "cognitive science," which he viewed as a throwback to early-twentieth-century introspectionism. Skinner died resisting the growing belief that cognitive processes—thoughts, perceptions, expectations—have a necessary place in the science of psychology and even in our understanding of conditioning. (He regarded thoughts and emotions as behaviors that follow the same laws as other behaviors.) Yet we have seen several hints that cognitive processes might be at work in operant learning. For example, animals on a fixed-interval reinforcement schedule respond more and more frequently as the time approaches when a response will produce a reinforcer. Although a strict behaviorist would object to talk of "expectations," the animals behave as if they expected that repeating the response would soon produce the reward.

Evidence of cognitive processes has also come from studying rats in mazes. Rats exploring a maze, with no obvious reward, are like people sightseeing in a new town. They seem to develop a **cognitive map**, a mental representation of the maze. When an experimenter then places food in the maze's goal box, the rats very soon run the maze as quickly as rats that have been reinforced with food for running the maze.

During their explorations, the rats have seemingly experienced **latent learning**—learning that becomes apparent only when there is some incentive to demonstrate it. Children, too, may learn from watching a parent but demonstrate the learning only much later, as needed. The point to remember: *There is more to learning than associating a response with a consequence; there is also cognition.* In Chapter 9 we will encounter more striking evidence of animals' cognitive abilities in solving problems and in using aspects of language.

Biological Predispositions

As with classical conditioning, an animal's natural predispositions constrain its capacity for operant conditioning. Using food as a reinforcer, you can easily condition a hamster to dig or to rear up because these actions are among the animal's natural

cognitive map a mental representation of the layout of one's environment. For example, after exploring a maze, rats act as if they have learned a cognitive map of it.

latent learning learning that occurs but is not apparent until there is an incentive to demonstrate it.

"Bathroom? Sure, it's just down the hall to the left, jog right, left, another left, straight past two more lefts, then right, and it's at the end of the third corridor on your right."

Will and Deni McIntyre/Photo Researchers

Latent learning Animals, like people, can learn from experience, with or without reinforcement. After exploring a maze for 10 days, rats received a food reward at the end of the maze. They quickly demonstrated their prior learning of the maze—by immediately completing it as quickly as (and even faster than) rats that had been reinforced each time they ran the maze. (From Tolman & Honzik, 1930.)

Natural athletes Animals can most easily learn and retain behaviors that draw on their biological predispositions, such as cats' inborn tendency to leap high and land on their feet.

For more information on animal behavior, see books by (I am not making this up) Robin Fox and Lionel Tiger.

"**Never try to teach a pig to sing. It wastes your time and annoys the pig.**"

—Mark Twain (1835–1910)

food-searching behaviors. But you won't be so successful if you use food as a reinforcer to shape other hamster behaviors, such as face washing, that aren't normally associated with food or hunger (Shettleworth, 1973). Similarly, you could easily teach pigeons to flap their wings to avoid being shocked, and to peck to obtain food, because fleeing with their wings and eating with their beaks are natural pigeon behaviors. However, they would have a hard time learning to peck to avoid a shock, or to flap their wings to obtain food (Foree & LoLordo, 1973). The principle: *Biological constraints predispose organisms to learn associations that are naturally adaptive.*

After witnessing the power of operant learning, Skinner's students Keller Breland and Marian Breland (1961; Bailey & Gillaspy, 2005) began training dogs, cats, chickens, parakeets, turkeys, pigs, ducks, and hamsters, and they eventually left their graduate studies to form an animal training company. Over the ensuing 47 years they trained more than 15,000 animals from 140 species for movies, traveling shows, corporations, amusement parks, and the government. They also trained animal trainers, including Sea World's first director of training.

At first, the Brelands presumed that operant principles would work on almost any response an animal could make. But along the way, they confronted the constraints of biological predispositions. In one act, pigs trained to pick up large wooden "dollars" and deposit them in a piggy bank began to drift back to their natural ways. They would drop the coin, push it with their snouts as pigs are prone to do, pick it up again, and then repeat the sequence—delaying their food reinforcer. This *instinctive drift* occurred as the animals reverted to their biologically predisposed patterns. Operant training works best when it builds on an animal's natural behavior tendencies.

Skinner's Legacy

B. F. Skinner was one of the most controversial intellectual figures of the late twentieth century. He stirred a hornet's nest with his outspoken beliefs. He repeatedly insisted that external influences (not internal thoughts and feelings) shape behavior. And he urged people to use operant principles to influence others' behavior at school, work, and home. Knowing that behavior is shaped by its results, he said we should use rewards to evoke more desirable behavior.

Skinner's critics objected, saying that he dehumanized people by neglecting their personal freedom and by seeking to control their actions. Skinner's reply: External consequences already haphazardly control people's behavior. Why not administer those consequences toward human betterment? Wouldn't reinforcers be more humane than the punishments used in homes, schools, and prisons? And if it is humbling to think that our history has shaped us, doesn't this very idea also give us hope that we can shape our future?

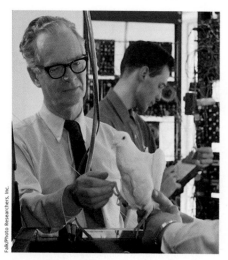

B. F. Skinner "I am sometimes asked, 'Do you think of yourself as you think of the organisms you study?' The answer is yes. So far as I know, my behavior at any given moment has been nothing more than the product of my genetic endowment, my personal history, and the current setting" (1983).

Applications of Operant Conditioning

12: **How might operant conditioning principles be applied at school, in sports, at work, and at home?**

In later chapters we will see how psychologists apply operant conditioning principles to help people moderate high blood pressure or gain social skills. Reinforcement technologies are also at work in schools, sports, workplaces, and homes (Flora, 2004).

AT SCHOOL A generation ago, Skinner and others worked toward a day when teaching machines and textbooks would shape learning in small steps, immediately reinforcing correct responses. Such machines and texts, they said, would revolutionize education and free teachers to focus on each student's special needs.

Stand in Skinner's shoes for a moment and imagine two math teachers, each with a class of students ranging from whiz kids to slow learners. Teacher A gives the whole class the same lesson, knowing that the bright kids will breeze through the math concepts, and the slower ones will be frustrated and fail. With so many different children, how could one teacher guide them individually? Teacher B, faced with a similar class, paces the material according to each student's rate of learning and provides prompt feedback, with positive reinforcement, to both the slow and the fast learners. Thinking as Skinner did, how might you achieve the individualized instruction of Teacher B?

Computers were Skinner's final hope. "Good instruction demands two things," he said. "Students must be told immediately whether what they do is right or wrong and, when right, they must be directed to the step to be taken next." Thus, the computer could be Teacher B—pacing math drills to the student's rate of learning, quizzing the student to find gaps in understanding, giving immediate feedback, and keeping flawless records. To the end of his life, Skinner (1986, 1988, 1989) believed his ideal was achievable. Although the predicted education revolution has not occurred, today's interactive student software, Web-based learning, and online testing bring us closer than ever before to achieving his ideal.

Computer-assisted learning Computers have helped realize Skinner's goal of individually paced instruction with immediate feedback.

IN SPORTS Reinforcement principles can enhance athletic performance as well. Again, the key is to shape behavior, by first reinforcing small successes and then gradually increasing the challenge. Thomas Simek and Richard O'Brien (1981, 1988) applied these principles to teaching golf and baseball by starting with easily reinforced responses. Golf students learn putting by starting with very short putts. As they build mastery, they eventually step back farther and farther. Likewise, novice batters begin with half swings at an oversized ball pitched from 10 feet away, giving them the immediate pleasure of smacking the ball. As the hitters' confidence builds with their success and they achieve mastery at each level, the pitcher gradually moves back—to 15, then 22, 30, and 40.5 feet—and eventually introduces a standard baseball. Compared with children taught by conventional methods, those trained by this behavioral method show, in both testing and game situations, faster skill improvement.

AT WORK Skinner's ideas have also shown up in the workplace. Knowing that reinforcers influence productivity, many organizations have invited employees to share the risks and rewards of company ownership. Others focus on reinforcing a job well done. Rewards are most likely to increase productivity if the desired performance has been well-defined and is achievable. The message for managers? *Reward specific, achievable behaviors, not vaguely defined "merit."* Even criticism triggers the least resentment and the greatest performance boost when specific and considerate (Baron, 1988).

Operant conditioning also reminds us that reinforcement should be *immediate.* IBM legend Thomas Watson understood. When he observed an achievement, he wrote the employee a check on the spot (Peters & Waterman, 1982). But rewards need not be material, or lavish. An effective manager may simply walk the floor and sincerely affirm people for good work, or write notes of appreciation for a completed project. As Skinner said, "How much richer would the whole world be if the reinforcers in daily life were more effectively contingent on productive work?"

AT HOME As we have seen, parents can apply operant conditioning practices. Parent-training researchers remind us that parents who say "Get ready for bed" but cave in to protests or defiance reinforce whining and

In 2009, we learned that huge bonuses were going to executives of companies bailed out with public tax dollars. Public outrage focused on the rewards following failure rather than achievement.

arguing (Wierson & Forehand, 1994). Exasperated, they may then yell or gesture menacingly. When the child, now frightened, obeys, that in turn reinforces the parents' angry behavior. Over time, a destructive parent-child relationship develops.

To disrupt this cycle, parents should remember the basic rule of shaping: *Notice people doing something right and affirm them for it.* Give children attention and other reinforcers when they are behaving *well* (Wierson & Forehand, 1994). Target a specific behavior, reward it, and watch it increase. When children misbehave or are defiant, don't yell at them or hit them. Simply explain the misbehavior and give them a time-out.

Finally, we can use operant conditioning in our own lives (see Close-Up: Training Our Partners). To reinforce your own desired behaviors and extinguish the undesired ones, psychologists suggest taking these steps:

1. *State your goal*—to stop smoking, eat less, or study or exercise more—in measurable terms, and announce it. You might, for example, aim to boost your study time by an hour a day and share that goal with some close friends.
2. *Monitor how often you engage in your desired behavior.* You might log your current study time, noting under what conditions you do and don't study. (When I began writing textbooks, I logged how I spent my time each day and was amazed to discover how much time I was wasting.)
3. *Reinforce the desired behavior.* To increase your study time, give yourself a reward (a snack or some activity you enjoy) only after you finish your extra hour of study. Agree with your friends that you will join them for weekend activities only if you have met your realistic weekly studying goal.
4. *Reduce the rewards gradually.* As your new behaviors become more habitual, give yourself a mental pat on the back instead of a cookie.

"I wrote another five hundred words. Can I have another cookie?"

"O! This learning, what a thing it is."

—William Shakespeare,
The Taming of the Shrew, 1597

Contrasting Classical and Operant Conditioning

Both classical and operant conditioning are forms of associative learning, and both involve acquisition, extinction, spontaneous recovery, generalization, and discrimination. The similarities are sufficient to make some researchers wonder if a single stimulus-response learning process might explain them both (Donahoe & Vegas,

Close-Up:

Training Our Partners   By Amy Sutherland

For a book I was writing about a school for exotic animal trainers, I started commuting from Maine to California, where I spent my days watching students do the seemingly impossible: teaching hyenas to pirouette on command, cougars to offer their paws for a nail clipping, and baboons to skateboard.

I listened, rapt, as professional trainers explained how they taught dolphins to flip and elephants to paint. Eventually it hit me that the same techniques might work on that stubborn but lovable species, the American husband.

The central lesson I learned from exotic animal trainers is that I should reward behavior I like and ignore behavior I

don't. After all, you don't get a sea lion to balance a ball on the end of its nose by nagging. The same goes for the American husband.

Back in Maine, I began thanking Scott if he threw one dirty shirt into the hamper. If he threw in two, I'd kiss him. Meanwhile, I would step over any soiled clothes on the floor without one sharp word, though I did sometimes kick them under the bed. But as he basked in my appreciation, the piles became smaller.

I was using what trainers call "approximations," rewarding the small steps toward learning a whole new behavior. . . . Once I started thinking this way, I couldn't stop. At the school in California, I'd be

scribbling notes on how to walk an emu or have a wolf accept you as a pack member, but I'd be thinking, "I can't wait to try this on Scott. . . ."

After two years of exotic animal training, my marriage is far smoother, my husband much easier to love. I used to take his faults personally; his dirty clothes on the floor were an affront, a symbol of how he didn't care enough about me. But thinking of my husband as an exotic species gave me the distance I needed to consider our differences more objectively.

Excerpted with permission from Sutherland, A., (2006, June 25). What Shamu taught me about a happy marriage, *New York Times*.

2004). Their procedural difference is this: Through classical (Pavlovian) conditioning, an organism associates different stimuli that it does not control and responds automatically (respondent behaviors) (**TABLE 7.4**). Through operant conditioning, an organism associates its operant behaviors—those that act on its environment to produce rewarding or punishing stimuli—with their consequences. Cognitive processes and biological predispositions influence both classical and operant conditioning.

TABLE 7.4 Comparison of Classical and Operant Conditioning

	Classical Conditioning	Operant Conditioning
Basic idea	Organism learns associations between events it doesn't control.	Organism learns associations between its behavior and resulting events.
Response	Involuntary, automatic.	Voluntary, operates on environment.
Acquisition	Associating events; NS is paired with US and becomes CS.	Associating response with a consequence (reinforcer or punisher).
Extinction	CR decreases when CS is repeatedly presented alone.	Responding decreases when reinforcement stops.
Spontaneous recovery	The reappearance, after a rest period, of an extinguished CR.	The reappearance, after a rest period, of an extinguished response.
Generalization	The tendency to respond to stimuli similar to the CS.	Organism's response to similar stimuli is also reinforced.
Discrimination	The learned ability to distinguish between a CS and other stimuli that do not signal a US.	Organism learns that certain responses, but not others, will be reinforced.
Cognitive processes	Organisms develop expectation that CS signals the arrival of US.	Organisms develop expectation that a response will be reinforced or punished; they also exhibit latent learning, without reinforcement.
Biological predispositions	Natural predispositions constrain what stimuli and responses can easily be associated.	Organisms best learn behaviors similar to their natural behaviors; unnatural behaviors instinctively drift back toward natural ones.

REHEARSE IT!

8. Salivating in response to a tone paired with food is a (an) _____; pressing a bar to obtain food is a (an) _____.
   a. primary reinforcer; conditioned reinforcer
   b. conditioned reinforcer; primary reinforcer
   c. operant behavior; respondent behavior
   d. respondent behavior; operant behavior

9. Thorndike's law of effect became the basis for operant conditioning and the "behavioral technology" developed by
   a. Ivan Pavlov.
   b. John Garcia.
   c. B. F. Skinner.
   d. John B. Watson.

10. One way to change behavior is to reward natural behaviors in small steps, as they get closer and closer to the desired behavior. This process is called
   a. shaping.
   b. punishment.
   c. taste aversion.
   d. classical conditioning.

11. Your dog is barking so loudly that it's making your ears ring. You clap your hands, the dog stops barking, your ears stop ringing, and you think to yourself, "I'll have to do that when he barks again." The end of the barking was for you a
   a. positive reinforcer.
   b. negative reinforcer.
   c. punishment.
   d. primary reinforcer.

12. The partial reinforcement schedule that reinforces a response at unpredictable times is a
   a. fixed-interval schedule.
   b. variable-interval schedule.
   c. fixed-ratio schedule.
   d. variable-ratio schedule.

13. A medieval proverb notes that "a burnt child dreads the fire." In operant conditioning, the burning would be an example of a
   a. primary reinforcer.
   b. negative reinforcer.
   c. punisher.
   d. positive reinforcer.

14. We now know that cognitive processes (thoughts, perceptions, and expectations) play an important role in learning. Evidence comes from studies in which rats
   a. spontaneously recover previously learned behavior.
   b. develop cognitive maps.
   c. exhibit respondent behavior.
   d. generalize responses.

15. Rats carried passively through a maze and given no reward later ran the maze as well as rats that had received food rewards for running the maze. The rats that had learned without reinforcement demonstrate
   a. modeling.
   b. biological predisposition.
   c. shaping.
   d. latent learning.

Answers: 8. d, 9. c, 10. a, 11. b, 12. b, 13. c, 14. b, 15. d.

observational learning learning by observing others.

modeling the process of observing and imitating a specific behavior.

mirror neurons frontal lobe neurons that fire when performing certain actions or when observing another doing so. The brain's mirroring of another's action may enable imitation and empathy.

Learning by Observation

13: What is observational learning, and how is it enabled by mirror neurons?

From drooling dogs, running rats, and pecking pigeons we have learned much about the basic processes of learning. But conditioning principles don't tell us the whole story. Higher animals, especially humans, can learn without direct experience, through **observational learning,** by observing and imitating others. A child who sees his sister burn her fingers on a hot stove learns not to touch it. And a monkey watching another selecting certain pictures to gain treats learns to imitate that behavior (**FIGURE 7.12**). We learn all kinds of specific behaviors by observing and imitating models, a process called **modeling.** Lord Chesterfield (1694–1773) had the idea: "We are, in truth, more than half what we are by imitation."

Imitation occurs in various animal species—monkey see, monkey do—but is most striking in humans. Our catch-phrases, hem lengths, ceremonies, foods, traditions, vices, and fads all spread by one person copying another. Even as 2½-year-olds, when many of our mental abilities were near those of chimpanzees, we considerably surpassed chimps at social tasks such as imitating another's solution to a problem (Hermann et al., 2007).

Mirrors in the Brain

On a 1991 hot summer day in Parma, Italy, a lab monkey awaited its researchers' return from lunch. The researchers had implanted wires next to its motor cortex, in a frontal lobe brain region that enabled the monkey to plan and enact movements. When the monkey moved a peanut into its mouth, for example, the monitoring device would buzz. That day, as one of the researchers reentered the lab, ice cream cone in hand, the monkey stared at him. As the student raised the cone to lick it, the monkey's monitor again buzzed—as if the motionless monkey had itself moved (Blakeslee, 2006; Iacoboni, 2008).

Having earlier observed the same weird result when the monkey watched humans or other monkeys move peanuts to their mouths, the flabbergasted researchers, led by Giacomo Rizzolatti (2002, 2006), eventually surmised that they had stumbled onto a previously unknown type of neuron: **mirror neurons,** whose activity provides a neural basis for imitation and observational learning. When a monkey grasps,

Monkey A's screen   Monkey B's screen

FIGURE 7.12 Cognitive imitation When Monkey A (above left) sees Monkey B touch four pictures on a display screen in a certain order to gain a banana, Monkey A learns to imitate that order, even when shown a different configuration (Subiaul et al., 2004).

holds, or tears something, these neurons fire. And they likewise fire when the monkey observes another doing so. When one monkey sees, these neurons mirror what another monkey does.

It's not just monkey business. Imitation shapes even very young humans' behavior. Shortly after birth, a baby may imitate an adult who sticks out his tongue. By 8 to 16 months, infants imitate various novel gestures (Jones, 2007). By age 12 months, they begin looking where an adult is looking (Brooks & Meltzoff, 2005). And by age 14 months (**FIGURE 7.13**), children imitate acts modeled on TV (Meltzoff, 1988; Meltzoff & Moore, 1989, 1997). Children see, children do.

PET scans of different brain areas reveal that humans, like monkeys, have a mirror neuron system that supports empathy and imitation (Iacoboni, 2008). As we observe another's action, our brain generates an inner simulation, enabling us to experience the other's experience within ourselves. Mirror neurons help give rise to children's empathy and to their ability to infer another's mental state, an ability called *theory of mind* (Chapter 5). People with autism display reduced imitative yawning and mirror neuron activity—"broken mirrors," some have said (Ramachandran & Oberman, 2006; Senju et al., 2007; Williams et al., 2006).

For most of us, however, our mirror neurons make emotions contagious. We grasp others' states of mind—often feeling what they feel—by mental simulation. We find it harder to frown when viewing a smile than when viewing a frown (Dimberg et al., 2000, 2002). We find ourselves yawning after observing another's yawn, laughing when others laugh. When watching a film of a scorpion crawling up someone's leg, we tighten up; observing a passionate kiss, we may notice our own lips puckering. Seeing a loved one's pain, our face mirrors their emotion. As **FIGURE 7.14** shows, so does our brain. In this fMRI scan, the pain imagined by an empathic romantic partner has triggered some of the same brain activity experienced by the loved one actually having the pain (Singer et al., 2004). Even fiction reading may trigger such activity, as we mentally simulate the experiences described (Mar & Oatley, 2008). The bottom line: *Our brain's mirror neurons underlie our intensely social nature.*

Bandura's Experiments

Picture this scene from a famous experiment by Albert Bandura, the pioneering researcher of observational learning (Bandura et al., 1961). A preschool child works on a drawing. An adult in another part of the room is building with Tinkertoys. As the child watches, the adult gets up and for nearly 10 minutes pounds, kicks, and throws around the room a large inflated Bobo doll, yelling, "Sock him in the nose. . . . Hit him down. . . . Kick him."

FIGURE 7.13 Learning from observation This 14-month-old boy in Andrew Meltzoff's laboratory is imitating behavior he has seen on TV. In the top photo the infant leans forward and carefully watches the adult pull apart a toy. In the middle photo he has been given the toy. In the bottom photo he pulls the toy apart, imitating what he has seen the adult do.

Pain   Empathy

FIGURE 7.14 Experienced and imagined pain in the brain Brain activity related to actual pain (left) is mirrored in the brain of an observing loved one (right). Empathy in the brain shows up in emotional brain areas, but not in the somatosensory cortex, which receives the physical pain input.

FIGURE 7.15 **The famous Bobo doll experiment** Notice how the children's actions directly imitate the adult's.

Albert Bandura "The Bobo doll follows me wherever I go. The photographs are published in every introductory psychology text and virtually every undergraduate takes introductory psychology. I recently checked into a Washington hotel. The clerk at the desk asked, 'Aren't you the psychologist who did the Bobo doll experiment?' I answered, 'I am afraid that will be my legacy.' He replied, 'That deserves an upgrade. I will put you in a suite in the quiet part of the hotel'" (2005).

prosocial behavior positive, constructive, helpful behavior. The opposite of antisocial behavior.

The child is then taken to another room filled with appealing toys. Soon the experimenter returns and tells the child she has decided to save these good toys "for the other children." She takes the now-frustrated child to a third adjacent room containing a few toys, including a Bobo doll. Left alone, what does the child do?

Compared with children not exposed to the adult model, those who viewed the model's actions were much more likely to lash out at the doll. Apparently, observing the aggressive outburst lowered their inhibitions. But something more was also at work, for the children imitated the very acts they had observed and used the very words they had heard (**FIGURE 7.15**).

What determines whether we will imitate a model? Bandura believes part of the answer is reinforcements and punishments—those received by the model as well as by the imitator. By watching, we learn to anticipate a behavior's consequences in situations like those we are observing. We are especially likely to imitate people we perceive as similar to ourselves, as successful, or as admirable.

Applications of Observational Learning

The big news from Bandura's studies is that we look and we learn. Models—in one's family or neighborhood, or on TV—may have effects, good or bad. Many business organizations effectively use *behavior modeling* to train communications, sales, and customer service skills (Taylor et al., 2005). Trainees gain skills faster when they not only are told the needed skills but also are able to observe the skills being modeled effectively by experienced workers (or actors simulating them).

Prosocial Observational Learning

14: What is the impact of prosocial modeling and of antisocial modeling?

The good news is that **prosocial** (positive, helpful) models can have prosocial effects. To encourage children to read, read to them and surround them with books and people who read. To increase the odds that your children will practice your religion, worship and attend religious activities with them. People who exemplify nonviolent, helpful behavior can prompt similar behavior in others. India's Mahatma Gandhi and America's Martin Luther King, Jr., both drew on the power of modeling, making nonviolent action a powerful force for social change in both countries.

Parents are also powerful models. European Christians who risked their lives to rescue Jews from the Nazis usually had a close relationship with at least one parent who modeled a strong moral or humanitarian concern; this was also true for U.S. civil rights activists in the 1960s (London, 1970; Oliner & Oliner, 1988). The observational learning of morality begins early. Socially responsive toddlers who readily imitate their parents tend to become preschoolers with a strong internalized conscience (Forman et al., 2004).

Models are most effective when their actions and words are consistent. Sometimes, however, models say one thing and do another. Many parents seem to operate according to the principle "Do as I *say,* not as I *do.*" Experiments have suggested that children learn to do both (Rice & Grusec, 1975; Rushton, 1975). Exposed to a hypocrite, they tend to imitate the hypocrisy by doing what the model did and saying what the model said.

A model grandma This boy is learning to cook by observing his grandmother. As the sixteenth-century proverb states, "Example is better than precept."

Antisocial Observational Learning

The bad news is that observational learning may also have *antisocial effects.* This helps us understand why abusive parents might have aggressive children, and why many men who beat their wives had wife-battering fathers (Stith et al., 2000). Critics note that being aggressive could be passed along by parents' genes. But with monkeys we know it can be environmental. In study after study, young monkeys separated from their mothers and subjected to high levels of aggression have grown up to be aggressive themselves (Chamove, 1980). The lessons we learn as children are not easily unlearned as adults, and they are sometimes visited on future generations.

Television is a powerful source of observational learning. While watching TV, children may "learn" that bullying is an effective way to control others, that free and easy sex brings pleasure without later misery or disease, or that men should be tough and women gentle. And they have ample time to learn such lessons. During their first 18 years, most children in developed countries spend more time watching TV than they spend in school. In the United States, where 9 in 10 teens watch TV daily, someone who lives to age 75 will have spent 9 years staring at the tube (Gallup, 2002; Kubey & Csikszentmihalyi, 2002). With more than 1 billion TV sets playing in homes worldwide, CNN reaching 150 countries, and MTV broadcasting in 17 languages, television has created a global pop culture (Gunderson, 2001; Lippman, 1992).

TV viewers are learning about life from a rather peculiar storyteller, one that reflects the culture's mythology but not its reality. During the late twentieth century, the average child viewed some 8000 TV murders and 100,000 other acts of violence before finishing elementary school (Huston et al., 1992). If we include cable programming and video rentals, the violence numbers escalate. An analysis of more than 3000 network and cable programs aired in the 1996–1997 season revealed that nearly 6 in 10 featured violence, that 74 percent of the violence went unpunished, that 58 percent did not show the victims' pain, that nearly half the incidents involved "justified" violence, and that nearly half involved an attractive perpetrator. These conditions define the recipe for the *violence-viewing effect* described in many studies (Donnerstein, 1998).

How much are we affected by repeated exposure to violent programs? Was the judge who in 1993 tried two British 10-year-olds for murdering a 2-year-old right to suspect that the pair had been influenced by "violent video films"? Were the American media right to think that the teen assassins who killed 13 of their Columbine High School classmates had been influenced by repeated exposure to *Natural Born Killers* and first-person shooter games such as *Doom?* To understand whether violence viewing leads to violent behavior, researchers have done some 600 correlational and experimental studies (Anderson & Gentile, 2008; Comstock, 2008; Murray, 2008).

"The problem with television is that the people must sit and keep their eyes glued to a screen: The average American family hasn't time for it. Therefore the showmen are convinced that . . . television will never be a serious competitor of [radio] broadcasting."

—*New York Times,* 1939

TV's greatest effect may stem from what it displaces. Children and adults who spend 4 hours a day watching TV spend 4 fewer hours in active pursuits—talking, studying, playing, reading, or socializing with friends. What would you have done with your extra time if you had never watched TV, and how might you therefore be different?

Correlational studies do support this link:

- In the United States and Canada, homicide rates doubled between 1957 and 1974, just when TV was introduced and spreading. Moreover, census regions with later dates for TV service also had homicide rates that jumped later.
- White South Africans were first introduced to TV in 1975. A similar near-doubling of the homicide rate began after 1975 (Centerwall, 1989).
- Elementary schoolchildren with heavy exposure to media violence (via TV, videos, and video games) also tend to get into more fights (**FIGURE 7.16**).

But as we know from Chapter 1, correlation does not imply causation. This is one reason why some researchers believe these studies do not prove that viewing violence causes aggression (Ferguson & Kilburn, 2009; Freedman, 1988). Maybe aggressive children prefer violent programs. Maybe abused or neglected children are both more aggressive and more often left in front of the TV. Maybe violent programs simply reflect, rather than affect, violent trends.

To pin down causation, psychologists use experiments. In this case, researchers randomly assigned some viewers to observe violence and others to watch entertaining nonviolence. Does viewing cruelty prepare people, when irritated, to react more cruelly? To some extent, it does. "The consensus among most of the research community," reported the National Institute of Mental Health (1982), "is that violence on television does lead to aggressive behavior by children and teenagers who watch the programs." This is especially so when an attractive person commits seemingly justified, realistic violence that goes unpunished and causes no visible pain or harm (Donnerstein, 1998).

The violence-viewing effect seems to stem from at least two factors. One is *imitation* (Geen & Thomas, 1986). As we noted earlier, children as young as 14 months will imitate acts they observe on TV. As they watch, their mirror neurons simulate the behavior, and after this inner rehearsal they become more likely to act it out. One research team observed a sevenfold increase in violent play immediately after children viewed *Power Rangers* (Boyatzis et al., 1995). These children, like those we saw earlier in the Bobo doll experiment, often precisely imitated the models' violent acts, including flying karate kicks. Imitation may also have played a role in

> "Thirty seconds worth of glorification of a soap bar sells soap. Twenty-five minutes worth of glorification of violence sells violence."
>
> —U.S. Senator Paul Simon, Remarks to the Communitarian Network, 1993

Violence viewing leads to violent play Research has shown that viewing media violence does lead to increased expression of aggression in the viewers, as with these boys imitating pro wrestlers.

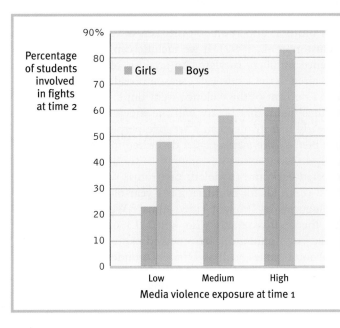

FIGURE 7.16 Media violence viewing predicts future aggressive behavior Douglas Gentile and his colleagues (2004) studied more than 400 third to fifth graders. After controlling for existing differences in hostility and aggression, the researchers reported increased aggression in those heavily exposed to violent television, videos, and video games.

the first eight days after the 1999 Columbine High School massacre, when every U.S. state except Vermont had to deal with copycat threats or incidents. Pennsylvania alone had 60 threats of school violence (Cooper, 1999).

Prolonged exposure to violence also *desensitizes* viewers; they become more indifferent to it when later viewing a brawl, whether on TV or in real life (Rule & Ferguson, 1986). Adult males who spent three evenings watching sexually violent movies became progressively less bothered by the rapes and slashings. Compared with those in a control group, the film watchers later expressed less sympathy for domestic violence victims, and they rated the victims' injuries as less severe (Mullin & Linz, 1995).

Indeed, suggested Edward Donnerstein and his co-researchers (1987), an evil psychologist could hardly imagine a better way to make people indifferent to brutality than to expose them to a graded series of scenes, from fights to killings to the mutilations in slasher movies. Watching cruelty fosters indifference.

* * *

Our knowledge of learning principles comes from the work of thousands of investigators. This chapter has focused on the ideas of a few pioneers—Ivan Pavlov, John Watson, B. F. Skinner, and Albert Bandura. They illustrate the impact that can result from single-minded devotion to a few well-defined problems and ideas. These researchers defined the issues and impressed on us the importance of learning. As their legacy demonstrates, intellectual history is often made by people who risk going to extremes in pushing ideas to their limits (Simonton, 2000).

"Don't you understand? This is life, this is what is happening. We can't switch to another channel."

REHEARSE IT!

16. Children learn many social behaviors by imitating parents and other models. This type of learning is called
    a. observational learning.
    b. reinforced learning.
    c. operant conditioning.
    d. classical conditioning.

17. Parents are powerful models of behavior. They are most effective in getting their children to imitate them if
    a. their words and actions are consistent.
    b. they have outgoing personalities.
    c. one parent works and the other stays home to care for the children.
    d. they carefully explain why a behavior is acceptable in adults but not in children.

18. Bandura believes that modeling is not automatic. Whether a child will imitate a model depends in part on the
    a. child's family connections to the model.
    b. child's ability to distinguish right from wrong.
    c. rewards and punishments received by the model.
    d. child's age in relation to that of the model.

19. There is considerable controversy about the effects of heavy exposure to TV programs showing violence. However, most experts agree that repeated viewing of TV violence
    a. makes all viewers significantly more aggressive.
    b. has little effect on viewers.
    c. dulls the viewer's sensitivity to violence.
    d. makes viewers angry and frustrated.

Answers: 16. a, 17. a, 18. c, 19. c.

CHAPTER REVIEW

Learning

How Do We Learn?

1 What distinguishes the basic forms of learning?

Learning is a relatively permanent change in an organism's behavior due to experience. In *associative learning,* we learn to associate two stimuli (as in classical conditioning) or a response and its consequences (as in operant conditioning). In observational learning, we learn by watching others' experiences and examples.

Classical Conditioning

2 How does a neutral stimulus become a conditioned stimulus?

In *classical conditioning*, a *UR* is an event that occurs naturally (such as salivation), in response to some stimulus. A *US* is something that naturally and automatically (without learning) triggers the unlearned response (as food in the mouth triggers salivation). An *NS* is a stimulus (such as a bell) that elicits no response before conditioning but, through learning, becomes a *CS* after being associated with some unlearned response (salivating). A *CR* is the learned response (salivating) to the originally irrelevant but now conditioned stimulus.

3 In classical conditioning, what are the processes of acquisition, extinction, spontaneous recovery, generalization, and discrimination?

In classical conditioning, *acquisition* is associating an initial NS with the US. Acquisition transforms an NS into a CS most readily when the stimulus is presented just before (ideally, about a half-second before) a US, thus preparing the organism for the upcoming event. This finding supports the view that classical conditioning is biologically adaptive. In *higher-order conditioning*, the CS in one conditioning experience is paired with a new NS, creating a second (often weaker) CS. *Extinction* is diminished responding when the CS no longer signals an impending US. *Spontaneous recovery* is the reappearance of a formerly extinguished response, following a rest period. *Generalization* is the tendency to respond to stimuli that are similar to a CS. *Discrimination* is the learned ability to distinguish between a CS and other irrelevant stimuli.

4 Do cognitive processes and biological constraints affect classical conditioning?

Despite early behaviorists' views, research has shown that cognition and biological predispositions place some limits on conditioning. Organisms may learn when to expect a US and may be aware of the link between stimuli and responses. Because of biological predispositions, some associations are easier to learn than others. Learning is adaptive: Each species learns behaviors that aid its survival.

5 Why is Pavlov's work important?

Pavlov taught us that significant psychological phenomena can be studied objectively, and that classical conditioning is a basic form of learning that applies to all species.

6 What have been some applications of classical conditioning?

Classical conditioning techniques have been used in drug-abuse treatment programs and in therapy for emotional disorders. The body's immune system also appears to respond to classical conditioning.

Operant Conditioning

7 What is operant conditioning, and how does it differ from classical conditioning?

In *operant conditioning*, an organism learns associations between its own behavior and resulting events; this form of conditioning involves *operant behavior* (behavior that operates on the environment, producing consequences). In classical conditioning, the organism forms associations between stimuli—behaviors it does not control; this form of conditioning involves *respondent behavior* (automatic responses to some stimulus).

Expanding on Thorndike's *law of effect*, Skinner and others found that the behavior of rats or pigeons placed in an *operant chamber* (Skinner box) can be *shaped* by reinforcing closer and closer approximations of the desired behavior.

8 What are the basic types of reinforcers?

A *reinforcer* is anything that strengthens the behavior it follows. *Positive reinforcement* adds something desirable to increase the frequency of a behavior. *Negative reinforcement* removes something undesirable to increase the frequency of a behavior. *Primary reinforcers* (receiving food when hungry, or having a headache go away) are innately satisfying—no learning is required. *Conditioned* (or secondary) *reinforcers* (such as cash) are satisfying because we have learned to associate them with more basic rewards (such as the food or medicine we buy with them). Immediate reinforcers (watching late-night TV) offer immediate payback; delayed reinforcers (feeling rested tomorrow) require the ability to delay gratification.

9 How do different reinforcement schedules affect behavior?

In *continuous reinforcement* (reinforcing desired responses every time they occur), learning is rapid, but so is extinction if rewards cease. In *partial (intermittent) reinforcement*, initial learning is slower, but resistance to extinction is greater. *Fixed-ratio schedules* offer rewards after a set number of responses; *variable-ratio schedules*, after an unpredictable number. *Fixed-interval schedules* offer rewards after set time periods; *variable-interval schedules*, after unpredictable time periods.

10 How does punishment affect behavior?

Punishment attempts to decrease the frequency of a behavior (a child's disobedience) by administering an undesirable consequence (spanking) or withdrawing something desirable (taking away a favorite toy). Undesirable side effects of physical punishment can include suppressing rather than changing unwanted behaviors, encouraging discrimination (the undesirable behavior appears when the punisher is not present), generalizing fear, and teaching aggression.

11 Do cognitive processes and biological constraints affect operant conditioning?

Skinner underestimated the limits that cognitive and biological constraints place on conditioning. Research on *cognitive maps* and *latent learning* demonstrate the importance of cognitive processes in learning. And when training attempts to override biological constraints, instinctive drift occurs as animals revert to predisposed patterns.

12 How might operant conditioning principles be applied at school, in sports, at work, and at home?

In school, teachers can use shaping techniques to guide students' behaviors, and they can use interactive software and Web sites to provide immediate feedback. In sports, coaches can build players' skills and self-confidence by rewarding small improvements. At work, managers can boost productivity and morale by rewarding well-defined and achievable behaviors. At home, parents can reward desirable behaviors, but not undesirable ones. We can shape our own behaviors by stating our goals, monitoring the frequency of desired behaviors, reinforcing desired behaviors, and gradually reducing incentives as the desired behaviors become habitual.

Learning by Observation

13 **What is observational learning, and how is it enabled by mirror neurons?**

In *observational learning*, we *model* others' behavior—we observe and imitate them. *Mirror neurons*, located in the brain's frontal lobes, demonstrate a neural basis for observational learning. They fire when we perform certain actions (such as yawning) or when we observe someone else performing those actions.

14 **What is the impact of prosocial modeling and of antisocial modeling?**

Children tend to imitate what a model does and says, whether the modeled behavior is *prosocial* (positive, constructive, and helpful) or antisocial. If a model's actions and words are inconsistent, children may imitate the hypocrisy they observe.

Terms and Concepts to Remember

learning, p. 225
associative learning, p. 226
classical conditioning, p. 227
behaviorism, p. 227
neutral stimulus (NS), p. 228
unconditioned response (UR), p. 228
unconditioned stimulus (US), p. 228
conditioned response (CR), p. 229
conditioned stimulus (CS), p. 229
acquisition, p. 230
higher-order conditioning, p. 230
extinction, p. 231
spontaneous recovery, p. 231
generalization, p. 231

discrimination, p. 232
respondent behavior, p. 236
operant conditioning, p. 236
operant behavior, p. 236
law of effect, p. 237
operant chamber, p. 237
shaping, p. 237
reinforcer, p. 238
positive reinforcement, p 239
negative reinforcement, p. 239
primary reinforcer, p. 239
conditioned reinforcer, p. 239
continuous reinforcement, p. 240

partial (intermittent) reinforcement, p. 240
fixed-ratio schedule, p. 240
variable-ratio schedule, p. 240
fixed-interval schedule, p. 240
variable-interval schedule, p. 241
punishment, p. 241
cognitive map, p. 243
latent learning, p. 243
observational learning, p. 248
modeling, p. 248
mirror neurons, p. 248
prosocial behavior, p. 250

Test for Success: Critical Thinking Exercises
By Amy Himsel, El Camino College

1. "Sex sells!" is a common saying in advertising. Using classical conditioning terms, explain how sexual images in advertisements can condition your response to a product.

2. Ethan constantly misbehaves at preschool even though his teacher scolds him several times each day. Why does his misbehavior continue, and what can his teacher do to stop it?

3. How could your psychology instructor use negative reinforcement to encourage your attentive behavior during class?

4. Why might a gymnastics coach encourage her students to improve their routines by watching recordings of Olympic gold medal gymnastics performances?

5. Jason's parents and older friends all smoke, but they advise him not to. Juan's parents and friends don't smoke, but they say nothing to deter him from doing so. Will Jason or Juan be more likely to start smoking?

The Test for Success exercises offer you a chance to apply your critical thinking skills to aspects of the material you have just read. Suggestions for answering these questions can be found in Appendix D at the back of the book.

Multiple-choice self-tests and more may be found at www.worthpublishers.com/myers.

Chapter Outline

- **The Phenomenon of Memory**

- **Studying Memory: Information-Processing Models**

- **Encoding: Getting Information In**
  How We Encode: Levels of Processing
  What We Encode

- **Storage: Retaining Information**
  Sensory Memory
  Working/Short-Term Memory
  Long-Term Memory
  Storing Information in the Brain

- **Retrieval: Getting Information Out**
  Retrieval Cues

- **Forgetting**
  Encoding Failure
  Storage Decay
  Retrieval Failure
  CLOSE-UP: Retrieving Passwords

- **Memory Construction**
  Misinformation and Imagination Effects
  Source Amnesia
  Children's Eyewitness Recall
  Repressed or Constructed Memories of Abuse?

- **Improving Memory**

8: Memory

Be thankful for memory. We take it for granted, except when it malfunctions. But it is our memory that accounts for time and defines our life. It is our memory that enables us to recognize family, speak our language, find our way home, and locate food and water. It is our memory that enables us to enjoy an experience and then mentally replay and enjoy it again. And it is our memory that occasionally pits us against those whose offenses we cannot forget.

In large part, you are what you remember. Without memory, your storehouse of accumulated learning, there would be no savoring of past joys, no guilt or anger over painful recollections. You would instead live in an enduring present, each moment fresh. But each person would be a stranger, every language foreign, every task—dressing, cooking, biking—a new challenge. You would even be a stranger to yourself, lacking that continuous sense of self that extends from your distant past to your momentary present. "If you lose the ability to recall your old memories then you have no life," suggested memory researcher James McGaugh (2003). "You might as well be a rutabaga or a cabbage."

"Waiter, I'd like to order, unless I've eaten, in which case bring me the check."

The Phenomenon of Memory

To a psychologist, **memory** is learning that has persisted over time, information that has been stored and can be retrieved.

Research on memory's extremes has helped us understand how memory works. At age 92, my father suffered a small stroke that had but one peculiar effect. His genial personality was intact. He was as mobile as before. He knew us and while poring over family photo albums could reminisce in detail about his past. But he had lost most of his ability to lay down new memories of conversations and everyday episodes. He could not tell me what day of the week it was. Told repeatedly of his brother-in-law's death, he expressed surprise each time he heard the news.

At the other extreme are people who would be medal winners in a memory Olympics, such as Russian journalist Shereshevskii, or S, who had merely to listen while other reporters scribbled notes (Luria, 1968). Where you and I could parrot back a string of about 7—maybe even 9—digits, S could repeat up to 70, provided they were read about 3 seconds apart in an otherwise silent room. Moreover, he could recall digits or words backward as easily as forward. His accuracy was unerring, even when recalling a list as much as 15 years later, after having memorized hundreds of others. "Yes, yes," he might recall. "This was a series you gave me once when we were in your apartment. . . . You were sitting at the table and I in the rocking chair. . . . You were wearing a gray suit and you looked at me like this. . . ."

Amazing? Yes, but consider your own pretty staggering capacity for remembering countless voices, sounds, and songs; tastes, smells, and textures; faces, places, and happenings. Imagine viewing more than 2500 slides of faces and places, for only 10

WELL, FOR CRYING OUT LOUD! AL TOWBRIDGE! WHAT IS IT, NINE YEARS, SEVEN MONTHS, AND TWELVE DAYS SINCE I LAST RAN INTO YOU? TEN-THIRTY-TWO A.M., A SATURDAY, FELCHER'S HARDWARE STORE. YOU WERE BUYING SEALER FOR YOUR BLACKTOP DRIVEWAY. TELL ME, AL, HOW DID THAT SEALER WORK? DID IT HOLD UP?

MR. TOTAL RECALL

memory the persistence of learning over time through the storage and retrieval of information.

FIGURE 8.1 What is this? People who had, 17 years earlier, seen the complete image (which you can see in Figure 8.3 by turning the next page) were more likely to recognize this fragment, even if they had forgotten the earlier experience (Mitchell, 2006).

encoding the processing of information into the memory system—for example, by extracting meaning.

storage the retention of encoded information over time.

retrieval the process of getting information out of memory storage.

sensory memory the immediate, very brief recording of sensory information in the memory system.

short-term memory activated memory that holds a few items briefly, such as the seven digits of a phone number while dialing, before the information is stored or forgotten.

long-term memory the relatively permanent and limitless storehouse of the memory system. Includes knowledge, skills, and experiences.

working memory a newer understanding of short-term memory that focuses on conscious, active processing of incoming auditory and visual-spatial information, and of information retrieved from long-term memory.

seconds each. Later you see 280 of these slides, paired with others not previously seen. If you are like the participants in this experiment by Ralph Haber (1970), you would recognize 90 percent of those you had seen before.

Or imagine yourself looking at a picture fragment, such as the one in **FIGURE 8.1**. Also imagine that you had seen the complete picture for a couple of seconds 17 years earlier. Given this experience in a real experiment (Mitchell, 2006), people were more likely to identify previously seen objects than were members of a control group who had not seen complete drawings. Moreover, like the cicada insect that reemerges every 17 years, the picture memory reappeared even for those who had no conscious recollection of participating in the long-ago experiment!

How do we accomplish such memory feats? How can we remember things we have not thought about for years, yet forget the name of someone we met a minute ago? How are memories stored in our brain? Why do some painful memories persist, like unwelcome houseguests, while other memories leave too quickly? How can two people's memories of the same event be so different? Why will you be likely later in this chapter to misrecall this sentence: *"The angry rioter threw the rock at the window"?* How can we improve our memories? These will be among the questions we consider as we review more than a century of research on memory.

Studying Memory: Information-Processing Models

1: How do psychologists describe the human memory system?

A model of how memory works can help us think about how we form and retrieve memories. One often-used model is a computer's information-processing system, which is in some ways similar to human memory. To remember any event, we must get information into our brain **(encoding)**, retain that information **(storage)**, and later get it back out **(retrieval)**. A computer also encodes, stores, and retrieves information. First, it translates input (keystrokes) into an electronic language, much as the brain encodes sensory information into a neural language. The computer permanently stores vast amounts of information on a drive, from which it can later be retrieved.

Like all analogies, the computer model has its limits. Our memories are less literal and more fragile than a computer's. Moreover, most computers process information speedily but sequentially, even while alternating between tasks. The brain is slower but does many things at once.

Psychologists have proposed several information-processing models of memory. One modern model, *connectionism,* views memories as emerging from interconnected neural networks. Specific memories arise from particular activation patterns within these networks. In an older but easier-to-picture model, Richard Atkinson and Richard Shiffrin (1968) proposed that we form memories in three stages:

1. We first record to-be-remembered information as a fleeting **sensory memory.**
2. From there, we process information into a **short-term memory** bin, where we encode it through *rehearsal.*
3. Finally, information moves into **long-term memory** for later retrieval.

Although historically important and helpfully simple, this three-step process is limited and fallible. In this chapter, we use a *modified version of the three-stage processing model of memory* (**FIGURE 8.2**). This updated model accommodates two important new concepts:

- Some information, as you will see later in this chapter, skips Atkinson and Shiffrin's first two stages and is processed directly and automatically into long-term memory, without our conscious awareness.

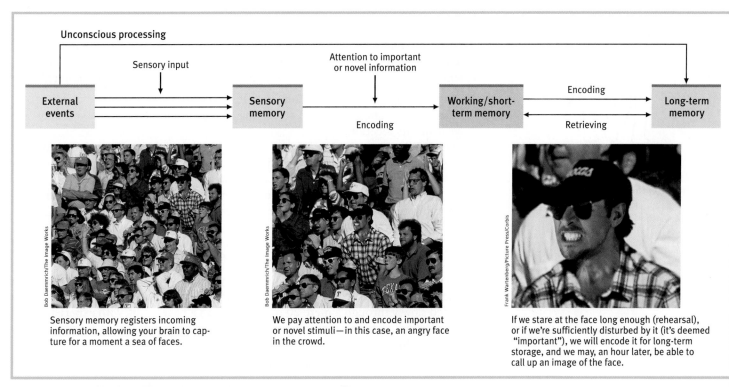

Sensory memory registers incoming information, allowing your brain to capture for a moment a sea of faces.

We pay attention to and encode important or novel stimuli—in this case, an angry face in the crowd.

If we stare at the face long enough (rehearsal), or if we're sufficiently disturbed by it (it's deemed "important"), we will encode it for long-term storage, and we may, an hour later, be able to call up an image of the face.

FIGURE 8.2 A modified three-stage processing model of memory Atkinson and Shiffrin's classic three-step model helps us to think about how memories are processed, but today's researchers recognize other ways long-term memories form. For example, some information slips into long-term memory via a "back door," without our consciously attending to it. And so much active processing occurs in the short-term memory stage that many now prefer the term *working memory*.

- **Working memory,** a newer understanding of Atkinson and Shiffrin's second stage, concentrates on the active processing of information in this intermediate stage. Because we cannot possibly focus on all the information bombarding our senses at once, we shine the flashlight beam of our attention on certain incoming stimuli—often those that are novel or important. We process these incoming stimuli, along with information we retrieve from long-term memory, in temporary working memory. Working memory associates new and old information and solves problems (Baddeley, 2001, 2002; Engle, 2002).

Let's use our updated model now to look more closely at how we encode, store, and retrieve information.

Encoding: Getting Information In

2: What information do we encode automatically? What information do we encode effortfully, and how does the distribution of practice influence retention?

How We Encode: Levels of Processing

Some information, such as the route you walked to your last class, you process with great ease, freeing your memory system to focus on less familiar events. But to retain novel information, such as a friend's new cell-phone number, you need to pay attention and try hard.

FIGURE 8.3 Now you know People who had seen this complete image were, 17 years later, more likely to recognize the fragment in Figure 8.1.

Automatic Processing

Thanks to your brain's capacity for simultaneous activity (for parallel processing), an enormous amount of multitasking goes on without your conscious attention. For example, without conscious effort you **automatically process** information about

- *space.* While studying, you often encode the place on a page where certain material appears; later, when struggling to recall that information, you may visualize its location.
- *time.* While going about your day, you unintentionally note the sequence of the day's events. Later, when you realize you've left your coat somewhere, you can re-create that sequence and retrace your steps.
- *frequency.* You effortlessly keep track of how many times things happen, thus enabling you to realize that "this is the third time I've run into her today."
- *well-learned material.* For example, when you see words in your native language, perhaps on the side of a delivery truck, you cannot help but register their meaning. At such times, automatic processing is so effortless that it is difficult to shut off.

Deciphering words was not always so easy. When you first learned to read, you sounded out individual letters to figure out what words they made. With effort, you plodded slowly through a mere 20 to 50 words on a page, until, with experience and practice, reading became automatic. Imagine now learning to read reversed sentences like this:

.citamotua emoceb nac gnissecorp luftroffE

At first, this requires effort, but after enough practice, you would also perform this task much more automatically. We develop many skills in this way. We learn to drive, to text message, to speak a new language first with full attention and great effort, then more automatically.

FIGURE 8.4 Automatic versus effortful processing Some information, such as where you ate dinner yesterday, you process automatically. Other information, such as this chapter's concepts, requires effort to encode and remember.

"He should test his memory by reciting the verses."

—Abdur-Rahman Abdul Khaliq, "Memorizing the Quran"

Effortful Processing

We encode and retain vast amounts of information automatically, but we remember other types of information, such as this chapter's concepts, only with effort and attention (**FIGURE 8.4**). **Effortful processing** often produces durable and accessible memories.

When learning novel information, such as names, we can boost our memory through **rehearsal,** or conscious repetition. The pioneering researcher of verbal memory, German philosopher Hermann Ebbinghaus (1850–1909), showed this after becoming impatient with philosophical speculations about memory. Ebbinghaus decided he would scientifically study his own learning and forgetting of novel verbal materials.

To create novel verbal material for his learning experiments, Ebbinghaus formed a list of all possible nonsense syllables by sandwiching one vowel between two consonants. He then randomly selected a sample of the syllables, practiced them, and tested himself. To get a feel for his experiments, rapidly read aloud, eight times over, the list at the top of the next page (from Baddeley, 1982). Then try to recall the items.

JIH, BAZ, FUB, YOX, SUJ, XIR, DAX, LEQ, VUM, PID, KEL, WAV, TUV, ZOF, GEK, HIW.

The day after learning such a list, Ebbinghaus could recall few of the syllables. But were they entirely forgotten? As **FIGURE 8.5** portrays, the more frequently he repeated the list aloud on day 1, the fewer repetitions he required to relearn the list on day 2. Here, then, was a simple beginning principle: *The amount remembered depends on the time spent learning.* Even after we learn material, additional rehearsal *(overlearning)* increases retention. *The point to remember:* For novel verbal information, practice—effortful processing—does indeed make perfect.

Later research revealed more about how to lay down enduring memories. To paraphrase Ebbinghaus (1885), those who learn quickly also forget quickly. We retain information better when our rehearsal is distributed over time (as when learning classmates' names), a phenomenon called the **spacing effect.** More than 300 experiments over the last century consistently reveal the benefits of spacing learning times (Cepeda et al., 2006). *Massed practice* (cramming) can produce speedy short-term learning and feelings of confidence. But *distributed study time* produces better long-term recall. After you've studied long enough to master the material, further study—overlearning—is most efficient if delayed (Rohrer & Pashler, 2007). Better to spend that extra reviewing time later—a day later if you need to remember something 10 days hence, or a month later if you need to remember something 6 months hence.

In a 9-year experiment, Harry Bahrick and three of his family members (1993) practiced foreign language word translations for a given number of times, at intervals ranging from 14 to 56 days. Their consistent finding: The longer the space between practice sessions, the better their retention up to 5 years later. The practical implication? Spreading out learning—over a semester or a year, rather than over a shorter term—should help you not only on comprehensive final exams, but also in retaining the information for a lifetime. Repeated quizzing of previously studied material also helps, a phenomenon that Henry Roediger and Jeffrey Karpicke (2006) call the *testing effect,* adding, "Testing is a powerful means of improving learning, not just assessing it." *So here is another point to remember:* Spaced study and self-assessment beat cramming.

Another phenomenon, the **serial position effect,** further illustrates the benefits of rehearsal. As an everyday parallel, imagine it's your first day in a new job, and your manager is introducing co-workers. As you meet each one, you repeat (rehearse) all their names, starting from the beginning. By the time you meet the last person, you will have spent more time rehearsing the earlier names than the later ones; thus, the next day you will probably more easily recall the earlier names. Also, learning the first few names may interfere with your learning the later ones.

Experimenters have demonstrated the serial position effect by showing people a list of items (words, names, dates, even odors) and then immediately asking them to recall the items in any order (Reed, 2000). Struggling to recall the list, people often remember the last and first items better than those in the middle (see **FIGURE 8.6** on the next page). Perhaps because the last items are still in working memory, people briefly recall them especially quickly and well *(a recency effect).* But after a delay—after they shift their attention from the last items—their recall is best for the first items *(a primacy effect).*

Sometimes, however, rehearsal is not enough to store new information for later recall (Craik & Watkins, 1973; Greene, 1987). To understand why this happens, we need to know more about how we encode information for processing into long-term memory.

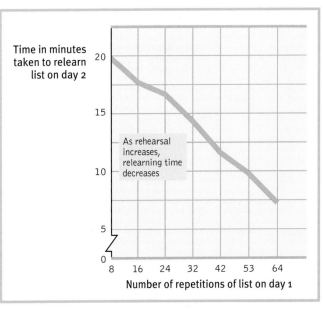

FIGURE 8.5 **Ebbinghaus' retention curve** Ebbinghaus found that the more times he practiced a list of nonsense syllables on day 1, the fewer repetitions he required to relearn it on day 2. Said simply, the more time we spend learning novel information, the more we retain. (From Baddeley, 1982.)

"The mind is slow in unlearning what it has been long in learning."

—Roman philosopher Seneca (4 B.C.E.–65 C.E.)

automatic processing unconscious encoding of incidental information, such as space, time, and frequency, and of well-learned information, such as word meanings.

effortful processing encoding that requires attention and conscious effort.

rehearsal the conscious repetition of information, either to maintain it in consciousness or to encode it for storage.

spacing effect the tendency for distributed study or practice to yield better long-term retention than is achieved through massed study or practice.

serial position effect our tendency to recall best the last and first items in a list.

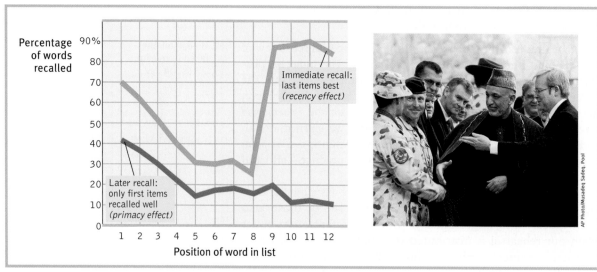

FIGURE 8.6 The serial position effect
Immediately after Australian Prime Minister Kevin Rudd introduces this long line of officials to Afghan President Hamid Karzai, President Karzai will probably recall the names of the last few people best. But he may later recall the first few people best. (From Craik & Watkins, 1973.)

Here is another sentence I will ask you about later: The fish attacked the swimmer.

What We Encode

3: What effortful processing methods aid in forming memories?

Processing our sensory input is like sorting through e-mail. Some items we instantly discard. Others we open, read, and retain. We process information by encoding its meaning, encoding its image, or mentally organizing it.

Encoding Meaning

When processing verbal information for storage, we usually encode its meaning, associating it with what we already know or imagine. Whether we hear *eye-screem* as "ice cream" or "I scream" depends on how the context and our experience guide us to interpret and encode the sounds. (Remember, our working memories interact with our long-term memories.)

Can you repeat the sentence about the rioter that I gave you at this chapter's beginning? ("The angry rioter threw . . .") Perhaps, like those in an experiment by William Brewer (1977), you recalled the rioter sentence by the meaning you encoded when you read it (for example, "The angry rioter threw the rock *through* the window") and not as it was written ("The angry rioter threw the rock *at* the window"). Referring to such recall, Gordon Bower and Daniel Morrow (1990) likened our minds to theater directors who, given a raw script, imagine a finished stage production. Asked later what we heard or read, we recall not the literal text but *what we encoded*. Thus, studying for an exam, you may remember your lecture notes rather than the lecture itself.

But given too raw a script, we have trouble creating a mental model. Put yourself in the place of the students who John Bransford and Marcia Johnson (1972) asked to remember the following recorded passage:

> The procedure is actually quite simple. First you arrange things into different groups. Of course, one pile may be sufficient depending on how much there is to do. . . . After the procedure is completed one arranges the materials into different groups again. Then they can be put into their appropriate places. Eventually they will be used once more and the whole cycle will then have to be repeated. However, that is part of life.

When the students heard the paragraph you have just read, without a meaningful context, they remembered little of it. When told the paragraph described washing clothes (something meaningful to them), they remembered much more of it—as you probably could now after rereading it.

Such research suggests the benefits of rephrasing what we read and hear into meaningful terms. People often ask actors how they learn "all those lines." They do it by first coming to understand the flow of meaning, report psychologist-actor team Helga Noice and Tony Noice (2006). "One actor divided a half-page of dialogue into three [intentions]: 'to flatter,' 'to draw him out,' and 'to allay his fears.'" With this meaningful sequence in mind, the actor more easily remembers the lines.

From his experiments on himself, Ebbinghaus estimated that, compared with learning nonsense material, learning meaningful material required one-tenth the effort. As memory researcher Wayne Wickelgren (1977, p. 346) noted, "The time you spend thinking about material you are reading and relating it to previously stored material is about the most useful thing you can do in learning any new subject matter."

The point to remember: The amount remembered depends both on the time spent learning and on your making it meaningful.

Visual Encoding

Why is it that we struggle to remember formulas, definitions, and dates, yet we can easily remember where we were yesterday, who was with us, where we sat, and what we wore? One difference is the greater ease of remembering mental pictures. Our earliest memories—probably of something that happened at age 3 or 4—involve visual **imagery.** We more easily remember concrete words, which lend themselves to visual mental images, than we do abstract, low-imagery words. (When I quiz you later, which three of these words—*typewriter, void, cigarette, inherent, fire, process*—will you most likely recall?) If you still recall the rock-throwing rioter sentence, it is probably not only because of the meaning you encoded but also because the sentence lent itself to a visual image. Memory for concrete nouns, such as *cigarette*, is aided by encoding *both* their meaning and their image (Marschark et al., 1987; Paivio, 1986). Two codes are better than one.

Thanks to this durability of vivid images, our memory of an experience is often colored by its best or worst moment—the best moment of pleasure or joy, and the worst moment of pain or frustration (Fredrickson & Kahneman, 1993). Recalling the high points while forgetting the mundane may explain the phenomenon of *rosy retrospection* (Mitchell et al., 1997): People tend to recall events such as a camping holiday more positively than they judged them at the time. The muggy heat and long lines of that visit to Disney World fade as we bask in our vivid recall of the surroundings, food, and rides.

Imagery is at the heart of many **mnemonic** (nih-MON-ik) devices (so named after the Greek word for "memory"). Ancient Greek scholars and orators developed mnemonics to help them retrieve lengthy memorized passages and speeches. Some modern mnemonic devices rely on both acoustic and visual codes. For example, the *peg-word system* requires you to memorize a jingle: *"One is a bun; two is a shoe; three is a tree; four is a door; five is a hive; six is sticks; seven is heaven; eight is a gate; nine is swine; ten is a hen."* Without much effort, you will soon be able to count by peg-words instead of numbers: *bun, shoe, tree* . . . and then to visually associate the peg-words with to-be-remembered items. Now you are ready to challenge anyone to give you a grocery list to remember. Carrots? Stick them into the imaginary bun. Milk? Fill the shoe with it. Paper towels? Drape them over the tree branch. Think *bun, shoe, tree* and you see their associated images: carrots, milk, paper towels. With few errors (Bugelski et al., 1968), you will be able to recall the items in any order and to name any given item. Memory whizzes understand the power of such systems. A study of star performers in the World Memory Championships showed them not to have exceptional intelligence, but rather to be superior at using spatial mnemonic strategies (Maguire et al., 2003).

How many Fs are in the following sentence? FINISHED FILES ARE THE RESULTS OF YEARS OF SCIENTIFIC STUDY COMBINED WITH THE EXPERIENCE OF YEARS. See inverted answer below.

Partly because your initial processing of the letters was primarily acoustic rather than visual, you probably missed some of the six Fs, especially those that sound like a V rather than an F.

imagery mental pictures; a powerful aid to effortful processing, especially when combined with encoding.

mnemonics [nih-MON-iks] memory aids, especially those techniques that use vivid imagery and organizational devices.

1. ⊲⊃⅁∾⅂N⊥
2. K L C I S N E

3. KLCISNE NVESE YNA NI CSTTIH TNDO
4. NICKELS SEVEN ANY IN STITCH DONT

5. NICKELS SEVEN ANY IN STITCH DONT SAVES AGO A SCORE TIME AND NINE WOODEN FOUR YEARS TAKE

6. DONT TAKE ANY WOODEN NICKELS FOUR SCORE AND SEVEN YEARS AGO A STITCH IN TIME SAVES NINE

FIGURE 8.7 Effects of meaningful chunking on memory When we organize information into meaningful units, such as letters, words, and phrases, we recall it more easily. (From Hintzman, 1978.)

春夏秋冬

FIGURE 8.8 An example of chunking—for those who read Chinese After looking at these characters, can you reproduce them exactly? If so, you are literate in Chinese.

- -

chunking organizing items into familiar, manageable units; often occurs automatically.

Organizing Information for Encoding

Mnemonic devices can also help organize material for our later retrieval. When Bransford and Johnson's laundry paragraph became meaningful, we could mentally organize its sentences into a sequence. We process information more easily when we can organize it into meaningful units or structures.

CHUNKING Glance for a few seconds at row 1 of **FIGURE 8.7**, then look away and try to reproduce what you saw. Impossible, yes? But you can easily reproduce the second row, which is no less complex. Similarly, you will probably find row 4 much easier to remember than row 3, although both contain the same letters. And you could remember the sixth cluster more easily than the fifth, although both contain the same words.

As these units demonstrate, we more easily recall information when we can organize it into familiar, manageable chunks. **Chunking** occurs so naturally that we take it for granted. If you are a native English speaker, you can reproduce perfectly the 150 or so line segments that make up the words in the three phrases of item 6 in Figure 8.7. It would astonish someone unfamiliar with the language.

I am similarly awed at the ability of someone literate in Chinese to glance at **FIGURE 8.8** and then to reproduce all of the strokes; or of a chess master who, after a 5-second look at the board during a game, can recall the exact positions of most of the pieces (Chase & Simon, 1973); or of a varsity basketball player who, given a 4-second glance at a basketball play, can recall the positions of the players (Allard & Burnett, 1985). We all remember information best when we can organize it into personally meaningful arrangements.

Chunking can also be used as a mnemonic technique to recall unfamiliar material. Want to remember the colors of the rainbow in order of wavelength? Think of the mnemonic ROY G. BIV (*r*ed, *o*range, *y*ellow, *g*reen, *b*lue, *i*ndigo, *v*iolet). Need to recall the names of North America's five Great Lakes? Just remember HOMES (*H*uron, *O*ntario, *M*ichigan, *E*rie, *S*uperior). In each case, we chunk information into a more familiar form by creating a word (called an *acronym*) from the first letters of the to-be-remembered items.

HIERARCHIES When people develop expertise in an area, they process information not only in chunks but also in *hierarchies* composed of a few broad concepts divided and subdivided into narrower concepts and facts. This chapter, for example, aims not only to teach you the elementary facts of memory but also to help you organize these facts around broad principles, such as *encoding;* subprinciples, such as *automatic* and *effortful processing;* and still more specific concepts, such as *meaning, imagery,* and *organization* (**FIGURE 8.9**).

FIGURE 8.9 Organization benefits memory When we organize words or concepts into hierarchical groups, as illustrated here with concepts in this chapter, we remember them better than when we see them presented randomly.

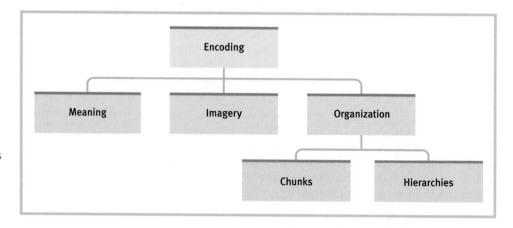

Organizing knowledge into hierarchies helps us retrieve information efficiently. Gordon Bower and his colleagues (1969) demonstrated this by presenting words either randomly or grouped into categories. When the words were organized into groups, recall was two to three times better. Such results show the benefits of organizing what you study—of giving special attention to chapter outlines, headings, preview questions, summaries, and self-test questions. If you can master a chapter's concepts within their overall organization, your recall should be effective at test time. Taking lecture and text notes in outline format—a type of hierarchical organization—may also prove helpful.

In the discussion of encoding imagery, I gave you six words and told you I would quiz you about them later. How many of these words can you now recall? Of these, how many are high-imagery words? How many are low-imagery? (You can check your list against the six inverted words below.)

Typewriter, void, cigarette, inherent, fire, process

REHEARSE IT!

1. The psychological terms for taking in information, retaining it, and later getting it back out are
   a. retrieval, encoding, and storage.
   b. encoding, storage, and retrieval.
   c. storage, encoding, and retrieval.
   d. retrieval, storage, and encoding.

2. Short-term memory is an intermediate memory stage where information is held before it is stored or forgotten. The newer concept of working memory
   a. clarifies the idea of short-term memory by focusing on the active processing that occurs in this stage.
   b. splits short-term memory into two substages—sensory memory and working memory.
   c. splits short-term memory into two areas—working (retrievable) memory and inaccessible memory.
   d. clarifies the idea of short-term memory by focusing on space, time, and frequency.

3. Rehearsal, the conscious repetition of information a person wants to remember, is part of
   a. automatic processing.
   b. effortful processing.
   c. forgetting.
   d. retrieval.

4. When tested immediately after viewing a list of words, people tend to recall the first and last items more readily than those in the middle. When retested after a delay, they are most likely to recall
   a. the first items on the list.
   b. the first and last items on the list.
   c. a few items at random.
   d. the last items on the list.

5. Memory aids that use visual imagery, peg-words, or other organizational devices are called
   a. encoders.
   b. nonsense material.
   c. acoustic clues.
   d. mnemonics.

6. Organizing information into broad categories, which are then divided into subcategories, is known as
   a. the serial position effect.
   b. the peg-word system.
   c. hierarchical organization.
   d. creating acronyms.

Answers: 1. b, 2. a, 3. b, 4. a, 5. d, 6. c.

Storage: Retaining Information

At the heart of memory is storage. If you later recall something you experienced, you must, somehow, have stored and retrieved it. Anything stored in long-term memory lies dormant, waiting to be reconstructed by a cue. What is our memory storage capacity? Let's start with the first memory store noted in the modified three-stage processing model (Figure 8.2)—our fleeting sensory memory.

Sensory Memory

4: **What are two components of sensory memory?**

How much of this page could you sense and recall with less exposure than a lightning flash? Researcher George Sperling (1960) asked people to do something similar when he showed them, for only one-twentieth of a second, three rows of three letters each (**FIGURE 8.10**). After the nine letters disappeared, people could recall only about half of them.

Was it because they had insufficient time to glimpse them? No, Sperling cleverly demonstrated that people actually *could* see and recall all the letters, but only momentarily. Rather than ask them to recall all nine letters at once, Sperling sounded a high, medium, or low tone immediately *after*

FIGURE 8.10 Momentary photographic memory When George Sperling flashed a group of letters similar to this for one-twentieth of a second, people could recall only about half of the letters. But when signaled to recall a particular row immediately after the letters had disappeared, they could do so with near-perfect accuracy.

K	Z	R
Q	B	T
S	G	N

iconic memory a momentary sensory memory of visual stimuli; a photographic or picture-image memory lasting no more than a few tenths of a second.

echoic memory a momentary sensory memory of auditory stimuli; if attention is elsewhere, sounds and words can still be recalled within 3 or 4 seconds.

flashing the nine letters. This cue directed participants to report only the letters of the top, middle, or bottom row, respectively. Now they rarely missed a letter, showing that all nine letters were momentarily available for recall.

Sperling's experiment revealed that we have a fleeting photographic memory called **iconic memory.** For a few tenths of a second, our eyes register an exact representation of a scene and we can recall any part of it in amazing detail. But if Sperling delayed the tone signal by more than half a second, the image faded and participants again recalled only about half the letters. Our visual screen clears quickly, as new images are superimposed over old ones.

We also have an impeccable, though fleeting, memory for auditory stimuli, called **echoic memory** (Cowan, 1988; Lu et al., 1992). Picture yourself in conversation, as your attention veers to the TV. If your mildly irked companion tests your attention by asking, "What did I just say?" you can recover their last few words from your mind's echo chamber. Auditory echoes tend to linger for 3 or 4 seconds. Experiments on echoic and iconic memory have helped us understand the initial recording of sensory information in the memory system.

Working/Short-Term Memory

5: What are the duration and capacity of short-term and of long-term memory?

Among the vast amounts of information registered by our sensory memory, we illuminate some with our attentional flashlight. We also retrieve information from long-term storage for "on-screen" display. But unless our working memory meaningfully encodes or rehearses that information, it quickly disappears from our short-term store. During your finger's trip from phone book to phone, a telephone number may evaporate.

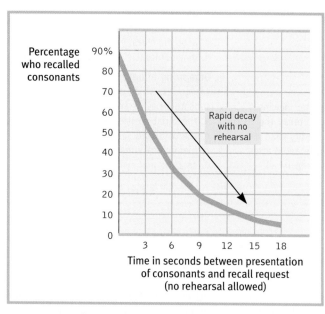

FIGURE 8.11 **Short-term memory decay** Unless rehearsed, verbal information may be quickly forgotten. (From Peterson & Peterson, 1959; see also Brown, 1958.)

The Magical Number Seven has become psychology's contribution to an intriguing list of magic sevens—the seven wonders of the world, the seven seas, the seven deadly sins, the seven primary colors, the seven musical scale notes, the seven days of the week—seven magical sevens.

To find out how quickly a short-term memory will disappear, Lloyd Peterson and Margaret Peterson (1959) asked people to remember three-consonant groups, such as CHJ. To prevent rehearsal, the researchers asked them, for example, to start at 100 and count aloud backward by threes. After 3 seconds, people recalled the letters only about half the time; after 12 seconds, they seldom recalled them at all (**FIGURE 8.11**). Without active processing, short-term memories have a limited life.

Short-term memory is limited not only in duration but also in capacity, typically storing about seven bits of information (give or take two). George Miller (1956) enshrined this recall capacity as the *Magical Number Seven, plus or minus two.* Not surprisingly, when some phone companies began requiring all callers to dial a three-digit area code in addition to a seven-digit number, many people reported trouble retaining the just-looked-up number.

Our short-term recall is slightly better for random digits (as in a phone number) than for random letters, which may have similar sounds. It is slightly better for what we hear than for what we see. Both children and adults have short-term recall for roughly as many words as they can speak in 2 seconds (Cowan, 1994; Hulme & Tordoff, 1989).

Without rehearsal, most of us actually retain in short-term memory only about four information chunks (for example, letters meaningfully grouped as BBC, FBI, KGB, CIA) (Cowan, 2001; Jonides et al., 2008). Suppressing rehearsal by saying *the, the, the* while hearing random digits also reduces memory to about four items. The basic principle: *At any given moment, we can consciously process only a very limited amount of information.*

Long-Term Memory

In Arthur Conan Doyle's *A Study in Scarlet,* Sherlock Holmes offers a popular theory of memory capacity:

> I consider that a man's brain originally is like a little empty attic, and you have to stock it with such furniture as you choose. . . . It is a mistake to think that that little room has elastic walls and can distend to any extent. Depend upon it, there comes a time when for every addition of knowledge you forget something that you knew before.

Contrary to Holmes' belief, our capacity for storing long-term memories is essentially limitless. Our brains are *not* like attics, which once filled can store more items only if we discard old ones.

The point is vividly illustrated by those who have performed phenomenal memory feats. Consider the 1990s tests of psychologist Rajan Mahadevan's memory. Given a block of 10 digits from the first 30,000 or so digits of pi, Rajan, after a few moments of mental searching for the string, would pick up the series from there, firing numbers like a machine gun (Delaney et al., 1999; Thompson et al., 1993). He could also repeat 50 random digits—backward. It is not a genetic gift, he said; anyone could learn to do it. But given the genetic influence on so many human traits, and knowing that Rajan's father memorized Shakespeare's complete works, one wonders. We are reminded that many psychological phenomena, including memory capacity, can be studied by means of different levels of analysis, including the biological.

Clark's nutcracker Among animals, one contender for champion memorist would be a mere birdbrain—the Clark's Nutcracker—which during winter and early spring can locate up to 6000 caches of pine seeds it had previously buried (Shettleworth, 1993).

Pi in the sky: The world record for memorizing pi has been held by Japan's Akira Haraguchi, who in 2006 reportedly recited the first 100,000 digits correctly (Associated Press, 2006).

Storing Information in the Brain

6: **How does the brain store our memories?**

I marveled at my aging mother-in-law, a retired pianist and organist. At age 88 her blind eyes could no longer read music. But let her sit at a keyboard and she would flawlessly play any of hundreds of hymns, including ones she had not thought of for 20 years. Where did her brain store those thousands of sequenced notes?

For a time, some surgeons and memory researchers believed that flashbacks triggered by brain stimulation during surgery indicated that our whole past, not just well-practiced music, is "in there," in complete detail, just waiting to be relived. But when Elizabeth Loftus and Geoffrey Loftus (1980) analyzed the vivid "memories" triggered by brain stimulation, they found that the seeming flashbacks appeared to have been invented, not relived. Psychologist Karl Lashley (1950) further demonstrated that memories do not reside in single, specific spots. He trained rats to find their way out of a maze, then cut out pieces of their brain's cortex and retested their memory. Amazingly, no matter what small section he removed, the rats retained at least a partial memory of how to navigate the maze. So, despite the brain's vast storage capacity, we do not store information as libraries store their books, in discrete, precise locations.

"Our memories are flexible and superimposable, a panoramic blackboard with an endless supply of chalk and erasers."

—Elizabeth Loftus and Katherine Ketcham, *The Myth of Repressed Memory,* 1994

Synaptic Changes

Looking for clues to the brain's storage system, contemporary memory researchers have searched for a *memory trace*. The quest to understand the physical basis of memory—for how information becomes incarnated in matter—has sparked study of the synaptic meeting places where neurons communicate with one another via their neurotransmitter messengers.

"The biology of the mind will be as scientifically important to this [new] century as the biology of the gene [was] to the twentieth century."

—Eric Kandel, acceptance remarks for the 2000 Nobel Prize

Aplysia The California sea slug, which neuro-scientist Eric Kandel studied for 45 years, has increased our understanding of the neural basis of learning.

We know that experience does modify the brain's neural networks; given increased activity in a particular pathway, neural interconnections form or strengthen (see Chapter 4). Eric Kandel and James Schwartz (1982) observed such changes in the sending neurons of a simple animal, the California sea slug, *Aplysia.* Its mere 20,000 or so nerve cells are unusually large and accessible, enabling the researchers to observe synaptic changes during learning. Chapter 7 noted how the sea slug can be classically conditioned (with electric shock) to reflexively withdraw its gills when squirted with water, much as a shell-shocked soldier jumps at the sound of a snapping twig. By observing the slugs' neural connections before and after conditioning, Kandel and Schwartz pinpointed changes. When learning occurs, the slug releases more of the neurotransmitter *serotonin* at certain synapses. These synapses then become more efficient at transmitting signals.

FIGURE 8.12 Doubled receptor sites
Electron microscope images show just one receptor site (gray) reaching toward a sending neuron before long-term potentiation (left), and two sites after LTP (right). A doubling of the receptor sites means that the receiving neuron has increased sensitivity for detecting the presence of the neurotransmitter molecules that may be released by the sending neuron. (From Toni et al., 1999.)

Increased synaptic efficiency makes for more efficient neural circuits. In experiments, rapidly stimulating certain memory-circuit connections has increased their sensitivity for hours or even weeks to come. The sending neuron now needs less prompting to release its neurotransmitter, and the receiving neuron's receptor sites may increase (**FIGURE 8.12**). This prolonged strengthening of potential neural firing, called **long-term potentiation (LTP)**, provides a neural basis for learning and remembering associations (Lynch, 2002; Whitlock et al., 2006). Several lines of evidence confirm that LTP is a physical basis for memory:

- Drugs that block LTP interfere with learning (Lynch & Staubli, 1991).
- Mutant mice engineered to lack an enzyme needed for LTP can't learn their way out of a maze (Silva et al., 1992).
- Rats given a drug that enhances LTP will learn a maze with half the usual number of mistakes (Service, 1994).
- Injecting rats with a chemical that blocks the preservation of LTP erases recent learning (Pastalkova et al., 2006).

Some memory-biology explorers have helped found pharmaceutical companies that are competing to develop and test memory-boosting drugs. Their target market includes millions of people with Alzheimer's disease, millions more with *mild cognitive impairment* that often becomes Alzheimer's, and countless millions who would love to turn back the clock on age-related memory decline. From expanding memories perhaps will come bulging profits.

After LTP has occurred, passing an electric current through the brain won't disrupt old memories. But the current will wipe out very recent memories. Such is the experience both of laboratory animals and of depressed people given electroconvulsive therapy (ECT). A blow to the head can do the same. Football players and boxers momentarily knocked unconscious typically have no memory of events just before the knock-out (Yarnell & Lynch, 1970). Their working memory had no time to consolidate the information into long-term memory before the lights went out.

Stress Hormones and Memory

Arousal can sear certain events into the brain, while disrupting memory for neutral events around the same time (Birnbaum et al., 2004; Brewin et al., 2007). When we are excited or stressed, emotion-triggered stress hormones make more glucose energy available to fuel brain activity, signaling the brain that something important has happened. Moreover, the amygdala, the two emotion-processing clusters in the limbic system, boosts activity and available proteins in the brain's memory-forming areas (Buchanan, 2007; Kensinger, 2007). The result? "Stronger emotional experiences make for stronger, more reliable memories," says James McGaugh (1994,

Although ECT for depression disrupts memory for recent experiences, it leaves most memories intact (see Chapter 14).

long-term potentiation (LTP) an increase in a synapse's firing potential after brief, rapid stimulation. Believed to be a neural basis for learning and memory.

flashbulb memory a clear memory of an emotionally significant moment or event.

amnesia the loss of memory.

Severe stress sears in memories
Significantly stressful events, such as the disastrous 2007 California wildfires, may be an indelible part of the memories of those who experienced them.

2003). After traumatic experiences—a wartime ambush, a house fire, a rape—vivid recollections of the horrific event may intrude again and again. It is as if they were burned in. This makes adaptive sense. Memory serves to predict the future and to alert us to potential dangers.

Conversely, weaker emotion means weaker memories. People given a drug that blocks the effects of stress hormones will later have more trouble remembering the details of an upsetting story (Cahill, 1994). That connection is appreciated by those working to develop drugs that, when taken after a traumatic experience, might blunt intrusive memories. In one experiment, victims of car accidents, rapes, and other traumas received, for 10 days afterward, either one such drug, propranolol, or a placebo. When tested three months later, half the placebo group but none of the drug-treated group showed signs of stress disorder (Pitman et al., 2002, 2005).

If you suffered a traumatic experience, would you want to take a drug to blunt that memory?

Emotion-triggered hormonal changes help explain why we long remember exciting or shocking events, such as our first kiss or our whereabouts when learning of a friend's death. In a 2006 Pew survey, 95 percent of American adults said they could recall exactly where they were or what they were doing when they first heard the news of the 9/11 attack. This perceived clarity of memories of surprising, significant events leads some psychologists to call them **flashbulb memories.** It's as if the brain commands, "Capture this!" The people who experienced a 1989 San Francisco earthquake did just that. A year and a half later, they had perfect recall of where they had been and what they were doing (verified by their recorded thoughts within a day or two of the quake). Others' memories for the circumstances under which they merely *heard* about the quake were more prone to errors (Neisser et al., 1991; Palmer et al., 1991).

Which is more important—your experiences or your memories of them?

Our flashbulb memories are noteworthy for their vividness and the confidence with which we recall them. But as we relive, rehearse, and discuss them, these memories may come to err, as misinformation seeps into them (Talarico et al., 2003; Talarico & Rubin, 2007).

Storing Implicit and Explicit Memories

A memory-to-be enters the cortex through the senses, then wends its way into the brain's depths. Precisely where it goes depends on the type of information, as dramatically illustrated by those who, as in the case of my father mentioned earlier, suffer from a type of **amnesia** in which they are unable to form new memories.

The most famous case, a patient known to every neuroscientist as H. M., experienced in 1953 the necessary surgical removal of a brain area involved in laying down new conscious memories of facts and experiences. The brain tissue loss left his older memories intact—many years later, he was still doing daily crossword puzzles. But converting new experiences to long-term storage was another matter. "I've known H. M. since 1962, and he still doesn't know who I am," noted his longtime researcher Suzanne Corkin (Adelson, 2005).

implicit memory retention independent of conscious recollection. (Also called *nondeclarative memory*.)

explicit memory memory of facts and experiences that one can consciously know and "declare." (Also called *declarative memory*.)

hippocampus a neural center that is located in the limbic system; helps process explicit memories for storage.

"The most important person in the history of brain science." So said the *New York Times* of H. M., revealed at his death in 2008 to be Henry Molaison. H. M. died at age 82 in a Connecticut nursing home.

http://www.nytimes.com/2008/12/05/us/05hm.html.

Neurologist Oliver Sacks (1985, pp. 26–27) described another such patient, Jimmie, who had brain damage. Jimmie had no memories—thus, no sense of elapsed time—beyond his injury in 1945. Asked in 1975 to name the U.S. President, he replied, "FDR's dead. Truman's at the helm."

When Jimmie gave his age as 19, Sacks set a mirror before him: "Look in the mirror and tell me what you see. Is that a 19-year-old looking out from the mirror?"

Jimmie turned ashen, gripped the chair, cursed, then became frantic: "What's going on? What's happened to me? Is this a nightmare? Am I crazy? Is this a joke?" When his attention was diverted to some children playing baseball, his panic ended, the dreadful mirror forgotten.

Sacks showed Jimmie a photo from *National Geographic*. "What is this?" he asked. "It's the Moon," Jimmie replied.

"No, it's not," Sacks answered. "It's a picture of the Earth taken from the Moon."

"Doc, you're kidding? Someone would've had to get a camera up there!"

"Naturally."

"Hell! You're joking—how the hell would you do that?" Jimmie's wonder was that of a bright young man from 60 years ago reacting with amazement to his travel back to the future.

Careful testing of these unique people reveals something even stranger: Although incapable of recalling new facts or anything they have done recently, Jimmie and others with similar conditions can learn. Shown hard-to-find figures in pictures (in the *Where's Waldo?* series), they can quickly spot them again later. They can find their way to the bathroom, though without being able to tell you where it is. They can learn to read mirror-image writing or do a jigsaw puzzle, and they have even been taught complicated job skills (Schacter, 1992, 1996; Xu & Corkin, 2001). And they can be classically conditioned. However, *they do all these things with no awareness of having learned them.* For example, over many practice sessions, H. M. became skilled at what is for anyone an initially difficult task: tracing the mirrored outline of a star. Yet, with no memory of having done the task in many practice trials, H. M. remarked to researcher Brenda Milner that "this was easier than I thought it would be" (Carey, 2008).

These amnesia victims are in some ways like people with brain damage who cannot consciously recognize faces but whose physiological responses to familiar faces reveal an *implicit* (unconscious) recognition. Their behaviors challenge the idea that memory is a single, unified, conscious system. Instead, we seem to have two memory systems operating in tandem (**FIGURE 8.13**). Whatever has destroyed *conscious* recall in these individuals with amnesia has not destroyed their *unconscious* capacity for learning. They can learn *how* to do something. Their **implicit memory** *(nondeclarative memory)* will be intact—having read a story once, they will read it faster a

FIGURE 8.13 Memory subsystems We process and store our explicit and implicit memories separately. Thus, people with brain damage may lose explicit memory (becoming amnesic), yet display implicit memory for material they cannot consciously recall.

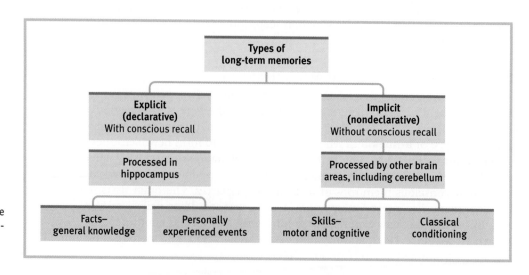

second time. But they may not know and declare that they know. There will be no **explicit memory** *(declarative memory)*, for they cannot recall having seen the story before. If repeatedly shown the word *perfume,* they will not recall having seen it. But if asked the first word that comes to mind in response to the letters *per,* they say *perfume,* readily displaying their learning. Using such tasks, even Alzheimer's patients, whose explicit memories for people and events are lost, display an ability to form new implicit memories (Lustig & Buckner, 2004).

These remarkable stories provoke us to wonder: Do our explicit and implicit memory systems involve separate brain regions? Research indicates that they do.

The two-track memory system reinforces an important principle introduced in Chapter 6's description of parallel processing: Mental feats such as vision, thinking, and memory may seem to be single abilities, but they are not. Rather, we split information into different components for separate and simultaneous processing.

THE HIPPOCAMPUS Brain scans, such as PET scans of people recalling words (Squire, 1992), and autopsies of people who had amnesia, reveal that new explicit memories of names, images, and events are laid down via the **hippocampus,** a temporal lobe neural center that also forms part of the brain's limbic system (**FIGURE 8.14**; Anderson et al., 2007).

Damage to the hippocampus therefore disrupts some types of memory. Chickadees and other birds can store food in hundreds of places and return to these unmarked caches months later, but not if their hippocampus has been removed (Kamil & Cheng, 2001; Sherry & Vaccarino, 1989). Like the brain's cortex, the hippocampus is lateralized. (You have two of them, one just above each ear and about an inch and a half straight in.) Damage to one or the other seems to produce different results. With left-hippocampus damage, people have trouble remembering verbal information, but they have no trouble recalling visual designs and locations. With right-hippocampus damage, the problem is reversed (Schacter, 1996).

New research also pinpoints the functions of subregions of the hippocampus. One part is active as people learn to associate names with faces (Zeineh et al., 2003). Another part is active as memory whizzes engage in spatial mnemonics (Maguire et al., 2003b). The rear area, which processes spatial memory, also grows bigger the longer a London cabbie has been navigating the maze of city streets (Maguire et al., 2003a).

The hippocampus is active during slow-wave sleep, as memories are processed and filed for later retrieval. The greater the hippocampus activity during sleep after a training experience, the better the next day's memory (Peigneux et al., 2004). But those memories are not permanently stored in the hippocampus. Instead, it seems to act as a loading dock where the brain registers and temporarily holds the elements of a remembered episode—its smell, feel, sound, and location. Then, like older files shifted to a basement storeroom, memories migrate for storage elsewhere. Sleep supports this memory consolidation. During sleep, our hippocampus and brain cortex display simultaneous activity rhythms, as if they were having a dialogue (Euston et al., 2007; Mehta, 2007). Researchers suspect that the brain is replaying the day's experiences as it transfers them to the cortex for long-term storage.

Once stored, our mental encores of these past experiences activate various parts of the frontal and temporal lobes (Fink et al., 1996; Gabrieli et al., 1996; Markowitsch, 1995). Recalling a telephone number and holding it in working memory, for example, would activate a region of the left frontal cortex; recalling a party scene would more likely activate a region of the right hemisphere.

"[Brain-scanning] technologies are revolutionizing the study of the brain and mind in the same way that the telescope revolutionized the study of the heavens."

—Endel Tulving (1996)

FIGURE 8.14 The hippocampus Explicit memories for facts and episodes are processed in the hippocampus and fed to other brain regions for storage.

Cerebellum The cerebellum plays an important part in our forming and storing of implicit memories.

Cerebellum

THE CEREBELLUM Although your hippocampus is a temporary processing site for your *explicit* memories, you could lose it and still lay down memories for skills and conditioned associations. Joseph LeDoux (1996) recounted the story of a brain-damaged patient whose amnesia left her unable to recognize her physician as, each day, he shook her hand and introduced himself. One day, after reaching for his hand, she yanked hers back, for the physician had pricked her with a tack in his palm. The next time he returned to introduce himself she refused to shake his hand but couldn't explain why. Having been classically conditioned, she just wouldn't do it.

The *cerebellum,* the brain region extending out from the rear of the brainstem, plays a key role in forming and storing the implicit memories created by classical conditioning. With a damaged cerebellum, people cannot develop certain conditioned reflexes, such as associating a tone with an impending puff of air—and thus do not blink in anticipation of the puff (Daum & Schugens, 1996; Green & Woodruff-Pak, 2000). By methodically disrupting the function of different pathways in the cortex and cerebellum of rabbits, researchers have shown that rabbits also fail to learn a conditioned eyeblink response when the cerebellum is temporarily deactivated (Krupa et al., 1993; Steinmetz, 1999). Implicit memory formation needs the cerebellum.

Our dual explicit-implicit memory system helps explain *infantile amnesia:* The implicit reactions and skills we learned during infancy reach far into our future, yet as adults we recall nothing (explicitly) of our first three years. Children's explicit memories have a seeming half-life. In one study, events experienced and discussed with one's mother at age 3 were 60 percent remembered at age 7 but only 34 percent remembered at age 9 (Bauer et al., 2007). As adults, our conscious memory of our first three years is blank because we index so much of our explicit memory by words that nonspeaking children have not learned, but also because the hippocampus is one of the last brain structures to mature.

recall a measure of memory in which the person must retrieve information learned earlier, as on a fill-in-the-blank test.

recognition a measure of memory in which the person need only identify items previously learned, as on a multiple-choice test.

relearning a measure of memory that assesses the amount of time saved when learning material for a second time.

REHEARSE IT!

7. Sensory information is initially recorded in our sensory memory. This memory may be visual (_____ memory) or auditory (_____ memory).
   a. implicit; explicit
   b. iconic; echoic
   c. declarative; nondeclarative
   d. long-term; short-term

8. Our short-term memory for new information is limited; its capacity is about
   a. 20 items.
   b. 18 items.
   c. 7 items.
   d. 3 items.

9. Long-term potentiation (LTP) seems to provide a neural basis for learning and memory. LTP refers to
   a. emotion-triggered hormonal changes.
   b. the role of the hippocampus in processing explicit memories.
   c. an increase in a synapse's firing potential after brief, rapid stimulation.
   d. aging people's potential for learning.

10. Amnesia following hippocampus damage typically leaves people unable to learn new facts or recall recent events. However, they may be able to learn new skills, such as riding a bicycle, which is an

   a. explicit memory.
   b. implicit memory.
   c. iconic memory.
   d. echoic memory.

11. The hippocampus seems to function as a
   a. temporary processing site for explicit memories.
   b. temporary processing site for implicit memories.
   c. permanent storage area for emotion-based memories.
   d. permanent storage area for iconic and echoic memories.

Answers: 7. b, 8. c, 9. c, 10. b, 11. a.

Retrieval: Getting Information Out

7: How do we get information out of memory?

To remember an event requires more than getting it in (encoding) and retaining it (storage). To most people, memory is **recall,** the ability to retrieve information not in conscious awareness. To a psychologist, memory is any sign that something learned has been retained. So **recognizing** or more quickly **relearning** information also indicates memory.

Long after you cannot recall most of the people in your high school graduating class, you may still be able to recognize their yearbook pictures from a photographic lineup and pick their names from a list of names. Harry Bahrick and his colleagues (1975) reported that people who had graduated 25 years earlier could not *recall* many of their old classmates, but they could *recognize* 90 percent of their pictures and names. If you are like most students, you, too, could likely recognize more names of the Seven Dwarfs than you could recall (Miserandino, 1991).

Our recognition memory is impressively quick and vast. "Is your friend wearing a new or old outfit?" "Old." "Is this five-second movie clip from a film you've ever seen?" "Yes." "Have you ever seen this person before—this minor variation on the same old human features (two eyes, one nose, and so on)?" "No." Before the mouth can form our answer to any of millions of such questions, the mind knows, and knows that it knows.

Our speed at relearning also reveals memory. If you once learned something and then forgot it, you probably will relearn it more quickly your second time around. When you study for a final exam or resurrect a language used in early childhood, the relearning is easier. Tests of recognition and of time spent relearning confirm the point: We remember more than we can recall.

Remembering things past Even if Oprah Winfrey and Brad Pitt had not become famous, their high school classmates would most likely still recognize their yearbook photos.

Multiple-choice questions test our
a. recall.
b. recognition.
c. relearning.

Fill-in-the-blank questions test our _____.
(See inverted answers below).

Fill-in-the-blank questions test recall.
Multiple-choice questions test recognition.

Retrieval Cues

Imagine a spider suspended in the middle of her web, held up by the many strands extending outward from her in all directions to different points (perhaps a window sill, a tree branch, a leaf on a shrub). If you were to trace a pathway to the spider, you would first need to create a path from one of these anchor points and then follow the strand down into the web.

The process of retrieving a memory follows a similar principle, because memories are held in storage by a web of associations, each piece of information interconnected with others. When you encode into memory a target piece of information, such as the name of the person sitting next to you in class, you associate with it other bits of information about your surroundings, mood, seating position, and so on. These bits can serve as *retrieval cues,* anchor points you can use to access the target information when you want to retrieve it later. The more retrieval cues you have, the better your chances of finding a route to the suspended memory.

Do you recall the gist of the second sentence I asked you to remember, in the discussion of what we encode? If not, does the word *shark* serve as a retrieval cue? Experiments show that *shark* (likely what you visualized) more readily retrieves the image you stored than does the sentence's actual word, *fish* (Anderson et al., 1976). (The sentence was "The fish attacked the swimmer.")

Mnemonic devices—ROY G. BIV; HOMES; bun, shoe, tree—provide us with handy retrieval cues. But the best retrieval cues come from associations we form at the time we encode a memory. Tastes, smells, and sights

> "Memory is not like a container that gradually fills up; it is more like a tree growing hooks onto which memories are hung."
>
> —Peter Russell, *The Brain Book*, 1979

"Let me refresh your memory. It was the night before Christmas and all through the house not a creature was stirring until you landed a sled, drawn by reindeer, on the plaintiff's home, causing extensive damage to the roof and chimney."

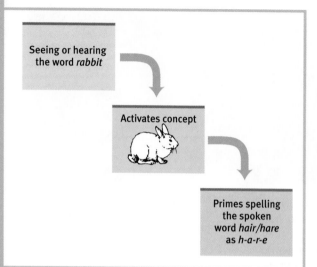

Seeing or hearing
the word *rabbit*

Activates concept

Primes spelling
the spoken
word *hair/hare*
as h-a-r-e

FIGURE 8.15 Priming—awakening associations After seeing or hearing *rabbit,* we are later more likely to spell the spoken word as h-a-r-e. The spreading of associations unconsciously activates related associations. This phenomenon is called priming. (Adapted from Bower, 1986.)

Ask a friend two rapid-fire questions: (a) How do you pronounce the word spelled by the letters s-h-o-p? *(b) What do you do when you come to a green light? If your friend answers "stop" to the second question, you have demonstrated priming.*

often evoke our recall of associated episodes. To call up visual cues when trying to recall something, we may mentally place ourselves in the original context. After losing his sight, John Hull (1990, p. 174) described his difficulty recalling such details: "I knew I had been somewhere, and had done particular things with certain people, but where? I could not put the conversations . . . into a context. There was no background, no features against which to identify the place. Normally, the memories of people you have spoken to during the day are stored in frames which include the background."

The features Hull was mourning are the strands we activate to retrieve a specific memory from its web of associations. Philosopher-psychologist William James referred to this process, which we call **priming,** as the "wakening of associations." Often our associations are activated, or primed, without our awareness. As **FIGURE 8.15** indicates, seeing or hearing the word *rabbit* primes associations with *hare,* even though we may not recall having earlier seen or heard *rabbit.*

Priming is often "memoryless memory"—invisible memory without explicit remembering. If, walking down a hallway, you see a poster of a missing child, you will then unconsciously be primed to interpret an ambiguous adult-child interaction as a possible kidnapping (James, 1986). Although you don't consciously remember the poster, it predisposes your interpretation.

Context Effects

8: **How do external contexts and internal emotions influence memory retrieval?**

Putting yourself back in the context where you experienced something can prime your memory retrieval. Duncan Godden and Alan Baddeley (1975) discovered this when they had scuba divers listen to a list of words in two different settings, either 10 feet underwater or sitting on the beach. As **FIGURE 8.16** illustrates, the divers recalled more words when they were tested in the same place.

You may have experienced similar context effects. Consider this scenario: While taking notes from this book, you realize you need to sharpen your pencil. You get up and walk downstairs, but then you cannot remember why. After returning to

FIGURE 8.16 The effects of context on memory Words heard underwater are best recalled underwater; words heard on land are best recalled on land. (Adapted from Godden & Baddeley, 1975.)

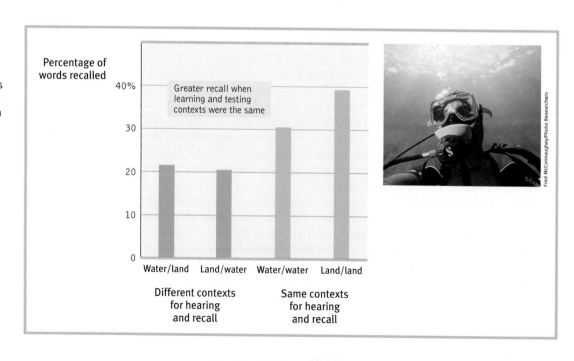

Percentage of words recalled

Greater recall when learning and testing contexts were the same

40%

30

20

10

0

Water/land   Land/water   Water/water   Land/land

Different contexts
for hearing
and recall

Same contexts
for hearing
and recall

Fred McConnaughey/Photo Researchers

your desk it hits you: "I wanted to sharpen this pencil!" What happens to create this frustrating experience? In one context (desk, reading psychology), you realize your pencil needs sharpening. When you go downstairs into a different context, you have few cues to lead you back to that thought. When you are once again at your desk, you are back in the context in which you encoded the thought ("This pencil is dull").

In several experiments, Carolyn Rovee-Collier (1993) found that a familiar context can activate memories even in 3-month-olds. After infants learned that kicking a crib mobile would make it move (via a connecting ribbon from the ankle), the infants kicked more when tested again in the same crib with the same bumper than when in a different context.

Sometimes, being in a context similar to one we've been in before may trigger the experience of **déjà vu** (French for "already seen"). Two-thirds of us have experienced this fleeting, eerie sense that "I've been in this exact situation before," but it happens most commonly to well-educated, imaginative young adults, especially when tired or stressed (Brown, 2003, 2004b; McAneny, 1996). Some wonder, "How could I recognize a situation I'm experiencing for the first time?" Others may think of reincarnation ("I must have experienced this in a previous life") or precognition ("I viewed this scene in my mind before experiencing it").

Posing the question differently ("Why do I feel as though I recognize this situation?"), we can see how our memory system might produce déjà vu (Alcock, 1981). The current situation may be loaded with cues that unconsciously retrieve an earlier, similar experience. (We take in and retain vast amounts of information while hardly noticing and often forgetting where it came from.) Thus, if in a similar context you see a stranger who looks and walks like one of your friends, the similarity may give rise to an eerie feeling of recognition. Having awakened a shadow of that earlier experience, you may think, "I've seen that person in this situation before."

Or perhaps, suggests James Lampinen (2002), a situation seems familiar when moderately similar to several events. Imagine you briefly encounter my dad, my brothers, my sister, my children, and a few weeks later meet me. You might think, "I've been with this guy before." Although no one in my family looks or acts just like me (lucky them), their looks and gestures are somewhat like mine and I might form a "global match" to what you had experienced.

Moods and Memories

Associated words, events, and contexts are not the only retrieval cues. Events in the past may have aroused a specific *emotion* that later primes us to recall its associated events. Cognitive psychologist Gordon Bower (1983) explained it this way: "An emotion is like a library room into which we place memory records. We best retrieve those records by returning to that emotional room." What we learn in one state—be it drunk or sober—may be more easily recalled when we are again in that state, a subtle phenomenon called *state-dependent memory*. What people learn when drunk they don't recall well in *any* state (alcohol disrupts storage). But they recall it slightly better when again drunk. Someone who hides money when drunk may forget the location until drunk again.

Our mood states provide an example of memory's state dependence. Emotions that accompany good or bad events become retrieval cues (Fiedler et al., 2001). Thus, our memories are somewhat **mood-congruent.** If you've had a bad evening—your date never showed, your Toledo Mud Hens hat disappeared, your TV went out 10 minutes before the end of a mystery—your gloomy mood may facilitate recalling other bad times. Being depressed sours memories by priming negative associations, which we then use to explain our current mood. If put in a buoyant mood—whether under hypnosis or just by the day's events (a World Cup soccer victory for the German participants in one study)—people recall the world through rose-colored glasses (DeSteno et al., 2000; Forgas et al., 1984; Schwarz

priming the activation, often unconsciously, of particular associations in memory.

déjà vu that eerie sense that "I've experienced this before." Cues from the current situation may subconsciously trigger retrieval of an earlier experience.

mood-congruent memory the tendency to recall experiences that are consistent with one's current good or bad mood.

"Do you ever get that strange feeling of vujà dé? Not déjà vu; vujà dé. It's the distinct sense that, somehow, something just happened that has never happened before. Nothing seems familiar. And then suddenly the feeling is gone. Vujà dé."

—George Carlin (1937–2008), *Funny Times*, 2001

"I can't remember what we're arguing about, either. Let's keep yelling, and maybe it will come back to us."

"When a feeling was there, they felt as if it would never go; when it was gone, they felt as if it had never been; when it returned, they felt as if it had never gone."

—George MacDonald,
What's Mine's Mine, 1886

Moods influence not only our memories but also how we interpret other people's behavior. In a bad mood we read someone's look as a glare and feel even worse; in a good mood we encode the same look as interest and feel even better. Passions exaggerate.

et al., 1987). They judge themselves competent and effective, other people benevolent, happy events more likely.

Knowing this mood-memory connection, we should not be surprised that adolescents' ratings of parental warmth in one week give little clue to how they will rate their parents six weeks later (Bornstein et al., 1991). When teens are down, their parents seem inhuman; as their mood brightens, their parents morph from devils into angels. You and I may nod our heads knowingly. Yet, in a good or bad mood, we persist in attributing to reality our own changing judgments and memories.

Our mood's effect on retrieval helps explain why our moods persist. When happy, we recall happy events and therefore see the world as a happy place, which helps prolong our good mood. When depressed, we recall sad events, which darkens our interpretations of current events. For those of us with a predisposition to depression, this process can help maintain a vicious, dark cycle.

REHEARSE IT!

12. A psychologist who asks you to write down as many objects as you can remember having seen a few minutes earlier is testing your
a. recall.
b. recognition.
c. recall and recognition.
d. relearning.

13. Specific odors, visual images, emotions, or other associations that help us access a memory are examples of

a. relearning.
b. déjà vu.
c. declarative memories.
d. retrieval cues.

14. When retrieval cues trigger the feeling that "I've been here before," you are experiencing
a. déjà vu.
b. mood-congruent memory.
c. relearning.
d. an explicit memory.

15. Our tendency to recall experiences consistent with our current emotions is called
a. mnemonics.
b. chunking.
c. repression.
d. mood-congruent memory.

Answers: 12. a, 13. d, 14. a, 15. d.

Forgetting

9: Why do we forget?

"Amnesia seeps into the crevices of our brains, and amnesia heals."

—Joyce Carol Oates, "Words Fail, Memory Blurs, Life Wins," 2001

Amid all the applause for memory—all the efforts to understand it, all the books on how to improve it—have any voices been heard in praise of forgetting? William James (1890, p. 680) was such a voice: "If we remembered everything, we should on most occasions be as ill off as if we remembered nothing." To discard the clutter of useless or out-of-date information—where we parked the car yesterday, a friend's old phone number, restaurant orders already cooked and served—is surely a blessing. The Russian memory whiz S, whom we met at the beginning of this chapter, was haunted by his junk heap of memories. They dominated his consciousness. He had difficulty thinking abstractly—generalizing, organizing, evaluating. After reading a story, he could recite it but would struggle to summarize its gist.

A more recent case of a life overtaken by memory is "A. J.," whose experience has been studied and verified by a University of California at Irvine research team (Parker et al., 2006). A. J., who has identified herself as Jill Price, describes her memory as "like a running movie

The woman who can't forget "A. J." in real life is Jill Price, who, with writer Bart Davis, told her story in a 2008 published memoir. Price remembers every day of her life since age 14 with detailed clarity, including both the joys and the unforgotten hurts.

Robert Hanashiro, USA Today

that never stops. It's like a split screen. I'll be talking to someone and seeing something else. . . . Whenever I see a date flash on the television (or anywhere for that matter) I automatically go back to that day and remember where I was, what I was doing, what day it fell on, and on and on and on and on. It is nonstop, uncontrollable, and totally exhausting." A good memory is helpful, but so is the ability to forget. If a memory-enhancing pill becomes available, it had better not be *too* effective.

More often, however, our memory dismays and frustrates us. Memories are quirky. My own memory can easily call up such episodes as that wonderful first kiss with the woman I love or trivial facts like the air mileage from London to Detroit. Then it abandons me when I discover I have failed to encode, store, or retrieve my new colleague's name or where I left my sunglasses.

Cellist Yo-Yo Ma forgot his 266-year-old, $2.5 million cello in a New York taxi. (He later recovered it.).

Encoding Failure

Much of what we sense we never notice, and what we fail to encode, we will never remember (**FIGURE 8.17**). Age can affect encoding efficiency. The brain areas that jump into action when young adults encode new information are less responsive in older adults. This slower encoding helps explain age-related memory decline (Grady et al., 1995).

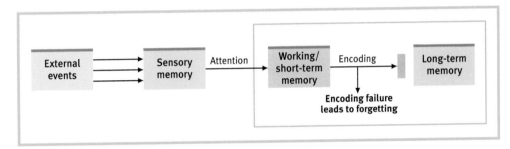

FIGURE 8.17 **Forgetting as encoding failure** We cannot remember what we have not encoded.

But no matter how young we are, we selectively attend to few of the myriad sights and sounds continually bombarding us. Consider something you have looked at countless times: What letters accompany the number 5 on your telephone? For people who don't text message, the question is surprisingly difficult. This detail is not personally meaningful, and few of us have made the effort to encode it. As we noted earlier, we encode some information—where we had dinner yesterday—automatically; other types of information—like the concepts in this chapter—require effortful processing. Without effort, many memories never form.

Storage Decay

Even after encoding something well, we sometimes later forget it. To study the durability of stored memories, Ebbinghaus (1885) learned more lists of nonsense syllables and measured how much he retained when relearning each list, from 20 minutes to 30 days later. The result, confirmed by later experiments, was his famous forgetting curve: The course of forgetting is initially rapid, then levels off with time (**FIGURE 8.18a** on the next page; Wixted & Ebbesen, 1991). One such experiment was Harry Bahrick's (1984) study of the forgetting curve for Spanish vocabulary learned in school. Compared with those just completing a high school or college Spanish course, people 3 years out of school had forgotten much of what they had learned (see Figure 8.18b on the next page). However, what people remembered then, they still remembered 25 and more years later. Their forgetting had leveled off.

One explanation for these forgetting curves is a gradual fading of the physical memory trace. Cognitive neuroscientists are getting closer to solving the mystery of the physical storage of memory and are increasing our understanding of how

"Each of us finds that in [our] own life every moment of time is completely filled. [We are] bombarded every second by sensations, emotions, thoughts . . . nine-tenths of which [we] must simply ignore. The past [is] a roaring cataract of billions upon billions of such moments: Any one of them too complex to grasp in its entirety, and the aggregate beyond all imagination. . . . At every tick of the clock, in every inhabited part of the world, an unimaginable richness and variety of 'history' falls off the world into total oblivion."

—English novelist-critic C. S. Lewis (1967)

FIGURE 8.18 Two forgetting curves
(a) After learning lists of nonsense syllables, Ebbinghaus studied how much he retained up to 30 days later. He found that memory for novel information fades quickly, then levels out. (Adapted from Ebbinghaus, 1885.)
(b) Compared with those just completing a Spanish course, people 3 years out of the course remembered much less. Compared with the 3-year group, however, those who studied Spanish even longer ago did not forget much more. (Adapted from Bahrick, 1984.)

(a)

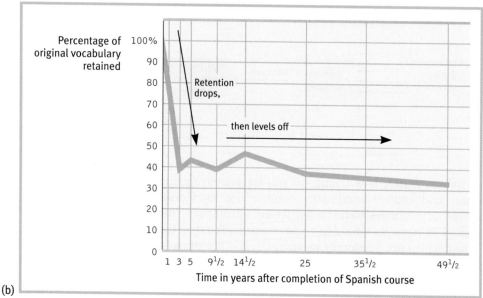

(b)

memory storage could decay. But memories fade for other reasons, including the accumulation of learning that disrupts our retrieval.

Retrieval Failure

Forgotten events are like books you can't find in your campus library—some because they were never acquired (not encoded), others because they were discarded (stored memories decay).

But there is a third possibility: The book may be there but inaccessible because we don't have enough information to look it up and retrieve it. How frustrating when we know information is "in there," but we cannot get it out (**FIGURE 8.19**), as when a name lies poised on the tip of our tongue, waiting to be retrieved. Given retrieval cues ("It begins with an *M*"), we may easily access the elusive memory. Retrieval problems contribute to the occasional memory failures of older adults, who more frequently are frustrated by tip-of-the-tongue forgetting (Abrams, 2008). Often, forgetting is not memories discarded but memories unretrieved.

Deaf persons fluent in sign language experience a parallel "tip of the fingers" phenomenon (Thompson et al., 2005).

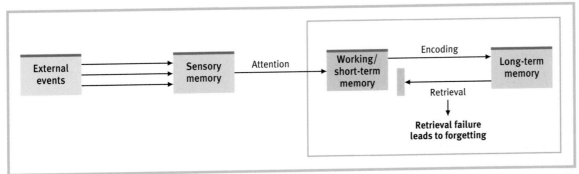

FIGURE 8.19 **Retrieval failure** We store in long-term memory what's important to us or what we've rehearsed. But sometimes even stored information cannot be accessed, which leads to forgetting.

Interference

Learning some items may interfere with retrieving others, especially when the items are similar. If someone gives you a phone number, you may be able to recall it later. But if two more people give you their numbers, each successive number will be more difficult to recall. Likewise, if you buy a new combination lock, your memory of the old one may interfere. Such **proactive** *(forward-acting)* **interference** occurs when something you learned earlier disrupts your recall of something you experience later. As you collect more and more information, your mental attic never fills, but it certainly gets cluttered.

Retroactive *(backward-acting)* **interference** occurs when new information makes it harder to recall something you learned earlier. It is rather like a second stone tossed in a pond, disrupting the waves rippling out from a first. (See Close-Up: Retrieving Passwords on the next page.)

Information presented in the hour before sleep is protected from retroactive interference because the opportunity for interfering events is minimized. Researchers John Jenkins and Karl Dallenbach (1924) discovered this in a now-classic experiment. Day after day, two people each learned some nonsense syllables, then tried to recall them after up to eight hours of being awake or asleep at night. As **FIGURE 8.20** shows, forgetting occurred more rapidly after being awake and involved with other activities. The investigators surmised that "forgetting is not so much a matter of the decay of old impressions and associations as it is a matter of interference, inhibition, or obliteration of the old by the new" (1924, p. 612). Later experiments have confirmed the benefits of sleep and found that the hour before a night's sleep is indeed a good time to commit information to memory (Benson & Feinberg, 1977; Fowler

proactive interference the disruptive effect of prior learning on the recall of new information.

retroactive interference the disruptive effect of new learning on the recall of old information.

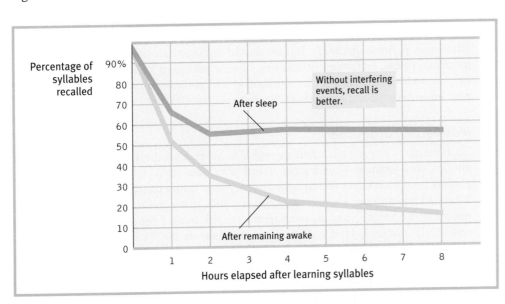

FIGURE 8.20 **Retroactive interference** More forgetting occurred when a person stayed awake and experienced other new material. (From Jenkins & Dallenbach, 1924.)

Close-Up:

Retrieving Passwords

There's something that you need lots of, and that your grandparents at your age didn't: passwords. To log into your e-mail, retrieve your voice mail, draw cash from a machine, access your phone card, use the copy machine, or persuade the keypad to open the building door, you need to remember your password. A typical student faces eight demands for passwords (Brown et al., 2004b).

With so many passwords needed, what's a person to do? As **FIGURE 8.21** illustrates, we are plagued by proactive interference from irrelevant old information and retroactive interference from other newly learned information.

Memory researcher Henry Roediger takes a simple approach to storing all the important phone, PIN, and code numbers in his life: "I have a sheet in my shirt pocket with all the numbers I need," says Roediger (2001), adding that he can't mentally store them all, so why bother? Other strategies may help those who do not want to lose their PINs in the wash. First, *duplicate*. The average student uses four different passwords to meet those eight needs. Second, *harness retrieval cues*. Surveys in Britain and the United States reveal that about half of our passwords harness a familiar name or date. Others often involve familiar phone or identification numbers.

Third, in online banking or other situations where security is essential, *use a mix of letters and numbers* (Brown et al., 2004). Rehearse that password, then rehearse it a day later, and continue rehearsing at increasing intervals. In such ways, long-term memories will form and be retrievable at the cash and copy machines.

FIGURE 8.21 Proactive and retroactive interference

et al., 1973; Nesca & Koulack, 1994). But not the seconds just before sleep; information presented then is seldom remembered (Wyatt & Bootzin, 1994). Nor is recorded information played during sleep, although the ears do register it (Wood et al., 1992).

Interference is an important cause of forgetting, and it may explain why ads viewed during attention-grabbing violent or sexual TV programs are so forgettable (Bushman & Bonacci, 2002). But we should not overstate the point. Sometimes old information can facilitate our learning of new information. Knowing Spanish may help us to learn Italian—a phenomenon called *positive transfer*. It is when old and new information compete with each other that interference occurs.

Motivated Forgetting

To remember our past is often to revise it. Years ago, the huge cookie jar in our kitchen was jammed with freshly baked chocolate chip cookies. Still more were cooling across racks on the counter. Twenty-four hours later, not a crumb was left. Who had taken them? During that time, my wife, three children, and I were the only people in the house. So while memories were still fresh, I conducted a little memory test. Andy acknowledged wolfing down as many as 20. Peter admitted eating 15. Laura guessed she had stuffed her then-6-year-old body with 15 cookies. My wife, Carol, recalled eating 6, and I remembered consuming 15 and taking 18 more to the office. We sheepishly accepted responsibility for 89 cookies. Still, we had not come close; there had been 160.

This would not have surprised Michael Ross and his colleagues (1981), who time and again showed that people unknowingly revise their own histories. One group of people, told the benefits of frequent toothbrushing, then recalled (more than others did) having frequently brushed their teeth in the preceding two weeks.

Why do our memories fail us? Why did my family and I not remember the number of cookies each of us had eaten? As **FIGURE 8.22** reminds us, we automatically encode sensory information in amazing detail. So was it an encoding problem? Or a storage problem—might our memories of cookies, like Ebbinghaus' memory of nonsense syllables, have vanished almost as fast as the cookies themselves? Or was the information still intact but irretrievable because it would be embarrassing to remember?[1]

Sigmund Freud might have argued that our memory systems self-censored this information. He proposed that we **repress** painful memories to protect our self-concept and to minimize anxiety. But the submerged memory will linger, he believed, to be retrieved by some later cue or during therapy. Here is a sample case. A woman had an intense, unexplained fear of running water. One day her aunt whispered, "I have never told." Like relighting a blown-out candle, these words cued the woman's memory of an incident when, as a disobedient young child, she had wandered away from a family picnic and become trapped under a waterfall—until being rescued by her aunt, who promised not to tell her parents (Kihlstrom, 1990).

Repression was central to Freud's psychology (see Chapter 12) and became part of psychology's lore. Most everyone—including 9 in 10 university students—believes that "memories for painful experiences are sometimes pushed into unconsciousness" (Brown et al., 1996). Therapists often assume it. *Yet increasing numbers of memory researchers think repression rarely, if ever, occurs.* People's efforts to intentionally forget neutral material often succeed, but not when the to-be-forgotten material is emotional (Payne & Corrigan, 2007). Thus, we may have intrusive memories of the very traumatic experiences we would most like to forget.

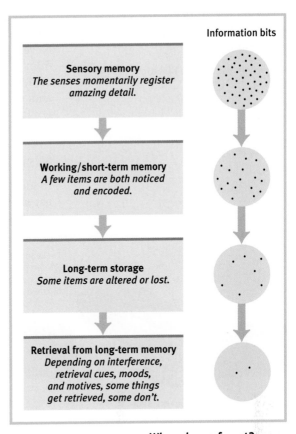

Information bits

Sensory memory
The senses momentarily register amazing detail.

Working/short-term memory
A few items are both noticed and encoded.

Long-term storage
Some items are altered or lost.

Retrieval from long-term memory
Depending on interference, retrieval cues, moods, and motives, some things get retrieved, some don't.

FIGURE 8.22 **When do we forget?** Forgetting can occur at any memory stage. As we process information, we filter, alter, or lose much of it.

Memory Construction

10: **How do misinformation, imagination, and source amnesia influence our memory construction?**

Picture yourself having this experience:

> You go to a fancy restaurant for dinner. You are seated at a table with a white tablecloth. You study the menu. You tell the server you want prime rib, medium rare, a baked potato with sour cream, and a salad with blue cheese dressing. You also order some red wine from the wine list. A few minutes later the server returns with your salad. Later the rest of the meal arrives. You enjoy it all, except the prime rib is a bit overdone.

Were I immediately to quiz you on this paragraph (adapted from Hyde, 1983), you could surely retrieve considerable detail. For example, without looking back, answer the following questions:

1. What kind of salad dressing did you order?
2. Was the tablecloth red checked?
3. What did you order to drink?
4. Did the server give you a menu?

---

[1] One of my cookie-scarfing sons, on reading this in his father's textbook years later, confessed he had fibbed "a little."

repression in psychoanalytic theory, the basic defense mechanism that banishes from consciousness anxiety-arousing thoughts, feelings, and memories.

"Memory isn't like reading a book; it's more like writing a book from fragmentary notes."

—Psychologist John F. Kihlstrom (1994)

You were probably able to recall exactly what you ordered, and maybe even the tablecloth color. But did the server give you a menu? Not in the paragraph given. Nevertheless, many answer *yes*. Like scientists who infer a dinosaur's appearance from its remains, we infer our past from stored information plus what we later imagined, expected, saw, and heard. We often construct our memories as we encode them and, as Daniel Gilbert noted (2007, p. 79), we don't just retrieve our memories, we reweave them: "Information acquired after an event alters memory of the event."

Misinformation and Imagination Effects

In more than 200 experiments, involving more than 20,000 people, Elizabeth Loftus has shown how eyewitnesses reconstruct their memories when later questioned. In one classic experiment, Loftus and John Palmer showed a film of a traffic accident

Leading question:
"About how fast were the cars going when they smashed into each other?"

Depiction of actual accident

Memory construction

and then quizzed people about what they had seen (Loftus & Palmer, 1974). Those asked, "How fast were the cars going when they *smashed* into each other?" gave higher speed estimates than those asked, "How fast were the cars going when they *hit* each other?" A week later, the researchers asked both groups if they recalled seeing any broken glass. Those who had heard *smashed* were more than twice as likely to report seeing glass fragments (**FIGURE 8.23**). In fact, the film showed no broken glass.

In many follow-up experiments around the world, people have demonstrated this **misinformation effect.** After exposure to subtle misinformation, they have misrecalled a yield sign as a stop sign, hammers as screwdrivers, Coke cans as peanut cans, *Vogue* magazine as *Mademoiselle*, "Dr. Henderson" as "Dr. Davidson," breakfast cereal as eggs, and a clean-shaven man as a man with a mustache (Loftus et al., 1992). One experiment showed people digitally altered photos depicting themselves (a pasted image from a childhood family album) taking a hot air balloon ride. After seeing this three times over two weeks, half the participants "remembered" the nonexistent experience often in rich detail (Wade et al., 2002). The human mind comes with built-in Photoshopping software.

So unwitting is the misinformation effect that we may later find it nearly impossible to discriminate between our memories of real and suggested events (Schooler et al., 1986). Perhaps you can recall recounting an experience and filling in memory gaps with plausible guesses and assumptions. We all do it, and after more retellings, we may recall the guessed details—now absorbed into our memories—as if we had actually observed them (Roediger et al., 1993). Others' vivid retelling of an event may also implant false memories.

Even repeatedly *imagining* nonexistent actions and events can create false memories. Students who repeatedly imagined simple acts (breaking a toothpick, picking up a stapler) were later more likely than others to think they had actually done such things during the experiment's first phase (Goff & Roediger, 1998; Seamon et al., 2006). Similarly, one in four American and British university students asked to imagine certain childhood events, such as breaking a window with their hand or having a skin sample removed from a finger, later recalled the imagined event as something that had really happened (Garry et al., 1996; Mazzoni & Memon, 2003).

This *imagination inflation* occurs partly because visualizing something and actually perceiving it activate similar brain areas (Gonsalves et al., 2004). Imagined events later seem more familiar, and familiar things seem more real. Thus, the more vividly we can imagine things, the more likely we are to inflate them into memories (Loftus, 2001; Porter et al., 2000). People who believe aliens transported them to spaceships

FIGURE 8.23 Memory construction When people who had seen the film of a car accident were later asked a leading question, they recalled a more serious accident than they had witnessed. (From Loftus, 1979.)

"Memory is insubstantial. Things keep replacing it. Your batch of snapshots will both fix and ruin your memory. . . . You can't remember anything from your trip except the wretched collection of snapshots."

—Annie Dillard, "To Fashion a Text," 1988

DOONESBURY

for medical exams tend to have powerful imaginations and, in memory tests, to be more susceptible to false memories (Clancy, 2005). Those who believe they have recovered memories of childhood sexual abuse likewise tend to have vivid imaginations and to score high on false memory tests (Clancy et al., 2000; McNally, 2003).

To see how far the mind's search for a fact will go in creating a fiction, Richard Wiseman and his University of Hertfordshire colleagues (1999) staged eight seances, each attended by 25 curious people. During each session, the medium—actually a professional actor and magician—urged everyone to concentrate on the moving table. Although it never moved, he suggested it had: "That's good. Lift the table up. That's good. Keep concentrating. Keep the table in the air." When questioned two weeks later, 1 in 3 participants recalled actually having seen the table levitate.

Memory construction may explain how faulty eyewitness identification could have helped convict 79 percent of 200 people later exonerated by DNA testing (Garrett, 2008). It explains why "hypnotically refreshed" memories of crimes so easily incorporate errors, some of which originate with the hypnotist's leading questions ("Did you hear loud noises?"). It explains why dating partners who fall in love *over*estimate their first impressions of one another ("It was love at first sight"), while those who break up *under*estimate their earlier liking ("We never really clicked") (McFarland & Ross, 1987). And it explains why people asked how they felt 10 years ago about marijuana or gender issues recall attitudes closer to their current views than to the views they had actually reported a decade earlier (Markus, 1986). How people feel today seems to be how they have always felt. What people know today seems to be what they have always known (Mazzoni & Vannucci, 2007; and recall from Chapter 1 our tendency to *hindsight bias*).

As George Vaillant (1977, p. 197) noted after following adult lives through time, "It is all too common for caterpillars to become butterflies and then to maintain that in their youth they had been little butterflies. Maturation makes liars of us all."

Source Amnesia

Among the frailest parts of a memory is its source. Thus, we may recognize someone but have no idea where we have seen the person. We may dream an event and later be unsure whether it really happened. We may hear something and later recall seeing it (Henkel et al., 2000). In all these cases of **source amnesia** (also called

misinformation effect incorporating misleading information into one's memory of an event.

source amnesia attributing to the wrong source an event we have experienced, heard about, read about, or imagined. (Also called *source misattribution*.) Source amnesia, along with the misinformation effect, is at the heart of many false memories.

U.S. Senator John McCain on the Iraq war:
2007 (on MSNBC): "When I voted to support this war I knew it was probably going to be long and hard and tough."
2002 (on Larry King): "I believe that the operation will be relatively short [and] that the success will be fairly easy."

"It isn't so astonishing, the number of things I can remember, as the number of things I can remember that aren't so."
—Mark Twain (1835–1910)

Authors and songwriters sometimes suffer source amnesia. They think an idea came from their own creative imagination, when in fact they are unintentionally plagiarizing something they earlier read or heard.

source misattribution), we retain the memory of the event but not of the context in which we acquired it.

Australian psychologist Donald Thompson found his own work on memory distortion haunting him when authorities brought him in for questioning about a rape. Although he was a near-perfect match to the victim's memory of the rapist, he had an airtight alibi. Just before the rape occurred, Thompson was being interviewed on live television. He could not possibly have made it to the crime scene. Then it came to light that the victim had been watching the interview—ironically about face recognition—and had experienced source amnesia, confusing her memories of Thompson with those of the rapist (Schacter, 1996).

Debra Poole and Stephen Lindsay (1995, 2001, 2002) demonstrated source amnesia among preschoolers. They had the children interact with "Mr. Science," who engaged them in activities such as blowing up a balloon with baking soda and vinegar. Three months later, on three successive days, their parents read them a story describing some things the children had experienced with Mr. Science and some they had not. When a new interviewer asked what Mr. Science had done with them—"Did Mr. Science have a machine with ropes to pull?"—4 in 10 children spontaneously recalled him doing things that had happened only in the story.

Children's Eyewitness Recall

If memories can be sincere, yet sincerely wrong, might children's recollections of sexual abuse be prone to error? Stephen Ceci (1993) thinks "it would be truly awful to ever lose sight of the enormity of child abuse." Yet, as we have seen, interviewers who ask leading questions can plant false memories. Ceci and Maggie Bruck's (1993, 1995) studies of children's memories have sensitized them to children's suggestibility. For example, they asked 3-year-olds to show on anatomically correct dolls where a pediatrician had touched them. Fifty-five percent of the children who had not received genital examinations pointed to either genital or anal areas. And when the researchers used suggestive interviewing techniques, they found that most preschoolers and many older children could be induced to report false events (Bruck & Ceci, 1999, 2004).

In experiments with adults, suggestive questions ("In fresh water, do snakes swim upside down for about half the time?") are often misremembered as statements (Pandelaere & Dewitte, 2006).

In one study, Ceci and Bruck had a child choose a card from a deck of possible happenings and an adult then read from the card. For example, "Think real hard, and tell me if this ever happened to you. Can you remember going to the hospital with a mousetrap on your finger?" After 10 weekly interviews, with the same adult repeatedly asking children to think about several real and fictitious events, a new adult asked the same question. The stunning result: 58 percent of preschoolers produced false (often vivid) stories regarding one or more events they had never experienced, as this little boy did (Ceci et al., 1994):

> My brother Colin was trying to get Blowtorch [an action figure] from me, and I wouldn't let him take it from me, so he pushed me into the wood pile where the mousetrap was. And then my finger got caught in it. And then we went to the hospital, and my mommy, daddy, and Colin drove me there, to the hospital in our van, because it was far away. And the doctor put a bandage on this finger.

"[The] research leads me to worry about the possibility of false allegations. It is not a tribute to one's scientific integrity to walk down the middle of the road if the data are more to one side."

—Stephen Ceci (1993)

Given such detailed stories, professional psychologists who specialize in interviewing children could not reliably separate real memories from false ones. Nor could the children themselves. The above child, reminded that his parents had told him several times that the mousetrap incident never happened—that he had imagined it—protested, "But it really did happen. I remember it!"

Does this mean that children can never be accurate eyewitnesses? No. If questioned about their experiences in neutral words they understand, children often accurately recall what happened and who did it (Goodman, 2006; Howe, 1997; Pipe, 1996). When interviewers use less suggestive, more effective techniques, even 4- to 5-year-old children produce more accurate recall (Holliday & Albon, 2004; Pipe et al., 2004). Children are especially accurate when they have not talked with involved adults prior to the interview and when their disclosure is made in a first interview with a neutral person who asks nonleading questions.

Repressed or Constructed Memories of Abuse?

11: **What is the controversy related to claims of repressed and recovered memories?**

There are two tragedies related to adult recollections of child abuse. One is trauma survivors being disbelieved when telling their secret. The other is innocent people being falsely accused. What, then, shall we say about clinicians who have guided people in "recovering" memories of childhood abuse? Are they triggering false memories that damage innocent adults? Or are they uncovering the truth?

Some therapists have reasoned with patients that "people who've been abused often have your symptoms, so you probably were abused. Let's see if, aided by hypnosis or drugs, or helped to dig back and visualize your trauma, you can recover it." As we might expect from the research on source amnesia and the misinformation effect, patients exposed to such techniques may form an image of a threatening person. With further visualization, the image grows more vivid, leaving the patient stunned, angry, and ready to confront or sue the equally stunned and devastated parent, relative, or clergy member, who then vigorously denies the accusation. After 32 therapy sessions, one woman recalled her father abusing her when she was 15 months old.

Without questioning the professionalism of most therapists, critics have charged that clinicians who use "memory work" techniques such as "guided imagery," hypnosis, and dream analysis to recover memories "are nothing more than merchants of mental chaos, and, in fact, constitute a blight on the entire field of psychotherapy" (Loftus et al., 1995). "Thousands of families were cruelly ripped apart," with "previously loving adult daughters" suddenly accusing fathers, noted Martin Gardiner (2006) in his commentary on North America's "greatest mental health scandal." Irate clinicians countered that those who dispute recovered memories of abuse add to abused people's trauma and play into the hands of child molesters.

In an effort to find a sensible common ground that might resolve this ideological battle—psychology's "memory war"—study panels have been convened and public statements made by the American Medical, American Psychological, and American Psychiatric Associations; the Australian Psychological Society; the British Psychological Society; and the Canadian Psychiatric Association. Those committed to protecting abused children and those committed to protecting wrongly accused adults agree on the following:

- **Sexual abuse happens.** And it happens more often than we once supposed. There is no characteristic "survivor syndrome" (Kendall-Tackett et al., 1993). However, sexual abuse is a traumatic betrayal that can leave its victims predisposed to problems ranging from sexual dysfunction to depression (Freyd et al., 2007).

- **Injustice happens.** Some innocent people have been falsely convicted. And some guilty people have evaded responsibility by casting doubt on their truth-telling accusers.

- **Forgetting happens.** Many of those actually abused were either very young when abused or may not have understood the meaning of their experience—circumstances under which forgetting is common. Forgetting isolated past events, both negative and positive, is an ordinary part of everyday life.

- **Recovered memories are commonplace.** Cued by a remark or an experience, we recover memories of long-forgotten events, both pleasant and unpleasant. What is debated is whether the unconscious mind sometimes *forcibly represses*

> "When memories are 'recovered' after long periods of amnesia, particularly when extraordinary means were used to secure the recovery of memory, there is a high probability that the memories are false."
>
> —Royal College of Psychiatrists Working Group on Reported Recovered Memories of Child Sexual Abuse (Brandon et al., 1998)

TODAY'S SPECIAL GUEST

BRUNDAGE MORNALD, OF BATTLE CREEK, MONTANA

UNDER HYPNOSIS, MR. MORNALD RECOVERED LONG-BURIED MEMORIES OF A PERFECTLY NORMAL, HAPPY CHILDHOOD.

> "Horror sears memory, leaving . . . the consuming memories of atrocity."
>
> —Robert Kraft, *Memory Perceived: Recalling the Holocaust*, 2002

painful experiences and, if so, whether these can be retrieved by certain therapist-aided techniques. (Memories that surface naturally are more likely to be corroborated than are therapist-assisted recollections [Geraerts et al., 2007].)

- **Memories of things happening before age 3 are unreliable.** Because people do not reliably recall happenings of any sort from their first three years, most psychologists—including most clinical and counseling psychologists—doubt "recovered" memories of abuse during infancy (Gore-Felton et al., 2000; Knapp & Vande Creek, 2000). The older the child was when suffering sexual abuse, and the more severe the abuse, the more likely it is to be remembered (Goodman et al., 2003).

- **Memories "recovered" under hypnosis or the influence of drugs are especially unreliable.** "Age-regressed" hypnotized subjects incorporate suggestions into their memories, even memories of "past lives."

- **Memories, whether real or false, can be emotionally upsetting.** Both the accuser and the accused may suffer when what was born of mere suggestion becomes, like an actual trauma, a stinging memory that drives bodily stress (McNally, 2003, 2007). People knocked unconscious in unremembered accidents have later developed stress disorders after being haunted by memories they constructed from photos, news reports, and friends' accounts (Bryant, 2001).

So, does repression ever occur? Or is this concept—the cornerstone of Freud's theory and of so much popular psychology—misleading? In Chapter 12, we will return to this hotly debated issue. As we will see, this much now appears certain: The most common response to a traumatic experience (witnessing a parent's murder, experiencing the horrors of a Nazi death camp, being terrorized by a hijacker or a rapist, escaping the collapsing World Trade Center towers, surviving an Asian tsunami) is not banishment of the experience into the unconscious. Rather, such experiences are typically etched on the mind as vivid, persistent, haunting memories (Porter & Peace, 2007). Playwright Eugene O'Neill understood. As one of the characters in his *Strange Interlude* (1928) exclaimed, "The devil! . . . What beastly incidents our memories insist on cherishing!"

REHEARSE IT!

16. When forgetting is due to encoding failure, meaningless information has not been transferred from
    a. the environment into sensory memory.
    b. sensory memory into long-term memory.
    c. long-term memory into short-term memory.
    d. short-term memory into long-term memory.

17. Ebbinghaus' "forgetting curve" shows that after an initial decline, memory for novel information tends to
    a. increase slightly.
    b. decrease noticeably.
    c. decrease greatly.
    d. level out.

18. The hour before sleep is a good time to memorize information because going to sleep after learning new material minimizes
    a. the misinformation effect.
    b. amnesia.
    c. retroactive interference.
    d. proactive interference.

19. Freud proposed that painful or unacceptable memories are self-censored, or blocked from consciousness, through a mechanism called
    a. repression.
    b. proactive interference.
    c. the misinformation effect.
    d. physical decay of the memory trace.

20. One reason false memories form is our tendency to fill in memory gaps with our assumptions about events. This tendency is an example of
    a. proactive interference.
    b. the misinformation effect.
    c. retroactive interference.
    d. the forgetting curve.

21. We may recognize a face in the crowd but be unable to recall where we know the person from. This is an example of
    a. the misinformation effect.
    b. proactive interference.
    c. source amnesia.
    d. repression.

Answers: 16. d, 17. d, 18. c, 19. a, 20. b, 21. c.

Improving Memory

12: How can an understanding of memory contribute to more effective study techniques?

Now and then we are dismayed at our forgetfulness—at our embarrassing inability to recall someone's name, at forgetting to bring up a point in conversation, at not bringing along something important, at finding ourselves standing in a room unable to recall why we are there (Herrmann, 1982). Is there anything we can do to minimize such memory misdeeds? Much as biology benefits medicine and botany benefits agriculture, so can the psychology of memory benefit education. Sprinkled throughout this chapter and summarized here for easy reference are concrete suggestions for improving memory. The SQ3R—Survey, Question, Read, Rehearse, Review—study technique introduced in Chapter 1 incorporates several of these strategies.

Study repeatedly. To master material, use distributed (spaced) practice. To learn a concept, provide yourself with many separate study sessions: Take advantage of life's little intervals—riding on the bus, walking across campus, waiting for class to start. To memorize specific facts or figures, suggests Thomas Landauer (2001), "rehearse the name or number you are trying to memorize, wait a few seconds, rehearse again, wait a little longer, rehearse again, then wait longer still and rehearse yet again. The waits should be as long as possible without losing the information." New memories are weak; exercise them and they will strengthen. Speed-reading (skimming) complex material—with minimal rehearsal—yields little retention. Rehearsal and critical reflection help more. It pays to study actively.

Make the material meaningful. To build a network of retrieval cues, take text and class notes in your own words. (Mindlessly repeating someone else's words is relatively ineffective.) To apply concepts to your own life, form images, understand and organize information, relate the material to what you already know or have experienced, and put it in your own words. Increase retrieval cues by forming associations. Without such cues, you may find yourself stuck when a question uses phrasing different from the rote forms you memorized.

Activate retrieval cues. Mentally re-create the situation and the mood in which your original learning occurred. Return to the same location. Jog your memory by allowing one thought to cue the next.

Use mnemonic devices. Associate items with peg words. Make up a story that incorporates vivid images of the items. Chunk information into acronyms. Create rhythmic rhymes ("*i* before *e*, except after *c*").

Minimize interference. Study before sleeping. Do not schedule back-to-back study times for topics that are likely to interfere with each other, such as French and Italian.

Sleep more. During sleep, the brain organizes and consolidates information for long-term memory. Sleep-deprivation disrupts this process.

Test your own knowledge, both to rehearse it and to help determine what you do not yet know. Don't be lulled into overconfidence by your ability to recognize information. Test your recall using the Preview Questions. Outline sections on a blank page. Define the terms and concepts listed at each chapter's end before turning back to their definitions. Take practice tests, including the Rehearse It questions at the end of main sections and the Test for Success exercises at the end of each chapter. The study guides that accompany this and many other texts are a good source for self-tests.

> "I have discovered that it is of some use when you lie in bed at night and gaze into the darkness to repeat in your mind the things you have been studying. Not only does it help the understanding, but also the memory."
>
> —Leonardo da Vinci (1452–1519)

> "Knit each new thing on to some acquisition already there."
>
> —William James,
> *Principles of Psychology,* 1890

Thinking and memory Most of what we know is not the result of efforts to memorize. We learn because we're curious and because we spend time thinking about our experiences. Actively thinking as we read, by rehearsing and relating ideas, yields the best retention.

Memory

Studying Memory: Information-Processing Models

1 How do psychologists describe the human memory system?

Memory is the persistence of learning over time. The Atkinson-Shiffrin classic three-stage memory model (*encoding, storage,* and *retrieval*) suggests that we (1) register fleeting *sensory memories,* some of which are (2) processed into on-screen *short-term memories,* a tiny fraction of which are (3) encoded for *long-term memory* and later retrieval. Two new concepts update the classic model: (a) We register some information automatically, directly into long-term memory. And (b) the term *working memory* (rather than *short-term memory*) emphasizes the active processing that occurs in the second stage.

Encoding: Getting Information In

2 What information do we encode automatically? What information do we encode effortfully, and how does the distribution of practice influence retention?

In *automatic processing,* we unconsciously absorb information about space, time, frequency, and well-learned material. *Effortful processing* (of meaning, imagery, organization) requires conscious attention and deliberate effort. We retain information more easily if we practice it repeatedly (the *spacing effect*) than if we practice it in one long cram session. The *serial position effect* is the tendency to recall best the first and last items in a list.

3 What effortful processing methods aid in forming memories?

We process information by encoding its meaning and by encoding *imagery,* as when using some *mnemonic* devices. We also mentally organize information through *chunking* and hierarchies, for easier retrieval.

Storage: Retaining Information

4 What are two components of sensory memory?

As information enters the memory system through our senses, we briefly register and store visual images via *iconic memory,* in which images last no more than a few tenths of a second. We register and store sounds via *echoic memory,* where sound echoes may linger as long as 3 or 4 seconds.

5 What are the duration and capacity of short-term and of long-term memory?

Without *rehearsal,* short-term memory is limited in duration (a few seconds) and in capacity (about seven items of information, either new or retrieved from our memory store). Our capacity for storing information permanently in long-term memory is essentially unlimited.

6 How does the brain store our memories?

Long-term potentiation (LTP) appears to be the neural basis for learning and memory. Stress triggers hormonal changes that arouse brain areas and can produce indelible memories. We are particularly likely to remember emotionally significant events that form *flashbulb memories.* We have a dual-track memory system. *Explicit* (declarative) *memories* of general knowledge, facts, and experiences are processed by the *hippocampus.* *Implicit* (nondeclarative) *memories* of skills and conditioned responses are processed by other parts of the brain, including the cerebellum.

Retrieval: Getting Information Out

7 How do we get information out of memory?

Recall is the ability to retrieve information not in conscious awareness; a fill-in-the-blank question tests recall. *Recognition* is the ability to identify items previously learned; a multiple-choice question tests recognition. *Relearning* is the ability to master previously stored information more quickly than you originally learned it. Retrieval cues catch our attention and tweak our web of associations, helping to move target information into conscious awareness. *Priming* is the process of activating associations (often unconsciously).

8 How do external contexts and internal emotions influence memory retrieval?

The context in which we originally experienced an event or encoded a thought can flood our memory with retrieval cues. Cues triggered by a different but similar context can trick us into believing we have had the experience before, a feeling known as *déjà vu.* Specific emotions can prime us to retrieve memories consistent with that state, a phenomenon known as *mood-congruent memory.*

Forgetting

9 Why do we forget?

We may fail to encode information for entry into our memory system. Memories may fade after storage—rapidly at first, and then leveling off, a trend known as the forgetting curve. We may experience retrieval failure, when old and new material compete, when we don't have adequate retrieval cues, or possibly, in rare instances, because of motivated forgetting, or *repression.* In *proactive interference,* something learned in the past interferes with our ability to recall something recently learned. In *retroactive interference,* something recently learned interferes with something learned in the past.

Memory Construction

10 How do misinformation, imagination, and source amnesia influence our memory construction?

If we are exposed to *misinformation* after an event, or if we repeatedly imagine and rehearse an event that never occurred, we may construct a false memory of what actually happened. We experience *source amnesia* when we attribute a memory to the wrong source.

11 What is the controversy related to claims of repressed and recovered memories?

Memory researchers and some well-meaning therapists have debated whether people repress memories of early childhood abuse

and can recover them by means of leading questions and/or hypnosis during therapy. Psychologists now tend to agree that: (1) Sexual abuse happens, and can leave lasting scars. (2) Some innocent people have been falsely convicted of abuse that never happened, and some true abusers have used the controversy over recovered memories to avoid punishment. (3) Forgetting isolated past events, good or bad, is an ordinary part of life. (4) Recovering good and bad memories, triggered by some memory cue, is commonplace. (5) Infantile amnesia—the inability to recall memories from the first three years of life—makes recovery of very early childhood memories unlikely. (6) Memories obtained under the influence of hypnosis or drugs or therapy are unreliable. (7) Both real and false memories cause stress and suffering.

Improving Memory

12 **How can an understanding of memory contribute to more effective study techniques?**

Memory research–based strategies include studying repeatedly, making material personally meaningful, activating retrieval cues, using mnemonic devices, minimizing interference, getting adequate sleep, and self-testing.

Terms and Concepts to Remember

memory, p. 257

encoding, p. 258

storage, p. 258

retrieval, p. 258

sensory memory, p. 258

short-term memory, p. 258

long-term memory, p. 258

working memory, p. 259

automatic processing, p. 260

effortful processing, p. 260

rehearsal, p. 260

spacing effect, p. 261

serial position effect, p. 261

imagery, p. 263

mnemonics [nih-MON-iks], p. 263

chunking, p. 264

iconic memory, p. 266

echoic memory, p. 266

long-term potentiation (LTP), p. 268

flashbulb memory, p. 269

amnesia, p. 269

implicit memory, p. 270

explicit memory, p. 271

hippocampus, p. 271

recall, p. 273

recognition, p. 273

relearning, p. 273

priming, p. 274

déjà vu, p. 275

mood-congruent memory, p. 275

proactive interference, p. 279

retroactive interference, p. 279

repression, p. 281

misinformation effect, p. 282

source amnesia, p. 283

Test for Success: Critical Thinking Exercises
By Amy Himsel, El Camino College

1. What would be the most effective strategy to learn and retain a list of names of key historical figures for a week? For a year?

2. Maria has always loved to wear winter clothing. The sensation of being bundled up makes her feel safe and secure. How might her preference be related to her January birth in Chicago?

3. When you feel sad, why might it help to look at pictures that reawaken some of your best memories?

4. What you know today seems to be what you have always known. Explain what this means.

5. Eliza's family loves to tell the story of how she "stole the show" as a 2-year-old, dancing at her aunt's wedding reception. Infantile amnesia should have prevented her from forming a memory, yet Eliza can recall the event clearly. How is this possible?

6. What—given the commonality of source amnesia—might life be like if we remembered all our waking experiences and all our dreams?

The Test for Success exercises offer you a chance to apply your critical thinking skills to aspects of the material you have just read. Suggestions for answering these questions can be found in Appendix D at the back of the book.

Multiple-choice self-tests and more may be found at www.worthpublishers.com/myers.

Chapter Outline

● **Thinking**
Concepts
Solving Problems
Making Decisions and Forming
Judgments
**THINKING CRITICALLY
ABOUT:** The Fear Factor—Do
We Fear the Right Things?

● **Language**
Language Development
Thinking and Language
Animal Thinking and Language

● **Intelligence**
What Is Intelligence?
Assessing Intelligence
CLOSE-UP: Extremes of
Intelligence
Genetic and Environmental
Influences on Intelligence
Group Differences in
Intelligence Test Scores

9: Thinking, Language, and Intelligence

Throughout history, we humans have both bemoaned our foolishness and celebrated our wisdom. The poet T. S. Eliot was struck by "the hollow men . . . Headpiece filled with straw." But Shakespeare's Hamlet extolled the human species as "noble in reason! . . . infinite in faculties! . . . in apprehension how like a god!" In the preceding chapters, we have likewise marveled at both our abilities and our errors.

We have studied the human brain—3 pounds of wet tissue the size of a small cabbage, yet containing circuitry more complex than the planet's telephone networks. We have marvelled at the competence of newborns. We have relished our sensory system, which disassembles visual stimuli into millions of nerve impulses, distributes them for parallel processing, and then reassembles them into colorful perceptions. We have pondered our memory's seemingly limitless capacity and the ease with which our two-track mind processes information, consciously and unconsciously. Little wonder that our species has had the collective genius to invent the camera, the car, and the computer; to unlock the atom and crack the genetic code; to travel out to space and into the oceans' depths.

Yet we have also seen that our species is kin to the other animals. We are influenced by the same principles that produce learning in rats and pigeons. As one pundit said, echoing Pavlov, "How like a dog!" We have noted that we assimilate reality into our preconceptions and succumb to perceptual illusions. We have seen how easily we deceive ourselves about hypnotic feats, pseudopsychic claims, and false memories.

In this chapter, we encounter further instances of these two images of the human condition—the rational and the irrational. We will consider how our cognitive system uses all the information it has received, perceived, stored, and retrieved. We will look at our flair for language and consider how and why it develops. And we will reflect on how deserving we are of our name, *Homo sapiens*—wise human.

cognition the mental activities associated with thinking, knowing, remembering, and communicating.

concept a mental grouping of similar objects, events, ideas, or people.

"The average newspaper boy in Pittsburgh knows more about the universe than did Galileo, Aristotle, Leonardo, or any of those other guys who were so smart they only needed one name."

—Daniel Gilbert,
Stumbling on Happiness, 2006

Thinking

Cognition refers to all the mental activities associated with thinking, knowing, remembering, and communicating. Cognitive psychologists study these activities, including the logical and sometimes illogical ways in which we create concepts, solve problems, make decisions, and form judgments.

Concepts

1: **What are the functions of concepts?**

To think about the countless events, objects, and people in our world, we simplify things. We form **concepts**—mental groupings of similar objects, events, ideas, and people. The concept *chair* includes many items—a baby's high chair, a reclining

"Attention, everyone! I'd like to introduce the newest member of our family."

A bird and a . . . ? It takes a bit longer to conceptualize a penguin as a bird because it doesn't match our prototype of a small, feathered, flying creature.

chair, a dentist's chair—all of which are for sitting. Chairs vary, but it is their common features (something with legs to sit on) that define the concept of *chair*.

Imagine life without concepts. We would need a different name for every object and idea. We could not ask a child to "throw the ball" because there would be no concept of *ball* (or *throw*). Instead of saying, "They were angry," we would have to describe expressions, intensities, and words. Such concepts as *ball* and *anger* give us much information with little cognitive effort.

To further simplify things, we organize concepts into category *hierarchies*. Cab drivers organize their cities into geographical sectors, which subdivide into neighborhoods, and again into blocks. Once our categories exist, we use them efficiently. Shown a bird, car, or food, people need no more time to identify an item's category than to perceive that something is there. "As soon as you know it is there, you know what it is," report Kalanit Grill-Spector and Nancy Kanwisher (2005).

We form some concepts by *definition*. Told that a triangle has three intersecting sides, we thereafter classify all three-sided geometric forms as triangles. More often, however, we form our concepts by developing **prototypes**—a mental image or best example that incorporates all the features we associate with a category (Rosch, 1978). The more closely something matches our prototype of a concept, the more readily we recognize it as an example of the concept. A robin and a penguin both satisfy our definition of *bird:* a two-footed animal that has wings and feathers and hatches from an egg. Yet people agree more quickly that "a robin is a bird" than that "a penguin is a bird." For most of us, the flying robin is the birdier bird; it more closely resembles our bird prototype.

Move away from our prototypes, and category boundaries may blur. Is a tomato a fruit? Is a 17-year-old female a girl or a woman? Is a whale a fish or a mammal? Because this marine animal fails to match our prototype, we are slower to recognize it as a mammal. Similarly, we are slow to perceive an illness when our symptoms don't fit one of our disease prototypes (Bishop, 1991). People whose heart attack symptoms (shortness of breath, exhaustion, a dull weight in the chest) don't match their prototype of a heart attack (sharp chest pain) may not seek help. So, like other mental shortcuts we will encounter, concepts speed and guide our thinking. But they don't always make us wise.

prototype a mental image or best example of a category. Matching new items to a prototype provides a quick and easy method for sorting items into categories (as when comparing feathered creatures to a prototypical bird, such as a robin).

algorithm a methodical, logical rule or procedure that guarantees solving a particular problem. Contrasts with the usually speedier—but also more error-prone—use of *heuristics*.

heuristic a simple thinking strategy that often allows us to make judgments and solve problems efficiently; usually speedier but also more error-prone than *algorithms*.

insight a sudden and often novel realization of the solution to a problem; it contrasts with strategy-based solutions.

confirmation bias a tendency to search for information that supports our preconceptions and to ignore or distort contradictory evidence.

Solving Problems

2: **What strategies assist our problem solving, and what obstacles hinder it?**

One tribute to our rationality is our problem-solving skill in coping with novel situations. What's the best route around this traffic jam? How shall we handle a friend's criticism? How can we get in the house without our keys?

Some problems we solve through *trial and error*. Thomas Edison tried thousands of lightbulb filaments before stumbling upon one that worked. For other problems, we use **algorithms,** step-by-step procedures that guarantee a solution. But step-by-step algorithms can be laborious and exasperating. For example, to find another word using all the letters in *SPLOYOCHYG*, we could try each letter in each position, but we would need to generate and examine the 907,200 resulting permutations. In such cases, we often resort to simpler strategies called **heuristics.** Thus, we might reduce the number of options in our *SPLOYOCHYG* example by excluding rare letter combinations, such as two Y's together. By using heuristics and then applying trial and error, we may hit upon the answer.[1]

Sometimes, the problem-solving strategy seems to be no strategy at all. We puzzle over a problem, and suddenly, the pieces fall together as we perceive the solution in a

[1]The answer: PSYCHOLOGY.

sudden flash of **insight.** Ten-year-old Johnny Appleton displayed insight in solving a problem that had stumped construction workers: how to rescue a young robin that had fallen into a narrow 30-inch-deep hole in a cement-block wall. Johnny's solution: Slowly pour in sand, giving the bird enough time to keep its feet on top of the constantly rising sand (Ruchlis, 1990).

Teams of researchers have identified brain activity associated with sudden flashes of insight (Jung-Beeman et al., 2004; Sandkühler & Bhattacharya, 2008). They gave people a problem: Think of a word that will form a compound word or phrase with each of three words in a set (such as *pine, crab,* and *sauce*), and press a button to sound a bell when you know the answer. (If you need a hint: The word is a fruit.[2]) To see what brain activity enables insight, the researchers mapped the problem solver's brain activity, using fMRIs (functional MRIs) or EEGs. In the first experiment, about half the solutions were by a sudden Aha! insight, which typically was preceded by frontal lobe activity involved in focusing attention and was accompanied by a burst of activity in the right temporal lobe, just above the ear (**FIGURE 9.1**).

As you perhaps experienced in solving the *pine-crab-sauce* problem, insight often pops into mind with striking suddenness, with no prior sense that one is "getting warmer" or feeling close to the answer (Knoblich & Oellinger, 2006; Metcalfe, 1986). When the "Eureka moment" hits us, we feel a sense of satisfaction, a feeling of happiness. The joy of a joke may similarly lie in our sudden comprehension of an unexpected ending or a double meaning.

Obstacles to Problem Solving

Inventive as we can be in solving problems, the correct answer may elude us. Two cognitive tendencies—*confirmation bias* and *fixation*—often lead us astray.

CONFIRMATION BIAS We seek evidence verifying our ideas more eagerly than we seek evidence that might refute them (Klayman & Ha, 1987; Skov & Sherman, 1986). This tendency, known as **confirmation bias,** is a major obstacle to problem solving. Peter Wason (1960) demonstrated the confirmation bias by giving British university students the three-number sequence 2-4-6 and asking them to guess the rule he had used to devise the series. (The rule was simple: any three ascending numbers.) Before submitting answers, students generated their own sets of three numbers, and Wason told them whether their sets conformed to his rule. Once they felt *certain* they had the rule, they were to announce it. The result? Seldom right but never in doubt. Most of Wason's students formed a wrong idea ("Maybe it's counting by twos") and then searched only for evidence confirming the wrong rule (by testing 6-8-10, 100-102-104, and so forth).

"Ordinary people," said Wason (1981), "evade facts, become inconsistent, or systematically defend themselves against the threat of new information relevant to the issue." The results are sometimes momentous. The United States launched its war against Iraq on the assumption that Saddam Hussein possessed weapons of mass destruction (WMD) that posed an immediate threat. When that assumption turned out to be false, confirmation bias was one of the flaws in the judgment process identified by the bipartisan U.S. Senate Select Committee on Intelligence (2004).

[2]The word is *apple:* pineapple, crabapple, applesauce.

Heuristic searching To search for guava juice, you could search every supermarket aisle (an algorithm), or check the bottled beverage, natural foods, and produce sections (heuristics). The heuristics approach is often speedier, but an algorithmic search guarantees you will find it eventually.

FIGURE 9.1 The Aha! moment A burst of right temporal lobe activity accompanies insight solutions to word problems (Jung-Beeman et al., 2004).

"The human understanding, when any proposition has been once laid down . . . forces everything else to add fresh support and confirmation."
—Francis Bacon, *Novum Organum,* 1620

FIGURE 9.2 The matchstick problem
How would you arrange six matches to form four equilateral triangles? (Turn the next page to see the solution in Figure 9.3.)

Administration analysts "had a tendency to accept information which supported [their presumptions] . . . more readily than information which contradicted" them. Sources denying such weapons were deemed "either lying or not knowledgeable about Iraq's problems, while those sources who reported ongoing WMD activities were seen as having provided valuable information."

FIXATION Once we incorrectly represent a problem, it's hard to restructure how we approach it. If the solution to the matchstick problem in **FIGURE 9.2** eludes you, you may be experiencing **fixation**—the inability to see a problem from a fresh perspective.

One example of fixation is *mental set*. As a perceptual set predisposes what we perceive, a **mental set** predisposes how we think. Mental set refers to our tendency to approach a problem with the mind-set of what has worked for us previously. Indeed, solutions that worked in the past often do work on new problems. Consider:

Given the sequence *O-T-T-F-?-?-?*, what are the final three letters?

Most people have difficulty recognizing that the three final letters are *F*(ive), *S*(ix), and *S*(even). But solving this problem may make the next one easier:

Given the sequence *J-F-M-A-?-?-?*, what are the final three letters? (If you don't get this one, ask yourself what month it is.)

Sometimes, however, a mental set based on what worked in the past precludes our finding a new solution to a new problem. Our mental set from our past experiences with matchsticks predisposes our arranging them in two dimensions.

Making Decisions and Forming Judgments

3: How do heuristics, overconfidence, and belief perseverance influence our decisions and judgments?

When making each day's hundreds of judgments and decisions *(Is it worth the bother to take an umbrella? Can I trust this person? Should I shoot the basketball or pass to the player who's hot?)* we seldom take the time and effort to reason systematically. We just follow our intuition. After interviewing policymakers in government, business, and education, social psychologist Irving Janis (1986) concluded that they "often do not use a reflective problem-solving approach. How do they usually arrive at their decisions? If you ask, they are likely to tell you . . . they do it mostly by *the seat of their pants*."

Using and Misusing Heuristics

When we need to act quickly, those mental shortcuts we call heuristics often do help us overcome analysis paralysis. Thanks to our mind's automatic information processing, intuitive judgments are instantaneous. But the price we sometimes pay for this efficiency—quick but bad judgments—can be costly. Research by cognitive psychologists Amos Tversky and Daniel Kahneman (1974) on the *representativeness* and *availability heuristics* showed how these generally helpful shortcuts can lead even the smartest people into dumb decisions. (Their joint work on decision making received a 2002 Nobel Prize, although sadly, only Kahneman was alive to receive the honor.)

THE REPRESENTATIVENESS HEURISTIC To judge the likelihood of things in terms of how well they represent particular prototypes is to use the **representativeness heuristic.** To illustrate, consider:

> A stranger tells you about a person who is short, slim, and likes to read poetry, and then asks you to guess whether this person is more likely to be a professor of classics at an Ivy League university or a truck driver. Which would be the better guess (adapted from Nisbett & Ross, 1980)?

fixation the inability to see a problem from a new perspective, by employing a different mental set.

mental set a tendency to approach a problem in one particular way, often a way that has been successful in the past.

representativeness heuristic judging the likelihood of things in terms of how well they seem to represent, or match, particular prototypes; may lead us to ignore other relevant information.

availability heuristic estimating the likelihood of events based on their availability in memory; if instances come readily to mind (perhaps because of their vividness), we presume such events are common.

"In creating these problems, we didn't set out to fool people. All our problems fooled us, too."
Amos Tversky (1985)

"Intuitive thinking [is] fine most of the time. . . . But sometimes that habit of mind gets us in trouble."
Daniel Kahneman (2005)

Did you answer "professor"? Many people do, because the description seems more *representative* of Ivy League scholars than of truck drivers. The representativeness heuristic enabled you to make a snap judgment. But it also led you to ignore other relevant information. When I help people think through this question, the conversation goes something like this:

> ***Question:*** *First, let's figure out how many professors fit the description. How many Ivy League universities do you suppose there are?*
> ***Answer:*** *Oh, about 10, I suppose.*
> ***Question:*** *How many classics professors would you guess there are at each?*
> ***Answer:*** *Maybe 4.*
> ***Question:*** *Okay, that's 40 Ivy League classics professors. What fraction of these are short and slim?*
> ***Answer:*** *Let's say half.*
> ***Question:*** *And, of these 20, how many like to read poetry?*
> ***Answer:*** *I'd say half—10 professors.*
> ***Question:*** *Okay, now let's figure how many truck drivers fit the description. How many truck drivers do you suppose there are?*
> ***Answer:*** *Maybe 400,000.*
> ***Question:*** *What fraction are short and slim?*
> ***Answer:*** *Not many—perhaps 1 in 8.*
> ***Question:*** *Of these 50,000, what percentage like to read poetry?*
> ***Answer:*** *Truck drivers who like poetry? Maybe 1 in 100—oh, oh, I get it—that leaves 500 short, slim, poetry-reading truck drivers.*
> ***Comment:*** *Yup. So, even if we accept your stereotype that the description is more representative of classics professors than of truck drivers, the odds are 50 to 1 that this person is a truck driver.*

The representativeness heuristic influences many of our daily decisions. To judge the likelihood of something, we intuitively compare it with our mental representation of that category—of, say, what truck drivers are like. If the two match, that fact usually overrides other considerations of statistics or logic.

THE AVAILABILITY HEURISTIC The **availability heuristic** operates when we base our judgments on the mental availability of information. Anything that enables information to "pop into mind" quickly and with little effort—its recency, vividness, or distinctiveness—can increase its perceived availability, making it seem commonplace. Casinos entice us to gamble by signaling even small wins with bells and lights—making them vividly memorable—while keeping big losses soundlessly invisible. And if someone from a particular ethnic group commits a terrorist act,

"The problem is I can't tell the difference between a deeply wise, intuitive nudge from the Universe and one of my own bone-headed ideas!"

FIGURE 9.3 Solution to the matchstick problem To solve this problem, you must view it from a new perspective, breaking the fixation of limiting solutions to two dimensions.

FIGURE 9.4 Risk of death from various causes in the United States, 2001 (Data assembled from various government sources by Randall Marshall et al., 2007.)

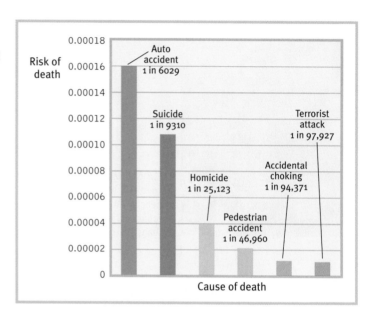

"Don't believe everything you think."

—Bumper sticker

"The human understanding is most excited by that which strikes and enters the mind at once and suddenly, and by which the imagination is immediately filled and inflated. It then begins almost imperceptibly to conceive and suppose that everything is similar to the few objects which have taken possession of the mind."

—Francis Bacon, *Novum Organum*, 1620

our readily available memory of the dramatic event may shape our impression of the whole group. When statistical reality is pitted against a single vivid case, the memorable case often wins. The mass killing of civilians may seem on the increase of late, thanks to memorably available terrorism and genocide. Actually, such horrors have declined sharply since the late 1980s (Pinker, 2007; U.S. Department of State, 2004).

Even during 9/11's horrific year, terrorist acts claimed comparatively few lives, note risk researchers (see **FIGURE 9.4**). Yet in 2007, a poll showed "terrorism" was Americans' top priority for Congress and the President, and that responding to global climate change—which some scientists regard as a future "Armageddon in slow motion"—was one of the lowest priorities (Pew, 2007). Emotion-laden images of terror exacerbate our fears of terrorism by harnessing the availability heuristic, notes political scientist Cass Sunstein (2007). We fear flying because we play in our heads a tape of 9/11 or some other air disaster. We fear letting our children walk to school because we play in our heads tapes of abducted and brutalized children. We fear swimming in ocean waters because we replay *Jaws* in our heads. And so, thanks to these readily available images, we come to fear extremely rare events. We overfeel and underthink. (For more on the power of vivid cases, turn the next page to see Thinking Critically About: The Fear Factor—Do We Fear the Right Things?)

Overconfidence

Our use of intuitive heuristics when forming judgments, our eagerness to confirm the beliefs we already hold, and our knack for explaining away failures combine to create **overconfidence,** a tendency to overestimate the accuracy of our knowledge and judgments. Across various tasks, people overestimate what their performance was, is, or will be (Metcalfe, 1998).

People are also more confident than correct when answering such questions as, "Is absinthe a liqueur or a precious stone?" (It's a licorice-flavored liqueur.) On questions where only 60 percent of people answer correctly, respondents typically feel 75 percent confident. Even those who feel 100 percent certain err about 15 percent of the time (Fischhoff et al., 1977).

Overconfidence plagues decisions outside the laboratory, too. It was an overconfident Lyndon Johnson who waged war with North Vietnam and an overconfident George W. Bush who marched into Iraq to eliminate supposed weapons of mass

overconfidence the tendency to be more confident than correct—to overestimate the accuracy of our beliefs and judgments.

belief perseverance clinging to one's initial conceptions after the basis on which they were formed has been discredited.

destruction. Overconfidence also drives stockbrokers and investment managers to market their ability to outperform stock market averages, despite overwhelming evidence to the contrary (Malkiel, 2004). A purchase of stock X, recommended by a broker who judges this to be the time to buy, is usually balanced by a sale made by someone who judges this to be the time to sell. Despite their confidence, buyer and seller cannot both be right.

Students are routinely overconfident about how quickly they can do assignments and write papers, typically expecting to finish ahead of schedule (Buehler et al., 1994). In fact, the projects generally take about twice the number of days predicted. Despite our painful underestimates, we remain overly confident of our next prediction. Moreover, anticipating how much we will accomplish, and believing we will have more free time in the future, we happily accept invitations, only to discover we're just as busy when the day rolls around (Zauberman & Lynch, 2005).

Failing to appreciate our potential for error can have serious consequences, but overconfidence does have adaptive value. People who err on the side of overconfidence live more happily, find it easier to make tough decisions, and seem more credible than those who lack self-confidence (Baumeister, 1989; Taylor, 1989). Moreover, given prompt and clear feedback—as weather forecasters receive after each day's predictions—we can learn to be more realistic about the accuracy of our judgments (Fischhoff, 1982). The wisdom to know when we know a thing and when we do not is born of experience.

Predict your own behavior When will you finish reading this chapter?

> "When you know a thing, to hold that you know it; and when you do not know a thing, to allow that you do not know it; this is knowledge."
>
> —Confucius (551–479 B.C.E.), *Analects*

The Belief Perseverance Phenomenon

Our readiness to fear the wrong things and to be overconfident in our judgments is startling. Equally startling is our tendency to cling to our beliefs in the face of contrary evidence. **Belief perseverance** often fuels social conflict, as it did in one study of people with opposing views of capital punishment (Lord et al., 1979). Those on both sides studied two supposedly new research findings, one supporting and the other refuting the claim that the death penalty deters crime. Each side was more impressed by the study supporting its own beliefs, and each readily disputed the other study. Thus, showing the pro– and anti–capital-punishment groups the *same* mixed evidence actually *increased* their disagreement.

If you want to rein in the belief perseverance phenomenon, a simple remedy exists: *Consider the opposite.* When Charles Lord and his colleagues (1984) repeated the capital-punishment study, they asked some participants to be "as *objective* and *unbiased* as possible." The plea did nothing to reduce biased evaluations of evidence. They asked another group to consider "whether you would have made the same high or low evaluations had exactly the same study produced results on the *other* side of the issue." Having imagined and pondered *opposite* findings, these people became much less biased in their evaluations of the evidence.

The more we come to appreciate why our beliefs might be true, the more tightly we cling to them. Once people have explained to themselves why they believe a child is "gifted" or "learning disabled," or why candidate X or Y will be a better commander-in-chief, or why company Z is a stock worth owning, they tend to ignore evidence undermining that belief. Prejudice persists. Once beliefs form and get justified, it takes more compelling evidence to change them than it did to create them.

"I'm happy to say that my final judgment of a case is almost always consistent with my prejudgment of the case."

Thinking Critically About:

The Fear Factor—Do We Fear the Right Things?

"Most people reason dramatically, not quantitatively," said Oliver Wendell Holmes. After 9/11, many people feared flying more than driving. (In a 2006 Gallup survey, only 40 percent reported being "not afraid at all" to fly.) Yet, for most people, the most dangerous aspect of airline flying is the drive to the airport. In the months between 2003 and 2005, mile for mile, Americans were 230 times more likely to die in an automobile crash than on a commercial flight (National Safety Council, 2008).

In a late-2001 essay, I calculated that if—because of 9/11—we flew 20 percent less and instead drove half those unflown miles, about 800 more people would die in traffic accidents in the year after 9/11 (Myers, 2001). In checking this estimate against actual accident data (why didn't I think of that?), German psychologist Gerd Gigerenzer (2004) found that the last three months of 2001 did indeed produce significantly more U.S. traffic fatalities than the three-month average in the previous five years (**FIGURE 9.5**). Long after

9/11, the dead terrorists were still killing Americans. As air travel gradually recovered during 2002 through 2005, U.S. commercial flights carried nearly 2.5 billion passengers, with no deaths on a major airline big jet (McMurray, 2006; Miller, 2005). Meanwhile, 172,000 Americans died in traffic accidents.

Why do we fear the wrong things? Why do we judge terrorism to be a greater risk than accidents—which kill nearly as many per *week* in just the United States as did terrorism (2527 deaths worldwide) in all of

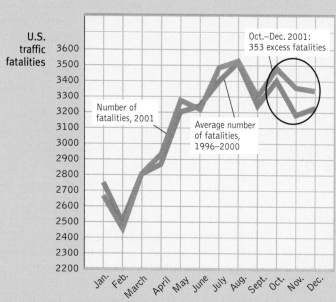

FIGURE 9.5 Still killing Americans Images of 9/11 etched a sharper image in our minds than did the millions of fatality-free flights on U.S. airlines during 2002 and after. Such dramatic events, being readily available to memory, shape our perceptions of risk. In the three months after 2001, those faulty perceptions led more people to travel, and some to die, by car. (Adapted from Gigerenzer, 2004.)

The Perils and Powers of Intuition

4: How do smart thinkers use intuition?

We have seen how our irrational thinking can plague our efforts to solve problems, make wise decisions, form valid judgments, and reason logically. Intuition also feeds our gut fears and prejudices. Moreover, these perils of **intuition** appear even when people are offered extra pay for thinking smart, even when they are asked to justify their answers, and even when they are expert physicians or clinicians (Shafir & LeBoeuf, 2002). From this you might conclude that our heads are indeed filled with straw.

But we must not abandon hope for human rationality. Today's cognitive scientists are also revealing intuition's powers, as you can see throughout this book. For

intuition an effortless, immediate, automatic feeling or thought, as contrasted with explicit, conscious reasoning.

the 1990s (Johnson, 2001)? Even with the horror of 9/11, more Americans in 2001 died of food poisoning (which scares few) than of terrorism (which scares many). Psychological science has identified four influences on our intuitions about risk. Together they explain why we sometimes fret over remote possibilities while ignoring much higher probabilities.

First, *we fear what our ancestral history has prepared us to fear.* Human emotions were road tested in the Stone Age. Our old brain prepares us to fear yesterday's risks: snakes, lizards, and spiders (which combined now kill relatively few in developed countries). And it prepares us to fear confinement and heights, and therefore flying.

Second, *we fear what we cannot control.* Driving we control, flying we do not.

Third, *we fear what is immediate.* Threats related to flying are mostly telescoped into the moments of takeoff and landing, while the dangers of driving are diffused across many moments to come, each trivially dangerous. Similarly, many smokers (whose habit shortens their life, on average, by about five years) fret openly before flying (which, averaged across people, shortens life by one day). Smoking's toxicity kills in the distant future.

Fourth, *we fear what is most readily available in memory.* Powerful, available memories—like the image of United Flight 175 slicing into the World Trade Center—serve as our measuring rods as we intuitively judge risks. Thousands of

Ian Berry/Magnum Photos

safe car trips have extinguished our anxieties about driving.

Vivid events also distort our comprehension of risks and probable outcomes. We comprehend disasters that have killed people dramatically, in bunches. But we fear too little those threats that will claim lives undramatically, one by one, and in the distant future. As Bill Gates has noted, each year a half-million children worldwide—the equivalent of four 747s full of children every day—die quietly, one by one, from rotavirus, and we hear nothing of it (Glass, 2004). Dramatic outcomes make us gasp; probabilities we hardly grasp.

The point to remember: It is perfectly normal to fear purposeful violence from those who hate us. When terrorists strike

Dramatic deaths in bunches breed concern and fear The memorable South Asian tsunami that killed some 300,000 people stirred an outpouring of concern and new tsunami-warning technology. Meanwhile, a "silent tsunami" of poverty-related malaria was killing about that many of the world's children every couple months, noted Jeffrey Sachs, the head of a United Nations project aiming to cut extreme poverty in half by 2015 (Dugger, 2005).

again, we will all recoil in horror. But smart thinkers will remember this: *Check your fears against the facts and resist those who serve their own purposes by cultivating a culture of fear.* By so doing, we can take away the terrorists' most omnipresent weapon: exaggerated fear.

"Fearful people are more dependent, more easily manipulated and controlled, more susceptible to deceptively simple, strong, tough measures and hard-line postures."

—Media researcher George Gerbner to U.S. Congressional Subcommittee on Communications, 1981

---

the most part, our cognition's instant, intuitive reactions enable us to react quickly and *usually* adaptively. They do so thanks, first, to our fast and frugal heuristics that enable us, for example, to intuitively assume that fuzzy-looking objects are far away, which they usually are (except on foggy mornings). Our learned associations also spawn the intuitions of our two-track mind. If a stranger looks like someone who previously harmed or threatened us, we may—without consciously recalling the earlier experience—react warily. (The learned association surfaces as a gut feeling.)

University of Amsterdam psychologist Ap Dijksterhuis and his colleagues (2006a,b) discovered the surprising powers of unconscious intuition in experiments that showed people complex information about potential apartments (or roommates or art posters). They invited some participants to state their immediate preference after reading a dozen pieces of information about each of four apartments.

Chick sexing When acquired expertise becomes an automatic habit, as it is for experienced chick sexers, it feels like intuition. At a glance, they just know.

A second group, given several minutes to analyze the information, tended to make slightly smarter decisions. But wisest of all, in study after study, was a third group, whose attention was distracted for a time. This enabled their minds to process the complex information unconsciously and to arrive at a more satisfying result. Faced with complex decisions involving many factors, the best advice may indeed be to take our time—to "sleep on it"—and to await the intuitive result of our unconscious processing.

Intuition is huge. More than we realize, thinking occurs off-screen, with the results occasionally displayed on-screen. Intuition feeds our expertise, our creativity, our love, and our spirituality. And intuition, smart intuition, is born of experience. Chess masters can look at a board and intuitively know the right move. Playing "blitz chess," where every move is made after barely more than a glance, they display a hardly diminished skill (Burns, 2004). Experienced chicken sexers can tell you a chick's sex at a glance, yet cannot tell you how they do it. In each case, the immediate insight describes acquired, speedy expertise that feels like instant intuition. Experienced nurses, firefighters, art critics, car mechanics, hockey players, and you, for anything in which you develop a deep and special knowledge, learn to size up many a situation in an eyeblink. Intuition is recognition, observed Nobel laureate psychologist-economist Herbert Simon (2001). It is analysis "frozen into habit."

So, intuition—fast, automatic, unreasoned feeling and thought—harvests our experience and guides our lives. Intuition is powerful, often wise, but sometimes perilous, and especially so when we overfeel and underthink, as we do when judging risks. Today's psychological science enhances our appreciation for intuition. But it also reminds us to check our intuitions against reality. Our two-track mind makes sweet harmony as smart, critical thinking listens to the creative whispers of our vast unseen mind, and builds upon it by evaluating evidence, testing conclusions, and planning for the future.

The Effects of Framing

5: What is framing?

A further test of rationality is whether the same issue, presented in two different but logically equivalent ways, will elicit the same answer. For example, one surgeon tells someone that 10 percent of people die while undergoing a particular surgery. Another tells someone that 90 percent survive. The information is the same. The effect is not. To both patients and physicians, the risk seems greater to those who hear that 10 percent will *die* (Marteau, 1989; McNeil et al., 1988; Rothman & Salovey, 1997).

The effects of **framing**, the way we present an issue, are sometimes striking. Nine in 10 college students rate a condom as effective if it has a supposed "95 percent success rate" in stopping the HIV virus that causes AIDS; only 4 in 10 think it successful given a "5 percent failure rate" (Linville et al., 1992). And people express more surprise when a 1-in-20 event happens than when an equivalent 10-in-200 event happens (Denes-Raj et al., 1995). To scare people, frame risks as numbers,

framing the way an issue is posed; how an issue is framed can significantly affect decisions and judgments.

not percentages. People told that a chemical exposure is projected to kill 10 of every 10 million people (imagine 10 dead people!) feel more frightened than if told the fatality risk is an infinitesimal .000001 (Kraus et al., 1992).

Consider how the framing effect influences political and business decisions. Politicians know to frame their position on public assistance as "aid to the needy" if they are for it and "welfare" if not. Merchants mark up their "regular prices" to appear to offer huge savings on "sale prices." A $100 coat marked down from $150 by Store X can seem like a better deal than the same coat priced regularly at $100 by Store Y (Urbany et al., 1988). And ground beef described as "75 percent lean" seems much more appealing than beef that is "25 percent fat" (Levin & Gaeth, 1988; Sanford et al., 2002). Likewise, a price difference between a credit-card purchase of gasoline versus a cash purchase feels better if framed as a "cash discount" rather than a "credit card fee."

Framing research also finds a powerful application in the definition of options, which can be posed in ways that nudge people toward better decisions (Thaler & Sunstein, 2008).

- *Why choosing to be an organ donor depends on where you live.* In many European countries as well as the United States, people can decide whether they want to be organ donors when renewing their driver's license. In countries where the default option is *yes,* but people can opt out, nearly 100 percent agree to be donors. In the United States, Britain, and Germany, where the default option is *no* but people can "opt in," only about 25 percent agree to be donors (Johnson & Goldstein, 2003).
- *How to help employees decide to save for their retirement.* A 2006 U.S. pension law recognized the huge effect of framing options. Previously, employees who wanted to defer part of their compensation to a 401(k) retirement plan typically had to elect to lower their take-home pay, which most people are averse to doing. Now companies are being encouraged to enroll their employees automatically but to allow them to opt out (thereby raising their take-home pay). In both plans, the choice was the employee's. But under the "opt-out" rather than "opt-in" option, enrollments soared from 49 to 86 percent (Madrian & Shea, 2001).

The point to remember: Those who understand the power of framing can use it to influence our decisions.

REHEARSE IT!

1. A concept is
   a. a mental grouping of similar things.
   b. an example of insight.
   c. a fixation on certain characteristics.
   d. a representativeness heuristic.

2. The most systematic procedure for solving a problem is a(n)
   a. heuristic.
   b. algorithm.
   c. insight.
   d. intuition.

3. A major obstacle to problem solving is fixation, which is a(n)
   a. tendency to base our judgments on vivid memories.
   b. art of framing the same question in two different ways.
   c. inability to view a problem from a new perspective.

   d. rule of thumb for judging the likelihood of an event in terms of our mental image of it.

4. You notice that your new next-door neighbor is very neatly dressed, wears glasses, and is reading a Greek play. Given a choice between her being a librarian and a store clerk, you incorrectly guess that she is a librarian. You were probably led astray by
   a. the availability heuristic.
   b. confirmation bias.
   c. overconfidence.
   d. the representativeness heuristic.

5. After the 9/11 attacks by foreign-born terrorists, some observers initially assumed that the 2003 East Coast black-out was probably also the work of

   foreign-born terrorists. This assumption illustrates
   a. belief perseverance.
   b. the availability heuristic.
   c. fixation.
   d. confirmation bias.

6. When consumers respond more positively to ground beef described as "75 percent lean" than to the same product labeled "25 percent fat," they have been influenced by
   a. belief perseverance.
   b. fixation.
   c. confirmation bias.
   d. framing.

Answers: 1. a, 2. b, 3. c, 4. d, 5. b, 6. d.

Language

The striking effects of framing illustrate the power of **language**—our spoken, written, or signed words and the ways we combine them as we think and communicate. Humans have long and proudly proclaimed that language sets us above all other animals. "When we study human language," asserted linguist Noam Chomsky (1972), "we are approaching what some might call the 'human essence,' the qualities of mind that are, so far as we know, unique [to humans]." Cognitive scientist Steven Pinker (1990) has called language "the jewel in the crown of cognition."

Imagine an alien species that could pass thoughts from one head to another merely by pulsating air molecules in the space between them. Perhaps these weird creatures could inhabit a future Spielberg movie? Actually, we are those creatures! When we speak, our brain and voice box conjure up air pressure waves that we send banging against another's eardrum—enabling us to transfer thoughts from our brain into theirs. As Pinker (1998) has noted, we sometimes sit for hours "listening to other people make noise as they exhale, because those hisses and squeaks contain *information*." And thanks to all those funny sounds created in our heads from the air pressure waves we send out, we get people's attention, we get them to do things, and we maintain relationships (Guerin, 2003). Depending on how you vibrate the air after opening your mouth, you may get slapped or kissed.

Thanks to language, we transfer meaning from one mind to another. Whether spoken, written, or signed, language enables us not only to communicate but to transmit civilization's accumulated knowledge across generations. Monkeys mostly know what they see. Thanks to language, we know much that we've never seen.

Language Development

Make a quick guess: How many words did you learn during the years between your first birthday and your high school graduation? The answer is about 60,000 (Bloom, 2000; McMurray, 2007). That averages (after age 1) to nearly 3500 words each year, or nearly 10 each day! How you did it—how the 3500 words a year you learned could so far outnumber the roughly 200 words a year that your schoolteachers consciously taught you—is one of the great human wonders.

Before you were able to add 2 + 2, you were creating your own original and grammatically appropriate sentences. Most of us would have trouble stating our language's rules for ordering words to form sentences. Yet as preschoolers, you comprehended and spoke with a facility that puts to shame your fellow college students now struggling to learn a foreign language.

We humans have an astonishing facility for language. With remarkable efficiency, we selectively sample tens of thousands of words in memory, effortlessly assemble them with near-perfect syntax, and spew them out at a rate of three words a second (Vigliocco & Hartsuiker, 2002). Seldom do we form sentences in our minds before speaking them. Rather they organize themselves on the fly as we speak. And while doing all this, we also adapt our utterances to our social and cultural context, following rules for speaking *(How far apart should we stand?)* and listening *(Is it OK to interrupt?)*. Given how many ways there are to mess up, it's amazing that we can master this social dance. So, when and how does it happen?

When Do We Learn Language?

6: What are the milestones in language development?

RECEPTIVE LANGUAGE Children's language development moves from simplicity to complexity. Infants start without language (*in fantis* means "not speaking"). Yet by 4 months of age, babies can discriminate speech sounds (Stager & Werker, 1997).

Although you probably know between 60,000 and 80,000 words, you use only 150 words for about half of what you say.

language our spoken, written, or signed words and the ways we combine them to communicate meaning.

babbling stage beginning at about 4 months, the stage of speech development in which the infant spontaneously utters various sounds at first unrelated to the household language.

one-word stage the stage in speech development, from about age 1 to 2, during which a child speaks mostly in single words.

two-word stage beginning about age 2, the stage in speech development during which a child speaks mostly two-word statements.

telegraphic speech early speech stage in which a child speaks like a telegram—"go car"—using mostly nouns and verbs.

They can also read lips: They prefer to look at a face that matches a sound, so we know they can recognize that *ah* comes from wide open lips and *ee* from a mouth with corners pulled back (Kuhl & Meltzoff, 1982). This period marks the beginning of the development of babies' *receptive language,* their ability to comprehend speech. At seven months and beyond, babies grow in their power to do what you and I find difficult when listening to an unfamiliar language: segmenting spoken sounds into individual words.

PRODUCTIVE LANGUAGE Babies' *productive language,* their ability to produce words, matures after their receptive language. Prior to this, around 4 months of age, babies enter the **babbling stage,** in which they spontaneously utter a variety of sounds, such as *ah-goo.* Babbling is not an imitation of adult speech, for it includes sounds from various languages, even those not spoken in the household. From this early babbling, a listener could not identify an infant as being, say, French, Korean, or Ethiopian. Deaf infants who observe their Deaf parents signing begin to babble more with their hands (Petitto & Marentette, 1991). Before nurture molds our speech, nature enables a wide range of possible sounds. Many of these natural babbling sounds are consonant-vowel pairs formed by simply bunching the tongue in the front of the mouth *(da-da, na-na, ta-ta)* or by opening and closing the lips *(ma-ma),* both of which babies do naturally for feeding (MacNeilage & Davis, 2000).

By the time infants are about 10 months old, their babbling has changed so that a trained ear can identify the language of the household (de Boysson-Bardies et al., 1989). Sounds and intonations outside that language begin to disappear. Without exposure to other languages, babies become functionally deaf to speech sounds outside their native language (Pallier et al., 2001). This explains why adults who speak only English cannot discriminate certain Japanese sounds within speech, and why Japanese adults with no training in English cannot distinguish between the English *r* and *l.* Thus, *la-la-ra-ra* may, to a Japanese-speaking adult, sound like the same syllable repeated. A Japanese-speaking person told that the train station is "just after the next light" may wonder, "The next what? After the street veering right, or farther down, after the traffic light?"

Around their first birthday (the exact age varies from child to child), most children enter the **one-word stage.** They have already learned that sounds carry meanings, and if repeatedly trained to associate, say, *fish* with a picture of a fish, 1-year-olds will look at a fish when a researcher says "Fish, fish! Look at the fish!" (Schafer, 2005). Not surprisingly, they now begin to use sounds—usually only one barely recognizable syllable, such as *ma* or *da*—to communicate meaning. But family members quickly learn to understand, and gradually the infant's language conforms more to the family's language. At this one-word stage, an inflected word may equal a sentence. "Doggy!" may mean "Look at the dog out there!"

At about 18 months, children's word learning explodes from about a word per week to a word per day. By their second birthday, most have entered the **two-word stage.** They start uttering two-word sentences (**TABLE 9.1**) in **telegraphic speech:** Like the old-fashioned telegrams (TERMS ACCEPTED. SEND MONEY), this early form of speech contains mostly nouns and verbs *(Want juice).* Also like telegrams, it follows rules of syntax; the words are in a sensible order. English-speaking children typically place adjectives before nouns—*big doggy* rather than *doggy big.*

Once children move out of the two-word stage, they quickly begin uttering longer phrases (Fromkin & Rodman, 1983). If they get a late start on learning a particular language, for example after receiving a cochlear implant or being an international adoptee, their language development still proceeds through the same sequence, although usually at a faster pace (Ertmer et al., 2007; Snedeker et al., 2007). By early elementary school, children understand complex sentences and begin to enjoy the humor conveyed by double meanings: "You never starve in the desert because of all the sand-which-is there."

"Got idea. Talk better. Combine words. Make sentences."

TABLE 9.1 Language Development

Month (approximate)	Stage
4	Babbling, variety of sounds.
10	Babbling, household language.
12	One-word stage.
24	Two-word, telegraphic speech.
24+	Rapid development, complex sentences.

Explaining Language Development

7: How do we learn language?

Attempts to explain how we acquire language have sparked a spirited intellectual controversy. The nature-nurture debate surfaces again and, here as elsewhere, appreciation for innate predispositions and nature-nuture interactions has grown.

SKINNER: OPERANT LEARNING Behaviorist B. F. Skinner (1957) believed we can explain language development with familiar learning principles, such as *association* (of the sights of things with the sounds of words); *imitation* (of the words and syntax modeled by others); and *reinforcement* (with smiles and hugs when the child says something right). Thus, Skinner (1985) argued, babies learn to talk in many of the same ways that animals learn to peck keys and press bars: "Verbal behavior evidently came into existence when, through a critical step in the evolution of the human species, the vocal musculature became susceptible to operant conditioning."

CHOMSKY: INBORN UNIVERSAL GRAMMAR Linguist Noam Chomsky (1959, 1987) rejected Skinner's ideas, arguing that children acquire untaught words and grammar at a rate too extraordinary to be explained solely by learning principles. They generate all sorts of sentences they have never heard, sometimes with novel errors. (No parent teaches the sentence, "I hate you, Daddy.") Moreover, many of the errors young children make result from overgeneralizing logical grammatical rules, such as adding -*ed* to form the past tense (de Cuevas, 1990): "My teacher holded the baby rabbits and we petted them."

Given adequate nurture, said Chomsky, language will naturally occur: It just "happens to the child." And the reason it happens is that we come prewired with a sort of switch box—a *language acquisition device*. It is as if the switches need to be turned either "on" or "off" for us to understand and produce language. As we hear language, the switches get set for the language we are to learn.

Chomsky also proposed that there is a *universal grammar* underlying human language. All human languages therefore have the same grammatical building blocks, such as nouns and verbs, subjects and objects, negations and questions. Thus, we readily learn the specific grammar of whatever language we experience, whether spoken or signed (Bavelier et al., 2003). And no matter what that language is, we start speaking mostly in nouns (*kitty, da-da*) rather than verbs and adjectives (Bornstein et al., 2004). It happens so naturally—as naturally as birds learning to fly—that training hardly helps.

Many psychologists believe we benefit from both Skinner's and Chomsky's views. Children's genes design complex brain wiring that prepares them to learn language as they interact with their caregivers. Skinner's emphasis on learning helps explain how infants acquire their language as they interact with others. Chomsky's emphasis on our built-in readiness to learn grammar rules helps explain why preschoolers acquire language so readily and use grammar so well. Once again, we see biology and experience working together.

CRITICAL PERIODS Childhood seems to represent a *critical* (or "sensitive") *period* for mastering certain aspects of language (Hernandez & Li, 2007). Deaf children who gain hearing with cochlear implants by age 2 develop better oral speech than do those who receive implants after age 4 (Greers, 2004). And whether children are deaf or hearing, later-than-usual exposure to language (at age 2 or 3) unleashes their brain's idle language capacity, producing a rush of language. But around age 7, a window in the mind closes, and children who have not been exposed to either a spoken or a signed language gradually lose their ability to master *any* language.

Creating a language Brought together as if on a desert island (actually a school), Nicaragua's young deaf children over time drew upon sign gestures from home to create their own Nicaraguan Sign Language, complete with words and intricate grammar. Our biological predisposition for language does not create language in a vacuum. But activated by a social context, nature and nurture work creatively together (Osborne, 1999; Sandler et al., 2005; Senghas & Coppola, 2001).

Susan Meiselas/Magnum Photos

"Childhood is the time for language, no doubt about it. Young children, the younger the better, are good at it; it is child's play. It is a onetime gift to the species."

—Lewis Thomas, *The Fragile Species*, 1992

Natively deaf children who learn sign language after age 9 never learn it as well as those who become deaf at age 9 after learning English. They also never learn English as well as other natively deaf children who learned sign in infancy (Mayberry et al., 2002). The striking conclusion: When a young brain does not learn *any* language, its language-learning capacity never fully develops.

After the window for learning language closes, learning a second language seems more difficult. People who learn a second language as adults usually speak it with the accent of their first. Grammar learning is similarly more difficult. Jacqueline Johnson and Elissa Newport (1991) asked Korean and Chinese immigrants to identify whether each of 276 English sentences (*"Yesterday the hunter shoots a deer"*) was grammatically correct or incorrect. Some test-takers had arrived in the United States in early childhood, others as adults, but all had been in the country for approximately 10 years. Nevertheless, as **FIGURE 9.6** reveals, those who learned their second language early learned it best. The older the age at which one emigrates to a new country, the harder it is to learn its language (Hakuta et al., 2003).

The impact of early experiences is also evident in language learning in the 90+ percent of deaf children born to hearing-nonsigning parents. These children typically do not experience language during their early years. Compared with children exposed to sign language from birth, those who learn to sign as teens or adults are like immigrants who learn English after childhood. They can master the basic words and learn to order them, but they never become as fluent as native signers in producing and comprehending subtle grammatical differences (Newport, 1990). Moreover, the late-learners show less brain activity in right hemisphere regions that are active as native signers read sign language (Newman et al., 2002). As a flower's growth will be stunted without nourishment, so, too, will children typically become linguistically stunted if isolated from language during the critical period for its acquisition.

* * *

Returning to our debate about how deserving we are of our name *Homo sapiens*, let's pause to issue an interim report card. On decision making and judgment, our error-prone species might rate a C+. On problem solving, where humans are inventive yet vulnerable to fixation, we would probably receive a better mark, perhaps a B. On cognitive efficiency, our fallible but quick heuristics earn us an A. And when it comes to learning and using language, the awestruck experts would surely award the human species an A+.

No means *no*—no matter how you say it! Deaf children of Deaf-signing parents and hearing children of hearing parents have much in common. They develop language skills at about the same rate, and they are equally effective at opposing parental wishes and demanding their way.

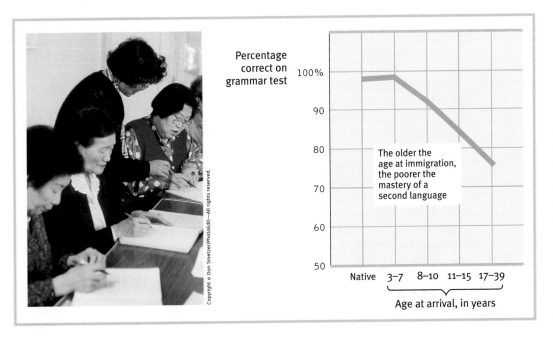

Percentage correct on grammar test

The older the age at immigration, the poorer the mastery of a second language

Age at arrival, in years

Native   3–7   8–10   11–15   17–39

FIGURE 9.6 **New language learning gets harder with age** Young children have a readiness to learn language. Ten years after coming to the United States, Asian immigrants took a grammar test. Although there is no sharply defined critical period for second language learning, those who arrived before age 8 understood American English grammar as well as native speakers did. Those who arrived later did not. (From Johnson & Newport, 1991.)

linguistic determinism Whorf's hypothesis that language determines the way we think.

"All words are pegs to hang ideas on."

—Henry Ward Beecher,
Proverbs from Plymouth Pulpit, 1887

"Learn a new language and get a new soul."

—Czech proverb

Before reading on, use a pen or pencil to sketch this idea: "The girl pushes the boy." Then see the inverted note below.

ʇɐ ʇǝ
(ꞁǝqoᗡ) ɯǝʇsᴧs ƃuᴉʇᴉɹʍ s,ǝɹnʇꞁnɔ ɹᴉǝɥʇ pǝuɹɐǝꞁ
ǝʌɐɥ oʇ ɥƃnouǝ pꞁo ǝsoɥʇ uᴉ ᴧꞁuo sɹɐǝddɐ
sɐᴉq ꞁɐᴉʇɐds sᴉɥꞱ ˙ʇɥƃᴉɹ ǝɥʇ uo ɹǝɥ ǝɔɐꞁd
ᴧꞁʇsoɯ 'ǝƃɐnƃuɐꞁ ʇɟǝꞁ-oʇ-ʇɥƃᴉɹ ɐ 'ɔᴉqɐɹⱯ ǝʇᴉɹʍ
puɐ pɐǝɹ oɥʍ ǝsoɥꞱ ˙ʇɟǝꞁ ǝɥʇ uo ꞁɹᴉƃ ƃuᴉɥsnd
ǝɥʇ uoᴉʇᴉsod oʇ ʇɥƃᴉɹ oʇ ʇɟǝꞁ ɯoɹɟ spɐǝɹ
ǝƃɐnƃuɐꞁ ǝsoɥʍ ǝꞁdoǝd ʇɐɥʇ ʇɹodǝɹ (Ɛ00ᘔ)
ossnᴚ ǝɹoʌnⱯ puɐ ssɐɐꟽ ǝuuⱯ ¿,,ᴧoq
ǝɥʇ sǝɥsnd ꞁɹᴉƃ ǝɥʇ,, ǝʇɐɹʇsnꞁꞁᴉ noᴧ pᴉp ʍoꞰ

Thinking and Language

8: What is the relationship between language and thinking?

Thinking and language intricately intertwine. Asking which comes first is one of psychology's chicken-and-egg questions. Do our ideas come first and we wait for words to name them? Or are our thoughts conceived in words and therefore unthinkable without them?

Language Influences Thinking

Linguist Benjamin Lee Whorf contended that language determines the way we think. According to Whorf's (1956) **linguistic determinism** hypothesis, different languages impose different conceptions of reality: "Language itself shapes a man's basic ideas." The Hopi, Whorf noted, have no past tense for their verbs. Therefore, he contended, a Hopi could not so readily *think* about the past.

To say that language *determines* the way we think is much too strong. But to those who speak two dissimilar languages, such as English and Japanese, it seems obvious that a person may think differently in different languages (Brown, 1986). Unlike English, which has a rich vocabulary for self-focused emotions such as anger, Japanese has more words for interpersonal emotions such as sympathy (Markus & Kitayama, 1991). Many bilinguals report that they have different senses of self, depending on which language they are using (Matsumoto, 1994). They may even reveal different personality profiles when taking the same test in their two languages (Dinges & Hull, 1992).

Michael Ross, Elaine Xun, and Anne Wilson (2002) demonstrated this by inviting China-born, bilingual University of Waterloo students to describe themselves in English or Chinese. English-language versions of self-descriptions fit typical Canadian profiles: Students expressed mostly positive self-statements and moods. Responding in Chinese, students gave typically Chinese self-descriptions: They reported more agreement with Chinese values and roughly equal positive and negative self-statements and moods. Their language use seemed to shape how they thought of themselves.

A similar personality change occurs as people shift between the cultural frames associated with English and Spanish. English speakers score higher than Spanish speakers on measures of extraversion, agreeableness, and conscientiousnous. But is this a language effect? Nairán Ramírez-Esparza and her co-workers (2006) wondered. So they had samples of bicultural, bilingual Americans and Mexicans take the tests in each language. Sure enough, when using English they expressed their somewhat more extraverted, agreeable, and conscientious selves (and the differences were not due to how the questionnaires were translated).

So our words may not *determine* what we think, but they do *influence* our thinking (Hardin & Banaji, 1993; Özgen, 2004). We use our language in forming categories. In Brazil, the isolated Piraha tribespeople have words for the numbers *1* and *2,* but numbers above that are simply "many." Thus, if shown 7 nuts in a row, they find it very difficult to lay out the same number from their own pile (Gordon, 2004).

Words also influence our thinking about colors. Whether we live in New Mexico, New South Wales, or New Guinea, we *see* colors much the same, but we use our native language to *classify* and *remember* colors (Davidoff, 2004; Roberson et al., 2004, 2005). If that language is English, you might view three colors and call two of them "yellow" and one of them "blue." Later you would likely see and recall the yellows as being more similar. But if you were a member of Papua New Guinea's Berinmo tribe, which has words for two different shades of yellow, you would better recall the distinctions between the two yellows.

Perceived differences grow when we assign different names to colors. On the color spectrum, blue blends into green—until we draw a dividing line between the portions we call "green" and "blue." Although equally different on the color spectrum

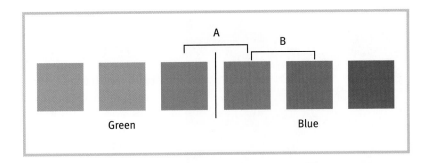

FIGURE 9.7 Language and perception
Emre Özgen (2004) reports that when people view blocks of equally different colors, they perceive those with different names as more different. Thus the "green" and "blue" in contrast A may appear to differ more than the two similarly different blues in contrast B.

(**FIGURE 9.7**), two different "blues" (or two different "greens") that share the same name are harder to distinguish than two items with the different names "green" and "blue" (Özgen, 2004).

Given words' subtle influence on thinking, we do well to choose our words carefully. Does it make any difference whether I write, "A child learns language as *he* interacts with *his* caregivers" or "Children learn language as *they* interact with *their* caregivers"? Many studies have found that it does. When hearing the generic *he* (as in "the artist and his work") people are more likely to picture a male (Henley, 1989; Ng, 1990). If *he* and *his* were truly gender-free, we shouldn't skip a beat when hearing that "man, like other mammals, nurses his young."

To expand language is to expand the ability to think. As Chapter 5 pointed out, young children's thinking develops hand in hand with their language (Gopnik & Meltzoff, 1986). Indeed, it is very difficult to think about or conceptualize certain abstract ideas (commitment, freedom, or rhyming) without language! And what is true for preschoolers is true for everyone: *It pays to increase your word power.* That's why most textbooks, including this one, introduce new words—to teach new ideas and new ways of thinking.

Increased word power helps explain what McGill University researcher Wallace Lambert (1992; Lambert et al., 1993) calls the *bilingual advantage.* Bilingual children, who learn to inhibit one language while using the other, are also better able to inhibit their attention to irrelevant information. If asked whether a sentence (*"Why is the cat barking so loudly?"*) is grammatically correct, they can more efficiently focus on the grammar alone (Bialystok, 2001; Carlson & Meltzoff, 2008).

Lambert helped devise a Canadian program that immerses English-speaking children in French. (From 1981 to 2001, the number of non-Quebec Canadian children immersed in French rose from 65,000 to 297,000 [Statistics Canada, 2007].) For most of their first three years in school, the English-speaking children are taught entirely in French, and thereafter gradually shift by the end of their schooling to classes mostly in English. Not surprisingly, the children attain a natural French fluency unrivaled by other methods of language teaching. Moreover, compared with similarly capable children in control groups, they do so without detriment to their English fluency, and with increased aptitude scores, creativity, and appreciation for French-Canadian culture (Genesee & Gándara, 1999; Lazaruk, 2007).

Whether we are deaf or hearing, minority or majority, language links us to one another. Language also connects us to the past and the future. "To destroy a people, destroy their language," observed poet Joy Harjo.

Perceived distances between cities also grow when two cities are in different countries rather than in the same country (Burris & Branscombe, 2005).

A safe sign We have outfielder William Hoy to thank for baseball sign language. The first deaf player to join the major leagues (1892), he invented hand signals for "Strike!" "Safe!" (shown here) and "Yerr Out!" (Pollard, 1992). Such gestures worked so well that referees in all sports now use invented signs, and fans are fluent in sports sign language.

Many native English speakers, including most Americans, are monolingual. Most humans are bilingual or multilingual. Does monolingualism limit people's ability to comprehend the thinking of other cultures?

Thinking in Images

Without a doubt, words convey ideas. But aren't there times when ideas precede words? To turn on the cold water in your bathroom, in which direction do you turn the handle? To answer this question, you probably thought not in words but with *nondeclarative* (procedural) memory—a mental picture of how you do it (see Chapter 8).

A thoughtful art Playing the piano engages thinking without language. In the absence of a piano, mental practice can sustain one's skill.

Indeed, we often think in images. Artists think in images. So do composers, poets, mathematicians, athletes, and scientists. Albert Einstein reported that he achieved some of his greatest insights through visual images and later put them into words. Pianist Liu Chi Kung showed the value of thinking in images. One year after placing second in the 1958 Tschaikovsky piano competition, Liu was imprisoned during China's cultural revolution. Soon after his release, after seven years without touching a piano, he was back on tour, the critics judging his musicianship better than ever. How did he continue to develop without practice? "I did practice," said Liu, "every day. I rehearsed every piece I had ever played, note by note, in my mind" (Garfield, 1986).

For someone who has learned a skill, such as ballet dancing, even *watching* the activity will activate the brain's internal simulation of it, reported one British research team after collecting fMRIs as people watched videos (Calvo-Merino et al., 2004). So, too, will imagining an activity. **FIGURE 9.8** shows an fMRI of a person imagining the experience of pain, activating neural networks that are active during actual pain (Grèzes & Decety, 2001). Small wonder, then, that mental practice is now a standard part of Olympic athletes' training (Suinn, 1997).

One experiment on mental practice and basketball foul shooting tracked the University of Tennessee women's team over 35 games (Savoy & Beitel, 1996). During that time, the team's free-throw shooting increased from approximately 52 percent in games following standard physical practice to some 65 percent after mental practice. Players had repeatedly imagined making foul shots under various conditions, including being "trash-talked" by their opposition. In a dramatic conclusion, Tennessee won the national championship game in overtime, thanks in part to their foul shooting.

Mental rehearsal can also help you achieve an academic goal, as Shelley Taylor and her UCLA colleagues (1998) demonstrated with two groups of introductory psychology students facing a midterm exam one week later. (Scores of other students formed a control group, not engaging in any mental simulation.) The first group was told to spend five minutes each day visualizing themselves scanning the posted grade list, seeing their A, beaming with joy, and feeling proud. This daily *outcome simulation* had little effect, adding only 2 points to their exam-scores average. Another group spent five minutes each day visualizing themselves effectively studying—reading the chapters, going over notes, eliminating distractions, declining an offer to go out. This daily *process simulation* paid off—this second group began studying sooner, spent more time at it, and beat the others' average by 8 points. *The*

FIGURE 9.8 The power of imagination Imagining a physical activity triggers action in the same brain areas that are triggered when actually performing that activity. These fMRIs show a person imagining the experience of pain, which activates some of the same areas in the brain as the actual experience of pain.

point to remember: It's better to spend your fantasy time planning how to get somewhere than to dwell on the imagined destination.

Experiments on thinking without language bring us back to a principle we've seen in earlier chapters: Much of our information processing occurs outside of consciousness and beyond language. Inside our ever-active brain, many streams of activity flow in parallel, function automatically, are remembered implicitly, and only occasionally surface as conscious words.

* * *

What, then, should we say about the relationship between thinking and language? As we have seen, language does influence our thinking. But if thinking did not also affect language, there would never be any new words. And new words and new combinations of old words express new ideas. The basketball term *slam dunk* was coined after the act itself had become fairly common. So, let us say that *thinking affects our language, which then affects our thought* (**FIGURE 9.9**).

Psychological research on thinking and language mirrors the mixed views of our species by those in fields such as literature and religion. The human mind is simultaneously capable of striking intellectual failures and of striking intellectual power. Misjudgments are common and can have disastrous consequences. So we do well to appreciate our capacity for error. Yet our efficient heuristics often serve us well. Moreover, our ingenuity at problem solving and our extraordinary power of language mark humankind as almost "infinite in faculties."

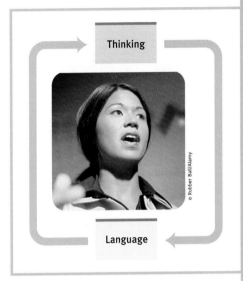

FIGURE 9.9 The interplay of thought and language The traffic runs both ways between thinking and language. Thinking affects our language, which affects our thought.

REHEARSE IT!

7. Children reach the one-word stage of speech development at about
   a. 4 months.   c. 1 year.
   b. 6 months.   d. 2 years.

8. Skinner's view that we learn language the same way we learn other behaviors—through association, imitation, and reinforcement—is most helpful in explaining
   a. the onset of babbling.
   b. the speech behavior of deaf infants.
   c. the seemingly effortless mastery of grammatical rules by very young children.

d. why children learn their household's language.

9. According to Chomsky, children are born with a readiness to learn the grammatical rules of language, and all they need to acquire language is
   a. instruction in grammar.
   b. exposure to some language in early childhood.
   c. reinforcement for babbling and other early verbal behaviors.
   d. imitation and drill.

10. Our language influences the way we perceive and think about the world. This

idea, adapted from Whorf's hypothesis, helps explain why
a. a person who learns a second language thinks differently in that language.
b. children have a built-in readiness to learn grammatical rules.
c. children's babbling contains sounds not found in the languages spoken in their homes.
d. artists, athletes, and others are able to think in visual images.

Answers: 7. c, 8. d, 9. b, 10. a.

Animal Thinking and Language

9: **What do we know about animal thinking? Do other animals share our capacity for language?**

If in our use of language we humans are, as the psalmist long ago rhapsodized, "little lower than God," where do other animals fit in the scheme of things? Are they "little lower than human"? Let's see what the research on animal thinking and language can tell us.

What Do Animals Think?

Animals are smarter than we may realize. Baboons know each voice in their 80-member troop (Jolly, 2007). Sheep can recognize and remember individual faces (Morell, 2008). Marmosets can learn from and imitate others. Great apes and even monkeys can *form concepts*. When monkeys learn to classify cats and dogs, certain frontal lobe neurons in their brains fire in response to new "catlike" images, others to new "doglike" images (Freedman et al., 2001). Even pigeons can sort objects (pictures of cars, cats, chairs, flowers). Shown a picture of a never-before-seen chair, pigeons will reliably peck a key that represents the category "chairs" (Wasserman, 1995).

We also are not the only creatures to *display insight*, as psychologist Wolfgang Köhler (1925) demonstrated in an experiment with Sultan, a chimpanzee. Köhler placed a piece of fruit and a long stick well beyond Sultan's reach, and a short stick inside his cage. Spying the short stick, Sultan grabbed it and tried to reach the fruit. After several unsuccessful attempts, Sultan dropped the stick and seemed to survey the situation. Then suddenly, as if thinking "Aha!" he jumped up, seized the short stick again, and used it to pull in the longer stick—which he then used to reach the fruit. This evidence of animal cognition, said Köhler, showed that there is more to learning than conditioning. What is more, in later research, apes have even exhibited foresight, by storing a tool that they can use to retrieve food the next day (Mulcahy & Call, 2006).

Some animals also display a surprising *numerical ability*. Until his death in 2007, the African Grey parrot, Alex, displayed jaw-dropping numerical skills (Pepperberg, 2006). He not only could name and categorize objects, he displayed a comprehension of numbers up to 6. Thus, he could speak the number of objects, add two small clusters of objects and announce the sum, and indicate which of two numbers was greater. And he could answer when shown various groups of objects and asked, for example, "What color four?" (meaning "What's the color of the objects of which there are four?").

Kyoto University researcher Tetsuro Matsuzawa (2007) has spent more than two decades studying chimpanzees' ability to remember and relate numbers. In one experiment, the chimpanzee Ai taps, in ascending order, numbers randomly displayed on a computer screen. If four or five of the numbers between 1 and 9 are flashed for no more than a second, and then replaced by white boxes, Ai, after much training, does what a human cannot: Remembering the flashed numbers, she again taps the boxes in numerical order (**FIGURE 9.10**).

Like humans, chimpanzees are shaped by reinforcement when they solve problems. Forest-dwelling chimpanzees have become *natural tool users* (Boesch-Achermann & Boesch, 1993). They break off a reed or a stick, strip the twigs and leaves, carry it to a termite mound, fish for termites by twisting it just so, and then carefully remove it without scraping off many termites. They even select different tools for different purposes—a heavy stick to puncture holes, a light, flexible stick for fishing (Sanz et al., 2004). One anthropologist, trying to mimic the chimpanzee's deft termite fishing, failed miserably.

Researchers have found at least 39 local customs related to chimpanzee tool use, grooming, and courtship (Whiten & Boesch, 2001). One group may slurp ants directly from the stick, while another group plucks them off individually. One group may break nuts with a stone hammer, another with a wooden hammer. Or picture this actual laboratory experiment with observational learning: Chimpanzee B observes Chimpanzee A as it obtains food, either by sliding or lifting a door. Then B follows the same lifting or sliding procedure. So does Chimpanzee C after observing B, and so forth. Chimp see, chimp do, unto the sixth generation (Bonnie et al., 2007; Horner et al., 2006).

The chimpanzee group differences, along with differing dialects and hunting styles, seem not to be genetic. Rather, they are the chimpanzee equivalent of cultural diversity. Like humans, chimpanzees invent behaviors and transmit cultural patterns to their peers and offspring (**FIGURE 9.11a**). And so do

FIGURE 9.10 Chimpanzee bests humans It is adaptive for chimpanzees to be able to monitor lots of information in their natural environment. This might explain how chimpanzee Ai can remember and tap numbers in ascending order, even when they are flashed for less than a second before being covered by white boxes.

(a)

(b)

FIGURE 9.11 Cultural transmission (a) On the western bank of one Ivory Coast river, a youngster watches as its mother uses a stone hammer to open a nut. On the river's other side, a few miles away, chimpanzees do not follow this custom. (b) This bottlenose dolphin in Shark Bay, Western Australia, is a member of a small group that uses marine sponges as protective gear when probing the sea floor for fish.

some Australian dolphins (Figure 9.11b), which have learned to break off sponges and wear them on their snouts while probing the sea floor for fish (Krützen et al., 2005). Thus animals, and chimpanzees in particular, display remarkable talents. But do they, like humans, exhibit language?

Do Animals Exhibit Language?

Without doubt, animals communicate. Vervet monkeys have different alarm cries for different predators: a barking call for a leopard, a cough for an eagle, and a chuttering for a snake. Hearing the leopard alarm, other vervets climb the nearest tree. Hearing the eagle alarm, they rush into the bushes. Hearing the snake chutter, they stand up and scan the ground (Byrne, 1991). Whales also communicate, with clicks and songs. Honeybees do a dance that informs other bees of the direction and distance of the food source.

And what shall we say of dogs' ability to understand us? Border collie Rico knows and can fetch 200 items by name. Moreover, reports a team of psychologists at Leipzig's Max Planck Institute, if he is asked to retrieve a novel toy with a name he has never heard, Rico will pick out the novel item from among a group of familiar items (Kaminski et al., 2004). Hearing that novel word for the second time four weeks later, he as often as not retrieves the object. Such feats show animals' comprehension and communication. But is this language?

Comprehending canine Rico, a border collie with a 200-word vocabulary, can infer that an unfamiliar sound refers to a novel object.

The Case of the Apes

The greatest challenge to our claim to be the only language-using species has come from one of our closest genetic relatives, the chimpanzees. Psychologists Allen Gardner and Beatrix Gardner (1969) aroused enormous scientific and public interest when they taught sign language to the chimpanzee Washoe (c. 1965–2007). After four years, Washoe could use 132 signs; by age 32, the number of signs had reached 181 (Sanz et al., 1998). One *New York Times* reporter, having learned sign language from his deaf parents, visited Washoe and exclaimed, "Suddenly I realized I was conversing with a member of another species in my native tongue."

Further evidence of gestured "ape language" surfaced during the 1970s. Usually apes sign just single words such as "that" or "gimme" (Bowman, 2003). But sometimes they string signs together to form intelligible sentences. Washoe signed, "You me go out, please." Apes even appear to combine words creatively. Washoe designated a swan as a "water bird." Koko, a gorilla trained by Francine Patterson (1978), reportedly described a long-nosed Pinocchio doll as an "elephant baby." Lana, a "talking" chimpanzee that punched a crude computer keyboard which translated her entries into English, improvised when she wanted her trainer's orange. She had no word for *orange*, but she did know her colors and the word for *apple*, so she punched in: "?Tim give apple which-is orange" (Rumbaugh, 1977).

"He says he wants a lawyer."

Seeing a doll floating in her water, Washoe signed, "Baby in my drink."

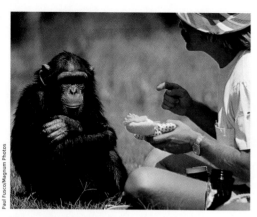

But is this language? Chimpanzees' ability to express themselves in American Sign Language (ASL) raises questions about the very nature of language. Here, the trainer is asking, "What is this?" The sign in response is "Baby." Does the response constitute language?

"Chimps do not develop language. But that is no shame on them; humans would surely do no better if trained to hoot and shriek like chimps, to perform the waggle-dance of the bee, or any of the other wonderful feats in nature's talent show."

—Steve Pinker (1995)

"[Our] view that [we are] unique from all other forms of animal life is being jarred to the core."

—Duane Rumbaugh and
Sue Savage-Rumbaugh (1978)

Granted, these vocabularies and sentences are simple, rather like those of a 2-year-old child (and nothing like your own 60,000 or so words, which you fluidly combine to create a limitless variety of sentences). Yet, as language reports accumulated, it seemed these apes might indeed be "little lower than human." Then, in the late 1970s, the fascination with "talking apes" turned toward cynicism: Were the chimps language champs or were the researchers chumps? The ape language researchers were making monkeys of themselves, said the skeptics. Consider:

- Unlike speaking or signing children, who effortlessly soak up dozens of new words a week, apes gain their limited vocabularies only with great difficulty (Wynne, 2004, 2008). Saying that apes can learn language because they can sign words is like saying humans can fly because they can jump.
- Chimpanzees can make signs or push buttons in sequence to get a reward, but pigeons, too, can peck a sequence of keys to get grain (Straub et al., 1979). After training a chimpanzee he named Nim Chimsky, Herbert Terrace (1979) concluded that much of apes' signing is nothing more than aping their trainers' signs and learning that certain arm movements produce rewards.
- Presented with ambiguous information, people, thanks to their perceptual set, tend to see what they want or expect to see. Interpreting chimpanzee signs as language may be little more than the trainers' wishful thinking, claimed Terrace. (When Washoe signed *water bird*, she perhaps was separately naming *water* and *bird*.)
- "Give orange me give eat orange me eat orange . . ." is a far cry from the exquisite syntax of a 3-year-old (Anderson, 2004; Pinker, 1995). To the child, "you tickle" and "tickle you" communicate different ideas. A chimpanzee, lacking human syntax, might sign the phrases interchangeably.

In science as in politics, controversy can stimulate progress. Further evidence confirmed chimpanzees' abilities to think and communicate. One surprising finding was of Washoe's training her adopted son in the signs she had learned. After her second infant died, Washoe became withdrawn when told, "Baby dead, baby gone, baby finished." Two weeks later, caretaker-researcher Roger Fouts (1992, 1997) signed better news: "I have baby for you." Washoe reacted with instant excitement, hair on end, swaggering and panting while signing over and again, "Baby, my baby." It took several hours for Washoe and the foster infant, Loulis, to warm to each other, whereupon she broke the ice by signing, "Come baby" and cuddling Loulis.

In the months that followed, Loulis picked up 68 signs simply by observing Washoe and three other language-trained chimpanzees. They went on to sign spontaneously, asking one another to *chase, tickle, hug, come,* or *groom.* People who sign were in near-perfect agreement about what the chimpanzees were saying, 90 percent of which pertained to social interaction, reassurance, or play (Fouts & Bodamer, 1987). The chimpanzees even proved to be modestly bilingual, translating spoken English words into signs (Shaw, 1989–1990).

Even more stunning was the report by Sue Savage-Rumbaugh and her colleagues (1993) of pygmy chimpanzees learning to *comprehend syntax* in English spoken to them. Kanzi, a pygmy chimpanzee with the seeming grammatical abilities of a human 2-year-old, happened onto language while observing his adoptive mother during language training. Kanzi has behaved intelligently whether asked, "Can you show me the light?" or "Can you bring me the [flash]light?" or "Can you turn the light on?" Kanzi also knows many spoken words, such as *snake, bite,* and *dog.* Given stuffed animals and asked—for the first time—to "make the dog bite the snake," he put the snake to the dog's mouth. For chimpanzees as for humans, early life is a critical time for learning language. Without early exposure to speech or word symbols, adults will not gain language competence (Rumbaugh & Savage-Rumbaugh, 1994).

The provocative claims that "apes share our capacity for language" and the skeptical counterclaims that "apes no use language" (as Washoe might have put it) have moved psychologists toward a greater appreciation of apes' remarkable abilities and of our own (Friend, 2004; Rumbaugh & Washburn, 2003). Most now agree that humans alone possess language, if by the term we mean verbal or signed expression of complex grammar. If we mean, more simply, an ability to communicate through a meaningful sequence of symbols, then apes are indeed capable of language.

Believing that animals could not think, French philosopher René Descartes and others argued that animals are living robots without any moral rights. Animals, it has been said at one time or another, cannot plan, conceptualize, count, use tools, show compassion, or use language (Thorpe, 1974). Today, we know better. Animal researchers have shown us that primates exhibit insight, show family loyalty, communicate with one another, display altruism, transmit cultural patterns across generations, and comprehend the syntax of human speech. Accepting and working out the moral implications of all this is an unfinished task for our own thinking species.

"Although humans make sounds with their mouths and occasionally look at each other, there is no solid evidence that they actually communicate with each other."

REHEARSE IT!

11. Of the examples discussed in this section, the problem-solving behavior that most closely resembled insight was
   a. Loulis the chimpanzee's ability to learn signs by observing Washoe.
   b. Sultan the chimpanzee's use of a short stick to pull in a long stick.
   c. Kanzi the pygmy chimpanzee's ability to understand grammatical differences in English sentences.
   d. Washoe the chimpanzee's use of sign language to request her baby.

12. Most researchers agree that apes can
   a. communicate through symbols.
   b. reproduce most human speech sounds.
   c. master language in adulthood.
   d. surpass a human 3-year-old in language skills.

Answers: 11. b, 12. a.

Intelligence

So far, we have considered how humans, in general, think and communicate. But do we humans not differ from one another in our intellectual capacities? No controversy in psychology has been more heated than the question of whether there exists in each person a general intellectual capacity that can be measured and quantified as a number. School boards, courts, and scientists debate the usefulness and fairness of intelligence and aptitude tests. Is it discriminatory to use such tests to rank individuals and determine whether to admit them to a particular educational program, university, or job? Do group differences reflect nature (heredity) or nurture (environment)? Let's consider findings from a century of research.

intelligence mental quality consisting of the ability to learn from experience, solve problems, and use knowledge to adapt to new situations.

What Is Intelligence?

Intelligence is a socially constructed concept: Cultures deem "intelligent" whatever attributes enable success in those cultures (Sternberg & Kaufman, 1998). In the Amazon rain forest, intelligence may be understanding the medicinal qualities of local plants; in an Ontario high school, it may be superior performance on cognitive tasks. In each context, **intelligence** is the ability to learn from experience, solve problems, and use knowledge to adapt to new situations. In research studies, intelligence is what intelligence tests measure. Historically, as we will see, that has been the sort of problem solving displayed as "school smarts."

Hands-on healing The socially constructed concept of intelligence varies from culture to culture. This folk healer in Peru displays his intelligence in his knowledge about his medicinal plants and understanding of the needs of the people he is helping.

Is Intelligence One General Ability or Several Specific Abilities?

10: What argues for and against considering intelligence as one general mental ability?

"g is one of the most reliable and valid measures in the behavioral domain . . . and it predicts important social outcomes such as educational and occupational levels far better than any other trait."

—Behavior geneticist Robert Plomin (1999)

general intelligence (g) a general intelligence factor that, according to Spearman and others, underlies specific mental abilities and is therefore measured by every task on an intelligence test.

factor analysis a statistical procedure that identifies clusters of related items (called *factors*) on a test; used to identify different dimensions of performance that underlie a person's total score.

savant syndrome a condition in which a person otherwise limited in mental ability has an exceptional specific skill, such as in computation or drawing.

You probably know some people with talents in science, others who excel at the humanities, and still others gifted in athletics, art, music, or dance. You may also know a talented artist who is dumbfounded by the simplest mathematical problems, or a brilliant math student with little aptitude for literary discussion. Are all these people intelligent? Could you rate their intelligence on a single scale? Or would you need several different scales?

Charles Spearman (1863–1945) believed we have one **general intelligence** (often shortened to **g**). He granted that people often have special abilities that stand out. Spearman had helped develop **factor analysis,** a statistical procedure that identifies clusters of related items. He had noted that those who score high in one area, such as verbal intelligence, typically score higher than average in other areas, such as spatial or reasoning ability. Spearman believed a common skill set, the g factor, underlies all of our intelligent behavior, from navigating the sea to excelling in school.

We might liken mental abilities to physical abilities. Athleticism is not one thing but many. The ability to run fast is distinct from the strength needed for power lifting, which is distinct from the eye-hand coordination required to throw a ball on target. A champion weightlifter rarely has the potential to be a skilled ice skater. Yet there remains some tendency for good things to come packaged together—for running speed and throwing accuracy to correlate, thanks to general athletic ability. So, too, with intelligence. Several distinct abilities tend to cluster together and to correlate enough to define a small general intelligence factor.

THEORIES OF MULTIPLE INTELLIGENCES Since the mid-1980s some psychologists have sought to extend the definition of *intelligence* beyond Spearman's and others' academic smarts.

GARDNER'S EIGHT INTELLIGENCES Howard Gardner (1983, 2006) views intelligence as multiple abilities that come in packages. Gardner finds evidence for this view in studies of people with diminished or exceptional abilities. Brain damage, for example, may destroy one ability but leave others intact. And consider people with **savant syndrome,** who often score low on intelligence tests but have an island of brilliance (Treffert & Wallace, 2002). Some have virtually no language ability, yet are able to compute numbers as quickly and accurately as an electronic calculator, or identify almost instantly the day of the week that corresponds to any given date in history, or render incredible works of art or musical performances (Miller, 1999).

Islands of genius: Savant syndrome
After a 30-minute helicopter ride and a visit to the top of a skyscraper, British savant artist Stephen Wiltshire began seven days of drawing that reproduced the Tokyo skyline.

About 4 in 5 people with savant syndrome are males, and many also have autism, a developmental disorder (see Chapter 5).

Memory whiz Kim Peek, a savant who does not have autism, was the inspiration for the movie *Rain Man*. In 8 to 10 seconds, he can read and remember a page, and he has learned 9000 books, including Shakespeare and the Bible, by heart. He learns maps from the front of phone books, and he can provide MapQuest-like travel directions within any major U.S. city. Yet he cannot button his clothes. And he has little capacity for abstract concepts. Asked by his father at a restaurant to "lower your voice," he slid lower in his chair to lower his voice box. Asked for Lincoln's Gettysburg Address, he responded, "227 North West Front Street. But he only stayed there one night—he gave the speech the next day" (Treffert & Christensen, 2005).

Using such evidence, Gardner argues that we do not have *an intelligence*, but rather *multiple intelligences*. He identifies a total of eight (**TABLE 9.2**), including the verbal and mathematical aptitudes assessed by standard tests. Thus, the computer programmer, the poet, the street-smart adolescent who becomes a crafty executive, and the basketball team's point guard exhibit different kinds of intelligence (Gardner, 1998):

> If a person is strong (or weak) in telling stories, solving mathematical proofs, navigating around unfamiliar terrain, learning an unfamiliar song, mastering a new game that entails dexterity, understanding others, or understanding himself, one simply does not know whether comparable strengths (or weaknesses) will be found in other areas.

A general intelligence score is therefore like the overall rating of a city—which tells you something but doesn't give you much specific information about its schools, streets, or nightlife.

Wouldn't it be wonderful if the world were so just, responded intelligence researcher Sandra Scarr (1989). Wouldn't it be nice if being weak in one area would be compensated by genius in some other area? Alas, the world is not just. General intelligence scores predict performance on various complex tasks, in various jobs, and in varied countries; *g* matters (Bertua et al., 2005; Gottfredson, 2002a,b; 2003a,b; Rindermann, 2007; see also **FIGURE 9.12**).

Even so, "success" is not a one-ingredient recipe. High intelligence may help you get into a profession (via the schools and training programs that take you there), but it won't make you successful once there. The recipe for success combines talent with *grit:* Those who become highly successful are also conscientious, well-connected, and

TABLE 9.2 Gardner's Eight Intelligences*

Aptitude	Exemplar
1. Linguistic	T. S. Eliot, poet
2. Logical-mathematical	Albert Einstein, scientist
3. Musical	Igor Stravinsky, composer
4. Spatial	Pablo Picasso, artist
5. Bodily-kinesthetic	Martha Graham, dancer
6. Intrapersonal (self)	Sigmund Freud, psychiatrist
7. Interpersonal (other people)	Mahatma Gandhi, leader
8. Naturalist	Charles Darwin, naturalist

*Gardner (1998) has also speculated about a ninth possible intelligence—*existential intelligence*—the ability "to ponder large questions about life, death, existence."

FIGURE 9.12 Smart and rich? Jay Zagorsky (2007) tracked 7403 participants in the U.S. National Longitudinal Survey of Youth across 25 years. As shown in this scatterplot, their intelligence scores correlated +.30, a modest positive correlation, with their later income.

Spatial intelligence genius In 1998, World Checkers Champion Ron "Suki" King of Barbados set a new record by simultaneously playing 385 players in 3 hours and 44 minutes. Thus, while his opponents often had hours to plot their game moves, King could only devote about 35 seconds to each game. Yet he still managed to win all 385 games!

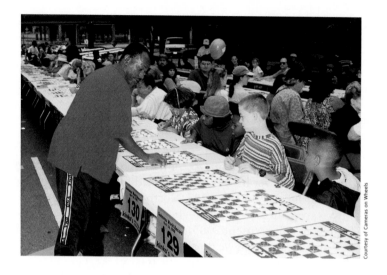

doggedly energetic. Anders Ericsson (2002, 2007; Ericsson et al., 2007) reports a *10-year rule:* A common ingredient of expert performance in chess, dancing, sports, computer programming, music, and medicine is "about 10 years of intense, daily practice."

"You have to be careful, if you're good at something, to make sure you don't think you're good at other things that you aren't necessarily so good at. . . . Because I've been very successful at [software development] people come in and expect that I have wisdom about topics that I don't."

—Bill Gates (1998)

STERNBERG'S THREE INTELLIGENCES Robert Sternberg (1985, 1999, 2003) agrees that there is more to success than traditional intelligence. And he agrees with Gardner's idea of multiple intelligences. But he proposes a *triarchic theory* of three, not eight, intelligences:

- *Analytical (academic problem-solving) intelligence* is assessed by intelligence tests, which present well-defined problems having a single right answer. Such tests predict school grades reasonably well and vocational success more modestly.
- *Creative intelligence* is demonstrated in reacting adaptively to novel situations and generating novel ideas.
- *Practical intelligence* is required for everyday tasks, which may be ill-defined, with multiple solutions. Sternberg and Richard Wagner's (1993, 1995) test of practical managerial intelligence measures skill at writing effective memos, motivating people, delegating tasks and responsibilities, reading people, and promoting one's own career. Business executives who score relatively high on this test have tended to earn high salaries and receive high performance ratings.

With support from the U.S. College Board (which administers the widely used SAT Reasoning Test to U.S. college and university applicants), Sternberg (2006, 2007) and a team of collaborators have developed new measures of creativity (such as thinking up a caption for an untitled cartoon) and practical thinking (such as figuring out how to move a large bed up a winding staircase). Their initial data indicate that these more comprehensive assessments improve prediction of American students' first-year college grades, and they do so with reduced ethnic-group differences.

Although Sternberg and Gardner differ on specific points, they agree that multiple abilities can contribute to life success and that the differing varieties of giftedness add spice to life and challenges for education. Under their influence, many teachers have been trained to appreciate the varieties of ability and to apply multiple intelligence theory in their classrooms.

Intelligence and Creativity

11:
What is creativity, and what fosters it?

Pierre de Fermat, a seventeenth-century mischievous genius, challenged mathematicians of his day to match his solutions to various number theory problems. His most famous challenge—*Fermat's last theorem*—baffled the greatest mathematical

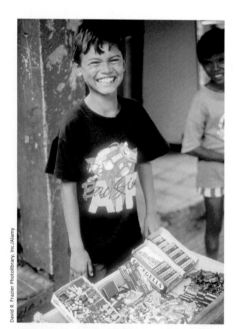

Street smarts This child selling candy on the streets of Manaus, Brazil, is developing practical intelligence at a very young age.

minds, even after a $2 million prize (in today's dollars) was offered in 1908 to whoever first created a proof.

Princeton mathematician Andrew Wiles had pondered the problem for more than 30 years and had come to the brink of a solution. Then, one morning, out of the blue, the final "incredible revelation" struck him. "It was so indescribably beautiful; it was so simple and so elegant. I couldn't understand how I'd missed it and I just stared at it in disbelief for 20 minutes. Then during the day I walked around the department, and I'd keep coming back to my desk looking to see if it was still there. It was still there. I couldn't contain myself, I was so excited. It was the most important moment of my working life" (Singh, 1997, p. 25).

Wiles' incredible moment illustrates **creativity**—the ability to produce ideas that are both novel and valuable. Studies suggest that a certain level of aptitude—a score of about 120 on a standard intelligence test—is necessary but not sufficient for creativity. Exceptionally creative architects, mathematicians, scientists, and engineers usually score not much higher on intelligence tests than do their less creative peers (MacKinnon & Hall, 1972; Simonton, 2000). So, clearly there is more to creativity than what intelligence tests reveal. Indeed, the two kinds of thinking engage different brain areas. Intelligence tests, which demand a single correct answer, require *convergent thinking*. Injury to the left parietal lobe damages this ability. Creativity tests *(How many uses can you think of for a brick?)* require *divergent thinking*. Injury to certain areas of the frontal lobes can leave reading, writing, and arithmetic skills intact but destroy imagination (Kolb & Whishaw, 2006).

Sternberg and his colleagues have identified five components of creativity (Sternberg, 1988, 2003; Sternberg & Lubart, 1991, 1992):

1. ***Expertise,*** a well-developed base of knowledge, furnishes the ideas, images, and phrases we use as mental building blocks. "Chance favors only the prepared mind," observed Louis Pasteur. The more blocks we have, the more chances we have to combine them in novel ways. Wiles' well-developed base of knowledge put the needed theorems and methods at his disposal.

2. ***Imaginative thinking skills*** provide the ability to see things in novel ways, to recognize patterns, and to make connections. Having mastered a problem's basic elements, we redefine or explore it in a new way. Copernicus first developed expertise regarding the solar system and its planets, and then creatively defined the system as revolving around the Sun, not the Earth. Wiles' imaginative solution combined two partial solutions.

3. ***A venturesome personality*** seeks new experiences, tolerates ambiguity and risk, and perseveres in overcoming obstacles. Inventor Thomas Edison tried countless substances before finding the right one for his lightbulb filament.

4. ***Intrinsic motivation*** is being driven more by interest, satisfaction, and challenge than by external pressures (Amabile & Hennessey, 1992). Creative people focus less on extrinsic motivators—meeting deadlines, impressing people, or making money—than on the pleasure and stimulation of the work itself.

creativity the ability to produce novel and valuable ideas.

After picking up a Nobel Prize in Stockholm, physicist Richard Feynman stopped in Queens, New York, to look at his high school record. "My grades were not as good as I remembered," he reported, "and my IQ was [a good, though unexceptional] 124" (Faber, 1987).

"If you would allow me any talent, it's simply this: I can, for whatever reason, reach down into my own brain, feel around in all the mush, find and extract something from my persona, and then graft it onto an idea."

—Cartoonist Gary Larson,
The Complete Far Side, 2003

Imaginative thinking Cartoonists display creativity as they see things in new ways or make unusual connections.

"For the love of God, is there a doctor in the house?"

Everyone held up their crackers as David threw the cheese log into the ceiling fan.

emotional intelligence the ability to perceive, understand, manage, and use emotions.

intelligence test a method for assessing an individual's mental aptitudes and comparing them with those of others, using numerical scores.

mental age a measure of intelligence test performance devised by Binet; the chronological age that most typically corresponds to a given level of performance. Thus, a child who does as well as the average 8-year-old is said to have a mental age of 8.

Stanford-Binet the widely used American revision (by Terman at Stanford University) of Binet's original intelligence test.

intelligence quotient (IQ) defined originally as the ratio of mental age *(ma)* to chronological age *(ca)* multiplied by 100 (thus, IQ = *ma/ca* × 100). On contemporary intelligence tests, the average performance for a given age is assigned a score of 100.

"You're wise, but you lack tree smarts."

"I worry about [intelligence] definitions that collapse assessments of our cognitive powers with statements about the kind of human beings we favor."

—Howard Gardner, "Rethinking the Concept of Intelligence," 2000

Asked how he solved such difficult scientific problems, Isaac Newton reportedly answered, "By thinking about them all the time." Wiles concurred: "I was so obsessed by this problem that for eight years I was thinking about it all the time—when I woke up in the morning to when I went to sleep at night" (Singh & Riber, 1997).

5. *A creative environment* sparks, supports, and refines creative ideas. After studying the careers of 2026 prominent scientists and inventors, Dean Keith Simonton (1992) noted that the most eminent among them were mentored, challenged, and supported by their relationships with colleagues. Even Wiles stood on the shoulders of others and wrestled his problem with the collaboration of a former student. Creativity-fostering environments often support contemplation. Jonas Salk solved a problem that led to the polio vaccine while in a monastery. Later, he designed the Salk Institute to provide contemplative spaces where other scientists could work without interruption (Sternberg, 2006).

Emotional Intelligence

12:
What makes up emotional intelligence?

Many creative people network effectively with peers because they are adept at processing and managing social information, a skill some rationally smart people lack (Cantor & Kihlstrom, 1987; Weis & Süß, 2007). Such skills are an aspect of *social intelligence,* a concept first proposed in 1920 by psychologist Edward Thorndike (Goleman, 2006). John Mayer, Peter Salovey, and David Caruso (2002, 2008) have developed a test that assesses four components of what they call **emotional intelligence:** the abilities to *perceive emotions* (to recognize them in faces, music, and stories); *understand emotions* (to predict them and how they change and blend); *manage emotions* (to know how to express them in varied situations); and *use emotions* to enable adaptive or creative thinking. In both the United States and Germany, those scoring high on managing emotions enjoy higher-quality interactions with friends (Lopes et al., 2004). They avoid being hijacked by overwhelming depression, anxiety, or anger. They can read others' emotions and know what to say to soothe a grieving friend, encourage a colleague, and manage a conflict. Across 69 studies in many countries, those scoring high in emotional intelligence also exhibit modestly better job performance (Van Rooy & Viswesvaran, 2004; Zeidner et al., 2008). They can override immediate impulses and delay gratification in pursuit of long-range rewards. Simply said, they are emotionally in tune with others, and thus they often succeed in career, marriage, and parenting situations where academically smarter (but emotionally less intelligent) people fail (Ciarrochi et al., 2006).

Brain damage reports have provided extreme examples of the results of diminished emotional intelligence in people with high general intelligence. Neuroscientist Antonio Damasio (1994) told of Elliot, who had a brain tumor removed: "I never saw a tinge of emotion in my many hours of conversation with him, no sadness, no impatience, no frustration." Shown disturbing pictures of injured people, destroyed communities, and natural disasters, Elliot showed—and realized he felt—no emotion. He knew but he could not feel. Unable to intuitively adjust his behavior in response to others' feelings, Elliot lost his job. He went bankrupt. His marriage collapsed. He remarried and divorced again. At last report, he was dependent on a disability check and custodial care from a sibling.

Some scholars are concerned that the concept of emotional intelligence pushes things too far. Mayer, Salovey, and Caruso have themselves cautioned against stretching "emotional intelligence" to include varied traits, such as self-esteem and optimism. Multiple-intelligence man Howard Gardner (1999) goes a step further. He welcomes our stretching the concept of intelligence into the realms of space, music, and information about ourselves and others. But let us also, he says, respect emotional sensitivity, creativity, and motivation as important but different. Stretch *intelligence* to include everything we prize and it will lose its meaning.

Assessing Intelligence

How do we assess intelligence? And what makes a test credible? Answering those questions begins with a look at why psychologists created **intelligence tests** and how they have used them.

The Origins of Intelligence Testing

13: When and why were intelligence tests created?

ALFRED BINET: PREDICTING SCHOOL ACHIEVEMENT The modern intelligence-testing movement began at the turn of the twentieth century, when France passed a law requiring that all children attend school. Some children, including many new-comers to Paris, seemed incapable of benefiting from the regular school curriculum and in need of special classes. But how could the schools objectively identify children with special needs?

The French government hesitated to trust teachers' subjective judgments of children's learning potential. Academic slowness might merely reflect inadequate prior education. Also, teachers might prejudge children on the basis of their social backgrounds. To minimize bias, France's minister of public education in 1904 commissioned Alfred Binet (1857–1911) and others to study the problem.

Binet and his collaborator, Théodore Simon, began by assuming that all children follow the same course of intellectual development but that some develop more rapidly. On tests, therefore, a "dull" child should perform as does a typical younger child, and a "bright" child as does a typical older child. Thus, their goal became measuring each child's **mental age,** the level of performance typically associated with a certain chronological age. The average 9-year-old, for example, has a mental age of 9. Children with below-average mental ages, such as 9-year-olds who perform at the level of a typical 7-year-old, would struggle with schoolwork considered normal for their age.

To measure mental age, Binet and Simon tested a variety of reasoning and problem-solving questions on Binet's two daughters, and then on "bright" and "backward" Parisian schoolchildren. They identified items that would predict how well French children would handle their schoolwork. Binet hoped his test would be used to improve children's education, but he also feared it would be used to label children and limit their opportunities (Gould, 1981).

LEWIS TERMAN: THE INNATE IQ Binet's fears were realized soon after his death in 1911, when others adapted his tests for use as a numerical measure of inherited intelligence. Stanford University professor Lewis Terman (1877–1956) adapted some of Binet's original items, added others, and established new age norms for California schoolchildren. Terman also extended the upper end of the test's range from teenagers to "superior adults." He gave his revision the name it retains today—the **Stanford-Binet.**

From such tests, German psychologist William Stern derived the famous **intelligence quotient,** or **IQ.** The IQ was simply a person's mental age divided by chronological age and multiplied by 100 to get rid of the decimal point:

$$IQ = \frac{\text{mental age}}{\text{chronological age}} \times 100$$

Thus, an average child, whose mental and chronological ages are the same, has an IQ of 100. But an 8-year-old who answers questions as would a typical 10-year-old has an IQ of 125.

The original IQ formula worked fairly well for children but not for adults. (Should a 40-year-old who does as well on the test as an average 20-year-old be assigned an IQ of only 50?) Most current intelligence tests, including the Stanford-Binet, no longer compute an IQ (though the term *IQ* still lingers in everyday vocabulary as a shorthand expression for "intelligence test score"). Instead, they

Alfred Binet "Some recent philosophers have given their moral approval to the deplorable verdict that an individual's intelligence is a fixed quantity, one which cannot be augmented. We must protest and act against this brutal pessimism" (Binet, 1909, p. 141).

"The IQ test was invented to predict academic performance, nothing else. If we wanted something that would predict life success, we'd have to invent another test completely."

—Social psychologist Robert Zajonc (1984b)

Mrs. Randolph takes mother's pride too far.

Wechsler Adult Intelligence Scale (WAIS)
the WAIS is the most widely used intelligence test; contains verbal and performance (nonverbal) subtests.

represent the test-taker's performance *relative* to the *average performance of others of the same age*. This average performance is arbitrarily assigned a score of 100, and about two-thirds of all test-takers fall between 85 and 115.

DAVID WECHSLER: VERBAL AND PERFORMANCE SUBTESTS Psychologist David Wechsler created what is now the most widely used intelligence test, the **Wechsler Adult Intelligence Scale (WAIS),** with a version for school-age children (the *Wechsler Intelligence Scale for Children [WISC]*), and another for preschool children. As illustrated in **FIGURE 9.13**, the WAIS consists of 11 subtests broken into verbal and performance areas. It yields not only an overall intelligence score, as does the Stanford-Binet, but also separate scores for verbal comprehension, perceptual organization, working memory, and processing speed. Striking differences among these scores can provide clues to cognitive strengths or weaknesses that teachers or therapists can build upon. For example, a low verbal comprehension score combined with high scores on other subtests could indicate a reading or language disability. Other comparisons can help a psychologist or psychiatrist establish a rehabilitation plan for a stroke patient. Such uses are possible, of course, only when we can trust the test results.

Principles of Test Construction

To be widely accepted, psychological tests must meet three criteria: They must be *standardized, reliable,* and *valid*. The Stanford-Binet and Wechsler tests meet these requirements.

FIGURE 9.13 Sample items from an earlier edition of Wechsler Adult Intelligence Scale (WAIS) subtests (Adapted from Thorndike & Hagen, 1977.)

VERBAL

General Information
What day of the year is Independence Day?

Similarities
In what way are *wool* and *cotton* alike?

Arithmetic Reasoning
If eggs cost 60 cents a dozen, what does 1 egg cost?

Vocabulary
Tell me the meaning of corrupt.

Comprehension
Why do people buy fire insurance?

Digit Span
Listen carefully, and when I am through, say the numbers right after me.

7   3   4   1   8   6

Now I am going to say some more numbers, but I want you to say them backward.

3   8   4   1   6

PERFORMANCE

Picture Completion
I am going to show you a picture with an important part missing. Tell me what is missing.

'85

SUN	MON	TUE	WED	THU	FRI	SAT
1	2	3	4	5	6	7
8	9	10	11	12	13	14
15	16	17	18	19	20	21
22	23	24	25	26	27	28
29	30					

Picture Arrangement
The pictures below tell a story. Put them in the right order to tell the story.

Block Design
Using the four blocks, make one just like this.

Object Assembly
If these pieces are put together correctly, they will make something. Go ahead and put them together as quickly as you can.

Getty Images/Stockdisc

Digit-Symbol Substitution

Code

△	○	▱	✕	◇
1	2	3	4	5

Test

1	5	4	2	1	3	5	4	1	5

STANDARDIZATION The number of questions you answer correctly on an intelligence test would tell us almost nothing. To evaluate your performance, we need a basis for comparing it with others' performance. To enable meaningful comparisons, test-makers first give the test to a large representative sample of people. When you later take the test following the same procedures, your score can be compared with the sample's scores to determine your position relative to others. This process of defining meaningful scores relative to a pretested group is called **standardization.**

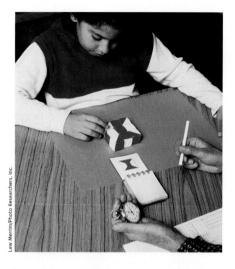

Matching patterns Block design puzzles test the ability to analyze patterns. Wechsler's individually administered intelligence test comes in forms suited for adults and children.

Group members' scores typically are distributed in a roughly symmetrical shape that forms the **normal curve** shown in **FIGURE 9.14**. No matter what we measure—heights, weights, or mental aptitudes—people's scores tend to form this *bell-shaped curve.* On an intelligence test, we call the midpoint, the average score, 100. Moving out from the average, toward either extreme, we find fewer and fewer people. For both the Stanford-Binet and the Wechsler tests, a person's score indicates whether that person's performance fell above or below the average. As Figure 9.14 shows, a performance higher than all but about 2 percent of all scores earns an intelligence score of 130. A performance lower than 98 percent of all scores earns an intelligence score of 70.

FIGURE 9.14 The normal curve Scores on aptitude tests tend to form a normal, or bell-shaped, curve around an average score. For the Wechsler scale, for example, the average score is 100.

RELIABILITY Knowing where you stand in comparison to a standardization group still won't tell us much about your intelligence unless the test has **reliability**—unless it yields dependably consistent scores. To check a test's reliability, researchers retest people. They may use the same test or they may split the test in half and see whether odd-question scores and even-question scores agree. If the two scores generally agree, or *correlate,* the test is reliable. The higher the correlation between the *test-retest* or the *split-half* scores, the higher the test's reliability. The tests we have considered so far—the Stanford-Binet, the WAIS, and the WISC—all have reliabilities of about +.9, which is very high. When retested, people's scores generally match their first score closely.

standardization defining meaningful scores by comparison with the performance of a pretested group.

normal curve the symmetrical bell-shaped curve that describes the distribution of many physical and psychological attributes. Most scores fall near the average, and fewer and fewer scores lie near the extremes.

reliability the extent to which a test yields consistent results, as assessed by the consistency of scores on two halves of the test, or on retesting.

validity the extent to which a test measures or predicts what it is supposed to. (See also *content validity* and *predictive validity*.)

content validity the extent to which a test samples the behavior that is of interest.

VALIDITY High reliability does not ensure a test's **validity**—the extent to which the test actually measures or predicts what it promises. If you use an inaccurate tape measure to measure people's heights, your height report would have high reliability (consistency) but low validity. It is enough for some tests that they have **content validity,** meaning the test taps the pertinent behavior, or criterion. The road test for a driver's license has content validity because it samples the tasks a driver routinely faces. Course exams have content validity if they assess one's

Close-Up:

Extremes of Intelligence

One way to glimpse the validity and significance of any test is to compare people who score at the two extremes of the normal curve. The two groups should differ noticeably, and they do.

Children with extraordinary academic gifts are sometimes more isolated, introverted, and in their own worlds (Winner, 2000). But most thrive. In one famous project begun in 1921, Lewis Terman studied more than 1500 California schoolchildren with IQ scores over 135. These high-scoring children, like others in later studies, were healthy, well-adjusted, and unusually successful academically (Lubinski & Benbow, 2006; Stanley, 1997). Over the next seven decades, most people in Terman's group attained high levels of education (Austin et al., 2002; Holahan & Sears, 1995). They included many doctors, lawyers, professors, scientists, and writers, but no Nobel Prize winners.

Terman did test two future Nobel laureates in physics but they failed to score above his gifted sample cutoff (Hulbert, 2005).

A more recent study focused on precocious youths who aced the math SAT at age 13—by scoring in the top quarter of 1 percent of their age group. At age 33, they were twice as likely to have patents as were those in the bottom quarter of the top 1 percent (Wai et al., 2005). These whiz kids were more likely to have earned a Ph.D.—1 in 3, compared with 1 in 5 for those in the bottom quarter.

Compared with the math aces, 13-year-olds scoring high on verbal aptitude were more likely to have become humanities professors or written a novel (Park et al., 2007).

At the other extreme of the normal curve are those whose intelligence test scores

> "Joining Mensa means that you are a genius. . . . I worried about the arbitrary 132 cutoff point, until I met someone with an IQ of 131 and, honestly, he was a bit slow on the uptake."
>
> —Steve Martin, 1997

The extremes of intelligence Sho Yano was playing Mozart by age 4, aced the SAT at age 8, and graduated summa cum laude from Loyola University at age 12, at which age he began combined Ph.D.–M.D. studies at the University of Chicago.

fall at 70 or below. To be labeled as having an **intellectual disability,** (formerly referred to as *mental retardation*), a child must have both a low test score and difficulty adapting to the normal demands of independent living. Only about 1 percent of the population meets both criteria, with males outnumbering females by 50 percent (American Psychiatric Association, 1994). As **TABLE 9.3** indicates, most of these individuals can, with support, live in mainstream society.

Intellectual disability sometimes has a known physical cause. **Down syndrome,** for example, is a disorder of varying severity caused by an extra chromosome 21 in the person's genetic makeup.

During the last two centuries, the pendulum of opinion about how best to care for Americans with such disabilities has made a complete swing. Until the mid-nineteenth century, they were cared for at home. Many of those with the most severe conditions died, but people with milder disabilities often found a place in a farm-based society. Then, residential schools for slow learners were established. By the twentieth century, many of these institutions had become warehouses, providing residents little attention, no privacy, and no hope. Parents often were told to separate themselves permanently from their impaired child before they became attached.

In the last half of the twentieth century, the pendulum swung back to normalization—encouraging people to live in their own communities as normally as their functioning permits. Children with mild impairments are educated in less restrictive environments, and many are

mastery of a representative sample of course material. But we expect intelligence tests to have **predictive validity:** They should predict the criterion of future performance, and to some extent they do. (See Close-Up: Extremes of Intelligence.)

Are general aptitude tests as predictive as they are reliable? As critics are fond of noting, the answer is plainly *no*. The predictive power of aptitude tests is fairly strong in the early school years, but later it weakens. Past grades, which reflect both aptitude and motivation, are better predictors of future achievements.

predictive validity the success with which a test predicts the behavior it is designed to predict; it is assessed by computing the correlation between test scores and the criterion behavior. (Also called *criterion-related validity.*)

TABLE 9.3 Degrees of Intellectual Disability

Level	Approximate Intelligence Scores	Adaptation to Demands of Life
Mild	50–70	May learn academic skills up to sixth-grade level. Adults may, with assistance, achieve self-supporting social and vocational skills.
Moderate	35–50	May progress to second-grade level academically. Adults may contribute to their own support by laboring in sheltered workshops.
Severe	20–35	May learn to talk and to perform simple work tasks under close supervision but are generally unable to profit from vocational training.
Profound	Below 20	Require constant aid and supervision.

Source: Reprinted with permission from the *Diagnostic and Statistical Manual of Mental Disorders,* Fourth Edition, text revision. Copyright 2000 American Psychiatric Association.

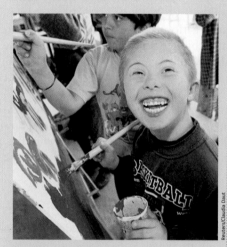

Mainstreaming in Chile Most Chilean children with Down syndrome attend separate schools for children with special needs. However, this boy is a student at The Altamira school, where children with differing abilities share the classrooms.

integrated, or *mainstreamed,* into regular classrooms. Most grow up with their own families, then move into a protected living arrangement, such as a group home. The hope, and often the reality, is a happier and more dignified life.

But consider another reason people diagnosed with a mild intellectual disability—those just below the 70 score—might be better able to live independently today than many decades ago. What if people who score near 70 are getting smarter?

For reasons no one quite understands, overall intelligence test performance has been rising during the twentieth century. (Is it greater test sophistication? Better nutrition? More stimulating environments? More education? Smaller families?) This worldwide phenomenon is called the *Flynn effect* in honor of New

Zealand researcher James Flynn (1987, 2007) who first calculated its magnitude. The average person's intelligence score 80 years ago was—by today's standard—only a 76! Such rising performance has been observed in 20 countries, from Canada to rural Australia (Daley et al., 2003).

Thanks to the Flynn effect, the tests have been periodically restandardized. As that happened, individuals who scored near 70 suddenly lost about 6 IQ points. Two people with the same ability level could thus be classified differently, depending on when they were tested (Kanaya et al., 2003). As the boundary shifts, more people become eligible for special education and for Social Security payments for those with a mental disability. And in the United States (one of only a few countries with the death penalty), fewer people are eligible for execution—the U.S. Supreme Court ruled in 2002 that the execution of people with an intellectual disability is "cruel and unusual punishment." For people near that score of 70, intelligence testing can be a high-stakes competition.

intellectual disability *(formerly referred to as mental retardation)* a condition of limited mental ability, indicated by an intelligence score of 70 or below and difficulty in adapting to the demands of life; varies from mild to profound.

Down syndrome a condition of mild to severe intellectual disability and associated physical disorders caused by an extra copy of chromosome 21.

REHEARSE IT!

13. The existence of savant syndrome—limited mental ability combined with an exceptional specific skill—seems to support
a. Sternberg's distinction among three aspects of intelligence.
b. Spearman's notion of general intelligence, or *g* factor.
c. Gardner's theory of multiple intelligences.
d. Thorndike's view of social intelligence.

14. Sternberg's three aspects of intelligence are
a. spatial, academic, and artistic.
b. musical, athletic, and academic.
c. academic, practical, and creative.
d. emotional, practical, and spatial.

15. Emotionally intelligent people tend to
a. seek immediate gratification.
b. understand their own emotions but not those of others.
c. understand others' emotions but not their own.
d. succeed in their careers.

16. Which of the following is NOT a characteristic of a creative person?
a. Expertise
b. Extrinsic motivation
c. A venturesome personality
d. Imaginative thinking skills

17. Intelligence quotient, or IQ, was originally defined as mental age divided by chronological age and multiplied by 100. By this definition, the IQ of a 6-year-old with a measured mental age of 9 would be
a. 67.   c. 86.
b. 133.   d. 150.

18. The Wechsler Adult Intelligence Scale (WAIS) yields an overall intelligence score as well as separate verbal and performance (nonverbal) scores. The WAIS is best able to tell us
a. what part of an individual's intelligence is determined by genetic inheritance.
b. whether the test-taker will succeed in a job.

c. how the test-taker compares with other adults in vocabulary and arithmetic reasoning.
d. whether the test-taker has specific skills for music and the performing arts.

19. The Stanford-Binet, the Wechsler Adult Intelligence Scale, and the Wechsler Intelligence Scale for Children are known to have very high reliability (about +.9). This means that
a. a pretest has been given to a representative sample.
b. the test yields consistent results, for example on retesting.
c. the test measures what it is supposed to measure.
d. the results of the test will predict future behavior, such as college grades or success in business.

Answers: 13. c, 14. c, 15. d, 16. b, 17. d, 18. c, 19. b.

"There are more studies addressing the genetics of *g* than any other human characteristic."

—Robert Plomin (1999)

"I told my parents that if grades were so important they should have paid for a smarter egg donor."

Genetic and Environmental Influences on Intelligence

14: **What does evidence reveal about hereditary and environmental influences on intelligence?**

Intelligence runs in families. But why? Are our intellectual abilities mostly inherited? Or are they molded by our environment?

Few issues arouse such passion or have such serious political implications. Consider: If we mainly inherit our differing mental abilities, and if success reflects those abilities, then people's socioeconomic standing will correspond to their inborn differences. This could lead to those on top believing that their intellectual birthright justifies their social positions.

But if mental abilities are primarily nurtured by the environments that raise and inform us, then children from disadvantaged environments can expect to lead disadvantaged lives. In this case, people's standing will result from their unequal opportunities.

For now, as best we can, let's set aside such political implications and examine the evidence.

Genetic Influences

Do people who share the same genes also share comparable mental abilities? Twin studies provide some clues. As you can see from **FIGURE 9.15**, which summarizes many studies, the answer is clearly *yes*. In support of the genetic contribution to intelligence, researchers cite three sets of findings:

- The intelligence test scores of identical twins reared together are virtually as similar as those of the same person taking the same test twice (Lykken, 1999; Plomin, 2001). (The scores of fraternal twins, who typically share only half their genes, are much less similar.) Likewise, the test scores of identical twins reared separately are similar enough to have led twin researcher Thomas

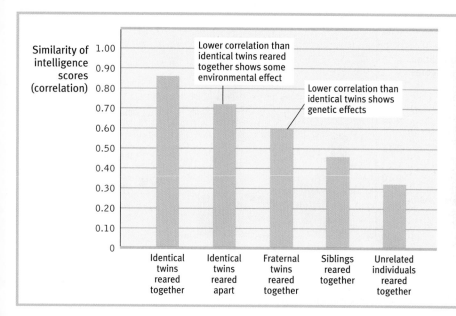

Lower correlation than identical twins reared together shows some environmental effect

Lower correlation than identical twins shows genetic effects

Similarity of intelligence scores (correlation)

Identical twins reared together

Identical twins reared apart

Fraternal twins reared together

Siblings reared together

Unrelated individuals reared together

FIGURE 9.15 **Intelligence: Nature and nurture** The most genetically similar people have the most similar intelligence scores. Remember: 1.0 indicates a perfect correlation; zero indicates no correlation at all. (Data from McGue et al., 1993.)

Bouchard (1996a) to estimate that "about 70 percent" of intelligence test score variation "can be attributed to genetic variation." Other estimates range from 50 to 75 percent (Devlin et al., 1997; Neisser et al., 1996; Plomin, 2003).

- Brain scans reveal that identical twins have very similar gray matter volume, and that their brains (unlike those of fraternal twins) are virtually the same in areas associated with verbal and spatial intelligence (Koten et al., 2009; Thompson et al., 2001).
- Are there genes for genius? Today's researchers have identified chromosomal regions important to intelligence, and they have pinpointed specific genes that seemingly influence variations in intelligence and learning disabilities (Dick et al., 2007; Plomin & Kovas, 2005; Posthuma & de Geus, 2006). Intelligence appears to be *polygenetic,* with many genes involved, each accounting for much less than 1 percent of intelligence variations (Butcher et al., 2008).

So it's clear that genes make a difference. But other evidence points to the effects of environment.

Environmental Influences

Even if we were all raised in the same intellectually stimulating environment, we would have differing aptitudes because of our genetic differences. Fraternal twins, who are genetically no more alike than any other siblings, are treated more alike because they are the same age. And they tend to score more alike than other siblings. Seeking to disentangle genes and environment, researchers have studied adopted children and their families.

ADOPTION STUDIES What have we learned from comparisons of intelligence test scores of adopted children with those of (a) their adoptive siblings; (b) their biological parents, the providers of their genes; and (c) their adoptive parents, the providers of their home environment? During childhood, the intelligence test scores of adoptive siblings correlate modestly. Over time, adopted children accumulate experience in their differing adoptive families. So would you expect the family environment effect to grow with age and the genetic legacy effect to shrink?

If you would, behavior geneticists have a surprise for you. Mental similarities between adopted children and their adoptive families wane with age, until the correlation approaches zero by adulthood (McGue et al., 1993). This is even true of

"Selective breeding has given me an aptitude for the law, but I still love fetching a dead duck out of freezing water."

FIGURE 9.16 Who do adopted children resemble? As the years went by in their adoptive families, children's verbal ability scores became modestly more like their *biological* parents' scores. (Adapted from Plomin & DeFries, 1998.)

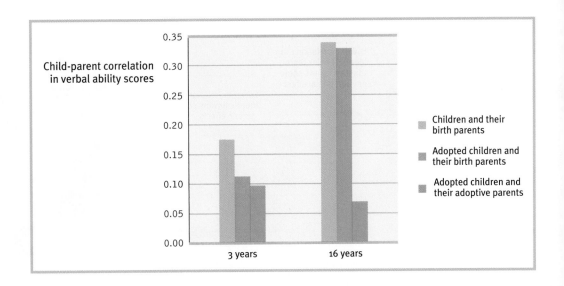

Child-parent correlation in verbal ability scores

- Children and their birth parents
- Adopted children and their birth parents
- Adopted children and their adoptive parents

3 years   16 years

Devastating neglect Romanian orphans who had minimal interaction with caregivers, such as this child in the Lagunul Pentro Copii orphanage in 1990, suffered delayed development.

virtual twins—same age, biologically unrelated siblings reared together from infancy (Segal et al., 2007). Genetic influences—not environmental ones—become more apparent as we accumulate life experience (Bouchard, 1995, 1996b). Identical twins' similarities, for example, continue or increase into their eighties (McClearn et al., 1997; Plomin et al., 1997). Similarly, adopted children's intelligence scores over time become more like those of their biological parents (**FIGURE 9.16**).

EARLY ENVIRONMENTAL INFLUENCES As we have so often seen, biology and experience intertwine in their influence on intellectual development. Human environments are rarely as impoverished as the dark and barren cages inhabited by deprived rats that develop thinner-than-normal brain cortexes (see Chapter 4). Yet severe deprivation does leave footprints on the brain, as J. McVicker Hunt (1982) observed in a destitute Iranian orphanage. The typical child Hunt observed there could not sit up unassisted at age 2 or walk at age 4. The little care infants received was not in response to their crying, cooing, or other behaviors, so the children developed little sense of personal control over their environment. Extreme deprivation was bludgeoning native intelligence, and these infants were becoming passive "glum lumps."

Aware of both the dramatic effects of early experiences and the impact of early intervention, Hunt began a program of *tutored human enrichment*. He trained caregivers to play language-fostering games with 11 infants, imitating the babies' babbling, then engaging them in vocal follow-the-leader, and finally teaching them sounds from the Persian language. The results were dramatic. By 22 months of age, the infants could name more than 50 objects and body parts and so charmed visitors that most were adopted—an unprecedented success for the orphanage. (Institutionalized Romanian orphans also benefited cognitively if transferred early to more enriched home care [Nelson et al., 2007].) Studies show that adoption enhances the intelligence scores of mistreated or neglected children (van IJzendoorn & Juffer, 2005, 2006).

Hunt's findings are an extreme case of a more general finding: Among the poor, environmental conditions can override genetic differences, depressing cognitive development. Unlike children of affluence, siblings within impoverished families have more similar intelligence scores (Turkheimer et al., 2003). Schools with lots of poverty-level children often have less-qualified teachers, as one study of 1450 Virginia schools found. And even after controlling for poverty, having less-qualified teachers predicted lower achievement scores (Tuerk, 2005). Malnutrition also plays a role. Relieve infant malnutrition with nutritional supplements, and poverty's effect on physical and cognitive development lessens (Brown & Pollitt, 1996).

Getting a Head Start Project Head Start offers educational activities designed to increase readiness for schoolwork and expand children's notions of where school might lead them. Here children in a classroom learn about colors, and children on a field trip prepare for the annual Head Start parade in Boston.

SCHOOLING AND INTELLIGENCE Schooling also pays dividends, boosting children's chances for success by developing their cognitive and social skills. Schooling and intelligence interact, and both enhance later income (Ceci & Williams, 1997).

Hunt's 1961 book, *Intelligence and Experience,* helped launch Project Head Start in 1965. This U.S. government-funded preschool program serves more than 900,000 children, most of whom come from families below the poverty level (Head Start, 2005). Does it succeed? Researchers study Head Start and other preschool programs such as Sure Start in Britain by comparing children who experience the program with their counterparts who don't. Quality programs, offering individual attention, increase children's school readiness, which decreases their likelihood of repeating a grade or being placed in special education. Although the aptitude benefits generally dissipate over time (reminding us that life experience *after* Head Start matters, too), there may be long-term effects (Ripple & Zigler, 2003; Zigler & Styfco, 2001). High-quality preschool programs provide at least a small boost to emotional intelligence—creating better attitudes toward learning and reducing school dropouts and criminality (Reynolds et al., 2001). And attitudes matter. What we accomplish with our intelligence depends also on our own beliefs and motivation (Dweck, 2006, 2007). Those who believe that intelligence is biologically fixed and unchanging tend to focus on proving and defending their identity. Those who instead believe that intelligence is changeable will focus more on learning and growing. Indeed, as we noted earlier, superior achievements in fields from sports to science to music arise from disciplined effort and sustained practice (Ericsson et al., 2007).

Heritability

So what portion of the variation in intelligence test scores can we attribute to genetic factors? Estimates of the **heritability** of intelligence put it at about 50 percent. Does this mean *your genes* are responsible for 50 percent of your intelligence and your environment for the rest? No. It means we credit heredity with 50 percent of the variation in intelligence *among people being studied.* This point is so often misunderstood that I repeat: Heritability never pertains to an individual, only to why people differ from one another.

Heritability differences among people due to genes can vary from study to study. Where environments vary widely, as they do among children of less-educated parents, environmental differences are more predictive of intelligence scores (Rowe et al., 1999; Turkheimer et al., 2003). To see why, consider Mark Twain's fantasy of raising boys in barrels to age 12, feeding them through a hole. Given the boys' equal environments, differences in their individual intelligence test scores at age 12 could be explained only by their heredity. Thus, heritability for their differences would be

"It is our choices . . . that show what we truly are, far more than our abilities."

—Professor Dumbledore to Harry Potter in J. K. Rowling's *Harry Potter and the Chamber of Secrets,* 1999

---

heritability the proportion of variation among individuals that we can attribute to genes. The heritability of a trait may vary, depending on the range of populations and environments studied.

A check on your understanding of heritability: If environments become more equal, the heritability of intelligence would

a. increase.

b. decrease.

c. be unchanged.

See inverted answer below.

Heritability—variation explained by genetic influences—will increase as environmental variation decreases.

Despite the gender equivalence in intelligence test scores, males are more likely than females to overestimate their own test scores. Both males and females tend to rate their father's scores higher than their mother's, their brothers' scores higher than their sisters', and their sons' scores higher than their daughters' (Furnham, 2001; Furnham et al., 2002a,b, 2004a,b,c).

nearly 100 percent. But if we raise people with similar heredities in drastically different environments (barrels versus advantaged homes), the environment effect will be huge, and heritability will therefore be lower. In a world of clones, heritability would be zero.

Remember, too, that genes and environment work together. If you try out for a basketball team and are just slightly taller and quicker than others, notes James Flynn (2003, 2007), you will more likely be picked, play more, and get more coaching. The same would be true for your separated identical twin—who might, *not just for genetic reasons,* also come to excel at basketball. Likewise, if you have a natural aptitude for academics, you will more likely stay in school, read books, and ask questions—all of which will amplify your cognitive brain power. Thanks to such gene-environment interactions, modest genetic advantages can be socially multiplied into big performance advantages. Our genes shape the experiences that shape us.

Group Differences in Intelligence Test Scores

15: How and why do gender and racial groups differ in mental ability scores?

If there were no group differences in aptitude scores, psychologists could politely debate hereditary and environmental influences in their ivory towers. But there are group differences. What are they? And what shall we make of them?

Gender Similarities and Differences

In science, as in everyday life, differences, not similarities, excite interest. Compared with the anatomical and physiological similarities between men and women, our differences are relatively minor. Yet it is the differences we find exciting. Similarly, in the psychological domain, our gender similarities vastly outnumber our gender differences. In a 1921 testing of all Scottish 11-year-olds, for example, girls' average intelligence score was 100.6 and boys was 100.5 (Deary et al., 2003). On a 2001 to 2003 Cognitive Ability Test administered to 324,000 British 11- and 12-year-olds, boys averaged 99.1 and girls a similar 99.9 (Strand et al., 2006). So far as g is concerned, boys and girls, men and women, are the same species. Yet, most people find differences more newsworthy. And here they are.

Spelling Females are better spellers: At the end of high school, only 30 percent of U.S. males spell better than the average female (Lubinski & Benbow, 1992).

Verbal ability Females excel at verbal fluency and remembering words (Halpern et al., 2007). And, year after year, among nearly 200,000 students taking Germany's Test for Medical Studies, young women have surpassed men in remembering facts from short medical cases (Stumpf & Jackson, 1994). (My wife, who remembers many of my experiences for me, tells me that if she died I'd be a man without a past.)

Nonverbal memory Females have an edge in remembering and locating objects (Voyer et al., 2007). In studies of more than 100,000 American adolescents, girls also modestly surpassed boys in memory for picture associations (Hedges & Nowell, 1995).

Sensation Females are more sensitive to touch, taste, and odor.

Emotion-detecting ability Females are better emotion detectors. Robert Rosenthal, Judith Hall, and their colleagues (1979; McClure, 2000) discovered this while studying sensitivity to emotional cues (an aspect of emotional intelligence). They showed hundreds of people brief film clips of portions of a person's emotionally expressive face or body, sometimes with a garbled voice added. For example, after showing a 2-second scene revealing only the face of an upset woman, the researchers asked people to guess whether the woman was criticizing someone for being late or was talking about her divorce. Some people, many of them women, detected emotions much better than others. Could such skills have helped

World Math Olympics champs After outscoring thousands of their U.S. peers, these young people became the U.S. Math Team in 2002 and placed third in the world-wide competition.

our ancestral mothers read emotions in their infants and would-be lovers, in turn fueling cultural tendencies to encourage women's empathic skills? Some evolutionary psychologists believe so.

Math and spatial aptitudes On math tests given to more than 3 million representatively sampled people in 100 independent studies, males and females obtained nearly identical average scores (Hyde et al., 1990, 2008). But again—despite greater diversity within the genders than between them—group differences make the news. In 20 of 21 countries, females displayed an edge in math computation, but males scored higher in math problem solving (Bronner, 1998; Hedges & Nowell, 1995). Gender score differences are sharpest at the extremes. Among 12- to 14-year-olds scoring extremely high on SAT math, boys have outnumbered girls 13 to 1, and within that precocious group, the boys have more often gone on to earn a degree in the inorganic sciences and engineering (Benbow et al., 2000).

The average male edge seems most reliable in spatial ability tests like the one shown in **FIGURE 9.17**, which involves speedily rotating three-dimensional objects in one's mind (Collins & Kimura, 1997; Halpern, 2000). Exposure to high levels of male sex hormones during the prenatal period does enhance spatial abilities (Berenbaum et al., 1995). So, one recent experiment indicates, does action video game playing (Feng et al., 2007).

Spatial abilities skills help when doing certain types of geometry problems, fitting suitcases into a car trunk, and playing chess. From an evolutionary perspective (Geary, 1995, 1996; Halpern et al., 2007), those skills may also have helped our ancestral fathers track prey and make their way home. The survival of our ancestral mothers may have benefited more from a keen memory for the location of edible plants—a legacy that lives today in women's superior memory for objects and their location.

In the first 56 years of the college Putnam Mathematical Competition, all of the nearly 300 awardees were men (Arenson, 1997). In 1997, a woman broke the male grip by joining 5 men in the winner's circle. In 1998, Melanie Wood became the first female member of a U.S. math Olympics team (Shulman, 2000). Her training began at an early age: When mall-shopping with her then-4-year-old daughter, Melanie's mother would alleviate her child's boredom by giving her linear equations to solve.

Among entering American collegians, 22 percent of men and 4 percent of women report having played video/computer games six or more hours a week (Pryor et al., 2006).

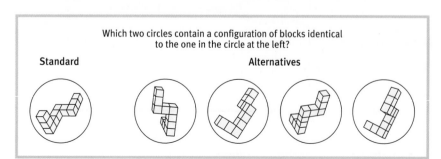

FIGURE 9.17 The mental rotation test This is a test of spatial abilities. (From Vandenberg & Kuse, 1978.) See inverted answer below.

The first and fourth alternatives.

Nature or nurture? At this 2005 Google Inc.-sponsored computer coding competition, programmers competed for cash prizes and possible jobs. What do you think accounted for the fact that only one of the 100 finalists was female?

Evolutionary psychologist Steven Pinker (2005) argues that biological as well as social influences appear to affect gender differences in life priorities (women's greater interest in people versus men's in money and things), in risk-taking (with men more reckless), and in math reasoning and spatial abilities. Such differences are, he notes, observed across cultures, stable over time, influenced by prenatal hormones, and observed in genetic boys raised as girls. Other researchers are exploring a brain basis for male-female cognitive differences (Halpern et al., 2007).

Elizabeth Spelke (2005), however, has urged caution in charting male-female intellectual worlds. It oversimplifies to say that women have more "verbal ability" and men more "math ability." Women excel at verbal fluency, men at verbal analogies. Women excel at rapid math calculations, men at rapid math reasoning. Women excel at remembering objects' spatial positions, men at remembering geometric layouts.

Other critics urge us to remember that social expectations and divergent opportunities shape boys' and girls' interests and abilities (Crawford et al., 1995; Eccles et al., 1990). Gender-equal cultures, such as Sweden and Iceland, exhibit little of the gender math gap found in gender-unequal cultures, such as Turkey and Korea (Guiso et al., 2008). In the United States, the male edge in math problem solving is detectable only after children begin school. As more parents encourage their daughters to develop their abilities in math and science, the gender gap is narrowing (Nowell & Hedges, 1998). In some fields, including psychology, women now earn most of the Ph.D.s. Yet, notes Diane Halpern (2005) with a twinkle in her eye, "no one has asked if men have the innate ability to succeed in those academic disciplines where *they* are underrepresented."

Greater male variability Finally, intelligence research consistently reports a peculiar tendency for males' mental ability scores to vary more than females' (Halpern et al., 2007). Thus, boys outnumber girls at both the low extreme and the high extreme (Kleinfeld, 1998; Strand et al., 2006; also see **FIGURE 9.18**). This peculiar phenomenon of greater male variability also is observed on reading and math test performance worldwide (Machin & Pekkarinen, 2008). Boys are, therefore, more often found in special education classes. They talk later. They stutter more.

FIGURE 9.18 Gender and variability In the 1932 intelligence testing of nearly 90,000 Scottish 11-year-olds, the average IQ scores for girls and boys was essentially identical. But as other studies have found, boys were overrepresented at the low and high extremes. (Adapted from Deary et al., 2003.)

Ethnic Similarities and Differences

Fueling the group-differences debate are two other disturbing but agreed-upon facts:

- Racial groups differ in their average intelligence test scores.
- High-scoring people (and groups) are more likely to attain high levels of education and income.

"The bell curve for Whites is centered roughly around IQ 100; the bell curve for American Blacks roughly around 85; and those for different subgroups of Hispanics roughly midway between those for Whites and Blacks," a statement by 52 intelligence researchers explained (Avery et al., 1994). Since that time, the Black-White test-score difference has diminished somewhat, dropping to 10 points among children in some studies (Dickens & Flynn, 2006). Yet the gap stubbornly persists, and other studies suggest the gap stopped narrowing among those born after 1970 (Murray, 2006, 2007).

There are differences between other groups as well. New Zealanders of European descent outscore native Maori New Zealanders. Israeli Jews outscore Israeli Arabs. Most Japanese outscore the stigmatized Burakumin minority in Japan. And those who can hear outscore those born deaf (Braden, 1994; Steele, 1990; Zeidner, 1990).

Everyone further agrees that such *group* differences provide little basis for judging *individuals*. Women outlive men by six years, but knowing someone's sex doesn't tell us with any precision how long that person will live. Even Charles Murray and Richard Herrnstein (1994), whose writings drew attention to Black-White differences, reminded us that "millions of Blacks have higher IQs than the average White."

Swedes and Bantus differ in complexion and language. That first factor is genetic, the second environmental. So what about intelligence scores?

As we have seen, heredity contributes to individual differences in intelligence. Does that mean it also contributes to group differences? Some psychologists believe it does, perhaps because of the world's differing climates and survival challenges (Herrnstein & Murray, 1994; Lynn, 1991, 2001; Rushton & Jensen, 2005, 2006).

But we have also seen that group differences in a heritable trait may be entirely environmental, as in our earlier barrel-versus-home–reared boys example. Consider one of nature's experiments: Allow some children to grow up hearing their culture's dominant language, while others, born deaf, do not. Then give both groups an intelligence test rooted in the dominant language, and (no surprise) those with expertise in that language will score highest. Although individual performance differences may be substantially genetic, the group difference is not (**FIGURE 9.19**).

Also consider: If each identical twin were exactly as tall as his or her co-twin, heritability would be 100 percent. Imagine that we then separated some young twins and gave only half of them a nutritious diet, and that the well-nourished twins all grew to be exactly 3 inches taller than their counterparts—an environmental effect

In prosperous country X everyone eats all they want. In country Y the rich are well fed, but the semistarved poor are often thin. In which country will the heritability of body weight be greater? See inverted answer below.

Heritability—differences due to genes—will be greater in country X, where environmental differences in nutrition are minimal.

FIGURE 9.19 Group differences and environmental impact Even if the variation between members within a group reflects genetic differences, the average difference between groups may be wholly due to the environment. Imagine that seeds from the same mixture are sown in different soils. Although height differences *within* each window box will be genetic, the height difference *between* the two groups will be environmental. (From Lewontin, 1976.)

comparable to that actually observed in both Britain and America, where adolescents are several inches taller than their counterparts were a half-century ago. What would the heritability of height now be for our well-nourished twins? Still 100 percent, because the variation in height within the group would remain entirely predictable from the heights of their malnourished identical siblings. So even perfect heritability within groups would not eliminate the possibility of a strong environmental impact on the group differences.

Might the racial gap be similarly environmental? Consider:

Genetics research reveals that under the skin, the races are remarkably alike (Cavalli-Sforza et al., 1994; Lewontin, 1982). Individual differences within a race are much greater than differences between races. The average genetic difference between two Icelandic villagers or between two Kenyans greatly exceeds the group difference between Icelanders and Kenyans. Moreover, looks can deceive. Light-skinned Europeans and dark-skinned Africans are genetically closer than are dark-skinned Africans and dark-skinned Aboriginal Australians.

Race is not a neatly defined biological category. Some scholars argue that there is a reality to race, noting that there are genetic markers for race (the continent of one's ancestry) and that medical risks (such as skin cancer or high blood pressure) vary by race. Behavioral traits may also vary by race. "No runner of Asian or European descent—a majority of the world's population—has broken 10 seconds in the 100-meter dash, but dozens of runners of West African descent have done so," observes psychologist David Rowe (2005). Many social scientists, though, see race primarily as a social construction without well-defined physical boundaries (Helms et al., 2005; Smedley & Smedley, 2005; Sternberg et al., 2005). People with varying ancestry may categorize themselves in the same race. Moreover, with increasingly mixed ancestries, more and more people defy neat racial categorization. (What race is Tiger Woods?)

The intelligence test performance of today's better-fed, better-educated, and more test-prepared population exceeds that of the 1930s population—by the same margin that the intelligence test score of the average White today exceeds that of the average Black. No one attributes the generational group difference to genetics.

White and Black infants have scored equally well on an infant intelligence measure (preference for looking at novel stimuli—a crude predictor of future intelligence scores [Fagan, 1992]).

When Blacks and Whites have or receive the same pertinent knowledge, they exhibit similar information-processing skill. "The data support the view that cultural differences in the provision of information may account for racial differences in IQ," report researchers Joseph Fagan and Cynthia Holland (2007).

In different eras, different ethnic groups have experienced golden ages—periods of remarkable achievement. Twenty-five-hundred years ago, it was the Greeks and the Egyptians, then the Romans; in the eighth and ninth centuries, genius seemed to reside in the Arab world; 500 years ago it was the Aztec Indians and the peoples of Northern Europe. Today, people marvel at Asians' technological genius. Cultures rise and fall over centuries; genes do not. That fact makes it difficult to attribute a natural superiority to any race.

Since 1830, the average Dutch man has grown from 5 feet 5 inches to nearly 6 feet.

Nature's own morphing
Nature draws no sharp boundaries between races, which blend gradually one into the next around the Earth. Thanks to the human urge to classify, however, people socially define themselves in racial categories, which become catch-all labels for physical features, social identity, and nationality.

© Paul Almasy/Corbis; © Rob Howard/ Corbis; © Barbara Bannister; Gallo Images/ Corbis; © David Turnley/Corbis; © Dave Bartruff/Corbis; © Haruyoshi Yamaguchi/Corbis; © Richard T. Nowitz/Corbis; © Owen Franken/Corbis; © Paul Almasy/Corbis; © John-Francis Bourke/zefa/Corbis

"Do not obtain your slaves from Britain, because they are so stupid and so utterly incapable of being taught."

—Cicero, 106–43 B.C.E.

The Question of Bias

16: Are intelligence tests inappropriately biased?

If one assumes that race is a meaningful concept, the debate over race differences in intelligence divides into three camps, note Earl Hunt and Jerry Carlson (2007):

- There are genetically disposed race differences in intelligence.
- There are socially influenced race differences in intelligence.
- There are race differences in test scores, but the tests are inappropriate or biased.

Are intelligence tests biased? The answer depends on which of two very different definitions of *bias* are used, and on an understanding of stereotypes.

TWO MEANINGS OF BIAS A test may be considered biased if it detects not only innate differences in intelligence but also performance differences caused by cultural experiences. This in fact happened to Eastern European immigrants in the early 1900s. Lacking the experience to answer questions about their new culture, many were classified as feeble-minded. (David Wechsler, who entered the United States as a 6-year-old Romanian just before this group, designed the WAIS.) In this popular sense, intelligence tests are biased. They measure your developed abilities, which reflect, in part, your education and experiences.

The *scientific* meaning of *bias* is different. It hinges on a test's validity—on whether it predicts future behavior only for some groups of test-takers. For example, if the U.S. SAT accurately predicted the college achievement of women but not of men, then the test would be biased. In this statistical meaning of the term, the near-consensus among psychologists (as summarized by the U.S. National Research Council's Committee on Ability Testing and the American Psychological Association's Task Force on Intelligence) is that the major U.S. aptitude tests are not biased (Hunt & Carlson, 2007; Neisser et al., 1996; Wigdor & Garner, 1982). The tests' predictive validity is roughly the same for women and men, for Blacks and Whites, and for rich and poor. If an intelligence test score of 95 predicts slightly below-average grades, that rough prediction usually applies equally to both genders and all ethnic and economic groups.

TEST-TAKERS' EXPECTATIONS Throughout this text, we have seen that our expectations and attitudes can influence our perceptions and behaviors. Once again, we find this effect in intelligence testing. When equally capable men and women took a difficult math test, women did not perform as well as men—except when they had been led to expect that women usually do as well as men on the test (Spencer et al., 1997). Otherwise, the women apparently felt apprehensive, and it affected their performance. This self-fulfilling **stereotype threat** appeared again when Black students, taking verbal aptitude tests under conditions designed to make them feel threatened, performed at a lower level (Steele et al., 2002). Critics note that stereotype threat does not fully account for the Black-White aptitude score difference (Sackett et al., 2004, 2008). But it does help explain why Blacks have scored higher when tested by Blacks than when tested by Whites (Danso & Esses, 2001; Inzlicht & Ben-Zeev, 2000). And it gives us insight into why women have scored higher on math tests when no male test-takers were in the group, and why women's chess play drops sharply when they *think* they are playing a male rather than female opponent (Maass et al., 2008).

Telling students they probably won't succeed (as is sometimes implied by remedial "minority support" programs) may function as a stereotype that erodes test and school performance (Steele, 1995, 1997). Over time, students hearing this message may detach their self-esteem from academics and look for recognition elsewhere. Indeed, from eighth to twelfth grade, some African-American boys have tended to

stereotype threat a self-confirming concern that one will be evaluated based on a negative stereotype.

"Math class is tough!"

—"Teen talk" talking Barbie doll (introduced February 1992, recalled October 1992)

What time is it now? When I asked you (in the section on overconfidence) to estimate how quickly you would finish this chapter, did you underestimate or overestimate?

underachieve as the disconnect between grades and self-esteem becomes pronounced (Osborne, 1997). One experiment challenged this trend by randomly assigning some seventh-graders to write for 15 minutes about their most important values (Cohen et al., 2006). This simple exercise in self-affirmation had the apparent effect of boosting their semester grade point average by 0.26 in a first experiment and 0.34 in a replication. Minority students in university programs that challenge them to believe in their potential, or to focus on the idea that intelligence is malleable and not fixed, have likewise produced markedly higher grades and had lower dropout rates (Wilson, 2006).

What, then, can we realistically conclude about aptitude tests and bias? The tests do seem biased (appropriately so, some would say) in one sense—sensitivity to performance differences caused by cultural experience. But they are not biased in the scientific sense of making valid statistical predictions for different groups.

Bottom line: Are the tests discriminatory? Again, the answer can be *yes* or *no*. In one sense, *yes,* their purpose is to discriminate—to distinguish among individuals. In another sense, *no,* their purpose is to reduce discrimination by reducing reliance on subjective criteria for school and job placement—who you know, how you dress, or whether you are the "right kind of person." Banning aptitude tests would lead those who decide on jobs and admissions to rely more on other considerations, such as their personal opinions.

Untestable compassion
Intelligence test scores are only one part of the picture of a whole person. They don't measure the abilities, talent, and commitment of, for example, people who devote their lives to helping others.

Perhaps, then, our goals for tests of mental abilities should be threefold. First, we should realize the benefits Alfred Binet envisioned—to enable schools to recognize who might profit most from early intervention. Second, we must remain alert to Binet's fear that intelligence test scores may be misinterpreted as literal measures of a person's worth and potential. And finally, we must remember that the competence that general intelligence tests sample is important; it helps enable success in some life paths. But it reflects only one aspect of personal competence. Our practical intelligence and emotional intelligence matter, too, as do other forms of creativity, talent, and character. The carpenter's spatial ability differs from the programmer's logical ability, which differs from the poet's verbal ability. Because there are many ways of being successful, our differences are variations of human adaptability.

"Almost all the joyful things of life are outside the measure of IQ tests."

—Madeleine L'Engle, *A Circle of Quiet*, 1972

REHEARSE IT!

20. The strongest support for heredity's influence on intelligence is the finding that
   a. identical twins, but not other siblings, have nearly identical intelligence test scores.
   b. the correlation between intelligence test scores of fraternal twins is higher than that for other siblings.
   c. mental similarities between adopted siblings increase with age.
   d. children in impoverished families have similar intelligence scores.

21. To say that the heritability of intelligence is about 50 percent means that 50 percent of
   a. an individual's intelligence is due to genetic factors.
   b. the similarities between men and women are attributable to genes.
   c. the variation in intelligence within a group of people is attributable to genetic factors.
   d. intelligence is due to the mother's genes and the rest is due to the father's genes.

22. The environmental influence that has the clearest, most profound effect on intellectual development is
   a. being enrolled in a Head Start program.
   b. growing up in an economically disadvantaged home or neighborhood.
   c. being raised in conditions of extreme deprivation.
   d. being an identical twin.

Answers: 20. a, 21. c, 22. c.

Thinking, Language, and Intelligence

Thinking

1 What are the functions of concepts?

Cognition refers to all the mental activities associated with thinking, knowing, remembering, and communicating. We use *concepts,* mental groupings of similar objects, events, ideas, or people, to simplify and order the world around us. In creating hierarchies, we organize concepts into smaller and more detailed units. We form some concepts, such as triangles, by definition (objects with three intersecting sides), but we form most around *prototypes,* mental images or best examples of a category.

2 What strategies assist our problem solving, and what obstacles hinder it?

An *algorithm* is a methodical, logical rule or procedure (such as a step-by-step description for evacuating a building during a fire) that guarantees a solution to a problem. A *heuristic* is a simpler thinking strategy (such as running for an exit if you smell smoke) that may provide faster—but sometimes incorrect—solutions. *Insight* is not a strategy-based solution, but rather a sudden flash of inspiration that solves a problem.

Problem-solving obstacles are the *confirmation bias* (which predisposes us to verify rather than challenge our hypotheses) and *fixation* (which may prevent us from taking a fresh perspective).

3 How do heuristics, overconfidence, and belief perseverance influence our decisions and judgments?

The *representativeness heuristic* leads us to judge the likelihood of things in terms of how well they match our prototypes. The *availability heuristic* may lead us to fear the wrong things by judging the likelihood of an event based on how readily it comes to mind. We are often *overconfident,* but right or wrong, we cling to our beliefs even when they have been discredited—a tendency known as *belief perseverance.*

4 How do smart thinkers use intuition?

Although it sometimes leads us astray, human *intuition*—effortless, immediate, automatic feeling or thought—can give us instant help when we need it. Experts in a field grow adept at making quick, shrewd judgments. Smart thinkers will welcome their intuitions but check them against available evidence.

5 What is framing?

Framing is the way a question or statement is worded. Subtle wording differences can tilt us in the direction of a questioner's preferred response.

6 What are the milestones in language development?

The timing varies from one child to another, but all children follow the same sequence. At about 4 months of age, infants *babble,* making a wide range of possible sounds. By about 10 months, babbling is limited to the sounds found in the child's household *language.* Around 12 months of age, children enter the *one-word stage,* which evolves into *two-word (telegraphic)* utterances before

their second birthday. Speaking in full sentences follows soon after.

7 How do we learn language?

Skinner proposed that we learn language by the familiar principles of operant conditioning—association (of sights of things with sounds of words), imitation (of words and syntax modeled by others), and reinforcement (with smiles and hugs after saying something right). Chomsky argued that we are biologically prepared to learn language, by means of a language acquisition device that equips us with a universal grammar, which we use to learn a specific language. Cognitive researchers find childhood to be a critical period for learning spoken and signed language.

8 What is the relationship between language and thinking?

Although Whorf's *linguistic determinism* hypothesis suggested that language determines thought, it is more accurate to say that language influences thought. Different languages embody different ways of thinking, and immersion in bilingual education can enhance thinking. We often think in images when we use procedural memory—our unconscious memory system for motor and cognitive skills and classically and operantly conditioned associations. Thinking in images can increase our skills when we mentally practice upcoming events.

9 What do we know about animal thinking? Do other animals share our capacity for language?

Primates and other animals demonstrate impressive abilities to think and communicate, including some abilities once thought possible only for humans, such as forming concepts, displaying insight, using and creating tools, exhibiting numerical abilities, and transmitting cultural innovations. Chimpanzees have learned to communicate with humans by signing or by pushing buttons wired to a computer and have taught their skills to younger animals. Pygmy chimpanzees have learned to comprehend syntax, but only humans possess true language—the ability to master the verbal or signed expression of complex grammar.

Intelligence

10 What argues for and against considering intelligence as one general mental ability?

Factor analysis is a statistical procedure that has revealed some underlying commonalities in different mental abilities. Spearman named this common factor the g factor for *general intelligence (g).* Gardner views *intelligence* as multiple abilities forming at least eight different aptitudes—linguistic, logical-mathematical, musical, spatial, bodily-kinesthetic, intrapersonal, interpersonal, and naturalist. Sternberg proposes a triarchic theory of three intelligences—analytical, creative, and practical.

11 What is creativity, and what fosters it?

Creativity is the ability to produce novel and valuable ideas. An intelligence test score of about 120 correlates with creativity but does not guarantee it. Expertise, imaginative thinking skills, a venturesome personality, intrinsic motivation, and the support offered by a creative environment are important components of creativity.

12 What makes up emotional intelligence?

Those with *emotional intelligence* are able to perceive, understand, manage, and use emotions, and they tend to achieve greater personal and professional success. However, critics question whether we stretch the idea of intelligence too far when we apply it to emotions.

13 When and why were intelligence tests created?

Binet started the modern *intelligence-testing* movement in France in 1904 by developing questions to predict children's future progress in the Paris school system. Terman's *Stanford-Binet* test revised Binet's work for use in the United States. More than Binet, Terman believed intelligence is inherited, and that test scores could be used to guide people toward appropriate opportunities. Weschler created the tests that are now most widely used—the *WAIS* and WISC. These and other psychological tests must meet three criteria to be useful. They must be *standardized, reliable,* and *valid.* Scores on a standardized test usually form a *normal curve.*

14 What does evidence reveal about hereditary and environmental influences on intelligence?

The *heritability* of intelligence is about 50 percent—this is the proportion of variation among individuals that can be attributed to genes. Genes and environment interact to influence intelligence. The effect of heredity can be seen in the intelligence test scores of family members, such as (a) fraternal twins raised together (more similar scores than those of other siblings), (b) identical twins raised together (nearly identical scores), and (c) identical twins raised apart (very slightly less similar than the scores of identical twins raised together). Other studies, of children from extremely impoverished environments or of children placed in enriched educational programs, indicate that life experiences can influence intelligence test performance.

15 How and why do gender and racial groups differ in mental ability scores?

Males and females' average scores are nearly identical in overall intelligence. Psychologists debate evolutionary, brain-based, and cultural explanations for the small gender differences found in specific abilities. Girls are better spellers, more verbally fluent, better at locating objects, better at detecting emotions, and more sensitive to touch, taste, and color. Boys outperform girls at spatial ability and math problem solving, though girls outperform boys in math computation. Boys also outnumber girls at the low and high extremes of mental abilities. As a group, Whites score higher than their Hispanic and Black counterparts, though the gap is narrowing. The evidence suggests that environmental differences are largely, perhaps entirely, responsible for these group differences.

16 Are intelligence tests inappropriately biased?

Intelligence tests are "biased" in the sense that they are designed to detect developed abilities, which reflect cultural experiences such as education and life experience. But these tests are not biased in the way psychologists commonly use the term—the tests do not predict less accurately for one group than for another. *Stereotype threat,* a self-confirming concern that one will be evaluated based on a negative stereotype, affects performance on all kinds of tests.

Terms and Concepts to Remember

cognition, p. 291
concept, p. 291
prototype, p. 292
algorithm, p. 292
heuristic, p. 292
insight, p. 293
confirmation bias, p. 293
fixation, p. 294
mental set, p. 294
representativeness heuristic, p. 294
availability heuristic, p. 295
overconfidence, p. 296
belief perseverance, p. 297
intuition, p. 298
framing, p. 300

language, p. 302
babbling stage, p. 303
one-word stage, p. 303
two-word stage, p. 303
telegraphic speech, p. 303
linguistic determinism, p. 306
intelligence, p. 313
general intelligence *(g)*, p. 314
factor analysis, p. 314
savant syndrome, p. 314
creativity, p. 317
emotional intelligence, p. 318
intelligence test, p. 319
mental age, p. 319
Stanford-Binet, p. 319

intelligence quotient (IQ), p. 319
Wechsler Adult Intelligence Scale (WAIS), p. 320
standardization, p. 321
normal curve, p. 321
reliability, p. 321
validity, p. 322
content validity, p. 322
intellectual disability, p. 322
Down syndrome, p. 322
predictive validity, p. 323
heritability, p. 327
stereotype threat, p. 333

Test for Success: Critical Thinking Exercises

By Amy Himsel, El Camino College

1. Oscar describes his political beliefs as "strongly liberal," but he has decided to explore opposing viewpoints. How might this influence his thinking?

2. It's been said that the development of language can be compared to the growth of a flower. Explain how, using the theories of Skinner and Chomsky.

3. A Czech proverb says, "Learn a new language and get a new soul." To what extent is this true?

4. When asked to report his IQ, Nobel Prize-winning physicist Stephen Hawking responded, "I have no idea. People who boast about their IQ are losers." How important are intelligence test scores to success in life?

5. How could mental rehearsal help your performance in this class?

6. As society succeeds in creating equality of opportunity, it will also increase the heritability of ability. The heritability of intelligence scores will be greater in a society marked by equal opportunity than in a society of peasants and aristocrats. Why?

The Test for Success exercises offer you a chance to apply your critical thinking skills to aspects of the material you have just read. Suggestions for answering these questions can be found in Appendix D at the back of the book.

Multiple-choice self-tests and more may be found at www.worthpublishers.com/myers.

Chapter Outline

● **Motivational Concepts**
  Instincts and Evolutionary
    Psychology
  Drives and Incentives
  Optimum Arousal
  A Hierarchy of Motives

● **Hunger**
  The Physiology of Hunger
  The Psychology of Hunger
  Obesity and Weight Control
  CLOSE-UP: Eating Disorders
  CLOSE-UP: Waist Management

● **Sexual Motivation**
  The Physiology of Sex
  The Psychology of Sex
  Adolescent Sexuality
  Sexual Orientation
  Sex and Human Values

● **The Need to Belong**

10 : Motivation

"What's my motivation?" the actor asks the director. In our everyday conversation, "What motivated you to do *that*?" is a way of asking "What *caused* your behavior?" To psychologists, a **motivation** is a need or desire that *energizes* behavior and *directs* it toward a goal.

After an ill-fated Saturday morning in the spring of 2003, experienced mountaineer Aron Ralston understands the extent to which motivation can energize and direct behavior. Having bagged nearly all of Colorado's tallest peaks, many of them solo and in winter, Ralston ventured some solo canyon hiking that seemed so risk-free he didn't bother to tell anyone where he was going. In Utah's narrow Bluejohn Canyon, just 150 yards above his final rappel, he was climbing over an 800-pound rock when disaster struck: It shifted and pinned his right wrist and arm. He was, as the title of his book says, caught *Between a Rock and a Hard Place*.

Realizing no one would be rescuing him, Ralston tried with all his might to dislodge the rock. Then, with his dull pocket knife, he tried chipping away at the rock. When that, too, failed, he rigged up ropes to lift the rock. Alas, nothing worked. Hour after hour, then cold night after cold night, he was stuck.

By Tuesday, he had run out of food and water. On Wednesday, as thirst and hunger gnawed, he began saving and sipping his own urine. Using his video recorder, he said his good-byes to family and friends, for whom he now felt intense love: "So again love to everyone. Bring love and peace and happiness and beautiful lives into the world in my honor. Thank you. Love you."

On Thursday, surprised to find himself still alive, Ralston had a seemingly divine insight into his reproductive future, a vision of a preschool boy being scooped up by a one-armed man. With this inspiration, he summoned his remaining strength and his enormous will to live and, over the next hour, willfully broke his bones and then proceeded to use that dull knife to cut off his arm. The moment after putting on a tourniquet, chopping the last piece of skin, and breaking free—and before rappelling with his bleeding half-arm down a 65-foot cliff and hiking 5 miles until finding someone—he was, in his own words, "just reeling with this euphoria . . . having been dead and standing in my grave, leaving my last will and testament, etching 'Rest in peace' on the wall, all of that, gone and then replaced with having my life again. It was undoubtedly the sweetest moment that I will ever experience" (Ralston, 2004).

Ralston's thirst and hunger, his sense of belonging to others, and his brute will to live and become a father highlight motivation's energizing and directing power. In this chapter, we explore how such motives arise from the interplay between nature (the physiological "push") and nurture (the cognitive and cultural "pulls").

Motivation personified
Aron Ralston's motivation to live and belong energized and directed his sacrificing half of his arm.

AP Photo/Rocky Mountain News, Judy Walgren

"What do you think . . . should we get started on that motivation research or not?"

Motivational Concepts

1: From what perspectives do psychologists view motivated behavior?

Let's step back now and consider four perspectives psychologists have used in their attempt to understand motivated behaviors. *Instinct theory* (now replaced by the *evolutionary perspective*) focuses on genetically predisposed behaviors. *Drive-reduction theory* focuses on how our inner pushes and external pulls interact. *Arousal theory* focuses on finding the right level of stimulation. And Abraham Maslow's *hierarchy of needs* describes how some of our needs take priority over others.

Instincts and Evolutionary Psychology

Early in the twentieth century, as the influence of Charles Darwin's evolutionary theory grew, it became fashionable to classify all sorts of behaviors as instincts. If people criticized themselves, it was because of their "self-abasement instinct." If they boasted, it reflected their "self-assertion instinct." After scanning 500 books, one sociologist compiled a list of 5759 supposed human instincts! Before long, this fad for naming instincts collapsed under its own weight. Rather than *explaining* human behaviors, the early instinct theorists were simply *naming* them. It was like "explaining" a bright child's low grades by labeling the child an "underachiever." To name a behavior is *not* to explain it.

To qualify as an **instinct,** a complex behavior must have a fixed pattern throughout a species and be unlearned (Tinbergen, 1951). Such behaviors are common in other species (recall imprinting in birds in Chapter 5 and the return of salmon to their birthplace in Chapter 7). Human behavior, too, exhibits certain unlearned fixed patterns, including infants' innate reflexes for rooting and sucking. Most psychologists, though, view human behavior as directed both by physiological needs and by psychological wants.

Although instinct theory failed to explain human motives, the underlying assumption that genes predispose species-typical behavior remains as strong as ever in *evolutionary psychology* today. We saw this in Chapter 4's evolutionary explanation of our human similarities. We saw this again in Chapter 7's discussion of animals' biological predispositions to learn certain behaviors. We will see this in this chapter's exploration of how our hunger, our taste, and our sexuality enable our survival and reproduction. And we will see this in later discussions of how evolution might influence our phobias, our helping behaviors, and our romantic attractions.

Same motive, different wiring The more complex the nervous system, the more adaptable the organism. Both humans and Weaver birds satisfy their need for shelter in ways that reflect their inherited capacities. Human behavior is flexible; we can learn whatever skills we need to build a house. The bird's behavior pattern is fixed; it can build only this kind of nest.

Drives and Incentives

When the original instinct theory of motivation collapsed, it was replaced by **drive-reduction theory**—the idea that a physiological need creates an aroused state that drives the organism to reduce the need by, say, eating or drinking. With few exceptions, when a physiological need increases, so does a psychological *drive*—an aroused, motivated state.

The physiological aim of drive reduction is **homeostasis**—the maintenance of a steady internal state. An example of homeostasis (literally "staying the same") is the body's temperature-regulation system, which works like a room thermostat. Both systems operate through feedback loops: Sensors feed temperature to a control center. If the room temperature cools, the thermostat's controls trigger a switch that turns on the furnace. Likewise, if our body temperature cools, blood vessels constrict to conserve warmth, and we feel driven to put on more clothes or seek a warmer environment.

Not only are we *pushed* by our "need" to reduce drives, we also are *pulled* by **incentives**—positive or negative stimuli that lure or repel us. This is one way our individual learning influences our motives. Depending on our learning history, the aroma of fresh roasted peanuts or toasted ants can motivate our behavior. So can the sight of those we find attractive or threatening.

When there is both a need and an incentive, we feel strongly driven. The food-deprived person who smells baking bread feels a strong hunger drive. In the presence of that drive, the baking bread becomes a compelling incentive. For each motive, we can therefore ask, "How is it pushed by our inborn physiological needs and pulled by incentives in the environment?"

Optimum Arousal

We are much more than homeostatic systems, however. Some motivated behaviors actually *increase* arousal. Well-fed animals will leave their shelter to explore and gain information, seemingly in the absence of any need-based drive. Curiosity drives monkeys to monkey around trying to figure out how to unlock a latch that opens nothing or how to open a window that allows them to see outside their room (Butler, 1954). It drives the 9-month-old infant who investigates every accessible corner of the house. It drives the scientists whose work this text discusses. And it drives explorers and adventurers such as Aron Ralston and George Mallory. Asked why he wanted to climb Mount Everest, Mallory answered, "Because it is there." Those who, like Mallory and Ralston, enjoy high arousal are most likely to enjoy intense music, novel foods, and risky behaviors (Zuckerman, 1979).

In our drive to experience stimulation, we hunger for information. We are *infovores,* say neuroscientists Irving Biederman and Edward Vessel (2006), after identifying brain mechanisms that reward us for acquiring information. Lacking stimulation, we feel bored and look for a way to increase arousal to some optimum level. However, given too much stimulation, we feel stressed and look for a way to decrease arousal.

instinct a complex behavior that is rigidly patterned throughout a species and is unlearned.

drive-reduction theory the idea that a physiological need creates an aroused tension state (a drive) that motivates an organism to satisfy the need.

homeostasis a tendency to maintain a balanced or constant internal state; the regulation of any aspect of body chemistry, such as blood glucose, around a particular level.

incentive a positive or negative environmental stimulus that motivates behavior.

Driven by curiosity Baby monkeys and young children are fascinated by things they've never handled before. Their drive to explore the relatively unfamiliar is one of several motives that do not fill any immediate physiological need.

hierarchy of needs Maslow's pyramid of human needs, beginning at the base with physiological needs that must first be satisfied before higher-level safety needs and then psychological needs become active.

"Hunger is the most urgent form of poverty."

—Alliance to End Hunger, 2002

A Hierarchy of Motives

Some needs take priority over others. Having all your biological needs satisfied, you seek increased levels of arousal. But let your need for water go unsatisfied and your thirst will preoccupy you. Just ask Aron Ralston. If you were deprived of air, your thirst would disappear.

Abraham Maslow (1970) described these priorities as a **hierarchy of needs** (**FIGURE 10.1**). At the base of this pyramid are our physiological needs, such as those for food and water. Only if these needs are met are we prompted to meet our need for safety, and then to satisfy the uniquely human needs to give and receive love and to enjoy self-esteem. Beyond this, said Maslow (1971), lies the need to actualize one's full potential. (More on self-esteem and self-actualization in Chapter 12.)

Near the end of his life, Maslow proposed that some people also reach a level of self-transcendence. At the self-actualization level, people seek to realize their own potential. At the self-transcendence level, people strive for meaning, purpose, and communion that is beyond the self, that is *transpersonal* (Koltko-Rivera, 2006).

Maslow's hierarchy is somewhat arbitrary; the order of such needs is not universally fixed. People have starved themselves to make a political statement. Nevertheless, the simple idea that some motives are more compelling than others provides a framework for thinking about motivation. Life-satisfaction surveys in 39 nations support this basic idea (Oishi et al., 1999). In poorer nations that lack easy access to money and the food and shelter it buys, financial satisfaction more strongly predicts feelings of well-being. In wealthy nations, where most are able to meet basic needs, home-life satisfaction is a better predictor. Self-esteem matters most in individualist nations, whose citizens tend to focus more on personal achievements than on family and community identity.

Let's now consider three representative motives, beginning at the physiological level with hunger and working up through sexual motivation to the higher-level need to belong. At each level, we shall see how experience interacts with biology.

FIGURE 10.1 Maslow's hierarchy of needs Once our lower-level needs are met, we are prompted to satisfy our higher-level needs. (From Maslow, 1970.) For survivors of the disastrous 2007 Bangladeshi flood, such as this man carefully carrying his precious load of clean water, satisfying very basic needs for water, food, and safety become top priority. Higher-level needs on Maslow's hierarchy, such as those for respect, self-actualization, and meaning tend to become far less important during such times.

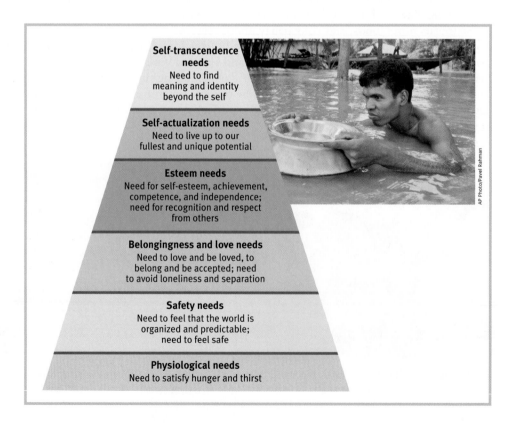

REHEARSE IT!

1. Today's evolutionary psychology shares an idea that was an underlying assumption of instinct theory. That idea is that
   a. physiological needs arouse psychological states.
   b. genes predispose species-typical behavior.
   c. physiological needs increase arousal.
   d. external needs energize and direct behavior.

2. In drive-reduction theory, the maintenance of a balanced internal state is called

   a. instinct.
   b. pursuit of stimulation.
   c. a hierarchy of needs.
   d. homeostasis.

3. _____theory attempts to explain behaviors that do NOT reduce physiological needs.
   a. Instinct
   b. Evolutionary
   c. Drive-reduction
   d. Arousal

4. The effects of external incentives, such as the smell of baking bread, are best explained in terms of

   a. biological needs.
   b. instinct.
   c. individual learning histories.
   d. homeostasis.

5. According to Maslow's hierarchy of needs, our most basic needs are physiological, including the need for food, water, and oxygen; just above these are _____ needs.
   a. safety
   b. self-esteem
   c. belongingness
   d. self-transcendence

Answers: 1. b, 2. d, 3. d, 4. c, 5. a.

Hunger

A vivid demonstration of the supremacy of physiological needs came from starvation experiences in World War II prison camps. David Mandel (1983), a Nazi concentration camp survivor, recalled how a starving "father and son would fight over a piece of bread. Like dogs." One father, whose 20-year-old son stole his bread from under his pillow while he slept, went into a deep depression, asking over and over how his son could do such a thing. The next day the father died. "Hunger does something to you that's hard to describe," Mandel explained.

To learn more about the results of semistarvation, a research team led by physiologist Ancel Keys (1950), the creator of World War II Army K rations, fed 36 male volunteers—all conscientious objectors to the war—just enough to maintain their initial weight. Then, for six months, they cut this food level in half. The effects soon became visible. Without thinking about it, the men began conserving energy; they appeared listless and apathetic. After dropping rapidly, their body weights eventually stabilized at about 25 percent below their starting weights. Especially dramatic were the psychological effects. Consistent with Maslow's idea of a needs hierarchy, the men became food-obsessed. They talked food. They daydreamed food. They collected recipes, read cookbooks, and feasted their eyes on delectable forbidden foods. Preoccupied with their unfulfilled basic need, they lost interest in sex and social activities. As one participant reported, "If we see a show, the most interesting part of it is contained in scenes where people are eating. I couldn't laugh at the funniest picture in the world, and love scenes are completely dull."

"Nobody wants to kiss when they are hungry."

—Dorothea Dix, 1801–1887

GARFIELD

glucose the form of sugar that circulates in the blood and provides the major source of energy for body tissues. When its level is low, we feel hunger.

"The full person does not understand the needs of the hungry."

—Irish proverb

The semistarved men's preoccupations illustrate how motives can hijack our consciousness. When we are hungry, thirsty, fatigued, or sexually aroused, little else may seem to matter. When we're not, food, water, sleep, or sex just doesn't seem like that big a thing in life, now or ever. (You may recall from Chapter 8 a parallel effect of our current good or bad mood on our memories.) In University of Amsterdam studies, Loran Nordgren and his colleagues (2006, 2007) found that people in a motivational "hot" state (from fatigue, hunger, or sexual arousal) become more aware of such feelings in their own past and as driving forces in others' behavior. Motives matter mightily. Grocery shop with an empty stomach and you are more likely to think that those jelly-filled doughnuts are just what you've always loved and will be wanting tomorrow.

The Physiology of Hunger

2: What physiological factors produce hunger?

Keys' semistarved volunteers felt their hunger in response to a homeostatic system designed to maintain normal body weight and an adequate nutrient supply. But what precisely triggers hunger? Is it the pangs of an empty stomach? To find out, A. L. Washburn, working with Walter Cannon (Cannon & Washburn, 1912), intentionally swallowed a balloon that, when inflated, filled his stomach and transmitted its contractions to a recording device (**FIGURE 10.2**). During this monitoring, Washburn pressed a key each time he felt hungry. The discovery: Washburn was indeed having stomach contractions whenever he felt hungry.

Would hunger persist without stomach pangs? To answer that question, researchers removed some rats' stomachs and attached their esophagi to their small intestines (Tsang, 1938). Did the rats continue to eat? Indeed they did. Some hunger persists similarly in humans whose ulcerated or cancerous stomachs have been removed.

If the pangs of an empty stomach are not the only trigger of hunger, what else matters?

Body Chemistry and the Brain

People and other animals automatically regulate their caloric intake to prevent energy deficits and maintain a stable body weight. This suggests that somehow, somewhere, the body is keeping tabs on its available resources. One such resource is the blood sugar **glucose.** Increases in the hormone *insulin* (secreted by the pancreas) diminish blood glucose, partly by converting it to stored fat. If your blood glucose level drops, you won't consciously feel this change. But your brain, which is automatically moni-

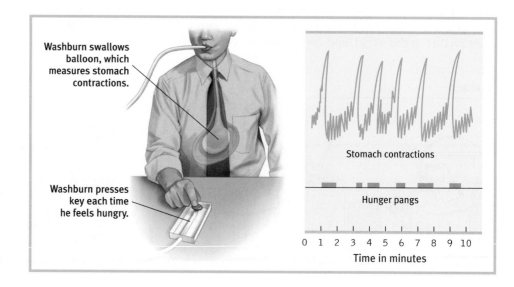

FIGURE 10.2 Monitoring stomach contractions Using this procedure, Washburn showed that stomach contractions (transmitted by the stomach balloon) accompany our feelings of hunger (indicated by a key press). (From Cannon, 1929.)

Washburn swallows balloon, which measures stomach contractions.

Washburn presses key each time he feels hungry.

Stomach contractions

Hunger pangs

0 1 2 3 4 5 6 7 8 9 10

Time in minutes

toring your blood chemistry and your body's internal state, will trigger hunger. Signals from your stomach, intestines, and liver (indicating whether glucose is being deposited or withdrawn) all signal your brain to motivate eating or not.

But how does the brain integrate and respond to these messages? More than a half-century ago, researchers began unraveling this puzzle when they located hunger controls within the *hypothalamus,* that small but complex neural traffic intersection deep in the brain (**FIGURE 10.3**).

Two distinct hypothalamic centers influence eating. Activity along the sides of the hypothalamus (the *lateral hypothalamus*) brings on hunger. If electrically stimulated there, well-fed animals begin to eat. (If the area is destroyed, even starving animals have no interest in food.) Recent research helps explain this behavior. When a rat is food-deprived, its blood sugar levels wane and the lateral hypothalamus churns out the hunger-triggering hormone *orexin.* When given orexin, rats become ravenously hungry (Sakurai et al., 1998).

Activity in the second center—the lower mid-hypothalamus (the *ventromedial hypothalamus*)—depresses hunger. Stimulate this area and an animal will stop eating; destroy it and the opposite occurs (Duggan & Booth, 1986; Hoebel & Teitelbaum, 1966). Rats with mid-hypothalamus lesions eat more often, produce more fat, and use less fat for energy, rather like a miser who runs every bit of extra money to the bank and resists taking any out (Pinel, 1993). This discovery helped explain why some patients with tumors near the base of the brain (in what we now realize is the hypothalamus) eat excessively and become very overweight (Miller, 1995).

In addition to producing orexin, the hypothalamus monitors levels of the body's other appetite hormones (**FIGURE 10.4**). *Ghrelin,* a hunger-arousing hormone, is secreted by an empty stomach. When people with severe obesity undergo surgery to seal off part of their stomach, the remaining stomach produces much less ghrelin, and their appetite lessens (Lemonick, 2002). *Obestatin,* a sister hormone to ghrelin,

FIGURE 10.3 The hypothalamus As we saw in Chapter 2, the hypothalamus (colored red) performs various body maintenance functions, including control of hunger. Blood vessels supply the hypothalamus, enabling it to respond to our current blood chemistry as well as to incoming neural information about the body's state.

Evidence for the brain's control of eating A lesion near the ventromedial area of the hypothalamus caused this rat to overeat, tripling its weight.

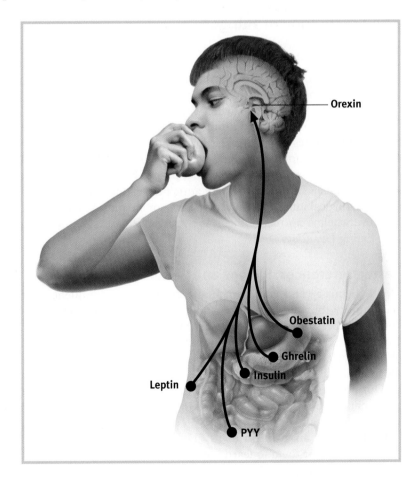

Orexin

Obestatin

Ghrelin

Insulin

Leptin

PYY

FIGURE 10.4 The appetite hormones
Insulin: Secreted by pancreas; controls blood glucose.
Orexin: Secreted by hypothalamus; triggers hunger.
Ghrelin: Secreted by empty stomach; sends "I'm hungry" signals to the brain.
Obestatin: Secreted by stomach; sends "I'm full" signals to the brain.
PYY: Secreted by digestive tract; sends "I'm *not* hungry" signals to the brain.
Leptin: Secreted by fat cells; sends signals to the brain diminishing the rewarding pleasure of food.

set point the point at which an individual's "weight thermostat" is supposedly set. When the body falls below this weight, an increase in hunger and a lowered metabolic rate may act to restore the lost weight.

basal metabolic rate the body's resting rate of energy expenditure.

Over the next 40 years you will eat about 20 tons of food. If, during those years you increase your daily intake by just .01 ounce more than required for your energy needs, you will gain 24 pounds (Martin et al., 1991).

sends out a fullness signal that suppresses hunger (Zhang et al., 2005). Other appetite-suppressants include *PYY,* a hormone secreted by the digestive tract, and *leptin,* a protein that is secreted by fat cells and acts to diminish the rewarding pleasure of food (Farooqi et al., 2007).

The complex interaction of appetite hormones and brain activity may help explain the body's apparent predisposition to maintain itself at a particular stable weight, or **set point** (Keesey & Corbett, 1983). When semistarved rats fall below their normal weight, this "weight thermostat" signals the body to restore the lost weight: Hunger increases and energy expenditure decreases. If body weight rises—as happens when rats are force-fed—hunger decreases and energy expenditure increases.

Heredity influences body type and set point, but our bodies also regulate weight by controlling food intake and energy output. At the end of their 24 weeks of semistarvation, the men who participated in Keys' experiment had stabilized at three-quarters of their normal weight, while taking in half their previous calories. How did they manage this? By reducing their energy expenditure, partly through inactivity but partly because of a 29 percent drop in their **basal metabolic rate**—the rate of energy expenditure for maintaining basic body functions when the body is at rest.

Noting that food intake and energy output are influenced by environment as well as biology, some researchers have abandoned the idea of a biologically fixed *set point* (Assanand et al., 1998). They point out that slow, sustained changes in body weight can alter set point, and that psychological factors also sometimes drive feelings of hunger. Given unlimited access to a wide variety of tasty foods, people and other animals tend to overeat and gain weight (Raynor & Epstein, 2001). For all these reasons, some psychologists use the term *settling point* to indicate the level at which a person's weight settles in response to caloric intake and expenditure.

The Psychology of Hunger

3: **What psychological and cultural factors influence hunger?**

Our eagerness to eat is indeed pushed by our physiological state—our body chemistry and hypothalamic activity. Yet there is more to hunger than meets the stomach. This was strikingly apparent when Paul Rozin and his trickster colleagues (1998) tested two patients who had no memory for events occurring more than a minute ago. If, 20 minutes after eating a normal lunch, the patients were offered another, both readily consumed it . . . and usually a third meal offered 20 minutes after the second was finished. This suggests that part of knowing when to eat is our memory of our last meal. As time passes, we anticipate eating again and start feeling hungry.

Psychological influences on eating behavior are most striking when the desire to be thin overwhelms normal homeostatic pressures. (Turn the next page to see Close-Up: Eating Disorders.)

Taste Preferences: Biology and Culture

Body chemistry and environmental factors together influence not only when we feel hungry, but also what we hunger for—our taste preferences. When feeling tense or depressed, do you crave starchy, carbohydrate-laden foods? Carbohydrates help boost levels of the neurotransmitter serotonin, which has calming effects. When stressed, even rats find it extra rewarding to scarf Oreos (Artiga et al., 2007; Boggiano et al., 2005).

Our preferences for sweet and salty tastes are genetic and universal. Other taste preferences are conditioned, as when people given highly salted foods develop a liking for excess salt (Beauchamp, 1987), or when people who have been sickened by a food develop an aversion to it. (The frequency of children's illnesses provides many chances for them to learn food aversions.)

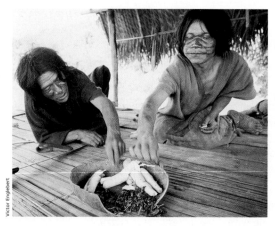

An acquired taste For Alaska Natives (left), but not for most other North Americans, whale blubber is a tasty treat. For these Campa Indians in Peru (right), roasted ants are similarly delicious. People everywhere learn to enjoy the foods prescribed by their culture.

Culture affects taste, too. Bedouins enjoy eating the eye of a camel, which most North Americans would find repulsive. But then North Americans and Europeans also shun horse, dog, and rat meat, all of which are prized elsewhere.

Rats tend to avoid unfamiliar foods (Sclafani, 1995). So do we, especially animal-based foods. Such *neophobia* (dislike of things unfamiliar) surely was adaptive for our ancestors, protecting them from potentially toxic substances. Nevertheless, in experiments people who repeatedly sample an initially novel fruit drink or ethnic food typically experience increasing appreciation for the new taste. Moreover, exposure to one set of novel foods increases a person's willingness to try another (Pliner, 1982; Pliner et al., 1993).

Other taste preferences are also adaptive. For example, the spices most commonly used in hot-climate recipes—where food, especially meat, spoils more quickly—inhibit the growth of bacteria (**FIGURE 10.5**). Pregnancy-related nausea is another example of adaptive taste preferences. Its associated food aversions peak about the tenth week, when the developing embryo is most vulnerable to toxins.

FIGURE 10.5 Hot cultures like hot spices Countries with hot climates, in which food historically spoiled more quickly, feature recipes with more bacteria-inhibiting spices (Sherman & Flaxman, 2001). India averages nearly 10 spices per meat recipe; Finland, 2 spices.

Obesity and Weight Control

4: **What factors predispose some people to become and remain obese?**

Why do some people gain weight while others eat the same amount and seldom add a pound? And why do so few overweight people win the battle of the bulge? Is there weight-loss hope for the 66 percent of Americans who, according to the Centers for Disease Control, are overweight?

Our bodies store fat for good reasons. Fat is an ideal form of stored energy—a high-calorie fuel reserve to carry the body through periods when food is scarce—a common occurrence in the feast-or-famine existence of our prehistoric ancestors. (Think of that spare tire around the middle as an energy storehouse—biology's counterpart to a hiker's waist-borne snack pack.) No wonder that wherever people haved faced famine—whether in developing societies today, or in Europe in earlier centuries—obesity has signaled affluence and social status (Furnham & Baguma, 1994).

Close-Up:

Eating Disorders

Our bodies are naturally disposed to maintain a normal weight, including stored energy reserves for times when food becomes unavailable. Yet sometimes psychological influences overwhelm biological wisdom. This becomes painfully clear in three eating disorders.

- **Anorexia nervosa** typically begins as a weight-loss diet. People with anorexia—usually adolescents and 3 out of 4 times females—drop significantly (typically 15 percent or more) below normal weight. Yet they feel fat, fear gaining weight, and remain obsessed with losing weight. About half display a binge-purge-depression cycle. Anorexia sufferers often have low self-evaluations, set perfectionist standards, fret about falling short of expectations, and are intensely concerned with how others perceive them (Pieters et al., 2007; Polivy & Herman,

Dying to be thin Anorexia was identified and named in the 1870s, when it appeared among affluent adolescent girls (Brumberg, 2000). This 1930s photo illustrates the physical condition.

2002; Striegel-Moore et al., 1993, 2007). Some of these factors also predict teen boys' pursuit of unrealistic muscularity (Ricciardelli & McCabe, 2004).

- Unlike anorexia, **bulimia nervosa** is marked by weight fluctuations within or above normal ranges, making the condition easy to hide. It, too, may be triggered by a weight-loss diet, broken by gorging on forbidden foods, sometimes in the company of friends who are also bingeing (Crandall, 1988). In a repeating cycle, overeating is followed by compensatory purging (through vomiting, laxative use), fasting, or excessive exercise (Wonderlich et al., 2007). Craving sweet and high-fat foods but fearful of becoming overweight, binge-purge eaters—mostly women in their late teens or early twenties—experience bouts of depression and anxiety, most severe during and following binges (Hinz & Williamson, 1987; Johnson et al., 2002).
- **Binge-eating disorder** is characterized by significant binge eating, followed by remorse—but not by purging, fasting, or excessive exercising.

A national study funded by the U.S. National Institute of Mental Health reports that, at some point during their lifetime, 0.6 percent of people meet the criteria for anorexia, 1 percent for bulimia, and 2.8 percent for binge-eating disorder (Hudson et al., 2007). So, how can we explain these disorders?

Genetics may influence susceptibility to eating disorders. Twins are somewhat more likely to share the disorder if they are identical rather than fraternal (Fairburn et al., 1999; Kaplan, 2004). In

follow-up molecular studies, scientists are searching for culprit genes, which may influence the body's available serotonin and estrogen (Klump & Culbert, 2007). But these disorders also have environmental components.

Eating disorders do *not* provide (as some have speculated) a telltale sign of childhood sexual abuse (Smolak & Murnen, 2002; Stice, 2002). However, the family environment may provide a fertile ground for the growth of eating disorders in other ways.

- Mothers of girls with eating disorders tend to focus on their own weight and on their daughters' weight and appearance (Pike & Rodin, 1991).
- Families of bulimia patients have a higher-than-usual incidence of childhood obesity and negative self-evaluation (Jacobi et al., 2004).
- Families of anorexia patients tend to be competitive, high-achieving, and protective (Pate et al., 1992; Yates, 1989, 1990).

Other environmental components include culture and gender. Body ideals, for example, vary across culture and time. In India, women students rate their ideal shape as close to their actual shape. In much of Africa—where plumpness means prosperity and thinness can signal poverty, AIDS, and hunger—bigger seems better (Knickmeyer, 2001).

Bigger does not seem better in Western cultures, where, according to 222 studies of 141,000 people, the rise in eating disorders over the last 50 years has coincided with a dramatic increase in women having a poor body image (Feingold & Mazzella, 1998). In one national survey, nearly one-half of all U.S. women reported feeling negative

In those parts of the world where food and sweets are now abundantly available, the rule that once served our hungry distant ancestors *(When you find energy-rich fat or sugar, eat it!)* has become dysfunctional.

Pretty much everywhere this book is being read, people have a growing problem. Worldwide, more than 1 billion people are overweight (WHO, 2007), and 300 million

about their appearance and preoccupied with being or becoming overweight (Cash & Henry, 1995).

Gender differences in body image have surfaced in several studies. In one study of New Zealand university students and 3500 British bank and university staff, men were more likely to *be* overweight and women were more likely to *perceive* themselves as overweight (Emslie et al., 2001; Miller & Halberstadt, 2005). In another study at the University of Michigan, men and women donned either a sweater or a swimsuit and completed a math test while alone in a changing room (Fredrickson et al., 1998). For the women but not the men, wearing the swimsuit triggered self-consciousness and shame that disrupted their math performance. That surely explains why a survey of 52,677 adults found that 16 percent of men and 31 percent of women avoid wearing a swimsuit in public (Frederick et al., 2006). In another informal survey of 60,000 people, 9 in 10 women said they would rather have a perfect body than have a mate with a perfect body; 6 of 10 men preferred the reverse (Lever, 2003).

Those most vulnerable to eating disorders are also those (usually women) who most idealize thinness and have the greatest body dissatisfaction (Striegel-Moore & Bulik, 2007). In one study, some adolescent girls (but not others) received a 15-month subscription to a U.S. teen-fashion magazine. Compared with their counterparts who had not received the magazine, girls defined as vulnerable—as already dissatisfied, idealizing thinness, and lacking social support—exhibited increased body dissatisfaction and eating disorder tendencies (Stice et al., 2001).

Viewing real and doctored images of unnaturally thin models and celebrities, women often feel ashamed, depressed, and dissatisfied with their own bodies—the very attitudes that predispose eating disorders (Grabe et al., 2008). But even ultra-thin models do not reflect the impossible standard of the classic Barbie doll, who had, when adjusted to a height of 5 feet 7 inches, a 32–16–29 figure (in centimeters, 82–41–73) (Norton et al., 1996).

It seems clear that the sickness of today's eating disorders lies in part within our weight-obsessed culture—a culture that says, in countless ways, "Fat is bad," that motivates millions of women to be "always dieting," and that encourages eating binges by pressuring women to live in a constant state of semistarvation.

"Skeletons on parade" A recent article used this headline in criticizing superthin models. Do such models make self-starvation fashionable?

> **"Why do women have such low self-esteem? There are many complex psychological and societal reasons, by which I mean Barbie."**
>
> —Dave Barry, 1999

"Thanks, but we don't eat."

If cultural learning contributes to eating disorders, then might prevention programs increase acceptance of one's body? From their review of 66 prevention studies, Eric Stice and his colleagues (2007) answer *yes*, especially if the programs are interactive and focused on girls over age 15.

---

anorexia nervosa an eating disorder in which a person (usually an adolescent female) diets and becomes significantly (15 percent or more) underweight, yet, still feeling fat, continues to starve.

bulimia nervosa an eating disorder characterized by episodes of overeating, usually of high-calorie foods, followed by vomiting, laxative use, fasting, or excessive exercise.

---

binge-eating disorder significant binge-eating episodes, followed by distress, disgust, or guilt, but without the compensatory purging, fasting, or excessive exercise that marks bulimia nervosa.

---

of them are clinically *obese* (defined as a body mass index of 30 or more—see **FIGURE 10.6** on the next page). The U.S. adult obesity rate has more than doubled in the last 40 years, reaching 34 percent, and child-teen obesity has quadrupled (CDC, 2007; NCHS, 2007). Australia classifies 54 percent of its population as overweight or obese, with Canada close behind at 49 percent, and France at 42 percent (Australian

> **"If we do nothing, in a few years the French will be as fat as Americans."**
>
> —Olivier Andrault, food expert with the French Union of Consumers, 2007

FIGURE 10.6 Obesity measured as body mass index (BMI) U.S. government guidelines encourage a BMI under 25. The World Health Organization and many countries define *obesity* as a BMI of 30 or more (although muscular bodies may also have a high BMI). The shading in this graph is based on BMI measurements for these heights and weights. BMI is calculated by using the following formula:

$$\frac{\text{Weight in kg (pounds} \times .45)}{\text{Squared height in meters (inches} \div 39.4)^2} = \text{BMI}$$

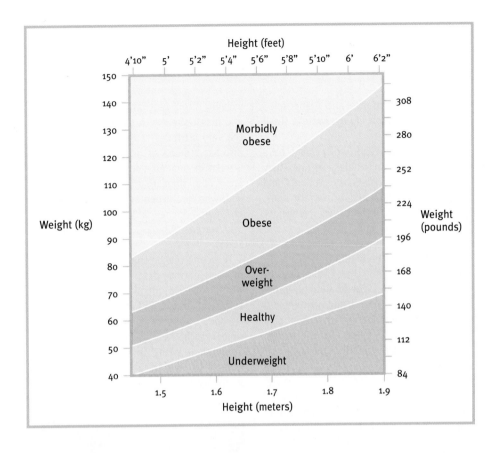

Obesity sterotype: "The [obesity lawsuit] bill says, 'Don't run off and file a lawsuit if you are fat.' It says, 'Look in the mirror because you're the one to blame.'"

—U.S. Senator F. James Sensenbrenner, 2004

Bureau of Statistics, 2007; Statistics Canada, 2007). In all these and many other countries, rising obesity rates trail the U.S. rates by just a few years and are projected to increase further, resulting in a "global epidemic" of diabetes (Yach et al., 2006).

Fitness matters more than being obese, which poses only modest health risks (Dolan et al., 2007; Gibbs, 2005). But significant obesity increases the risk of diabetes, high blood pressure, heart disease, gallstones, arthritis, and certain types of cancer (Olshansky et al., 2005). The risks are greater for apple-shaped people who carry their weight in pot bellies than for pear-shaped people with ample hips and thighs (Greenwood, 1989; Price et al., 2006). Research also links women's obesity to their risk of late-life Alzheimer's disease and brain tissue loss (Gustafson et al., 2003, 2004).

Not surprisingly, then, one 14-year study (Calle et al., 1999) of more than 1 million Americans revealed that being significantly overweight can cut life short. Those overweight at age 40 die three years earlier than their slim counterparts, reports another long-term study (Peeters et al., 2003). The death rate is especially high among very overweight men. Understandably, in 2004 the U.S. Medicare system began recognizing obesity as an illness. And in 2008 in Japan, a new national law mandated waistline measurements as part of annual checkups for those ages 40 to 74, with dieting guidance and re-education for those persistently over 33.5 inches for men and 35.4 inches for women (Onishi, 2008).

The Social Effects of Obesity

Obesity can also be socially toxic, by affecting both how you are treated and how you feel about yourself. Obese people know the stereotype: slow, lazy, and sloppy (Crandall, 1994, 1995; Ryckman et al., 1989). Widen people's images on a video monitor (making them look fatter) and observers suddenly rate them as less sincere, less friendly, meaner, and more obnoxious (Gardner & Tockerman, 1994). The

social effects of obesity were clear in a study that followed 370 obese 16- to 24-year-old women (Gortmaker et al., 1993). When restudied seven years later, two-thirds of the women were still obese. They also were making less money—$7000 a year less—than an equally intelligent comparison group of some 5000 nonobese women. And they were less likely to be married. In personal ads, men often state their preference for, and women often advertise, slimness (Miller et al., 2000; Smith et al., 1990).

Regina Pingitore and her colleagues (1994) demonstrated weight discrimination in a clever experiment. They filmed mock job interviews in which professional actors appeared either as normal-weight or as overweight applicants (wearing makeup and prostheses to make them look 30 pounds heavier). When appearing overweight, the same person—using the same lines, intonations, and gestures—was rated less worthy of hiring (**FIGURE 10.7**). The weight bias was especially strong against women. Other studies reveal that weight discrimination, though hardly discussed, is greater than race and gender discrimination. It occurs at every stage of the employment cycle—hiring, placement, promotion, compensation, discipline, and discharge—and is, indeed, much more likely to affect women (Roehling et al., 1999, 2007). Anti-fat prejudice even extends to applicants who are *seen* with an obese person (Hebl & Mannix, 2003)! This prejudice appears early. Children scorn fat children and express less liking of normal-weight children who are seen with an obese child (Penny & Haddock, 2007; Puhl & Latner, 2007).

Obesity has been associated with lower psychological well-being in Western cultures, especially among women, and with a 25 percent increase in depression and anxiety (Bookwala & Boyar, 2008; Petry et al., 2008; Simon et al., 2006). In studies of patients who had been especially unhappy with their weight and had lost an average of 100 pounds after short-cutting digestion with intestinal bypass surgery, 4 in 5 said their children had asked them not to attend school functions. And 9 in 10 said they would rather have a leg amputated than be obese again (Rand & Macgregor, 1990, 1991).

Why don't obese people drop their excess baggage and free themselves of all this pain? An answer lies in the physiology of fat.

The Physiology of Obesity

Research on the physiology of obesity challenges the stereotype of severely overweight people being weak-willed gluttons. First, consider the arithmetic of weight gain: People get fat by consuming more calories than they expend. The energy equivalent of a pound of fat is 3500 calories; therefore, dieters have been told they will lose a pound for every 3500-calorie reduction in their diet. Surprise: This conclusion is false. (Read on.)

FAT CELLS The immediate determinants of body fat are the size and number of fat cells. A typical adult has 30 to 40 billion of these miniature fuel tanks, half of which lie near the skin's surface. A fat cell can vary from relatively empty, like a deflated balloon, to overly full. In an obese person, fat cells may swell to two or three times their normal size and then divide or trigger nearby immature fat cells to divide—resulting in up to 75 billion fat cells (Hirsch, 2003). Once the number of fat cells increases—due to genetic predisposition, early childhood eating patterns, or adult overeating—it never decreases (**FIGURE 10.8**). During a diet, fat cells may shrink, but their number does not (Sjöstrum, 1980; Spalding et al., 2008).

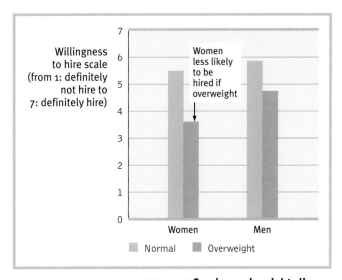

FIGURE 10.7 **Gender and weight discrimination** When women applicants were made to look overweight, university students were less willing to think they would hire them. Among men applicants, weight mattered less. (Data from Pingitore et al., 1994.)

"For fat students, the school experience is one of almost constant harassment."

—Report on Size Discrimination, National Education Association, 1994

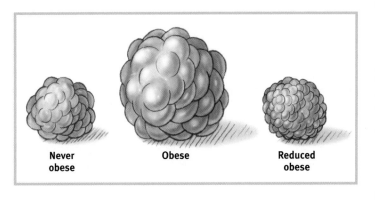

FIGURE 10.8 **Fat cells** We store energy in fat cells, which become larger and more numerous if we are obese, and smaller (but still more numerous) if we then lose weight. (Adapted from Jules Hirsch, 2003.)

SET POINT AND METABOLISM Once we become fat, we require less food to maintain our weight than we did to attain it. Why? Because compared with other tissue, fat has a lower metabolic rate—it takes less food energy to maintain. When an overweight person's body drops below its previous set point (or settling point), the person's hunger increases and metabolism decreases. Thus, the body adapts to starvation by burning off fewer calories.

In a classic month-long experiment (Bray, 1969), obese patients whose daily food intake was reduced from 3500 to 450 calories lost only 6 percent of their weight—partly because their bodies reacted as though they were being starved, and their metabolic rates dropped about 15 percent (**FIGURE 10.9**). That is why reducing your food intake by 3500 calories may not reduce your weight by 1 pound. That is also why further weight loss comes slowly following the rapid losses during the initial three weeks or so of a rigorous diet. And that is why amounts of food that worked to maintain weight before a diet began may increase it when a diet ends— the body is still conserving energy. Given two people who weigh and look the same, the formerly overweight one will likely need to eat fewer calories to maintain that weight than will the never-overweight one. (Who said life is fair?)

Thirty years after the Bray study, researchers performed a reverse experiment (Levine et al., 1999). They overfed volunteers an extra 1000 calories a day for eight weeks. Those who gained the least weight tended to spend the extra caloric energy by fidgeting more. Lean people are naturally disposed to fidget and move about more, and to burn more calories, than are energy-conserving overweight people who tend to sit still longer, report James Levine and his colleagues (2005). (How did the

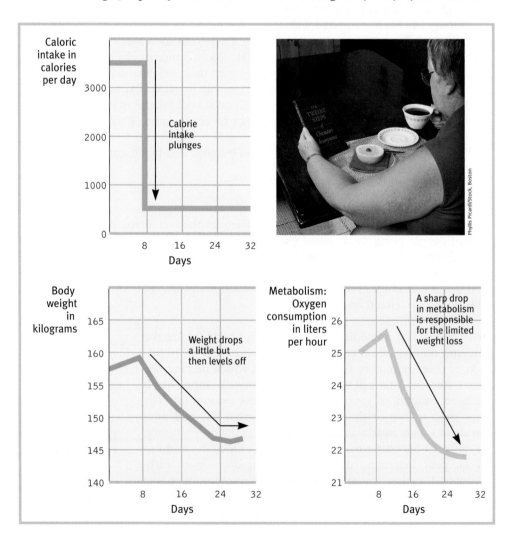

FIGURE 10.9 The effects of a severe diet on obese patients' body weight and metabolism After 7 days on a 3500-calorie diet, six obese patients were given only 450 calories a day for the next 24 days. Body weight declined only 6 percent and then leveled off, because metabolism dropped about 15 percent. (From Bray, 1969.)

researchers know this? They outfitted people with undergarments that for 10 days monitored their movements every half-second.) These individual differences in resting metabolism help explain why two people of the same height, age, and activity level can maintain the same weight, even if one of them eats much less than the other does.

GENETIC INFLUENCES Do our genes predispose us to fidget or sit still? Possibly. Studies do reveal a genetic influence on body weight. Consider:

- Despite shared family meals, adoptive siblings' body weights are uncorrelated with one another or with those of their adoptive parents. Rather, people's weights resemble those of their biological parents (Grilo & Pogue-Geile, 1991).
- Identical twins have closely similar weights, even when reared apart (Plomin et al., 1997; Stunkard et al., 1990). Across studies, their weight correlates +.74. The much lower +.32 correlation among fraternal twins suggests that genes explain two-thirds of our varying body mass (Maes et al., 1997).
- Given an obese parent, a boy is three times, and a girl six times, more likely to be obese than their counterparts with normal-weight parents (Carrière, 2003).
- Scientists have discovered many different genes that influence body weight. One gene scan of 40,000 people worldwide identified a variant of a gene called *FTO*, which nearly doubles the risk of becoming obese (Flier & Maratos-Flier, 2007; Frayling et al., 2007). Researchers hope that identifying such culprit genes will lead them to the trail of the hunger-signaling proteins encoded by those genes.

So, the specifics of our genes predispose the size of our jeans. But the genetic influence is surely complex, with different genes, like differing band members, making music by playing together. Some genes might influence when our intestines signal "full," with others dictating how efficiently we burn calories or convert extra calories to fat, and, yes, still others prompting us to fidget or sit still.

Environmental Influences on Obesity

Genes tell an important part of the obesity story. But research reveals that environmental factors are mighty important, too.

Social influence is one such factor. One research team followed the social networks of 12,067 people whom they had closely studied for 32 years (Christakis & Fowler, 2007). Their discovery: People were most likely to become obese when a friend became obese. If that friend was a close mutual friend, the odds almost tripled. Moreover, the correlation among friends' weights was not simply a matter of seeking out similar people as friends. Friends matter.

Sleep loss also matters. Studies in France, Japan, Spain, the United States, and Switzerland show that children and adults who skimp on sleep are more vulnerable to obesity (Keith et al., 2006; Taheri, 2004a,b). With sleep deprivation, the levels of leptin (which reports body fat to the brain) fall and ghrelin (the stomach hormone that stimulates appetite) rise.

The strongest evidence that environment influences weight comes from our fattening world. Although the developed nations lead the trend, people *across the globe* are getting heavier. Since 1989, the percentage of overweight people in Mexico has expanded from 1 in 10 to today's nearly 7 in 10 (Popkin, 2007). Changing *activity levels* are partly to blame, as activity-inhibiting TV watching spreads across the world. One massive long-term study of 50,000 North American nurses found—even after controlling for exercise, smoking, age, and diet—that each two-hour increase in daily TV watching predicted a 23 percent obesity increase and a 7 percent diabetes increase (Hu et al., 2003). Energy-saving tools, trucks, and cars also play a role. Among Ontario's Old Order Amish, where farming and gardening is labor intensive and pedometers reveal that men walk nine miles a day and women seven miles, the obesity rate is one-seventh the U.S. rate (Bassett et al., 2004). And within the United States, people living in walking-dependent communities such as Manhattan tend to weigh less than more sedentary folks in car-dependent suburbs (Ewing et al., 2003).

Too much food, and too little It is ironic that in a world where 800 million still live with hunger, obesity rates continue to rise in Western countries, endangering the lives of the severely overweight (Pinstrup-Andersen & Cheng, 2007; Popkin, 2007).

Western cultures have become like animal feedlots (where farmers fatten inactive animals). But *food consumption* patterns are also changing, as sugar-laden soft drinks, energy-rich cooking oils, and ever-larger portions of high-calorie foods compound inactivity. Compared with their counterparts in the early 1900s, North Americans are eating a higher-fat, higher-sugar diet, expending fewer calories, and suffering higher rates of diabetes at younger ages (Popkin, 2007). Just since 1971, women are eating 300 more calories a day and men nearly 200 calories more (O'Connor, 2004). And they are eating three times as many meals in fast-food restaurants (Farley & Cohen, 2001). Small wonder that your parents and grandparents at age 30 likely weighed less than you did or will. Since 1960, the average adult American has grown one inch and gained 23 pounds (Ogden et al., 2004).

Today's teens consume twice as much soda as milk—the reverse of a quarter-century ago (Brownell & Nestle, 2004). And when it's time for college, they'll find limitless soft drinks in campus food buffets, along with multiple serving stations offering all-you-can-eat entrees and make-your-own waffles (Brody, 2003). For many, the understandable result will be the "freshman 5" (Holm-Denoma et al., 2008).

Taken together, Big Macs, Double Whoppers, sugar-laden drinks, sleep loss, and inactivity form a weapon of mass destruction. And they've produced a new "bottom" line: Stadiums, theaters, and subway cars are widening their own seats to accommodate this population growth (Hampson, 2000). Washington State Ferries abandoned a 50-year-old standard of 18 inches per person: "Eighteen-inch butts are a thing of the past," explained a spokesperson (Shepherd, 1999). New York City, facing a large problem with Big Apple bottoms, has mostly replaced 17.5-inch bucket-style subway seats with bucketless seats (Hampson, 2000). In the end, today's people need more room.

If the changing environment explains the expanding obesity problem, then environmental reform is part of the remedy, reasoned the 53 European health ministers who signed a new World Health Organization anti-obesity charter (Cheng, 2006). The charter beckons the private sector to "substantially reduce" its advertising of fatty, sugary foods to children and commits governments to increasing the availability of healthy foods and roadways that promote cycling and walking. Psychologist Kelly Brownell (2002) has campaigned for these and other U.S. environmental reforms, such as establishing a fast-food–free zone around schools and slapping a "Twinkie Tax" (modeled on existing cigarette taxes) on calorie-laden junk food and soft drinks, with revenues used to subsidize healthy foods and to finance health-supportive nutritional advertising.

Note how research on global obesity reinforces a familiar lesson from Chapter 9's study of intelligence: There can be high levels of heritability (genetic influence on individual differences) without heredity explaining group differences. Genes mostly determine why one person today is heavier than another. Environment mostly determines why people today are heavier than their counterparts 50 years ago. Our eating behavior again demonstrates the familiar interaction among biological, psychological, and social-cultural factors.

Losing Weight

Perhaps you are shaking your head: "Slim chance I have of becoming and staying thin. If I lose weight on a diet, my metabolism slows and my hungry fat cells cry out, 'Feed me!' I'm fated for fat!" Indeed, the condition of an obese person's body reduced to average weight is much like that of a semistarved body. Held under its normal settling point, the body "thinks" it is starving. Having lost weight, formerly obese people look normal, but their fat cells may be abnormally small, their metabolism slowed, and their minds obsessed with food.

A losing battle Ryan Benson lost 122 pounds to win the first season of the TV reality show, *The Biggest Loser*. But then, like so many, he found maintaining the loss an even bigger challenge.

The battle of the bulge rages on as intensely as ever, and it is most intense among those with two X chromosomes. Nearly two-thirds of women and half of men say they want to lose weight; about half of those women and men say they are "seriously trying" (Moore, 2006). Asked if they would rather "be five years younger or weigh 15 pounds less," 29 percent of men and 48 percent of women said they would prefer losing the weight (Responsive Community, 1996).

With fat cells, settling points, metabolism, and genetic and environmental factors all tirelessly conspiring against shedding excess pounds, what advice can psychology offer these people? Perhaps the most important point is that permanent weight loss is not easy. Millions can vouch that it is possible to lose weight; they have done it lots of times. But short of drastic surgery to tie off part of the stomach and small intestine, most who succeed on a weight-loss program eventually regain the lost weight or more (Mann et al., 2007).

Those who do manage to keep pounds off set realistic and moderate goals, undertaking programs that modify their life-style and ongoing eating behavior. They realize that being moderately heavy is less risky than being extremely thin (Ernsberger & Koletsky, 1999). They lose weight gradually: "A reasonable time line for a 10 percent reduction in body weight is six months," advised the National Institutes of Health (1998). And they exercise regularly. For other helpful hints, see Close-Up: Waist Management, on the next page.

"Some people daydream heroic deeds or sex scenes or tropical vacations. I daydream crab legs dipped in hot butter."

—Judith Moore, *Fat Girl,* 2005

REHEARSE IT!

6. Hunger occurs in response to high blood insulin and
a. high blood glucose and low levels of ghrelin.
b. low blood glucose and high levels of ghrelin.
c. a low basal metabolic rate.
d. a high basal metabolic rate.

7. According to set point theory, our body maintains itself at a particular weight level. This "weight thermostat" is an example of
a. homeostasis.
b. an eating disorder.
c. individual learning.
d. binge-purge episodes.

8. Which of the following is a genetically disposed response to food?
a. An aversion to eating cats and dogs
b. An interest in novel foods
c. A preference for sweet and salty foods
d. An aversion to carbohydrates

9. Which of the following statements is true of bulimia nervosa?
a. People with bulimia continue to want to lose weight even when they are underweight.
b. Bulimia is marked by weight fluctuations within or above normal ranges.
c. Bulimia patients often come from middle-class families that are competitive, high-achieving, and protective.

d. If one twin is diagnosed with bulimia, the chances of the other twin's sharing the disorder are greater if they are fraternal rather than identical twins.

10. Obese people find it very difficult to lose weight permanently. This is due to several factors, including the fact that
a. with dieting, fat cells shrink and then disappear.
b. the set point of obese people is lower than average.
c. with dieting, basal metabolic rate increases.
d. there is a genetic influence on body weight.

Answers: 6. b, 7. a, 8. c, 9. b, 10. d.

Close-Up:

Waist Management

People struggling with obesity are well advised to seek medical evaluation and guidance. For others who wish to take off a few pounds, researchers have offered these tips.

Begin only if you feel motivated and self-disciplined. For most people, permanent weight loss requires making a career of staying thin—a lifelong change in eating habits combined with gradually increased exercise.

Minimize exposure to tempting food cues. Keep tempting foods out of the house or out of sight. Shop only on a full stomach, and avoid the sweets and chips aisles. Eat simple meals, with only a few different foods; given more variety, people consume more.

Take steps to boost your metabolism. Inactive people are often overweight (**FIGURE 10.10**). In studies of thousands of young people ages 8 through 17, obesity was more common among those who watched the most TV (Andersen et al., 1998; Dietz & Gortmaker, 1985). Of course, overweight people may avoid activity, preferring to sit and watch TV. But the association between TV watching and obesity remained when many other factors were controlled, suggesting that inactivity and snacking while watching TV do contribute to obesity. The good news is that one of the few predictors of successful long-term weight loss is exercise, both during and after changing your eating patterns (Jeffery et al., 2000; McGuire et al., 1999; Wadden et al., 1998). Exercise, supported by 7 to 8 hours sleep a night, empties fat cells, builds muscle, speeds up metabolism, and helps lower your settling point (Bennett, 1995; Kolata, 1987; Thompson et al., 1982).

Eat healthy foods. Whole grains, fruits, vegetables, and healthy fats such as those found in olive oil and fish help regulate appetite and artery-clogging cholesterol (Taubes, 2001, 2002). Better crispy greens than Krispy Kremes.

A successful loser After losing 110 pounds, former Arkansas governor and U.S. presidential candidate Mike Huckabee posed with a girl who weighs what he lost. "Look at Huckabee," said his longtime adversary, former U.S. president Bill Clinton. "You've got to consume less and burn more. There is no other alternative. And to do that, you've got to change the culture."

Don't starve all day and eat one big meal at night. This eating pattern, common among overweight people, slows metabolism. Moreover, those who eat a balanced breakfast are, by late morning, more alert and less fatigued (Spring et al., 1992).

Beware of the binge. Especially for men, eating more slowly leads to eating less (Martin et al., 2007). Among people who do consciously restrain their eating, drinking alcohol or feeling anxious or depressed can unleash the urge to eat (Herman & Polivy, 1980). So can being distracted from monitoring your eating (Ward & Mann, 2000). (Ever notice that you eat more when out with friends?) Once the diet is broken, the person often thinks "What the heck" and then binges (Polivy & Herman, 1985, 1987). A lapse need not become a full collapse: Remember, most people occasionally lapse.

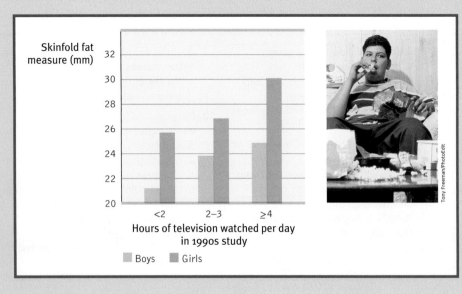

Skinfold fat measure (mm)

Hours of television watched per day in 1990s study

■ Boys   ■ Girls

FIGURE 10.10 American idle: Couch potatoes beware—TV watching correlates with obesity As life-styles have become more sedentary and TV watching has increased, so has the percentage of overweight people in Britain, North America, and elsewhere. When California children were placed in a TV-reduction educational program, they watched less—and lost weight (Robinson, 1999).

Sexual Motivation

Sex is part of life. Had this not been so for all your ancestors, you would not be reading this book. Sexual motivation is nature's clever way of making people procreate, thus enabling their genes' survival. When two people feel attracted, they hardly stop to think of themselves as guided by their genes. As the pleasure we take in eating is nature's inventive method of getting our body nourishment, so the desires and pleasures of sex are our genes' way of preserving and spreading themselves. Life is sexually transmitted.

The Physiology of Sex

Like hunger, sexual arousal depends on the interplay of internal and external stimuli. To understand sexual motivation, we must consider both.

The Sexual Response Cycle

5: **What stages mark the human sexual response cycle?**

In the 1960s, gynecologist-obstetrician William Masters and his collaborator Virginia Johnson (1966) made headlines by recording the physiological responses of volunteers who masturbated or had intercourse. With the help of 382 female and 312 male volunteers—a somewhat atypical sample, consisting only of people able and willing to display arousal and orgasm while being observed in a laboratory—Masters and Johnson monitored or filmed more than 10,000 sexual "cycles." Their description of the **sexual response cycle** identified four stages, similar in men and women. During the initial *excitement phase,* men's and women's genital areas become engorged with blood, a woman's vagina expands and secretes lubricant, and her breasts and nipples may enlarge.

In the *plateau phase,* excitement peaks as breathing, pulse, and blood pressure rates continue to increase. The penis becomes fully engorged and some fluid—frequently containing enough live sperm to enable conception—may appear at its tip. Vaginal secretion continues to increase, the clitoris retracts, and orgasm feels imminent.

Masters and Johnson observed muscle contractions all over the body during *orgasm;* these were accompanied by further increases in breathing, pulse, and blood pressure rates. A woman's arousal and orgasm facilitate conception by helping propel semen from the penis, positioning the uterus to receive sperm, and drawing the sperm further inward. A woman's orgasm therefore not only reinforces intercourse, which is essential to natural reproduction, it also increases retention of deposited sperm (Baker & Bellis, 1995). In the excitement of the moment, men and women are hardly aware of all this as their rhythmic genital contractions create a pleasurable feeling of sexual release.

The feeling apparently is much the same for both sexes. In one study, a panel of experts could not reliably distinguish between descriptions of orgasm written by men and those written by women (Vance & Wagner, 1976). University of Groningen neuroscientist Gerg Holstege and his colleagues (2003a,b) understand why. They discovered that when men and women undergo PET scans while having orgasms, the same subcortical brain regions glow. And when people who are passionately in love undergo fMRI (functional MRI) scans while viewing photos of their beloved or of a stranger, men's and women's brain responses to their partner are pretty similar (Fisher et al., 2002).

The body gradually returns to its unaroused state as the engorged genital blood vessels release their accumulated blood—relatively quickly if orgasm has occurred, relatively slowly otherwise. (It's like the nasal tickle that goes away rapidly if you have sneezed, slowly otherwise.) During this *resolution phase,* the male enters a **refractory period,** lasting from a few minutes to a day or more, during which he is incapable of

"I love the idea of there being two sexes, don't you?"

A nonsmoking 50-year-old male has about a 1-in-a-million chance of a heart attack during any hour. This increases to merely 2-in-a-million during the hour following sex (with no increase for those who exercise regularly). Compared with risks associated with heavy exertion or anger (see Chapter 11), this risk seems not worth losing sleep (or sex) over (Muller et al., 1996).

sexual response cycle the four stages of sexual responding described by Masters and Johnson—excitement, plateau, orgasm, and resolution.

refractory period a resting period after orgasm, during which a man cannot achieve another orgasm.

sexual disorder a problem that consistently impairs sexual arousal or functioning.

estrogens sex hormones, such as estradiol, secreted in greater amounts by females than by males and contributing to female sex characteristics. In nonhuman female mammals, estrogen levels peak during ovulation, promoting sexual receptivity.

testosterone the most important of the male sex hormones. Both males and females have it, but the additional testosterone in males stimulates the growth of the male sex organs in the fetus and the development of the male sex characteristics during puberty.

another orgasm. The female's much shorter refractory period may enable her to have more orgasms if restimulated during or soon after resolution.

Masters and Johnson sought not only to describe the human sexual response cycle but also to understand and treat the inability to complete it. **Sexual disorders** are problems that consistently impair sexual arousal or functioning. Some involve sexual motivation, especially lack of sexual energy and arousability. For men, others include *premature ejaculation* and *erectile dysfunction* (inability to have or maintain an erection). For women, the problem may be *orgasmic dysfunction* (infrequently or never experiencing orgasm). Most women who experience sexual distress relate it to their emotional relationship with the partner during sex, not to physical aspects of the activity (Bancroft et al., 2003).

Men or women with sexual disorders can often be helped by receiving therapy. In behaviorally oriented therapy, for example, men learn ways to control their urge to ejaculate, and women are trained to bring themselves to orgasm. Starting with the introduction of Viagra in 1998, erectile dysfunction has been routinely treated by taking a pill.

Hormones and Sexual Behavior

6: Do hormones influence human sexual motivation?

Sex hormones have two effects: They direct the physical development of male and female sex characteristics, and (especially in nonhuman animals) they activate sexual behavior. In most mammals, nature neatly synchronizes sex with fertility. The female becomes sexually receptive ("in heat") when secretion of the female hormones, the **estrogens** (such as estradiol), peaks during ovulation. In experiments, researchers can stimulate receptivity by injecting female animals with estrogen. Male hormone levels are more constant, and researchers cannot so easily manipulate the sexual behavior of male animals with hormones (Feder, 1984). Nevertheless, castrated male rats—having lost their testes, which manufacture the male sex hormone **testosterone**—gradually lose much of their interest in receptive females. They gradually regain it if injected with testosterone.

In humans, hormones more loosely influence sexual behavior, although sexual desire rises slightly at ovulation among women with mates (Pillsworth et al., 2004). One study invited partnered women not at risk for pregnancy to keep a diary of their sexual activity. (These women were either using intrauterine devices or had undergone surgery to prevent pregnancy.) On the days around ovulation, intercourse was 24 percent more frequent (Wilcox et al., 2004). Other studies find that women fantasize more about sex with desirable partners and wear more sexually attractive clothing around ovulation (Haselton et al., 2006; Pillsworth & Haselton, 2006; Sheldon et al., 2006). In a study of 5300 strip-club lap dancers, hourly tips almost doubled on the days near ovulation, compared with days during menstruation (Miller et al., 2007).

Women's sexuality differs from that of other mammalian females in being more responsive to testosterone level than to estrogen levels (Meston & Frohlich, 2000; Reichman, 1998). If a woman's natural testosterone level drops, as happens with removal of the ovaries or adrenal glands, her sexual interest may wane. But testosterone-replacement therapy sometimes restores diminished sexual appetite. That is the finding of experiments with hundreds of surgically or naturally menopausal women, for whom a testosterone-replacement patch restored sexual activity, arousal, and desire more than did a placebo (Braunstein et al., 2005; Buster et al., 2005; Davis et al., 2003; Kroll et al., 2004).

In men, normal fluctuations in testosterone levels, from man to man and hour to hour, have little effect on sexual drive (Byrne, 1982). Indeed, fluctuations in male hormones are partly a *response* to sexual stimulation. When James Dabbs and his colleagues (1987, 2000) had heterosexual male collegians converse separately with another male student and with a female student, the men's testosterone levels rose with the social arousal, but especially after talking with the female. Thus, sexual arousal can be a cause as well as a consequence of increased testosterone levels. At the other end of the mating spectrum, studies in both North America and China find that married fathers tend to have lower testosterone levels than do bachelors and married men without children (Gray et al., 2006).

Although normal short-term hormonal changes have little effect on men's and women's desire, large hormonal shifts over the life span have a greater effect. A person's interest in dating and sexual stimulation usually increases with the pubertal surge in sex hormones, as happens with male testosterone levels during puberty. If the hormonal surge is precluded—as it was during the 1600s and 1700s for prepubertal boys who were castrated to preserve their soprano voices for Italian opera—the normal development of sex characteristics and sexual desire does not occur (Peschel & Peschel, 1987). When adult men are castrated, sex drive typically falls as testosterone levels decline (Hucker & Bain, 1990). Male sex offenders taking Depo-Provera, a drug that reduces testosterone level to that of a prepubertal boy, similarly lose much of their sexual urge (Money et al., 1983).

In later life, as sex hormone levels decline, the frequency of sexual fantasies and intercourse declines as well (Leitenberg & Henning, 1995). For men with abnormally low testosterone levels, testosterone-replacement therapy often increases sexual desire and also energy and vitality (Yates, 2000).

To summarize: We might compare human sex hormones, especially testosterone, to the fuel in a car. Without fuel, a car will not run. But if the fuel level is minimally adequate, adding more fuel to the gas tank won't change how the car runs. The analogy is imperfect, because hormones and sexual motivation interact. However, the analogy correctly suggests that biology is a necessary but not sufficient explanation of human sexual behavior. The hormonal fuel is essential, but so are the psychological stimuli that turn on the engine, keep it running, and shift it into high gear.

"Fill'er up with testosterone."

In a National Center for Health Statistics survey of adult Americans, using computer-assisted self-interviews that guaranteed privacy, nearly 98 percent of 30- to 59-year-olds reported having had sex (Fryar et al., 2007).

The Psychology of Sex

7 : **How do internal and external stimuli influence sexual motivation?**

Hunger and sex are different sorts of motivations. Hunger responds to a *need*. If we do not eat, we die. Sex is not in this sense a need. If we do not have sex, we may feel like dying, but we do not. Nevertheless, there are similarities between hunger and sexual motivation. Both depend on internal physiological factors. And both are influenced by external and imagined stimuli, as well as cultural expectations (see **FIGURE 10.11** on the next page). Thus, despite the shared biology that underlies sexual motivation, the 281 expressed reasons for having sex (at last count) range widely—from "to get closer to God" to "to get my boyfriend to shut up" (Buss, 2008; Meston & Buss, 2007).

External Stimuli

Many studies confirm that men become aroused when they see, hear, or read erotic material. Surprising to many (because sexually explicit materials are sold mostly to men) is that most women—at least the less-inhibited women who volunteer to participate in such studies—report or exhibit nearly as much arousal to the same stimuli (Heiman, 1975; Stockton & Murnen, 1992). (Their brains do, however, respond differently, with fMRI scans revealing a more active amygdala in men viewing erotica [Hamann et al., 2004].)

People may find such arousal either pleasing or disturbing. (Those who find it disturbing often limit their exposure to such materials, just as those wishing to control

FIGURE 10.11 **Levels of analysis for sexual motivation** Compared with our motivation for eating, our sexual motivation is less influenced by biological factors. Psychological and social-cultural factors play a bigger role.

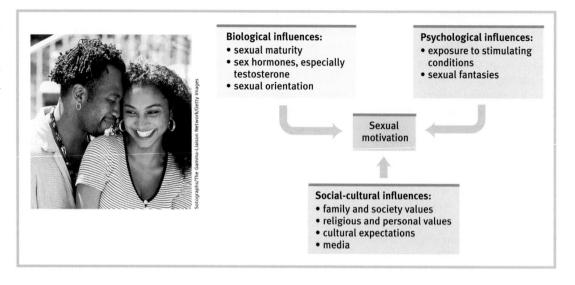

"There is no difference between being raped and being run over by a truck except that afterward men ask if you enjoyed it."

—Marge Piercy, "Rape Poem," 1976

Sexually explicit TV programs also divert attention from TV ads, making the ads more forgettable. Ads embedded in nonsexual and nonviolent programs more often produce memory for the products (Bushman & Bonacci, 2002).

hunger limit their exposure to tempting cues.) With repeated exposure, the emotional response to any erotic stimulus often lessens, or *habituates*. During the 1920s, when Western women's hemlines first reached the knee, an exposed leg was a mildly erotic stimulus, as were modest (by today's standards) two-piece swimsuits and movie scenes of a mere kiss.

Can sexually explicit material have adverse effects? Research indicates that it can. Depictions of women being sexually coerced—and enjoying it—tend to increase viewers' acceptance of the false idea that women enjoy rape, and they tend to increase male viewers' willingness to hurt women (Malamuth & Check, 1981; Zillmann, 1989). Viewing images of sexually attractive women and men may also lead people to devalue their own partners and relationships. After male collegians view TV or magazine depictions of sexually attractive women, they often find an average woman, or their own girlfriend or wife, less attractive (Kenrick & Gutierres, 1980; Kenrick et al., 1989; Weaver et al., 1984). Viewing X-rated sex films similarly tends to diminish people's satisfaction with their own sexual partner (Zillmann, 1989). Some sex researchers suspect that reading or watching erotica may create expectations that few men and women can fulfill.

Imagined Stimuli

The brain, it has been said, is our most significant sex organ. The stimuli inside our heads—our imagination—can influence sexual arousal and desire. People who, because of a spinal cord injury, have no genital sensation can still feel sexual desire (Willmuth, 1987).

Wide-awake people become sexually aroused not only by memories of prior sexual activities but also by fantasies. In one survey of masturbation-related fantasies (Hunt, 1974), 19 percent of women and 10 percent of men reported imagining being "taken" by someone overwhelmed with desire for them. Fantasy is not reality, however. To paraphrase Susan Brownmiller (1975), there's a big difference between fantasizing that Christian Bale just won't take no for an answer and having a hostile person actually force himself on you.

About 95 percent of both men and women say they have had sexual fantasies. Men (whether gay or straight) fantasize about sex more often, more physically, and less romantically. They also prefer less personal and faster-paced sexual content in books and videos (Leitenberg & Henning, 1995). Fantasizing about sex does *not* indicate a sexual problem or dissatisfaction. If anything, sexually active people have more sexual fantasies.

Adolescent Sexuality

8: **What factors influence teen pregnancy and risk of sexually transmitted infections?**

Sexual expression varies dramatically with time and culture. Among American women born before 1900, a mere 3 percent had experienced premarital sex by age 18 (Smith, 1998). In 2005, 47 percent of high school students acknowledged having had sexual intercourse (CDC, 2006). Teen intercourse rates are roughly similar in Western Europe and in Latin America but are much lower in Arab and Asian countries and among North Americans of Asian descent (McLaughlin et al., 1997; Wellings et al., 2006). Given the wide variation across time and place, it's no surprise that a recent twin study found that environmental factors accounted for almost three-fourths of the individual variation in age of sexual initiation (Bricker et al., 2006). Family and cultural values matter.

Teen Pregnancy

Sex during the teen years is often unprotected, leading to risks of pregnancy and *sexually transmitted infections* (*STIs;* also called *STDs* for *sexually transmitted diseases*). Compared with European teens, American teens have a lower rate of contraceptive use and thus a higher rate of teen pregnancy and abortion (Call et al., 2002). Why?

Ignorance One survey of Canadian teens revealed gaps in knowledge about sex and sexual health (Ipsos, 2006). For example, although 9 in 10 claimed to be knowledgeable, many were unaware that STIs can be transmitted through oral sex (which two-thirds had engaged in). Most teens also overestimate their peers' sexual activity, a misperception that may influence their own behavior (Child Trends, 2001). A World Health Organization report found that contraceptive sex education increases the "intention to practice safer sex," and may even *delay* "rather than hasten the onset of sexual activity" (Wellings et al., 2006).

Minimal communication about birth control Many teenagers are uncomfortable discussing contraception with their parents, partners, and peers. Teens who talk freely with parents and are in an exclusive relationship with a partner with whom they communicate openly are more likely to use contraceptives (Aspy et al., 2007; Milan & Kilmann, 1987).

Guilt related to sexual activity In one survey, 72 percent of sexually active 12- to 17-year-old American girls said they regretted having had sex (Reuters, 2000). Sexual inhibitions or ambivalence can reduce sexual activity, but they may also reduce attempts at birth control if passion overwhelms intentions (Gerrard & Luus, 1995; MacDonald & Hynie, 2008).

Alcohol use Sexually active teens are typically alcohol-using teens (Albert et al., 2003; CASA, 2004), and those who use alcohol prior to sex are less likely to use condoms (Kotchick et al., 2001). By depressing the brain centers that control judgment, inhibition, and self-awareness, alcohol tends to break down normal restraints, a phenomenon well known to sexually coercive males.

Mass media norms of unprotected promiscuity Media help write the "social scripts" that affect our perceptions and actions. So what sexual scripts do today's media write on our minds? An average hour of prime-time television on the three major U.S. networks contains approximately 15 sexual acts, words, and innuendos. The partners are usually unmarried, with no prior romantic relationship, and few communicate any concern for birth control or sexually transmitted infections (Brown et al., 2002; Kunkel, 2001; Sapolsky & Tabarlet, 1991). The more sexual content adolescents view (even when controlling for other predictors of early sexual activity), the more likely they are to perceive their peers as sexually active, to develop sexually permissive attitudes, and to experience early intercourse (Escobar-Chaves et al., 2005; Martino et al., 2005; Ward & Friedman, 2006).

"Will your child learn to multiply before she learns to subtract?"

—Anti–teen-pregnancy poster, Children's Defense Fund

"Condoms should be used on every conceivable occasion."

—Anonymous

"All of us who make motion pictures are teachers, teachers with very loud voices."

—Film producer George Lucas, Academy Award ceremonies, 1992

Teens and STIs

Unprotected sex has led to increased rates of sexually transmitted infections. Two-thirds of new infections occur in people under 25 (CASA, 2004). Teenage girls, because of their not yet fully mature biological development and lower levels of protective antibodies, seem especially vulnerable (Dehne & Riedner, 2005; Guttmacher, 1994). A recent Centers for Disease Control study of sexually experienced 14- to 19-year-old U.S. females found 39.5 percent had STIs (Forhan et al., 2008).

To comprehend the mathematics of transmitting these infections, imagine this scenario: Over the course of a year, Pat has sex with 9 people, each of whom over the same period has sex with 9 other people, who in turn have sex with 9 others. How many "phantom" sex partners (past partners of partners) will Pat have? Laura Brannon and Timothy Brock (1993) report that the actual number—511—is more than five times the estimate given by the average student.

Given these odds, the rapid spread of STIs is not surprising. Condoms offer little protection against certain skin-to-skin STIs (Medical Institute, 1994; NIH, 2001). Across the available studies, condoms have, however, been 80 percent effective in preventing transmission of HIV (human immunodeficiency virus—the virus that causes AIDS) from an infected partner (Weller & Davis-Beaty, 2002; WHO, 2003). The effects were clear when Thailand promoted 100 percent condom use by commercial sex workers. Over a four-year period, as condom use soared from 14 to 94 percent, the annual number of bacterial STIs plummeted from 410,406 to 27,362 (WHO, 2000).

In the United States, STI facts of life have led to another response: a greater emphasis on teen abstinence within some comprehensive sex-education programs. A National Longitudinal Study of Adolescent Health among 12,000 teens found several predictors of sexual restraint:

High intelligence Teens with high rather than average intelligence test scores more often delay sex, evidently because they appreciate possible negative consequences and are more focused on future achievement than on here-and-now pleasures (Halpern et al., 2000).

Religious engagement Actively religious teens and adults more often reserve sex for marital commitment (Rostosky et al., 2004; Smith, 1998).

Father presence In studies following hundreds of New Zealand and U.S. girls from age 5 to 18, a father's absence was linked to sexual activity before age 16 and teen pregnancy (Ellis et al., 2003). These associations held even after adjusting for other adverse influences, such as poverty.

Participation in service learning programs Several experiments have found lower pregnancy rates among teens volunteering as tutors or teachers' aides or participating in community projects, than found among comparable teens randomly assigned to control conditions (Kirby, 2002; O'Donnell et al., 2002). Researchers are unsure why. Does service learning promote a sense of personal competence, control, and responsibility? Does it encourage more future-oriented thinking? Or does it simply reduce opportunities for unprotected sex?

* * *

In recent history, the pendulum of sexual values has swung from the European eroticism of the early 1800s to the conservative Victorian era of the late 1800s, from the libertine flapper era of the 1920s to the family values period of the 1950s. The pendulum may have begun a new swing toward commitment in the twenty-first century, with declining teen birth rates since 1991. This decline reflects both increasing condom use among sexually active high school students (from 46 to 63 percent between 1991 and 2005) and decreasing sexual intercourse (from 54 to 47 percent) (CDC, 2006).

Sexual Orientation

9: What has research taught us about sexual orientation?

To motivate is to energize and direct behavior. So far, we have considered the energizing of sexual motivation but not its direction. We express the direction of our sexual interest in our **sexual orientation**—our enduring sexual attraction toward members of our own sex *(homosexual orientation)* or the other sex *(heterosexual orientation)*. Cultures vary in their attitudes toward homosexuality. In Chile, 32 percent of people say homosexuality "is never justified," as do 50 percent of Americans and 98 percent of Kenyans and Nigerians (Pew, 2006). Yet, as far as we know, all cultures in all times have been predominantly heterosexual (Bullough, 1990). Whether a culture condemns or accepts homosexuality, heterosexuality prevails and homosexuality survives.

Gay men and lesbians often recall childhood play preferences like those of the other sex (Bailey & Zucker, 1995). But most homosexual people report not becoming aware of same-sex attraction until during or shortly after puberty, and not thinking of themselves as gay or lesbian (their socially influenced identity) until later in their teens or twenties (Garnets & Kimmel, 1990; Hammack, 2005). As adolescents, their friendship quality is similar to that of "straight" teenagers, and as adults, their partnerships are "remarkably similar" in love and satisfaction to those of heterosexual couples (Busseri et al., 2006; Peplau & Fingerhut, 2007).

Sexual Orientation Statistics

How many people are exclusively homosexual? About 10 percent, as the popular press has often assumed? A little more than 20 percent, as average Americans estimated in a 2002 Gallup survey (Robinson, 2002)? Not according to more than a dozen national surveys that explored sexual orientation in Europe and the United States in the early 1990s, using methods protecting the respondents' anonymity. The most accurate figure seems to be about 3 or 4 percent of men and 1 or 2 percent of women (Laumann et al., 1994; Mosher et al., 2005; Smith, 1998). Estimates derived from the sexual activity of unmarried partners reported in the 2000 U.S. Census suggest that 2.5 percent of the population is gay or lesbian (Tarmann, 2002). Fewer than 1 percent of survey respondents—for example, 12 people out of 7076 Dutch adults in one survey (Sandfort et al., 2001)—reported being actively bisexual. A larger number of adults in that study reported having had an isolated homosexual experience. And most people report having had an occasional homosexual fantasy. Health experts find it helpful to know sexual statistics, but numbers do not decide issues of human rights.

What does it feel like to be homosexual in a heterosexual culture? If you are heterosexual, one way to understand is to imagine how you would feel if you were shunned or fired for openly admitting or displaying your feelings toward someone of the other sex; if you overheard people making crude jokes about heterosexual people; if most movies, TV shows, and advertisements portrayed (or implied) homosexuality; and if your family members were pleading with you to change your heterosexual life-style and to enter into a homosexual marriage.

Sexual orientation is not an indicator of mental health. "Homosexuality, in and of itself, is not associated with mental disorders or emotional or social problems," declares the American Psychological Association (2007). Moreover, same-sex civil unions provide emotional, social, and health benefits similar to those of heterosexual unions (Herek, 2006; King & Bartlett, 2006; Kurdek, 2005). But some homosexual individuals, especially during adolescence, struggle with their sexual attractions and are at increased risk for thinking about and attempting suicide (Balsam et al., 2005; Kitts, 2005; Plöderl & Fartacek, 2005). They may at first try to ignore or deny their desires, hoping they will go away. But they don't. Then they

sexual orientation an enduring sexual attraction toward members of either one's own sex (homosexual orientation) or the other sex (heterosexual orientation).

In one British survey, of the 18,876 people contacted, 1 percent were seemingly asexual, having "never felt sexually attracted to anyone at all" (Bogaert, 2004, 2006).

In a study of self-described heterosexual, bisexual, and homosexual men, those who described themselves as bisexual responded as did homosexual men—with genital arousal primarily to same-sex erotic stimuli (Rieger et al., 2005). They also exhibit interests and traits more like gay than heterosexual men (Lippa, 2005).

"Efforts to change sexual orientation are unlikely to be successful and involve some risk of harm."

—American Psychological Association, 2009

Personal values affect sexual orientation less than they affect other forms of sexual behavior. Compared with people who rarely attend religious services, for example, those who attend regularly are one-third as likely to have cohabited before marriage, and they report having had many fewer sex partners. But (if male) they are just as likely to be homosexual (Smith, 1998).

Note that the scientific question is not "What causes homosexuality?" (or "What causes heterosexuality?") but "What causes differing sexual orientations?" In pursuit of answers, psychological science compares the backgrounds and physiology of people whose sexual orientations differ.

may try to change, through psychotherapy, willpower, or prayer. But the feelings typically persist, as do those of heterosexual people—who are similarly incapable of becoming homosexual (Haldeman, 1994, 2002; Myers & Scanzoni, 2005). Most of today's psychologists therefore view sexual orientation as neither willfully chosen nor willfully changed. Sexual orientation in some ways is like handedness: Most people are one way, some the other. A very few are truly ambidextrous. Regardless, the way one is endures.

This conclusion is most strongly established for men. Compared with men's sexual orientation, women's tends to be less strongly felt and potentially more fluid and changing (Chivers, 2005; Diamond, 2007; Peplau & Garnets, 2000). Men's lesser sexual variability is apparent in many ways, notes Roy Baumeister (2000). Across time, across cultures, across situations, and across differing levels of education, religious observance, and peer influence, adult women's sexual drive and interests are more flexible and varying than are adult men's. Women, more than men, for example, prefer to alternate periods of high sexual activity with periods of almost none, and they are somewhat more likely than men to feel and act on bisexual attractions (Mosher et al., 2005).

In men, a high sex drive is associated with increased attraction to women (if heterosexual) or men (if homosexual). In women, a high sex drive is associated with increased attraction to both men and women (Lippa, 2006, 2007). When shown pictures of heterosexual couples, in either erotic or nonerotic contexts, heterosexual men look mostly at the woman; heterosexual women look more equally at both the man and the woman (Lykins et al., 2008). And when shown sexually explicit film clips, men's genital and subjective sexual arousal is mostly to preferred sexual stimuli (for heterosexual viewers, depictions of women). Women respond more nonspecifically to depictions of sexual activity involving males or females (Chivers et al., 2007). Baumeister calls this phenomenon the gender difference in *erotic plasticity.*

Gays and lesbians suffer elevated rates of depression and risk of suicide attempts, which researchers suspect result from their experiences with bullying, harassment, and discrimination (Sandfort et al., 2001; Warner et al., 2004). Most people, whether straight or gay, accept their orientation—by electing celibacy, by engaging in promiscuous sex (a choice more commonly made by gay men than by lesbian women), or by entering into a committed, long-term love relationship (a choice more often made by lesbians than by gays) (Kulkin et al., 2000; Peplau, 1982; Remafedi, 1999; Weinberg & Williams, 1974). Mental health professionals are now more accepting of clients' sexual orientation. The American Psychiatric Association dropped homosexuality from its list of "mental illnesses" in 1973, as did the World Health Organization in 1993, and Japan's and China's psychiatric associations in 1995 and 2001.

Origins of Sexual Orientation

If our sexual orientation is indeed something we do not choose and seemingly cannot change (most clearly so for males), then where do these preferences—heterosexual or homosexual—come from? See if you can anticipate the consensus that has emerged from hundreds of research studies by responding *yes* or *no* to the following questions:

1. Is homosexuality linked with problems in a child's relationships with parents, such as with a domineering mother and an ineffectual father, or a possessive mother and a hostile father?
2. Does homosexuality involve a fear or hatred of people of the other gender, leading individuals to direct their sexual desires toward members of their own sex?
3. Is sexual orientation linked with levels of sex hormones currently in the blood?
4. As children, were many homosexuals molested, seduced, or otherwise sexually victimized by an adult homosexual?

The answer to all these questions appears to be *no* (Storms, 1983). In interviews with nearly 1000 homosexuals and 500 heterosexuals, Kinsey Institute investigators assessed nearly every imaginable psychological cause of homosexuality—parental relationships, childhood sexual experiences, peer relationships, dating experiences (Bell et al., 1981; Hammersmith, 1982). Their findings: Homosexuals are no more likely than heterosexuals to have been smothered by maternal love, neglected by their father, or sexually abused. And consider this: If "distant fathers" were more likely to produce homosexual sons, then shouldn't boys growing up in father-absent homes more often be gay? (They are not.) And shouldn't the rising number of such homes have led to a noticeable increase in the gay population? (It has not.)

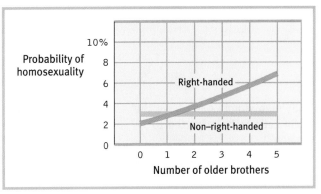

FIGURE 10.12 The fraternal birth-order effect Researcher Ray Blanchard (2008) offers these approximate curves depicting a man's likelihood of homosexuality as a function of his number of older brothers. This correlation has been found in several studies, but only among right-handed men.

Homosexual people do, however, appear more often in certain populations. One study (Ludwig, 1995) of the biographies of 1004 eminent people found homosexual and bisexual people overrepresented, especially among poets (24 percent), fiction writers (21 percent), and artists and musicians (15 percent). Gay more than straight men also express interest in occupations that attract many women, such as decorator, florist, and flight attendant (Lippa, 2002). (Given that some 96 percent of men are not gay, most men in such occupations may nevertheless be straight.)

Men who have older brothers are also somewhat more likely to be gay, report Ray Blanchard (1997, 2008) and Anthony Bogaert (2003)—about one-third more likely for each additional older brother. If the odds of homosexuality are roughly 2 percent among first sons, they would rise to nearly 3 percent among second sons, 4 percent for third sons, and so on for each additional older brother (see **FIGURE 10.12**). The reason for this curious phenomenon—the *fraternal birth-order effect*—is unclear. Blanchard suspects a defensive maternal immune response to foreign substances produced by male fetuses. With each pregnancy with a male fetus, the maternal antibodies may become stronger and may prevent the fetus' brain from developing in a male-typical pattern. Consistent with this biological explanation, the fraternal birth-order effect occurs only in men with older brothers born to the same mother (whether reared together or not). Sexual orientation is unaffected by adoptive brothers (Bogaert, 2006). The birth-order effect on sexual orientation is not found among women with older sisters, women who were womb-mates of twin brothers, and men who are not right-handed (Rose et al., 2002).

So, what else might influence sexual orientation? One theory has proposed that people develop same-sex erotic attachments if segregated by gender at the time their sex drive matures (Storms, 1981). Indeed, gay men tend to recall going through puberty somewhat earlier, when peers are more likely to be all males (Bogaert et al., 2002). But even in tribal cultures in which homosexual behavior is expected of all boys before marriage, heterosexuality prevails (Hammack, 2005; Money, 1987). (As this illustrates, homosexual *behavior* does not always indicate a homosexual *orientation*.)

The bottom line from a half-century's theory and research: If there are environmental factors that influence sexual orientation, we do not yet know what they are. This reality has motivated researchers to consider more carefully the possible biological influences on orientation, including evidence of homosexuality in the animal world, and the influences of differing brain centers, genetics, and prenatal hormone exposure.

Juliet and Juliet Boston's beloved swan couple, "Romeo and Juliet," were discovered actually to be, as are many other animal partners, a same-sex pair.

SAME-SEX ATTRACTION IN ANIMALS Biologist Bruce Bagemihl (1999) has identified several hundred species in which at least occasional same-sex relations have been observed. Grizzlies, gorillas, monkeys, flamingos, and owls are all on the long list. Among rams, for example, some 6 to 10 percent—to sheep-breeding ranchers, the "duds"—display same-sex attraction by shunning ewes and seeking to mount other males (Perkins & Fitzgerald, 1997). Some degree of homosexuality seems to be a natural part of the animal world.

"Gay men simply don't have the brain cells to be attracted to women."

—Simon LeVay, *The Sexual Brain*, 1993

Gay and lesbian humans also differ from their straight counterparts in brain responses to sex-related sweat odors and to pictures of male and female faces (Kranz & Ishai, 2006; Martins et al., 2005; Savic et al., 2005).

"Studies indicate that male homosexuality is more likely to be transmitted from the mother's side of the family."

—Robert Plomin, John DeFries,
    Gerald McClearn, and Michael Rutter,
    Behavioral Genetics, 1997

THE BRAIN AND SEXUAL ORIENTATION Researcher Simon LeVay (1991) studied sections of the hypothalamus taken from deceased heterosexual and homosexual people. As a gay scientist, LeVay wanted to do "something connected with my gay identity." To avoid biasing the results, he did a *blind study,* not knowing which donors were gay. For nine months he peered through his microscope at a cell cluster he thought might be important. Then, one morning, he broke the codes: One cell cluster was reliably larger in heterosexual men than in women and homosexual men. "I was almost in a state of shock," LeVay said (1994). "I took a walk by myself on the cliffs over the ocean. I sat for half an hour just thinking what this might mean."

It should not surprise us that brains differ with sexual orientation. Remember our maxim: *Everything psychological is simultaneously biological.* But when do such brain differences begin? At conception? In the womb? During childhood or adolescence? Does experience produce these differences? Or is it genes or prenatal hormones (or genes via prenatal hormones)?

LeVay does not view the hypothalamic center as a sexual orientation center; rather, he sees it as an important part of the neural pathway engaged in sexual behavior. He acknowledges that sexual behavior patterns may influence the brain's anatomy. In fish, birds, rats, and humans, brain structures vary with experience—including sexual experience (Breedlove, 1997). But LeVay believes it more likely that brain anatomy influences sexual orientation. His hunch seems confirmed by the discovery of a similar hypothalamic difference between male sheep that display same-sex attraction and those attracted to females (Larkin et al., 2002; Roselli et al., 2002, 2004). Moreover, report University of London psychologists Qazi Rahman and Glenn Wilson (2003), "the neuroanatomical correlates of male homosexuality differentiate very early postnatally, if not prenatally."

GENES AND SEXUAL ORIENTATION Are these sexuality-related brain differences genetically influenced? Some evidence suggests they are. "First, homosexuality does appear to run in families," note Brian Mustanski and Michael Bailey (2003). "Second, twin studies have established that genes play a substantial role in explaining individual differences in sexual orientation." Identical twins are somewhat more likely than fraternal twins to share a homosexual orientation (Långström et al., 2008). (Because sexual orientations differ in many identical twin pairs, especially female twins, we know that other factors besides genes are at work.)

Experimenters have also, by genetic manipulations, created female fruit flies that during courtship act like males (pursuing other females) and males that act like females (Demir & Dickson, 2005). "We have shown that a single gene in the fruit fly is sufficient to determine all aspects of the flies' sexual orientation and behavior," explained Barry Dickson (2005). With humans, it's likely that multiple genes, possibly in interaction with other influences, shape sexual orientation. One study financed by the U.S. National Institutes of Health is analyzing the genes of more than 1000 gay brothers in search of such genetic markers.

Researchers have speculated about possible reasons why "gay genes" might exist. Given that same-sex couples cannot naturally reproduce, how could such genes have survived in the human gene pool? Evolutionary psychologists suggest two possible answers. The first is kin selection. Because many of our genes also reside in our biological relatives, gay people's genes could live on through their supporting the survival and reproductive success of relatives—nieces, nephews, and others—who carry many of those same genes.

Or second, and perhaps more likely, maternal genetics is at work (Bocklandt et al., 2006). Recent Italian studies (Camperio-Ciani et al., 2004, 2008) confirm what others have found—that homosexual men have more homosexual relatives on their mother's side than on their father's. And, compared with the maternal relatives of heterosexual men, the maternal relatives of homosexual men produce more offspring. Perhaps, surmise the researchers, the genes that make women more likely to have children (such as by strongly attracting them to men) also produce sons and nephews who are attracted to men.

PRENATAL HORMONES AND SEXUAL ORIENTATION Elevated rates of homosexual orientation in identical *and* fraternal twins suggest that not just shared genetics but also a shared prenatal environment may be a factor. In animals and some exceptional human cases, abnormal prenatal hormone conditions have altered a fetus' sexual orientation. German researcher Gunter Dorner (1976, 1988) pioneered research on the influence of prenatal hormones by manipulating a fetal rat's exposure to male hormones, thereby "inverting" its sexual orientation. In other studies, when pregnant sheep were injected with testosterone during a critical period of fetal development, their female offspring later showed homosexual behavior (Money, 1987).

A critical period for the human brain's neural-hormonal control system may exist between the middle of the second and fifth months after conception (Ellis & Ames, 1987; Gladue, 1990; Meyer-Bahlburg, 1995). Exposure to the hormone levels typically experienced by female fetuses during this time appears to predispose the person (whether female or male) to be attracted to males in later life.

On several traits influenced by prenatal hormones, gays and lesbians appear to fall midway between straight females and males (**TABLE 10.1**). For example, lesbians' cochlea and hearing systems develop in a way that is intermediate between those of heterosexual females and heterosexual males (McFadden, 2002). Fingerprint ridges, which are complete by the sixteenth fetal week, may also differ. Although most people have more fingerprint ridges on their right hand than on their left, some studies find a greater right-left difference in heterosexual males than in females and gay males (Hall & Kimura, 1994; Mustanski et al., 2002; Sanders et al., 2002). Handedness also differs. Data from 20 studies reveals that "homosexual participants had 39 percent greater odds of being non–right-handed" (Lalumière et al., 2000).

Another you-never-would-have-guessed-it gay-straight difference appears in studies showing that gay men's spatial abilities resemble those typical of straight women (Cohen, 2002; Gladue, 1994; McCormick & Witelson, 1991; Sanders &

> "Modern scientific research indicates that sexual orientation is . . . partly determined by genetics, but more specifically by hormonal activity in the womb."
>
> —Glenn Wilson and Qazi Rahman, *Born Gay: The Psychobiology of Sex Orientation*, 2005

TABLE 10.1 Biological Correlates of Sexual Orientation

On average (the evidence is strongest for males), various biological and behavioral traits of gays and lesbians fall between those of straight men and straight women. Tentative findings—some in need of replication—include these:

Brain differences

- Brain asymmetry is greater in straight men and lesbian women.
- One hypothalamic cell cluster is larger in straight men than in women and gay men; same difference is found in male sheep displaying other-sex versus same-sex attraction.
- Gay men's hypothalamus reacts as does a straight woman's to the smell of sex-related hormones and pictures of male and female faces.

Genetic influences

- Shared sexual orientation is higher among identical twins than among fraternal twins.
- Sexual attraction in fruit flies can be genetically manipulated.

Prenatal hormonal influences

- Altered prenatal hormone exposure may lead to homosexuality in humans and other animals.
- Right-handed men with several older biological brothers are more likely to be gay.

These brain differences and genetic and prenatal influences may contribute to observed gay-straight differences in

- spatial abilities.
- fingerprint ridge counts.
- auditory system development.
- occupational preferences.
- relative finger lengths.
- male eating disorders.
- gender nonconformity.
- age of onset of puberty in males.
- male body size.
- sleep length.
- physical aggression.

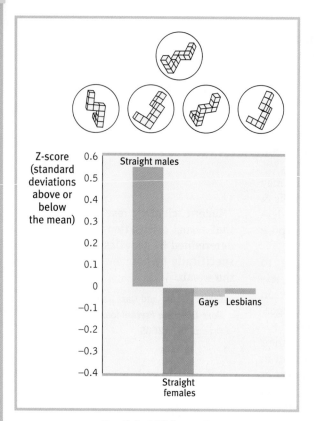

Z-score (standard deviations above or below the mean)

FIGURE 10.13 **Spatial abilities and sexual orientation** Which of the four figures can be rotated to match the target figure at the top? Straight males tend to find this an easier task than do straight females, with gays and lesbians intermediate. (From Rahman et al., 2003, with 60 people tested in each group.)

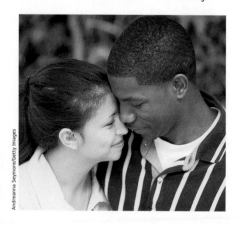

A sharing of love For most adults, a sexual relationship fulfills not only a biological motive but also a social need for intimacy.

Wright, 1997). On mental rotation tasks such as the one illustrated in **FIGURE 10.13**, straight men tend to outscore women. Studies by Qazi Rahman and colleagues (2003, 2008) find that, as on a number of other measures, the scores of gays and lesbians fall between those of heterosexual males and females. But straight women and gays both outperform straight men at remembering objects' spatial locations in tasks like those found in memory games (Hassan & Rahman, 2007).

Because the physiological evidence is preliminary and controversial, some scientists remain skeptical. Rather than specifying sexual orientation, they suggest, biological factors may predispose a *temperament* that influences sexuality "in the context of individual learning and experience" (Byne & Parsons, 1993). Daryl Bem (1996, 1998, 2000) has theorized that genes code for prenatal hormones and brain anatomy, which predispose temperaments that lead children to prefer gender-typical or gender-atypical activities and friends. These preferences may later lead children to feel attracted to whichever sex feels different from their own. The dissimilar-seeming sex (whether or not it conforms to one's own anatomy) becomes associated with anxiety and other forms of arousal, which are eventually transformed into romantic arousal. The exotic becomes erotic.

Regardless of the process, the consistency of the brain, genetic, and prenatal findings has swung the pendulum toward a biological explanation of sexual orientation (Rahman & Wilson, 2003). This helps explain why sexual orientation is so difficult to change, and why a BBC Internet study of more than 200,000 people found the same gay-straight differences in personality and interests worldwide (Lippa, 2007a,b, 2008). Still, some people wonder: Should the cause of sexual orientation matter? Perhaps it shouldn't, but people's assumptions matter. Those who believe—as do 41 percent of Americans and most gays and lesbians—that sexual orientation is biologically disposed also tend to express more accepting attitudes toward homosexual people (Allen et al., 1996; Gallup polls; Haslam & Levy, 2006; Kaiser, 2001; Whitley, 1990).

To gay and lesbian activists, the new biological research is a double-edged sword (Diamond, 1993). If sexual orientation, like skin color and sex, is genetically influenced, that offers a further rationale for civil rights protection. Moreover, it may alleviate parents' concerns about their children being unduly influenced by gay teachers and role models. At the same time, this research raises the troubling possibility that genetic markers of sexual orientation could someday be identified through fetal testing, and a fetus could be aborted simply for being predisposed to an unwanted orientation.

Sex and Human Values

10: **Is scientific research on sexual motivation value free?**

Recognizing that values are both personal and cultural, most sex researchers and educators strive to keep their writings on sexual behavior and its motivation value free. But the very words we use to describe behavior can reflect our personal values. Whether we label certain sexual behaviors as "perversions" or as part of an "alternative sexual life-style" depends on our attitude toward the behaviors. Labels describe, but they also evaluate.

Sex education separated from the context of human values may also give some students the idea that sexual intercourse is simply a recreational activity. Child-rearing expert Diana Baumrind (1982) has observed that an implication that adults are neutral about adolescent sexual activity is unfortunate, because "promiscuous recreational sex poses certain psychological, social, health, and moral problems that must be faced realistically."

Perhaps we can agree that the knowledge provided by sex research is preferable to ignorance, and yet also agree that researchers' values should be stated openly, enabling us to debate them and to reflect on our own values. We should remember that scientific research on sexual motivation does not aim to define the personal meaning of sex in our own lives. You could know every available fact about sex—that the initial spasms of male and female orgasm come at 0.8-second intervals, that the female nipples expand 10 millimeters at the peak of sexual arousal, that systolic blood pressure rises some 60 points and the respiration rate to 40 breaths per minute—but fail to understand the human significance of sexual intimacy.

Surely one significance of sexual intimacy is its expression of our profoundly social nature. Sex is a socially significant act. Men and women can achieve orgasm alone, yet most people find greater satisfaction—and experience a much greater surge in the prolactin hormone associated with sexual satisfaction and satiety—after intercourse and orgasm with their loved one (Brody & Tillmann, 2005). With the satisfaction of intimacy and relationship surpassing the satisfaction of self-stimulation, there is a yearning for closeness in sexual motivation. Sex at its human best is life-uniting and love-renewing.

REHEARSE IT!

11. In describing the sexual response cycle, Masters and Johnson noted that
a. a plateau phase followed orgasm.
b. men experience a refractory period during which they cannot experience orgasm.
c. the feeling that accompanies orgasm is stronger in men than in women.
d. testosterone is released in the female as well as in the male.

12. One striking effect of hormonal changes on human sexual behavior is the
a. arousing influence of erotic materials.
b. sharp rise in sexual interest at puberty.
c. decrease in women's sexual desire at the time of ovulation.
d. increase in testosterone levels in castrated males.

13. Sexual behavior is motivated by internal biological factors, by external stimuli, and by imagined stimuli. An example of an external stimulus that might influence sexual behavior is
a. blood level of testosterone.
b. the onset of puberty.
c. a sexually explicit film.
d. an erotic fantasy or dream.

14. Factors contributing to teen pregnancies include ignorance about reproduction and contraception, guilt about sexual behavior, mass media norms of promiscuity, insufficient communication about contraception, and
a. the "just say no" attitude.
b. the unavailability of abortion.

c. the decreased rates of sexually transmitted diseases.
d. alcohol use.

15. Current research suggests several possible contributors to sexual orientation. Which of the following is NOT one of those contributors?
a. Certain cell clusters in the hypothalamus
b. A domineering mother and ineffectual father
c. Multiple genes interacting with other influences
d. Exposure to hormone levels typically experienced by female fetuses

Answers: 11. b, 12. b, 13. c, 14. d, 15. b.

The Need to Belong

11: **What evidence points to our human need to belong?**

Separated from friends or family—isolated in prison, alone at a new school, living in a foreign land—most people feel keenly their lost connections with important others. We are what Aristotle called the *social animal*. "Without friends," wrote Aristotle in his *Nichomachean Ethics*, "no one would choose to live, though he had all other goods." We have a need to affiliate with others, even to become strongly attached to certain others in enduring, close relationships. Human beings, contended the personality theorist Alfred Adler, have an "urge to community" (Ferguson, 1989, 2001). Roy Baumeister and Mark Leary (1995) have assembled evidence for this deep need to belong.

Aiding Survival

Social bonds boosted our ancestors' survival rate. By keeping children close to their caregivers, attachments served as a powerful survival impulse. As adults, those who formed attachments were more likely to reproduce and to co-nurture their offspring to maturity. To be "wretched" literally means, in its Middle English origin *(wrecche)*, to be without kin nearby.

Survival also was enhanced by cooperation. In solo combat, our ancestors were not the toughest predators. But as hunters, they learned that six hands were better

"We must love one another or die."

—W. H. Auden "September 1, 1939"

"The only thing that really matters in life are your relationships to other people."

—George Vaillant, 2009, when asked what he had learned from his study following 238 Harvard University men from the 1930s to the end of their lives.

Separation amplifies the felt need to belong In the film *Cast Away*, Chuck Noland (played by Tom Hanks) combats social starvation by talking with his girlfriend's snapshot and a volleyball he named Wilson.

than two. As foragers, they gained protection from predators and enemies by traveling in groups. Those who felt a need to belong survived and reproduced most successfully, and their genes now predominate. We are innately social creatures. People in every society on Earth belong to groups (and, as Chapter 15 explains, prefer and favor "us" over "them").

Wanting to Belong

The need to belong colors our thoughts and emotions. We spend a great deal of time thinking about actual and hoped-for relationships. When relationships form, we often feel joy. Falling in mutual love, people have been known to feel their cheeks ache from their irrepressible grins. Asked, "What is necessary for your happiness?" or "What is it that makes your life meaningful?" most people mention—before anything else—close, satisfying relationships with family, friends, or romantic partners (Berscheid, 1985). Happiness hits close to home.

Pause a moment to consider: What was your most satisfying moment in the past week? Kennon Sheldon and his colleagues (2001) asked that question of American and South Korean collegians, then asked them to rate how much this peak experience had satisfied various needs. In both countries, the satisfaction of self-esteem and relatedness-belonging needs were the top two contributors to the peak moment. Another study found that *very* happy university students are not distinguished by their money but by their "rich and satisfying close relationships" (Diener & Seligman, 2002). The need to belong runs deeper, it seems, than any need to be rich. When our need for relatedness is satisfied in balance with two other basic psychological needs—*autonomy* and *competence*—the result is a deep sense of well-being (Deci & Ryan, 2002; Patrick et al., 2007; Sheldon & Niemiec, 2006). To feel connected, free, and capable is to enjoy a good life.

South Africans have a word for the human bonds that define us all. *Ubuntu* (oo-BOON-too), explained Desmond Tutu (1999), expresses the fact that "my humanity is caught up, is inextricably bound up, in yours." A Zulu maxim captures the idea: *Umuntu ngumuntu ngabantu*—"a person is a person through other persons."

When we feel included, accepted, and loved by those important to us, our self-esteem rides high. Indeed, say Mark Leary and his colleagues (1998), self-esteem is a gauge of how valued and accepted we feel. Much of our social behavior therefore aims to increase our belonging—our social acceptance and inclusion. To avoid rejection, we generally conform to group standards and seek to make favorable impressions (more on this in Chapter 15). To win friendship and esteem, we monitor our behavior, hoping to create the right impressions. Seeking love and belonging, we spend billions on clothes, cosmetics, and diet and fitness aids—all motivated by our quest for acceptance.

Like sexual motivation, which feeds both love and exploitation, the need to belong feeds both deep attachments and menacing threats. Out of our need to define a "we" come loving families, faithful friendships, and team spirit, but also teen gangs, ethnic rivalries, and fanatic nationalism.

Sustaining Relationships

For most of us, familiarity breeds liking, not contempt. Thrown together in groups at school, at summer camp, on a vacation cruise, we later resist breaking those social bonds—we promise to call, to write, to come back for reunions. Parting, we feel distress. You don't need to look far to see people spending hours on smart phones and computers, sustaining their relationships with absent people by talking, text messaging, and e-mailing. Two-thirds of entering American collegians report spending one to five or more hours per week on social networking sites such as Facebook and MySpace (Pryor et al., 2007).

When the fear of being alone seems worse than the pain of emotional or physical abuse, attachments can keep people in abusive relationships. Even when bad relationships break, people suffer. After separations, feelings of loneliness and anger—and sometimes even a strange desire to be near the former partner—linger. In one 16-nation survey, and repeated in U.S. surveys, separated and divorced people have been half as likely as married people to say they were "very happy" (Inglehart, 1990; NORC, 2007).

Our fear of being alone has some basis in reality. Children who move through a series of foster homes, with repeated disruption of budding attachments, may come to have difficulty forming deep attachments. And children reared in institutions without a sense of belonging to anyone, or locked away at home under extreme neglect, become pathetic creatures—withdrawn, frightened, speechless.

When something threatens or dissolves our social ties, negative emotions—anxiety, loneliness, jealousy, guilt—overwhelm us. The bereaved often feel life is empty, pointless. Even the first weeks living on a college campus away from home can be distressing. For immigrants and refugees moving alone to new places, the stress and loneliness can be depressing. But if feelings of acceptance and connection build, so do self-esteem, positive feelings, and desires to help rather than hurt others (Buckley & Leary, 2001). After years of placing individual refugee and immigrant families in isolated communities, U.S. policies today encourage *chain migration* (Pipher, 2002). The second refugee Sudanese family settling in a town generally has an easier adjustment than the first.

The need to connect Six days a week, women from the Philippines work as "domestic helpers" in 154,000 Hong Kong households. On Sundays, they throng to the central business district to picnic, dance, sing, talk, and laugh. "Humanity could stage no greater display of happiness," reported one observer (*Economist*, 2001).

The Pain of Ostracism

Sometimes, though, the need to belong is denied. Perhaps you can recall such a time, when you felt excluded or ignored or shunned. Perhaps you received the silent treatment. Perhaps others avoided you, or averted their eyes in your presence, or even mocked you behind your back.

Social psychologist Kipling Williams (2007) and his colleagues have studied such experiences of *ostracism*—of social exclusion—in both natural and laboratory settings. Worldwide, humans control social behavior via the punishing effects of severe ostracism—of exile, imprisonment, and solitary confinement. For children, even a brief time-out in isolation can be punishing. Asked to describe personal episodes that made them feel especially good about themselves, people often think of some achievement. But asked what made them feel especially *bad* about themselves, they will—about four times in five—describe a relationship difficulty (Pillemer et al., 2007).

To be shunned—given the cold shoulder or the silent treatment, with others' eyes avoiding yours—is to have one's need to belong threatened (Williams & Zadro, 2001). "It's the meanest thing you can do to someone, especially if you know they can't fight back. I never should have been born," said Lea, a lifelong victim of the silent treatment by her mother and grandmother. Like Lea, people often respond to social ostracism with depressed moods, initial efforts to restore their acceptance, and then withdrawal. After two years of silent treatment by his employer, Richard reported, "I came home every night and cried. I lost 25 pounds, had no self-esteem, and felt that I wasn't worthy."

Rejected and unable to remedy the situation, people may seek new friends—or they may turn nasty. In a series of experiments, Jean Twenge and her collaborators (2001, 2002, 2007; Baumeister et al., 2002; Maner et al., 2007) told some students (who had taken a personality test) that they were "the type likely to end up alone later in life," or that people they had met didn't want them in a group that was forming. They told other students that they would have "rewarding relationships throughout life," or that "everyone chose you as someone they'd like to work with." Those excluded became much more likely to engage in self-defeating behaviors and to underperform on aptitude tests. The rejection also interfered with their empathy for others and made them more likely to act in disparaging or aggressive ways against those who had excluded them (blasting them with noise, for example). "If intelligent, well-adjusted, successful university students can turn aggressive in response to a small

A violent response to social exclusion Most socially excluded teens do not commit violence, but some do. Charles "Andy" Williams, described by a classmate as someone his peers derided as "freak, dork, nerd, stuff like that," went on a shooting spree at his suburban California high school, killing 2 and wounding 13 (Bowles & Kasindorf, 2001).

Note: The researchers later debriefed and reassured the participants.

laboratory experience of social exclusion," noted the research team, "it is disturbing to imagine the aggressive tendencies that might arise from a series of important rejections or chronic exclusion from desired groups in actual social life." Indeed, reports Williams (2007), ostracism "weaves through case after case of school violence."

REHEARSE IT!

16. Which of the following is NOT part of the evidence presented to support the view that humans are strongly motivated by a need to belong?
   a. Students who rated themselves as "very happy" also tended to have satisfying close relationships.
   b. Social exclusion—such as exile or solitary confinement—is considered a severe form of punishment.
   c. As adults, adopted children tend to resemble their biological parents and to yearn for an affiliation with them.
   d. Children who are extremely neglected become withdrawn, frightened, and speechless.

Answer: 16. c.

CHAPTER REVIEW

Motivation

Motivational Concepts

1 From what perspectives do psychologists view motivated behavior?

The *instinct*/evolutionary perspective explores genetic influences on complex behaviors, including *motivation*. *Drive-reduction theory* explores how physiological needs create aroused tension states (drives) that direct us to satisfy those needs. Arousal theory proposes that we are motivated to maintain an optimum level of arousal, which explains behaviors that do not reduce physiological needs. Maslow's *hierarchy of needs* proposes a pyramid of human needs, from basic needs such as hunger and thirst up to higher-level needs such as actualization and transcendence.

Hunger

2 What physiological factors produce hunger?

Hunger's pangs correspond to the stomach's contractions. Appetite hormones that influence hunger include insulin, leptin, orexin, ghrelin, obestatin, and PYY. Two hypothalamus areas regulate the body's weight by affecting feelings of hunger and satiety. The body may have a *set point* (a biologically fixed tendency to maintain an optimum weight) or a looser settling point (also influenced by the environment).

3 What psychological and cultural factors influence hunger?

Hunger also reflects individual learning and cultural expectations of what and when we should eat. Some tastes (such as sweet and salty) are species-wide, and some taste preferences (such as the avoidance of new foods or of foods that have made us ill) have survival value.

4 What factors predispose some people to become and remain obese?

Twin and adoption studies indicate that body weight is genetically influenced (in the number of fat cells and *basal metabolic rate*). Lack of exercise, combined with abundant high-calorie food, has led to increased rates of obesity, showing the influence of environment. Losing weight requires a lifelong change in habits, minimizing exposure to tempting food cues, exercising to expend energy, eating healthy foods, spacing meals throughout the day, avoiding binges, and forgiving the occasional lapses.

Sexual Motivation

5 What stages mark the human sexual response cycle?

Masters and Johnson described four stages in the human *sexual response cycle*: excitement, plateau, orgasm (which seems to involve similar feelings and brain activity in males and females), and resolution. In the resolution phase, males experience a *refractory period*, during which renewed arousal and orgasm are impossible. *Sexual disorders* (problems that consistently impair sexual arousal or functioning) can be successfully treated, often by behaviorally oriented therapy or drug therapy.

6 Do hormones influence human sexual motivation?

Sex hormones direct sexual development and activate sexual behavior. The female *estrogen* and male *testosterone* hormones influence sexual behavior less directly in humans than in other animals. Unlike other mammalian females, women's sexuality is more responsive to testosterone level than to estrogen level. Short-term shifts in testosterone level are normal in men and have little effect on sexual drive.

7 How do internal and external stimuli influence sexual motivation?

Erotic material and other external stimuli can trigger sexual arousal in both men and women. Sexually explicit material may lead people to perceive their partners as comparatively less appealing and to devalue their relationships. Sexually coercive material tends to increase viewers' acceptance of rape and violence toward women. Fantasies (imagined stimuli) also influence sexual arousal.

8 **What factors influence teen pregnancy and risk of sexually transmitted infections?**

Factors contributing to teen pregnancy include ignorance; minimal communication about contraception with parents, partners, and peers; guilt related to sexual activity; alcohol use; and mass media norms of unprotected and impulsive sexuality. Attempts to protect teens from STIs—sexually transmitted infections—through comprehensive sex-education programs include contraceptive and abstinence education. High intelligence, religiosity, father presence, and participation in service learning programs are predictors of teen sexual restraint.

9 **What has research taught us about sexual orientation?**

Surveys can tell us how many people (about 3 percent) are attracted to their own sex, but statistics cannot decide issues of human rights. There is no evidence that environmental influences determine *sexual orientation*. Evidence of biological influences comes from same-sex behaviors in many animal species, straight-gay differences in body and brain characteristics, higher rates of homosexuality in certain families, shared orientation in some identical twins, and the effects of prenatal exposure to certain hormones during critical periods of development.

10 **Is scientific research on sexual motivation value free?**

Scientific research on sexual motivation does not attempt to define the personal meaning of sex in our lives, but sex research and education are not value free.

The Need to Belong

11 **What evidence points to our human need to belong?**

The need to affiliate or belong had survival value for our ancestors. Humans in every society live in groups, and societies everywhere control behavior with the threat of ostracism—excluding or shunning others. When socially excluded, people may engage in self-defeating behaviors (performing below their ability) or in antisocial behaviors.

Terms and Concepts to Remember

motivation, p. 339

instinct, p. 340

drive-reduction theory, p. 340

homeostasis, p. 341

incentive, p. 341

hierarchy of needs, p. 342

glucose, p. 344

set point, p. 346

basal metabolic rate, p. 346

anorexia nervosa, p. 348

bulimia nervosa, p. 348

binge-eating disorder, p. 348

sexual response cycle, p. 357

refractory period, p. 357

sexual disorder, p. 358

estrogens, p. 358

testosterone, p. 358

sexual orientation, p. 363

Test for Success: Critical Thinking Exercises

By Amy Himsel, El Camino College

1. Dorothea Dix (1801–1887) once remarked, "Nobody wants to kiss when they are hungry." Which theory of motivation best supports her statement?

2. Sanjay recently adopted the typical college diet high in fat and sugar. He knows he may gain weight, but he figures it's no big deal because he can lose the extra pounds in the future. How would you evaluate Sanjay's plan?

3. Everything psychological is simultaneously biological. How is this true of sexual orientation?

4. To what extent might social networking Web sites like Facebook satisfy or thwart our need to belong?

The Test for Success exercises offer you a chance to apply your critical thinking skills to aspects of the material you have just read. Suggestions for answering these questions can be found in Appendix D at the back of the book.

Multiple-choice self-tests and more may be found at www.worthpublishers.com/myers.

Chapter Outline

- **Theories of Emotion**

- **Embodied Emotion**
  Emotions and the Autonomic Nervous System
  Brain and Other Physiological Indicators of Emotions
  Cognition and Emotion
  THINKING CRITICALLY ABOUT: Lie Detection

- **Expressed Emotion**
  Detecting Emotion
  Gender, Emotion, and Nonverbal Behavior
  Culture and Emotional Expression
  The Effects of Facial Expressions

- **Experienced Emotion**
  Anger
  Happiness
  CLOSE-UP: How to Be Happier

- **Stress and Health**
  Stress and Illness
  Stress and the Heart
  Stress and Susceptibility to Disease
  THINKING CRITICALLY ABOUT: Complementary and Alternative Medicine

- **Promoting Health**
  Coping With Stress
  CLOSE-UP: Pets Are Friends, Too
  Managing Stress
  CLOSE-UP: The Relaxation Response

11: Emotions, Stress, and Health

No one needs to tell you that feelings add color to your life, or that in times of stress they can disrupt your life or save it. Of all the species, we seem the most emotional (Hebb, 1980). More often than any other creature, we express fear, anger, sadness, joy, and love, and these psychological states often entail physical reactions. Nervous about an important encounter, we feel butterflies in our stomach. Anxious over speaking in public, we frequent the bathroom. Smoldering over a conflict with a family member, we get a splitting headache.

You can surely recall a time when you were overcome with emotion. I retain a flashbulb memory for the day I went to a huge store to drop off film and brought along Peter, my toddler first-born child. As I set Peter down on his feet and prepared to complete the paperwork, a passerby warned, "You'd better be careful or you'll lose that boy!" Not more than a few breaths later, after dropping the film in the slot, I turned and found no Peter beside me.

With mild anxiety, I peered around one end of the counter. No Peter in sight. With slightly more anxiety, I peered around the other end. No Peter there, either. Now, heart accelerating, I circled the neighboring counters. Still no Peter anywhere. As anxiety turned to panic, I began racing up and down the store aisles. He was nowhere to be found. Apprised of my alarm, the store manager used the public-address system to ask customers to assist in looking for a missing child. Soon after, I passed the customer who had warned me. "I told you that you were going to lose him!" he scorned. With visions of kidnapping (strangers routinely adored that beautiful child), I braced for the possibility that my negligence had caused me to lose what I loved above all else, and that I might have to return home and face my wife without our only child.

But then, as I passed the customer service counter yet again, there he was, having been found and returned by some obliging customer! In an instant, the arousal of terror spilled into ecstasy. Clutching my son, with tears suddenly flowing, I found myself unable to speak my thanks and stumbled out of the store awash in grateful joy.

Where do such emotions come from? Why do we have them? What are they made of? Emotions are our body's adaptive response. They exist not to give us interesting experiences but to enhance our survival. When we face challenges, emotions focus our attention and energize our action. Our heart races. Our pace quickens. All our senses go on high alert. Receiving unexpected good news, we may find our eyes tearing. We raise our hands triumphantly. We feel exuberance and a newfound confidence. Yet when prolonged and experienced as stress, emotions can also have a damaging effect on our health, as we will see.

Not only emotion, but most psychological phenomena (vision, sleep, memory, sex, and so forth) can be approached these three ways—physiologically, behaviorally, and cognitively.

Theories of Emotion

1: What are the components of an emotion?

As my anguished search for Peter illustrates, **emotions** are a mix of (1) physiological arousal (heart pounding), (2) expressive behaviors (quickened pace), and (3) consciously experienced thoughts *(Is this a kidnapping?)* and feelings (a sense of fear, and later joy). The puzzle for psychologists has been figuring out how these three pieces fit together.

There are two controversies over the interplay of physiology, expressions, and thoughts in emotions:

- Does our physiological arousal precede or follow our emotional experience? (Did I first notice my heart racing and my faster step, and then feel anxious dread about losing Peter? Or did my sense of fear come first, stirring my heart and legs to respond?)
- Does cognition always precede emotion? Or can we experience emotion apart from or after thinking? (Did I *think* about the kidnapping threat before reacting emotionally? Or did I react first and then interpret my reaction?)

Common sense tells most of us that we cry because we are sad, lash out because we are angry, tremble because we are afraid. First comes conscious awareness, then the physiological trimmings. But to pioneering psychologist William James, this commonsense view of emotion was backward. According to James, "We feel sorry because we cry, angry because we strike, afraid because we tremble" (1890, p. 1066). James' idea, also proposed by Danish physiologist Carl Lange, is called the **James-Lange theory.** First comes a distinct physiological response, then (as we observe that response) comes our experienced emotion.

This James-Lange theory struck U.S. physiologist Walter Cannon as implausible, in part because he thought the body's responses are not distinct enough to evoke the different emotions. Does a racing heart signal fear, anger, or love? Also, changes in heart rate, perspiration, and body temperature seemed too slow to trigger sudden emotion. Cannon, and later another physiologist, Philip Bard, concluded that our physiological arousal and our emotional experience occur *simultaneously.* According to this **Cannon-Bard theory,** the emotion-triggering stimulus is routed separately but simultaneously to the brain's cortex, causing the *subjective awareness* of emotion, and to the sympathetic nervous system, causing the body's arousal. Thus, your heart begins pounding *as* you experience fear; one does not cause the other.

Let's check your understanding of the James-Lange and Cannon-Bard theories. Imagine that your brain could not sense your heart pounding or your stomach churning. According to each theory, how would this affect your experienced emotions?

Cannon and Bard would have expected you to experience emotions normally because they believed emotions occur separately from (though simultaneously with) the body's arousal. James and Lange would have expected greatly diminished emotions because they believed that to experience emotion you must first perceive your body's arousal.

The James-Lange theory finds support in studies of people with severed spinal cords, including a survey of 25 soldiers who suffered such injuries in World War II (Hohmann, 1966). Those with lower-spine injuries, who had lost sensation only in their legs, reported little change in the intensity of their emotions before and after their spinal injuries. Those with high spinal-cord injury, who could feel nothing below the neck, reported a difference, however. After their injury, the intensity of some reactions had decreased considerably, as James and Lange would have expected. Anger, one man confessed, "just doesn't have the heat to it that it used to. It's a mental kind of anger." But other emotions, those expressed mostly in body areas above the neck—such as weeping while watching a touching film—were felt more intensely by the men with high spinal-cord injury.

Joy expressed According to the James-Lange theory, we don't just smile because we share our teammates' joy. We also share the joy because we are smiling with them.

AP Photo/Charlie Neibergall

So, with James and Lange we can say that our body's reactions are an important ingredient of emotion. Some researchers now view feelings as "mostly shadows" of our bodily responses and behaviors (Damasio, 2003).

But most researchers agree with Cannon and Bard on another point: There is more to the experience of emotion than reading our body's responses. Our experienced emotions also involve cognition (Averill, 1993). Whether we fear the man behind us on the dark street depends entirely on whether we interpret his actions as threatening or friendly.

Stanley Schachter and Jerome Singer (1962) proposed a third theory: Our physiology and our cognitions—perceptions, memories, and interpretations—together create emotion. In their **two-factor theory,** emotions therefore have two ingredients: physical arousal and a cognitive label (**FIGURE 11.1**). Like James and Lange, Schachter and Singer presumed that our experience of emotion grows from our awareness of our body's arousal. Yet like Cannon and Bard, Schachter and Singer also believed that emotions are physiologically similar. Thus, in their view, an emotional experience requires a conscious interpretation of the arousal.

To assess the James-Lange, Cannon-Bard, and two-factor theories, we'll consider some answers contemporary researchers have gleaned to two questions:

- Are different emotions marked by distinct physiological responses?
- What is the connection between what we *think* and how we *feel*?

Then, in the remainder of this chapter, we'll consider two specific emotions—anger and happiness—and how prolonged negative emotion can lead to stress and illness.

emotion a response of the whole organism, involving (1) physiological arousal, (2) expressive behaviors, and (3) consciously experienced thoughts and feelings.

James-Lange theory the theory that our experience of emotion is our awareness of our physiological responses to emotion-arousing stimuli.

Cannon-Bard theory the theory that an emotion-arousing stimulus simultaneously triggers (1) physiological responses and (2) the subjective experience of emotion.

two-factor theory the Schachter-Singer theory that to experience emotion one must (1) be physically aroused and (2) cognitively label the arousal.

FIGURE 11.1 Theories of emotion

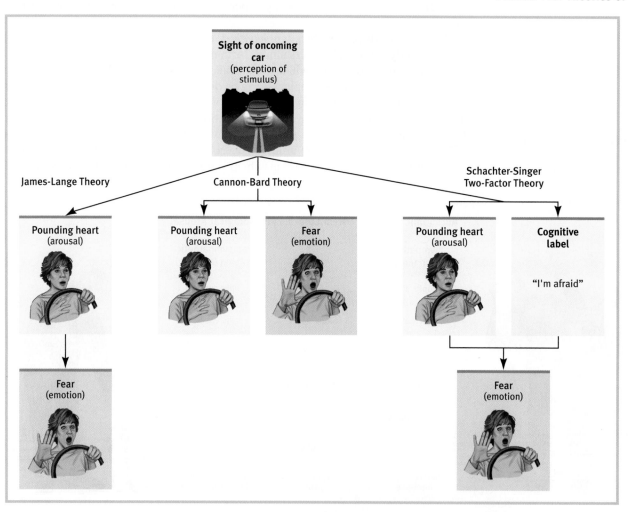

Embodied Emotion

Whether you are eagerly anticipating a long-awaited vacation, falling in love, or grieving a death, you need little convincing that emotions involve the body. Feeling without a body is like breathing without lungs. Some physical responses are easy to notice, others—many taking place at the level of brain neurons—happen without your awareness.

Emotions and the Autonomic Nervous System

2: **What is the link between emotional arousal and the autonomic nervous system?**

In a crisis, it is your autonomic nervous system (ANS) that mobilizes your body for action and calms it when the crisis passes (**FIGURE 11.2**; see also Chapter 2). Without any conscious effort, your body's response to danger is wonderfully coordinated and adaptive—preparing you to fight or flee.

The *sympathetic division* of your ANS directs your adrenal glands to release the stress hormones epinephrine (adrenaline) and norepinephrine (noradrenaline). To provide energy, your liver, influenced by this hormonal surge, pours extra sugar into your bloodstream. To help burn the sugar, your respiration increases to supply needed oxygen. Your heart rate and blood pressure increase. Your digestion slows, diverting blood from your internal organs to your muscles. With blood sugar driven into the large muscles, running becomes easier. Your pupils dilate, letting in more light. To cool your stirred-up body, you perspire. If wounded, your blood would clot more quickly.

When the crisis passes, the *parasympathetic division* of your ANS takes over, calming your body. Its neural centers inhibit further release of stress hormones, but those already in your bloodstream will linger awhile, so arousal diminishes gradually.

Too little arousal (think sleepiness) can be disruptive. In many situations, arousal is adaptive. Performance peaks at higher levels of arousal for easy or well-learned tasks. Thus, runners excel when aroused by competition. But when we are facing difficult tasks, high anxiety can disrupt performance. When you're taking an exam, for example, it pays to be moderately aroused—alert but not trembling with nervousness. Learning to relax before an exam may help you to perform better (Hembree, 1988).

"Fear lends wings to his feet."

—Virgil, *Aeneid*, 19 B.C.E.

FIGURE 11.2 Emotional arousal Like a crisis control center, the autonomic nervous system arouses the body in a crisis and calms it when danger passes.

Autonomic Nervous System Controls Physiological Arousal

Sympathetic division (arousing)		Parasympathetic division (calming)
Pupils dilate	EYES	Pupils contract
Decreases	SALIVATION	Increases
Perspires	SKIN	Dries
Increases	RESPIRATION	Decreases
Accelerates	HEART	Slows
Inhibits	DIGESTION	Activates
Secrete stress hormones	ADRENAL GLANDS	Decrease secretion of stress hormones

(Later in this chapter, you'll hear more about relaxation techniques, and also about the dangers of prolonged high arousal, which can tax the body.)

Brain and Other Physiological Indicators of Emotions

3: **Do different emotions activate different physiological or brain responses?**

Imagine conducting this experiment: In each of four rooms, you have someone watching a movie: In the first, the person is viewing a horror show; in the second, an anger-provoking film; in the third, a sexually arousing film; in the fourth, an utterly boring movie. From the control center, you are monitoring each person's physiological responses, measuring heart rates, breathing, and perspiration. Do you think you could tell who is frightened? Who is angry? Who is sexually aroused? Who is bored?

With training, you could probably pick out the bored viewer. But discerning physiological differences among fear, anger, and sexual arousal would be much more difficult (Barrett, 2006). Different emotions do not have sharply distinct biological signatures. Nevertheless, to you and me, sexual arousal, fear, and anger *feel* different. And, despite similar arousal, emotions often *look* different. People may appear "paralyzed with fear" or "ready to explode."

Although we can't easily see differences in emotions from tracking heart rate, breathing, and perspiration, researchers have found some real, though subtle, physiological distinctions among the emotions. For example, the finger temperatures and hormone secretions that accompany fear and rage sometimes differ (Ax, 1953; Levenson, 1992). And, though fear and joy can prompt similar increased heart rate, they stimulate different facial muscles. During fear, brow muscles tense. During joy, muscles in the cheeks and under the eyes pull into a smile (Witvliet & Vrana, 1995).

Emotions differ much more in the brain circuits they use (Panksepp, 2007). Compared with observers watching angry faces, those watching (and subtly mimicking) fearful faces show more activity in their amygdala, the emotional control center in the brain's limbic system (Whalen et al., 2001). (The amygdala also offers a shortcut for some of our emotional responses, as you'll see later in this chapter.) Brain scans and EEG recordings show that emotions also activate different areas of the brain's cortex, with some tendency for negative emotions to be linked to the right hemisphere and positive emotions to the left. Disgust, for example, triggers more activity in the right prefrontal cortex than in the left. Depression-prone people, and those with generally negative personalities, also show more right frontal lobe activity (Harmon-Jones et al., 2002).

Positive moods tend to trigger more left frontal lobe activity. (When you're happy and you know it, your brain will surely show it.) People with positive personalities—exuberant infants and alert, enthusiastic, energized, and persistently goal-directed adults—also show more activity in the left frontal lobe than in the right (Davidson, 2000, 2003; Urry et al., 2004). Indeed, the more a person's baseline frontal lobe activity tilts left—or is made to tilt left by perceptual activity—the more upbeat the person typically is (Drake & Myers, 2006).

Given the physical indicators of emotion, might we, like Pinocchio, give some telltale signs when we lie? See Thinking Critically About: Lie Detection on the next page.

Cognition and Emotion

4: **To experience emotions, must we consciously interpret and label them?**

Do our thoughts define our feelings? It sometimes seems that way when our arousal response to one event spills over into our response to the next event. Imagine arriving home after an invigorating run and finding a message that you got a longed-for

Emotional arousal Elated excitement and panicky fear involve similar physiological arousal. That allows us to flip rapidly between the two emotions.

"No one ever told me that grief felt so much like fear. I am not afraid, but the sensation is like being afraid. The same fluttering in the stomach, the same restlessness, the yawning. I keep on swallowing."

—C. S. Lewis, *A Grief Observed*, 1961

In 1966, a young man named Charles Whitman killed his wife and mother and then climbed to the top of a tower at the University of Texas and shot 38 people. An autopsy later revealed a tumor pressing against his amygdala, which may have contributed to his violence.

Thinking Critically About:

Lie Detection

Can polygraph tests like this identify liars? To learn more, read on.

For those who believe in them, *lie detectors,* or **polygraphs,** have offered a way to eavesdrop on the brain and detect lies as they are told. But as our understanding of physiological measures of emotion has grown, the reputation of lie detectors has shrunk.

Polygraphs measure the changes in breathing, cardiovascular activity, and perspiration that accompany emotion. An examiner monitors these responses as you answer questions. Some items, called *control questions,* aim to make anyone a little nervous. If asked, "In the last 20 years, have you ever taken something that didn't belong to you?" many people will tell a white lie and say *no,* and the polygraph will detect arousal. If your physiological reactions to *critical ques-*

polygraph a machine, commonly used in attempts to detect lies, that measures several of the physiological responses accompanying emotion (such as perspiration and cardiovascular and breathing changes).

tions ("Did you ever steal anything from your previous employer?") are weaker than to control questions, the examiner infers you are telling the truth.

But there are two problems: First, our physiological arousal is much the same from one emotion to another—anxiety, irritation, and guilt all prompt similar physiological reactivity. Second, these tests err about one-third of the time, especially when innocent people respond with heightened tension to the accusations implied by the critical questions (**FIGURE 11.3**). Many rape victims, for example, "fail" lie detector tests when reacting emotionally while telling the truth about their assailant (Lykken, 1991).

A 2002 U.S. National Academy of Sciences report noted that "no spy has ever been caught [by] using the polygraph." It is not for lack of trying. The FBI, CIA, and Departments of Defense and Energy in the United States have spent

FIGURE 11.3 How often do lie detectors lie? Benjamin Kleinmuntz and Julian Szucko (1984) had polygraph experts study the polygraph data of 50 theft suspects who later confessed to being guilty and 50 suspects whose innocence was later established by someone's confession. Had the polygraph experts been the judges, more than one-third of the innocent would have been declared guilty, and almost one-fourth of the guilty would have been declared innocent.

millions of dollars testing tens of thousands of employees. Meanwhile Aldrich Ames, who enjoyed an unexplained lavish life-style as a Russian spy within the CIA, went undetected. Ames "took scores of polygraph tests and passed them all," noted Robert Park (1999). "Nobody thought to investigate the source of his sudden wealth—after all, he was passing the lie detector tests." The truth is, lie detectors can lie.

A more effective approach to lie detection uses the *guilty knowledge test,* which assesses a suspect's physiological responses to crime-scene details known only to the police and the guilty person (Ben-Shakhar & Elaad, 2003). If a camera and computer had been stolen, for example, presumably only a guilty person would react strongly to the specific brand names of these items. Given enough such specific probes, an innocent person will seldom be wrongly accused.

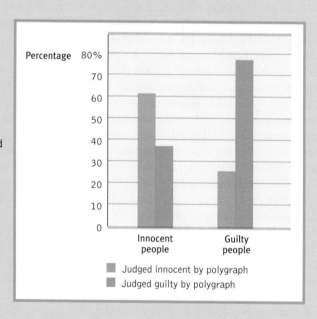

job. With arousal lingering from the run, would you feel more elated than if you received this news after awakening from a nap?

To find out whether this *spillover effect* exists, Stanley Schachter and Jerome Singer (1962) aroused college men with injections of the hormone epinephrine. Picture yourself as one of their participants: After receiving the injection, you go to a waiting room, where you find yourself with another person (actually an accomplice of the experimenters) who is acting either euphoric or irritated. As you observe this person, you begin to feel your heart race, your body flush, and your breathing become more rapid. If told to expect these effects from the injection, what would you feel? Schachter and Singer's volunteers felt little emotion—because they attributed their arousal to the drug. But if told the injection would produce no effects, what would you feel? Perhaps you would react, as another group of participants did, by "catching" the apparent emotion of the person you are with—becoming happy if the accomplice is acting euphoric, and testy if the accomplice is acting irritated.

This discovery—that a stirred-up state can be experienced as one emotion or another very different one, depending on how we interpret and label it—has been replicated in dozens of experiments. Insult people who have just been aroused by pedaling an exercise bike or watching rock videos and they will find it easy to misattribute their arousal to the provocation. Their anger will exceed that of people similarly provoked but not previously aroused. Likewise, sexually aroused people react with more hostility in anger-provoking situations. And, vice versa—the arousal that lingers after an intense argument or a frightening experience may intensify sexual passion (Palace, 1995). Just as the Schachter-Singer two-factor theory predicts, arousal + label = emotion. Emotional arousal may not be as undifferentiated as Schachter and Singer believed, but arousal from emotions as diverse as anger, fear, and sexual excitement can indeed spill from one emotion to another (Reisenzein, 1983; Sinclair et al., 1994; Zillmann, 1986). *The point to remember:* Arousal fuels emotion; cognition channels it.

The spillover effect Arousal from a soccer match can fuel anger, which can descend into rioting or other violent confrontations.

"Feelings that one interprets as fear in the presence of a sheer drop may be interpreted as lust in the presence of a sheer blouse."

—Daniel Gilbert,
Stumbling on Happiness, 2006

Emotion and the Two-Track Brain

Is the heart *always* subject to the mind? Robert Zajonc (pronounced ZI-yence; 1980, 1984a) has contended that we actually have many emotional reactions apart from, or even before, our interpretations of a situation. Imagine receiving some unsettling news. You discover that you've forgotten an important deadline, or that you've hurt someone's feelings. As the ongoing conversation distracts your attention, you lose awareness of the bad news. Yet the feeling still churns. You feel a little bad. You know there's a reason, but for the moment you can't put your finger on it.

Arousal can linger without a label. Without being consciously aware of having seen it, we can be influenced by a stimulus flashed too briefly to interpret, much less label. A subliminally flashed stimulus, such as a smiling or angry face or a disgusting scene can prime a mood or specific emotion and lead us to feel better or worse about a follow-up stimulus (Murphy et al., 1995; Ruys & Stapel, 2008). In one set of experiments, thirsty people were given a fruit-flavored drink after viewing a subliminally flashed (thus unperceived) face. Those exposed to a happy face drank about 50 percent more than those exposed to a neutral face (Berridge & Winkielman, 2003). Those flashed an angry face drank substantially less.

Neuroscience research helps us understand these surprising findings. Like speedy reflexes that operate apart from the brain's thinking cortex, some emotions take what Joseph LeDoux (2002) calls the "low road," via neural pathways that bypass the cortex (which offers the alternative "high road" pathway). One low-road pathway runs from the eye or ear via the thalamus to the amygdala, bypassing the cortex (see **FIGURE 11.4** on the next page). This shortcut enables our greased-lightning emotional response before our intellect intervenes. So speedy is the amygdala reaction that we may be unaware of what's transpired (Dimberg et al., 2000). In one fascinating experiment, Paul Whalen and his colleagues (2004) used fMRI

Can you recall liking something or someone immediately, without knowing why?

"Oh! ye'll tak' the high road and I'll tak' the low road, An' I'll be in Scotland afore ye."

—Traditional Scottish song, "Bonnie Banks o' Loch Lomond"

FIGURE 11.4 The brain's shortcut for emotions In the two-track brain, sensory input may be routed (a) directly to the amygdala (via the thalamus) for an instant emotional reaction, or (b) to the cortex for analysis.

(a) The speedy low road

(b) The thinking high road

Fearful   Happy

FIGURE 11.5 The brain's sensitivity to threats Even when fearful eyes (left) were flashed too briefly for people to consciously perceive them, fMRI scans revealed that their hypervigilant amygdala was alerted (Whalen et al., 2004). The happy eyes on the right did not have this effect.

Courtesy of Paul J. Whalen, PhD, Dartmouth College, www.whalenlab.info

scans to observe the amygdala's response to subliminally presented fearful eyes (**FIGURE 11.5**). Compared with a control condition that presented the whites of happy eyes, the fearful eyes triggered increased amygdala activity (despite no one's being aware of seeing them).

The amygdala sends more neural projections up to the cortex than it receives back. This makes it easier for our feelings to hijack our thinking than for our thinking to rule our feelings, noted LeDoux and Jorge Armony (1999). In the forest, we jump at the sound of rustling bushes nearby, leaving the cortex to decide later whether the sound was made by a predator or just the wind. Such an experience supports Zajonc's belief that *some* of our emotional reactions involve no deliberate thinking.

Emotion researcher Richard Lazarus (1991, 1998) has conceded that our brains process and react to vast amounts of information without our conscious awareness, and he willingly granted that some emotional responses do not require *conscious* thinking. Much of our emotional life operates via the automatic, effortless, speedy low road. But, without some sort of cognitive appraisal, how would we *know* what we are reacting to? The appraisal may be effortless and we may not be conscious of it, but it is still a mental function. To know whether something is good or bad, the brain must have some idea of what it is (Storbeck et al., 2006). Thus, emotions arise when we *appraise* an event as beneficial or harmful to our well-being, whether we truly know it is or not. We appraise the sound of the rustling bushes as the presence of a threat. Later, we realize that it was "just the wind."

To sum up, as Zajonc and LeDoux have demonstrated, some emotional responses—especially simple likes, dislikes, and fears (imagine a large spider falling on you)—involve no conscious thinking (**FIGURE 11.6**). Such responses are difficult to alter by changing our thinking. The emotional brain even influences people's political decisions, leading many to vote for

FIGURE 11.6 Another example of dual processing: two routes to emotion Zajonc and LeDoux have emphasized that some emotional responses are immediate, before any conscious appraisal. Lazarus, Schachter, and Singer emphasized that our appraisal and labeling of events also determine our emotional responses.

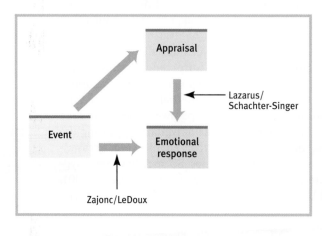

Appraisal

Lazarus/
Schachter-Singer

Event

Emotional
response

Zajonc/LeDoux

candidates they automatically *like* over a candidate expressing positions closer to their own (Westen, 2007).

But like other emotions—including moods such as depression and complex feelings such as hatred, guilt, happiness, and love—our feelings about politics are, as Lazarus, Schachter, and Singer predicted, greatly influenced by our memories, expectations, and interpretations. Highly emotional people are intense partly because of their interpretations. They may *personalize* events as being somehow directed at them, and they may *generalize* their experiences by blowing single incidents out of proportion (Larsen et al., 1987). In dealing with complex emotions, learning to *think* more positively can help people *feel* better. Even though the emotional low road functions automatically, the thinking high road allows us to retake some control over our emotional life.

REHEARSE IT!

1. The Cannon-Bard theory of emotion proposes that the physiological response (like heart pounding) and the subjective experience of, say, fear
   a. are unrelated.
   b. occur simultaneously.
   c. occur in the opposite order (with feelings of fear first).
   d. are regulated by the thalamus.

2. With a challenging task, such as taking a difficult exam, performance is likely to peak when arousal is
   a. very high.
   b. moderate.
   c. low.
   d. absent.

3. Assume that after spending an hour on a treadmill, you receive a letter saying that your scholarship request has been approved. The two-factor theory of emotion would predict that your physical arousal will
   a. weaken your happiness.
   b. intensify your happiness.
   c. transform your happiness into relief.
   d. have no particular effect on your happiness.

4. If physically aroused by swimming, then heckled by an onlooker, we may interpret our arousal as anger and
   a. become less physically aroused.
   b. feel angrier than usual.
   c. feel less angry than usual.
   d. act euphoric.

5. Zajonc and LeDoux maintain that some emotional reactions occur before we have had the chance to label or interpret them. Lazarus disagreed. These psychologists differ about whether emotional responses occur in the absence of
   a. physical arousal.
   b. the hormone epinephrine.
   c. cognitive processing.
   d. learning.

Answers: 1. b, 2. b, 3. b, 4. b, 5. c.

Expressed Emotion

5: How do we communicate nonverbally?

There is a simpler method of deciphering people's emotions: We read their bodies, listen to their tone of voice, and study their faces. People's expressive behavior reveals their emotion. Does this nonverbal language vary with culture, or is it universal? And do our expressions influence our experienced emotions?

> "Your face, my thane, is a book where men may read strange matters."
>
> —Lady Macbeth to her husband, in William Shakespeare's *Macbeth*

Detecting Emotion

All of us communicate nonverbally as well as verbally. To Westerners, a firm handshake immediately conveys an outgoing, expressive personality (Chaplin et al., 2000). With a gaze, an averted glance, or a stare we can communicate intimacy, submission, or dominance (Kleinke, 1986). Among those passionately in love, gazing into each other's eyes is typically prolonged and mutual (Rubin, 1970). Joan Kellerman, James Lewis, and James Laird (1989) wondered if intimate gazes would stir such feelings between strangers. To find out, they asked unacquainted male-female pairs to gaze intently for two minutes either at each other's hands or into each other's eyes. After separating, the eye gazers reported feeling a tingle of attraction and affection.

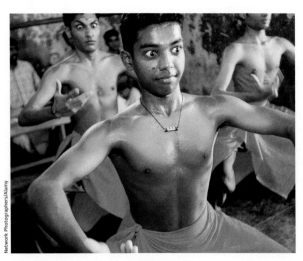

A silent language of emotion Hindu classic dance uses the face and body to effectively convey 10 different emotions (Hejmadi et al., 2000).

Which of researcher Paul Ekman's smiles is feigned, which natural? The smile on the right engages the facial muscles of a natural smile.

FIGURE 11.7 Experience influences how we perceive emotions Viewing the morphed middle face, evenly mixing fear with anger, physically abused children were more likely than nonabused children to perceive the face as angry (Pollak & Kistler, 2002; Pollak & Tolley-Schell, 2003).

Most of us are good enough at reading nonverbal cues to decipher the emotions in an old silent film. We are especially good at detecting threats. Even when hearing emotions conveyed in another language, people most readily detect anger (Scherer et al., 2001). When viewing subliminally flashed words, we more often sense the presence of a negative word, such as *snake* or *bomb* (Dijksterhuis & Aarts, 2003). And in a crowd of faces, a single angry face will "pop out" faster than a single happy one (Fox et al., 2000; Hansen & Hansen, 1988; Öhman et al., 2001).

Experience can sensitize us to particular emotions, as shown by experiments using a series of faces (like those in **FIGURE 11.7**) that morphed from fear (or sadness) to anger. Viewing such faces, physically abused children are much quicker than other children to spot the signals of anger. Shown a face that is 60 percent fear and 40 percent anger, they are as likely to perceive anger as fear. Their perceptions become sensitively attuned to glimmers of danger that nonabused children miss.

Hard-to-control facial muscles reveal signs of emotions you may be trying to conceal. Lifting just the inner part of your eyebrows, which few people do consciously, reveals distress or worry. Eyebrows raised and pulled together signal fear. Activated muscles under the eyes and raised cheeks suggest a natural smile. A feigned smile, such as one we make for a photographer, often continues for more than 4 or 5 seconds. Most authentic expressions have faded by that time. Feigned smiles are also switched on and off more abruptly than is a genuine happy smile (Bugental, 1986).

Our brains are rather amazing detectors of subtle expressions. Elisha Babad, Frank Bernieri, and Robert Rosenthal (1991) discovered just *how* amazing after filming teachers talking to unseen schoolchildren. A mere 10-second clip of either the teacher's voice or face provided enough clues for both young and old viewers to determine whether the teacher liked and admired the child he or she was addressing. In another experiment, a glimpse of a face for even one-tenth of a second was enough for people to judge someone's trustworthiness (Willis & Todorov, 2006).

Despite our brain's emotion-detecting skill, we find it difficult to detect deceiving expressions (Porter & ten Brinke, 2008). In one digest of 206 studies of discerning truth from lies, people were just 54 percent accurate—barely better than a coin toss (Bond & DePaulo, 2006). Moreover, contrary to claims that some experts can spot lies, the available research indicates that virtually no one beats chance by much (Bond & DePaulo, 2008).

Some of us are, however, more sensitive than others to physical cues. In one study (Rosenthal et al., 1979), hundreds of people viewed brief film clips of an emotionally expressive face or body, sometimes accompanied by a garbled voice, and reported on the emotions they had observed. For example, after a 2-second scene revealing only the face of an upset woman, the viewers would decide whether the woman was criticizing someone for being late or was talking about her divorce. Given such *thin slices*, some people were much better than others at detecting emotion. Introverts tend to excel at reading others' emotions, and extraverts' emotions are generally easier to read (Ambady et al., 1995).

Nonverbal cues—gestures, facial expressions, tones of voice—are absent in computer-based communication, except for occasional sideways *emoticons*, such as ;-) for a knowing wink and :-(for a frown. In e-mails and Internet discussions, nobody knows what you look or sound like, or anything about your status, personality, age, or background; you are judged solely on your words. When first meeting face to face, e-mail pen pals are often surprised at the person they encounter.

It's also easy to misread computer-based communications. The absence of expressive e-motion, including the vocal nuances by which we signal that a statement is serious, kidding, or sarcastic, can make for ambiguous emotion. Communicators may think their "just kidding" intent is equally clear, whether e-mailed or spoken, but they commonly exhibit egocentrism by not foreseeing misinterpretations (Krueger et al., 2005).

Botox injections paralyze facial muscles that create wrinkles, allowing the overlying skin to relax and smooth. By erasing the subtle expressions of frown lines or smiling eyes, might this cosmetic procedure hide subtle emotions?

Gender, Emotion, and Nonverbal Behavior

Is women's intuition, as so many believe, superior to men's? Consider: As Jackie Larsen left her Grand Marais, Minnesota, church prayer group one April 2001 morning, she encountered Christopher Bono, a clean-cut, well-mannered youth. Bono's car had broken down, and he said he was looking for a ride to meet friends in Thunder Bay. When Bono later appeared in Larsen's shop, where she had promised to help him phone his friends, she felt a pain in her stomach. Sensing that something was very wrong with this young man, she insisted they talk outside on the sidewalk. "I said, 'I am a mother and I have to talk to you like a mother. . . . I can tell by your manners that you have a nice mother.'" At the mention of his mother, Bono's eyes fixed on her. "I don't know where my mother is," he said.

As the conversation ended, Larsen directed Bono back to the church to meet the pastor. She also called the police and suggested that they trace his license plates. The car was registered to his mother in southern Illinois. When police went to her apartment, they found blood all over and Lucia Bono dead in the bathtub. Christopher Bono, 16, was charged with first-degree murder (Biggs, 2001).

Was it a coincidence that Larsen, who had seen through Bono's calm exterior, was a woman? Some psychologists would say *no*. In her analysis of 125 studies of sensitivity to nonverbal cues, Judith Hall (1984, 1987) discerned that women generally surpass men at reading people's emotional cues in thin slices of behavior. And women have surpassed men in discerning whether a male-female couple is a genuine romantic couple or a posed phony couple, and in discerning which of two people in a photo is the other's supervisor (Barnes & Sternberg, 1989).

Women's nonverbal sensitivity helps explain their greater emotional literacy. Invited by Lisa Feldman Barrett and her colleagues (2000) to describe how they would feel in certain situations, men described simpler emotional reactions. You might like to try this yourself: Ask some people how they might feel when saying good-bye to friends after graduation. Barrett's work suggests you are more likely to hear men say, simply, "I'll feel bad," and to hear women express more complex emotions: "It will be bittersweet; I'll feel both happy and sad."

In both positive and negative situations, women tend to display greater emotional responsiveness (Grossman & Wood, 1993; Sprecher & Sedikides, 1993; Stoppard & Gruchy, 1993). Studies of 23,000 people from 26 cultures around the world have found that women more than men report themselves open to feelings (Costa et al., 2001). That helps explain the extremely strong perception that emotionality is "more true of women"—a perception expressed by nearly 100 percent of 18- to 29-year-old Americans (Newport, 2001).

One exception: Anger strikes most people as a more masculine emotion. Ask someone to imagine an angry face, then ask them: What gender is the person? For three in four Arizona State University students, the imagined angry person was male (Becker et al., 2007). The researchers also found that if a gender-neutral face

FIGURE 11.8 **Male or Female?** When Vaughn Becker and his colleagues (2007) manipulated a gender-neutral face, people were more likely to see it as a male when it wore an angry expression, and as a female when it wore a smile.

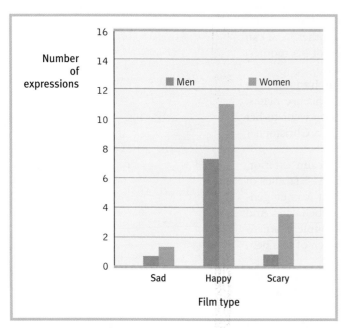

FIGURE 11.9 **Gender and expressiveness** Although male and female students did not differ dramatically in self-reported emotions or physiological responses while viewing emotional films, the women's faces *showed* much more emotion. (From Kring & Gordon, 1998.)

is made to look angry, most people will perceive it as male. If the face is smiling, they will more likely perceive it as female (**FIGURE 11.8**).

Women and men also differ in whether they describe themselves as empathic. If you have *empathy,* you identify with others and imagine what it must be like to walk in their shoes. You rejoice with those who rejoice and weep with those who weep. Physiological measures of empathy, such as heart rate while seeing another's distress, reveal a much smaller gender gap than is found in self-reports in surveys (Eisenberg & Lennon, 1983).

Nevertheless, females are more likely to *express* empathy—to cry and to report distress when observing someone in distress. Ann Kring and Albert Gordon (1998) observed this gender difference in videotapes of men and women students watching film clips that were sad (children with a dying parent), happy (slapstick comedy), or frightening (a man nearly falling off the ledge of a tall building). As **FIGURE 11.9** shows, the women reacted more visibly to each film type. Women also tend to experience emotional events (such as viewing pictures of mutilation) more deeply—with more brain activation in areas sensitive to emotion—and then to remember the scenes better three weeks later (Canli et al., 2002).

In another exploration of gender and facial expression, Harold Hill and Alan Johnston (2001) animated an image of an average head with expressions (smirks, head tosses, raised eyebrows) that had been digitally captured from the faces of London University students as they read a joke. Despite having no anatomical clues to gender, observers could usually detect gender in the telltale expressions.

Culture and Emotional Expression

6: Are nonverbal expressions of emotion universally understood?

The meaning of gestures varies with the culture. Some years ago, psychologist Otto Klineberg (1938) observed that in Chinese literature people clapped their hands to express worry or disappointment, laughed a great "Ho-Ho" to express anger, and stuck out their tongues to show surprise. Similarly, the North American "thumbs up" and "A-OK" signs are considered insults in certain other cultures. (When former U.S. President Richard Nixon made the latter sign in Brazil, he didn't realize he was making a crude insult.) Just how important cultural definitions of gestures can be was demonstrated in 1968, when North Korea publicized photos of supposedly happy officers from a captured U.S. Navy spy ship. In the photo, three of the men raised their middle fingers; they had told captors it was a "Hawaiian good luck sign" (Fleming & Scott, 1991).

Do facial expressions also have different meanings in different cultures? To find out, two investigative teams—one led by Paul Ekman, Wallace Friesen, and others (1975, 1987, 1994), the other by Carroll Izard (1977, 1994)— showed photographs of various facial expressions to people in different parts of the world and asked them to guess the emotion. You can try this matching task yourself by pairing the six emotions with the six faces of **FIGURE 11.10**.

Regardless of your cultural background, you probably did pretty well. A smile's a smile the world around. Ditto for anger, and to a lesser extent the other basic expressions (Elfenbein & Ambady, 1999). (There is no culture where people frown when they are happy.) Thus, a glimpse at competitors' spontaneous expressions following an Olympic judo competition gives a very good clue to who won, no matter their country (Matsumoto & Willingham, 2006).

Do people from different cultures share these similarities because they share experiences, such as American movies or the BBC and CNN broadcasts? Apparently not. Ekman and his team asked people in isolated parts of New Guinea to display various emotions in response to such statements as, "Pretend your child has died." When the researchers showed tapes of the New Guineans' facial reactions to North American collegians, the students read them easily.

Facial expressions do contain some nonverbal accents that provide clues to one's culture (Marsh et al., 2003). So it's not surprising that data from 182 studies show slightly enhanced accuracy when people judge emotions from their own culture (Elfenbein & Ambady, 2002, 2003a,b). Still, the telltale signs of emotion generally cross cultural boundaries.

People blind from birth spontaneously exhibit the common facial expressions associated with such emotions as joy, sadness, fear, and anger (Galati et al., 1997). Even blind children who have never seen a face, display these facial expressions (Eibl-Eibesfeldt, 1971). The world over, children cry when distressed, shake their heads when defiant, and smile when they are happy.

The discovery that facial muscles speak a fairly universal language would not have surprised pioneering emotion researcher Charles Darwin (1809–1882). He speculated that before our prehistoric ancestors communicated in words, their ability to convey threats, greetings, and submission with facial expressions helped them survive. That shared heritage, he believed, is why all humans express the basic emotions with similar facial expressions. A sneer, for example, retains elements of an animal baring its teeth in a snarl. Emotional expressions may enhance our survival in other ways, too. Surprise raises the eyebrows and widens the eyes, enabling us to take in more information. Disgust wrinkles the nose, closing it from foul odors.

Smiles, too, are social phenomena as well as emotional reflexes. Bowlers seldom smile when they score a strike—they smile when they turn to face their companions (Jones et al., 1991; Kraut & Johnston, 1979). Even euphoric winners of Olympic gold medals typically don't smile when they are awaiting their ceremony but do when interacting with officials and facing the crowd and cameras (Fernández-Dols & Ruiz-Belda, 1995).

Ekman & Matsumoto, Japanese and Caucasian Facial Expression of Emotion

FIGURE 11.10 Culture-specific or culturally universal expressions? As people of differing cultures and races, do our faces speak differing languages? Which face expresses disgust? Anger? Fear? Happiness? Sadness? Surprise? (From Matsumoto & Ekman, 1989.) See inverted answers below.

From left to right, top to bottom: happiness, surprise, fear, sadness, anger, disgust.

"For news of the heart, ask the face."
—Guinean proverb

While weightless, astronauts' internal bodily fluids move toward their upper body and their faces become puffy. This makes nonverbal communication more difficult, increasing the risks of misunderstanding, especially among multinational crews (Gelman, 1989).

It has been adaptive for us to interpret faces in particular contexts. (Recall the aggressive or frightened monsters from Chapter 6.) People judge an angry face set in a frightening situation as afraid. They judge a fearful face set in a painful situation as pained (Carroll & Russell, 1996). Movie directors harness this phenomenon by creating contexts and soundtracks that amplify our perceptions of particular emotions.

Although cultures share a universal facial language for basic emotions, they differ in how *much* emotion they express. Cultures that encourage individuality, as in Western Europe, Australia, New Zealand, and North America, display mostly visible emotions (van Hemert et al., 2007). In Chinese culture, which encourages people to adjust to others, personal emotions are less visibly displayed (Tsai et al., 2007). Ditto Japan, where people infer emotion more from the surrounding context, and where the difficult-to-control eyes convey more emotion than the mouth, which is so expressive in North America (Masuda et al., 2008; Yuki et al., 2007).

Cultural differences also exist within nations. The Irish and their Irish-American descendants tend to be more expressive than Scandinavians and their Scandinavian-American descendants (Tsai & Chentsova-Dutton, 2003). And that reminds us of a familiar lesson: Like most psychological events, emotion is best understood not only as a biological and cognitive phenomenon, but also as a social-cultural phenomenon (**FIGURE 11.11**).

FIGURE 11.11 Levels of analysis for the study of emotion As with other psychological phenomena, researchers explore emotion at biological, psychological, and social-cultural levels.

Biological influences:
• physiological arousal
• evolutionary adaptiveness
• brain pathways
• spillover effect

Psychological influences:
• cognitive labeling
• gender differences

Emotion

Social-cultural influences:
• expressiveness
• presence of others
• cultural expectations

"Whenever I feel afraid
I hold my head erect
And whistle a happy tune."

—Richard Rodgers and Oscar Hammerstein, *The King and I*, 1958

A request from your author: Smile often as you read this book.

The Effects of Facial Expressions

7: Do our facial expressions influence our feelings?

As William James struggled with feelings of depression and grief, he came to believe that we can control emotions by going "through the outward movements" of any emotion we want to experience. "To feel cheerful," he advised, "sit up cheerfully, look around cheerfully, and act as if cheerfulness were already there."

Studies of emotional effects of facial expressions reveal precisely what James might have predicted. Expressions not only communicate emotion, they also amplify and regulate it. In his 1872 book, *The Expression of the Emotions in Man and Animals*, Darwin contended that "the free expression by outward signs of an emotion intensifies it. . . . He who gives way to violent gestures will increase his rage."

Was Darwin right? Let's test Darwin's hypothesis: Fake a big grin. Now scowl. Can you feel the "smile therapy" difference? Participants in dozens of experiments have felt a difference. For example, James Laird and his colleagues (1974, 1984, 1989) subtly induced students to make a frowning expression by asking them to "contract these muscles" and "pull your brows together" (supposedly to help the researchers attach facial electrodes). The results? The students reported feeling a little angry. People instructed to mold their faces in ways that express other basic emotions also experienced those emotions (**FIGURE 11.12**). For example, they reported feeling more fear than anger, disgust, or sadness when made to construct a fearful expression: "Raise your eyebrows. And open your eyes wide. Move your whole head back, so that your chin is tucked in a little bit, and let your mouth relax and hang open a little" (Duclos et al., 1989). The face is more than a billboard that displays our feelings; *it also feeds our feelings*.

In the absence of competing emotions, this *facial feedback* effect is subtle yet detectable. Students induced to smile have felt happier and recalled happier memories than did frowners. Just activating one of the smiling muscles by holding a pen in the teeth (rather than with the lips, which activates a frowning muscle) is enough to make cartoons seem more amusing (Strack et al., 1988). A heartier smile—made not just with the mouth but with raised cheeks that crinkle the eyes—enhances positive feelings even more when you are reacting to something pleasant or funny (Soussignan, 2001). Smile warmly on the outside and you feel better on the inside. Scowl and the whole world seems to scowl back.

Sara Snodgrass and her associates (1986) observed the *behavior feedback* phenomenon with walking. You can duplicate the participants' experience: Walk for a few minutes with short, shuffling steps, keeping your eyes downcast. Now walk around taking long strides, with your arms swinging and your eyes looking straight ahead. Can you feel your mood shift? Going through the motions awakens the emotions.

One small way to become more empathic is to let your own face mimic another person's expression (Vaughn & Lanzetta, 1981). Acting as another acts helps us feel what another feels. Indeed, natural mimicry of others' emotions helps explain why emotions are contagious (Dimberg et al., 2000; Neumann & Strack, 2000).

FIGURE 11.12 How to make people frown without telling them to frown Randy Larsen, Margaret Kasimatis, and Kurt Frey's (1992) solution: Attach two golf tees above people's eyebrows and ask them to make the tee tips touch. Participants felt sad while viewing scenes of war, sickness, and starvation, and even sadder with their "sad face" muscles activated.

Courtesy of Louis Schakel/Michael Kausman/The New York Times Pictures

---

REHEARSE IT!

6. People in different cultures are most likely to differ in their interpretations of
   a. adults' facial expressions.
   b. children's facial expressions.
   c. frowns.
   d. postures and gestures.

7. When people are induced to assume fearful expressions, they often report feeling a little fearful. This result is known as the _____ effect.
   a. facial feedback
   b. culture-specific
   c. natural mimicry
   d. emotional contagion

Answers: 6. d, 7. a.

Experienced Emotion

How many distinct emotions are there? Carroll Izard (1977) isolated 10 basic emotions (joy, interest-excitement, surprise, sadness, anger, disgust, contempt, fear, shame, and guilt), most of which are present in infancy (see **FIGURE 11.13** on the next page). Jessica Tracey and Richard Robins (2004) believe that pride is also a distinct emotion, signaled by a small smile, head slightly tilted back, and an open posture. And Phillip Shaver and his colleagues (1996) believe that love, too, may be a basic emotion. But Izard has argued that other emotions are combinations of these 10, with love, for example, being a mixture of joy and interest-excitement.

Let's take a closer look at two of these emotions: anger and happiness. What influences our experience of each? What functions do they serve?

Anger

8: **What are the causes and consequences of anger?**

Anger, the sages have said, is "a short madness" (Horace, 65–8 B.C.E.) that "carries the mind away" (Virgil, 70–19 B.C.E.) and can be "many times more hurtful than the injury that caused it" (Thomas Fuller, 1654–1734). But they have also said that "noble anger" (William Shakespeare, 1564–1616) "makes any coward brave" (Cato, 234–149 B.C.E.) and "brings back . . . strength" (Virgil).

What makes us angry? Sometimes anger is a response to a friend or loved one's perceived misdeed, especially when the act seems willful, unjustified, and avoidable (Averill, 1983). But small hassles and blameless annoyances—foul odors, high

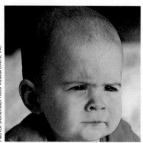

(a) Joy (mouth forming smile, cheeks lifted, twinkle in eye)

(b) Anger (brows drawn together and downward, eyes fixed, mouth squarish)

(c) Interest (brows raised or knitted, mouth softly round-ed, lips may be pursed)

(d) Disgust (nose wrinkled, upper lip raised, tongue pushed outward)

FIGURE 11.13 Infants' naturally occurring emotions To identify the emotions present from birth, Carroll Izard analyzed infants' facial expressions.

(e) Surprise (brows raised, eyes widened, mouth rounded in oval shape)

(f) Sadness (brow's inner cor-ners raised, mouth corners drawn down)

(g) Fear (brows level, drawn in and up, eyelids lifted, mouth corners retracted)

temperatures, a traffic jam, aches and pains—also have the power to make us angry (Berkowitz, 1990).

Anger, especially chronic hostility, can harm us. How, then, can we rid ourselves of our anger?

When irritated, should we lash out at the offender rather than internalizing our angry feelings? Are advice columnists right in urging us to teach children to vent their anger? Are "recovery" therapists right in encouraging us to rage at our dead parents, imaginatively curse the boss, or confront our childhood abuser?

Although common in individualized cultures, such advice would seldom be heard in cultures where people's identity is centered more on the group. People who keenly sense their *inter*dependence see anger as a threat to group harmony (Markus & Kitayama, 1991). In Tahiti, for instance, people learn to be considerate and gentle. In Japan, from infancy on, angry expressions are less frequent than in Western cultures.

A cool culture Domestic violence is rare in Micronesia. This photo of community life on Pulap Island suggests one possible reason: Family life takes place in the open. Relatives and neighbors who witness angry outbursts can step in before the emotion escalates into child, spouse, or elder abuse.

The idea of "venting your anger" presumes that through aggressive action or fantasy you can achieve emotional release, or **catharsis.** Experimenters report that *sometimes* when people retaliate against a provoker, they may indeed calm down. But this tends to be true only *if* their counterattack is directed against the provoker, *if* their retaliation seems justifiable, and *if* their target is not intimidating (Geen & Quanty, 1977; Hokanson & Edelman, 1966). In short, expressing anger can be *temporarily* calming *if* it does not leave you feeling guilty or anxious.

More often, however, catharsis fails to cleanse rage and instead breeds more anger. For one thing, expressing anger may provoke further retaliation, escalating minor conflicts into major confrontations. For another, expressing anger can magnify anger. (Recall the *behavior feedback* research: Acting angry can make us feel angrier.) In a now-classic study (Ebbesen et al., 1975), researchers interviewed 100 people recently laid off by an aerospace company during an economic downturn, and they asked them to fill out a questionnaire assessing their attitudes toward the

catharsis emotional release. The catharsis hypothesis maintains that "releasing" aggressive energy (through action or fantasy) relieves aggressive urges.

company. First, however, they asked some workers questions that released hostility, such as, "What instances can you think of where the company has not been fair with you?" Did this opportunity to "drain off" hostility reduce it? Quite the contrary. Those who had vented their anger exhibited *more* hostility.

Even when provoked people hit a punching bag *believing* it will be cathartic, the effect is the opposite—leading them to exhibit *more* cruelty (Bushman et al., 1999). And when they wallop a punching bag while ruminating about the person who angered them, they become even more aggressive when given a chance for revenge. "Venting to reduce anger is like using gasoline to put out a fire," concluded researcher Brad Bushman (2002). When anger fuels physically or verbally aggressive acts we later regret, it becomes maladaptive. Anger primes prejudice. After 9/11, Americans who responded with anger more than fear displayed intolerance for immigrants and Muslims (DeSteno et al., 2004; Skitka et al., 2004).

Angry outbursts that temporarily calm us are dangerous in another way: They may be reinforcing and therefore habit forming. If stressed managers find they can drain off some of their tension by berating an employee, then the next time they feel irritated and tense they may be more likely to explode again. Think about it: The next time you are angry you are likely to do whatever has relieved your anger in the past.

What, then, is the best way to handle our anger? Experts offer two suggestions. First, wait. You can bring down the level of physiological arousal of anger by waiting. "It is true of the body as of arrows," noted Carol Tavris (1982), "what goes up must come down. Any emotional arousal will simmer down if you just wait long enough." Second, deal with anger in a constructive way. Being chronically angry over every little annoyance or ruminating inwardly about the causes of your anger serves only to increase it (Rusting & Nolen-Hoeksema, 1998). Instead, calm yourself by exercising, playing an instrument, or talking it through with a friend. One Gallup survey indicated that teens found these tactics successful. Boys more than girls reported walking away from the situation or working it off with exercise. Girls more often reported talking with a friend, listening to music, or writing (Ray, 2005).

Civility means not only keeping silent about trivial irritations but also communicating important ones clearly and assertively. Anger can communicate strength and competence (Tiedens, 2001). Controlled expressions of anger are more adaptive than either hostile outbursts or pent-up angry feelings. When James Averill (1983) asked people to recall or keep careful records of their experiences with anger, they often recalled reacting assertively rather than hurtfully. Their anger frequently led them to discuss the conflicts with the offender, thereby lessening the aggravation. A nonaccusing statement of feeling—perhaps letting one's housemate know that "I get irritated when the dirty dishes are left for me to clean up"—can help resolve the conflicts that cause anger. Grievances expressed in ways that promote reconciliation rather than retaliation can benefit a relationship.

What if such tactics fail, but someone else's behavior has really hurt you? Research recommends the age-old response of forgiveness. Without letting the offender off the hook or inviting further harm, forgiveness releases anger and calms the body. To explore the bodily effects of forgiveness, Charlotte Witvliet and her co-researchers (2001) invited college students to recall an incident in which someone had hurt them. As the students mentally rehearsed forgiveness, their negative feelings—and their perspiration, blood pressure, heart rate, and facial tension—all were lower than when they rehearsed their grudges.

SIX CHIX

The catharsis myth: Is it true?

"Anger will never disappear so long as thoughts of resentment are cherished in the mind."

—The Buddha, 500 B.C.E.

Happiness

9: **What are the causes and consequences of happiness?**

"How to gain, how to keep, how to recover happiness is in fact for most men at all times the secret motive for all they do," observed William James (1902, p. 76). Understandably so, for one's state of happiness or unhappiness colors everything. People

feel-good, do-good phenomenon people's tendency to be helpful when already in a good mood.

subjective well-being self-perceived happiness or satisfaction with life. Used along with measures of objective well-being (for example, physical and economic indicators) to evaluate people's quality of life.

who are happy perceive the world as safer, feel more confident, make decisions more easily, rate job applicants more favorably, are more cooperative and tolerant, and live healthier and more energized and satisfied lives (Briñol et al., 2007; Lyubomirsky et al., 2005; Pressman & Cohen, 2005). When your mood is gloomy and your thinking preoccupied, life as a whole seems depressing and meaningless. Let your mood brighten, and your thinking broadens and becomes more playful and creative (Amabile et al., 2005; Fredrickson, 2006; King et al., 2006). Your relationships, your self-image, and your hopes for the future also seem more promising. Positive emotions fuel upward spirals.

This helps explain why college students' happiness helps predict their life course. In one study, women who smiled happily in 1950s college yearbook photos were more likely to be married, and happily so, in middle age (Harker & Keltner, 2001). In another study, which surveyed thousands of U.S. college students in 1976 and restudied them at age 37, happy students had gone on to earn significantly more money than their less-happy-than-average peers (Diener et al., 2002).

Moreover—and this is one of psychology's most consistent findings—happiness doesn't just feel good, it does good. In study after study, a mood-boosting experience (finding money, succeeding on a challenging task, recalling a happy event) has made people more likely to give money, pick up someone's dropped papers, volunteer time, and do other good deeds. Psychologists call it the **feel-good, do-good phenomenon** (Salovey, 1990). (Doing good also promotes good feeling, a phenomenon harnessed by some happiness coaches as they assign people to perform a daily "random act of kindness" and to record the results.)

Despite the significance of happiness, psychology throughout its history has more often focused on negative emotions. Since 1887, *Psychological Abstracts* (a guide to psychology's literature) has included, as of this writing, 16,150 articles mentioning anger and 130,520 mentioning depression, but only 6895 on happiness. There is, of course, good reason to focus on negative emotions; they can make our lives miserable and drive us to seek help. But researchers are becoming increasingly interested in **subjective well-being,** assessed either as feelings of happiness (sometimes defined as a high ratio of positive to negative feelings) or as a sense of satisfaction with life. A new *positive psychology* is on the rise (see Chapter 12).

The Short Life of Emotional Ups and Downs

Happiness research has focused on both our temporary moods and our long-term life satisfaction. Even over the course of an average day, our emotions vary (**FIGURE 11.14**), with positive emotion rising over the early to middle hours (Kahneman et al., 2004; Watson, 2000). Stressful events—an argument, a sick child, a car

FIGURE 11.14 Moods across the day
When psychologist David Watson (2000) sampled nearly 4500 mood reports from 150 people, he found this pattern of variation from the average levels of positive and negative emotions.

problem—can trigger a bad day. No surprise there. But by the next day, the gloom nearly always lifts (Affleck et al., 1994; Bolger et al., 1989; Stone & Neale, 1984). If anything, people tend to rebound from a bad day to a *better-than-usual* good mood the following day. (When in a bad mood, can you usually depend on rebounding within a day or two? Are your times of elation similarly hard to sustain?)

Over the long run, our emotional ups and downs tend to balance. After being struck by a severe disability, we may not rebound all the way back to our former emotions (Diener et al., 2006). But consider our remarkable adaptiveness and resilience:

- Learning that one is HIV-positive is devastating. But after five weeks of adapting to the grim news, those who have tested positive have reported feeling less emotionally distraught than they had expected (Sieff et al., 1999).
- Kidney dialysis patients recognize that their health is relatively poor, yet in their moment-to-moment experiences they report being just as happy as healthy nonpatients (Riis et al., 2005).
- European 8- to 12-year-olds with cerebral palsy experience normal psychological well-being (Dickinson et al., 2007).

A major disability often leaves people less happy than average, yet happier than able-bodied people with depression (Kübler et al., 2005; Lucas, 2007a,b; Oswald & Powdthavee, 2006; Schwartz & Estrin, 2004). "If you are a paraplegic," explains Daniel Kahneman (2005), "you will gradually start thinking of other things, and the more time you spend thinking of other things the less miserable you are going to be." Even patients "locked in" a motionless body "rarely want to die," report Eimar Smith and Mark Delargy (2005), which "counters a popular misconception that such patients would have been better off dead."

In less life-threatening contexts, the pattern continues. Faculty members up for tenure expect their lives would be deflated by a negative decision. Actually, 5 to 10 years later, those denied were not noticeably less happy than those who were awarded tenure (Gilbert et al., 1998). The same is true of romantic breakups, which feel devastating. The surprising reality: *We overestimate the duration of our emotions and underestimate our capacity to adapt.*

> "Weeping may tarry for the night, but joy comes with the morning."
>
> —Psalm 30:5

Wealth and Well-Being

"Do you think you would be happier if you made more money?" *Yes*, replied 73 percent of Americans in a 2006 Gallup poll. How important is "Being very well off financially"? *Very*, say many entering U.S. collegians (**FIGURE 11.15**). Some 3 in 4 students rate their top two objectives (among 21 possible) as being "very well off" and "raising a family," and they grade them "extremely important" or "essential."

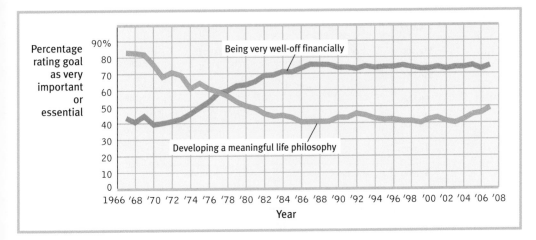

FIGURE 11.15 The changing materialism of entering collegians Surveys of more than 200,000 entering U.S. collegians per year have revealed an increasing desire for wealth after 1970. (From *The American Freshman* surveys, UCLA, 1966 to 2007.)

In World Values Surveys in 97 countries (Inglehart, 2008) and in Gallup (2008) surveys in 130 countries, the highest self-reported happiness was found in Denmark.

"Money won't make you happy, Waldron. So instead of a raise, I'm giving a Prozac."

"Australians are three times richer than their parents and grandparents were in the 1950s, but they are not happier."

—The Australia Institute, *A Well-Being Manifesto*, 2005

FIGURE 11.16 Does money buy happiness? It surely helps us to avoid certain types of pain. Yet, though buying power has almost tripled since the 1950s, the average American's reported happiness has remained almost unchanged. (Happiness data from National Opinion Research Center surveys; income data from *Historical Statistics of the United States* and *Economic Indicators*.)

And, to a point, wealth does correlate with well-being. Consider:

- Within most countries, though especially in poor countries, individuals with lots of money are typically happier than those who struggle to afford life's basic needs (Diener & Biswas-Diener, 2009; Howell & Howell, 2008). They also, as we will see later in this chapter, often enjoy better health than those stressed by poverty and lack of control over their lives.
- People in rich countries are also somewhat happier than those in poor countries (Inglehart, 2009).
- Those who have experienced a recent windfall from a lottery, an inheritance, or a surging economy typically feel some elation (Diener & Oishi, 2000; Gardner & Oswald, 2007).

So, it seems that money enough to buy your way out of hunger and hopelessness also buys some happiness. But once one has enough money for comfort and security, piling up more and more affects happiness less and less.

And consider this: During the last four decades, the average U.S. citizen's buying power almost tripled. Did this greater wealth—enabling twice as many cars per person, not to mention iPods, laptops, and camera cell phones—also buy more happiness? As **FIGURE 11.16** shows, the average American, though certainly richer, is not a bit happier. In 1957, some 35 percent said they were "very happy," as did slightly fewer—32 percent—in 2008. Much the same has been true of Europe, Australia, and Japan, where people enjoy better nutrition, health care, education, and science, and they are somewhat happier than those in very poor countries (Diener & Biswas-Diener, 2002, 2009; Speth, 2008). Yet their increasing real incomes have *not* produced increasing happiness. This finding lobs a bombshell at modern materialism: *Economic growth in affluent countries has provided no apparent boost to morale or social well-being.*

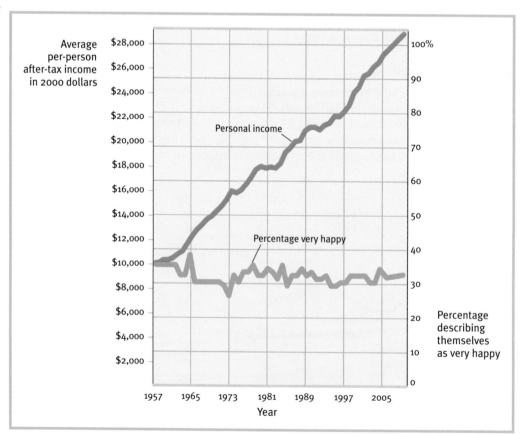

Ironically, in every culture, those who strive hardest for wealth tend to live with lower well-being (Ryan, 1999), especially when those hard-driving people are seeking money to prove themselves, gain power, or show off rather than support their families (Srivastava et al., 2001). Those who instead strive for intimacy, personal growth, and contribution to the community experience a higher quality of life (Kasser, 2000, 2002).

Two Psychological Phenomena: Adaptation and Comparison

Two psychological principles explain why, for those who are not poor, more money buys little more than a temporary surge of happiness and why our emotions seem attached to elastic bands that pull us back from highs or lows. In its own way, each principle suggests that happiness is relative.

HAPPINESS AND PRIOR EXPERIENCE The **adaptation-level phenomenon** describes our tendency to judge various stimuli relative to those we have previously experienced. As psychologist Harry Helson (1898–1977) explained, we adjust our *neutral levels*—the points at which sounds seem neither loud nor soft, temperatures neither hot nor cold, events neither pleasant nor unpleasant—based on our prior experience. We then notice and react to variations up or down from these levels.

So, could we ever create a permanent social paradise? Social psychologist Donald Campbell (1975) answered *no:* If you woke up tomorrow to your utopia—perhaps a world with no bills, no ills, perfect scores, someone who loves you unreservedly—you would feel euphoric, for a time. But then you would gradually recalibrate your adaptation level. Before long, you would again sometimes feel gratified (when achievements surpass expectations), sometimes feel deprived (when they fall below), and sometimes feel neutral. *The point to remember:* Satisfaction and dissatisfaction, success and failure—all are relative to our recent experience. Satisfaction, as Richard Ryan (1999) said, "has a short half-life."

HI & LOIS

HAPPINESS AND OTHERS' ATTAINMENTS Happiness is relative not only to our past experience but also to our comparisons with others (Lyubomirsky, 2001). We are always comparing ourselves with others. And whether we feel good or bad depends on who those others are. We are slow-witted or clumsy only when others are smarter or more agile.

Two examples: To explain the frustration expressed by U.S. Air Corps soldiers during World War II, researchers formulated the concept of **relative deprivation**—the sense that we are worse off than others with whom we compare ourselves. Despite a relatively rapid promotion rate for the group, many soldiers were frustrated about their own promotion rates (Merton & Kitt, 1950). Apparently, seeing so many others being promoted inflated the soldiers' expectations. And when expectations soar above attainments, the result is disappointment. Alex Rodriguez's 10-year, $275 million baseball contract surely made him temporarily happy, but it likely also diminished other star players' satisfaction with their lesser, multimillion-dollar contracts. Likewise, the economic surge that has made some urban Chinese

"But on the positive side, money can't buy happiness—so who cares?"

"No happiness lasts for long."
—Seneca, *Agamemnon,* C.E. 60

"Continued pleasures wear off. . . . Pleasure is always contingent upon change and disappears with continuous satisfaction."
—Dutch psychologist Nico Frijda (1988)

"I have a 'fortune cookie maxim' that I'm very proud of: Nothing in life is quite as important as you think it is while you are thinking about it. So, nothing will ever make you as happy as you think it will."
—Nobel laureate psychologist Daniel Kahneman, Gallup interview, "What Were They Thinking?" 2005

adaptation-level phenomenon our tendency to form judgments (of sounds, of lights, of income) relative to a neutral level defined by our prior experience.

relative deprivation the perception that we are worse off relative to those with whom we compare ourselves.

The effect of comparison with others helps explain why students of a given level of academic ability tend to have a higher academic self-concept if they attend a school where most other students are not exceptionally able (Marsh & Parker, 1984). If you were near the top of your graduating class, you might feel inferior upon entering a college or university where all students were near the top of their class.

"Researchers say I'm not happier for being richer, but do you know how much researchers make?"

Studies of chimpanzees in zoos reveal that happiness in chimpanzees, as rated by 200 employees, is also genetically influenced (Weiss et al., 2000, 2002).

newly affluent appears to have fueled among others a sense of relative deprivation (Burkholder, 2005a,b).

Such comparisons help us understand why the middle- and upper-income people in a given country, who can compare themselves with the relatively poor, tend to be slightly more satisfied with life than their less fortunate compatriots. Nevertheless, once people reach a moderate income level, further increases buy little more happiness. Why? Because as people climb the ladder of success they mostly compare themselves with peers who are at or above their current level (Gruder, 1977; Suls & Tesch, 1978). "Beggars do not envy millionaires, though of course they will envy other beggars who are more successful," noted Bertrand Russell (1930, p. 90). Thus, "Napoleon envied Caesar, Caesar envied Alexander, and Alexander, I daresay, envied Hercules, who never existed. You cannot, therefore, get away from envy by means of success alone, for there will always be in history or legend some person even more successful than you are" (pp. 68–69).

"Shortly after I realized I had plenty, I realized there was plenty more."

Just as comparing ourselves with those who are better off creates envy, so counting our blessings as we compare ourselves with those worse off boosts our contentment. Marshall Dermer and his colleagues (1979) demonstrated this by asking University of Wisconsin-Milwaukee women to study others' deprivation and suffering. After viewing vivid depictions of how grim life was in Milwaukee in 1900, or after imagining and then writing about various personal tragedies, such as being burned and disfigured, the women expressed greater satisfaction with their own lives. Similarly, when mildly depressed people read about someone who is even more depressed, they feel somewhat better (Gibbons, 1986). "I cried because I had no shoes," states a Persian saying, "until I met a man who had no feet."

Predictors of Happiness

If, as the adaptation-level phenomenon implies, our emotions tend to rebound toward our normal, why are some people normally so joyful and others so gloomy? The answers vary somewhat by culture. Self-esteem matters more to individualistic Westerners, social acceptance matters more to those in communal cultures (Diener et al., 2003). But across many countries, research does reveal several predictors of happiness (**TABLE 11.1**).

Although tasks and relationships affect our happiness, genes matter, too. From their study of 254 identical and fraternal twins, David Lykken and Auke Tellegen

TABLE 11.1 **Happiness Is . . .**

Researchers Have Found That Happy People Tend to	However, Happiness Seems Not Much Related to Other Factors, Such as
Have high self-esteem (in individualistic countries).	Age.
Be optimistic, outgoing, and agreeable.	Gender (women are more often depressed, but also more often joyful).
Have close friendships or a satisfying marriage.	Parenthood (having children or not).
Have work and leisure that engage their skills.	Physical attractiveness.
Have a meaningful religious faith.	
Sleep well and exercise.	

Sources: Summarized from DeNeve & Cooper (1998), Diener et al. (2003), Lucas et al. (2004), Myers (1993, 2000), Myers & Diener (1995, 1996), and Steel et al. (2008).

(1996) estimated that 50 percent of the difference among people's happiness ratings is heritable. Thus, even identical twins raised apart are often similarly happy.

The point is not that, so far as long-term happiness goes, nothing really matters. After following thousands of lives over two decades, researchers have observed that people's "happiness set point" is not fixed (Lucas, 2008; Lucas & Donnellan, 2007). Satisfaction may rise or fall, and happiness can be influenced by factors that are under our control. A striking example: In a long-term German study, married partners were as similarly satisfied with their lives as were identical twins (Schimmack & Lucas, 2007). Genes matter. But as this study hints, relationship quality matters, too. (For research-based hints on enhancing your own happiness, see Close-Up: How to Be Happier.)

* * *

Our studies of happiness remind us that emotions combine physiological activation (left hemisphere especially), expressive behaviors (smiles), and conscious thoughts ("I was so ready for that test!") and feelings (pride, satisfaction). Fear, anger, happiness, and so much else have this in common: They are biopsychosocial phenomena. Our genetic predispositions, brain activity, outlooks, experiences, relationships, and cultures jointly form us.

"I could cry when I think of the years I wasted accumulating money, only to learn that my cheerful disposition is genetic."

Close-Up:

How to Be Happier

Happiness, like cholesterol level, is a genetically influenced trait. Yet as cholesterol is also influenced by diet and exercise, so our happiness is to some extent under our personal control. Here are some research-based suggestions for improving your mood and increasing your satisfaction with life.

1. ***Realize that enduring happiness may not come from financial success.*** People adapt to changing circumstances. Thus, wealth is like health: Its utter absence breeds misery, but having it (or any circumstance we long for) doesn't guarantee happiness.

2. ***Take control of your time.*** Happy people feel in control of their lives. To master your use of time, set goals and break them into daily aims. Although we often overestimate how much we will accomplish in any given day (leaving us frustrated), we generally underestimate how much we can accomplish in a year, given just a little progress every day.

3. ***Act happy.*** Manipulated into a smiling expression, people feel better, so put on a happy face. Talk as *if* you feel positive self-esteem, are optimistic, and are outgoing. Going

through the motions can trigger the emotions.

4. ***Seek work and leisure that engage your skills.*** Happy people often are in a zone called *flow*—absorbed in tasks that challenge but don't overwhelm them. Passive forms of leisure (watching TV) often provide less flow experience than gardening, socializing, or craft work. Take time to savor such pleasant experiences.

5. ***Join the "movement" movement.*** Aerobic exercise can relieve mild depression and anxiety and promote health and energy. Sound minds reside in sound bodies. Off your duffs, couch potatoes.

6. ***Give your body the sleep it wants.*** Happy people live active, vigorous lives yet reserve time for renewing sleep and solitude. Many people suffer from sleep debt, with resulting fatigue, diminished alertness, and gloomy moods.

7. ***Give priority to close relationships.*** Intimate friendships with those who care deeply about you can help you weather difficult times. Confiding is good for soul and body. Resolve to nurture your closest relationships by *not* taking your loved ones for

granted, by displaying to them the sort of kindness you display to others, by affirming them, by playing together and sharing together.

8. ***Focus beyond self.*** Reach out to those in need. Happiness increases helpfulness (those who feel good do good). But doing good also makes us feel good.

9. ***Count your blessings and record your gratitude.*** Keeping a gratitude journal heightens well-being (Emmons, 2007; Seligman et al., 2005). Try pausing each day to record positive events and why they occurred. Express your gratitude to others.

10. ***Nurture your spiritual self.*** For many people, faith provides a support community, a reason to focus beyond self, and a sense of purpose and hope. That helps explain why people active in faith communities report greater-than-average happiness and often cope well with crises.

Digested from David G. Myers, *The Pursuit of Happiness* (Harper, 1993).

Stress and Health

What happens when our emotional experiences are both negative and prolonged? How does the human body respond to such experiences?

Stress and Illness

10: What is stress?

You think roller coasters are scary? Imagine being 21-year-old Ben Carpenter on the world's wildest and fastest wheelchair ride. As he crossed an intersection on a sunny summer afternoon in 2007, the light changed. A large truck, whose driver didn't see him, started moving into the intersection. As they bumped, the wheelchair turned to face forward, its handles becoming stuck in the grille. And off they went, the driver unable to hear Ben's cries for help. As they sped down the highway about an hour from my home, passing motorists caught the bizarre sight of a truck pushing a wheelchair at 50 mph and started calling 911. (The first caller: "You are not going to believe this. There is a semi truck pushing a guy in a wheelchair on Red Arrow highway!") One passerby was an undercover police officer, who did a quick U-turn, followed the truck to its destination a couple of miles from where the incident started, and informed the disbelieving driver that he had a passenger hooked in his grille. "It was very scary," said Ben, who has muscular dystrophy.

Extreme stress Ben Carpenter experienced the wildest of rides after his wheelchair got stuck in a truck's grille.

Stress is a slippery concept. We sometimes use the word informally to describe threats or challenges ("Ben was under a lot of stress"), and at other times, to describe our responses ("Ben experienced acute stress"). To a psychologist, the dangerous truck ride was a *stressor*. Ben's physical and emotional responses were a *stress reaction*. And the process by which he related to the threat was *stress*.

Thus, **stress** is not just a stimulus or a response. It is the process by which we appraise and cope with environmental threats and challenges (**FIGURE 11.17**). Stress arises less from events themselves than from how we appraise them (Lazarus, 1998). One person, alone in a house, dismisses its creaking sounds and experiences no stress; someone else suspects an intruder and becomes alarmed.

When short-lived, or when perceived as challenges, stressors can have positive effects. A momentary stress can mobilize your immune system to fend off infection and heal a wound (Segerstrom, 2007). Stress can also arouse and motivate us to

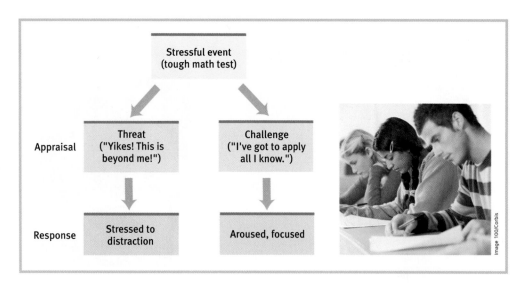

FIGURE 11.17 Stress appraisal
The events of our lives flow through a psychological filter. How we appraise an event influences how much stress we experience and how effectively we respond.

conquer problems. Championship athletes, successful entertainers, and great teachers and leaders all thrive and excel when aroused by a challenge (Blascovich et al., 2004). Having conquered cancer or rebounded from a lost job, some people emerge with stronger self-esteem and a deepened spirituality and sense of purpose. Indeed, some stress early in life is conducive to later emotional resilience (Landauer & Whiting, 1979). Adversity can beget growth.

But stressors can also threaten us. And experiencing severe or prolonged stress may harm us. Children's physiological responses to severe abuse put them at later risk of chronic disease (Repetti et al., 2002). Adults who had post-traumatic stress reactions to heavy combat in the Vietnam war went on to suffer greatly elevated rates of circulatory, digestive, respiratory, and infectious diseases (Boscarino, 1997).

The Stress Response System

Medical interest in stress dates back to Hippocrates (460–377 B.C.E.). But it was not until the 1920s that Walter Cannon (1929) confirmed that the stress response is part of a unified mind-body system. He observed that extreme cold, lack of oxygen, and emotion-arousing incidents all trigger an outpouring of the stress hormones epinephrine and norepinephrine from the central core of the adrenal glands. This is but one part of the sympathetic nervous system's response as it prepares the body for the wonderfully adaptive response Cannon called *fight or flight* (see Figure 11.2 and discussion in Chapter 2).

There are alternatives to fight or flight. Faced with an extreme disaster, such as a ship sinking, some people become paralyzed by fear. Faced with a loved one's death, some withdraw, pull back, conserve energy.

Facing stress, men more often than women tend to socially withdraw, turn to alcohol, or become aggressive. Women more often respond to stress by nurturing and banding together for support (Taylor et al., 2000). Shelley Taylor (2006) attributes this *tend-and-befriend* response partly to *oxytocin*, a stress-moderating hormone associated with pair-bonding in animals and released by cuddling, massage, and breastfeeding in humans.

Canadian scientist Hans Selye (1936, 1976) devoted 40 years to understanding the body's response to stress. In studies of animals' reactions to various stressors, such as electric shock, surgical trauma, and immobilizing restraint, he discovered that the body's adaptive response is so general—like a single burglar alarm that sounds no matter what intrudes—that it merits the name **general adaptation syndrome (GAS).**

---

stress the process by which we perceive and respond to certain events, called *stressors*, that we appraise as threatening or challenging.

---

general adaptation syndrome (GAS) Selye's concept of the body's adaptive response to stress in three phases—alarm, resistance, exhaustion.

High

The body's resistance to stress can only last so long before exhaustion sets in

Stress resistance

Stressor occurs

Low

| Phase 1 | Phase 2 | Phase 3 |
| Alarm reaction (mobilize resources) | Resistance (cope with stressor) | Exhaustion (reserves depleted) |

EPA/ Yuri Kochetkov/Landov

FIGURE 11.18 Selye's general adaptation syndrome This girl being carried to freedom and medical attention managed to escape her terrorist captors in a three-day school holdup in North Ossetia in 2004. After such a trauma, the body enters an alarm phase of temporary shock. From this it rebounds, as stress resistance rises. If the stress is prolonged, as it was for the 400 school hostages and their waiting loved ones, wear and tear may lead to exhaustion.

Selye saw the GAS as having three phases (**FIGURE 11.18**). Let's say you suffer a physical or emotional trauma. In Phase 1, you experience an *alarm reaction* due to the sudden activation of your sympathetic nervous system. Your heart rate zooms. Blood is diverted to your skeletal muscles. You feel the faintness of shock. With your resources mobilized, you are now ready to fight the challenge during Phase 2, *resistance*. Your temperature, blood pressure, and respiration remain high, and there is a sudden outpouring of hormones. If persistent, the stress may eventually deplete your body's reserves during Phase 3, *exhaustion*. With exhaustion, you are more vulnerable to illness or even, in extreme cases, collapse and death.

Selye's work extended Cannon's findings and helped make stress a major concept in both psychology and medicine. Few today would quarrel with his basic point: Although the human body comes designed to cope with temporary stress, prolonged stress can produce physical deterioration. Even fearful, easily stressed rats have been found to die sooner (after about 600 days) than their more confident siblings, which average 700-day life spans. Still, questions remain: What stressors threaten us most? And how does stress harm us?

Stressful Life Events

11 : **What events provoke stress responses?**

Research has focused on our responses to three types of stressors: catastrophes, significant life changes, and daily hassles.

CATASTROPHES Catastrophes are unpredictable large-scale events, such as war and natural disasters, that nearly everyone appraises as threatening. Although people often provide one another with aid as well as comfort after such events, the health consequences can be significant. In the three weeks after the 9/11 terrorist attacks, two-thirds of Americans surveyed by University of Michigan researchers said they were having some trouble concentrating and sleeping (Wahlberg, 2001). In another national survey, New Yorkers were especially likely to report such symptoms (NSF, 2001). Sleeping pill prescriptions rose by a reported 28 percent in the New York area (HMHL, 2002).

Do other community disasters usually produce effects this great? After digesting data from 52 studies of catastrophic floods, hurricanes, and fires, Anthony Rubonis and Leonard Bickman (1991) found the typical effect more modest but nonetheless genuine. In disaster's wake, rates of psychological disorders such as depression and anxiety rose an average 17 percent. In the four months after Hurricane Katrina, New Orleans reportedly experienced a tripled suicide rate (Saulny, 2006). Refugees fleeing their homeland also suffer increased rates of psychological disorders. Their stress is twofold: the trauma of uprooting and family separation, and the challenges of adjusting to a foreign culture's new language, ethnicity, climate, and social norms (Pipher, 2002; Williams & Berry, 1991). In years to come, relocations necessitated by climate change may also produce such effects.

Toxic stress On the day of its 1994 earthquake, Los Angeles experienced a fivefold increase in sudden-death heart attacks—especially in the first two hours after the quake and near its epicenter. Physical exertion (running, lifting debris) was a factor in only 13 percent of the deaths, leaving stress as the likely trigger for the others (Muller & Verier, 1996).

SIGNIFICANT LIFE CHANGES The second type of life-event stressor is a significant personal life change—the death of a loved one, the loss of a job, leaving home, a marriage, a divorce. Life transitions and insecurities are often keenly felt during young adulthood. That helps explain why, when 15,000 Canadian adults were asked whether "You are trying to take on too many things at once," responses indicated highest stress levels among the youngest adults. The same is true of Americans: Half of adults under age 50 report "frequent" stress, as do fewer than 30 percent of those over 50 (Saad, 2001).

Some psychologists study the health effects of life changes by following people over time to see if such events precede illnesses. Others compare the life changes recalled by those who have or have not suffered a specific health problem, such as a heart attack. A review of these studies commissioned by the U.S. National Academy of Sciences revealed that people recently widowed, fired, or divorced are more vulnerable to disease (Dohrenwend et al., 1982). A Finnish study of 96,000 widowed people confirmed the phenomenon: Their risk of death doubled in the week following their partner's death (Kaprio et al., 1987). Experiencing a cluster of crises puts one even more at risk.

DAILY HASSLES As we noted earlier, our happiness stems less from enduring good fortune than from our response to daily events—a hoped-for medical result, a perfect exam score, a gratifying e-mail, your team's winning the big game.

This principle works for negative events, too. Everyday annoyances—rush-hour traffic, aggravating housemates, long lines at the store, too many things to do, e-mail spam, and obnoxious cell-phone talkers—may be the most significant sources of stress (Kohn & Macdonald, 1992; Lazarus, 1990; Ruffin, 1993). Although some people can simply shrug off such hassles, others are "driven up the wall" by them. People's difficulties in letting go of unattainable goals is another everyday stressor with health consequences (Miller & Wrosch, 2007).

Over time, these little stressors can add up and take a toll on our health and well-being. Hypertension rates are high among residents of impoverished areas where the stresses that accompany inadequate income, unemployment, solo parenting, and overcrowding are part of daily life for many people. In Europe, hypertension rates are likewise highest in countries where people express the least satisfaction with their lives (Blanchflower & Oswald, 2008).

For minority populations, daily pressures may be compounded by racism, which—like other stressors—can have both psychological and physical consequences. Thinking that some of the people you encounter each day will distrust you, dislike you, or doubt your abilities makes daily life stressful. Such stress takes a toll on the health of many African-Americans, driving up blood pressure levels (Clark et al., 1999; Mays et al., 2007).

A 2009 Pew survey of 2969 American adults asked, "Is the recession causing stress in your family?"

Age	"Yes" responses
18–49	52%
50–64	58%
65+	38%

coronary heart disease the clogging of the vessels that nourish the heart muscle; the leading cause of death in North America.

Type A Friedman and Rosenman's term for competitive, hard-driving, impatient, verbally aggressive, and anger-prone people.

Type B Friedman and Rosenman's term for easygoing, relaxed people.

psychophysiological illness literally, "mind-body" illness; any stress-related physical illness, such as hypertension and some headaches.

lymphocytes the two types of white blood cells that are part of the body's immune system: *B lymphocytes* form in the *b*one marrow and release antibodies that fight bacterial infections; *T lymphocytes* form in the *t*hymus and other lymphatic tissue and attack cancer cells, viruses, and foreign substances.

In both India and America, Type A bus drivers are literally hard-driving: They brake, pass, and honk their horns more often than their more easygoing Type B colleagues (Evans et al., 1987).

Stress and the Heart

12: **Why are some of us more prone than others to coronary heart disease?**

Elevated blood pressure is just one of the factors that increase the risk of **coronary heart disease,** the closing of the vessels that nourish the heart muscle. Although infrequent before 1900, this condition became by the 1950s North America's leading cause of death, and it remains so today. In addition to hypertension and a family history of the disease, many behavioral and physiological factors—smoking, obesity, a high-fat diet, physical inactivity, and an elevated cholesterol level—increase the risk of heart disease. The psychological factors of stress and personality also play a big role.

In a now-famous study, Meyer Friedman, Ray Rosenman, and their colleagues tested the idea that stress increases vulnerability to heart disease (Friedman & Ulmer, 1984). They measured the blood cholesterol level and clotting speed of 40 U.S. tax accountants. From January through March, both of these coronary warning indicators registered completely normal. Then, as the accountants began scrambling to finish their clients' tax returns before the April 15 filing deadline, their cholesterol and clotting measures rose to dangerous levels. In May and June, with the deadline past, the measures returned to normal. The researchers' hunch had paid off: Stress predicted heart attack risk.

The stage was set for Friedman and Rosenman's classic nine-year study of more than 3000 healthy men aged 35 to 59. At the start of the study, they interviewed each man for 15 minutes about his work and eating habits. During the interview, they noted the man's manner of talking and other behavioral patterns. Those who seemed the most reactive, competitive, hard-driving, impatient, time-conscious, supermotivated, verbally aggressive, and easily angered they called **Type A.** The roughly equal number who were more easygoing they called **Type B.** Which group do you suppose turned out to be the most coronary prone?

By the time the study was complete, 257 men had suffered heart attacks; 69 percent of them were Type A. Moreover, not one of the "pure" Type Bs—the most mellow and laid-back of their group—had suffered a heart attack.

As often happens in science, this exciting and revolutionary discovery provoked enormous public interest. But after the honeymoon period, researchers began asking new questions: Is the finding reliable? If so, what is the toxic component of the Type A profile: Time-consciousness? Competitiveness? Anger?

Type A's toxic core was revealed to be negative emotions, especially the anger associated with an aggressively reactive temperament (Smith, 2006; Williams, 1993). Type A individuals are more often "combat ready," as their aroused sympathetic nervous systems redistribute bloodflow to their muscles and away from internal organs such as the liver, which normally removes cholesterol and fat from the blood.

Thus, excess cholesterol and fat may continue to circulate in their bloodstream and later be deposited around their heart. Further stress—sometimes conflicts brought on by the Type A person's own abrasiveness—may trigger the altered heart rhythms that, in those with weakened hearts, can cause sudden death (Kamarck & Jennings, 1991). In important ways, people's minds and hearts interact.

The effect of an anger-prone personality appears most noticeably in studies in which interviewers assess verbal assertiveness and emotional intensity. (If you pause in the middle of a sentence, an intense, anger-prone person may jump in and finish it for you.) One study of young and middle-aged adults found that those who react with anger over little things are the most prone to coronary problems, and that suppressing negative emotions only heightens the risk (Kupper & Denollet, 2007). Another study (Williams et al., 2000) that followed 13,000 middle-aged people for 5 years found that among those with normal blood pressure, people who had

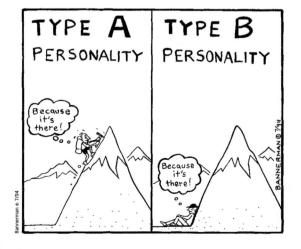

scored high on anger were three times more likely to have had heart attacks. Those odds held even after researchers controlled for smoking and weight, which, along with drinking, tend to correlate with hostility (Bunde & Suls, 2006). The link between anger and heart attacks also appeared in a study that followed 1055 male medical students over an average of 36 years. Those who had reported being hot-tempered were five times more likely to have had a heart attack by age 55 (Chang et al., 2002). As Charles Spielberger and Perry London (1982) put it, rage "seems to lash back and strike us in the heart muscle."

Pessimism seems to be similarly toxic. Laura Kubzansky and her colleagues (2001) studied 1306 initially healthy men who a decade earlier had scored as optimists, pessimists, or neither. Even after other risk factors such as smoking had been ruled out, pessimists were more than twice as likely as optimists to develop heart disease (**FIGURE 11.19**).

Depression, too, can be lethal. The accumulated evidence from 57 studies suggests that "depression substantially increases the risk of death, especially death by unnatural causes and cardiovascular disease" (Wulsin et al., 1999). One study of 7406 women age 67 or older found that among those with no depressive symptoms, 7 percent died within six years, as did 24 percent of those with six or more depressive symptoms (Whooley & Browner, 1998). In the years following a heart attack, people with high scores for depression are four times more likely than their low-scoring counterparts to develop further heart problems (Frasure-Smith & Lesperance, 2005). Depression is disheartening.

Stress and Susceptibility to Disease

13: **How does stress make us more vulnerable to disease?**

Not so long ago, the term *psychosomatic* described psychologically caused physical symptoms. To laypeople, the term implied that the symptoms were unreal— "merely" psychosomatic. To avoid such connotations and to better describe the genuine physiological effects of psychological states, most experts today refer instead to stress-related **psychophysiological illnesses,** such as hypertension and some headaches. Stress also affects our disease-fighting immune system.

Stress and the Immune System

Hundreds of experiments have revealed the nervous and endocrine systems' influences on the immune system (Sternberg, 2001). Your immune system is a complex surveillance system that defends your body by isolating and destroying bacteria, viruses, and other foreign substances. This system includes two types of white blood cells, called **lymphocytes.** *B lymphocytes* form in the *b*one marrow and release antibodies that fight bacterial infections. *T lymphocytes* form in the *t*hymus and other lymphatic tissue and attack cancer cells, viruses, and foreign substances—even "good" ones, such as transplanted organs. Two other important agents of the immune system are the *macrophage* ("big eater"), which identifies, pursues, and ingests harmful invaders and worn-out cells (**FIGURE 11.20**), and the *natural killer cells* (NK cells), which pursue diseased cells (such as those infected by viruses or cancer).

Age, nutrition, genetics, body temperature, and stress all influence the immune system's activity, which can err in two directions. Responding too strongly, it may attack the body's own tissues, causing arthritis or an allergic reaction. Underreacting, it may allow a dormant herpes virus to erupt or cancer cells to multiply. Women are immunologically stronger than men, making them less susceptible to infections (Morell, 1995). But this very strength also makes them more susceptible to self-attacking diseases, such as lupus and multiple sclerosis.

"The fire you kindle for your enemy often burns you more than him."

—Chinese proverb

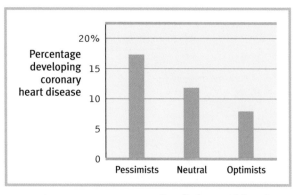

FIGURE 11.19 Pessimism and heart disease A Harvard School of Public Health team found pessimistic adult men at doubled risk of developing heart disease over a 10-year period. (From Kubzansky et al., 2001.)

"A cheerful heart is a good medicine, but a downcast spirit dries up the bones."

—Proverbs 17:22

FIGURE 11.20 The immune system in action A large macrophage (at top) is about to trap and ingest a tiny bacterium (lower right). Macrophages constantly patrol our bodies in search of invaders—such as this *Escherichia coli* bacterium—and debris, such as worn-out red blood cells.

Your immune system is not a headless horseman. The brain regulates the secretion of stress hormones, which supress the disease-fighting lymphocytes. Thus, when animals are physically restrained, given unavoidable electric shocks, or subjected to noise, crowding, cold water, social defeat, or maternal separation, their immune systems become less active (Maier et al., 1994). One study monitored immune responses in 43 monkeys over six months (Cohen et al., 1992). Twenty-one were stressed by being housed with new roommates—three or four new monkeys—each month. (To empathize with the monkeys, recall the stress of leaving home to attend school or summer camp, and imagine having to repeat this experience monthly.) Compared with monkeys left in stable groups, the socially disrupted monkeys experienced weakened immune systems. Stress similarly depresses the immune system of humans:

- *Slower healing of wounds.* In one experiment, dental students received punch wounds (precise small holes punched in the skin). Compared with wounds placed during summer vacation, those placed three days before a major exam healed 40 percent more slowly (Kiecolt-Glaser et al., 1998).

- *Greater vulnerability to infection.* After a virus was dropped in their nose, 47 percent of people living stress-filled lives developed colds, as did only 27 percent of those living relatively free of stress (**FIGURE 11.21**). In follow-up research, the happiest and most relaxed people were likewise markedly less vulnerable to an experimentally delivered cold virus (Cohen et al., 2003, 2006).

The stress effect on immunity makes physiological sense (Maier et al., 1994). It takes energy to fight infections and maintain fevers. Thus, when diseased, our bodies reduce muscular energy output by inactivity and increased sleep. But stress creates a competing energy need. Stress triggers an aroused fight-or-flight response, diverting energy from the disease-fighting immune system to the muscles and brain, rendering us more vulnerable to illness (see Figure 11.2). Perhaps it's not surprising, then, that one personality trait shared by 169 centenarians (people over 100) was their ability to manage stress well (Perls et al., 1999). *The bottom line:* Stress does not make us sick, but it does alter our immune functioning, making us less able to heal rapidly or to resist infection.

Stress and AIDS

AIDS has become the world's fourth leading cause of death and the number one killer in Africa. As its name tells us, AIDS is an immune disorder—an *acquired immune deficiency syndrome* caused by the *human immunodeficiency virus (HIV)*, which is spread by the exchange of bodily fluids, primarily semen and blood. When a disease spread by human contact kills slowly, as AIDS does, it ironically can be lethal

> "When the heart is at ease, the body is healthy."
>
> —Chinese proverb

FIGURE 11.21 Stress and colds
In an experiment by Sheldon Cohen and colleagues (1991), people with the highest life stress scores were also most vulnerable when exposed to an experimentally delivered cold virus.

to more people. Those who carry the virus have time to spread it, often without realizing they are infected. When the HIV infection manifests itself as AIDS, some years after the initial infection, the person has difficulty fighting off other diseases, such as pneumonia. Worldwide, reports the United Nations, more than 20 million people have died of AIDS (UNAIDS, 2008). (In the United States, where "only" a half-million of these fatalities have occurred, AIDS has killed more people than did combat in all the twentieth-century wars.) In 2007, worldwide some 2.7 million—half of them women—were infected with HIV, often without their awareness (UNAIDS, 2008).

So if stress restrains the immune system's response to infections, could it also exacerbate the *course* of AIDS? Researchers have found that stress and negative emotions do correlate with (a) a progression from HIV infection to AIDS, and (b) the speed of decline in those infected (Bower et al., 1998; Kiecolt-Glaser & Glaser, 1995; Leserman et al., 1999). HIV-infected men faced with stressful life circumstances, such as the loss of a partner, exhibit somewhat greater immune suppression and a faster disease progression.

Would efforts to reduce stress help control the disease? Although the benefits are small compared with available drug treatments, the answer appears again to be *yes*. Educational initiatives, bereavement support groups, cognitive therapy, relaxation training, and exercise programs that reduce distress have all had positive consequences for HIV-positive individuals (Baum & Posluszny, 1999; McCain et al., 2008; Schneiderman, 1999). Better yet is preventing HIV infection, which is the focus of many educational programs, such as the ABC (*a*bstinence, *b*eing faithful, *c*ondom use) program used in many countries, with seeming success in Uganda (Altman, 2004; USAID, 2004).

In North America and Western Europe, 75 percent of people with AIDS are men. In Sub-Saharan Africa, 60 percent of people with AIDS are women (and among 15- to 24-year-olds, 75 percent are women). Girls' thin layer of cervical cells makes them especially vulnerable (Altman, 2004; UNAIDS, 2005).

Africa is ground zero for AIDS Part of the AIDS prevention effort in Lesotho and elsewhere is the "ABC" Campaign—Abstinence, Be faithful, and use Condoms.

Stress and Cancer

Some investigators have reported that people are at increased risk for cancer within a year after experiencing depression, helplessness, or bereavement. One large Swedish study revealed that people with a history of workplace stress had 5.5 times greater risk of colon cancer than those who reported no such problems, a difference not attributable to differing age, smoking, drinking, or physical characteristics (Courtney et al., 1993).

Other researchers, however, have found no link between stress and human cancer (Edelman & Kidman, 1997; Fox, 1998; Petticrew et al., 1999, 2002). Concentration camp survivors and former prisoners of war, for example, have not exhibited elevated cancer rates.

One danger in hyping reports on stress management and cancer is that some patients may then blame themselves for their illness—"If only I had been more expressive, relaxed, and hopeful." A corollary danger is a "wellness macho" among the healthy, who take credit for their "healthy character" and lay a guilt trip on the ill: "She has cancer? That's what you get for holding your feelings in and being so nice." Dying thus becomes the ultimate failure.

The emerging view seems to be that stress does *not* create cancer cells. At worst, it may affect their growth by weakening the body's natural defenses against proliferating malignant cells (Antoni & Lutgendorf, 2007). Although a relaxed, hopeful state may enhance these defenses, we should be aware of the thin line that divides science from wishful thinking. The powerful biological processes at work in advanced cancer or AIDS are not likely to be completely derailed by avoiding stress or maintaining a relaxed but determined spirit (Anderson, 2002; Kessler et al., 1991). Often, however, patients or their friends and families look to less certain sources for help in preventing or defeating illnesses (turn the page to see Thinking Critically About: Complementary and Alternative Medicine).

"I didn't give myself cancer."

—Mayor Barbara Boggs Sigmund, 1939–1990, Princeton, New Jersey

When organic causes of illness are unknown, it is tempting to invent psychological explanations. Before the germ that causes tuberculosis was discovered, personality explanations of TB were popular (Sontag, 1978).

* * *

Thinking Critically About:

Complementary and Alternative Medicine

One health care growth market is **complementary and alternative medicine (CAM)**, which includes relaxation, acupuncture, massage therapy, homeopathy, spiritual healing, herbal remedies, chiropractic, and aromatherapy. In Germany, herbal remedies and homeopathy are enormously popular. In China, herbal therapies have long flourished, as have acupuncture and acupressure therapies that claim to correct "imbalances of energy flow" (called *Qi* or *Chi*) at identifiable points close to the skin. Andrew Weil's many books on alternative medicine have sold millions of copies, putting him on the cover of *Time* magazine.

Facing political pressure to explore these techniques, the U.S. National Institutes of Health (NIH) established the National Center for Complementary and Alternative Medicine, which the center defines as health care treatments not taught widely in medical schools, not usually reimbursed by insurance companies, and not used in hospitals (**TABLE 11.2**).

So what shall we make of CAM? Some aspects, such as life-style changes and stress management, have acknowledged validity. And certain techniques have proved useful for specific ailments, such as acupuncture, massage therapy, and aromatherapy for pain relief in cancer patients (Fellowes et al., 2004). Do the other aspects offer, as some believe, a new medical paradigm?

Critics point out that people consult physicians for diagnosable, curable diseases and turn to CAM techniques either for incurable illnesses or when well but feeling subpar. Thus, an otherwise healthy person with a cold may try an herbal remedy and then credit the subsequent return to good

complementary and alternative medicine (CAM) as yet unproven health care treatments intended to supplement (complement) or serve as alternatives to conventional medicine, and which typically are not widely taught in medical schools, used in hospitals, or reimbursed by insurance companies. When research shows a therapy to be safe and effective, it usually then becomes part of accepted medical practice.

health to CAM, rather than to the body's natural return to normal. CAM will seem especially effective with cyclical diseases, such as arthritis and allergies, as people seek therapy during the downturn and presume its effectiveness during the ensuing upturn. Add to this the healing power of belief—the *placebo effect*—plus the natural disappearance *(spontaneous remission)* of many diseases, and CAM practices are bound to seem effective, whether they are or not. One study of 302 migraine headache patients in Germany found that 51 percent of those receiving acupuncture treatment found relief, as did only 15 percent of those in a waiting list control group. But among a third group that received "sham acupuncture" (needles inserted at nonacupuncture points), 53 percent enjoyed relief. Such results, the investigators suspected, may indicate "a powerful placebo effect" (Linde et al., 2005).

As always, the way to discern what works and what does not is to experiment: Randomly assign patients to receive the therapy or a placebo control. Then ask the critical question: When neither the therapist nor the patient knows who is getting the real therapy, is the real therapy effective?

Much of today's mainstream medicine began as yesterday's alternative medicine.

Natural botanical life has given us digitalis (from purple foxglove), morphine (from the opium poppy), and penicillin (from penicillium mold). In each case, the active ingredient was verified in controlled trials. We have medical and public health science to thank for the antibiotics, vaccines, surgical procedures, sanitation, and emergency medicine that helped lengthen our life expectancy by three decades during the last century.

"CAM changes continually," notes the National Center for Complementary and Alternative Medicine (2006), "as those therapies that are proven to be safe and effective become adopted into conventional health care." Indeed, said *New England Journal of Medicine* editors Marcia Angell and Jerome Kassirer (1998), "There cannot be two kinds of medicine—conventional and alternative. There is only medicine that has been adequately tested and medicine that has not, medicine that works and medicine that may or may not work. Once a treatment has been tested rigorously, it no longer matters whether it was considered alternative at the outset."

"In God we trust. All others must have data."

—**George Lundberg, Editor, *Journal of the American Medical Association*, 1998**

TABLE 11.2 Five Domains of Complementary and Alternative Medicine

Alternative medical systems	Therapies used in place of conventional medicine, including homeopathy in Western cultures and traditional practices in non-Western cultures, such as those native to China and India.
Mind-body interventions	Techniques designed to enhance the mind's capacity to affect bodily functions and symptoms, including meditation, prayer, mental healing, and therapies that use creative outlets such as art, music, or dance.
Biologically based therapies	Therapies using natural substances such as herbs, foods, and vitamins.
Manipulative and body-based methods	Based on manipulation and/or movement of one or more parts of the body, including chiropractic or osteopathic manipulation, and massage.
Energy therapies	Theories using presumed energy fields. Biofield therapies, such as qi gong, Reiki, and therapeutic touch, are intended to affect energy fields that purportedly surround and penetrate the human body. Bioelectromagnetic-based therapies involve the unconventional use of electromagnetic fields, such as pulsed or magnetic fields.

Source: Adapted from the National Center for Complementary and Alternative Medicine, NIH http://nccam.nih.gov/health/whatiscam.

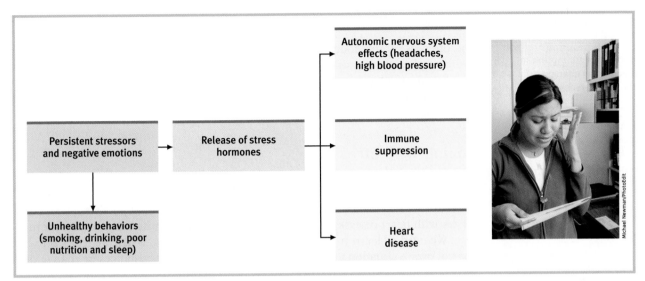

Michael Newman/PhotoEdit

FIGURE 11.22 Stress can have a variety of health-related consequences This is especially so when experienced by "disease-prone" angry, depressed, or anxious persons.

We can view the stress effect on our disease resistance as a price we pay for the benefits of stress. Stress invigorates our lives by arousing and motivating us. An unstressed life would hardly be challenging or productive. Moreover, it pays to spend our resources in fighting or fleeing an external threat. But we do so at the cost of diminished resources for fighting internal threats to health. When the stress is momentary, the cost is negligible. When uncontrollable aggravations persist, the cost may become considerable (**FIGURE 11.22**).

The interplay between stress and health provides yet another reminder of one of contemporary psychology's overriding themes: *Mind and body interact; everything psychological is simultaneously physiological.* Psychological states are physiological events that influence other parts of our physiological system. Just pausing to *think* about biting into an orange section—the sweet, tangy juice from the pulpy fruit flooding across your tongue—can trigger salivation. As the Indian sage Santi Parva recognized more than 4000 years ago, "Mental disorders arise from physical causes, and likewise physical disorders arise from mental causes." We are biopsychosocial systems.

REHEARSE IT!

12. Selye's general adaptation syndrome (GAS) consists of an alarm reaction followed by
    a. fight or flight.
    b. resistance then exhaustion.
    c. challenge then recovery.
    d. stressful life events.

13. The number of short-term illnesses and stress-related psychological disorders was higher than usual in the months following an earthquake. Such findings suggest that
    a. daily hassles have adverse health consequences.
    b. experiencing a very stressful event increases a person's vulnerability to illness.
    c. the amount of stress a person feels is directly related to the number of stressors experienced.
    d. small, bad events don't cause stress, but large ones can be toxic.

14. Research suggests that the most significant sources of stress are
    a. catastrophes.
    b. traumatic events, such as the loss of a loved one.
    c. daily hassles.
    d. threatening events that we witness.

15. The component of Type A behavior linked most closely to coronary heart disease is
    a. living a fast-paced life-style.
    b. working in a competitive area.
    c. meeting deadlines and challenges.
    d. feeling angry and negative much of the time.

16. Stress hormones suppress lymphocytes, which ordinarily attack bacteria, viruses, cancer cells, and other foreign substances. The stress hormones are released mainly in response to a signal from the

    a. lymphocytes and macrophages.
    b. brain.
    c. upper respiratory tract.
    d. adrenal glands.

17. Research has shown that people are at increased risk for cancer a year or so after experiencing depression, helplessness, or bereavement. In describing this link, researchers are quick to point out that
    a. accumulated stress causes cancer.
    b. anger is the negative emotion most closely linked to cancer.
    c. stress does not create cancer cells, but it weakens the body's natural defenses against them.
    d. feeling optimistic about chances of survival ensures that a cancer patient will get well.

Answers: 12. b, 13. b, 14. c, 15. d, 16. b, 17. c.

coping alleviating stress using emotional, cognitive, or behavioral methods.

problem-focused coping attempting to alleviate stress directly—by changing the stressor or the way we interact with that stressor.

emotion-focused coping attempting to alleviate stress by avoiding or ignoring a stressor and attending to emotional needs related to one's stress reaction.

Promoting Health

Too often, we think about our health only when something goes wrong, and then rush to a physician for diagnosis and treatment. That strategy is like ignoring a car's maintenance and going to a mechanic only when the car breaks down. A wiser tactic is maintaining our health by alleviating stress, preventing illness, and promoting well-being.

Coping With Stress

14: **What factors affect our ability to cope with stress?**

Stressors are unavoidable. This fact, coupled with the fact that persistent stress correlates with heart disease, depression, and lowered immunity, sends us a clear message. We need to learn to **cope** with the stress in our lives. When we feel a sense of control over a situation and think we can change the circumstances or change ourselves, we may address stressors directly, with **problem-focused coping.** For example, if our impatience leads to a family fight, we may go directly to that family member to work things out. When we cannot—or believe we cannot—change a situation, we may turn to **emotion-focused coping.** If, despite our best efforts, we cannot get along with that family member, we may reach out to friends to help address our own emotional needs.

Emotion-focused strategies can be nonadaptive, as when students worried about not keeping up with the reading in class go out and party to clear their mind. A problem-focused strategy (catching up with the reading) would more effectively reduce stress and promote long-term health and satisfaction. But when challenged, some people tend to respond more with cool problem-focused coping, others with emotion-focused coping (Connor-Smith & Flachsbart, 2007). Several factors affect the ability to cope successfully, including feelings of personal control, outlook, and supportive connections.

Perceived Control

Studies indicate that uncontrollable threats trigger the strongest stress responses (Dickerson & Kemeny, 2004). If two rats receive simultaneous shocks, but one can turn a wheel to stop the shocks, the helpless rat will be more susceptible to ulcers and lowered immunity to disease (Laudenslager & Reite, 1984). In humans, a bacterial infection often combines with uncontrollable stress to produce the most severe ulcers (Overmier & Murison, 1997). To cure the ulcer, kill the bug with antibiotics and control the stomach's acid secretions with reduced stress.

Perceiving a loss of control, we become more vulnerable to ill health. Elderly nursing home residents with little perceived control over their activities tend to decline faster and die sooner than do those given more control (Rodin, 1986). Workers who can control their work environment—by adjusting office furnishings and controlling interruptions and distractions—also experience less stress (O'Neill, 1993). This helps explain why Finnish workers with low job stress are less than half as likely to die of cardiovascular disease as are those with a demanding job and little control. The more control workers have, the longer they live (Bosma et al., 1997, 1998; Kivimaki et al., 2002; Marmot et al., 1997).

Control may also help explain a well-established link between economic status and longevity. In one study, inhabitants of Scottish regions with the least overcrowding and unemployment outlived less affluent Scots. There and elsewhere, high economic status predicts a lower risk of heart and respiratory diseases (Sapolsky, 2005). Wealthy predicts healthy among children, too, with reduced risks of infant mortality, low birth weight, smoking, and violence (Chen, 2004). Even among other primates, those at the top of the social pecking order are less likely than their lower-status companions to become sick when exposed to a coldlike virus (Cohen et al., 1997). But high status also entails stress for baboons and monkeys who frequently have to physically defend their dominant position (Sapolsky, 2005).

Why does perceived loss of control predict health problems? Animal studies show—and human studies confirm—that losing control provokes an outpouring of stress hormones. When rats cannot control shock or when primates or humans feel unable to control their environment, stress hormone levels rise, blood pressure increases, and immune responses drop (Rodin, 1986; Sapolsky, 2005). Captive animals therefore experience more stress and are more vulnerable to disease than are wild animals (Roberts, 1988). The crowding that occurs in high-density neighborhoods, prisons, and college and university dorms is another source of diminished feelings of control—and of elevated levels of stress hormones and blood pressure (Fleming et al., 1987; Ostfeld et al., 1987).

Optimism and Health

Can our basic outlook influence our ability to cope with stress? Studies indicate that it can. Compared with pessimists, *optimists*—people who agree with statements such as, "In uncertain times, I usually expect the best"—perceive more control, cope better with stressful events, and enjoy better health (Scheier & Carver, 1992). During the stressful first few weeks of law school, students who are optimistic ("It's unlikely that I will fail") enjoy better moods and stronger infection-thwarting immune systems (Segerstrom et al., 1998).

Consider the consistency and startling magnitude of the optimism and positive emotions factor in several other studies:

- One research team followed 941 Dutch people, ages 65 to 85, for nearly a decade (Giltay et al., 2004, 2007). Among those in the lowest optimism quartile, 57 percent died, as did only 30 percent of the top optimism quartile.
- Another study asked 795 Americans, ages 64 to 79 years, if they were "hopeful about the future." When the researchers checked up on these folks about 5 years later, 29 percent of those answering *no* had died—more than double the 11 percent of deaths among those who said *yes* (Stern et al., 2001).
- A now-famous study followed up on 180 Catholic nuns who had written brief autobiographies at about 22 years of age. Despite living thereafter with similar life-styles and status, those who had expressed happiness, love, and other positive feelings lived an average 7 years longer than their more dour counterparts (Danner et al., 2001). By age 80, some 54 percent of those expressing few positive emotions had died, as had only 24 percent of the most positive-spirited.

Social Support

More than 50 studies reveal that social support calms the cardiovascular system, lowering blood pressure and stress hormones (Graham et al., 2006; Uchino et al., 1996, 1999). James Coan and his colleagues (2006) observed the soothing benefit of social support when they subjected happily married women to the threat of electric shock to an ankle while lying in an fMRI machine. During the experiment, some women held their husband's hand. Others held the hand of an anonymous person or no hand at all. While awaiting the occasional shocks, the women's brains were less active in threat-responsive areas if they held their husband's hand. The benefit was greatest for those reporting the highest-quality marriages.

Social ties also foster stronger immune functioning, as Sheldon Cohen and his colleagues (1997, 2004) demonstrated by putting 276 healthy volunteers in quarantine for five days after administering nasal drops laden with a cold virus, and then repeating the experiment with 334 more volunteers. (In both experiments, the volunteers were paid $800 each to endure this experience.) The cold fact is that the effect of social ties is nothing to sneeze at. Age, race, sex, smoking, and other health habits being equal, those with the most social ties were least likely to catch a cold, and if they caught one, they produced less mucus.

We should not be surprised, then, that seven massive investigations, each following thousands of people for several years have revealed that close relationships—with friends, family, fellow workers, members of a faith community, or other support groups—predict health and a lower risk of premature death (Cohen, 1988; House et al., 1988; Nelson, 1988). Even pets can help us cope with stress. (See Close-Up: Pets Are Friends, Too.)

As in the Coan study, many people find social support in their marriage. In a seven-decades-long Harvard study, a good marriage at age 50 predicted healthy aging better than did a low cholesterol level at 50 (Vaillant, 2002). Many other carefully controlled studies also indicate that married people live longer, healthier lives than the unmarried (Kaplan & Kronick, 2006; National Center for Health Statistics, 2004; Wilson & Oswald, 2002). But, as Coan's study also indicated, marital *functioning* matters. Positive, happy, supportive marriages are conducive to health; conflict-laden ones are not (De Vogli et al., 2007; Kiecolt-Glaser & Newton, 2001). Moreover, middle-aged and older adults living alone are more likely to smoke, be obese, and have high cholesterol—and to have a doubled risk of heart attacks (Nielsen et al., 2006).

Close relationships give us an opportunity to confide painful feelings (Frattaroli, 2006). When researchers (Pennebaker & O'Heeron, 1984) contacted the surviving spouses of people who had committed suicide or died in car accidents, those who bore their grief alone had more health problems than those who could express it openly. Confiding in others can be "open heart therapy."

Talking about a stressful event can temporarily arouse people, but in the long run it calms them, by calming limbic system activity (Lieberman et al., 2007; Mendolia & Kleck, 1993). When James Pennebaker and his colleagues (1989) invited 33 Holocaust survivors to spend two hours recalling their experiences, many did so in intimate detail never before disclosed. In the weeks following, most watched a tape of their recollections and showed it to family and friends. Those who were most self-disclosing had the most improved health 14 months later. Confiding is good for the body and the soul.

> "Woe to one who is alone and falls and does not have another to help."
>
> —Ecclesiastes 4:10

Close-Up:

Pets Are Friends, Too

Have you ever wished for a friend who would love you just as you are, who is nonjudgmental, and who is always there for you, no matter your mood? For many tens of millions of people that friend exists, and it is a loyal dog or a friendly cat.

Many people describe their pet as a cherished family member who helps them feel calm, happy, and valued. Can pets also help people handle stress? If so, might pets have healing power? Karen Allen reports that the answers are *yes* and *yes*. For example, women's blood pressure rises as they struggle with challenging math problems in the presence of a best friend or even a spouse, but much less so in the presence of their dog (Allen, 2003). And pets have been found to increase the

odds of survival after a heart attack, to relieve depression among AIDS patients, and to lower the level of blood lipids that contribute to cardiovascular risk.

So, would pets be good medicine for people who do not have pets? To find out, Allen studied a group of stockbrokers who lived alone, described their work as stressful, and had high blood pressure. She randomly selected half to adopt an animal shelter cat or dog. When later facing stress, these new pet owners exhibited less than half the blood pressure increase of their counterparts without pets. The effect was greatest for those with few social contacts or friends. Allen's conclusion: For lowering blood pressure, pets are no substitute for effective drugs and exercise. But for those who enjoy animals, and especially for those who live alone, they are a healthy pleasure.

Managing Stress

15:

What tactics can we use to manage stress and reduce stress-related ailments?

Having a sense of control, developing more optimistic thinking, and building social support can help us *experience* less stress and thus improve our health. Moreover, these factors interrelate: People who are upbeat about themselves and their future tend also to enjoy health-promoting social ties (Stinson et al., 2008). But sometimes we cannot alleviate stress and simply need to *manage* our stress, lessening its effects. Aerobic exercise, relaxation, meditation, and spirituality may help.

"Is there anyone here who specializes in stress management?"

Aerobic Exercise

Aerobic exercise is sustained exercise, such as jogging, swimming, and biking that increases heart and lung fitness. Does it also boost the spirit?

EXERCISE AND MOOD With less physical activity demanded of us to provide food, shelter, and mobility (machines do much of the work for us), our more sedentary life-style contributes to today's high rate of depression. Less exercise means less brain activity in areas essential for reward, motivation, and effective coping (Ilardi et al., 2007; Lambert, 2005, 2008). Many studies have suggested that aerobic exercise can reduce stress, depression, and anxiety. For example, 3 in 10 American and Canadian people, and 2 in 10 British people who do aerobic exercise at least three times a week also manage stressful events better, exhibit more self-confidence, feel more vigor, and feel depressed and fatigued less often than those who exercise less (McMurray, 2004). In a Gallup survey, nonexercisers were twice as likely as exercisers to report being "not too happy" (Brooks, 2002). But if we state this observation the other way around—that stressed and depressed people exercise less—cause and effect become unclear.

Experiments have resolved this ambiguity by randomly assigning stressed, depressed, or anxious people either to aerobic exercise or to other treatments. In one classic experiment, Lisa McCann and David Holmes (1984) assigned one-third of a group of mildly depressed female college students to a program of aerobic exercise, one-third to a treatment of relaxation exercises, and the remaining third (a control group) to no treatment. Ten weeks later, those in the aerobic exercise program reported the greatest decrease in depression (**FIGURE 11.23**). Many had, quite literally, run away from their troubles. Vigorous exercise provides a "substantial" immediate mood boost, reports David Watson (2000) from his monitoring of university students. Even a 10-minute walk stimulates two hours of increased well-being by raising energy levels and lowering tension (Thayer, 1987, 1993).

Researchers are now wondering *why* aerobic exercise alleviates negative emotions. Exercise orders up mood-boosting chemicals from our body's internal pharmacy—neurotransmitters such as norepinephrine,

aerobic exercise sustained exercise that increases heart and lung fitness; may also reduce stress, depression, and anxiety.

FIGURE 11.23 Aerobic exercise and depression Mildly depressed college women who participated in an aerobic exercise program showed markedly reduced depression, compared with those who did relaxation exercises or received no treatment. (From McCann & Holmes, 1984.)

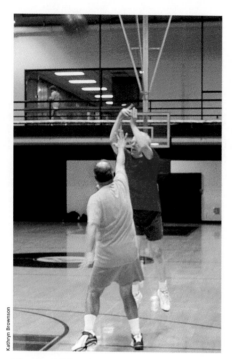

The mood boost When one's energy or spirits are sagging, few things reboot the day better than exercising (as I can vouch from my daily noontime basketball). Aerobic exercise appears to counteract depression partly by increasing arousal (replacing depression's low-arousal state) and by doing naturally what Prozac does—increasing the brain's serotonin activity.

Meditation is a modern phenomenon with a long history: "Sit down alone and in silence. Lower your head, shut your eyes, breathe out gently, and imagine yourself looking into your own heart. . . . As you breathe out, say 'Lord Jesus Christ, have mercy on me.' . . . Try to put all other thoughts aside. Be calm, be patient, and repeat the process very frequently" (Gregory of Sinai, died 1346).

serotonin, and the endorphins (Jacobs, 1994; Salmon, 2001). In mice, exercise causes their brains to produce a molecule that acts as a natural antidepressant by stimulating the production of new neurons (Hunsberger et al., 2007). Perhaps the emotional benefits of exercise are also a side effect of increased warmth and body arousal (counteracting depression's low arousal state), or of the muscle relaxation and sounder sleep that occur afterward. Or perhaps a sense of accomplishment and an improved physique enhance one's emotional state.

EXERCISE AND HEALTH By one estimate, moderate exercise adds not only quality of life (more energy and better mood) but also quantity of life—two additional years, on average. "Perhaps God does not subtract the time spent exercising from your allotted time on Earth," jested Martin Seligman (1994, p. 193). Exercise strengthens the heart, increases bloodflow, keeps blood vessels open, and lowers both blood pressure and the blood pressure reaction to stress (Ford, 2002; Manson, 2002). Compared with inactive adults, people who exercise suffer half as many heart attacks (Powell et al., 1987). Exercise makes the muscles hungry for the "bad fats" that, if not used by the muscles, contribute to clogged arteries (Barinaga, 1997). One study following adult Finnish twins for nearly 20 years revealed that, other things being equal, occasional exercise (compared with no exercise) reduced the risk of death by 29 percent. Daily conditioning exercise reduced death risk by 43 percent (Kujala et al., 1998). In later life, regular exercise also predicts better cognitive functioning and reduced risk of dementia and Alzheimer's disease (Kramer & Erickson, 2007).

Relaxation and Meditation

Knowing the damaging effects of stress, could we train people to counteract stress, bringing their heart rate and blood pressure under conscious control? Dozens of studies have found that relaxation procedures can help alleviate hypertension, anxiety, headaches, and insomnia (Nestoriuc et al., 2008; Stetter & Kupper, 2002). Such findings would not surprise Meyer Friedman and his colleagues. To find out whether teaching Type A heart attack victims to relax might reduce their risk of another attack, those researchers randomly assigned hundreds of middle-aged, male heart-attack survivors to one of two groups. The first group received standard advice from cardiologists concerning medications, diet, and exercise habits. The second group received similar advice plus continuing counseling on modifying their life-style—how to slow down and relax by walking, talking, and eating more slowly; by smiling at others and laughing at themselves; by admitting mistakes; by taking time to enjoy life; and by renewing their religious faith. As **FIGURE 11.24** indicates, during the ensuing three years, the second group experienced half as many repeat heart attacks as the first group. This, wrote the exuberant Friedman, was an unprecedented, spectacular reduction in heart-attack recurrence. A smaller-scale British study similarly divided heart-attack–prone people into control and life-style modification groups (Eysenck & Grossarth-Maticek, 1991). During the next 13 years, it also found a 50 percent reduction in death rate among those trained to alter their thinking and life-style. After suffering a heart attack at age 55, Friedman started taking his own behavioral medicine—and lived to age 90 (Wargo, 2007).

Cardiologist Herbert Benson (1996) became intrigued with meditative relaxation when he found that experienced meditators could decrease their blood pressure, heart rate, and oxygen consumption and could raise their fingertip temperature. His study led him to what he calls the *relaxation response,* described in Close-Up: The Relaxation Response.

Tibetan Buddhists deep in meditation and Franciscan nuns deep in centering prayer report a diminished sense of self, space, and time. Brain scans reveal the neural footprints of such spiritual feelings during these mystical experiences: A part of the parietal lobe that tracks where we are in space is less active than usual, and a

FIGURE 11.24 **Recurrent heart attacks and life-style modification** The San Francisco Recurrent Coronary Prevention Project offered counseling from a cardiologist to survivors of heart attacks. Those who were also guided in modifying their Type A life-style suffered fewer repeat heart attacks. (From Friedman & Ulmer, 1984.)

frontal lobe area involved in focused attention is more active (Cahn & Polich, 2006; Newberg & D'Aquili, 2001).

Buddhist monks experienced in meditation display elevated levels of the left frontal lobe activity associated with positive emotions. To explore whether such activity is a result of meditation, psychologist Richard Davidson and his colleagues (2003) ran baseline brain scans of volunteers who were *not* experienced meditators, and then randomly assigned them either to a control group or to an eight-week course in "mindfulness meditation." Compared with both the control group and their own baseline, the meditation participants exhibited noticeably more left-hemisphere activity, and also improved immune functioning after the training. Such effects may help explain the astonishing results of a study that randomly assigned 73 residents of homes for the elderly either to daily meditation or to none. After three years, one-fourth of the nonmeditators had died, but all the meditators were still alive (Alexander et al., 1989). A more recent study found that hypertension patients assigned to meditation training had (compared with other treatment groups) a 30 percent lower cardiovascular death rate over the ensuing 19-year study period (Schneider et al., 2005).

Spirituality and Health

More than a thousand studies have examined the relationship between health and healing. From those studies, a curious correlation, called the *faith factor*, has

And then there are the mystics who seek to use the mind's power to enable novocaine-free cavity repair. Their aim: To transcend dental medication.

Close-Up:

The Relaxation Response

The relaxation response is a state of calm marked by relaxed muscles, slowed breathing and heart rate, and decreased blood pressure. Advocates such as cardiologist Herbert Benson claim lasting stress-reducing benefits when relaxation is practiced once or twice daily. For those who want to experience the relaxation response, the Benson-Henry Institute for Mind-Body Medicine has recommended these steps:

Sit quietly in a comfortable position. Close your eyes. Relax your muscles, starting with your feet, then your calves, and upward through your thighs, shoulders, neck, and head. Breathe slowly. As you exhale each breath, repeat a focus word, phrase, or prayer—something drawn from your own belief system. When other thoughts intrude, don't worry. Just return to your repetition and continue for 10 to 20 minutes. When finished, sit quietly for another minute or two, then open your eyes and sit for a few more moments.

emerged: Religiously active people tend to live longer than those who are not religiously active. For example, one 16-year study (Kark et al., 1996) compared the death rates for 3900 Israelis either in one of 11 religiously orthodox or in one of 11 matched, nonreligious collective settlements (kibbutz communities). The researchers reported that "belonging to a religious collective was associated with a strong protective effect" not explained by age or economic differences. In every age group, religious community members were about half as likely to have died as were their nonreligious counterparts. This is roughly comparable to the gender difference in mortality.

Richard Sloan and his skeptical colleagues (1999, 2000, 2002, 2005) remind us that mere correlations can leave many factors uncontrolled. Consider one obvious possibility for such findings: Women are more religiously active than men, and women outlive men. Perhaps religious involvement is merely an expression of the gender effect on longevity.

The correlation between religious involvement and life expectancy is stronger among women. One 8-year study by the National Institutes of Health, for example, followed 92,395 women, ages 50 to 79. Even after controlling for many factors, women attending religious services weekly (or more often) experienced an approximately 20 percent reduced risk of death during the study period (Schnall et al., 2008). But the correlation also appears among men alone (McCullough et al., 2000, 2005). A 28-year study that followed 5286 Californians, controlling for age, gender, ethnicity, and education, found that frequent religious attenders were 36 percent less likely to have died in any year (Oman et al., 2002; Strawbridge et al., 1997, 1999). As a predictor of lowered risk of death, regular religious attendance rivaled the effects of nonsmoking and regular exercise.

After controlling for age, sex, race, and region, a U.S. National Health Interview Survey (of 21,204 people over 8 years) found that nonattenders were 1.87 times more likely to have died than were those attending more than weekly (Hummer, et al., 1999). This translated into a life expectancy at age 20 of 83 years for frequent attenders and 75 years for infrequent attenders (**FIGURE 11.25**). These findings do not indicate that nonattenders who start attending services and change nothing else will live 8 years longer. But they do indicate that religious involvement is a *predictor* of health and longevity.

Such findings demand explanation. Can you imagine what intervening variables might account for the correlation?

First, religiously active people tend to have healthier life-styles; for example, they smoke and drink less (Lyons, 2002; Park, 2007; Strawbridge et al., 2001). Health-oriented, vegetarian Seventh Day Adventists have a longer-than-usual life expectancy (Berkel & de Waard, 1983). Religiously orthodox Israelis eat less fat than do their nonreligious compatriots. But these differences are not great enough to explain the dramatically reduced mortality that was found in studies that controlled for unhealthy behaviors such as inactivity and smoking (Musick et al., 1999).

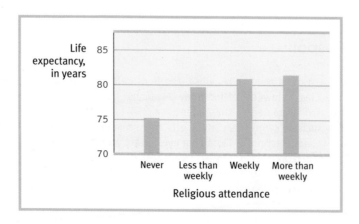

FIGURE 11.25 Religious attendance and life expectancy In a national health survey financed by the U.S. Centers for Disease Control and Prevention, religiously active people had longer life expectancies. (Data from Hummer et al., 1999.)

Could social support help explain the faith factor (Ai et al., 2007; George et al., 2002)? For Judaism, Christianity, and Islam, faith is not solo spirituality but a communal experience, providing support networks for their active participants—people who are there for one another when misfortune strikes. Moreover, religion encourages another predictor of health and longevity—marriage. In the religious kibbutzim, for example, divorce has been almost nonexistent.

Even after controlling for social ties, gender, unhealthy behaviors, and preexisting health problems, however, researchers find much of the mortality reduction remains (George et al., 2000; Powell et al., 2003). They therefore speculate that a third set of intervening variables is the stress protection and enhanced well-being associated with a coherent worldview, a sense of hope for the long-term future, feelings of ultimate acceptance, and the relaxed meditation of prayer or Sabbath observance (**FIGURE 11.26**). These variables might also help to explain other recent findings among the religiously active, such as healthier immune functioning, fewer hospital admissions, and, for AIDS patients, fewer stress hormones and longer survival (Ironson et al., 2002; Koenig & Larson, 1998; Lutgendorf et al., 2004).

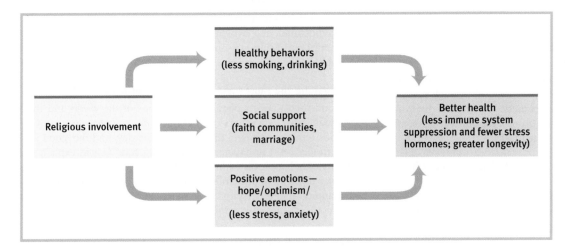

FIGURE 11.26 Possible explanations for the correlation between religious involvement and health/longevity

REHEARSE IT!

18. To cope with stress, we tend to use _____ strategies when we feel in control of our world, and to use _____ strategies when we believe we cannot change a situation.
    a. emotion-focused; problem-focused
    b. problem-focused; emotion-focused
    c. positive-emotion; negative-emotion
    d. negative-emotion; positive-emotion

19. Aerobic exercise raises energy levels and may reduce stress, depression, and anxiety by triggering the release of mood-boosting neurotransmitters, such as norepinephrine, serotonin, and the
    a. placebos.
    b. endorphins.
    c. B lymphocytes.
    d. T lymphocytes.

20. People who have close relationships—a strong social support system—are less likely to die prematurely than those who do not, supporting the idea that

    a. social ties can be a source of stress.
    b. gender influences longevity.
    c. Type A behavior is responsible for many premature deaths.
    d. social support has a beneficial effect on health.

Answers: 18. b, 19. b, 20. d.

CHAPTER REVIEW

Emotions, Stress, and Health

Theories of Emotion

1 What are the components of an emotion?

Emotions are psychological responses of the whole organism involving an interplay among (1) physiological arousal, (2) expressive behaviors, and (3) conscious experience.

The *James-Lange theory* maintains that our emotional feelings follow our body's response to the emotion-inducing stimuli. The *Cannon-Bard theory* proposes that our body responds to emotion at the same time that we experience the emotion (one does not cause the other). The Schachter-Singer *two-factor theory* holds that our emotions have two ingredients: physical arousal and a cognitive label.

Embodied Emotion

2 What is the link between emotional arousal and the autonomic nervous system?

Emotions are both psychological and physiological. The autonomic nervous system controls physiological arousal through its sympathetic (arousing) and parasympathetic (calming) divisions. Performance peaks at lower levels of arousal for difficult tasks, and at higher levels for easy or well-learned tasks.

3 Do different emotions activate different physiological or brain responses?

Emotions may be similarly arousing, but subtle differences in physiological responses and brain activity are associated with different emotions. *Polygraphs* measure several physiological indicators of emotion, but they are not accurate enough to justify their widespread use. The use of guilty knowledge questions may produce better results.

4 To experience emotions, must we consciously interpret and label them?

Schachter and Singer's two-factor theory of emotion contended that the cognitive labels we put on our states of arousal are an essential ingredient of emotion. Lazarus agreed that cognition is essential: Many important emotions arise from our interpretations or inferences. Zajonc and LeDoux, however, believe that some simple emotional responses occur instantly, outside our conscious awareness and before any cognitive processing occurs. The interplay between emotion and cognition illustrates our dual-track mind.

Expressed Emotion

5 How do we communicate nonverbally?

Nonverbal communication includes gestures, facial expressions, and voice tones. Even very thin (seconds-long) filmed slices of behavior can reveal feelings. Women tend to be better at reading people's emotional cues, and their faces tend to express more emotion.

6 Are nonverbal expressions of emotion universally understood?

The meaning of gestures varies from culture to culture. Facial expressions, such as those of happiness and fear, are common the world over. Cultures differ in the amount of emotion they express.

7 Do our facial expressions influence our feelings?

Our facial expressions can amplify the emotions we are displaying and signal our body to respond accordingly. This is known as the facial feedback effect.

Experienced Emotion

8 What are the causes and consequences of anger?

Anger is most often evoked by events that are interpreted as willful, unjustified, and avoidable. Blowing off steam *(catharsis)* may be temporarily calming, but in the long run expressing anger can actually make us angrier.

9 What are the causes and consequences of happiness?

A good mood boosts people's perceptions of the world and their willingness to help others (the *feel-good, do-good phenomenon*). Our moods tend to vary over the course of the day, and our good and bad moods tend to balance over the long run. We can explain the relativity of happiness with the *adaptation-level phenomenon* and the *relative deprivation* principle. Nevertheless, some people are usually happier than others, and researchers have identified factors that predict such *subjective well-being*.

Stress and Health

10 What is stress?

Stress is the process by which we appraise and respond to stressors, events that challenge or threaten us. Cannon viewed stress as a "fight or flight" system. Selye saw it as a three-phase (alarm-resistance-exhaustion) *general adaptation syndrome (GAS)*.

11 What events provoke stress responses?

There are three main categories of life-event stressors: catastrophic events, significant life changes, and daily hassles. Each type has the ability to have harmful effects on health and well-being.

12 Why are some of us more prone than others to coronary heart disease?

Coronary heart disease, North America's number one cause of death, has been linked with the competitive, hard-driving, impatient, and (especially) anger-prone *Type A* personality. More frequent bouts of anger may trigger increased cholesterol levels and altered heart rhythms. *Type B* personalities, who are more relaxed and easygoing, are less prone to coronary attacks. Pessimism and depression are also correlated with higher-than-normal risks of heart disease.

13 **How does stress make us more vulnerable to disease?**

Stress diverts energy from the immune system, inhibiting the activities of its B and T *lymphocytes,* macrophages, and NK cells. Stress does not cause diseases such as AIDS and cancer, but it may weaken the body's natural defenses to fight these and other diseases.

Promoting Health

14 **What factors affect our ability to cope with stress?**

We *cope* with stress emotionally, cognitively, and behaviorally. *Problem-focused coping* strategies alleviate stress directly, by changing the stressor or the way we interact with it; *emotion-focused coping* tries to alleviate stress indirectly by attending to emotional needs. Those with a sense of control, an optimistic outlook, and a base of social support seem to cope more successfully with stress and enjoy better health.

15 **What tactics can we use to manage stress and reduce stress-related ailments?**

Stress-management programs may include *aerobic exercise,* relaxation, and meditation. Researchers are working toward understanding the active components of the religion-health correlation.

Terms and Concepts to Remember

emotion, p. 376

James-Lange theory, p. 376

Cannon-Bard theory, p. 376

two-factor theory, p. 377

polygraph, p. 380

catharsis, p. 390

feel-good, do-good phenomenon, p. 392

subjective well-being, p. 392

adaptation-level phenomenon, p. 395

relative deprivation, p. 395

stress, p. 398

general adaptation syndrome (GAS), p. 399

coronary heart disease, p. 402

Type A, p. 402

Type B, p. 402

psychophysiological illness, p. 403

lymphocytes, p. 403

complementary and alternative medicine (CAM), p. 406

coping, p. 408

problem-focused coping, p. 408

emotion-focused coping, p. 408

aerobic exercise, p. 411

Test for Success: Critical Thinking Exercises

By Amy Himsel, El Camino College

1. Christine is holding her 8-month-old baby when a fierce dog appears out of nowhere and, with teeth bared, leaps for the baby's face. Christine immediately ducks for cover to protect the baby, screams at the dog, then notices that her heart is banging in her chest and she's broken out in a cold sweat. How would the James-Lange, Cannon-Bard, and two-factor theories explain Christine's emotional reaction?

2. How might mountain climbing on a first date influence your emotional reaction to the person?

3. You are happy to have earned a B on an exam until you learn that most of your friends received an A. How can you explain your drop in mood?

4. A self-help book declares that you can prevent cancer through "the power of positive thinking." How would you evaluate this claim?

5. A Chinese proverb warns, "The fire you kindle for your enemy often burns you more than him." How is this true of Type A individuals?

The Test for Success exercises offer you a chance to apply your critical thinking skills to aspects of the material you have just read. Suggestions for answering these questions can be found in Appendix D at the back of the book.

Multiple-choice self-tests and more may be found at www.worthpublishers.com/myers.

Chapter Outline

● **The Psychoanalytic Perspective**
Exploring the Unconscious
The Neo-Freudian and Psychodynamic Theorists
Assessing Unconscious Processes
Evaluating the Psychoanalytic Perspective

● **The Humanistic Perspective**
Abraham Maslow's Self-Actualizing Person
Carl Rogers' Person-Centered Perspective
Assessing the Self
Evaluating the Humanistic Perspective

● **The Trait Perspective**
Exploring Traits
Assessing Traits
THINKING CRITICALLY ABOUT: How to Be a "Successful" Astrologer or Palm Reader
The Big Five Factors
Evaluating the Trait Perspective

● **The Social-Cognitive Perspective**
Reciprocal Influences
Personal Control
CLOSE-UP: Toward a More Positive Psychology
Assessing Behavior in Situations
Evaluating the Social-Cognitive Perspective

● **Exploring the Self**
The Benefits of Self-Esteem
Self-Serving Bias

12: Personality

Lord of the Rings hobbit-hero Frodo Baggins knew that throughout his difficult journey there was one who would never fail him—his loyal and ever-cheerful companion, Sam Gamgee. Even before they left their beloved hometown, Frodo warned Sam that the journey would not be easy.

> "It is going to be very dangerous, Sam. It is already dangerous. Most likely neither of us will come back."
>
> "If you don't come back, sir, then I shan't, that's certain," said Sam. "[The Elves told me] 'Don't you leave him!' Leave him! I said. I never mean to. I am going with him, if he climbs to the Moon; and if any of those Black Riders try to stop him, they'll have Sam Gamgee to reckon with." (J.R.R. Tolkien, *The Fellowship of the Ring*, p. 96)

And so they did! Later in the story, when it becomes clear that Frodo's path will lead him into the land of Mordor, it is Sam who insists he will be at Frodo's side, come what may. It is Sam who lifts Frodo's spirits with songs and stories from their boyhood. And it is Sam whom Frodo leans upon when he can barely take another step. When Frodo is overcome by the evil of the ring he carries, it is Sam who saves him. In the end, it is Sam who helps Frodo successfully reach the end of his journey. Sam Gamgee—cheerful, optimistic, emotionally stable—never falters in his faithfulness or his belief that they will overcome the threatening darkness.

As he appears and reappears throughout the series, Tolkien's Sam Gamgee exhibits the distinctive and enduring behaviors that define **personality**—a person's characteristic pattern of thinking, feeling, and acting.

Much of this book deals with personality. In earlier chapters, we considered biological influences on personality, personality development across the life span, and personality-related aspects of learning, motivation, emotion, and health. In later chapters, we will study disorders of personality and social influences on personality.

Those chapters all focus on our shared paths. In this chapter, we focus on what makes us each unique. We begin with two historically significant perspectives that helped establish the field of personality psychology and raised key issues still being addressed in today's research and clinical work. The first, Sigmund Freud's *psychoanalytic* theory, proposed that childhood sexuality and unconscious motivations influence personality. The second, the *humanistic* approach, focused on our inner capacities for growth and self-fulfillment.

These classic theories, which offer sweeping perspectives on human nature, have become part of our cultural legacy. They are complemented by today's more focused and down-to-earth scientific research on specific aspects of personality. Contemporary personality researchers study the basic dimensions of personality, the biological roots of these basic dimensions, and the interaction of persons and environments. They also study self-esteem, self-serving bias, and cultural influences on one's sense of self. And they study the unconscious mind—with findings that probably would have surprised Freud himself.

personality an individual's characteristic pattern of thinking, feeling, and acting.

419

Sigmund Freud, 1856–1939 "I was the only worker in a new field."

The Psychoanalytic Perspective

1: What was Freud's view of personality and its development?

Love him or hate him, Sigmund Freud has profoundly influenced Western culture. Ask 100 people on the street to name a notable deceased psychologist, suggested Keith Stanovich (1996, p. 1), and "Freud would be the winner hands down." In the popular mind, he is to psychology's history what Elvis Presley is to rock music's history. Freud's influence lingers in literary and film interpretation, psychiatry, and clinical psychology. So, who was Freud, and what did he teach?

Long before entering the University of Vienna in 1873, a youthful Sigmund Freud showed signs of independence and brilliance. He had a prodigious memory and so loved reading plays, poetry, and philosophy that he once ran up a bookstore debt beyond his means. As a teen he often took his evening meal in his tiny bedroom in order to lose no time from his studies. After medical school he set up a private practice, specializing in nervous disorders. Before long, however, he faced patients whose disorders made no neurological sense. For example, a patient might have lost all feeling in a hand—yet there is no sensory nerve that, if damaged, would numb the entire hand and nothing else. Freud's search for a cause for such disorders set his mind running in a direction destined to change human self-understanding.

Exploring the Unconscious

Might some neurological disorders have psychological causes? Observing patients led Freud to speculate that lost feeling in one's hand might be caused by a fear of touching one's genitals; that unexplained blindness or deafness might be caused by not wanting to see or hear something that aroused intense anxiety. After some early unsuccessful trials with hypnosis, Freud turned to **free association,** in which he told the patient to relax and say whatever came to mind, no matter how embarrassing or trivial. He assumed that a line of mental dominoes had fallen from his patients' distant past to their troubled present. Free association, he believed, would allow him to retrace that line, following a chain of thought leading into the patient's **unconscious** mind, where painful memories, often from childhood, could be retrieved and released.

Freud called his theory of personality and the associated treatment techniques **psychoanalysis.** Basic to his theory was the belief that the mind is mostly hidden (**FIGURE 12.1**). Our conscious awareness is like the part of an iceberg that floats above the surface. Beneath our awareness is the larger unconscious mind with its thoughts, wishes, feelings, and memories. Some of these thoughts we store temporarily in a *preconscious* area, from which we can retrieve them into conscious awareness. Of greater interest to Freud was the mass of unacceptable passions and thoughts that he believed we *repress,* or forcibly block from consciousness because they would be too unsettling to acknowledge. Nevertheless, these feelings and ideas lurking outside our awareness can powerfully influence us, sometimes gaining expression in disguised forms—the work we choose, the beliefs we hold, our daily habits, our troubling symptoms.

For Freud the determinist, nothing was ever accidental. He believed he could glimpse the unconscious seeping not only into people's free associations, beliefs, habits, and symptoms but also into slips of the tongue

free association in psychoanalysis, a method of exploring the unconscious in which the person relaxes and says whatever comes to mind, no matter how trivial or embarrassing.

unconscious according to Freud, a reservoir of mostly unacceptable thoughts, wishes, feelings, and memories. According to contemporary psychologists, information processing of which we are unaware.

psychoanalysis Freud's theory of personality that attributes thoughts and actions to unconscious motives and conflicts; the techniques used in treating psychological disorders by seeking to expose and interpret unconscious tensions.

id contains a reservoir of unconscious psychic energy that, according to Freud, strives to satisfy basic sexual and aggressive drives. The id operates on the *pleasure principle*, demanding immediate gratification.

ego the largely conscious, "executive" part of personality that, according to Freud, mediates among the demands of the id, superego, and reality. The ego operates on the *reality principle*, satisfying the id's desires in ways that will realistically bring pleasure rather than pain.

superego the part of personality that, according to Freud, represents internalized ideals and provides standards for judgment (the conscience) and for future aspirations.

"*Good morning, beheaded—uh, I mean beloved.*"

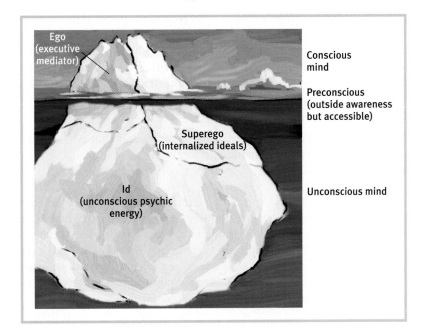

Ego
(executive
mediator)

Conscious
mind

Preconscious
(outside awareness
but accessible)

Superego
(internalized ideals)

Id
(unconscious psychic
energy)

Unconscious mind

FIGURE 12.1 Freud's idea of the mind's structure Psychologists have used an iceberg image to illustrate Freud's idea that the mind is mostly hidden beneath the conscious surface. Note that the id is totally unconscious, but ego and superego operate both consciously and unconsciously. Unlike the parts of a frozen iceberg, however, the id, ego, and superego interact.

and pen. He illustrated with a financially stressed patient who, not wanting any large pills, said, "Please do not give me any bills, because I cannot swallow them." Similarly, Freud viewed jokes as expressions of repressed sexual and aggressive tendencies, and dreams as the "royal road to the unconscious." The remembered content of dreams (their *manifest content*) he believed to be a censored expression of the dreamer's unconscious wishes (the dream's *latent content*). In his dream analyses, Freud searched for patients' inner conflicts.

Personality Structure

In Freud's view, human personality—including its emotions and strivings—arises from a conflict between impulse and restraint—between our aggressive, pleasure-seeking biological urges and our internalized social controls over these urges. Freud believed personality is the result of our efforts to resolve this basic conflict—by expressing these impulses in ways that bring satisfaction without also bringing guilt or punishment. To understand the mind's dynamics during this conflict, Freud proposed three interacting systems: the *id, ego,* and *superego* (Figure 12.1).

The **id's** unconscious psychic energy constantly strives to satisfy basic drives to survive, reproduce, and aggress. The id operates on the *pleasure principle:* It seeks immediate gratification. To envision an id-dominated person, think of a newborn infant crying out for satisfaction, caring nothing for the outside world's conditions and demands. Or think of adults who often use tobacco, alcohol, and other drugs and would sooner party now than sacrifice today's pleasure for future success and happiness (Keough et al., 1999).

As the **ego** develops, the young child responds to the real world. The ego, operating on the *reality principle,* seeks to gratify the id's impulses in realistic ways that will bring long-term pleasure. (Imagine what would happen if, lacking an ego, we expressed all our unrestrained sexual or aggressive impulses.) The ego contains our partly conscious perceptions, thoughts, judgments, and memories.

Around age 4 or 5, Freud theorized, a child's ego recognizes the demands of the **superego,** the newly emerging moral compass *(conscience)* that forces the ego to consider the *ideal*—how we *ought* to behave. The superego strives for perfection, judging actions and producing positive feelings of pride or negative feelings of guilt. Someone with an exceptionally strong superego may be virtuous yet guilt-ridden; another with a weak superego may be wantonly self-indulgent and remorseless.

INSTANT CASH

"Fifty is plenty."   *"Hundred and fifty."*

The ego struggles to reconcile the demands of superego and id, said Freud.

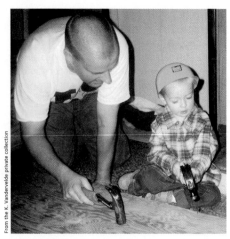

Identification Freud believed that children cope with threatening feelings of competition with their same-sex parent by identifying with that parent.

"Oh, for goodness' sake! Smoke!"

psychosexual stages the childhood stages of development (oral, anal, phallic, latency, genital) during which, according to Freud, the id's pleasure-seeking energies focus on distinct erogenous zones.

Oedipus [ED-uh-puss] **complex** according to Freud, a boy's sexual desires toward his mother and feelings of jealousy and hatred for the rival father.

identification the process by which, according to Freud, children incorporate their parents' values into their developing superegos.

fixation according to Freud, a lingering focus of pleasure-seeking energies at an earlier psychosexual stage, in which conflicts were unresolved.

Because the superego's demands often oppose the id's, the ego struggles to reconcile the two. It is the personality "executive," mediating the impulsive demands of the id, the restraining demands of the superego, and the real-life demands of the external world. If chaste Jane feels sexually attracted to John, she may satisfy both id and superego by joining a volunteer organization that John attends regularly.

Personality Development

Analysis of his patients' histories convinced Freud that personality forms during life's first few years. He concluded that children pass through a series of **psychosexual stages,** during which the id's pleasure-seeking energies focus on distinct *erogenous zones,* or pleasure-sensitive areas (**TABLE 12.1**). For example, during the *phallic stage,* Freud said, boys seek genital stimulation. They develop both unconscious sexual desires for their mother and jealousy and hatred for their father, whom they consider a rival. They then experience guilt and a lurking fear of punishment, perhaps by castration, from their father. Freud called this collection of feelings the **Oedipus complex** after the Greek legend of Oedipus, who unknowingly killed his father and married his mother. Some psychoanalysts in Freud's era believed that girls experience a parallel *Electra complex.*

Children eventually cope with the threatening feelings, said Freud, by repressing them and by identifying with (trying to become like) the rival parent. It's as though something inside the child decides, "If you can't beat 'em [the parent of the same sex], join 'em." Through this **identification** process, children's superegos gain strength as they incorporate many of their parents' values. Freud believed that identification with the same-sex parent provides what psychologists now call *gender identity*—the sense of being male or female. Freud presumed that our early childhood relations—with parents, caregivers, and everything else—influence our developing identity, personality, and frailties.

In Freud's view, conflicts unresolved during earlier psychosexual stages could surface as maladaptive behavior in the adult years. At any point in the oral, anal, or phallic stages, strong conflict could lock, or **fixate,** the person's pleasure-seeking energies in that stage. A person who had been either orally overindulged or deprived (perhaps by abrupt, early weaning) might fixate at the oral stage. This orally fixated adult could exhibit either passive dependence (like that of a nursing infant) or an exaggerated denial of this dependence (by acting tough or uttering biting sarcasm). Or the person might continue to seek oral gratification by smoking or excessive eating. In such ways, Freud suggested, the twig of personality is bent at an early age.

TABLE 12.1 Freud's Psychosexual Stages

Stage	Focus
Oral (0–18 months)	Pleasure centers on the mouth—sucking, biting, chewing
Anal (18–36 months)	Pleasure focuses on bowel and bladder elimination; coping with demands for control
Phallic (3–6 years)	Pleasure zone is the genitals; coping with incestuous sexual feelings
Latency (6 to puberty)	Dormant sexual feelings
Genital (puberty on)	Maturation of sexual interests

Defense Mechanisms

Anxiety, said Freud, is the price we pay for civilization. As members of social groups, we must control our sexual and aggressive impulses, not act them out. But sometimes the ego fears losing control of this inner war between the id and superego. The presumed result is a dark cloud of unfocused anxiety that leaves us feeling unsettled but unsure why.

He proposed that the ego protects itself with **defense mechanisms**—tactics that function indirectly and unconsciously, reducing anxiety by disguising some threatening impulse. Just as the body unconsciously defends itself against disease, so also, believed Freud, does the ego unconsciously defend itself against anxiety. For example, **repression** banishes anxiety-arousing wishes from consciousness. According to Freud, *repression underlies all the other defense mechanisms*, each of which disguises threatening impulses and keeps them from reaching consciousness. Freud believed that repression is often incomplete, with repressed urges seeping out in dream symbols and slips of the tongue. **TABLE 12.2** describes six other well-known defense mechanisms.

defense mechanisms in psychoanalytic theory, the ego's protective methods of reducing anxiety by unconsciously distorting reality.

repression in psychoanalytic theory, the basic defense mechanism that banishes anxiety-arousing thoughts, feelings, and memories from consciousness.

TABLE 12.2 Six Defense Mechanisms

Freud believed that *repression,* the basic defense mechanism that banishes anxiety-arousing impulses, enables other defense mechanisms.

Defense mechanism	Unconscious process employed to avoid anxiety-arousing thoughts or feelings	Example
Regression	Retreating to a more infantile psychosexual stage, where some psychic energy remains fixated.	A little boy reverts to the oral comfort of thumb sucking in the car on the way to his first day of school.
Reaction formation	Switching unacceptable impulses into their opposites.	Repressing angry feelings, a person displays exaggerated friendliness.
Projection	Disguising one's own threatening impulses by attributing them to others.	An El Salvadoran saying captures the idea: "The thief thinks everyone else is a thief."
Rationalization	Offering self-justifying explanations in place of the real, more threatening unconscious reasons for one's actions.	A habitual drinker says she drinks with her friends "just to be sociable."
Displacement	Shifting sexual or aggressive impulses toward a more acceptable or less threatening object or person.	A little girl kicks the family dog after her mother sends her to her room.
Denial	Refusing to believe or even perceive painful realities.	A partner denies evidence of his loved one's affair.

The Neo-Freudian and Psychodynamic Theorists

2:
Which of Freud's ideas did his followers accept or reject?

Freud's writings were controversial, but they soon attracted followers, mostly young, ambitious physicians who formed an inner circle around their strong-minded leader. These pioneering psychoanalysts and others, whom we now call *neo-Freudians,* accepted Freud's basic ideas: the personality structures of id, ego, and superego; the importance of the unconscious; the shaping of personality in childhood; and the dynamics of anxiety and the defense mechanisms. But they veered away from Freud in two important ways. First, they placed more emphasis on the conscious mind's role in interpreting experience and in coping with the environment. And second, they doubted that sex and aggression were all-consuming motivations. Instead, they tended to emphasize loftier motives and social interactions. The following examples illustrate.

Alfred Adler "The individual feels at home in life and feels his existence to be worthwhile just so far as he is useful to others and is overcoming feelings of inferiority" (*Problems of Neurosis,* 1964).

Karen Horney "The view that women are infantile and emotional creatures, and as such, incapable of responsibility and independence is the work of the masculine tendency to lower women's self-respect" (*Feminine Psychology,* 1932).

Carl Jung "From the living fountain of instinct flows everything that is creative; hence the unconscious is the very source of the creative impulse" (*The Structure and Dynamics of the Psyche,* 1960).

"The female . . . acknowledges the fact of her castration, and with it, too, the superiority of the male and her own inferiority; but she rebels against this unwelcome state of affairs."

—Sigmund Freud, *Female Sexuality,* 1931

collective unconscious Carl Jung's concept of a shared, inherited reservoir of memory traces from our species' history.

projective test a personality test, such as the Rorschach inkblot test, that provides ambiguous stimuli designed to trigger projection of one's inner dynamics.

Rorschach inkblot test the most widely used projective test, a set of 10 inkblots, designed by Hermann Rorschach; seeks to identify people's inner feelings by analyzing their interpretations of the blots.

Alfred Adler and Karen Horney [HORN-eye] agreed with Freud that childhood is important. But they believed that childhood *social,* not sexual, tensions are crucial for personality formation (Ferguson, 2003). Adler (who proposed the still-popular idea of the *inferiority complex*) had himself struggled to overcome childhood illnesses and accidents. He believed that much of our behavior is driven by efforts to conquer childhood feelings of inferiority, feelings that trigger our strivings for superiority and power. Horney said childhood anxiety, caused by the dependent child's sense of helplessness, triggers our desire for love and security. Horney also attempted to balance the masculine bias she detected in Freud's view of psychology, such as the assumptions that women have weak superegos and suffer "penis envy."

Unlike other neo-Freudians, Carl Jung—Freud's disciple-turned-dissenter—placed less emphasis on social factors and agreed with Freud that the unconscious exerts a powerful influence. But to Jung (pronounced *Yoong*), the unconscious contains more than our repressed thoughts and feelings. He believed we also have a **collective unconscious,** a common reservoir of images derived from our species' universal experiences. This collective unconscious, said Jung, explains why people in different cultures share certain spiritual concerns, myths, and images, such as mother as a symbol of nurturance. (Today's psychologists discount the idea of inherited experiences. But many do believe that our shared evolutionary history shaped some universal dispositions.)

Freud died in 1939. Since then, some of his ideas have been incorporated into *psychodynamic theory.* "Most contemporary dynamic theorists and therapists are not wedded to the idea that sex is the basis of personality," noted Drew Westen (1996). They "do not talk about ids and egos, and do not go around classifying their patients as oral, anal, or phallic characters." What they do assume, with Freud, is that much of our mental life is unconscious; that we often struggle with inner conflicts among our wishes, fears, and values; and that childhood shapes our personality and ways of becoming attached to others.

Assessing Unconscious Processes

3: What are projective tests, and how are they used?

Personality assessment tools are useful to those who study personality or provide therapy. Such tools differ because they are tailored to specific theories. How might clinicians working in the Freudian tradition attempt to assess personality characteristics?

The first requirement would be some sort of a road into the unconscious. Objective assessment tools, such as agree-disagree or true-false questionnaires, would be inadequate because they would merely tap the conscious surface. To track down residue from early childhood experiences, a test would need to move beyond surface pretensions and reveal hidden conflicts and impulses.

Projective tests aim to provide this "psychological X-ray," by asking test-takers to describe an ambiguous stimulus or tell a story about it. The stimulus has no inherent significance, so any meaning people read into it is presumably a projection of their interests and conflicts.

The most widely used projective test is the famous **Rorschach inkblot test,** in which people describe what they see in a series of inkblots (**FIGURE 12.2**). Swiss psychiatrist Hermann Rorschach [ROAR-shock] based it on a childhood game in which he and his friends dripped ink on a paper, folded it, and then said what they saw in the resulting blot (Sdorow, 2005). Do you see predatory animals or weapons? Perhaps you have aggressive tendencies. But is this a reasonable assumption?

Clinicians' and critics' answers differ. Some clinicians cherish the Rorschach, even offering Rorschach-based assessments of criminals' violence potential to judges. Others view it as a helpful diagnostic tool, a source of suggestive leads, or an icebreaker and a revealing interview technique. The Society for Personality Assessment (2005) commends "its responsible use" (which would *not* include inferring past childhood sexual abuse). And—in response to past criticisms of test scoring and interpretation (Sechrest et al, 1998)—a research-based, computer-aided tool has been designed to improve agreement among raters and enhance the test's validity (Erdberg, 1990; Exner, 2003).

But the evidence is insufficient to its revilers, who insist the Rorschach is no emotional MRI. They argue that only a few of the many Rorschach-derived scores, such as ones for hostility and anxiety, have demonstrated *validity* (Wood, 2006). Moreover, they say, these tests are not *reliable*. Inkblot assessments diagnose many normal adults as pathological (Wood et al., 2003, 2006). Alternative projective assessment techniques fare little better. "Even seasoned professionals can be fooled by their intuitions and their faith in tools that lack strong evidence of effectiveness," warned Scott Lilienfeld, James Wood, and Howard Garb (2001).

"The forward thrust of the antlers shows a determined personality, yet the small sun indicates a lack of self-confidence. . . ."

"We don't see things as they are; we see things as we are."

—The Talmud

Recall the difference:
Validity *is the extent to which a test measures or predicts what it is supposed to.*
Reliability *is the extent to which a test yields consistent results.*

"The Rorschach Inkblot Test has been resoundingly discredited . . . I call it the Dracula of psychological tests, because no one has been able to drive a stake through the cursed thing's heart."

—Carol Tavris, "Mind Games: Psychological Warfare Between Therapists and Scientists," 2003

FIGURE 12.2 The Rorschach test In this projective test, people tell what they see in a series of symmetrical inkblots. Some who use this test are confident that the interpretation of ambiguous stimuli will reveal unconscious aspects of the test-taker's personality. Others use it as an icebreaker or to supplement other information.

"When a substantial body of research demonstrates that old intuitions are wrong, it is time to adopt new ways of thinking." Freud himself might have agreed. He probably would have been more interested in the therapist–patient interactions that take place during the testing process.

Evaluating the Psychoanalytic Perspective

4 : How do contemporary psychologists view Freud and the unconscious?

Freud did not have access to neurotransmitter or DNA studies, or to all that we have since learned about human development, thinking, and emotion. To criticize his theory by comparing it with current concepts, some say, is like criticizing Henry Ford's Model T by comparing it with today's hybrid cars. (How tempting it always is to judge people in the past from our perspective in the present, a perspective that itself will be subject to revision in the future.) But both Freud's admirers and his critics agree that recent research contradicts many of his specific ideas. For example, history has failed to support Freud's belief that suppressed sexuality causes psychological disorders. From Freud's time to ours, sexual inhibition has diminished; psychological disorders have not. Consider, too, some other contradictory research.

DOES DEVELOPMENTAL RESEARCH SUPPORT FREUD'S VIEWS OF CHILDHOOD? Developmental psychologists now see our development as lifelong, not fixed in childhood. They doubt that infants' neural networks are mature enough to sustain as much emotional trauma as Freud assumed. Some think Freud overestimated parental influence and underestimated peer influence (and abuse). They also doubt that conscience and gender identity form as the child resolves the Oedipus complex at age 5 or 6. We gain our gender identity earlier and become strongly masculine or feminine even without a same-sex parent present. And they note that Freud's ideas about childhood sexuality arose from his skepticism of stories of childhood sexual abuse told by his female patients—stories that some scholars believe he attributed to their own childhood sexual wishes and conflicts (Esterson, 2001; Powell & Boer, 1994). Today, we understand how Freud's questioning might have created false memories of abuse, but we also know that childhood sexual abuse does happen.

DOES MEMORY RESEARCH SUPPORT FREUD'S IDEA OF REPRESSION? Freud's entire psychoanalytic theory rests on his assumption that the human mind often *represses* offending wishes, banishing them into the unconscious until they resurface, like long-lost books in a dusty attic. Recover and resolve childhood's conflicted wishes, and emotional healing should follow. Under Freud's influence, repression became a widely accepted concept, used to explain hypnotic phenomena and psychological disorders. Freud's followers extended repression to explain apparently lost and recovered memories of childhood traumas (Boag, 2006; Cheit, 1998; Erdelyi, 2006). In one survey, 88 percent of university students believed that painful experiences commonly get pushed out of awareness and into the unconscious (Garry et al., 1994).

Today's researchers acknowledge that we sometimes spare our egos by neglecting threatening information (Green et al., 2008). Yet, many contend that repression, if it ever occurs, is a rare mental response to terrible trauma. "Repression folklore is . . . partly refuted, partly untested, and partly untestable," said Elizabeth Loftus (1995). Even those who have witnessed a parent's murder or survived Nazi death camps retain their unrepressed memories of the horror (Helmreich, 1992, 1994; Malmquist, 1986; Pennebaker, 1990). "Dozens of formal studies have yielded not a single convincing case of repression in the entire literature on trauma," concludes personality researcher John Kihlstrom (2006).

"Many aspects of Freudian theory are indeed out of date, and they should be: Freud died in 1939, and he has been slow to undertake further revisions."

—Psychologist Drew Westen (1998)

Some researchers believe that extreme, prolonged stress, such as the stress some severely abused children experience, might disrupt memory by damaging the hippocampus (Schacter, 1996). But the far more common reality is that high stress and associated stress hormones enhance memory (see Chapter 8). Indeed, rape, torture, and other traumatic events haunt survivors, who experience unwanted flashbacks. They are seared onto the soul. "You see the babies," said Holocaust survivor Sally H. (1979). "You see the screaming mothers. You see hanging people. You sit and you see that face there. It's something you don't forget."

DOES COGNITIVE RESEARCH SUPPORT FREUD'S VIEW OF THE UNCONSCIOUS? As we saw in Chapter 3, new ideas about why we dream dispute Freud's belief that dreams disguise and fulfill wishes lurking in our unconscious. And slips of the tongue can be explained as competition between similar verbal choices in our memory network. Someone who says "I don't want to do that—it's a lot of brothel" may simply be blending *bother* and *trouble* (Foss & Hakes, 1978). But Freud was right about at least one thing: We indeed have limited access to all that goes on in our minds (Erdelyi, 1985, 1988, 2006; Kihlstrom, 1990). Research confirms the reality of unconscious *implicit learning* (Fletcher et al., 2005; Frensch & Rünger, 2003). In experiments, people have learned to anticipate where on a computer screen a character will appear next, even before being able to articulate the underlying rule (Lewicki, 1992, 1997). Our two-track mind has a vast out-of-sight realm.

But the "iceberg" notion held by today's researchers differs from Freud's (Greenwald, 1992). Many now think of the unconscious not as seething passions and repressive censoring but as cooler information processing that occurs without our awareness, such as

- the right-hemisphere activity that enables the split-brain patient's left hand to carry out an instruction the patient cannot verbalize (Chapter 2).
- the parallel processing of different aspects of vision and thinking, and the schemas that automatically control our perceptions and interpretations (Chapters 6 and 9).
- the implicit memories that operate without our conscious recall, and even among those with amnesia (Chapter 8).
- the emotions that activate instantly, before conscious analysis (Chapter 11).
- the self-concept and stereotypes that automatically and unconsciously influence how we process information about ourselves and others (Chapter 15).

More than we realize, we fly on autopilot, guided by off-screen, out-of-sight, unconscious information processing. The unconscious mind is huge. This understanding of unconscious information processing is more like the pre-Freudian view of an underground, unattended stream of thought from which spontaneous behavior and creative ideas surface (Bargh & Morsella, 2008).

Researchers find little support for Freud's idea that defense mechanisms disguise sexual and aggressive impulses. More evidence exists for defenses that defend self-esteem. For example, Roy Baumeister and his colleagues (1998) found that people tend to see their foibles and attitudes in others, a phenomenon that Freud called projection and that today's researchers call the *false consensus effect*, the tendency to overestimate the extent to which others share our beliefs and behaviors. Although our cognitive gymnastics do work to support our self-esteem, supportive evidence is meager for other defenses, such as displacement, that are tied to instinctual energy. Defense mechanisms, Baumeister concluded, are motivated less by the seething impulses that Freud presumed than by our need to protect our self-image.

CAN FREUD'S THEORY BE TESTED SCIENTIFICALLY? Recall from Chapter 1 that good scientific theories explain observations and offer testable hypotheses. Freud's critics note that his theory rests on few objective observations, and parts of it offer few testable hypotheses. (For Freud, his own recollections and interpretations of patients' free associations, dreams, and slips were evidence enough.)

"During the Holocaust, many children . . . were forced to endure the unendurable. For those who continue to suffer [the] pain is still present, many years later, as real as it was on the day it occurred."

—Eric Zillmer, Molly Harrower, Barry Ritzler, and Robert Archer, *The Quest for the Nazi Personality*, 1995

"For seven and a half years I've worked alongside President Reagan. We've had triumphs. Made some mistakes. We've had some sex . . . uh . . . setbacks."

—George H. W. Bush, 1988

"I remember your name perfectly but I just can't think of your face."

—Oxford professor W. A. Spooner, 1844–1930, famous for his linguistic flip-flops *(spoonerisms)*. Spooner rebuked one student for "fighting a liar in the quadrangle" and another who "hissed my mystery lecture," adding "You have tasted two worms."

"We are arguing like a man who should say, 'If there were an invisible cat in that chair, the chair would look empty; but the chair does look empty; therefore there is an invisible cat in it.'"

—C. S. Lewis, *Four Loves*, 1958

What is the most serious problem with Freud's theory? It offers after-the-fact explanations of any characteristic (of one person's smoking, another's fear of horses, another's sexual orientation) yet fails to *predict* such behaviors and traits. If you feel angry at your mother's death, you illustrate his theory because "your unresolved childhood dependency needs are threatened." If you do not feel angry, you again illustrate his theory because "you are repressing your anger." That, said Calvin Hall and Gardner Lindzey (1978, p. 68), "is like betting on a horse after the race has been run." A good theory makes testable predictions.

For such reasons, some of Freud's critics offer harsh words. They see a decaying Freudian edifice built on the swamplands of childhood sexuality, repression, dream analysis, and after-the-fact speculation. "When we stand on [Freud's] shoulders, we only discover that we're looking further in the wrong direction," said John Kihlstrom (1997). To Freud's most searing critic, Frederick Crews (1998), what is original about Freud's ideas is not good, and what is good is not original (the unconscious mind is an idea that dates back to Plato).

So, should psychology post a "Do Not Resuscitate" order on this old theory? Freud's supporters object. To criticize Freudian theory for not making testable predictions is, they say, like criticizing baseball for not being an aerobic exercise, something it was never intended to be. Freud never claimed that psychoanalysis was predictive science. He merely claimed that, looking back, psychoanalysts could find meaning in our state of mind (Rieff, 1979).

Supporters also note that some of Freud's ideas *are* enduring. It was Freud who drew our attention to the unconscious and the irrational, to our self-protective defenses, to the importance of human sexuality, and to the tension between our biological impulses and our social well-being. It was Freud who challenged our self-righteousness, punctured our pretensions, and reminded us of our potential for evil.

In science, Darwin's legacy lives while Freud's is waning (Bornstein, 2001). But in the popular culture, Freud's legacy lives on. Some ideas that many people assume to be true—that childhood experiences mold personality, that dreams have meaning, that many behaviors have disguised motives—are part of that legacy. His early twentieth-century concepts penetrate our twenty-first-century language. Without realizing their source, we may speak of *ego, repression, projection, complex* (as in "inferiority complex"), *sibling rivalry, Freudian slips,* and *fixation.* "Freud's premises may have undergone a steady decline in currency within academia for many years," noted Martin Seligman (1994), "but Hollywood, the talk shows, many therapists, and the general public still love them."

REHEARSE IT!

1. Freud believed that we may block from consciousness the thoughts, wishes, feelings, or memories that are unbearably painful or unacceptable. He called this unconscious process
   a. free association.
   b. repression.
   c. anxiety.
   d. identification.

2. According to Freud's view of personality structure, the "executive" system, the _____, seeks to gratify the impulses of the _____ in more acceptable ways.
   a. id; ego
   b. ego; superego
   c. ego; id
   d. id; superego

3. Freud proposed that the development of the "voice of conscience" is related to the _____, which internalizes ideals and provides standards for judgments.
   a. ego
   b. superego
   c. id
   d. collective unconscious

4. According to the psychoanalytic view of development, we all pass through a

series of psychosexual stages, such as the oral, anal, and phallic stages. Conflicts unresolved at any of these stages may lead to
   a. dormant sexual feelings.
   b. fixation in that stage.
   c. preconscious blocking of impulses.
   d. a distorted gender identity.

5. Freud believed that all defense mechanisms distort or disguise reality, and all are
   a. conscious.
   b. unconscious.
   c. preconscious.
   d. rationalizations.

6. Projective tests ask test-takers to respond to an ambiguous stimulus, for example, by describing it or telling a story about it. The creator of the well-known projective test that uses inkblots as stimuli was
   a. Alfred Adler.
   b. Karen Horney.
   c. Sigmund Freud.
   d. Hermann Rorschach.

7. In general, neo-Freudians such as Adler and Horney accepted many of Freud's views but placed more emphasis on

a. development throughout the life span.
b. the collective unconscious.
c. the role of the id.
d. social interactions.

8. Psychodynamic theorists and therapists tend to reject Freud's view that sex is the basis of personality. But they would agree with Freud about
   a. the existence of unconscious mental processes.
   b. the Oedipus and Electra complexes.
   c. the predictive value of Freudian theory.
   d. the superego's role as the executive part of personality.

9. Which of the following is not part of the CONTEMPORARY view of the unconscious?
   a. Repressed memories of anxiety-provoking events.
   b. Schemas that influence our perceptions and interpretations.
   c. Parallel processing that occurs without our conscious knowledge.
   d. Instantly activated emotions and implicit memories of learned skills.

Answers: 1. b, 2. c, 3. b, 4. b, 5. b, 6. d, 7. d, 8. a, 9. a.

The Humanistic Perspective

5: How did humanistic psychologists view personality, and what was their goal in studying personality?

By the 1960s, some personality psychologists had become discontented with the negativity of Freudian theory and the mechanistic psychology of B. F. Skinner's behaviorism. In contrast to Freud's study of the base motives of "sick" people, these *humanistic psychologists* focused on the ways "healthy" people strive for self-determination and self-realization. In contrast to behaviorism's scientific objectivity, they studied people through their own self-reported experiences and feelings.

Two pioneering theorists—Abraham Maslow (1908–1970) and Carl Rogers (1902–1987)—instead emphasized human potential.

Abraham Maslow's Self-Actualizing Person

Maslow proposed that we are motivated by a hierarchy of needs (Chapter 10). If our physiological needs are met, we become concerned with personal safety; if we achieve a sense of security, we can then seek to love, to be loved, and to love ourselves; with our love needs satisfied, we can seek self-esteem. Having achieved self-esteem, we can then ultimately seek **self-actualization** (the process of fulfilling our potential) and *self-transcendence* (meaning, purpose, and communion beyond the self).

self-actualization according to Maslow, one of the ultimate psychological needs that arises after basic physical and psychological needs are met and self-esteem is achieved; the motivation to fulfill one's potential.

Abraham Maslow *"Any theory of motivation that is worthy of attention must deal with the highest capacities of the healthy and strong person as well as with the defensive maneuvers of crippled spirits"* (*Motivation and Personality,* 1970).

Maslow (1970) developed his ideas by studying healthy, creative people rather than troubled clinical cases. He based his description of self-actualization on a study of those who seemed notable for their rich and productive lives—among them, Abraham Lincoln, Thomas Jefferson, and Eleanor Roosevelt. Maslow reported that these people shared certain characteristics: They were self-aware and self-accepting, open and spontaneous, loving and caring, and not paralyzed by others' opinions. They were secure in their sense of who they were, and their interests were problem-centered rather than self-centered. They focused their energies on a particular task, one they often regarded as their mission in life. Most enjoyed a few deep relationships rather than many superficial ones. Many had been moved by spiritual or personal *peak experiences* that surpassed ordinary consciousness.

These, said Maslow, are mature adult qualities, ones found in those who have learned enough about life to be compassionate, to have outgrown their mixed feelings toward their parents, to have found their calling, to have "acquired enough courage to be unpopular, to be unashamed about being openly virtuous, etc." Maslow's work with college students led him to speculate that those likely to become self-actualizing adults were likable, caring, "privately affectionate to those of their elders who deserve it," and "secretly uneasy about the cruelty, meanness, and mob spirit so often found in young people."

Carl Rogers' Person-Centered Perspective

Fellow humanistic psychologist Carl Rogers agreed with much of Maslow's thinking. Rogers believed that people are basically good and are endowed with self-actualizing tendencies. Unless thwarted by an environment that inhibits growth, each of us, like an acorn, is primed for growth and fulfillment. For Rogers (1980), a growth-promoting climate required three conditions:

- *Genuineness:* When people are *genuine,* they are open with their own feelings, drop their facades, and are transparent and self-disclosing.
- *Acceptance:* When people are *accepting,* they offer **unconditional positive regard,** an attitude of grace that values us even knowing our failings. It is a profound relief to drop our pretenses, confess our worst feelings, and discover that we are still accepted. In a good marriage, a close family, or an intimate friendship, we are free to be spontaneous without fearing the loss of others' esteem.
- *Empathy:* When people are *empathic,* they share and mirror others' feelings and reflect their meanings. "Rarely do we listen with real understanding, true empathy," said Rogers. "Yet listening, of this very special kind, is one of the most potent forces for change that I know."

Genuineness, acceptance, and empathy are the water, sun, and nutrients that enable people to grow like vigorous oak trees, according to Rogers. For "as persons are accepted and prized, they tend to develop a more caring attitude toward themselves" (Rogers, 1980, p. 116). As persons are empathically heard, "it becomes possible for them to listen more accurately to the flow of inner experiencings."

Writer Calvin Trillin (2006) recalls an example of parental genuineness and acceptance at a camp for children with severe disorders, where his wife, Alice, worked. L., a "magical child," had genetic diseases that meant she had to be tube-fed and could walk only with difficulty. Alice recalled,

> One day, when we were playing duck-duck-goose, I was sitting behind her and she asked me to hold her mail for her while she took her turn to be chased around the circle. It took her a while to make the circuit, and I had time to see that on top of the pile [of mail] was a note from her mom. Then I did something truly awful. . . . I simply had to know what this child's parents could have done to make her so spectacular, to make her the most optimistic, most enthusiastic, most hopeful human being I had ever encountered.

A father *not* offering unconditional positive regard:

"Just remember, son, it doesn't matter whether you win or lose—unless you want Daddy's love."

I snuck a quick look at the note, and my eyes fell on this sentence: "If God had given us all of the children in the world to choose from, L., we would only have chosen you." Before L. got back to her place in the circle, I showed the note to Bud, who was sitting next to me. "Quick. Read this," I whispered. "It's the secret of life."

Although today's science sees children as formed by much more than parental nurture, Maslow and Rogers would have smiled knowingly. For them a central feature of personality is one's **self-concept**—all the thoughts and feelings we have in response to the question, "Who am I?" If our self-concept is positive, we tend to act and perceive the world positively. If it is negative—if in our own eyes we fall far short of our *ideal self*—said Rogers, we feel dissatisfied and unhappy. A worthwhile goal for therapists, parents, teachers, and friends is therefore, he said, to help others know, accept, and be true to themselves.

The picture of empathy Being open and sharing confidences is easier when the listener shows real understanding. Within such relationships people can relax and fully express their true selves.

Assessing the Self

6: How did humanistic psychologists assess a person's sense of self?

Humanistic psychologists sometimes assessed personality by asking people to fill out questionnaires that would evaluate their self-concept. One questionnaire, inspired by Carl Rogers, asked people to describe themselves both as they would *ideally* like to be and as they *actually* are. When the ideal and the actual self are nearly alike, said Rogers, the self-concept is positive. Assessing his clients' personal growth during therapy, he looked for successively closer ratings of actual and ideal selves.

Some humanistic psychologists believed that any standardized assessment of personality, even a questionnaire, is depersonalizing. Rather than forcing the person to respond to narrow categories, these humanistic psychologists presumed that interviews and intimate conversation would provide a better understanding of each person's unique experiences.

Evaluating the Humanistic Perspective

7: How has the humanistic perspective influenced psychology? What criticisms has it faced?

One thing said of Freud can also be said of the humanistic psychologists: Their impact has been pervasive. Maslow's and Rogers' ideas have influenced counseling, education, child-rearing, and management.

They have also influenced—sometimes in ways they did not intend—much of today's popular psychology. Is a positive self-concept the key to happiness and success? Do acceptance and empathy nurture positive feelings about oneself? Are people basically good and capable of self-improvement? Many people answer *yes, yes, and yes*. Responding to a 1992 *Newsweek* Gallup poll, 9 in 10 people rated self-esteem as very important for "motivating a person to work hard and succeed." Humanistic psychology's message has been heard.

The prominence of the humanistic perspective set off a backlash of criticism. First, said the critics, its concepts are vague and *subjective*. Consider Maslow's description of self-actualizing people as open, spontaneous, loving, self-accepting, and productive. Is this a scientific description? Isn't it merely a description of the theorist's own values and ideals? Maslow, noted M. Brewster Smith (1978), offered impressions of his own personal heroes. Imagine another theorist who began with a different set of heroes—perhaps Napoleon, John D. Rockefeller, Sr., and former U.S. Vice President Dick Cheney. This theorist would likely describe self-actualizing people as "undeterred by others' needs and opinions," "motivated to achieve," and "comfortable with power."

unconditional positive regard according to Rogers, an attitude of total acceptance toward another person.

self-concept all our thoughts and feelings about ourselves, in answer to the question, "Who am I?"

"We do pretty well when you stop to think that people are basically good."

Critics have also objected to the idea that, as Rogers put it, "The only question which matters is, 'Am I living in a way which is deeply satisfying to me, and which truly expresses me?'" (quoted by Wallach & Wallach, 1985). The *individualism* encouraged by humanistic psychology—trusting and acting on one's feelings, being true to oneself, fulfilling oneself—can, the critics have said, lead to self-indulgence, selfishness, and an erosion of moral restraints (Campbell & Specht, 1985; Wallach & Wallach, 1983). Indeed, it is those who focus beyond themselves who are most likely to experience social support, to enjoy life, and to cope effectively with stress.

Humanistic psychologists reply that a secure, nondefensive self-acceptance is actually the first step toward loving others. Indeed, people who feel intrinsically liked and accepted—for who they are, not just for their achievements—exhibit less-defensive attitudes (Schimel et al., 2001).

A final accusation leveled against humanistic psychology is that it is *naive*, that it fails to appreciate the reality of our human capacity for evil. Faced with global climate change, overpopulation, terrorism, and the spread of nuclear weapons, we may become apathetic from either of two rationalizations. One is a naive optimism that denies the threat ("People are basically good; everything will work out"). The other is a dark despair ("It's hopeless; why try?"). Action requires enough realism to fuel concern and enough optimism to provide hope. Humanistic psychology, say the critics, encourages the needed hope but not the equally necessary realism about evil.

REHEARSE IT!

10. Maslow's hierarchy of needs proposes that we must satisfy basic physiological and psychological needs before we seek self-actualization. Maslow based his ideas on
a. Freudian theory.
b. his experiences with patients.
c. a series of laboratory experiments.
d. his study of healthy, creative people.

11. The total acceptance Rogers advocated as part of a growth-promoting environment is called
a. self-concept.
b. unconditional positive regard.
c. self-actualization.
d. the "ideal self."

Answers: 10. d, 11. b.

The Trait Perspective

8: How do psychologists use traits to describe personality?

Rather than focusing on unconscious forces and thwarted growth opportunities, some researchers attempt to define personality in terms of stable and enduring behavior patterns, such as Sam Gamgee's loyalty and optimism. This perspective can be traced in part to a remarkable meeting in 1919, when Gordon Allport, a curious 22-year-old psychology student, interviewed Sigmund Freud in Vienna. Allport soon discovered just how preoccupied the founder of psychoanalysis was with finding hidden motives, even in Allport's own behavior during the interview. That experience ultimately led Allport to a new approach to personality. Meeting Freud, he said, "taught me that [psychoanalysis], for all its merits, may plunge too deep, and that psychologists would do well to give full recognition to manifest motives before probing the unconscious." Allport came to define personality in terms of fundamental **traits**—people's characteristic behavior patterns and conscious motives (such as the curiosity that actually motivated Allport to see Freud). He was concerned less with *explaining* individual traits than with *describing* them.

Exploring Traits

Classifying people as one or another distinct personality type fails to capture their full individuality. We are each a unique complex of multiple traits. So how else could we describe our personalities? We might describe an apple by placing it along several

trait a characteristic pattern of behavior or a disposition to feel and act, as assessed by self-report inventories and peer reports.

trait dimensions—relatively large or small, red or yellow, sweet or sour. By placing people on several trait dimensions simultaneously, psychologists can describe countless individual personality variations. (Remember from Chapter 6 that variations on just three color dimensions—hue, saturation, and brightness—create many thousands of colors.)

What trait dimensions describe personality? If you had an upcoming blind date, what personality traits might give you an accurate sense of the person? Allport and his associate H. S. Odbert (1936) counted all the words in an unabridged dictionary with which one could describe people. How many were there? Almost 18,000! How, then, could psychologists condense the list to a manageable number of basic traits?

One way has been to propose traits, such as anxiety, that some theory regards as basic. A newer technique is *factor analysis*, the statistical procedure described in Chapter 9 to identify clusters of test items that tap basic components of intelligence (such as spatial ability or verbal skill). Imagine that people who describe themselves as outgoing also tend to say that they like excitement and practical jokes and dislike quiet reading. Such a statistically correlated cluster of behaviors reflects a basic *factor*, or trait—in this case, *extraversion*.

Brain-activity scans indicate that extraverts seek stimulation because their normal *brain arousal* is relatively low. PET scans, for example, show that a frontal lobe area involved in behavior inhibition is less active in extraverts than in introverts (Johnson et al., 1999).

Our biology influences our personality in other ways as well. Twin and adoption studies indicate that our *genes* have much to say about our temperament and behavioral style, which help define our personality (Chapter 4). Jerome Kagan, for example, has attributed differences in children's shyness and inhibition to their *autonomic nervous system reactivity*. Given a reactive autonomic nervous system, we respond to stress with greater anxiety and inhibition. The fearless, curious child may become the rock-climbing or fast-driving adult.

Samuel Gosling and his colleagues (2003; Jones & Gosling, 2005) report that personality differences among dogs (in energy, affection, reactivity, and curious intelligence) are as evident, and as consistently judged, as personality differences among humans. Monkeys, chimpanzees, orangutans, and even birds have stable personalities (Weiss et al., 2006). Among the Great Tit (a European relative of the American chickadee), bold birds more quickly inspect new objects and explore trees (Groothuis & Carere, 2005; Verbeek et al., 1994). By selective breeding, researchers can produce bold or shy birds. Both have their place in natural history. In lean years, bold birds are more likely to find food; in abundant years, shy birds feed with less risk.

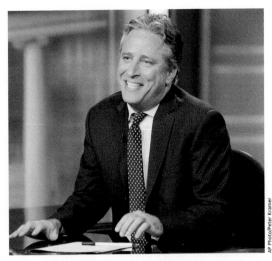

Jon Stewart: The extravert Trait labels such as *extraversion* can describe our temperament and typical behaviors.

Assessing Traits

9: What are personality inventories, and what are their strengths and weaknesses as trait-assessment tools?

If stable and enduring traits guide our actions, can we devise valid and reliable tests of them? Several trait assessment techniques exist—some more valid than others (turn the page to see Thinking Critically About: How to Be a "Successful" Astrologer or Palm Reader). Some profile a person's behavior patterns—often providing quick assessments of a single trait, such as extraversion, anxiety, or self-esteem. **Personality inventories**—longer questionnaires covering a wide range of feelings and behaviors—are designed to assess several traits at once.

The classic personality inventory is the **Minnesota Multiphasic Personality Inventory (MMPI).** Although it assesses "abnormal" personality tendencies rather than normal personality traits, the MMPI illustrates a good way of developing a personality inventory. One of its creators, Starke Hathaway (1960), compared his effort to that of Alfred Binet. Binet, as you may recall from Chapter 9, developed

personality inventory a questionnaire (often with *true-false* or *agree-disagree* items) on which people respond to items designed to gauge a wide range of feelings and behaviors; used to assess selected personality traits.

Minnesota Multiphasic Personality Inventory (MMPI) the most widely researched and clinically used of all personality tests. Originally developed to identify emotional disorders (still considered its most appropriate use), this test is now used for many other screening purposes.

Thinking Critically About:

How to Be a "Successful" Astrologer or Palm Reader

Can we discern people's traits from the alignment of the stars and planets at the time of their birth? From their handwriting? From lines on their palms?

Astronomers scoff at the naiveté of astrology—the constellations have shifted in the millennia since astrologers formulated their predictions (Kelly, 1997, 1998). Humorists mock it: "No offense," wrote Dave Barry, "but if you take the horoscope seriously your frontal lobes are the size of Raisinets." Psychologists instead ask questions: Does it work? Can astrologers surpass chance when given someone's birth date and asked to identify the person from a short lineup of different personality descriptions? Can people pick out their own horoscopes from a lineup of horoscopes?

The consistent answers have been *no*, *no*, and *no* (British Psychological Society, 1993; Carlson, 1985; Kelly, 1997). For example, one researcher examined census data from 20 million married people in England and Wales and found that "astrological sign has no impact on the probability of marrying—and staying married to—someone of any other sign" (Voas, 2008).

Graphologists, who make predictions from handwriting samples, have similarly been found to do no better than chance when trying to discern people's occupations from examining several pages of their handwriting (Beyerstein & Beyerstein, 1992; Dean et al., 1992). Nevertheless, graphologists—and introductory psychology students—will

often *perceive* correlations between personality and handwriting even where there are none (King & Koehler, 2000).

If all these perceived correlations evaporate under close scrutiny, how do astrologers, palm readers, and crystal-ball gazers persuade millions of people worldwide to buy their services? Ray Hyman (1981), palm reader turned research psychologist, has revealed some of their suckering methods.

The first technique, the "stock spiel," builds on the observation that each of us is in some ways like no one else and in

other ways just like everyone. That some things are true of us all enables the "seer" to offer statements that seem impressively accurate: "I sense that you worry about things more than you let on, even to your best friends." A number of such generally true statements can be combined into a personality description. Imagine that you take a personality test and then receive the following character sketch:

You have a strong need for other people to like and to admire you. You have a tendency to be critical of yourself. . . . You pride yourself on

---

the first intelligence test by selecting items that identified children who would probably have trouble progressing normally in French schools. The MMPI items, too, were **empirically derived.** That is, from a large pool of items, Hathaway and his colleagues selected those on which particular diagnostic groups differed. They then grouped the questions into 10 clinical scales, including scales that assess depressive tendencies, masculinity-femininity, and introversion-extraversion.

Hathaway and others initially gave hundreds of true-false statements ("No one seems to understand me"; "I get all the sympathy I should"; "I like poetry") to groups of psychologically disordered patients and to "normal" people. They retained any statement—no matter how silly it sounded—on which the patient group's answer differed from that of the normal group. "Nothing in the newspaper interests me except the comics" may seem senseless, but it just so happened that depressed people were more likely to answer *True*. (Nevertheless, people have had fun

empirically derived test a test (such as the MMPI) developed by testing a pool of items and then selecting those that discriminate between groups.

being an independent thinker and do not accept other opinions without satisfactory proof. You have found it unwise to be too frank in revealing yourself to others. At times you are extraverted, affable, sociable; at other times you are introverted, wary, and reserved. Some of your aspirations tend to be pretty unrealistic (Davies, 1997; Forer, 1949).

In experiments, college students have received stock assessments like this one, drawn from statements in a newsstand astrology book. When they think the bogus, generic feedback was prepared just for them and when it is favorable, they nearly always rate the description as either "good" or "excellent" (Davies, 1997). Even skeptics given a flattering description attributed to an astrologer, begin to think that "maybe there's something to this astrology stuff after all" (Glick et al., 1989). An astrologer, it has been said, is someone "prepared to tell you what you think of yourself" (Jones, 2000).

French psychologist Michael Gauguelin offered a free personal horoscope in an ad he placed in a Paris newspaper. Ninety-four percent of those receiving the horoscope praised the description as accurate. Whose horoscope had they all received? That of France's Dr. Petiot, a notorious mass murderer (Kurtz, 1983). This acceptance of stock, positive descriptions is called the *Barnum effect*, named in honor of master showman P. T. Barnum's dictum, "There's a sucker born every minute."

"Madame Zelinski can provide an even more accurate reading with your date of birth and Social Security number."

A second technique used by seers is to "read" our clothing, physical features, nonverbal gestures, and reactions to what they are saying. No wonder, say the skeptics, that when mediums cannot see the person who has come to them, their clients cannot recognize the reading that was meant for them from among other readings (O'Keeffe & Wiseman, 2005).

If you are not as shrewd as most character readers, Hyman says it hardly matters. If people seek you out for a reading, start with some safe sympathy: "I sense you're having some problems lately. You seem unsure what to do. I get the feeling another person is involved." Then tell them what they want to hear. Memorize some Barnum statements from astrology and fortune-telling manuals and use them liberally. Tell people it is their responsibility to cooperate by relating your message to their specific experiences. Later they will recall that you predicted those specific details. Phrase statements as questions, and when you detect a positive response assert the statement strongly. Finally, be a good listener, and later, in different words, reveal to people what they earlier revealed to you. If you dupe them, they will come.

Better yet, beware of those who, by exploiting people with these techniques, are fortune takers rather than fortune tellers.

spoofing the MMPI with their own mock items: "Weeping brings tears to my eyes," "Frantic screams make me nervous," and "I stay in the bathtub until I look like a raisin" [Frankel et al., 1983].) Today's MMPI-2 also has scales assessing, for instance, work attitudes, family problems, and anger.

In contrast to the subjectivity of most projective tests, personality inventories are scored objectively—so objectively that a computer can administer and score them. (The computer can also provide descriptions of people who previously responded similarly.) Objectivity does not, however, guarantee validity. For example, individuals taking the MMPI for employment purposes can give socially desirable answers to create a good impression. But in so doing they may also score high on a *lie scale* that assesses faking (as when people respond *False* to a universally true statement such as "I get angry sometimes"). The objectivity of the MMPI has contributed to its popularity and to its translation into more than 100 languages.

The Big Five Factors

10: Which traits seem to provide the most useful information about personality variation?

Today's trait researchers believe that simple trait factors are important, but they do not tell the whole story. A slightly expanded set of factors—dubbed the *Big Five*—does a better job (Costa & McCrae, 2006; John & Srivastava, 1999). If a test specifies where you are on the five dimensions (conscientiousness, agreeableness, neuroticism, openness, and extraversion, as in TABLE 12.3), it has said much of what there is to say about your personality. Around the world—across 56 nations and 29 languages in one study (Schmitt et al., 2007)—people describe others in terms roughly consistent with this list. The Big Five may not be the last word, but for now, at least, it is the winning number in the personality lottery. The Big Five—today's "common currency for personality psychology" (Funder, 2001)—has been the most active personality research topic since the early 1990s and is currently our best approximation of the basic trait dimensions.

The recent wave of Big Five research explores various questions, including these:

- *How stable are these traits?* In adulthood, the Big Five traits are quite stable, with some tendencies (neuroticism, extraversion, and openness) waning a bit during early and middle adulthood, and others (agreeableness and conscientiousness) rising (McCrae et al., 1999; Vaidya et al., 2002). Conscientiousness increases the most during people's twenties, as people mature and learn to manage their jobs and relationships. Agreeableness increases the most during people's thirties and continues to increase through their sixties (Srivastava et al., 2003).

- *How heritable are they?* Heritability of individual differences varies with the diversity of people studied, but it generally runs about 50 percent for each dimension. Genetic influences are similar in different nations (Loehlin et al., 1998; Yamagata et al., 2006).

By exploring such questions, Big Five research has sustained trait psychology and renewed appreciation for the importance of personality.

TABLE 12.3 The "Big Five" Personality Factors

(*Memory tip:* Picturing a **CANOE** will help you recall these.)

Trait Dimension	Endpoints of the Dimension		
Conscientiousness	Organized	←——→	Disorganized
	Careful	←——→	Careless
	Disciplined	←——→	Impulsive
Agreeableness	Soft-hearted	←——→	Ruthless
	Trusting	←——→	Suspicious
	Helpful	←——→	Uncooperative
Neuroticism	Calm	←——→	Anxious
(emotional stability	Secure	←——→	Insecure
vs. instability)	Self-satisfied	←——→	Self-pitying
Openness	Imaginative	←——→	Practical
	Preference for variety	←——→	Preference for routine
	Independent	←——→	Conforming
Extraversion	Sociable	←——→	Retiring
	Fun-loving	←——→	Sober
	Affectionate	←——→	Reserved

Source: Adapted from McCrae & Costa (1986, p. 1002).

Evaluating the Trait Perspective

11: **Does research support the consistency of personality traits over time and across situations?**

Are our personality traits stable and enduring? Or does our behavior depend on where and with whom we find ourselves? Both. Our behavior is influenced by the interaction of our inner disposition with our environment. Still, the question lingers: Which is more important?

The Person-Situation Controversy

To explore this *person-situation controversy*, we look for genuine personality traits that persist over time and across situations. Are some people dependably conscientious and others unreliable, some cheerful and others dour, some friendly and outgoing and others shy? If we are to consider friendliness a trait, friendly people must act friendly at different times and places. Do they?

In Chapter 5, we considered research that has followed lives through time. We noted that some scholars (especially those who study infants) are impressed with personality change; others are struck by personality stability during adulthood. As **FIGURE 12.3** illustrates, data from 152 long-term studies reveal that personality trait scores are positively correlated with scores obtained seven years later, and that as people grow older their personality stabilizes. Interests may change—the avid collector of tropical fish may become an avid gardener. Careers may change—the determined salesperson may become a determined social worker. Relationships may change—the hostile spouse may start over with a new partner. But most people recognize their traits as their own, noted Robert McCrae and Paul Costa (1994), "and it is well that they do. A person's recognition of the inevitability of his or her one and only personality is . . . the culminating wisdom of a lifetime." Moreover, our traits are socially significant. They influence our health, our thinking, and our job performance (Deary & Matthews, 1993; Hogan, 1998). Studies that follow lives through time show that personality traits rival socioeconomic status and cognitive ability as predictors of mortality, divorce, and occupational attainment (Roberts et al., 2007).

Although our personality *traits* may be both stable and potent, the consistency of our specific *behaviors* from one situation to the next is another matter. As Walter Mischel (1968, 1984, 2004) has pointed out, people do not act with predictable consistency. Mischel's studies of college students' conscientiousness revealed but a modest relationship between a student's being conscientious on one occasion (say, showing up for class on time) and being similarly conscientious on another occasion (say, turning in assignments on time). If you've noticed how outgoing you are in some situations and how reserved you are in others, perhaps you're not surprised. Being a different person to different people, you perhaps are content to have your boss or your family members *not* become your Facebook friends.

Roughly speaking, the temporary, external influences on behavior are the focus of social psychology, and the enduring, inner influences are the focus of personality psychology. In actuality, behavior always depends on the interaction of persons with situations.

Change and consistency can co-exist. If all people were to become somewhat less shy with age, there would be personality change, but also relative stability and predictability.

"Mr. Coughlin over there was the founder of one of the first motorcycle gangs."

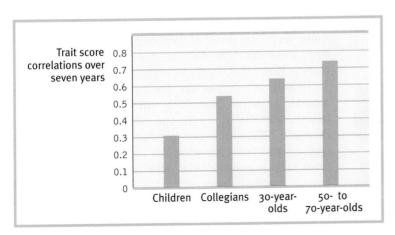

FIGURE 12.3 Personality stability With age, personality traits become more stable. Thus, as people age, their trait scores increasingly correlate with follow-up scores seven years later. (Data from Roberts & DelVecchio, 2000.)

"I'm going to France—I'm a different person in France."

This inconsistency in behaviors also makes personality test scores weak predictors of behaviors. People's scores on an extraversion test, for example, do not neatly predict how sociable they actually will be on any given occasion. If we remember such results, says Mischel, we will be more cautious about labeling and pigeonholing individuals. Years in advance, science can tell us the phase of the Moon for any given date. A day in advance, meteorologists can often predict the weather. But we are much further from being able to predict how *you* will feel and act tomorrow.

However, people's *average* outgoingness, happiness, or carelessness over many situations is predictable (Epstein, 1983a,b). This consistency enables people who know someone well to agree in their ratings of the person's shyness or agreeableness (Kenrick & Funder, 1988).

By collecting snippets of people's daily experience via body-worn recording devices, Matthias Mehl and his colleagues (2006) have confirmed that extraverts really do talk more. (I have repeatedly vowed to cut back on my jabbering and joking during my noontime pickup basketball games with friends. Alas, moments later, the irrepressible chatterbox inevitably reoccupies my body.) As our best friends can verify, we do have genetically influenced personality traits. And those traits even lurk, report Samuel Gosling and his colleagues in a series of studies, in our

- *music preferences.* Classical, jazz, blues, and folk music lovers tend to be open to experience and verbally intelligent; country, pop, and religious music lovers tend to be cheerful, outgoing, and conscientious (Rentfrow & Gosling, 2003, 2006).
- *dorm rooms and offices.* Our personal spaces display our identity and leave a behavioral residue (in our scattered laundry or neat desktop). And that helps explain why just a few minutes' inspection of our living and working spaces can enable someone to assess with reasonable accuracy our conscientiousness, our openness to new experiences, and even our emotional stability (Gosling et al., 2002).
- *personal Web sites.* Is a personal Web site or a Facebook profile also a canvas for self-expression? Or is it an opportunity for people to present themselves in false or misleading ways? It's more the former (Gosling et al., 2007; Marcus et al., 2006; Vazire & Gosling, 2004). Visitors to personal Web sites quickly gain important clues to the owner's extraversion, conscientiousness, and openness to experience.
- *e-mail.* If you have ever felt you could detect someone's personality from the writing voice in their e-mail, you are right. People's ratings of others' personalities based solely on their e-mails correlate with actual personality scores on measures such as extraversion and neuroticism (Gill et al., 2006; Oberlander & Gill, 2006). Extraverts, for example, use more adjectives. (What a cool, exciting finding!!!)

In unfamiliar, formal situations—perhaps as a guest in the home of a person from another culture—our traits remain hidden as we carefully attend to social cues. In familiar, informal situations—just hanging out with friends—we feel less constrained, allowing our traits to emerge (Buss, 1989). In these informal situations, our expressive styles—our animation, manner of speaking, and gestures—are impressively consistent. That's why those very thin slices of someone's behavior—even just three 2-second clips of a teacher—can be revealing (Ambady & Rosenthal, 1992, 1993).

To sum up, we can say that at any moment the immediate situation powerfully influences a person's behavior, especially when the situation makes clear demands. We can better predict drivers' behavior at traffic lights from knowing the color of the lights than from knowing the drivers' personalities. Averaging our behavior across many occasions does, however, reveal distinct personality traits. Traits exist. We differ. And our differences matter.

Our spaces express our personalities
Even at "zero acquaintance," people can discern something of others' personality from glimpsing their Web site, dorm room, or office. So, what is your read on University of Texas researcher Samuel Gosling?

12. Trait theory describes personality in terms of characteristic behavior patterns, or traits, such as agreeableness or extra-version. A pioneering trait theorist was
    a. Sigmund Freud.
    b. Alfred Adler.
    c. Gordon Allport.
    d. Carl Rogers.

13. Personality inventories are long ques-tionnaires that ask people to report their characteristic feelings and behaviors. One famous personality inventory is the
    a. Extraversion-Introversion Scale.
    b. Person-Situation Inventory.
    c. MMPI.
    d. Rorschach.

14. Which of the following is NOT one of the Big Five personality factors?
    a. Conscientiousness
    b. Anxiety
    c. Extraversion
    d. Agreeableness

15. People's scores on personality tests are only mildly predictive of their behavior. Such tests best predict
    a. a person's behavior on a specific occasion.
    b. a person's average behavior across many situations.
    c. behavior involving a single trait, such as conscientiousness.
    d. behavior that depends on the situation or context.

Answers: 12. c, 13. c, 14. b, 15. b.

The Social-Cognitive Perspective

12: In the view of social-cognitive psychologists, what mutual influences shape an individual's personality?

Much as nature and nurture always work together, so do individuals and their situa-tions. Albert Bandura (1986, 2006, 2008) emphasized this interaction of our traits with our situations when he proposed the **social-cognitive perspective** on personality.

Social-cognitive theorists believe we learn many of our behaviors either through conditioning or by observing others and modeling our behavior after theirs. (That is the "social" part.) But mental processes are also important: What we *think* about our situation affects our behavior. (That is the "cognitive" part.) Instead of focusing solely on how our environment *controls* us (behaviorism), social-cognitive theorists focus on how we and our environment *interact:* How do we interpret and respond to external events? How do our schemas, our memories, and our expectations influ-ence our behavior patterns?

Reciprocal Influences

Bandura (1986, 2006) views the person-environment interaction as **reciprocal determinism.** "Behavior, internal personal factors, and environmental influ-ences," he has said, "all operate as interlocking determinants of each other" (**FIGURE 12.4** on the next page). For example, children's TV-viewing habits (past behavior) influence their viewing preferences (internal factor), which influence how television (environmental factor) affects their current behavior. The influences are mutual.

Consider three specific ways in which individuals and environments interact:

1. **Different people choose different environments.** The school you attend, the material you read, the programs you watch, the Web sites you visit, the music you listen to, the friends you associate with—all are parts of an environment you have chosen, based partly on your dispositions (Ickes et al., 1997). You choose your environment and it then shapes you.

2. **Our personalities shape how we interpret and react to events.** Anxious peo-ple, for example, are attuned to potentially threatening events (Eysenck et al., 1987). Thus, they perceive the world as threatening, and they react accordingly.

3. **Our personalities help create situations to which we react.** Many experi-ments reveal that how we view and treat people influences how they in turn treat us. If we expect someone to be angry with us, we may give the person a cold shoulder, touching off the very anger we expect. If we have an easygoing, positive disposition, we will likely enjoy close, supportive friendships (Donnellan et al., 2005; Kendler, 1997).

In such ways, we are both the products and the architects of our environments.

social-cognitive perspective views behav-ior as influenced by the interaction between people's traits (including their thinking) and their social context.

reciprocal determinism the interacting influences of behavior, internal cognition, and environment.

FIGURE 12.4 Reciprocal determinism The social-cognitive perspective proposes that our personalities are shaped by the interaction of our personal traits (including our thoughts and feelings), our environment, and our behaviors.

If all this has a familiar ring, it may be because it parallels and reinforces a pervasive theme in psychology and in this book: *Behavior emerges from the interplay of external and internal influences.* Boiling water turns an egg hard and a potato soft. A threatening environment turns one person into a hero, another into a scoundrel. *At every moment,* our behavior is influenced by our biology, our social and cultural experiences, and our cognition and dispositions, including our feelings about our control over our environment (**FIGURE 12.5**).

FIGURE 12.5 The biopsychosocial approach to the study of personality As with other psychological phenomena, personality is fruitfully studied at multiple levels.

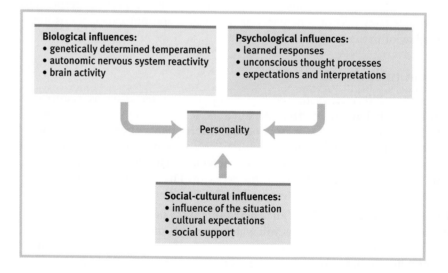

Personal Control

13: What are the causes and consequences of personal control?

Consider your own feelings of **personal control.** Do you believe that your life is beyond your control? That the world is run by a few powerful people? That getting a good job depends mainly on being in the right place at the right time? Or do you more strongly believe that what happens to you is your own doing? That the average person can influence government decisions? That being a success is a matter of hard work?

Hundreds of studies have compared people who differ in their perceptions of control. On the one side are those who have what psychologist Julian Rotter called

We can study the effect of personal control (or any personality factor) in two ways:
1. Correlate people's feelings of control with their behaviors and achievements.
2. Experiment, by raising or lowering people's sense of control and noting the effects.

an **external locus of control**—the perception that chance or outside forces determine their fate. On the other are those who perceive an **internal locus of control,** who believe that they control their own destiny.

In study after study, "internals" achieve more in school and work, act more independently, enjoy better health, and feel less depressed than do "externals" (Lefcourt, 1982; Ng et al., 2006). Moreover, they score higher on measures of *self-control*—the ability to control impulses and delay gratification (Miller et al., 1986). Self-control in turn predicts good adjustment, better grades, and social success (Tangney et al., 2004). Students who plan their day's activities and then live out their day as planned tend to be at low risk for depression (Nezlek, 2001).

None of us experiences unvarying self-control; like a muscle, self-control temporarily weakens after an exertion. Exercising willpower can deplete your mental energy and even the blood sugar and neural activity associated with mental focus (Inzlicht & Gutsell, 2007). Hungry people who had resisted the temptation to eat chocolate chip cookies gave up sooner on a tedious task in one experiment. In others, people who had expended willpower on laboratory tasks, such as stifling prejudice or saying the color of words (for example, "red" even if the red-colored word was *green*), later became less restrained in their aggressive responses to provocation and in their sexual behavior (DeWall et al., 2007; Gaillot & Baumeister, 2007).

In the long run, self-control requires attention and energy. Giving people energy-boosting sugar (in a naturally rather than an artificially sweetened lemonade)—as experimenters did in another experiment—strengthened their effortful thinking (Masicampo & Baumeister, 2008). Self-control also replenishes with rest and becomes stronger with exercise (Baumeister & Exline, 2000). People who practice self-regulation through physical exercise and time-managed study programs develop strengthened self-control, as seen both in their performance on laboratory tasks and in their improved self-management of eating, drinking, smoking, and household chores (Oaten & Cheng, 2006a,b). Develop your self-discipline in one area of your life and your strengthened self-control may spill over into other areas as well.

Personal Control, Learned Helplessness, and Empowerment

People who feel helpless and oppressed often perceive control as external. This perception may then deepen their feelings of resignation. In fact, this is precisely what researcher Martin Seligman (1975, 1991) and others found in experiments with both animals and people. Dogs strapped in a harness and given repeated shocks, with no opportunity to avoid them, developed a sense of passive resignation now called **learned helplessness.** Later placed in another situation where they *could* escape the punishment by simply leaping a hurdle, the dogs cowered as if without hope. In contrast, animals able to escape the first shocks learned personal control and easily escaped the shocks in the new situation (**FIGURE 12.6**).

personal control the extent to which people perceive control over their environment rather than feeling helpless.

external locus of control the perception that chance or outside forces beyond your personal control determine your fate.

internal locus of control the perception that you control your own fate.

learned helplessness the hopelessness and passive resignation an animal or human learns when unable to avoid repeated aversive events.

```
┌─────────────────┐
│ Uncontrollable  │
│ bad events      │
└─────────────────┘
         ↓
    ┌──────────────┐
    │ Perceived    │
    │ lack of control │
    └──────────────┘
              ↓
         ┌──────────────┐
         │ Generalized  │
         │ helpless behavior │
         └──────────────┘
```

FIGURE 12.6 Learned helplessness
When animals and people experience no control over repeated bad events, they often learn helplessness.

"Happy are those who choose their own path" These happy East Berliners, crossing over to West Berlin after the wall came down in 1989, seem to personify this sentiment from the Roman philosopher Seneca.

People, too, when repeatedly faced with traumatic events over which they have no control, come to feel helpless, hopeless, and depressed. As researcher Ellen Langer (1983, p. 291) has concluded, "perceived control is basic to human functioning." People given little control over their world in prisons, factories, colleges, and nursing homes experience lower morale and increased stress. Measures that increase control—allowing prisoners to move chairs and control room lights and the TV, having workers participate in decision making, offering nursing home patients choices about their environment—noticeably improve health and morale (Humphrey et al., 2007; Ruback et al., 1986; Wener et al., 1987). In one famous study of nursing home patients, 93 percent of those encouraged to exert more control became more alert, active, and happy (Rodin, 1986). "For the young and old alike," noted Langer, it is important to create environments that enhance a sense of control and personal efficacy. No wonder so many people like their iPods and TiVos, which give them control of the content and timing of their entertainment.

The verdict of such studies is reassuring: Under conditions of personal freedom and empowerment, people thrive. Small wonder that the citizens of stable democracies report higher levels of happiness (Inglehart, 1990, 2009). Shortly before the democratic revolution in the former East Germany, psychologists Gabriele Oettingen and Martin Seligman (1990) studied the telltale body language of working-class men in East and West Berlin bars. Compared with their counterparts on the other side of the Wall, the empowered West Berliners much more often laughed, sat upright rather than slumped, and had upward- rather than downward-turned mouths.

Some freedom and control is better than none, notes Barry Schwartz (2000, 2004). But does ever-increasing choice breed ever-happier lives? Actually not. Schwartz notes that the "excess of freedom" in today's Western cultures contributes to decreasing life satisfaction, increased depression, and sometimes paralysis. Increased consumer choices, as when buying a car or phone, are not an unmixed blessing. After choosing among 30 brands of jam or chocolate, people express less satisfaction than those choosing among a half-dozen options (Iyengar & Lepper, 2000). This *tyranny of choice* brings information overload and a greater likelihood that we will feel regret over some of the unchosen options.

Optimism Versus Pessimism

One measure of how helpless or effective you feel is where you stand on optimism-pessimism. How do you characteristically explain negative and positive events? Perhaps you have known students whose *attributional style* is pessimistic—who attribute poor performance to their lack of ability ("I can't do this") or to situations enduringly beyond their control ("There is nothing I can do about it"). Such students are more likely to persist in getting low grades than are students who adopt the more hopeful attitude that effort, good study habits, and self-discipline can make a difference (Noel et al., 1987; Peterson & Barrett, 1987). Mere fantasies do not fuel motivation and success, but realistic positive expectations do (Oettingen & Mayer, 2002).

Attributional style also matters when dating couples wrestle with conflicts. Optimists and their partners see each other as engaging constructively, and they then tend to feel more supported and satisfied with the resolution and with their relationship (Srivastava et al., 2006). Expect good things from others, and often you will get what you expect. Such studies helped point Seligman toward proposing a more positive psychology (see Close-Up: Toward a More Positive Psychology).

Positive expectations often motivate eventual success.

"We just haven't been flapping them hard enough."

Close-Up:

Toward a More Positive Psychology

During its first century, psychology understandably focused much of its attention on understanding and alleviating negative states. Psychologists have studied abuse and anxiety, depression and disease, prejudice and poverty. Articles on selected negative emotions since 1887 have outnumbered those on positive emotions by 17 to 1.

In ages past, notes American Psychological Association past-president Martin Seligman (2002), times of relative peace and prosperity have enabled cultures to turn their attention from repairing weakness and damage to promoting "the highest qualities of life." Prosperous fifth-century Athens nurtured philosophy and democracy. Flourishing fifteenth-century Florence nurtured great art. Victorian England, flush with the bounty of the British empire, nurtured honor, discipline, and duty. In this millennium, Seligman believes, thriving Western cultures have a parallel opportunity to create, as a "humane, scientific monument," a more **positive psychology**—a psychology concerned not only with weakness and damage but also with strength and virtue. Thanks to his own leadership and to some $30 million in funding, the new positive psychology movement has gained strength (Seligman, 2004).

Positive psychology shares with humanistic psychology an interest in advancing human fulfillment, but its methodology is scientific. From these

Martin E. P. Seligman "The main purpose of a positive psychology is to measure, understand, and then build the human strengths and the civic virtues."

Courtesy of Martin E. P. Seligman, Ph.D. Director, Positive Psychology Center/University of Pennsylvania

roots have grown not only the new studies of happiness and health (Chapter 11), but also the shift in emphasis from learned helplessness and depression to optimism and thriving. "Positive psychology," say Seligman and colleagues (2005) "is an umbrella term for the study of positive emotions, positive character traits, and enabling institutions."

Taken together, satisfaction with the past, happiness with the present, and optimism about the future define the movement's first pillar: *positive emotions*. Happiness, Seligman argues, is a by-product of a pleasant, engaged, and meaningful life.

Positive psychology is about building not just a pleasant life, says Seligman, but also a *good life* that engages one's

skills, and a *meaningful life* that points beyond oneself. Thus, the second pillar, *positive character*, focuses on exploring and enhancing creativity, courage, compassion, integrity, self-control, leadership, wisdom, and spirituality. Current research examines the roots and fruits of such characteristics, sometimes by studying individuals who exemplify them in extraordinary ways.

The third pillar, *positive groups, communities, and cultures*, seeks to foster a positive social ecology, including healthy families, communal neighborhoods, effective schools, socially responsible media, and civil dialogue.

Will psychology have a more positive mission in this century? Without slighting the need to repair damage and cure disease, positive psychology's proponents hope so. With *American Psychologist* and *British Psychologist* special issues devoted to positive psychology, with lots of books, with networked scientists working in worldwide research groups, and with prizes, research awards, summer institutes, and a graduate program promoting positive psychology scholarship, these psychologists have reason to be positive.

positive psychology the scientific study of optimal human functioning; aims to discover and promote strengths and virtues that enable individuals and communities to thrive.

Positive thinking in the face of adversity can pay dividends, but so, too, can a dash of realism (Schneider, 2001). Realistic anxiety over possible *future* failures can fuel energetic efforts to avoid the dreaded fate rather than depress ambition (Goodhart, 1986; Norem, 2001; Showers, 1992). Concerned about failing an upcoming exam, students may study thoroughly and outperform their equally able but more confident peers. Asian-American students express somewhat greater pessimism than their European-American counterparts, which Edward Chang (2001) suspects helps explain their impressive academic achievements. Success requires enough optimism to provide hope and enough pessimism to prevent complacency. We want our airline pilots to be mindful of worst-possible outcomes.

Excessive optimism, however, can blind us to real risks. Neil Weinstein (1980, 1982, 1996) has shown how our natural positive-thinking bias can promote "an unrealistic optimism about future life events." Most late adolescents see themselves as much less vulnerable than their peers to the HIV virus that causes AIDS (Abrams,

"O God, give us grace to accept with serenity the things that cannot be changed, courage to change the things which should be changed, and the wisdom to distinguish the one from the other."

—Reinhold Niebuhr, "The Serenity Prayer," 1943

Ignorance of one's incompetence Assessing one's competence often requires getting others' feedback, as sometimes happens for naïve would-be contestants for *American Idol.*

"I didn't think it could happen to me."

—Earvin "Magic" Johnson, *My Life,* 1993 (after contracting HIV)

1991). Most college students perceive themselves as less likely than their average classmate to develop drinking problems, drop out of school, have a heart attack by age 40, or go deeply into debt on their high-interest credit cards (Yang et al., 2006).

Like pride, blind optimism may go before a fall. And so may blindness to our own incompetence. Ironically, we are often most overconfident when most incompetent. That's because it often takes competence to recognize competence (Kruger & Dunning, 1999). This helps explain why so many low-scoring students are dumbfounded after doing badly on an exam. If you don't know all the Scrabble word possibilities you've overlooked, you may feel pretty smart—until someone points them out. Our ignorance of what we don't know helps sustain our confidence in our own abilities (Caputo & Dunning, 2005).

This phenomenon has a parallel, as I can vouch, in hard-of-hearing people's difficulty recognizing their own hearing loss. We're not so much "in denial" as we are simply unaware of what we don't hear. If I fail to hear my friend calling my name, the friend notices my inattention. But for me it's a nonevent. I hear what I hear—which, to me, seems pretty normal. But my family tells a different story.

DOONESBURY

Assessing Behavior in Situations

14: What underlying principle guides social-cognitive psychologists in their assessment of people's behavior and beliefs?

To judge one's competence and predict one's future performance, it often pays to invite others' assessments, notes David Dunning (2006). Based on studies in which both individuals and their acquaintances predict their future, we can hazard some advice: If you're a junior doctor and want to predict how well you will do on a surgical skills exam, don't rate yourself—ask your peers for their candid prediction. If you're a Naval officer and need to assess your leadership ability—don't rate yourself, ask your fellow officers. And if you're in love and want to predict whether it will last, don't listen to your heart—ask your roommate.

To predict people's behavior, social-cognitive psychologists often observe them in action in realistic situations. The idea, though effective, is not new. One ambitious example was the U.S. Army's World War II strategy for assessing candidates for spy missions. Rather than using paper-and-pencil tests, Army psychologists subjected the candidates to simulated undercover conditions. They tested their ability to handle stress, solve problems, maintain leadership, and withstand intense interrogation without blowing their cover. Although time-consuming and expensive, this assessment of behavior in a realistic situation helped predict later success on actual spy missions (OSS Assessment Staff, 1948).

Military and educational organizations and many Fortune 500 companies are adopting assessment center strategies in their evaluations of hundreds of thousands of people each year (Bray et al., 1991, 1997; Thornton & Rupp, 2005). Most American cities with populations of 50,000 or more have used assessment centers in evaluating police and fire officers (Lowry, 1997). These procedures exploit the principle that the best means of predicting future behavior is neither a personality test nor an interviewer's intuition. Rather, it is the person's past behavior patterns in similar situations (Mischel, 1981; Ouellette & Wood, 1998; Schmidt & Hunter, 1998). As long as the situation and the person remain much the same, the best predictor of future job performance is past job performance; the best predictor of future grades is past grades; the best predictor of future aggressiveness is past aggressiveness; the best predictor of drug use in young adulthood is drug use in high school. If you can't check the person's past behavior, the next-best thing is to create an assessment situation that simulates the task so you can see how the person handles it.

Assessing behavior in situations Reality TV shows, such as Donald Trump's *The Apprentice,* may take "show me" job interviews to the extreme, but they do illustrate a valid point. Seeing how a potential employee behaves in a job-relevant situation helps predict job performance.

A New York Times analysis of 100 rampage murders over the last half-century revealed that 55 of the killers had regularly exploded in anger and 63 had threatened violence (Goodstein & Glaberson, 2000). Most didn't, out of the blue, "just snap."

Evaluating the Social-Cognitive Perspective

15: What has the social-cognitive perspective contributed to the study of personality, and what criticisms has it faced?

The social-cognitive perspective on personality sensitizes researchers to how situations affect, and are affected by, individuals. More than other perspectives, it builds from psychological research on learning and cognition.

Critics charge that the social-cognitive perspective focuses so much on the situation that it fails to appreciate the person's inner traits. Where is the person in this view of personality, ask the dissenters, and where are human emotions? True, the situation does guide our behavior. But, say the critics, in many instances our unconscious motives, our emotions, and our pervasive traits shine through. Personality traits have been shown to predict behavior at work, love, and play. Our biologically influenced traits really do matter. Consider Percy Ray Pridgen and Charles Gill. Each faced the same situation: They had jointly won a $90 million lottery jackpot (Harriston, 1993). When Pridgen learned of the winning numbers, he began trembling uncontrollably, huddled with a friend behind a bathroom door while confirming the win, then sobbed. When Gill heard the news, he told his wife and then went to sleep.

REHEARSE IT!

16. The social-cognitive perspective proposes that interacting with our environment involves reciprocal determinism, or mutual influences among personal factors, environmental factors, and behavior. An example of an environmental factor is
    a. the presence of books in a home.
    b. a preference for outdoor play.
    c. the ability to read at a fourth-grade level.
    d. the fear of violent action on television.

17. When elderly patients take an active part in managing their own care and surroundings, their morale and health tend to improve. Such findings indicate that people do better when they experience
    a. learned helplessness.
    b. an external locus of control.
    c. an internal locus of control.
    d. reciprocal determinism.

18. Seligman's research showed that a dog will respond with learned helplessness if it has received repeated shocks and has had
    a. the opportunity to escape.
    b. no control over the shocks.
    c. pain or discomfort.
    d. no food or water prior to the shocks.

19. Critics say that _____ personality theory is very sensitive to the way people interact with particular situations, but it says little about their enduring traits.
    a. psychoanalytic
    b. humanistic
    c. trait
    d. social-cognitive

Answers: 16. a, 17. c, 18. b, 19. d.

Exploring the Self

16: Are we helped or hindered by high self-esteem?

Psychology's concern with people's sense of self dates back at least to William James, who devoted more than 100 pages of his 1890 *Principles of Psychology* to the topic. By 1943, Gordon Allport lamented that the self had become "lost to view." Although humanistic psychology's emphasis on the self did not instigate much scientific research, it did help renew the concept of self and keep it alive. Now, more than a century after James, the self is one of Western psychology's most vigorously researched topics. Every year, new studies galore appear on self-esteem, self-disclosure, self-awareness, self-schemas, self-monitoring, and so forth. Underlying this research is an assumption that the **self,** as organizer of our thoughts, feelings, and actions, is the center of personality.

One example of thinking about self is the concept of *possible selves* put forth by Hazel Markus and her colleagues (Cross & Markus, 1991; Markus & Nurius, 1986). Your possible selves include your visions of the self you dream of becoming—the rich self, the successful self, the loved and admired self. They also include the self you fear becoming—the unemployed self, the lonely self, the academically failed self. Such possible selves motivate us by laying out specific goals and calling forth the energy to work toward them. University of Michigan students in a combined undergraduate/medical school program earn higher grades if they undergo the program with a clear vision of themselves as successful doctors. Dreams do often give birth to achievements.

Our self-focused perspective may motivate us, but it can also lead us to presume too readily that others are noticing and evaluating us. Thomas Gilovich (1996) demonstrated this **spotlight effect** by having individual Cornell University students don Barry Manilow T-shirts before entering a room with other students. Feeling self-conscious, the T-shirt wearers guessed that nearly half their peers would take note of the shirt as they walked in. In reality, only 23 percent did. This absence of attention applies not only to our dorky clothes and bad hair but also to our nervousness, irritation, or attraction: Fewer people notice than we presume (Gilovich & Savitsky, 1999). Others are also less aware than we suppose of the variability—the ups and downs—of our appearance and performance (Gilovich et al., 2002). Even after a blunder (setting off a library alarm, showing up in the wrong clothes), we stick out like a sore thumb less than we imagine (Savitsky et al., 2001). Knowing about the spotlight effect can be empowering. Help public speakers to understand that their natural nervousness is not so apparent to their audience and their speaking performance improves (Savitsky & Gilovich, 2003).

"The first step to better times is to imagine them."

—Chinese fortune cookie

Possible selves By giving them a chance to try out many possible selves, pretend games offer children important opportunities to grow emotionally, socially, and cognitively. This young boy may or may not grow up to be a physician, but playing adult roles will certainly bear fruit in terms of an expanded vision of what he might become.

Sybil Shackman

The Benefits of Self-Esteem

How we feel about ourselves is also important. High **self-esteem**—a feeling of self-worth—pays dividends. People who feel good about themselves (who strongly agree with self-affirming questionnaire statements such as, "I am fun to be with") have fewer sleepless nights; succumb less easily to pressures to conform; are more persistent at difficult tasks; are less shy, anxious, and lonely; and are just plain happier (Greenberg, 2008; Leary, 1999; Murray et al., 2002; Watson et al., 2002). Moreover, today's self-esteem sometimes predicts tomorrow's achievements. In one study of 297 Finnish university students, self-esteem scores predicted employment, salary, and job satisfaction a decade later (Salmela-Aro & Nurmi, 2007).

Is high self-esteem really "the armor that protects kids" from life's problems? Some psychologists have their doubts (Baumeister, 2006; Dawes, 1994; Leary, 1999; Seligman, 1994, 2002). Children's *academic self-concept*—their confidence that they can do well in a subject—predicts school achievement. But *general self-image* does not (Marsh & Craven, 2006; Swann et al., 2007; Trautwein et al., 2006). Maybe self-esteem simply reflects reality. Maybe feeling good *follows* doing well. Maybe it's a side effect of meeting challenges and surmounting difficulties. Maybe self-esteem is a gauge that reads out the state of our relationships with others. If so, isn't pushing the gauge artificially higher akin to forcing a car's low fuel gauge to display "full"? And if problems and failures cause low self-esteem, won't the best boost therefore come not so much from our repeatedly telling children how wonderful they are as from their own effective coping and hard-won achievements?

However, experiments do reveal an *effect* of low self-esteem. Temporarily deflate people's self-image (say, by telling them they did poorly on an aptitude test or by disparaging their personality) and they will be more likely to disparage others or to express heightened racial prejudice (Ybarra, 1999). Those who are negative about themselves also tend to be thin-skinned and judgmental (Baumgardner et al., 1989; Pelham, 1993). In experiments, people made to feel insecure often become excessively critical, as if to impress others with their own brilliance (Amabile, 1983). Such findings are consistent with Maslow's and Rogers' presumptions that a healthy self-image pays dividends. Accept yourself and you'll find it easier to accept others. Disparage yourself and you will be prone to the floccinaucinihilipilification[1] of others. Said more simply, some "love their neighbors as themselves"; others loathe their neighbors as themselves.

Self-Serving Bias

Carl Rogers (1958) once objected to the religious doctrine that humanity's problems arise from excessive self-love, or pride. He noted that most people he had known "despise themselves, regard themselves as worthless and unlovable." Mark Twain had a similar idea: "No man, deep down in the privacy of his heart, has any considerable respect for himself."

Actually, most of us have a good reputation with ourselves. In studies of self-esteem, even those who score low respond in the midrange of possible scores. (A low–self-esteem person responds to statements such as "I have good ideas" with qualifying adjectives such as *somewhat* or *sometimes.*) Moreover, one of psychology's most provocative and firmly established recent conclusions concerns our potent **self-serving bias**—our readiness to perceive ourselves favorably (Mezulis et al., 2004; Myers, 2008). Consider these findings:

People accept more responsibility for good deeds than for bad, and for successes than for failures. Athletes often privately credit their victories to their

---

self in contemporary psychology, assumed to be the center of personality, the organizer of our thoughts, feelings, and actions.

spotlight effect overestimating others' noticing and evaluating our appearance, performance, and blunders (as if we presume a spotlight shines on us).

self-esteem one's feelings of high or low self-worth.

self-serving bias a readiness to perceive oneself favorably.

"There's a lot of talk about self-esteem these days. It seems pretty basic to me. If you want to feel proud of yourself, you've got to do things you can be proud of."

—Oseola McCarty, Mississippi laundry worker, after donating $150,000 to the University of Southern Mississippi

Dear diary, Sorry to bother you again.

LOW SELF-ESTEEM

---

[1]I couldn't resist throwing that in. But don't worry, you won't be tested on floccinaucinihilipilification, which is the act of estimating something as worthless (and was the longest nontechnical word in the first edition of the *Oxford English Dictionary*).

PEANUTS

own prowess, and their losses to bad breaks, lousy officiating, or the other team's exceptional performance. People are quick to credit themselves as good drivers, but on insurance forms, they have explained accidents in such words as: "An invisible car came out of nowhere, struck my car, and vanished." "As I reached an intersection, a hedge sprang up, obscuring my vision, and I did not see the other car." "A pedestrian hit me and went under my car." The question "What have I done to deserve this?" is one we usually ask of our troubles, not our successes—those, we assume we deserve.

Most people see themselves as better than average. This is true for nearly any commonplace behavior that is subjectively assessed and socially desirable. In national surveys, most business executives say they are more ethical than their average counterpart. In several studies, 90 percent of business managers and more than 90 percent of college professors rated their performance as superior to that of their average peer. In Australia, 86 percent of people rate their job performance as above average, and only 1 percent as below average. The phenomenon, which reflects the overestimation of self rather than the underestimation of others (Epley & Dunning, 2000), is less striking in Asia, where people value modesty (Heine & Hamamura, 2007). Yet self-serving biases have been observed worldwide: among Dutch, Australian, and Chinese students; Japanese drivers; Indian Hindus; and French people of most walks of life. In every one of 53 countries surveyed, people expressed self-esteem above the midpoint of the most widely used scale (Schmitt & Allik, 2005).

Ironically, people even see themselves as more immune than others to self-serving bias (Pronin, 2007). The world, it seems, is Garrison Keillor's Lake Wobegon writ large—a place where "all the women are strong, all the men are good-looking, and all the children are above average." And so are the pets. Three in four owners believe their pet is smarter than average (Nier, 2004).

After tracking self-importance across the last several decades, psychologist Jean Twenge (2006; Twenge et al., 2008) reports that today's new generation—*Generation Me*, she calls it—expresses more *narcissism* (by agreeing more often with statements such as, "If I ruled the world, it would be a better place," or "I think I am a special person"). Agreement with such statements correlates with materialism, the desire to be famous, inflated expectations, more hookups with fewer committed relationships, more gambling, and more cheating, all of which have been on the rise as narcissism has increased.

As religion and literature together remind us, pride does often go before a fall. Self-serving perceptions underlie conflicts ranging from blaming one's spouse for marital discord to arrogantly promoting one's own ethnic superiority. Finding their self-esteem threatened, people with large egos may do more than put others down; they may react violently. "Aryan pride" fueled Nazi atrocities. "These biases have the effect of making wars more likely to begin and more difficult to end," note Daniel Kahneman and Jonathan Renshon (2007).

Brad Bushman and Roy Baumeister (1998; Bushman et al., 2009) experimented with the "dark side of high self-esteem" by having 540 undergraduate volunteers write a paragraph, in response to which another supposed student gave them either praise ("Great essay!") or stinging criticism ("One of the worst essays I have read!").

"To love oneself is the beginning of a life-long romance."

—Oscar Wilde, *An Ideal Husband*, 1895

Then the essay writers played a reaction-time game in which, after wins, they could assault an opponent with noise of any intensity for any duration. Can you anticipate the result? After criticism, those with narcissism were "exceptionally aggressive." They delivered three times the auditory torture of those with normal self-esteem. Threatened egotism, more than low self-esteem, it seems, predisposes aggression. "Encouraging people to feel good about themselves when they haven't earned it" poses problems, Baumeister (2001) concluded. "Conceited, self-important individuals turn nasty toward those who puncture their bubbles of self-love."

Despite the demonstrated perils of pride, many people reject the idea of self-serving bias, insisting it overlooks those who feel worthless and unlovable and seem to despise themselves. If self-serving bias prevails, why do so many people disparage themselves? For four reasons: Some self-disparaging thoughts—"How could I have been so stupid!"—*protect us from repeating mistakes.* Sometimes self-directed put-downs are *subtly strategic:* They elicit reassuring strokes. Saying "No one likes me" may at least elicit "But not everyone has met you!" Other times, such as before a game or an exam, self-disparaging comments *prepare us for possible failure.* The coach who extols the superior strength of the upcoming opponent makes a loss understandable, a victory noteworthy. And finally, self-disparagement also frequently *pertains to one's old self.* People are much more critical of their distant past selves than of their current selves—even when they have not changed (Wilson & Ross, 2001). "At 18, I was a jerk; today I'm more sensitive." In their own eyes, chumps yesterday, champs today.

Even so, it's true: All of us some of the time, and some of us much of the time, do feel inferior—especially when we compare ourselves with those who are a step or two higher on the ladder of status, looks, income, or ability. The deeper and more frequently we have such feelings, the more unhappy, even depressed, we are. But for most people, thinking has a naturally positive bias. And positive self-esteem correlates with happiness, initiative, and persistence after failure (Baumeister et al., 2003).

While recognizing the dark side of self-serving bias and self-esteem, some researchers prefer isolating the effects of two types of self-esteem—defensive and secure (Kernis, 2003; Lambird & Mann, 2006; Ryan & Deci, 2004). *Defensive self-esteem* is fragile. It focuses on sustaining itself, which makes failures and criticism feel threatening. Such egotism exposes one to perceived threats, which feed anger and disorder, note Jennifer Crocker and Lora Park (2004).

Secure self-esteem is less fragile, because it is less contingent on external evaluations. To feel accepted for who we are, and not for our looks, wealth, or acclaim, relieves pressures to succeed and enables us to focus beyond ourselves. By losing ourselves in relationships and purposes larger than self, Crocker and Park add, we may achieve a more secure self-esteem and greater quality of life.

> "The enthusiastic claims of the self-esteem movement mostly range from fantasy to hogwash. The effects of self-esteem are small, limited, and not all good."
>
> —Roy Baumeister (1996)

> "If you compare yourself with others, you may become vain and bitter; for always there will be greater and lesser persons than yourself."
>
> —Max Ehrmann, "Desiderata," 1927

REHEARSE IT!

20. The *spotlight effect* is our tendency to
    a. perceive ourselves favorably and perceive others unfavorably.
    b. try out many possible selves.
    c. become excessively critical when made to feel insecure.
    d. overestimate others' attention to and evaluation of our appearance, performance, and blunders.

21. Researchers have found that low self-esteem tends to be linked with life problems. How should this link be interpreted?
    a. Life problems cause low self-esteem.
    b. The answer isn't clear because the link is correlational and does not indicate cause and effect.
    c. Low self-esteem leads to life problems.
    d. Because of the self-serving bias, we must assume that external factors cause low self-esteem.

22. People tend to accept responsibility for their successes or good qualities and blame circumstances or luck for their failures. This is an example of
    a. low self-esteem.
    b. self-actualization.
    c. self-serving bias.
    d. narcissism.

Answers: 20. d, 21. b, 22. c.

Personality

The Psychoanalytic Perspective

1 What was Freud's view of personality and its development?

Freud believed that emotional disorders spring from *unconscious dynamics*, which he sought to analyze through *free association* and dreams. He referred to his theory and techniques as *psychoanalysis*. He saw *personality* as composed of pleasure-seeking psychic impulses (the *id*), a reality-oriented executive (the *ego*), and an internalized set of ideals (the *superego*). He believed that children develop through *psychosexual stages*, and that failure to resolve conflicts associated with a particular stage may result in *fixation* at that stage. To ward off free-floating anxiety, the ego employs *defense mechanisms*, especially *repression*.

2 Which of Freud's ideas did his followers accept or reject?

Neo-Freudians Adler and Horney accepted many of Freud's ideas, but they argued for motives other than sex and aggression and for greater conscious control than Freud supposed. Jung also accepted many of Freud's ideas but also proposed a *collective unconscious*. Psychodynamic theorists share Freud's view that unconscious mental processes, inner conflicts, and childhood experiences are important influences on personality.

3 What are projective tests, and how are they used?

Projective tests attempt to assess personality by presenting ambiguous stimuli designed to reveal the unconscious. The most famous projective test, the *Rorschach inkblot test*, has questionable reliability and validity.

4 How do contemporary psychologists view Freud and the unconscious?

Freud's critics note that his theory offers only after-the-fact explanations, and that repression rarely occurs. Current information-processing research confirms that our access to all that goes on in our mind is very limited, but it does not support Freud's view of the unconscious. Rather, the unconscious consists of schemas that control our perceptions; parallel processing that occurs without our conscious knowledge; implicit memories of learned skills; instantly activated emotions; and self-concepts and stereotypes that filter information about ourselves and others. With the exception of projection and reaction formation, there is little support for Freud's proposed defense mechanisms.

Nevertheless, Freud drew psychology's attention to the unconscious, to the struggle to cope with anxiety and sexuality, and to the conflict between biological impulses and social restraints. His cultural impact has been enormous.

The Humanistic Perspective

5 How did humanistic psychologists view personality, and what was their goal in studying personality?

Humanistic psychologists sought to turn psychology's attention toward the growth potential of healthy people. Maslow believed that if basic human needs are fulfilled, people will strive toward *self-actualization* and self-transcendence. To nurture growth in others,

Rogers advised being genuine, accepting, and empathic. In this climate of *unconditional positive regard,* he believed, people can develop a deeper self-awareness and a more realistic and positive *self-concept.*

6 How did humanistic psychologists assess a person's sense of self?

Some humanistic psychologists assessed personality through questionnaires on which people reported their self-concept. Others believed the only acceptable approach is understanding others' subjective personal experiences in face-to-face situations.

7 How has the humanistic perspective influenced psychology? What criticisms has it faced?

Humanistic psychology helped to renew psychology's interest in the concept of self. Its critics have complained that its concepts are vague and subjective, its values self-centered, and its assumptions naively optimistic.

The Trait Perspective

8 How do psychologists use traits to describe personality?

Rather than explain the hidden aspects of personality, *trait* theorists attempt to describe our stable and enduring characteristics. Through factor analysis, researchers have isolated important dimensions of personality. Genetic predispositions influence many traits.

9 What are personality inventories, and what are their strengths and weaknesses as trait-assessment tools?

Personality inventories (like the *MMPI*) are questionnaires on which people respond to items designed to gauge a wide range of feelings and behaviors. Items on the test are *empirically derived*, and the tests are objectively scored.

10 Which traits seem to provide the most useful information about personality variation?

The Big Five personality dimensions—conscientiousness, agreeableness, neuroticism, openness, and extaversion—offer a reasonably comprehensive picture of personality. They have been tested worldwide.

11 Does research support the consistency of personality traits over time and across situations?

People's traits persist over time, but their behaviors vary widely from situation to situation. A person's average behavior across different situations tends to be fairly consistent.

The Social-Cognitive Perspective

12 In the view of social-cognitive psychologists, what mutual influences shape an individual's personality?

The *social-cognitive perspective* applies principles of learning, cognition, and social behavior to personality, with particular emphasis on the ways in which personality influences and is influenced by interactions with the environment. It assumes *reciprocal determinism*—that personal-cognitive factors interact with the environment to influence people's behavior.

13 What are the causes and consequences of personal control?

By studying how people vary in their perceived *locus of control* (*external* or *internal*), researchers have found that a sense of *personal control* helps people to cope with life. Research on *learned helplessness* evolved into research on the effects of optimism and pessimism, which led to a broader *positive psychology* movement.

14 What underlying principle guides social-cognitive psychologists in their assessment of people's behavior and beliefs?

Social-cognitive researchers tend to believe that the best way to predict someone's behavior in a given situation is to observe that person's behavior in similar situations.

15 What has the social-cognitive perspective contributed to the study of personality, and what criticisms has it faced?

The social-cognitive perspective builds on psychology's well-established concepts of learning and cognition and reminds us of the power of social situations. It has been faulted for underemphasizing the importance of inner traits.

Exploring the Self

16 Are we helped or hindered by high self-esteem?

In contemporary psychology, the *self* is assumed to be the center of personality, the organizer of our thoughts, feelings, and actions. Research confirms the benefits of high *self-esteem*, but it also warns of the dangers of narcissism. The *self-serving bias* leads us to perceive ourselves favorably, often causing us to overestimate our abilities and underestimate our faults.

Terms and Concepts to Remember

personality, p. 419
free association, p. 420
unconscious, p. 420
psychoanalysis, p. 420
id, p. 421
ego, p. 421
superego, p. 421
psychosexual stages, p. 422
Oedipus [ED-uh-puss] complex, p. 422
identification, p. 422
fixation, p. 422
defense mechanisms, p. 423

repression, p. 423
collective unconscious, p. 424
projective test, p. 425
Rorschach inkblot test, p. 425
self-actualization, p. 429
unconditional positive regard, p. 430
self-concept, p. 431
trait, p. 432
personality inventory, p. 433
Minnesota Multiphasic Personality Inventory (MMPI), p. 433
empirically derived test, p. 434

social-cognitive perspective, p. 439
reciprocal determinism, p. 439
personal control, p. 440
external locus of control, p. 441
internal locus of control, p. 441
learned helplessness, p. 441
positive psychology, p. 443
self, p. 446
spotlight effect, p. 446
self-esteem, p. 447
self-serving bias, p. 447

Test for Success: Critical Thinking Exercises
By Amy Himsel, El Camino College

1. How might Freud and Rogers differ in their explanations of how the environment influences the development of a criminal?

2. In *Essays*, Michel de Montaigne (1588) suggested, "There is as much difference between us and ourselves, as between us and others." Does research on the trait perspective support his claim?

3. You think you are talented enough to compete on *American Idol*, but you don't want to make a fool of yourself on TV.

What is the best way to accurately assess your talent beforehand?

4. A fortune cookie advises, "Love yourself and happiness will follow." Is this good advice?

The Test for Success exercises offer you a chance to apply your critical thinking skills to aspects of the material you have just read. Suggestions for answering these questions can be found in Appendix D at the back of the book.

Multiple-choice self-tests and more may be found at www.worthpublishers.com/myers.

Chapter Outline

● **Perspectives on Psychological Disorders**
Defining Psychological Disorders
THINKING CRITICALLY ABOUT: ADHD—Normal High Energy or Genuine Disorder?
Understanding Psychological Disorders
Classifying Psychological Disorders
CLOSE-UP: The "un-DSM": A Diagnostic Manual of Human Strengths
Labeling Psychological Disorders
THINKING CRITICALLY ABOUT: Insanity and Responsibility

● **Anxiety Disorders**
Generalized Anxiety Disorder
Panic Disorder
Phobias
Obsessive-Compulsive Disorder
Post-Traumatic Stress Disorder
Understanding Anxiety Disorders

● **Somatoform Disorders**

● **Dissociative Disorders**
Dissociative Identity Disorder
Understanding Dissociative Identity Disorder

● **Mood Disorders**
Major Depressive Disorder
Bipolar Disorder
Understanding Mood Disorders
CLOSE-UP: Suicide

● **Schizophrenia**
Symptoms of Schizophrenia
Onset and Development of Schizophrenia
Understanding Schizophrenia

● **Personality Disorders**
Antisocial Personality Disorder
Understanding Antisocial Personality Disorder

● **Rates of Psychological Disorders**

13: Psychological Disorders

I felt the need to clean my room at home in Indianapolis every Sunday and would spend four to five hours at it. I would take every book out of the bookcase, dust and put it back. At the time I loved doing it. Then I didn't want to do it anymore, but I couldn't stop. The clothes in my closet hung exactly two fingers apart. . . . I made a ritual of touching the wall in my bedroom before I went out because something bad would happen if I didn't do it the right way. I had a constant anxiety about it as a kid, and it made me think for the first time that I might be nuts.

Marc, diagnosed with obsessive-compulsive disorder (from Summers, 1996)

Whenever I get depressed it's because I've lost a sense of self. I can't find reasons to like myself. I think I'm ugly. I think no one likes me. . . . I become grumpy and short-tempered. Nobody wants to be around me. I'm left alone. Being alone confirms that I am ugly and not worth being with. I think I'm responsible for everything that goes wrong.

Greta, diagnosed with depression (from Thorne, 1993, p. 21)

Voices, like the roar of a crowd came. I felt like Jesus; I was being crucified. It was dark. I just continued to huddle under the blanket, feeling weak, laid bare and defenseless in a cruel world I could no longer understand.

Stuart, diagnosed with schizophrenia (from Emmons et al., 1997)

People are fascinated by the exceptional, the unusual, the abnormal. "The sun shines and warms and lights us and we have no curiosity to know why this is so," observed Ralph Waldo Emerson, "but we ask the reason of all evil, of pain, and hunger, and [unusual] people." But why such fascination with disturbed people? Do we see in them something of ourselves? At various moments, all of us feel, think, or act the way disturbed people do much of the time. We, too, get anxious, depressed, withdrawn, suspicious, or deluded, just less intensely and more briefly. It's no wonder that studying psychological disorders may at times evoke an eerie sense of self-recognition, one that illuminates the dynamics of our own personality. "To study the abnormal is the best way of understanding the normal," proposed William James (1842–1910).

Another reason for our curiosity is that so many of us have felt, either personally or through friends or family, the bewilderment and pain of a psychological disorder that may bring unexplained physical symptoms, irrational fears, or a feeling that life is not worth living. Indeed, as members of the human family, most of us will at some point encounter a psychologically disturbed person.

The World Health Organization reports that, worldwide, some 450 million people have psychological disorders (WHO, 2008). These disorders account for 15.4 percent of the years of life lost due to death or disability—scoring slightly below cardiovascular conditions and slightly above cancer (Murray & Lopez, 1996). Rates and symptoms of psychological disorders vary by culture, but no known society is free of two terrible maladies: depression and schizophrenia (Baumeister & Härter, 2007; Draguns, 1990a,b, 1997). Before we examine disorders in depth, however, let's consider some more basic questions.

Perspectives on Psychological Disorders

Most people would agree that someone too depressed to get out of bed for weeks at a time has a psychological disorder. But what about those who, having experienced a loss, are unable to resume their usual social activities? Where should we draw the line between sadness and depression? Between zany creativity and bizarre irrationality? Between normality and abnormality? Let's start with three questions. How should we *define* psychological disorders? How should we *understand* disorders—as sicknesses that need to be diagnosed and cured, or as natural responses to a troubling environment? How should we *classify* psychological disorders? And can we do so in a way that allows us to help people without stigmatizing them with labels?

Defining Psychological Disorders

1: **How should we draw the line between normality and disorder?**

psychological disorder deviant, distressful, and dysfunctional patterns of thoughts, feelings, and actions.

Mental health workers view **psychological disorders** as ongoing patterns of thoughts, feelings, and actions that are deviant, distressful, and dysfunctional (Comer, 2004).

Being different *(deviant)* from most other people in one's culture is *part* of what it takes to define a psychological disorder. As the reclusive poet Emily Dickinson observed in 1862,

Assent—and you are sane—

Demur—you're straightaway dangerous—

and handled with a Chain.

Standards for deviant behavior vary by context and by culture. In one context—wartime—mass killing may be viewed as normal and even heroic. In some contexts, people are presumed deranged when they hear voices. But in cultures practicing ancestor worship, people may claim to talk with the dead and not be seen as disordered because other people find them rational (Friedrich, 1987).

Standards for deviance also vary with time. From 1952 through December 9, 1973, homosexuality was classified as an illness. By day's end on December 10, it was not. The American Psychiatric Association had dropped homosexuality as a disorder because more and more of its members no longer viewed it as a psychological problem. Also in 1952, a distractible, fidgety, and impulsive 8-year-old would have been considered rambunctious. Today, she—but more often he—may be diagnosed with *attention-deficit hyperactivity disorder* (see Thinking Critically About: ADHD—Normal High Energy or Genuine Disorder?).

Culture and normality Men of the West African Wodaabe tribe put on elaborate makeup and costumes to attract women. In Western society, the same behavior would break behavioral norms and might be judged abnormal.

Carol Beckwith

Thinking Critically About:

ADHD—Normal High Energy or Genuine Disorder?

Eight-year-old Todd has always been energetic. At home, he chatters away and darts from one activity to the next, rarely settling down to read a book or focus on a game. At play, he is reckless and over-reacts when playmates bump into him or take one of his toys. At school, his exasperated teacher complains that fidgety Todd doesn't listen, follow instructions, or stay in his seat and do his lessons.

If taken for a psychological evaluation, Todd may be diagnosed with **attention-deficit hyperactivity disorder (ADHD),** as are some 4 percent of children who display at least one of its key symptoms (extreme inattention, hyperactivity, and impulsivity) (NIMH, 2003).

To skeptics, being distractible, fidgety, and impulsive sounds like a "disorder" caused by a single genetic variation: a Y chromosome. And sure enough, ADHD is diagnosed two to three times more often in boys than in girls.

Critics note that in the decade after 1987 the proportion of American children being treated for ADHD nearly quadrupled (Olfson et al., 2003). By 2005, a Gallup survey showed that 10 percent of American 13- to 17-year-olds were being medicated for ADHD (Mason, 2005). The diagnosis depends in part on teacher referrals. Some refer lots of kids for ADHD assessment, others none. ADHD rates have therefore varied widely—in New York State, for example, by a factor of 10 in different counties (Carlson, 2000).

Others argue that the more frequent diagnoses of ADHD today reflect increased awareness of the disorder, especially in those areas where rates are highest. They acknowledge that diagnoses can be inconsistent—ADHD is not as objectively defined as is a broken arm. Nevertheless, declared the World Federation for Mental Health (2005), "there is strong agreement among the international scientific community that ADHD is a real neurobiological disorder whose existence should no longer be debated." In neuroimaging studies, ADHD has associations with certain brain activity patterns, notes a consensus statement by 75 researchers (Barkley et al., 2002).

What, then, is known about ADHD's causes? It is not caused by too much sugar or poor schools. (Researchers have found, however, that toddlers who watch lots of TV are, at age 7, more likely than average to display ADHD symptoms [Christakis et al., 2004].) It often coexists with a learning disorder or with defiant and temper-prone behavior. The U.S. National Institute of Mental Health (1999, 2003) reports that ADHD is heritable, and research teams are sleuthing the culprit genes (Brookes et al., 2006). It is treatable with nonaddictive medications such as Ritalin and Adderall, which are stimulants but help calm hyperactivity and increase one's ability to sit and focus on a task. Psychological therapies, such as those focused on shaping behaviors in the classroom and at home, have also helped address the distress of ADHD. Finally, many children diagnosed with ADHD exhibit delayed brain maturation. Thus, many fidgety, hyperactive 5-year-olds mature into normal teens.

The bottom line: Extreme inattention, hyperactivity, and impulsivity can derail social, academic, and vocational achievements, and these symptoms can be treated with medication and other treatment. But the debate continues over whether normal rambunctiousness is too often diagnosed as a psychiatric disorder, and whether there is a cost to the long-term use of stimulant drugs in treating ADHD.

---

attention-deficit hyperactivity disorder (ADHD) a psychological disorder marked by the appearance by age 7 of one or more of three key symptoms: extreme inattention, hyperactivity, and impulsivity.

But there is more to a disorder than being deviant. Olympic gold medalists deviate from the norm in their physical abilities, and society honors them. To be considered disordered, deviant behavior usually causes the person *distress*. Marc, Greta, and Stuart were all clearly distressed by their behaviors.

Deviant and distressful behaviors are more likely to be considered disordered when also judged to be a *harmful dysfunction* (Wakefield, 1992, 2006). Marc's distracting obsessive behaviors, for example, interfered with his work and leisure. By this measuring stick, even typical behaviors, such as the occasional despondency many college students feel, may signal a psychological disorder *if they become disabling*. Dysfunction is key to defining a disorder: An intense fear of spiders may be deviant, but if it doesn't impair your life it is not a disorder.

Understanding Psychological Disorders

2: What perspectives can help us understand psychological disorders?

To explain puzzling behavior, people in earlier times often presumed that strange forces—the movements of the stars, godlike powers, or evil spirits—were at work.

Had you lived during the Middle Ages, you might have said "The devil made him do it," and you might have approved of an exorcism to get rid of the evil demon. Until the last two centuries, "mad" people were sometimes caged in zoolike conditions or given "therapies" appropriate to a demon: beatings, burning, or castration. In other times, therapy included trephination (drilling holes in the skull), pulling teeth, removing lengths of intestines, cauterizing the clitoris, or giving transfusions of animal blood (Farina, 1982).

The Medical Model

In opposition to brutal treatments, reformers, including Philippe Pinel (1745–1826) in France, insisted that madness is not demon possession but a sickness of the mind caused by severe stresses and inhumane conditions. For Pinel and others, "moral treatment" included boosting patients' morale by unchaining them and talking with them, and by replacing brutality with gentleness, isolation with activity, and filth with clean air and sunshine.

By the 1800s, the discovery that syphilis infects the brain and distorts the mind provided the impetus for further reform. Hospitals replaced asylums, and the medical world began searching for physical causes of mental disorders, and for treatments that would cure them. Today, this **medical model** is recognizable in the terminology of the mental *health* movement: A mental *illness* (also called a psycho*pathology*) needs to be *diagnosed* on the basis of its *symptoms* and *cured* through *therapy*, which may include *treatment* in a psychiatric *hospital*.

The medical perspective has gained credibility from recent discoveries that genetically influenced abnormalities in brain structure and biochemistry contribute to many disorders. But as we will see, psychological factors, such as enduring or traumatic stress, also play an important role.

"Moral treatment" Under Philippe Pinel's influence, hospitals sometimes sponsored patient dances, such as the "Lunatic Ball" depicted in this painting by George Bellows (*Dance in a Madhouse*).

George Wesley Bellows, Dance in a Madhouse, 1907. © 1997 The Art Institute of Chicago

In Malaysia, amok *describes a sudden outburst of violent behavior (thus the phrase "run amok").*

The Biopsychosocial Approach

Today's psychologists believe that the medical model gives an incomplete understanding of disorders. To presume that a person is "mentally ill," they say, attributes the condition to a "sickness" that must be identified and cured. But instead or additionally, there may be a difficulty in the person's environment, in the person's current interpretations of events, or in the person's bad habits and poor social skills.

Evidence of such effects comes from links between specific disorders and cultures (Beardsley, 1994; Castillo, 1997). Cultures differ in their sources of stress, and they produce different ways of coping. The eating disorders anorexia nervosa and bulimia nervosa, for example, occur mostly in Western cultures. Latin America lays claim to *susto,* a condition marked by severe anxiety, restlessness, and a fear of black magic. *Taijin-kyofusho,* social anxiety about one's appearance combined with a readiness to blush and a fear of eye contact, appears in Japan. Such disorders may share an underlying dynamic (such as anxiety) while differing in the symptoms (an eating problem or a type of fear) manifested in a particular culture. But not all disorders are culture-bound. As noted earlier, depression and schizophrenia occur worldwide. From Asia to Africa and across the Americas, schizophrenia's symptoms often include irrationality and incoherent speech.

To assess the whole set of interacting influences—genetic predispositions and physiological states; inner psychological dynamics; and social and cultural circumstances—the biopsychosocial model helps (**FIGURE 13.1**). This approach recognizes that mind and body are inseparable. Negative emotions contribute to physical illness, and physical abnormalities contribute to negative emotions. We are mind embodied.

FIGURE 13.1 The biopsychosocial approach to psychological disorders
Today's psychology studies how biological, psychological, and social-cultural factors interact to produce specific psychological disorders.

Classifying Psychological Disorders

3: How and why do clinicians classify psychological disorders?

In biology and the other sciences, classification creates order. To classify an animal as a "mammal" says a great deal—that it is warm-blooded, has hair or fur, and nourishes its young with milk. In psychiatry and psychology, too, classification orders and describes symptoms. To classify a person's disorder as "schizophrenia" suggests that the person talks incoherently; has hallucinations (false sensory experiences) or delusions (bizarre beliefs); shows either little emotion or inappropriate emotion; or is socially withdrawn. "Schizophrenia" provides a handy shorthand for describing a complex disorder.

Diagnostic classification aims not only to describe a disorder but also to predict its future course, imply appropriate treatment, and stimulate research into its causes. Indeed, to study a disorder we must first name and describe it. A current authoritative scheme for classifying psychological disorders is the **DSM-IV-TR.** This volume is the American Psychiatric Association's *Diagnostic and Statistical Manual of Mental Disorders,* Fourth Edition, updated as a 2000 "text revision"; a more substantially revised DSM-V will appear in 2012. (A book of case illustrations accompanying DSM-IV-TR provides the basis for much of this chapter.) DSM-IV-TR was developed in coordination with the tenth edition of the World Health Organization's *International Classification of Diseases* (ICD-10), which covers both medical and psychological disorders.

Despite its medical terminology *(diagnosing, symptoms, illness),* most practitioners find the DSM-IV-TR a helpful and practical tool. It is also financially necessary: North American health insurance companies usually require a DSM-IV-TR diagnosis before they pay for therapy.

The DSM-IV-TR defines a diagnostic process and 16 clinical syndromes (**TABLE 13.1** on the next page). Without presuming to explain their causes, it describes various disorders. To be helpful and useful, these categories and diagnostic guidelines must be reliable, and to a reasonable extent they are. If one psychiatrist or psychologist diagnoses someone as having, say, catatonic schizophrenia, the chances are good that another mental health worker will independently give the same diagnosis. Following these guidelines, clinicians answer a series of objective questions about observable behaviors, such as, "Is the person afraid to leave home?" In one study, 16 psychologists used this structured-interview procedure to diagnose 75 psychiatric patients as

"I'm always like this, and my family was wondering if you could prescribe a mild depressant."

medical model the concept that diseases, in this case psychological disorders, have physical causes that can be *diagnosed, treated,* and, in most cases, *cured,* often through treatment in a hospital.

DSM-IV-TR the American Psychiatric Association's *Diagnostic and Statistical Manual of Mental Disorders,* Fourth Edition, updated as a 2000 "text revision"; a widely used system for classifying psychological disorders.

TABLE 13.1 How Are Psychological Disorders Diagnosed?

Based on assessments, interviews, and observations, many clinicians diagnose by answering the following questions from the five levels, or *axes,* of the DSM-IV-TR. (Chapters in parentheses locate the topics in this text.)

Axis I Is a *Clinical Syndrome* present?

Using specifically defined criteria, clinicians may select none, one, or more syndromes from the following list:

- Disorders usually first diagnosed in infancy, childhood, and adolescence
- Delirium, dementia, amnesia, and other cognitive disorders (Chapters 5 and 8)
- Mental disorders due to a general medical condition
- Substance-related disorders (Chapter 3)
- Schizophrenia and other psychotic disorders (this chapter)
- Mood disorders (this chapter)
- Anxiety disorders (this chapter)
- Somatoform disorders (this chapter)
- Factitious disorders, intentionally faked
- Dissociative disorders (this chapter)
- Eating disorders (Chapter 10)
- Sexual disorders and gender identity disorder (Chapter 10)
- Sleep disorders (Chapter 3)
- Impulse-control disorders not classified elsewhere
- Adjustment disorders
- Other conditions that may be a focus of clinical attention

Axis II Is a *Personality Disorder* or *Mental Retardation* present?
Clinicians may or may not also select one of these two conditions.

Axis III Is a *General Medical Condition,* such as diabetes, hypertension, or arthritis, also present?

Axis IV Are *Psychosocial* or *Environmental Problems,* such as school or housing issues, also present?

Axis V What is the *Global Assessment* of this person's functioning?
Clinicians assign a code from 0–100.

experiencing (1) depression, (2) generalized anxiety, or (3) some other disorder (Riskind et al., 1987). Without knowing the first psychologist's diagnosis, another psychologist viewed a videotape of each interview and offered a second opinion. For 83 percent of the patients, the two opinions agreed.

Some critics have faulted the manual for casting too wide a net. As the number of disorder categories has swelled (from 60 in the 1950s DSM to 400 today), so has the number of adults who meet the criteria for at least one of them—26 percent in any year, according to the U.S. National Institute of Mental Health (2008), and 46 percent at some time in their lives (Kessler et al., 2005). The number of children diagnosed with psychological disorders has also mushroomed, tripling to 6 million children since the early 1990s, according to some reports (Carey, 2006). Today's adolescent mood swings are more often taken to be bipolar disorder. Temper tantrums, arguing, touchiness, and spitefulness are more often taken to be oppositional defiant disorder.

Psychologists Christopher Peterson and Martin Seligman (2004) have noted the usefulness of the DSM-IV-TR in ordering and defining dysfunctions. Would it not also be useful, they ask, to have a companion catalog of the thinking-feeling-action tendencies that contribute to the *good* life, for self and others? As a complement to the DSM, they therefore have offered a diagnostic manual of human strengths (see Close-Up: The "un-DSM": A Diagnostic Manual of Human Strengths).

Close-Up:

The "un-DSM": A Diagnostic Manual of Human Strengths

The Values in Action Classification of Strengths is an expression of the *positive psychology movement* (Chapter 12). Psychological science seeks to understand and help alleviate human ills and evils, agree positive psychology advocates, but also to understand and promote human strengths and virtues. Their complementary classification resembles the DSM-IV-TR in proposing a research-based common vocabulary. A questionnaire, taken by some 1 million people worldwide (at viastrengths.org), assesses six clusters of 24 strengths:

- *Wisdom and knowledge*—creativity; curiosity; judgment and open-mindedness; love of learning; and perspective (wisdom)
- *Courage (overcoming opposition)*— bravery; perseverance; honesty; and zest
- *Humanity*—love; kindness; and social intelligence
- *Justice*—teamwork; fairness; and leadership

Building strengths In their work for Habitat for Humanity, former U.S. President Jimmy Carter and First Lady Rosalynn Carter model strengths related to humanity and justice.

- *Temperance*—forgiveness and mercy; modesty and humility; prudence; and self-regulation
- *Transcendence*—appreciation of beauty and excellence; gratitude; hope; humor; and religiousness and spirituality

Mental health workers have used these categories to get their clients to consider what makes for a good life—a life of engagement, meaning, and purpose—and to identify their own signature strengths. Researchers have studied the development of each strength and its associations with health and well-being. Consultants have assisted organizations in identifying and enhancing their collective strengths (Niemiec, 2009).

Labeling Psychological Disorders

4: **Why do some psychologists criticize the use of diagnostic labels?**

Let us remember the *benefits* of diagnostic labels. Mental health professionals use labels to communicate about their cases, to comprehend the underlying causes, and to discern effective treatment programs.

But the DSM has critics who register a fundamental complaint about these diagnostic labels—that they are at best arbitrary and at worst value judgments masquerading as science. Once we label a person, we view that person differently (Farina, 1982). Labels can bias perceptions and change reality. When teachers are told certain students are "gifted," when students expect someone to be "hostile," or when interviewers check to see whether someone is "extraverted," they may act in ways that elicit the very behavior expected (Snyder, 1984). Labels can serve as self-fulfilling prophecies.

In a now-classic study, David Rosenhan (1973) and seven others went to hospital admissions offices, complaining of "hearing voices" saying *empty, hollow,* and *thud.* Apart from this complaint and giving false names and occupations, they answered questions truthfully. All eight normal people were misdiagnosed with disorders. Should we be surprised? As one psychiatrist noted, if someone swallows blood, goes to an emergency room, and spits it up, should we fault the doctor for diagnosing a bleeding ulcer? Surely not. But what followed the diagnosis in the Rosenhan study was startling. Until being released an average of 19 days later, the "patients" exhibited no further symptoms. Yet after analyzing their (quite normal) life histories, clinicians were able to "discover" the causes of their disorders, such as

"What's the use of their having names," the Gnat said, "if they won't answer to them?"
"No use to *them,*" said Alice; "but it's useful to the people that name them, I suppose."

—Lewis Carroll,
Through the Looking Glass, 1871

"One of the unpardonable sins, in the eyes of most people, is for a man to go about unlabeled. The world regards such a person as the police do an unmuzzled dog, not under proper control."

—T. H. Huxley, *Evolution and Ethics,* 1893

reacting with mixed emotions about a parent. Even the routine behavior of taking notes was misinterpreted as a symptom. A label can, as Rosenhan discovered, have "a life and an influence of its own."

Surveys in Europe and North America have demonstrated the stigmatizing power of labels (Page, 1977). Getting a job or finding a place to rent can be a challenge for those known to be just released from prison—or a mental hospital. But as we are coming to understand that many psychological disorders are diseases of the brain, not failures of character, the stigma seems to be lifting (Solomon, 1996). Public figures are feeling freer to "come out" and speak with candor about their struggles with disorders. And the more contact people have with individuals with disorders, the more accepting their attitudes are (Kolodziej & Johnson, 1996).

© Mario Anzuoni/Reuters/Corbis

OCD advocate Comedian and TV host Howie Mandel knows the reality of obsessive-compulsive disorder. He has used humor to deal with his own challenges and to help others understand the disorder. Mandel also suffers a germ phobia that prompted him to shave his head to "feel cleaner."

Nevertheless, stereotypes linger in media portrayals of psychological disorders. Some are reasonably accurate and sympathetic. But too often people with disorders are portrayed as objects of humor or ridicule (*As Good as It Gets*), as homicidal maniacs (Hannibal Lecter in *Silence of the Lambs*), or as freaks (Nairn, 2007). Apart from the few who experience threatening delusions and hallucinated voices that command a violent act, mental disorders seldom lead to violence (Harris & Lurigio, 2007). In real life, people with disorders are more likely to be the victims of violence, rather than the perpetrators (Marley & Bulia, 2001). Indeed, reports the U.S. Surgeon General's Office (1999, p. 7), "There is very little risk of violence or harm to a stranger from casual contact with an individual who has a mental disorder." (Although most people with psychological disorders are not violent, those who are create a moral dilemma for society. For more on this topic, see Thinking Critically About: Insanity and Responsibility.

REHEARSE IT!

1. Although some psychological disorders are culture-bound, others are universal. For example, in every known culture some people have
   a. bulimia nervosa.
   b. anorexia nervosa.
   c. schizophrenia.
   d. susto.

2. If a lawyer washes his hands 100 times a day for no apparent reason and has no time left to meet with his clients, the hand washing will probably be labeled disordered because it is, among other things,
   a. distressing and dysfunctional.
   b. not explained by the medical model.

   c. harmful to others.
   d. untreatable.

3. A therapist says that psychological disorders are sicknesses and people with these disorders should be treated as patients in a hospital. This therapist believes in the
   a. social-cultural perspective.
   b. psychological model.
   c. medical model.
   d. diagnostic model.

4. Many psychologists reject the "disorders-as-illness" view and contend that other factors may also be involved—for example, the person's bad habits and poor social skills. This view represents the _____ approach.

   a. medical
   b. positive psychology
   c. biopsychosocial
   d. diagnostic labels

5. One study found that psychologists using the DSM-IV agreed on a diagnosis for more than 80 percent of patients. The DSM-IV's reliability stems in part from its reliance on
   a. structured-interview procedures.
   b. in-depth histories of the patients.
   c. input from patients' family and friends.
   d. the theories of Pinel, Freud, and others.

Answers: 1. c, 2. a, 3. c, 4. c, 5. a.

Thinking Critically About:

Insanity and Responsibility

"My brain . . . my genes . . . my bad upbringing made me do it." Such defenses were anticipated by Shakespeare's *Hamlet*. If I wrong someone when not myself, he explained, "then Hamlet does it not, Hamlet denies it. Who does it then? His madness." Such is the essence of a legal insanity defense, created in 1843 after a deluded Scotsman tried to shoot the prime minister (who he thought was persecuting him) but killed an assistant by mistake. Like U.S. President Ronald Reagan's near-assassin, John Hinckley, Scotsman Daniel M'Naughten was sent to a mental hospital rather than to prison.

In both cases, the public was outraged. "Hinckley Insane, Public Mad," declared one headline. And they were mad again when a deranged Jeffrey Dahmer in 1991 admitted murdering 15 young men and eating parts of their bodies. They were mad in 1998 when 15-year-old Kip Kinkel, driven by "those voices in my head," killed his parents and 2 fellow Springfield, Oregon, students and wounded 25 others. And they were mad in 2002 when Andrea Yates, after being taken off her antipsychotic medication, was tried in Texas for drowning her five children. All

Jail or hospital? Two weeks after being taken off antipsychotic medication by her psychiatrist, Andrea Yates drowned her five children, ages 7, 5, 3, 2, and 6 months, in her bathtub, apparently believing she was sparing them "the fires of hell." Although Yates was irrational and had lost contact with reality, one jury rejected the insanity defense, believing she still could have discerned right from wrong. On retrial, a second jury found her not guilty by reason of insanity.

of these people were sent to jails, not hospitals, following their arrests (though later, after another trial, Yates was instead hospitalized).

Most people with psychological disorders are not violent. But what should

society do with those who are? A 1999 U.S. Justice Department study found that about 16 percent of U.S. jail and prison inmates had severe mental disorders. This is roughly 100,000 more than the 183,000 psychiatric inpatients in all types of U.S. hospitals (Bureau of the Census, 2004; Butterfield, 1999). Many people who have been executed or are now on death row have been motivated by delusional voices or limited by intellectual disability (formerly called mental retardation). The State of Arkansas forcibly medicated one murderer with schizophrenia, Charles Singleton, with antipsychotic drugs—in order to make him mentally competent, so that he could then be put to death.

Which of Yates' two juries made the right decision? The first, which decided that people who commit such rare but terrible crimes should be held responsible? Or the second, which decided to blame the "madness" that clouds their vision? As we come to better understand the biological and environmental basis for all human behavior, from generosity to vandalism, when should we—and should we not—hold people accountable for their actions?

Anxiety Disorders

5: What are anxiety disorders, and how do they differ from ordinary worries and fears?

Anxiety is part of life. Speaking in front of a class, peering down from a ledge, or waiting to play in a big game, any one of us might feel anxious. At times we may feel enough anxiety to avoid making eye contact or talking with someone—"shyness," we call it. Fortunately for most of us, our uneasiness is not intense and persistent. If it becomes so, we may have one of the **anxiety disorders,** marked by distressing, persistent anxiety or dysfunctional anxiety-reducing behaviors. Let's consider these five:

- *Generalized anxiety disorder,* in which a person is unexplainably and continually tense and uneasy
- *Panic disorder,* in which a person experiences sudden episodes of intense dread
- *Phobias,* in which a person feels irrationally and intensely afraid of a specific object or situation
- *Obsessive-compulsive disorder,* in which a person is troubled by repetitive thoughts or actions
- *Post-traumatic stress disorder,* in which a person has lingering memories, nightmares, and other symptoms for weeks after a severely threatening, uncontrollable event

In its own way, each anxiety disorder harms quality of life (Olatunji et al., 2007).

anxiety disorders psychological disorders characterized by distressing, persistent anxiety or maladaptive behaviors that reduce anxiety.

Generalized Anxiety Disorder

For the past two years, Tom, a 27-year-old electrician, has been bothered by dizziness, sweating palms, heart palpitations, and ringing in his ears. He feels edgy and sometimes finds himself shaking. With reasonable success, he hides his symptoms from his family and co-workers. But he allows himself few other social contacts, and occasionally he has to leave work. His family doctor and a neurologist can find no physical problem.

Tom's unfocused, out-of-control, negative feelings suggest **generalized anxiety disorder.** The symptoms of this disorder are commonplace; their persistence is not. People with this condition (two-thirds are women) worry continually, and they are often jittery, agitated, and sleep-deprived. Concentration is difficult as attention switches from worry to worry, and their tension and apprehension may leak out through furrowed brows, twitching eyelids, trembling, perspiration, or fidgeting.

One of the worst characteristics of this disorder is that the person cannot identify, and therefore cannot deal with or avoid, its cause. To use Sigmund Freud's term, the anxiety is *free-floating.* Generalized anxiety disorder is often accompanied by depressed mood, but even without depression it tends to be disabling (Hunt et al., 2004; Moffitt et al., 2007b). Moreover, it may lead to physical problems, such as high blood pressure.

Many people with generalized anxiety disorder were maltreated and inhibited as children (Moffitt et al., 2007a). As time passes, however, emotions tend to mellow, and by age 50, generalized anxiety disorder becomes rare (Rubio & López-Ibor, 2007).

Panic Disorder

Panic disorder is an anxiety tornado. It strikes suddenly, wreaks havoc, and disappears. For the 1 person in 75 with this disorder, anxiety suddenly escalates into a terrifying *panic attack*—a minutes-long episode of intense fear that something horrible is about to happen. Heart palpitations, shortness of breath, choking sensations, trembling, or dizziness typically accompany the panic, which may be misperceived as a heart attack or other serious physical ailment. Smokers have at least a doubled risk of panic disorder (Zvolensky & Bernstein, 2005). Because nicotine is a stimulant, lighting up doesn't lighten up.

One woman recalled suddenly feeling "hot and as though I couldn't breathe. My heart was racing and I started to sweat and tremble and I was sure I was going to faint. Then my fingers started to feel numb and tingly and things seemed unreal. It was so bad I wondered if I was dying and asked my husband to take me to the emergency room. By the time we got there (about 10 minutes) the worst of the attack was over and I just felt washed out" (Greist et al., 1986).

Phobias

Phobias are anxiety disorders in which an irrational fear causes the person to avoid some object, activity, or situation. Many people accept their phobias and live with them, but others are incapacitated by their efforts to avoid the feared situation. Marilyn, an otherwise healthy and happy 28-year-old, so fears thunderstorms that she feels anxious as soon as a weather forecaster mentions possible storms later in the week. If her husband is away and a storm is forecast, she may stay with a close relative. During a storm, she hides from windows and buries her head to avoid seeing the lightning.

Other *specific phobias* may focus on animals, insects, heights, blood, or close spaces (**FIGURE 13.2**). People avoid the stimulus that arouses the fear, hiding during thunderstorms or avoiding high places.

Not all phobias have such specific triggers. *Social phobia* is shyness taken to an extreme. Those with a social phobia, an intense fear of being scrutinized by others, avoid potentially embarrassing social situations, such as speaking up, eating out, or going to parties—or will sweat, tremble, or have diarrhea when doing so.

generalized anxiety disorder an anxiety disorder in which a person is continually tense, apprehensive, and in a state of autonomic nervous system arousal.

panic disorder an anxiety disorder marked by unpredictable minutes-long episodes of intense dread in which a person experiences terror and accompanying chest pain, choking, or other frightening sensations.

phobia an anxiety disorder marked by a persistent, irrational fear and avoidance of a specific object, activity, or situation.

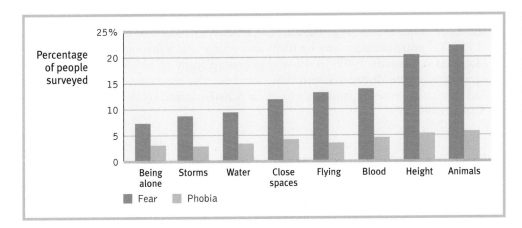

FIGURE 13.2 **Some common and uncommon specific fears** This national interview study identified the commonality of various specific fears. A strong fear becomes a phobia if it provokes a compelling but irrational desire to avoid the dreaded object or situation. (From Curtis et al., 1998.)

People who have experienced several panic attacks may come to fear the fear itself and avoid situations where the panic has struck before. If the fear is intense enough, it may become *agoraphobia,* fear or avoidance of situations in which escape might be difficult or help unavailable when panic strikes. Given such fear, people may avoid being outside the home, in a crowd, on a bus, or on an elevator.

After spending five years sailing the world, Charles Darwin began suffering panic attacks at age 28. He moved to the country, avoided social gatherings, and traveled only in his wife's company. But the relative seclusion did free him to focus on developing his evolutionary theory. "Even ill health," he reflected, "has saved me from the distraction of society and its amusements" (quoted in Ma, 1997).

Obsessive-Compulsive Disorder

As with generalized anxiety and phobias, we can see aspects of our own behavior in **obsessive-compulsive disorder (OCD).** We may at times be obsessed with senseless or offensive thoughts that will not go away. Or we may engage in compulsive behaviors, rigidly checking, ordering, and cleaning before guests arrive, or lining up books and pencils "just so" before studying.

Obsessive thoughts and compulsive behaviors cross the fine line between normality and disorder when they persistently interfere with everyday living and cause the person distress. Checking to see that you locked the door is normal; checking 10 times is not. Washing your hands is normal; washing so often that your skin becomes raw is not. (**TABLE 13.2** offers more examples.) At some time during their lives, often during their late teens or twenties, 2 to 3 percent of people cross that line from normal preoccupations and fussiness to debilitating disorder (Karno et

Snapshots

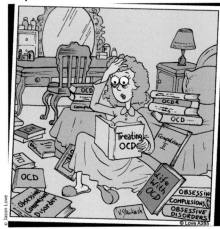

Obsessing about obsessive-compulsive disorder.

obsessive-compulsive disorder (OCD) an anxiety disorder characterized by unwanted repetitive thoughts (obsessions) and/or actions (compulsions).

TABLE 13.2 Common Obsessions and Compulsions Among Children and Adolescents With Obsessive-Compulsive Disorder

Thought or Behavior	Percentage Reporting Symptom
Obsessions *(repetitive thoughts)*	
Concern with dirt, germs, or toxins	40
Something terrible happening (fire, death, illness)	24
Symmetry, order, or exactness	17
Compulsions *(repetitive behaviors)*	
Excessive hand washing, bathing, tooth brushing, or grooming	85
Repeating rituals (in/out of a door, up/down from a chair)	51
Checking doors, locks, appliances, car brakes, homework	46

Source: Adapted from Rapoport, 1989.

al., 1988). The obsessive thoughts become so haunting, the compulsive rituals so senselessly time-consuming, that effective functioning becomes impossible.

OCD is more common among teens and young adults than among older people (Samuels & Nestadt, 1997). A 40-year follow-up study of 144 Swedish people diagnosed with the disorder found that, for most, the obsessions and compulsions had gradually lessened, though only 1 in 5 had completely recovered (Skoog & Skoog, 1999).

Post-Traumatic Stress Disorder

As an Army infantry scout during the Iraq War, Jesse "saw the murder of children, women. It was just horrible for anyone to experience." After calling in a helicopter strike on one house where he had seen ammunition crates carried in, he heard the screams of children from within. "I didn't know there were kids there," he recalls. Back home in Texas, he suffered "real bad flashbacks" (Welch, 2005).

Our memories exist in part to protect us in the future. So there is biological wisdom in not being able to forget our most emotional or traumatic experiences—our greatest embarrassments, our worst accidents, our most horrid experiences. But sometimes, for some of us, the unforgettable takes over our lives. The complaints of battled-scarred veterans such as Jesse—recurring haunting memories and nightmares, a numbed social withdrawal, jumpy anxiety, and/or insomnia—are typical of what once was called "shellshock" or "battle fatigue" and now is called **post-traumatic stress disorder (PTSD)** (Hoge et al., 2004; Kessler, 2000).

PTSD symptoms have also been reported by survivors of accidents, disasters, and violent and sexual assaults (including an estimated two-thirds of prostitutes) (Brewin et al., 1999; Farley et al., 1998; Taylor et al., 1998). A month after the 9/11 terrorist attacks, a survey of Manhattan residents indicated that 8.5 percent were suffering PTSD, most as a result of the attack (Galea et al., 2002). Among those living near the World Trade Center, 20 percent reported such telltale signs as nightmares, severe anxiety, and fear of public places (Susser et al., 2002).

To pin down the frequency of this disorder, the U.S. Centers for Disease Control (1988) compared 7000 Vietnam combat veterans with 7000 noncombat veterans who served during the same years. On average, according to a recent reanalysis, 19 percent of all Vietnam veterans reported PTSD symptoms. The rate varied from 10 percent among those who had never seen combat to 32 percent among those who had experienced heavy combat (Dohrenwend et al., 2006). Similar variations in rates have been found among people who have experienced a natural disaster or have been kidnapped, held captive, tortured, or raped (Brewin et al., 2000; Brody, 2000; Kessler, 2000; Stone, 2005).

The toll seems at least as high for veterans of the Iraq war, where 1 in 6 U.S. combat infantry personnel has reported symptoms of PTSD, depression, or severe anxiety in the months after returning home (Hoge et al., 2006, 2007). In one study of 103,788 veterans returning from Iraq and Afghanistan, 1 in 4 was diagnosed with a psychological disorder, most frequently PTSD (Seal et al., 2007).

So what determines whether a person develops PTSD after a traumatic event? Research indicates that the greater one's emotional distress during a trauma, the higher the risk for post-traumatic symptoms (Ozer et al., 2003). Among New Yorkers who witnessed the 9/11 attacks, PTSD was doubled for survivors who were inside rather than outside the World Trade Center (Bonanno et al., 2006). And the more frequent an assault experience, the more adverse the long-term outcome tends to be (Golding, 1999).

A sensitive limbic system seems to increase vulnerability, by flooding the body with stress hormones again and again as images of the traumatic experience erupt into consciousness (Kosslyn, 2005; Ozer & Weiss, 2004). Genes may also play a role. Some combat-exposed men have identical twins who did not experience

Gender and anxiety: Eight months after 9/11, more U.S. women (34 percent) than men (19 percent) told Gallup (2002) they were still less willing than before 9/11 to go into skyscrapers or fly on planes. In early 2003, more women (57 percent) than men (36 percent) were "somewhat worried" about becoming a terrorist victim (Jones, 2003).

Bringing the war home Many war veterans, such as this sergeant at a Veteran's Administration hospital, have recently been treated for post-traumatic stress disorder.

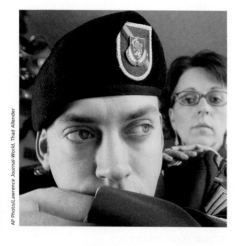

combat. But these nonexposed co-twins tend to share their brother's risk for cognitive difficulties, such as unfocused attention. Such findings suggest that some PTSD symptoms may actually be genetically predisposed (Gilbertson et al., 2006).

Some psychologists believe that PTSD has been overdiagnosed, due partly to a broadening definition of *trauma* (which originally meant direct exposure to threatened death or serious injury, as during combat or rape [McNally, 2003]). Well-intentioned attempts to help people avoid PTSD by reliving the trauma may exacerbate their emotions. "Debriefing" survivors right after a trauma by getting them to revisit the experience and vent emotions has actually proven generally ineffective and may pathologize normal stress reactions (Devilly et al., 2006; McNally et al., 2003; Rose et al., 2003; Wakefield & Spitzer, 2002).

Other researchers are interested in the impressive *survivor resiliency* of those who do *not* develop PTSD (Bonanno, 2004, 2005). About half of adults experience at least one traumatic event in their lifetime, but only about 1 in 10 women and 1 in 20 men develop PTSD (Olff et al., 2007; Ozer & Weiss, 2004; Tolin & Foa, 2006). More than 9 in 10 New Yorkers, although stunned and grief-stricken by 9/11, did *not* respond pathologically. By the following January, the stress symptoms of the rest had mostly subsided (Galea et al., 2002). Similarly, most combat-stressed veterans and most political dissidents who survive dozens of episodes of torture do not later exhibit PTSD (Mineka & Zinbarg, 1996).

Psychologist Peter Suedfeld (1998, 2000; Cassel & Suedfeld, 2006), who as a boy survived the Holocaust under deprived conditions while his mother died in Auschwitz, has documented the resilience of Holocaust survivors, most of whom lived productive lives. "It is not always true that 'What doesn't kill you makes you stronger,' but it is often true," he reports. And "what doesn't kill you may reveal to you just how strong you really are."

Indeed, suffering can lead to "benefit finding" (Helgeson et al., 2006), what Richard Tedeschi and Lawrence Calhoun (2004) call **post-traumatic growth.** Tedeschi and Calhoun have found that the struggle with challenging crises, such as facing cancer, often leads people later to report an increased appreciation for life, more meaningful relationships, increased personal strength, changed priorities, and a richer spiritual life. This idea—that suffering has transformative power—is also found in Judaism, Christianity, Hinduism, Buddhism, and Islam. Out of even our worst experiences some good can come. Like the body, the mind has great recuperative powers.

> "'Tis an ill wind that blows no good."
>
> —English proverb

Understanding Anxiety Disorders

6: **What produces the thoughts and feelings that mark anxiety disorders?**

Anxiety is both a feeling and a cognition, a doubt-laden appraisal of one's safety or social skill. How do these anxious feelings and cognitions arise? Freud's psychoanalytic theory proposed that, beginning in childhood, people *repress* intolerable impulses, ideas, and feelings and that this submerged mental energy sometimes produces mystifying symptoms, such as anxiety. Today's psychologists have turned to two contemporary perspectives—learning and biological.

The Learning Perspective

FEAR CONDITIONING When bad events happen unpredictably and uncontrollably, anxiety often develops (Field, 2006; Mineka & Zinbarg, 2006). Recall from Chapter 7 that dogs learn to fear neutral stimuli associated with shock and that infants have learned to fear furry objects associated with frightening noises. Using classical conditioning, researchers have also created chronically anxious, ulcer-prone rats by giving them unpredictable electric shocks (Schwartz, 1984). Like assault victims who report feeling anxious when returning to the scene of the crime,

post-traumatic stress disorder (PTSD) an anxiety disorder characterized by haunting memories, nightmares, social withdrawal, jumpy anxiety, and/or insomnia that lingers for four weeks or more after a traumatic experience.

post-traumatic growth positive psychological changes as a result of struggling with extremely challenging circumstances and life crises.

the rats become apprehensive in their lab environment. This link between conditioned fear and general anxiety helps explain why anxious people are hyperattentive to possible threats, and how panic-prone people come to associate anxiety with certain cues (Bar-Haim et al., 2007; Bouton et al., 2001). In one survey, 58 percent of those with social phobia experienced their disorder after a traumatic event (Ost & Hugdahl, 1981).

Two specific learning processes can contribute to such anxiety. The first is *stimulus generalization*. My car was once struck by another whose driver missed a stop sign. For months afterward, I felt a twinge of unease when any car approached from a side street. The second learning process, *reinforcement*, helps maintain our phobias and compulsions after they arise. Avoiding or escaping the feared situation reduces anxiety, thus reinforcing the phobic behavior. Feeling anxious during a thunderstorm, Marilyn may have fled to a relative's home and been reinforced by feeling calmer (Antony et al., 1992). Compulsive behaviors operate similarly. If washing your hands relieves your feelings of anxiety, you may wash your hands again when those feelings return.

OBSERVATIONAL LEARNING We may also learn fear through observational learning—by observing others' fears. As Susan Mineka (1985) demonstrated, wild monkeys transmit their fear of snakes to their watchful offspring. Human parents similarly transmit fears to their children. Moreover, just observing someone receiving a mild electric shock after a conditioned stimulus produces fear learning similar to that produced by direct experience (Olsson & Phelps, 2004).

The Biological Perspective

There is, however, more to anxiety than conditioning and observational learning. The biological perspective can help us understand why few people develop lasting phobias after suffering traumas, why we learn some fears more readily, and why some individuals are more vulnerable.

NATURAL SELECTION We humans seem biologically prepared to fear threats faced by our ancestors. Our phobias focus on such specific fears: spiders, snakes, and other animals; close spaces and heights; storms and darkness. (Those fearless about these occasional threats were less likely to survive and leave descendants.) Preschool children more speedily detect snakes in a scene than they do flowers, caterpillars, or frogs (LoBue & DeLoache, 2008). And even in Britain, with only one poisonous snake species, people often fear snakes. It is easy to condition and hard to extinguish fears of such stimuli (Davey, 1995; Öhman, 1986).

Our *modern* fears can also have an evolutionary explanation. For example, a fear of flying may come from our biological predisposition to fear confinement and heights. Moreover, consider what people tend *not* to learn to fear. World War II air raids produced remarkably few lasting phobias. As the air blitzes continued, the British, Japanese, and German populations became not more panicked, but rather more indifferent to planes outside their immediate neighborhoods (Mineka & Zinbarg, 1996). Evolution has not prepared us to fear bombs dropping from the sky.

Just as our phobias focus on dangers faced by our ancestors, our compulsive acts typically exaggerate behaviors that contributed to our species' survival. Grooming gone wild becomes hair pulling. Washing up becomes ritual hand washing. Checking territorial boundaries becomes rechecking an already locked door (Rapoport, 1989).

GENES Pair a traumatic event with a sensitive, high-strung temperament and the result may be a new phobia. Genes matter.

Among monkeys, fearfulness runs in families. Individual monkeys react more strongly to stress if their close biological relatives are anxiously reactive (Suomi, 1986). Some humans, too, seem more predisposed than others to anxiety. Vulnerability to

An emotional high Fearing heights is certainly an adaptive response. The biological perspective helps us understand why most people would be terrified in this situation, and why some individuals—like this construction worker—seem relatively free of that fear.

John Coletti/Stock, Boston

anxiety disorder rises when an afflicted relative is an identical twin (Hettema et al., 2001; Kendler et al., 1992, 1999, 2002a,b). Identical twins also may develop similar phobias, even when raised separately (Carey, 1990; Eckert et al., 1981). One pair of 35-year-old female identical twins independently became so afraid of water that each would wade in the ocean backward and only up to the knees.

Researchers sleuthing specific genes that put people at risk have identified 17 that appear to be expressed with typical anxiety disorder symptoms (Hovatta et al., 2005). Another team found genes associated specifically with OCD (Hu et al., 2006). Genes influence disorders by regulating neurotransmitters. One anxiety gene affects brain levels of serotonin, which influences sleep and mood (Canli, 2008). Other genes regulate the neurotransmitter glutamate (Lafleur et al., 2006; Welch et al., 2007). With too much glutamate, the brain's alarm centers become overactive.

THE BRAIN Generalized anxiety, panic attacks, PTSD, and even obsessions and compulsions are manifested biologically as an overarousal of brain areas involved in impulse control and habitual behaviors. When the disordered brain detects that something is amiss, it seems to generate a mental hiccup of repeating thoughts or actions (Gehring et al., 2000). Brain scans of people with OCD reveal elevated activity in specific brain areas during behaviors such as compulsive hand washing, checking, ordering, or hoarding (Mataix-Cols et al., 2004, 2005). As **FIGURE 13.3** shows, the *anterior cingulate cortex*, a brain region that monitors our actions and checks for errors, seems especially likely to be hyperactive in those with OCD (Ursu et al., 2003). Fear-learning experiences that traumatize the brain can also create fear circuits within the amygdala (Etkin & Wager, 2007; Kolassa & Elbert, 2007; Maren, 2007). Some antidepressant drugs dampen this fear-circuit activity and its associated obsessive-compulsive behavior.

The biological perspective cannot by itself explain all aspects of anxiety disorders, such as the sharp increase in the anxiety levels of both children and college students over the last half-century, which appears to be related to fraying social support accompanying family breakup (Twenge, 2006). It is nevertheless clear that biology underlies anxiety.

S. Ursu, V. A. Stenger, M. K. Shear, M. R. Jones, & C. S. Carter (2003). Overactive action monitoring in obsessive-compulsive disorder. *Psychological Science, 14,* 347–353.

FIGURE 13.3 An obsessive-compulsive brain Neuroscientist Stefan Ursu and his colleagues (2003) used functional magnetic resonance imaging (fMRI) scans to compare the brains of those with and without OCD as they engaged in a challenging cognitive task. The fMRI scans showed elevated activity in the anterior cingulate cortex in the brain's frontal area of those with OCD.

REHEARSE IT!

6. An episode of intense dread, accompanied by trembling, dizziness, chest pains, or choking sensations and by feelings of terror, is called
   a. a specific phobia.
   b. compulsion.
   c. a panic attack.
   d. an obsessive fear.

7. Anxiety that takes the form of an irrational and maladaptive fear of a specific object or situation is called
   a. a phobia.
   b. a panic attack.
   c. generalized anxiety.
   d. an obsessive-compulsive disorder.

8. Marina became consumed with the need to clean the entire house and refused to participate in any other activities. A therapist Marina consulted diagnosed her as having
   a. obsessive-compulsive disorder.
   b. generalized anxiety disorder.
   c. a phobia.
   d. a panic attack.

9. Rats subjected to unpredictable shocks in the laboratory become chronically anxious. To the learning researcher this suggests that anxiety is a response to
   a. a phobia.
   b. biological factors.
   c. a genetic predisposition.
   d. fear conditioning.

10. The learning perspective proposes that phobias are
   a. the result of individual genetic makeup.
   b. a way of repressing unacceptable impulses.
   c. conditioned fears.
   d. a symptom of having been abused as a child.

Answers: 6. c, 7. a, 8. a, 9. d, 10. c.

Somatoform Disorders

7: What are somatoform disorders?

Among the most common problems bringing people into doctors' offices are "medically unexplained illnesses" (Johnson, 2008). Ellen becomes dizzy and nauseated in the late afternoon—shortly before she expects her husband home. Neither her primary care physician nor the neurologist he sent her to could identify a physical cause. They suspect her symptoms have an unconscious psychological origin, possibly triggered by her mixed feelings about her husband. In **somatoform disorders,** such as Ellen's, the distressing symptoms take a somatic (bodily) form without apparent physical causes. One person may have a variety of complaints—vomiting, dizziness, blurred vision, difficulty in swallowing. Another may experience severe and prolonged pain.

Culture has a big effect on people's physical complaints and how they explain them (Kirmayer & Sartorius, 2007). In China, psychological explanations of anxiety and depression are socially less acceptable than in many Western countries. People express the emotional aspects of distress less often, and they appear more sensitive to—and more willing to report—the physical symptoms of their distress (Ryder et al., 2008). Mr. Wu, a 36-year-old technician in Hunan, illustrates one of China's most common psychological disorders (Spitzer & Skodol, 2000). He finds work difficult because of his insomnia, fatigue, weakness, and headaches. Chinese herbs and Western medicines provide no relief. To his Chinese clinician, who treats the bodily symptoms, Mr. Wu seems not so much depressed as exhausted.

Even to people in the West, somatic symptoms are familiar. To a lesser extent, we have all experienced inexplicable physical symptoms under stress. It is little comfort to be told that the problem is "all in your head." Although the symptoms may be psychological in origin, they are nevertheless genuinely felt.

One type of somatoform disorder, more common in Freud's day than in ours, is **conversion disorder,** so called because anxiety presumably is converted into a physical symptom, such as unexplained paralysis, blindness, or an inability to swallow. (As we noted in Chapter 12, Freud's effort to treat and understand psychological disorders stemmed from his puzzlement over ailments that had no physiological basis.) In each case, the physical symptoms would be real, although no physiological basis could be found.

As you can imagine, somatoform disorders send people not to a psychologist or psychiatrist but to a physician. This is especially true of those who experience **hypochondriasis.** In this relatively common somatoform disorder, people interpret normal sensations (a stomach cramp today, a headache tomorrow) as symptoms of a dreaded disease. Sympathy or temporary relief from everyday demands may reinforce such complaints. No amount of reassurance by any physician convinces the patient not to worry. So the patient moves on to another physician, seeking and receiving more medical attention—but failing to confront the disorder's psychological root.

Dissociative Disorders

8: What are dissociative disorders, and why are they controversial?

Among the most bewildering disorders are the rare **dissociative disorders.** These are disorders of consciousness, in which a person appears to experience a sudden loss of memory or change in identity, often in response to an overwhelmingly stressful situation. One Vietnam veteran who was haunted by his comrade's deaths, and who had left his World Trade Center office shortly before the 9/11 attack, disappeared en route to work one day and was discovered six months later in a Chicago

somatoform disorder psychological disorder in which the symptoms take a somatic (bodily) form without apparent physical cause. (See *conversion disorder* and *hypochondriasis.*)

conversion disorder a rare somatoform disorder in which a person experiences very specific genuine physical symptoms for which no physiological basis can be found.

hypochondriasis a somatoform disorder in which a person interprets normal physical sensations as symptoms of a disease.

dissociative disorders disorders in which conscious awareness becomes separated (dissociated) from previous memories, thoughts, and feelings.

dissociative identity disorder (DID) a rare dissociative disorder in which a person exhibits two or more distinct and alternating personalities. Formerly called *multiple personality disorder.*

homeless shelter, reportedly with no memory of his identity or family (Stone, 2006). In such cases, the person's conscious awareness is said to *dissociate* (become separated) from painful memories, thoughts, and feelings. (Note that this explanation presumes the existence of repressed memories, which, as we noted in Chapters 8 and 12, have been questioned by memory researchers.)

Dissociation itself is not so rare. Now and then, many people may have a sense of being unreal, of being separated from their body, of watching themselves as if in a movie. Sometimes we may say, "I was not myself at the time." Perhaps you can recall getting in your car and driving to some unintended location while your mind was preoccupied elsewhere. Facing trauma, such detachment may actually protect a person from being overwhelmed by emotion.

Dissociative Identity Disorder

A massive dissociation of self from ordinary consciousness characterizes those with **dissociative identity disorder** (**DID;** formerly called *multiple personality disorder*), in which two or more distinct identities are said to alternately control the person's behavior. Each personality has its own voice and mannerisms. Thus, the person may be prim and proper one moment, loud and flirtatious the next. Typically, the original personality denies any awareness of the other(s).

Understanding Dissociative Identity Disorder

Skeptics question whether DID is a genuine disorder or an extension of our normal capacity for personality shifts. Nicholas Spanos (1986, 1994, 1996) asked college students to pretend they were accused murderers being examined by a psychiatrist. Given a hypnotic treatment that "called forth" a second personality, most spontaneously expressed such. This discovery made Spanos wonder: Are dissociative identities simply a more extreme version of our capacity to vary the "selves" we present—as when we display a goofy, loud self while hanging out with friends, and a subdued, respectful self around grandparents? Are clinicians who discover multiple personalities merely triggering role-playing by fantasy-prone people? Do these patients, like actors who commonly report "losing themselves" in their roles, then convince themselves of the authenticity of their own role enactments?

Skeptics also find it suspicious that the disorder is so localized in time and space. Between 1930 and 1960, the number of DID diagnoses in North America was 2 per decade. In the 1980s, when the DSM contained the first formal code for this disorder, the number of reported cases had exploded to more than 20,000 (McHugh, 1995a). The average number of displayed personalities also mushroomed—from 3 to 12 per patient (Goff & Simms, 1993). Outside North America, the disorder is much less prevalent, although in other cultures some people are said to be "possessed" by an alien spirit (Aldridge-Morris, 1989; Kluft, 1991). In Britain, DID—which some consider "a wacky American fad" (Cohen, 1995)—is rare. In India and Japan, it is essentially nonexistent.

Such findings, skeptics say, point to a cultural phenomenon—a disorder created by therapists in a particular social context (Merskey, 1992). Patients do not enter therapy saying "Allow me to introduce myselves." Rather, note skeptics, some therapists—often practitioners of hypnosis (Goff, 1993; Piper, 1998)—go fishing for multiple personalities: "Have you ever felt like another part of you does things you can't control? Does this part of you have a name? Can I talk to the angry part of you?" Once patients permit a therapist to talk, by name, "to the part of you that says those angry things" they have begun acting out the fantasy. The result may be a real phenomenon, which vulnerable patients may experience as another self.

Other psychologists disagree, finding support for DID as a genuine disorder in the distinct brain and body states associated with differing personalities (Putnam,

Multiple personalities Chris Sizemore's story, *The Three Faces of Eve,* gave early visibility to what is now called *dissociative identity disorder.*

"Pretense may become reality."

—Chinese proverb

"Would it be possible to speak with the personality that pays the bills?"

1991). Handedness, for example, sometimes switches with personality (Henninger, 1992). Ophthalmologists have detected shifting visual acuity and eye-muscle balance as patients switched personalities, changes that did not occur among control group members trying to simulate DID (Miller et al., 1991).

Researchers and clinicians from psychoanalytic and learning perspectives do, however, agree that DID symptoms are ways of dealing with anxiety. Psychoanalysts see them as defenses against the anxiety caused by the eruption of unacceptable impulses; a wanton second personality enables the discharge of forbidden impulses. Learning theorists see dissociative disorders as behaviors reinforced by anxiety reduction.

Other clinicians include dissociative disorders under the umbrella of posttraumatic disorders—a natural, protective response to "histories of childhood trauma" (Putnam, 1995; Spiegel, 2008). Many DID patients recall suffering physical, sexual, or emotional abuse as children (Gleaves, 1996; Lilienfeld et al., 1999). In one study of 12 murderers diagnosed with DID, 11 had suffered severe, torturous child abuse (Lewis et al., 1997). One was set afire by his parents. Another was used in child pornography and was scarred from being made to sit on a stove burner. Some critics wonder, however, whether vivid imagination or therapist suggestions contribute to such recollections (Kihlstrom, 2005).

So the debate continues. On one side are those who believe multiple personalities are the desperate efforts of the traumatized to detach from a horrific existence. On the other are the skeptics who think DID is a condition contrived by fantasy-prone, emotionally vulnerable people, and constructed out of the therapist-patient interaction. If the skeptics' view wins, predicted psychiatrist Paul McHugh (1995b), "this epidemic will end in the way that the witch craze ended in Salem. The [multiple personality phenomenon] will be seen as manufactured."

> "Though this be madness, yet there is method in 't."
>
> —William Shakespeare, *Hamlet,* 1600

REHEARSE IT!

11. One relatively common disorder is
a. conversion disorder.
b. hypochondriasis.
c. dissociative identity disorder.
d. multiple personality disorder.

12. Dissociative identity disorder is relatively rare. This disorder is controversial because
a. criminals have used it as a defense.
b. it was reported frequently in the 1920s but rarely today.
c. it is almost never reported outside North America.
d. its symptoms are nearly identical to those of obsessive-compulsive disorder.

Answers: 11. b, 12. c.

Mood Disorders

9: What are mood disorders, and what forms do they take?

The emotional extremes of **mood disorders** take two principal forms: (1) *major depressive disorder,* with its prolonged hopelessness and lethargy, and (2) *bipolar disorder* (formerly called *manic-depressive disorder*), in which a person alternates between depression and *mania,* an overexcited, hyperactive state.

Major Depressive Disorder

Joy, contentment, sadness, and despair are different points on a continuum, points at which any of us may be found at any given moment. If you are like most college students, at some time during this year—more likely the dark months of winter than the bright days of summer—you will probably experience a few of depression's symptoms. You may feel deeply discouraged about the future, dissatisfied with your life, or socially isolated. You may lack the energy to get things done or even to force

For some people, recurring depression during winter's dark months constitutes a seasonal affective disorder. *For others, winter darkness means more blue moods. When asked "Have you cried today?" Americans answered "Yes" more often in the winter.*

Percentage answering yes

	Men	Women
August	*4%*	*7%*
December	*8%*	*21%*

Source: Time/CNN survey, 1994

yourself out of bed; be unable to concentrate, eat, or sleep normally; or even wonder if you would be better off dead. Perhaps academic success came easily to you in high school, and now you find that disappointing grades jeopardize your goals. Maybe social stresses, such as feeling you don't belong or experiencing the end of a romance, have plunged you into despair. And maybe brooding has at times only worsened your self-torment. You are not alone. In one survey of 90,000 American college and university students, 44 percent reported that on one or more occasions within the last school year, they had felt "so depressed it was difficult to function" (ACHA, 2006).

Depression has been called the "common cold" of psychological disorders—an expression that effectively describes its pervasiveness but not its seriousness. Although phobias are more common, depression is the number-one reason people seek mental health services. At some point during their lifetime, 12 percent of Canadian adults and 13 percent of U.S. adults have experienced a depressive disorder (Hasin et al., 2005; Patten et al., 2006). Moreover, depression is the leading cause of disability worldwide (WHO, 2002). In any given year, a depressive episode plagues 5.8 percent of men and 9.5 percent of women, reports the World Health Organization.

As anxiety is a response to the threat of future loss, depressed mood is often a response to past and current loss. To feel bad in reaction to profoundly sad events is to be in touch with reality. In such times, depression is like a car's low–oil-pressure light—a signal that warns us to stop and take protective measures. Recall that, biologically speaking, life's purpose is not happiness but survival and reproduction. Coughing, vomiting, and various forms of pain protect the body from dangerous toxins. Similarly, depression is a sort of psychic hibernation: It slows us down, defuses aggression, and restrains risk taking (Allen & Badcock, 2003). To grind temporarily to a halt and ruminate, as depressed people do, is to reassess one's life when feeling threatened and to redirect energy in more promising ways (Watkins, 2008). There is sense to suffering.

But prolonged, this response can become seriously maladaptive. The difference between a blue mood after bad news and a mood disorder is like the difference between gasping for breath after a hard run and being chronically short of breath.

Major depressive disorder occurs when at least five signs of depression (including lethargy, feelings of worthlessness, or loss of interest in family, friends, and activities) last two or more weeks and are not caused by drugs or a medical condition. To sense what major depression feels like, suggest some clinicians, imagine combining the anguish of grief with the sluggishness of jet lag.

Bipolar Disorder

With or without therapy, episodes of major depression usually end, and people temporarily or permanently return to a more normal state. However, some people rebound to, or sometimes start with, the opposite emotional extreme—the euphoric, hyperactive, wildly optimistic state of **mania**. If depression is living in slow motion, mania is fast forward. Alternating between depression and mania signals **bipolar disorder.**

Adolescent mood swings, from rage to bubbly, can, when prolonged, produce a bipolar diagnosis. Between 1994 and 2003, U.S. National Center for Health Statistics annual physician surveys revealed an astonishing 40-fold increase in diagnoses of bipolar disorder in those 19 and under—from an estimated 20,000 to 800,000 (Carey, 2007; Moreno et al., 2007). The new popularity of the diagnosis, given in two-thirds of the cases to boys, has been a boon to companies whose drugs are prescribed to lessen mood swings.

During the manic phase, people with bipolar disorder are typically overtalkative, overactive, and elated (though easily irritated if crossed); have little need for sleep;

"My life had come to a sudden stop. I was able to breathe, to eat, to drink, to sleep. I could not, indeed, help doing so; but there was no real life in me."

—Leo Tolstoy, *My Confession*, 1887

"If someone offered you a pill that would make you permanently happy, you would be well advised to run fast and run far. Emotion is a compass that tells us what to do, and a compass that is perpetually stuck on NORTH is worthless."

—Daniel Gilbert, "The Science of Happiness," 2006

mood disorders psychological disorders characterized by emotional extremes. See *major depressive disorder, mania,* and *bipolar disorder.*

major depressive disorder a mood disorder in which a person experiences, in the absence of drugs or a medical condition, two or more weeks of significantly depressed moods, feelings of worthlessness, and diminished interest or pleasure in most activities.

mania a mood disorder marked by a hyperactive, wildly optimistic state.

bipolar disorder a mood disorder in which the person alternates between the hopelessness and lethargy of depression and the overexcited state of mania. (Formerly called *manic-depressive disorder.*)

Creativity and bipolar disorders History has given us many creative artists, composers, and writers with bipolar disorder, including (left to right) Walt Whitman, Virginia Woolf, Samuel Clemens (Mark Twain), and Ernest Hemingway.

"All the people in history, literature, art, whom I most admire: Mozart, Shakespeare, Homer, El Greco, St. John, Chekhov, Gregory of Nyssa, Dostoevsky, Emily Brontë: not one of them would qualify for a mental-health certificate."

—Madeleine L'Engle, *A Circle of Quiet*, 1972

and show fewer sexual inhibitions. Speech is loud, flighty, and hard to interrupt. They find advice irritating, yet they need protection from their own poor judgment, which may lead to reckless spending or unsafe sex.

In milder forms, mania's energy and free-flowing thinking does fuel creativity. George Frideric Handel (1685–1759), who may have suffered from a mild form of bipolar disorder, composed his nearly four-hour-long *Messiah* during three weeks of intense, creative energy (Keynes, 1980). Robert Schumann composed 51 musical works during two years of mania (1840 and 1849) and none during 1844, when he was severely depressed (Slater & Meyer, 1959). Those who rely on precision and logic, such as architects, designers, and journalists, are less likely to have bipolar disorder than are those who rely on emotional expression and vivid imagery (Ludwig, 1995). Composers, artists, poets, novelists, and entertainers seem especially prone (Jamison, 1993, 1995; Kaufman & Baer, 2002; Ludwig, 1995).

It is as true of emotions as of everything else: What goes up comes down. Before long, the elated mood either returns to normal or plunges into a depression. Though bipolar disorder is much less common than major depressive disorder, it is often more dysfunctional, claiming twice as many lost workdays yearly (Kessler et al., 2006). Among adults, it afflicts men and women about equally.

Understanding Mood Disorders

10: What causes mood disorders, and what might explain the Western world's rising incidence of depression among young people?

In thousands of studies, psychologists have been accumulating evidence to help explain mood disorders and suggest more effective ways to treat and prevent them. Researcher Peter Lewinsohn and his colleagues (1985, 1998, 2003) have summarized the facts that any theory of depression must explain, including the following:

- *Many behavioral and cognitive changes accompany depression.* People trapped in a depressed mood are inactive and feel unmotivated. They are sensitive to negative happenings, more often recall negative information, and expect negative outcomes (my team will lose, my grades will fall, my love will fail). When the mood lifts, these behavioral and cognitive accompaniments disappear. Nearly half the time, people also exhibit symptoms of another disorder, such as anxiety or substance abuse.
- *Depression is widespread.* Its commonality suggests that its causes, too, must be common.
- *Compared with men, women are nearly twice as vulnerable to major depression* (FIGURE 13.4). This gender gap begins in adolescence; preadolescent girls are not more depression-prone than boys (Hyde et al., 2008). The factors that put women at risk for depression (genetic predispositions, child abuse, low

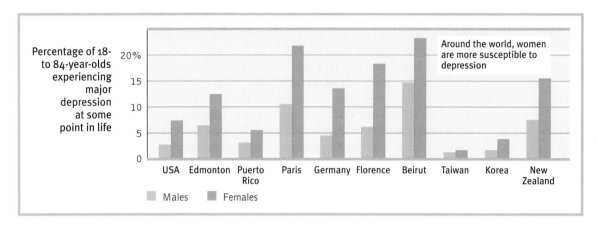

Percentage of 18- to 84-year-olds experiencing major depression at some point in life

Around the world, women are more susceptible to depression

USA Edmonton Puerto Rico Paris Germany Florence Beirut Taiwan Korea New Zealand

■ Males   ■ Females

FIGURE 13.4 **Gender and major depression**
Interviews with 38,000 adults in 10 countries confirm what many smaller studies have found: Women's risk of major depression is nearly double that of men's. Lifetime risk of depression also varies by culture—from 1.5 percent in Taiwan to 19 percent in Beirut. (Data from Weissman et al., 1996.)

self-esteem, marital problems, and so forth) similarly put men at risk (Kendler et al., 2006). Yet women are more vulnerable to disorders involving internalized states, such as depression, anxiety, and inhibited sexual desire. Men's disorders tend to be more external—alcohol abuse, antisocial conduct, lack of impulse control. When women get sad, they often get sadder than men do. When men get mad, they often get madder than women do.

- ***Most major depressive episodes self-terminate.***
  Therapy tends to speed recovery, yet most people suffering major depression eventually return to normal even without professional help. The plague of depression comes and, a few weeks or months later, it goes, though it sometimes recurs (Burcusa & Iacono, 2007). About 50 percent of those who recover from depression will experience another episode within two years. Recovery is more likely to be permanent the later the first episode strikes, the longer the person stays well, the fewer the previous episodes, the less stress experienced, and the more social support received (Belsher & Costello, 1988; Fergusson & Woodward, 2002; Kendler et al., 2001).

- ***Stressful events related to work, marriage, and close relationships often precede depression.*** A family member's death, a job loss, a marital crisis, or a physical assault increase one's risk of depression. If stress-related anxiety is a "crackling, menacing brushfire," notes biologist Robert Sapolsky (2003), "depression is a suffocating heavy blanket thrown on top of it." One long-term study (Kendler, 1998) tracked rates of depression in 2000 people. The risk of depression ranged from less than 1 percent among those who had experienced no stressful life event in the preceding month to 24 percent among those who had experienced three such events in that month.

- ***With each new generation, depression is striking earlier (now often in the late teens) and affecting more people.*** This is true in Canada, the United States, England, France, Germany, Italy, Lebanon, New Zealand, Puerto Rico, and Taiwan (Collishaw et al., 2007; Cross-National Collaborative Group, 1992; Twenge et al., 2008). In one study, 12 percent of Australian adolescents reported symptoms of depression (Sawyer et al., 2000). Most hid it from their parents; almost 90 percent of those parents perceived their depressed teen as *not* suffering depression. In North America, today's young adults are three times more likely than their grandparents to report having recently—or ever—suffered depression (despite the grandparents' many more years of being at risk). The increase appears partly authentic, but it may also reflect today's young adults' greater willingness to disclose depression.

The emotional lives of men and women?

"I see depression as the plague of the modern era."

—Lewis Judd, former chief, National Institute of Mental Health, 2000

Researchers may accept these facts without agreeing how best to explain them. For example, proponents of Sigmund Freud's psychoanalytic theory (or the more modern psychodynamic approach) have an idea: Depression often occurs when significant losses, such as the breakup of a current romantic relationship, evoke feelings associated with losses experienced in childhood (the intimate relationship with one's mother, for example). Alternatively, these theorists may view depression as unresolved anger toward one's parents, turned inward against oneself.

Most contemporary researchers propose biological and cognitive explanations of depression, often combined in a biopsychosocial perspective.

> "Could bad cognitions be the hex, instead of conflicts over sex?"
>
> —Psychiatrist Robert L. Spitzer et al. (1982)

The Biological Perspective

Most recent mental health research dollars have funded explorations of biological influences on mood disorders. Areas of interest have been genetic predispositions, brain activity, and biochemical imbalances.

GENETIC INFLUENCES We have long known that mood disorders run in families. As one researcher noted, emotions are "postcards from our genes" (Plotkin, 1994).

Close-Up:

Suicide

> "But life, being weary of these worldly bars, Never lacks power to dismiss itself."
>
> —William Shakespeare, *Julius Caesar*, 1599

Each year nearly 1 million despairing people worldwide will elect a permanent solution to what might have been a temporary problem (WHO, 2008). Comparing the suicide rates of different groups, researchers have found

- *national differences:* Britain's, Italy's, and Spain's suicide rates are little more than half those of Canada, Australia, and the United States. Austria's and Finland's are about double (WHO, 2008). Within Europe, the most suicide-prone people (Lithuanians) have been 14 times more likely to kill themselves than the least (Greeks).
- *racial differences:* Within the United States, Whites are nearly twice as likely as Blacks to kill themselves (NIMH, 2002).
- *gender differences:* Women are much more likely than men to attempt suicide (WHO, 2008). But men are two to four times more likely (depending on the country) to succeed (Figure 13.5). Men use more lethal methods, such as firing

a bullet into the head, the method of choice in 6 of 10 U.S. suicides.

- *age differences and trends:* In late adulthood, rates increase, dramatically so among men (**FIGURE 13.5**). In the last half of the twentieth century, the global rate of annual suicide deaths rose from 10 to 18 per 100,000 (WHO, 2008).
- *other group differences:* Suicide rates are much higher among the rich, the nonreligious, and those who are single, widowed, or divorced (Hoyer & Lund, 1993; Stack, 1992; Stengel, 1981). Gay and lesbian youth much more often suffer distress and attempt suicide than do their heterosexual peers (Goldfried, 2001). Among 1.3 million Swedish military conscripts at age 18, the thinner men were more likely than their rounder age-mates to later commit suicide (Magnusson et al., 2006).

The risk of suicide is at least five times greater for those who have been depressed than for the general population

(Bostwick & Pankratz, 2000). People seldom commit suicide while in the depths of depression, when energy and initiative are lacking. It is when they begin to rebound and become capable of following through that the risk increases. Compared with people who suffer no disorder, those with alcohol dependency are roughly 100 times more likely to commit suicide; some 3 percent of them do (Murphy & Wetzel, 1990; Sher, 2006). Even among people who have attempted suicide, those who abuse alcohol are five times more likely than others to kill themselves eventually (Beck & Steer, 1989). Teenage suicides are often linked with drug and alcohol abuse; the final act may follow a traumatic event, such as a romantic breakup or a guilt-provoking antisocial act (Fowler et al., 1986; Kolata, 1986). Because suicide is so often an impulsive act, environmental barriers (such as jump barriers on high bridges and the unavailability of loaded guns) can reduce suicides (Anderson, 2008). Although common sense might suggest that a determined person would simply find another way to complete the act, such restrictions give time for self-destructive impulses to subside.

Social suggestion can act as a trigger. Following highly publicized suicides in

The risk of major depression and bipolar disorder increases if you have a parent or sibling with the disorder (Sullivan et al., 2000). If one identical twin is diagnosed with major depressive disorder, the chances are about 1 in 2 that at some time the other twin will be, too. If one identical twin has bipolar disorder, the chances are 7 in 10 that the other twin will at some point be diagnosed similarly. Among fraternal twins, the corresponding odds are just under 2 in 10 (Tsuang & Faraone, 1990). The greater similarity among identical twins holds even among twins reared apart (DiLalla et al., 1996). Summarizing the major twin studies, Kenneth Kendler and his co-researchers (2006) estimate that the heritability of major depression is 35 to 40 percent.

Moreover, adopted people with mood disorders often have close biological relatives who have mood disorders, become dependent on alcohol, or commit suicide (Wender et al., 1986). (See Close-Up: Suicide.)

To tease out the genes that put people at risk for depression, some researchers have turned to *linkage analysis*. After finding families in which the disorder appears across several generations, geneticists examine DNA from affected and unaffected family members, looking for differences. Linkage analysis points us to a chromosome neighborhood, note behavior genetics researchers Robert Plomin and Peter

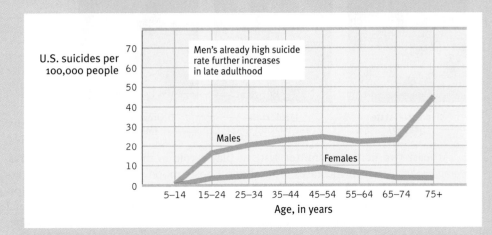

FIGURE 13.5 Suicide rates by gender and age Worldwide suicide rates are higher among males than among females. The highest rates of all are found among older men. (From *Statistical Abstract*, 2008.)

real life or in TV programs, known suicides increase. So do fatal auto and private airplane "accidents." One six-year study tracked suicide cases among all 1.2 million people who lived in metropolitan Stockholm at any time during the 1990s (Hedström et al., 2008). Men exposed to a co-worker's suicide were 3.5 times more likely to kill themselves than were nonexposed men.

Suicide is not necessarily an act of hostility or revenge. The elderly sometimes choose death as an alternative to current or future suffering. During the recent economic crisis, calls for help increased— from 42,406 calls to the National Suicide Prevention Lifeline[1] in April 2008, to 51,465 in April 2009.

People of all ages may view suicide as a way of switching off unendurable pain and relieving a perceived burden on family members. "People desire death when two fundamental needs are frustrated to the point of extinction," notes Thomas Joiner (2006, p. 47): "The need to belong with or connect to others, and the need to feel effective with or to influence others."

In retrospect, families and friends may recall signs that they believe should have

[1] 1-800-273-TALK (in USA)

forewarned them—verbal hints, giving possessions away, or withdrawal and preoccupation with death. But few who talk or think of suicide (a number that includes one-third of all adolescents and college students) actually attempt it, and only about 1 in 25 who make the attempt will complete the act (AAS, 2009). But about 30,000 do succeed, one-third of whom have tried to kill themselves previously. Most discussed it beforehand. So, if a friend talks suicide to you, it's important to listen and to direct the person to professional help. Anyone who threatens suicide is at least sending a signal of feeling desperate or despondent.

Gene-hunters' pursuit of bipolar-DNA links Linkage studies seek to identify aberrant genes in family members suffering a disorder. These Pennsylvania Amish family members—an isolated population sharing a common life-style and some vulnerability to bipolar disorder—have volunteered for such studies.

McGuffin (2003); "a house-to-house search is then needed to find the culprit gene." Such studies are reinforcing the view that depression is a complex condition. Many genes probably work together, producing a mosaic of small effects that interact with other factors to put some people at greater risk.

THE DEPRESSED BRAIN Using modern technology, researchers are also gaining insight into brain activity during depressed and manic states, and into the effects of certain neurotransmitters during these states. Many studies have found less activity in the brain during slowed-down depressive states, and more activity during periods of mania (**FIGURE 13.6**). The left frontal lobe, which is active during positive emotions, is likely to be inactive during depressed states (Davidson et al., 2002). In one study of people with severe depression, MRI scans found their frontal lobes 7 percent smaller than normal (Coffey et al., 1993). Other studies show that the *hippocampus,* the memory-processing center linked with the brain's emotional circuitry, is vulnerable to stress-related damage.

FIGURE 13.6 The ups and downs of bipolar disorder These top-facing PET scans show that brain energy consumption rises and falls with the patient's emotional switches. Red areas are where the brain rapidly consumes glucose.

| Depressed state (May 17) | Manic state (May 18) | Depressed state (May 27) |

At least two neurotransmitter systems play a role in mood disorders. The first, *norepinephrine,* which increases arousal and boosts mood, is scarce during depression and overabundant during mania. (Drugs that alleviate mania reduce norepinephrine.) Most people with a history of depression also have a history of habitual smoking. This may indicate an attempt to self-medicate with inhaled nicotine, which can temporarily increase norepinephrine and boost mood (HMHL, 2002).

The second neurotransmitter, *serotonin,* is also scarce during depression. Some genes now under scrutiny provide codes for a protein that controls serotonin activity (Plomin & McGuffin, 2003). A widely publicized study of New Zealand young adults seemed to identify a serotonin-controlling gene that, in combination with significant stress, formed a recipe for depression (Caspi et al., 2003; Moffitt et al., 2006). Alas, other recent studies failed to replicate the finding (Risch et al., 2009). But stay tuned: Science grows by fits and starts.

Drugs that relieve depression tend to increase norepinephrine or serotonin supplies by blocking either their reuptake (as Prozac, Zoloft, and Paxil do with serotonin) or their chemical breakdown. Repetitive physical exercise, such as jogging, reduces depression as it increases serotonin (Ilardi et al., 2007; Jacobs, 1994). Boosting serotonin may promote recovery from depression by stimulating hippocampus neuron growth (Airan et al., 2007; Jacobs et al., 2000).

The Social-Cognitive Perspective

Depression is a whole-body disorder resulting from the interaction of many factors (**FIGURE 13.7**). Biological influences contribute to depression but don't fully explain it. The social-cognitive perspective explores the roles of thinking and acting.

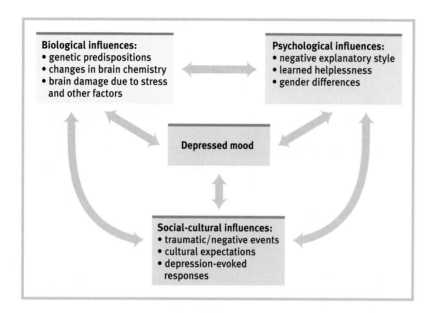

FIGURE 13.7 **Biopsychosocial approach to depression** Seriously depressed moods result from a combination of interacting factors. Altering any one component can alter the others.

Depressed people view life through dark glasses. Their intensely negative assumptions about themselves, their situation, and their future lead them to magnify bad experiences and minimize good ones. Listen to Norman, a Canadian college professor, recalling his depression:

> I [despaired] of ever being human again. I honestly felt subhuman, lower than the lowest vermin. Furthermore, I was self-deprecatory and could not understand why anyone would want to associate with me, let alone love me. . . . I was positive that I was a fraud and a phony and that I didn't deserve my Ph.D. I didn't deserve to have tenure; I didn't deserve to be a Full Professor. . . . I didn't deserve the research grants I had been awarded; I couldn't understand how I had written books and journal articles. . . . I must have conned a lot of people. (Endler, 1982, pp. 45–49)

Research reveals how s*elf-defeating beliefs* and a *negative explanatory style* feed depression's vicious cycle.

NEGATIVE THOUGHTS AND NEGATIVE MOODS INTERACT Self-defeating beliefs may arise from *learned helplessness.* As we saw in Chapter 12, both dogs and humans act depressed, passive, and withdrawn after experiencing uncontrollable painful events. Learned helplessness is more common in women than in men, and women may respond more strongly to stress (Hankin & Abramson, 2001; Mazure et al., 2002; Nolen-Hoeksema, 2001, 2003). For example, 38 percent of women and 17 percent of men entering American colleges and universities report feeling "frequently overwhelmed by all I have to do" (Pryor et al., 2006). (Men report spending more of their time in "light anxiety" activities such as sports, TV watching, and partying, possibly avoiding activities that might make them feel overwhelmed.) This may help explain why, beginning in their early teens, women are nearly twice as vulnerable to depression (Kessler, 2001). Susan Nolen-Hoeksema (2003) believes women's higher risk of depression may also be related to what she describes as their tendency to *overthink,* to ruminate. Women often have vivid recall for both wonderful and horrid experiences; men more vaguely recall such experiences (Seidlitz & Diener, 1998). The gender difference in emotional memory may feed women's greater rumination over negative events and explain why fewer men than women report being frequently overwhelmed on entering college.

But why do life's unavoidable failures lead some people—women or men—and not others to become depressed? The answer lies partly in their *explanatory style*— who or what they blame for their failures. Think how you might feel if you failed a

Susan Nolen-Hoeksema "This epidemic of morbid meditation is a disease that women suffer much more than men. Women can ruminate about anything and everything—our appearance, our families, our career, our health." (*Women Who Think Too Much: How to Break Free of Overthinking and Reclaim Your Life,* 2003)

"I have learned to accept my mistakes by referring them to a personal history which was not of my making."

—B. F. Skinner (1983)

From 1985 to 2004, Americans indeed reported fewer close relationships with co-workers, extended family, and neighbors, and thus had fewer people with whom they could discuss meaningful matters. The number of people with no confidantes increased from 10 to 25 percent (McPherson et al., 2006).

test. If you can externalize the blame ("What an unfair test!"), you are more likely to feel angry. But if you blame yourself, you probably will feel stupid and depressed.

So it is with depressed people, who tend to explain bad events in terms that are *stable* ("It's going to last forever"), *global* ("It's going to affect everything I do"), and *internal* ("It's all my fault") (**FIGURE 13.8**). Depression-prone people respond to bad events in an especially self-focused, self-blaming way (Mor & Winquist, 2002; Pyszczynski et al., 1991; Wood et al., 1990a,b). Their self-esteem fluctuates more rapidly up with boosts and down with threats (Butler et al., 1994).

The result of these pessimistic, overgeneralized, self-blaming attributions may be a depressing sense of hopelessness (Abramson et al., 1989; Panzarella et al., 2006). As Martin Seligman has noted, "A recipe for severe depression is preexisting pessimism encountering failure" (1991, p. 78). What then might we expect of new college students who are not depressed but do exhibit a pessimistic explanatory style? Lauren Alloy and her collaborators (1999) monitored Temple University and University of Wisconsin students every 6 weeks for 2.5 years. Among those identified as having a pessimistic thinking style, 17 percent had a first episode of major depression, as did only 1 percent of those who began college with an optimistic thinking style. Follow-up research has found that students who exhibit optimism as they begin college develop more social support, which contributes to a lowered risk of depression (Brissette et al., 2002).

Seligman (1991, 1995) contends that depression is common among young Westerners because the rise of individualism and the decline of commitment to religion and family have forced young people to take personal responsibility for failure or rejection. In non-Western cultures, where close-knit relationships and cooperation are the norm, major depression is less common and less tied to self-blame over personal failure (WHO, 2004). In Japan, for example, depressed people instead tend to report feeling shame over letting others down (Draguns, 1990a).

There is, however, a chicken-and-egg problem with the social-cognitive explanation of depression. Self-defeating beliefs, negative attributions, and self-blame surely do support depression. Peter Barnett and Ian Gotlib (1988) have noted that such cognitions *coincide* with a depressed mood and are *indicators* of depression. But

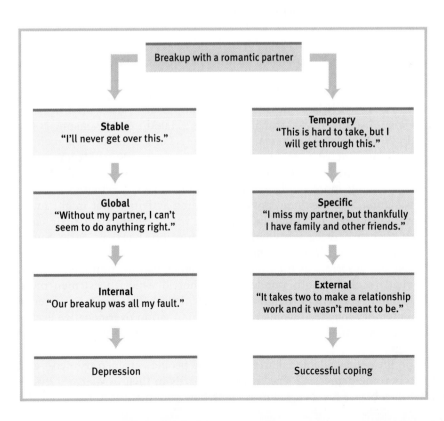

FIGURE 13.8 Explanatory style and depression

PEANUTS

Might Charlie Brown be helped by an optimism-training program?

do they *cause* depression, any more than a speedometer's reading of 70 mph causes a car's speed? Before or after being depressed, people's thoughts are less negative. Perhaps this is because, as we noted in our discussion of state-dependent memory (Chapter 8), a depressed mood triggers negative thoughts. If you temporarily put people in a bad or sad mood, their memories, judgments, and expectations suddenly become more pessimistic.

DEPRESSION'S VICIOUS CYCLE Depression, as we have seen, is often brought on by stressful experiences—losing a job, getting divorced or rejected, suffering physical trauma—by anything that disrupts our sense of who we are and why we are worthy human beings. This disruption in turn leads to brooding, which amplifies negative feelings. But being withdrawn, self-focused, and complaining can by itself elicit rejection (Furr & Funder, 1998; Gotlib & Hammen, 1992). In one study, researchers Stephen Strack and James Coyne (1983) noted that "depressed persons induced hostility, depression, and anxiety in others and got rejected. Their guesses that they were not accepted were not a matter of cognitive distortion." Indeed, people in the throes of depression are at high risk for divorce, job loss, and other stressful life events. Weary of the person's fatigue, hopeless attitude, and lethargy, a spouse may threaten to leave or a boss may begin to question the person's competence. The losses and stress only serve to compound the original depression. Rejection and depression feed each other. Misery may love another's company, but company does not love another's misery.

We can now assemble some of the pieces of the depression puzzle (**FIGURE 13.9**): (1) Negative, stressful events interpreted through (2) a ruminating, pessimistic explanatory style create (3) a hopeless, depressed state that (4) hampers the way the person thinks and acts. This, in turn, fuels (1) negative stressful experiences such as rejection.

It is a cycle we can all recognize. Bad moods feed on themselves: When we *feel* down, we *think* negatively and remember bad experiences. On the brighter side, we can break the cycle of depression at any of these points—by moving to a different environment, by reversing our self-blame and negative attributions, by turning our attention outward, or by engaging in more pleasant activities and more competent behavior.

> "Man never reasons so much and becomes so introspective as when he suffers, since he is anxious to get at the cause of his sufferings."
>
> —Luigi Pirandello, *Six Characters in Search of an Author*, 1922

FIGURE 13.9 The vicious cycle of depressed thinking Cognitive therapists attempt to break this cycle, as we will see in Chapter 14, by changing the way depressed people process events. Psychiatrists attempt to alter with medication the biological roots of persistently depressed moods.

Diagram:
1 Stressful experiences → 2 Negative explanatory style → 3 Depressed mood → 4 Cognitive and behavioral changes → (back to 1)

Winston Churchill called depression a "black dog" that periodically hounded him. Poet Emily Dickinson was so afraid of bursting into tears in public that she spent much of her adult life in seclusion (Patterson, 1951). As these lives reminds us, people can and do struggle through depression. Most regain their capacity to love, to work, and even to succeed at the highest levels.

REHEARSE IT!

13. The disorder that is so common it has been called the "common cold" of psychological disorders is
    a. mania.
    b. depression.
    c. bipolar disorder.
    d. suicide.

14. Although bipolar disorder is as maladaptive as depression, it is much less common and it affects
    a. more women than men.
    b. more men than women.
    c. women and men equally.
    d. primarily scientists and doctors.

15. Depression affects many people, often following a stressful event, such as divorce or job change. The rate of depression is
    a. increasing among young people.
    b. decreasing among young people.
    c. increasing among elderly women.
    d. decreasing among elderly women.

16. Depression can often be alleviated by drugs that increase supplies of the neurotransmitters
    a. acetylcholine and dopamine.
    b. glycine and GABA.

    c. endorphin and glutamate.
    d. norepinephrine and serotonin.

17. Psychologists who emphasize the importance of negative perceptions, beliefs, and thoughts in depression are working within the _____ perspective.
    a. psychoanalytic
    b. biological
    c. behavioral
    d. social-cognitive

Answers: 13. b, 14. c, 15. a, 16. d, 17. d.

Schizophrenia

11: What patterns of thinking, perceiving, feeling, and behaving characterize schizophrenia?

If depression is the common cold of psychological disorders, chronic schizophrenia is the cancer. Nearly 1 in 100 people will develop schizophrenia, joining the estimated 24 million across the world who suffer one of humanity's most dreaded disorders (WHO, 2008). Schizophrenia is a disease of the brain exhibited in symptoms of the mind.

Symptoms of Schizophrenia

Literally translated, **schizophrenia** means "split mind." It refers not to a multiple-personality split but rather to a split from reality that shows itself in disorganized thinking, disturbed perceptions, and inappropriate emotions and actions. As such, it is the chief example of a **psychotic disorder,** a disorder marked by irrationality and lost contact with reality.

Disorganized Thinking

Imagine trying to communicate with Maxine, a young woman whose thoughts spill out in no logical order. Her biographer, Susan Sheehan (1982, p. 25), observed her saying aloud to no one in particular, "This morning, when I was at Hillside [Hospital], I was making a movie. I was surrounded by movie stars. . . . I'm Mary Poppins. Is this room painted blue to get me upset? My grandmother died four weeks after my eighteenth birthday."

As this strange monologue illustrates, the thinking of a person with schizophrenia is fragmented, bizarre, and often distorted by false beliefs called **delusions** ("I'm Mary Poppins"). Those with *paranoid* tendencies are particularly prone to delusions of persecution. Even within sentences, jumbled ideas may create what is called *word salad*. One young man begged for "a little more allegro in the treatment," and suggested that "liberationary movement with a view to the widening of the horizon" will "ergo extort some wit in lectures."

schizophrenia a group of severe disorders characterized by disorganized and delusional thinking, disturbed perceptions, and inappropriate emotions and actions.

psychotic disorder a psychological disorder in which a person loses contact with reality, experiencing irrational ideas and distorted perceptions.

delusions false beliefs, often of persecution or grandeur, that may accompany psychotic disorders.

Disorganized thoughts may result from a breakdown in *selective attention,* the normal ability to give undivided attention to one set of sensory stimuli while filtering out others. For someone with schizophrenia, irrelevant, minute stimuli, such as the grooves on a brick or the inflections of a voice, may distract attention from a bigger event. As one former patient recalled, "What had happened to me . . . was a breakdown in the filter, and a hodge-podge of unrelated stimuli were distracting me from things which should have had my undivided attention" (MacDonald, 1960, p. 218). This selective-attention difficulty is but one of dozens of cognitive differences associated with schizophrenia (Reichenberg & Harvey, 2007).

Disturbed Perceptions

A person with schizophrenia may have *hallucinations* (sensory experiences without sensory stimulation), seeing, feeling, tasting, or smelling things that are not there. One of this book's reviewers recalls a psychiatric ward experience with two patients: One *believed* he was Jesus Christ (a delusion), while the other *saw* Jesus (a hallucination). Most often, however, hallucinations are auditory, frequently voices making insulting remarks or giving orders. The voices may tell the patient that she is bad or that she must burn herself with a cigarette lighter. Imagine your own reaction if a dream broke into your waking consciousness. When the unreal seems real, the resulting perceptions are at best bizarre, at worst terrifying.

Inappropriate Emotions and Actions

The emotions of schizophrenia are often utterly inappropriate, split off from reality. Maxine laughed after recalling her grandmother's death. On other occasions, she cried when others laughed, or became angry for no apparent reason. Others with schizophrenia lapse into an emotionless state of *flat affect.*

Motor behavior may also be inappropriate. Some perform senseless, compulsive acts, such as continually rocking or rubbing an arm. Others, who exhibit *catatonia,* may remain motionless for hours and then become agitated.

As you can imagine, such disorganized thinking, disturbed perceptions, and inappropriate emotions and actions profoundly disrupt social relationships and make it difficult to hold a job. Given a supportive environment, some eventually recover to enjoy a normal life or experience bouts of schizophrenia only intermittently. Others remain in their private inner world, withdrawn and isolated throughout much of their lives.

Onset and Development of Schizophrenia

Schizophrenia typically strikes as young people are maturing into adulthood. It knows no national boundaries, and it affects both males and females—though men tend to be struck earlier, more severely, and slightly more often (Aleman et al.,

"When someone asks me to explain schizophrenia I tell them, you know how sometimes in your dreams you are in them yourself and some of them feel like real nightmares? My schizophrenia was like I was walking through a dream. But everything around me was real. At times, today's world seems so boring and I wonder if I would like to step back into the schizophrenic dream, but then I remember all the scary and horrifying experiences."

—Stuart Emmons, with Craig Geisler, Kalman J. Kaplan, and Martin Harrow, *Living With Schizophrenia,* 1997

Art by people diagnosed with schizophrenia Commenting on the kind of art work shown here, poet and art critic John Ashbery wrote: "The lure of the work is strong, but so is the terror of the unanswerable riddles it proposes."

2003; Picchioni & Murray, 2007). Studies of Swedish and Danish male populations reveal that thin young men, and those who were not breast-fed, are more vulnerable (Sørensen et al., 2005, 2006; Zammit et al., 2007).

Schizophrenia patients with *positive symptoms* may experience hallucinations, talk in disorganized and deluded ways, and exhibit inappropriate laughter, tears, or rage. Those with *negative symptoms* have toneless voices, expressionless faces, or mute and rigid bodies. Thus, positive symptoms are the *presence* of inappropriate behaviors, and negative symptoms are the *absence* of appropriate behaviors.

For some, schizophrenia will appear suddenly, seemingly as a reaction to stress. For others, as was the case with Maxine, schizophrenia develops gradually, emerging from a long history of social inadequacy (which helps explain why those predisposed to schizophrenia often end up in the lower socioeconomic levels, or even homeless).

One rule holds true around the world: When schizophrenia is a slow-developing process (called *chronic*, or *process*, *schizophrenia*), recovery is doubtful (WHO, 1979, 2009). Those with chronic schizophrenia often exhibit the persistent and incapacitating negative symptom of social withdrawal (Kirkpatrick et al., 2006). Men, whose schizophrenia develops on average four years earlier than women's, more often exhibit negative symptoms and chronic schizophrenia (Räsänen et al., 2000). When previously well-adjusted people develop schizophrenia rapidly (called *acute*, or *reactive*, *schizophrenia*) following particular life stresses, recovery is much more likely. They more often have the positive symptoms that are more likely to respond to drug therapy (Fenton & McGlashan, 1991, 1994; Fowles, 1992).

Understanding Schizophrenia

12: **What causes schizophrenia?**

We have thus far described schizophrenia as if it were a single disorder. Actually, it is a cluster of disorders. The subtypes share some common features, but they also have some distinguishing symptoms (**TABLE 13.3**). Schizophrenia is not only the most dreaded psychological disorder but also one of the most heavily researched. Because it is a cluster of disorders, its varied symptoms could have more than one cause. Most of the new research studies link these disorders with brain abnormalities and genetic predispositions.

TABLE 13.3 **Subtypes of Schizophrenia**

Paranoid:	Preoccupation with delusions or hallucinations, often with themes of persecution or grandiosity
Disorganized:	Disorganized speech or behavior, or flat or inappropriate emotion
Catatonic:	Immobility (or excessive, purposeless movement), extreme negativism, and/or parrotlike repeating of another's speech or movements
Undifferentiated:	Many and varied symptoms
Residual:	Withdrawal, after hallucinations and delusions have disappeared

Brain Abnormalities

Might imbalances in brain chemistry underlie schizophrenia? Scientists have long known that strange behavior can have strange chemical causes. The saying "mad as a hatter" refers to the psychological deterioration of British hatmakers whose brains, it was later discovered, were slowly poisoned as they moistened the brims of mercury-laden felt hats with their lips (Smith, 1983). Research on neurotransmitters, including studies on the mechanism by which chemicals such as LSD produce hallucinations, hint that schizophrenia symptoms might have a biochemical key.

DOPAMINE OVERACTIVITY Researchers discovered one such key when they examined schizophrenia patients' brains after death and found an excess of receptors for *dopamine*—a sixfold excess for the so-called D4 dopamine receptor (Seeman et al., 1993; Wong et al., 1986). They speculate that such a high level may intensify brain signals in schizophrenia, creating positive symptoms such as hallucinations and paranoia. As we might therefore expect, drugs that block dopamine receptors often lessen these symptoms; drugs that increase dopamine levels, such as amphetamines and cocaine, sometimes intensify them (Swerdlow & Koob, 1987). Dopamine overactivity may underlie patients' overreactions to irrelevant external and internal stimuli.

About 60 percent of schizophrenia patients smoke, often heavily. Nicotine apparently stimulates certain brain receptors, which helps focus attention (Javitt & Coyle, 2004).

ABNORMAL BRAIN ACTIVITY AND ANATOMY Modern brain-scanning techniques reveal that many people with chronic schizophrenia have abnormal activity in multiple brain areas. Some have abnormally low activity in the frontal lobes, which are critical for reasoning, planning, and problem solving (Morey et al., 2005; Pettegrew et al., 1993; Resnick, 1992). People diagnosed with schizophrenia also display a noticeable decline in the brain waves that reflect synchronized neural firing in the frontal lobes (Spencer et al., 2004; Symond et al., 2005). Out-of-sync neurons may disrupt the integrated functioning of neural networks, possibly contributing to schizophrenia symptoms.

One study took PET scans of brain activity while people were hallucinating (Silbersweig et al., 1995). When participants heard a voice or saw something, their brain became vigorously active in several core regions, including the thalamus, a structure deep in the brain that filters incoming sensory signals and transmits them to the cortex. Another PET scan study of people with paranoia found increased activity in the amygdala, a fear-processing center (Epstein et al., 1998).

Many studies have found enlarged, fluid-filled areas and a corresponding shrinkage of cerebral tissue in people with schizophrenia (Wright et al., 2000). Some studies have even found such abnormalities in the brains of people who would *later* develop this disorder, and in their close relatives (Boos et al., 2007; Job et al., 2006). The greater the shrinkage, the more severe the thought disorder (Collinson et al., 2003; Nelson et al., 1998; Shenton, 1992). One smaller-than-normal area is the cortex. Another is the thalamus, which may explain why people with schizophrenia have difficulty filtering sensory input and focusing attention (Andreasen et al., 1994). The bottom line of various studies is that schizophrenia involves not one isolated brain abnormality but problems with several brain regions and their interconnections (Andreasen, 1997, 2001).

Naturally, scientists wonder what causes these abnormalities. Some suspect a mishap during prenatal development or delivery. Two known risk factors for schizophrenia are low birth weight and oxygen deprivation during delivery (Buka et al., 1999; Zornberg et al., 2000). Famine may also increase risks. People conceived during the peak of the Dutch wartime famine later displayed a doubled rate of schizophrenia, as did those conceived during the famine of 1959 to 1961 in eastern China (St. Clair et al., 2005; Susser et al., 1996).

MATERNAL VIRUS DURING MIDPREGNANCY Consider another possible culprit: a midpregnancy viral infection that impairs fetal brain development (Patterson, 2007). Can you imagine some ways to test this fetal-virus idea? Scientists have asked the following:

- *Are people at increased risk of schizophrenia if, during the middle of their fetal development, their country experienced a flu epidemic?* The repeated answer is *yes* (Mednick et al., 1994; Murray et al., 1992; Wright et al., 1995).
- *Are people born in densely populated areas, where viral diseases spread more readily, at greater risk for schizophrenia?* The answer, confirmed in a study of 1.75 million Danes, is *yes* (Jablensky, 1999; Mortensen, 1999).

Studying the neurophysiology of schizophrenia Psychiatrist E. Fuller Torrey is collecting the brains of hundreds of those who died as young adults and suffered disorders such as schizophrenia and bipolar disorder. Torrey is making tissue samples available to researchers worldwide.

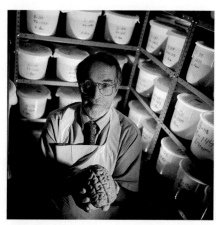

Chris Usher

- *Are those born during the winter and spring months—after the fall-winter flu season—also at increased risk?* The answer is again *yes*, at 5 to 8 percent increased risk (Torrey et al., 1997, 2002).
- *In the Southern Hemisphere, where the seasons are the reverse of the Northern Hemisphere, are the months of above-average schizophrenia births similarly reversed?* Again, the answer is *yes*, though somewhat less so. In Australia, for example, people born between August and October are at greater risk—*unless* they migrated from the Northern Hemisphere, in which case their risk is greater if they were born between January and March (McGrath et al., 1995, 1999).
- *Are mothers who report being sick with influenza during pregnancy more likely to bear children who develop schizophrenia?* In one study of nearly 8000 women, the answer was *yes*. The schizophrenia risk increased from the customary 1 percent to about 2 percent—but only when infections occurred during the second trimester (Brown et al., 2000).
- *Does blood drawn from pregnant women whose offspring develop schizophrenia show higher-than-normal levels of antibodies that suggest a viral infection?* In one study of 27 women whose children later developed schizophrenia, the answer was *yes* (Buka et al., 2001). And the answer was again *yes* in a huge California study, which collected blood samples from some 20,000 pregnant women during the 1950s and 1960s. Some children born of those pregnancies were later diagnosed with schizophrenia. When antibodies in the mother's blood indicated she had been exposed to influenza during the first half of the pregnancy, the child's risk of developing schizophrenia tripled. Flu during the second half of the pregnancy produced no such increase (Brown et al., 2004).

These converging lines of evidence suggest that fetal-virus infections play a contributing role in the development of schizophrenia. They also strengthen the recommendation that "women who will be more than three months pregnant during the flu season" have a flu shot (CDC, 2003).

Why might a second-trimester maternal flu bout put fetuses at risk? Is it the virus itself? The mother's immune response to it? Medications taken? (Wyatt et al., 2001). Does the infection weaken the brain's supportive glial cells, leading to reduced synaptic connections (Moises et al., 2002)? In time, answers may become available.

Genetic Factors

Fetal-virus infections do appear to increase the odds that a child will develop schizophrenia. But this theory cannot tell us why only 2 percent of women who catch the flu during their second trimester of pregnancy bear children who develop schizophrenia. Might people also inherit a predisposition to this disorder? The evidence strongly suggests that, *yes*, some do. The nearly 1-in-100 odds of any person's being diagnosed with schizophrenia become about 1 in 10 among those whose sibling or parent has the disorder, and close to 1 in 2 if the affected sibling is an identical twin (**FIGURE 13.10**). And, although only a dozen or so such cases are on record, the co-twin of an identical twin with schizophrenia retains that 1-in-2 chance when the twins are reared apart (Plomin et al., 1997).

Nevertheless, the fact remains: Some identical twins, despite their shared genes, do not share a schizophrenia diagnosis (**FIGURE 13.11**). This difference tells us that genes are not the whole story.

Remember that identical twins also share a prenatal environment. About two-thirds also share a placenta and the blood it supplies; the other one-third have two single placentas, as do

FIGURE 13.10 Risk of developing schizophrenia The lifetime risk of developing schizophrenia varies with one's genetic relatedness to someone having this disorder. Across countries, barely more than 1 in 10 fraternal twins, but some 5 in 10 identical twins, share a schizophrenia diagnosis. (Adapted from Gottesman, 2001.)

No schizophrenia   Schizophrenia

FIGURE 13.11 Different but identical twins When twins differ, only the one afflicted with schizophrenia typically has enlarged, fluid-filled cranial cavities (right) (Suddath et al., 1990). The difference between the twins implies some non-genetic factor, such as a virus, is also at work.

fraternal twins. If an identical twin has schizophrenia, the co-twin's chances of being similarly afflicted are 6 in 10 if they shared a placenta. If they had separate placentas, the chances are only 1 in 10 (Davis et al., 1995a,b; Phelps et al., 1997). Twins who share a placenta are more likely to experience the same prenatal viruses. So it is possible that shared germs as well as shared genes produce identical twin similarities.

Adoption studies, however, confirm that the genetic link is real (Gottesman, 1991). Children adopted by someone who develops schizophrenia seldom "catch" the disorder. Rather, adopted children have an elevated risk if a biological parent is diagnosed with schizophrenia.

With the genetic factor established, researchers are now sleuthing specific genes that, in some combination, might predispose schizophrenia-inducing brain abnormalities (Marx, 2007; Millar et al., 2005; Williams et al., 2007). (It is not our genes but our brains that directly control our behavior.) Some of these genes influence the effects of dopamine and other neurotransmitters in the brain. Others affect the production of *myelin*, a fatty substance that coats the axons of some nerve cells and lets impulses travel at high speed through neural networks.

Although the genetic contribution to schizophrenia is beyond question, the genetic formula is not as straightforward as the inheritance of eye color. A complex cluster of disorders such as those found in schizophrenia is surely influenced by multiple genes with small effects, but identifying these genes has proven difficult (McClellan et al., 2007; Sanders et al., 2008; Walsh et al., 2008). And even within this context, other factors—such as the prenatal viral infections, nutritional deprivation, and oxygen deprivation at birth mentioned earlier—may somehow help to "turn on" the genes that predispose some of us to this disease. As we have so often seen, nature and nurture interact. Neither hand claps alone.

Our knowledge of human genetics and of genetic influences on maladies such as schizophrenia is exploding, thanks partly to millions of new U.S. National Institute of Mental Health dollars focused on solving the schizophrenia riddle. In 2007, one privately funded new research center announced its ambitious aim: "To unambiguously diagnose patients with psychiatric disorders based on their DNA sequence in 10 years' time" (Holden, 2007). So, can scientists develop genetic tests that reveal who is at risk? If so, will people in the future subject their embryos to genetic testing (and gene repair or abortion) if they are at risk for this or some other psychological or physical malady? Might they take their egg and sperm to a genetics lab for screening before combining them to produce an embryo? Or will children be tested for genetic risks and given appropriate preventive treatments? In this brave new twenty-first-century world, such questions await answers.

The Genain quadruplets The odds of any four people picked at random all being diagnosed with schizophrenia are 1 in 100 million. But genetically identical sisters Nora, Iris, Myra, and Hester Genain all have the disease. Two of the sisters have more severe forms of the disorder than the others, suggesting the influence of environmental as well as biological factors.

Psychological Factors

If prenatal viruses and genetic predispositions do not, by themselves, cause schizophrenia, neither do family or social factors alone. Psychologists who once attributed schizophrenia to cold and capricious "refrigerator mothers" have long since abandoned this idea. It remains true, as Susan Nicol and Irving Gottesman (1983) noted almost three decades ago, that "no environmental causes have been discovered that will invariably, or even with moderate probability, produce schizophrenia in persons who are not related to" a person with schizophrenia.

Personality Disorders

13: What characteristics are typical of personality disorders?

Personality disorders are disruptive, inflexible, and enduring behavior patterns that impair people's social functioning. One cluster of these disorders expresses eccentric behaviors, such as the emotionless disengagement of *schizoid personality disorder*. A second cluster expresses anxiety, such as a fearful sensitivity to rejection that predisposes the withdrawn *avoidant personality disorder*. A third cluster exhibits dramatic or impulsive behaviors, such as the attention-getting *histrionic personality disorder* and the self-focused and self-inflating *narcissistic personality disorder*. The personality disorders categories are not sharply distinguished, however, and likely will be reworked in the next DSM revision (Clark, 2007; Widiger & Trull, 2007).

Antisocial Personality Disorder

The most troubling and heavily researched personality disorder is the **antisocial personality disorder.** The person (formerly called a *sociopath* or a *psychopath*) is typically a male whose lack of conscience becomes plain before age 15, as he begins to lie, steal, fight, or display unrestrained sexual behavior (Cale & Lilienfeld, 2002). About half of such children become antisocial adults—unable to keep a job, irresponsible as a spouse and parent, and assaultive or otherwise criminal (Farrington, 1991). When the antisocial personality combines a keen intelligence with amorality, the result may be a charming and clever con artist—or worse.

Despite their antisocial behavior, many criminals do not fit the description of antisocial personality disorder. Why? Because they actually show responsible concern for their friends and family members. Antisocial personalities feel and fear little, and in extreme cases, the results can be horrifyingly tragic. Henry Lee Lucas confessed that during his 32 years of crime, he had bludgeoned, suffocated, stabbed, shot, or mutilated some 360 women, men, and children—the first (a woman) at age 13. During the last 6 years of his reign of terror, Lucas teamed with Elwood Toole,

Antisocial personality? Dennis Rader, known as the "BTK killer" in Kansas, was convicted in 2005 of killing 10 people over a 30-year span. Rader exhibited the extreme lack of conscience that marks antisocial personality disorder.

EPA/Jeff Tuttle/Landov

who reportedly slaughtered about 50 people he "didn't think was worth living anyhow." It ended when Lucas confessed to stabbing and dismembering his 15-year-old common-law wife, who was Toole's niece.

The antisocial personality expresses little regret over violating others' rights. "Once I've done a crime, I just forget it," said Lucas. Toole was equally matter-of-fact: "I think of killing like smoking a cigarette, like another habit" (Darrach & Norris, 1984).

"Thursday is out. I have jury duty."

Many criminals, like this one, exhibit a sense of conscience and responsibility in other areas of their life, and thus do **not** exhibit antisocial personality disorder.

Understanding Antisocial Personality Disorder

Antisocial personality disorder is woven of both biological and psychological strands. No single gene codes for a complex behavior such as crime, but twin and adoption studies reveal that biological relatives of those with antisocial and unemotional tendencies are at increased risk for antisocial behavior (Larsson et al., 2007; Livesley & Jang, 2008). The genetic vulnerability of people with antisocial and unemotional tendencies appears as a fearless approach to life. Awaiting aversive events, such as electric shocks or loud noises, they show little autonomic nervous system arousal (Hare, 1975; van Goozen et al., 2007). Even as youngsters, before committing any crime, they react with lower levels of stress hormones than do others their age (**FIGURE 13.12**).

Some studies have detected the early signs of antisocial behavior in children as young as ages 3 to 6 (Caspi et al., 1996; Tremblay et al., 1994). Boys who later became aggressive or antisocial adolescents tended, as young children, to have been impulsive, uninhibited, and unconcerned with social rewards, and they showed low levels of anxiety. If channeled in more productive directions, such fearlessness may lead to courageous heroism, adventurism, or star-level athleticism (Poulton & Milne, 2002). The genes that put people at risk for antisocial behavior also put people at risk for dependence on alcohol and other drugs, which helps explain why these disorders often appear in combination (Dick, 2007).

Genetic influences help wire the brain. Adrian Raine (1999, 2005) compared PET scans of 41 murderers' brains with those from people of similar age and sex. The scans showed reduced activity in the murderers' frontal lobes, an area of the cortex that helps control impulses (see **FIGURE 13.13** on the next page). This reduction was especially apparent in those who murdered impulsively. Violent repeat offenders had 11 percent less frontal lobe tissue than normal (Raine et al., 2000). This helps explain why people with antisocial personality disorder exhibit marked deficits in frontal lobe cognitive functions, such as planning, organization, and inhibition (Morgan & Lilienfeld, 2000). Compared with people who feel and display empathy, their brains also respond less to facial displays of others' distress (Deeley et al., 2006).

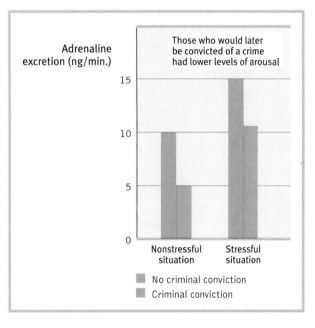

FIGURE 13.12 Cold-blooded arousability and risk of crime
Levels of the stress hormone adrenaline were measured in two groups of 13-year-old Swedish boys. In both stressful and nonstressful situations, those who would later be convicted of a crime (as 18- to 26-year-olds) showed relatively low arousal. (From Magnusson, 1990.)

personality disorders psychological disorders characterized by inflexible and enduring behavior patterns that impair social functioning.

antisocial personality disorder a personality disorder in which the person (usually a man) exhibits a lack of conscience for wrongdoing, even toward friends and family members. May be aggressive and ruthless or a clever con artist.

FIGURE 13.13 Murderous minds These top-facing PET scans illustrate reduced activation (less red and yellow) in a murderer's frontal cortex—a brain area that helps brake impulsive, aggressive behavior. (From Raine, 1999.)

Normal   Murderer

Genetics alone is hardly the whole story of antisocial crime, however. Relative to 1960, the average American in 1995 (before an ensuing crime decline) was twice as likely to be murdered, four times as likely to report being raped, four times as likely to report being robbed, and five times as likely to report being assaulted (FBI, *Uniform Crime Reports*). Violent crime was also surging in other Western nations. Yet the human gene pool had hardly changed. Or consider the British social experiment begun in 1787, exiling 160,000 criminals to Australia. The descendants of these exiles, carrying their ancestors' supposed "criminal genes," helped create a civilized democracy whose crime rate is similar to Britain's. Genetic predispositions do put some individuals more at risk for antisocial conduct than others; biological as well as environmental influences explain why 5 to 6 percent of offenders commit 50 to 60 percent of crimes (Lyman, 1996). But we must look to social-cultural factors to explain variations in violent crime over time.

REHEARSE IT!

21. A personality disorder, such as antisocial personality, is characterized by
    a. depression.
    b. hallucinations.
    c. enduring and inflexible behavior patterns that impair social functioning.
    d. an elevated level of autonomic nervous system arousal.

22. Pet scans of murderers' brains have revealed
    a. higher-than-normal activation in the frontal lobes.
    b. lower-than-normal activation in the frontal lobes.
    c. more frontal lobe tissue than normal.
    d. no differences in brain structures or activity.

Answers: 21. c, 22. b.

Rates of Psychological Disorders

14: How many people have, or have had, a psychological disorder?

Does a full Moon trigger "madness" in some people? James Rotton and I. W. Kelly (1985) examined data from 37 studies that related lunar phase to crime, homicides, crisis calls, and mental hospital admissions. Their conclusion: There is virtually no evidence of "Moon madness." Nor does lunar phase correlate with suicides, assaults, emergency room visits, or traffic disasters (Martin et al., 1992; Raison et al., 1999).

Who is most vulnerable to psychological disorders? At what times of life? To answer such questions, various countries have conducted lengthy, structured interviews with representative samples of thousands of their citizens. After asking hundreds of questions that probed for symptoms—"Has there ever been a period of two weeks or more when you felt like you wanted to die?"—the researchers have estimated the current, prior-year, and lifetime prevalence of various disorders.

How many people have, or have had, a psychological disorder? More than most of us suppose:

- The U.S. National Institute of Mental Health (2008, based on Kessler et al., 2005) estimates that 26 percent of adult Americans "suffer from a diagnosable mental disorder in a given year" (**TABLE 13.4**).
- National population surveys reveal differing annual rates in Australia (16 percent), Germany (31 percent), and The Netherlands (23 percent) (Baumeister & Härter, 2007).
- A twenty-first-century World Health Organization (2004) study—based on 90-minute interviews of 60,463 people—estimated the number of prior-year mental disorders in 20 countries. As **FIGURE 13.14** displays, the lowest rate of reported mental disorders was in Shanghai, the highest rate in the United States. Moreover, immigrants to the United States from Mexico, Africa, and Asia average better mental health than their native-born U.S. counterparts (Breslau et al., 2007). For example, compared with people who have recently immigrated from Mexico, Mexican-Americans born in the United States are at greater risk of mental disorder.

TABLE 13.4 Percentage of Americans Reporting Selected Psychological Disorders in the Past Year

Psychological Disorder	Percentage
Generalized anxiety	3.1
Social phobia	6.8
Phobia of specific object or situation	8.7
Mood disorder	9.5
Obsessive-compulsive disorder	1.0
Schizophrenia	1.1
Post-traumatic stress disorder (PTSD)	3.5
Attention-deficit hyperactivity disorder (ADHD)	4.1
Any mental disorder	26.2

Source: National Institute of Mental Health, 2008.

Who is most vulnerable to mental disorders? As we have seen, the answer varies with the disorder. One predictor of mental disorder, poverty, crosses ethnic and gender lines. The incidence of serious psychological disorders is doubly high among those below the poverty line (Centers for Disease Control, 1992). Like so many other correlations, the poverty-disorder association raises a chicken-and-egg question: Does poverty cause disorders? Or do disorders cause poverty? It is both, though the answer varies with the disorder. Schizophrenia understandably leads to poverty. Yet the stresses and demoralization of poverty can also precipitate disorders, especially depression in women and substance abuse in men (Dohrenwend et al., 1992). In one natural experiment on the poverty-pathology link, researchers tracked rates of behavior problems in North Carolina Native American children as economic development enabled a dramatic reduction in their community's poverty rate. As the study began, children of poverty exhibited more deviant and aggressive behaviors. After four years, children whose families had moved above the poverty line exhibited a 40 percent decrease in the behavior problems, while those who continued in their previous positions below or above the poverty line exhibited no change (Costello et al., 2003).

At what times of life do disorders strike? Usually by early adulthood. "Over 75 percent of our sample with any disorder had experienced its first symptoms by age 24," reported Lee Robins and Darrel Regier (1991, p. 331). The symptoms of antisocial personality disorder and of phobias are among the earliest to appear, at a median age of 8 and 10, respectively. Symptoms of alcohol dependency, obsessive-compulsive disorder, bipolar disorder, and schizophrenia appear at a median age near 20. Major depression often hits somewhat later, at a median age of 25. Such findings make clear the need for research and treatment to help the growing number of people, especially teenagers and young adults, who suffer the bewilderment and pain of a psychological disorder.

Although mindful of the pain, we can also be encouraged by the many successful people—including Leonardo da Vinci, Isaac Newton, and Leo Tolstoy—who pursued brilliant careers while enduring psychological difficulties. So have 18 U.S. presidents, including the periodically depressed Abraham Lincoln, according to one psychiatric analysis of their biographies (Davidson et al., 2006). The bewilderment, fear, and sorrow caused by psychological disorders are real. But, as Chapter 14 shows, hope, too, is real.

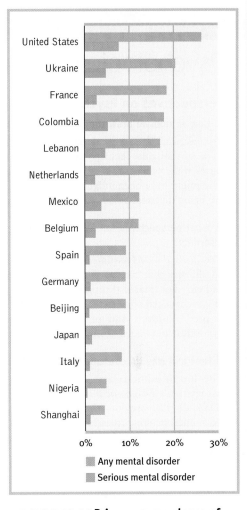

FIGURE 13.14 Prior-year prevalence of disorders in selected areas From World Health Organization (2004b) interviews in 20 countries.

REHEARSE IT!

23. One predictor of psychiatric disorders that crosses ethnic and gender lines is
a. age.
b. education.
c. poverty.
d. religious faith.

24. Most psychological disorders strike by early adulthood. The symptoms of _____ appear around age 10; _____ tends to appear later, around age 25.

a. schizophrenia; bipolar disorder
b. bipolar disorder; schizophrenia
c. major depression; phobias
d. phobias; major depression

Answers: 23. c, 24. d.

Psychological Disorders

Perspectives on Psychological Disorders

1 How should we draw the line between normality and disorder?

Psychological disorders are deviant, distressful, and dysfunctional patterns of thoughts, feelings, and actions. The definition of deviant varies with context, culture, and time. For example, some children who might have been judged rambunctious a few decades ago now are being diagnosed with *attention-deficit hyperactivity disorder.*

2 What perspectives can help us understand psychological disorders?

The *medical model* assumes that psychological disorders are mental illnesses that can be diagnosed on the basis of their symptoms and cured or treated through therapy, sometimes in a hospital. The biopsychosocial approach assumes that disorders arise from genetic predispositions and physiological states; inner psychological dynamics; and social-cultural circumstances.

3 How and why do clinicians classify psychological disorders?

The fourth edition (text revised) of the American Psychiatric Association's *Diagnostic and Statistical Manual of Mental Disorders (DSM-IV-TR)* provides diagnostic guidelines and categories that aid mental health professionals by providing a common language and shared concepts for communication and research. Most U.S. health insurance organizations require DSM-IV-TR diagnoses before they will pay for therapy.

4 Why do some psychologists criticize the use of diagnostic labels?

Labels can create preconceptions that bias our perceptions of a person's past and present behavior. The insanity defense raises moral and ethical questions about how a society should treat people who have disorders and have committed crimes.

Anxiety Disorders

5 What are anxiety disorders, and how do they differ from ordinary worries and fears?

Anxiety is classified as a psychological disorder only when it becomes distressing or persistent, or is characterized by maladaptive behaviors intended to reduce it. People with *generalized anxiety disorder* feel persistently and uncontrollably tense and apprehensive, for no apparent reason. In *panic disorder,* anxiety escalates into periodic episodes of intense dread. Those with a *phobia* may be irrationally afraid of an object or situation. Persistent and repetitive thoughts (obsessions) and actions (compulsions) characterize *obsessive-compulsive disorder.* Symptoms of *post-traumatic stress disorder* include four or more weeks of haunting memories, nightmares, social withdrawal, jumpy anxiety, and sleep problems following some traumatic and uncontrollable event.

6 What produces the thoughts and feelings that mark anxiety disorders?

Freud viewed *anxiety disorders* as the manifestation of mental energy associated with the discharge of repressed impulses. Psychologists working from the learning perspective view anxiety disorders as a product of fear conditioning, stimulus generalization, reinforcement of fearful behaviors, and observational learning of others' fear. Those working from the biological perspective consider the role that fears of life-threatening animals, objects, or situations played in natural selection and evolution; the genetic inheritance of a high level of emotional reactivity; and abnormal responses in the brain's fear circuits.

Somatoform Disorders

7 What are somatoform disorders?

Somatoform disorders present a somatic (bodily) symptom—some physiologically unexplained but genuinely felt ailment. With *conversion disorder,* anxiety appears converted to a physical symptom that has no reasonable physiological basis. *Hypochondriasis* is the more common interpretation of normal sensations as a dreaded disorder.

Dissociative Disorders

8 What are dissociative disorders, and why are they controversial?

Dissociative disorders are conditions in which conscious awareness seems to become separated from previous memories, thoughts, and feelings. Skeptics note that *dissociative identity disorder (DID),* formerly known as multiple personality disorder, was rarely found before the late twentieth century or outside North America, and that it may reflect role-playing by people who are vulnerable to therapists' suggestions. Others view DID symptoms as ways of handling anxiety.

Mood Disorders

9 What are mood disorders, and what forms do they take?

Mood disorders are characterized by emotional extremes. A person with *major depressive disorder* experiences two or more weeks of seriously depressed moods, feelings of worthlessness, and diminished interest and pleasure in most activities. These feelings are not caused by drugs or a medical condition. People with the less common condition of *bipolar disorder* experience not only depression but also *mania,* episodes of hyperactive and wildly optimistic impulsive behavior.

10 What causes mood disorders, and what might explain the Western world's rising incidence of depression among young people?

The biological perspective on depression focuses on genetic predispositions, abnormalities in brain structures and functions, and neurotransmitter imbalances. The social-cognitive perspective examines the influence of self-defeating beliefs, learned helplessness, negative attributions, and stressful experiences. The biopsychosocial approach considers the interaction of these and other influences. Increased rates of depression among young Westerners may be due to the rise of individualism and the decline of commitment to religion and family, but this is a correlational finding, so the cause-effect relationship is not yet clear.

Schizophrenia

11 What patterns of thinking, perceiving, feeling, and behaving characterize schizophrenia?

Schizophrenia typically strikes during late adolescence, affects men very slightly more than women, and seems to occur in all cultures. Symptoms include disorganized and delusional thinking, disturbed perceptions, and inappropriate emotions and actions. *Delusions* are false beliefs; hallucinations are sensory experiences without sensory stimulation. Symptoms may be positive (the presence of inappropriate behaviors) or negative (the absence of appropriate behaviors). Chronic schizophrenia emerges gradually (and the outlook for recovery is dim). Acute or reactive schizophrenia appears suddenly (and prospects for recovery are brighter).

12 What causes schizophrenia?

Schizophrenia is a cluster of disorders. Dopamine may intensify the positive symptoms of schizophrenia, and people with schizophrenia have increased receptors for this neurotransmitter. Brain abnormalities include enlarged, fluid-filled cerebral cavities and corresponding decreases in the cortex. Brain scans reveal abnormal activity in the frontal lobes, thalamus, and amygdala. Malfunctions in multiple brain regions and their connections apparently interact to produce symptoms. A mid-pregnancy viral infection may be a causal factor. Twin and adoption studies also point to a genetic predisposition that interacts with environmental factors to produce schizophrenia.

Personality Disorders

13 What characteristics are typical of personality disorders?

Personality disorders are enduring, maladaptive patterns of behavior that impair social functioning. *Antisocial personality disorder* is characterized by a lack of conscience and, sometimes, aggressive and fearless behavior. Genetic predispositions may interact with environment to produce the altered brain activity associated with this disorder.

Rates of Psychological Disorders

14 How many people have, or have had, a psychological disorder?

About 26 percent of adult Americans experience mental disorders annually, according to one recent estimate. Mental health surveys provide varying estimates of the rates of psychological disorders in many countries. Poverty is a predictor of mental illness. Conditions and experiences associated with poverty contribute to the development of mental disorders, but some mental disorders, such as schizophrenia, can drive people into poverty.

Terms and Concepts to Remember

psychological disorder, p. 454

attention-deficit hyperactivity disorder (ADHD), p. 455

medical model, p. 456

DSM-IV-TR, p. 457

anxiety disorders, p. 461

generalized anxiety disorder, p. 462

panic disorder, p. 462

phobia, p. 462

obsessive-compulsive disorder (OCD), p. 463

post-traumatic stress disorder (PTSD), p. 464

post-traumatic growth, p. 465

somatoform disorder, p. 468

conversion disorder, p. 468

hypochondriasis, p. 468

dissociative disorders, p. 468

dissociative identity disorder (DID), p. 469

mood disorders, p. 470

major depressive disorder, p. 471

mania, p. 471

bipolar disorder, p. 471

schizophrenia, p. 480

psychotic disorder, p. 480

delusions, p. 480

personality disorders, p. 486

antisocial personality disorder, p. 486

Test for Success: Critical Thinking Exercises
By Amy Himsel, El Camino College

1. Anna is embarrassed that it takes her several minutes to parallel park her car. She usually gets out of the car once or twice to inspect her distance both from the curb and from the cars nearby. Should she worry about having a psychological disorder?

2. A full-figured body is the traditional cultural ideal for women in the South Pacific island of Fiji. After the introduction of American TV programs to the island in 1995, however, eating disorder diagnoses increased rapidly. How can the biopsychosocial approach explain this phenomenon?

3. When women get sad, they often get sadder than men do. When men get mad, they often get madder than women do. How does this correspond to gender differences in psychological disorders?

4. What does it mean to say that depression is the "common cold" of psychological disorders?

5. Victor exclaimed, "The weather has been so schizophrenic lately: It's hot one day and freezing the next!" Is this an accurate analogy? Why or why not?

The Test for Success exercises offer you a chance to apply your critical thinking skills to aspects of the material you have just read. Suggestions for answering these questions can be found in Appendix D at the back of the book.

Chapter Outline

- **The Psychological Therapies**
  Psychoanalysis
  Humanistic Therapies
  Behavior Therapies
  Cognitive Therapies
  Group and Family Therapies

- **Evaluating Psychotherapies**
  Is Psychotherapy Effective?
  The Relative Effectiveness of Different Therapies
  Evaluating Alternative Therapies
  Commonalities Among Psychotherapies
  Culture and Values in Psychotherapy
  CLOSE-UP: A Consumer's Guide to Psychotherapists

- **The Biomedical Therapies**
  Drug Therapies
  Brain Stimulation
  Psychosurgery
  Therapeutic Life-Style Change

- **Preventing Psychological Disorders**

We have treated psychological disorders with a bewildering array of harsh and gentle methods: by cutting holes in the head and by giving warm baths and massages; by restraining, bleeding, or "beating the devil" out of people and by placing them in sunny, serene environments; by administering drugs and electric shocks and by talking—talking about childhood experiences, about current feelings, about maladaptive thoughts and behaviors.

The transition from brutal to gentler treatments occurred thanks to the efforts of reformers such as Philippe Pinel in France and Dorothea Dix in the United States, Canada, and Scotland. Both advocated constructing mental hospitals to offer more humane methods of treatment. But times have once again changed, and the introduction of therapeutic drugs and community-based treatment programs has largely emptied mental health hospitals since the mid-1950s.

Today's favored treatments depend on both the disorder and the therapist's viewpoint. Learning-related disorders, such as phobias, are likely candidates for *psychotherapy,* in which a trained therapist uses psychological techniques to assist someone seeking to overcome difficulties or achieve personal growth. Biologically influenced disorders, such as schizophrenia, will often be treated with *biomedical therapy*—a prescribed medication or medical procedure that acts directly on the patient's nervous system.

Depending on the client and the problem, some therapists—particularly the many using a biopsychosocial approach—draw from a variety of techniques. Many patients receive drug therapy in combination with psychotherapy. Half of all psychotherapists describe themselves as taking an **eclectic approach,** using a blend of therapies (Beitman et al., 1989; Castonguay & Goldfried, 1994). *Psychotherapy integration* attempts to combine a selection of assorted techniques into a single, coherent system.

Dorothea Dix (1802–1887) "I . . . call your attention to the state of the Insane Persons confined within this Commonwealth, in cages."

eclectic approach an approach to psychotherapy that, depending on the client's problems, uses techniques from various forms of therapy.

The history of treatment As William Hogarth's (1697–1764) painting of London's St. Mary of Bethlehem hospital (commonly called Bedlam) depicts, visitors to eighteenth-century mental hospitals paid to gawk at patients, as though they were viewing zoo animals. Benjamin Rush (1746–1813), a founder of the movement for more humane treatment of the mentally ill, designed the chair on the left "for the benefit of maniacal patients." He believed the restraints would help them regain their sensibilities.

psychotherapy treatment involving psychological techniques; consists of interactions between a trained therapist and someone seeking to overcome psychological difficulties or achieve personal growth.

"You say, 'Off with her head' but what I'm hearing is, 'I feel neglected.'"

"Your problems make my fee seem insignificant."

"I haven't seen my analyst in 200 years. He was a strict Freudian. If I'd been going all this time, I'd probably almost be cured by now."

—Woody Allen, after awakening from suspended animation in the movie *Sleeper*

The Psychological Therapies

Among the dozens of types of **psychotherapy,** we will look at only the most influential. Each is built on one or more of psychology's major theories: psychoanalytic, humanistic, behavioral, and cognitive. Most of these techniques can be used one-on-one or in groups.

Psychoanalysis

1: What are the aims and methods of psychoanalysis, and how have they been adapted in psychodynamic therapy?

Sigmund Freud's **psychoanalysis** was the first of the psychological therapies. Few clinicians today practice therapy as Freud did, but his work deserves discussion as part of the foundation for treating psychological disorders.

Aims

Psychoanalytic theory presumes that healthier, less anxious living becomes possible when people release the energy they had previously devoted to id-ego-superego conflicts (see Chapter 12). Freud's therapy aimed to bring patients' repressed feelings into conscious awareness, giving them *insight* into the origins of their disorders and helping them take responsibility for their own growth.

Methods

Psychoanalysis is historical reconstruction. Psychoanalytic theory emphasizes the formative power of childhood experiences, and thus aims to excavate the past in the hope of unmasking the present. After discarding hypnosis as an unreliable excavator, Freud turned to *free association.*

Imagine yourself as a patient using free association. First, you relax, perhaps by lying on a couch. As the psychoanalyst sits out of your line of vision, you say aloud whatever comes to your mind—at one moment a childhood memory, at another a dream or recent experience. It sounds easy, but soon you notice how often you edit your thoughts as you speak. You pause momentarily before uttering an embarrassing thought. You omit what seems trivial, irrelevant, or shameful. Sometimes your mind goes blank or you clutch, unable to remember important details. You may joke or change the subject to something less threatening.

To the analyst, these blocks in the flow of your free associations indicate **resistance.** They hint that anxiety lurks and you are defending against sensitive material. The analyst will note your resistances and then provide insight into their meaning. If offered at the right moment, this **interpretation**—of, say, your not wanting to talk about your mother—may illuminate the underlying wishes, feelings, and conflicts you are avoiding. The analyst may also offer an explanation of how this resistance fits with other pieces of your psychological puzzle, including those based on analysis of your dream content.

Over many such sessions, you may find yourself experiencing strong positive or negative feelings for your analyst. The analyst may suggest you are **transferring** feelings, such as dependency or mingled love and anger, that you experienced in earlier relationships with family members or other important people. By exposing such feelings, you may gain insight into your current relationships, not just those of your past childhood.

Relatively few U.S. therapists now offer traditional psychoanalysis. Its underlying theory is not supported by scientific research (Chapter 12). Analysts' interpretations cannot be proven or disproven. And psychoanalysis takes time and money, often years of several expensive sessions each week. Some of these problems have been addressed in a contemporary psychodynamic perspective that has evolved from psychoanalysis.

Psychodynamic Therapy

Influenced by Freud, **psychodynamic therapists** try to help people understand their current symptoms by focusing on themes across important relationships, including childhood experiences and the therapist relationship. In face-to-face meetings (rather than on a couch, with the therapist out of their line of vision), patients explore and gain perspective on defended-against thoughts and feelings. But these meetings take place once a week (rather than several times weekly) for only a few weeks or months (rather than several years).

No brief excerpt can exemplify the way psychodynamic therapy interprets a patient's conflict. But the following interaction between therapist David Malan (1978, pp. 133–134) and a depressed patient illustrates the goal of enabling self-insight by looking for common, recurring themes, especially in relationships.

> **Malan:** *I get the feeling that you're the sort of person who needs to keep active. If you don't keep active, then something goes wrong. Is that true?*
>
> **Patient:** *Yes.*
>
> **Malan:** *I get a second feeling about you and that is that you must, underneath all this, have an awful lot of very strong and upsetting feelings. Somehow they're there but you aren't really quite in touch with them. Isn't this right? I feel you've been like that as long as you can remember.*
>
> **Patient:** *For quite a few years, whenever I really sat down and thought about it I got depressed, so I tried not to think about it.*
>
> **Malan:** *You see, you've established a pattern, haven't you? You're even like that here with me, because in spite of the fact that you're in some trouble and you feel that the bottom is falling out of your world, the way you're telling me this is just as if there wasn't anything wrong.*

Notice how Malan interpreted the woman's earlier remarks (when she did most of the talking) and suggested that her relationship with him reveals a characteristic pattern of behavior? He was suggesting insights into her problems.

Humanistic Therapies

2: What are the basic themes of humanistic therapy, such as Rogers' client-centered approach?

Psychoanalytic and humanistic therapies are often referred to as **insight therapies** because both attempt to help troubled people by reducing inner conflicts and increasing self-understanding. Humanistic therapists aim to boost people's inherent potential for self-fulfillment by helping them grow in self-awareness and self-acceptance (Chapter 12). Humanistic therapists differ from psychoanalysts in other ways as well. They focus on

- the *present* and *future* more than the past. They explore feelings as they occur, rather than delving into the childhood origins of the feelings.
- *conscious* rather than unconscious thoughts.
- taking immediate *responsibility* for one's feelings and actions, rather than uncovering hidden determinants.
- promoting growth instead of curing illness. Thus, those in therapy became *clients* rather than *patients* (a change many therapists have since adopted).

"Look, making you happy is out of the question, but I can give you a compelling narrative for your misery."

Face-to-face therapy In this type of therapy session, the couch has disappeared. But the influence of psychoanalytic theory may not have, especially if the therapist probes for the origin of the patient's symptoms by seeking information from the patient's childhood.

Photofusion Picture Library/Alamy

psychoanalysis Sigmund Freud's therapeutic technique. Freud believed the patient's free associations, resistances, dreams, and transferences—and the therapist's interpretations of them—release previously repressed feelings, allowing the patient to gain self-insight.

resistance in psychoanalysis, the blocking from consciousness of anxiety-laden material.

interpretation in psychoanalysis, the analyst's noting supposed dream meanings, resistances, and other significant behaviors and events in order to promote insight.

transference in psychoanalysis, the patient's transfer to the analyst of emotions linked with other relationships (such as love or hatred for a parent).

psychodynamic therapy therapy deriving from the psychoanalytic tradition that views individuals as responding to unconscious forces and childhood experiences, and that seeks to enhance self-insight.

insight therapies a variety of therapies which aim to improve psychological functioning by increasing the client's awareness of underlying motives and defenses.

Active listening Carl Rogers (right) empathized with a client during this group therapy session.

Carl Rogers (1902–1987) developed the widely used humanistic technique he called **client-centered therapy.** In this *nondirective therapy,* the therapist listens to the person's conscious self-perceptions without judging, interpreting, or directing the client toward certain insights.

Believing that most people already possess the resources for growth, Rogers (1961, 1980) encouraged therapists to exhibit *genuineness, acceptance,* and *empathy.* When therapists drop their facades and genuinely express their true feelings, when they enable their clients to feel unconditionally accepted, and when they empathically sense and reflect their clients' feelings, the clients may deepen their self-understanding and self-acceptance (Hill & Nakayama, 2000). As Rogers (1980, p. 10) explained,

> Hearing has consequences. When I truly hear a person and the meanings that are important to him at that moment, hearing not simply his words, but him, and when I let him know that I have heard his own private personal meanings, many things happen. There is first of all a grateful look. He feels released. He wants to tell me more about his world. He surges forth in a new sense of freedom. He becomes more open to the process of change. . . . Almost always, when a person realizes he has been deeply heard, his eyes moisten. I think in some real sense he is weeping for joy. It is as though he were saying, "Thank God, somebody heard me. Someone knows what it's like to be me."

"Hearing" refers to Rogers' technique of **active listening**—echoing, restating, and seeking clarification of what the person expresses (verbally or nonverbally) and acknowledging the expressed feelings. Rogers believed that the therapist's most important contribution is to accept and understand the client. Given a nonjudgmental, grace-filled environment that provides **unconditional positive regard,** people may accept even their worst traits and feel valued and whole.

Active listening is now an accepted part of therapeutic counseling practices in many schools, colleges, and clinics. The counselor listens attentively and interrupts only to restate and confirm feelings, to accept what is being expressed, or to seek clarification. The following brief excerpt between Rogers and a male client illustrates how he sought to provide a psychological mirror that would help clients see themselves more clearly.

Rogers: *Feeling that now, hm? That you're just no good to yourself, no good to anybody. Never will be any good to anybody. Just that you're completely worthless, huh?—Those really are lousy feelings. Just feel that you're no good at all, hm?*

Client: Yeah. (Muttering in low, discouraged voice) *That's what this guy I went to town with just the other day told me.*

Rogers: *This guy that you went to town with really told you that you were no good? Is that what you're saying? Did I get that right?*

"We have two ears and one mouth that we may listen the more and talk the less."

—Zeno, 335–263 B.C.E., *Diogenes Laertius*

To listen more actively in your own relationships, try this:

1. Paraphrase. *Rather than saying "I know how you feel," check your understandings by summarizing the speaker's words in your own words.*

2. Invite clarification. *"What might be an example of that?" may encourage the speaker to say more.*

3. Reflect feelings. *"It sounds frustrating" might mirror what you're sensing from the speaker's body language and intensity.*

Client: *M-hm.*

Rogers: *I guess the meaning of that if I get it right is that here's somebody that—meant something to you and what does he think of you? Why, he's told you that he thinks you're no good at all. And that just really knocks the props out from under you.* (Client weeps quietly.) *It just brings the tears.* (Silence of 20 seconds)

Client: (Rather defiantly) *I don't care though.*

Rogers: *You tell yourself you don't care at all, but somehow I guess some part of you cares because some part of you weeps over it.*

(Meador & Rogers, 1984, p. 167)

* * *

The insight therapies assume that many psychological problems diminish as self-awareness grows. Their influence has waned, although aspects of their approaches can be found in some contemporary approaches to therapy. But now, rather than delving deeply below the surface looking for inner causes, twenty-first-century therapists tend to view maladaptive symptoms as learned behaviors that can be replaced by new and more constructive responses.

client-centered therapy a humanistic therapy, developed by Carl Rogers, in which the therapist uses techniques such as active listening within a genuine, accepting, empathic environment to facilitate clients' growth. (Also called *person-centered therapy.*)

active listening empathic listening in which the listener echoes, restates, and clarifies. A feature of Rogers' client-centered therapy.

unconditional positive regard a caring, accepting, nonjudgmental attitude, which Carl Rogers believed would help clients to develop self-awareness and self-acceptance.

behavior therapy therapy that applies learning principles to the elimination of unwanted behaviors.

REHEARSE IT!

1. A therapist who helps patients search for the unconscious roots of their problems and offers interpretations of their behaviors, feelings, and dreams, is drawing from
   a. psychoanalysis.
   b. humanistic therapies.
   c. client-centered therapy.
   d. nondirective therapy.

2. According to psychoanalytic theory, important relationships in a patient's life—for example, an early relationship with a parent—may be reflected in strong feelings for the analyst. This process is called
   a. transference.
   b. resistance.
   c. interpretation.
   d. empathy.

3. Compared with psychoanalysts, humanistic therapists are more likely to emphasize
   a. hidden or repressed feelings.
   b. childhood experiences.
   c. psychological disorders.
   d. self-fulfillment and growth.

4. Especially important to Rogers' client-centered therapy is the technique of active listening. The therapist who practices active listening
   a. engages in free association.
   b. exposes the patient's resistances.
   c. restates and clarifies the client's statements.
   d. directly challenges the client's self-perceptions.

Answers: 1. a, 2. a, 3. d, 4. c.

Behavior Therapies

3: **What are the assumptions and techniques of the behavior therapies?**

Behavior therapists doubt the healing power of self-awareness. (You can become aware of why you are highly anxious during exams and still be anxious.) They assume that problem behaviors *are* the problems, and the application of learning principles can eliminate them.

Classical Conditioning Techniques

As Pavlov and others showed, we learn various behaviors and emotions through classical conditioning (Chapter 7). Could maladaptive symptoms be examples of conditioned responses? If so, might reconditioning be a solution? Learning theorist O. H. Mowrer thought so and developed a successful conditioning therapy for chronic bed-wetters. The child sleeps on a liquid-sensitive pad connected to an alarm. Moisture on the pad triggers the alarm, waking the child. With sufficient repetition, this association of urinary relaxation with waking up stops the bed-wetting in three out of four cases, boosting the child's self-image at the same time (Christophersen & Edwards, 1992; Houts et al., 1994).

What might a psychoanalyst say about Mowrer's therapy for bed-wetting? How might a behavior therapist reply?

counterconditioning a behavior therapy procedure that uses classical conditioning to evoke new responses to stimuli that are triggering unwanted behaviors; includes *exposure therapies* and *aversive conditioning*.

exposure therapies behavioral techniques, such as systematic desensitization, that treat anxieties by exposing people (in imagination or actuality) to the things they fear and avoid.

systematic desensitization a type of exposure therapy that associates a pleasant relaxed state with gradually increasing anxiety-triggering stimuli. Commonly used to treat phobias.

aversive conditioning a type of counterconditioning that associates an unpleasant state (such as nausea) with an unwanted behavior (such as drinking alcohol).

Other psychologists wondered, might one unlearn an aversion to certain stimuli by undergoing another round of conditioning to replace the fear response? In **counterconditioning,** the therapist pairs the trigger stimulus with a new response that is incompatible with fear. They use two specific counterconditioning techniques—*exposure therapy* and *aversive conditioning*—to replace unwanted responses.

EXPOSURE THERAPIES Picture this scene reported in 1924 by behaviorist psychologist Mary Cover Jones: Three-year-old Peter is petrified of rabbits and other furry objects. Jones plans to replace Peter's fear of rabbits with a conditioned response incompatible with fear. Her strategy is to associate the fear-evoking rabbit with the pleasurable, relaxed response associated with eating.

As Peter begins his midafternoon snack, Jones introduces a caged rabbit on the other side of the huge room. Peter, eagerly munching away on his crackers and drinking his milk, hardly notices. On succeeding days, she gradually moves the rabbit closer and closer. Within two months, Peter is tolerating the rabbit in his lap, even stroking it while he eats. Moreover, his fear of other furry objects subsides as well, having been *countered*, or replaced, by a relaxed state that cannot coexist with fear (Fisher, 1984; Jones, 1924).

Unfortunately, Jones' story of Peter and the rabbit did not become part of psychology's lore for more than 30 years, when psychiatrist Joseph Wolpe (1958; Wolpe & Plaud, 1997) refined her techniques into what are now the most widely used types of behavior therapies: **exposure therapies.** As people can habituate to the sound of a train passing their new apartment, so, with repeated exposure, can they become less anxiously responsive to things that once petrified them (Deacon & Abramowitz, 2004).

One widely used exposure therapy is **systematic desensitization.** If you can repeatedly relax when facing anxiety-provoking stimuli, you can gradually eliminate your anxiety. (You cannot be simultaneously anxious and relaxed.) The trick is to proceed gradually. Let's see how this might work. Imagine yourself with a common phobia—fear of public speaking. A behavior therapist might first ask for your help in constructing a hierarchy of anxiety-triggering speaking situations, ranging perhaps from the mildly anxiety-provoking situation of speaking up in a small group of friends, to the panic-provoking situation of addressing a large audience. Using *progressive relaxation*, the therapist would train you to relax one muscle group after another, until you achieve a drowsy state of complete relaxation and comfort. Then the therapist would ask you to imagine, with your eyes closed, a mildly anxiety-arousing situation: You are having coffee with a group of friends and are trying to decide whether to speak up. If imagining the scene causes you to feel any anxiety, you would signal your tension by raising your finger, and the therapist would instruct you to switch off the mental image and go back to deep relaxation. This imagined scene is repeatedly paired with relaxation until you feel no trace of anxiety.

The therapist would progress up the constructed anxiety hierarchy, using the relaxed state to desensitize you to each imagined situation. After several sessions, you move to actual situations, beginning with relatively easy tasks and gradually moving to more anxiety-filled ones. Conquering your anxiety in an actual situation, not just in your imagination, raises your self-confidence (Foa & Kozak, 1986; Williams, 1987). Eventually, you may even become a confident public speaker.

When an anxiety-arousing situation is too expensive, difficult, or embarrassing to re-create, *virtual reality exposure therapy* may offer an alternative (**FIGURE 14.1**). Experiments led by several research teams have treated many different people with many different fears—flying, heights, particular animals, and public speaking (Gregg & Tarrier, 2007; Powers & Emmelkamp, 2008; Rothbaum, 2006). Those experiencing virtual reality exposure therapy have had greater relief from their fears—in real life—than have those in control groups.

THE FAR SIDE® BY GARY LARSON

Professor Gallagher and his controversial technique of simultaneously confronting the fear of heights, snakes, and the dark.

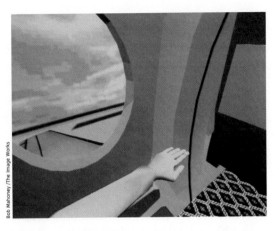

Bob Mahoney /The Image Works

Bob Mahoney /The Image Works

FIGURE 14.1 Virtual reality exposure therapy Virtual reality technology exposes people to vivid simulations of feared stimuli. The head-mounted display unit projects a three-dimensional, lifelike series of scenes. As the client's head turns, motion sensors adjust the scene. People who fear flying can peer out a "window," feel vibrations, and hear the engine roar as the plane taxis down the run- way and takes off.

AVERSIVE CONDITIONING In systematic desensitization, the goal is substituting a positive (relaxed) response for a negative (fearful) response to a *harmless* stimulus. **Aversive conditioning** is the reverse of systematic desensitization—its goal is to substitute a negative (aversive) response for a positive response to a *harmful* stimu- lus. The procedure is simple: It associates the unwanted behavior with unpleasant feelings. To treat nail biting, one can paint the fingernails with a nasty-tasting nail polish (Baskind, 1997). To treat alcohol dependency, an aversion therapist offers the client appealing drinks laced with a drug that produces severe nausea. By linking alcohol with violent nausea (recall the taste-aversion experiments with rats and coy- otes in Chapter 7), the therapist seeks to transform the person's reaction to alcohol from positive to negative (**FIGURE 14.2**).

Does aversive conditioning work? In the short run it may. Arthur Wiens and Carol Menustik (1983) studied 685 patients with alcohol dependency who com- pleted an aversion therapy program at a Portland, Oregon, hospital. One year later, after returning for several booster treatments of alcohol-sickness pairings,

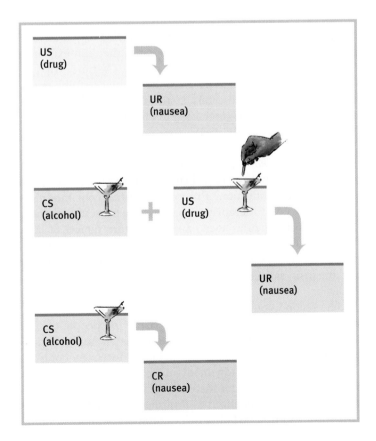

FIGURE 14.2 Aversion therapy for alcohol dependency After repeatedly imbibing an alcoholic drink mixed with a drug that produces severe nausea, some people with a history of alcohol abuse develop at least a temporary conditioned aversion to alcohol.

63 percent were still successfully abstaining. But after three years, only 33 percent had remained abstinent.

The problem, as we saw in Chapter 7, is that cognition influences conditioning. People know that outside the therapist's office they can drink without fear of nausea. Their ability to discriminate between the aversive conditioning situation and all other situations can limit the treatment's effectiveness. Thus, therapists often use aversive conditioning in combination with other treatments.

Operant Conditioning

A basic concept in operant conditioning (Chapter 7) is that voluntary behaviors are strongly influenced by their consequences. Knowing this, behavior therapists can practice *behavior modification*—reinforcing desired behaviors and withholding reinforcement for, or punishing, undesired behaviors. Using operant conditioning, children with an intellectual disability have been taught to care for themselves. Socially withdrawn children with autism have learned to interact. People with schizophrenia have been helped to behave more rationally in their hospital ward. In such cases, therapists use positive reinforcers to shape behavior in a step-by-step manner, rewarding closer and closer approximations of the desired behavior.

In extreme cases, treatment must be intensive. One study worked with 19 withdrawn, uncommunicative 3-year-olds with autism. Each participated in a 2-year program in which their parents spent 40 hours a week attempting to shape their behavior (Lovaas, 1987). The combination of positively reinforcing desired behaviors, and ignoring or punishing aggressive and self-abusive behaviors, worked wonders for some. By first grade, 9 of the 19 children were functioning successfully in school and exhibiting normal intelligence. In a group of 40 comparable children not undergoing this treatment (which involves sustained effort), only one showed similar improvement.

Rewards used to modify behavior vary. For some people, the reinforcing power of attention or praise is sufficient. Others require concrete rewards, such as food. In institutional settings, therapists may create a **token economy.** When people display appropriate behavior, such as getting out of bed, washing, dressing, eating, talking coherently, cleaning up their rooms, or playing cooperatively, they receive a token or plastic coin as a positive reinforcer. Later, they can exchange their accumulated tokens for various rewards, such as candy, TV time, trips to town, or better living quarters. Token economies have been successfully applied in various settings (homes, classrooms, hospitals, institutions for the delinquent) and among members of various populations (including disturbed children and people with schizophrenia and other mental disabilities).

Critics of behavior modification express two concerns. The first is practical: *How durable are the behaviors?* Will people become so dependent on extrinsic rewards that the appropriate behaviors will stop when the reinforcers stop, as may happen when they leave the institution? Proponents of behavior modification believe the behaviors will endure if therapists wean patients from the tokens by shifting them toward other rewards, such as social approval, more typical of life outside the institution. They also point out that the appropriate behaviors themselves can be intrinsically rewarding. For example, as a withdrawn person becomes more socially competent, the intrinsic satisfactions of social interaction may help the person maintain the behavior.

The second concern is ethical: *Is it right for one human to control another's behavior?* To critics, the whole process of depriving people of something they desire and deciding which behaviors to reinforce has an authoritarian taint. Advocates reply that some patients request the therapy. Moreover, control already exists; rewards and punishers are already maintaining destructive behavior patterns. So why not reinforce adaptive behavior instead? Treatment with positive rewards is more humane than being institutionalized or punished, they argue, and the right to effective treatment and an improved life justifies temporary deprivation.

token economy an operant conditioning procedure in which people earn a token of some sort for exhibiting a desired behavior and can later exchange the tokens for various privileges or treats.

cognitive therapy therapy that teaches people new, more adaptive ways of thinking and acting; based on the assumption that thoughts intervene between events and our emotional reactions.

Cognitive Therapies

4: What are the goals and techniques of the cognitive therapies?

We have seen how behavior therapists treat specific fears and problem behaviors. But how do they deal with major depression? Or with generalized anxiety, in which anxiety has no focus and developing a hierarchy of anxiety-triggering situations is difficult? Behavior therapists treating these less clearly defined psychological problems have had help from the same *cognitive revolution* that has profoundly changed other areas of psychology during the last five decades.

Cognitive therapy for eating disorders aided by journaling Cognitive therapists guide people toward new ways of explaining their good and bad experiences. By recording each day's positive events and how one enabled them, for example, people may become more mindful of their self-control.

The **cognitive therapies** assume that our thinking colors our feelings (**FIGURE 14.3**). Between the event and our response lies the mind. Self-blaming and overgeneralized explanations of bad events are often an integral part of the vicious cycle of depression (see Chapter 13). The depressed person interprets a suggestion as criticism, disagreement as dislike, praise as flattery, friendliness as pity. Ruminating on such thoughts sustains the bad mood. If such thinking patterns can be learned, then surely they can be replaced. Cognitive therapists therefore try in various ways to teach people new, more constructive ways of thinking.

"Life does not consist mainly, or even largely, of facts and happenings. It consists mainly of the storm of thoughts that are forever blowing through one's mind."

—Mark Twain, 1835–1910

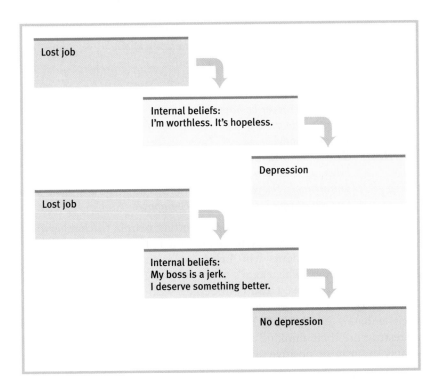

FIGURE 14.3 **A cognitive perspective on psychological disorders** The person's emotional reactions are produced not directly by the event but by the person's thoughts in response to the event.

Beck's Therapy for Depression

If people are miserable, they can be helped to change their minds. As therapist Aaron Beck applied his training in Freudian techniques to the dreams of depressed people, he found recurring negative themes of loss, rejection, and abandonment that extended into their waking thoughts. Beck and his colleagues (1979) came to believe that cognitive therapy could reverse people's *catastrophizing* beliefs about themselves, their situations, and their futures. Such negativity even extends into

cognitive-behavioral therapy a popular integrative therapy that combines cognitive therapy (changing self-defeating thinking) with behavior therapy (changing behavior).

family therapy therapy that treats the family as a system. Views an individual's unwanted behaviors as influenced by, or directed at, other family members.

therapy, as clients recall and rehearse their failings and worst impulses (Kelly, 2000). Gentle questioning seeks to reveal irrational thinking and then to persuade people to remove the dark glasses through which they view life (Beck et al., 1979, pp. 145–146):

> **Client:** *I agree with the descriptions of me but I guess I don't agree that the way I think makes me depressed.*
>
> **Beck:** *How do you understand it?*
>
> **Client:** *I get depressed when things go wrong. Like when I fail a test.*
>
> **Beck:** *How can failing a test make you depressed?*
>
> **Client:** *Well, if I fail I'll never get into law school.*
>
> **Beck:** *So failing the test means a lot to you. But if failing a test could drive people into clinical depression, wouldn't you expect everyone who failed the test to have a depression? . . . Did everyone who failed get depressed enough to require treatment?*
>
> **Client:** *No, but it depends on how important the test was to the person.*
>
> **Beck:** *Right, and who decides the importance?*
>
> **Client:** *I do.*
>
> **Beck:** *And so, what we have to examine is your way of viewing the test (or the way that you think about the test) and how it affects your chances of getting into law school. Do you agree?*
>
> **Client:** *Right.*
>
> **Beck:** *Do you agree that the way you interpret the results of the test will affect you? You might feel depressed, you might have trouble sleeping, not feel like eating, and you might even wonder if you should drop out of the course.*
>
> **Client:** *I have been thinking that I wasn't going to make it. Yes, I agree.*
>
> **Beck:** *Now what did failing mean?*
>
> **Client:** *(tearful) That I couldn't get into law school.*
>
> **Beck:** *And what does that mean to you?*
>
> **Client:** *That I'm just not smart enough.*
>
> **Beck:** *Anything else?*
>
> **Client:** *That I can never be happy.*
>
> **Beck:** *And how do these thoughts make you feel?*
>
> **Client:** *Very unhappy.*
>
> **Beck:** *So it is the meaning of failing a test that makes you very unhappy. In fact, believing that you can never be happy is a powerful factor in producing unhappiness. So, you get yourself into a trap—by definition, failure to get into law school equals "I can never be happy."*

We often think in words. Therefore, getting people to change what they say to themselves is an effective way to change their thinking. Perhaps you can identify with the anxious students who before an exam make matters worse with self-defeating thoughts: "This exam's probably going to be impossible. All these other students seem so relaxed and confident. I wish I were better prepared. Anyhow, I'm so nervous I'll forget everything." To change such negative self-talk, Donald Meichenbaum (1977, 1985) has offered *stress inoculation training*: teaching people to restructure their thinking in stressful situations. Sometimes it may be enough simply to say more positive things to oneself: "Relax. The exam may be hard, but it

PEANUTS

will be hard for everyone else, too. I studied harder than most people. Besides, I don't need a perfect score to get a good grade." After being trained to dispute their negative thoughts, depression-prone children and college students exhibit a halved rate of future depression (Seligman, 2002). To a great extent, it *is* the thought that counts.

Cognitive-Behavioral Therapy

The widely practiced **cognitive-behavioral therapy** aims not only to alter the way people think (*cognitive* therapy), but also to alter the way they act (*behavior* therapy). It seeks to make people aware of their irrational negative thinking, to replace it with new ways of thinking, *and to practice* the more positive approach in everyday settings.

Many studies confirm cognitive-behavioral therapy's effectiveness for those suffering anxiety or depression (Covin et al., 2008; Mitte, 2005; Norton & Price, 2007). Anxiety and mood disorders share a common problem: emotion regulation. An effective treatment program for these emotional disorders trains people both to replace their catastrophizing thinking with more realistic appraisals, and to practice behaviors that are incompatible with their problem (Moses & Barlow, 2006). A person with a fear of social situations, for example, might learn new ways of thinking, but also practice approaching people.

In one study, people with obsessive-compulsive behaviors learned to relabel their compulsive thoughts (Schwartz et al., 1996). Feeling the urge to wash their hands again, they would tell themselves, "I'm having a compulsive urge," and attribute it to their brain's abnormal activity, as previously viewed in their PET scans. Instead of giving in to the urge, they would then spend 15 minutes in an enjoyable, alternative behavior, such as practicing an instrument, taking a walk, or gardening. This helped "unstick" the brain by shifting attention and engaging other brain areas. For two or three months, the weekly therapy sessions continued, with relabeling and refocusing practice at home. By the study's end, most participants' symptoms had diminished and their PET scans revealed normalized brain activity. Behavioral practice plus cognitive relabeling equaled relief.

> "The trouble with most therapy is that it helps you to feel better. But you don't get better. You have to back it up with action, action, action."
>
> —Therapist Albert Ellis (1913–2007)

Group and Family Therapies

5: What are the aims and benefits of group and family therapy?

Except for traditional psychoanalysis, most therapies may also occur in small groups. Group therapy can save therapists' time and clients' money, and it often is no less effective than individual therapy (Fuhriman & Burlingame, 1994). It does not provide the same degree of therapist involvement with each client, but the social context of the sessions offers other unique benefits. Up to 90 minutes a week, the therapist guides the interactions of 6 to 10 people as they confront issues and react to one another. It can be a relief to find that others, despite their apparent composure, have problems similar to yours and share your troublesome feelings. Group members can also give and receive feedback on new ways of behaving. Hearing that you look poised, even though you feel anxious and self-conscious, can be very reassuring. Hearing how and why your behavior distresses others can help you learn new behaviors.

Therapists frequently suggest group therapy for people who are having family conflicts. **Family therapy** assumes that no person is an island, that we live and grow in relation to others. Two opposing tendencies—working to find an identity outside our family, yet needing to connect with family

Family therapy The therapist helps family members understand how their ways of relating to one another create problems. The treatment's emphasis is not on changing the individuals but on changing their relationships and interactions.

members emotionally—can create stress for the individual and the family. Thus, therapists tend to view families as systems, in which each person's actions trigger reactions from others. To break that pattern, the therapist often attempts to guide family members toward positive relationships and improved communication. This type of therapy often acts as a preventive mental health strategy.

* * *

For a synopsis of the main forms of psychotherapy we've been discussing, see **TABLE 14.1**.

TABLE 14.1 Comparison of a Sample of Major Psychotherapies

Therapy	Assumed Problem	Therapy Aims	Method
Psychodynamic	Unconscious forces and childhood experiences	Reduced anxiety through self-insight	Analysis and interpretation
Client-centered	Barriers to self-understanding and self-acceptance	Personal growth through self-insight	Active listening and unconditional positive regard
Behavior	Maladaptive behavior	Extinction and relearning	Counterconditioning, exposure, desensitization, aversive conditioning, and operant conditioning
Cognitive	Negative, self-defeating thinking	Healthier thinking and self-talk	Reveal and reverse self-blaming
Family	Stressful relationships	Relationship healing	Understanding family social system; exploring roles; improving communication

REHEARSE IT!

5. Behavior therapists apply learning principles to the treatment of problems such as phobias and alcohol dependency. In such treatment, the goal is to
a. identify and treat the underlying causes of the problem.
b. improve learning and insight.
c. eliminate the unwanted behavior.
d. improve communication and social sensitivity.

6. Behavior therapists often use counterconditioning to produce new responses to old stimuli. Two counterconditioning techniques are systematic desensitization and
a. resistance.
b. aversive conditioning.
c. transference.
d. active listening.

7. Systematic desensitization, which teaches people to relax in the presence of progressively more anxiety-provoking stimuli, has been especially effective in the treatment of
a. phobias.
b. depression.
c. alcohol dependency.
d. bed-wetting.

8. In token economies, people who display a desired behavior earn tokens that they can later exchange for other rewards. Token economies are an application of
a. classical conditioning.
b. counterconditioning.
c. cognitive therapy.
d. operant conditioning.

9. Cognitive therapy has been shown to be especially effective in treating
a. bed-wetting.
b. phobias.
c. alcohol dependency.
d. depression.

10. In family therapy, the therapist assumes that
a. only one family member needs to change.
b. each person's actions trigger reactions from other family members.
c. dysfunctional families must improve their interactions or give up their children.
d. all of these statements are true.

Answers: 5. c, 6. b, 7. a, 8. d, 9. d, 10. b.

Evaluating Psychotherapies

Advice columnists frequently urge their troubled letter writers to get professional help: "Don't give up. Find a therapist who can help you. Make an appointment." Statistics show that many Americans share this confidence in psychotherapy's effectiveness. In 2004, for example, 7.4 percent of Americans reported "undergoing counseling for mental or emotional problems," a 25 percent increase since 1991 (Smith, 2005). With such an enormous outlay of time as well as money, effort, and hope, it is important to ask: Are the millions of people worldwide justified in placing such hope in psychotherapy?

Is Psychotherapy Effective?

6: **Does psychotherapy work? Who decides?**

The question, though simply put, is not simply answered. Measuring therapy's effectiveness is not like taking your body's temperature to see if your fever has gone away. If you and I were to undergo psychotherapy, how would we assess its effectiveness? By how we feel about our progress? How our friends and family feel about it? How our therapist feels about it? How our behavior has changed?

Clients' Perceptions

If clients' testimonials were the only measuring stick, we could strongly affirm the effectiveness of psychotherapy. When 2900 *Consumer Reports* readers (1995; Kotkin et al., 1996; Seligman, 1995) related their experiences with mental health professionals, 89 percent said they were at least "fairly well satisfied." Among those who recalled feeling *fair* or *very poor* when beginning therapy, 9 in 10 now were feeling *very good, good,* or at least *so-so.* We have their word for it—and who should know better?

We should not dismiss these testimonials lightly. But for several reasons, client testimonials do not persuade psychotherapy's skeptics:

- *People often enter therapy in crisis.* When, with the normal ebb and flow of events, the crisis passes, people may attribute their improvement to the therapy.
- *Clients may need to believe the therapy was worth the effort.* To admit investing time and money in something ineffective is like admitting to having one's car serviced repeatedly by a mechanic who never fixes it. Self-justification is a powerful human motive.
- *Clients generally speak kindly of their therapists.* Even if the problems remain, say the critics, clients "work hard to find something positive to say. The therapist had been very understanding, the client had gained a new perspective, he learned to communicate better, his mind was eased, anything at all so as not to have to say treatment was a failure" (Zilbergeld, 1983, p. 117).

Clinicians' Perceptions

Do clinicians' perceptions give us any more reason to celebrate? Case studies of successful treatment abound. The problem is that clients justify entering psychotherapy by emphasizing their unhappiness, justify leaving by emphasizing their well-being, and stay in touch only if satisfied. Therapists treasure compliments from clients as they say good-bye or later express their gratitude, but they hear little from clients who experience only temporary relief and seek out new therapists for their recurring problems. Thus, the same person—with the same recurring anxieties, depression, or marital difficulty—may be a "success" story in several therapists' files.

Because people enter therapy when they are extremely unhappy, and usually leave when they are less extremely unhappy, most therapists, like most clients, testify to therapy's success—regardless of the treatment.

Outcome Research

How, then, can we objectively measure the effectiveness of psychotherapy? How can we determine what types of people and problems are best helped, and by what type of psychotherapy? In search of answers, psychologists have turned to controlled research studies.

In the 1800s, the field of medicine faced a similar challenge. Physicians, skeptical of many of the fashionable treatments (bleeding, purging, infusions of plant and metal substances) began to realize that many patients got better on their own, without these treatments, and that others died in spite of them. Sorting fact from superstition required following patients with and without a particular treatment. Typhoid fever patients, for example, often improved after being bled, convincing most physicians that the treatment worked. Not until a control group was given mere bed rest—and 70 percent were observed to improve after five weeks of fever—did physicians learn, to their shock, that the bleeding was worthless (Thomas, 1992).

In the twentieth century, psychology, with its many diverse therapy options, faced a similar challenge. British psychologist Hans Eysenck (1952) launched a spirited debate when he summarized 24 studies of psychotherapy outcomes and found that two-thirds of those receiving psychotherapy for nonpsychotic disorders improved markedly. To this day, no one disputes that optimistic estimate.

Why, then, are we still debating psychotherapy's effectiveness? Because Eysenck also reported similar improvement among *untreated* persons, such as those who were on waiting lists. With or without psychotherapy, he said, roughly two-thirds improved noticeably. Time was a great healer.

Eysenck's sample was small, but later summaries have analyzed hundreds of studies (Kopta et al., 1999; Shadish et al., 2000). Many of these studies were *randomized clinical trials*, in which researchers randomly assign people on a waiting list to therapy or to no therapy, and later evaluate everyone, using tests and the reports of people who don't know whether therapy was given. The first statistical summary, of some 475 psychotherapy outcome studies (Smith et al., 1977, 1980), showed that the average therapy client ends up better off than 80 percent of the untreated individuals on waiting lists. The claim is modest—by definition, about 50 percent of untreated people also are better off than the average untreated person. Nevertheless, Mary Lee Smith and her colleagues exulted that "psychotherapy benefits people of all ages as reliably as schooling educates them, medicine cures them, or business turns a profit" (p. 183). Later summaries echoed the results: *Those not undergoing therapy often improve, but those undergoing therapy are more likely to improve.*

Is psychotherapy also cost-effective? Again, the answer is *yes*. When people seek psychological treatment, their search for other medical treatment drops—by 16 percent in one summary of 91 studies (Chiles et al., 1999). Given the staggering annual cost of psychological disorders and substance abuse—including crime, accidents, lost work, and treatment—this is a good investment, much like money spent on prenatal and well-baby care. Both *reduce* long-term costs. Boosting employees' psychological well-being, for example, can lower medical costs, improve work efficiency, and diminish absenteeism.

But note that the claim—that psychotherapy, *on average*, is somewhat effective—refers to no one therapy in particular. It is like reassuring lung-cancer patients that "on average," medical treatment of health problems is effective. What people want to know is the effectiveness of a *particular* treatment for their *specific* problem.

> "Fortunately, [psycho]analysis is not the only way to resolve inner conflicts. Life itself still remains a very effective therapist."
>
> —Karen Horney, *Our Inner Conflicts*, 1945

The Relative Effectiveness of Different Therapies

7: Are some therapies more effective than others?

The statistical summaries and surveys have failed to pinpoint any one type of therapy as generally superior (Smith et al., 1977, 1980). So, was the dodo bird in *Alice in Wonderland* right: "Everyone has won and all must have prizes"? Not quite. Some forms of therapy do get prizes for particular problems.

Behavioral conditioning therapies, for example, have achieved especially favorable results with specific behavior problems, such as bed-wetting, phobias, compulsions, marital problems, and sexual disorders (Bowers & Clum, 1988; Hunsley & DiGiulio, 2002; Shadish & Baldwin, 2005). Studies confirm cognitive therapy's effectiveness in coping with depression and reducing suicide risk (Brown et al., 2005; DeRubeis et al., 2005; Hollon et al., 2005).

Moreover, we can say that therapy is most effective when the problem is clear-cut (Singer, 1981; Westen & Morrison, 2001). Those who experience phobias or panic, who are unassertive, or who are frustrated by sexual performance problems can

> "Whatever differences in treatment efficacy exist, they appear to be extremely small, at best."
>
> —Bruce Wampold et al. (1997)

> "Different sores have different salves."
>
> —English proverb

hope for improvement. Those with less-focused problems, such as depression and anxiety, usually benefit in the short term but often relapse later. And those with the negative symptoms of chronic schizophrenia or a desire to change their entire personality are unlikely to benefit from psychotherapy alone (Pfammatter et al., 2006; Zilbergeld, 1983). The more specific the problem, the greater the hope.

But no prizes—and little or no scientific support—go to certain other therapies (Arkowitz & Lilienfeld, 2006):

- **Energy therapies** propose to manipulate people's invisible energy fields.
- **Recovered-memory therapies** aim to unearth "repressed memories" of early childhood abuse (Chapter 8).
- **Rebirthing therapies** engage people in reenacting the supposed trauma of their birth.
- **Facilitated communication** has an assistant touch the typing hand of a child with autism.
- **Crisis debriefing** forces people to verbalize, rehearse, and "process" their traumatic experiences.

The question—Which therapies get prizes and which do not?—lies at the heart of a serious controversy some call psychology's civil war. To what extent should science guide both clinical practice and the willingness of health care providers and insurers to pay for psychotherapy? On the one side are research psychologists using scientific methods to extend the list of well-defined and validated therapies for various disorders. On the other side are nonscientist therapists who view their practices as more art than science, saying that people are too complex and therapy too intuitive to describe in a manual or test in an experiment. Between these two factions stand the science-oriented clinicians, who advocate **evidence-based practice,** the integration of the best available research with clinical expertise and patient preferences and characteristics. These clinicians believe that by basing practice on evidence and making mental health professionals accountable for effectiveness, therapy will only gain in credibility. Moreover, the public will be protected from pseudotherapies, and therapists will be protected from accusations of sounding like snake-oil salespeople—"Trust me, I know it works, I've seen it work."

To encourage evidence-based practice in psychology, the American Psychological Association (2006; Spring, 2007) has followed the Institute of Medicine's lead, advocating that available therapies "should be rigorously evaluated" and then applied by clinicians who are mindful of their skills and of each patient's unique situation (**FIGURE 14.4**). Increasingly, insurer and government support for mental health services requires evidence-based practice. In late 2007, for example, Britain's National Health Service announced that it would pour the equivalent of $600 million into training new mental health workers in evidence-based practices (such as cognitive-behavioral therapy) and to disseminating information about such treatments (DeAngelis, 2008).

Evaluating Alternative Therapies

8: **How do alternative therapies fare under scientific scrutiny?**

Bolstered by anecdotes, heralded by the media, and praised on the Internet, alternative therapies can spread like wildfire. In one national survey, 57 percent of those with a history of anxiety attacks and 54 percent of those with a history of depression had used alternative treatments, such as herbal medicine, massage, and spiritual healing (Kessler et al., 2001).

Natural or spontaneous recovery (the tendency of many abnormal states of mind to return to normal), combined with the placebo effect (a result caused by expectations alone), creates fertile soil for pseudotherapies. Testimonials aside, what does the evidence say? This is a tough question, because there is no evidence for or

evidence-based practice clinical decision making that integrates the best available research with clinical expertise and patient characteristics and preferences.

FIGURE 14.4 Evidence-based clinical decision making Ideal clinical decision making is a three-legged stool, upheld by knowledge of the patient, clinical expertise, and research evidence.

against most alternative therapies. Some, however, have been the subject of controlled research. Let's consider two of them. As we do, remember that sifting sense from nonsense requires the scientific attitude: being skeptical but not cynical, open to surprises but not gullible.

Eye Movement Desensitization and Reprocessing (EMDR)

EMDR (eye movement desensitization and reprocessing) is a therapy adored by thousands and dismissed by thousands more as a sham—"an excellent vehicle for illustrating the differences between scientific and pseudoscientific therapy techniques," suggested James Herbert and seven others (2000). Francine Shapiro (1989, 2007) developed EMDR one day while walking in a park and observing that anxious thoughts vanished as her eyes spontaneously darted about. Offering her novel anxiety treatment to others, she had people imagine traumatic scenes while she triggered eye movements by waving her finger in front of their eyes, supposedly enabling them to unlock and reprocess previously frozen memories. After she tried this on 22 people haunted by old traumatic memories, and all reported marked reductions in their distress after just one therapeutic session, the extraordinary result evoked an enormous response from mental health professionals. To date, nearly 70,000 of them, from more than 75 countries, have undergone training (EMDR, 2008). Not since the similarly charismatic Franz Anton Mesmer introduced *animal magnetism* (hypnosis) more than two centuries ago (also after feeling inspired by an outdoor experience) has a new therapy attracted so many devotees so quickly.

Does EMDR work? For 84 to 100 percent of single-trauma victims participating in four studies, the answer was *yes,* reported Shapiro (1999, 2002). (When EMDR did not fare well in other trials, Shapiro argued that the therapists were not properly trained.) Moreover, the treatment need take no more than three 90-minute sessions. The Society of Clinical Psychology task force on empirically validated treatments has acknowledged that the treatment is "probably efficacious" for the treatment of nonmilitary post-traumatic stress disorder (Chambless et al., 1997; see also Bisson & Andrew, 2007; Seidler & Wagner, 2006). Encouraged by their seeming successes, EMDR therapists have applied the technique to other anxiety disorders, such as panic disorder, and, with Shapiro's (1995, 2002) encouragement, to a wide range of complaints, including pain, grief, paranoid schizophrenia, rage, and guilt.

Why, wonder the skeptics, should rapidly moving one's eyes while recalling traumas be therapeutic? Indeed, controlled trials have indicated that eye movements are *not* the therapeutic ingredient: Whether people imagined traumatic scenes and tapped a finger, or just stared straight ahead while the therapist's finger wagged, the therapeutic results were the same (Devilly, 2003). EMDR does work better than doing nothing, acknowledge the skeptics (Lilienfeld & Arkowitz, 2007), but many suspect that what is therapeutic is the combination of exposure therapy—repeatedly

> "Studies indicate that EMDR is just as effective with fixed eyes. If that conclusion is right, what's useful in the therapy (chiefly behavioral desensitization) is not new, and what's new is superfluous."
>
> —*Harvard Mental Health Letter,* 2002

EMDR Eye movement desensitization and reprocessing is a controversial therapy procedure that may provide a form of exposure therapy for trauma survivors.

Bianca Moscatelli/Worth Publishers

associating traumatic memories with a safe and reassuring context that provides some emotional distance from the experience—and a robust placebo effect. Had Mesmer's pseudotherapy been compared with no treatment at all, it, too (thanks to the healing power of positive belief), could have been found "probably efficacious," observed Richard McNally (1999).

Light Exposure Therapy

Have you ever found yourself oversleeping, gaining weight, and feeling lethargic during the dark mornings and overcast days of winter? There likely was a survival advantage to your distant ancestors' slowing down and conserving energy during the dark days of winter. For some people, however, especially women and those liv-

ing far from the equator, the wintertime blahs constitute a form of depression known as *seasonal affective disorder*, for which the appropriate acronym is SAD. To counteract these dark spirits, National Institute of Mental Health researchers in the early 1980s had an idea: Give SAD people a timed daily dose of intense light. Sure enough, people reported they felt better.

Was this a bright idea, or another dim-witted example of the placebo effect, attributable to people's expectations? Recent studies shed some light. One exposed some people with SAD to 90 minutes of bright light and others to a sham placebo treatment—a "negative ion generator" about which the staff ex-

Courtesy of Christine Brune

Light therapy To counteract winter depression, some people spend time each morning exposed to intense light that mimics natural outdoor light. Light boxes to counteract SAD are available from health supply and lighting stores.

pressed similar enthusiasm (but which, unknown to the participants, was not turned on). After four weeks of treatment, 61 percent of those exposed to morning light had greatly improved, as had 50 percent of those exposed to evening light and 32 percent of those exposed to the placebo (Eastman et al., 1998). Other studies have found that 30 minutes of exposure to 10,000-lux white fluorescent light produced relief for more than half the people receiving morning light therapy and for one-third receiving evening light therapy (Terman et al., 1998, 2001). From 20 carefully controlled trials we have a verdict (Golden et al., 2005): Morning bright light does indeed dim SAD symptoms for many people. Moreover, it does so as effectively as taking antidepressant drugs or undergoing cognitive-behavioral therapy (Lam et al., 2006; Rohan et al., 2007). The effects are clear in brain scans; this therapy sparks activity in a brain region that influences the body's arousal and hormones (Ishida et al., 2005).

Commonalities Among Psychotherapies

9: **What three elements are shared by all forms of psychotherapy?**

The scientific attitude helps us sift sense from nonsense as we consider new forms of therapy. Might it also help explain another curious finding: There is little correlation between clinicians' experience, training, supervision, and licensing and their clients' outcomes. Clients in the *Consumer Reports* survey, for example, seemed equally satisfied whether treated by a psychiatrist, psychologist, or social worker; whether seen in a group or individual context; whether the therapist had extensive or relatively limited training and experience (Seligman, 1995). Other studies concur.

In search of some answers, researchers have studied the common ingredients of various therapies (Frank, 1982; Goldfried & Padawer, 1982; Strupp, 1986; Wampold, 2001, 2007). They suggest they all offer at least three benefits: *hope for demoralized people; a new perspective on oneself and the world;* and *an empathic, trusting, caring relationship.*

Hope for Demoralized People

People seeking therapy typically feel anxious, depressed, devoid of self-esteem, and incapable of turning things around. What any therapy offers is the expectation that, with commitment from the therapy seeker, things can and will get better. This belief, apart from any therapeutic technique, may function as a placebo, improving morale, creating feelings of self-efficacy, and diminishing symptoms (Prioleau et al., 1983). Statistical analyses showing that improvement is greater for placebo-treated people than for untreated people suggest that one way therapies help is by harnessing the client's own healing powers. And that, said psychiatrist Jerome Frank (1982), helps us understand why all sorts of treatments—including some folk healing rites that are powerless apart from the participants' belief—may in their own time and place produce cures.

A New Perspective

Every therapy also offers people a plausible explanation of their symptoms and an alternative way of looking at themselves or responding to their world. Armed with a believable fresh perspective, they may approach life with a new attitude, open to making changes in their behaviors and their views of themselves.

An Empathic, Trusting, Caring Relationship

To say that therapy outcome is unrelated to training and experience is not to say all *therapists* are equally effective. No matter what technique they use, effective therapists are empathic people who seek to understand another's experience; who communicate their care and concern to the client; and who earn the client's trust and respect through respectful listening, reassurance, and advice. Marvin Goldfried and his associates (1998) found these qualities in taped therapy sessions from 36 recognized master therapists. Some were cognitive-behavioral therapists, others were psychodynamic-interpersonal therapists. Regardless, the striking finding was how *similar* they were during the parts of their sessions they considered most significant. At key moments, the empathic therapists of both persuasions would help clients evaluate themselves, link one aspect of their life with another, and gain insight into their interactions with others.

The emotional bond between therapist and client—the *therapeutic alliance*—is a key aspect of effective therapy (Klein et al., 2003; Wampold, 2001). One U.S. National Institute of Mental Health depression-treatment study confirmed that the most effective therapists were those who were perceived as most empathic and caring and who established the closest therapeutic bonds with their clients (Blatt et al., 1996).

That all therapies offer hope through a fresh perspective offered by a caring person is what also enables paraprofessionals (briefly trained caregivers) to assist so many troubled people so effectively (Christensen & Jacobson, 1994). These three common elements are also part of what the growing numbers of self-help and support groups offer their members. And they are part of what traditional healers have offered (Jackson, 1992). Healers everywhere—special people to whom others disclose their suffering, whether psychiatrists, witch doctors, or shamans—have listened in order to understand and to empathize, reassure, advise, console, interpret, or explain (Torrey, 1986). Such qualities may also explain why

"I utilize the best from Freud, the best from Jung, and the best from my Uncle Marty, a very smart fellow."

A caring relationship Effective therapists form a bond of trust with their patients.

people who feel supported by close relationships—who enjoy the fellowship and friendship of caring people—are less likely to need or seek therapy (Frank, 1982; O'Connor & Brown, 1984).

* * *

To recap, people who seek help usually improve. So do many of those who do not undergo psychotherapy, and that is a tribute to our human resourcefulness and our capacity to care for one another. Nevertheless, though the therapist's orientation and experience appear not to matter much, people who receive some psychotherapy usually improve more than those who do not. People with clear-cut, specific problems tend to improve the most.

Culture and Values in Psychotherapy

10: How do culture and values influence the therapist-client relationship?

All therapies offer hope, and nearly all therapists attempt to enhance their clients' sensitivity, openness, personal responsibility, and sense of purpose (Jensen & Bergin, 1988). But in matters of culture and values, therapists differ from one another and may differ from their clients (Delaney et al., 2007; Kelly, 1990).

These differences can become significant when a therapist from one culture meets a client from another. In North America, Europe, and Australia, for example, most therapists reflect their culture's individualism, which often gives priority to personal desires and identity. Clients who are immigrants from Asian countries, where people are mindful of others' expectations, may have trouble relating to therapies that require them to think only of their own well-being. Such differences help explain the reluctance of some minority populations to use mental health services (Sue, 2006). In one experiment, Asian-American clients matched with counselors who shared their cultural values (rather than mismatched with those who did not) perceived more counselor empathy and felt a stronger alliance with the counselor (Kim et al., 2005). Recognizing that therapists and clients may differ in their values, communication styles, and language, many therapy training programs now provide training in cultural sensitivity and recruit members of underrepresented cultural groups.

Another area of potential value conflict is religion. Highly religious people may prefer and benefit from religiously similar therapists (Smith et al., 2007; Wade et al., 2006; Worthington et al., 1996). They may have trouble establishing an emotional bond with a therapist who does not share their values. Albert Ellis, who advocated an aggressive *rational-emotive therapy*, and Allen Bergin, co-editor of the *Handbook of Psychotherapy and Behavior Change*, illustrated how sharply such differences can affect a therapist's view of a healthy person. Ellis (1980) assumed that "no one and nothing is supreme," that "self-gratification" should be encouraged, and that "unequivocal love, commitment, service, and . . . fidelity to any interpersonal commitment, especially marriage, leads to harmful consequences." Bergin (1980) assumed the opposite—that "because God is supreme, humility and the acceptance of divine authority are virtues," that "self-control and committed love and self-sacrifice are to be encouraged," and that "infidelity to any interpersonal commitment, especially marriage, leads to harmful consequences."

Bergin and Ellis disagreed more radically than most therapists on what values are healthiest. In so doing, however, they agreed on a more general point: Psychotherapists' personal beliefs influence their practice. Because clients tend to adopt their therapists' values (Worthington et al., 1996), some psychologists believe therapists should divulge those values more openly. (For those thinking about seeking therapy, Close-Up: A Consumer's Guide to Psychotherapists on the next page offers some tips on when to seek help and how to start searching for a therapist who shares your perspective and goals.)

A Consumer's Guide to Psychotherapists

Life for everyone is marked by a mix of serenity and stress, blessing and bereavement, good moods and bad. So, when should we seek a mental health professional's help? The American Psychological Association offers these common trouble signals:

- Feelings of hopelessness
- Deep and lasting depression
- Self-destructive behavior, such as alcohol and drug abuse
- Disruptive fears
- Sudden mood shifts
- Thoughts of suicide
- Compulsive rituals, such as hand washing
- Sexual difficulties

Before 1950, psychiatrists were the primary providers of mental health care. Today, surging demands for psychotherapy also occupy the time and attention of clinical and counseling psychologists; clinical and psychiatric social workers; pastoral, marital, abuse, and school counselors; and psychiatric nurses (**TABLE 14.2**). In looking for a therapist, you may want to have a preliminary consultation with two or three. You can describe your problem and learn each therapist's treatment approach. You can ask questions about the therapist's values, credentials, and fees. And, knowing the importance of the emotional bond between therapist and client, you can assess your own feelings about each of them.

TABLE 14.2 Therapists and Their Training

Type	Description
Counselors	Marriage and family counselors specialize in problems arising from family relations. Pastoral and school counselors provide counseling to countless people. Abuse counselors work with substance abusers and with spouse and child abusers and their victims.
Clinical or psychiatric social workers	A two-year master of social work graduate program plus postgraduate supervision prepares some social workers to offer psychotherapy, mostly to people with everyday personal and family problems. About half have earned the National Association of Social Workers' designation of clinical social worker.
Clinical psychologists	Most are psychologists with a Ph.D. or Psy.D. and expertise in research, assessment, and therapy, supplemented by a supervised internship and, often, postdoctoral training. About half work in agencies and institutions, half in private practice.
Psychiatrists	Psychiatrists are physicians who specialize in the treatment of psychological disorders. Not all psychiatrists have had extensive training in psychotherapy, but as M.D.s they can prescribe medications. Thus, they tend to see those with the most serious problems. Many have their own private practice.

11. The most enthusiastic or optimistic view of the effectiveness of psychotherapy comes from
a. outcome research.
b. randomized clinical trials.
c. reports of clinicians and clients.
d. a government study of treatment for depression.

12. On average, troubled people who undergo therapy are more likely to improve than those who do not. Studies show that _____ therapy is most effective overall.
a. behavior
b. humanistic
c. psychodynamic
d. no one type of

13. The three ingredients of evidence-based practice are
a. research evidence, clinical expertise, and knowledge of the patient.
b. hope, a fresh perspective, and a caring relationship.
c. biological, psychological, and social-cultural influences.
d. the client, the clinician, and their shared values.

14. One alternative therapy that has passed the test of critical evaluation is
a. rebirthing therapy.
b. light exposure therapy.
c. facilitated communication.
d. energy therapy.

Answers: 11. c, 12. d, 13. a, 14. b.

The Biomedical Therapies

Psychotherapy is one way to treat psychological disorders. The other, often used with serious disorders, is **biomedical therapy**—physically changing the brain's functioning by altering its chemistry with drugs, or affecting its circuitry with various kinds of direct stimulation or psychosurgery. Psychologists can provide psychological therapies. But with a few exceptions, only psychiatrists (as medical doctors) offer biomedical therapies.

biomedical therapy prescribed medications or medical procedures that act directly on the patient's nervous system.

Drug Therapies

11: What are the drug therapies? What criticisms have been leveled against drug therapies?

By far the most widely used biomedical treatments today are the drug therapies. Since the 1950s, discoveries in **psychopharmacology** (the study of drug effects on mind and behavior) have revolutionized the treatment of people with severe disorders, liberating hundreds of thousands from hospital confinement. Thanks to drug therapy—and to efforts to minimize involuntary hospitalization and to support people with community mental health programs—the resident population of U.S. state and county mental hospitals is a small fraction of what it was a half-century ago (**FIGURE 14.5**).

FIGURE 14.5 The emptying of U.S. mental hospitals After the widespread introduction of antipsychotic drugs, starting in about 1955, the number of residents in state and county mental hospitals declined sharply. But in the rush to deinstitutionalize the mentally ill, many people who were ill-equipped to care for themselves were left homeless on city streets. (Data from the U.S. National Institute of Mental Health and Bureau of the Census, 2004.)

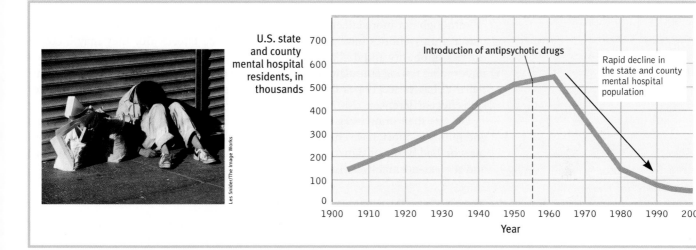

Almost any new treatment, including drug therapy, is greeted by an initial wave of enthusiasm as many people apparently improve. But that enthusiasm often diminishes after researchers subtract the rates of (1) spontaneous recovery, normal recovery among untreated persons, and (2) recovery due to the *placebo effect*, which arises from the positive expectations of patients and mental health workers alike. So, to evaluate the effectiveness of any new drug, researchers give half the patients the drug, and the other half a similar-appearing placebo. Because neither the staff nor the patients know who gets which, this is called a *double-blind technique*. The good news: In double-blind studies, several types of drugs have proven useful in treating psychological disorders.

"Our psychopharmacologist is a genius."

Drug or placebo effect?
For many people, depression lifts while taking an antidepressant drug. But people given a placebo may experience the same effect. Double-blind clinical trials suggest that, especially for those with severe depression, antidepressant drugs do have at least a modest clinical effect.

Antipsychotic Drugs

The revolution in drug therapy for psychological disorders began with the accidental discovery that certain drugs, used for other medical purposes, calmed patients with *psychoses* (disorders in which hallucinations or delusions indicate some loss of contact with reality). These **antipsychotic drugs,** such as chlorpromazine (sold as Thorazine), dampened responsiveness to irrelevant stimuli. Thus, they provided the most help to patients experiencing positive symptoms of schizophrenia, such as auditory hallucinations and paranoia (Lehman et al., 1998; Lenzenweger et al., 1989).

psychopharmacology the study of the effects of drugs on mind and behavior.

antipsychotic drugs drugs used to treat schizophrenia and other forms of severe thought disorder.

Perhaps you can guess an occasional side effect of L-dopa, a drug that raises dopamine levels for Parkinson's patients: hallucinations.

The molecules of most conventional antipsychotic drugs are similar enough to molecules of the neurotransmitter dopamine to occupy its receptor sites and block its activity. This finding reinforces the idea that an overactive dopamine system contributes to schizophrenia (Chapter 13). Antipsychotics are powerful drugs. Some can produce sluggishness, tremors, and twitches similar to those of Parkinson's disease, which is marked by too little dopamine (Kaplan & Saddock, 1989). Long-term use of these medications can also produce *tardive dyskinesia* with involuntary movements of the facial muscles (such as grimacing), tongue, and limbs.

Patients exhibiting the negative symptoms of schizophrenia, such as apathy and withdrawal, often do not respond well to conventional antipsychotic drugs. Newer *atypical antipsychotics,* such as clozapine (marketed since 1989 as Clozaril), target both dopamine and serotonin receptors. This helps alleviate negative symptoms, sometimes enabling "awakenings" in these individuals. Atypical antipsychotics may also help those who have positive symptoms but have not responded to other drugs.

Although not more effective in controlling schizophrenia symptoms, many of the newer antipsychotics have fewer conventional side effects. But they may increase the risk of obesity and diabetes (Lieberman et al., 2005, 2006). One new drug now undergoing testing stimulates receptors for the amino acid called glutamate. An initial trial has raised hopes that it may reduce schizophrenia symptoms with fewer side effects (Berenson, 2007).

Despite their drawbacks, antipsychotic drugs, combined with life-skills programs and family support, have enabled hundreds of thousands of people with schizophrenia who had been consigned to the back wards of mental hospitals to return to work and to near-normal lives (Leucht et al., 2003).

Antianxiety Drugs

Like alcohol, **antianxiety** agents, such as Xanax or Ativan, depress central nervous system activity (and so should not be used in combination with alcohol). Antianxiety drugs are often used in combination with psychological therapy. A new antianxiety drug, the antibiotic D-cycloserine, acts upon a receptor that facilitates the extinction of learned fears. Experiments indicate that the drug enhances the benefits of exposure therapy and helps relieve the symptoms of post-traumatic stress disorder and obsessive-compulsive disorder (Davis, 2005; Kushner et al., 2007).

A criticism sometimes made of the behavior therapies—that they reduce symptoms without resolving underlying problems—is also made of antianxiety drugs. Unlike the behavior therapies, however, these substances may be used as an ongoing treatment. "Popping a Xanax" at the first sign of tension can produce psychological dependence; the immediate relief reinforces a person's tendency to take drugs when anxious. Antianxiety drugs can also cause physiological dependence. After heavy use, people who stop taking them may experience increased anxiety, insomnia, and other withdrawal symptoms.

On U.S. college campuses, the 9 percent of counseling center visitors taking psychiatric medication in 1994 nearly tripled, to 24.5 percent in 2004 (Duenwald, 2004).

Over the dozen years at the end of the twentieth century, the rate of outpatient treatment for anxiety disorders nearly doubled. The proportion of psychiatric patients receiving medication during that time increased from 52 to 70 percent (Olfson et al., 2004). And the new standard drug treatment for anxiety disorders? Antidepressants.

Antidepressant Drugs

The **antidepressants** were named for their ability to lift people up from a state of depression, and this was their main use until recently. The label is a bit of a misnomer now that these drugs are increasingly being used to successfully treat anxiety disorders such as obsessive-compulsive disorder. They work by increasing the availability of norepinephrine or serotonin, neurotransmitters that elevate arousal and mood and appear scarce during depression. Fluoxetine, which tens of millions of users worldwide have known as Prozac, partially blocks the reabsorption and removal of serotonin from

antianxiety drugs drugs used to control anxiety and agitation.

antidepressant drugs drugs used to treat depression; also increasingly prescribed for anxiety. Different types work by altering the availability of various neurotransmitters.

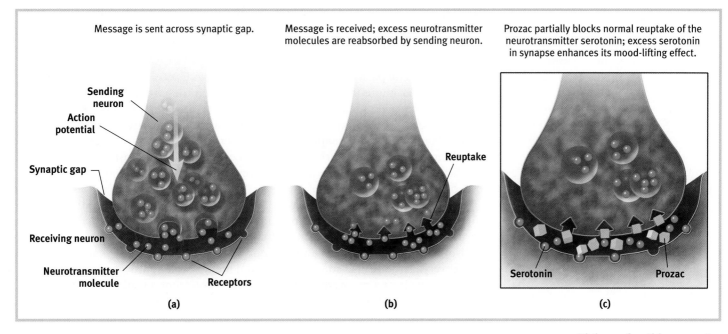

Message is sent across synaptic gap.

Message is received; excess neurotransmitter molecules are reabsorbed by sending neuron.

Prozac partially blocks normal reuptake of the neurotransmitter serotonin; excess serotonin in synapse enhances its mood-lifting effect.

FIGURE 14.6 Biology of antidepressants
Shown here is the action of Prozac, which partially blocks the reuptake of serotonin.

synapses (**FIGURE 14.6**). Because they slow the synaptic vacuuming up of serotonin, Prozac, and its cousins Zoloft and Paxil, are called *selective-serotonin-reuptake-inhibitors (SSRIs)*. Other antidepressants work by blocking the reabsorption or breakdown of both norepinephrine and serotonin. Though effective, these dual-action drugs have more potential side effects, such as dry mouth, weight gain, hypertension, or dizzy spells (Anderson, 2000; Mulrow, 1999). Administering them by means of a patch, bypassing the intestines and liver, helps reduce such side effects (Bodkin & Amsterdam, 2002).

After the introduction of SSRI drugs, the percentage of patients receiving medication for depression jumped dramatically, from 70 percent in 1987, the year before SSRIs were introduced, to 89 percent in 2001 (Olfson et al., 2003; Stafford et al., 2001). In the United States, 11 percent of women and 5 percent of men are now taking antidepressants (Barber, 2008).

Be advised: Patients with depression who begin taking antidepressants do not wake up the next day singing "Oh, what a beautiful morning!" Although the drugs begin to influence neurotransmission within hours, their full psychological effect often requires four weeks (and may involve a side effect of diminished sexual desire). One possible reason for the delay is that increased serotonin promotes *neurogenesis*—the birth of new brain cells, perhaps reversing stress-induced loss of neurons (Becker & Wojtowicz, 2007; Jacobs, 2004).

Antidepressant drugs are not the only way to give the body a lift. Aerobic exercise, which helps calm people who feel anxious and energize those who feel depressed, does about as much good for some people with mild to moderate depression, and has additional positive side effects (more on this topic later in this chapter). Cognitive therapy, by helping people reverse their habitual negative thinking style, can boost the drug-aided relief from depression and reduce the post-treatment risk of relapse (Hollon et al., 2002; Keller et al., 2000; Vittengl et al., 2007). Better yet, some studies suggest, is to attack depression from both above and below (Goldapple et al., 2004; TADS, 2004). Use antidepressant drugs (which work, bottom-up, on the emotion-forming limbic system) in conjunction with cognitive-behavioral therapy (which works, top-down, starting with changed frontal lobe activity).

Everyone agrees that people with depression often improve after a month on antidepressants. But drug effects, like psychotherapy effects, can be inflated by other influences. After allowing for natural recovery and the placebo effect,

"If this doesn't help you don't worry, it's a placebo."

electroconvulsive therapy (ECT) a biomedical therapy for severely depressed patients in which a brief electric current is sent through the brain of an anesthetized patient.

"No twisted thought without a twisted molecule."

—Attributed to psychologist Ralph Gerard

"First of all I think you should know that last quarter's sales figures are interfering with my mood-stabilizing drugs."

"Lithium prevents my seductive but disastrous highs, diminishes my depressions, clears out the wool and webbing from my disordered thinking, slows me down, gentles me out, keeps me from ruining my career and relationships, keeps me out of a hospital, alive, and makes psychotherapy possible."

—Kay Redfield Jamison, *An Unquiet Mind*, 1995

The medical use of electricity is an ancient practice. Physicians treated the Roman Emperor Claudius (10 B.C.E.–C.E. 54) for headaches by pressing electric eels to his temples.

how big is the drug effect? Not big, report Irving Kirsch and his colleagues (1998, 2002). Their analyses of double-blind clinical trials indicate that placebos accounted for about 75 percent of the active drug's effect. In a follow-up review that included unpublished clinical trials, the antidepressant drug effect was again modest (Kirsch et al., 2008). The placebo effect was less for those with severe depression, who benefited somewhat more from taking the drug. "Given these results, there seems little reason to prescribe antidepressant medication to any but the most severely depressed patients, unless alternative treatments have failed," Kirsch concluded (BBC, 2008). For about 1 in 4 people who do not respond to a particular antidepressant, switching to another does bring relief (Rush et al., 2006). Scientists dream of a not-too-far-off day when patients may be screened for genetic variations that will indicate drugs to use or avoid.

The effects of drug therapy may be less exciting than many TV ads suggest, but they also are less frightening than other stories have warned. Some people taking Prozac, for example, have committed suicide, but their numbers seem fewer than we would expect from the millions of depressed people now taking that medication. Moreover, a large British study revealed that the ups and downs of adolescent SSRI prescriptions over time were unrelated to the adolescent suicide rate (Wheeler et al., 2008). Prozac users who commit suicide are like cell-phone users who get brain cancer. Given the millions of people taking Prozac and using cell phones, alarming anecdotes tell us nothing.

The question critical thinkers want answered is this: Do these groups suffer an elevated *rate* of suicide and brain cancer? The answer in each case appears to be *no* (Grunebaum et al., 2004; Paulos, 1995; Tollefson et al., 1993, 1994). Three recent studies of between 70,000 and 439,000 patients concur that, in the long run, patients attempt fewer suicides if treated with antidepressants (Gibbons et al., 2007; Simon & Savarino, 2007; Sønergård et al., 2006).

Mood-Stabilizing Medications

In addition to antipsychotic, antianxiety, and antidepressant drugs, psychiatrists have *mood-stabilizing drugs* in their arsenal. The simple salt *lithium* can be an effective mood stabilizer for those suffering the emotional highs and lows of bipolar disorder. Australian physician John Cade discovered this in the 1940s when he administered lithium to a patient with severe mania. Although Cade's reasoning was misguided—he thought lithium had calmed excitable guinea pigs when actually it had made them sick—his patient became perfectly well in less than a week (Snyder, 1986). After suffering mood swings for years, about 7 in 10 people with bipolar disorder benefit from a long-term daily dose of this cheap salt (Solomon et al., 1995). Their risk of suicide is but one-sixth that of bipolar patients not taking lithium (Tondo et al., 1997).

Although we do not fully understand why, lithium works. And so does Depakote, a drug originally used to treat epilepsy and more recently found effective in the control of manic episodes associated with bipolar disorder.

Brain Stimulation

12: How effective is electroconvulsive therapy, and what other brain-stimulation options may offer relief from severe depression?

Electroconvulsive Therapy

A more controversial brain manipulation occurs through shock treatment, or **electroconvulsive therapy (ECT)**. When ECT was first introduced in 1938, the wide-awake patient was strapped to a table and jolted with roughly 100 volts of electricity to the brain, producing racking convulsions and brief unconsciousness.

ECT therefore gained a barbaric image, one that lingers. Today, however, it is administered with briefer pulses, sometimes only to the brain's right side and with less memory disruption (HMHL, 2007). The patient receives a general anesthetic and a muscle relaxant (to prevent injury from convulsions) before a psychiatrist delivers 30 to 60 seconds of electrical current to the patient's brain (**FIGURE 14.7**). Within 30 minutes, the patient awakens and remembers nothing of the treatment or of the preceding hours. After three such sessions each week for two to four weeks, 80 percent or more of people receiving ECT improve markedly, showing no discernible brain damage. Study after study has confirmed that ECT is an effective treatment for severe depression in patients who have not responded to drug therapy (Pagnin et al., 2004; UK ECT Review Group, 2003). ECT reduces suicidal thoughts and is credited with saving many from suicide (Kellner et al., 2005). One leading medical journal has concluded that "the results of ECT in treating severe depression are among the most positive treatment effects in all of medicine" (Glass, 2001).

How does ECT alleviate severe depression? After more than 50 years, no one knows for sure. One recipient likened ECT to the smallpox vaccine, which was saving lives before we knew how it worked. Perhaps the shock-induced seizures calm neural centers where overactivity produces depression. ECT, like antidepressant drugs and exercise, also appears to boost the production of new brain cells (Bolwig & Madsen, 2007).

ECT's results are not always long lasting. About 4 in 10 ECT-treated patients relapse into depression within six months (Kellner et al., 2006). Nevertheless, in the minds of many psychiatrists and patients, ECT is a lesser evil than severe depression's misery, anguish, and risk of suicide. As research psychologist Norman Endler (1982) reported after ECT alleviated his deep depression, "A miracle had happened in two weeks."

FIGURE 14.7 Electroconvulsive therapy Although controversial, ECT is often an effective treatment for depression that does not respond to drug therapy.

Alternative Neurostimulation Therapies

Some patients with chronic depression have found relief through a chest implant that intermittently stimulates the vagus nerve, which sends signals to the brain's mood-related limbic system (Fitzgerald & Daskalakis, 2008; George & Belmaker, 2007; Marangell et al., 2007). Two other techniques—deep-brain stimulation and magnetic stimulation—are also raising hopes for gentler alternatives that jump-start neural circuits in the depressed brain.

DEEP-BRAIN STIMULATION Patients whose depression has resisted both drugs that flood the body and ECT that jolts at least half the brain have benefited from an experimental treatment pinpointing at a brain depression center. Neuroscientist Helen Mayberg and her colleagues (2005, 2006, 2007; Dobbs, 2006) have been focusing on a cortex area that bridges the thinking frontal lobes to the limbic system. They have discovered that this area, which is overactive in the brain of a depressed or temporarily sad person, becomes calm when treated by ECT or antidepressants.

To experimentally excite neurons that inhibit this negative emotion-feeding activity, Mayberg drew upon the deep-brain stimulation technology sometimes used to treat tremors associated with Parkinson's disease. Among an initial 12 patients receiving implanted electrodes and a pacemaker stimulator, 8 experienced relief. Some felt suddenly more aware and became more talkative and engaged; others improved only slightly if at all. Future research will explore

A depression switch?
By comparing the brains of patients with and without depression, researcher Helen Mayberg identified a brain area that appears active in people who are depressed or sad, and whose activity may be calmed by deep-brain stimulation.

whether Mayberg has discovered a switch that can lift depression. Other researchers are following up on reports that deep-brain stimulation can offer relief to people with obsessive-compulsive disorder.

MAGNETIC STIMULATION Depressed moods also seem to improve when repeated pulses surge through a magnetic coil held close to a person's skull (**FIGURE 14.8**). Unlike deep-brain stimulation, the magnetic energy penetrates only to the brain's surface (though tests are under way with a higher energy field that penetrates more deeply). The painless procedure—called **repetitive transcranial magnetic stimulation (rTMS)**—is performed on wide-awake patients over several weeks. Unlike ECT, the rTMS procedure produces no seizures, memory loss, or other side effects.

In one double-blind experiment, 67 Israelis with major depression were randomly assigned to two groups (Klein et al., 1999). One group received rTMS daily for two weeks, while the other received sham treatments (without magnetic stimulation). At the end of the two weeks, half the stimulated patients showed at least a 50 percent improvement in their scores on a depression scale, as did only a quarter of the placebo group.

FIGURE 14.8 Magnets for the mind
Repetitive transcranial magnetic stimulation (rTMS) sends a painless magnetic field through the skull to the surface of the cortex. Pulses can be used to stimulate or dampen activity in various cortical areas. (From George, 2003.)

One possible explanation is that the stimulation energizes depressed patients' relatively inactive left frontal lobe (Helmuth, 2001). When repeatedly stimulated, nerve cells can form functioning circuits through long-term potentiation (LTP), a process described in Chapter 8.

Other clinical experiments have had mixed results. Some have found little effect of rTMS treatment. However, several recent studies using the latest techniques have produced significant relief from depression, as compared with sham treatments (George & Belmaker, 2007; Gross et al., 2007; O'Reardon et al., 2007).

Psychosurgery

13: What is psychosurgery?

Because its effects are irreversible, **psychosurgery**—surgery that removes or destroys brain tissue—is the most drastic and the least-used biomedical intervention for changing behavior. In the 1930s, Portuguese physician Egas Moniz developed what became the best-known psychosurgical operation: the **lobotomy.** Moniz found that cutting the nerves connecting the frontal lobes with the emotion-controlling centers of the inner brain calmed uncontrollably emotional and violent patients. In a crude but easy and inexpensive procedure that took only about 10 minutes, a neurosurgeon would shock the patient into a coma, hammer an icepick-like instrument through each eye socket into the brain, and then wiggle it to sever connections running up to the frontal lobes. Tens of thousands of severely disturbed people—including President John F. Kennedy's sister, Rosemary—were "lobotomized" between 1936 and 1954, and Moniz was honored with a Nobel Prize (Valenstein, 1986).

Although the intention was simply to disconnect emotion from thought, a lobotomy's effect was often more drastic: It usually decreased the person's misery or tension, but it also produced a permanently lethargic, immature, uncreative person. During the 1950s, after some 35,000 people had been lobotomized in the United States alone, calming drugs became available and psychosurgery was largely abandoned. Today, lobotomies are history, and other psychosurgery is used only in extreme cases. For example, if a patient suffers uncontrollable seizures, surgeons can deactivate the specific nerve clusters that cause or transmit the convulsions. MRI-guided precision surgery is also occasionally done to cut the circuits involved in severe obsessive-compulsive disorder (Sachdev & Sachdev, 1997). Because these procedures are irreversible, however, neurosurgeons perform them only as a last resort.

Therapeutic Life-Style Change

14: How, by caring for their bodies with a healthy life-style, might people find some relief from depression?

The effectiveness of the biomedical therapies reminds us of a fundamental lesson: We find it convenient to talk of separate psychological and biological influences, but everything psychological is also biological (**FIGURE 14.9**). Every thought and feeling depends on the functioning brain. Every creative idea, every moment of joy or anger, every period of depression emerges from the electrochemical activity of the living brain. The influence is two-way: When psychotherapy relieves obsessive-compulsive behavior, PET scans reveal a calmer brain (Schwartz et al., 1996).

For years, we have trusted our bodies to physicians and our minds to psychiatrists and psychologists. That neat separation no longer seems valid. Stress affects body chemistry and health. And chemical imbalances, whatever their cause, can produce psychological disorders.

repetitive transcranial magnetic stimulation (rTMS) the application of repeated pulses of magnetic energy to the brain; used to stimulate or suppress brain activity.

psychosurgery surgery that removes or destroys brain tissue in an effort to change behavior.

lobotomy a now-rare psychosurgical procedure once used to calm uncontrollably emotional or violent patients. The procedure cut the nerves connecting the frontal lobes to the emotion-controlling centers of the inner brain.

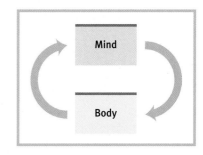

FIGURE 14.9 Mind-body interaction The biomedical therapies assume that mind and body are a unit: Affect one and you will affect the other.

That lesson is being applied by Stephen Ilardi and his colleagues (2008) in their training seminars promoting *therapeutic life-style change.* Human brains and bodies were designed for physical activity and social engagement, they note. Our ancestors hunted, gathered, and built in groups, with little evidence of disabling depression. Indeed, those whose way of life entails strenuous physical activity, strong community ties, sunlight exposure, and plenty of sleep (think of foraging bands in Papua, New Guinea, or Amish farming communities in North America) rarely experience major depression. "Simply put: Humans were never designed for the sedentary, disengaged, socially isolated, poorly nourished, sleep-deprived pace of twenty-first-century American life."

Other studies confirm that exercise reduces depression and anxiety and is therefore a useful adjunct to antidepressant drugs and psychotherapy (Dunn et al., 2005; Stathopoulou et al., 2006). Not only is exercise about as effective as drugs, some research suggests it better prevents symptom recurrence (Babyak et al., 2000; Salmon, 2001).

The Ilardi team was impressed by this research showing that regular aerobic exercise and a complete night's sleep boost mood and energy. So they invited small groups of people with depression to undergo a 12-week training program with the following goals:

- *Aerobic exercise,* 30 minutes a day, at least three times weekly (increases fitness and vitality, stimulates endorphins)
- *Adequate sleep,* with a goal of 7 to 8 hours a night (increases energy and alertness, boosts immunity)
- *Light exposure,* at least 30 minutes each morning with a light box (amplifies arousal, influences hormones)
- *Social connection,* with less alone time and at least two meaningful social engagements weekly (helps satisfy the human need to belong)
- *Anti-rumination,* by identifying and redirecting negative thoughts (enhances positive thinking)
- *Nutritional supplements,* including a daily fish oil supplement with omega-3 fatty acids (aids in healthy brain functioning)

In one study of 74 people, 77 percent of those who completed the program experienced relief from depressive symptoms, compared with a 19 percent rate in those assigned to a treatment-as-usual control condition. Future research will seek to replicate this striking result of life-style change and to identify which of the treatment components (some of which are part of other therapies) produce the therapeutic effect. But there seems little reason to doubt the truth of the Latin adage, *Mens sana in corpore sano:* "A healthy mind in a healthy body."

Preventing Psychological Disorders

15: **What is the rationale for preventive mental health programs?**

Psychotherapies and biomedical therapies tend to locate the cause of psychological disorders within the person with the disorder. We infer that people who act cruelly must be cruel and that people who act "crazy" must be "sick." We attach labels to such people, thereby distinguishing them from "normal" folks. It follows, then, that we try to treat "abnormal" people by giving them insight into their problems, by changing their thinking, by helping them gain control with drugs.

There is an alternative viewpoint: We could interpret many psychological disorders as understandable responses to a disturbing and stressful society. According to this view, it is not just the person who needs treatment, but also the person's social context. Better to prevent a problem by reforming a sick situation and by developing people's coping competencies than to wait for a problem to arise and then treat it.

A story about the rescue of a drowning person from a rushing river illustrates this viewpoint: Having successfully administered first aid to the first victim, the rescuer spots another struggling person and pulls her out, too. After a half-dozen repetitions, the rescuer suddenly turns and starts running away while the river sweeps yet another floundering person into view. "Aren't you going to rescue that fellow?" asks a bystander. "Heck no," the rescuer replies. "I'm going upstream to find out what's pushing all these people in."

Preventive mental health is upstream work. It seeks to prevent psychological casualties by identifying and alleviating the conditions that cause them. As George Albee (1986) pointed out, there is abundant evidence that poverty, meaningless work, constant criticism, unemployment, racism, and sexism undermine people's sense of competence, personal control, and self-esteem. Such stresses increase their risk of depression, alcohol dependency, and suicide.

We who care about preventing psychological casualties should, Albee contended, support programs that alleviate these demoralizing situations. We eliminated smallpox not by treating the afflicted but by inoculating the unafflicted. We conquered yellow fever by controlling mosquitoes. Preventing psychological problems means empowering those who have learned an attitude of helplessness, changing environments that breed loneliness, renewing the disintegrating family, and bolstering parents' and teachers' skills at nurturing children's achievements and resulting self-esteem. Indeed, "Everything aimed at improving the human condition, at making life more fulfilling and meaningful, may be considered part of primary prevention of mental or emotional disturbance" (Kessler & Albee, 1975, p. 557). That includes the cognitive training that promotes positive thinking in children at risk for depression (Gillham et al., 2006).

> "It is better to prevent than to cure."
>
> —Peruvian folk wisdom

> "Mental disorders arise from physical ones, and likewise physical disorders arise from mental ones."
>
> —*The Mahabharata*, C.E. 200

REHEARSE IT!

15. Some antipsychotic drugs, used to calm schizophrenia patients, can have unpleasant side effects, most notably
    a. hyperactivity.
    b. convulsions and momentary memory loss.
    c. sluggishness, tremors, and twitches.
    d. paranoia.

16. Xanax and Ativan, which depress central nervous system activity, are often used as ongoing treatment and can lead to dependency. These drugs are referred to as _____ drugs.
    a. antipsychotic
    b. antianxiety
    c. antidepressant
    d. antineurotic

17. One substance that often brings relief to patients suffering the highs and lows of bipolar disorder is
    a. rTMS.
    b. Xanax.
    c. lithium.
    d. clozapine.

18. Lobotomy, once used to treat uncontrollably violent patients, is no longer an accepted biomedical treatment. ECT, however, remains in use as a treatment for
    a. severe obsessive-compulsive disorder.
    b. severe depression.
    c. schizophrenia.
    d. anxiety disorders.

19. An approach that seeks to identify and alleviate conditions that put people at high risk for developing psychological disorders is called
    a. deep-brain stimulation.
    b. the mood-stabilizing perspective.
    c. spontaneous recovery.
    d. preventive mental health.

Answers: 15. c, 16. b, 17. c, 18. b, 19. d.

Therapy

The Psychological Therapies

Psychotherapy consists of interactions between a trained therapist and someone seeking to overcome psychological difficulties or achieve personal growth. The major psychotherapies derive from psychology's psychoanalytic, humanistic, behavioral, and cognitive perspectives. Today, many therapists combine aspects of these perspectives in an *eclectic approach* or psychotherapy integration.

1 What are the aims and methods of psychoanalysis, and how have they been adapted in psychodynamic therapy?

Freud believed that *psychoanalysis* would help people achieve healthier, less anxious lives by gaining insight into the unconscious origins of their disorders and by taking responsibility for their own growth. Techniques included free association, dream analysis, and *interpretation* of *resistances* and *transference* to the therapist of long-repressed feelings. Contemporary *psychodynamic therapy* is briefer and less expensive than traditional psychoanalysis, and it focuses on current symptoms and themes common to many past and present important relationships.

2 What are the basic themes of humanistic therapy, such as Rogers' client-centered approach?

Humanistic therapists have focused on clients' current conscious feelings and on their taking responsibility for their own growth. Rogers' *client-centered therapy* proposed that therapists' most important contributions are to exhibit genuineness, acceptance, and empathy. These qualities, plus the technique of *active listening* provide a growth-fostering environment of *unconditional positive regard*. The humanistic and psychoanalytic therapies are known as *insight therapies* because they attempt to improve functioning by increasing awareness of underlying motives and defenses.

3 What are the assumptions and techniques of the behavior therapies?

Behavior therapists do not attempt to explain the origin of problems or to promote self-awareness. Instead, they attempt to modify the problem behaviors themselves. Thus, they may *countercondition* behaviors through *exposure therapies*, such as *systematic desensitization* or virtual reality exposure therapy, or through *aversive conditioning*. Or they may apply operant conditioning principles with behavior modification techniques, such as *token economies*.

4 What are the goals and techniques of the cognitive therapies?

The *cognitive therapies*, such as Beck's cognitive therapy for depression, aim to change unwanted behaviors by teaching people new and more adaptive ways of thinking and behaving. The widely researched and practiced *cognitive-behavioral therapy* combines cognitive and behavior therapies to help clients learn new ways of thinking and to practice the more positive approach in their actions.

5 What are the aims and benefits of group and family therapy?

Group therapy sessions can help more people and cost less per person than individual therapy would. Clients may benefit from knowing others have similar problems and from getting feedback and reassurance. *Family therapy* views a family as an interactive system and attempts to help members discover the roles they play and to learn to communicate more openly and directly.

Evaluating Psychotherapies

6 Does psychotherapy work? Who decides?

Neither the positive testimonials of clients nor those of therapists can prove that therapy is effective. Statistical summaries of hundreds of outcome studies of psychotherapy's effectiveness indicate that people who remain untreated often improve, but those who receive psychotherapy are more likely to improve.

7 Are some therapies more effective than others?

No one type of psychotherapy has been found to be generally superior to all others. Therapy is most effective for those with clear-cut, specific problems. Some therapies—such as behavioral conditioning for treating phobias and compulsions—are more effective for specific disorders. *Evidence-based practice* integrates the best available research with clinicians' expertise and patients' characteristics and preferences.

8 How do alternative therapies fare under scientific scrutiny?

Controlled research has not supported the therapeutic power of eye movements during eye movement desensitization and reprocessing (EMDR) therapy. Light exposure therapy does seem to relieve the symptoms of seasonal affective disorder (SAD).

9 What three elements are shared by all forms of psychotherapy?

All psychotherapies offer new hope for demoralized people; a fresh perspective; and (if the therapist is effective) an empathic, trusting, and caring relationship.

10 How do culture and values influence the therapist-client relationship?

Therapists differ in the values that influence their aims. These differences may create problems when therapists work with clients with different cultural or religious perspectives. A person seeking therapy may want to ask about the therapist's treatment approach, values, credentials, and fees.

The Biomedical Therapies

The *biomedical therapies* treat psychological disorders with medications or medical procedures that act directly on the nervous system.

11 What are the drug therapies? What criticisms have been leveled against drug therapies?

Drug therapy, the most widely used biomedical therapy, alters brain chemistry, often by decreasing or increasing the available supply of particular neurotransmitters. Many *antipsychotic drugs,* used in treating schizophrenia, block dopamine activity, and some can have serious side effects. *Antianxiety drugs,* which depress central nervous system activity, are used to treat anxiety disorders. These drugs can

be physically and psychologically addictive. *Antidepressant drugs,* which increase the availability of serotonin and norepinephrine, are now used to treat anxiety as well as depression. Their full effect may not be felt for several weeks, and their effect is generally modest. Lithium and Depakote are mood stabilizers prescribed for those with bipolar disorder.

12 How effective is electroconvulsive therapy, and what other brain-stimulation options may offer relief from severe depression?

Electroconvulsive therapy (ECT), in which a brief electric current is sent through the brain of an anesthetized patient, is an effective, last-resort treatment for severely depressed people who have not responded to other therapy. Newer alternative treatments being considered for chronic depression include deep brain stimulation, which has calmed an overactive brain region linked with negative emotions, and *repetitive transcranial magnetic stimulation (rTMS),* which is used to alter activity in cortical areas.

13 What is psychosurgery?

Psychosurgery removes or destroys brain tissue in hopes of modifying behavior. The once-popular psychosurgery known as *lobotomy* proved to be dangerous and too radical. Neurosurgeons now rarely perform brain surgery to change behavior or moods. Brain surgery is a treatment of last resort because its effects are irreversible.

14 How, by caring for their bodies with a healthy life-style, might people find some relief from depression?

Mind and body interact. In early studies, people who completed a program of aerobic exercise, adequate sleep, light exposure, social engagement, negative-thought reduction, and better nutrition have experienced relief from depressive symptoms.

Preventing Psychological Disorders

15 What is the rationale for preventive mental health programs?

Preventive mental health programs are based on the idea that many psychological disorders could be prevented by changing oppressive, esteem-destroying environments into more benevolent, nurturing environments that foster individual growth and self-confidence.

Terms and Concepts to Remember

eclectic approach, p. 493
psychotherapy, p. 494
psychoanalysis, p. 494
resistance, p. 494
interpretation, p. 494
transference, p. 494
psychodynamic therapy, p. 495
insight therapies, p. 495
client-centered therapy, p. 496
active listening, p. 496
unconditional positive regard, p. 496

behavior therapy, p. 497
counterconditioning, p. 498
exposure therapies, p. 498
systematic desensitization, p. 498
aversive conditioning, p. 499
token economy, p. 500
cognitive therapy, p. 501
cognitive-behavioral therapy, p. 503
family therapy, p. 503
evidence-based practice, p. 507
biomedical therapy, p. 512

psychopharmacology, p. 513
antipsychotic drugs, p. 513
antianxiety drugs, p. 514
antidepressant drugs, p. 514
electroconvulsive therapy (ECT), p. 516
repetitive transcranial magnetic stimulation (rTMS), p. 518
psychosurgery, p. 519
lobotomy, p. 519

Test for Success: Critical Thinking Exercises
By Amy Himsel, El Camino College

1. American playwright August Wilson (1945–2005) advised, "Your willingness to wrestle with your demons will cause your angels to sing." Which psychological therapy best matches this quote, and why?

2. After a near-fatal car accident, Rico developed an intense fear of driving on the freeway. In fact, his anxious response to the freeway has become so intense that he must take lengthy alternative routes to work each day. Which psychological therapy might best help Rico overcome his phobia, and why?

3. How can we apply the knowledge that *everything psychological is simultaneously biological* to the treatment of depression?

4. Talia is convinced the "anxiety-relief" herbal tea she ordered online has improved her mental health over the past few weeks. What other explanations might account for Talia's improvement?

The Test for Success exercises offer you a chance to apply your critical thinking skills to aspects of the material you have just read. Suggestions for answering these questions can be found in Appendix D at the back of the book.

Multiple-choice self-tests and more may be found at www.worthpublishers.com/myers.

Chapter Outline

● **Social Thinking**
  Attributing Behavior to Persons
    or to Situations
  Attitudes and Actions
  CLOSE-UP: Abu Ghraib Prison:
    An "Atrocity-Producing
    Situation"?

● **Social Influence**
  Conformity and Obedience
  Group Influence
  The Power of Individuals

● **Social Relations**
  Prejudice
  CLOSE-UP: Automatic Prejudice
  Aggression
  **THINKING CRITICALLY
    ABOUT:** Do Video Games
    Teach, or Release, Violence?
  Attraction
  CLOSE-UP: Online Matchmaking
  Altruism
  Conflict and Peacemaking

Social Psychology

Although still young, this twenty-first century has dramatically reminded us that we are social animals whose lives and cultures revolve around how we think about, influence, and relate to one another.

On September 11, 2001, nineteen men with box cutters achieved an act of catastrophic violence that triggered fright, outrage, and a lust for revenge. But it also triggered an outpouring of compassion and care. What drives people to feel such hatred that they would destroy thousands of innocent lives? And what motivates the heroic altruism of those who died trying to save others and of the many more who reached out—with gifts of money, food, clothing, shelter, and love—to those coping with loss?

Echoes of these questions resurfaced after genocide plagued the Sudan's Darfur region beginning in 2003. And they resurfaced again during the war in Iraq, where survey-based estimates of deaths ranged from 151,000 to more than 1 million from 2002 through 2006 (Iraq Family Study, 2008; ORB, 2008). What factors affect the decision making of our world leaders? And how can we transform the closed fists of international conflict into the open arms of peace and cooperation?

As each day's news brings updates on acts of hate or heroism, defeats or victories, many of us live out our own experiences with love and loss. What spurs friendship and romance? And why do we help some but not others?

Human connections are powerful and can be perilous. Yet "we cannot live for ourselves alone," remarked the novelist Herman Melville. "Our lives are connected by a thousand invisible threads." **Social psychologists** explore these connections by *scientifically studying* how we *think about, influence,* and *relate to* one another.

Social Thinking

Our social behavior arises from our social cognition—our attitudes and our explanations of people's sometimes unexpected actions. Does her warmth reflect romantic interest, or is that how she relates to everyone? Does his absenteeism signify illness or laziness? Was the bar fight a hate crime or a drunken brawl?

Attributing Behavior to Persons or to Situations

1 : **How do we tend to explain others' behavior and our own?**

Attribution theory proposes that we usually attribute others' behavior either to their internal dispositions or to their external situations (Heider, 1958). In class, we notice that Juliette seldom talks; over coffee, Jack talks nonstop. Attributing their behaviors to their personal dispositions, we decide Juliette is shy and Jack is outgoing.

social psychology the scientific study of how we think about, influence, and relate to one another.

attribution theory the theory that we explain someone's behavior by crediting either the situation or the person's disposition.

The fundamental attribution error If our new friend acts grouchy, we may decide she's a grouchy person. Her grouchiness may actually reflect her current situation—losing sleep over a financial worry, getting a flat tire on the way to work, or having a fight with a family member.

Because people do have enduring personality traits, these *dispositional attributions* are sometimes valid. However, we often fall prey to the **fundamental attribution error,** by overestimating the influence of personality and underestimating the influence of situations. In class, Jack may be as quiet as Juliette. Catch Juliette at a party and you may hardly recognize your quiet classmate. Explanations stressing these external influences are *situational attributions.*

A now-classic experiment illustrated the fundamental attribution error. David Napolitan and George Goethals (1979) had Williams College students talk, one at a time, with a young woman who acted either aloof and critical or warm and friendly. Beforehand, they told half the students that the woman's behavior would be spontaneous. They told the other half the truth—that she had been instructed to *act* friendly (or unfriendly). What do you suppose was the effect of being told the truth?

There was no effect. If the woman acted friendly, they inferred she *really was* a warm person. If she acted unfriendly, they inferred she *really was* a cold person. In other words, they attributed her behavior to her personal disposition *even when told that her behavior was situational*—that she was merely acting that way for the purposes of the experiment. Although the fundamental attribution error occurs in all cultures studied, this tendency to explain people's behavior in terms of their personal traits runs especially strong in individualistic Western countries. In East Asian cultures, for example, people are more sensitive to the power of the situation (Masuda & Kitayama, 2004).

You have surely committed the fundamental attribution error. In judging whether your psychology instructor is shy or outgoing, you have perhaps by now inferred that he or she has an outgoing personality. But you know your instructor only from the classroom, a situation that demands outgoing behavior. Catch the instructor in a different situation and you might be surprised. Outside their assigned roles, professors seem less professorial, presidents less presidential, servants less servile.

The instructor, however, might say, "Me, outgoing? It all depends on the situation. In class or with good friends, yes, I'm outgoing. But at conventions I'm really rather shy." When explaining *our own* behavior, which we observe in many different situations, or the behavior of those we know well and also see in varied situations, we are sensitive to how behavior changes with the situation (Idson & Mischel, 2001). (An important exception is our own intentional and admirable actions, which we more often attribute to our own good reasons than to situational causes [Malle, 2006; Malle et al., 2007].)

When explaining *others'* behavior, particularly the behavior of strangers we have observed in only one type of situation, we often commit the fundamental attribution error: We disregard the situation and leap to unwarranted conclusions about their personality traits.

Actor and observer perspectives make for differing attributions During their contentious U.S. presidential primaries in 2008, Barack Obama was criticized for seeming—in this camera perspective that faces him—to turn a cold shoulder to his opponent, Hillary Clinton. Obama later explained that he had greeted her earlier, and here was turning to speak to (as a picture shot from behind him might have shown) the unseen person to his left. In laboratory experiments, when a camera shows the actor's perspective, observers better appreciate the situation's influence.

If we could take the observer's point of view, would we become more aware of our own personal style? To test this idea, researchers have reversed the perspectives of actor and observer. They filmed some interactions and then had participants view a replay of the situation—filmed from the other person's perspective. It worked. The viewers reversed their explanations of the behaviors (Lassiter & Irvine, 1986; Storms, 1973). Seeing the world from the actor's perspective, the observers better appreciated the situation.

As we act, our eyes look outward; we see others' faces, not our own. Reflecting on our past selves of 5 or 10 years ago also switches our perspective. Our present self adopts the observer's perspective and attributes our past behavior mostly to our traits (Pronin & Ross, 2006). In another 5 or 10 years, your today's self may seem like another person.

The Effects of Attribution

Our attributions—either to the person or to the situation—have important consequences in everyday life, as we struggle to explain others' actions (Fincham & Bradbury, 1993; Fletcher et al., 1990). A jury must decide whether a shooting was malicious or in self-defense. An interviewer must judge whether the applicant's geniality is genuine. A person must decide whether to attribute another's friendliness to sexual interest. Attributions matter. Happily married couples attribute a spouse's tart-tongued remark to a temporary situation ("She must have had a bad day at work"). Unhappily married couples attribute the same remark to a mean disposition ("Why did I marry such a hostile person?").

Consider the political effects of attribution. How do you explain poverty or unemployment? Researchers in Britain, India, Australia, and the United States (Furnham, 1982; Pandey et al., 1982; Wagstaff, 1982; Zucker & Weiner, 1993) report that political conservatives tend to attribute such social problems to the personal dispositions of the poor and unemployed themselves: "People generally get what they deserve. Those who don't work are often freeloaders. Anybody who takes the initiative can still get ahead." Political liberals (and social scientists) are more likely to blame past and present situations: "If you or I had to live with the same poor education, lack of opportunity, and discrimination, would we be any better off?" To understand and prevent terrorism, they say, consider the situations that breed terrorists. Better to drain the swamps than swat the mosquitoes.

The point to remember: Our attributions—to individuals' dispositions or to their situations—should be made carefully. They have real consequences.

Some 7 in 10 college women report having experienced a man misattributing her friendliness as a sexual come-on (Jacques-Tiura et al., 2007).

"Otis, shout at that man to pull himself together."

Attitudes and Actions

2: **Does what we think affect what we do, or does what we do affect what we think?**

Attitudes are feelings, often influenced by our beliefs, that predispose our reactions to objects, people, and events. If we *believe* someone is mean, we may *feel* dislike for the person and *act* unfriendly.

Attitudes Affect Actions

Our attitudes often predict our behavior. Attitudes are especially likely to affect behavior when external influences are minimal, and when the attitude is stable, specific to the behavior, and easily recalled (Glasman & Albarracín, 2006). One experiment used vivid, easily recalled information to persuade people that sustained tanning put them at risk for future skin cancer. One month later, 72 percent of the participants, and only 16 percent of those in a waitlist control group, had lighter skin (McClendon & Prentice-Dunn, 2001).

fundamental attribution error the tendency for observers, when analyzing another's behavior, to underestimate the impact of the situation and to overestimate the impact of personal disposition.

attitude feelings, often influenced by our beliefs, that predispose us to respond in a particular way to objects, people, and events.

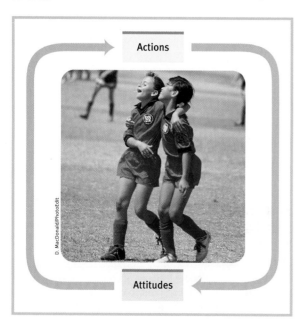

Persuasive celebrity Long an environmental advocate, Leonardo DiCaprio has persuaded many to consider his cause by way of the peripheral route thanks to his celebrated-actor status. Yet in 2007 he wrote, produced, and narrated a feature film documentary, *The 11th Hour*, which may also have persuaded others through the central route.

On a larger scale, former Vice President Al Gore's movie *An Inconvenient Truth,* and the Alliance for Climate Protection it spawned, are based on a similar premise: People's views of the reality and dangers of global climate change can change, and those changed attitudes can affect both personal behaviors and public policies. Indeed, by the end of 2007, an analysis of international opinion surveys by WorldPublicOpinion.org showed "widespread and growing concern about climate change. Large majorities believe that human activity causes climate change and favor policies designed to reduce emissions." Thanks to the mass persuasion campaign, many corporations, as well as campuses, are "going green."

This tidal wave of change is an example of attitude change through **central route persuasion:** Interested people have focused on scientific evidence and arguments and responded with favorable thoughts. This type of persuasion occurs mostly when people are naturally analytical or involved in the issue. When issues don't engage systematic thinking, persuasion may still change attitudes through a faster **peripheral route.** In such cases, people respond to incidental cues, such as celebrity endorsements, and make snap judgments. Because central route persuasion is deeper—more thoughtful and less superficial—it is more durable and more likely to influence behavior.

So, our attitudes can change our behaviors. Sometimes, however, strong social pressures can weaken the attitude-behavior connection (Wallace et al., 2005). For example, after 9/11, the American public overwhelmingly supported President George W. Bush's preparation to attack Iraq. This support formed a social pressure that motivated Democratic leaders to vote for Bush's war plan, despite their private reservations (Nagourney, 2002). Nevertheless, when external influences are minimal, our attitudes influence our actions.

Actions Affect Attitudes

Now consider a more surprising principle: Not only will people sometimes stand up for what they believe, they will also come to believe in the idea they have supported. Many streams of evidence confirm that *attitudes follow behavior* (**FIGURE 15.1**).

THE FOOT-IN-THE-DOOR PHENOMENON Inducing people to act against their beliefs can affect their attitude. During the Korean war, many captured U.S. soldiers were imprisoned in war camps run by Chinese communists. Without using brutality, the captors secured the prisoners' collaboration in various activities. Some merely ran errands or accepted favors. Others made radio appeals and false confessions. Still others informed on fellow prisoners and divulged military information. When the war ended, 21 prisoners chose to stay with the communists, and many more returned home convinced that communism was good for Asia.

A key ingredient of the Chinese "brain-washing" program was its effective use of the **foot-in-the-door phenomenon**—a tendency for people who agree to a small action to comply later with a larger one. The Chinese began with harmless requests but gradually escalated their demands (Schein, 1956). Having "trained" the prisoners to speak or write trivial statements, the communists then asked them to copy or create something more important—noting, perhaps, the flaws of capitalism. Then, perhaps to gain privileges, the prisoners participated in group discussions, wrote self-criticisms, or uttered public confessions. After doing so, they often adjusted their beliefs toward consistency with their public acts. This chicken-and-egg spiral, of actions-feeding-attitudes-feeding-actions, enables behavior to escalate. A trivial act makes the next act easier.

In dozens of experiments, people have been coaxed into acting against their attitudes or violating their moral standards. The nearly inevitable result: Doing becomes believing. When people are induced to harm an

FIGURE 15.1 Attitudes follow behavior Cooperative actions, such as those performed by people on sports teams, feed mutual liking. Such attitudes, in turn, promote positive behavior.

innocent victim—by making nasty comments or delivering electric shocks—they then begin to disparage their victim. If induced to speak or write on behalf of a position they have qualms about, they begin to believe their own words. The point is simple: To get people to agree to something big, "start small and build," said Robert Cialdini (1993). Knowing this, you can be wary of those who would exploit you with the tactic. Succumb to a temptation and you will find the next temptation harder to resist.

Fortunately, the attitudes-follow-behavior principle works as well for good deeds as for bad. In one experiment, researchers posing as safe-driving volunteers asked Californians to permit the installation of a large, poorly lettered "Drive Carefully" sign in their front yards. Only 17 percent consented. They approached other home owners with a small request first: Would they display a 3-inch-high "Be a Safe Driver" sign? Nearly all readily agreed. When reapproached two weeks later to allow the large, ugly sign in their front yards, 76 percent consented (Freedman & Fraser, 1966). To secure a big commitment—whether a charitable contribution, blood donation, or product sale—it often pays to put your foot in the door: Start small and build.

ROLE-PLAYING AFFECTS ATTITUDES When you adopt a new **role**—when you become a college student, marry, or begin a new job—you strive to follow the social prescriptions. At first, your behaviors may feel phony, because you are *acting* a role. The first weeks in the military feel artificial—as if one is pretending to be a soldier. The first weeks of a marriage may feel like "playing house." Before long, however, what began as play-acting in the theater of life becomes *you*.

One famous laboratory study dramatically demonstrated the way actions—in this case, role-playing—can change attitudes. In the Stanford Prison experiment, male college students volunteered to spend time in a simulated prison devised by psychologist Philip Zimbardo (1972). Some he randomly designated as guards; he gave them uniforms, billy clubs, and whistles and instructed them to enforce certain rules. The remainder became prisoners; they were locked in barren cells and forced to wear humiliating outfits. After a day or two in which the volunteers self-consciously "played" their roles, the simulation became real—too real. Most of the guards developed disparaging attitudes, and some devised cruel and degrading routines. One by one, the prisoners broke down, rebelled, or became passively resigned, causing Zimbardo to call off the study after only six days.

Psychologists add a cautionary note: In Zimbardo's prison simulation and in other atrocity-producing situations, some people succumb to the situation and others do not (Carnahan & McFarland, 2007; Haslam & Reicher, 2007; Mastroianni & Reed, 2006; Zimbardo, 2007). Person and situation interact. Water has the power to dissolve some substances, notes John Johnson (2007), but not all. In a watery situation, salt dissolves, sand does not (see Close-Up: Abu Ghraib Prison: An "Atrocity-Producing Situation"? on the next page).

"If the King destroys a man, that's proof to the King it must have been a bad man."
—Thomas Cromwell, in Robert Bolt's *A Man for All Seasons,* 1960.

"Fake it until you make it."
—Alcoholics Anonymous saying

central route to persuasion attitude-change path in which interested people focus on the arguments and respond with favorable thoughts.

peripheral route to persuasion attitude-change path in which people are influenced by incidental cues, such as a speaker's attractiveness.

foot-in-the-door phenomenon the tendency for people who have first agreed to a small request to comply later with a larger request.

role a set of expectations (norms) about a social position, defining how those in the position ought to behave.

The power of the situation
In Philip Zimbardo's Stanford Prison simulation, a toxic situation triggered degrading behaviors among those assigned to the guard role.

Philip G. Zimbardo, Inc.

Close-Up:

Abu Ghraib Prison: An "Atrocity-Producing Situation"?

As the first photos emerged in 2004 from Iraq's Abu Ghraib prison, the civilized world was shocked. The photos showed U.S. military guards stripping prisoners naked, placing hoods on them, stacking them in piles, prodding them with electricity, taunting them with attack dogs, and subjecting them to sleep deprivation, humiliation, and extreme stress. Was the problem, as so many people initially supposed, a few bad apples—a few irresponsible or sadistic guards? That was the U.S. Army's seeming verdict when it court-martialed and imprisoned some of the guards, and then cleared four of the five top commanding officers responsible for Abu Ghraib's policies and operations. The lower-level military guards were "sick bastards," explained the defense attorney for one of the commanding officers (Tarbert, 2004).

Many social psychologists, however, reminded us that a toxic situation can make even good apples go bad (Fiske et al., 2004). "When ordinary people are put in a novel, evil place, such as most prisons, Situations Win, People Lose," offered

Bad apples or bad barrels? Like the Stanford Prison Experiment in 1972, the real-life Abu Ghraib Prison fiasco in 2004 was a powerfully toxic situation, contended social psychologist Philip Zimbardo.

Philip Zimbardo (2004), adding, "That is true for the majority of people in all the relevant social psychological research done over the past 40 years."

Consider the situation, explained Zimbardo. The guards, some of them model soldier-reservists with no prior criminal or sadistic history, were exhausted from working 12-hour shifts, seven days a week. They were dealing with an enemy, and their prejudices were heightened by fears of lethal attacks and by the violent deaths of many fellow soldiers. They were put in an understaffed guard role, with minimal training and supervision. With support from high ranking people, they were then encouraged to "soften up" for interrogation detainees who had been denied access to the Red Cross. "When you put that set of horrendous work conditions and external factors together, it creates an evil barrel. You could put virtually anybody in it and you're going to get this kind of evil behavior" (Zimbardo, 2005).

Atrocious behaviors often emerge in atrocious situations. But remember also that people and situations interact. When put in with rotten apples, some people, but not others, become bad apples.

Originally published in the New Yorker

COGNITIVE DISSONANCE: WHEN ACTIONS AND ATTITUDES CLASH So far, we have seen that actions can affect attitudes, sometimes turning prisoners into collaborators, doubters into believers, and compliant guards into abusers. But why?

One explanation is that when we become aware that our attitudes and actions don't coincide, we experience tension, or *cognitive dissonance.* To relieve this tension, according to the **cognitive dissonance theory** proposed by Leon Festinger, we often bring our attitudes into line with our actions. Dozens of experiments have explored this idea by having people perform some small act that they otherwise would not have supported. As a participant in one of these experiments, you might agree for a measly $2 to help a researcher by writing an essay that supports something you don't believe in (perhaps a tuition increase). Later, thinking that an administrator would be reading your essay, and feeling responsible for what you've done, you would probably feel uncomfortable about the inconsistency of your action (asking for a hike in tuition) and your attitudes ("Tuition is already too expensive!"). How could you reduce the dissonance? One way would be to start believing your phony words. At such times, it is as if we rationalize, "If I chose to do it (or write it), I must believe in it."

The greater the dissonance, the more motivated we are to find consistency, such as changing our attitudes to help justify the act. The U.S. invasion of Iraq was mainly premised on the presumed threat of Saddam Hussein's weapons of mass destruction (WMD). As the war began, only 38 percent of Americans surveyed said the war was justified even if Iraq did not have WMD (Gallup, 2003). Nearly 80 percent believed such weapons would be found (Duffy, 2003; Newport et al., 2003).

cognitive dissonance theory the theory that we act to reduce the discomfort (dissonance) we feel when two of our thoughts (cognitions) are inconsistent. For example, when our awareness of our attitudes and of our actions clash, we can reduce the resulting dissonance by changing our attitudes.

When no WMD were found, many Americans felt dissonance, which was heightened by their awareness of the war's financial and human costs, by scenes of chaos in Iraq, and by inflamed anti-American and pro-terrorist sentiments in some parts of the world.

To reduce this dissonance, some people revised their memories of the main rationale for going to war, convincing themselves that the goal had been liberating an oppressed people and promoting democracy in the Middle East. Before long, 58 percent of Americans—a majority—said they supported the war even if there were no WMD (Gallup, 2003). It was not until late 2004, when hopes for a flourishing peace waned, that Americans' support for the war dropped below 50 percent.

The attitudes-follow-behavior principle has a heartening implication: Although we cannot directly control all our feelings, we can influence them by altering our behavior. (Recall from Chapter 11 the emotional effects of facial expressions and of body postures.) If we are down in the dumps, we can do as cognitive therapists advise and talk in more positive, self-accepting ways with fewer self–put-downs. If we are unloving, we can become more loving by behaving as if we were so—by doing thoughtful things, expressing affection, giving affirmation. "Assume a virtue, if you have it not," says Hamlet to his mother. "For use can almost change the stamp of nature."

Racial attitudes in the United States have followed this pattern. In the years immediately after the introduction of school desegregation and the passage of the Civil Rights Act of 1964, White Americans expressed diminishing racial prejudice, enabling, 45 years later, Barack Obama's inauguration. As Americans in different regions came to act more alike—thanks to more uniform national standards against discrimination—they began to think more alike.

The point to remember: Cruel acts shape the self. But so do acts of good will. Act as though you like someone, and you soon will. Changing our behavior can change how we think about others and how we feel about ourselves.

"Look, I have my misgivings, too, but what choice do we have except stay the course?"

"Sit all day in a moping posture, sigh, and reply to everything with a dismal voice, and your melancholy lingers. . . . If we wish to conquer undesirable emotional tendencies in ourselves, we must . . . go through the outward movements of those contrary dispositions which we prefer to cultivate."

—William James, *Principles of Psychology,* 1890

REHEARSE IT!

1. If we encounter a person who appears to be high on drugs, and we make the fundamental attribution error, we will probably attribute the person's behavior to
   a. moral weakness or an addictive personality.
   b. peer pressure.
   c. the easy availability of drugs on city streets.
   d. society's acceptance of drug use.

2. We tend to agree to a larger request more readily if we have already agreed to a small request. This tendency is called
   a. the fundamental attribution error.
   b. the foot-in-the-door phenomenon.
   c. the behavior-follows-attitudes principle.
   d. role-playing.

3. Cognitive dissonance theory predicts that we will act to reduce the discomfort we feel when our actions and attitudes clash. The theory explains why
   a. people who act against their attitudes tend to change their attitudes.
   b. attitudes predict actions when social pressures are minimized.
   c. changing an attitude—through persuasion—often fails to result in behavioral changes.
   d. people are hypocritical, talking one way and acting another.

Answers: 1. a, 2. b, 3. a.

Social Influence

Social psychology's great lesson is the enormous power of social influence. This influence can be seen in our conformity, our compliance, and our group behavior. On campus, jeans are the dress code; on New York's Wall Street or London's Bond Street, dress suits are the norm. When we know how to act, how to groom, how to talk, life functions smoothly. Armed with social influence principles, advertisers, fund-raisers, and campaign workers aim to sway our decisions to buy, to donate, to vote. Isolated with others who share their grievances, dissenters may gradually become rebels, and rebels may become terrorists. Let's examine the pull of these social strings. How strong are they? How do they operate?

Niche conformity Are these students asserting their individuality or identifying themselves with others of the same microculture?

Conformity and Obedience

3: **What do experiments on conformity and compliance reveal about the power of social influence?**

Behavior is contagious. Consider:

- A cluster of people stand gazing upward, and passersby pause to do likewise.
- Baristas and street musicians know to "seed" their tip containers with money to suggest that others have given.
- One person laughs, coughs, or yawns, and others in the group soon do the same. Chimpanzees, too, are more likely to yawn after observing another chimpanzee yawn (Anderson et al., 2004).
- "Sickness" can also be psychologically contagious. In the anxious 9/11 aftermath, more than two dozen elementary and middle schools had outbreaks of children reporting red rashes, sometimes causing parents to wonder whether biological terrorism was at work (Talbot, 2002). Some cases may have been stress-related, but mostly, health experts concluded, people were just noticing normal early acne, insect bites, eczema, and dry skin from overheated classrooms.

We are natural mimics—an effect Tanya Chartrand and John Bargh (1999) have called the *chameleon effect*—an effect they demonstrated by having students work in a room alongside a person who, unknown to the students, was working for the experimenter. Sometimes the persons rubbed their face; on other occasions, they shook their foot. Sure enough, the students tended to rub their own face when with the face-rubbing person and shake their own foot when with the foot-shaking person.

Unconsciously mimicking others' expressions, postures, and voice tones helps us feel what they are feeling. This helps explain why we feel happier around happy people than around depressed ones. Just hearing someone reading a neutral text in either a happy- or sad-sounding voice creates "mood contagion" in listeners (Neumann & Strack, 2000). Such automatic mimicry is part of empathy. Empathic people yawn more after seeing others yawn (Morrison, 2007). And empathic, mimicking people are liked more. Those most eager to fit in with a group seem intuitively to know this, for they are especially prone to unconscious mimicry (Lakin & Chartrand, 2003).

Sometimes the effects of suggestibility are more serious. Suicides, bomb threats, airplane hijackings, and school violence all have a curious tendency to come in clusters. In the eight days following the 1999 shooting rampage at Colorado's Columbine High School, every U.S. state except Vermont experienced threats of copycat violence. Pennsylvania alone recorded 60 such threats (Cooper, 1999). And in the wake of screen idol Marilyn Monroe's reported suicide on August 6, 1962, the number of suicides in the United States exceeded the usual August count by 200 (Phillips et al., 1985, 1989).

What causes clusters of violence? Do people act similarly because of their influence on one another? Or because they are simultaneously exposed to the same events and conditions? Seeking answers, social psychologists have conducted experiments on group pressure and conformity.

NON SEQUITUR   by WILEY

Group Pressure and Conformity

Suggestibility is a subtle type of **conformity**—adjusting our behavior or thinking toward some group standard. To study conformity, Solomon Asch (1955) devised a simple test. As a participant in what you believe is a study of visual perception, you arrive at the experiment location in time to take a seat at a table where five people are already seated. The experimenter asks which of three comparison lines is identical to a standard line. You see clearly that the answer is Line 2 and await your turn to say so after the others. Your boredom with this experiment begins to show when the next set of lines proves equally easy.

Now comes the third trial, and the correct answer seems just as clear-cut, but the first person gives what strikes you as a wrong answer: "Line 3" (**FIGURE 15.2**). When the second person and then the third and fourth give the same wrong answer, you sit up straight and squint. When the fifth person agrees with the first four, you feel your heart begin to pound. The experimenter then looks to you for your answer. Torn between the unanimity of your five fellow respondents and the evidence of your own eyes, you feel tense and much less sure of yourself than you were moments ago. You hesitate before answering, wondering whether you should suffer the discomfort of being the oddball. What answer do you give?

> **conformity** adjusting one's behavior or thinking to coincide with a group standard.

FIGURE 15.2 Asch's conformity experiments Which of the three comparison lines is equal to the standard line? What do you suppose most people would say after hearing five others say, "Line 3"? In this photo from one of Asch's experiments, the student in the center shows the severe discomfort that comes from disagreeing with the responses of other group members (in this case, confederates of the experimenter).

Standard line   Comparison lines   1 2 3

In the experiments conducted by Asch and others after him, thousands of college students have experienced this conflict. Answering such questions alone, they erred less than 1 percent of the time. But the odds were quite different when several others—confederates working for the experimenter—answered incorrectly. Although most people went with their eyes even when others did not, Asch nevertheless was disturbed by his result: More than one-third of the time, these "intelligent and well-meaning" college-student participants were then "willing to call white black" by going along with the group.

CONDITIONS THAT STRENGTHEN CONFORMITY Asch's procedure became the model for later investigations. Although experiments have not always found so much conformity, they do reveal that conformity increases when

- one is made to feel incompetent or insecure.
- the group has at least three people.
- the group is unanimous. (The dissent of just one other person greatly increases social courage.)
- one admires the group's status and attractiveness.
- one has made no prior commitment to any response.
- others in the group observe one's behavior.
- one's culture strongly encourages respect for social standards.

Thus, we might predict the behavior of Austin, an enthusiastic but insecure new fraternity member: Noting that the 40 other members appear unanimous in their plans for a fund-raiser, Austin is unlikely to voice his dissent.

> "Have you ever noticed how one example—good or bad—can prompt others to follow? How one illegally parked car can give permission for others to do likewise? How one racial joke can fuel another?"
>
> —Marian Wright Edelman, *The Measure of Our Success*, 1992

normative social influence influence resulting from a person's desire to gain approval or avoid disapproval.

informational social influence influence resulting from one's willingness to accept others' opinions about reality.

"Those who never retract their opinions love themselves more than they love truth."

—Joseph Joubert, eighteenth-century French essayist

"*I love the little ways you're identical to everyone else.*"

REASONS FOR CONFORMING Fish swim in schools. Birds fly in flocks. And humans, too, tend to go with their group, to think what it thinks and do what it does. Researchers have seen this in college residence halls, where over time students' attitudes become more similar to those living near them (Cullum & Harton, 2007). But why? Why do we clap when others clap, eat as others eat, believe what others believe, even see what others see? Social psychologists invite us to consider two reasons.

Sometimes we conform because we are responding to **normative social influence,** trying to avoid rejection or to gain social approval. The price we pay for violating social norms—understood rules for accepted and expected behavior—may be severe.

At other times, we are responding to **informational social influence.** Groups may provide valuable information, and only an uncommonly stubborn person will never listen to others. As Rebecca Denton demonstrated in 2004, sometimes it pays to assume others are right and to follow their lead. Denton set a record for the furthest distance driven on the wrong side of a British divided highway—30 miles, with only one minor sideswipe, before the motorway ran out and police were able to puncture her tires. Denton later explained that she thought the hundreds of other drivers coming at her were all on the wrong side of the road (Woolcock, 2004).

Social influence experiments conducted in 17 countries demonstrate that cultures vary in the extent to which they value conformity. As we have seen throughout this text, Western Europeans and people in most English-speaking countries tend to prize individualism more than conformity and obedience, and in those cultures, conformity rates are lower than in cultures that stress collectivist values (Bond & Smith, 1996). American university students, for example, tend to see themselves, in domains ranging from consumer purchases to political views, as less conforming than others (Pronin et al., 2007). We are, in our own eyes, individuals amid a crowd of sheep. Thus, tattoos, once a symbol of nonconformity, may lose their appeal if they become too popular.

Obedience

Social psychologist Stanley Milgram (1963, 1974), a student of Solomon Asch, knew that people often comply with social pressures. But how would they respond to outright commands? To find out, he undertook what have become social psychology's most famous and controversial experiments. Imagine yourself as one of the nearly 1000 participants in Milgram's 20 experiments.

Responding to an advertisement, you come to Yale University's psychology department to participate in an experiment. Professor Milgram's assistant explains that the study concerns the effect of punishment on learning. You and another person draw slips from a hat to see who will be the "teacher" (which your slip says) and who will be the "learner." The learner is then led to an adjoining room and strapped into a chair that is wired through the wall to an electric shock machine. You sit in front of the machine, which has switches labeled with voltages. Your task: to teach and then test the learner on a list of word pairs. You are to punish the learner for wrong answers by delivering brief electric shocks, beginning with a switch labeled "15 Volts—Slight Shock." After each of the learner's errors, you are to move up to the next higher voltage. With each flick of a switch, lights flash, relay switches click on, and an electric buzzing fills the air.

Stanley Milgram (1933–1984) This social psychologist's obedience experiments "belong to the self-understanding of literate people in our age" (Sabini, 1986).

Complying with the experimenter's instructions, you hear the learner grunt when you flick the third, fourth, and fifth switches. After you activate the eighth switch (labeled "120 Volts—Moderate Shock"), the learner shouts that the shocks are painful. After the tenth switch ("150 Volts—Strong Shock"), he cries, "Get me out of here! I won't be in the experiment anymore! I refuse to go on!" Hearing these pleas, you draw back. But the experimenter prods you: "Please continue—the experiment requires that you continue." If you still resist, he insists, "It is absolutely essential that you continue," or "You have no other choice, you *must* go on."

Obeying, you hear the learner's protests escalate to shrieks of agony as you continue to raise the shock level with each succeeding error. After the 330-volt level, the learner refuses to answer and falls silent. Still, the experimenter pushes you toward the final, 450-volt switch, ordering you to ask the questions and, if no correct answer is given, to administer the next shock level.

How far do you think you would follow the experimenter's commands? In a survey Milgram conducted before the experiment, most people declared they would stop playing such a sadistic-seeming role soon after the learner first indicated pain and certainly before he shrieked in agony. This also was the prediction made by each of 40 psychiatrists Milgram asked to guess the outcome. When Milgram actually conducted the experiment with men aged 20 to 50, he was astonished to find that 63 percent complied fully—right up to the last switch. Ten later studies that included women found women's compliance rates were similar to men's (Blass, 1999).

Did the teachers figure out the hoax—that no shock was being delivered? Did they correctly guess the learner was a confederate who only pretended to feel the shocks? Did they realize the experiment was really testing their willingness to comply with commands to inflict punishment? No. The teachers typically displayed genuine distress: They perspired, trembled, laughed nervously, and bit their lips.

Wondering whether the participants obeyed because the learners' protests were unconvincing, Milgram repeated the experiment with 40 new teachers. This time his confederate mentioned a "slight heart condition" while being strapped into the chair, and then he complained and screamed more intensely as the shocks became more punishing. Still, 65 percent of the new teachers complied fully (**FIGURE 15.3**).

"Drive off the cliff, James, I want to commit suicide."

Milgram's use of deception and stress triggered a debate over his research ethics. In response, Milgram cited participants' statements that they did not regret taking part, and psychiatrists' opinions (based on interviews of 40 "teachers") that there were no apparent emotional aftereffects. The experiments, he said, provoked less enduring stress than university students experience when facing and failing big exams (Blass, 1996).

FIGURE 15.3 Milgram's follow-up obedience experiment In a repeat of the earlier experiment, 65 percent of the adult male "teachers" fully obeyed the experimenter's commands to continue. They did so despite the "learner's" earlier mention of a heart condition and despite hearing cries of protest after 150 volts and agonized protests after 330 volts. (Data from Milgram, 1974.)

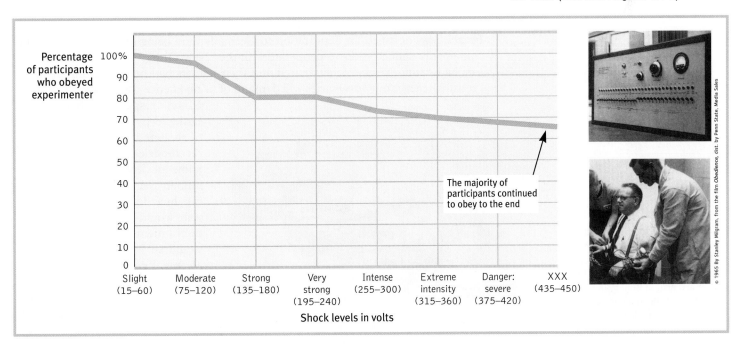

Percentage of participants who obeyed experimenter

The majority of participants continued to obey to the end

Shock levels in volts

| Slight (15–60) | Moderate (75–120) | Strong (135–180) | Very strong (195–240) | Intense (255–300) | Extreme intensity (315–360) | Danger: severe (375–420) | XXX (435–450) |

In later experiments, Milgram discovered that subtle details of a situation powerfully influence people. When he varied the social conditions, the proportion of fully compliant participants varied from 0 to 93 percent. Obedience was highest when

- the person giving the orders was close at hand and was perceived to be a legitimate authority figure. (Such was the case in 2005 when Temple University's basketball coach sent a 250-pound bench player, Nehemiah Ingram, into a game with instructions to commit "hard fouls." Following orders, Ingram fouled out in four minutes after breaking an opposing player's right arm.)
- the authority figure was supported by a prestigious institution. Compliance was somewhat lower when Milgram dissociated his experiments from Yale University.
- the victim was depersonalized or at a distance, even in another room. (Similarly, in combat with an enemy they can see, many soldiers either do not fire their rifles or do not aim them properly. Such refusals to kill are rare among those who operate more distant artillery or aircraft weapons [Padgett, 1989].)
- there were no role models for defiance; that is, no other participants were seen disobeying the experimenter.

The power of legitimate, close-at-hand authorities is dramatically apparent in stories of those who complied with orders to carry out the Holocaust atrocities, and those who didn't. Obedience alone does not explain the Holocaust; anti-Semitic ideology produced eager killers as well (Mastroianni, 2002). But obedience was a factor. In the summer of 1942, nearly 500 middle-aged German reserve police officers were dispatched to German-occupied Jozefow, Poland. On July 13, the group's visibly upset commander informed his recruits, mostly family men, that they had been ordered to round up the village's Jews, who were said to be aiding the enemy. Able-bodied men were to be sent to work camps, and all the rest were to be shot on the spot. Given a chance to refuse participation in the executions, only about a dozen immediately did so. Within 17 hours, the remaining 485 officers killed 1500 helpless women, children, and elderly by shooting them in the back of the head as they lay face down. Hearing the pleas of the victims, and seeing the gruesome results, some 20 percent of the officers did eventually dissent, managing either to miss their victims or to wander away and hide until the slaughter was over (Browning, 1992). But in real life, as in Milgram's experiments, the disobedient were the minority.

Another story was being played out in the French village of Le Chambon, where French Jews destined for deportation to Germany were being sheltered by villagers who openly defied orders to cooperate with the "New Order." The villagers' ancestors had themselves been persecuted and their pastors had been teaching them to "resist whenever our adversaries will demand of us obedience contrary to the orders of the Gospel" (Rochat, 1993). Ordered by police to give a list of sheltered Jews, the head pastor modeled defiance: "I don't know of Jews, I only know of human beings." Without realizing how long and terrible the war would be, or how much punishment and poverty they would suffer, the resisters made an initial commitment to resist. Supported by their beliefs, their role models, their interactions with one another, and their own initial acts, they remained defiant to the war's end.

Standing up for democracy
Some individuals—roughly one in three in Milgram's experiments—resist social coercion, as did this unarmed man in Beijing, by single-handedly challenging an advancing line of tanks the day after the 1989 Tiananmen Square student uprising was suppressed.

AP/Wide World Photos

Lessons From the Conformity and Obedience Studies

What do the Asch and Milgram experiments teach us about ourselves? How does judging the length of a line or flicking a shock switch relate to everyday social behavior? Recall from Chapter 1 that psychological experiments aim not to re-create the literal behaviors of everyday life but to capture and explore the underlying processes that shape those behaviors. Asch and Milgram devised experiments in which the participants had to choose between adhering to their own standards and being responsive to others, a dilemma we all face frequently.

In Milgram's experiments and its later replications (Burger, 2009), participants were also torn. Their moral sense warned them not to harm another, yet it also prompted them to obey the experimenter and to be a good research participant. With kindness and obedience on a collision course, obedience usually won.

Such experiments demonstrate that strong social influences can make people conform to falsehoods or capitulate to cruelty. "The most fundamental lesson of our study," Milgram noted, is that "ordinary people, simply doing their jobs, and without any particular hostility on their part, can become agents in a terrible destructive process" (1974, p. 6). Milgram did not entrap his teachers by asking them first to zap learners with enough electricity to make their hair stand on end. Rather, he exploited the foot-in-the-door effect, beginning with a little tickle of electricity and escalating step by step. In the minds of those throwing the switches, the small action became justified, making the next act tolerable. In Jozefow, in Le Chambon, and in Milgram's experiments, those who resisted usually did so early. After the first acts of compliance or resistance, attitudes began to follow and justify behavior.

So it happens when people succumb, gradually, to evil. In any society, great evils sometimes grow out of people's compliance with lesser evils. The Nazi leaders suspected that most German civil servants would resist shooting or gassing Jews directly, but they found them surprisingly willing to handle the paperwork of the Holocaust (Silver & Geller, 1978). Likewise, when Milgram asked 40 men to administer the learning test while someone else did the shocking, 93 percent complied. Contrary to images of devilish villains, cruelty does not require monstrous characters; all it takes is ordinary people corrupted by an evil situation—ordinary soldiers who follow orders to torture prisoners, ordinary students who follow orders to haze initiates into their group, ordinary employees who follow orders to produce and market harmful products. Before leading the 9/11 attacks, Mohammed Atta reportedly was a sane, rational person who had been a "good boy" and an excellent student from a close-knit family—not someone who fits our image of a barbaric monster.

> "I was only following orders."
>
> —Adolf Eichmann, Director of Nazi deportation of Jews to concentration camps

> "The normal reaction to an abnormal situation is abnormal behavior."
>
> —James Waller, *Becoming Evil: How Ordinary People Commit Genocide and Mass Killing*, 2007

Group Influence

When we conform, when we comply, we are reacting to the power of social influence. How do groups affect our behavior? To find out, social psychologists study the various influences that operate in the simplest of groups—one person in the presence of another—and those that operate in more complex groups, such as families, teams, and committees.

Individual Behavior in the Presence of Others

4: How is our behavior affected by the presence of others or by being part of a group?

Appropriately, social psychology's first experiments focused on the simplest of all questions about social behavior: How are we influenced by people watching us or joining us in various activities?

SOCIAL FACILITATION Having noticed that cyclists' racing times were faster when they competed against each other than when they competed with a clock, Norman Triplett (1898) hypothesized that the presence of others boosts performance.

Social facilitation Skilled athletes often find they are "on" before an audience. What they do well, they do even better when people are watching.

Courtesy Hope College Public Relations

To test his hypothesis, Triplett had adolescents wind a fishing reel as rapidly as possible. He discovered that they wound the reel faster in the presence of someone doing the same thing. This phenomenon of stronger performance in others' presence is called **social facilitation.** For example, after a light turns green, drivers take about 15 percent less time to travel the first 100 yards when another car is beside them at the intersection than when they are alone (Towler, 1986).

But on tougher tasks (learning nonsense syllables or solving complex multiplication problems), people perform *less* well when observers or others working on the same task are present. Further studies revealed why the presence of others sometimes helps and sometimes hinders performance (Guerin, 1986; Zajonc, 1965). When others observe us, we become aroused. This arousal strengthens the most *likely* response—the correct one on an easy task, an incorrect one on a difficult task. Thus, when we are being observed, we perform well-learned tasks more quickly and accurately, and unmastered tasks less quickly and accurately.

James Michaels and his associates (1982) found that expert pool players who made 71 percent of their shots when alone made 80 percent when four people came to watch them. Poor shooters, who made 36 percent of their shots when alone, made only 25 percent when watched. The energizing effect of an enthusiastic audience probably contributes to the home advantage enjoyed by various sports teams. Studies of more than 80,000 college and professional athletic events in Canada, the United States, and England reveal that home teams win about 6 in 10 games (somewhat fewer for baseball and football, somewhat more for basketball and soccer—see **TABLE 15.1**).

The point to remember: What you do well, you are likely to do even better in front of an audience, especially a friendly audience; what you normally find difficult may seem all but impossible when you are being watched.

TABLE 15.1 Home Advantage in Major Team Sports

Sport	Games Studied	Home Team Winning Percentage
Baseball	23,034	53.5%
Football	2,592	57.3
Ice hockey	4,322	61.1
Basketball	13,596	64.4
Soccer	37,202	69.0

From Courneya & Carron (1992).

SOCIAL LOAFING Social facilitation experiments test the effect of others' presence on performance on an *individual task,* such as shooting baskets. But what happens to performance when people perform the task as a group? In a team tug-of-war, for example, do you suppose your effort would be more than, less than, or the same as the effort you would exert in a one-on-one tug-of-war? If you are like a group of blindfolded University of Massachusetts students told to pull as hard as you can on a rope, you would exert only 82 percent as much effort when you thought three others were pulling with you (Ingham et al., 1974).

Bibb Latané (1981; Jackson & Williams, 1988) has described this diminished effort as **social loafing.** In 78 experiments conducted in the United States, India, Thailand, Japan, China, and Taiwan, social loafing occurred on various tasks, though it was especially common among men in individualistic cultures (Karau & Williams, 1993). In one of Latané's experiments, blindfolded people seated in a group clapped or shouted as loud as they could while listening through headphones to the sound of loud clapping or shouting. When told they were doing it with the others, the participants produced about one-third less noise than when they thought their individual efforts were identifiable.

Why this social loafing? First, people acting as part of a group feel less accountable and therefore worry less about what others think. Second, they may view their contribution as dispensable (Harkins & Szymanski, 1989; Kerr & Bruun, 1983). As many leaders of organizations know—and as you have perhaps observed on student group assignments—if group members share equally in the benefits regardless of how much they contribute, some may slack off. Unless highly motivated and identified with their group, they may free-ride on the other group members' efforts.

Working hard, or hardly working? In group projects, such as car washes, social loafing often occurs, as individuals free-ride on the efforts of others.

DEINDIVIDUATION So, the presence of others can arouse people (as in the social facilitation experiments) or can diminish their feelings of responsibility (as in the social loafing experiments). But sometimes the presence of others both arouses people *and* diminishes their sense of responsibility. The result can be uninhibited behavior ranging from screaming at a basketball referee to political rioting in the streets.

This diminished self-consciousness and loss of normal restraints in a group situation is termed **deindividuation.** It often occurs when group participation makes people feel aroused and anonymous. In one experiment, New York University women dressed in depersonalizing Ku Klux Klan–style hoods delivered twice as much electric shock to a victim as did identifiable women (Zimbardo, 1970). (As in all such experiments, the "victim" did not actually receive the shocks.) Similarly, tribal warriors who depersonalize themselves with face paints or masks are more likely than those with exposed faces to kill, torture, or mutilate captured enemies (Watson, 1973). Whether in a mob, at a rock concert, at a ballgame, or at worship, to lose self-consciousness (to become deindividuated) is to become more responsive to the group experience.

Effects of Group Interaction

5: What are group polarization and groupthink?

We have examined the conditions under which being in the *presence* of others can make easy tasks easier and difficult tasks harder, motivate people to exert themselves or tempt them to free-ride on the efforts of others, and enhance team spirit or fuel mob violence. Research shows that *interacting* with others can similarly have both bad and good effects.

GROUP POLARIZATION Over time, initial differences between groups of college students tend to grow. If the first-year students at College X tend to be more intellectually oriented than those at College Y, that difference will probably be amplified by the time they are seniors. And if the political conservatism of students who join fraternities and sororities is greater than that of students who do not, the gap in the political attitudes of the two groups will probably widen as they progress through college (Wilson et al., 1975). Similarly, notes Eleanor Maccoby (2002) from her decades of observing gender development, gender differences—girls talking more intimately than boys and playing and fantasizing less aggressively—widen over time as children interact mostly with their own gender.

This enhancement of a group's prevailing tendencies—called **group polarization**—occurs when people within a group discuss an idea that most of them either favor or oppose. Group polarization can have beneficial results, as when it reinforces the resolve of those in a self-help group. But it can also have dire consequences. George Bishop and I discovered that when high-prejudice students discussed racial issues, they

social facilitation stronger responses on simple or well-learned tasks in the presence of others.

social loafing the tendency for people in a group to exert less effort when pooling their efforts toward attaining a common goal than when individually accountable.

deindividuation the loss of self-awareness and self-restraint occurring in group situations that foster arousal and anonymity.

group polarization the enhancement of a group's prevailing inclinations through discussion within the group.

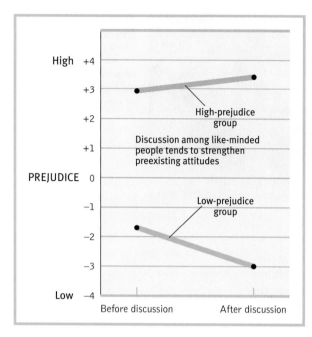

FIGURE 15.4 Group polarization If a group is like-minded, discussion strengthens its prevailing opinions. Talking over racial issues increased prejudice in a high-prejudice group of high school students and decreased it in a low-prejudice group (Myers & Bishop, 1970).

became *more* prejudiced (**FIGURE 15.4**). (Low-prejudice students became even more accepting.) The experiment's ideological separation and polarization finds a seeming parallel in the growing polarization of American politics. The percentage of landslide counties—voting 60 percent or more for one presidential candidate—increased from 26 percent in 1976 to 48 percent in 2004 (Bishop, 2004). More and more, people are living near and learning from others who think as they do. One experiment brought together small groups of citizens in liberal Boulder, Colorado, and other groups down in conservative Colorado Springs, to discuss global climate change, affirmative action, and same-sex unions. Although the discussions increased agreement within groups, those in Boulder generally moved further left and those in Colorado Springs moved further right (Schkade et al., 2006). Thus, ideological separation + deliberation = polarization between groups.

The polarizing effect of interaction among the like-minded applies also to suicide terrorists. Analyses of terrorist organizations around the world reveal that the terrorist mentality does not erupt suddenly (McCauley, 2002; McCauley & Segal, 1987). Rather, it usually arises among people who get together because of a grievance and then become more and more extreme as they interact in isolation from any moderating influences. Increasingly, group members (who may be isolated with other "brothers" and "sisters" in camps) categorize the world as "us" against "them" (Moghaddam, 2005; Qirko, 2004). Suicide terrorism is virtually never done on a personal whim (Merari, 2002). The like-minded echo chamber will continue to polarize people, speculates the 2006 U.S. National Intelligence Estimate: "We assess that the operational threat from self-radicalized cells will grow."

The Internet provides a medium for group polarization. Its tens of thousands of virtual groups enable bereaved parents, peacemakers, and teachers to find solace and support from kindred spirits. But the Internet also enables people who share interests in government conspiracy, extraterrestrial visitors, White supremacy, or citizen militias to find one another and to find support for their shared suspicions (McKenna & Bargh, 1998).

GROUPTHINK Does group interaction ever distort important decisions? Social psychologist Irving Janis began to think so as he read historian Arthur M. Schlesinger Jr.'s account of how President John F. Kennedy and his advisers blundered into an ill-fated plan to invade Cuba with 1400 CIA-trained Cuban exiles. When the invaders were easily captured and soon linked to the U.S. government, Kennedy wondered in hindsight, "How could we have been so stupid?"

To find out, Janis (1982) studied the decision-making procedures that led to the fiasco. He discovered that the soaring morale of the recently elected president and his advisers fostered undue confidence in the plan. To preserve the good group feeling, any dissenting views were suppressed or self-censored, especially after President Kennedy voiced his enthusiasm for the scheme. Since no one spoke strongly against the idea, everyone assumed support was unanimous. To describe this harmonious but unrealistic group thinking, Janis coined the term **groupthink.**

Janis and others then examined other historical fiascos—the failure to anticipate the 1941 Japanese attack on Pearl Harbor, the escalation of the Vietnam war, the U.S. Watergate cover-up, the Chernobyl nuclear reactor accident (Reason, 1987), and the U.S. space shuttle *Challenger* explosion (Esser & Lindoerfer, 1989). They discovered that in these cases, too, groupthink was fed by overconfidence, conformity, self-justification, and group polarization.

Groupthink surfaced again, reported the bipartisan U.S. Senate Intelligence Committee (2004), when "personnel involved in the Iraq WMD issue demonstrated several aspects of groupthink: examining few alternatives, selective gathering of information, pressure to conform within the group or withhold criticism, and

groupthink the mode of thinking that occurs when the desire for harmony in a decision-making group overrides a realistic appraisal of alternatives.

collective rationalization." This groupthink led analysts to "interpret ambiguous evidence as conclusively indicative of a WMD program as well as ignore or minimize evidence that Iraq did not have [WMD] programs."

Despite such fiascos and tragedies, two heads are better than one in solving some types of problems. Knowing this, Janis also studied instances in which U.S. presidents and their advisers collectively made good decisions, such as when the Truman administration formulated the Marshall Plan, which offered assistance to Europe after World War II, and when the Kennedy administration worked to keep the Soviets from installing missiles in Cuba. In such instances—and in the business world, too, Janis believed—groupthink is prevented when a leader welcomes various opinions, invites experts' critiques of developing plans, and assigns people to identify possible problems. Just as the suppression of dissent bends a group toward bad decisions, so open debate often shapes good ones. This is especially so with diverse groups, whose varied perspectives enable creative or superior outcomes (Nemeth & Ormiston, 2007; Page, 2007). None of us is as smart as all of us.

The Power of Individuals

6: **How much power do we have as individuals? Can a minority sway a majority?**

In affirming the power of social influence, we must not overlook our power as individuals. *Social control* (the power of the situation) and *personal control* (the power of the individual) interact. People aren't billiard balls. When feeling pressured, we may react by doing the opposite of what is expected, thereby reasserting our sense of freedom (Brehm & Brehm, 1981).

Three individual soldiers asserted their personal control at the Abu Ghraib prison (O'Connor, 2004). Lt. David Sutton put an end to one incident, which he reported to his commanders. Navy dog-handler William Kimbro refused pressure to participate in improper interrogations using his attack dogs. Specialist Joseph Darby brought those visual images of the horrors into the light of day, providing incontestable evidence of the atrocities. Each risked ridicule or even court-martial for not following orders.

Committed individuals can sway the majority and make social history. Were this not so, communism would have remained an obscure theory, Christianity would be a small Middle Eastern sect, and Rosa Parks' refusal to sit at the back of the bus would not have ignited the U.S. civil rights movement. Technological history, too, is often made by innovative individuals who overcome the majority's resistance to change. To many, the railroad was a nonsensical idea; some farmers even feared that train noise would prevent hens from laying eggs.

European social psychologists have sought to better understand *minority influence*—the power of one or two individuals to sway majorities (Moscovici, 1985). They investigated groups in which one or two individuals consistently expressed a controversial attitude or an unusual perceptual judgment. They repeatedly found that a minority that unswervingly holds to its position is far more successful in swaying the majority than is a minority that waffles. Holding consistently to a minority opinion will not make you popular, but it may make you influential. This is especially so if your self-confidence stimulates others to consider why you react as you do. Although people often follow the majority view publicly, they may privately develop sympathy for the minority view. Even when a minority's influence is not yet visible, it may be persuading some members of the majority to rethink their views (Wood et al., 1994). The powers of social influence are enormous, but so are the powers of the committed individual.

> "Truth springs from argument among friends."
>
> —Philosopher David Hume, 1711–1776

> "One of the dangers in the White House, based on my reading of history, is that you get wrapped up in groupthink and everybody agrees with everything and there's no discussion and there are no dissenting views. So I'm going to be welcoming a vigorous debate inside the White House."
>
> —President-elect Barack Obama, press conference, December 1, 2008

Gandhi As the life of Hindu nationalist and spiritual leader Mahatma Gandhi powerfully testifies, a consistent and persistent minority voice can sometimes sway the majority. Gandhi's nonviolent appeals and fasts were instrumental in winning India's independence from Britain in 1947.

Margaret Bourke-White/Life Magazine. © 1946 Time Warner, Inc.

REHEARSE IT!

4. Researchers have found that a person is most likely to conform to a group if
   a. the group members have diverse opinions.
   b. the person feels competent and secure.
   c. the person admires the group's status.
   d. no one else will observe the person's behavior.

5. In Milgram's experiments, the rate of compliance was highest when
   a. the victim was at a distance from the "teacher."
   b. the victim was close at hand.
   c. other "teachers" refused to go along with the experimenter.
   d. the "teacher" disliked the victim.

6. Social facilitation—improved performance in the presence of others—occurs with

   a. any physical task.
   b. new learning.
   c. a well-learned task.
   d. competitive sports or activities only.

7. When people are part of a group working toward a common goal, their individual efforts are diminished. Latané and his colleagues called this
   a. minority influence.
   b. social facilitation.
   c. social loafing.
   d. group polarization.

8. In a group situation that fosters arousal and anonymity, a person sometimes loses self-consciousness and self-control. This phenomenon is called
   a. social loafing.
   b. deindividuation.

   c. groupthink.
   d. group polarization.

9. If a group is like-minded, discussion strengthens its prevailing opinion. This effect is called
   a. groupthink.
   b. minority influence.
   c. group polarization.
   d. social facilitation.

10. When a group's desire for harmony overrides its realistic appraisal of alternatives, _____ has occurred.
   a. group polarization
   b. groupthink
   c. social facilitation
   d. deindividuation

Answers: 4. c, 5. a, 6. c, 7. c, 8. b, 9. c, 10. b.

Social Relations

We have sampled how we think about and influence one another. Now we come to social psychology's third focus—how we relate to one another. What causes us to harm or to help or to fall in love? How can we move a destructive conflict toward a just peace? We will ponder the bad and the good: from prejudice and aggression to attraction, altruism, and peacemaking.

Prejudice

7: What is prejudice?

Prejudice means "prejudgment." It is an unjustifiable and usually negative attitude toward a group—often a different cultural, ethnic, or gender group. Like all attitudes, **prejudice** is a mixture of *beliefs* (in this case called **stereotypes**), *emotions* (hostility, envy, or fear), and predispositions to *action* (to **discriminate**). To *believe* that obese people are gluttonous, to *feel* dislike for an obese person, and to be hesitant to hire or date an obese person is to be prejudiced. Prejudice is a negative *attitude;* discrimination is a negative *behavior.*

How Prejudiced Are People?

To learn about levels of prejudice, we can assess what people say and what they do. Judging by what Americans say, gender and racial attitudes have changed dramatically in the last half-century. The one-third of Americans who in 1937 told Gallup they would vote for a qualified woman whom their party nominated for president soared to 89 percent in 2007. Support for all forms of racial contact, including interracial marriage, has also dramatically increased. And nearly everyone agrees that children of all races should attend the same schools and that women and men should receive the same pay for the same job.

Yet as *overt* prejudice wanes, *subtle* prejudice lingers. A slew of recent experiments illustrates that prejudice can be not only subtle but also automatic and unconscious (see Close-Up: Automatic Prejudice). Despite increased verbal support for interracial marriage, many people admit that in socially intimate settings (dating, dancing, marrying) they would feel uncomfortable with someone of another race.

prejudice an unjustifiable (and usually negative) attitude toward a group and its members. Prejudice generally involves stereotyped beliefs, negative feelings, and a predisposition to discriminatory action.

stereotype a generalized (sometimes accurate but often overgeneralized) belief about a group of people.

discrimination unjustifiable negative behavior toward a group and its members.

Close-Up:

Automatic Prejudice

As we have seen throughout this book, we process information on two levels: conscious and unconscious. To some extent, our thinking, our memories, and our attitudes are *explicit*—on the radar screen of our awareness. And to an even greater extent, today's researchers believe, they are *implicit*—below the radar, out of sight. Modern studies of implicit, automatic attitudes indicate that prejudice is often more of an unthinking knee-jerk response than a decision. Consider these findings on U.S. racial prejudice:

Implicit racial associations Asked to tap keys to associate words and images, people more quickly associate positive words such as *happy* or *peace* with positive objects such as flowers, and negative words such as *rotten* or *ugly* with insects. Extending these Implicit Association Tests, Anthony Greenwald and his colleagues (1998) showed that even people who deny harboring racial prejudice may carry negative associations. For example, 9 in 10 White respondents took longer to identify pleasant words (such as *peace* and *paradise*) as "good" when presented with Black-sounding names (such as *Latisha* and *Darnell*) rather than White-sounding names (such as *Katie* and *Ian*). Moreover, people who more quickly associate good things with White names or faces also are the quickest to perceive anger and apparent threat in Black faces (Hugenberg & Bodenhausen, 2003). (By 2008, more than 6 million people had taken the Implicit Association Test, as you can, at implicit.harvard.edu.)

Unconscious patronization Kent Harber (1998) asked White university women to evaluate a flawed essay said to be written by a Black or a White fellow student. When they believed the writer was Black, the women gave markedly higher ratings and never expressed the harsh criticisms they assigned to White-authored essays, such as "When I read college work this bad I just want to lay my head down on the table and cry." Did the evaluators calibrate their evaluations

to their racial stereotypes, Harber wondered, leading them to patronize the Black writers with less exacting standards? If used in real-world evaluations, such low expectations and the resulting "inflated praise and insufficient criticism" could hinder minority student achievement. (To preclude such bias, many teachers read essays while "blind" to their authors.)

> **"There are still barriers and biases out there, often unconscious."**
>
> —Senator Hillary Rodham Clinton, 2008 U.S. presidential primary concession speech

Race-influenced perceptions Two research teams were interested in the shooting of an unarmed man in the doorway of his Bronx apartment building by officers who mistook his wallet for a gun. Each research team reenacted the situation with a video, asking viewers to press buttons quickly to "shoot" or not shoot men who suddenly appeared on screen holding either a gun or a harmless object such as a flashlight or bottle (Correll et al., 2002, 2007; Greenwald et al., 2003). People (both Blacks and Whites, in one of the studies) more often mistakenly shot targets who were Black. Priming people with a flashed Black rather than White face also makes them more likely then to misperceive a flashed tool as a gun (**FIGURE 15.5**).

Seeing Black Several studies show that the more a person's features are perceived as typical of their racial category, the more likely they are to elicit race-based

responding (Maddox, 2004). In one study of 182 police officers, Jennifer Eberhardt and her collaborators (2004; 2006) found that "Black faces looked more criminal to police officers; the more Black, the more criminal." In a follow-up study, they found people more willing to give the death sentence to Black defendants having the most stereotypically Black features.

Reflexive bodily responses Today's biopsychosocial approach has stimulated neuroscience studies that measure people's instant responses to viewing White and Black faces. These studies have detected implicit prejudice in people's facial-muscle responses and in the activation of their amygdala, the emotion-processing center (Cunningham et al., 2004; Eberhardt, 2005; Vanman et al., 2004). Even people who consciously express little prejudice may give off tell-tale signals as their body responds selectively to another's race.

If your own gut check sometimes reveals feelings you would rather not have about other people, be assured that you are not alone. It is what we do with our feelings that matters. By monitoring our feelings and actions, and by replacing old habits with new ones based on new friendships, we can work to free ourselves from prejudice.

FIGURE 15.5 Race primes perceptions In experiments by Keith Payne (2006), people viewed a White or Black face, immediately followed by a gun or hand tool, which was then followed by a visual mask that obscured the images. Participants were more likely to misperceive a tool as a gun when it was preceded by a Black rather than White face.

— Visual mask

And in Western Europe, where many "guest workers" and refugees settled at the end of the twentieth century, "modern prejudice"—an indirect racial prejudice that, for example, rejects immigrant minority job applicants for supposedly nonracial reasons—has been replacing blatant prejudice (Jackson et al., 2001; Lester, 2004; Pettigrew, 1998, 2006).

In most places in the world, gays and lesbians cannot comfortably acknowledge who they are and whom they love. Gender prejudice and discrimination persist, too. Despite gender equality in intelligence scores, people have tended to perceive their fathers as more intelligent than their mothers (Furnham & Rawles, 1995). In Saudi Arabia, women are not allowed to drive. In Western countries, we pay more to those (usually men) who drive machines that take care of our streets than to those (usually women) who take care of our children. Worldwide, women are more likely to live in poverty (Lipps, 1999), and their 69 percent literacy rate is well below men's 83 percent (PRB, 2002).

Female infants are no longer left out on a hillside to die of exposure, as was the practice in ancient Greece. Yet even today boys are often valued more than their sisters. With testing that enables sex-selective abortions, several south Asian countries, including certain regions of China and India, have experienced a shortfall in female births. Natural female mortality and the normal male-to-female newborn ratio (105-to-100) hardly explain why 95 percent of children in Chinese orphanages have reportedly been girls (Webley, 2009). Nor do they explain the world's estimated 101 million (say that number slowly) "missing women" (Sen, 2003). In 2005, China's newborn sex ratio reportedly reached 118 boys for every 100 girls (AP, 2007). With demographic predictions of 40 million Chinese bachelors unable to find mates, China has declared that sex-selective abortions—gender genocide—are now a criminal offense.

Suppose that you could only have one child. Would you prefer that it be a boy or a girl? When Gallup asked that question of Americans, two-thirds expressed a gender preference, and for two-thirds of those—in 2003 as in 1941—it was for a boy (Lyons, 2003).

But the news isn't all bad for girls and women. Researchers have found that most people also *feel* more positively about women in general than they do about men (Eagly, 1994; Haddock & Zanna, 1994). People worldwide see women as having some traits (such as nurturance, sensitivity, and less aggressiveness) that most people prefer (Glick et al., 2004; Swim, 1994). That may explain why women tend to like women more than men like men (Rudman & Goodwin, 2004). And perhaps that is also why people prefer slightly feminized computer-generated faces—men's and women's—to slightly masculinized faces. Researcher David Perrett and his colleagues (1998) have speculated that a slightly feminized male face connotes kindness, cooperativeness, and other traits of a good father. When the British Broadcasting Company invited 18,000 women to guess which of the men in FIGURE 15.6 was most likely to place a personal ad seeking a "special lady to love and cherish forever," which one do you think they picked?

FIGURE 15.6 **Who do you like best?** Which one placed an ad seeking "a special lady to love and cherish forever?" See inverted answer below.

Research suggests that subtly feminized features convey a likeable image, which people tend to associate more with committed dads than with promiscuous cads. Thus, 66 percent of the women picked computer-generated face b in response to both of these questions.

(a)

(b)

Professor Dave Perrett, St. Andrews University

Social Roots of Prejudice

8: What are the social and emotional roots of prejudice?

Why does prejudice arise? Inequalities, social divisions, and emotional scapegoating are partly responsible.

SOCIAL INEQUALITIES When some people have money, power, and prestige and others do not, the "haves" usually develop attitudes that justify things as they are. In the extreme case, slave "owners" perceived slaves as innately lazy, ignorant, and irresponsible—as having the very traits that "justified" enslaving them. More commonly, women have been perceived as unassertive but sensitive and therefore suited for the caretaking tasks they have traditionally performed (Hoffman & Hurst, 1990). In short, stereotypes rationalize inequalities.

Discrimination also increases stereotyping and prejudice through the reactions it provokes in its victims. In his classic 1954 book, *The Nature of Prejudice,* Gordon Allport noted that being a victim of discrimination can produce either self-blame or anger. Both reactions may create new grounds for prejudice through the classic *blame-the-victim* dynamic, if observers assume the world is just and "people get what they deserve." In experiments, merely watching someone receive painful shocks has led many people to think less of the victim (Lerner, 1980). This **just-world phenomenon** reflects an idea we commonly teach our children—that good is rewarded and evil is punished. From this it is but a short leap to assume that those who succeed must be good and those who suffer must be bad. Such reasoning enables the rich to see both their own wealth and the poor's misfortune as justly deserved. As one German civilian is said to have remarked when visiting the Bergen-Belsen concentration camp shortly after World War II, "What terrible criminals these prisoners must have been to receive such treatment."

US AND THEM: INGROUP AND OUTGROUP We are a group-bound species. Our ancestors, living in a world where neighboring tribes occasionally raided and pillaged one another's camps, knew that there was safety in solidarity (those who didn't band together left fewer descendants). Whether defending, attacking, or hunting, 10 hands were better than 2. Dividing the world into "us" and "them" entails racism and war, but it also provides the benefits of communal solidarity. Thus, we cheer for our groups, kill for them, die for them. Indeed, we define who we are—our identities—partly in terms of our groups.

And that social definition of who we are also implies who we are not. Mentally drawing a circle that defines "us" (the **ingroup**) excludes "them" (the **outgroup**).

just-world phenomenon the tendency for people to believe the world is just and that people therefore get what they deserve and deserve what they get.

ingroup "Us"—people with whom we share a common identity.

outgroup "Them"—those perceived as different or apart from our ingroup.

French fury Members of France's marginalized ethnic groups reached the tipping point for tolerance in 2005, when they began destructive rioting.

The ingroup Scotland's famed "Tartan Army" soccer fans, shown here during a match against archrival England, share a social identity that defines "us" (the Scottish ingroup) and "them" (the English outgroup).

ingroup bias the tendency to favor our own group.

Australian psychologists John Turner (1987, 2007) and Michael Hogg (1996, 2006) note that through our *social identities* we associate ourselves with certain groups and contrast ourselves with others. When Nicholas identifies himself as a man, an Aussie, a Labourite, a University of Sydney student, a Catholic, and a MacGregor, he knows who he is, and so do we. Such group identifications typically promote an **ingroup bias**—a favoring of one's own group. Even arbitrarily creating an us-them distinction—by grouping people with the toss of a coin—leads people to show favoritism to their own group when dividing any rewards (Tajfel, 1982; Wilder, 1981).

Ironically, we often reserve our most intense dislike for outgroup rivals most like us. In surveys, 7 in 10 Japanese express an unfavorable view of China, and 7 in 10 Chinese similarly dislike Japan (Pew, 2006). Hostilities between the Iraqi Sunni and Shia, the Rwandan Hutu and Tutsi, and the Northern Ireland Protestant and Catholic have pitted ingroups against outgroups who, on a world diversity scale, are much more alike than different. Consider Scotland. As an occasional resident there, I've witnessed many examples of *The Xenophobe's Guide to the Scots* observation— that Scots divide non-Scots "into two main groups: (1) The English; (2) The Rest." As rabid Chicago Cubs fans are happy if either the Cubs win or the Chicago White Sox lose, so rabid Scottish soccer fans rejoice in either a Scotland victory or an England defeat. "Phew! They lost," rejoiced one Scottish tabloid's front-page headline after England's 1996 Euro Cup defeat—by Germany, no less.

Numerical minorities, such as the Scots in Britain, are especially conscious of their social identities. The 5 million Scots are more conscious of their national identity vis-á-vis the neighboring 51 million English than vice versa. Likewise, the 4 million New Zealanders are more conscious of their identity vis-á-vis the 21 million Australians, and they are more likely to root for Australia's sports opponents (Halberstadt et al., 2006).

The urge to distinguish enemies from friends and to have one's group be dominant appears even among children: Most believe their school is better than all other schools in town. Many high school students form cliques—jocks, goths, skaters, gangsters, freaks, geeks—and disparage those outside their own group. Even chimpanzees have been seen to wipe clean the spot where they were touched by a chimpanzee from another group (Goodall, 1986). Ingroup bias predisposes prejudice against strangers (Whitley, 1999).

Emotional Roots of Prejudice

Prejudice springs not only from the divisions of society but also from the passions of the heart. Facing the terror of death tends to heighten patriotism and produce loathing and aggression toward "them"—those who threaten one's world (Pyszczynski et al., 2002). Recalling such terror may alter attitudes, as happened to participants when Mark Landau and eight others (2004) reminded them of their own mortality or of the terror of 9/11. This terror reminder led to their expressing increased support for President George W. Bush.

"All good people agree,
And all good people say
All nice people, like Us, are We
And every one else is They.
But if you cross over the sea
Instead of over the way
You may end by (think of it)
Looking on We
As only a sort of They."

—Rudyard Kipling, "We and They," 1926

Prejudice may also express anger. According to the **scapegoat theory** of prejudice, finding someone to blame when things go wrong can provide a target for one's anger. This may help explain why prejudice levels are high among economically frustrated people. And why, in laboratory experiments, students who experience failure or are made to feel insecure often restore their self-esteem by disparaging a rival school or another person (Cialdini & Richardson, 1980; Crocker et al., 1987). Following 9/11, some outraged people similarly lashed out at innocent Arab-Americans, about whom negative stereotypes blossomed. Calls to eliminate Saddam Hussein, whom Americans had been grudgingly tolerating, also increased. "Fear and anger create aggression, and aggression against citizens of different ethnicity or race creates racism and, in turn, new forms of terrorism," noted Philip Zimbardo (2001).

In short, to boost our own sense of status, it helps to have others to denigrate. That is why a rival's misfortune sometimes provides a twinge of pleasure. By contrast, those made to feel loved and supported become more open to and accepting of others who differ (Mikulincer & Shaver, 2001).

Cognitive Roots of Prejudice

9: **What are the cognitive roots of prejudice?**

Prejudice springs not only from a culture's divisions and the heart's passions, but also from the mind's natural workings. Stereotyped beliefs are a by-product of how we cognitively simplify the world.

CATEGORIZATION One way we simplify our world is to categorize. A chemist categorizes molecules as organic and inorganic. A mental health professional categorizes psychological disorders by types. In categorizing people into groups, however, we often stereotype them, overlooking their diversity. We recognize that "we" are diverse, but "they"—the members of some other group—seem to look and act alike (Bothwell et al., 1989). To those in one ethnic group, members of another often seem more alike than they really are in attitudes, personality, and appearance. This greater recognition for own-race faces—called the **other-race effect,** or *own-race bias*—emerges during infancy, between 3 and 9 months of age (Kelly et al., 2007).

With experience, however, people get better at recognizing individual faces from another group (Li et al., 1996). For example, the longer Chinese people reside in a Western country, the less they exhibit the other-race effect (Hancock & Rhodes, 2008).

VIVID CASES In judging other groups, we often overgeneralize from vivid, memorable cases. In one classic experiment (Rothbart et al., 1978), researchers divided University of Oregon student volunteers into two groups, then showed them information about 50 men. The first group's list included 10 men arrested for nonviolent crimes, such as forgery. The second group's list included 10 men arrested for violent crimes, such as assault. Later, when both groups recalled how many men on their list had committed any sort of crime, the second group overestimated the number. Vivid (violent) cases come readily to mind and therefore influence our judgments of a group (**FIGURE 15.7**).

"If the Tiber reaches the walls, if the Nile does not rise to the fields, if the sky doesn't move or the Earth does, if there is famine, if there is plague, the cry is at once: 'The Christians to the lion!'"

—Tertullian, *Apologeticus,* A.D. 197

One seeming antidote to prejudice is intelligence. In a large national study, British children with high intelligence scores at age 10 typically expressed low prejudice at age 30 (Deary et al., 2008).

scapegoat theory the theory that prejudice offers an outlet for anger by providing someone to blame.

other-race effect the tendency to recall faces of one's own race more accurately than faces of other races. Also called the *cross-race effect* and the *own-race bias.*

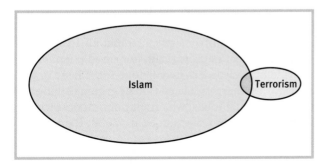

FIGURE 15.7 Vivid cases feed stereotypes The 9/11 Muslim terrorists created, in many minds, an exaggerated stereotype of Muslims as terror-prone. Actually, reported a U.S. National Research Council panel on terrorism, when offering the inexact illustration at left, most terrorists are not Muslim and "the vast majority of Islamic people have no connection with and do not sympathize with terrorism" (Smelser & Mitchell, 2002).

aggression any physical or verbal behavior intended to hurt or destroy.

In the last 40 years in the United States, well over 1 million people—more than all deaths in all wars in American history—have been killed by firearms in nonwar settings. Compared with people of the same sex, race, age, and neighborhood, those who keep a gun in the home (ironically, often for protection) are nearly three times more likely to be murdered in the home—nearly always by a family member or close acquaintance. For every self-defense use of a gun in the home, there are 4 unintentional shootings, 7 criminal assaults or homicides, and 11 attempted or completed suicides (Kellermann et al., 1993, 1997, 1998).

"It's a guy thing."

Aggression

The most destructive force in our social relations is aggression. In psychology, *aggression* has a more precise meaning than it does in everyday usage. The assertive, persistent salesperson is not aggressive. Nor is the dentist who makes you wince with pain. But the person who passes along a vicious rumor about you, the person who verbally assaults you, and the attacker who mugs you are aggressive. Thus, to a psychologist, **aggression** is any physical or verbal behavior intended to hurt or destroy, whether done reactively out of hostility or proactively as a calculated means to an end. Thus, murders and assaults that occurred as hostile outbursts are aggression. So were the 110 million war-related deaths that took place during this and the last century, many of which were cool and calculated.

Aggression research shows that behavior emerges from the interaction of biology and experience. For a gun to fire, the trigger must be pulled; with some people, as with hair-trigger guns, it doesn't take much to trip an explosion. Let us look first at biological factors that influence our thresholds for aggressive behavior, then at the psychological factors that pull the trigger.

The Biology of Aggression

10: What biological factors make us more prone to hurt one another?

Aggression varies too widely from culture to culture, era to era, and person to person to be considered an unlearned instinct. But biology does *influence* aggression. Stimuli that trigger aggressive behavior operate through our biological system. We can look for biological influences at three levels—genetic, neural, and biochemical. Our genes engineer our individual nervous systems, which operate electrochemically.

GENETIC INFLUENCES Animals have been bred for aggressiveness—sometimes for sport, sometimes for research. Pit bulls and cocker spaniels are formed by differing genes. Twin studies suggest that genes influence human aggression as well (Miles & Carey, 1997; Rowe et al., 1999). If one identical twin admits to "having a violent temper," the other twin will often independently admit the same. Fraternal twins are much less likely to respond similarly. This story is still unfolding, as researchers search for genetic markers found in those who commit the most violence. (One is already well known and is carried by half the human race: the Y chromosome.)

NEURAL INFLUENCES Animal and human brains have neural systems that, when stimulated, either inhibit or produce aggressive behavior (Moyer, 1983). Consider:

- The domineering leader of a caged monkey colony had a radio-controlled electrode implanted in a brain area that, when stimulated, inhibits aggression. When researchers placed the button that activated the electrode in the colony's cage, one small monkey learned to push it every time the boss became threatening.
- A mild-mannered woman had an electrode implanted in her brain's limbic system (in the amygdala) by neurosurgeons seeking to diagnose a disorder. Because the brain has no sensory receptors, she was unable to feel the stimulation. But at the flick of a switch she snarled, "Take my blood pressure. Take it now," then stood up and began to strike the doctor.
- One intensive evaluation of 15 death-row inmates revealed that all 15 had suffered a severe head injury. Although most neurologically impaired people are not violent, unrecognized neurological disorders may be one ingredient in the violence recipe (Lewis et al., 1986). Other studies of violent criminals have revealed diminished activity in the frontal lobes, which play an important role in controlling impulses (Amen et al., 1996; Davidson et al., 2000; Raine, 1999, 2005).

No one spot in the brain functions as a "violence center" that controls aggression. Rather, the brain has neural systems that, given provocation, will *facilitate* aggression. And it has a frontal lobe system for inhibiting aggression, making aggression more likely if this system is damaged, inactive, disconnected, or not yet fully mature.

BIOCHEMICAL INFLUENCES Hormones, alcohol, and other substances in the blood influence the neural systems that control aggression. A raging bull will become a gentle creature when castration reduces its testosterone level. The same is true of aggressive mice. When injected with testosterone, however, the castrated mice once again become aggressive.

Although humans are less sensitive to hormonal changes, violent criminals tend to be muscular young males with lower-than-average intelligence scores, low levels of the neurotransmitter serotonin, and higher-than-average testosterone levels (Dabbs et al., 2001a; Pendick, 1994). Drugs that sharply reduce their testosterone levels also subdue their aggressive tendencies. High testosterone correlates with irritability, assertiveness, impulsiveness, and low tolerance for frustration—qualities that predispose somewhat more aggressive responses to provocation (Dabbs et al., 2001b; Harris, 1999). Among both teenage boys and adult men, high testosterone levels correlate with delinquency, hard drug use, and aggressive-bullying responses to frustration (Berman et al., 1993; Dabbs & Morris, 1990; Olweus et al., 1988). With age, testosterone levels—and aggressiveness—diminish. Hormonally charged, aggressive 17-year-olds mature into hormonally quieter and gentler 70-year-olds.

For both biological and psychological reasons, alcohol unleashes aggressive responses to frustration (Bushman, 1993; Ito et al., 1996; Taylor & Chermack, 1993). Just *thinking* you've imbibed alcohol has some effect; but so, too, does unknowingly ingesting alcohol slipped into a drink. Police data and prison surveys reinforce conclusions drawn from experiments on alcohol and aggression: Aggression-prone people are more likely to drink and to become violent when intoxicated (White et al., 1993). People who have been drinking commit 4 in 10 violent crimes and 3 in 4 acts of spousal abuse (Greenfeld, 1998).

> "We could avoid two-thirds of all crime simply by putting all able-bodied young men in cryogenic sleep from the age of 12 through 28."
>
> —David T. Lykken, *The Antisocial Personalities*, 1995

A lean, mean, fighting machine—the testosterone-laden female hyena The hyena's unusual embryology pumps testosterone into female fetuses. The result is revved-up young female hyenas who seem born to fight.

Psychological and Social-Cultural Factors in Aggression

11: What psychological factors may trigger aggressive behavior?

Biological factors influence the ease with which aggression is triggered. But aggression is a complex behavior that occurs in particular contexts. What psychological factors pull the trigger?

AVERSIVE EVENTS Although suffering sometimes builds character, it may also bring out the worst in us. Being blocked short of a goal may increase our readiness to aggress. This phenomenon is called the **frustration-aggression principle:** Frustration creates anger, which may in some people generate aggression, especially in the presence of an aggressive cue, such as a gun—or a baseball. One study analyzed 27,667 hit-by-pitch major league baseball incidents between 1960 and 2004. It found that pitchers were most likely to hit batters when frustrated by the previous batter's hitting a home run, by the current batter's hitting a home run the last time at bat, or by a teammate's having been hit by a pitch in the previous half inning (Timmerman, 2007).

frustration-aggression principle the principle that frustration—the blocking of an attempt to achieve some goal—creates anger, which can generate aggression.

When we experience frustration and stress, we often respond with a *fight-or-flight reaction* (Chapter 11). After 9/11, Americans responded with a readiness to fight. Terrorism similarly may spring from a desire for revenge, sometimes after a friend or family member has been killed or injured. Contrary to the popular idea that poverty breeds terrorists, studies indicate that suicide bombers and those who support them tend to be neither uneducated nor desperately poor (Krueger, 2007). The 9/11 suicide bombers, for example, were mostly educated men from wealthy Saudi Arabia (McDermott, 2005). Frustration (and aggression) arise less from deprivation than from the gap between reality and expectations, which may rise with education and attainments.

Like frustration, other aversive stimuli—physical pain, personal insults, foul odors, hot temperatures, cigarette smoke, and a host of others—can also evoke hostility. And studies in which animals or humans experience unpleasant events reveal that those made miserable will often make others miserable (Berkowitz, 1983, 1989). Violent crime and spousal abuse rates are higher during hotter years, seasons, months, and days (**FIGURE 15.8**). When overheated, people think, feel, and act more aggressively. From the available data, Craig Anderson and his colleagues (2000) have projected that, other things being equal, global warming of 4 degrees Fahrenheit (about 2 degrees centigrade) would induce more than 50,000 additional assaults and murders in the United States alone.

SOCIAL AND CULTURAL INFLUENCES Aggression may be a natural response to aversive events, but learning can alter natural reactions. We are likely to be more aggressive in situations where experience has taught us that aggression pays. Children whose aggression successfully intimidates other children may become more aggressive. Animals that have successfully fought to get food or mates become increasingly ferocious. Rewards and punishments can shape our behavior.

Rejection often intensifies aggression (Catanese & Tice, 2005; Gaertner & Iuzzini, 2005). In a series of studies, Jean Twenge and her collaborators (2001, 2002, 2003) told some people that others whom they had met didn't want them in their group, or that a personality test indicated they "were likely to end up alone later in life." People led to feel socially excluded were later more likely to disparage or even deliver a blast of noise to someone who had insulted them. This rejection-induced aggression brings to mind various North American and European school shootings, committed by youths who had been shunned, mocked, and sometimes bullied by peers. Ostracism, as we noted in Chapter 10, can be a real pain.

FIGURE 15.8 Uncomfortably hot weather and aggressive reactions
Between 1980 and 1982 in Houston, murders and rapes were more common on days over 91 degrees Fahrenheit (33 degrees centigrade), as shown in the graph. This finding is consistent with those from laboratory experiments in which people working in a hot room react to provocations with greater hostility. (From Anderson & Anderson, 1984.)

Different cultures model, reinforce, and evoke different tendencies toward violence. For example, crime rates are higher (and average happiness is lower) in countries marked by a great disparity between rich and poor (Triandis, 1994). With great disparity may come, for those who have less, feelings of *relative deprivation*. Richard Nisbett and Dov Cohen (1996) have shown how violence can vary by culture within a country. They analyzed violence among White Americans in southern towns settled by Scots-Irish herders whose tradition emphasized "manly honor," the use of arms to protect one's flock, and a history of coercive slavery. Their cultural descendants, Nisbett and Cohen found, have triple the homicide rates and are more supportive of physically punishing children, of warfare initiatives, and of uncontrolled gun ownership than are their White counterparts in New England towns settled by the more traditionally peaceful Puritan, Quaker, and Dutch farmer-artisans.

Social influence also appears in high violence rates among cultures and families that experience minimal father care (Triandis, 1994). Even after controlling for parental education, race, income, and teen motherhood, American male youths from father-absent homes have double their peers' incarceration rate (Harper & McLanahan, 2004).

It is important, however, to note how many people are leading gentle, even heroic lives amid social stresses, reminding us again that individuals differ. The person matters. That people differ over time and place reminds us that environments also differ, and situations matter. Yesterday's plundering Vikings have become today's peace-promoting Scandinavians. Like all behavior, aggression arises from the interaction of persons and situations.

OBSERVING MODELS OF AGGRESSION Observational learning also influences our natural reactions. Modeling violence—screaming and hitting—is precisely what exasperated parents often do. Parents of delinquent youngsters typically discipline with beatings, thus modeling aggression as a method of dealing with problems (Patterson et al., 1982, 1992). They also frequently cave into (reward) their children's tears and temper tantrums. Parent-training programs advise a more positive approach. They encourage parents to discipline without modeling violence, to reinforce desirable behaviors, and to frame statements positively ("When you finish loading the dishwasher you can go play," rather than "If you don't load the dishwasher, there'll be no playing"). One *aggression-replacement program* has brought down re-arrest rates of juvenile offenders and gang members by teaching the youths and their parents communication skills, training them to control anger, and encouraging more thoughtful moral reasoning (Goldstein et al., 1998).

But parents are hardly the only aggression models. As we noted in Chapter 7, observing TV violence tends to desensitize people to cruelty and prime them to respond aggressively when provoked. If, as research has shown, passively viewing violence elevates aggressive responses to provocation and lowers sensitivity to cruelty, what will be the effect of actively role-playing aggression? Social psychologists attribute the media's influence partly to the *social scripts* (mental tapes for how to act, provided by our culture) they portray (see Thinking Critically About: Do Video Games Teach, or Release, Violence? on the next page). When we find ourselves in new situations, uncertain how to act, we rely on social scripts. After so many action films, youngsters may acquire a script that gets played when they face real-life conflicts. Challenged, they may "act like a man" by intimidating or eliminating the threat.

Does this media influence extend to sexual violence? We do know that sexually coercive men typically are sexually promiscuous and hostile in their relationships with women (**FIGURE 15.9**). We also know from surveys of American and Australian teens and university students that viewing X-rated films and Internet pornography is several times higher among males than among females (Carroll et al., 2008; Flood, 2007; Wolak et al., 2007). Might sexually explicit media models contribute to sexually aggressive tendencies?

"Why do we kill people who kill people to show that killing people is wrong?"

—National Coalition to Abolish the Death Penalty, 1992

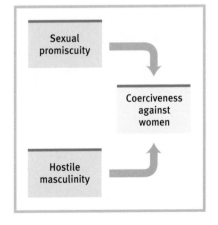

FIGURE 15.9 Men who sexually coerce women The recipe for coercion against women combines an impersonal approach to sex with a hostile masculinity. (Adapted from Malamuth, 1996.)

Thinking Critically About:

Do Video Games Teach, or Release, Violence?

Violent video games became an issue for public debate after teen assassins in more than a dozen places seemed to mimic the carnage in the splatter games they had so often played (Anderson, 2004a). In 2002, two Grand Rapids, Michigan, teens and a man in his early twenties spent part of a night drinking beer and playing *Grand Theft Auto III,* using cars to run down simulated pedestrians, before beating them with fists and leaving a bloody body behind (Kolker, 2002). Then they went out on a real drive, spotted a 38-year-old man on a bicycle, ran him down with their car, got out, stomped and punched him, and returned home to play the game some more. (The man, a father of three, died six days later.)

Interactive games transport the player into their own vivid reality. When youths play *Grand Theft Auto: San Andreas,* they can carjack vehicles; run down pedestrians; do drive-by shootings; pick up a prostitute, have sex with her, and then kill her. When youths play such games, do they learn social scripts?

Most abused children don't become abusive adults. Most social drinkers don't become alcohol dependent. And most youths who spend hundreds of hours in these mass murder simulators don't become teen assassins. Still, we wonder: Although very few will commit slaughter, how many will become desensitized to violence and more open to violent acts?

Thirty-eight studies of more than 7000 people offer some answers (Anderson et al., 2004). In one study, people with extensive experience in violent video gaming also display desensitization to violent images, as shown by blunted brain responses (Bartholow et al., 2006). Another study observed a rising level of arousal and feelings of hostility in college men as they played *Mortal Kombat* (Ballard & Wiest, 1998). Others have

Mark C. Burnett/Stock, Boston

Desensitizing people to violence

found that video games can prime aggressive thoughts and increase aggression. Consider this report from Craig Anderson and Karen Dill (2000): University men who have spent the most hours playing violent video games tend to be the most physically aggressive (for example, to acknowledge having hit or attacked someone else). In one experiment, people randomly assigned to play a game involving bloody murders with groaning victims (rather than to play nonviolent *Myst*) became more hostile. On a follow-up task, they also were more likely to blast intense noise at a fellow student.

Studies of young adolescents by Douglas Gentile and his co-researchers (2004; 2007) further reveal that kids who play a lot of violent video games see the world as more hostile, get into more arguments and fights, and get worse grades (those hours aren't spent reading or studying). Ah, but is this merely because

naturally hostile kids are drawn to such games? *No,* says Gentile. Even among violent-game players scoring low in hostility, 38 percent had been in fights. That figure is nearly 10 times the rate (4 percent) found among their nongaming counterparts. Moreover, over time, the nongamers became more likely to have fights only if they started playing the violent games. Anderson and his colleagues (2007) believe that, due partly to the more active participation and rewarded violence of game play, violent video games have even greater effects on aggressive behavior and cognition than do violent television and movies.

"We are what we repeatedly do."

—Aristotle

Although much remains to be learned, these studies again disconfirm the *catharsis hypothesis*—the idea that we feel better if we "blow off steam" by venting our emotions (Chapter 11). Playing violent video games *increases* aggressive thoughts, emotions, and behaviors. One video game company's CEO rationalized that we are "violent by nature [and] need release valves." "It's a way to process violent feelings and anxieties through a fantasy medium," added a prominent civil liberties lawyer in explaining her hunch that playing violent games calms violent tendencies (Heins, 2004). Actually, expressing anger breeds more anger, and practicing violence breeds more violence.

Tomorrow's games may have even greater effects. Social psychologists Susan Persky and Jim Blascovich (2005) created a violent video game for students to play on either a desktop computer or by putting on a headset and stepping into a virtual reality. As they predicted, the virtual reality more dramatically heightened aggressive feelings and behavior during and after the play.

Content analyses reveal that most X-rated films have depicted quick, casual sex between strangers, but that scenes of rape and sexual exploitation of women by men are also common (Cowan et al., 1988; NCTV, 1987; Yang & Linz, 1990). In less graphic form, the same unrealistic script—she resists her attacker, he persists, she melts and is finally driven to ecstasy—is commonplace in movies, TV programs, and romance novels. Most rapists accept this *rape myth*—the idea that some women invite or enjoy rape and get "swept away" while being "taken" (Brinson, 1992). And—compared with those who watch little TV—men and women who watch a great deal are also more likely to accept the rape myth (Kahlor & Morrison, 2007). (In actuality, rape is traumatic, and it frequently harms women's reproductive and psychological health [Golding, 1996].)

Other studies have also found that repeatedly watching X-rated films (even if nonviolent) later makes one's own partner seem less attractive, makes a woman's friendliness seem more sexual, and makes sexual aggression seem less serious (Harris, 1994). In one such experiment, undergraduates were asked to suggest an appropriate prison term for a man convicted of raping a hitchhiker. Participants who had viewed sexually explicit films for six weeks recommended sentences half as long as those recommended by a control group that had viewed nonerotic films (Zillmann & Bryant, 1984).

Experiments cannot elicit actual sexual violence, but they can assess a man's willingness to hurt a woman. Often the research gauges the effect of violent versus nonviolent erotic films on men's willingness to deliver supposed electric shocks to women who had earlier provoked the men. These experiments suggest that it's not the eroticism but rather the depictions of sexual *violence* (whether in R-rated slasher films or X-rated films) that most directly affect men's acceptance and performance of aggression against women. A conference of 21 social scientists, including many of the researchers who conducted these experiments, produced a consensus (Surgeon General, 1986): "Pornography that portrays sexual aggression as pleasurable for the victim increases the acceptance of the use of coercion in sexual relations." Contrary to much popular opinion, viewing such depictions does not provide an outlet for bottled-up impulses. Rather, "in laboratory studies measuring short-term effects, exposure to violent pornography increases punitive behavior toward women."

Significant behaviors, such as violence, usually have many determinants, making any single explanation an oversimplification. Asking what causes violence is therefore like asking what causes cancer. Those who study the effects of asbestos exposure on cancer rates may remind us that asbestos is indeed a cancer cause, albeit only one among many. Factors that can create a predisposition to sexual violence include the media but also dominance motives, disinhibition by alcohol, and a history of childhood abuse (Malamuth et al., 1991, 1995). Still, if media depictions of violence can disinhibit and desensitize; if viewing sexual violence fosters hostile, domineering attitudes and behaviors; and if viewing pornography leads viewers to trivialize rape, devalue their partners, and engage in uncommitted sex, then media influence is not a minor issue.

In sexual aggression, as in other forms of aggression, the media provide social scripts. After viewing the multiple sexual innuendoes and acts found in most prime-time TV hours—often involving impulsive or short-term relationships—youths may acquire sexual scripts they later enact in real-life relationships (Kunkel et al., 2001; Sapolsky & Tabarlet, 1991). Music lyrics also write social scripts. In one set of experiments, German university men who listened to women-hating song lyrics administered the most hot chili sauce to a woman and recalled more negative feelings and beliefs about women. Man-hating song lyrics had a similar effect on the aggressive behavior of women listeners (Fischer & Greitemeyer, 2006).

Might public consciousness be raised by making people aware of the information you have just been reading? In the 1950s, movies often depicted attractive actors enjoying a cigarette. Today, after decades of education in the dangers of smoking, the entertainment industry now more often avoids such images. Researchers Brad Bushman and Craig Anderson (2001) have noted that the correlation between viewing violence and behaving aggressively nearly equals the correlation between smoking and lung cancer. They also noted other parallels, such as desensitization with continued exposure; severe long-term cumulative effects; and industry opposition to regulation of these products.

In follow-up studies, Zillmann (1989) found that after massive exposure to X-rated sexual films, men and women became more accepting of extramarital sex, of women's sexual submission to men, and of a man's seducing a 12-year-old girl. As people heavily exposed to televised crime perceive the world as more dangerous, so people heavily exposed to pornography see the world as more sexual.

FIGURE 15.10 Biopsychosocial understanding of aggression Because many factors contribute to aggressive behavior, there are many ways to change such behavior, including learning anger management and communication skills, and avoiding violent media and video games.

Biological influences:
• genetic influences
• biochemical influences, such as testosterone and alcohol
• neural influences, such as severe head injuries

Psychological influences:
• dominating behavior (which boosts testosterone levels in the blood)
• believing you've drunk alcohol (whether you actually have or not)
• frustration
• aggressive role models
• rewards for aggressive behavior

Aggressive behavior

Social-cultural influences:
• deindividuation from being in a crowd
• challenging environmental factors, such as crowding, heat, and direct provocations
• parental models of aggression
• minimal father involvement
• being rejected from a group
• exposure to violent media

In response to growing public concern about violence in the media, television violence levels declined in the early 1990s (Gerbner et al., 1993). The growing sensitivity to violence has raised hopes that entertainers, producers, and audiences might someday look back with embarrassment on the days when movies "entertained" people with scenes of torture, mutilation, and sexual coercion.

* * * * *

To sum up, research reveals biological, psychological, and social-cultural influences on aggressive behavior. Like so much else, aggression is a biopsychosocial phenomenon (**FIGURE 15.10**).

REHEARSE IT!

11. When we are frustrated, prejudice provides an outlet for our anger and gives us someone to blame. This effect is best described by
a. ingroup bias.
b. scapegoat theory.
c. vivid-case theory.
d. the just-world phenomenon.

12. If several well-publicized murders are committed by members of a particular group, we may tend to react with fear and suspicion toward all members of that group. In other words, we
a. blame the victim.
b. overgeneralize from vivid, memorable cases.
c. view the world as just.
d. rationalize inequality.

13. Aggression is influenced by biology at the genetic, neural, and biochemical

levels. Evidence of a biochemical influence on aggression is the finding that
a. aggressive behavior varies widely from culture to culture.
b. animals can be bred for aggressiveness.
c. stimulation of an area of the brain's limbic system produces aggressive behavior.
d. a higher-than-average level of the hormone testosterone is associated with violent behavior in males.

14. Studies show that parents of delinquent young people tend to use beatings to enforce discipline. This demonstrates that aggression can be
a. learned through direct rewards.
b. triggered by exposure to violent media.
c. learned through observation of aggressive models.

d. caused by hormonal changes at puberty.

15. A conference of social scientists studying the effects of pornography unanimously agreed that violent pornography
a. has little effect on most viewers.
b. is the primary cause of reported and unreported rapes.
c. leads viewers to be more accepting of coercion in sexual relations.
d. has no effect, other than short-term arousal and entertainment.

16. The aspect of X-rated films that most directly influences men's aggression toward women seems to be the
a. length of the film.
b. eroticism portrayed.
c. depictions of sexual violence.
d. attractiveness of the actors.

Answers: 11. b, 12. b, 13. d, 14. c, 15. c, 16. c.

Attraction

Pause a moment and think about your relationships with two people—a close friend, and someone who stirs in you feelings of romantic love. What is the psychological chemistry that binds us together in these special sorts of attachments that help us cope with all other relationships? Social psychology suggests some answers.

The Psychology of Attraction

12: **Why do we befriend or fall in love with some people but not with others?**

We endlessly wonder how we can win others' affection and what makes our own affections flourish or fade. Does familiarity breed contempt, or does it intensify our affection? Do birds of a feather flock together, or do opposites attract? Is beauty only skin deep, or does attractiveness matter greatly? Consider three ingredients of our liking for one another: proximity, physical attractiveness, and similarity.

PROXIMITY Before friendships become close, they must begin. *Proximity*—geographic nearness—is friendship's most powerful predictor. Proximity provides opportunities for aggression, but much more often it breeds liking. Study after study reveals that people are most inclined to like, and even to marry, those who live in the same neighborhood, who sit nearby in class, who work in the same office, who share the same parking lot, who eat in the same dining hall. Look around. (For a twenty-first-century technology that connects people not in physical proximity, see Close-Up: Online Matchmaking.)

Why is proximity so conducive to liking? Obviously, part of the answer is the greater availability of those we often meet. But there is more to it than that. For one thing, repeated exposure to novel stimuli—be they nonsense syllables, musical selections, geometric figures, Chinese characters, human faces, or the letters of our own name—increases our liking for them (Moreland & Zajonc, 1982; Nuttin, 1987; Zajonc, 2001). People are even somewhat more likely to marry someone whose familiar-sounding first or last name resembles their own (Jones et al., 2004).

Familiarity breeds acceptance When this rare white penguin was born in the Sydney, Australia, zoo, his tuxedoed peers ostracized him. Zookeepers thought they would need to dye him black to gain acceptance. But after three weeks of contact, the other penguins came to accept him.

Close-Up:

Online Matchmaking

If you have not found a romantic partner in your immediate proximity, why not cast a wider net? In the United States, 16 million people have tried online dating and matchmaking services, as have an estimated 14 million more in China, 10 million in India, and tens of millions in other countries (Cullen & Masters, 2008).

Although published research on the effectiveness of Internet matchmaking services is sparse, this much seems well established: Some people dishonestly represent their age, attractiveness, occupation, or other details, and thus are not who they seem to be. Nevertheless, Katelyn McKenna and John Bargh and their colleagues have offered a surprising

"I can't wait to see what you're like online."

finding: Compared with relationships formed in person, Internet-formed friendships and romantic relationships are more likely to last beyond two years (Bargh et al., 2002, 2004; McKenna et al., 2002; McKenna & Bargh, 1998, 2000). In one of their studies, people disclosed more, with less posturing, to those whom they met online. When conversing online with someone for 20 minutes, they felt more liking for that person than they did for someone they had met and talked with face to face. This was true even when (unknown to them) it was the same person! Small wonder that Internet friendships often feel as real and important to people as in-person relationships.

The mere exposure effect The mere exposure effect applies even to ourselves. Because the human face is not perfectly symmetrical, the face we see in the mirror is not the same face our friends see. Most of us prefer the familiar mirror image, while our friends like the reverse (Mita et al., 1977). The Bill Gates known to us all is at left. The person he sees in the mirror each morning is shown at right, and that's the photo he would probably prefer.

This phenomenon is the **mere exposure effect.** Within certain limits (Bornstein, 1989, 1999), familiarity breeds fondness. Richard Moreland and Scott Beach (1992) demonstrated this by having four equally attractive women silently attend a 200-student class for zero, 5, 10, or 15 class sessions. At the end of the course, students were shown slides of each woman and asked to rate each one's attractiveness. The most attractive? The ones they'd seen most often. The phenomenon will come as no surprise to the young Taiwanese man who wrote more than 700 letters to his girlfriend, urging her to marry him. She did marry—the mail carrier (Steinberg, 1993).

No face is more familiar than one's own. And that helps explain an interesting finding from Lisa DeBruine's research (2004): Men liked other men, and women liked other women, when their faces incorporated some morphed features of their own. When DeBruine (2002) had McMaster University students play a game with a supposed other player, they also were more trusting and cooperative when the other person's image had some features of their own face morphed into it. In me I trust. (See also **FIGURE 15.11**.)

For our ancestors, the mere exposure effect was adaptive. What was familiar was generally safe and approachable. What was unfamiliar was more often dangerous and threatening. Evolution seems to have hard-wired into us the tendency to bond with those who are familiar and to be wary of those who are unfamiliar (Zajonc, 1998). Gut-level prejudice against those who are culturally different may thus be a primitive, automatic emotional response (Devine, 1995). It's what we do with our knee-jerk prejudice that matters, suggest researchers. Do we let those feelings control our behavior? Or do we monitor our feelings and act in ways that reflect our conscious valuing of human equality?

PHYSICAL ATTRACTIVENESS Once proximity affords you contact, what most affects your first impressions: The person's sincerity? Intelligence? Personality? Hundreds of experiments reveal that it is something far more superficial: Appearance.

In one study, Elaine Hatfield and her co-workers (Walster et al., 1966) randomly matched new University of Minnesota students for a Welcome Week dance. Before the dance, each student took a battery of personality and aptitude tests. On the night of the blind date, the couples danced and talked for more than two hours and then took a brief intermission to rate their dates. What determined whether they liked each other? As far as the researchers could determine, only one thing mattered: Physical attractiveness (which had been rated by the researchers beforehand).

mere exposure effect the phenomenon that repeated exposure to novel stimuli increases liking of them.

FIGURE 15.11 I like the candidate who looks a bit like dear old me Jeremy Bailenson and his colleagues (2005) incorporated morphed features of voters' faces into the faces of 2004 U.S. presidential candidates George Bush and John Kerry. Without conscious awareness that they were viewing some of their own features, the participants were more likely to favor the candidate whose face incorporated some of their own features.

Voter

Candidate George Bush

60:40 Blend

Both the men and the women liked good-looking dates best. Have people changed since that early experiment? Apparently not. Recent speed-dating experiments confirm that attractiveness influences first impressions for both sexes (Belot & Francesconi, 2006; Finkel & Eastwick, 2008). Although women are more likely than men to say that another's looks don't affect them (Lippa, 2007), a man's looks do affect women's behavior (Feingold, 1990; Sprecher, 1989; Woll, 1986).

People's physical attractiveness also predicts their frequency of dating, their feelings of popularity, and others' initial impressions of their personalities. We perceive attractive people to be healthier, happier, more sensitive, more successful, and more socially skilled, though not more honest or compassionate (Eagly et al., 1991; Feingold, 1992; Hatfield & Sprecher, 1986). Attractive, well-dressed people are more likely to make a favorable impression on potential employers and to enjoy occupational success (Cash & Janda, 1984; Langlois et al., 2000; Solomon, 1987). Income analyses show a penalty for plainness or obesity and a premium for beauty (Engemann & Owyang, 2005).

An analysis of 100 top-grossing films since 1940 found that attractive characters were portrayed as morally superior to unattractive characters (Smith et al., 1999). But Hollywood modeling doesn't explain why, to judge from their gazing times, even babies prefer attractive over unattractive faces (Langlois et al., 1987). So do some blind people, as University of Birmingham professor John Hull (1990, p. 23) discovered after going blind. A colleague's remarks on a woman's beauty would strangely affect his feelings. He found this "deplorable. . . . What can it matter to me what sighted men think of women . . . yet I do care what sighted men think, and I do not seem able to throw off this prejudice."

For people taught that "beauty is only skin deep" and that "appearances can be deceiving," the power of physical attractiveness seems unfair and unenlightened. Why should it matter? Two thousand years ago the Roman statesman Cicero felt the same way: "The final good and the supreme duty of the wise person is to resist appearance." Cicero might be reassured by two other findings.

First, people's attractiveness is surprisingly unrelated to their self-esteem and happiness (Diener et al., 1995; Major et al., 1984). One reason may be that, except after comparing themselves with superattractive people, few people (thanks, perhaps, to the mere exposure effect) view themselves as unattractive (Thornton & Moore, 1993). Another reason is that strikingly attractive people are sometimes suspicious that praise for their work may simply be a reaction to their looks. When less attractive people are praised, they are more likely to accept it as sincere (Berscheid, 1981).

Cicero might also find comfort in knowing that attractiveness judgments are relative. The standards by which judges crown Miss Universe hardly apply to the whole planet. Rather, beauty is in the eye of the culture—our standards for beauty reflect our time and place. Hoping to look attractive, people in different cultures have pierced their noses, lengthened their necks, bound their feet, and dyed or painted their skin and hair. They have gorged themselves to achieve a full figure or

When Neanderthals fall in love.

"Personal beauty is a greater recommendation than any letter of introduction."
—Aristotle, *Apothegems*, 330 B.C.

Percentage of Men and Women Who "Constantly Think About Their Looks"

	Men	Women
Canada	18%	20%
United States	17	27
Mexico	40	45
Venezuela	47	65

From Roper Starch survey, reported by McCool (1999).

In the eye of the beholder
Conceptions of attractiveness vary by culture. Moreover, the current concept of attractiveness in Morocco, Kenya, and Scandinavia may well change in the future.

Extreme makeover In affluent, beauty-conscious cultures, increasing numbers of people, such as this woman from the American TV show *Extreme Makeover,* have turned to cosmetic surgery to improve their looks. If money were no concern, might you ever do the same?

New York Times *columnist Maureen Dowd on liposuction (January 19, 2000): "Women in the 50's vacuumed. Women in the 00's are vacuumed. Our Hoovers have turned on us!"*

Women have 91 percent of cosmetic procedures (ASAPS, 2008). Women also recall others' appearance better than do men (Mast & Hall, 2006).

liposuctioned fat to achieve a slim one, applied chemicals hoping to rid themselves of unwanted hair or to regrow wanted hair, strapped on leather garments to make their breasts seem smaller or surgically filled their breasts with silicone and put on Wonderbras to make them look bigger.

For women in North America, the ultra-thin ideal of the Roaring Twenties gave way to the soft, voluptuous Marilyn Monroe ideal of the 1950s, only to be replaced by today's lean yet busty ideal. Americans now spend more on beauty supplies than on education and social services combined. Still not satisfied, they line up for 12 million cosmetic medical treatments each year, including plastic surgery, Botox skin smoothing, and laser hair removal—not even counting procedures for teeth capping or whitening (ASAPS, 2008). But the result of the beauty race since 1970 has been that more and more women feel *un*happy with their appearance (Feingold & Mazella, 1998).

Some aspects of attractiveness, however, do cross place and time (Cunningham et al., 2005; Langlois et al., 2000). You may recall from Chapter 4 that men in a wide variety of cultures, from Australia to Zambia, judge women as more attractive if they have a youthful appearance. Women feel attracted to healthy-looking men, but especially to those who seem mature, dominant, and affluent.

Beauty grows with mere exposure
Herman Miller, Inc.'s famed Aeron chair initially received high comfort ratings but abysmal beauty ratings. To some it looked like "lawn furniture" or "a giant prehistoric insect" (Gladwell, 2005). But then, with design awards, media visibility, and imitators, the ugly duckling came to be the company's bestselling chair ever and to be seen as beautiful. With people, too, beauty lies partly in the beholder's eye and can grow with exposure.

Cultural standards aside, attractiveness also depends on our feelings about the person. If led to believe that someone has appealing traits (such as being honest, humorous, and polite rather than rude, unfair, and abusive) people perceive the person as more physically attractive (Lewandowski et al., 2007). In a Rodgers and Hammerstein musical, Prince Charming asks Cinderella, "Do I love you because you're beautiful, or are you beautiful because I love you?" Chances are it's both. As we see our loved ones again and again, their physical imperfections grow less noticeable and their attractiveness grows more apparent (Beaman & Klentz, 1983; Gross & Crofton, 1977). Shakespeare said it in *A Midsummer Night's Dream:* "Love looks not with the eyes, but with the mind." Come to love someone and watch beauty grow.

"Love has ever in view the absolute loveliness of that which it beholds."

—George MacDonald, *Unspoken Sermons,* 1867

SIMILARITY Let's say that proximity has brought you into contact with someone and that your appearance has made an acceptable first impression. What now influences whether acquaintances develop into friends? For example, as you get to know someone better, is the chemistry better if you are opposites or if you are alike?

It makes a good story—extremely different types living in harmonious union: Rat, Mole, and Badger in *The Wind in the Willows*, Frog and Toad in Arnold Lobel's books. The stories delight us by expressing what we seldom experience, for we tend *not* to like dissimilar people (Rosenbaum, 1986). In real life, opposites retract. Birds that flock together usually *are* of a feather. Friends and couples are far more likely to share common attitudes, beliefs, and interests (and, for that matter, age, religion, race, education, intelligence, smoking behavior, and economic status) than are randomly paired people. Similarity breeds content.

Proximity, attractiveness, and similarity are not the only determinants of attraction. We also like those who like us. This is especially so when our self-image is low. When we believe someone likes us, we feel good and respond to them warmly, which leads them to like us even more (Curtis & Miller, 1986). To be liked is powerfully rewarding.

Indeed, a simple *reward theory of attraction*—that we will like those whose behavior is rewarding to us and that we will continue relationships that offer more rewards than costs—can explain all the findings we have considered so far. When a person lives or works in close proximity with someone else, it costs less time and effort to develop the friendship and enjoy its benefits. Attractive people are aesthetically pleasing, and associating with them can be socially rewarding. Those with similar views reward us by validating our own.

Romantic Love

13: How does romantic love typically change as time passes?

Occasionally, people move quickly from initial impressions, to friendship, to the more intense, complex, and mysterious state of romantic love. Elaine Hatfield (1988) has distinguished two types of love: temporary passionate love and a more enduring companionate love.

PASSIONATE LOVE Noting that arousal is a key ingredient of **passionate love,** Hatfield suggested that the two-factor theory of emotion (Chapter 11) can help us understand this intense positive absorption in another. The theory assumes that (1) emotions have two ingredients—physical arousal plus cognitive appraisal—and that (2) arousal from any source can enhance one emotion or another, depending on how we interpret and label the arousal.

In tests of this theory, college men have been aroused by fright, by running in place, by viewing erotic materials, or by listening to humorous or repulsive monologues. They were then introduced to an attractive woman and asked to rate her (or their girlfriend). Unlike unaroused men, those who were stirred up attributed some of their arousal to the woman or girlfriend and felt more attracted to her (Carducci et al., 1978; Dermer & Pyszczynski, 1978; White & Kight, 1984).

Outside the laboratory, Donald Dutton and Arthur Aron (1974, 1989) went to two bridges across British Columbia's rocky Capilano River. One, a swaying footbridge, was 230 feet above the rocks; the other was low and solid. An attractive young female accomplice intercepted men coming off each bridge, sought their help

Snapshots

Bill looked at Susan, Susan at Bill. Suddenly death didn't seem like an option. This was love at first sight.

HI & LOIS

passionate love an aroused state of intense positive absorption in another, usually present at the beginning of a love relationship.

ƎGAIЯ MATRIMONY

COURTSHIP

Sometimes passionate love becomes enduring companionate love, sometimes not (invert the picture) What, in addition to similar attitudes and interests, predicts long-term loving attachment?

"When two people are under the influence of the most violent, most insane, most delusive, and most transient of passions, they are required to swear that they will remain in that excited, abnormal, and exhausting condition continuously until death do them part."

—George Bernard Shaw, "Getting Married," 1908

Love is an ancient thing In 2007, a 5000- to 6000-year-old "Romeo and Juliet" young couple was unearthed locked in embrace, near Rome.

in filling out a short questionnaire, and then offered her phone number in case they wanted to hear more about her project. Far more of those who had just crossed the high bridge—which left their hearts pounding—accepted the number and later called the woman. To be revved up and to associate some of that arousal with a desirable person is to feel the pull of passion. Adrenaline makes the heart grow fonder.

COMPANIONATE LOVE Although the spark of romantic love often endures, the intense absorption in the other, the thrill of the romance, the giddy "floating on a cloud" feeling typically fades. Does this mean the French are correct in saying that "love makes the time pass and time makes love pass"? Or can friendship and commitment keep a relationship going after the passion cools?

Hatfield noted that as love matures it becomes a steadier **companionate love**—a deep, affectionate attachment. There may be adaptive wisdom to this change from passion to attachment (Reis & Aron, 2008). Passionate love often produces children, whose survival is aided by the parents' waning obsession with one another. Social psychologist Ellen Berscheid and her colleagues (1984) observed that the failure to appreciate passionate love's limited half-life can doom a relationship: "If the inevitable odds against eternal passionate love in a relationship were better understood, more people might choose to be satisfied with the quieter feelings of satisfaction and contentment." Indeed, recognizing the short duration of passionate love, some societies have deemed such feelings an irrational reason for marrying. Better, such cultures say, to choose (or have someone choose for you) a partner with a compatible background and interests. Non-Western cultures, where people rate love less important for marriage, do have lower divorce rates (Levine et al., 1995).

One key to a gratifying and enduring relationship is **equity:** Both partners receive in proportion to what they give. When equity exists—when both partners freely give and receive, when they share decision making—their chances for sustained and satisfying companionate love are good (Gray-Little & Burks, 1983; Van Yperen & Buunk, 1990). In one national survey, "sharing household chores" ranked third, after "faithfulness" and a "happy sexual relationship," on a list of nine things people associated with successful marriages. "I like hugs. I like kisses. But what I really love is help with the dishes," summarized the Pew Research Center (2007).

Another vital ingredient of loving relationships is **self-disclosure,** the revealing of intimate details about ourselves—our likes and dislikes, our dreams and worries, our proud and shameful moments. "When I am with my friend," noted the Roman statesman Seneca, "me thinks I am alone, and as much at liberty to speak anything as to think it." Self-disclosure breeds liking, and liking breeds self-disclosure (Collins & Miller, 1994). As one person reveals a little, the other reciprocates, the first then reveals more, and on and on, as friends or lovers move to deeper intimacy. Each increase in intimacy rekindles passion (Baumeister & Bratslavsky, 1999).

One experiment marched pairs of volunteer students through 45 minutes of increasingly self-disclosing conversation—from "When did you last sing to yourself?" to "When did you last cry in front of another person? By yourself?" By the experiment's end, those experiencing the escalating intimacy felt remarkably close to their conversation partner, much closer than others who had spent the time with small-talk questions, such as "What was your high school like?" (Aron et al., 1997). Given self-disclosing intimacy plus mutually supportive equality, the odds favor enduring companionate love.

Altruism

14: When are we most—and least—likely to help?

Carl Wilkens, a Seventh Day Adventist missionary, was living with his family in Kigali, Rwanda, when Hutu militia began to slaughter the Tutsi in 1994. The U.S. government, church leaders, and friends all implored Wilkens to leave. He refused. After evacuating his family, and even after every other American had left Kigali, he alone stayed and contested the 800,000-person genocide. When the militia came to kill him and his Tutsi servants, Wilkens' Hutu neighbors deterred them. Despite repeated death threats, he spent his days running roadblocks to take food and water to orphanages and to negotiate, plead, and bully his way through the bloodshed, saving lives time and again. "It just seemed the right thing to do," he later explained (Kristof, 2004).

Such selfless goodness exemplifies **altruism**—the unselfish regard for the welfare of others. Altruism became a major concern of social psychologists after an especially vile act of sexual violence. On March 13, 1964, a stalker repeatedly stabbed Kitty Genovese, then raped her as she lay dying outside her Queens, New York, apartment at 3:30 A.M. "Oh, my God, he stabbed me!" Genovese screamed into the early morning stillness. "Please help me!" Windows opened and lights went on as neighbors—38 of them, according to an initial *New York Times* report, though the number was later contested—heard her screams. Her attacker fled and then returned to stab and rape her again. Not until he had fled for good did anyone so much as call the police, at 3:50 A.M.

Bystander Intervention

Reflecting on initial reports of the Genovese murder, most commentators were outraged by the bystanders' "apathy" and "indifference." Rather than blaming the onlookers for their inaction, social psychologists John Darley and Bibb Latané (1968b) searched for an explanation. The answer, they suspected, was an important situational factor—the presence of others.

After staging emergencies under various conditions, Darley and Latané assembled their findings into a decision scheme: We will help only if the situation enables us first to *notice* the incident, then to *interpret* it as an emergency, and finally to *assume responsibility* for helping (**FIGURE 15.12**). At each step, the presence of other bystanders can turn us away from the path that leads to helping. In the laboratory and on the street, people in a group of strangers are more likely than solitary individuals to keep their eyes focused on what they themselves are doing or where they are going. If they notice an unusual situation, they may infer from the blasé reactions of the other passersby that the situation is not an emergency. "The person lying on the sidewalk must be drunk," they think, and move on.

But sometimes the emergency is unambiguous and people still fail to help. The witnesses looking out through their windows noticed the incident, correctly

companionate love the deep affectionate attachment we feel for those with whom our lives are intertwined.

equity a condition in which people receive from a relationship in proportion to what they give to it.

self-disclosure revealing intimate aspects of oneself to others.

altruism unselfish regard for the welfare of others.

> "Probably no single incident has caused social psychologists to pay as much attention to an aspect of social behavior as Kitty Genovese's murder."
>
> —R. Lance Shotland (1984)

FIGURE 15.12 The decision-making process for bystander intervention
Before helping, we must first notice an emergency, then correctly interpret it, and then feel responsible. (From Darley & Latané, 1968b.)

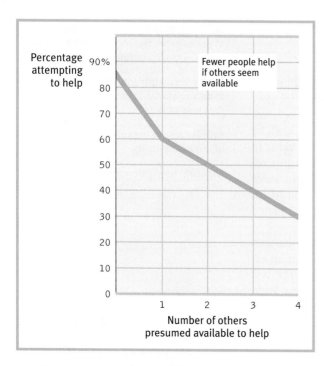

Percentage
attempting
to help

Fewer people help
if others seem
available

Number of others
presumed available to help

FIGURE 15.13 Responses to a simulated physical emergency When people thought they alone heard the calls for help from a person they believed to be having an epileptic seizure, they usually helped. But when they thought four others were also hearing the calls, fewer than a third responded. (From Darley & Latané, 1968a.)

"Oh, make us happy and you make us good!"

—Robert Browning, *The Ring and the Book,* 1868

---

bystander effect the tendency for any given bystander to be less likely to give aid if other bystanders are present.

---

social exchange theory the theory that our social behavior is an exchange process, the aim of which is to maximize benefits and minimize costs.

interpreted the emergency, and yet failed to assume responsibility. Why? To find out, Darley and Latané (1968a) simulated a physical emergency in their laboratory. University students participated in a discussion over an intercom. Each student was in a separate cubicle, and only the person whose microphone was switched on could be heard. One of the students was an accomplice of the experimenters. When his turn came, he made sounds as though he were having an epileptic seizure and called for help.

How did the other students react? As **FIGURE 15.13** shows, those who believed only they could hear the victim—and therefore thought they bore total responsibility for helping him—usually went to his aid. Those who thought others also could hear were more likely to react as did Kitty Genovese's neighbors. When more people shared responsibility for helping—when there was a *diffusion of responsibility*—any single listener was less likely to help.

In hundreds of additional experiments, psychologists have studied the factors that influence bystanders' willingness to relay an emergency phone call, aid a stranded motorist, donate blood, contribute money, give time, and pick up dropped books and pencils (Eagly & Crowley, 1986; Latané & Dabbs, 1975). The major finding that emerged was the **bystander effect**—any particular bystander is less likely to give aid with other bystanders present. When alone with the person in need, about 40 percent help; in the presence of five other bystanders, only 20 percent help.

Observations of behavior in tens of thousands of such situations, indicate that the *best* odds of our helping occur when

- the person appears to need and deserve help.
- the person is in some way similar to us.
- we have just observed someone else being helpful.
- we are not in a hurry.
- we are in a small town or rural area.
- we are feeling guilty.
- we are focused on others and not preoccupied.
- we are in a good mood.

This last result, that happy people are helpful people, is one of the most consistent findings in all of psychology. No matter how people are cheered—whether by being made to feel successful and intelligent, by thinking happy thoughts, by finding money, or even by receiving a posthypnotic suggestion—they become more generous and more eager to help (Carlson et al., 1988).

The Norms for Helping

Why do we help? One widely held view is that self-interest underlies all human interactions, that our constant goal is to maximize our rewards and minimize our costs. Accountants call it *cost-benefit analysis.* Philosophers call it *utilitarianism.* Social psychologists call it **social exchange theory.** If you are pondering whether to donate blood, you may weigh the costs of doing so (time, discomfort, and anxiety) against the benefits (reduced guilt, social approval, and good feelings). If the rewards you anticipate from helping exceed the costs, you will help.

For most people, helping is intrinsically rewarding. Making charitable donations activates brain areas associated with reward (Harbaugh et al., 2007). That helps explain some findings by Elizabeth Dunn and her colleagues (2008). People who give more money away are happier than those who spend their money almost entirely on themselves. Employees who receive a windfall bonus, for example, are later happier if they have done something for other people with it. In one experiment, researchers gave people an envelope with cash and told them either to spend it on themselves or on others. Which group do you suppose was happiest at the day's end? It was, indeed, those assigned to the spend-it-on-others condition.

But why do we leave tips or give directions to total strangers—people we will never see again? In part, we have been socialized to do so, through norms that prescribe how we *ought* to behave, often to our mutual benefit. The **reciprocity norm,** for example, is the expectation that we should return help, not harm, to those who have helped us. In our relations with others of similar status, the reciprocity norm compels us to give (in favors, gifts, or social invitations) about as much as we receive. We also learn a **social-responsibility norm:** We should help those who need our help—young children and others who cannot give as much as they receive—even if the costs outweigh the benefits. In repeated Gallup surveys, people who each week attend religious services often exhibit the social responsibility norm: They report volunteering more than twice as many hours in helping the poor and infirm than do those who rarely or never attend religious services (Hodgkinson & Weitzman, 1992; Independent Sector, 2002). They also give away three times as much money.

Conflict and Peacemaking

15: **How do social traps and mirror-image perceptions fuel social conflict?**

We live in surprising times. With astonishing speed, late-twentieth-century democratic movements swept away totalitarian rule in Eastern European countries, and hopes for a new world order displaced the Cold War chill. And yet, the twenty-first century began with terrorist acts and war, and the world continued to spend $2 billion every day for arms and armies—money that could have been used for housing, nutrition, education, and health care. Knowing that wars begin in human minds, psychologists have wondered: What in the human mind causes destructive conflict? How might the perceived threats of social diversity be replaced by a spirit of cooperation?

To a social psychologist, a **conflict** is a perceived incompatibility of actions, goals, or ideas. The elements of conflict are much the same at all levels, from nations at war, to cultural disputes within a society, to individuals in a marital dispute. In each situation, people become enmeshed in a potentially destructive social process that can produce results no one wants. Among the destructive processes are *social traps* and *distorted perceptions.*

Social Traps

In some situations, we support our collective well-being by pursuing our personal interests. As capitalist Adam Smith wrote in *The Wealth of Nations* (1776), "It is not from the benevolence of the butcher, the brewer, or the baker that we expect our dinner, but from their regard to their own interest."

In other situations, we harm our collective well-being by pursuing our personal interests. Such situations are **social traps.** Consider the simple game matrix in **FIGURE 15.14.** Pretend you are Person 1, and that you and Person 2 will each receive the amount shown after you separately choose either A or B. (You might invite someone to look at the matrix with you and take the role of Person 2.) Which do you choose—A or B?

You and Person 2 are caught in a dilemma, because both sides can win or both can lose, depending on the players' individual choices. If you both choose A, you both benefit, making $5 each. If you both choose B, neither of you makes anything. Nevertheless, on any single trial you would serve your own interests if you choose B: You can't lose, and you might make $10. But the same is true for the other person. Hence, the social trap: As long as you both pursue your own immediate best interest and choose B, you will both end up with nothing—the typical result—when you could have made $5.

reciprocity norm an expectation that people will help, not hurt, those who have helped them.

social-responsibility norm an expectation that people will help those dependent upon them.

conflict a perceived incompatibility of actions, goals, or ideas.

social trap a situation in which the conflicting parties, by each rationally pursuing their self-interest, become caught in mutually destructive behavior.

FIGURE 15.14 Social-trap game matrix By pursuing our self-interest and not trusting others, we can end up losers. To illustrate this, imagine playing the game below. The pink triangles show the outcomes for Person 1, which depend on the choices made by both players. If you were Person 1, would you choose A or B? (This game is called a *non–zero-sum game* because the outcomes need not add up to zero; both sides can win or both can lose.)

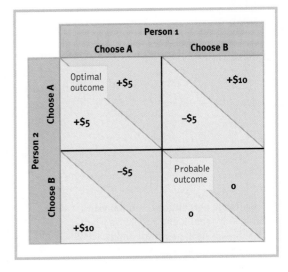

Not in my ocean! Many people support alternative energy sources, including wind turbines. But proposals to construct wind farms in real-world neighborhoods elicit debate over the future benefits of clean energy versus the costs of altering treasured ocean views and, possibly, migratory bird routes.

AP Photo/Lisa Poole

Many real-life situations similarly pit our individual interests against our communal well-being. Individual whalers reasoned that the few whales they took would not threaten the species and that if they didn't take them others would anyway. The result: Some species of whales became endangered. Ditto for the buffalo hunters of yesterday and the elephant-tusk hunters of today. Individual car owners and home owners reason, "It would cost me comfort or money to buy a more fuel-efficient car and furnace. Besides, the fossil fuels I burn don't noticeably add to the greenhouse gases." When enough of us reason this way, the collective result threatens disaster—global climate change, rising seas, and more extreme weather.

Social traps challenge us to find ways of cooperating for our mutual betterment, through *agreed-upon regulations, better communication,* and *increased awareness of our responsibilities* toward community, nation, and the whole of humanity. Whether playing a laboratory game or the real game of life, people more often cooperate when these three factors are present (Dawes, 1980; Linder, 1982; Sato, 1987).

Enemy Perceptions

Psychologists have noted that those in conflict have a curious tendency to form diabolical images of each other. These distorted images are ironically similar, so similar in fact that we call them **mirror-image perceptions:** As we see "them"—as untrustworthy and evil intentioned—so "they" see us. Each demonizes the other.

Mirror-image perceptions often become self-fulfilling prophecies, feeding a vicious cycle of hostility. If Juan believes Maria is annoyed with him, he may snub her, causing her to act in ways that justify his perception. As with individuals, so with countries. When perceiving Country A as hostile, Country B may react in ways that seem justified. And, seeing their own actions as responses to provocation (tit for tat), not as the causes of what happens, they often hit back harder. In one experiment, University College London volunteers used a mechanical device to press on another volunteer's finger, after feeling pressure on their own finger. Although their task was to reciprocate with the same amount of pressure, they typically responded with about 40 percent more force than they had just experienced. Despite seeking to respond only in kind, their touches soon escalated to hard presses, much as when each child after a fight claims that "I just poked him, but he hit me harder" (Shergill et al., 2003).

In the early twenty-first century, many Americans came to loathe Saddam Hussein. Like the "evil" Saddam Hussein, "some of today's tyrants are gripped by an implacable hatred of the United States of America," declared then-President George W. Bush (2001). "They hate our friends, they hate our values, they hate democracy and freedom and individual liberty. Many care little for the lives of their own people." Hussein (2002) reciprocated the perception, seeing the United States as "an evil tyrant" that, with Satan as its protector, lusted for oil and aggressively attacked those who "defend what is right."

mirror-image perceptions mutual views often held by conflicting people, as when each side sees itself as ethical and peaceful and views the other side as evil and aggressive.

The point is not that truth must lie midway between two such views (one may be more accurate). The point is that enemy perceptions often form mirror images. Moreover, as enemies change, so do perceptions. In American minds and media, the "bloodthirsty, cruel, treacherous" Japanese of World War II later became our "intelligent, hardworking, self-disciplined, resourceful allies" (Gallup, 1972).

Can contact, cooperation, communication, and conciliation transform the antagonisms fed by prejudice and conflicts into attitudes that promote peace? In some cases, the answer is *yes*.

Contact

16: How can we transform feelings of prejudice, aggression, and conflict into attitudes that promote peace?

Does it help to put two conflicting parties into close contact? It depends. When such contact is noncompetitive and between parties of equal status, such as retail clerks working the same shift, it typically helps. Initially prejudiced co-workers of different races have, in such circumstances, usually come to accept one another.

This finding is confirmed by a statistical digest of more than 500 studies of face-to-face contact with outgroups (such as ethnic minorities, the elderly, and those with disabilities). Among the quarter-million people studied across 38 nations, contact has been correlated with, or in experimental studies has led to, more positive attitudes (Pettigrew & Tropp, 2006). Some examples:

- With interracial contact, South African Whites' and Blacks' "attitudes [have moved] into closer alignment" (Dixon et al, 2007).
- Heterosexuals' personal contact with gay people correlates with accepting attitudes. In one national survey, those who knowingly had a gay family member or close friend were twice as likely to support gay marriage as those who didn't—55 percent versus 25 percent (Neidorf & Morin, 2007).
- Even indirect contact with a member of an outgroup (via story reading or through a friend who has an outgroup friend) tends to reduce prejudice (Cameron & Rutland, 2006; Pettigrew et al., 2007).

However, mere contact is not always enough. In most desegregated schools, ethnic groups resegregate themselves in the lunchrooms and on the school grounds (Clack et al., 2005; Schofield, 1986). People in each group often think they would welcome more contact with the other group, but they assume the other group does not reciprocate the wish (Richeson & Shelton, 2007). "I don't reach out to them, because I don't want to be rebuffed; they don't reach out to me, because they're just not interested." When such mirror-image misperceptions are corrected, friendships may then form and prejudices melt.

Cooperation

To see if enemies could overcome their differences, researcher Muzafer Sherif (1966) first instigated conflict. He placed 22 Oklahoma City boys in two separate areas of a Boy Scout camp. He then put the two groups through a series of competitive activities, with prizes going to the victors. Before long, each group became intensely proud of itself and hostile to the other group's "sneaky," "smart-alecky stinkers." Food wars, ransacked cabins, and fistfights were commonplace. When Sherif brought the two groups together, they avoided one another, except to taunt and threaten.

Nevertheless, within a few days Sherif transformed these young enemies into jovial comrades. He gave them **superordinate goals**—shared goals that overrode their differences and that could be achieved only through cooperation. A planned disruption of the camp water supply necessitated that all 22 boys work together to restore water. Renting a movie in those pre-DVD days required their pooled resources. A stalled truck needed the combined force of all the boys pulling and pushing together to get it

superordinate goals shared goals that override differences among people and require their cooperation.

"You cannot shake hands with a clenched fist."

—Indira Gandhi, 1971

Superordinate goals override differences Cooperative efforts to achieve shared goals are an effective way to break down social barriers.

moving. Having used isolation and competition to make strangers into enemies, Sherif used shared predicaments and goals to reconcile the enemies and make them friends. What reduced conflict was not mere contact, but *cooperative* contact.

A shared predicament—a fearsome external threat and a superordinate desire to overcome it—likewise had a powerfully unifying effect in the weeks after 9/11. Patriotism soared as Americans felt that "we" were under attack. Gallup-surveyed approval of "our President" (George W. Bush) shot up from 51 percent the week before the attack to a highest-ever level of 90 percent ten days after, just surpassing the previous approval record of 89 percent enjoyed by his father, George H. W. Bush, at the climax of the 1991 Persian Gulf war (Newport, 2002). In chat groups and everyday speech, even the word *we* (relative to *I*) surged in the immediate aftermath (Pennebaker, 2002).

Cooperation has especially positive effects when it leads people to define a new, inclusive group that dissolves their former subgroups (Dovidio & Gaertner, 1999). Seat the members of two groups not on opposite sides, but alternately around the table. Give them a new, shared name. Have them work together. Such experiences change "us" and "them" into "we." Those once perceived as being in another group now are seen as part of one's own group. One 18-year-old New Jersey man would not be surprised. After 9/11, he explained a shift in his social identity: "I just thought of myself as Black. But now I feel like I'm an American, more than ever" (Sengupta, 2001). In one experiment, White Americans who read a newspaper article about a terrorist threat against all Americans subsequently expressed reduced prejudice against African-Americans (Dovidio et al., 2004).

The unifying effects of cooperative contacts has led thousands of teachers to introduce interracial cooperative learning into their classrooms with great success. Experiments with adolescents from 11 countries confirm that cooperative classroom situations and cooperative learning lead to interracial friendships and may even enhance student achievement (Roseth, Johnson, & Johnson, 2008). Members of interracial groups who work together on projects and play together on athletic teams typically come to feel friendly toward those of another race.

The power of cooperative activity to make friends of former enemies has led psychologists to urge increased international exchange and cooperation (Klineberg, 1984). As we engage in mutually beneficial trade, as we work to protect our common destiny on this fragile planet, and as we become more aware that our hopes and fears are shared, we can change misperceptions that feed conflict into a solidarity based on common interests.

Communication

When real-life conflicts become intense, a third-party mediator—a marriage counselor, labor mediator, diplomat, community volunteer—may facilitate much-needed communication (Rubin et al., 1994). Mediators help each party to voice its viewpoint and to understand the other's. By leading each side to think about the other's underlying needs and goals, the mediator aims to replace a competitive *win-lose* orientation with a cooperative *win-win* orientation that aims at a mutually beneficial resolution. A classic example: Two friends, after quarreling over an orange, agreed to split it. One squeezed his half for juice. The other used the peel from her half to make a cake. If only the two had understood each other's motives, they could have hit on the win-win solution of one having all the juice, the other all the peel.

Conciliation

GRIT Graduated and Reciprocated Initiatives in Tension-Reduction—a strategy designed to decrease international tensions.

Understanding and cooperative resolution is most needed, yet least likely, in times of anger or crisis (Bodenhausen et al., 1994; Tetlock, 1988). When conflicts intensify, images become more stereotyped, judgments more rigid, and communication more difficult, or even impossible. Each party is likely to threaten, coerce, or retaliate. In the weeks before the Persian Gulf war, the first President George Bush threatened, in the full glare of publicity, to "kick Saddam's ass." Saddam Hussein communicated in kind, threatening to make Americans "swim in their own blood."

Under such conditions, is there an alternative to war or surrender? Social psychologist Charles Osgood (1962, 1980) advocated a strategy of *Graduated and Reciprocated Initiatives in Tension-Reduction*, nicknamed **GRIT.** In applying GRIT, one side first announces its recognition of mutual interests and its intent to reduce tensions. It then initiates one or more small, conciliatory acts. Without weakening one's retaliatory capability, this modest beginning opens the door for reciprocity by the other party. Should the enemy respond with hostility, one reciprocates in kind. But so, too, with any conciliatory response. Thus, U.S. President John Kennedy's gesture of stopping atmospheric nuclear tests began a series of reciprocated conciliatory acts that culminated in the 1993 atmospheric test-ban treaty.

In laboratory experiments, GRIT has been an effective strategy for increasing trust and cooperation (Lindskold et al., 1978, 1988). Even during intense personal conflict, when communication has been nonexistent, a small conciliatory gesture—a smile, a touch, a word of apology—may work wonders. Conciliations allow both parties to begin edging down the tension ladder to a safer rung where communication and mutual understanding can begin.

And how good that such can happen, for civilization advances not by cultural isolation—maintaining walls around ethnic enclaves—but by tapping the knowledge, the skills, and the arts that are each culture's legacy to the whole human race. Thomas Sowell (1991) observed that, thanks to cultural sharing, every modern society is enriched by a cultural mix. We have China to thank for paper and printing and for the magnetic compass that opened the great explorations. We have Egypt to thank for trigonometry. We have the Islamic world and India's Hindus to thank for our Arabic numerals. While celebrating and claiming these diverse cultural legacies, we can also welcome the enrichment of today's social diversity. We can view ourselves as instruments in a human orchestra. And we can therefore affirm our own culture's heritage while building bridges of communication, understanding, and cooperation across cultural traditions as we think about, influence, and relate to one another.

Conciliatory gestures In hopes of encouraging steps down the tension ladder, President Barack Obama in 2009 spoke to the Muslim world from the University of Cairo, proposing" a new beginning" in relations between Muslim nations and the United States.

Chris Bouroncle/AFP/Getty Images

"Most of us have overlapping identities which unite us with very different groups. We *can* love what we are, without hating what—and who—we are *not*. We can thrive in our own tradition, even as we learn from others."

—Former U.N. Secretary General Kofi Annan, Nobel Prize Lecture, 2001

REHEARSE IT!

17. The mere exposure effect helps explain why proximity is a powerful predictor of friendship and marriage, and why, for example, people tend to marry someone
  a. about as attractive as themselves.
  b. who lives or works nearby.
  c. with whom they enjoy self-disclosure.
  d. with whom they have an equitable relationship.

18. After vigorous exercise, you meet an attractive person, and you are suddenly seized by romantic feelings for that person. This event supports the two-factor theory of emotion, which assumes that emotions such as passionate love consist of physical arousal plus

  a. a reward.
  b. proximity.
  c. companionate love.
  d. our interpretation of that arousal.

19. Two vital ingredients in the deep, affectionate attachment of companionate love are
  a. equity and self-disclosure.
  b. proximity and privacy.
  c. attractiveness and self-absorption.
  d. altruism and excitement.

20. The bystander effect states that a particular bystander is less likely to give aid if
  a. the victim is similar to the bystander in appearance.
  b. no one else is present.

  c. other people are present.
  d. the incident occurs in a deserted or rural area.

21. Social psychologists have attempted to define the circumstances that facilitate conflict resolution. One way of resolving conflicts and fostering cooperation is by giving rival groups superordinate goals, which are
  a. the goals of friendly competition.
  b. shared goals that override differences.
  c. goals for winning at negotiations.
  d. goals for increasing conflict through reduced contact.

Answers: 17, b, 18, d, 19, a, 20, c, 21, b.

CHAPTER REVIEW

Social Psychology

Social psychologists study how people think about, influence, and relate to one another.

Social Thinking

1 How do we tend to explain others' behavior and our own?

We generally explain people's behavior by *attributing* it to internal dispositions and/or to external situations. In committing the *fundamental attribution error*, we underestimate the influence of the situation on others' actions. When explaining our own behavior, we more often point to the situation.

2 Does what we think affect what we do, or does what we do affect what we think?

Attitudes—feelings influenced by beliefs—affect our behavior when other influences are minimal, and when the attitude is stable, specific to the behavior, and easily recalled. Attempts to change behaviors by changing attitudes may follow a *central route to persuasion* or *peripheral route to persuasion*.

Studies of the *foot-in-the-door phenomenon* and of *role*-playing reveal that our actions (especially those we feel responsible for) can also modify our attitudes. *Cognitive dissonance theory* proposes that behavior shapes attitudes because we feel discomfort when our actions and attitudes differ. We reduce the discomfort by bringing our attitudes more into line with what we have done.

Social Influence

3 What do experiments on conformity and compliance reveal about the power of social influence?

Asch's *conformity* studies demonstrated that under certain conditions people will adopt a group's judgment even when it is clearly incorrect. We may conform either to gain social approval (*normative social influence*) or because we welcome the information that others provide (*informational social influence*). In Milgram's famous experiments, people torn between obeying an experimenter and responding to another's pleas to stop the apparent shocks usually chose to obey orders. People most often obeyed when the person giving orders was nearby and was perceived as a legitimate authority figure; when the person giving orders was supported by a prestigious institution; when the victim was depersonalized or at a distance; and when no other person modeled defiance by disobeying.

4 How is our behavior affected by the presence of others or by being part of a group?

Social facilitation experiments reveal that the presence of either observers or co-actors can arouse individuals, boosting their performance on easy tasks but hindering it on difficult ones. When people pool their efforts toward a group goal, *social loafing* may occur as individuals free-ride on others' efforts. *Deindividuation*—becoming less self-aware and self-restrained in a group situation—may happen when people are both aroused and made to feel anonymous.

5 What are group polarization and groupthink?

Discussions among like-minded members often produces *group polarization*, as prevailing attitudes intensify. *Groupthink* is the tendency to suppress unwelcome information and make unrealistic decisions for the sake of group harmony. To prevent groupthink, leaders can welcome a variety of opinions, invite experts' critiques, and assign people to identify possible problems in developing plans.

6 How much power do we have as individuals? Can a minority sway a majority?

The power of the group is great, but even a small minority may sway group opinion, especially when the minority expresses its views consistently.

Social Relations

7 What is prejudice?

Prejudice is a mixture of beliefs (often *stereotypes*), negative emotions, and predispositions to action. Prejudice may be explicit (such as openly and consciously denying a particular ethnic group the right to vote) or implicit (such as feeling fearful when alone in an elevator with a stranger from a different racial or ethnic group).

8 What are the social and emotional roots of prejudice?

Social inequalities may trigger prejudice as people in power attempt to justify the status quo, which sometimes involves blaming the victim. Favored social groups often rationalize their higher status with the *just-world phenomenon*. Group identifications (*ingroup* versus *outgroup*) leads to *ingroup bias*. Fear and anger feed prejudice, and, when frustrated, we may focus our anger on a *scapegoat*.

9 What are the cognitive roots of prejudice?

In processing information, we tend to recognize diversity in our own groups but to overestimate similarities in other groups, as in the *other-race effect*. We also notice and remember vivid cases. These trends help create stereotypes.

10 What biological factors make us more prone to hurt one another?

Biology influences *aggression* at three levels: genetic, neural, and biochemical. Genes influence our temperament, making us more or less likely to respond aggressively when frustrated in specific situations. Neural systems in the brain can facilitate or inhibit aggression. Biochemical influences, such as testosterone and other hormones; alcohol (which disinhibits); and other substances also contribute to aggression.

11 What psychological factors may trigger aggressive behavior?

The *frustration-aggression principle* states that frustration and other aversive events (such as heat, crowding, and provocation) can evoke hostility. This is especially likely in those who have been rewarded for aggression or have learned aggression from role models, including those seen in the media, who teach social scripts that are later enacted in real life. Enacting violence in video games or viewing it in the media can desensitize people to cruelty and prime them to behave aggressively when provoked, or to view sexual aggression as more acceptable.

12 Why do we befriend or fall in love with some people but not with others?

Three factors affect our liking for one another. Proximity—geographical nearness—is conducive to attraction, partly because *mere exposure* to novel stimuli enhances liking. Physical attractiveness increases social opportunities and influences the way we are perceived. As acquaintanceship moves toward friendship, similarity of attitudes and interests greatly increases liking.

13 How does romantic love typically change as time passes?

Passionate love is an aroused state that we cognitively label as love. The strong affection of *companionate love*, which often emerges as passionate love subsides, is enhanced by an *equitable* relationship and by intimate *self-disclosure*.

14 When are we most—and least—likely to help?

Altruism is unselfish regard for the well-being of others. We are less likely to help if others are present. This *bystander effect* is especial-ly apparent in situations where the presence of others inhibits our noticing the event, interpreting it as an emergency, or assuming responsibility for offering help. Explanations of our willingness to help others focus on *social exchange theory* (the costs and benefits of helping); the intrinsic rewards of helping others; the *reciprocity norm* (we help those who help us); and the *social-responsibility norm* (we help those who need our help).

15 How do social traps and mirror-image perceptions fuel social conflict?

Conflicts are situations in which people perceive their actions, goals, or ideas to be incompatible. In *social traps*, two or more individuals engage in mutually destructive behavior by rationally pursuing their individual self-interests. People in conflict tend to expect the worst of each other, producing *mirror-image perceptions* that can become self-fulfilling prophecies.

16 How can we transform feelings of prejudice, aggression, and conflict into attitudes that promote peace?

Enemies sometimes become friends, especially when the circumstances favor equal-status contact, cooperation to achieve *superordinate goals,* understanding through communication, and reciprocated conciliatory gestures.

Terms and Concepts to Remember

social psychology, p. 525
attribution theory, p. 525
fundamental attribution error, p. 526
attitude, p. 527
central route to persuasion, p. 528
peripheral route to persuasion, p. 528
foot-in-the-door phenomenon, p. 528
role, p. 529
cognitive dissonance theory, p. 530
conformity, p. 533
normative social influence, p. 534
informational social influence, p. 534
social facilitation, p. 538
social loafing, p. 538
deindividuation, p. 539

group polarization, p. 539
groupthink, p. 540
prejudice, p. 542
stereotype, p. 542
discrimination, p. 542
just-world phenomenon, p. 545
ingroup, p. 545
outgroup, p. 545
ingroup bias, p. 546
scapegoat theory, p. 547
other-race effect, p. 547
aggression, p. 548
frustration-aggression principle, p. 549
mere exposure effect, p. 556

passionate love, p. 559
companionate love, p. 560
equity, p. 560
self-disclosure, p. 560
altruism, p. 561
bystander effect, p. 562
social exchange theory, p. 562
reciprocity norm, p. 563
social-responsibility norm, p. 563
conflict, p. 563
social trap, p. 563
mirror-image perceptions, p. 564
superordinate goals, p. 565
GRIT, p. 567

Test for Success: Critical Thinking Exercises
By Amy Himsel, El Camino College

1. Driving to school one wintry day, Marco narrowly misses a car that slides through a red light. "Slow down! What a terrible driver," he thinks to himself. Moments later, Marco himself slips through an intersection and yelps, "Wow! These roads are awful. The city snow plows need to get out here." What social psychology principle has Marco just demonstrated? Explain.

2. Jamal's therapist has suggested that Jamal should "act as if" he is confident, even though he feels insecure and shy. Which social psychological theory would best support this suggestion, and what might the therapist be hoping to achieve?

3. Dr. Huang, a popular music professor whose classes are always jam-packed, delivers riveting lectures on music history but gets nervous and often makes mistakes when describing exam statistics in front of the class. Why does his performance vary by task?

4. Stacy, a Chicago Cubs fan who is normally a very calm and softhearted person, becomes wild with joy whenever the White Sox, a rival baseball team, loses a game. Why does Stacy take pleasure in their losses?

5. Brittany, the president of the Psychology Club, needs assistance preparing for an upcoming fund-raising event. She made a plea for help in an e-mail she sent in a mass mailing to all 60 club members. So far, however, nobody has responded—either to help or not help. What might be the problem, and how could Brittany change her approach in the hope of getting people to respond and help?

The Test for Success exercises offer you a chance to apply your critical thinking skills to aspects of the material you have just read. Suggestions for answering these questions can be found in Appendix D at the back of the book.

→ Multiple-choice self-tests and more may be found at www.worthpublishers.com/myers.

Appendix A

Statistical Reasoning in Everyday Life

● **Describing Data**
Measures of Central Tendency
Measures of Variation
Correlation: A Measure of Relationships

● **Making Inferences**
When Is an Observed Difference Reliable?
CLOSE-UP: Cross-Sectional and Longitudinal Studies
When Is a Difference Significant?

In descriptive, correlational, and experimental research, statistics are tools that help us see and interpret what the unaided eye might miss. But statistical understanding benefits more than just researchers. To be an educated person today is to be able to apply simple statistical principles to everyday reasoning. One needn't memorize complicated formulas to think more clearly and critically about data.

1: What is the first important point to remember when assessing studies that use statistical reasoning?

Off-the-top-of-the-head estimates often misread reality and then mislead the public. Someone throws out a big, round number. Others echo it, and before long the big, round number becomes public misinformation. A few examples:

● *Ten percent of people are lesbians or gay men.* Or is it 2 to 3 percent, as suggested by various national surveys (Chapter 10)?
● *We ordinarily use but 10 percent of our brain.* Or is it closer to 100 percent (Chapter 2)?
● *The human brain has 100 billion nerve cells.* Or is it more like 40 billion, as suggested by extrapolation from sample counts (Chapter 2)?

The point to remember: Doubt big, round, undocumented numbers. Rather than swallowing top-of-the-head estimates, focus on thinking smarter by applying simple statistical principles to everyday reasoning.

"Figures can be misleading—so I've written a song which I think expresses the real story of the firm's performance this quarter."

Describing Data

2: How can we describe data with measures of central tendency and variation?

Once researchers have gathered their data, they must organize them in some meaningful way. One way to do this is to convert the data into a simple *bar graph,* as in **FIGURE A.1** on the next page, which displays a distribution of different brands of trucks still on the road after a decade. When reading statistical graphs such as this, take care. It's easy to design a graph to make a difference look big (Figure A.1a) or small (Figure A.1b). The secret lies in how you label the vertical scale *(the Y-axis).*

The point to remember: Think smart. When viewing figures in magazines and on television, read the scale labels and note their range.

Measures of Central Tendency

The next step is to summarize the data using some *measure of central tendency,* a single score that represents a whole set of scores. The simplest measure is the **mode,** the most frequently occurring score or scores. The most commonly reported is the **mean,** or arithmetic average—the total sum of all the scores divided by the number of scores. On a divided highway, the median is the middle. So, too, with data: The **median** is the midpoint—the 50th percentile. If you arrange all the scores in order from the highest to the lowest, half will be above the median and half will be below it.

mode the most frequently occurring score(s) in a distribution.

mean the arithmetic average of a distribution, obtained by adding the scores and then dividing by the number of scores.

median the middle score in a distribution; half the scores are above it and half are below it.

FIGURE A.1 **Read the scale labels** An American truck manufacturer offered graph a—with actual brand names included—to suggest the much greater durability of its trucks. Note, however, how the apparent difference shrinks as the vertical scale changes (graph b).

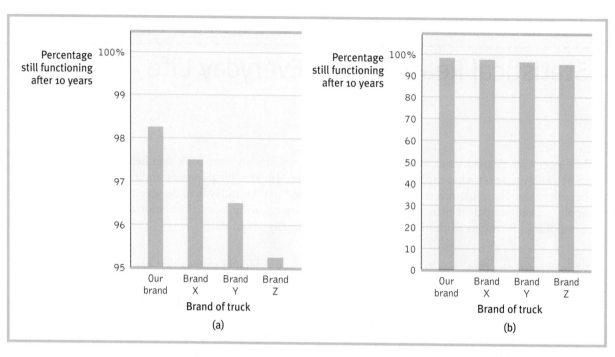

The average person has one ovary and one testicle.

FIGURE A.2 **A skewed distribution** This graphic representation of the distribution of a village's incomes illustrates the three measures of central tendency—mode, median, and mean. Note how just a few high incomes make the mean—the fulcrum point that balances the incomes above and below—deceptively high.

Measures of central tendency neatly summarize data. But consider what happens to the mean when a distribution is lopsided or *skewed*. With income data, for example, the mode, median, and mean often tell very different stories (**FIGURE A.2**). This happens because the mean is biased by a few extreme scores. When Microsoft co-founder Bill Gates sits down in an intimate café, its average (mean) customer instantly becomes a billionaire. But the customer's median wealth remains unchanged. Understanding this, you can see how a British newspaper could accurately run the headline "Income for 62% Is Below Average" (Waterhouse, 1993). Because the bottom *half* of British income earners receive only a *quarter* of the national income cake, most British people, like most people everywhere, make less than the mean. In the United States, Republicans tended to tout the economy's solid growth from 2000 to 2006 using average income; Democrats lamented the economy's lackluster growth using median income (Paulo, 2006). Mean and median tell different true stories.

The point to remember: Always note which measure of central tendency is reported. Then, if it is a mean, consider whether a few atypical scores could be distorting it.

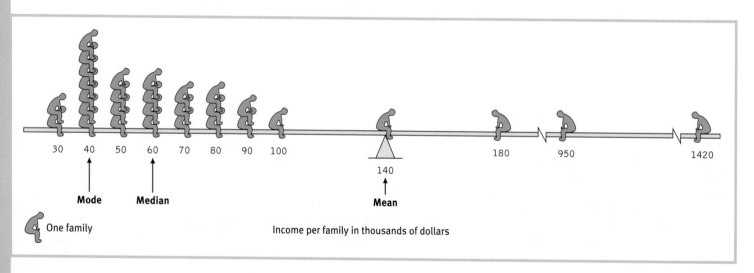

Measures of Variation

Knowing the value of an appropriate measure of central tendency can tell us a great deal. But the single number omits other information. It helps to know something about the amount of *variation* in the data—how similar or diverse the scores are. Averages derived from scores with low variability are more reliable than averages based on scores with high variability. Consider a basketball player who scored between 13 and 17 points in each of her first 10 games in a season. Knowing this, we would be more confident that she would score near 15 points in her next game than if her scores had varied from 5 to 25 points.

"The poor are getting poorer, but with the rich getting richer it all averages out in the long run."

The **range** of scores—the gap between the lowest and highest scores—provides only a crude estimate of variation because a couple of extreme scores in an otherwise uniform group, such as the $950,000 and $1,420,000 incomes in Figure A.2, will create a deceptively large range.

The more useful standard for measuring how much scores deviate from one another is the **standard deviation.** It better gauges whether scores are packed together or dispersed, because it uses information from each score (**TABLE A.1**). The computation assembles information about how much individual scores differ from the mean. If your college or university attracts students of a certain ability level, their intelligence scores will have a relatively small standard deviation compared with the more diverse community population outside your school.

You can grasp the meaning of the standard deviation if you consider how scores tend to be distributed in nature. Large numbers of data—heights, weights, intelligence scores, grades (though not incomes)—often form a symmetrical, *bell-shaped* distribution. Most cases fall near the mean, and fewer cases fall near either extreme. This bell-shaped distribution is so typical that we call the curve it forms the **normal curve.**

range the difference between the highest and lowest scores in a distribution.

standard deviation a computed measure of how much scores vary around the mean score.

normal curve (*normal distribution*) a symmetrical, bell-shaped curve that describes the distribution of many types of data; most scores fall near the mean (68 percent fall within one standard deviation of it) and fewer and fewer near the extremes.

TABLE A.1 Standard Deviation Is Much More Informative Than Mean Alone

Note that the test scores in Class A and Class B have the same mean (80), but very different standard deviations, which tell us more about how the students in each class are really faring.

Test Scores in Class A				Test Scores in Class B		
Score	Deviation from the Mean	Squared Deviation		Score	Deviation from the Mean	Squared Deviation
72	−8	64		60	−20	400
74	−6	36		60	−20	400
77	−3	9		70	−10	100
79	−1	1		70	−10	100
82	+2	4		90	+10	100
84	+4	16		90	+10	100
85	+5	25		100	+20	400
87	+7	49		100	+20	400
Total = 640		Sum of (deviations)² = 204		Total = 640		Sum of (deviations)² = 2000
Mean = 640 ÷ 8 = 80				Mean = 640 ÷ 8 = 80		

Standard deviation =

$$\sqrt{\frac{\text{Sum of (deviations)}^2}{\text{Number of scores}}} = \sqrt{\frac{204}{8}} = 5.0$$

Standard deviation =

$$\sqrt{\frac{\text{Sum of (deviations)}^2}{\text{Number of scores}}} = \sqrt{\frac{2000}{8}} = 15.8$$

FIGURE A.3 **The normal curve** Scores on aptitude tests tend to form a normal, or bell-shaped, curve, with most scores falling near the mean. For example, the Wechsler Adult Intelligence Scale calls the mean score 100.

A a useful property of the normal curve is that roughly 68 percent of the cases fall within one standard deviation on either side of the mean. As **FIGURE A.3** shows, about 95 percent of cases fall within two standard deviations. Thus, as Chapter 9 notes, about 68 percent of people taking an intelligence test will score within ±15 points of 100. About 95 percent will score within ±30 points.

FIGURE A.4 **How to read a correlation coefficient**

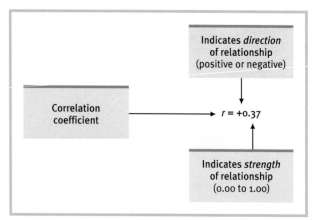

Correlation: A Measure of Relationships

3: What does it mean when we say that two things are correlated?

Throughout this book we often ask how strongly two things are related: For example, how closely related are the personality scores of identical twins? How well do intelligence test scores predict achievement? How closely is stress related to disease?

As we saw in Chapter 1, describing behavior is a first step toward predicting it. When surveys and naturalistic observations reveal that one trait or behavior accompanies another, we say the two *correlate*. A **correlation coefficient** is a statistical measure of a relationship (**FIGURE A.4**).

FIGURE A.5 contains three **scatterplots,** illustrating the range of possible correlations from a perfect positive to a perfect negative. (Perfect correlations rarely occur in the real world.) Each dot in a scatterplot represents the scattered values of two variables. A correlation is positive if two sets of scores, such as height and weight, tend to rise or fall together. Saying that a correlation is "negative" says nothing about its strength or weakness. A correlation is negative if two sets of scores relate inversely, one set going up as the other goes down.

FIGURE A.5 **Scatterplots, showing patterns of correlation** Correlations can range from +1.00 (scores on one measure increase in direct proportion to scores on another) to −1.00 (scores on one measure decrease precisely as scores rise on the other).

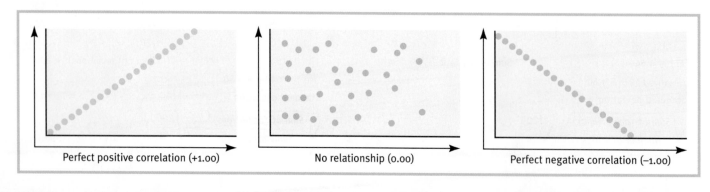

Toothbrushing and decay correlate negatively. As brushing goes up from zero, tooth decay goes down. A weak correlation, indicating little relationship, has a coefficient near zero.

Statistics can help us see what the naked eye sometimes misses. To demonstrate this for yourself, try an imaginary project. Wondering if tall men are more or less easygoing, you collect two sets of scores: men's heights and men's temperaments. You measure the heights of 20 men, and you have someone else independently assess their temperaments (from zero for extremely calm to 100 for highly reactive).

With all the relevant data right in front of you (**TABLE A.2**), can you tell whether there is (1) a positive correlation between height and reactive temperament, (2) very little or no correlation, or (3) a negative correlation?

Comparing the columns in Table A.2, most people detect very little relationship between height and temperament. In fact, the correlation in this imaginary example is moderately positive, +0.63, as we can see if we display the data as a scatterplot. In **FIGURE A.6**, moving from left to right, the upward, oval-shaped slope of the cluster of points shows that our two imaginary sets of scores (height and reactivity) tend to rise together.

If we fail to see a relationship when data are presented as systematically as in Table A.2, how much less likely are we to notice them in everyday life? To see what is right in front of us, we sometimes need statistical illumination. We can easily see evidence of gender discrimination when given statistically summarized information about job level, seniority, performance, gender, and salary. But we often see no discrimination when the same information dribbles in, case by case (Twiss et al., 1989).

The point to remember: Although the correlation coefficient tells us nothing about cause and effect, it can help us see the world more clearly by revealing the actual extent to which two things relate.

TABLE A.2 Height and Temperament of 20 Men

Person	Height in Inches	Temperament
1	80	75
2	63	66
3	61	60
4	79	90
5	74	60
6	69	42
7	62	42
8	75	60
9	77	81
10	60	39
11	64	48
12	76	69
13	71	72
14	66	57
15	73	63
16	70	75
17	63	30
18	71	57
19	68	84
20	70	39

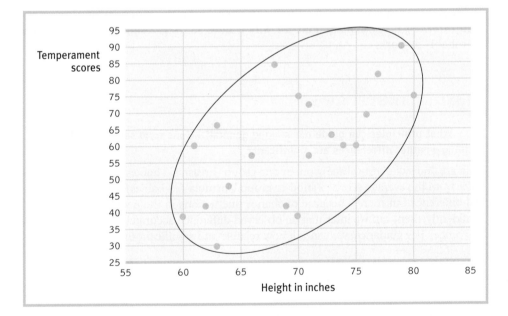

FIGURE A.6 Scatterplot for height and temperament This display of data from 20 imagined men (each represented by a data point) reveals an upward slope, indicating a positive correlation. The considerable scatter of the data indicates the correlation is much lower than +1.0.

---

correlation coefficient a statistical measure of the extent to which two factors vary together, and thus of how well either factor predicts the other. Scores with a *positive correlation coefficient* move up and down together (as with high school and college GPAs). A *negative correlation coefficient* indicates that one score falls as the other rises (as in the relationship between self-esteem and depression).

---

scatterplots a graphed cluster of dots, each of which represents the values of two variables. The slope of the points suggests the direction of the relationship between the two variables. The amount of scatter suggests the strength of the correlation (little scatter indicates high correlation).

4: What is regression toward the mean?

Correlations not only make visible the relationships we might otherwise miss, they also restrain our "seeing" nonexistent relationships. As Chapter 1 explained, a perceived correlation that does not really exist is an *illusory correlation.* When we believe there is a relationship between two things, we are likely to notice and recall instances that confirm our belief. If we believe that dreams are forecasts of actual events, we may notice and recall confirming instances more than disconfirming instances. The result is an illusory correlation.

Illusory correlations feed an illusion of control—that chance events are subject to our personal control. Gamblers, remembering their lucky rolls, may come to believe they can influence the roll of the dice by again throwing gently for low numbers and hard for high numbers. The illusion that uncontrollable events correlate with our actions is also fed by a statistical phenomenon called **regression toward the mean.** Average results are more typical than extreme results. Thus, after an unusual event, things tend to return toward their average level; extraordinary happenings tend to be followed by more ordinary ones.

"Once you become sensitized to it, you see regression everywhere."

—Psychologist Daniel Kahneman (1985)

The point may seem obvious, yet we regularly miss it: We sometimes attribute what may be a normal regression (the expected return to normal) to something we have done. Consider:

- Students who score much lower or higher on an exam than they usually do are likely, when retested, to return to their average.
- Unusual ESP subjects who defy chance when first tested nearly always lose their "psychic powers" when retested (a phenomenon parapsychologists have called the "decline effect").
- Coaches often yell at their players after an unusually bad first half. They may then feel rewarded for having done so when the team's performance improves (returns to normal) during the second half.

Failure to recognize regression is the source of many superstitions and of some ineffective practices as well. When day-to-day behavior has a large element of chance fluctuation, we may notice that others' behavior improves (regresses toward average) after we criticize them for very bad performance, and that it worsens (regresses toward average) after we warmly praise them for an exceptionally fine performance. Ironically, then, regression toward the average can mislead us into feeling rewarded for having criticized others and into feeling punished for having praised them (Tversky & Kahneman, 1974).

The point to remember: When a fluctuating behavior returns to normal, there is no need to invent fancy explanations for why it does so. Regression toward the mean is probably at work.

Making Inferences

5: What principles can guide our making generalizations from samples and deciding whether differences are significant?

Data are "noisy." The average score in one group (breast-fed babies) could conceivably differ from the average score in another group (formula-fed babies) not because of any real difference but merely because of chance fluctuations in the people sampled. How confidently, then, can we infer that an observed difference accurately estimates the true difference? For guidance, we can ask how reliable and significant the differences are.

When Is an Observed Difference Reliable?

In deciding when it is safe to generalize from a sample, we should keep three principles in mind.

1. **Representative samples are better than biased samples.** The best basis for generalizing is not from the exceptional and memorable cases one finds at the extremes but from a representative sample of cases. Research never randomly samples the whole human population. Thus, it pays to keep in mind what population a study has sampled. (To see how an unrepresentative sample can lead you astray, see Close-Up: Cross-Sectional and Longitudinal Studies.)

regression toward the mean the tendency for extreme or unusual scores or events to fall back (regress) toward the average.

Close-Up:

Cross-Sectional and Longitudinal Studies

6: **What are cross-sectional studies and longitudinal studies, and why is it important to know which method was used?**

When interpreting research results, smart thinkers consider how researchers arrived at their conclusions. One way studies vary is in the time period for gathering data.

In **cross-sectional studies**, researchers compare different groups at the same time. For example, they might compare intelligence test scores among people in differing age groups. In those studies, older adults, on average, give fewer correct answers than do younger adults. This could suggest that mental ability declines with age, and indeed, that was the conclusion drawn from many early cross-sectional studies of intelligence.

In **longitudinal studies**, researchers study and restudy the same group at different times in their life span. After colleges began giving intelligence tests to entering students about 1920, several psychologists saw their chance to study intelligence longitudinally. What they expected to find was a decrease in intelligence after about age 30 (Schaie & Geiwitz, 1982). What they actually found was a surprise: Until late in life, intelligence remained stable. On some tests, it even increased.

Why did these new results differ from the earlier cross-sectional findings? In retrospect, researchers realized that cross-sectional studies that compared 70-year-olds and 30-year-olds were comparing people not only of two different ages but also of two different eras. They were comparing generally less-educated people (born, say, in the early 1900s) with better-educated people (born after 1950); people raised in large families with people raised in smaller families; people from less-affluent families with people from more-affluent families.

Others have since pointed out that longitudinal studies have their own pitfalls. Participants who survive to the end of longitudinal studies may be the healthiest (and brightest) people. When researchers adjust for the loss of participants, as did one study following more than 2000 people over 75 in Cambridge, England, they find a steeper intelligence decline, especially as people age after 85 (Brayne et al., 1999).

The point to remember: When interpreting research results, pay attention to the methodology used, such as whether it was a longitudinal or cross-sectional study.

2. **Less-variable observations are more reliable than those that are more variable.** As we noted in the example of the basketball player whose game-to-game points were consistent, an average is more reliable when it comes from scores with low variability.

3. **More cases are better than fewer.** An eager prospective student visits two university campuses, each for a day. At the first, the student randomly attends two classes and discovers both instructors to be witty and engaging. At the next campus, the two sampled instructors seem dull and uninspiring. Returning home, the student (discounting the small sample size of only two teachers at each institution) tells friends about the "great teachers" at the first school, and the "bores" at the second. Again, we know it but we ignore it: *Averages based on many cases are more reliable* (less variable) than averages based on only a few cases.

The point to remember: Don't be overly impressed by a few anecdotes. Generalizations based on a few unrepresentative cases are unreliable.

When Is a Difference Significant?

Statistical tests also help us determine whether differences are meaningful. Here is the underlying logic: When averages from two samples are each reliable measures of their respective populations (as when each is based on many observations that have small variability), then their *difference* is likely to be reliable as well. (Example: The lower the variability in women's and in men's aggression scores, the more confidence we would have that any observed gender difference is reliable.) And when the difference between the sample averages is *large*, we have even more confidence that the difference between them reflects a real difference in their populations.

In short, when the sample averages are reliable, and when the difference between them is relatively large, we say the difference has **statistical significance.** This means that the observed difference is probably not due to chance variation between the samples.

---

cross-sectional study a study in which people of different ages are compared with one another.

---

longitudinal study research in which the same people are restudied and retested over a long period of time.

---

statistical significance a statistical statement of how likely it is that an obtained result occurred by chance.

PEANUTS

In judging statistical significance, psychologists are conservative. They are like juries who must presume innocence until guilt is proven. For most psychologists, proof beyond a reasonable doubt means not making much of a finding unless the odds of its occurring by chance are less than 5 percent (an arbitrary criterion).

When reading about research, you should remember that, given large enough or homogeneous enough samples, a difference between them may be "statistically significant" yet have little practical significance. For example, comparisons of intelligence test scores among hundreds of thousands of first-born and later-born individuals indicate a highly significant tendency for first-born individuals to have higher average scores than their later-born siblings (Kristensen & Bjerkedal, 2007; Zajonc & Markus, 1975). But because the scores differ by only one to three points, the difference has little practical importance. Such findings have caused some psychologists to advocate alternatives to significance testing (Hunter, 1997). Better, they say, to use other ways to express a finding's *effect* size—its magnitude and reliability.

The point to remember: Statistical significance indicates the *likelihood* that a result will happen by chance. But this does not say anything about the *importance* of the result.

REHEARSE IT!

1. Which of the three measures of central tendency is most easily distorted by a few very large or very small scores?
   a. The mode
   b. The mean
   c. The median
   d. They are all equally vulnerable to distortion from atypical scores.

2. The standard deviation is the most useful measure of variation in a set of data because it tells us
   a. the difference between the highest and lowest scores in the set.
   b. the extent to which the sample being used deviates from the bigger population it represents.
   c. how much individual scores differ from the mode.
   d. how much individual scores differ from the mean.

3. A correlation coefficient is a statistical measure of the extent to which two factors, such as two sets of scores, vary together. In a _____ correlation, the scores would travel up and down together; in a(n) _____ correlation, one score would fall as the other rises.
   a. positive; negative
   b. positive; illusory
   c. negative; inverse
   d. strong; weak

4. When sample averages are _____ and the difference between them is _____, we can say the difference has statistical significance.
   a. reliable; large
   b. reliable; small
   c. due to chance; large
   d. due to chance; small

Answers: 1. b, 2. d, 3. a, 4. a.

APPENDIX REVIEW

Statistical Reasoning in Everyday Life

Describing Data

1 What is the first important point to remember when assessing studies that use statistical reasoning?

Doubt big, round, undocumented numbers. Think smarter by applying simple statistical reasoning.

2 How can we describe data with measures of central tendency and variation?

Three measures of central tendency are the *mode* (the most frequently occurring score), the *mean* (the arithmetic average), and the *median* (the middle score in a group of data). Measures of variation tell us how similar or diverse data are. A *range* describes the gap between the highest and lowest scores. The more useful measure, the *standard deviation*, states how much scores vary around the mean, or average, score. The *normal curve* is a bell-shaped curve that describes the distribution of many types of data.

3 What does it mean when we say that two things are correlated?

A *correlation coefficient* is a statistical measure that tells us the extent to which two things relate. In *scatterplots*, the amount of scatter suggests the correlation's strength, and the slope of the points suggests the direction of the relationship. Correlation coefficients cannot tell cause and effect, but they do tell us how well one variable predicts the other, and they also restrain us from seeing nonexistent relationships.

4 What is regression toward the mean?

Regression toward the mean is the tendency of extreme scores to return to normal.

Making Inferences

5 What principles can guide our making generalizations from samples and deciding whether differences are significant?

Three principles are worth remembering: (1) Representative samples are better than biased samples. (2) Less-variable observations are more reliable than those that are more variable. (3) More cases are better than fewer. We can assume that a result is *statistically significant*—that it did not occur by chance alone—when averages from two samples are each reliable measures of their own populations, and the difference between them is relatively large.

6 What are cross-sectional studies and longitudinal studies, and why is it important to know which method was used?

Cross-sectional studies compare people of different ages at the same time; *longitudinal studies* retest the same people over time. The two methods give different perspectives. Cross-sectional studies show the effects of time and environment on many different individuals; longitudinal studies show those effects on the same people.

Terms and Concepts to Remember

mode, p. A-1

mean, p. A-1

median, p. A-1

range, p. A-3

standard deviation, p. A-3

normal curve, p. A-3

correlation coefficient, p. A-4

scatterplots, p. A-4

regression toward the mean, p. A-6

cross-sectional study, p. A-7

longitudinal study, p. A-7

statistical significance, p. A-7

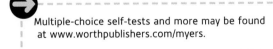

Multiple-choice self-tests and more may be found at www.worthpublishers.com/myers.

Gallup researchers Marcus Buckingham and Donald Clifton (2001) have argued that the first step to a stronger organization is instituting a strengths-based selection system. Thus, as a manager, you would first identify a group of the most effective people in any role—the ones you would want to hire more of—and compare their strengths with those of a group of the least effective people in that role.

In defining these groups, you would try to measure performance as objectively as possible. In one Gallup study of more than 5000 telecommunications customer-service representatives, those evaluated most favorably by their managers were strong in "harmony" and "responsibility," while those actually rated most effective by customers were strong in energy, assertiveness, and eagerness to learn.

Consider an example. Suppose you needed to hire new people in software development, and you have discovered that your best software developers are analytical, disciplined, and eager to learn. When writing your employment ads, you would focus less on experience than on the strengths you have identified: "Do you take a logical and systematic approach to problem solving *[analytical]*? Are you a perfectionist who strives for timely completion of your projects *[disciplined]*? Do you want to learn to use Java, C++, and PHP *[eager to learn]*? If you can say *yes* to these questions, then please call . . ."

Identifying people's strengths and matching strengths to work is a first step toward workplace effectiveness. Personnel managers use various tools to assess applicants' strengths and decide who is best-suited to the job (Sackett & Lievens, 2008). In Chapter 9, we saw how psychologists assess candidates using ability tests. And in Chapter 12, we explored personality testing. For now, let's consider the job interview.

Do Interviews Predict Performance?

Interviewers tend to feel confident in their ability to predict long-term job performance from an unstructured, get-acquainted interview. What's therefore shocking is how error-prone those predictions are.

Whether predicting job or graduate school success, interviewers' judgments are weak predictors. From their review of 85 years of personnel-selection research, I/O psychologists Frank Schmidt and John Hunter (1998; Schmidt, 2002) determined that for all but less-skilled jobs, general mental ability best predicts on-the-job performance. Subjective overall evaluations from informal interviews are more useful than handwriting analysis (which is worthless). But informal interviews are less informative than aptitude tests, work samples, job knowledge tests, and past job performance. If there's a contest between what our gut tells us about someone and what test scores, work samples, and past performance tell us, we should distrust our gut.

> "Interviews are a terrible predictor of performance."
>
> —Laszlo Bock, Google's Vice President, People Operations, 2007

The Interviewer Illusion

Interviewers often overrate their discernment, a phenomenon psychologist Richard Nisbett (1987) labeled the *interviewer illusion*. "I have excellent interviewing skills, so I don't need reference checking as much as someone who doesn't have my ability to read people," is a comment sometimes heard by I/O consultants. Four factors explain this gap between interviewers' intuition and the resulting reality:

- *Interviews disclose the interviewee's good intentions, which are less revealing than habitual behaviors* (Ouellette & Wood, 1998). Intentions matter. People can change. But the best predictor of the person we will be is the person we have been. Wherever we go, we take ourselves along.
- *Interviewers more often follow the successful careers of those they have hired than the successful careers of those they have rejected and lost track of.* This missing feedback prevents interviewers from getting a reality check on their hiring ability.

Personnel Psychology

1: How do personnel psychologists help organizations with employee selection, work placement, and performance appraisal?

Psychologists can assist organizations at various stages of selecting and assessing employees. They may help identify needed job skills, decide upon selection methods, recruit and evaluate applicants, introduce and train new employees, and appraise their performance.

Harnessing Strengths

As a recently hired AT&T human resource executive, psychologist Mary Tenopyr (1997) was assigned to solve a problem: Customer service representatives were failing at a high rate. Tenopyr's solution was a data-driven test that better identified likely-to-succeed customer representatives. To develop this new selection instrument, she

1. asked new applicants to respond to various questions (without as yet making any use of their responses).
2. followed up later to assess which of the applicants excelled on the job.
3. identified the individual items on the earlier test that best predicted who would succeed.

Personnel selection techniques such as this one aim to match people's strengths with work that enables them and their organization to flourish. Marry the strengths of people with the tasks of organizations and the result is often prosperity and profit for the organization and greater satisfaction for workers (see Close-Up: Discovering Your Strengths).

Close-Up:

Discovering Your Strengths

Your strengths are any enduring qualities that can be productively applied. Are you naturally curious? Persuasive? Charming? Persistent? Competitive? Analytical? Empathic? Organized? Articulate? Neat? Mechanical? Any such trait, if matched with suitable work, can function as a strength (Buckingham, 2007). To identify your strengths and pinpoint types of work that will likely prove satisfying and successful, Gallup researchers Marcus Buckingham and Donald Clifton (2001) have suggested asking yourself:

- What activities give me pleasure? (Bringing order out of chaos? Playing host? Helping others? Challenging sloppy thinking?)
- What activities leave me wondering, "When can I do this again?" (Rather than "When will this be over?")
- What sorts of challenges do I relish? (And which do I dread?)
- What sorts of tasks do I learn easily? (And which do I struggle with?)

Artistic strengths At age 21, Henri Matisse was a sickly and often depressed lawyer's clerk. When his mother gave him a box of paints to cheer him up one day, he felt the darkness lift and his energy surge. He began to fill his days with painting and drawing and went on to art school and a life as one of the world's great painters. For Matisse, doing art felt like "a comfortable armchair." That is how exercising our strengths often feels.

Satisfied and successful people devote far less time to correcting their deficiencies than to accentuating their strengths. Top performers are "rarely well rounded"; instead, they have sharpened their existing skills (Buckingham & Clifton, 2001, p. 26). Given the persistence of our traits and temperaments, we should focus not on our deficiencies, but rather on identifying and employing our talents. There may be limits to the benefits of assertiveness training if you are shy, for public speaking courses if you tend to be nervous and soft-spoken, or for drawing classes if you express your artistic side in stick figures.

But identifying your talents can help you recognize the activities you learn quickly and find absorbing. Knowing your strengths, you can develop them further.

As Robert Louis Stevenson said in *Familiar Studies of Men and Books* (1882), "To be what we are, and to become what we are capable of becoming, is the only end of life."

Have you ever noticed that when you are immersed in an activity, time flies? And that when you are watching the clock, it seems to move more slowly? French researchers have confirmed that the more we attend to an event's duration, the longer it seems to last (Couli et al., 2004).

Csikszentmihalyi's later observations—of dancers, chess players, surgeons, writers, parents, mountain climbers, sailors, and farmers; of Australians, North Americans, Koreans, Japanese, and Italians; of people from their teens to their golden years—confirmed an overriding principle: It's exhilarating to flow with an activity that fully engages our skills. Flow experiences boost our sense of self-esteem, competence, and well-being. When the researchers beeped people at random intervals and asked them to report what they were doing and how much they were enjoying themselves, those who were vegetating usually reported little sense of flow and little satisfaction. People reported more positive feelings when interrupted while doing something active, something that engaged their skills, be it play or work.

In industrialized nations, work has been changing, from farming to manufacturing to *knowledge work.* More and more work is *outsourced* to temporary employees and consultants who communicate electronically from virtual workplaces in remote locations. (This book and its teaching package are developed and produced by a team of people in a dozen cities, from Alaska to Florida.) As work changes, will our attitudes toward our work also change? Will our satisfaction with work increase or decrease? Will the *psychological contract*—the subjective sense of mutual obligations between workers and employers—become more or less trusting and secure? These are among the questions that fascinate psychologists who study work-related behavior.

Industrial-organizational (I/O) psychology is a fast-growing profession that applies psychology's principles to the workplace (see Close-Up: I/O Psychology at Work). Here we consider three main subfields:

- **Personnel psychology,** which applies psychology's methods and principles to selecting and evaluating workers. Personnel psychologists match people with jobs, by identifying and placing well-suited candidates.
- **Organizational psychology,** which considers how work environments and management styles influence worker motivation, satisfaction, and productivity. Organizational psychologists modify jobs and supervision in ways that boost morale and productivity.
- **Human factors psychology,** which explores how machines and environments can be optimally designed to fit human abilities and expectations. Human factors psychologists help to design appliances, machines, Web sites, and work settings that fit our natural perception.

industrial-organizational (I/O) psychology the application of psychological concepts and methods to optimizing human behavior in workplaces.

personnel psychology a subfield of I/O psychology that focuses on employee recruitment, selection, placement, training, appraisal, and development.

organizational psychology a subfield of I/O psychology that examines organizational influences on worker satisfaction and productivity and facilitates organizational change.

human factors psychology a branch of psychology that explores how people and machines interact and how machines and physical environments can be made safe and easy to use.

Close-Up:

I/O Psychology at Work

As scientists, consultants, and management professionals, industrial-organizational psychologists are found working in varied areas:

PERSONNEL PSYCHOLOGY
Selecting and placing employees
- Developing and validating assessment tools for selecting, placing, and promoting workers
- Analyzing job content
- Optimizing worker placement

Training and developing employees
- Identifying needs
- Designing training programs
- Evaluating training programs

Appraising performance
- Developing criteria
- Measuring individual performance
- Measuring organizational performance

ORGANIZATIONAL PSYCHOLOGY
Developing organizations
- Analyzing organizational structures
- Maximizing worker satisfaction and productivity
- Facilitating organizational change

Enhancing quality of worklife
- Expanding individual productivity
- Identifying elements of satisfaction
- Redesigning jobs

HUMAN FACTORS (ENGINEERING) PSYCHOLOGY
- Designing optimum work environments
- Optimizing person-machine interactions
- Developing systems technologies

Source: Adapted from the Society of Industrial and Organizational Psychology (siop.org).

Appendix B

Psychology at Work

● **Personnel Psychology**
  CLOSE-UP: I/O Psychology at Work
  Harnessing Strengths
  CLOSE-UP: Discovering Your Strengths
  Appraising Performance

● **Organizational Psychology**
  Satisfaction and Engagement
  CLOSE-UP: Doing Well While Doing
    Good: "The Great Experiment"
  Managing Well

● **Human Factors Psychology**

The healthy life, said Sigmund Freud, is filled by love and by work. For most of us, work is life's biggest single waking activity. To live is to work. Work supports us. Work connects us. Work defines us. Meeting someone for the first time, and wondering "Who are you?" we may ask, "So, what do you do?"

If we feel dissatisfied with our work-related pay, relationships, or identity, we may change where or for whom we work, as 16 percent of Australians did in just the year 2000 (Trewin, 2001). Most people therefore have neither a single vocation nor a predictable career path. Two decades from now, most of you reading this book will be doing work you cannot now imagine. To prepare you and others for this unknown future, many colleges and universities focus less on training your job skills and more on enlarging your capacities for understanding, thinking, and communicating in any work environment.

Amy Wrzesniewski and her colleagues (1997, 2001) have identified person-to-person variations in people's attitudes toward their work. Across various occupations, some people view their work as a *job,* an unfulfilling but necessary way to make money. Others view their work as a *career,* an opportunity to advance from one position to a better position. The rest—those who view their work as a *calling,* a fulfilling and socially useful activity—report the highest satisfaction with their work and with their lives. Other research indicates that people have reported markedly lower well-being if unemployed (**FIGURE B.**1). Idleness may sound like bliss, but purposeful work enriches our lives.

This finding would not surprise Mihaly Csikszentmihalyi (1990, 1999), who has observed that people's quality of life increases when they are purposefully engaged. Between the anxiety of being overwhelmed and stressed, and the apathy of being underwhelmed and bored, lies a zone in which people experience **flow.** Csikszentmihalyi (chick-SENT-me-hi) formulated the flow concept after studying artists who spent hour after hour painting or sculpting with enormous concentration. Immersed in a project, they worked as if nothing else mattered, and then, when finished, they promptly forgot about it. The artists seemed driven less by the external rewards of producing art—money, praise, promotion—than by the intrinsic rewards of creating the work. Internet-related distractions can disrupt such flow. It takes time to refocus mental concentration after the distraction of an e-mail or instant message.

Sometimes, noted Gene Weingarten (2002), a humor writer knows "when to just get out of the way." Here are some sample job titles from the U.S. Department of Labor Dictionary of Occupational Titles: Animal impersonator, human projectile, banana ripening-room supervisor, impregnator, impregnator helper, dope sprayer, finger waver, rug scratcher, egg smeller, bottom buffer, cookie breaker, brain picker, hand pouncer, bosom presser, and mother repairer.

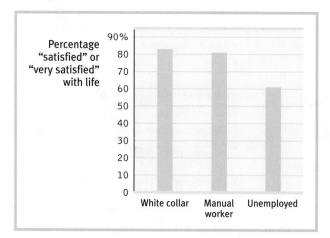

FIGURE B.1 **The bane of unemployment** To want work but not have it is to feel less satisfied with life. These data are from 169,776 adults in 16 nations (Inglehart, 1990).

flow a completely involved, focused state of consciousness, with diminished awareness of self and time, resulting from optimal engagement of one's skills.

- *Interviewers presume that people are what they seem to be in the interview situation.* As Chapter 15 explains, when meeting others, we discount the enormous influence of varying situations and mistakenly presume that what we see is what we will get. But mountains of research on everything from chattiness to conscientiousness reveal that how we behave reflects not only our enduring traits, but also the details of the particular situation (such as wanting to impress in a job interview).

- *Interviewers' preconceptions and moods color how they perceive interviewees' responses* (Cable & Gilovich, 1998; Macan & Dipboye, 1994). If interviewers instantly like a person who perhaps is similar to themselves, they may interpret the person's assertiveness as indicating "confidence" rather than "arrogance." If told certain applicants have been prescreened, interviewers are disposed to judge them more favorably.

Traditional *unstructured interviews* do provide a sense of someone's personality—their expressiveness, warmth, and verbal ability, for example. But this information reveals less about the person's behavior toward others in different situations than most people suppose. Hoping to improve prediction and selection, personnel psychologists have put people in simulated work situations, scoured sources for information on past performance, aggregated evaluations from multiple interviews, administered tests, and developed job-specific interviews.

Structured Interviews

Unlike casual conversation aimed at getting a feel for someone, **structured interviews** offer a disciplined method of collecting information. A personnel psychologist may analyze a job, script questions, and train interviewers. The interviewers then put the same questions, in the same order, to all applicants, and rate each applicant on established scales.

In an unstructured interview, someone might ask, "How organized are you?" "How well do you get along with people?" or "How do you handle stress?" Street-smart applicants know how to score high: "Although I sometimes drive myself too hard, I handle stress by prioritizing and delegating, and by making sure I leave time for sleep and exercise."

By contrast, structured interviews pinpoint strengths (attitudes, behaviors, knowledge, and skills) that distinguish high performers in a particular line of work. The process includes outlining job-specific situations and asking candidates to explain how they would handle them, and how they handled similar situations in their prior employment. "Tell me about a time when you were caught between conflicting demands, without time to accomplish both. How did you handle that?"

To reduce memory distortions and bias, the interviewer takes notes and makes ratings as the interview proceeds and avoids irrelevant and follow-up questions. The structured interview therefore feels less warm, but that can be explained to the applicant: "This conversation won't typify how we relate to each other in this organization."

A review of 150 findings revealed that structured interviews had double the predictive accuracy of unstructured seat-of-the-pants interviews (Schmidt & Hunter, 1998; Wiesner & Cronshaw, 1988). Structured interviews also reduce bias, such as against overweight applicants (Kutcher & Bragger, 2004). Thanks partly to its greater reliability and partly to its job-analysis focus, the predictive power of one structured interview is roughly equal to that of the average judgment from three or four unstructured interviews (Huffcutt et al., 2001; Schmidt & Zimmerman, 2004).

Appraising Performance

Performance appraisal serves organizational purposes: It helps decide who to retain and lay off, how to appropriately reward and pay people, and how to better harness employee strengths, sometimes with job shifts or promotions. Performance

"Between the idea and reality . . . falls the shadow."

—T. S. Eliot, *The Hollow Men,* 1925

structured interviews interview process that asks the same job-relevant questions of all applicants, each of whom is rated on established scales.

FIGURE B.2 **360-degree feedback** With multisource 360-degree feedback, one's knowledge, skills, and behaviors are rated by self and surrounding others. Professors, for example, may be rated by their department chairs, their students, and their colleagues. After receiving all these ratings, professors discuss the 360-degree feedback with their department chair.

appraisal also serves individual purposes: Feedback affirms workers' strengths and helps motivate needed improvements.

Performance appraisal methods include

- *checklists* on which supervisors simply check specific behaviors that describe the worker ("always attends to customers' needs," "takes long breaks").
- *graphic rating scales* on which a supervisor checks, perhaps on a five-point scale, how often a worker is dependable, productive, and so forth.
- *behavior rating scales* on which a supervisor checks scaled behaviors that describe a worker's performance. If rating the extent to which a worker "follows procedures," the supervisor might mark the employee somewhere between "often takes shortcuts" and "always follows established procedures" (Levy, 2003).

In some organizations, performance feedback comes not only from supervisors but also from all organizational levels. If you join an organization that practices *360-degree feedback* (**FIGURE B.2**), you will rate yourself, your manager, and your other colleagues, and you will be rated by your manager, other colleagues, and customers (Green, 2002). The net result is often more open communication and more complete appraisal.

To recap, personnel psychologists assist organizations in analyzing jobs, recruiting well-suited applicants, selecting and placing employees, and appraising their performance (**FIGURE B.3**).

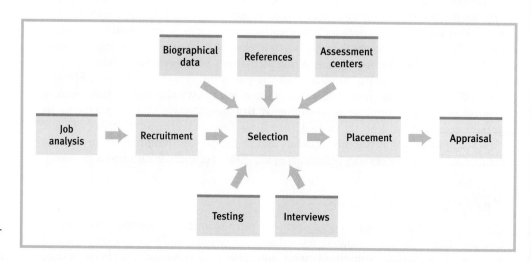

FIGURE B.3 **Personnel psychologists' tasks** Personnel psychologists consult in human resources activities, from job definition to employee appraisal.

Organizational Psychology

2: What is the role of organizational psychologists?

The appraisal of work and the matching of talents to work matter, but so does overall motivation. Before considering how organizational psychologists assist with efforts to motivate employees and keep them engaged, let's take a closer look at why any employee might want to pursue high standards or difficult goals.

Think of someone you know who strives to succeed by excelling at any task where evaluation is possible. Now think of someone who is less driven. Psychologist Henry Murray (1938) defined the first person's **achievement motivation** as a desire for significant accomplishment, for mastering skills or ideas, for control, and for rapidly attaining a high standard.

As you might expect from their persistence and eagerness for realistic challenges, people with high achievement motivation do achieve more. One study followed the lives of 1528 California children whose intelligence test scores were in the top 1 percent. Forty years later, when researchers compared those who were most and least successful professionally, they found a motivational difference. Those most successful were more ambitious, energetic, and persistent. As children, they had more active hobbies. As adults, they participated in more groups and favored being sports participants to being spectators (Goleman, 1980). Gifted children are able learners. Accomplished adults are tenacious doers.

In other studies of both secondary school and university students, self-discipline has been a better predictor of school performance, attendance, and graduation honors than intelligence scores have been. "Discipline outdoes talent," concluded researchers Angela Duckworth and Martin Seligman (2005, 2006), and it explains why girls get higher school grades than equally capable boys.

But discipline also refines talent. By their early twenties, top violinists have accumulated some 10,000 lifetime practice hours—double the practice time of other violin students aiming to be teachers (Ericsson et al., 2001, 2006, 2007). From his studies, Herbert Simon (1998), a psychologist who won a Nobel Prize in Economics, formed what Chapter 9 called the *10-year rule:* That world-class experts in a field typically have invested "at least 10 years of hard work—say, 40 hours a week for 50 weeks a year." A study of outstanding scholars, athletes, and artists found that all were highly motivated and self-disciplined, willing to dedicate hours every day to the pursuit of their goals (Bloom, 1985). These superstar achievers were distinguished not so much by their extraordinary natural talent as by their extraordinary daily discipline. Great achievement, it seems, mixes a teaspoon of inspiration with a gallon of perspiration.

What distinguishes extremely successful individuals from their equally talented peers, note Duckworth and Seligman, is *grit*—passionate dedication to an ambitious, long-term goal. Although intelligence is distributed in a bell curve, achievements are not. That tells us that achievement involves much more than raw ability. And that is why organizational psychologists seek ways to engage and motivate ordinary people doing ordinary jobs.

Disciplined motivation feeds achievement Aware that he was far behind other students when beginning his graduate education in psychology, B. F. Skinner devised a daily discipline of rising at 6:00 A.M., studying until breakfast, then going to classes, labs, and the library. After dinner he studied some more, leaving no more than 15 unscheduled minutes each day, and later continued a disciplined daily routine as he became one of the twentieth century's most influential psychologists.

achievement motivation a desire for significant accomplishment; for mastery of things, people, or ideas; for rapidly attaining a high standard.

Satisfaction and Engagement

Because work is such a big part of life, employee satisfaction is a priority concern for I/O psychologists. Satisfaction with work feeds satisfaction with life (see Close-Up: Doing Well While Doing Good). Moreover, as we saw in Chapter 11, decreased job stress feeds improved health.

Does employee satisfaction also contribute to successful organizations? Positive moods at work do contribute to creativity, persistence, and helpfulness (Brief & Weiss, 2002). But are engaged, happy workers also less often absent? Less likely to

"The only place success comes before work is in the dictionary."

—Former Green Bay Packers football coach Vince Lombardi

Close-Up:

Doing Well While Doing Good: "The Great Experiment"

At the end of the 1700s, the more than 1000 workers in the cotton mill at New Lanark, Scotland—many of them children drawn from Glasgow's poorhouses—worked 13-hour days and lived in grim conditions. Their education and sanitation were neglected, theft and drunkenness were commonplace, and most families occupied just one room.

On a visit to Glasgow, Welsh-born Robert Owen—an idealistic young cotton-mill manager—chanced to meet and fall in love with the mill owner's daughter. After their marriage, Owen, with several partners, purchased the mill and on the first day of the 1800s took control as its manager. Before long, he began what he said was "the most important experiment for the happiness of the human race that had yet been instituted at any time in any part of the world" (Owen, 1814). The exploitation of child and adult labor was, he observed, producing unhappy and inefficient workers. Believing that better working and living conditions could pay economic dividends, he undertook (with some resistance from his partners, whom he ultimately bought out) numerous innovations: a nursery for preschool children, education (with

Courtesy of New Lanark World Heritage Site

The great experiment New Lanark Mills, which today is preserved as a World Heritage Site (www.newlanark.org), provided an influential demonstration of how industries could do well while doing good. In its heyday, New Lanark was visited by many European royals and reformers who came to observe its vibrant work force and prosperous business.

encouragement rather than corporal punishment), Sundays off, health care, paid sick days, unemployment pay for days when the mill could not operate, and a company store selling goods at reduced prices.

Owen also innovated a goals and worker-assessment program that included detailed records of daily productivity and costs. By each employee's workstation, one of four colored boards indicated that person's performance for the previous day. Owen could walk through the mill and at a glance see how individuals were performing. There was, he said, "no beating, no abusive language. . . . I merely looked at the person and then at the color. . . . I could at once see by the expression [which color] was shown."

The commercial success that followed was essential to sustaining what became a movement toward humanitarian reforms. By 1816, with decades of profitability still ahead, Owen believed he had demonstrated "that society may be formed so as to exist without crime, without poverty, with health greatly improved, with little if any misery, and with intelligence and happiness increased a hundredfold." Although his Utopian vision has not been fulfilled, Owen's great experiment did lay the groundwork for employment practices that have today become accepted in much of the world.

quit? Less prone to theft? More punctual? More productive? Conclusive evidence of satisfaction's benefits is, some have said, the holy grail of I/O psychology. Statistical digests of prior research have found a modest positive correlation between individual job satisfaction and performance (Judge et al., 2001; Parker et al., 2003). In one analysis of 4500 employees at 42 British manufacturing companies, the most productive workers tended to be those in satisfying work environments (Patterson et al., 2004). But does satisfaction *produce* better job performance? The debate continues.

Nevertheless, some organizations do have a knack for cultivating more engaged and productive employees. In the United States, the *Fortune* "100 Best Companies to Work For" have also produced markedly higher-than-average returns for their investors (Fulmer et al., 2003). Other positive data come from the biggest-ever study, an analysis of Gallup data from more than 198,000 employees (**TABLE B.1**) in nearly 8000 business units of 36 large companies (including some 1100 bank branches, 1200 stores, and 4200 teams or departments). James Harter, Frank Schmidt, and Theodore Hayes (2002) explored correlations between various measures of organizational success and *employee engagement*—the extent of workers' involvement, enthusiasm, and identification with their organizations. They found

TABLE B.1 The Gallup Workplace Audit

Overall satisfaction—On a 5-point scale, where 5 is extremely satisfied and 1 is extremely dissatisfied, how satisfied are you with *(name of company)* as a place to work? _____
On a scale of 1 to 5, where 1 is strongly disagree and 5 is strongly agree, please indicate your agreement with the following items.

1. I know what is expected from me at work.
2. I have the materials and equipment I need to do my work right.
3. At work, I have the opportunity to do what I do best every day.
4. In the last seven days, I have received recognition or praise for doing good work.
5. My supervisor, or someone at work, seems to care about me as a person.
6. There is someone at work who encourages my development.
7. At work, my opinions seem to count.
8. The mission/purpose of my company makes me feel my job is important.
9. My associates (fellow employees) are committed to doing quality work.
10. I have a best friend at work.
11. In the last six months, someone at work has talked to me about my progress.
12. This last year, I have had opportunities at work to learn and grow.

Note: These statements are proprietary and copyrighted by The Gallup Organization. They may not be printed or reproduced in any manner without the written consent of The Gallup Organization. Reprinted here by permission.

that engaged workers (compared with not-engaged workers who are just putting in time) know what's expected of them, have what they need to do their work, feel fulfilled in their work, have regular opportunities to do what they do best, perceive that they are part of something significant, and have opportunities to learn and develop. They also found that business units with engaged employees have more loyal customers, less turnover, higher productivity, and greater profits. A follow-up analysis compared companies with top-quartile versus below-average employee engagement levels. Over a three-year period, earnings grew 2.6 times faster for the companies with highly engaged workers (Ott, 2007).

Three types of employees *(Crabtree, 2005):*
Engaged: *working with passion and feeling a profound connection to their company or organization.*
Not-engaged: *putting in the time, but investing little passion or energy into their work.*
Actively disengaged: *unhappy workers undermining what their colleagues accomplish.*

Managing Well

Every leader dreams of managing in ways that enhance people's satisfaction, engagement, and productivity and their organization's success. Effective leaders harness job-relevant strengths, set goals, and choose an appropriate leadership style.

Harnessing Job-Relevant Strengths

"The major challenge for CEOs over the next 20 years will be the effective deployment of human assets," observed Marcus Buckingham (2001). That challenge is

FIGURE B.4 **On the right path** The Gallup Organization path to organizational success (adapted from Fleming, 2001).

"about psychology. It's about getting [individuals] to be more productive, more focused, more fulfilled than [they were] yesterday." To do so, he and others have maintained, effective leaders want first to select the right people. Then, they aim to discern their employees' natural talents, adjust their work roles to suit their talents, and develop those talents into great strengths (**FIGURE B.4**). For example, should every professor at a given college or university be expected to teach the same load, advise the same number of students, serve on the same number of

Positive coaching Larry Brown, an adviser to the youth sports organization The Positive Coaching Alliance, was observed during practices to offer his players 4 to 5 positive comments for every negative comment (Insana, 2005). In 2004, his underdog Detroit Pistons won the National Basketball Association championship.

committees, and engage in the same amount of research? Or should each job description be tailored to harness a specific person's unique strengths?

As noted earlier in the discussion of personnel psychologists, our temperament and our traits tend to follow us throughout our lives. Managers who excel spend less time trying to instill talents that are not there and more time developing and drawing out what is there. Kenneth Tucker (2002) has noted that great managers

- start by helping people identify and measure their talents.
- match tasks to talents and then give people freedom to do what they do best.
- care how their people feel about their work.
- reinforce positive behaviors through recognition and reward.

Thus, rather than focusing on weaknesses and packing people off to training seminars to fix those problems, good managers focus training time on educating people about their strengths and building upon them (which means not promoting people into roles ill-suited to their strengths). In Gallup surveys, 77 percent of engaged workers, and only 23 percent of not-engaged workers, strongly agreed that "my supervisor focuses on my strengths or positive characteristics" (Krueger & Killham, 2005).

Celebrating engaged and productive employees in every organizational role builds upon a basic principle of operant conditioning (Chapter 7): To teach a behavior, catch a person doing something right and reinforce it. It sounds simple, but many managers are like parents who, when a child returns home with perfect scores, focus on the one low score in a troublesome biology class and ignore the rest. "Sixty-five percent of Americans received NO praise or recognition in the workplace last year," reported the Gallup Organization (2004).

Setting Specific, Challenging Goals

In everyday life, our achievement goals sometimes involve approaching high levels of mastery or performance (perhaps mastering the material for this class and getting a high grade) and sometimes involve avoiding failure (Elliot & McGregor, 2001). In many situations, specific, challenging goals motivate achievement, especially when combined with progress reports (Johnson et al., 2006; Latham & Locke, 2007). Thus, a specific, measurable objective—"finish gathering information for the history paper by Friday"—serves to direct our attention, promote our effort, motivate persistence, and stimulate creative strategies.

Work is more focused and on-time completion becomes more likely when our goal statements include *subgoals* and *implementation intentions*—action plans that specify when, where, and how we will march toward achieving those goals (Burgess et al., 2004; Fishbach et al., 2006; Koestner et al., 2002). Before beginning each new edition of this book, for example, my editor, my associates, and I *manage by objectives*—we agree on target dates for the completion, reviewing, and editing of each chapter draft. To motivate high productivity, effective leaders work with people to define explicit goals, subgoals, and implementation plans, and then provide feedback on progress.

Choosing an Appropriate Leadership Style

Leadership varies from a boss-focused directive style to a democratic style that empowers workers in setting goals and strategies. Which works best may depend on the situation and the leader. The best leadership style for leading a discussion may not be the best style for leading troops on a charge (Fiedler, 1981). Moreover, different leaders are suited to different styles. Some excel at **task leadership**—setting standards, organizing work, and focusing attention on goals. Being goal-oriented, task leaders are good at keeping a group centered on its mission. Typically, they have a directive style, which can work well if the leader is bright enough to give good orders (Fiedler, 1987).

Other managers excel at **social leadership**—explaining decisions, mediating conflicts, and building high-achieving teams (Evans & Dion, 1991). Social leaders often have a democratic style: They delegate authority and welcome the participation of team members. Many experiments show that social leadership is good for morale. Subordinates usually feel more satisfied and motivated and perform better when they participate in decision making (Cawley et al., 1998; Pereira & Osburn, 2007).

Because effective leadership styles vary with the situation and the person, the once-popular *great person theory of leadership*—that all great leaders share certain traits—now seems overstated (Vroom & Jago, 2007; Wielkiewicz & Stelzner, 2005). The same coach may seem great or inferior depending on the strength of the team and its competition. But a leader's personality does matter (Zaccaro, 2007). Effective leaders tend to be neither extremely assertive (impairing social relationships) or unassertive (limiting task leadership) (Ames & Flynn, 2007). Effective leaders of laboratory groups, work teams, and large corporations also tend to exude *charisma*, a blend of goal-based *vision*, clear *communication*, and optimism that *inspires* others to follow (House & Singh, 1987; Shamir et al., 1993). In one study of 50 Dutch companies, the highest morale was at those firms with chief executives who most inspired their colleagues "to transcend their own self-interests for the sake of the collective" (de Hoogh et al., 2004). *Transformational leadership* of this kind motivates others to identify with and commit themselves to the group's mission. Transformational leaders, many of whom are natural extraverts, articulate high standards, inspire people to share their vision, and offer personal attention (Bono & Judge, 2004). The frequent result is more engaged, trusting, and effective workers (Turner et al., 2002). Women more than men tend to exhibit transformational leadership qualities. Alice Eagly (2007) believes this helps explain why companies with women in top management have recently tended to enjoy superior financial results, even after controlling for such variables as company size.

Peter Smith and Monir Tayeb (1989) compiled data from studies in India, Taiwan, and Iran indicating that effective managers—whether in coal mines, banks, or government offices—often exhibit a high degree of *both* task and social leadership. As achievement-minded people, effective managers certainly care about how well work is done, yet at the same time they are sensitive to their subordinates' needs. In one national survey of American workers, those in family-friendly organizations offering flexible-time hours reported feeling greater loyalty to their employers (Roehling et al., 2001).

task leadership goal-oriented leadership that sets standards, organizes work, and focuses attention on goals.

social leadership group-oriented leadership that builds teamwork, mediates conflict, and offers support.

"Good leaders don't ask more than their constituents can give, but they often ask—and get—more than their constituents intended to give or thought it was possible to give."

—John W. Gardner, *Excellence*, 1984

Sharing vision and decisions As CEO, Jeffrey Bleustein helped Harley-Davidson thrive, in part by replacing the organization's command-and-control management style with one based on company-wide consensus planning and decision making.

Many successful businesses have also increased employee participation in making decisions, a management style common in Sweden and Japan and increasingly elsewhere (Naylor, 1990; Sundstrom et al., 1990). Although managers often think better of work they have directly supervised, studies reveal a *voice effect*: If given a chance to voice their opinion during a decision-making process, people will respond more positively to the decision (van den Bos & Spruijt, 2002). And, as we noted earlier, positive, engaged employees are a mark of thriving organizations.

The rags-to-riches Harley-Davidson story illustrates the potential of inviting workers to participate in decision making (Teerlink & Ozley, 2000). In 1987, the struggling company began transforming its *command-and-control* management process to a *joint-vision process*. The aim: "To push decision making, planning, and strategizing from a handful of people at the top, down throughout the organization. We wanted all the employees to think every day about how to improve the company," reported CEO Jeffrey Bleustein (2002). In the mid-1990s, Harley signed a cooperative agreement with its unions that included them "in decision making in virtually every aspect of the business." Consensus decision making can take longer, but "when the decision is made, it gets implemented quickly and the commitment is by the group," said Bleustein. The result has been more engaged workers and also more satisfied stockholders. Every $1 of Harley-Davidson stock purchased at the beginning of 1988 was worth $40 by mid-2009.

* * * * *

We have considered *personnel psychology* (the I/O subfield that focuses on employee selection, placement, appraisal, and development). And we have considered *organizational psychology* (the I/O subfield that focuses on worker satisfaction and productivity, and on organizational change). Finally, we turn to *human factors psychology*, which explores the human-machine interface.

Human Factors Psychology

3: How do human factors psychologists work to create user-friendly machines and work settings?

Designs sometimes neglect the human factor. Psychologist Donald Norman, an MIT alumnus with a Ph.D., bemoaned the complexity of assembling his new high-definition TV, receiver, speakers, digital recorder, DVD player, VCR, and seven remotes into a usable home theater system: "I was VP of Advanced Technology at Apple. I can program dozens of computers in dozens of languages. I understand television, really, I do. . . . It doesn't matter: I am overwhelmed."

How much easier life might be if engineers would routinely work with *human factors psychologists* to test their designs and instructions on real people. Human factors psychologists help to design appliances, machines, and work settings that fit our natural perceptions and inclinations. ATM machines are internally more complex than VCRs ever were, yet, thanks to human factors psychologists working with engineers, ATMs are easier to operate. TiVo has solved the TV-recording problem with a simple select-and-click menu system ("record that one"). Apple has similarly engineered easy usability with the iPod and iPhone.

Norman (2001) hosts a Web site (jnd.org) that illustrates good designs that fit people (see **FIGURE B.5**). Human factors psychologists also work at designing safe and efficient environments. An ideal kitchen layout, researchers have found, stores needed items close to their usage point and near eye level. It locates work areas to enable doing tasks in order, such as placing a refrigerator, stove, and sink in a triangle or

Courtesy www.rideoncarryon.com

Courtesy OXO Good Grips

Courtesy The London Teapot Company Ltd.

FIGURE B.5 Designing products that fit people Human factors psychologist Donald Norman offers these and other examples of effectively designed new products (see www.jnd.org). The Ride On Carry On foldable chair attachment "designed by a flight attendant mom," enables a small suitcase to double as a stroller. The Oxo measuring cup allows the user to see the quantity from above. The Chatsford Tea Pot comes with a built-in strainer.

L-shaped area. It creates counters that enable hands to work at or slightly below elbow height (Boehm-Davis, 2005).

Understanding human factors can do more than enable us to design for reduced frustration; it can help prevent accidents and avoid disaster (Boehm-Davis, 2005). Two-thirds of commercial air accidents, for example, have been caused by human error (Nickerson, 1998). After beginning commercial flights in the late 1960s, the Boeing 727 was involved in several landing accidents caused by pilot error. Psychologist Conrad Kraft (1978) noted a common setting for these accidents: All took place at night, and all involved landing short of the runway after crossing a dark stretch of water or unilluminated ground. Kraft reasoned that, beyond the runway, city lights would project a larger retinal image if on a rising terrain. This would make the ground seem farther away than it was. By re-creating these conditions in flight simulations, Kraft discovered that pilots were deceived into thinking they were flying higher than their actual altitudes. Aided by Kraft's finding, the airlines began requiring the co-pilot to monitor the altimeter—calling out altitudes during the descent—and the accidents diminished.

Later Boeing psychologists worked on other human factors problems (Murray, 1998): How should airlines best train and manage mechanics to reduce the maintenance errors that underlie about 50 percent of flight delays and 15 percent of accidents? What illumination and typeface would make on-screen flight data easiest to read? How could warning messages be most effectively worded—as an action statement ("Pull Up") rather than a problem statement ("Ground Proximity")?

In studying human factors issues, psychologists' most powerful tool is theory-aided research. If an organization wonders what sort of Web design (Emphasizing content? Speed? Graphics?) would most effectively draw in visitors and entice them to return, the psychologist will want to test responses to several alternatives. If NASA (National Aeronautics and Space Administration) wonders what sort of

AP Photo/Steven Day

The human factor in safe landings Advanced cockpit design and rehearsed emergency procedures aided pilot Chesley "Sully" Sullenberger, a U.S. Air Force Academy graduate who studied psychology and human factors. In January 2009, Sullenberger's instantaneous decisions safely guided his disabled airliner onto New York City's Hudson River, where all 155 of the passengers and crew were evacuated safely.

FIGURE B.6 How not to go mad while going to Mars Future astronauts headed to Mars will be confined in conditions of monotony, stress, and weightlessness for months on end. To help design and evaluate a workable human environment, such as for this Transit Habitation (Transhab) Module, NASA engages human factors psychologists (Weed, 2001; Wichman, 1992).

spacecraft design would best facilitate sleeping, work, and morale, their human factors psychologists will also want to test the alternatives (**FIGURE B.6**).

Consider, finally, the available *assistive listening* technologies in various theaters, auditoriums, and places of worship. One technology, commonly available in the United States, requires a headset attached to a pocket-sized receiver that detects infrared or FM signals from the room's sound system. The well-meaning people who design, purchase, and install these systems correctly understand that the technology puts sound directly into the user's ears. Alas, few people with hearing loss undergo the hassle and embarrassment of locating, requesting, wearing, and returning a conspicuous headset. Most such units therefore sit in closets. Britain, the Scandinavian countries, and Australia have instead installed *loop systems* (see hearingloop.org) that broadcast customized sound directly through a person's own hearing aid. When suitably equipped, a hearing aid can be transformed by a discrete touch of a switch into an in-the-ear loudspeaker. Offered convenient, inconspicuous, personalized sound, many more people elect to use assistive listening.

Designs that enable safe, easy, and effective interactions between people and technology often seem obvious after the fact. Why, then, aren't they more common? Technology developers sometimes mistakenly assume that others share their expertise—that what's clear to them will similarly be clear to others (Camerer et al., 1989; Nickerson, 1999). When people rap their knuckles on a table to convey a familiar tune (try this with a friend), they often expect their listener to recognize it. But for the listener, this is a near-impossible task (Newton, 1991). When you know a thing, it's hard to mentally simulate what it's like not to know, and that is called the *curse of knowledge*.

The point to remember: Designers and engineers should consider human abilities and behaviors by designing things to fit people, user-testing their inventions before production and distribution, and being mindful of the curse of knowledge.

REHEARSE IT!

1. People who view their work as a calling often experience _____, a focused state of consciousness, with diminished awareness of themselves and of time.
   a. stress
   b. apathy
   c. flow
   d. facilitation

2. The three main divisions within I/0 psychology are _____, _____, and _____ psychology.
   a. motivational; management; small group
   b. personnel; organizational; human factors
   c. motivational; personnel; human factors
   d. personnel; management; small group

3. A personnel psychologist scripted a set of questions to ask all applicants for a job opening. She then trained the firm's interviewers to ask only these questions, to take notes, and to rate applicants' responses. This technique is known as a(n)
   a. structured interview.
   b. unstructured interview.
   c. performance appraisal checklist.
   d. behavior rating scale.

4. In your job, you rate your own performance, your manager's, and your peers'. Your manager, your peers, and your customers also rate your performance. Your organization is using a form of performance appraisal called
   a. flow procedure.
   b. graphic feedback.
   c. structured interviews.
   d. 360-degree feedback.

5. Task leadership is goal-oriented, whereas social leadership is group-oriented. Research indicates that effective managers exhibit
   a. only task leadership.
   b. only social leadership.
   c. both task and social leadership, depending on the situation and the person.
   d. task leadership for building teams and social leadership for setting standards.

6. To reduce users' frustration and to avoid accidents, human factors psychologists help organizations avoid the curse of knowledge, which is
   a. the idea that a little bit of knowledge is dangerous for the user.
   b. users' tendencies to override machines and resort to familiar habits.
   c. engineers' and designers' tendencies to assume that users are idiots and need overly detailed instructions.
   d. engineers' and designers' tendencies to assume that others share their knowledge.

Answers: 1. c, 2. b, 3. a, 4. d, 5. c, 6. d.

APPENDIX REVIEW

Psychology at Work

Personnel Psychology

1 How do personnel psychologists help organizations with employee selection, work placement, and performance appraisal?

Personnel psychologists help devise selection methods for new employees, recruit and evaluate applicants, design and evaluate training programs, identify people's strengths, analyze job content, and appraise individual and organizational performance. Subjective interviews foster the interviewer illusion; *structured interviews* pinpoint job-relevant strengths and are better predictors of performance.

Organizational Psychology

2 What is the role of organizational psychologists?

Organizational psychologists examine influences on workers' *achievement motivation*, satisfaction, and productivity, and they facilitate organizational change. Employee engagement tends to correlate with organizational success. Leadership style may be goal oriented *(task leadership)*, group oriented *(social leadership)*, or some combination of the two.

Human Factors Psychology

3 How do human factors psychologists work to create user-friendly machines and work settings?

Human factors psychologists contribute to safety and improved design by exploring ways that machines and physical environments can be adapted to human behaviors. They encourage developers and designers to consider human perceptual abilities, to test users to reveal perception-based problems, and to avoid the curse of knowledge.

Terms and Concepts to Remember

flow, p. B-1

industrial-organizational (I/O) psychology, p. B-2

personnel psychology, p. B-2

organizational psychology, p. B-2

human factors psychology, p. B-2

structured interviews, p. B-5

achievement motivation, p. B-7

task leadership, p. B-11

social leadership, p. B-11

Multiple-choice self-tests and more may be found at www.worthpublishers.com/myers.

Appendix C

Careers in Psychology

Jennifer Zwolinski
University of San Diego

● **Preparing for a Career in Psychology**
The Bachelor's Degree
Postgraduate Degrees

● **Subfields of Psychology**

● **Preparing Early for Graduate Study in Psychology**

● **For More Information**

What can you do with a degree in psychology? Lots!

As a psychology major, you will graduate with a scientific mind-set and an awareness of basic principles of human behavior (biological mechanisms, development, cognition, psychological disorders, social interaction). This background will prepare you for success in many areas, including business, the helping professions, health services, marketing, law, sales, and teaching. You may even go on to graduate school for specialized training to become a psychology professional. This appendix describes the various levels of psychology education and some jobs available at those levels; psychology's specialized subfields; and ways you can improve your chances of admission to graduate school.[1]

Preparing for a Career in Psychology

Psychology is the second most popular major in the United States, second only to business (Princeton Review, 2005). Recent data show that more than 88,000 psychology majors graduate annually from U.S. colleges and universities (National Center for Education Statistics, 2007a,b). An undergraduate degree in psychology can prepare you for a broad array of jobs in numerous fields after graduation. For a career that is more closely related to the field of psychology, you will need a graduate degree.

The Bachelor's Degree

If you major in psychology, you will have several possible career paths to follow (Cannon, 2005). First, you might consider employment after graduation in a variety of professional settings. Most students who graduate with psychology majors find work in for-profit organizations, especially in management, sales, and administration. **TABLE C.1** on the next page shows the top 10 occupations that employ people with a bachelor's degree in psychology.[2] If you choose to work more directly in the field of psychology, a bachelor's degree will qualify you to work as an assistant to psychologists, researchers, or other professionals in community mental health centers, vocational rehabilitation offices, and correctional programs (U.S. Bureau of Labor Statistics, 2008). A second option for psychology majors after graduation is to pursue a graduate degree in psychology. Approximately 42 percent of U.S. psychology majors go on to graduate school in psychology (Fogg et al., 2004). A third option is to pursue advanced training in other disciplines, such as law, business, education, or medicine.

Clearly, psychology majors are marketable beyond the boundaries of psychology. Their sought-after skills include an ability to work and get along with others, a

---

[1]Although this text covers the world of psychology for students in many countries, this appendix draws primarily from available U.S. data. Its descriptions of psychology's subfields and its suggestions for preparing to enter the profession are, however, also applicable in many other countries.

[2]For a more comprehensive list of job titles, see Appleby (2006).

TABLE C.1 Top 10 U.S. Occupations That Employ People With a Bachelor's Degree in Psychology

1. Top- and mid-level managers, executives, administrators
2. Sales occupations, including retail
3. Social workers
4. Other management-related occupations
5. Personnel, training, labor relations specialists
6. Other administrative occupations
7. Insurance, securities, real estate, business services
8. Other marketing and sales occupations
9. Registered nurses, pharmacists, therapists, physician assistants
10. Accountants, auditors, other financial specialists

Source: Fogg et al. (2004).

desire and willingness to learn new things, adaptability to changing situations, and a capacity for problem solving (Landrum, 2001). Psychology majors also have a number of methodological skills that result from the focus on the scientific study of human and animal behavior. The study of statistics and research methodology contributes to a scientific mind-set that emphasizes exploring and managing uncertainty, critical and analytical skills, and logical thinking abilities. The ability to analyze data using statistics, conduct database searches, and integrate multiple sources of information would be helpful in a number of professional settings. Prospective employers will also appreciate the excellent written and oral communication skills among students who present their research projects at conferences and master American Psychological Association (APA) style.

There are some things that all psychology majors can do to maximize success in the job market. Employers who hire people with only a bachelor's degree tend to favor individuals with strong interpersonal skills and practical experience as well as a good education (Cannon, 2005). Betsy Morgan and Ann Korschgen (1998) have offered the following helpful tips for increasing your chances of getting a job after graduation. Many of these tools will benefit students who plan to apply to graduate school as well.

1. *Get to know your instructors.* Talk with them about the field of psychology and get their advice on your career plan. Ask them to support you on an independent study internship or research project. By learning more about your skills and future aims, faculty members can help you accomplish your goals. This may even result in an enthusiastic reference for future employment.
2. *Take courses that support your interests.* Although the psychology major offers a range of skills that will benefit you in the job market, don't assume the psychology curriculum will offer all the skills necessary to get a job in your area of interest. Add courses to increase your knowledge base and skills. This will also show prospective employers that your specific interests are in line with the demands of the job.
3. *Familiarize yourself with available resources, such as campus career services and alumni.* Career services can help you identify and market your job skills and emphasize the knowledge and abilities you have in your resume. They can also help you to network with other alumni who are working in your area of interest and who can help you to prepare for the career that you want.
4. *Participate in at least one internship experience.* Many employers want students to gain relevant experience outside the classroom. Internships are offered during the school year as well as the summer break. Some are paid and others are

not, but you may be able to earn course credit while completing your internship. In addition to gaining relevant work experience before you graduate, you will increase your support network of mentors who can provide supervision and support for your career goals as well as letters of support when you apply for jobs.

5. *Volunteer some of your time and talent to campus or community organizations, such as Psi Chi (the national honor society in psychology) or your school's psychology club.* In addition to showing that you are an active citizen in your department, you will gain important skills, such as meeting and event planning, how to work with a group, and improved communication skills, all of which enhance your marketability.

Postgraduate Degrees

A graduate degree in psychology will give you proficiency in an area of psychological specialization. According to the U.S. Bureau of Labor Statistics (2008), psychologists with advanced degrees held approximately 166,000 jobs in 2006. Employment for psychologists is expected to grow 15 percent from 2006 to 2016, which is faster than the average for all occupations. The work settings for psychologists vary somewhat by type of graduate degree. As shown in **FIGURE C.1**, psychologists with a doctorate work primarily in universities and colleges; most people with a master's degree work in other educational institutions (such as elementary and middle schools) and in for-profit companies. Among advanced degree recipients in 2005–2006, a total of 19,770 had master's degrees and 4921 earned doctoral degrees (National Center for Education Statistics, 2007a,b).

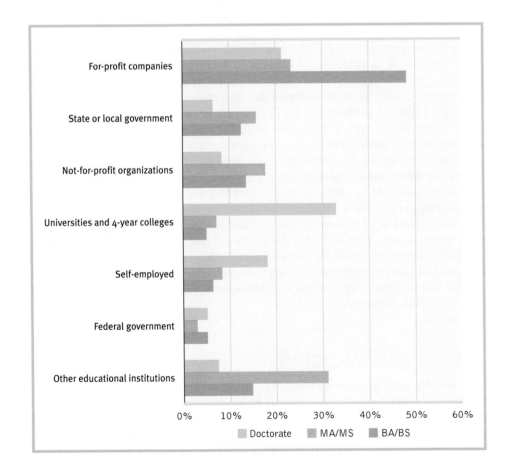

FIGURE C.1 **Work settings for psychology-degree recipients**
Source: Fogg et al., 2004.

The Master's Degree

A master's degree in psychology requires at least two years of full-time graduate study in a specific subfield of psychology. In addition to specialized course work in psychology, requirements usually include practical experience in an applied setting and/or a master's thesis reporting on an original research project. You might acquire a master's degree to do specialized work in psychology. As a graduate with a master's degree, you might handle research and data collection and analysis in a university, government, or private industry setting. You might work under the supervision of a psychologist with a doctorate, providing some clinical service such as therapy or testing. Or you might find a job in the health, government, industry, or education field. You might also acquire a master's degree as a stepping stone for more advanced study in a doctoral program in psychology, which will considerably expand the number of employment opportunities available to you (Super & Super, 2001).

Doctoral Degrees

You will probably need five to seven years of graduate study in a specific subfield of psychology to get your doctoral degree. The degree you choose to pursue will depend on your career goals. You will probably choose to earn a doctor of philosophy (Ph.D.) in psychology if your career goals are geared toward conducting research, or a doctor of psychology (Psy.D.) if you are more interested in pursuing professional practice. Training for the Ph.D. culminates in a dissertation (an extensive research paper you will be required to defend orally) based on original research. Courses in quantitative research methods, which include the use of computer-based analysis, are an important part of graduate study and are necessary to complete the dissertation. Psy.D. training may be based on clinical (therapeutic) work and examinations rather than a dissertation. It is important to note, however, that psychologists with Psy.D. degrees are not the only ones who work in professional practice. Many psychologists who earn a Ph.D. in clinical or counseling psychology conduct research and work in professional settings. If you pursue clinical and counseling psychology programs, you should expect at least a one-year internship in addition to the regular course work, clinical practice, and research.

FIGURE C.2 lists by subfield the Ph.D.s earned in the United States in a recent year. Clinical psychology is the most popular specialty area among those with doctorates in psychology. The largest employment growth areas for doctoral graduates have been in the for-profit and self-employment sectors, including health services providers, industrial-organizational psychology, and educational psychology. About one-third of doctoral-level psychologists are employed in academic settings (Fogg et al., 2004).

In 2001, a total of 73 percent of new doctoral respondents and 55 percent of new master's respondents indicated that their primary occupational position was their first choice. Most new graduates with a master's degree or a Ph.D. are fairly satisfied with their current positions overall in terms of salary, benefits, opportunities for personal development, supervisors, colleagues, and working conditions (Kohout & Wicherski, 2004; Singleton et al., 2003).

Prescription privileges Many psychologists would like the opportunity to prescribe medicines (normally reserved for *physicians* only) in order to expand the scope of clinical practice and to meet the need for psychiatric services in many parts of the United States. Psychologists in the U.S. military and in the states of New Mexico and Louisiana currently have prescription privileges.

Subfields of Psychology

If you are like most psychology students, you may be unaware of the wide variety of specialties and work settings available in psychology (Terre & Stoddart, 2000). To date, the American Psychological Association (APA) has formed 56 divisions (turn the next page to see TABLE C.2). An alphabetical list of some of these careers, in the main specialty areas of psychology, follows. Most require a graduate degree in psychology.

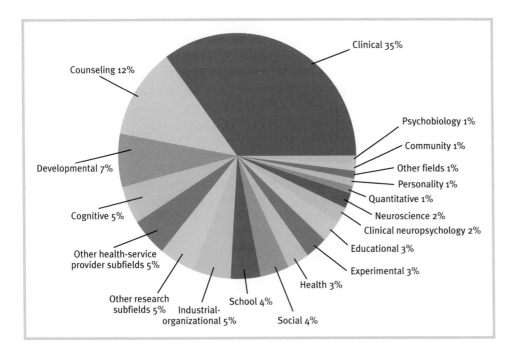

FIGURE C.2 **U.S. Ph.D.s by subfield, 2001** *Source:* National Science Foundation 2001 Survey of Doctorate Recipients. Compiled by the American Psychological Association.

Clinical psychologists promote psychological health in individuals, groups, and organizations. Some clinical psychologists specialize in specific psychological disorders. Others treat a range of disorders, from adjustment difficulties to severe psychopathology. Clinical psychologists might engage in research, teaching, assessment, and consultation. Some hold workshops and lectures on psychological issues for other professionals or for the public. Clinical psychologists work in a variety of settings, including private practice, mental health service organizations, schools, universities, industries, legal systems, medical systems, counseling centers, government agencies, and military services.

To become a clinical psychologist, you will need to earn a doctorate from a clinical psychology program. The APA sets the standards for clinical psychology graduate programs, offering accreditation (official recognition) to those who meet their standards. In all U.S. states, clinical psychologists working in independent practice must obtain a license to offer services such as therapy and testing.

Cognitive psychologists study thought processes and focus on such topics as perception, language, attention, problem solving, memory, judgment and decision making, forgetting, and intelligence. Recent areas of research interest include designing computer-based models of thought processes and identifying biological correlates of cognition. As a cognitive psychologist, you might work as a professor, industrial consultant, or human factors specialist in an educational or business setting.

Community psychologists move beyond focusing on specific individuals or families and deal with broad problems of mental health in community settings. These psychologists believe that human behavior is powerfully influenced by the interaction between people and their physical, social, political, and economic environments. They seek to improve individual functioning by enhancing environmental settings to promote psychological health. Community psychologists focus on prevention, promotion of positive mental health, and crisis intervention, with special attention to the problems of underserved groups and ethnic minorities. Given the

Cognitive consulting Cognitive psychologists may advise businesses on how to operate more effectively by understanding the human factors involved.

TABLE C.2 APA Divisions by Number and Name

1. Society for General Psychology
2. Society for the Teaching of Psychology
3. Experimental Psychology
4. There is no Division 4.
5. Evaluation, Measurement, and Statistics
6. Behavioral Neuroscience and Comparative Psychology
7. Developmental Psychology
8. Society for Personality and Social Psychology
9. Society for the Psychological Study of Social Issues (SPSSI)
10. Society for the Psychology of Aesthetics, Creativity, and the Arts
11. There is no Division 11.
12. Society of Clinical Psychology
13. Society of Consulting Psychology
14. Society for Industrial and Organizational Psychology
15. Educational Psychology
16. School Psychology
17. Society of Counseling Psychology
18. Psychologists in Public Service
19. Society for Military Psychology
20. Adult Development and Aging
21. Applied Experimental and Engineering Psychology
22. Rehabilitation Psychology
23. Society for Consumer Psychology
24. Society for Theoretical and Philosophical Psychology
25. Behavior Analysis
26. Society for the History of Psychology
27. Society for Community Research and Action: Division of Community Psychology
28. Psychopharmacology and Substance Abuse
29. Psychotherapy
30. Society of Psychological Hypnosis
31. State, Provincial, and Territorial Psychological Association Affairs
32. Society for Humanistic Psychology
33. Intellectual and Developmental Disabilities
34. Population and Environmental Psychology
35. Society for the Psychology of Women
36. Psychology of Religion
37. Society for Child and Family Policy and Practice
38. Health Psychology
39. Psychoanalysis
40. Clinical Neuropsychology
41. American Psychology-Law Society
42. Psychologists in Independent Practice
43. Society for Family Psychology
44. Society for the Psychological Study of Lesbian, Gay, and Bisexual Issues
45. Society for the Psychological Study of Ethnic Minority Issues
46. Media Psychology
47. Exercise and Sport Psychology
48. Society for the Study of Peace, Conflict, and Violence: Peace Psychology Division
49. Group Psychology and Group Psychotherapy
50. Addictions
51. Society for the Psychological Study of Men and Masculinity
52. International Psychology
53. Society of Clinical Child and Adolescent Psychology
54. Society of Pediatric Psychology
55. American Society for the Advancement of Pharmacotherapy
56. Trauma Psychology

Source: American Psychological Association.

shared emphasis on prevention, some community psychologists collaborate with professionals in other areas, such as public health. As a community psychologist, your work settings could include federal, state, and local departments of mental health, corrections, and welfare systems. You might conduct research or help evaluate research in health service settings, serve as an independent consultant for a private or government agency, or teach and consult as a college or university faculty member.

Counseling psychologists help people adjust to life transitions or make lifestyle changes. This field is very similar to clinical psychology, except that counseling psychologists typically help people with adjustment problems rather than severe psychopathology. Like clinical psychologists, counseling psychologists conduct therapy and provide assessments to individuals and groups. As a counseling psychologist, you would emphasize your clients' strengths, helping clients cope during a transitional time using their own skills, interests, and abilities. You might find yourself working in an academic setting as a faculty member or administrator or in a university counseling center, community mental health center, business, or private practice. As with clinical psychology, if you plan to work in independent practice you will need to obtain a state license to provide counseling services to the public.

Developmental psychologists conduct research in age-related behavioral changes and apply their scientific knowledge to educational, child-care, policy, and related settings. As a developmental psychologist, you would investigate change across a broad range of topics, including the biological, social, psychological, and cognitive aspects of development. Developmental psychology informs a number of applied fields, including educational psychology, school psychology, child psychopathology, and gerontology. The field also informs public policy in areas such as education and child-care reform, maternal and child health, and attachment and adoption. You would probably specialize in behavior during infancy, childhood, adolescence, or middle or late adulthood. Your work setting could be an educational institution, day-care center, youth group program, or senior center.

Coping with disaster After Peru's deadly August 2007 earthquake, this community psychologist working with Médecins Sans Frontières (Doctors Without Borders) helped survivors cope with the loss of their homes and (for many) the deaths of family members and friends.

Educational psychologists study the relationship between learning and our physical and social environments. They study the psychological processes involved in learning and develop strategies for enhancing the learning process. As an educational psychologist, you might work in a university—in a psychology department or a school of education. You might conduct basic research on topics related to learning or develop innovative methods of teaching to enhance the learning process. You might design effective tests including measures of aptitude and achievement. You might be employed by a school or government agency or charged with designing and implementing effective employee-training programs in a business setting.

Experimental psychologists are a diverse group of scientists who investigate a variety of basic behavioral processes in research involving humans and other animals. Prominent areas of study in experimental research include comparative methods of science, motivation, learning, thought, attention, memory, perception, and language. Most experimental psychologists identify with a particular subfield, such as cognitive psychology, depending on their area of study. It is also important to note that the experimental method for conducting research studies is not limited to the field of experimental psychology, as many other subfields rely on experimental methodology to conduct studies. As an experimental psychologist, you would most likely work in an academic setting, teaching courses and supervising students' research in addition to conducting your own research using experimental methodology. Or you might be employed by a research institution, zoo, business, industry affiliate, or government agency.

Forensic psychologists apply psychological principles to legal issues. They conduct research on the interface of law and psychology, help to create public policies related to mental health, help law-enforcement agencies in criminal investigations, or assist in forensic consultation involving jury selection and deliberation research. They also provide therapy and assessment to assist the legal community. Some forensic psychologists hold law degrees and provide clients with legal services as well. Although most

Criminal profiling On the popular U.S. TV show *Law and Order: Special Victims Unit,* Dr. George Huang (played by B. D. Wong) is an FBI agent and psychiatrist who uses his background in forensic psychology to conduct criminal investigations.

forensic psychologists are clinical psychologists, they might have expertise in other areas of psychology, such as social or cognitive psychology. As a forensic psychologist, you might work in a university psychology department, law school, research organization, community mental health agency, law-enforcement agency, court, or correctional setting.

Health psychologists are researchers and practitioners concerned with psychology's contribution to promoting health and preventing disease. As applied psychologists or clinicians, they may help individuals lead healthier lives by designing, conducting, and evaluating programs to stop smoking, lose weight, improve sleep, manage pain, treat psychosocial problems associated with chronic and terminal illness, or prevent the spread of sexually transmitted infections. As researchers and clinicians, they identify conditions and practices associated with health and illness to help create effective interventions. In public service, health psychologists study and work to improve government policies and health care systems. As a health psychologist, you could be employed in a hospital, medical school, rehabilitation center, public health agency, college or university, or, if you are also a clinical psychologist, in private practice.

Industrial-organizational (I/O) psychologists study the relationship between people and their working environments. They may develop new ways to increase productivity, improve personnel selection, or promote job satisfaction in a business setting. Their interests include organizational structure and change, consumer behavior, and personnel selection and training. As an I/O psychologist, you might conduct workplace training or provide organizational analysis and development. You may find yourself working in business, industry, the government, or a college or university. Or you may be self-employed as a consultant or work for a management consulting firm.

Neuropsychologists investigate the relationship between neurological processes (structure and function of the brain) and behavior. As a neuropsychologist you might assess, diagnose, or treat disorders related to the central nervous system, such as Alzheimer's disease or stroke. You might also evaluate individuals for evidence of head injuries, learning and developmental disabilities (such as autism), and other psychiatric disorders (including attention-deficit hyperactivity disorder [ADHD]). If you are a *clinical neuropsychologist,* you might work in the neurology, neurosurgery, or psychiatric unit of a hospital. Neuropsychologists also work in academic settings, where they conduct research and teach.

Psychometric and *quantitative psychologists* study the methods and techniques used to acquire psychological knowledge. A psychometrician may update existing neurocognitive or personality tests or devise new tests for use in clinical and school settings or in business and industry. These psychologists also administer, score, and interpret such tests. Quantitative psychologists collaborate with researchers to design, analyze, and interpret the results of research programs. As a psychometric or quantitative psychologist, you will need to be well trained in research methods, statistics, and computer technology. You will most likely be employed by a university or college, testing company, private research firm, or government agency.

Rehabilitation psychologists are researchers and practitioners who work with people who have lost optimal functioning after an accident, illness, or other event. As a rehabilitation psychologist, you would probably work in a medical rehabilitation institution or hospital. You might also work in a medical school, university, state or federal vocational rehabilitation agency, or in private practice serving people with physical disabilities.

School psychologists are involved in the assessment of and intervention for children in educational settings. They diagnose and treat cognitive, social, and emotional problems that may negatively influence children's learning or overall functioning at school. As a school psychologist, you would collaborate with teachers, parents, and administrators, making recommendations to improve student learning. You would work in an academic setting, a federal or state government agency, a child guidance center, or a behavioral research laboratory.

Social psychologists are interested in our interactions with others. Social psychologists study how our beliefs, feelings, and behaviors are affected by and influence other people. They study topics such as attitudes, aggression, prejudice, interpersonal attraction, group behavior, and leadership. As a social psychologist, you would probably be a college or university faculty member. You might also work in organizational consultation, marketing research, or other applied psychology fields including social neuroscience. Some social psychologists work for hospitals, federal agencies, or businesses performing applied research.

As a ***sports psychologist,*** you would study the psychological factors that influence, and are influenced by, participation in sports and other physical activities. Professional activities of sports psychologists include coach education and athlete preparation, as well as research and teaching. Sports psychologists who also have a clinical or counseling degree can apply those skills to working with individuals with psychological problems such as anxiety or substance-abuse problems that might interfere with optimal performance. If you were not working in an academic or research setting, you would most likely work as part of a team or organization or in a private capacity.

Preparing Early for Graduate Study in Psychology

Competition for the openings for advanced degrees in psychology is keen. If you choose to go to graduate school, there are a number of things you can do now to maximize your chances of gaining admission to the school of your choice.

If possible, begin preparing during your first year on campus to maximize opportunities and obtain the experience needed to gain admission to a competitive program. Kristy Arnold and Kelly Horrigan (2002) have offered a number of suggestions to facilitate this process.

1. *Network.* Get to know faculty members and the psychology department by attending activities and meetings. This will be especially helpful when you apply to graduate school or for a professional position, because many applications require two to three letters of reference. Become involved in psychology clubs and in Psi Chi, the national honor society in psychology. These meetings connect students with similar interests and expose them to a broader study of the field.
2. *Become actively involved in research as early as possible.* Start by doing simple tasks such as data entry and data collection, and over time you will be prepared to conduct your own research project under the supervision of a research mentor. Consider applying for summer research positions through your university or from other organizations such as the American Psychological Association Summer Science Institute (SSI) or the National Science Foundation Research Experiences for Undergraduates (REU) Program to test your interest in academic careers and to build your skills for future study in psychology.
3. *Volunteer or get a job in a psychology-related field.* Getting involved will show your willingness to apply psychological concepts to real-world settings. Further, it will showcase your ability to juggle a number of tasks successfully, such as work and school—an important skill for graduate school success.
4. *Maintain good grades.* Demonstrate the ability to do well in graduate school with successful completion of challenging courses, especially those related to your interests. (See Chapters 1 and 8 for tips on how to do well in this and other courses, and how to improve your retention of the information you are learning.)

Membership benefits Members of the Psi Chi Honor Society, such as those meeting here, enjoy educational and professional benefits. They may attend special Psi Chi sessions at psychological conventions, apply for research grants in psychology or other academic awards, and read about research advances in the society's journal *Eye on Psi Chi*. (See www.psichi.org for more information.)

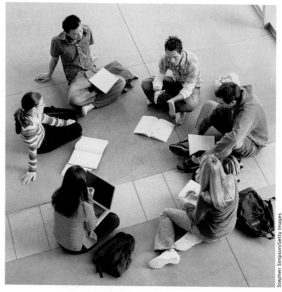

Stephen Simpson/Getty Images

In your junior year, you should begin studying for the Graduate Record Exam (GRE), the standardized test that applicants to graduate school must complete. Many graduate programs in psychology require both the General GRE and the Psychology subject tests. If you start preparing early, you will be ready for success in your graduate school application and study.

* * *

So, the next time someone asks you what you will do with your psychology degree, tell them you have a lot of options. You might use your acquired skills and understanding to get a job and succeed in any number of fields, or you might pursue graduate school and then career opportunities in associated professions. In any case, what you have learned about behavior and mental processes will surely enrich your life (Hammer, 2003).

For More Information

www.apa.org (Web site for the American Psychological Association)

Actkinson, T. R. (2000). Master's and myth. *Eye on Psi Chi, 4,* 19–25.

American Psychological Association (2003). *Careers for the twenty-first century.* Washington, DC: Author.

American Psychological Association (2005). *Graduate study in psychology.* Washington, DC: Author.

Appleby, D. C. (2002). *The savvy psychology major.* Dubuque, IA: Kendall/Hunt.

Appleby, D. C. (2006). Occupations of interest to psychology majors from the Dictionary of Occupational Titles. *Eye on Psi Chi, 10,* 28–29.

Arnold, K., & Horrigan, K. (2002). Gaining admission into the graduate program of your choice. *Eye on Psi Chi, 7,* 1, 30–33.

Aubrecht, L. (2001). What can you do with a BA in psychology? *Eye on Psi Chi, 5,* 29–31.

Cannon, J. (2005). Career planning and opportunities: The bachelor's degree in psychology, *Eye on Psi Chi, 9,* 26–28.

Huss, M. (1996). Secrets to standing out from the pile: Getting into graduate school. *Psi Chi Newsletter,* 6–7.

Koch, G. (2001). Utilizing Psi Chi's programs to maximize learning and success. *Eye on Psi Chi, 10,* 22.

Kracen, A. C., & Wallace, I. J. (Eds.) (2008). *Applying to graduate school in psychology: Advice from successful students and prominent psychologists.* Washington, DC: American Psychological Association.

Lammers, B. (2000). Quick tips for applying to graduate school in psychology. *Eye on Psi Chi, 4,* 40–42.

Landrum, E. (2001). I'm getting my bachelor's degree in psychology. What can I do with it? *Eye on Psi Chi, 6,* 22–24.

LaRoche, K. (2004). Advantages of undergraduate research: A student's perspective. *Eye on Psi Chi, 8,* 20–21.

Morgan, B., & Korschgen, A. (2001). Psychology career exploration made easy. *Eye on Psi Chi, 5,* 35–36.

Schultheiss, D. E. P. (2008). *Psychology as a major: Is it right for me and what can I do with my degree?* Washington, DC: American Psychological Association.

Sternberg, R. (Ed.) (2002). *Career paths in psychology: Where your degree can take you.* Washington, DC: American Psychological Association.

Answers to *Test for Success: Critical Thinking Exercises*

By Amy Himsel
El Camino College

CHAPTER 1 Thinking Critically With Psychological Science

1. **"Nurture works on what nature endows." Describe what this means.**
   ANSWER: The environment (nurture) has an influence on us, but that influence is constrained by our biology (nature). Nature and nurture interact. If I am predisposed to be very tall (nature), for example, I am unlikely to become an Olympic gymnast, no matter how hard I work (nurture).

2. **How can you use your knowledge of the scientific attitude to help you evaluate claims in the media, even if you're not a scientific expert on the issue?**
   ANSWER: One of the most important tips is to realize that hoping something is true has nothing to do with whether or not it is true. Sensible ideas, ideas that seem reasonable and likely, may nevertheless be false. The scientific attitude teaches us to look for evidence instead of relying on our often fallible intuition. In evaluating a claim in the media, look for any signs of empirical evidence, presumably from several studies. Are claims based on scientific findings? Have several studies replicated the findings and confirmed them? Are any experts cited? If so, research their background. Are they affiliated with a credible university, college, or institution? Have they conducted or written about scientific findings?

3. **Here are some recently reported correlations, with interpretations drawn by journalists. Further research, often including experiments, has clarified cause and effect in each case. Knowing just these correlations, can you come up with other possible explanations for each of these?**
   ANSWER:
   a. *Alcohol use is associated with violence. (One interpretation: Drinking triggers or unleashes aggressive behavior.)* Perhaps anger triggers drinking, or perhaps the same genes or rearing predispose both drinking and aggression. (Here researchers have learned that drinking does indeed trigger aggressive behavior.)
   b. *Educated people live longer, on average, than less-educated people. (One interpretation: Education lengthens life and enhances health.)* Perhaps richer people can afford more education and better health care. (Research supports this conclusion.)
   c. *Teens engaged in team sports are less likely to use drugs, smoke, have sex, carry weapons, and eat junk food than are teens who do not engage in team sports. (One interpretation: Team sports encourage healthy living.)* Perhaps some third factor explains this correlation—teens who use drugs, smoke, have sex, carry weapons, and eat junk food may be "loners" who do not enjoy playing on any team.
   d. *Adolescents who frequently see smoking in movies are more likely to smoke. (One interpretation: Movie stars' behavior influences impressionable teens.)* Perhaps adolescents who smoke and attend movies frequently have less parental supervision and more access to spending money than other adolescents.

4. **As you watch an Orlando Magic basketball game with your friend, he says that Dwight Howard really has a hot hand right now and the other players should give him the ball as soon as possible. Based on your knowledge of our tendency toward illusory thinking, how should you respond?**
   ANSWER: Your friend is perceiving order where none exists. He sees Dwight Howard make several shots in a row, and he misinterprets the streak as a special phenomenon

("the hot hand"). The same thing happens when we toss a coin and happen to get a string of heads in a row. The coin hasn't changed; it's just that the random pattern doesn't always look random. Streaks are to be expected.

5. **Foot pads purported to draw toxins out of the body during sleep have become popular lately. Testimonials suggest that foot pads remove toxins from the body and also help alleviate a variety of health problems, including fatigue and backaches. How can we determine whether foot pads are actually effective?**
ANSWER: To determine whether the foot pads are truly effective, we have to experiment. It doesn't matter how convinced we are that the pads work; what matters is how well the pads actually do work. A double-blind experiment is the best method to determine this. We would give the experimental group the real foot pads and give the control group a placebo (something physically similar, but without any active agent). Participants would be randomly assigned to these groups, and they would be unaware of which group they are in. We would then monitor the health of all participants to see if the foot pads (the independent variable) actually do have an impact on health (the dependent variable). Are the foot pads likely to be effective? Health experts say *no*. Our body already has effective ways of releasing toxins, and we do not excrete enough toxins through our skin to have an impact on our health. So, the result we expect may be that the foot pads will have no effect. Yet only a well-run experiment can give us confidence in this finding.

CHAPTER 2 The Biology of Mind

1. **In *The Astonishing Hypothesis* (1994, p. 49), Sir Francis Crick noted, "What one neuron tells another neuron is simply how much it is excited." Using terms from this chapter, compare the neural communication when we are (a) tapped gently on the arm, and (b) slapped across the face.**
ANSWER: Whether we are tapped or slapped, communications between neurons would be at the same level of intensity because neurons fire in an all-or-nothing fashion. In each case, axon terminal/dendrite pairs would "chat" across a synapse about how excited or inhibited they are. If "I'm excited" chats outnumber "I'm inhibited" ones, a threshold would be reached, sending an impulse (the action potential) down the axon. Reaching the axon terminal, the impulse would launch a message, in the form of a neurotransmitter, across the synapse to the dendrite of the receiving neuron. Compared with a tap, a slap would involve more of these chats.

2. **Which area of the human brain is most similar to that of primitive animals? Which part of the human brain distinguishes us the most from primitive animals?**
ANSWER: The human brainstem is most similar to that of primitive animals, and the cerebral cortex is most different.

3. **We are not conscious of many brain processes that help create our experiences. To appreciate how much is going on outside of our awareness, we can imagine functioning without certain brain areas. For example, what would it be like to talk on the phone with your mother if you didn't have the temporal lobe association areas? What would you hear? What would you understand?**
ANSWER: You would hear sounds, but without the temporal lobe association areas you would be unable to make sense of what you were hearing. With no memories of the sound of your mother's voice, you would not realize, "It's my mother!" With no memories of the meaning of the words she was speaking, you could not understand what she was saying.

4. **Neurons bunch together in networks, just as people tend to congregate in cities—in each case, shorter distances enable efficient communication. Yet your brain somehow integrates information transmitted from distant regions. How do different neural networks communicate with one another to let you, for example, respond when a friend greets you at a party?**
ANSWER: In the real estate of your brain, the various neural networks are connected by billions of interneurons, whose job is to form connections between other neurons. Each

specialized area in the cerebral cortex resides next to an association area that helps integrate information across the cortex. The visual cortex, for example, is a neural network of sensory neurons that is connected via interneurons to other neural networks. This explains how you can integrate visual and auditory information to respond when a friend you recognize greets you at a party.

5. **In what brain region would damage be most likely to disrupt your ability to skip rope? Your ability to sense tastes and sounds? In what brain region would damage perhaps leave you in a coma? Without the very breath and heartbeat of life?**
   ANSWER: These regions are, respectively, the *cerebellum,* the *thalamus,* the *reticular formation,* and the *medulla.* These questions assess your understanding of the essential functions of the lower-level brain areas.

CHAPTER 3 Consciousness and the Two-Track Mind

1. **Research on the two-track mind shows that we know more than we know we know. Might we function better if we were completely conscious of all of our thought processes?**
   ANSWER: It is actually adaptive that our mind operates at two levels simultaneously. With an unconscious mind running largely on auto-pilot, our conscious thought processes can focus on executive-level, important decisions. While reading this textbook, for example, you don't have to remind yourself to inhale and exhale. Capable "assistants" in your unconscious mind—in this case, your medulla—are handling these tasks. Thanks to selective attention, you can focus consciously on only a fraction of the several billion bits of sensory information your mind processes in any given moment. Without this dual-processing ability, your information-processing system would be completely overwhelmed.

2. **In the discussion of sleep stages, a man in a cartoon states, "Boy, are my eyes tired! I had REM sleep all night long!" In reality, how tiring is REM sleep, and how much time do we spend in it?**
   ANSWER: In reality, REM sleep involves a mix of activity (bursts of eye movement and brain activity similar to alpha waves) and inactivity (body paralysis as the brainstem prevents cortex activity from reaching the rest of the body). This activity-paralysis mix gives REM sleep its other name: paradoxical sleep. Adults tend to spend about 20 to 25 percent of an average night in REM sleep. The man in the cartoon would be more likely to be exhausted by too little REM sleep than by too much.

3. **Sleep researcher William Dement said that a large sleep debt "makes you stupid" (1999, p. 231). What are some of the ways sleep deprivation can affect cognitive performance?**
   ANSWER: Chronic sleep deprivation can "make you stupid" by impairing your ability to concentrate, slowing reaction time, increasing irritability, and decreasing creativity and productivity. Lack of sleep can have disastrous effects on memory consolidation, which occurs during REM sleep. Chronic sleep deprivation also inhibits the nightly repair process of the brain and other body tissues, which sets the stage for impaired cognition.

4. **"For what one has dwelt on by day, these things are seen in visions of the night" (Menander of Athens [342–292 B.C.E.], *Fragments*). Consider this quote from the wish-fulfillment, information-processing, and activation-synthesis perspectives on dreaming.**
   ANSWER: *Freud's wish-fulfillment* explanation proposes that our thoughts *(what one has dwelt on by day)* do appear in our dreams (our *visions of the night*), but in deeply disguised form (the dream's latent content), not in the dream's actual story line (the manifest content). The *information-processing* explanation proposes that brain activity during REM sleep enables us to sift through *what one has dwelt on by day* and to commit that information to memory. The *activation-synthesis* explanation proposes that our frontal cortex weaves a story from random bursts of brain activity (influenced by our past experiences, including *what one has dwelt on by day*) emanating from the brainstem during REM sleep, creating our dreams.

5. **Fourth-century-B.C.E. philosopher Plato observed, "How strange would appear to be this thing that men call pleasure! And how curiously it is related to what is thought to be its opposite, pain! . . . Wherever the one is found, the other follows up behind." Explain how this pleasure-pain description applies to the neurotransmitter activity underlying repeated use of heroin.**

   ANSWER: In general, psychoactive drugs create pleasure by altering brain chemistry. With repeated use, the brain undergoes neuroadaptation, changing the way it functions. Tolerance results as the amount of the drug needed to achieve the desired effect increases. Once the body becomes dependent, discontinuing use of the substance produces painful withdrawal symptoms because the brain's neurochemistry has changed. The opiate heroin creates a sense of *pleasure* by depressing neural functioning and making the user less responsive to physical pain. The *pain* that follows results from the neuroadaptation that decreases or stops the brain's production of natural opiates, the endorphins. Heroin abuse may permanently damage the endorphin production system.

CHAPTER 4 Nature, Nurture, and Human Diversity

1. **If heredity is a primary influence on personality, how can we explain why some siblings, who have different combinations of their parents' genes, have very similar personalities?**

   ANSWER: When siblings have strikingly similar personalities, it is tempting to credit the influence of the family environment. But it's important to keep in mind that biological siblings share half their genes. By chance alone, couples could produce a few children with very similar genetic predispositions toward certain personality characteristics. Of course, genes also interact with the environment, so that two cheerful and outgoing siblings are likely to evoke positive reactions from others, further reinforcing their bubbly personalities. Conversely, children who differ greatly may evoke (and later recall) very different experiences in that "same" family environment. We must also keep in mind that this research focuses on personality. Other characteristics, including attitudes and values, are strongly influenced by the family environment.

2. **"Use it or lose it" is a phrase often used when discussing strategies to stave off brain aging and decline in adulthood. In reality, this rule is just as critical during infancy. Explain why.**

   ANSWER: Infancy is the time when the brain is most plastic (changeable). The human brain continues to produce new neurons and connections throughout the life span, but no time is more critical than infancy. During the first years of life, surplus neural connections form in the brain of an infant experiencing a healthy family environment and adequate levels of stimulation through seeing, hearing, touching, being touched, and having things to do. Without these normal experiences—for example, in severely deprived environments—the pathways in a child's brain won't develop, and the normal pruning process will eliminate underused neural connections. Another milder wave of surplus building and pruning occurs across childhood and adolescence, but if damage has been extensive during the first years of life, later recovery may be impaired.

3. **It's been said that our female ancestors most often sent their genes into the future by pairing wisely, and our male ancestors by pairing widely. How does the evolutionary psychology perspective explain why these adaptive patterns are still seen in the behaviors and priorities of contemporary men and women who have more choices about when and whether they will have children?**

   ANSWER: Our interests and motivations have been shaped by the genetic legacy (carried in our DNA) of our species. As evolutionary psychologist David Buss said, "Humans are living fossils—collections of mechanisms produced by prior selection pressures." From an evolutionary perspective, human sexual motivation is directed toward the goal of survival of the species, which requires passing our genes on to future generations. In our evolutionary past, men could ensure the survival of their genes by mating with, and impregnating, several women, especially those who were young, healthy, and fertile. Our female ancestors, capable of sustaining only one pregnancy at a time, were more likely to leave surviving descendents if they focused more on quality of partners rather than quantity—thus, say evolutionary psychologists, women were attracted to partners able to protect and support offspring.

4. **Primatologist Frans B. M. de Waal (1999) observed that "genes, by themselves, are like seeds dropped onto pavement: powerless to produce anything." Explain what this means, in terms of our human characteristics.**

   ANSWER: Genes certainly are important because they trigger the development of the protein molecules that help form all our physical characteristics (including the brain). But to do this work, genes need housing (the environment provided by the cells in which our genetic code—our DNA—lives). Genes also need other genes because groups of genes work in concert to produce our complex psychological characteristics, such as intelligence. Finally, genes are self-regulating and some (like a gene that predisposes a person to depression) need environmental influences (such as major life stress) to trigger their expression. Genes and environment interact.

5. **Consider the Chinese saying, "One needs to cultivate the spirit of sacrificing the *little me* to achieve the benefits of the *big me*." What is the *little me*? The *big me*? How might a staunch individualist react to this saying?**

   ANSWER: This saying reflects a central feature of collectivism: that one's identity is formed in connection with group goals. The *little me* is the individual, separate from others; the *big me* is the sense of self in connection to the group—the individual's family, friends, society, and so on. If the needs of the group and the individual collide, the *big me* must take priority in order to maintain harmony and bring honor to the group. A staunch individualist would likely struggle to understand this saying. The *little me* looms large in individualist cultures, where the *big me* may be sacrificed or compromised in service to the goals and desires of the *little me*. Staunch individualists might even struggle to comprehend the meaning of *big me* because their concept of self is defined as separate from that of the group.

CHAPTER 5 Developing Through the Life Span

1. **"Nature is all that a man brings with him into the world; nurture is every influence that affects him after his birth," said Francis Galton (*English Men of Science*, 1874). What part of this quote would need to be updated to reflect current research?**

   ANSWER: The second half of Galton's quote would need to be updated because we now know that nurture includes not only all that we experience *after* birth, but also all that we experience in the womb *prior* to birth. The importance of the prenatal environment, our first experience of nurture, is clearly illustrated by the effects of *teratogens,* substances like viruses and drugs that can reach the developing organism and cause harm.

2. **We all learned to walk as infants, and we retain that learning as adults. Yet we would be unable to consciously recall just how we achieved this feat. Why can't we reconstruct those memories?**

   ANSWER: Although our brain is processing information and we are learning from our experiences, our brain is not equipped to form conscious memories before the age of 3, a concept known as infantile amnesia. The baby in Rovee-Collier's study demonstrated this idea when he showed that he had learned from his experience of moving a mobile by kicking her foot. Although our nervous system is processing information and creating memories during the phase of infantile amnesia, we cannot access those memories consciously.

3. **A counselor has advised a teenager's frustrated parents that his behavior may improve when his brain matures. What evidence supports the counselor's suggestion?**

   ANSWER: The immaturity of the adolescent brain is so well established that the U.S. Supreme Court ruled it unconstitutional to sentence adolescents to the death penalty. The frontal lobes of a teenager's cerebral cortex continue to develop during adolescence and may not reach full maturity until his mid-twenties. As frontal lobe neurons become increasingly myelinated, the teen will slowly gain more control over his emotions and impulses. Heavy drinking during adolescence can, however, interfere with frontal lobe development.

4. **"I hope I die before I get old," sang rock star Peter Townshend—when he was 20. What could you tell other 20-year-olds to make them feel more optimistic about aging?**

ANSWER: You could remind 20-year-olds that aging is more than a series of losses. For most people, the rapid-processing skills of fluid intelligence will decrease steadily, but their vocabulary and knowledge of crystallized intelligence will increase well into older adulthood. Negative emotions will likely be less intense than in young adulthood, and the risk of depression often decreases with age.

5. **Research has shown that living together before marriage predicts an increased likelihood of future divorce. Can you imagine two possible explanations for his correlation?**

ANSWER: Will Axinn and Arland Thornton (1992) reported data that support two explanations. (1) The first explanation is an example of a *selection effect*—our tendency to seek out others who are similar to us. Cohabitation attracts people who are more open to terminating unsatisfying relationships. People who cohabit bring a more individualistic ethic to marriage, are more likely to see close relationships as temporary and fragile, are more accepting of divorce, and are about three times more likely after marriage to have an affair (Forste & Tanfer, 1996). (2) Axinn and Thornton's second explanation illustrates the *causal effect* of the experience of cohabitation. Over time, those who cohabit tend to become more approving of dissolving an unfulfilling union. This divorce-accepting attitude increases the odds of later divorce.

CHAPTER 6 Sensation and Perception

1. **Before reading this question, you probably didn't notice the sensation of your shoes touching your feet. Yet it's likely you notice them now. Why?**

ANSWER: Before this question brought the touch of your shoes into your conscious awareness, you were experiencing sensory adaptation. The shoes provide constant stimulation, which triggers fewer and fewer neurons to fire, until the sensation recedes into the background, unnoticed. Sensory adaptation allows us to focus on changing stimuli, which are typically most important for survival. Without this adaptive reaction, we would be bombarded with incoming information and would have difficulty functioning.

2. **Why do you feel a little dizzy immediately after a roller coaster ride?**

ANSWER: The same sensory features that allow you to perceive the world accurately can also, on occasion, generate false perceptions. Your vestibular sense regulates balance and body positioning through kinesthetic receptors triggered by fluid in your inner ear. Wobbly legs and a spinning world are signs that these receptors are still responding to the ride's turbulence. As your vestibular sense adjusts to solid ground, your balance will be restored.

3. **Why might it be helpful for people with chronic pain to meditate or exercise?**

ANSWER: Because we feel pain in our brain, we may diminish the experience of pain by changing the messages sent to the brain. Gate-control theory proposes that our pain sensory receptors send signals to the spinal cord, which relays messages to the brain. Small fibers in the spinal cord open the gate to pain; large fibers close the gate, blocking those signals. Meditation triggers large-fiber activity by shifting our attention elsewhere (toward the breath or repeated word); exercise triggers that activity by generating competing stimulation and endorphin release.

4. **What mental processes allow you to perceive a lemon as yellow?**

ANSWER: The lemon itself has no color; your brain constructs this perception of color in two stages. First, the lemon reflects light energy into your eyes, where it is transformed into neural messages. Three sets of cones, each sensitive to a different light frequency (red, blue, and green) process color. In this case, the light energy stimulates both red-sensitive and green-sensitive cones. In the second stage, a network of opponent-process cells sensitive to paired opposites of color (red/green and yellow/blue) evaluates the incoming neural messages as they pass through your optic nerve to the thalamus and visual cortex. When the yellow-sensitive opponent-process cells are stimulated, you identify the lemon as yellow.

CHAPTER 7 Learning

1. **"Sex sells!" is a common saying in advertising. Using classical conditioning terms, explain how sexual images in advertisements can condition your response to a product.**

   ANSWER: The sexual image is a US that triggers the UR of interest or arousal. The product is an NS. An advertisement pairs the product with a sexual image. Over time, the product becomes a CS that triggers the CR of interest or arousal.

2. **Ethan constantly misbehaves at preschool even though his teacher scolds him several times each day. Why does his misbehavior continue, and what can his teacher do to stop it?**

   ANSWER: Ethan probably enjoys the attention; if so, he is experiencing the scolding as a positive reinforcement instead of a punishment. To stop the misbehavior, he needs a mild punishment (such as a time out) to teach him what *not* to do, followed by reinforcement (such as praise) to teach him what *to* do. Reinforcement is most effective for long-term learning, but initially, it may be challenging for the teacher to find any behavior to praise. The teacher might encourage Ethan toward increasingly appropriate behavior by shaping with successive approximations. Another option is to rephrase rules as rewards instead of as punishments, perhaps saying, "You can have a snack if you play nicely with the other children" (reward) instead of "You will not get a snack if you misbehave!" (punishment).

3. **How could your psychology instructor use negative reinforcement to encourage your attentive behavior during class?**

   ANSWER: Your instructor could reinforce your attentive behavior by taking away something you dislike. If you detest writing, the promise of shortening the required length of a paper might be an effective reward. If you are easily bored, an engaging lecture might be rewarding. If you dislike lectures, a reward could be an in-class video or activity. In each case, the instructor would remove something aversive in order to negatively reinforce your focused attention.

4. **Why might a gymnastics coach encourage her students to improve their routines by watching recordings of Olympic gold medal gymnastics performances?**

   ANSWER: The coach may realize that mirror neurons influence observational learning. Mirror neurons in the students' frontal lobes will mimic the Olympic gymnasts' movements, and this "brain rehearsal" will help prepare the students for learning when they practice their own routines later.

5. **Jason's parents and older friends all smoke, but they advise him not to. Juan's parents and friends don't smoke, but they say nothing to deter him from doing so. Will Jason or Juan be more likely to start smoking?**

   ANSWER: Although both saying and doing can influence people, experiments suggest that children more often do as others do and say as they say. Generalizing this finding to smoking, we can expect that Jason will be more likely to start smoking.

CHAPTER 8 Memory

1. **What would be the most effective strategy to learn and retain a list of names of key historical figures for a week? For a year?**

   ANSWER: For a week: Make the names personally meaningful. For a year: Overlearn the list and space out rehearsals over the course of several weeks.

2. **Maria has always loved to wear winter clothing. The sensation of being bundled up makes her feel safe and secure. How might her preference be related to her January birth in Chicago?**

ANSWER: Maria's first few months of life were spent wrapped in warm clothing in the bitter cold of a Chicago winter. As an infant, she may have learned to associate winter clothing with her parents' sensitive caregiving (feeling safe and secure). Maria could not form explicit memories of these experiences because of her immature hippocampus and verbal skills. Instead, an implicit memory retrieved from her cerebellum may be triggering this vague sense of comfort.

3. **When you feel sad, why might it help to look at pictures that reawaken some of your best memories?**

ANSWER: Memories are stored within a web of many associations, one of which is mood. When you recall fond moments from your past, you stimulate the "happy-memories" associations. By deliberately activating these threads of the web, you may experience mood-congruent memory and recall other happy moments, which will likely improve your mood and positively influence your interpretation of current events.

4. **What you know today seems to be what you have always known. Explain what this means.**

ANSWER: Our memories are often modified by our subsequent experiences, thoughts, and expectations. We tend to fill in gaps with reasonable guesses that eventually feel like real memories. Misinformation may color the construction of retrieved memories. If you have a vivid imagination, you may be especially susceptible to incorporating imagined events into your memories. In addition, motivated forgetting may lead you to revise memories to align them with your current self-concept. We are largely unaware of this memory revision process, which is why "what we remember today" seems to be "what we have always remembered."

5. **Eliza's family loves to tell the story of how she "stole the show" as a 2-year-old, dancing at her aunt's wedding reception. Infantile amnesia should have prevented her from forming a memory, yet Eliza can recall the event clearly. How is this possible?**

ANSWER: Eliza's immature hippocampus and lack of verbal skills prevented her from encoding an explicit memory of her aunt's wedding reception at the age of two. Instead, it's likely that Eliza learned information (from hearing the story repeatedly) that she eventually constructed into a very convincing (yet false) explicit memory.

6. **What—given the commonality of source amnesia—might life be like if we remembered all our waking experiences and all our dreams?**

ANSWER: Real experiences would be confused with those we dreamed. When meeting someone, we might therefore be unsure whether we were reacting to something they previously had done or to something we dreamed they had done. William Dement (1999, p. 298) noted that this "would put a great burden on your sanity. . . . I truly believe that the wall of memory is a blessed protection."

CHAPTER 9 Thinking, Language, and Intelligence

1. **Oscar describes his political beliefs as "strongly liberal," but he has decided to explore opposing viewpoints. How might this influence his thinking?**

ANSWER: Oscar is guarding against confirmation bias by seeking out opposing viewpoints, but he is likely to find fault with these views and grow overconfident in his liberal beliefs. Even if Oscar encounters new information that disproves his liberal beliefs, belief perseverance may lead him to cling to these views anyway. It will take more compelling evidence to change his political beliefs than it took to create them.

2. **It's been said that the development of language can be compared to the growth of a flower. Explain how, using the theories of Skinner and Chomsky.**

ANSWER: The growth of a flower is influenced by sunlight, water, and soil. Skinner argued that language also develops from environmental stimulation, as children learn associations between words and objects or actions; imitate observed language behaviors; and receive reinforcement for their speech. The growth of a flower is also influenced by the innate components of the seed. Chomsky argued that inborn skills (such as the language acquisition device) permit language development to "just happen," provided children receive adequate stimulation during a critical period early in life. Contemporary psychologists tend to believe that each viewpoint explains part of the language development process.

3. **A Czech proverb says, "Learn a new language and get a new soul." To what extent is this true?**

   ANSWER: Words do not *determine* how you think (as the linguistic determinism theory suggests), but they do *influence* your thinking. A newly learned language may alter your thoughts, personality, and sense of self. In addition, the vocabulary of the new language widens your perspective and allows you to think more like the members of that culture.

4. **When asked to report his IQ, Nobel Prize-winning physicist Stephen Hawking (2004) responded, "I have no idea. People who boast about their IQ are losers." How important are intelligence test scores to success in life?**

   ANSWER: Standard intelligence test scores best predict school performance and analytic intelligence ("school smarts"), but they only modestly predict other factors that influence success in life, such as common sense, creativity, or self-motivation. Other types of intelligence, such as those proposed by Gardner, Sternberg, and others, address a variety of mental abilities that may also influence success in life, such as practical, musical, or emotional intelligence.

5. **How could mental rehearsal help your performance in this class?**

   ANSWER: Studying is a skill that improves with practice. You can improve your study skills by using visual imagery as mental rehearsal for future behaviors. Visualizing yourself engaged in the *process* of achieving your goals—effective study behaviors, such as rehearsing information and eliminating distractions—is more effective than dreaming about your desired *outcome*.

6. **As society succeeds in creating equality of opportunity, it will also increase the heritability of ability. The heritability of intelligence scores will be greater in a society marked by equal opportunity than in a society of peasants and aristocrats. Why?**

   ANSWER: Perfect environmental equality would create 100 percent heritability—because genes alone would account for any remaining human differences.

CHAPTER 10 Motivation

1. **Dorothea Dix (1801–1887) once remarked, "Nobody wants to kiss when they are hungry." Which theory of motivation best supports her statement?**

   ANSWER: Maslow's hierarchy of needs best supports this statement because it addresses the primacy of some motives over others. Physiological needs (such as hunger) trump all others. Once those basic needs are met, safety concerns are addressed next, followed by belongingness and love needs (such as the desire to kiss).

2. **Sanjay recently adopted the typical college diet high in fat and sugar. He knows he may gain weight, but he figures it's no big deal because he can lose the extra pounds in the future. How would you evaluate Sanjay's plan?**

   ANSWER: Sanjay's plan is problematic. Yes, he could someday lose his "college weight" by expending more calories than he consumes; however, weight gain now could make weight loss and maintenance in the future more challenging. With weight gain, his fat cells may increase in number; even if he tries to lose weight later, those cells will shrink in size but will never be eliminated entirely. Sanjay would be better off to maintain his current, healthy weight by adopting a balanced diet and exercising regularly.

3. **Everything psychological is simultaneously biological. How is this true of sexual orientation?**

   ANSWER: Sexual orientation involves both psychology (mental processes and behaviors) and biology (genetics, prenatal hormones, and the brain). Researchers have not yet found that environmental factors outside of the womb determine sexual orientation, but the influence of biology has been demonstrated in several studies. For example, sexual orientation correlates with differences in the structure and functioning of the hypothalamus. Other research indicates that biological factors (such as genetic influences and prenatal hormonal activity) may predispose these brain-related differences. Biological factors may also predispose a temperament that motivates the child toward gender-atypical behavior, which may gradually develop into a homosexual orientation.

4. **To what extent might social networking Web sites like Facebook satisfy or thwart our need to belong?**

   ANSWER: During social networking, healthy relationships (which increase self-esteem and happiness) may grow stronger because of increased contact with important others, and we may make new friends online, satisfying our need to belong. But electronic contact may not confer the same benefit as face-to-face or telephone contact. We risk being deceived or misled by others who misrepresent themselves. We may even experience social rejection (ostracism and cyberbullying, for example), which could trigger depression, withdrawal, and even aggressive retaliation. Thus, social networking sites may satisfy *and* thwart our need to belong.

CHAPTER 11 Emotions, Stress, and Health

1. **Christine is holding her 8-month-old baby when a fierce dog appears out of nowhere and, with teeth bared, leaps for the baby's face. Christine immediately ducks for cover to protect the baby, screams at the dog, then notices that her heart is banging in her chest and she's broken out in a cold sweat. How would the James-Lange, Cannon-Bard, and two-factor theories explain Christine's emotional reaction?**

   ANSWER: The James-Lange theory would say that Christine's emotional reaction consists of her awareness of her physiological responses to the dog attack. The Cannon-Bard theory would say that her fear experience happened simultaneously with her physiological arousal. Schacter's two-factor theory would presume that her emotional reaction stemmed from her interpreting and labeling the arousal.

2. **How might mountain climbing on a first date influence your emotional reaction to the person?**

   ANSWER: Mountain climbing increases physiological arousal, which may spill over and intensify your emotions. So, if your date might otherwise seem slightly annoying, you may feel intense dislike. If your date is mildly interesting, you may feel strong attraction. A quiet dinner will give you a more accurate read without intensifying your emotions.

3. **You are happy to have earned a B on an exam until you learn that most of your friends received an A. How can you explain your drop in mood?**

   ANSWER: You experienced *relative deprivation*, the sense that you fared more poorly than others with whom you compared yourself. When you compare upward, focusing on those who did better (in this case, those who received an A), your happiness decreases. If you compare downward (with those who received a C), your happiness will likely rebound.

4. **A self-help book declares that you can prevent cancer through "the power of positive thinking." How would you evaluate this claim?**

   ANSWER: Positive thinking may boost immune functioning and slow the growth of tumors, but it won't prevent the formation of cancer cells, which are the product of various biological and environmental influences. Nevertheless, negative thinking can exacerbate our health problems by triggering a fight-or-flight reaction, stress hormone activity, and the reduction of T lymphocyte and natural killer cells. As a result, tumors may grow faster. So, although positive thinking doesn't prevent cancer, it may enhance the immune system's fight against the disease.

5. A Chinese proverb warns, "The fire you kindle for your enemy often burns you more than him." How is this true of Type A individuals?

ANSWER: During their frequent bouts of hostility, Type A individuals put themselves greatly at risk for health problems, including heart disease. Their sympathetic nervous system diverts blood away from the liver, leaving fat and cholesterol circulating in the bloodstream for deposit near the heart and other organs. Hostility also correlates with unhealthy habits, such as smoking, drinking, and obesity. Ultimately, the Type A individual harms himself greatly by kindling a fire for his enemy.

CHAPTER 12 Personality

1. How might Freud and Rogers differ in their explanations of how the environment influences the development of a criminal?

ANSWER: Freud might argue that the environment failed to trigger the superego, which moderates the id's dangerous urges (inherent selfishness and aggression). Lacking proper guidance as a child, the criminal may have developed a weak superego, allowing the id free rein. Rogers might assert that the environment failed to nurture self-actualizing potential. Thus, the criminal was likely raised in an environment lacking genuineness, acceptance (unconditional positive regard), and empathy, which inhibited psychological growth and led to a negative self-concept.

2. In *Essays*, Michel de Montaigne (1588) suggested, "There is as much difference between us and ourselves, as between us and others." Does research on the trait perspective support his claim?

ANSWER: Trait researchers have found significant *differences between us and others* on the Big Five personality characteristics. These traits are stable (especially in adulthood), moderately heritable, and documented worldwide. Nevertheless, situational variations in our behavior indicate *differences between us and ourselves* as well. Personality assessments, designed to measure behavior averaged across many situations, are weak predictors of behavior in a given moment because the demands of the situation may overpower our stable traits.

3. You think you are talented enough to compete on *American Idol*, but you don't want to make a fool of yourself on TV. What is the best way to accurately assess your talent beforehand?

ANSWER: The least competent individuals have the most difficulty recognizing their incompetence, so the more talented you are, the better your chances of accurately judging yourself. But to be safe, ask peers to evaluate your singing; they are likely to be more objective than you.

4. A fortune cookie advises, "Love yourself and happiness will follow." Is this good advice?

ANSWER: Loving yourself can lead to happiness *or* sorrow. High levels of secure self-esteem promote a focus beyond the self and correlate with a high quality of life. In contrast, low self-esteem involves negativity directed not only toward the self, but toward others as well. Furthermore, narcissism and the self-serving bias may prompt self-esteem that is artificially high (not based on one's behaviors) or defensive (erected to protect the self), which may lead to sorrow, especially when negative external feedback triggers anger or aggression.

CHAPTER 13 Psychological Disorders

1. Anna is embarrassed that it takes her several minutes to parallel park her car. She usually gets out of the car once or twice to inspect her distance both from

the curb and from the cars nearby. Should she worry about having a psychological disorder?

ANSWER: Anna's behaviors are similar to some symptoms of obsessive-compulsive disorder, but she does not have a psychological disorder. Her behavior is unusual, causes her distress, and may make her a few minutes late on occasion, but it does not appear to significantly disrupt her ability to function. Like most of us, Anna demonstrates some unusual behaviors that are not disabling or dysfunctional.

2. A full-figured body is the traditional cultural ideal for women in the South Pacific island of Fiji. After the introduction of American TV programs to the island in 1995, however, eating disorder diagnoses increased rapidly. How can the biopsychosocial approach explain this phenomenon?

ANSWER: In the past, the cultural ideal of full figures helped protect Fijian women from developing eating disorders. American TV programs, with their emphasis on thinness, introduced a competing social-cultural ideal, which also probably triggered changes in psychological factors (such as perceptions and thoughts about weight). These social-cultural and psychological influences, in combination with biological factors (such as genetic predispositions), increased Fijian women's risk of eating disorders.

3. When women get sad, they often get sadder than men do. When men get mad, they often get madder than women do. How does this correspond to gender differences in psychological disorders?

ANSWER: Women tend to have strong emotional memories and to ruminate over negative events, leaving them more vulnerable to anxiety and depression. Men, who tend to direct their negative emotions outward, show higher rates of substance abuse disorder or antisocial personality disorder than are found among women.

4. What does it mean to say that depression is the "common cold" of psychological disorders?

ANSWER: Saying that depression is the "common cold" of psychological disorders is a quick way to state that this serious disorder is the most common condition in those seeking mental health treatment—with almost 6 percent of men and nearly 10 percent of women reporting a depressive episode each year. Worldwide, depression is the leading cause of disability.

5. Victor exclaimed, "The weather has been so schizophrenic lately: It's hot one day and freezing the next!" Is this an accurate analogy? Why or why not?

ANSWER: This analogy is inaccurate; it reflects a common misunderstanding—that schizophrenia involves rapid changes in mood or identity. Schizophrenia is a disorder involving the altered perceptions, emotions, and behaviors of a mind split from reality. Perhaps Victor is confusing schizophrenia with dissociative identity disorder (DID), in which a person may display distinctly different identities from one moment to the next.

CHAPTER 14 Therapy

1. American playwright August Wilson (1945–2005) advised, "Your willingness to wrestle with your demons will cause your angels to sing." Which psychological therapy best matches this quote, and why?

ANSWER: Psychoanalysis is the best fit for this quote because it proposes that unpleasant, repressed conflicts and urges will fester and cause psychological disorders. To help the patient increase awareness of unwanted, hidden aspects of the self (*wrestling with demons*), the psychoanalyst encourages free association, explores resistance, and offers interpretations. As a result, the patient hopefully gains insight and improved psychological functioning (*causing angels to sing*).

2. After a near-fatal car accident, Rico developed an intense fear of driving on the freeway. In fact, his anxious response to the freeway has become so intense that he must take lengthy alternative routes to work each day. Which psychological therapy might best help Rico overcome his phobia, and why?

ANSWER: Behavior therapies are often the best choice for treating phobias and other anxiety disorders. A behavior therapist would view Rico's fear of the freeway as a learned response that can be changed. Using counterconditioning (such as systematic desensitization, an exposure therapy), the therapist would teach Rico to replace his anxious response to freeway driving with a relaxation response. Over time, Rico should be able to resume freeway driving without intense anxiety.

3. **How can we apply the knowledge that *everything psychological is simultaneously biological* to the treatment of depression?**
   ANSWER: Depression's feelings of worthlessness and distorted thoughts correlate with brain activity. Biomedical treatments (such as antidepressants or neurostimulation) affect the limbic system, working from the bottom up to influence neurotransmitter activity and the growth of new neurons. As a result, distorted thoughts and negative emotions often subside. But changes in thoughts and feelings triggered by psychological therapies (such as cognitive-behavioral therapy) work from the top down as well, influencing the brain activity of the frontal lobes.

4. **Talia is convinced the "anxiety-relief" herbal tea she ordered online has improved her mental health over the past few weeks. What other explanations might account for Talia's improvement?**
   ANSWER: This untested alternative therapy may seem effective for many reasons. Talia's relief from anxiety may be due to her strong expectation that the tea would work (the *placebo effect*). She may have ordered the tea during a particularly tough time, and her anxiety may now have lessened naturally *(spontaneous recovery)*. And feeling the need to self-justify the money and time she has spent on this alternative remedy, Talia may be convincing herself it was worth the effort. Ultimately, a controlled research study (such as a randomized clinical trial) would be needed to objectively measure the effectiveness of this or any other alternative therapy.

CHAPTER 15 Social Psychology

1. **Driving to school one wintry day, Marco narrowly misses a car that slides through a red light. "Slow down! What a terrible driver," he thinks to himself. Moments later, Marco himself slips through an intersection and yelps, "Wow! These roads are awful. The city snow plows need to get out here." What social psychology principle has Marco just demonstrated? Explain.**
   ANSWER: By attributing the other person's behavior to the person ("he's a terrible driver") and his own to the situation ("these roads are awful"), Marco has exhibited the fundamental attribution error.

2. **Jamal's therapist has suggested that Jamal should "act as if" he is confident, even though he feels insecure and shy. Which social psychological theory would best support this suggestion, and what might the therapist be hoping to achieve?**
   ANSWER: Cognitive dissonance theory best supports this suggestion. If Jamal acts confident, his behavior will contradict his negative self-thoughts, creating cognitive dissonance. To relieve the tension, Jamal may realign his attitudes with his actions by viewing himself as more outgoing and confident.

3. **Dr. Huang, a popular music professor whose classes are always jam-packed, delivers riveting lectures on music history but gets nervous and often makes mistakes when describing exam statistics in front of the class. Why does his performance vary by task?**
   ANSWER: The presence of a large audience generates arousal and strengthens Dr. Huang's most likely response: enhanced performance on a task he has mastered (expertise in music history) and impaired performance on a task he finds difficult (statistics).

4. **Stacy, a Chicago Cubs fan who is normally a very calm and soft-hearted person, becomes wild with joy whenever the White Sox, a rival baseball team, loses a game. Why does Stacy take such pleasure in their losses?**

ANSWER: In this situation, social identity forces are influencing Stacy's thoughts and emotions, even more so than her enduring personality traits. As a Chicago Cubs fan, Stacy is a member of an ingroup that sets itself apart from an outgroup (White Sox fans). In such cases, ingroup bias tends to develop, leading to prejudice and the view that the outgroup is worthy of misfortune. This tendency is particularly strong when the two groups share many similarities, as is the case with these two Chicago baseball teams. So, when something bad happens to the White Sox (they lose a game), Stacy and other Cubs fans take pleasure in denigrating the Sox and viewing their failure as justified.

5. **Brittany, the president of the Psychology Club, needs assistance preparing for an upcoming fund-raising event. She made a plea for help in an e-mail she sent in a mass mailing to all 60 club members. So far, however, nobody has responded—either to help or not help. What might be the problem, and how could Brittany change her approach in the hope of getting people to respond and help?**

    ANSWER: People are less likely to help when they are part of a group. By sending one e-mail addressed to all members of the club, Brittany has created conditions that will foster diffusion of responsibility. With responsibility spread across all 60 members, each of them will feel less responsible for assisting Brittany—much as individuals feel less responsible for helping when they are in the presence of many other bystanders. Brittany may receive the assistance she needs if she sends a personal e-mail to each club member, which will make each person notice the problem, interpret it as a cry for help, and—hopefully—take responsibility for finding a solution.

A

absolute threshold the minimum stimulation needed to detect a particular stimulus 50 percent of the time. (p. 181)

accommodation adapting our current understandings (schemas) to incorporate new information. (p. 143)

accommodation the process by which the eye's lens changes shape to focus near or far objects on the retina. (p. 186)

achievement motivation a desire for significant accomplishment; for mastery of things, people, or ideas; for rapidly attaining a high standard. (p. B-7)

acquisition in classical conditioning, the initial stage, when one links a neutral stimulus and an unconditioned stimulus so that the neutral stimulus begins triggering the conditioned response. In operant conditioning, the strengthening of a reinforced response. (p. 230)

action potential a neural impulse; a brief electrical charge that travels down an axon. (p. 36)

active listening empathic listening in which the listener echoes, restates, and clarifies. A feature of Rogers' client-centered therapy. (p. 496)

adaptation-level phenomenon our tendency to form judgments (of sounds, of lights, of income) relative to a neutral level defined by our prior experience. (p. 395)

addiction compulsive drug craving and use, despite adverse consequences. (p. 88)

adolescence the transition period from childhood to adulthood, extending from puberty to independence. (p. 154)

adrenal [ah-DREEN-el] **glands** a pair of endocrine glands that sit just above the kidneys and secrete hormones (epinephrine and norepinephrine) that help arouse the body in times of stress. (p. 43)

aerobic exercise sustained exercise that increases heart and lung fitness; may also alleviate depression and anxiety. (p. 411)

aggression any physical or verbal behavior intended to hurt or destroy someone. (pp. 127, 548)

algorithm a methodical, logical rule or procedure that guarantees solving a particular problem. Contrasts with the usually speedier—but also more error-prone—use of *heuristics*. (p. 292)

alpha waves the relatively slow brain waves of a relaxed, awake state. (p. 72)

altruism unselfish regard for the welfare of others. (p. 561)

amnesia the loss of memory. (p. 269)

amphetamines drugs that stimulate neural activity, causing speeded-up body functions and associated energy and mood changes. (p. 91)

amygdala [uh-MIG-duh-la] two lima-bean-sized neural clusters in the limbic system; linked to emotion. (p. 48)

anorexia nervosa an eating disorder in which a person (usually an adolescent female) diets and becomes significantly (15 percent or more) underweight, yet, still feeling fat, continues to starve. (p. 348)

antianxiety drugs drugs used to control anxiety and agitation. (p. 514)

antidepressant drugs drugs used to treat depression; also increasingly prescribed for anxiety. Different types work by altering the availability of various neurotransmitters. (p. 514)

antipsychotic drugs drugs used to treat schizophrenia and other forms of severe thought disorder. (p. 513)

antisocial personality disorder a personality disorder in which the person (usually a man) exhibits a lack of conscience for wrongdoing, even toward friends and family members. May be aggressive and ruthless or a clever con artist. (p. 486)

anxiety disorders psychological disorders characterized by distressing, persistent anxiety or maladaptive behaviors that reduce anxiety. (p. 461)

aphasia impairment of language, usually caused by left-hemisphere damage either to Broca's area (impairing speaking) or to Wernicke's area (impairing understanding). (p. 54)

applied research scientific study that aims to solve practical problems. (p. 8)

assimilation interpreting our new experiences in terms of our existing schemas. (p. 143)

association areas areas of the cerebral cortex that are not involved in primary motor or sensory functions; rather, they are involved in higher mental functions such as learning, remembering, thinking, speaking, and integrating information. (p. 53)

associative learning learning that certain events occur together. The events may be two stimuli (as in classical conditioning) or a response and its consequences (as in operant conditioning). (p. 226)

attachment an emotional tie with another person; shown in young children by their seeking closeness to the caregiver and showing distress on separation. (p. 149)

attention-deficit hyperactivity disorder (ADHD) a psychological disorder marked by the appearance by age 7 of one or more of three key symptoms: extreme inattention, hyperactivity, and impulsivity. (p. 455)

attitude feelings, often influenced by our beliefs, that predispose us to respond in a particular way to objects, people, and events. (p. 527)

attribution theory the theory that we explain someone's behavior by crediting either the situation or the person's disposition. (p. 525)

audition the sense or act of hearing. (p. 193)

autism a disorder that appears in childhood and is marked by deficient communication, social interaction, and understanding of others' states of mind. (p. 146)

automatic processing unconscious encoding of incidental information, such as space, time, and frequency, and of well-learned information, such as word meanings. (p. 260)

autonomic [aw-tuh-NAHM-ik] **nervous system** the part of the peripheral nervous system that controls the glands and the muscles of the internal organs (such as the heart). Its sympathetic division arouses; its parasympathetic division calms. (p. 40)

availability heuristic estimating the likelihood of events based on their availability in memory; if instances come readily to mind (perhaps because of their vividness), we presume such events are common. (p. 295)

aversive conditioning a type of counterconditioning that associates an unpleasant state (such as nausea) with an unwanted behavior (such as drinking alcohol). (p. 499)

axon the neuron's extension that passes messages through its branching terminal fibers that form junctions with other neurons, muscles, or glands. (p. 35)

B

babbling stage beginning at about 4 months, the stage of speech development in which the infant spontaneously utters various sounds at first unrelated to the household language. (p. 303)

barbiturates drugs that depress the activity of the central nervous system, reducing anxiety but impairing memory and judgment. (p. 91)

basal metabolic rate the body's resting rate of energy expenditure. (p. 346)

basic research pure science that aims to increase the scientific knowledge base. (p. 8)

basic trust according to Erik Erikson, a sense that the world is predictable and trustworthy; said to be formed during infancy by appropriate experiences with responsive caregivers. (p. 152)

behavior genetics the study of the relative power and limits of genetic and environmental influences on behavior. (p. 105)

behavior therapy therapy that applies learning principles to the elimination of unwanted behaviors. (p. 497)

behaviorism the view that psychology (1) should be an objective science that (2) studies behavior without reference to mental processes. Most research psychologists today agree with (1) but not with (2). (pp. 4, 227)

belief perseverance clinging to one's initial conceptions after the basis on which they were formed has been discredited. (p. 297)

binge-eating disorder significant binge-eating episodes, followed by distress, disgust, or guilt, but without the compensatory purging, fasting, or excessive exercise that marks bulimia nervosa. (p. 348)

binocular cues depth cues, such as retinal disparity, that depend on the use of two eyes. (p. 207)

biological psychology the scientific study of the links between biological (genetic, neural, hormonal) and psychological processes. (Some biological psychologists call themselves *behavioral neuroscientists, neuropsychologists, behavior geneticists, physiological psychologists,* or *biopsychologists.*) (p. 35)

biomedical therapy prescribed medications or medical procedures that act directly on the patient's nervous system. (p. 512)

biopsychosocial approach an integrated approach that incorporates biological, psychological, and social-cultural levels of analysis. (p. 6)

bipolar disorder a mood disorder in which the person alternates between the hopelessness and lethargy of depression and the overexcited state of mania. (Formerly called *manic-depressive disorder.*) (p. 471)

blind spot the point at which the optic nerve leaves the eye, creating a "blind" spot because no receptor cells are located there. (p. 187)

bottom-up processing analysis that begins with the sensory receptors and works up to the brain's integration of sensory information. (p. 180)

brainstem the oldest part and central core of the brain, beginning where the spinal cord swells as it enters the skull; the brainstem is responsible for automatic survival functions. (p. 44)

Broca's area controls language expression; an area of the frontal lobe, usually in the left hemisphere, that directs the muscle movements involved in speech. (p. 54)

bulimia nervosa an eating disorder characterized by episodes of overeating, usually of high-calorie foods, followed by vomiting, laxative use, fasting, or excessive exercise. (p. 348)

bystander effect the tendency for any given bystander to be less likely to give aid if other bystanders are present. (p. 562)

C

Cannon-Bard theory the theory that an emotion-arousing stimulus simultaneously triggers (1) physiological responses and (2) the subjective experience of emotion. (p. 376)

case study an observation technique in which one person is studied in depth in the hope of revealing universal principles. (p. 15)

catharsis emotional release. In psychology, the catharsis hypothesis maintains that "releasing" aggressive energy (through action or fantasy) relieves aggressive urges. (p. 390)

central nervous system (CNS) the brain and spinal cord. (p. 39)

central route to persuasion occurs when interested people focus on the arguments and respond with favorable thoughts. (p. 528)

cerebellum [sehr-uh-BELL-um] the "little brain" at the rear of the brainstem; functions include some nonverbal learning, processing sensory input, and coordinating movement output and balance. (p. 46)

cerebral [seh-REE-bruhl] **cortex** the intricate fabric of interconnected neural cells covering the cerebral hemispheres; the body's ultimate control and information-processing center. (p. 50)

change blindness failing to notice changes in the environment. (p. 69)

chromosomes threadlike structures made of DNA molecules that contain the genes. (p. 106)

chunking organizing items into familiar, manageable units; often occurs automatically. (p. 264)

circadian [ser-KAY-dee-an] **rhythm** the biological clock; regular bodily rhythms (for example, of temperature and wakefulness) that occur on a 24-hour cycle. (p. 71)

classical conditioning a type of learning in which one learns to link two or more stimuli and anticipate events. (p. 227)

client-centered therapy a humanistic therapy, developed by Carl Rogers, in which the therapist uses techniques such as active listening within a genuine, accepting, empathic environment to facilitate clients' growth. (Also called *person-centered therapy.*) (p. 496)

clinical psychology a branch of psychology that studies, assesses, and treats people with psychological disorders. (p. 8)

cochlea [KOHK-lee-uh] a coiled, bony, fluid-filled tube in the inner ear through which sound waves trigger nerve impulses. (p. 194)

cognition the mental activities associated with thinking, knowing, remembering, and communicating. (pp. 142, 291)

cognitive dissonance theory the theory that we act to reduce the discomfort (dissonance) we feel when two of our thoughts (cognitions) are inconsistent. For example, when our awareness of our attitudes and of our actions clash, we can reduce the resulting dissonance by changing our attitudes. (p. 530)

cognitive map a mental representation of the layout of one's environment. For example, after exploring a maze, rats act as if they have learned a cognitive map of it. (p. 243)

cognitive neuroscience the interdisciplinary study of the brain activity linked with cognition (including perception, thinking, memory, and language). (p. 4)

cognitive therapy therapy that teaches people new, more adaptive ways of thinking and acting; based on the assumption that thoughts intervene between events and our emotional reactions. (p. 501)

cognitive-behavioral therapy a popular integrative therapy that combines cognitive therapy (changing self-defeating thinking) with behavior therapy (changing behavior). (p. 503)

collective unconscious Carl Jung's concept of a shared, inherited reservoir of memory traces from our species' history. (p. 424)

collectivism giving priority to group goals (often those of the extended family or work group) and defining one's identity accordingly. (p. 123)

color constancy perceiving familiar objects as having consistent color, even if changing illumination alters the wavelengths reflected by the object. (p. 212)

companionate love the deep affectionate attachment we feel for those with whom our lives are intertwined. (p. 560)

complementary and alternative medicine (CAM) as yet unproven health care treatments intended to supplement (complement) or serve as alternatives to conventional medicine, and which typically are not widely taught in medical schools, used in hospitals, or reimbursed by insurance companies. When research shows a therapy to be safe and effective, it usually then becomes part of accepted medical practice. (p. 406)

concept a mental grouping of similar objects, events, ideas, or people. (p. 291)

concrete operational stage in Piaget's theory, the stage of cognitive development (from about 6 or 7 to 11 years of age) during which children gain the mental operations that enable them to think logically about concrete events. (p. 146)

conditioned reinforcer a stimulus that gains its reinforcing power through its association with a primary reinforcer; also known as a *secondary reinforcer.* (p. 239)

conditioned response (CR) in classical conditioning, the learned response to a previously neutral (but now conditioned) stimulus (CS). (p. 229)

conditioned stimulus (CS) in classical conditioning, a previously neutral stimulus that, after association with an unconditioned stimulus (US), comes to trigger a conditioned response. (p. 229)

cones retinal receptor cells that are concentrated near the center of the retina and that function in daylight or in well-lit conditions. The cones detect fine detail and give rise to color sensations. (p. 186)

confirmation bias a tendency to search for information that supports our preconceptions and to ignore or distort contradictory evidence. (p. 293)

conflict a perceived incompatibility of actions, goals, or ideas. (p. 563)

conformity adjusting one's behavior or thinking to coincide with a group standard. (p. 533)

consciousness our awareness of ourselves and our environment. (p. 65)

conservation the principle (which Piaget believed to be a part of concrete operational reasoning) that properties such as mass, volume, and number remain the same despite changes in the forms of objects. (p. 144)

content validity the extent to which a test samples the behavior that is of interest. (p. 322)

continuous reinforcement reinforcing the desired response every time it occurs. (p. 240)

control group in an experiment, the group that is *not* exposed to the treatment; contrasts with the experimental group and serves as a comparison for evaluating the effect of the treatment. (p. 22)

conversion disorder a rare somatoform disorder in which a person experiences very specific genuine physical symptoms for which no physiological basis can be found. (p. 468)

coping alleviating stress using emotional, cognitive, or behavioral methods. (p. 408)

coronary heart disease the clogging of the vessels that nourish the heart muscle; the leading cause of death in many developed countries. (p. 402)

corpus callosum [KOR-pus kah-LOW-sum] the large band of neural fibers connecting the two brain hemispheres and carrying messages between them. (p. 57)

correlation coefficient a statistical measure of the extent to which two factors vary together, and thus of how well either factor predicts the other. Scores with a positive correlation coefficient go up and down together (as with high school and college GPAs). A negative correlation coefficient indicates that one score falls as the other rises (as in the relationship between self-esteem and depression). (pp. 18, A-4)

correlation the extent to which two factors vary together, and thus of how well either factor predicts the other. The *correlation coefficient* is the mathematical expression of the relationship, ranging from -1 to +1. (p. 18)

counseling psychology a branch of psychology that assists people with problems in living (often related to school, work, or marriage) and in achieving greater well-being. (p. 8)

counterconditioning a behavior therapy procedure that uses classical conditioning to evoke new responses to stimuli that are triggering unwanted behaviors; includes *exposure therapies* and *aversive conditioning*. (p. 498)

creativity the ability to produce novel and valuable ideas. (p. 317)

critical period an optimal period shortly after birth when an organism's exposure to certain stimuli or experiences produces proper development. (p. 150)

critical thinking thinking that does not blindly accept arguments and conclusions. Rather, it examines assumptions, discerns hidden values, evaluates evidence, and assesses conclusions. (p. 13)

cross-sectional study a study in which people of different ages are compared with one another. (p. A-7)

crystallized intelligence our accumulated knowledge and verbal skills; tends to increase with age. (p. 167)

culture the enduring behaviors, ideas, attitudes, values, and traditions shared by a group of people and transmitted from one generation to the next. (pp. 25, 121)

D

defense mechanisms in psychoanalytic theory, the ego's protective methods of reducing anxiety by unconsciously distorting reality. (p. 423)

deindividuation the loss of self-awareness and self-restraint occurring in group situations that foster arousal and anonymity. (p. 539)

déjà vu that eerie sense that "I've experienced this before." Cues from the current situation may subconsciously trigger retrieval of an earlier experience. (p. 275)

delta waves the large, slow brain waves associated with deep sleep. (p. 73)

delusions false beliefs, often of persecution or grandeur, that may accompany psychotic disorders. (p. 480)

dendrite the neuron's bushy, branching extensions that receive messages and conduct impulses toward the cell body. (p. 35)

dependent variable the outcome factor; the variable that may change in response to manipulations of the independent variable. (p. 23)

depressants drugs (such as alcohol, barbiturates, and opiates) that reduce neural activity and slow body functions. (p. 89)

depth perception the ability to see objects in three dimensions although the images that strike the retina are two-dimensional; allows us to judge distance. (p. 207)

developmental psychology a branch of psychology that studies physical, cognitive, and social change throughout the life span. (p. 137)

difference threshold the minimum difference between two stimuli required for detection 50 percent of the time. We experience the difference threshold as a *just noticeable difference* (or *jnd*). (p. 182)

discrimination in classical conditioning, the learned ability to distinguish between a conditioned stimulus and stimuli that do not signal an unconditioned stimulus. (p. 232)

discrimination unjustifiable negative behavior toward a group and its members. (p. 542)

dissociation a split in consciousness, which allows some thoughts and behaviors to occur simultaneously with others. (p. 86)

dissociative disorders disorders in which conscious awareness becomes separated (dissociated) from previous memories, thoughts, and feelings. (p. 468)

dissociative identity disorder (DID) a rare dissociative disorder in which a person exhibits two or more distinct and alternating personalities. Formerly called *multiple personality disorder*. (p. 469)

DNA (deoxyribonucleic acid) a complex molecule containing the genetic information that makes up the chromosomes. (p. 106)

double-blind procedure an experimental procedure in which both the research participants and the research staff are ignorant (blind) about whether the research participants have received the treatment or a placebo. Commonly used in drug-evaluation studies. (p. 22)

Down syndrome a condition of mild to severe intellectual disability and associated physical disorders caused by an extra copy of chromosome 21. (p. 322)

dream a sequence of images, emotions, and thoughts passing through a sleeping person's mind. Dreams are notable for their hallucinatory imagery, discontinuities, and incongruities, and for the dreamer's delusional acceptance of the content and later difficulties remembering it. (p. 80)

drive-reduction theory the idea that a physiological need creates an aroused tension state (a drive) that motivates an organism to satisfy the need. (p. 340)

DSM-IV-TR the American Psychiatric Association's *Diagnostic and Statistical Manual of Mental Disorders,* Fourth Edition, with an updated "text revision"; a widely used system for classifying psychological disorders. (p. 457)

dual processing the principle that information is often simultaneously processed on separate conscious and unconscious tracks. (p. 67)

E

echoic memory a momentary sensory memory of auditory stimuli; if attention is elsewhere, sounds and words can still be recalled within 3 or 4 seconds. (p. 266)

eclectic approach an approach to psychotherapy that, depending on the client's problems, uses techniques from various forms of therapy. (p. 493)

Ecstasy (MDMA) a synthetic stimulant and mild hallucinogen. Produces euphoria and social intimacy, but with short-term health risks and longer-term harm to serotonin-producing neurons and to mood and cognition. (p. 95)

effortful processing encoding that requires attention and conscious effort. (p. 260)

ego the largely conscious, "executive" part of personality that, according to Freud, mediates among the demands of the id, superego, and reality. The ego operates on the *reality principle*, satisfying the id's desires in ways that will realistically bring pleasure rather than pain. (p. 421)

egocentrism in Piaget's theory, the preoperational child's difficulty taking another's point of view. (p. 145)

electroconvulsive therapy (ECT) a biomedical therapy for severely depressed patients in which a brief electric current is sent through the brain of an anesthetized patient. (p. 516)

electroencephalogram (EEG) an amplified recording of the waves of electrical activity that sweep across the brain's surface. These waves are measured by electrodes placed on the scalp. (p. 45)

embryo the developing human organism from about 2 weeks after fertilization through the second month. (p. 138)

emerging adulthood for some people in modern cultures, a period from the late teens to mid-twenties, bridging the gap between adolescent dependence and full independence and responsible adulthood. (p. 162)

emotion a response of the whole organism, involving (1) physiological arousal, (2) expressive behaviors, and (3) consciously experienced thoughts and feelings. (p. 376)

emotion-focused coping attempting to alleviate stress by avoiding or ignoring a stressor and attending to emotional needs related to one's stress reaction. (p. 408)

emotional intelligence the ability to perceive, understand, manage, and use emotions. (p. 318)

empirically derived test a test (such as the MMPI) developed by testing a pool of items and then selecting those that discriminate between groups. (p. 434)

encoding the processing of information into the memory system—for example, by extracting meaning. (p. 258)

endocrine [EN-duh-krin] **system** the body's "slow" chemical communication system; a set of glands that secrete hormones into the bloodstream. (p. 42)

endorphins [en-DOR-fins] "morphine within"—natural, opiatelike neurotransmitters linked to pain control and to pleasure. (p. 38)

environment every nongenetic influence, from prenatal nutrition to the people and things around us. (p. 105)

equity a condition in which people receive from a relationship in proportion to what they give to it. (p. 560)

estrogens sex hormones, such as estradiol, secreted in greater amounts by females than by males and contributing to female sex characteristics. In nonhuman female mammals, estrogen levels peak during ovulation, promoting sexual receptivity. (p. 358)

evidence-based practice clinical decision-making that integrates the best available research with clinical expertise and patient characteristics and preferences. (p. 507)

evolutionary psychology the study of the roots of behavior and mental processes, using the principles of natural selection. (p. 113)

experiment a research method in which an investigator manipulates one or more factors (independent variables) to observe the effect on some behavior or mental process (the dependent variable). By *random assignment* of participants, the experimenter aims to control other relevant factors. (p. 22)

experimental group in an experiment, the group that is exposed to the treatment, that is, to one version of the independent variable. (p. 22)

explicit memory memory of facts and experiences that one can consciously know and "declare." (Also called *declarative memory*.) (p. 271)

exposure therapies behavioral techniques, such as systematic desensitization, that treat anxieties by exposing people (in imagination or actuality) to the things they fear and avoid. (p. 498)

external locus of control the perception that chance or outside forces beyond your personal control determine your fate. (p. 441)

extinction the diminishing of a conditioned response; occurs in classical conditioning when an unconditioned stimulus (US) does not follow a conditioned stimulus (CS); occurs in operant conditioning when a response is no longer reinforced. (p. 231)

extrasensory perception (ESP) the controversial claim that perception can occur apart from sensory input; includes telepathy, clairvoyance, and precognition. (p. 218)

F

factor analysis a statistical procedure that identifies clusters of related items (called *factors*) on a test; used to identify different dimensions of performance that underlie a person's total score. (p. 314)

family therapy therapy that treats the family as a system. Views an individual's unwanted behaviors as influenced by, or directed at, other family members. (p. 188)

feature detectors nerve cells in the brain that respond to specific features of a stimulus, such as shape, angle, or movement. (p. 188)

feel-good, do-good phenomenon people's tendency to be helpful when already in a good mood. (p. 392)

fetal alcohol syndrome (FAS) physical and cognitive abnormalities in children caused by a pregnant woman's heavy drinking. In severe cases, symptoms include noticeable facial misproportions. (p. 139)

fetus the developing human organism from 9 weeks after conception to birth. (p. 138)

figure-ground the organization of the visual field into objects (the *figures*) that stand out from their surroundings (the *ground*). (p. 205)

fixation according to Freud, a lingering focus of pleasure-seeking energies at an earlier psychosexual stage, in which conflicts were unresolved. (p. 422)

fixation the inability to see a problem from a new perspective, by employing a different mental set. (p. 294)

fixed-interval schedule in operant conditioning, a reinforcement schedule that reinforces a response only after a specified time has elapsed. (p. 240)

fixed-ratio schedule in operant conditioning, a reinforcement schedule that reinforces a response only after a specified number of responses. (p. 240)

flashbulb memory a clear memory of an emotionally significant moment or event. (p. 269)

flow a completely involved, focused state of consciousness, with diminished awareness of self and time, resulting from optimal engagement of one's skills. (p. B-1)

fluid intelligence our ability to reason speedily and abstractly; tends to decrease during late adulthood. (p. 167)

fMRI (functional MRI) a technique for revealing bloodflow and, therefore, brain activity by comparing successive MRI scans. fMRI scans show brain function. (p. 45)

foot-in-the-door phenomenon the tendency for people who have first agreed to a small request to comply later with a larger request. (p. 528)

formal operational stage in Piaget's theory, the stage of cognitive development (normally beginning about age 12) during which people begin to think logically about abstract concepts. (p. 148)

fovea the central focal point in the retina, around which the eye's cones cluster. (p. 188)

framing the way an issue is posed; how an issue is framed can significantly affect decisions and judgments. (p. 300)

fraternal twins twins who develop from separate fertilized eggs. They are genetically no closer than brothers and sisters, but they share a fetal environment. (p. 107)

free association in psychoanalysis, a method of exploring the unconscious in which the person relaxes and says whatever comes to mind, no matter how trivial or embarrassing. (p. 420)

frequency the number of complete wavelengths that pass a point in a given time (for example, per second). (p. 193)

frontal lobes portion of the cerebral cortex lying just behind the forehead; involved in speaking and muscle movements and in making plans and judgments. (p. 50)

frustration-aggression principle the principle that frustration—the blocking of an attempt to achieve some goal—creates anger, which can generate aggression. (p. 549)

fundamental attribution error the tendency for observers, when analyzing another's behavior, to underestimate the impact of the situation and to overestimate the impact of personal disposition. (p. 526)

G

gate-control theory the theory that the spinal cord contains a neurological "gate" that blocks pain signals or allows them to pass on to the brain. The "gate" is opened by the activity of pain signals traveling up small nerve fibers and is closed by activity in larger fibers or by information coming from the brain. (p. 199)

gender identity our sense of being male or female. (p. 131)

gender in psychology, the biologically and socially influenced characteristics by which people define *male* and *female*. (p. 115)

gender role a set of expected behaviors for males or for females. (p. 130)

gender-typing the acquisition of a traditional masculine or feminine role. (p. 131)

general adaptation syndrome (GAS) Selye's concept of the body's adaptive response to stress in three states—alarm, resistance, exhaustion. (p. 399)

general intelligence *(g)* a general intelligence factor that, according to Spearman and others, underlies specific mental abilities and is therefore measured by every task on an intelligence test. (p. 314)

generalization the tendency, once a response has been conditioned, for stimuli similar to the conditioned stimulus to elicit similar responses. (p. 231)

generalized anxiety disorder an anxiety disorder in which a person is continually tense, apprehensive, and in a state of autonomic nervous system arousal. (p. 462)

genes the biochemical units of heredity that make up the chromosomes; a segment of DNA capable of synthesizing a protein. (p. 106)

gestalt an organized whole. Gestalt psychologists emphasized our tendency to integrate pieces of information into meaningful wholes. (p. 205)

glucose the form of sugar that circulates in the blood and provides the major source of energy for body tissues. When its level is low, we feel hunger. (p. 344)

GRIT Graduated and Reciprocated Initiatives in Tension—Reduction—a strategy designed to decrease international tensions. (p. 567)

group polarization the enhancement of a group's prevailing inclinations through discussion within the group. (p. 539)

grouping the perceptual tendency to organize stimuli into coherent groups. (p. 206)

groupthink the mode of thinking that occurs when the desire for harmony in a decision-making group overrides a realistic appraisal of alternatives. (p. 540)

H

hallucinations false sensory experiences, such as seeing something in the absence of an external visual stimulus. (p. 72)

hallucinogens psychedelic ("mind-manifesting") drugs, such as LSD, that distort perceptions and evoke sensory images in the absence of sensory input. (p. 95)

heritability the proportion of variation among individuals that we can attribute to genes. The heritability of a trait may vary, depending on the range of populations and environments studied. (p. 327)

heuristic a simple thinking strategy that often allows us to make judgments and solve problems efficiently; usually speedier but also more error-prone than *algorithms*. (p. 292)

hierarchy of needs Maslow's pyramid of human needs, beginning at the base with physiological needs that must first be satisfied before higher-level safety needs and then psychological needs become active. (p. 342)

higher-order conditioning a procedure in which the conditioned stimulus in one conditioning experience is paired with a new neutral stimulus, creating a second (often weaker) conditioned stimulus. For example, an animal that has learned that a tone predicts food might then learn that a light predicts the tone and begin responding to the light alone. (Also called *second-order conditioning*.) (p. 230)

hindsight bias the tendency to believe, after learning an outcome, that we would have foreseen it. (Also known as the *I-knew-it-all-along phenomenon*.) (p. 10)

hippocampus a neural center that is located in the limbic system; helps process explicit memories for storage. (p. 271)

homeostasis a tendency to maintain a balanced or constant internal state; the regulation of any aspect of body chemistry, such as blood glucose, around a particular level. (p. 341)

hormones chemical messengers that are manufactured by the endocrine glands, travel through the bloodstream, and affect other tissues. (p. 42)

hue the dimension of color that is determined by the wavelength of light; what we know as the color names *blue, green,* and so forth. (p. 185)

human factors psychology a branch of psychology that explores how people and machines interact and how machines and physical environments can be made safe and easy to use. (p. B-2)

humanistic psychology historically significant perspective that emphasized the growth potential of healthy people and the individual's potential for personal growth. (p. 4)

hypnosis a social interaction in which one person (the hypnotist) suggests to another (the subject) that certain perceptions, feelings, thoughts, or behaviors will spontaneously occur. (p. 84)

hypochondriasis a somatoform disorder in which a person interprets normal physical sensations as symptoms of a disease. (p. 468)

hypothalamus [hi-po-THAL-uh-muss] a neural structure lying below *(hypo)* the thalamus; it directs several maintenance activities (eating, drinking, body temperature), helps govern the endocrine system via the pituitary gland, and is linked to emotion and reward. (p. 48)

hypothesis a testable prediction, often implied by a theory. (p. 14)

I

iconic memory a momentary sensory memory of visual stimuli; a photographic or picture-image memory lasting no more than a few tenths of a second. (p. 266)

id contains a reservoir of unconscious psychic energy that, according to Freud, strives to satisfy basic sexual and aggressive drives. The id operates on the *pleasure principle*, demanding immediate gratification. (p. 421)

identical twins twins who develop from a single fertilized egg that splits in two, creating two genetically identical organisms. (p. 107)

identification the process by which, according to Freud, children incorporate their parents' values into their developing superegos. (p. 422)

identity our sense of self; according to Erikson, the adolescent's task is to solidify a sense of self by testing and integrating various roles. (p. 159)

illusory correlation the perception of a relationship where none exists. (p. 19)

imagery mental pictures; a powerful aid to effortful processing, especially when combined with encoding. (p. 263)

implicit memory retention independent of conscious recollection. (Also called *nondeclarative memory*.) (p. 270)

imprinting the process by which certain animals form attachments during a critical period very early in life. (p. 150)

inattentional blindness failing to see visible objects when our attention is directed elsewhere. (p. 69)

incentive a positive or negative environmental stimulus that motivates behavior. (p. 341)

independent variable the experimental factor that is manipulated; the variable whose effect is being studied. (p. 22)

individualism giving priority to one's own goals over group goals and defining one's identity in terms of personal attributes rather than group identifications. (p. 123)

industrial-organizational (I/O) psychology the application of psychological concepts and methods to optimizing human behavior in workplaces. (p. B-2)

informational social influence influence resulting from one's willingness to accept others' opinions about reality. (p. 534)

ingroup "Us"—people with whom we share a common identity. (p. 545)

ingroup bias the tendency to favor our own group. (p. 546)

inner ear the innermost part of the ear, containing the cochlea, semicircular canals, and vestibular sacs. (p. 194)

insight a sudden and often novel realization of the solution to a problem; it contrasts with strategy-based solutions. (p. 292)

insight therapies a variety of therapies which aim to improve psychological functioning by increasing the client's awareness of underlying motives and defenses. (p. 495)

insomnia recurring problems in falling or staying asleep. (p. 78)

instinct a complex behavior that is rigidly patterned throughout a species and is unlearned. (p. 340)

intellectual disability (formerly called mental retardation) a condition of limited mental ability, indicated by an intelligence score of 70 or below and difficulty in adapting to the demands of life; varies from mild to profound. (p. 322)

intelligence mental quality consisting of the ability to learn from experience, solve problems, and use knowledge to adapt to new situations. (p. 313)

intelligence quotient (IQ) defined originally as the ratio of mental age *(ma)* to chronological age *(ca)* multiplied by 100 (thus, IQ = *ma/ca* × 100). On contemporary intelligence tests, the average performance for a given age is assigned a score of 100. (p. 319)

intelligence test a method for assessing an individual's mental aptitudes and comparing them with those of others, using numerical scores. (p. 319)

intensity the amount of energy in a light or sound wave, which we perceive as brightness or loudness, as determined by the wave's amplitude. (p. 185)

interaction the interplay that occurs when the effect of one factor (such as environment) depends on another factor (such as heredity). (p. 111)

internal locus of control the perception that you control your own fate. (p. 441)

interneurons neurons within the brain and spinal cord that communicate internally and intervene between the sensory inputs and motor outputs. (p. 39)

interpretation in psychoanalysis, the analyst's noting supposed dream meanings, resistances, and other significant behaviors and events in order to promote insight. (p. 494)

intuition an effortless, immediate, automatic feeling or thought, as contrasted with explicit, conscious reasoning. (p. 298)

J

James-Lange theory the theory that our experience of emotion is our awareness of our physiological responses to emotion-arousing stimuli. (p. 376)

just-world phenomenon the tendency for people to believe the world is just and that people therefore get what they deserve and deserve what they get. (p. 545)

K

kinesthesis [kin-ehs-THEE-sehs] the system for sensing the position and movement of individual body parts. (p. 197)

L

language our spoken, written, or signed words and the ways we combine them to communicate meaning. (p. 302)

latent content according to Freud, the underlying meaning of a dream (as distinct from its manifest content). (p. 81)

latent learning learning that occurs but is not apparent until there is an incentive to demonstrate it. (p. 243)

law of effect Thorndike's principle that behaviors followed by favorable consequences become more likely. (p. 237)

learned helplessness the hopelessness and passive resignation an animal or human learns when unable to avoid repeated aversive events. (p. 441)

learning a relatively permanent change in an organism's behavior due to experience. (p. 225)

lesion [LEE-zhuhn] tissue destruction. A brain lesion is a naturally or experimentally caused destruction of brain tissue. (p. 44)

levels of analysis the differing complementary views, from biological to psychological to social-cultural, for analyzing any given phenomenon. (p. 6)

limbic system neural system (including the *hippocampus, amygdala,* and *hypothalamus*) located below the cerebral hemispheres; associated with emotions and drives. (p. 47)

linguistic determinism Whorf's hypothesis that language determines the way we think. (p. 306)

lobotomy a now-rare psychosurgical procedure once used to calm uncontrollably emotional or violent patients. The procedure cut the nerves connecting the frontal lobes to the emotion-controlling centers of the inner brain. (p. 519)

longitudinal study research in which the same people are restudied and retested over a long period of time. (p. A-7)

long-term memory the relatively permanent and limitless storehouse of the memory system. Includes knowledge, skills, and experiences. (p. 258)

long-term potentiation (LTP) an increase in a synapse's firing potential after brief, rapid stimulation. Believed to be a neural basis for learning and memory. (p. 268)

LSD a powerful hallucinogenic drug; also known as acid *(lysergic acid diethylamide)*. (p. 95)

lymphocytes the two types of white blood cells that are part of the body's immune system: *B lymphocytes* form in the *b*one marrow and release antibodies that fight bacterial infections; *T lymphocytes* form in the *t*hymus and other lymphatic tissue and attack cancer cells, viruses, and foreign substances. (p. 403)

M

major depressive disorder a mood disorder in which a person experiences, in the absence of drugs or a medical condition, two or more weeks of significantly depressed moods, feelings of worthlessness, and diminished interest or pleasure in most activities. (p. 471)

mania a mood disorder marked by a hyperactive, wildly optimistic state. (p. 471)

manifest content according to Freud, the remembered story line of a dream (as distinct from its latent, or hidden, content). (p. 81)

maturation biological growth processes that enable orderly changes in behavior, relatively uninfluenced by experience. (p. 140)

mean the arithmetic average of a distribution, obtained by adding the scores and then dividing by the number of scores. (p. A-1)

median the middle score in a distribution; half the scores are above it and half are below it. (p. A-1)

medical model the concept that diseases, in this case psychological disorders, have physical causes that can be *diagnosed, treated,* and, in most cases, *cured,* often through *treatment* in a hospital. (p. 456)

medulla [muh-DUL-uh] the base of the brainstem; controls heartbeat and breathing. (p. 45)

memory the persistence of learning over time through the storage and retrieval of information. (p. 257)

menarche [meh-NAR-key] the first menstrual period. (p. 155)

menopause the time of natural cessation of menstruation; also refers to the biological changes a woman experiences as her ability to reproduce declines. (p. 164)

mental age a measure of intelligence test performance devised by Binet; the chronological age that most typically corresponds to a given level of performance. Thus, a child who does as well as the average 8-year-old is said to have a mental age of 8. (p. 319)

mental set a tendency to approach a problem in one particular way, often a way that has been successful in the past. (p. 294)

mere exposure effect the phenomenon that repeated exposure to novel stimuli increases liking of them. (p. 556)

methamphetamine a powerfully addictive drug that stimulates the central nervous system, with speeded-up body functions and associated energy and mood changes; over time, appears to reduce baseline dopamine levels. (p. 91)

middle ear the chamber between the eardrum and cochlea containing three tiny bones (hammer, anvil, and stirrup) that concentrate the vibrations of the eardrum on the cochlea's oval window. (p. 194)

Minnesota Multiphasic Personality Inventory (MMPI) the most widely researched and clinically used of all personality tests. Originally developed to identify emotional disorders (still considered its most appropriate use), this test is now used for many other screening purposes. (p. 433)

mirror neurons frontal lobe neurons that fire when performing certain actions or when observing another doing so. The brain's mirroring of another's action may enable imitation and empathy. (p. 248)

mirror-image perceptions mutual views often held by conflicting people, as when each side sees itself as ethical and peaceful and views the other side as evil and aggressive. (p. 564)

misinformation effect incorporating misleading information into one's memory of an event. (p. 282)

mnemonics [nih-MON-iks] memory aids, especially those techniques that use vivid imagery and organizational devices. (p. 263)

mode the most frequently occurring score(s) in a distribution. (p. A-1)

modeling the process of observing and imitating a specific behavior. (p. 248)

monocular cues depth cues, such as interposition and linear perspective, available to either eye alone. (p. 208)

mood disorders psychological disorders characterized by emotional extremes. See *major depressive disorder, mania,* and *bipolar disorder.* (p. 470)

mood-congruent memory the tendency to recall experiences that are consistent with one's current good or bad mood. (p. 275)

motivation a need or desire that energizes and directs behavior. (p. 339)

motor cortex an area at the rear of the frontal lobes that controls voluntary movements. (p. 51)

motor neurons neurons that carry outgoing information from the brain and spinal cord to the muscles and glands. (p. 39)

MRI (magnetic resonance imaging) a technique that uses magnetic fields and radio waves to produce computer-generated images of soft tissue. MRI scans show brain anatomy. (p. 45)

mutation a random error in gene replication that leads to a change. (p. 113)

N

narcolepsy a sleep disorder characterized by uncontrollable sleep attacks. The sufferer may lapse directly into REM sleep, often at inopportune times. (p. 78)

natural selection the principle that, among the range of inherited trait variations, those that lead to increased reproduction and survival will most likely be passed on to succeeding generations. (p. 113)

naturalistic observation observing and recording behavior in naturally occurring situations without trying to manipulate and control the situation. (p. 17)

nature-nurture issue the longstanding controversy over the relative contributions that genes and experience make to the development of psychological traits and behaviors. Today's science sees traits and behaviors arising from the interaction of nature and nurture. (p. 5)

near-death experience an altered state of consciousness reported after a close brush with death (such as through cardiac arrest); often similar to drug-induced hallucinations. (p. 95)

negative reinforcement increasing behaviors by stopping or reducing negative stimuli. A negative reinforcer is any stimulus that, when *removed* after a response, strengthens the response. (Note: negative reinforcement is not punishment.) (p. 239)

nerves bundled axons that form neural "cables" connecting the central nervous system with muscles, glands, and sense organs. (p. 39)

nervous system the body's speedy, electrochemical communication network, consisting of all the nerve cells of the peripheral and central nervous systems. (p. 39)

neurogenesis the formation of new neurons. (p. 57)

neuron a nerve cell; the basic building block of the nervous system. (p. 35)

neurotransmitters chemical messengers that cross the synaptic gaps between neurons. When released by the sending neuron, neurotransmitters travel across the synapse and bind to receptor sites on the receiving neuron, thereby influencing whether that neuron will generate a neural impulse. (p. 37)

neutral stimulus (NS) in classical conditioning, a stimulus that elicits no response before conditioning. (p. 228)

night terrors a sleep disorder characterized by high arousal and an appearance of being terrified; unlike nightmares, night terrors occur during Stage 4 sleep, within two or three hours of falling asleep, and are seldom remembered. (p. 79)

norm an understood rule for accepted and expected behavior. Norms prescribe "proper" behavior. (p. 122)

normal curve (*normal distribution*) a symmetrical, bell-shaped curve that describes the distribution of many types of data; most scores fall near the mean (68 percent fall within one standard deviation of it) and fewer and fewer near the extremes. (pp. 321, A-3)

normal curve the symmetrical bell-shaped curve that describes the distribution of many physical and psychological attributes. Most scores fall near the average, and fewer and fewer scores lie near the extremes. (p. 321)

normative social influence influence resulting from a person's desire to gain approval or avoid disapproval. (p. 534)

O

object permanence the awareness that things continue to exist even when not perceived. (p. 144)

observational learning learning by observing others. (p. 248)

obsessive-compulsive disorder (OCD) an anxiety disorder characterized by unwanted repetitive thoughts (obsessions) and/or actions (compulsions). (p. 463)

occipital [ahk-SIP-uh-tuhl] **lobes** portion of the cerebral cortex lying at the back of the head; includes areas that receive information from the visual fields. (p. 50)

Oedipus [ED-uh-puss] **complex** according to Freud, a boy's sexual desires toward his mother and feelings of jealousy and hatred for the rival father. (p. 422)

one-word stage   the stage in speech development, from about age 1 to 2, during which a child speaks mostly in single words. (p. 303)

operant behavior   behavior that operates on the environment, producing consequences. (p. 236)

operant chamber   in operant conditioning research, a chamber (also known as a *Skinner box*) containing a bar or key that an animal can manipulate to obtain a food or water reinforcer; attached devices record the animal's rate of bar pressing or key pecking. (p. 237)

operant conditioning   a type of learning in which behavior is strengthened if followed by a reinforcer or diminished if followed by a punisher. (p. 236)

operational definition   a statement of the procedures (operations) used to define research variables. For example, *human intelligence* may be operationally defined as "what an intelligence test measures." (p. 15)

opiates   opium and its derivatives, such as morphine and heroin; they depress neural activity, temporarily lessening pain and anxiety. (p. 91)

opponent-process theory   the theory that opposing retinal processes (red-green, yellow-blue, white-black) enable color vision. For example, some cells are stimulated by green and inhibited by red; others are stimulated by red and inhibited by green. (p. 192)

optic nerve   the nerve that carries neural impulses from the eye to the brain. (p. 187)

organizational psychology   a subfield of I/O psychology that examines organizational influences on worker satisfaction and productivity and facilitates organizational change. (p. B-2)

other-race effect   the tendency to recall faces of one's own race more accurately than faces of other races. Also called the *cross-race effect* and the *own-race bias*. (p. 547)

outgroup   "Them"—those perceived as different or apart from our ingroup. (p. 545)

overconfidence   the tendency to be more confident than correct—to overestimate the accuracy of our beliefs and judgments. (p. 296)

P

panic disorder   an anxiety disorder marked by unpredictable minutes-long episodes of intense dread in which a person experiences terror and accompanying chest pain, choking, or other frightening sensations. (p. 462)

parallel processing   the processing of many aspects of a problem simultaneously; the brain's natural mode of information processing for many functions, including vision. Contrasts with the step-by-step (serial) processing of most computers and of conscious problem solving. (p. 190)

parapsychology   the study of paranormal phenomena, including ESP and psychokinesis. (p. 218)

parasympathetic nervous system   the division of the autonomic nervous system that calms the body, conserving its energy. (p. 40)

parietal [puh-RYE-uh-tuhl] **lobes**   portion of the cerebral cortex lying at the top of the head and toward the rear; receives sensory input for touch and body position. (p. 50)

partial (intermittent) reinforcement   reinforcing a response only part of the time; results in slower acquisition of a response but much greater resistance to extinction than does continuous reinforcement. (p. 240)

passionate love   an aroused state of intense positive absorption in another, usually present at the beginning of a love relationship. (p. 559)

perception   the process of organizing and interpreting sensory information, enabling us to recognize meaningful objects and events. (p. 180)

perceptual adaptation   in vision, the ability to adjust to an artificially displaced or even inverted visual field. (p. 214)

perceptual constancy   perceiving objects as unchanging (having consistent shapes, size, lightness, and color) even as illumination and retinal images change. (p. 210)

perceptual set   a mental predisposition to perceive one thing and not another. (p. 215)

peripheral nervous system (PNS)   the sensory and motor neurons that connect the central nervous system (CNS) to the rest of the body. (p. 39)

peripheral route to persuasion   occurs when people are influenced by incidental cues, such as a speaker's attractiveness. (p. 528)

personal control   the extent to which people perceive control over their environment rather than feeling helpless. (p. 440)

personal space   the buffer zone we like to maintain around our bodies. (p. 122)

personality   an individual's characteristic pattern of thinking, feeling, and acting. (p. 419)

personality disorders   psychological disorders characterized by inflexible and enduring behavior patterns that impair social functioning. (p. 486)

personality inventory   a questionnaire (often with *true-false* or *agree-disagree* items) on which people respond to items designed to gauge a wide range of feelings and behaviors; used to assess selected personality traits. (p. 433)

personnel psychology   a subfield of I/O psychology that focuses on employee recruitment, selection, placement, training, appraisal, and development. (p. B-2)

PET (positron emission tomography) scan   a visual display of brain activity that detects where a radioactive form of glucose goes while the brain performs a given task. (p. 45)

phobia   an anxiety disorder marked by a persistent, irrational fear and avoidance of a specific object or situation. (p. 462)

physical dependence   a physiological need for a drug, marked by unpleasant withdrawal symptoms when the drug is discontinued. (p. 88)

pitch   a tone's experienced highness or lowness; depends on frequency. (p. 193)

pituitary gland   the endocrine system's most influential gland. Under the influence of the hypothalamus, the pituitary regulates growth and controls other endocrine glands. (p. 43)

placebo [pluh-SEE-bo; Latin for "I shall please"] **effect**   experimental results caused by expectations alone; any effect on behavior caused by the administration of an inert substance or condition, which the recipient assumes is an active agent. (p. 22)

plasticity   the brain's ability to change, especially during childhood, by reorganizing after damage or by building new pathways based on experience. (p. 56)

polygraph   a machine, commonly used in attempts to detect lies, that measures several of the physiological responses accompanying emotion (such as perspiration and cardiovascular and breathing changes). (p. 380)

population   all the cases in a group being studied, from which samples may be drawn. (*Note:* Except for national studies, this does *not* refer to a country's whole population.) (p. 16)

positive psychology   the scientific study of optimal human functioning; aims to discover and promote strengths and virtues that enable individuals and communities to thrive. (p. 443)

positive reinforcement   increasing behaviors by presenting positive stimuli, such as food. A positive reinforcer is any stimulus that, when *presented* after a response, strengthens the response. (p. 239)

post-traumatic growth   positive psychological changes as a result of struggling with extremely challenging circumstances and life crises. (p. 465)

post-traumatic stress disorder (PTSD)   an anxiety disorder characterized by haunting memories, nightmares, social withdrawal, jumpy anxiety, and/or insomnia that lingers for four weeks or more after a traumatic experience. (p. 464)

posthypnotic suggestion   a suggestion, made during a hypnosis session, to be carried out after the subject is no longer hypnotized; used by some clinicians to help control undesired symptoms and behaviors. (p. 88)

predictive validity   the success with which a test predicts the behavior it is designed to predict; it is assessed by computing the correlation between test scores and the criterion behavior. (Also called *criterion-related validity*.) (p. 323)

prejudice   an unjustifiable (and usually negative) attitude toward a group and its members. Prejudice generally involves stereotyped beliefs, negative feelings, and a predisposition to discriminatory action. (p. 542)

preoperational stage   in Piaget's theory, the stage (from about 2 to 6 or 7 years of age) during which a child learns to use language but does not yet comprehend the mental operations of concrete logic. (p. 144)

primary reinforcer   an innately reinforcing stimulus, such as one that satisfies a biological need. (p. 239)

primary sex characteristics   the body structures (ovaries, testes, and external genitalia) that make sexual reproduction possible. (p. 155)

priming   the activation, often unconsciously, of certain associations, thus predisposing one's perception, memory, or response. (pp. 182, 274)

proactive interference   the disruptive effect of prior learning on the recall of new information. (p. 279)

problem-focused coping   attempting to alleviate stress directly—by changing the stressor or the way we interact with that stressor. (p. 408)

projective test   a personality test, such as the Rorschach or TAT, that provides ambiguous stimuli designed to trigger projection of one's inner dynamics. (p. 425)

prosocial behavior   positive, constructive, helpful behavior. The opposite of antisocial behavior. (p. 250)

prototype   a mental image or best example of a category. Matching new items to a prototype provides a quick and easy method for sorting items into categories (as when comparing feathered creatures to a prototypical bird, such as a robin). (p. 292)

psychiatry   a branch of medicine dealing with psychological disorders; practiced by physicians who sometimes provide medical (for example, drug) treatments as well as psychological therapy. (p. 8)

psychoactive drug   a chemical substance that alters perceptions and moods. (p. 88)

psychoanalysis   Freud's theory of personality and therapeutic techniques that attributes thoughts and actions to unconscious motives and conflicts. Freud believed the patient's free associations, resistances, dreams, and transferences—and the therapist's interpretations of them—release previously repressed feelings, allowing the patient to gain self-insight. (p. 494)

psychodynamic therapy   therapy deriving from the psychoanalytic tradition that views individuals as responding to unconscious forces and childhood experiences, and that seeks to enhance self-insight. (p. 495)

psychological dependence   a psychological need to use a drug, such as to relieve negative emotions. (p. 88)

psychological disorder   deviant, distressful, and dysfunctional patterns of thoughts, feelings, and actions. (p. 454)

psychology   the science of behavior and mental processes. (p. 4)

psychopharmacology   the study of the effects of drugs on mind and behavior. (p. 513)

psychophysics   the study of relationships between the physical characteristics of stimuli, such as their intensity, and our psychological experience of them. (p. 181)

psychophysiological illness   literally, "mind-body" illness; any stress-related physical illness, such as hypertension and some headaches. (p. 403)

psychosexual stages   the childhood stages of development (oral, anal, phallic, latency, genital) during which, according to Freud, the id's pleasure-seeking energies focus on distinct erogenous zones. (p. 422)

psychosurgery   surgery that removes or destroys brain tissue in an effort to change behavior. (p. 519)

psychotherapy   treatment involving psychological techniques; consists of interactions between a trained therapist and someone seeking to overcome psychological difficulties or achieve personal growth. (p. 494)

psychotic disorder   a psychological disorder in which a person loses contact with reality, experiencing irrational ideas and distorted perceptions. (p. 480)

puberty   the period of sexual maturation, during which a person becomes capable of reproducing. (p. 155)

punishment   an event that *decreases* the behavior it follows. (p. 241)

R

random assignment   assigning participants to experimental and control groups by chance, thus minimizing preexisting differences between those assigned to the different groups. (p. 22)

random sample   a sample that fairly represents a population because each member has an equal chance of inclusion. (p. 16)

range   the difference between the highest and lowest scores in a distribution. (p. A-3)

recall   a measure of memory in which the person must retrieve information learned earlier, as on a fill-in-the-blank test. (p. 273)

reciprocal determinism   the interacting influences of behavior, internal cognition, and environment. (p. 439)

reciprocity norm   an expectation that people will help, not hurt, those who have helped them. (p. 563)

recognition   a measure of memory in which the person need only identify items previously learned, as on a multiple-choice test. (p. 273)

reflex   a simple, automatic response to a sensory stimulus, such as the knee-jerk response. (p. 41)

refractory period   a resting period after orgasm, during which a man cannot achieve another orgasm. (p. 357)

regression toward the mean   the tendency for extreme or unusual scores or events to fall back (regress) toward the average. (p. A-6)

rehearsal   the conscious repetition of information, either to maintain it in consciousness or to encode it for storage. (p. 260)

reinforcer   in operant conditioning, any event that *strengthens* the behavior it follows. (p. 238)

relative deprivation   the perception that one is worse off relative to those with whom one compares oneself. (p. 395)

relearning   a measure of memory that assesses the amount of time saved when learning material for a second time. (p. 273)

reliability   the extent to which a test yields consistent results, as assessed by the consistency of scores on two halves of the test, or on retesting. (p. 321)

REM rebound   the tendency for REM sleep to increase following REM sleep deprivation (created by repeated awakenings during REM sleep). (p. 83)

REM sleep   rapid eye movement sleep; a recurring sleep stage during which vivid dreams commonly occur. Also known as *paradoxical sleep*, because the muscles are relaxed (except for minor twitches) but other body systems are active. (p. 72)

repetitive transcranial magnetic stimulation (rTMS)   the application of repeated pulses of magnetic energy to the brain; used to stimulate or suppress brain activity. (p. 518)

replication   repeating the essence of a research study, usually with different participants in different situations, to see whether the basic finding extends to other participants and circumstances. (p. 15)

representativeness heuristic   judging the likelihood of things in terms of how well they seem to represent, or match, particular prototypes; may lead us to ignore other relevant information. (p. 294)

repression   in psychoanalytic theory, the basic defense mechanism that banishes anxiety-arousing thoughts, feelings, and memories from consciousness. (pp. 281, 423)

resistance   in psychoanalysis, the blocking from consciousness of anxiety-laden material. (p. 494)

respondent behavior   behavior that occurs as an automatic response to some stimulus. (p. 236)

reticular formation   a nerve network in the brainstem that plays an important role in controlling arousal. (p. 46)

retina   the light-sensitive inner surface of the eye, containing the receptor rods and cones plus layers of neurons that begin the processing of visual information. (p. 186)

retinal disparity   a binocular cue for perceiving depth: By comparing images from the retinas in the two eyes, the brain computes distance—the greater the disparity (difference) between the two images, the closer the object. (p. 207)

retrieval the process of getting information out of memory storage. (p. 258)

retroactive interference the disruptive effect of new learning on the recall of old information. (p. 279)

rods retinal receptors that detect black, white, and gray; necessary for peripheral and twilight vision, when cones don't respond. (p. 186)

role a set of explanations (norms) about a social position, defining how those in the position ought to behave. (pp. 130, 529)

Rorschach inkblot test the most widely used projective test, a set of 10 inkblots, designed by Hermann Rorschach; seeks to identify people's inner feelings by analyzing their interpretations of the blots. (p. 425)

S

savant syndrome a condition in which a person otherwise limited in mental ability has an exceptional specific skill, such as in computation or drawing. (p. 314)

scapegoat theory the theory that prejudice offers an outlet for anger by providing someone to blame. (pp. 314, 547)

scatterplots a graphed cluster of dots, each of which represents the values of two variables. The slope of the points suggests the direction of the relationship between the two variables. The amount of scatter suggests the strength of the correlation (little scatter indicates high correlation). (p. A-4)

schema a concept or framework that organizes and interprets information. (p. 143)

schizophrenia a group of severe disorders characterized by disorganized and delusional thinking, disturbed perceptions, and inappropriate emotions and actions. (p. 480)

secondary sex characteristics nonreproductive sexual characteristics, such as female breasts and hips, male voice quality, and body hair. (p. 155)

selective attention the focusing of conscious awareness on a particular stimulus. (p. 68)

self in contemporary psychology, assumed to be the center of personality, the organizer of our thoughts, feelings, and actions. (p. 446)

self-actualization according to Maslow, one of the ultimate psychological needs that arises after basic physical and psychological needs are met and self-esteem is achieved; the motivation to fulfill one's potential. (p. 429)

self-concept all our thoughts and feelings about ourselves, in answer to the question, "Who am I?" (p. 431)

self-disclosure revealing intimate aspects of oneself to others. (p. 560)

self-esteem one's feelings of high or low self-worth. (p. 447)

self-serving bias a readiness to perceive oneself favorably. (p. 447)

sensation the process by which our sensory receptors and nervous system receive and represent stimulus energies from our environment. (p. 180)

sensorimotor stage in Piaget's theory, the stage (from birth to about 2 years of age) during which infants know the world mostly in terms of their sensory impressions and motor activities. (p. 144)

sensory adaptation diminished sensitivity as a consequence of constant stimulation. (p. 183)

sensory cortex area at the front of the parietal lobes that registers and processes body touch and movement sensations. (p. 52)

sensory interaction the principle that one sense may influence another, as when the smell of food influences its taste. (p. 202)

sensory memory the immediate, very brief recording of sensory information in the memory system. (p. 258)

sensory neurons neurons that carry incoming information from the sensory receptors to the brain and spinal cord. (p. 39)

serial position effect our tendency to recall best the last and first items in a list. (p. 261)

set point the point at which an individual's "weight thermostat" is supposedly set. When the body falls below this weight, an increase in hunger and a lowered metabolic rate may act to restore the lost weight. (p. 346)

sexual disorder a problem that consistently impairs sexual arousal or functioning. (p. 358)

sexual orientation an enduring sexual attraction toward members of either one's own sex (homosexual orientation) or the other sex (heterosexual orientation). (p. 363)

sexual response cycle the four stages of sexual responding described by Masters and Johnson—excitement, plateau, orgasm, and resolution. (p. 357)

shaping an operant conditioning procedure in which reinforcers guide behavior toward closer and closer approximations of the desired behavior. (p. 237)

short-term memory activated memory that holds a few items briefly, such as the seven digits of a phone number while dialing, before the information is stored or forgotten. (p. 258)

sleep apnea a sleep disorder characterized by temporary cessations of breathing during sleep and repeated momentary awakenings. (p. 79)

sleep periodic, natural loss of consciousness—as distinct from unconsciousness resulting from a coma, general anesthesia, or hibernation. (Adapted from Dement, 1999.) (p. 72)

social clock the culturally preferred timing of social events such as marriage, parenthood, and retirement. (p. 168)

social exchange theory the theory that our social behavior is an exchange process, the aim of which is to maximize benefits and minimize costs. (p. 562)

social facilitation stronger responses on simple or well-learned tasks in the presence of others. (p. 538)

social identity the "we" aspect of our self-concept; the part of our answer to "Who am I?" that comes from our group memberships. (p. 159)

social leadership group-oriented leadership that builds teamwork, mediates conflict, and offers support. (p. B-11)

social learning theory the theory that we learn social behavior by observing and imitating and by being rewarded or punished. (p. 131)

social loafing the tendency for people in a group to exert less effort when pooling their efforts toward attaining a common goal than when individually accountable. (p. 538)

social psychology the scientific study of how we think about, influence, and relate to one another. (p. 525)

social trap a situation in which the conflicting parties, by each rationally pursuing their self-interest, become caught in mutually destructive behavior. (p. 563)

social-cognitive perspective views behavior as influenced by the interaction between people's traits (including their thinking) and their social context. (p. 439)

social-responsibility norm an expectation that people will help those dependent upon them. (p. 563)

somatic nervous system the division of the peripheral nervous system that controls the body's skeletal muscles. Also called the *skeletal nervous system*. (p. 39)

somatoform disorder psychological disorder in which the symptoms take a somatic (bodily) form without apparent physical cause. (See *conversion disorder* and *hypochondriasis*.) (p. 468)

source amnesia attributing to the wrong source an event we have experienced, heard about, read about, or imagined. (Also called *source misattribution*.) Source amnesia, along with the misinformation effect, is at the heart of many false memories. (p. 283)

spacing effect the tendency for distributed study or practice to yield better long-term retention than is achieved through massed study or practice. (p. 261)

split brain a condition resulting from surgery that isolates the brain's two hemispheres by cutting the fibers (mainly those of the corpus callosum) connecting them. (p. 58)

spontaneous recovery the reappearance, after a pause, of an extinguished conditioned response. (p. 231)

spotlight effect overestimating others' noticing and evaluating our appearance, performance, and blunders (as if we presume a spotlight shines on us). (p. 446)

SQ3R a study method incorporating five steps: *Survey, Question, Read, Rehearse, Review.* (p. 29)

standard deviation a computed measure of how much scores vary around the mean score. (p. A-3)

standardization defining meaningful scores by comparison with the performance of a pretested group. (p. 321)

Stanford-Binet the widely used American revision (by Terman at Stanford University) of Binet's original intelligence test. (p. 319)

statistical significance a statistical statement of how likely it is that an obtained result occurred by chance. (p. A-7)

stereotype a generalized (sometimes accurate but often overgeneralized) belief about a group of people. (p. 542)

stereotype threat a self-confirming concern that one will be evaluated based on a negative stereotype. (p. 333)

stimulants drugs (such as caffeine, nicotine, amphetamines, and the even more powerful cocaine, Ecstasy, and methamphetamine) that excite neural activity and speed up body functions. (p. 91)

storage the retention of encoded information over time. (p. 258)

stranger anxiety the fear of strangers that infants commonly display, beginning by about 8 months of age. (p. 149)

stress the process by which we perceive and respond to certain events, called *stressors,* that we appraise as threatening or challenging. (p. 398)

structured interviews interview process that asks the same job-relevant questions of all applicants, each of whom is rated on established scales. (p. B-5)

subjective well-being self-perceived happiness or satisfaction with life. Used along with measures of objective well-being (for example, physical and economic indicators) to evaluate people's quality of life. (p. 392)

subliminal below one's absolute threshold for conscious awareness. (p. 181)

superego the part of personality that, according to Freud, represents internalized ideals and provides standards for judgment (the conscience) and for future aspirations. (p. 421)

superordinate goals shared goals that override differences among people and require their cooperation. (p. 565)

survey a technique for ascertaining the self-reported attitudes or behaviors of a particular group, usually by questioning a representative, random sample of the group. (p. 16)

sympathetic nervous system the division of the autonomic nervous system that arouses the body, mobilizing its energy in stressful situations. (p. 40)

synapse [SIN-aps] the junction between the axon tip of the sending neuron and the dendrite or cell body of the receiving neuron. The tiny gap at this junction is called the *synaptic gap* or *synaptic cleft.* (p. 37)

systematic desensitization a type of exposure therapy that associates a pleasant relaxed state with gradually increasing anxiety-triggering stimuli. Commonly used to treat phobias. (p. 498)

T

task leadership goal-oriented leadership that sets standards, organizes work, and focuses attention on goals. (p. B-11)

telegraphic speech early speech stage in which a child speaks like a telegram— "go car"—using mostly nouns and verbs. (p. 303)

temperament a person's characteristic emotional reactivity and intensity. (p. 110)

temporal lobes portion of the cerebral cortex lying roughly above the ears; includes the auditory areas, each receiving information primarily from the opposite ear. (p. 50)

teratogens agents, such as chemicals and viruses, that can reach the embryo or fetus during prenatal development and cause harm. (p. 138)

testosterone the most important of the male sex hormones. Both males and females have it, but the additional testosterone in males stimulates the growth of the male sex organs in the fetus and the development of the male sex characteristics during puberty. (pp. 129, 358)

thalamus [THAL-uh-muss] the brain's sensory switchboard, located on top of the brainstem; it directs messages to the sensory receiving areas in the cortex and transmits replies to the cerebellum and medulla. (p. 46)

THC the major active ingredient in marijuana; triggers a variety of effects, including mild hallucinations. (p. 96)

theory an explanation using an integrated set of principles that organizes observations and predicts behaviors or events. (p. 14)

theory of mind people's ideas about their own and others' mental states—about their

feelings, perceptions, and thoughts, and the behaviors these might predict. (p. 145)

threshold the level of stimulation required to trigger a neural impulse. (p. 36)

token economy an operant conditioning procedure in which people earn a token of some sort for exhibiting a desired behavior and can later exchange the tokens for various privileges or treats. (p. 500)

tolerance the diminishing effect with regular use of the same dose of a drug, requiring the user to take larger and larger doses before experiencing the drug's effect. (p. 88)

top-down processing information processing guided by higher-level mental processes, as when we construct perceptions drawing on our experience and expectations. (p. 180)

trait a characteristic pattern of behavior or a disposition to feel and act, as assessed by self-report inventories and peer reports. (p. 432)

transference in psychoanalysis, the patient's transfer to the analyst of emotions linked with other relationships (such as love or hatred for a parent). (p. 494)

two-factor theory the Schachter-Singer theory that to experience emotion one must (1) be physically aroused and (2) cognitively label the arousal. (p. 377)

two-word stage beginning about age 2, the stage in speech development during which a child speaks mostly two-word statements. (p. 303)

Type A Friedman and Rosenman's term for competitive, hard-driving, impatient, verbally aggressive, and anger-prone people. (p. 402)

Type B Friedman and Rosenman's term for easygoing, relaxed people. (p. 402)

U

unconditional positive regard a caring, accepting, nonjudgmental attitude of total acceptance toward another person; Carl Rogers believed that this attitude, used in therapy, would help clients develop self-awareness and self-acceptance. (pp. 430, 496)

unconditioned response (UR) in classical conditioning, the unlearned, naturally occurring response to the unconditioned stimulus (US), such as salivation when food is in the mouth. (p. 228)

unconditioned stimulus (US) in classical conditioning, a stimulus that unconditionally— naturally and automatically—triggers a response. (p. 228)

unconscious according to Freud, a reservoir of mostly unacceptable thoughts, wishes, feelings, and memories. According to contemporary psychologists, information processing of which we are unaware. (p. 420)

V

validity the extent to which a test measures or predicts what it is supposed to. (See also *content validity* and *predictive validity*). (p. 322)

variable-interval schedule in operant conditioning, a reinforcement schedule that reinforces a response at unpredictable time intervals. (p. 240)

variable-ratio schedule in operant conditioning, a reinforcement schedule that reinforces a response after an unpredictable number of responses. (p. 240)

vestibular sense the sense of body movement and position, including the sense of balance. (p. 197)

visual cliff a laboratory device for testing depth perception in infants and young animals. (p. 207)

W

wavelength the distance from the peak of one light or sound wave to the peak of the next. Electromagnetic wavelengths vary from the short blips of cosmic rays to the long pulses of radio transmission. (p. 185)

Weber's law the principle that, to be perceived as different, two stimuli must differ by a constant minimum percentage (rather than a constant amount). (p. 183)

Wechsler Adult Intelligence Scale (WAIS) the WAIS is the most widely used intelligence test; contains verbal and performance (nonverbal) subtests. (p. 320)

Wernicke's area controls language reception; a brain area, usually in the left temporal lobe, that is involved in language comprehension and expression. (p. 54)

withdrawal the discomfort and distress that follow discontinuing the use of an addictive drug. (p. 88)

working memory a newer understanding of short-term memory that focuses on conscious, active processing of incoming auditory and visual-spatial information, and of information retrieved from long-term memory. (p. 259)

X

X chromosome the sex chromosome found in both men and women. Females have two X chromosomes; males have one. An X chromosome from each parent produces a female child. (p. 129)

Y

Y chromosome the sex chromosome found only in males. When paired with an X chromosome from the mother, it produces a male child. (p. 129)

Young-Helmholtz trichromatic (three-color) theory the theory that the retina contains three different color receptors—one most sensitive to red, one to green, one to blue—which, when stimulated in combination, can produce the perception of any color. (p. 191)

Z

zygote the fertilized egg; it enters a 2-week period of rapid cell division and develops into an embryo. (p. 138)

AAS (2009, April 25). USA suicide: 2006 final data. Prepared for the American Association of Suicidology by J. L. McIntosh (www.suicidology.org). (p. 475)

Abrams, D. B. (1991). AIDS: What young people believe and what they do. Paper presented at the British Association for the Advancement of Science conference. (p. 444)

Abrams, D. B., & Wilson, G. T. (1983). Alcohol, sexual arousal, and self-control. *Journal of Personality and Social Psychology, 45*, 188–198. (p. 90)

Abrams, L. (2008). Tip-of-the-tongue states yield language insights. *American Scientist, 96*, 234–239. (p. 278)

Abrams, M. (2002, June). Sight unseen—Restoring a blind man's vision is now a real possibility through stem-cell surgery. But even perfect eyes cannot see unless the brain has been taught to use them. *Discover, 23*, 54–60. (p. 213)

Abramson, L. Y., Metalsky, G. I., & Alloy, L. B. (1989). Hopelessness depression: A theory-based subtype. *Psychological Review, 96*, 358–372. (p. 478)

ACHA (2006). American College Health Association National College Health Assessment. Baltimore, MD: American College Health Association (acha-ncha.org). (p. 471)

Ackerman, D. (2004). *An alchemy of mind: The marvel and mystery of the brain.* New York: Scribner. (p. 37)

Adelmann, P. K., Antonucci, T. C., Crohan, S. F., & Coleman, L. M. (1989). Empty nest, cohort, and employment in the well-being of midlife women. *Sex Roles, 20*, 173–189. (p. 170)

Adelson, R. (2005, September). Lessons from H. M. *Monitor on Psychology*, p. 59. (p. 269)

Ader, R., & Cohen, N. (1985). CNS-immune system interactions: Conditioning phenomena. *Behavioral and Brain Sciences, 8*, 379–394. (p. 235)

Affleck, G., Tennen, H., Urrows, S., & Higgins, P. (1994). Person and contextual features of daily stress reactivity: Individual differences in relations of undesirable daily events with mood disturbance and chronic pain intensity. *Journal of Personality and Social Psychology, 66*, 329–340. (p. 393)

Ai, A. L., Park, C. L., Huang, B., Rodgers, W., & Tice, T. N. (2007). Psychosocial mediation of religious coping styles: A study of short-term psychological distress following cardiac surgery. *Personality and Social Psychology Bulletin, 33*, 867–882. (p. 415)

Ainsworth, M. D. S. (1973). The development of infant-mother attachment. In B. Caldwell & H. Ricciuti (Eds.), *Review of child development research* (Vol. 3). Chicago: University of Chicago Press. (p. 151)

Ainsworth, M. D. S. (1979). Infant-mother attachment. *American Psychologist, 34*, 932–937. (p. 151)

Ainsworth, M. D. S. (1989). Attachments beyond infancy. *American Psychologist, 44*, 709–716. (p. 151)

Airan, R. D., Meltzer, L. A., Roy, M., Gong, Y., Chen, H., & Deisseroth, K. (2007). High-speed imaging reveals neurophysiological links to behavior in an animal model of depression. *Science, 317*, 819–823. (p. 476)

Åkerstedt, T., Kecklund, G., & Axelsson, J. (2007). Impaired sleep after bedtime stress and worries. *Biological Psychology, 76*, 170–173. (p. 78)

Albee, G. W. (1986). Toward a just society: Lessons from observations on the primary prevention of psychopathology. *American Psychologist, 41*, 891–898. (p. 521)

Albert, B., Brown, S., & Flanigan, C. M. (Eds.). (2003). *14 and younger: The sexual behavior of young adolescents.* Washington, DC: National Campaign to Prevent Teen Pregnancy. (p. 361)

Alcock, J. E. (1981). *Parapsychology: Science or magic?* Oxford: Pergamon. (p. 275)

Aldrich, M. S. (1989). Automobile accidents in patients with sleep disorders. *Sleep, 12*, 487–494. (p. 79)

Aldridge-Morris, R. (1989). *Multiple personality: An exercise in deception.* Hillsdale, NJ: Erlbaum. (p. 469)

Aleman, A., Kahn, R. S., & Selten, J-P. (2003). Sex differences in the risk of schizophrenia: Evidence from meta-analysis. *Archives of General Psychiatry, 60*, 565–571. (p. 482)

Alexander, C. N., Langer, E. J., Newman, R. I., Chandler, H. M., & Davies, J. L. (1989). Transcendental meditation, mindfulness, and longevity: An experimental study with the elderly. *Journal of Personality and Social Psychology, 57*, 950–964. (p. 413)

Allard, F., & Burnett, N. (1985). Skill in sport. *Canadian Journal of Psychology, 39*, 294–312. (p. 264)

Allen, J. B., Repinski, D. J., Ballard, J. C., & Griffin, B. W. (1996). Beliefs about the etiology of homosexuality may influence attitudes toward homosexuals. Paper presented to the American Psychological Society convention. (p. 368)

Allen, K. (2003). Are pets a healthy pleasure? The influence of pets on blood pressure. *Current Directions in Psychological Science, 12*, 236–239. (p. 410)

Allen, N. B., & Badcock, P. B. T. (2003). The social risk hypothesis of depressed mood: Evolutionary, psychosocial, and neurobiological perspectives. *Psychological Bulletin, 129*, 887–913. (p. 471)

Alloy, L. B., Abramson, L. Y., Whitehouse, W. G., Hogan, M. E., Tashman, N. A., Steinberg, D. L., Rose, D. T., & Donovan, P. (1999). Depressogenic cognitive styles: Predictive validity, information processing and personality characteristics, and developmental origins. *Behaviour Research and Therapy, 37*, 503–531. (p. 478)

Allport, G. W. (1954). *The nature of prejudice.* New York: Addison-Wesley. (p. 15)

Allport, G. W., & Odbert, H. S. (1936). Trait-names: A psycho-lexical study. *Psychological Monographs, 47*(1). (p. 433)

Altman, L. K. (2004, November 24). Female cases of HIV found rising worldwide. *New York Times* (www.nytimes.com). (p. 405)

Alwin, D. F. (1990). Historical changes in parental orientations to children. In N. Mandell (Ed.), *Sociological studies of child development* (Vol. 3). Greenwich, CT: JAI Press. (p. 125)

Amabile, T. M. (1983). *The social psychology of creativity.* New York: Springer-Verlag. (p. 447)

Amabile, T. M., Barsade, S. G., Mueller, J. S., & Staw, B. M. (2005). Affect and creativity at work. *Administrative Science Quarterly, 50*, 367–403. (p. 392)

Amabile, T. M., & Hennessey, B. A. (1992). The motivation for creativity in children. In A. K. Boggiano & T. S. Pittman (Eds.), *Achievement and motivation: A social-developmental perspective.* New York: Cambridge University Press. (p. 317)

Amato, P. R., Booth, A., Johnson, D. R., & Rogers, S. J. (2007). *Alone together: How marriage in America is changing.* Cambridge, MA: Harvard University Press. (p. 130)

Ambady, N., Hallahan, M., & Rosenthal, R. (1995). On judging and being judged accurately in zero-acquaintance situations. *Journal of Personality and Social Psychology, 69*, 518–529. (p. 384)

Ambady, N., & Rosenthal, R. (1992). Thin slices of expressive behavior as predictors of interpersonal consequences: A meta-analysis. *Psychological Bulletin, 111*, 256–274. (p. 438)

Ambady, N., & Rosenthal, R. (1993). Half a minute: Predicting teacher evaluations from thin slices of nonverbal behavior and physical attractiveness. *Journal of Personality and Social Psychology, 64*, 431–441. (p. 438)

Amedi, A., Floel, A., Knect, S., Zohary, E., & Cohen, L. (2004). Transcranial magnetic stimulation of the occipital pole interferes with verbal processing in blind subjects. *Nature Neuroscience, 7*, 1266–1270. (p. 56)

Amedi, A., Merabet, L. B., Bermpohl, F., & Pascual-Leone, A. (2005). The occipital cortex in the blind: Lessons about plasticity and vision. *Current Directions in Psychological Science, 14*, 306–311. (p. 56)

Amen, D. G., Stubblefield, M., Carmichael, B., & Thisted, R. (1996). Brain SPECT findings and aggressiveness. *Annals of Clinical Psychiatry, 8*, 129–137. (p. 548)

American Enterprise. (1992, January/February). Women, men, marriages & ministers. p. 106. (p. 124)

American Psychiatric Association. (1994). *Diagnostic and statistical manual of mental disorders* (4th ed.). Washington, DC: American Psychiatric Press. (p. 322)

American Psychological Association. (1992). Ethical principles of psychologists and code of conduct. *American Psychologist, 47*, 1597–1611. (p. 27)

American Psychological Association. (2002). *Ethical principles of psychologists and code of conduct.* Washington, DC: Author. (p. 27)

American Psychological Association. (2006). Evidence-based practice in psychology (from APA Presidential Task Force on Evidence-Based Practice). *American Psychologist, 61*, 271–285. (p. 507)

American Psychological Association. (2007). Answers to your questions about sexual orientation and homosexuality (www.apa.org. Accessed December 6, 2007). (p. 363)

Andersen, R. E., Crespo, C. J., Bartlett, S. J., Cheskin, L. J., & Pratt, M. (1998). Relationship of physical activity and television watching with body weight and level of fatness among children. *Journal of the American Medical Association, 279,* 938–942. (p. 356)

Andersen, S. M. (1998). *Service learning: A national strategy for youth development.* A position paper issued by the Task Force on Education Policy. Washington, DC: Institute for Communitarian Policy Studies, George Washington University. (p. 158)

Anderson, A. K., & Phelps, E. A. (2000). Expression without recognition: Contributions of the human amygdala to emotional communication. *Psychological Science, 11,* 106–111. (p. 48)

Anderson, B. L. (2002). Biobehavioral outcomes following psychological interventions for cancer patients. *Journal of Consulting and Clinical Psychology, 70,* 590–610. (p. 405)

Anderson, C. A. (2004a). An update on the effects of playing violent video games. *Journal of Adolescence, 27,* 113–122. (p. 552)

Anderson, C. A., & Anderson, D. C. (1984). Ambient temperature and violent crime: Tests of the linear and curvilinear hypotheses. *Journal of Personality and Social Psychology, 46,* 91–97. (p. 550)

Anderson, C. A., Anderson, K. B., Dorr, N., DeNeve, K. M., & Flanagan, M. (2000). Temperature and aggression. In M. P. Zanna (Ed.), *Advances in Experimental Social Psychology.* San Diego: Academic Press. (p. 550)

Anderson, C. A., Carnagey, N. L., Flanagan, M., Benjamin, A. J., Jr., Eubanks, J., & Valentine, J. C. (2004). Violent video games: Specific effects of violent content on aggressive thoughts and behavior. *Advances in Experimental Social Psychology, 36,* 199–249. (p. 552)

Anderson, C. A., & Dill, K. E. (2000). Video games and aggressive thoughts, feelings, and behavior in the laboratory and in life. *Journal of Personality and Social Psychology, 78,* 772–790. (p. 552)

Anderson, C. A., & Gentile, D. A. (2008). Media violence, aggression, and public policy. In E. Borgida & S. Fiske (Eds.), *Beyond common sense: Psychological science in the courtroom.* Malden, MA: Blackwell. (p. 251)

Anderson, C. A., Gentile, D. A., & Buckley, K. E. (2007). *Violent video game effects on children and adolescents: Theory, research, and public policy.* New York: Oxford University Press. (pp. 271, 552)

Anderson, C. A., Lindsay, J. J., & Bushman, B. J. (1999). Research in the psychological laboratory: Truth or triviality? *Current Directions in Psychological Science, 8,* 3–9. (p. 25)

Anderson, I. M. (2000). Selective serotonin reuptake inhibitors versus tricyclic antidepressants: A meta-analysis of efficacy and tolerability. *Journal of Affective Disorders, 58,* 19–36. (p. 515)

Anderson, J. R., Myowa-Yamakoshi, M., & Matsuzawa, T. (2004). Contagious yawning in chimpanzees. *Biology Letters, 271,* S468–S470. (p. 532)

Anderson, R. C., Pichert, J. W., Goetz, E. T., Schallert, D. L., Stevens, K. V., & Trollip, S. R. (1976). Instantiation of general terms. *Journal of Verbal Learning and Verbal Behavior, 15,* 667–679. (p. 273)

Anderson, S. (2008, July 6). The urge to end it. *New York Times* (www.nytimes.com). (p. 474)

Anderson, S. E., Dallal, G. E., & Must, A. (2003). Relative weight and race influence average age at menarche: Results from two nationally representative surveys of U.S. girls studied 25 years apart. *Pediatrics, 111,* 844–850. (p. 155)

Anderson, S. R. (2004). *Doctor Dolittle's delusion: Animals and the uniqueness of human language.* New Haven: Yale University Press. (p. 312)

Andreasen, N. C. (1997). Linking mind and brain in the study of mental illnesses: A project for a scientific psychopathology. *Science, 275,* 1586–1593. (p. 483)

Andreasen, N. C. (2001). *Brave new brain: Conquering mental illness in the era of the genome.* New York: Oxford University Press. (p. 483)

Andreasen, N. C., Arndt, S., Swayze, V., II, Cizadlo, T., & Flaum, M. (1994). Thalamic abnormalities in schizophrenia visualized through magnetic resonance image averaging. *Science, 266,* 294–298. (p. 483)

Angell, M., & Kassirer, J. P. (1998). Alternative medicine: The risks of untested and unregulated remedies. *New England Journal of Medicine, 17,* 839–841. (p. 406)

Angelsen, N. K., Vik, T., Jacobsen, G., & Bakketeig, L. S. (2001). Breast feeding and cognitive development at age 1 and 5 years. *Archives of Disease in Childhood, 85,* 183–188. (p. 21)

Annan, K. A. (2001). We can love what we are, without hating who—and what—we are not. Nobel Peace Prize lecture. (p. 567)

Antoni, M. H., & Lutgendorf, S. (2007). Psychosocial factors and disease progression in cancer. *Current Directions in Psychological Science, 16,* 42–46. (p. 405)

Antony, M. M., Brown, T. A., & Barlow, D. H. (1992). Current perspectives on panic and panic disorder. *Current Directions in Psychological Science, 1,* 79–82. (p. 466)

Antrobus, J. (1991). Dreaming: Cognitive processes during cortical activation and high afferent thresholds. *Psychological Review, 98,* 96–121. (p. 82)

AP (2007). AP-Ipsos poll of 1,013 U.S. adults taken October 16–18, 2007 and distributed via Associated Press. (p. 218)

AP (2007, January 12). China facing major gender imbalance. Associated Press release. (p. 544)

APA. (2003, November). *Psychology careers for the twenty-first century.* Washington, DC: American Psychological Association. (p. 8)

Archer, J. (2004). Sex differences in aggression in real-world settings: A meta-analytic review. *Review of General Psychology, 8,* 291–322. (p. 127)

Archer, J. (2006). Cross-cultural differences in physical aggression between partners: A social-role analysis. *Personality and Social Psychology Review, 10,* 133–153. (p. 127)

Arenson, K. W. (1997, May 4). Romanian woman breaks male grip on top math prize. *New York Times* News Service (in *Grand Rapids Press,* p. A7). (p. 329)

Aries, E. (1987). Gender and communication. In P. Shaver & C. Henrick (Eds.), *Review of Personality and Social Psychology, 7,* 149–176. (p. 127)

Arkowitz, H., & Lilienfeld, S. O. (2006, April/May). Psychotherapy on trial. *Scientific American: Mind,* pp. 42–49. (p. 507)

Armel, K. C., & Ramachandran, V. S. (2003). Projecting sensations to external objects: Evidence from skin conductance response. *Proceedings of the Royal Society of London. Series B. Biological Sciences, 270,* 1499–1506. (p. 199)

Arnett, J. J. (1999). Adolescent storm and stress, reconsidered. *American Psychologist, 54,* 317–326. (p. 155)

Arnett, J. J. (2006). Emerging adulthood: Understanding the new way of coming of age. In J. J. Arnett & J. L. Tanner (Eds.), *Emerging adults in America: Coming of age in the 21st century.* Washington, DC: American Psychological Association. (p. 162)

Arnett, J. J. (2007). Socialization in emerging adulthood: From the family to the wider world, from socialization to self-socialization. In J. E. Grusec & P. D. Hastings (Eds.), *Handbook of socialization: Theory and research.* New York: Guilford Press. (p. 162)

Aron, A., Melinat, E., Aron, E. N., Vallone, R. D., & Bator, R. J. (1997). The experimental generation of interpersonal closeness: A procedure and some preliminary findings. *Personality and Social Psychology Bulletin, 23,* 363–377. (p. 560)

Aronson, E. (2001, April 13). Newsworthy violence. E-mail to SPSP discussion list, drawing from *Nobody Left to Hate.* New York: Freeman, 2000. (p. 161)

Artiga, A. I., Viana, J. B., Maldonado, C. R., Chandler-Laney, P. C., Oswald, K. D., & Boggiano, M. M. (2007). Body composition and endocrine status of long-term stress-induced binge-eating rats. *Physiology and Behavior, 91,* 424–431. (p. 346)

ASAPS. (2008). Cosmetic procedures in 2007. American Society for Aesthetic Plastic Surgery (www.surgery.org). (p. 558)

Asch, S. E. (1955). Opinions and social pressure. *Scientific American, 193,* 31–35. (p. 533)

Aserinsky, E. (1988, January 17). Personal communication. (p. 72)

Askay, S. W., & Patterson, D. R. (2007). Hypnotic analgesia. *Expert Review of Neurotherapeutics, 7,* 1675–1683. (p. 86)

Aspy, C. B., Vesely, S. K., Oman, R. F., Rodine, S., Marshall, L., & McLeroy, K. (2007). Parental communication and youth sexual behaviour. *Journal of Adolescence, 30,* 449–466. (p. 361)

Assanand, S., Pinel, J. P. J., & Lehman, D. R. (1998). Personal theories of hunger and eating. *Journal of Applied Social Psychology, 28,* 998–1015. (p. 346)

Associated Press. (2006, October 4). Man recites pi to 100,000 places. (p. 267)

Astin, A. W., Astin, H. S., & Lindholm, J. A. (2004). *Spirituality in higher education: A national study of college students' search for meaning and purpose.* Los Angeles: Higher Education Research Institute, UCLA. (p. 160)

Atkinson, R. C., & Shiffrin, R. M. (1968). Human memory: A control system and its control processes. In K. Spence (Ed.), *The psychology of learning and motivation* (Vol. 2). New York: Academic Press. (p. 258)

Austin, E. J., Deary, I. J., Whiteman, M. C., Fowkes, F. G. R., Pedersen, N. L., Rabbitt, P., Bent, N., & McInnes, L. (2002). Relationships between ability and personality: Does intelligence contribute positively to personal and social adjustment? *Personality and Individual Differences, 32,* 1391–1411. (p. 322)

Australian Bureau of Statistics (2007, July 8). Overweight and obesity (www.abs.gov.au). (p. 350)

Averill, J. R. (1983). Studies on anger and aggression: Implications for theories of emotion. *American Psychologist, 38,* 1145–1160. (pp. 389, 391)

Averill, J. R. (1993). William James's other theory of emotion. In M. E. Donnelly (Ed.), *Reinterpreting the legacy of William James.* Washington, DC: American Psychological Association. (p. 377)

Avery, R. D., & others. (1994, December 13). Mainstream science on intelligence. *Wall Street Journal,* p. A-18. (p. 331)

Ax, A. F. (1953). The physiological differentiation of fear and anger in humans. *Psychosomatic Medicine, 15,* 433–442. (p. 379)

Axiss. (2007). Immigration and foreign population as percentage of total population: 1992 and 2003. Axiss Australia, Australian Government (www.axiss.gov.au). (p. 122)

Azar, B. (1998, June). Why can't this man feel whether or not he's standing up? *APA Monitor* (www.apa.org/monitor/jun98/touch.html). (p. 197)

Babad, E., Bernieri, F., & Rosenthal, R. (1991). Students as judges of teachers' verbal and nonverbal behavior. *American Educational Research Journal, 28,* 211–234. (p. 384)

Babyak, M., Blumenthal, J. A., Herman, S., Khatri, P., Doraiswamy, M., Moore, K., Craighead, W. W., Baldewics, T. T., & Krishnan, K. R. (2000). Exercise treatment for major depression: Maintenance of therapeutic benefit at ten months. *Psychosomatic Medicine, 62,* 633–638. (p. 520)

Bachman, J., O'Malley, P. M., Schulenberg, J. E., Johnston, L. D., Freedman-Doan, P., & Messersmith, E. E. (2007). *The education-drug use connection: How successes and failures in school relate to adolescent smoking, drinking, drug use, and delinquency.* Mahwah, NJ: Erlbaum. (p. 99)

Backman, L., & MacDonald, S. W. S. (2006). Death and cognition: Synthesis and outlook. *European Psychologist, 11,* 224–235. (p. 168)

Baddeley, A. D. (1982). *Your memory: A user's guide.* New York: Macmillan. (pp. 260, 261)

Baddeley, A. D. (2001). Is working memory still working? *American Psychologist, 56,* 849–864. (p. 259)

Baddeley, A. D. (2002, June). Is working memory still working? *European Psychologist, 7,* 85–97. (p. 259)

Bagemihl, B. (1999). *Biological exuberance: Animal homosexuality and natural diversity.* New York: St. Martins. (p. 365)

Bahrick, H. P. (1984). Semantic memory content in permastore: 50 years of memory for Spanish learned in school. *Journal of Experimental Psychology: General, 111,* 1–29. (pp. 277, 278)

Bahrick, H. P., Bahrick, L. E., Bahrick, A. S., & Bahrick, P. E. (1993). Maintenance of foreign language vocabulary and the spacing effect. *Psychological Science, 4,* 316–321. (p. 261)

Bahrick, H. P., Bahrick, P. O., & Wittlinger, R. P. (1975). Fifty years of memory for names and faces: A cross-sectional approach. *Journal of Experimental Psychology: General, 104,* 54–75. (p. 273)

Bailenson, J. N., Iyengar, S., & Yee, N. (2005). Facial identity capture and presidential candidate preference. Paper presented at the Annual Conference of the International Communication Association. (p. 556)

Bailey, J. M., Gaulin, S., Agyei, Y., & Gladue, B. A. (1994). Effects of gender and sexual orientation on evolutionary relevant aspects of human mating psychology. *Journal of Personality and Social Psychology, 66,* 1081–1093. (p. 115)

Bailey, J. M., Kirk, K. M., Zhu, G., Dunne, M. P., & Martin, N. G. (2000). Do individual differences in sociosexuality represent genetic or environmentally contingent strategies? Evidence from the Australian twin registry. *Journal of Personality and Social Psychology, 78,* 537–545. (p. 115)

Bailey, J. M., & Zucker, K. J. (1995). Childhood sex-typed behavior and sexual orientation: A conceptual analysis and quantitative review. *Developmental Psychology, 31,* 43–55. (p. 363)

Bailey, R. E., & Gillaspy, J. A., Jr. (2005). Operant psychology goes to the fair: Marian and Keller Breland in the popular press, 1947–1966. *The Behavior Analyst, 28,* 143–159. (p. 244)

Baillargeon, R. (1995). A model of physical reasoning in infancy. In C. Rovee-Collier & L. P. Lipsitt (Eds.), *Advances in infancy research* (Vol. 9). Stamford, CT: Ablex. (p. 144)

Baillargeon, R. (2008). Innate ideas revisited: For a principle of persistence in infants' physical reasoning. *Perspectives in Psychological Science, 3,* 2–13. (p. 144)

Baird, G., Simonoff, E., Pickles, A., Chandler, S., Loucas, T., Meldrum, D., & Charman, T. (2006). Prevalence of disorders of the autism spectrum in a population cohort of children in South Thames: The special needs and autism project (SNAP). *Lancet, 368,* 210–215. (p. 146)

Baker, E. L. (1987). The state of the art of clinical hypnosis. *International Journal of Clinical and Experimental Hypnosis, 35,* 203–214. (p. 85)

Baker, R. R., & Bellis, M. A. (1995). *Human sperm competition.* London: Chapman & Hall. (p. 357)

Baker, T. B., Piper, M. E., McCarthy, D. E., Majeskie, M. R., & Fiore, M. C. (2004). Addiction motivation reformulated: An affective processing model of negative reinforcement. *Psychological Review, 111,* 33–51. (p. 239)

Bakermans-Kranenburg, M. J., van IJzendoorn, M. H., & Juffer, F. (2003). Less is more: Meta-analyses of sensitivity and attachment interventions in early childhood. *Psychological Bulletin, 129,* 195–215. (p. 151)

Ballard, M. E., & Wiest, J. R. (1998). Mortal Kombat: The effects of violent videogame play on males' hostility and cardiovascular responding. *Journal of Applied Social Psychology, 26,* 717–730. (p. 552)

Balsam, K. F., Beauchaine, T. P., Mickey, R. M., & Rothblum, E. D. (2005). Mental health of lesbian, gay, bisexual, and heterosexual siblings: Effects of gender, sexual orientation, and family. *Journal of Abnormal Psychology, 114,* 471–476. (p. 363)

Balsam, K. F., Beauchaine, T. P., Rothblum, E. S., & Solomon, S. E. (2008). Three-year follow-up of same-sex couples who had civil unions in Vermont, same-sex couples not in civil unions, and heterosexual married couples. *Developmental Psychology, 44,* 102–116. (p. 169)

Bancroft, J., Loftus, J., & Long, J. S. (2003). Distress about sex: A national survey of women in heterosexual relationships. *Archives of Sexual Behavior, 32,* 193–208. (p. 358)

Bandura, A. (1986). *Social foundations of thought and action: A social-cognitive theory.* Englewood Cliffs, NJ: Prentice-Hall. (p. 439)

Bandura, A. (2005). The evolution of social cognitive theory. In K. G. Smith & M. A. Hitt (Eds.), *Great minds in management: The process of theory development.* Oxford: Oxford University Press. (p. 250)

Bandura, A. (2006). Toward a psychology of human agency. *Perspectives on Psychological Science, 1,* 164–180. (p. 439)

Bandura, A. (2008). An agentic perspective on positive psychology. In S. J. Lopez (Ed.), *The science of human flourishing.* Westport, CT: Praeger. (p. 439)

Bandura, A., Ross, D., & Ross, S. A. (1961). Transmission of aggression through imitation of aggressive models. *Journal of Abnormal and Social Psychology, 63,* 575–582. (p. 249)

Barash, D. P. (2006, July 14). I am, therefore I think. *Chronicle of Higher Education,* pp. B9, B10. (p. 66)

Barber, C. (2008, February/March). The medicated American. *Scientific American Mind,* pp. 45–51. (p. 515)

Barber, T. X. (2000). A deeper understanding of hypnosis: Its secrets, its nature, its essence. *American Journal of Clinical Hypnosis, 42,* 208–272. (p. 86)

Bargh, J. A., & Chartrand, T. L. (1999). The unbearable automaticity of being. *American Psychologist, 54,* 462–479. (p. 67)

Bargh, J. A., & McKenna, K. Y. A. (2004). The Internet and social life. *Annual Review of Psychology, 55,* 573–590. (p. 555)

Bargh, J. A., McKenna, K. Y. A., & Fitzsimons, G. M. (2002). Can you see the real me? Activation and expression of the "true self" on the Internet. *Journal of Social Issues, 58,* 33–48. (p. 555)

Bargh, J. A., & Morsella, E. (2008). The unconscious mind. *Perspectives on Psychological Science, 3,* 73–79. (p. 427)

Bar-Haim, Y., Lamy, D., Pergamin, L., Bakermans-Kranenburg, M. J., & van IJzendoorn, M. H. (2007). Threat-related attentional bias in anxious and nonanxious individuals: A meta-analytic study. *Psychological Bulletin, 133,* 1–24. (p. 466)

Barinaga, M. B. (1992a). The brain remaps its own contours. *Science, 258,* 216–218. (p. 56)

Barinaga, M. B. (1997). How exercise works its magic. *Science, 276,* 1325. (p. 412)

Barkley, R. A., & 74 others. (2002). International consensus statement (January 2002). *Clinical Child and Family Psychology Review, 5,* 2. (p. 455)

Barnes, M. L., & Sternberg, R. J. (1989). Social intelligence and decoding of nonverbal cues. *Intelligence, 13,* 263–287. (p. 385)

Barnett, P. A., & Gotlib, I. H. (1988). Psychosocial functioning and depression: Distinguishing among antecedents, concomitants, and consequences. *Psychological Bulletin, 104,* 97–126. (p. 478)

Barnier, A. J., & McConkey, K. M. (2004). Defining and identifying the highly hypnotizable person. In M. Heap, R. J. Brown, & D. A. Oakley (Eds.), *High hypnotisability: Theoretical, experimental and clinical issues.* London: Brunner-Routledge. (p. 84)

Baron, R. A. (1988). Negative effects of destructive criticism: Impact on conflict, self-efficacy, and task performance. *Journal of Applied Psychology, 73,* 199–207. (p. 245)

Baron-Cohen, S. (2008). Autism, hypersystemizing, and truth. *Quarterly Journal of Experimental Psychology, 61,* 64–75. (p. 146)

Baron-Cohen, S., Golan, O., Chapman, E., & Granader, Y. (2007). Transported to a world of emotion. *The Psychologist, 20,* 76–77. (p. 147)

Barrett, L. F. (2006). Are emotions natural kinds? *Perspectives on Psychological Science, 1,* 28–58. (p. 379)

Barrett, L. F., Lane, R. D., Sechrest, L., & Schwartz, G. E. (2000). Sex differences in emotional awareness. *Personality and Social Psychology Bulletin, 26,* 1027–1035. (p. 385)

Barry, D. (1995, September 17). Teen smokers, too, get cool, toxic, waste-blackened lungs. *Asbury Park Press,* p. D3. (p. 92)

Bartholow, B. C., Bushman, B. J., & Sestir, M. A. (2006). Chronic violent video game exposure and desensitization to violence: Behavioral and event-related brain potential data. *Journal of Experimental Social Psychology, 42,* 532–539. (p. 552)

Bashore, T. R., Ridderinkhof, K. R., & van der Molen, M. W. (1997). The decline of cognitive processing speed in old age. *Current Directions in Psychological Science, 6,* 163–169. (p. 165)

Baskind, D. E. (1997, December 14). Personal communication, from Delta College. (p. 499)

Bassett, D. R., Schneider, P. L., & Huntington, G. E. (2004). Physical activity in an Old Order Amish community. *Medicine and Science in Sports and Exercise, 36,* 79–85. (p. 353)

Bauer, P. J. (2002). Long-term recall memory: Behavioral and neurodevelopmental changes in the first 2 years of life. *Current Directions in Psychology, 11,* 137–141. (p. 141)

Bauer, P. J. (2007). Recall in infancy: A neurodevelopmental account. *Current Directions in Psychological Science, 16,* 142–146. (p. 141)

Bauer, P. J., Burch, M. M., Scholin, S. E., & Güler, O. E. (2007). Using cue words to investigate the distribution of autobiographical memories in childhood. *Psychological Science, 18,* 910–916. (p. 272)

Baum, A., & Posluszny, D. M. (1999). Health psychology: Mapping biobehavioral contributions to health and illness. *Annual Review of Psychology, 50,* 137–163. (p. 405)

Baumeister, H., & Härter, M. (2007). Prevalence of mental disorders based on general population surveys. *Social Psychiatry and Psychiatric Epidemiology, 42,* 537–546. (pp. 488, 453)

Baumeister, R. F. (1989). The optimal margin of illusion. *Journal of Social and Clinical Psychology, 8,* 176–189. (p. 297)

Baumeister, R. F. (1996). Should schools try to boost self-esteem? Beware the dark side. *American Educator, 20,* 43. (p. 449)

Baumeister, R. F. (2000). Gender differences in erotic plasticity: The female sex drive as socially flexible and responsive. *Psychological Bulletin, 126,* 347–374. (p. 364)

Baumeister, R. F. (2001, April). Violent pride: Do people turn violent because of self-hate, or self-love? *Scientific American,* pp. 96–101. (p. 449)

Baumeister, R. F. (2005). *The cultural animal: Human nature, meaning, and social life.* New York: Oxford University Press. (p. 121)

Baumeister, R. F. (2006, August/September). Violent pride. *Scientific American Mind,* pp. 54–59. (p. 447)

Baumeister, R. F., & Bratslavsky, E. (1999). Passion, intimacy, and time: Passionate love as a function of change in intimacy. *Personality and Social Psychology Review, 3,* 49–67. (p. 560)

Baumeister, R. F., Campbell, J., Krueger, J. I., & Vohs, K. D. (2003). Does high self-esteem cause better performance, interpersonal success, happiness, or healthier lifestyles? *Psychological Science in the Public Interest, 4*(1), 1–44. (p. 449)

Baumeister, R. F., Catanese, K. R., & Vohs, K. D. (2001). Is there a gender difference in strength of sex drive? Theoretical views, conceptual distinctions, and a review of relevant evidence. *Personality and Social Psychology Review, 5,* 242–273. (p. 115)

Baumeister, R. F., Dale, K., & Sommer, K. L. (1998). Freudian defense mechanisms and empirical findings in modern personality and social psychology: Reaction formation, projection, displacement, undoing, isolation, sublimation, and denial. *Journal of Personality, 66,* 1081–1125. (p. 427)

Baumeister, R. F., & Exline, J. J. (2000). Self-control, morality, and human strength. *Journal of Social and Clinical Psychology, 19,* 29–42. (p. 441)

Baumeister, R. F., & Leary, M. R. (1995). The need to belong: Desire for interpersonal attachments as a fundamental human motivation. *Psychological Bulletin, 117,* 497–529. (p. 369)

Baumeister, R. F., & Tice, D. M. (1986). How adolescence became the struggle for self: A historical transformation of psychological development. In J. Suls & A. G. Greenwald (Eds.), *Psychological perspectives on the self* (Vol. 3). Hillsdale, NJ: Erlbaum. (p. 162)

Baumeister, R. F., Twenge, J. M., & Nuss, C. K. (2002). Effects of social exclusion on cognitive processes: Anticipated aloneness reduces intelligent thought. *Journal of Personality and Social Psychology, 83,* 817–827. (p. 371)

Baumgardner, A. H., Kaufman, C. M., & Levy, P. E. (1989). Regulating affect interpersonally: When low esteem leads to greater enhancement. *Journal of Personality and Social Psychology, 56,* 907–921. (p. 447)

Baumrind, D. (1982). Adolescent sexuality: Comment on Williams' and Silka's comments on Baumrind. *American Psychologist, 37,* 1402–1403. (p. 368)

Baumrind, D. (1996). The discipline controversy revisited. *Family Relations, 45,* 405–414. (p. 154)

Baumrind, D., Larzelere, R. E., & Cowan, P. A. (2002). Ordinary physical punishment: Is it harmful? Comment on Gershoff (2002). *Psychological Bulletin, 128,* 602–611. (p. 242)

Bavelier, D., Newport, E. L., & Supalla, T. (2003). Children need natural languages, signed or spoken. *Cerebrum, 5*(1), 19–32. (p. 304)

BBC (2006, June 14). Crystal meth to be Class A drug. *BBC News* (www.news.bbc.co.uk). (p. 92)

BBC (2008, February 26). Anti-depressants 'of little use.' *BBC News* (www.news.bbc.co.uk). (p. 516)

Beaman, A. L., & Klentz, B. (1983). The supposed physical attractiveness bias against supporters of the women's movement: A meta-analysis. *Personality and Social Psychology Bulletin, 9,* 544–550. (p. 558)

Beardsley, L. M. (1994). Medical diagnosis and treatment across cultures. In W. J. Lonner & R. Malpass (Eds.), *Psychology and culture.* Boston: Allyn & Bacon. (p. 456)

Beauchamp, G. K. (1987). The human preference for excess salt. *American Scientist, 75,* 27–33. (p. 346)

Beck, A. T., Rush, A. J., Shaw, B. F., & Emery, G. (1979). *Cognitive therapy of depression.* New York: Guilford Press. (pp. 501, 502)

Beck, A. T., & Steer, R. A. (1989). Clinical predictors of eventual suicide: A 5- to 10–year prospective study of suicide attempters. *Journal of Affective Disorders, 17,* 203–209. (p. 474)

Becker, D. V., Kenrick, D. T., Neuberg, S. L., Blackwell, K. C., & Smith, D. M. (2007). The confounded nature of angry men and happy women. *Journal of Personality and Social Psychology, 92,* 179–190. (pp. 385, 386)

Becker, S., & Wojtowicz, J. M. (2007). A model of hippocampal neurogenesis in memory and mood disorders. *Trends in Cognitive Sciences, 11,* 70–76. (p. 515)

Becklen, R., & Cervone, D. (1983). Selective looking and the noticing of unexpected events. *Memory and Cognition, 11,* 601–608. (p. 69)

Beckman, M. (2004). Crime, culpability, and the adolescent brain. *Science, 305,* 596–599. (p. 156)

Beeman, M. J., & Chiarello, C. (1998). Complementary right- and left-hemisphere language comprehension. *Current Directions in Psychological Science, 7,* 2–8. (p. 60)

Beilin, H. (1992). Piaget's enduring contribution to developmental psychology. *Developmental Psychology, 28,* 191–204. (p. 148)

Beitman, B. D., Goldfried, M. R., & Norcross, J. C. (1989). The movement toward integrating the psychotherapies: An overview. *American Journal of Psychiatry, 146,* 138–147. (p. 493)

Bell, A. P., Weinberg, M. S., & Hammersmith, S. K. (1981). *Sexual preference: Its development in men and women.* Bloomington: Indiana University Press. (p. 365)

Belot, M., & Francesconi, M. (2006, November). *Can anyone be 'the one'? Evidence on mate selection from speed dating.* London: Centre for Economic Policy Research (www.cepr.org). (p. 557)

Belsher, G., & Costello, C. G. (1988). Relapse after recovery from unipolar depression: A critical review. *Psychological Bulletin, 104,* 84–96. (p. 473)

Bem, D. J. (1984). Quoted in *The Skeptical Inquirer, 8,* 194. (p. 220)

Bem, D. J. (1996). Exotic becomes erotic: A developmental theory of sexual orientation. *Psychological Review, 103,* 320–335. (p. 368)

Bem, D. J. (1998). Is EBE theory supported by the evidence? Is it androcentric? A reply to Peplau et al. (1998). *Psychological Review, 105,* 395–398. (p. 368)

Bem, D. J. (2000). Exotic becomes erotic: Interpreting the biological correlates of sexual orientation. *Archives of Sexual Behavior, 29,* 531–548. (p. 368)

Bem, D. J., & Honorton, C. (1994). Does psi exist? Replicable evidence for an anomalous process of information transfer. *Psychological Bulletin, 115,* 4–18. (p. 220)

Bem, D. J., Palmer, J., & Broughton, R. S. (2001). Updating the Ganzfeld database: A victim of its own success? *Journal of Parapsychology, 65,* 207–218. (p. 220)

Bem, S. L. (1987). Masculinity and femininity exist only in the mind of the perceiver. In J. M. Reinisch, L. A. Rosenblum, & S. A. Sanders (Eds.), *Masculinity/femininity: Basic perspectives.* New York: Oxford University Press. (p. 131)

Bem, S. L. (1993). *The lenses of gender.* New Haven, CT: Yale University Press. (p. 131)

Benbow, C. P., Lubinski, D., Shea, D. L., & Eftekhari-Sanjani, H. (2000). Sex differences in mathematical reasoning ability at age 13: Their status 20 years later. *Psychological Science, 11,* 474–2000. (p. 329)

Bennett, W. I. (1995). Beyond overeating. *New England Journal of Medicine, 332,* 673–674. (p. 356)

Ben-Shakhar, G., & Elaad, E. (2003). The validity of psychophysiological detection of information with the guilt knowledge test: A meta-analytic review. *Journal of Applied Psychology, 88,* 131–151. (p. 380)

Benson, H. (1996). *Timeless healing: The power and biology of belief.* New York: Scribner. (p. 412)

Benson, K., & Feinberg, I. (1977). The beneficial effect of sleep in an extended Jenkins and Dallenbach paradigm. *Psychophysiology, 14,* 375–384. (p. 279)

Berenbaum, S. A., Korman, K., & Leveroni, C. (1995). Early hormones and sex differences in cognitive abilities. *Learning and Individual Differences, 7,* 303–321. (p. 329)

Berenson, A. (2007, September 3). New schizophrenia drug shows promise in trials. *New York Times* (www.nytimes.com). (p. 514)

Berghuis, P., & 16 others (2007). Hardwiring the brain: Endocannabinoids shape neuronal connectivity. *Science, 316,* 1212–1216. (p. 96)

Bergin, A. E. (1980). Psychotherapy and religious values. *Journal of Consulting and Clinical Psychology, 48,* 95–105. (p. 511)

Berkel, J., & de Waard, F. (1983). Mortality pattern and life expectancy of Seventh-Day Adventists in the Netherlands. *International Journal of Epidemiology, 12,* 455–459. (p. 414)

Berkowitz, L. (1983). Aversively stimulated aggression: Some parallels and differences in research with animals and humans. *American Psychologist, 38,* 1135–1144. (p. 550)

Berkowitz, L. (1989). Frustration-aggression hypothesis: Examination and reformulation. *Psychological Bulletin, 106,* 59–73. (p. 550)

Berkowitz, L. (1990). On the formation and regulation of anger and aggression: A cognitive-neoassociationistic analysis. *American Psychologist, 45,* 494–503. (p. 390)

Berman, M., Gladue, B., & Taylor, S. (1993). The effects of hormones, Type A behavior pattern, and provocation on aggression in men. *Motivation and Emotion, 17,* 125–138. (p. 549)

Berndt, T. J., & Murphy, L. M. (2002). Influences of friends and friendships: Myths, truths, and research recommendations. *Advances in Child Development and Behavior, 30,* 275–310. (p. 161)

Berridge, K. C., & Winkielman, P. (2003). What is an unconscious emotion? (The case of unconscious "liking"). *Cognition and Emotion, 17,* 181–211. (p. 381)

Berry, D. S., & McArthur, L. Z. (1986). Perceiving character in faces: The impact of age-related craniofacial changes on social perception. *Psychological Bulletin, 100,* 3–18. (p. 231)

Berscheid, E. (1981). An overview of the psychological effects of physical attractiveness and some comments upon the psychological effects of knowledge of the effects of physical attractiveness. In G. W. Lucker, K. Ribbens, & J. A. McNamara (Eds.), *Psychological aspects of facial form* (Craniofacial growth series). Ann Arbor: Center for Human Growth and Development, University of Michigan. (p. 557)

Berscheid, E. (1985). Interpersonal attraction. In G. Lindzey & E. Aronson (Eds.), *The handbook of social psychology.* New York: Random House. (p. 370)

Berscheid, E., Gangestad, S. W., & Kulakowski, D. (1984). Emotion in close relationships: Implications for relationship counseling. In S. D. Brown & R. W. Lent (Eds.), *Handbook of counseling psychology.* New York: Wiley. (p. 560)

Berti, A., Cottini, G., Gandola, M., Pia, L., Smania, N., Stracciari, A., Castiglioni, I., Vallar, G., & Paulesu, E. (2005). Shared cortical anatomy for motor awareness and motor control. *Science, 309,* 488–491. (p. 60)

Bertua, C., Anderson, N., & Salgado, J. F. (2005). The predictive validity of cognitive ability tests: A UK meta-analysis. *Journal of Occupational and Organizational Psychology, 78,* 387–409. (p. 315)

Bettencourt, B. A., & Kernahan, C. (1997). A meta-analysis of aggression in the presence of violent cues: Effects of gender differences and aversive provocation. *Aggressive Behavior, 23,* pp. 447–457. (p. 127)

Beyerstein, B., & Beyerstein, D. (Eds.). (1992). *The write stuff: Evaluations of graphology.* Buffalo, NY: Prometheus Books. (p. 434)

Bhatt, R. S., Wasserman, E. A., Reynolds, W. F., Jr., & Knauss, K. S. (1988). Conceptual behavior in pigeons: Categorization of both familiar and novel examples from four classes of natural and artificial stimuli. *Journal of Experimental Psychology: Animal Behavior Processes, 14,* 219–234. (p. 238)

Bialystok, E. (2001). *Bilingualism in development, language, literacy, and cognition.* New York: Cambridge University Press. (p. 307)

Biederman, I., & Vessel, E. A. (2006). Perceptual pleasure and the brain. *American Scientist, 94,* 247–253. (p. 341)

Biggs, V. (2001, April 13). Murder suspect captured in Grand Marais. *Cook County News-Herald.* (p. 385)

Binet, A. (1909). *Les idées modernes sur les enfants.* Paris: Flammarion (quoted by A. Clarke & A. Clarke, Born to be bright. *The Psychologist, 19,* 409. (p. 319)

Birnbaum, G. E., Reis, H. T., Mikulincer, M., Gillath, O., & Orpaz, A. (2006). When sex is more than just sex: Attachment orientations, sexual experience, and relationship quality. *Journal of Personality and Social Psychology, 91,* 929–943. (p. 152)

Birnbaum, S. G., Yuan, P. X., Wang, M., Vijayraghavan, S., Bloom, A. K., Davis, D. J., Gobeski, K. T., Sweatt, J. D., Manhi, H. K., & Arnsten, A. F. T. (2004). Protein kinase C overactivity impairs prefrontal cortical regulation of working memory. *Science, 306,* 882–884. (p. 268)

Bishop, G. (2004, November 22). Personal correspondence, and earlier articles on "The great divide" in the *Austin Statesman.* (p. 540)

Bishop, G. D. (1991). Understanding the understanding of illness: Lay disease representations. In J. A. Skelton & R. T. Croyle (Eds.), *Mental representation in health and illness.* New York: Springer-Verlag. (p. 292)

Bisson, J., & Andrew, M. (2007). Psychological treatment of post-traumatic stress disorder (PTSD). *Cochrane Database of Systematic Reviews 2007,* Issue 3. Art. No: CD003388. (p. 508)

Bjork, R. A. (2000, July/August). Toward one world of psychological science. *APS Observer,* p. 3. (p. 5)

Bjorklund, D. F., & Green, B. L. (1992). The adaptive nature of cognitive immaturity. *American Psychologist, 47,* 46–54. (p. 148)

Blakemore, S-J., Wolpert, D. M., & Frith, C. D. (1998). Central cancellation of self-produced tickle sensation. *Nature Neuroscience, 1,* 635–640. (p. 197)

Blakeslee, S. (2006, January 10). Cells that read minds. *New York Times* (www.nytimes.com). (p. 248)

Blanchard, R. (1997). Birth order and sibling sex ratio in homosexual versus heterosexual males and females. *Annual Review of Sex Research, 8,* 27–67. (p. 365)

Blanchard, R. (2008). Review and theory of handedness, birth order, and homosexuality in men. *Laterality, 13,* 51–70. (p. 365)

Blanchard-Fields, F. (2007). Everyday problem solving and emotion: An adult developmental perspective. *Current Directions in Psychological Science, 16,* 26–31. (p. 167)

Blanchflower, D. G., & Oswald, A. J. (2008). Hypertension and happiness across nations. *Journal of Health Economics, 27,* 218–233. (pp. 171, 401)

Blank, H., Musch, J., & Pohl, R. F. (2007). Hindsight bias: On being wise after the event. *Social Cognition, 25,* 1–9. (p. 10)

Blankenburg, F., Taskin, B., Ruben, J., Moosmann, M., Ritter, P., Curio, G., & Villringer, A. (2003). Imperceptive stimuli and sensory processing impediment. *Science, 299,* 1864. (p. 182)

Blascovich, J., Seery, M. D., Mugridge, C. A., Norris, R. K., & Weisbuch, M. (2004). Predicting athletic performance from cardiovascular indexes of challenge and threat. *Journal of Experimental Social Psychology, 40,* 683–688. (p. 399)

Blass, T. (1996). Stanley Milgram: A life of inventiveness and controversy. In G. A. Kimble, C. A. Boneau, & M. Wertheimer (Eds.), *Portraits of pioneers in psychology* (Vol. II). Washington, DC, and Mahwah, NJ: American Psychological Association and Lawrence Erlbaum Publishers. (p. 535)

Blass, T. (1999). The Milgram paradigm after 35 years: Some things we now know about obedience to authority. *Journal of Applied Social Psychology, 29,* 955–978. (p. 535)

Blatt, S. J., Sanislow, C. A., III, Zuroff, D. C., & Pilkonis, P. (1996). Characteristics of effective therapists: Further analyses of data from the National Institute of Mental Health Treatment of Depression Collaborative Research Program. *Journal of Consulting and Clinical Psychology, 64,* 1276–1284. (p. 510)

Bloom, F. E. (1993, January/February). What's new in neurotransmitters. *BrainWork,* pp. 7–9. (p. 38)

Bloom, P. (2000). *How children learn the meanings of words.* Cambridge, MA: MIT Press. (p. 302)

Blum, K., Cull, J. G., Braverman, E. R., & Comings, D. E. (1996). Reward deficiency syndrome. *American Scientist, 84,* 132–145. (p. 49)

Boag, S. (2006). Freudian repression, the common view, and pathological science. *Review of General Psychology, 10,* 74–86. (p. 426)

Bocklandt, S., Horvath, S., Vilain, E., & Hamer, D. H. (2006). Extreme skewing of X chromosome inactivation in mothers of homosexual men. *Human Genetics, 118,* 691–694. (p. 366)

Bodenhausen, G. V., Sheppard, L. A., & Kramer, G. P. (1994). Negative affect and social judgment: The differential impact of anger and sadness. *European Journal of Social Psychology, 24,* 45–62. (p. 566)

Bodkin, J. A., & Amsterdam, J. D. (2002). Transdermal selegiline in major depression: A double-blind, placebo-controlled, parallel-group study in outpatients. *American Journal of Psychiatry, 159,* 1869–1875. (p. 515)

Boehm, K. E., Schondel, C. K., Marlowe, A. L., & Manke-Mitchell, L. (1999). Teens' concerns: A national evaluation. *Adolescence, 34,* 523–528. (p. 161)

Boesch-Achermann, H., & Boesch, C. (1993). Tool use in wild chimpanzees: New light from dark forests. *Current Directions in Psychological Science, 2,* 18–21. (p. 310)

Bogaert, A. F. (2003). Number of older brothers and sexual orientation: New texts and the attraction/behavior distinction in two national probability samples. *Journal of Personality and Social Psychology, 84,* 644–652. (p. 365)

Bogaert, A. F. (2004). Asexuality: Prevalence and associated factors in a national probability sample. *Journal of Sex Research, 41,* 279–287. (p. 363)

Bogaert, A. F. (2006). Biological versus nonbiological older brothers and men's sexual orientation. *Proceedings of the National Academy of Sciences, 103,* 10771–10774. (p. 365)

Bogaert, A. F. (2006). Toward a conceptual understanding of asexuality. *Review of General Psychology, 10,* 241–250. (p. 363)

Bogaert, A. F., Friesen, C., & Klentrou, P. (2002). Age of puberty and sexual orientation in a national probability sample. *Archives of Sexual Behavior, 31,* 73–81. (p. 365)

Boggiano, M. M., Chandler, P. C., Viana, J. B., Oswald, K. D., Maldonado, C. R., & Wauford, P. K. (2005). Combined dieting and stress evoke exaggerated responses to opioids in binge-eating rats. *Behavioral Neuroscience, 119,* 1207–1214. (p. 346)

Bohman, M., & Sigvardsson, S. (1990). Outcome in adoption: Lessons from longitudinal studies. In D. Brodzinsky & M. Schechter (Eds.), *The psychology of adoption.* New York: Oxford University Press. (p. 110)

Bolger, N., DeLongis, A., Kessler, R. C., & Schilling, E. A. (1989). Effects of daily stress on negative mood. *Journal of Personality and Social Psychology, 57,* 808–818. (p. 393)

Bolwig, T. G., & Madsen, T. M. (2007). Electroconvulsive therapy in melancholia: The role of hippocampal neurogenesis. *Acta Psychiatrica Scandinavica, 115,* 130–135. (p. 517)

Bonanno, G. A. (2001). Grief and emotion: Experience, expression, and dissociation. In M. Stroebe, W. Stroebe, R. O. Hansson, & H. Schut (Eds.), *New handbook of bereavement: Consciousness, coping, and care.* Cambridge: Cambridge University Press. (p. 172)

Bonanno, G. A. (2004). Loss, trauma, and human resilience: Have we underestimated the human capacity to thrive after extremely aversive events? *American Psychologist, 59,* 20–28. (p. 465)

Bonanno, G. A. (2004). Loss, trauma, and human resilience: Have we underestimated the human capacity to thrive after extremely aversive events? *American Psychologist, 59,* 20–28. (p. 172)

Bonanno, G. A. (2005). Adult resilience to potential trauma. *Current Directions in Psychological Science, 14,* 135–137. (p. 465)

Bonanno, G. A., Galea, S., Bucciarelli, A., & Vlahov, D. (2006). Psychological resilience after disaster. *Psychological Science, 17,* 181–186. (p. 464)

Bonanno, G. A., & Kaltman, S. (1999). Toward an integrative perspective on bereavement. *Psychological Bulletin, 125,* 760–777. (p. 172)

Bond, C. F., Jr., & DePaulo, B. M. (2006). Accuracy of deception judgments. *Personality and Social Psychology Review, 10,* 214–234. (p. 384)

Bond, C. F., Jr., & DePaulo, B. M. (2008). Individual differences in detecting deception: Accuracy and bias. *Psychological Bulletin, 134,* 477–492. (p. 384)

Bond, M. H. (1988). Finding universal dimensions of individual variation in multi-cultural studies of values: The Rokeach and Chinese values surveys. *Journal of Personality and Social Psychology, 55,* 1009–1015. (p. 124)

Bond, R., & Smith, P. B. (1996). Culture and conformity: A meta-analysis of studies using Asch's (1952b, 1956) line judgment task. *Psychological Bulletin, 119,* 111–137. (p. 534)

Bonnie, K. E., Horner, V., Whiten, A., & de Waal, F. B. M. (2007). Spread of arbitrary conventions among chimpanzees: A controlled experiment. *Proceedings of the Royal Society, 274,* 367–372. (p. 310)

Bookwala, J., & Boyar, J. (2008). Gender, excessive body weight, and psychological well-being in adulthood. *Psychology of Women Quarterly, 32,* 188–195. (p. 351)

Boos, H. B. M., Aleman, A., Cahn, W., Hulshoff, H., & Kahn, R. S. (2007). Brain volumes in relatives of patients with schizophrenia. *Archives of General Psychiatry, 64,* 297–304. (p. 483)

Boring, E. G. (1930). A new ambiguous figure. *American Journal of Psychology, 42,* 444–445. (p. 215)

Bornstein, M. H., Cote, L. R., Maital, S., Painter, K., Park, S-Y., Pascual, L., Pecheux, M-G., Ruel, J., Venute, P., & Vyt, A. (2004). Cross-linguistic analysis of vocabulary in young children: Spanish, Dutch, French, Hebrew, Italian, Korean, and American English. *Child Development, 75,* 1115–1139. (p. 304)

Bornstein, M. H., Tal, J., Rahn, C., Galperin, C. Z., Pecheux, M-G., Lamour, M., Toda, S., Azuma, H., Ogino, M., & Tamis-LeMonda, C. S. (1992a). Functional analysis of the contents of maternal speech to infants of 5 and 13 months in four cultures: Argentina, France, Japan, and the United States. *Developmental Psychology, 28,* 593–603. (p. 125)

Bornstein, M. H., Tamis-LeMonda, C. S., Tal, J., Ludemann, P., Toda, S., Rahn, C. W., Pecheux, M-G., Azuma, H., & Vardi, D. (1992b). Maternal responsiveness to infants in three societies: The United States, France, and Japan. *Child Development, 63,* 808–821. (p. 125)

Bornstein, R. F. (1989). Exposure and affect: Overview and meta- analysis of research, 1968–1987. *Psychological Bulletin, 106,* 265–289. (pp. 150, 556)

Bornstein, R. F. (1999). Source amnesia, misattribution, and the power of unconscious perceptions and memories. *Psychoanalytic Psychology, 16,* 155–178. (p. 556)

Bornstein, R. F. (2001). The impending death of psychoanalysis. *Psychoanalytic Psychology, 18,* 3–20. (p. 428)

Bornstein, R. F., Galley, D. J., Leone, D. R., & Kale, A. R. (1991). The temporal stability of ratings of parents: Test-retest reliability and influence of parental contact. *Journal of Social Behavior and Personality, 6,* 641–649. (p. 276)

Boron, J. B., Willis, S. L., & Schaie, K. W. (2007). Cognitive training gain as a predictor of mental status. *Journal of Gerontology: Series B: Psychological Sciences and Social Sciences, 62B(1),* 45–52. (p. 168)

Boscarino, J. A. (1997). Diseases among men 20 years after exposure to severe stress: Implications for clinical research and medical care. *Psychosomatic Medicine, 59,* 605–614. (p. 399)

Bosma, H., Marmot, M. G., Hemingway, H., Nicolson, A. C., Brunner, E., & Stansfeld, S. A. (1997). Low job control and risk of coronary heart disease in Whitehall II (prospective cohort) study. *British Medical Journal, 314,* 558–565. (p. 408)

Bosma, H., Peter, R., Siegrist, J., & Marmot, M. (1998). Two alternative job stress models and the risk of coronary heart disease. *American Journal of Public Health, 88,* 68–74. (p. 408)

Bostwick, J. M., & Pankratz, V. S. (2000). Affective disorders and suicide risk: A re-examination. *American Journal of Psychiatry, 157,* 1925–1932. (p. 474)

Bosworth, R. G., & Dobkins, K. R. (1999). Left-hemisphere dominance for motion processing in deaf signers. *Psychological Science, 10,* 256–262. (p. 56)

Bothwell, R. K., Brigham, J. C., & Malpass, R. S. (1989). Cross-racial identification. *Personality and Social Psychology Bulletin, 15,* 19–25. (p. 547)

Bouchard, T. J., Jr. (1981, December 6). Interview on Nova: Twins [program broadcast by the Public Broadcasting Service]. (p. 108)

Bouchard, T. J., Jr. (1995). Longitudinal studies of personality and intelligence: A behavior genetic and evolutionary psychology perspective. In D. H. Saklofske & M. Zeidner (Eds.), *International handbook of personality and intelligence.* New York: Plenum. (p. 326)

Bouchard, T. J., Jr. (1996a). IQ similarity in twins reared apart: Finding and responses to critics. In R. Sternberg & C. Grigorenko (Eds.), *Intelligence: Heredity and environment.* New York: Cambridge University Press. (p. 325)

Bouchard, T. J., Jr. (1996b). Behavior genetic studies of intelligence, yesterday and today: The long journey from plausibility to proof. *Journal of Biosocial Science, 28,* 527–555. (p. 326)

Bouchard, T. J., Jr., & McGue, M. (1990). Genetic and rearing environmental influences on adult personality: An analysis of adopted twins reared apart. *Journal of Personality, 58,* 263. (p. 109)

Bouchard, T. J., Jr., McGue, M., Hur, T-M., & Horn, J. M. (1990). A genetic and environmental analysis of the California Psychological Inventory using adult twins reared apart and together. *European Journal of Personality, 12,* 307–320. (p. 108)

Bouton, M. E., Mineka, S., & Barlow, D. H. (2001). A modern learning theory perspective on the etiology of panic disorder. *Psychological Review, 108,* 4–32. (p. 466)

Bowden, E. M., & Beeman, M. J. (1998). Getting the right idea: Semantic activation in the right hemisphere may help solve insight problems. *Psychological Science, 9,* 435–440. (p. 60)

Bower, B. (2003, November 22). Vision seekers. *Science News, 164,* pp. 331, 332. (p. 214)

Bower, G. H. (1983). Affect and cognition. *Philosophical Transaction: Royal Society of London, Series B, 302,* 387–402. (p. 275)

Bower, G. H. (1986). Prime time in cognitive psychology. In P. Eelen (Ed.), *Cognitive research and behavior therapy: Beyond the conditioning paradigm.* Amsterdam: North Holland Publishers. (p. 274)

Bower, G. H., Clark, M. C., Lesgold, A. M., & Winzenz, D. (1969). Hierarchical retrieval schemes in recall of categorized word lists. *Journal of Verbal Learning and Verbal Behavior, 8,* 323–343. (p. 265)

Bower, G. H., & Morrow, D. G. (1990). Mental models in narrative comprehension. *Science, 247,* 44–48. (p. 262)

Bower, J. E., Kemeny, M. E., Taylor, S. E., & Fahey, J. L. (1998). Cognitive processing, discovery of meaning, CD4 decline, and AIDS-related mortality among bereaved HIV-seropositive men. *Journal of Consulting and Clinical Psychology, 66,* 979–986. (p. 405)

Bower, J. M., & Parsons, L. M. (2003, August). Rethinking the "lesser brain." *Scientific American,* pp. 50–57. (p. 46)

Bowers, K. S. (1984). Hypnosis. In N. Endler & J. M. Hunt (Eds.), *Personality and behavioral disorders* (2nd ed.). New York: Wiley. (pp. 84, 85)

Bowers, K. S. (1987, July). Personal communication. (p. 85)

Bowers, T. G., & Clum, G. A. (1988). Relative contribution of specific and nonspecific treatment effects: Meta-analysis of placebo-controlled behavior therapy research. *Psychological Bulletin, 103,* 315–323. (p. 506)

Bowles, S., & Kasindorf, M. (2001, March 6). Friends tell of picked-on but 'normal' kid. *USA Today,* p. 4A. (p. 371)

Bowman, H. (2003, Fall). Interactions between chimpanzees and their human caregivers in captive settings: The effects of gestural communication on reciprocity. *Friends of Washoe, 25(1),* 7–16. (p. 311)

Boyatzis, C. J., Matillo, G. M., & Nesbitt, K. M. (1995). Effects of the "Mighty Morphin Power Rangers" on children's aggression with peers. *Child Study Journal, 25,* 45–55. (p. 252)

Boynton, R. M. (1979). *Human color vision.* New York: Holt, Rinehart & Winston. (p. 191)

Braden, J. P. (1994). *Deafness, deprivation, and IQ.* New York: Plenum. (p. 331)

Bradley, D. R., Dumais, S. T., & Petry, H. M. (1976). Reply to Cavonius. *Nature, 261,* 78. (p. 205)

Bradley, R. B., & 15 others (2008). Influence of child abuse on adult depression: Moderation by the corticotropin-releasing hormone receptor gene. *Archives of General Psychiatry, 65,* 190–200. (p. 153)

Braiker, B. (2005, October 18). A quiet revolt against the rules on SIDS. *New York Times* (www.nytimes.com). (p. 141)

Brainerd, C. J. (1996). Piaget: A centennial celebration. *Psychological Science, 7,* 191–195. (p. 142)

Brandon, S., Boakes, J., Glaser, & Green, R. (1998). Recovered memories of childhood sexual abuse: Implications for clinical practice. *British Journal of Psychiatry, 172,* 294–307. (p. 286)

Brannon, L. A., & Brock, T. C. (1993). Comment on report of HIV infection in rural Florida: Failure of instructions to correct for gross underestimation of phantom sex partners in perception of AIDS risk. *New England Journal of Medicine, 328,* 1351–1352. (p. 362)

Bransford, J. D., & Johnson, M. K. (1972). Contextual prerequisites for understanding: Some investigations of comprehension and recall. *Journal of Verbal Learning and Verbal Behavior, 11,* 717–726. (p. 262)

Braun, S. (1996). New experiments underscore warnings on maternal drinking. *Science, 273,* 738–739. (p. 138)

Braun, S. (2001, Spring). Seeking insight by prescription. *Cerebrum,* pp. 10–21. (p. 95)

Braunstein, G. D., Sundwall, D. A., Katz, M., Shifren, J. L., Buster, J. E., Simon, J. A., Bachman, G., Aguirre, O. A., Lucas, J. D., Rodenberg, C., Buch, A., & Watts, N. B. (2005). Safety and efficacy of a testosterone patch for the treatment of hypoactive sexual desire disorder in surgically menopausal women: A randomized, placebo-controlled trial. *Archives of Internal Medicine, 165,* 1582–1589. (p. 358)

Bray, D. W., & Byham, W., interviewed by Mayes, B. T. (1997). Insights into the history and future of assessment centers: An interview with Dr. Douglas W. Bray and Dr. William Byham. *Journal of Social Behavior and Personality, 12,* 3–12. (p. 445)

Bray, D. W., & Byham, W. C. (1991, Winter). Assessment centers and their derivatives. *Journal of Continuing Higher Education,* pp. 8–11. (p. 445)

Bray, G. A. (1969). Effect of caloric restriction on energy expenditure in obese patients. *Lancet, 2,* 397–398. (p. 352)

Breedlove, S. M. (1997). Sex on the brain. *Nature, 389,* 801. (p. 366)

Brehm, S., & Brehm, J. W. (1981). *Psychological reactance: A theory of freedom and control.* New York: Academic Press. (p. 541)

Breland, K., & Breland, M. (1961). The misbehavior of organisms. *American Psychologist, 16,* 661–664. (p. 244)

Breslau, J., Aguilar-Gaxiola, S., Borges, G., Kendler, K. S., Su, M., & Kessler, R. C. (2007). Risk for psychiatric disorder among immigrants and their US-born descendants. *Journal of Nervous and Mental Disease, 195,* 189–195. (p. 488)

Bressan, P., & Dal Martello, M. F. (2002). Talis pater, talis filius: Perceived resemblance and the belief in genetic relatedness. *Psychological Science, 13,* 213–218. (p. 215)

Brewer, C. L. (1990). Personal correspondence. (pp. 6, 112)

Brewer, M. B., & Chen, Y-R. (2007). Where (who) are collectives in collectivism? Toward conceptual clarification of individualism and collectivism. *Psychological Review, 114,* 133–151. (p. 123)

Brewer, W. F. (1977). Memory for the pragmatic implications of sentences. *Memory & Cognition, 5,* 673–678. (p. 262)

Brewin, C. R., Andrews, B., Rose, S., & Kirk, M. (1999). Acute stress disorder and posttraumatic stress disorder in victims of violent crime. *American Journal of Psychiatry, 156,* 360–366. (p. 464)

Brewin, C. R., Andrews, B., & Valentine, J. D. (2000). Meta-analysis of risk factors for posttraumatic stress disorder in trauma-exposed adults. *Journal of Consulting and Clinical Psychology, 68,* 748–766. (p. 464)

Brewin, C. R., Kleiner, J. S., Vasterling J. J., & Field, A. P. (2007). Memory for emotionally neutral information in posttraumatic stress disorder: A meta-analytic investigation. *Journal of Abnormal Psychology, 116,* 448–463. (p. 268)

Bricker, J. B., Stallings, M. C., Corley, R. P., Wadsworth, S. J., Bryan, A., Timberlake, D. S., Hewitt, J. K., Caspi, A., Hofer, S. M., Rhea, S. A., & DeFries, J. C. (2006). Genetic and environmental influences on age at sexual initiation in the Colorado Adoption Project. *Behavior Genetics, 36,* 820–832. (p. 361)

Briers, B., Pandelaere, M., Dewitte, S., & Warlop, L. (2006). Hungry for money: The desire for caloric resources increases the desire for financial resources and vice versa. *Psychological Science, 17,* 939–943. (p. 239)

Briñol, P., Petty, R. E., & Barden, J. (2007). Happiness versus sadness as a determinant of thought confidence in persuasion: A self-validation analysis. *Journal of Personality and Social Psychology, 93,* 711–727. (p. 392)

Brinson, S. L. (1992). The use and opposition of rape myths in prime-time television dramas. *Sex Roles, 27,* 359–375. (p. 553)

Brislin, R. W. (1988). Increasing awareness of class, ethnicity, culture, and race by expanding on students' own experiences. In I. Cohen (Ed.), *The G. Stanley Hall Lecture Series.* Washington, DC: American Psychological Association. (p. 121)

Brissette, I., & Cohen, S. (2002). The contribution of individual differences in hostility to the associations between daily interpersonal conflict, affect, and sleep. *Personality and Social Psychology Bulletin, 28,* 1265–1274. (p. 78)

Brissette, I., Scheier, M. F., & Carver, C. S. (2002). The role of optimism in social network development, coping, and psychological adjustment during a life transition. *Journal of Personality and Social Psychology, 82,* 102–111. (p. 478)

British Psychological Society. (1993). Ethical principles for conducting research with human participants. *The Psychologist: Bulletin of the British Psychological Society, 6,* 33–36. (pp. 27, 434)

Brody, J. E. (1999, November 30). Yesterday's precocious puberty is norm today. *New York Times* (www.nytimes.com). (p. 155)

Brody, J. E. (2000, March 21). When posttraumatic stress grips youth. *New York Times* (www.nytimes.com). (p. 464)

Brody, J. E. (2002, November 26). When the eyelids snap shut at 65 miles an hour. *New York Times* (www.nytimes.com). (p. 76)

Brody, J. E. (2003, September). Addiction: A brain ailment, not a moral lapse. *New York Times* (www.nytimes.com). (p. 88)

Brody, J. E. (2003, December 23). Stampede of diabetes as U.S. races to obesity. *New York Times* (www.nytimes.com). (p. 354)

Brody, N. (2001, December 11). An old enemy, smoking, hangs tough. *New York Times* (www.nytimes.com). (p. 93)

Brody, S., & Tillmann, H. C. (2006). The postorgasmic prolactin increase following intercourse is greater than following masturbation and suggests greater satiety. *Biological Psychology, 71,* 312–315. (p. 369)

Bronner, E. (1998, February 25). U.S. high school seniors among worst in math and science. *New York Times* (www.nytimes.com). (p. 329)

Brookes, K., & 61 others (2006). The analysis of 51 genes in DSM-IV combined type attention deficit hyperactivity disorder: Association signals in DRD4, DAT1 and 16 other genes. *Molecular Psychiatry, 11,* 935–953. (p. 455)

Brooks, D. J. (2002, October 8). Running down the road to happiness. *Gallup Tuesday Briefing* (www.gallup.com). (p. 411)

Brooks, R., & Meltzoff, A. N. (2005). The development of gaze following and its relation to language. *Developmental Science, 8,* 535–543. (p. 249)

Brown, A. S. (2003). A review of the déjà vu experience. *Psychological Bulletin, 129,* 394–413. (p. 275)

Brown, A. S. (2004b) Getting to grips with déja vu. *The Psychologist, 17,* 694–696. (p. 275)

Brown, A. S., Begg, M. D., Gravenstein, S., Schaefer, C. A., Wyatt, R. J., Bresnahan, M., Babulas, V. P., & Susser, E. S. (2004). Serologic evidence of prenatal influenza in the etiology of schizophrenia. *Archives of General Psychiatry, 61,* 774–780. (p. 484)

Brown, A. S., Bracken, E., Zoccoli, S., & Douglas, K. (2004). Generating and remembering passwords. *Applied Cognitive Psychology, 18,* 641–651. (p. 280)

Brown, A. S., Schaefer, C. A., Wyatt, R. J., Goetz, R., Begg, M. D., Gorman, J. M., & Susser, E. S. (2000). Maternal exposure to respiratory infections and adult schizophrenia spectrum disorders: A prospective birth cohort study. *Schizophrenia Bulletin, 26,* 287–295. (p. 484)

Brown, E. L., & Deffenbacher, K. (1979). *Perception and the senses.* New York: Oxford University Press. (p. 196)

Brown, G. K., Ten Have, T., Henriques, G. R., Xie, S. X., Hollander, J. E., & Beck, A. T. (2005). Cognitive therapy for the prevention of suicide attempts. *Journal of the American Medical Association, 294,* 563–570. (p. 506)

Brown, J. A. (1958). Some tests of the decay theory of immediate memory. *Quarterly Journal of Experimental Psychology, 10,* 12–21. (p. 266)

Brown, J. D., Steele, J. R., & Walsh-Childers, K. (2002). *Sexual teens, sexual media: Investigating media's influence on adolescent sexuality.* Mahwah, NJ: Erlbaum. (p. 361)

Brown, J. L., & Pollitt, E. (1996, February). Malnutrition, poverty and intellectual development. *Scientific American,* pp. 38–43. (p. 326)

Brown, R. (1986). Linguistic relativity. In S. H. Hulse & B. F. Green, Jr. (Eds.), *One hundred years of psychological research in America.* Baltimore: Johns Hopkins University Press. (p. 306)

Brown, S. L., Brown, R. M., House, J. S., & Smith, D. M. (2008). Coping with spousal loss: Potential buffering effects of self-reported helping behavior. *Personality and Social Psychology Bulletin, 34,* 849–861. (p. 172)

Brown, S. W., Garry, M., Loftus, E., Silver, B., DuBois, K., & DuBreuil, S. (1996). People's beliefs about memory: Why don't we have better memories? Paper presented at the American Psychological Society convention. (p. 281)

Brownell, K. D. (2002). Public policy and the prevention of obesity. In C. G. Fairburn & K. D. Brownell (Eds.), *Eating disorders and obesity: A comprehensive handbook* (2nd ed.). New York: Guilford. (p. 354)

Brownell, K. D., & Nestle, M. (2004, June 7). Are you responsible for your own weight? *Time,* p. 113. (p. 354)

Browning, C. (1992). *Ordinary men: Reserve police battalion 101 and the final solution in Poland.* New York: HarperCollins. (p. 536)

Brownmiller, S. (1975). *Against our will: Men, women, and rape.* New York: Simon & Schuster. (p. 360)

Bruce, D., Dolan, A., & Phillips-Grant, K. (2000). On the transition from childhood amnesia to the recall of personal memories. *Psychological Science, 11,* 360–364. (p. 141)

Bruck, M., & Ceci, S. (2004). Forensic developmental psychology: Unveiling four common misconceptions. *Current Directions in Psychological Science, 15,* 229–232. (p. 284)

Bruck, M., & Ceci, S. J. (1999). The suggestibility of children's memory. *Annual Review of Psychology, 50,* 419–439. (p. 284)

Brumberg, J. J. (2000). *Fasting girls: The history of anorexia nervosa.* New York: Vintage. (p. 348)

Bryant, A. N. & Astin, H. A. (2007). The spiritual struggles of college students. *Journal of Higher Education,* in press. (p. 160)

Bryant, R. A. (2001). Posttraumatic stress disorder and traumatic brain injury: Can they co-exist? *Clinical Psychology Review, 21,* 931–948. (p. 286)

Buchanan, T. W. (2007). Retrieval of emotional memories. *Psychological Bulletin, 133,* 761–779. (p. 268)

Buck, L. B., & Axel, R. (1991). A novel multi-gene family may encode odorant receptors: A molecular basis for odor recognition. *Cell, 65,* 175–187. (p. 203)

Buckley, K. E., & Leary, M. R. (2001). Perceived acceptance as a predictor of social, emotional, and academic outcomes. Paper presented at the Society of Personality and Social Psychology annual convention. (p. 371)

Buehler, R., Griffin, D., & Ross, M. (1994). Exploring the "planning fallacy": Why people underestimate their task completion times. *Journal of Personality and Social Psychology, 67,* 366–381. (p. 297)

Bugelski, B. R., Kidd, E., & Segmen, J. (1968). Image as a mediator in one-trial paired-associate learning. *Journal of Experimental Psychology, 76,* 69–73. (p. 263)

Bugental, D. B. (1986). Unmasking the "polite smile": Situational and personal determinants of managed affect in adult-child interaction. *Personality and Social Psychology Bulletin, 12,* 7–16. (p. 384)

Buka, S. L., Goldstein, J. M., Seidman, L. J., Zornberg, G., Donatelli, J-A. A., Denny, L. R., & Tsuang, M. T. (1999). Prenatal complications, genetic vulnerability, and schizophrenia: The New England longitudinal studies of schizophrenia. *Psychiatric Annals, 29,* 151–156. (p. 483)

Buka, S. L., Tsuang, M. T., Torrey, E. F., Klebanoff, M. A., Wagner, R. L., & Yolken, R. H. (2001). Maternal infections and subsequent psychosis among offspring. *Archives of General Psychiatry, 58,* 1032–1037. (p. 484)

Bullough, V. (1990). The Kinsey scale in historical perspective. In D. P. McWhirter, S. A. Sanders, & J. M. Reinisch (Eds.), *Homosexuality/heterosexuality: Concepts of sexual orientation.* New York: Oxford University Press. (p. 363)

Bunde, J., & Suls, J. (2006). A quantitative analysis of the relationship between the Cook-Medley Hostility Scale and traditional coronary artery disease risk factors. *Health Psychology, 25,* 493–500. (p. 403)

Buquet, R. (1988). Le rêve et les deficients visuels [Dreams and the visually-impaired]. *Psychanalyse-à-l'Université, 13,* 319–327. (p. 80)

Burcusa, S. L., & Iacono, W. G. (2007). Risk for recurrence in depression. *Clinical Psychology Review, 27,* 959–985. (p. 473)

Bureau of Labor Statistics. (2004, September 14). *American time-user survey summary.* Washington, DC: United States Department of Labor (www.bls.gov). (p. 130)

Bureau of the Census. (2004). *Statistical abstract of the United States 2004.* Washington, DC: U.S. Government Printing Office. (pp. 461, 513)

Bureau of the Census. (2007). *Statistical abstract of the United States 2007.* Washington, DC: U.S. Government Printing Office. (p. 169)

Burger, J. M. (2009). Replicating Milgram: Would people still obey today? *American Psychologist, 64,* 1–11. (p. 537)

Buri, J. R., Louiselle, P. A., Misukanis, T. M., & Mueller, R. A. (1988). Effects of parental authoritarianism and authoritativeness on self-esteem. *Personality and Social Psychology Bulletin, 14,* 271–282. (p. 154)

Burke, D. M., & Shafto, M. A. (2004). Aging and language production. *Current Directions in Psychological Science, 13,* 21–24. (p. 167)

Burkholder, R. (2005a, January 11). Chinese far wealthier than a decade ago—but are they happier? *Gallup Poll News Service* (www.gallup.com). (p. 396)

Burkholder, R. (2005b, January 18). China's citizens optimistic, yet not entirely satisfied. *Gallup Poll News Service* (www.gallup.com). (p. 396)

Burns, B. C. (2004). The effects of speed on skilled chess performance. *Psychological Science, 15,* 442–447. (p. 300)

Burris, C. T., & Branscombe, N. R. (2005). Distorted distance estimation induced by a self-relevant national boundary. *Journal of Experimental Social Psychology, 41,* 305–312. (p. 307)

Bush, G. W. (2001). Quoted in various places, including BBC News (bbc.co.uk), June 16, 2001. (p. 564)

Bushman, B. J. (1993). Human aggression while under the influence of alcohol and other drugs: An integrative research review. *Current Directions in Psychological Science, 2,* 148–152. (p. 549)

Bushman, B. J. (2002). Does venting anger feed or extinguish the flame? Catharsis, rumination, distraction, anger, and aggressive responding. *Personality and Social Psychology Bulletin, 28,* 724–731. (p. 391)

Bushman, B. J., & Anderson, C. A. (2001). Media violence and the American public: Scientific facts versus media misinformation. *American Psychologist, 56,* 477–489. (p. 553)

Bushman, B. J., & Baumeister, R. F. (1998). Threatened egotism, narcissism, self-esteem, and direct and displaced aggression: Does self-love or self-hate lead to violence? *Journal of Personality and Social Psychology, 75,* 219–229. (p. 448)

Bushman, B. J., Baumeister, R. F., & Stack, A. D. (1999). Catharsis, aggression, and persuasive influence: Self-fulfilling or self-defeating prophecies? *Journal of Personality and Social Psychology, 76,* 367–376. (p. 391)

Bushman, B. J., Baumeister, R. F., Thomaes, S., Ryu, E., Begeer, S., & West, S. G. (2009). Looking again, and harder, for a link between low self-esteem and aggression. *Journal of Personality, 11,* 427–446. (p. 448)

Bushman, B. J., & Bonacci, A. M. (2002). Violence and sex impair memory for television ads. *Journal of Applied Psychology, 87,* 557–564. (pp. 280, 360)

Buss, A. H. (1989). Personality as traits. *American Psychologist, 44,* 1378–1388. (p. 438)

Buss, D. M. (1991). Evolutionary personality psychology. *Annual Review of Psychology, 42,* 459–491. (p. 111)

Buss, D. M. (1994). The strategies of human mating: People worldwide are attracted to the same qualities in the opposite sex. *American Scientist, 82,* 238–249. (p. 116)

Buss, D. M. (1995). Evolutionary psychology: A new paradigm for psychological science. *Psychological Inquiry, 6,* 1–30. (p. 116)

Buss, D. M. (1996). Sexual conflict: Evolutionary insights into feminism and the "battle of the sexes." In D. M. Buss & N. M. Malamuth (Eds.), *Sex, power, conflict: Evolutionary and feminist perspectives.* New York: Oxford University Press. (p. 116)

Buss, D. M. (2000). *The dangerous passion: Why jealousy is as necessary as love and sex.* New York: Free Press. (p. 116)

Buss, D. M. (2008). Female sexual psychology. World Question Center 2008 (edge.org). (p. 359)

Busseri, M. A., Willoughby, T., Chalmers, H., & Bogaert, A. R. (2006). Same-sex attraction and successful adolescent development. *Journal of Youth and Adolescence, 35,* 563–575. (p. 363)

Buster, J. E., Kingsberg, S. A., Aguirre, O., Brown, C., Breaux, J. G., Buch, A., Rodenberg, C. A., Wekselman, K., & Casson, P. (2005). Testosterone patch for low sexual desire in surgically menopausal women: A randomized trial. *Obstetrics and Gynecology, 105*(5), 944–952. (p. 358)

Butcher, L. M., Davis, O. S. P., Craig, I. W., & Plomin, R. (2008). Genome-wide quantitative trait locus association scan of general cognitive ability using pooled DNA and 500K single nucleotide polymorphism microarrays. *Genes, Brain and Behavior, 7,* 435–446. (p. 325)

Butler, A. C., Hokanson, J. E., & Flynn, H. A. (1994). A comparison of self-esteem lability and low trait self-esteem as vulnerability factors for depression. *Journal of Personality and Social Psychology, 66,* 166–177. (p. 478)

Butler, R. A. (1954, February). Curiosity in monkeys. *Scientific American,* pp. 70–75. (p. 341)

Butterfield, F. (1999, July 12). Experts say study confirms prison's new role as mental hospital. *New York Times* (www.nytimes.com). (p. 461)

Byne, W., & Parsons, B. (1993). Human sexual orientation: The biologic theories reappraised. *Archives of General Psychiatry, 50,* 228–239. (p. 368)

Bynum, R. (2004, November 1). Associated Press article. (p. 198)

Byrne, D. (1982). Predicting human sexual behavior. In A. G. Kraut (Ed.), *The G. Stanley Hall Lecture Series* (Vol. 2). Washington, DC: American Psychological Association. (pp. 230, 358)

Byrne, J. (2003, September 21). From correspondence reported by Michael Shermer, E-Skeptic for September 21, 2003, from The Skeptics Society. (p. 219)

Byrne, R. W. (1991, May/June). Brute intellect. *The Sciences,* pp. 42–47. (p. 311)

Byrne, R. W., & Corp, N. (2004). Neocortex size predicts deception in primates. *Proceedings of the Royal Society B, 271,* 1693–1699. (p. 17)

Cahill, L. (1994). (Beta)-adrenergic activation and memory for emotional events. *Nature, 371,* 702–704. (p. 269)

Cahill, L. (2005, May). His brain, her brain. *Scientific American,* pp. 40–47. (p. 129)

Cahn, B. R., & Polich, J. (2006). Meditation states and traits: EEG, ERP, and neuroimaging studies. *Psychological Bulletin, 132,* 180–211. (p. 413)

Cale, E. M., & Lilienfeld, S. O. (2002). Sex differences in psychopathy and antisocial personality disorder: A review and integration. *Clinical Psychology Review, 22,* 1179–1207. (p. 486)

Call, K. T., Riedel, A. A., Hein, K., McLoyd, V., Petersen, A., & Kipke, M. (2002). Adolescent health and well-being in the twenty-first century: A global perspective. *Journal of Research on Adolescence, 12,* 69–98. (p. 361)

Callaghan, T., Rochat, P., Lillard, A., Claux, M. L., Odden, H., Itakura, S., Tapanya, S., & Singh, S. (2005). Synchrony in the onset of mental-state reasoning. *Psychological Science, 16,* 378–384. (p. 145)

Calle, E. E., Thun, M. J., Petrelli, J. M., Rodriguez, C., & Health, C. W., Jr. (1999). Body-mass index and mortality in a prospective cohort of U.S. adults. *New England Journal of Medicine, 341,* 1097–1105. (p. 350)

Calvo-Merino, B., Glaser, D. E., Grèzes, J., Passingham, R. E., & Haggard, P. (2004). Action observation and acquired motor skills: An fMRI study with expert dancers. *Cerebral Cortex, 15,* 1243–1249. (p. 308)

Cameron, L., & Rutland, A. (2006). Extended contact through story reading in school: Reducing children's prejudice toward the disabled. *Journal of Social Issues, 62,* 469–488. (p. 565)

Campbell, D. T. (1975). On the conflicts between biological and social evolution and between psychology and moral tradition. *American Psychologist, 30,* 1103–1126. (p. 395)

Campbell, D. T., & Specht, J. C. (1985). Altruism: Biology, culture, and religion. *Journal of Social and Clinical Psychology, 3*(1), 33–42. (p. 432)

Campbell, S. (1986). *The Loch Ness Monster: The evidence.* Willingborough, Northamptonshire, U.K.: Acquarian Press. (p. 215)

Camper, J. (1990, February 7). Drop pompom squad, U. of I. rape study says. *Chicago Tribune,* p. 1. (p. 90)

Camperio-Ciani, A., Cermelli, P., & Zanzott, G. (2008). Sexually antagonistic selection in human male homosexuality. *PloS One, 3,* e2282, 1–8. (p. 366)

Camperio-Ciani, A., Corna, F., & Capiluppi, C. (2004). Evidence for maternally inherited factors favouring male homosexuality and promoting female fecundity. *Proceedings of the Royal Society of London B, 271,* 2217–2221. (p. 366)

Campos, J. J., Bertenthal, B. I., & Kermoian, R. (1992). Early experience and emotional development: The emergence of wariness and heights. *Psychological Science, 3,* 61–64. (p. 207)

Canli, T. (2008, February/March). The character code. *Scientific American Mind,* pp. 53–57. (p. 467)

Canli, T., Desmond, J. E., Zhao, Z., & Gabrieli, J. D. E. (2002). Sex differences in the neural basis of emotional memories. *Proceedings of the National Academy of Sciences, 99,* 10789–10794. (p. 386)

Cannon, W. B. (1929). *Bodily changes in pain, hunger, fear, and rage.* New York: Branford. (pp. 344, 399)

Cannon, W. B., & Washburn, A. (1912). An explanation of hunger. *American Journal of Physiology, 29,* 441–454. (p. 344)

Cantor, N., & Kihlstrom, J. F. (1987). *Personality and social intelligence.* Englewood Cliffs, NJ: Prentice-Hall. (p. 318)

Caplan, N., Choy, M. H., & Whitmore, J. K. (1992, February). Indochinese refugee families and academic achievement. *Scientific American,* pp. 36–42. (p. 119)

Caputo, D., & Dunning, D. (2005). What you don't know: The role played by errors of omission in imperfect self-assessments. *Journal of Experimental Social Psychology,* 488–505. (p. 444)

Carducci, B. J., Cosby, P. C., & Ward, D. D. (1978). Sexual arousal and interpersonal evaluations. *Journal of Experimental Social Psychology, 14,* 449–457. (p. 559)

Carey, B. (2006, November 11). What's wrong with a child? Psychiatrists often disagree. *New York Times* (www.nytimes.com). (p. 458)

Carey, B. (2007, September 4). Bipolar illness soars as a diagnosis for the young. *New York Times* (www.nytimes.com). (p. 471)

Carey, B. (2008, December 4). H. M., an unforgettable amnesiac, dies at 82. *New York Times* (www.nytimes.com). (p. 270)

Carey, G. (1990). Genes, fears, phobias, and phobic disorders. *Journal of Counseling and Development, 68,* 628–632. (p. 467)

Carlson, C. L. (2000). ADHD is overdiagnosed. In R. L. Atkinson, R. C. Atkinson, E. E. Smith, D. J. Bem, & S. Nolen-Hoeksema (Eds.), *Hilgard's introduction to psychology* (13th ed.). Fort Worth: Harcourt. (p. 455)

Carlson, M. (1995, August 29). Quoted by S. Blakeslee, In brain's early growth, timetable may be crucial. *New York Times,* pp. C1, C3. (p. 152)

Carlson, M., Charlin, V., & Miller, N. (1988). Positive mood and helping behavior: A test of six hypotheses. *Journal of Personality and Social Psychology, 55,* 211–229. (p. 562)

Carlson, S. (1985). A double-blind test of astrology. *Nature, 318,* 419–425. (p. 434)

Carlson, S. M., & Meltzoff, A. N. (2008). Bilingual experience and executive functioning in young children. *Developmental Science, 11,* 282–298. (p. 307)

Carnahan, T., & McFarland, S. (2007). Revisiting the Stanford Prison Experiment: Could participant self-selection have led to the cruelty? *Personality and Social Psychology Bulletin, 33,* 603–614. (p. 529)

Carnelley, K. B., Wortman, C. B., Bolger, N., & Burke, C. T. (2006). The time course of grief reactions to spousal loss: Evidence from a national probability sample. *Journal of Personality and Social Psychology, 91,* 476–492. (p. 172)

Carpusor, A., & Loges, W. E. (2006). Rental discrimination and ethnicity in names. *Journal of Applied Social Psychology, 36,* 934–952. (p. 23)

Carrière, G. (2003). Parent and child factors associated with youth obesity. *Statistics Canada, Catalogue 82–003,* Supplement to Health Reports, 2003. (p. 353)

Carroll, J. M., & Russell, J. A. (1996). Do facial expressions signal specific emotions? Judging emotion from the face in context. *Journal of Personality and Social Psychology, 70,* 205–218. (p. 388)

Carroll, J. S., Padilla-Walker, L. M., Nelson, L. J., Olson, C. D., Barry, C. M., & Madsen, S. D. (2008). Generation XXX: Pornography acceptance and use among emerging adults. *Journal of Adolescent Research, 23,* 6–30. (p. 551)

Carskadon, M. (2002). *Adolescent sleep patterns: Biological, social, and psychological influences.* New York: Cambridge University Press. (p. 76)

Carstensen, L. I., & Mikels, J. A. (2005). At the intersection of emotion and cognition: Aging and the positivity effect. *Current Directions in Psychological Science, 14,* 117–121. (pp. 167, 171)

Carter, R. (1998). *Mapping the mind.* Berkeley: University of California Press. (p. 38)

Cartwright, R. D. (1978). *A primer on sleep and dreaming.* Reading, MA: Addison-Wesley. (p. 74)

CASA. (2003). *The formative years: Pathways to substance abuse among girls and young women ages 8–22.* New York: National Center on Addiction and Substance Use, Columbia University. (pp. 90, 98)

CASA. (2004). CASA 2004 teen survey. National Center on Addiction and Substance Abuse, Columbia University (www.casacolumbia.org). (pp. 361, 362)

Casey, B. J., Getz, S., & Galvan, A. (2008). The adolescent brain. *Developmental Review, 28,* 62–77. (p. 156)

Cash, T., & Janda, L. H. (1984, December). The eye of the beholder. *Psychology Today,* pp. 46–52. (p. 557)

Cash, T. F., & Henry, P. E. (1995). Women's body images: The results of a national survey in the U.S.A. *Sex Roles, 33,* 19–28. (p. 349)

Caspi, A. (2000). The child is father of the man: Personality continuities from childhood to adulthood. *Journal of Personality and Social Psychology, 78,* 158–172. (p. 111)

Caspi, A., Harrington, H., Milne, B., Amell, J. W., Theodore, R. F., & Moffitt, T. E. (2003). Children's behavioral styles at age 3 are linked to their adult personality traits at age 26. *Journal of Personality, 71,* 496–513. (pp. 174, 476)

Caspi, A., Moffitt, T. E., Newman, D. L., & Silva, P. A. (1996). Behavioral observations at age 3 years predict adult psychiatric disorders: Longitudinal evidence from a birth cohort. *Archives of General Psychiatry, 53,* 1033–1039. (p. 487)

Caspi, A., Williams, B., Kim-Cohen, J., Craig, I. W., Milne, B. J., Poulton, R., Schalkwyk, L. C., Taylor, A., Werts, H., & Moffitt, T. E. (2007). Moderation of breastfeeding effects on the IQ by genetic variation in fatty acid metabolism. *Proceedings of the National Academy of Sciences, 104,* 18860–18865. (p. 106)

Cassel, L., & Suedfeld, P. (2006). Salutogenesis and autobiographical disclosure among Holocaust survivors. *The Journal of Positive Psychology, 1,* 212–225. (p. 465)

Cassidy, J., & Shaver, P. R. (1999). *Handbook of attachment.* New York: Guilford. (p. 150)

Castillo, R. J. (1997). *Culture and mental illness: A client-centered approach.* Pacific Grove, CA: Brooks/Cole. (p. 456)

Castonguay, L. G., & Goldfried, M. R. (1994). Psychotherapy integration: An idea whose time has come. *Applied & Preventive Psychology, 3,* 159–172. (p. 493)

Catanese, K. R., & Tice, D. M. (2005). The effect of rejection on anti-social behaviors: Social exclusion produces aggressive behaviors. In K. D. Williams, J. P. Forgas, & W. Von Hippel (Eds.), *The social outcast: Ostracism, social exclusion, rejection, and bullying.* New York: Psychology Press. (p. 550)

Cattell, R. B. (1963). Theory of fluid and crystallized intelligence: A critical experiment. *Journal of Educational Psychology, 54,* 1–22. (p. 167)

Cavalli-Sforza, L., Menozzi, P., & Piazza, A. (1994). *The history and geography of human genes.* Princeton, NJ: Princeton University Press. (p. 332)

CDC. (2003). Who should get a flu shot (influenza vaccine). National Center for Infectious Diseases (http://www.cdc.gov/ncidod/diseases/flu/who.htm). (p. 484)

CDC. (2006, June 9). Youth risk behavior surveillance: United States, 2005. *Morbidity and Mortality Weekly Report, 55,* No. SS-5, Centers for Disease Control and Prevention. (pp. 361, 362)

CDC. (2007, February 8). CDC releases new data on autism spectrum disorders (ASDs) from multiple communities in the United States. Centers for Disease Control and Prevention (www.cdc.gov). (p. 146)

CDC. (2007, November). Obesity among adults in the United States—No change since 2003–2004. NCHS Data Brief, Centers for Disease Control and Prevention (www.cdc.gov/nchs/data/databriefs/db01.pdf). (p. 349)

Ceci, S. J. (1993). Cognitive and social factors in children's testimony. Master lecture, American Psychological Association convention. (p. 284)

Ceci, S. J., & Bruck, M. (1993). Child witnesses: Translating research into policy. *Social Policy Report* (Society for Research in Child Development), *7*(3), 1–30. (p. 284)

Ceci, S. J., & Bruck, M. (1995). *Jeopardy in the courtroom: A scientific analysis of children's testimony.* Washington, DC: American Psychological Association. (p. 284)

Ceci, S. J., & Williams, W. M. (1997). Schooling, intelligence, and income. *American Psychologist, 52,* 1051–1058. (p. 327)

Ceci, S. J., Huffman, M. L. C., Smith, E., & Loftus, E. F. (1994). Repeatedly thinking about a non-event: Source misattributions among preschoolers. *Consciousness and Cognition, 3,* 388–407. (p. 284)

Centers for Disease Control Vietnam Experience Study. (1988). Health status of Vietnam veterans. *Journal of the American Medical Association, 259,* 2701–2709. (p. 464)

Centers for Disease Control. (1992, September 16). Serious mental illness and disability in the adult household population: United States, 1989. *Advance Data* No. 218 from *Vital and Health Statistics,* National Center for Health Statistics. (p. 489)

Centerwall, B. S. (1989). Exposure to television as a risk factor for violence. *American Journal of Epidemiology, 129,* 643–652. (p. 252)

Cepeda, N. J., Pashler, H., Vul, E., Wixted, J. T., & Rohrer, D. (2006). Distributed practice in verbal recall tasks: A review and quantitative synthesis. *Psychological Bulletin, 132,* 354–380. (p. 261)

Cerella, J. (1985). Information processing rates in the elderly. *Psychological Bulletin, 98,* 67–83. (p. 165)

CFI. (2003, July). International developments. Report. Amherst, NY: Center for Inquiry International. (p. 220)

Chambless, D. L., Baker, M. J., Baucom, D. H., Beutler, L. E., Calhoun, K. S., Crits-Christoph, P., Daiuto, A., DeRubeis, R., Detweiler, J., Haaga, D. A. F., Johnson, S. B., McCurry, S., Mueser, K. T., Pope, K. S., Sanderson, W. C., Shoham, V., Stickle, T., Williams, D. A., & Woody, S. R. (1997). Update on empirically validated therapies, II. *The Clinical Psychologist, 51*(1), 3–16. (p. 508)

Chamove, A. S. (1980). Nongenetic induction of acquired levels of aggression. *Journal of Abnormal Psychology, 89,* 469–488. (p. 251)

Chance News (1997, 25 November). More on the frequency of letters in texts. Dart.Chance@Dartmouth.edu. (p. 16)

Chang, E. C. (2001). Cultural influences on optimism and pessimism: Differences in Western and Eastern construals of the self. In E. C. Chang (Ed.), *Optimism and pessimism.* Washington, DC: APA Books. (p. 443)

Chang, P. P., Ford, D. E., Meoni, L. A., Wang, N-Y., & Klag, M. J. (2002). Anger in young men and subsequent premature cardiovascular disease: The precursors study. *Archives of Internal Medicine, 162,* 901–906. (p. 403)

Chaplin, W. F., Phillips, J. B., Brown, J. D., Clanton, N. R., & Stein, J. L. (2000). Handshaking, gender, personality, and first impressions. *Journal of Personality and Social Psychology, 79,* 110–117. (p. 383)

Charles, S. T., Reynolds, C. A., & Gatz, M. (2001). Age-related differences and change in positive and negative affect over 23 years. *Journal of Personality and Social Psychology, 80,* 136–151. (p. 170)

Charpak, G., & Broch, H. (2004). *Debunked! ESP, telekinesis, and other pseudoscience.* Baltimore, MD: Johns Hopkins University Press. (p. 219)

Chartrand, T. L., & Bargh, J. A. (1999). The chameleon effect: The perception-behavior link and social interaction. *Journal of Personality and Social Psychology, 76,* 893–910. (p. 532)

Chase, W. G., & Simon, H. A. (1973). Perception in chess. *Cognitive Psychology, 4,* 55–81. (p. 264)

Cheek, J. M., & Melchior, L. A. (1990). Shyness, self-esteem, and self-consciousness. In H. Leitenberg (Ed.), *Handbook of social and evaluation anxiety.* New York: Plenum. (p. 124)

Cheit, R. E. (1998). Consider this, skeptics of recovered memory. *Ethics & Behavior, 8,* 141–160. (p. 426)

Chen, E. (2004). Why socioeconomic status affects the health of children: A psychosocial perspective. *Current Directions in Psychological Science, 13,* 112–115. (p. 408)

Chen, X., Beydoun, M. A., & Wang, Y. (2008). Is sleep duration associated with childhood obesity? A systematic review and meta-analysis. *Obesity, 16,* 265–274. (p. 76)

Cheng, M. (2006, November 16). Europeans OK anti-obesity charter. Associated Press. (p. 354)

Chess, S., & Thomas, A. (1987). *Know your child: An authoritative guide for today's parents.* New York: Basic Books. (pp. 111, 151)

Child Trends. (2001, August). Facts at a glance. (www.childtrends.org). (p. 361)

Chiles, J. A., Lambert, M. J., & Hatch, A. L. (1999). The impact of psychological interventions on medical cost offset: A meta-analytic review. *Clinical Psychology: Science and Practice, 6,* 204–220. (p. 506)

Chisholm, K. (1998). A three year follow-up of attachment and indiscriminate friendliness in children adopted from Romanian orphanages. *Child Development, 69,* 1092–1106. (p. 152)

Chivers, M. L. (2005). A brief review and discussion of sex differences in the specificity of sexual arousal. *Sexual and Relationship Therapy, 20,* 377–390. (p. 364)

Chivers, M. L., Seto, M. C., & Blanchard, R. (2007). Gender and sexual orientation differences in sexual response to sexual activities versus gender of actors in sexual films. *Journal of Personality and Social Psychology, 93,* 1108–1121. (p. 364)

Choi, C. Q. (2008, March). Do you need only half your brain? *Scientific American,* p. 104. (p. 56)

Choi, I., & Choi, Y. (2002). Culture and self-concept flexibility. *Personality and Social Psychology Bulletin, 28,* 1508–1517. (p. 123)

Chomsky, N. (1959). [Review of B. F. Skinner's *Verbal behavior*]. *Language, 35,* 26–58. (p. 304)

Chomsky, N. (1972). *Language and mind.* New York: Harcourt Brace. (p. 302)

Chomsky, N. (1987). *Language in a psychological setting* (Sophia Linguistic Working Papers in Linguistics, No. 22). Sophia University, Tokyo. (p. 304)

Christakis, D. S., Zimmerman, F. J., DiGiuseppe, D. L., & McCarty, C. A. (2004). Early television exposure and subsequent attentional problems in children. *Pediatrics, 113,* 708–713. (p. 455)

Christakis, N. A., & Fowler, J. H. (2007). The spread of obesity in a large social network over 32 years. *New England Journal of Medicine, 357,* 370–379. (p. 353)

Christakis, N. A., & Fowler, J. H. (2008, May). The collective dynamics of smoking in a large social network. *New England Journal of Medicine, 358*(21), 2249–2258. (p. 100)

Christensen, A., & Jacobson, N. S. (1994). Who (or what) can do psychotherapy: The status and challenge of nonprofessional therapies. *Psychological Science, 5,* 8–14. (p. 510)

Christophersen, E. R., & Edwards, K. J. (1992). Treatment of elimination disorders: State of the art 1991. *Applied & Preventive Psychology, 1,* 15–22. (p. 497)

Chugani, H. T., & Phelps, M. E. (1986). Maturational changes in cerebral function in infants determined by 18FDG positron emission tomography. *Science, 231,* 840–843. (p. 140)

Cialdini, R. B. (1993). *Influence: Science and practice* (3rd ed.). New York: HarperCollins. (p. 529)

Cialdini, R. B., & Richardson, K. D. (1980). Two indirect tactics of image management: Basking and blasting. *Journal of Personality and Social Psychology, 39,* 406–415. (p. 547)

Ciarrochi, J., Forgas, J. P., & Mayer, J. D. (2006). *Emotional intelligence in everyday life* (2nd ed.). New York: Psychology Press. (p. 318)

Cin, S. D., Gibson, B., Zanna, M. P., Shumate, R., & Fong, G. T. (2007). Smoking in movies, implicit associations of smoking with the self, and intentions to smoke. *Psychological Science, 18,* 559–563. (p. 92)

Clack, B., Dixon, J., & Tredoux, C. (2005). Eating together apart: Patterns of segregation in a multi-ethnic cafeteria. *Journal of Community and Applied Social Psychology, 15,* 1–16. (p. 565)

Clancy, S. A. (2005). *Abducted: How people come to believe they were kidnapped by aliens.* Cambridge, MA: Harvard University Press. (pp. 73, 283)

Clancy, S. A., Schacter, D. L., McNally, R. J., & Pitman, R. K. (2000). False recognition in women reporting recovered memories of sexual abuse. *Psychological Science, 11,* 26–31. (p. 283)

Clark, K. B., & Clark, M. P. (1947). Racial identification and preference in Negro children. In T. M. Newcomb & E. L. Hartley (Eds.), *Readings in social psychology.* New York: Holt. (p. 28)

Clark, L. A. (2007). Assessment and diagnosis of personality disorder: Perennial issues and an emerging reconceptualization. *Annual Review of Psychology, 58,* 227–257. (p. 486)

Clark, R., Anderson, N. B., Clark, V. R., & Williams, D. R. (1999). Racism as a stressor for African Americans: A biopsychosocial model. *American Psychologist, 54,* 805–816. (p. 401)

Coan, J. A., Schaefer, H. S., & Davidson, R. J. (2006). Lending a hand: Social regulation of the neural response to threat. *Psychological Science, 17,* 1032–1039. (p. 409)

Coffey, C. E., Wilkinson, W. E., Weiner, R. D., Parashos, I. A., Djang, W. T., Webb, M. C., Figiel, G. S., & Spritzer, C. E. (1993). Quantitative cerebral anatomy in depression: A controlled magnetic resonance imaging study. *Archives of General Psychiatry, 50,* 7–16. (p. 476)

Cogan, J. C., Bhalla, S. K., Sefa-Dedeh, A., & Rothblum, E. D. (1996). A comparison study of United States and African students on perceptions of obesity and thinness. *Journal of Cross-Cultural Psychology, 27,* 98–113. (p. 347)

Cohen, D. (1995, June 17). Now we are one, or two, or three. *New Scientist,* pp. 14–15. (p. 469)

Cohen, G. L., Garcia, J., Apfel, N., & Master, A. (2006). Reducing the racial achievement gap: A social-psychological intervention. *Science, 313,* 1307–1310. (p. 334)

Cohen, K. M. (2002). Relationships among childhood sex-atypical behavior, spatial ability, handedness, and sexual orientation in men. *Archives of Sexual Behavior, 31,* 129–143. (p. 367)

Cohen, S. (1988). Psychosocial models of the role of social support in the etiology of physical disease. *Health Psychology, 7,* 269–297. (p. 410)

Cohen, S. (2004). Social relationships and health. *American Psychologist, 59,* 676–684. (p. 409)

Cohen, S., Alper, C. M., Doyle, W. J., Treanor, J. J., & Turner, R. B. (2006). Positive emotional style predicts resistance to illness after experimental exposure to rhinovuros or influenza A virus. *Psychosomatic Medicine, 68,* 809–815. (p. 404)

Cohen, S., Doyle, W. J., Skoner, D. P., Rabin, B. S., & Gwaltney, J. M., Jr. (1997). Social ties and susceptibility to the common cold. *Journal of the American Medical Association, 277,* 1940–1944. (p. 409)

Cohen, S., Doyle, W. J., Turner, R., Alper, C. M., & Skoner, D. P. (2003). Sociability and susceptibility to the common cold. *Psychological Science, 14,* 389–395. (p. 404)

Cohen, S., Kaplan, J. R., Cunnick, J. E., Manuck, S. B., & Rabin, B. S. (1992). Chronic social stress, affiliation, and cellular immune response in nonhuman primates. *Psychological Science, 3,* 301–304. (p. 404)

Cohen, S., Line, S., Manuck, S. B., Rabin, B. S., Heise, E. R., & Kaplan, J. R. (1997). Chronic social stress, social status, and susceptibility to upper respiratory infections in nonhuman primates. *Psychosomatic Medicine, 59,* 213–221. (p. 409)

Cohen, S., Tyrrell, D. A. J., & Smith, A. P. (1991). Psychological stress and susceptibility to the common cold. *New England Journal of Medicine, 325,* 606–612. (p. 404)

Colapinto, J. (2000). *As nature made him: The boy who was raised as a girl.* New York: HarperCollins. (p. 129)

Colarelli, S. M., & Dettman, J. R. (2003). Intuitive evolutionary perspectives in marketing. *Psychology and Marketing, 20,* 837–865. (p. 114)

Colarelli, S. M., Spranger, J. L., & Hechanova, M. R. (2006). Women, power, and sex composition in small groups: An evolutionary perspective. *Journal of Organizational Behavior, 27,* 163–184. (p. 127)

Colcombe, S., & Kramer, A. F. (2003). Fitness effects on the cognitive function of older adults: A meta-analytic study. *Psychological Science, 14,* 125–130. (p. 166)

Colcombe, S. J., Kramer, A. F., Erickson, K. I., Scalf, P., McAuley, E., Cohen, N. J., Webb, A., Jerome, G. J., Marquex, D. X., & Elavsky, S. (2004). Cardiovascular fitness, cortical plasticity, and aging. *Proceedings of the National Academy of Sciences, 101,* 3316–3321. (p. 166)

Cole, K. C. (1998). *The universe and the teacup: The mathematics of truth and beauty.* New York: Harcourt Brace. (p. 92)

Collins, D. W., & Kimura, D. (1997). A large sex difference on a two-dimensional mental rotation task. *Behavioral Neuroscience, 111,* 845–849. (p. 329)

Collins, F. (2006). *The language of God.* New York: Free Press. (p. 133)

Collins, N. L., & Miller, L. C. (1994). Self-disclosure and liking: A meta-analytic review. *Psychological Bulletin, 116,* 457–475. (p. 560)

Collins, R. L., Elliott, M. N., Berry, S. H., Danouse, D. E., Kunkel, D., Hunter, S. B., & Miu, A. (2004). Watching sex on television predicts adolescent initiation of sexual behavior. *Pediatrics, 114,* 280–289. (p. 18)

Collinson, S. L., MacKay, C. E., James, A. C., Quested, D. J., Phillips, T., Roberts, N., & Crow, T. J. (2003). Brain volume, asymmetry and intellectual impairment in relation to sex in early-onset schizophrenia. *British Journal of Psychiatry, 183,* 114–120. (p. 483)

Collishaw, S., Pickles, A., Natarajan, L., & Maughan, B. (2007, June). 20-year trends in depression and anxiety in England. Paper presented at the Thirteenth Scientific Meeting on The Brain and the Developing Child, London. (p. 473)

Colombo, J. (1982). The critical period concept: Research, methodology, and theoretical issues. *Psychological Bulletin, 91,* 260–275. (p. 150)

Comer, R. J. (2004). *Abnormal psychology.* New York: Worth Publishers. (p. 454)

Comstock, G. (2008). A sociological perspective on television violence and aggression. *American Behavioral Scientist, 51,* 1184–1211. (p. 251)

Connor-Smith, J. K., & Flachsbart, C. (2007). Relations between personality and coping: A meta-analysis. *Journal of Personality and Social Psychology, 93,* 1080–1107. (p. 408)

Consumer Reports. (1995, November). Does therapy help? Pp. 734–739. (p. 505)

Conway, M. A., Wang, Q., Hanyu, K., & Haque, S. (2005). A cross-cultural investigation of autobiographical memory. On the universality and cultural variation of the reminiscence bump. *Journal of Cross-Cultural Psychology, 36,* 739–749. (p. 166)

Cooke, L. J., Wardle, J., & Gibson, E. L. (2003). Relationship between parental report of food neophobia and everyday food consumption in 2–6-year-old children. *Appetite, 41,* 205–206. (p. 201)

Cooper, K. J. (1999, May 1). This time, copycat wave is broader. *Washington Post* (www.washingtonpost.com). (pp. 253, 532)

Cooper, M. L. (2006). Does drinking promote risky sexual behavior? A complex answer to a simple question. *Current Directions in Psychological Science, 15,* 19–23. (p. 91)

Coopersmith, S. (1967). *The antecedents of self-esteem.* San Francisco: Freeman. (p. 154)

Coren, S. (1996). *Sleep thieves: An eye-opening exploration into the science and mysteries of sleep.* New York: Free Press. (pp. 75, 77, 78)

Corey, D. P., & 15 others (2004). TRPA1 is a candidate for the mechanosensitive transduction channel of vertebrate hair cells. *Nature* (advance online publication, October 13, at www.nature.com). (p. 194)

Corina, D. P. (1998). The processing of sign language: Evidence from aphasia. In B. Stemmer & H. A. Whittaker (Eds.), *Handbook of neurolinguistics.* San Diego: Academic Press. (p. 60)

Corina, D. P., Vaid, J., & Bellugi, U. (1992). The linguistic basis of left hemisphere specialization. *Science, 255,* 1258–1260. (p. 60)

Correll, J., Park, B., Judd, C. M., & Wittenbrink, B. (2002). The police officer's dilemma: Using ethnicity to disambiguate potentially threatening individuals. *Journal of Personality and Social Psychology, 83,* 1314–1329. (p. 543)

Correll, J., Park, B., Judd, C. M., Wittenbrink, B., Sadler, M. S., & Keesee, T. (2007). Across the thin blue line: Police officers and racial bias in the decision to shoot. *Journal of Personality and Social Psychology, 92,* 1006–1023. (p. 543)

Costa, P. T., Jr., & McCrae, R. R. (2006). Trait and factor theories. In J. C. Thomas, D. L. Segal, & M. Hersen (Eds.), *Comprehensive handbook of personality and psychopathology: Vol. 1. Personality and everyday functioning.* Hoboken, NJ: Wiley. (p. 436)

Costa, P. T., Jr., Terracciano, A., & McCrae, R. R. (2001). Gender differences in personality traits across cultures: Robust and surprising findings. *Journal of Personality and Social Psychology, 81,* 322–331. (p. 385)

Costello, E. J., Compton, S. N., Keeler, G., & Angold, A. (2003). Relationships between poverty and psychopathology: A natural experiment. *Journal of the American Medical Association, 290,* 2023–2029. (p. 489)

Coughlin, J. F., Mohyde, M., D'Ambrosio, L. A., & Gilbert, J. (2004). *Who drives older driver decisions?* Cambridge, MA: MIT Age Lab. (p. 166)

Courneya, K. S., & Carron, A. V. (1992). The home advantage in sports competitions: A literature review. *Journal of Sport and Exercise Psychology, 14,* 13–27. (p. 538)

Courtney, J. G., Longnecker, M. P., Theorell, T., & de Verdier, M. G. (1993). Stressful life events and the risk of colorectal cancer. *Epidemiology, 4,* 407–414. (p. 405)

Covin, R., Ouimet, A. J., Seeds, P. M., & Dozois, D. J. A. (2008). A meta-analysis of CBT for pathological worry among clients with GAD. *Journal of Anxiety Disorders, 22,* 108–116. (p. 503)

Cowan, G., Lee, C., Levy, D., & Snyder, D. (1988). Dominance and inequality in X-rated videocassettes. *Psychology of Women Quarterly, 12,* 299–311. (p. 552)

Cowan, N. (1988). Evolving conceptions of memory storage, selective attention, and their mutual constraints within the human information-processing system. *Psychological Bulletin, 104,* 163–191. (p. 266)

Cowan, N. (1994). Mechanisms of verbal short-term memory. *Current Directions in Psychological Science, 3,* 185–189. (p. 266)

Cowan, N. (2001). The magical number 4 in short-term memory: A reconsideration of mental storage capacity. *Behavioral and Brain Sciences, 24,* 87–185. (p. 266)

Cowart, B. J. (1981). Development of taste perception in humans: Sensitivity and preference throughout the life span. *Psychological Bulletin, 90,* 43–73. (p. 202)

Cowart, B. J. (2005). Taste, our body's gustatory gatekeeper. *Cerebrum, 7*(2), 7–22. (pp. 201, 202)

Cox, J., & 18 others (2006). An *SCN9A* channelopathy causes congenital inability to experience pain. *Nature, 444,* 894–898. (p. 199)

Crabbe, J. C. (2002). Genetic contributions to addiction. *Annual Review of Psychology, 53,* 435–462. (p. 97)

Craik, F. I. M., & Watkins, M. J. (1973). The role of rehearsal in short-term memory. *Journal of Verbal Learning and Verbal Behavior, 12,* 599–607. (pp. 261, 262)

Crandall, C. S. (1988). Social contagion of binge eating. *Journal of Personality and Social Psychology, 55,* 588–598. (p. 348)

Crandall, C. S. (1994). Prejudice against fat people: Ideology and self-interest. *Journal of Personality and Social Psychology, 66,* 882–894. (p. 350)

Crandall, C. S. (1995). Do parents discriminate against their heavyweight daughters? *Personality and Social Psychology Bulletin, 21,* 724–735. (p. 350)

Crawford, M., Chaffin, R., & Fitton, L. (1995). Cognition in social context. Learning and Individual Differences, Special Issue: Psychological and psychobiological perspectives on sex differences in cognition: 1. Theory and Research, 7, 341–362. (p. 330)

Crawley, J. N. (2007). Testing hypotheses about autism. Science, 318, 56–57. (p. 146)

Crews, F. (Ed.). (1998). Unauthorized Freud: Doubters confront a legend. New York: Viking. (p. 428)

Crews, F. T., Mdzinarishvilli, A., Kim, D., He, J., & Nixon, K. (2006). Neurogenesis in adolescent brain is potently inhibited by ethanol. Neuroscience, 137, 437–445. (p. 90)

Crews, F., He, J., & Hodge, C. (2007). Adolescent cortical development: A critical period of vulnerability for addiction. Pharmacology, Biochemistry and Behavior, 86, 189–199. (pp. 90, 156)

Crocker, J., & Park, L. E. (2004). The costly pursuit of self-esteem. Psychological Bulletin, 130, 392–414. (p. 449)

Crocker, J., Thompson, L. L., McGraw, K. M., & Ingerman, C. (1987). Downward comparison, prejudice, and evaluation of others: Effects of self-esteem and threat. Journal of Personality and Social Psychology, 52, 907–916. (p. 547)

Croft, R. J., Klugman, A., Baldeweg, T., & Gruzelier, J. H. (2001). Electrophysiological evidence of serotonergic impairment in long-term MDMA ("Ecstasy") users. American Journal of Psychiatry, 158, 1687–1692. (p. 95)

Crook, T. H., & West, R. L. (1990). Name recall performance across the adult life-span. British Journal of Psychology, 81, 335–340. (p. 166)

Cross, S., & Markus, H. (1991). Possible selves across the life span. Human Development, 34, 230–255. (p. 446)

Cross-National Collaborative Group. (1992). The changing rate of major depression. Journal of the American Medical Association, 268, 3098–3105. (p. 473)

Crowell, J. A., & Waters, E. (1994). Bowlby's theory grown up: The role of attachment in adult love relationships. Psychological Inquiry, 5, 1–22. (p. 150)

Csikszentmihalyi, M., & Hunter, J. (2003). Happiness in everyday life: The uses of experience sampling. Journal of Happiness Studies, 4, 185–199. (p. 160)

Cullen, L. T., & Masters, C. (2008, January 28). We just clicked. Time, pp. 84–89. (p. 555)

Cullum, J., & Harton, H. C. (2007). Cultural evolution: Interpersonal influence, issue importance, and the development of shared attitudes in college residence halls. Personality and Social Psychology Bulletin, 33, 1327–1339. (p. 534)

Cunningham, M. R., & others. (2005). "Their ideas of beauty are, on the whole, the same as ours": Consistency and variability in the cross-cultural perception of female physical attractiveness. Journal of Personality and Social Psychology, 68, 261–279. (p. 558)

Cunningham, W. A., Johnson, M. K., Raye, C. L., Gatenby, J. C., Gore, J. C., & Banaji, M. R. (2004). Separable neural components in the processing of Black and White faces. Psychological Science, 15, 806–813. (p. 543)

Curtis, G. C., Magee, W. J., Eaton, W. W., Wittchen, H-U., & Kessler, R. C. (1998). Specific fears and phobias: Epidemiology and classification. British Journal of Psychiatry, 173, 212–217. (p. 463)

Curtis, R. C., & Miller, K. (1986). Believing another likes or dislikes you: Behaviors making the beliefs come true. Journal of Personality and Social Psychology, 51, 284–290. (p. 559)

Czeisler, C. A., Allan, J. S., Strogatz, S. H., Ronda, J. M., Sanchez, R., Rios, C. D., Freitag, W. O., Richardson, G. S., & Kronauer, R. E. (1986). Bright light resets the human circadian pacemaker independent of the timing of the sleep-wake cycle. Science, 233, 667–671. (p. 71)

Czeisler, C. A., Duffy, J. F., Shanahan, T. L., Brown, E. N., Mitchell, J. F., Rimmer, D. W., Ronda, J. M., Silva, E. J., Allan, J. S., Emens, J. S., Dijk, D-J., & Kronauer, R. E. (1999). Stability, precision, and near-24-hour period of the human circadian pacemaker. Science, 284, 2177–2181. (p. 71)

Czeisler, C. A., Kronauer, R. E., Allan, J. S., & Duffy, J. F. (1989). Bright light induction of strong (type O) resetting of the human circadian pacemaker. Science, 244, 1328–1333. (p. 71)

Dabbs, J. M., Jr. (2000). Heroes, rogues, and lovers: Testosterone and behavior. New York: McGraw-Hill. (p. 358)0

Darwin, C. (1859). On the origin of species by means of natural selection. London: John Murray. (p. 114)

Daum, I., & Schugens, M. M. (1996). On the cerebellum and classical conditioning. Psychological Science, 5, 58–61. (p. 272)

Davey, G. C. L. (1995). Preparedness and phobias: Specific evolved associations or a generalized expectancy bias? Behavioral and Brain Sciences, 18, 289–297. (p. 466)

Davidoff, J. (2004). Coloured thinking. The Psychologist, 17, 570–572. (p. 306)

Davidson, J. R. T., Connor, K. M., & Swartz, M. (2006). Mental illness in U.S. presidents between 1776 and 1974: A review of biographical sources. Journal of Nervous and Mental Disease, 194, 47–51. (p. 489)

Davidson, R. J. (2000). Affective style, psychopathology, and resilience: Brain mechanisms and plasticity. American Psychologist, 55, 1196–1209. (pp. 379, 548)

Davidson, R. J. (2003). Affective neuroscience and psychophysiology: Toward a synthesis. Psychophysiology, 40, 655–665. (p. 379)

Davidson, R. J., Kabat-Zinn, J., Schumacher, J., Rosenkranz, M., Muller, D., Santorelli, S. F., Urbanowski, F., Harrington, A., Bonus, K., & Sheridan, J. F. (2003). Alterations in brain and immune function produced by mindfulness meditation. Psychosomatic Medicine, 65, 564–570. (p. 413)

Davidson, R. J., Pizzagalli, D., Nitschke, J. B., & Putnam, K. (2002). Depression: Perspectives from affective neuroscience. Annual Review of Psychology, 53, 545–574. (p. 476)

Davies, D. R., Matthews, G., & Wong, C. S. K. (1991). Aging and work. International Review of Industrial and Organizational Psychology, 6, 149–211. (p. 168)

Davies, M. F. (1997). Positive test strategies and confirmatory retrieval processes in the evaluation of personality feedback. Journal of Personality and Social Psychology, 73, 574–583. (p. 435)

Davies, P. (2007). Cosmic jackpot: Why our universe is just right for life. Boston: Houghton Mifflin. (p. 134)

Davis, B. E., Moon, R. Y., Sachs, H. C., & Ottolini, M. C. (1998). Effects of sleep position on infant motor development. Pediatrics, 102, 1135–1140. (p. 141)

Davis, J. O., & Phelps, J. A. (1995a). Twins with schizophrenia: Genes or germs? Schizophrenia Bulletin, 21, 13–18. (p. 485)

Davis, J. O., Phelps, J. A., & Bracha, H. S. (1995b). Prenatal development of monozygotic twins and concordance for schizophrenia. Schizophrenia Bulletin, 21, 357–366. (p. 485)

Davis, M. (2005). Searching for a drug to extinguish fear. Cerebrum, 7(3), 47–58. (p. 514)

Davis, S., Rees, M., Ribot, J., Moufarege, A., Rodenberg, C., & Purdie, D. (2003, October 1–15). Efficacy and safety of testosterone patches for the treatment of low sexual desire in surgically menopausal women. Paper presented to the American Society for Reproductive Medicine, San Antonio. (p. 358)

Dawes, R. M. (1980). Social dilemmas. Annual Review of Psychology, 31, 169–193. (p. 564)

Dawes, R. M. (1994). House of cards: Psychology and psychotherapy built on myth. New York: Free Press. (p. 447)

Dawkins, R. (1998). Unweaving the rainbow. Boston: Houghton Mifflin. (p. 133)

Dawkins, R. (2007, July 1). Inferior design. New York Times (www.nytimes.com). (p. 113)

de Boysson-Bardies, B., Halle, P., Sagart, L., & Durand, C. (1989). A cross linguistic investigation of vowel formats in babbling. Journal of Child Language, 16, 1–17. (p. 303)

de Courten-Myers, G. M. (2005, February 4). Personal correspondence (estimating total brain neurons, extrapolating from her carefully estimated 20 to 23 billion cortical neurons). (pp. 40, 50)

de Cuevas, J. (1990, September-October) "No, she held them loosely." Harvard Magazine, pp. 60–67. (p. 304)

De Koninck, J. (2000). Waking experiences and dreaming. In M. Kryger, T. Roth, & W. Dement (Eds.), Principles and practice of sleep medicine (3rd ed.). Philadelphia: Saunders. (p. 80)

De Vogli, R., Chandola, T., & Marmot, M. G. (2007). Negative aspects of close relationships and heart disease. Archives of Internal Medicine, 167, 1951–1957. (p. 410)

de Waal, F. (2005, September 23). We're all Machiavellians. Chronicle of Higher Education. (p. 17)

de Waal, F. B. M. (1999, December). The end of nature versus nurture. Scientific American, pp. 94–99. (pp. 130, 135)

Deacon, B. J., & Abramowitz, J. S. (2004). Cognitive and behavioral treatments for anxiety disorders: A review of meta-analytic findings. Journal of Clinical Psychology, 60, 429–441. (p. 498)

Dean, G. A., Kelly, I. W., Saklofske, D. H., & Furnham, A. (1992). Graphology and human judgment. In B. Beyerstein & D. Beyerstein (Eds.), The write stuff: Evaluations of graphology. Buffalo, NY: Prometheus Books. (p. 434)

DeAngelis, T. (2008, February). U.K. gives huge boost to psychologists. Monitor on Psychology, p. 51. (p. 507)

Deary, I. J., Batty, G. D., & Gale, C. R. (2008). Bright children become enlightened adults. *Psychological Science, 19,* 1–6. (p. 547)

Deary, I. J., & Matthews, G. (1993). Personality traits are alive and well. *The Psychologist: Bulletin of the British Psychological Society, 6,* 299–311. (p. 437)

Deary, I. J., Thorpe, G., Wilson, V., Starr, J. M., & Whalley, L. J. (2003). Population sex differences in IQ at age 11: The Scottish mental survey 1932. *Intelligence, 31,* 533–541. (pp. 328, 330)

DeBruine, L. M. (2002). Facial resemblance enhances trust. *Proceedings of the Royal Society of London, 269,* 1307–1312. (p. 556)

DeBruine, L. M. (2004). Facial resemblance increases the attractiveness of same-sex faces more than other-sex faces. *Proceedings of the Royal Society of London B, 271,* 2085–2090. (p. 556)

Deci, E. L., & Ryan, R. M. (Eds.). (2002). *Handbook of self-determination research.* Rochester, NY: University of Rochester Press. (p. 370)

Deeley, Q., Daly, E., Surguladze, S., Tunstall, N., Mezey, G., Beer, D., Ambikapathy, A., Robertson, D., Giampietro, V., Brammer, M. J., Clarke, A., Dowsett, J., Fahy, T., Phillips, M. L., & Murphy, D. G. (2006). Facial emotion processing in criminal psychopathy. *British Journal of Psychiatry, 189,* 533–539. (p. 487)

Dehne, K. L., & Riedner, G. (2005). *Sexually transmitted infections among adolescents: The need for adequate health services.* Geneva: World Health Organization. (p. 362)

DeLamater, J. D., & Sill, M. (2005). Sexual desire in later life. *Journal of Sex Research, 42,* 138–149. (p. 164)

Delaney, H. D., Miller, W. R., & Bisonó, A. M. (2007). Religiosity and spirituality among psychologists: A survey of clinician members of the American Psychological Association. *Professional Psychology: Research and Practice, 38,* 538–546. (p. 511)

Delaney, P. F., Ericsson, K. A., Weaver, G. E., & Mahadevan, S. (1999). Accounts of the memorist Rajan's exceptional performance: Comparing three theoretical proposals. Paper presented to the American Psychological Society convention. (p. 267)

Delgado, J. M. R. (1969). *Physical control of the mind: Toward a psychocivilized society.* New York: Harper & Row. (p. 51)

DeLoache, J. S. (1987). Rapid change in the symbolic functioning of very young children. *Science, 238,* 1556–1557. (p. 144)

DeLoache, J. S. (1995). Early understanding and use of symbols: The model model. *Current Directions in Psychological Science, 4,* 109–113. (p. 144)

DeLoache, J. S., Uttal, D. H., & Rosengren, K. S. (2004). Scale errors offer evidence for a perception-action dissociation early in life. *Science, 304,* 1027–1029. (p. 142)

Dement, W. C. (1978). *Some must watch while some must sleep.* New York: Norton. (pp. 72, 73, 78)

Dement, W. C. (1997, September). *What all undergraduates should know about how their sleeping lives affect their waking lives.* Stanford University: www.leland.stanford.edu/~dement/sleepless.html. (p. 76)

Dement, W. C. (1999). *The promise of sleep.* New York: Delacorte Press. (pp. 71, 72, 73, 75, 76, 78, 79, 103)

Dement, W. C., & Wolpert, E. A. (1958). The relation of eye movements, body mobility, and external stimuli to dream content. *Journal of Experimental Psychology, 55,* 543–553. (p. 81)

Demir, E., & Dickson, B. J. (2005). Fruitless splicing specifies male courtship behavior in *Drosophila. Cell, 121,* 785–794. (p. 366)

Denes-Raj, V., Epstein, S., & Cole, J. (1995). The generality of the ratio-bias phenomenon. *Personality and Social Psychology Bulletin, 21,* 1083–1092. (p. 300)

DeNeve, K. M., & Cooper, H. (1998). The happy personality: A meta-analysis of 137 personality traits and subjective well-being. *Psychological Bulletin, 124,* 197–229. (p. 396)

Dennett, D. C. (1991). *Consciousness explained.* Boston: Little, Brown. (p. 232)

Denton, K., & Krebs, D. (1990). From the scene to the crime: The effect of alcohol and social context on moral judgment. *Journal of Personality and Social Psychology, 59,* 242–248. (p. 90)

Der, G., Batty, G. D., & Deary, I. J. (2006). Effect of breast feeding on intelligence in children: Prospective study, sibling pairs analysis, and meta-analysis. *British Medical Journal, 333,* 945. (p. 21)

Dermer, M., Cohen, S. J., Jacobsen, E., & Anderson, E. A. (1979). Evaluative judgments of aspects of life as a function of vicarious exposure to hedonic extremes. *Journal of Personality and Social Psychology, 37,* 247–260. (p. 396)

Dermer, M., & Pyszczynski, T. A. (1978). Effects of erotica upon men's loving and liking responses for women they love. *Journal of Personality and Social Psychology, 36,* 1302–1309. (p. 559)

Deroche-Garmonet, V., Belin, D., & Piazza, P. V. (2004). Evidence for addiction-like behavior in the rat. *Science, 305,* 1014–1017. (p. 89)

DeRubeis, R. J., & 10 others. (2005). Cognitive therapy vs. medications in the treatment of moderate to severe depression. *Archives of General Psychiatry, 62,* 409–416. (p. 506)

DeSteno, D., Dasgupta, N., Bartlett, M. Y., & Cajdric, A. (2004). Prejudice from thin air: The effect of emotion on automatic intergroup attitudes. *Psychological Science, 15,* 319–324. (p. 391)

DeSteno, D., Petty, R. E., Wegener, D. T., & Rucker, D. D. (2000). Beyond valence in the perception of likelihood: The role of emotion specificity. *Journal of Personality and Social Psychology, 78,* 397–416. (p. 275)

Deutsch, J. A. (1972, July). Brain reward: ESP and ecstasy. *Psychology Today,* 46–48. (p. 49)

DeValois, R. L., & DeValois, K. K. (1975). Neural coding of color. In E. C. Carterette & M. P. Friedman (Eds.), *Handbook of perception: Vol. V. Seeing.* New York: Academic Press. (p. 192)

Devilly, G. J. (2003). Eye movement desensitization and reprocessing: A chronology of its development and scientific standing. *Scientific Review of Mental Health Practice, 1,* 113–118. (p. 508)

Devilly, G. J., Gist, R., & Cotton, P. (2006). Ready! Fire! Aim! The status of psychological debriefing and therapeutic interventions: In the work place and after disasters. *Review of General Psychology, 10,* 318–345. (p. 465)

Devine, P. G. (1995). Prejudice and outgroup perception. In A. Tesser (Ed.), *Advanced social psychology.* New York: McGraw-Hill. (p. 556)

Devlin, B., Daniels, M., & Roeder, K. (1997). The heritability of IQ. *Nature, 388,* 468–471. (p. 325)

Dew, M. A., Hoch, C. C., Buysse, D. J., Monk, T. H., Begley, A. E., Houck, P. R., Hall, M., Kupfer, D. J., Reynolds, C. F., III (2003). Healthy older adults' sleep predicts all-cause mortality at 4 to 19 years of follow-up. *Psychosomatic Medicine, 65,* 63–73. (p. 76)

DeWall, C. N., Baumeister, R. F., Stillman, T. F., & Gaillot, M. T. (2007). Violence restrained: Effects of self-regulation and its depletion on aggression. *Journal of Experimental Social Psychology, 43,* 62–76. (p. 441)

Diaconis, P. (2002, August 11). Quoted by L. Belkin, The odds of that. *New York Times* (www.nytimes.com). (p. 21)

Diaconis, P., & Mosteller, F. (1989). Methods for studying coincidences. *Journal of the American Statistical Association, 84,* 853–861. (p. 21)

Diamond, L. M. (2007). A dynamical systems approach to the development and expression of female same-sex sexuality. *Perspectives on Psychological Science, 2,* 142–161. (p. 364)

Diamond, R. (1993). Genetics and male sexual orientation (letter). *Science, 261,* 1258. (p. 368)

Dick, D. M. (2007). Identification of genes influencing a spectrum of externalizing psychopathology. *Current Directions in Psychological Science, 16,* 331–335. (p. 487)

Dick, D. M., & 14 others (2007). Association of *CHRM2* with IQ: Converging evidence for a gene influencing intelligence. *Behavior Genetics, 37,* 265–272. (p. 325)

Dickens, W. T., & Flynn, J. R. (2006). Black Americans reduce the racial IQ gap: Evidence from standardization samples. *Psychological Science, 17,* 913–920. (p. 331)

Dickerson, S. S., & Kemeny, M. E. (2004). Acute stressors and cortisol responses: A theoretical integration and synthesis of laboratory research. *Psychological Bulletin, 130,* 355–391. (p. 408)

Dickinson, H. O., Parkinson, K. M., Ravens-Sieberer, U., Schirripa, G., Thyen, U., Arnaud, C., Beckung, E., Fauconnier, J., McManus, V., Michelsen, S. I., Parkes, J., & Colver, A. F. (2007). Self-reported quality of life of 8–12-year-old children with cerebral palsy: A cross-sectional European study. *Lancet, 369,* 2171–2178. (p. 393)

Dickson, B. J. (2005, June 3). Quoted in E. Rosenthal, For fruit flies, gene shift tilts sex orientation. *New York Times* (www.nytimes.com). (p. 366)

Diener, E., & Biswas-Diener, R. (2002). Will money increase subjective well-being? A literature review and guide to needed research. *Social Indicators Research, 57,* 119–169. (p. 394)

Diener, E., & Biswas-Diener, R. (2009). *Rethinking happiness: The science of psychological wealth.* Malden, MA: Wiley Blackwell. (p. 394)

Diener, E., & Oishi, S. (2000). Money and happiness: Income and subjective well-being across nations. In E. Diener & E. M. Suh (Eds.), *Subjective well-being across cultures.* Cambridge, MA: MIT Press. (p. 394)

Diener, E., & Seligman, M. E. P. (2002). Very happy people. *Psychological Science, 13,* 81–84. (p. 370)

Diener, E., Lucas, R. E., & Scollon, C. N. (2006). Beyond the hedonic treadmill: Revising the adaptation theory of well-being. *American Psychologist, 61,* 305–314. (p. 393)

Diener, E., Nickerson, C., Lucas, R. E., & Sandvik, E. (2002). Dispositional affect and job outcomes. *Social Indicators Research, 59,* 229–259. (p. 392)

Diener, E., Oishi, S., & Lucas, R. E. (2003). Personality, culture, and subjective well-being: Emotional and cognitive evaluations of life. *Annual Review of Psychology, 54,* 403–425. (p. 396)

Diener, E., Wolsic, B., & Fujita, F. (1995). Physical attractiveness and subjective well-being. *Journal of Personality and Social Psychology, 69,* 120–129. (p. 557)

Dietz, W. H., Jr., & Gortmaker, S. L. (1985). Do we fatten our children at the television set? Obesity and television viewing in children and adolescents. *Pediatrics, 75,* 807–812. (p. 356)

DiFranza, J. R. (2008, May). Hooked from the first cigarette. *Scientific American,* pp. 82–87. (p. 92)

Dijksterhuis, A., & Aarts, H. (2003). On wilde-beests and humans: The preferential detection of negative stimuli. *Psychological Science, 14,* 14–18. (p. 384)

Dijksterhuis, A., Bos, M. W., Nordgren, L. F., & van Baaren, R. B. (2006b). Complex choices better made unconsciously? *Science, 313,* 760–761. (p. 299)

Dijksterhuis, A., & Nordgren, L. F. (2006a). A theory of unconscious thought. *Perspectives on Psychological Science, 1,* 95–109. (p. 299)

DiLalla, D. L., Carey, G., Gottesman, I. I., & Bouchard, T. J., Jr. (1996). Heritability of MMPI personality indicators of psychopathology in twins reared apart. *Journal of Abnormal Psychology, 105,* 491–499. (pp. 109, 475)

Dimberg, U., Thunberg, M., & Elmehed, K. (2000). Unconscious facial reactions to emotional facial expressions. *Psychological Science, 11,* 86–89. (pp. 249, 381, 389)

Dimberg, U., Thunberg, M., & Grunedal, S. (2002). Facial reactions to emotional stimuli: Automatically controlled emotional responses. *Cognition and Emotion, 16,* 449–472. (p. 249)

Dinges, N. G., & Hull, P. (1992). Personality, culture, and international studies. In D. Lieberman (Ed.), *Revealing the world: An interdisciplinary reader for international studies.* Dubuque, IA: Kendall-Hunt. (p. 306)

Dion, K. K., & Dion, K. L. (1993). Individualistic and collectivistic perspectives on gender and the cultural context of love and intimacy. *Journal of Social Issues, 49,* 53–69. (p. 124)

Dion, K. K., & Dion, K. L. (2001). Gender and cultural adaptation in immigrant families. *Journal of Social Issues, 57,* 511–521. (p. 130)

Discover (1996, May). A fistful of risks. Pp. 82–83. (p. 92)

Dixon, J., Durrheim, K., & Tredoux, C. (2007). Intergroup contact and attitudes toward the principle and practice of racial equality. *Psychological Science, 18,* 867–872. (p. 565)

Dobbs, D. (2006, August/September). Turning off depression. *Scientific American Mind,* pp. 26–31. (p. 518)

Dobel, C., Diesendruck, G., & Bölte, J. (2007). How writing system and age influence spatial representations of actions: A developments, cross-linguistic study. *Psychological Science, 18,* 487–491. (p. 306)

Doherty, E. W., & Doherty, W. J. (1998). Smoke gets in your eyes: Cigarette smoking and divorce in a national sample of American adults. *Families, Systems, and Health, 16,* 393–400. (p. 93)

Dohrenwend, B., Pearlin, L., Clayton, P., Hamburg, B., Dohrenwend, B. P., Riley, M., & Rose, R. (1982). Report on stress and life events. In G. R. Elliott & C. Eisdorfer (Eds.), *Stress and human health: Analysis and implications of research* (a study by the Institute of Medicine/National Academy of Sciences). New York: Springer. (p. 401)

Dohrenwend, B. P., Levav, I., Shrout, P. E., Schwartz, S., Naveh, G., Link, B. G., Skodol, A. E., & Stueve, A. (1992). Socioeconomic status and psychiatric disorders: The causation-selection issue. *Science, 255,* 946–952. (p. 489)

Dohrenwend, B. P., Turner, J. B., Turse, N. A., Adams, B. G., Koenen, K. C., & Marshall, R. (2006). The psychological risks of Vietnam for U.S. veterans: A revisit with new data and methods. *Science, 313,* 979–982. (p. 464)

Dolan, C. M., Kraemer, H., Browner, W., Ensrud, K., & Kelsey, J. L. (2007). Associations between body composition, anthropometry and mortality in women of age 65 and older. *American Journal of Public Health, 97,* 913–918. (p. 350)

Dolezal, H. (1982). *Living in a world transformed.* New York: Academic Press. (p. 215)

Domhoff, G. W. (1996). *Finding meaning in dreams: A quantitative approach.* New York: Plenum. (p. 80)

Domhoff, G. W. (2003). The scientific study of dreams: Neural networks, cognitive development, and content analysis. Washington, DC: APA Books. (pp. 82, 83)

Domhoff, G. W. (2007). Realistic simulations and bizarreness in dream content: Past findings and suggestions for future research. In D. Barrett & P. McNamara (Eds.), *The new science of dreaming: Content, recall, and personality characteristics.* Westport, CT: Praeger. (p. 80)

Domjan, M. (1992). Adult learning and mate choice: Possibilities and experimental evidence. *American Zoologist, 32,* 48–61. (p. 230)

Domjan, M. (1994). Formulation of a behavior system for sexual conditioning. *Psychonomic Bulletin & Review, 1,* 421–428. (p. 230)

Domjan, M. (2005). Pavlovian conditioning: A functional perspective. *Annual Review of Psychology, 56.* (p. 230)

Donahoe, J. W., & Vegas, R. (2004). Pavlovian conditioning: The CS-UR relation. *Journal of Experimental Psychology: Animal Behavior, 30,* 17–33. (p. 247)

Donnellan, M. B., Trzesniewski, K. H., Robins, R. W., Moffitt, T. E., & Caspi, A. (2005). Low self-esteem is related to aggression, antisocial behavior, and delinquency. *Psychological Science, 16,* 328–335. (p. 439)

Donnerstein, E. (1998). Why do we have those new ratings on television. Invited address to the National Institute on the Teaching of Psychology. (pp. 251, 252)

Donnerstein, E., Linz, D., & Penrod, S. (1987). *The question of pornography.* New York: Free Press. (p. 253)

Dorner, G. (1976). *Hormones and brain differentiation.* Amsterdam: Elsevier Scientific. (p. 367)

Dorner, G. (1988). Neuroendocrine response to estrogen and brain differentiation in heterosexuals, homosexuals, and transsexuals. *Archives of Sexual Behavior, 17,* 57–75. (p. 367)

Doty, R. L., Shaman, P., Applebaum, S. L., Giberson, R., Siksorski, L., & Rosenberg, L. (1984). Smell identification ability: Changes with age. *Science, 226,* 1441–1443. (p. 165)

Dovidio, J. F., & Gaertner, S. L. (1999). Reducing prejudice: Combating intergroup biases. *Current Directions in Psychological Science, 8,* 101–105. (p. 566)

Dovidio, J. F., ten Vergert, M., Stewart, T. L., Gaertner, S. L., Johnson, J. D., Esses, V. M., Riek, B. M., & Pearson, A. R. (2004). Perspective and prejudice: Antecedents and mediating mechanisms. *Personality and Social Psychology Bulletin, 30,* 1537–1549. (p. 566)

Downing, P. E., Jiang, Y., & Shuman, M. (2001). A cortical area selective for visual processing of the human body. *Science, 293,* 2470–2473. (p. 189)

Doyle, R. (2005, March). Gay and lesbian census. *Scientific American,* p. 28. (p. 115)

Draguns, J. G. (1990a). Normal and abnormal behavior in cross-cultural perspective: Specifying the nature of their relationship. *Nebraska Symposium on Motivation 1989, 37,* 235–277. (pp. 453, 478)

Draguns, J. G. (1990b). Applications of cross-cultural psychology in the field of mental health. In R. W. Brislin (Ed.), *Applied cross-cultural psychology.* Newbury Park, CA: Sage. (p. 453)

Draguns, J. G. (1997). Abnormal behavior patterns across cultures: Implications for counseling and psychotherapy. *International Journal of Intercultural Relations, 21,* 213–248. (p. 453)

Drake, R. A., & Myers, L. R. (2006). Visual attention, emotion, and action tendency: Feeling active or passive. *Cognition and Emotion, 20,* 608–622. (p. 379)

Druckman, D., & Bjork, R. A. (Eds.). (1994). *Learning, remembering, believing: Enhancing human performance.* Washington, DC: National Academy Press. (p. 85)

Duclos, S. E., Laird, J. D., Sexter, M., Stern, L., & Van Lighten, O. (1989). Emotion-specific effects of facial expressions and postures on emotional experience. *Journal of Personality and Social Psychology, 57,* 100–108. (p. 388)

Duenwald, M. (2004, October 26). The dorms may be great, but how's the counseling? *New York Times* (www.nytimes.com). (p. 514)

Duffy, M. (2003, June 9). Weapons of mass disappearance. *Time,* pp. 28–33. (p. 530)

Duggan, J. P., & Booth, D. A. (1986). Obesity, overeating, and rapid gastric emptying in rats with ventromedial hypothalamic lesions. *Science, 231,* 609–611. (p. 345)

Dugger, C. W. (2005, January 18). U.N. proposes doubling of aid to cut poverty. *New York Times* (www.nytimes.com). (p. 299)

Dumont, K. A., Widom, C. S., & Czaja, S. J. (2007). Predictors of resilience in abused and neglected children grown-up: The role of individual and neighborhood characteristics. *Child Abuse & Neglect, 31,* 255–274. (p. 153)

Dunn, A. L., Trivedi, M. H., Kampert, J. B., Clark, C. G., & Chambliss, H. O. (2005). Exercise treatment for depression: Efficacy and dose response. *American Journal of Preventive Medicine, 28,* 1–8. (p. 520)

Dunn, E. W., Aknin, L. B., & Norton, M. I. (2008). Spending money on others promotes happiness. *Science, 319,* 1687–1688. (p. 562)

Dunning, D. (2006). Strangers to ourselves? *The Psychologist, 19,* 600–603. (p. 445)

Dunson, D. B., Colombo, B., & Baird, D. D. (2002). Changes with age in the level and duration of fertility in the menstrual cycle. *Human Reproduction, 17,* 1399–1403. (p. 164)

Durgin, F. H., Evans, L., Dunphy, N., Klostermann, S., & Simmons, K. (2007). Rubber hands feel the touch of light. *Psychological Science, 18,* 152–157. (p. 197)

Dush, C. M. K, Cohan, C. L., & Amato, P. R. (2003). The relationship between cohabitation and marital quality and stability: Change across cohorts? *Journal of Marriage and Family, 65,* 539–549. (p. 169)

Dutton, D. G., & Aron, A. P. (1974). Some evidence for heightened sexual attraction under conditions of high anxiety. *Journal of Personality and Social Psychology, 30,* 510–517. (p. 559)

Dutton, D. G., & Aron, A. P. (1989). Romantic attraction and generalized liking for others who are sources of conflict-based arousal. *Canadian Journal of Behavioural Sciences, 21,* 246–257. (p. 559)

Dweck, C. S. (2006). *Mindset: The new psychology of success.* New York: Random House. (p. 327)

Dweck, C. S. (2007, November 28). The secret to raising smart kids. *Scientific American Mind,* pp. 36–43 (http: //www.sciam.com). (p. 327)

Eagly, A., & Carli, L. (2007). *Through the labyrinth: The truth about how women become leaders.* Cambridge, MA: Harvard University Press. (p. 127)

Eagly, A. H. (1994). Are people prejudiced against women? Donald Campbell Award invited address, American Psychological Association convention. (p. 544)

Eagly, A. H., Ashmore, R. D., Makhijani, M. G., & Kennedy, L. C. (1991). What is beautiful is good, but ... : A meta-analytic review of research on the physical attractiveness stereotype. *Psychological Bulletin, 110,* 109–128. (p. 557)

Eagly, A. H., & Crowley, M. (1986). Gender and helping behavior: A meta-analytic review of the social psychological literature. *Psychological Bulletin, 100,* 283–308. (p. 562)

Eastman, C. L., Boulos, Z., Terman, M., Campbell, S. S., Dijk, D-J., & Lewy, A. J. (1995). Light treatment for sleep disorders: Consensus report. VI. Shift work. *Journal of Biological Rhythms, 10,* 157–164. (p. 71)

Eastman, C. L., Young, M. A., Fogg, L. F., Liu, L., & Meaden, P. M. (1998). Bright light

treatment of winter depression: A placebo-controlled trial. *Archives of General Psychiatry, 55,* 883–889. (p. 509)

Ebbesen, E. B., Duncan, B., & Konecni, V. J. (1975). Effects of content of verbal aggression on future verbal aggression: A field experiment. *Journal of Experimental Social Psychology, 11,* 192–204. (p. 390)

Ebbinghaus, H. (1885). Über das Gedächtnis. Leipzig: Duncker & Humblot. Cited in R. Klatzky (1980), *Human memory: Structures and processes.* San Francisco: Freeman. (p. 261)

Ebbinghaus, H. (1885/1964). *Memory: A contribution to experimental psychology* (H. A. Ruger & C. E. Bussenius, Trans.). New York: Dover. (pp. 277, 278)

Eberhardt, J. L. (2005). Imaging race. *American Psychologist, 60,* 181–190. (p. 543)

Eberhardt, J. L., Davies, P. G., Purdie-Vaughns, V. J., & Johnson, S. L. (2006). Looking deathworthy: Perceived stereotypicality of Black defendants predicts capital-sentencing outcomes. *Psychological Science, 17,* 383–386. (p. 543)

Eberhardt, J. L., Goff, P. A., Purdie, V. J., & Davies, P. G. (2004). Seeing Black: Race, crime, and visual processing. *Journal of Personality and Social Psychology, 87,* 876–893. (p. 543)

Eccles, J. S., Jacobs, J. E., & Harold, R. D. (1990). Gender role stereotypes, expectancy effects, and parents' socialization of gender differences. *Journal of Social Issues, 46,* 183–201. (p. 330)

Eckensberger, L. H. (1994). Moral development and its measurement across cultures. In W. J. Lonner & R. Malpass (Eds.), *Psychology and culture.* Boston: Allyn & Bacon. (p. 158)

Eckert, E. D., Heston, L. L., & Bouchard, T. J., Jr. (1981). MZ twins reared apart: Preliminary findings of psychiatric disturbances and traits. In L. Gedda, P. Paris, & W. D. Nance (Eds.), *Twin research: Vol. 3. Pt. B. Intelligence, personality, and development.* New York: Alan Liss. (p. 467)

Economist. (2001, December 20). An anthropology of happiness. *The Economist* (www.economist.com/world/asia). (p. 371)

Edelman, S., & Kidman, A. D. (1997). Mind and cancer: Is there a relationship? A review of the evidence. *Australian Psychologist, 32,* 1–7. (p. 405)

Edison, T. A. (1948). *The diary and sundry observations of Thomas Alva Edison,* edited by D. D. Runes. New York: Philosophical Library. Cited by S. Coren (1996). *Sleep Thieves.* New York: Free Press. (p. 75)

Eibl-Eibesfeldt, I. (1971). *Love and hate: The natural history of behavior patterns.* New York: Holt, Rinehart & Winston. (p. 387)

Eich, E. (1990). Learning during sleep. In R. B. Bootzin, J. F. Kihlstrom, & D. L. Schacter (Eds.), *Sleep and cognition.* Washington, DC: American Psychological Association. (p. 81)

Eisenberg, N., & Lennon, R. (1983). Sex differences in empathy and related capacities. *Psychological Bulletin, 94,* 100–131. (p. 386)

Eiser, J. R. (1985). Smoking: The social learning of an addiction. *Journal of Social and Clinical Psychology, 3,* 446–457. (p. 92)

Ekman, P. (1994). Strong evidence for universals in facial expressions: A reply to Russell's mistak-

en critique. *Psychological Bulletin, 115,* 268–287. (p. 387)

Ekman, P., & Friesen, W. V. (1975). *Unmasking the face.* Englewood Cliffs, NJ: Prentice-Hall. (p. 387)

Ekman, P., Friesen, W. V., O'Sullivan, M., Chan, A., Diacoyanni-Tarlatzis, I., Heider, K., Krause, R., LeCompte, W. A., Pitcairn, T., Ricci-Bitti, P. E., Scherer, K., Tomita, M., & Tzavaras, A. (1987). Universals and cultural differences in the judgments of facial expressions of emotion. *Journal of Personality and Social Psychology, 53,* 712–717. (p. 387)

Elbert, T., Pantev, C., Wienbruch, C., Rockstroh, B., & Taub, E. (1995). Increased cortical representation of the fingers of the left hand in string players. *Science, 270,* 305–307. (p. 118)

Elfenbein, H. A., & Ambady, N. (1999). *Does it take one to know one? A meta-analysis of the universality and cultural specificity of emotion recognition.* Unpublished manuscript, Harvard University. (p. 387)

Elfenbein, H. A., & Ambady, N. (2002). On the universality and cultural specificity of emotion recognition: A meta-analysis. *Psychological Bulletin, 128,* 203–235. (p. 387)

Elfenbein, H. A., & Ambady, N. (2003a). When familiarity breeds accuracy: Cultural exposure and facial emotion recognition. *Journal of Personality and Social Psychology, 85,* 276–290. (P. 387)

Elfenbein, H. A., & Ambady, N. (2003b). Universals and cultural differences in recognizing emotions. *Current Directions in Psychological Science, 12,* 159–164. (p. 387)

Elkind, D. (1970). The origins of religion in the child. *Review of Religious Research, 12,* 35–42. (p. 157)

Elkind, D. (1978). *The child's reality: Three developmental themes.* Hillsdale, NJ: Erlbaum. (p. 157)

Ellenbogen, J. M., Hu, P. T., Payne, J. D., Titone, D., & Walker, M. P. (2007). Human relational memory requires time and sleep. *Proceedings of the National Academy of Sciences, 104,* 7723–7728. (p. 78)

Elliot, A. J., & Niesta, D. (2008). Romantic red: Red enhances men's attraction to women. *Journal of Personality and Social Psychology, 95,* 1150–1164. (p. 234)

Ellis, A. (1980). Psychotherapy and atheistic values: A response to A. E. Bergin's "Psychotherapy and religious values." *Journal of Consulting and Clinical Psychology, 48,* 635–639. (p. 511)

Ellis, A., & Becker, I. M. (1982). *A guide to personal happiness.* North Hollywood, CA: Wilshire Book Co. (p. 235)

Ellis, B. J. (2004). Timing of pubertal maturation in girls: An integrated life history approach. *Psychological Bulletin, 130,* 920–958. (p. 162)

Ellis, B. J., Bates, J. E., Dodge, K. A., Fergusson, D. M., John, H. L., Pettit, G. S., & Woodward, L. (2003). Does father absence place daughters at special risk for early sexual activity and teenage pregnancy? *Child Development, 74,* 801–821. (p. 362)

Ellis, L., & Ames, M. A. (1987). Neurohormonal functioning and sexual orientation: A theory of homosexuality-heterosexuality. *Psychological Bulletin, 101,* 233–258. (p. 367)

EMDR. (2008). E-mail correspondence from Robbie Dunton, EMDR Institute (www.emdr.org). (p. 508)

Emerging Trends. (1997, September). *Teens turn more to parents than friends on whether to attend church.* Princeton, NJ: Princeton Religion Research Center. (p. 161)

Emery, G. (2004). Psychic predictions 2004. Committee for the Scientific Investigation of Claims of the Paranormal (www.csicop.org). (p. 218)

Emmons, R. A. (2007). *Thanks! How the new science of gratitude can make you happier.* Boston: Houghton Mifflin. (p. 397)

Emmons, S., Geisler, C., Kaplan, K. J., & Harrow, M. (1997). *Living with schizophrenia.* Muncie, IN: Taylor and Francis (Accelerated Development). (pp. 453, 481)

Empson, J. A. C., & Clarke, P. R. F. (1970). Rapid eye movements and remembering. *Nature, 227,* 287–288. (p. 82)

Emslie, C., Hunt, K., & Macintyre, S. (2001). Perceptions of body image among working men and women. *Journal of Epidemiology and Community Health, 55,* 406–407. (p. 349)

Endler, N. S. (1982). *Holiday of darkness: A psychologist's personal journey out of his depression.* New York: Wiley. (pp. 477, 517)

Engemann, K. M., & Owyang, M. T. (2005, April). So much for that merit raise: The link between wages and appearance. *Regional Economist* (www.stlouisfed.org). (p. 557)

Engen, T. (1987). Remembering odors and their names. *American Scientist, 75,* 497–503. (p. 204)

Engle, R. W. (2002). Working memory capacity as executive attention. *Current Directions in Psychological Science, 11,* 19–23. (p. 259)

Epley, N., & Dunning, D. (2000). Feeling "holier than thou": Are self-serving assessments produced by errors in self- or social prediction? *Journal of Personality and Social Psychology, 79,* 861–875. (p. 448)

Epley, N., & Huff, C. (1998). Suspicion, affective response, and educational benefit as a result of deception in psychology research. *Personality and Social Psychology Bulletin, 24,* 759–768. (p. 28)

Epley, N., Keysar, B., Van Boven, L., & Gilovich, T. (2004). Perspective taking as egocentric anchoring and adjustment. *Journal of Personality and Social Psychology, 87,* 327–339. (p. 145)

EPOCH. (2000). Legal reforms: Corporal punishment of children in the family (www.stophitting.com/laws/legalReform.php). (p. 242)

Epstein, J., Stern, E., & Silbersweig, D. (1998). Mesolimbic activity associated with psychosis in schizophrenia: Symptom-specific PET studies. In J. F. McGinty (Ed.), *Advancing from the ventral striatum to the extended amygdala: Implications for neuropsychiatry and drug use: In honor of Lennart Heimer. Annals of the New York Academy of Sciences, 877,* 562–574. (p. 483)

Epstein, S. (1983a). Aggregation and beyond: Some basic issues on the prediction of behavior. *Journal of Personality, 51,* 360–392. (p. 438)

Epstein, S. (1983b). The stability of behavior across time and situations. In R. Zucker, J. Aronoff, & A. I. Rabin (Eds.), *Personality and the prediction of behavior.* San Diego: Academic Press. (p. 438)

Erdberg, P. (1990). Rorschach assessment. In G. Goldstein & M. Hersen (Eds.), *Handbook of psychological assessment* (2nd ed.). New York: Pergamon. (p. 425)

Erdelyi, M. H. (1985). *Psychoanalysis: Freud's cognitive psychology.* New York: Freeman. (p. 427)

Erdelyi, M. H. (1988). Repression, reconstruction, and defense: History and integration of the psychoanalytic and experimental frameworks. In J. Singer (Ed.), *Repression: Defense mechanism and cognitive style.* Chicago: University of Chicago Press. (p. 427)

Erdelyi, M. H. (2006). The unified theory of repression. *Behavioral and Brain Sciences, 29,* 499–551. (pp. 426, 427)

Erel, O., & Burman, B. (1995). Interrelatedness of marital relations and parent-child relations: A meta-analytic review. *Psychological Bulletin, 118,* 108–132. (p. 170)

Erickson, M. F., & Aird, E. G. (2005). *The motherhood study: Fresh insights on mothers' attitudes and concerns.* New York: The Motherhood Project, Institute for American Values. (p. 169)

Ericsson, K. A. (2002). Attaining excellence through deliberate practice: Insights from the study of expert performance. In C. Desforges & R. Fox (Eds.), *Teaching and learning: The essential readings.* Malden, MA: Blackwell Publishers. (p. 316)

Ericsson, K. A. (2007). Deliberate practice and the modifiability of body and mind: Toward a science of the structure and acquisition of expert and elite performance. *International Journal of Sport Psychology, 38,* 4–34. (p. 316)

Ericsson, K. A., Roring, R. W., & Nandagopal, K. (2007). Giftedness and evidence for reproducibly superior performance: An account based on the expert performance framework. *High Ability Studies, 18,* 3–56. (pp. 316, 327)

Erikson, E. H. (1963). *Childhood and society.* New York: Norton. (p. 159)

Erikson, E. H. (1983, June). A conversation with Erikson (by E. Hall). *Psychology Today,* pp. 22–30. (p. 152)

Ernsberger, P., & Koletsky, R. J. (1999). Biomedical rationale for a wellness approach to obesity: An alternative to a focus on weight loss. *Journal of Social Issues, 55,* 221–260. (p. 355)

Ertmer, D. J., Young, N. M., & Nathani, S. (2007). Profiles of focal development in young cochlear implant recipients. *Journal of Speech, Language, and Hearing Research, 50,* 393–407. (p. 303)

Escobar-Chaves, S. L., Tortolero, S., Markham, C., Low, B., Eitel, P., & Thickstun, P. (2005). Impact of the media on adolescents attitudes and behaviors. *Pediatrics, 116,* 303–326. (p. 361)

ESPAD. (2003). Summary of the 2003 findings. European School Survey Project on Alcohol and Other Drugs (www.espad.org). (p. 99)

Esser, J. K., & Lindoerfer, J. S. (1989). Groupthink and the space shuttle Challenger accident: Toward a quantitative case analysis. *Journal of Behavioral Decision Making, 2,* 167–177. (p. 540)

Esterson, A. (2001). The mythologizing of psychoanalytic history: Deception and self-deception in Freud's accounts of the seduction theory episode. *History of Psychiatry, 12,* 329–352. (p. 426)

Etkin, A., & Wager, T. D. (2007). Functional neuroimaging of anxiety: A meta-analysis of emotional processing in PTSD, social anxiety disorder, and specific phobia. *American Journal of Psychiatry, 164,* 1476–1488. (p. 467)

Euston, D. R., Tatsuno, M., & McNaughton, B. L. (2007). Fast-forward playback of recent memory sequences in prefrontal cortex during sleep. *Science, 318,* 1147–1150. (p. 271)

Evans, G. W., Palsane, M. N., & Carrere, S. (1987). Type A behavior and occupational stress: A cross-cultural study of blue-collar workers. *Journal of Personality and Social Psychology, 52,* 1002–1007. (p. 402)

Evans, R. I., Dratt, L. M., Raines, B. E., & Rosenberg, S. S. (1988). Social influences on smoking initiation: Importance of distinguishing descriptive versus mediating process variables. *Journal of Applied Social Psychology, 18,* 925–943. (p. 92)

Ewing, R., Schmid, T., Killingsworth, R., Zlot, A., & Raudenbush, S. (2003). Relationship between urban sprawl and physical activity, obesity, and morbidity. *American Journal of Health Promotion, 18,* 47–57. (p. 353)

Exner, J. E. (2003). *The Rorschach: A comprehensive system* (4th ed.). Hoboken, NJ: Wiley. (p. 425)

Eysenck, H. J. (1952). The effects of psychotherapy: An evaluation. *Journal of Consulting Psychology, 16,* 319–324. (p. 506)

Eysenck, H. J., & Grossarth-Maticek, R. (1991). Creative novation behaviour therapy as a prophylactic treatment for cancer and coronary heart disease: Part II—Effects of treatment. *Behaviour Research and Therapy, 29,* 17–31. (p. 412)

Eysenck, M. W., MacLeod, C., & Mathews, A. (1987). Cognitive functioning and anxiety. *Psychological Research, 49,* 189–195. (p. 439)

Faber, N. (1987, July). Personal glimpse. *Reader's Digest,* p. 34. (p. 317)

Fagan, J. F., & Holland, C. R. (2007). Racial equality in intelligence: Predictions from a theory of intelligence as processing. *Intelligence, 35,* 319–334. (p. 332)

Fagan, J. F., III. (1992). Intelligence: A theoretical viewpoint. *Current Directions in Psychological Science, 1,* 82–86. (p. 332)

Fairburn, C. G., Cowen, P. J., & Harrison, P. J. (1999). Twin studies and the etiology of eating disorders. *International Journal of Eating Disorders, 26,* 349–358. (p. 348)

Fantz, R. L. (1961, May). The origin of form perception. *Scientific American,* pp. 66-72. (p. 139)

Farah, M. J., Rabinowitz, C., Quinn, G. E., & Liu, G. T. (2000). Early commitment of neural substrates for face recognition. *Cognitive Neuropsychology, 17,* 117–124. (p. 56)

Farina, A. (1982). The stigma of mental disorders. In A. G. Miller (Ed.), *In the eye of the beholder.* New York: Praeger. (pp. 456, 459)

Farley, M., Baral, I., Kiremire, M., & Sezgin, U. (1998). Prostitution in five countries: Violence and post-traumatic stress disorder. *Feminism and Psychology, 8,* 405–426. (p. 464)

Farley, T., & Cohen, D. (2001, December). Fixing a fat nation. *Washington Monthly* (www.washingtonmonthly.com/features/2001/0112.farley.cohen. html). (p. 354)

Farooqi, I. S., Bullmore, E., Keogh, J., Gillard, J., O'Rahilly, S., & Fletcher, P. C. (2007). Leptin regulates striatal regions and human eating behavior. *Science, 317,* 1355. (p. 346)

Farrington, D. P. (1991). Antisocial personality from childhood to adulthood. *The Psychologist: Bulletin of the British Psychological Society, 4,* 389–394. (p. 486)

FBI. (2008). *Murder offenders by age, sex, and race, 2008.* (Expanded Homicide Data, Table 3). (p. 127)

Feder, H. H. (1984). Hormones and sexual behavior. *Annual Review of Psychology, 35,* 165–200. (p. 358)

Feeney, D. M. (1987). Human rights and animal welfare. *American Psychologist, 42,* 593–599. (p. 27)

Feeney, J. A., & Noller, P. (1990). Attachment style as a predictor of adult romantic relationships. *Journal of Personality and Social Psychology, 58,* 281–291. (p. 152)

Feinberg, T. E., & Keenan, J. P. (Eds.). (2005). *The lost self: Pathologies of the brain and identity.* New York: Oxford University Press. (p. 60)

Feingold, A. (1990). Gender differences in effects of physical attractiveness on romantic attraction: A comparison across five research paradigms. *Journal of Personality and Social Psychology, 59,* 981–993. (p. 557)

Feingold, A. (1992). Good-looking people are not what we think. *Psychological Bulletin, 111,* 304–341. (p. 557)

Feingold, A., & Mazzella, R. (1998). Gender differences in body image are increasing. *Psychological Science, 9,* 190–195. (pp. 348, 558)

Fellowes, D., Barnes, K., & Wilkinson, S. (2004). Aromatherapy and massage for symptom relief in patients with cancer. *The Cochrane Library, 3.* Oxford, England: Update Software. (p. 406)

Feng, J., Spence, I., & Pratt, J. (2007). Playing an action video game reduces gender differences in spatial cognition. *Psychological Science, 18,* 850–855. (p. 329)

Fenton, W. S., & McGlashan, T. H. (1991). Natural history of schizophrenia subtypes: II. Positive and negative symptoms and long-term course. *Archives of General Psychiatry, 48,* 978–986. (p. 482)

Fenton, W. S., & McGlashan, T. H. (1994). Antecedents, symptom progression, and long-term outcome of the deficit syndrome in schizophrenia. *American Journal of Psychiatry, 151,* 351–356. (p. 482)

Ferguson, C. J., & Kilburn, J. (2009). The public health risks of media violence: A meta-analytic review. *Journal of Pediatrics,* in press. (p. 252)

Ferguson, E. D. (1989). Adler's motivational theory: An historical perspective on belonging and the fundamental human striving. *Individual Psychology, 45,* 354–361. (p. 369)

Ferguson, E. D. (2001). Adler and Dreikurs: Cognitive-social dynamic innovators. *Journal of Individual Psychology, 57,* 324–341. (p. 369)

Ferguson, E. D. (2003). Social processes, personal goals, and their intertwining: Their importance in Adlerian theory and practice. *Journal of Individual Psychology, 59,* 136–144. (p. 424)

Fergusson, D. M., & Woodward, L. G. (2002). Mental health, educational, and social role outcomes of adolescents with depression. *Archives of General Psychiatry, 59,* 225–231. (p. 473)

Fernandez, E., & Turk, D. C. (1989). The utility of cognitive coping strategies for altering pain perception: A meta-analysis. *Pain, 38,* 123–135. (p. 201)

Fernandez-Dols, J-M., & Ruiz-Belda, M-A. (1995). Are smiles a sign of happiness? Gold medal winners at the Olympic Games. *Journal of Personality and Social Psychology, 69,* 1113–1119. (p. 387)

Ferris, C. F. (1996, March). The rage of innocents. *The Sciences,* pp. 22–26. (p. 153)

Fiedler, K., Nickel, S., Muehlfriedel, T., & Unkelbach, C. (2001). Is mood congruency an effect of genuine memory or response bias? *Journal of Experimental Social Psychology, 37,* 201–214. (p. 275)

Field, A. P. (2006). Is conditioning a useful framework for understanding the development and treatment of phobias? *Clinical Psychology Review, 26,* 857–875. (p. 465)

Field, T., Diego, M., & Hernandez-Reif, M. (2007). Massage therapy research. *Developmental Review, 27,* 75–89. (p. 118)

Field, T., Hernandez-Reif, M., Feijo, L., & Freedman, J. (2006). Prenatal, perinatal and neonatal stimulation: A survey of neonatal nurseries. *Infant Behavior & Development, 29,* 24–31. (p. 118)

Fincham, F. D., & Bradbury, T. N. (1993). Marital satisfaction, depression, and attributions: A longitudinal analysis. *Journal of Personality and Social Psychology, 64,* 442–452. (p. 527)

Fink, G. R., Markowitsch, H. J., Reinkemeier, M., Bruckbauer, T., Kessler, J., & Heiss, W-D. (1996). Cerebral representation of one's own past: Neural networks involved in autobiographical memory. *Journal of Neuroscience, 16,* 4275–4282. (p. 271)

Finkel, E. J., & Eastwick, P. W. (2008). Speed-dating. *Current Directions in Psychological Science, 17,* 193–197. (p. 557)

Fischer, P., & Greitemeyer, T. (2006). Music and aggression: The impact of sexual-aggressive song lyrics on aggression-related thoughts, emotions, and behavior toward the same and the opposite sex. *Personality and Social Psychology Bulletin, 32,* 1165–1176. (p. 553)

Fischhoff, B. (1982). Debiasing. In D. Kahneman, P. Slovic, & A. Tversky (Eds.), *Judgment under uncertainty: Heuristics and biases.* New York: Cambridge University Press. (p. 297)

Fischhoff, B., Slovic, P., & Lichtenstein, S. (1977). Knowing with certainty: The appropriateness of extreme confidence. *Journal of Experimental Psychology: Human Perception and Performance, 3,* 552–564. (p. 296)

Fischtein, D. S., Herold, E. S., & Desmarais, S. (2007). How much does gender explain in sexual attitudes and behaviors? A survey of Canadian adults. *Archives of Sexual Behavior, 36,* 451–461. (p. 115)

Fisher, H. E. (1993, March/April). After all, maybe it's biology. *Psychology Today,* pp. 40–45. (p. 169)

Fisher, H. E., Aron, A., Mashek, D., Li, H., & Brown, L. L. (2002). Defining the brain systems of lust, romantic attraction, and attachment. *Archives of Sexual Behavior, 31,* 413–419. (p. 357)

Fisher, H. T. (1984). Little Albert and Little Peter. *Bulletin of the British Psychological Society, 37,* 269. (p. 498)

Fisher, K., Egerton, M., Gershuny, J. I., & Robinson, J. P. (2006). Gender convergence in the American Heritage Time Use Study (AHTUS). *Social Indicators Research, 82,* 1–33. (p. 130)

Fiske, S. T., Harris, L. T., & Cuddy, A. J. C. (2004). Why ordinary people torture enemy prisoners. *Science, 306,* 1482–1483. (p. 530)

Fitzgerald, P. B., & Daskalakis, Z. J. (2008). The use of repetitive transcranial magnetic stimulation and vagal nerve stimulation in the treatment of depression. *Current Opinion in Psychiatry, 21,* 25–29. (p. 517)

Fleming, I., Baum, A., & Weiss, L. (1987). Social density and perceived control as mediator of crowding stress in high-density residential neighborhoods. *Journal of Personality and Social Psychology, 52,* 899–906. (p. 409)

Fleming, J. H., & Scott, B. A. (1991). The costs of confession: The Persian Gulf War POW tapes in historical and theoretical perspective. *Contemporary Social Psychology, 15,* 127–138. (p. 387)

Fletcher, G. J. O., Fitness, J., & Blampied, N. M. (1990). The link between attributions and happiness in close relationships: The roles of depression and explanatory style. *Journal of Social and Clinical Psychology, 9,* 243–255. (p. 527)

Fletcher, P. C., Zafiris, O., Frith, C. D., Honey, R. A. E., Corlett, P. R., Zilles, K., & Fink, G. R. (2005). On the benefits of not trying: Brain activity and connectivity reflecting the interactions of explicit and implicit sequence learning. *Cerebral Cortex, 7,* 1002–1015. (p. 427)

Flier, J. S., & Maratos-Flier, E. (2007, September). What fuels fat. *Scientific American,* pp. 72–81. (p. 353)

Flood, M. (2007). Exposure to pornography among youth in Australia. *Journal of Sociology, 43,* 45–60. (p. 551)

Flora, S. R. (2004). *The power of reinforcement.* Albany, NJ: SUNY Press. (p. 244)

Flouri, E., & Buchanan, A. (2004). Early father's and mother's involvement and child's later educational outcomes. *British Journal of Educational Psychology, 74,* 141–153. (p. 152)

Flynn, J. R. (1987). Massive IQ gains in 14 nations: What IQ tests really measure. *Psychological Bulletin, 101,* 171–191. (p. 323)

Flynn, J. R. (2003). Movies about intelligence: The limitations of g. *Current Directions in Psychological Science, 12,* 95–99. (p. 328)

Flynn, J. R. (2007). *What is intelligence?* New York: Cambridge University Press. (pp. 323, 328)

Foa, E. B., & Kozak, M. J. (1986). Emotional processing of fear: Exposure to corrective information. *Psychological Bulletin, 99,* 20–35. (p. 498)

Ford, E. S. (2002). Does exercise reduce inflammation? Physical activity and B-reactive protein among U.S. adults. *Epidemiology, 13,* 561–569. (p. 412)

Foree, D. D., & LoLordo, V. M. (1973). Attention in the pigeon: Differential effects of food-getting versus shock-avoidance procedures. *Journal of Comparative and Physiological Psychology, 85,* 551–558. (p. 244)

Forer, B. R. (1949). The fallacy of personal validation: A classroom demonstration of gullibility. *Journal of Abnormal and Social Psychology, 44,* 118–123. (p. 435)

Forgas, J. P., Bower, G. H., & Krantz, S. E. (1984). The influence of mood on perceptions of social interactions. *Journal of Experimental Social Psychology, 20,* 497–513. (p. 275)

Forhan, S. E., Gottlieb, S. L., Sternberg, M. R., Xu, F., Datta, D., Berman, S., & Markowitz, L. (2008). Prevalence of sexually transmitted infections and bacterial vaginosis among female adolescents in the United States: Data from the National Health and Nutrition Examination Survey (NHANES) 2003–2004. Paper presented to the 2008 National STD Prevention Conference, Chicago, Illinois. (p. 362)

Forman, D. R., Aksan, N., & Kochanska, G. (2004). Toddlers' responsive imitation predicts preschool-age conscience. *Psychological Science, 15,* 699–704. (p. 251)

Foss, D. J., & Hakes, D. T. (1978). *Psycholinguistics: An introduction to the psychology of language.* Englewood Cliffs, NJ: Prentice-Hall. (p. 427)

Foster, R. G. (2004). Are we trying to banish biological time? *Cerebrum, 6*(2), 7–26. (p. 71)

Foulkes, D. (1999). *Children's dreaming and the development of consciousness.* Cambridge, MA: Harvard University Press. (p. 83)

Fouts, R. (1997). *Next of kin: What chimpanzees have taught me about who we are.* New York: Morrow. (p. 312)

Fouts, R. S. (1992). Transmission of a human gestural language in a chimpanzee mother-infant relationship. *Friends of Washoe, 12/13,* 2–8. (p. 312)

Fouts, R. S., & Bodamer, M. (1987). Preliminary report to the National Geographic Society on: "Chimpanzee intrapersonal signing." *Friends of Washoe, 7*(1), 4–12. (p. 312)

Fowler, M. J., Sullivan, M. J., & Ekstrand, B. R. (1973). Sleep and memory. *Science, 179,* 302–304. (p. 280)

Fowler, R. C., Rich, C. L., & Young, D. (1986). San Diego suicide study: II. Substance abuse in young cases. *Archives of General Psychiatry, 43,* 962–965. (p. 474)

Fowles, D. C. (1992). Schizophrenia: Diathesis-stress revisited. *Annual Review of Psychology, 43,* 303–336. (p. 482)

Fox, B. H. (1998). Psychosocial factors in cancer incidence and prognosis. In P. M. Cinciripini & others (Eds.), *Psychological and behavioral factors in cancer risk.* New York: Oxford University Press. (p. 405)

Fox, E., Lester, V., Russo, R., Bowles, R. J., Pichler, A., & Dutton, K. (2000). Facial expression of emotion: Are angry faces detected more efficiently? *Cognition and Emotion, 14,* 61–92. (p. 384)

Fox, J. L. (1984). The brain's dynamic way of keeping in touch. *Science, 225,* 820–821. (p. 57)

Fozard, J. L., & Popkin, S. J. (1978). Optimizing adult development: Ends and means of an applied psychology of aging. *American Psychologist, 33,* 975–989. (p. 164)

Fracassini, C. (2000, August 27). Holidaymakers led by the nose in sales quest. *Scotland on Sunday.* (p. 204)

Fraley, R. C. (2002). Attachment stability from infancy to adulthood: Meta-analysis and dynamic modeling of developmental mechanisms. *Personality and Social Psychology Review, 6,* 123–151. (p. 152)

Frank, J. D. (1982). Therapeutic components shared by all psychotherapies. In J. H. Harvey & M. M. Parks (Eds.), *The Master Lecture Series: Vol. 1. Psychotherapy research and behavior change.* Washington, DC: American Psychological Association. (pp. 510, 511)

Frank, R. (1999). *Luxury fever: Why money fails to satisfy in an era of excess.* New York: Free Press. (p. 123)

Frank, S. J. (1988). Young adults' perceptions of their relationships with their parents: Individual differences in connectedness, competence, and emotional autonomy. *Developmental Psychology, 24,* 729–737. (p. 162)

Frankel, A., Strange, D. R., & Schoonover, R. (1983). CRAP: Consumer rated assessment procedure. In G. H. Scherr & R. Liebmann-Smith (Eds.), *The best of The Journal of Irreproducible Results.* New York: Workman Publishing. (p. 435)

Frankenburg, W., Dodds, J., Archer, P., Shapiro, H., & Bresnick, B. (1992). The Denver II: A major revision and restandardization of the Denver Developmental Screening Test. *Pediatrics, 89,* 91–97. (p. 141)

Franz, E. A., Waldie, K. E., & Smith, M. J. (2000). The effect of callosotomy on novel versus familiar bimanual actions: A neural dissociation between controlled and automatic processes? *Psychological Science, 11,* 82–85. (p. 59)

Frasure-Smith, N., & Lespérance, F. (2005). Depression and coronary heart disease: Complex synergism of mind, body, and environment. *Current Directions in Psychological Science, 14,* 39–43. (p. 403)

Frattaroli, J. (2006). Experimental disclosure and its moderators: A meta-analysis. *Psychological Bulletin, 132,* 823–865. (p. 410)

Frayling, T. M., & 41 others (2007, April 12). A common variant in the *FTO* gene is associated with body mass index and predisposes to childhood and adult obesity. *Science, 316,* 889–894. (p. 353)

Frederick, D. A., Peplau, L. A., & Lever, J. (2006). The swimsuit issue: Correlates of body image in a sample of 52,667 heterosexual adults. *Body Image, 3,* 413–419. (p. 349)

Fredrickson, B. L. (2006). The broaden-and-build theory of positive emotions. In M. Csikszentmihalyi & I. S. Csikszentmihalyi (Eds.), *A life worth living: Contributions to positive psychology.* New York: Oxford University Press. (p. 392)

Fredrickson, B. L., & Kahneman, D. (1993). Duration neglect in retrospective evaluations of affective episodes. *Journal of Personality and Social Psychology, 65,* 45–55. (p. 263)

Fredrickson, B. L., Roberts, T-A., Noll, S. M., Quinn, D. M., & Twenge, J. M. (1998). That swimsuit becomes you: Sex differences in self-objectification, restrained eating, and math performance. *Journal of Personality and Social Psychology, 75,* 269–284. (p. 349)

Freedman, D. J., Riesenhuber, M., Poggio, T., & Miller, E. K. (2001). Categorical representation of visual stimuli in the primate prefrontal cortex. *Science, 291,* 312–316. (p. 310)

Freedman, J. L. (1988). Television violence and aggression: What the evidence shows. In S. Oskamp (Ed.), *Television as a social issue.* Newbury Park, CA: Sage. (p. 252)

Freedman, J. L., & Fraser, S. C. (1966). Compliance without pressure: The foot-in-the-door technique. *Journal of Personality and Social Psychology, 4,* 195–202. (p. 529)

Freeman, W. J. (1991, February). The physiology of perception. *Scientific American,* pp. 78–85. (p. 193)

Frensch, P. A., & Rünger, D. (2003). Implicit learning. *Current Directions in Psychological Science, 12,* 13–18. (p. 427)

Freud, S. (1935; reprinted 1960). *A general introduction to psychoanalysis.* New York: Washington Square Press. (p. 169)

Freyd, J. J., DePrince, A. P., & Gleaves, D. H. (2007). The state of betrayal trauma theory: Reply to McNally—Conceptual issues and future directions. *Memory, 15,* 295–311. (p. 285)

Freyd, J. J., Putnam, F. W., Lyon, T. D., Becker-Blease, K. A., Cheit, R. E., Siegel, N. B., & Pezdek, K. (2005). The science of child sexual abuse. *Science, 308,* 501. (p. 153)

Friedman, M., & Ulmer, D. (1984). *Treating Type A behavior—and your heart.* New York: Knopf. (pp. 402, 413)

Friedrich, O. (1987, December 7). New age harmonies. *Time,* pp. 62–72. (p. 454)

Friend, T. (2004). *Animal talk: Breaking the codes of animal language.* New York: Free Press. (p. 313)

Frijda, N. H. (1988). The laws of emotion. *American Psychologist, 43,* 349–358. (p. 395)

Frith, U., & Frith, C. (2001). The biological basis of social interaction. *Current Directions in Psychological Science, 10,* 151–155. (p. 146)

Fromkin, V., & Rodman, R. (1983). *An introduction to language* (3rd ed.). New York: Holt, Rinehart & Winston. (p. 303)

Fry, A. F., & Hale, S. (1996). Processing speed, working memory, and fluid intelligence: Evidence for a developmental cascade. *Psychological Science, 7,* 237–241. (p. 165)

Fryar, C., Hirsch, R., Porter, K. S., Kottiri, B., Brody, D. J., & Louis, T. (2007, June 28). Drug use and sexual behavior reported by adults: United States, 1999–2002. *Advance Data: From Vital and Health Statistics,* Number 384 (Centers for Disease Control and Prevention). (p. 359)

Fuhriman, A., & Burlingame, G. M. (1994). Group psychotherapy: Research and practice. In A. Fuhriman & G. M. Burlingame (Eds.), *Handbook of group psychotherapy.* New York: Wiley. (p. 503)

Fuller, M. J., & Downs, A. C. (1990). Spermarche is a salient biological marker in men's development. Poster presented at the American Psychological Society convention. (p. 155)

Funder, D. C. (2001). Personality. *Annual Review of Psychology, 52,* 197–221. (p. 436)

Funder, D. C., & Block, J. (1989). The role of ego-control, ego-resiliency, and IQ in delay of gratification in adolescence. *Journal of Personality and Social Psychology, 57,* 1041–1050. (p. 158)

Furnham, A. (1982). Explanations for unemployment in Britain. *European Journal of Social Psychology, 12,* 335–352. (p. 527)

Furnham, A. (2001). Self-estimates of intelligence: Culture and gender difference in self and other estimates of both general (g) and multiple intelligences. *Personality and Individual Differences, 31,* 1381–1405. (p. 328)

Furnham, A., & Baguma, P. (1994). Cross-cultural differences in the evaluation of male and female body shapes. *International Journal of Eating Disorders, 15,* 81–89. (p. 347)

Furnham, A., Callahan, I., & Akande, D. (2004a). Self-estimates of intelligence: A study in two African countries. *Journal of Psychology, 138,* 265–285. (p. 328)

Furnham, A., Hosoe, T., & Tang, T. L-P. (2002a). Male hubris and female humility? A cross-cultural study of ratings of self, parental, and sibling multiple intelligence in America, Britain, and Japan. *Intelligence, 30,* 101–115. (p. 328)

Furnham, A., & Mottabu, R. (2004b). Sex and culture differences in the estimates of general and multiple intelligence: A study comparing British and Egyptian students. *Individual Differences Research, 3,* 82–96. (p. 328)

Furnham, A., & Rawles, R. (1995). Sex differences in the estimation of intelligence. *Journal of Social Behavior and Personality, 10,* 741–748. (p. 544)

Furnham, A., Reeves, E., & Bughani, S. (2002b). Parents think their sons are brighter than their daughters: Sex differences in parental self-estimations and estimations of their children's multiple intelligences. *Journal of Genetic Psychology, 163,* 24–39. (p. 328)

Furnham, A., & Thomas, C. (2004c). Parents' gender and personality and estimates of their own and their children's intelligence. *Personality and Individual Differences, 37,* 887–903. (p. 328)

Furr, R. M., & Funder, D. C. (1998). A multimodal analysis of personal negativity. *Journal of Personality and Social Psychology, 74,* 1580–1591. (p. 479)

Gable, S. L., Gonzaga, G. C., & Strachman, A. (2006). Will you be there for me when things go right? Supportive responses to positive event disclosures. *Journal of Personality and Social Psychology, 91,* 904–917. (p. 170)

Gabrieli, J. D. E., Desmond, J. E., Demb, J. E., Wagner, A. D., Stone, M. V., Vaidya, C. J., & Glover, G. H. (1996). Functional magnetic resonance imaging of semantic memory processes in the frontal lobes. *Psychological Science, 7,* 278–283. (p. 271)

Gaertner, L., & Iuzzini, J. (2005). Rejection and entitativity: A synergistic model of mass violence. In K. D. Williams, J. P. Forgas, & W. von Hippel (Eds.). *The social outcast: Ostracism, social exclusion, rejection, and bullying.* New York: Psychology Press. (p. 550)

Gage, F. H. (2003, September). Repair yourself. *Scientific American,* pp. 46–53. (p. 57)

Gaillot, M. T., & Baumeister, R. F. (2007). Self-regulation and sexual restraint: Dispositionally and temporarily poor self-regulatory abilities contribute to failures at restraining sexual behavior. *Personality and Social Psychology Bulletin, 33,* 173–186. (p. 441)

Galambos, N. L. (1992). Parent-adolescent relations. *Current Directions in Psychological Science, 1,* 146–149. (p. 161)

Galambos, N. L., Barker, E. T., & Krahn, H. J. (2006). Depression, self-esteem, and anger in emerging adulthood: Seven-year trajectories. *Developmental Psychology, 42,* 350–365. (p. 162)

Galanter, E. (1962). Contemporary psychophysics. In R. Brown, E. Galanter, E. H. Hess, & G. Mandler (Eds.), *New directions in psychology.* New York: Holt Rinehart & Winston. (p. 181)

Galati, D., Scherer, K. R., & Ricci-Bitti, P. E. (1997). Voluntary facial expression of emotion: Comparing congenitally blind with normally sighted encoders. *Journal of Personality and Social Psychology, 73,* 1363–1379. (p. 387)

Galea, S., Boscarino, J., Resnick, H., & Vlahov, D. (2002). Mental health in New York City after the September 11 terrorist attacks: Results from two population surveys. In R. W. Manderscheid & M. J. Henderson (Eds.), *Mental-Health, United States, 2001.* Washington, DC: U.S. Government Printing Office. (pp. 464, 465)

Galinsky, A. D., Magee, J. C., Inesi, M. E., & Gruenfeld, D. H. (2006). Power and perspectives not taken. *Psychological Science, 17,* 1068–1074. (p. 145)

Gallup Organization. (2003, July 8). American public opinion about Iraq. *Gallup Poll News Service* (www.gallup.com). (pp. 530, 531)

Gallup, G., Jr. (2002, April 30). Education and youth. *Gallup Tuesday Briefing* (www.gallup.com/poll/tb/educaYouth/20020430.asp). (p. 251)

Gallup, G. H. (1972). *The Gallup poll: Public opinion 1935–1971* (Vol. 3). New York: Random House. (p. 565)

Gallup. (2002, June 11). Poll insights: The gender gap—post Sept. 11th fear. The Gallup Organization (www.gallup.com/poll/pollInsights). (p. 464)

Gallup. (2008, February 27). Worldwide, residents of richer nations more satisfied. The Gallup Organization (http://www.gallup.com/poll/104608/Worldwide-Residents-Richer-Nations-More-Satisfied.aspx). (p. 394)

Gangestad, S. W., & Simpson, J. A. (2000). The evolution of human mating: Trade-offs and strategic pluralism. *Behavioral and Brain Sciences, 23,* 573–587. (p. 116)

Garber, K. (2007). Autism's cause may reside in abnormalities at the synapse. *Science, 317,* 190–191. (p. 146)

Garcia, J., & Gustavson, A. R. (1997, January). Carl R. Gustavson (1946–1996): Pioneering wildlife psychologist. *APS Observer,* pp. 34–35. (p. 233)

Garcia, J., & Koelling, R. A. (1966). Relation of cue to consequence in avoidance learning. *Psychonomic Science, 4,* 123–124. (p. 232)

Gardner, H. (1983). *Frames of mind: The theory of multiple intelligences.* New York: Basic Books. (p. 314)

Gardner, H. (1998, March 19). An intelligent way to progress. *The Independent* (London), p. E4. (p. 315)

Gardner, H. (1998, November 5). Do parents count? *New York Review of Books* (www.nybooks.com). (p. 120)

Gardner, H. (1999). *Multiple views of multiple intelligence.* New York: Basic Books. (p. 318)

Gardner, H. (2006). *The development and education of the mind: The selected works of Howard Gardner.* New York: Routledge/Taylor & Francis. (p. 314)

Gardner, J., & Oswald, A. J. (2007). Money and mental well-being: A longitudinal study of medium-sized lottery wins. *Journal of Health Economics, 6,* 49–60. (p. 394)

Gardner, M. (2006, January/February). The memory wars, part one. *Skeptical Inquirer, 30,* 28–31. (p. 285)

Gardner, R. A., & Gardner, B. I. (1969). Teaching sign language to a chimpanzee. *Science, 165,* 664–672. (p. 311)

Gardner, R. M., & Tockerman, Y. R. (1994). A computer-TV video methodology for investigating the influence of somatotype on perceived personality traits. *Journal of Social Behavior and Personality, 9,* 555–563. (p. 350)

Garfield, C. (1986). *Peak performers: The new heroes of American business.* New York: Morrow. (p. 308)

Garnets, L., & Kimmel, D. (1990). Lesbian and gay dimensions in the psychological study of human diversity. Master lecture, American Psychological Association convention. (p. 363)

Garon, N., Bryson, S. E., & Smith, I. M. (2008). Executive function in preschoolers: A review using an integrative framework. *Psychological Bulletin, 134,* 31–60. (p. 140)

Garrett, B. L. (2008). Judging innocence. *Columbia Law Review, 108,* 55–142. (p. 283)

Garry, M., Loftus, E. F., & Brown, S. W. (1994). Memory: A river runs through it. *Consciousness and Cognition, 3,* 438–451. (p. 426)

Garry, M., Manning, C. G., Loftus, E. F., & Sherman, S. J. (1996). Imagination inflation: Imagining a childhood event inflates confidence that it occurred. *Psychonomic Bulletin & Review, 3,* 208–214. (p. 282)

Gatchel, R. J., Peng, Y. B., Peters, M. L., Fuchs, P. N., & Turk, D. C. (2007). The biopsychosocial approach to chronic pain: Scientific advances and future directions. *Psychological Bulletin, 133,* 581–624. (p. 198)

Gates, W. (1998, July 20). Charity begins when I'm ready (interview). *Fortune* (www.pathfinder.com/fortune/1998/980720/bil7.html). (p. 316)

Gawande, A. (1998, September 21). The pain perplex. *The New Yorker,* pp. 86–94. (p. 200)

Gawin, F. H. (1991). Cocaine addiction: Psychology and neurophysiology. *Science, 251,* 1580–1586. (p. 94)

Gazzaniga, M. S. (1967, August). The split brain in man. *Scientific American,* pp. 24–29. (p. 58)

Gazzaniga, M. S. (1983). Right hemisphere language following brain bisection: A 20-year perspective. *American Psychologist, 38,* 525–537. (p. 59)

Gazzaniga, M. S. (1988). Organization of the human brain. *Science, 245,* 947–952. (pp. 60, 89)

Gazzaniga, M. S. (1997). Brain, drugs, and society. *Science, 275,* 459. (p. 89)

Geary, D. C. (1995). Sexual selection and sex differences in spatial cognition. *Learning and Individual Differences, 7,* 289–301. (p. 329)

Geary, D. C. (1996). Sexual selection and sex differences in mathematical abilities. *Behavioral and Brain Sciences, 19,* 229–247. (p. 329)

Geary, D. C. (1998). *Male, female: The evolution of human sex differences.* Washington, DC: American Psychological Association. (p. 116)

Geen, R. G., & Quanty, M. B. (1977). The catharsis of aggression: An evaluation of a hypothesis. In L. Berkowitz (Ed.), *Advances in experimental social psychology* (Vol. 10). New York: Academic Press. (p. 390)

Geen, R. G., & Thomas, S. L. (1986). The immediate effects of media violence on behavior. *Journal of Social Issues, 42*(3), 7–28. (p. 252)

Gehring, W. J., Wimke, J., & Nisenson, L. G. (2000). Action monitoring dysfunction in obsessive-compulsive disorder. *Psychological Science, 11*(1), 1–6. (p. 467)

Geldard, F. A. (1972). *The human senses* (2nd ed.). New York: Wiley. (p. 191)

Gelman, D. (1989, May 15). Voyages to the unknown. *Newsweek*, pp. 66–69. (p. 387)

Genesee, F., & Gándara, P. (1999). Bilingual education programs: A cross-national perspective. *Journal of Social Issues, 55*, 665–685. (p. 307)

Genevro, J. L. (2003). *Report on bereavement and grief research.* Washington, DC: Center for the Advancement of Health. (p. 172)

Gentile, D. A., Lynch, P. J., Linder, J. R., & Walsh, D. A. (2004). The effects of violent video game habits on adolescent hostility, aggressive behaviors, and school performance. *Journal of Adolescence, 27*, 5–22. (pp. 252, 552)

Gentile, D. A., Saleem, M., & Anderson, C. A. (2007). Public policy and the effects of media violence on children. *Social Issues and Policy Review, 1*, 15–61. (p. 552)

George, L. K., Ellison, C. G., & Larson, D. B. (2002). Explaining the relationships between religious involvement and health. *Psychological Inquiry, 13*, 190–200. (p. 415)

George, L. K., Larson, D. B., Koenig, H. G., & McCullough, M. E. (2000). Spirituality and health: What we know, what we need to know. *Journal of Social and Clinical Psychology, 19*, 102–116. (p. 415)

George, M. S. (2003, September). Stimulating the brain. *Scientific American*, pp. 67–73. (p. 518)

George, M. S., & Belmaker, R. H. (Eds.). (2007). *Transcranial magnetic stimulation in clinical psychiatry.* Washington, DC: American Psychiatric Publishing. (pp. 517, 519)

Geraerts, E., Schooler, J. W., Merckelbach, H., Jelicic, M., Hauer, B. J. A., & Ambadar, Z. (2007). The reality of recovered memories: Corroborating continuous and discontinuous memories of childhood sexual abuse. *Psychological Science, 18*, 564–568. (p. 286)

Gerbner, G. (1990). Stories that hurt: Tobacco, alcohol, and other drugs in the mass media. In H. Resnik (Ed.), *Youth and drugs: Society's mixed messages.* Rockville, MD: Office for Substance Abuse Prevention, U.S. Department of Health and Human Services. (p. 97)

Gerbner, G., Morgan, M., & Signorielli, N. (1993). *Television violence profile no. 16: The turning point from research to action.* Philadelphia: Annenberg School for Communication, University of Pennsylvania. (p. 554)

Gernsbacher, M. A., Dawson, M., & Goldsmith, H. H. (2005). Three reasons not to believe in an autism epidemic. *Current Directions in Psychological Science, 14*, 55–58. (p. 146)

Gerrard, M., & Luus, C. A. E. (1995). Judgments of vulnerability to pregnancy: The role of risk factors and individual differences. *Personality and Social Psychology Bulletin, 21*, 160–171. (p. 361)

Gershoff, E. T. (2002). Parental corporal punishment and associated child behaviors and experiences: A meta-analytic and theoretical review. *Psychological Bulletin, 128*, 539–579. (p. 242)

Geschwind, N. (1979, September). Specializations of the human brain. *Scientific American, 241*, 180–199. (p. 54)

Gest, S. D., Rulison, K. L., Davidson, A. J., & Welsh, J. A. (2008). A reputation for success (or failure): The association of peer academic reputations with academic self-concept, effort, and performance across the upper elementary grades. *Developmental Psychology, 44*, 625–636. (p. 161)

Gfeller, J. D., Lynn, S. J., & Pribble, W. E. (1987). Enhancing hypnotic susceptibility: Interpersonal and rapport factors. *Journal of Personality and Social Psychology, 52*, 586–595. (p. 86)

Gibbons, F. X. (1986). Social comparison and depression: Company's effect on misery. *Journal of Personality and Social Psychology, 51*, 140–148. (p. 396)

Gibbons, R. D., Brown, C. H., Hur, K., Marcus, S. M., Bhaumik, D. K., & Mann, J. J. (2007). Relationship between antidepressants and suicide attempts: An analysis of the Veterans Health Administration data sets. *American Journal of Psychiatry, 164*, 1044–1049. (p. 516)

Gibbs, J. C., Basinger, K. S., Grime, R. L., & Snarey, J. R. (2007). Moral judgment development across cultures: Revisiting Kohlberg's universality claims. *Developmental Review, 27*, 443–500. (p. 158)

Gibbs, W. W. (1996, June). Mind readings. *Scientific American*, pp. 34–36. (p. 51)

Gibbs, W. W. (2005, June). Obesity: An overblown epidemic? *Scientific American*, pp. 70–77. (p. 350)

Gibson, E. J., & Walk, R. D. (1960, April). The "visual cliff." *Scientific American*, pp. 64–71. (p. 207)

Gibson, H. B. (1995, April). Recovered memories. *The Psychologist*, pp. 153–154. (p. 85)

Gigerenzer, G. (2004). Dread risk, September 11, and fatal traffic accidents. *Psychological Science, 15*, 286–287. (p. 298)

Gilbert, D. T. (2006). *Stumbling on happiness.* New York: Knopf. (pp. 170, 282, 291, 381)

Gilbert, D. T., Pelham, B. W., & Krull, D. S. (2003). The psychology of good ideas. *Psychological Inquiry, 14*, 258–260. (p. 11)

Gilbert, D. T., Pinel, E. C., Wilson, T. D., Blumberg, S. J., & Wheatley, T. P. (1998). Immune neglect: A source of durability bias in affective forecasting. *Journal of Personality and Social Psychology, 75*, 617–638. (p. 393)

Gilbertson, M. W., Paulus, L. A., Williston, S. K., Gurvits, T. V., Lasko, N. B., Pitman, R. K., & Orr, S. P. (2006). Neurocognitive function in monozygotic twins discordant for combat exposure: Relationship to posttraumatic stress disorder. *Journal of Abnormal Psychology, 115*, 484–495. (p. 465)

Giles, D. E., Dahl, R. E., & Coble, P. A. (1994). Childbearing, developmental, and familial aspects of sleep. In J. M. Oldham & M. B. Riba (Eds.), *Review of psychiatry* (Vol. 13). Washington, DC: American Psychiatric Press. (p. 73)

Gill, A. J., Oberlander, J., & Austin, E. (2006). Rating e-mail personality at zero acquaintance. *Personality and Individual Differences, 40*, 497–507. (p. 438)

Gillham, J.E., Hamilton, J., Freres, D.R., Patton, K. & Gallop, R. (2006). Preventing depression among early adolescents in the primary care setting: A randomized controlled study of the Penn Resiliency Program. *Journal of Abnormal Child Psychology, 34*, 195-211. (p. 521)

Gilligan, C. (1982). *In a different voice: Psychological theory and women's development.* Cambridge, MA: Harvard University Press. (p. 128)

Gilligan, C., Lyons, N. P., & Hanmer, T. J. (Eds.). (1990). *Making connections: The relational worlds of adolescent girls at Emma Willard School.* Cambridge, MA: Harvard University Press. (p. 128)

Gilovich, T. (1991). *How we know what isn't so: The fallibility of human reason in everyday life.* New York: Free Press. (p. 19)

Gilovich, T., Kruger, J., & Medvec, V. H. (2002). The spotlight effect revisted: Overestimating the manifest variability of our actions and appearance. *Journal of Experimental Social Psychology, 38*, 93–99. (p. 446)

Gilovich, T., & Medvec, V. H. (1995). The experience of regret: What, when, and why. *Psychological Review, 102*, 379–395. (p. 170)

Gilovich, T., & Savitsky, K. (1999). The spotlight effect and the illusion of transparency: Egocentric assessments of how we are seen by others. *Current Directions in Psychological Science, 8*, 165–168. (p. 446)

Gilovich, T., Vallone, R., & Tversky, A. (1985). The hot hand in basketball: On the misperception of random sequences. *Cognitive Psychology, 17*, 295–314. (p. 20)

Gilovich, T. D. (1996). *The spotlight effect: Exaggerated impressions of the self as a social stimulus.* Unpublished manuscript, Cornell University. (p. 446)

Giltay, E. J., Geleijnse, J. M., Zitman, F. G., Buijsse, B., & Kromhout, D. (2007). Lifestyle and dietary correlates of dispositional optimism in men: The Zutphen Elderly Study. *Journal of Psychosomatic Research, 63*, 483–490. (p. 409)

Giltay, E. J., Geleijnse, J. M., Zitman, F. G., Hoekstra, T., & Schouten, E. G. (2004). Dispositional optimism and all-cause and cardiovascular mortality in a prospective cohort of elderly Dutch men and women. *Archives of General Psychiatry, 61*, 1126–1135. (p. 409)

Gingerich, O. (1999, February 6). Is there a role for natural theology today? *The Real Issue* (www.origins.org/real/n9501/natural.html). (p. 133)

Gladue, B. A. (1990). Hormones and neuroendocrine factors in atypical human sexual behavior. In J. R. Feierman (Ed.), *Pedophilia: Biosocial dimensions.* New York: Springer-Verlag. (p. 367)

Gladue, B. A. (1994). The biopsychology of sexual orientation. *Current Directions in Psychological Science, 3*, 150–154. (p. 367)

Gladwell, M. (2005). *Blink: The power of thinking without thinking.* New York: Little, Brown. (p. 558)

Glasman, L. R., & Albarracin, D. (2006). Forming attitudes that predict future behavior: A meta-analysis of the attitude-behavior relation. *Psychological Bulletin, 132*, 778–822. (p. 527)

Glass, R. I. (2004). Perceived threats and real killers. *Science, 304,* 927. (p. 299)

Glass, R. M. (2001). Electroconvulsive therapy: Time to bring it out of the shadows. *Journal of the American Medical Association, 285,* 1346–1348. (p. 517)

Gleaves, D. H. (1996). The sociocognitive model of dissociative identity disorder: A reexamination of the evidence. *Psychological Bulletin, 120,* 42–59. (p. 470)

Glenn, N. D. (1975). Psychological well-being in the postparental stage: Some evidence from national surveys. *Journal of Marriage and the Family, 37,* 105–110. (p. 170)

Glick, P., & 15 others. (2004). Bad but bold: Ambivalent attitudes toward men predict gender inequality in 16 nations. *Journal of Personality and Social Psychology, 86,* 713–728. (p. 544)

Glick, P., Gottesman, D., & Jolton, J. (1989). The fault is not in the stars: Susceptibility of skeptics and believers in astrology to the Barnum effect. *Personality and Social Psychology Bulletin, 15,* 572–583. (p. 435)

Godden, D. R., & Baddeley, A. D. (1975). Context-dependent memory in two natural environments: On land and underwater. *British Journal of Psychology, 66,* 325–331. (p. 274)

Goel, V., & Dolan, R. J. (2001). The functional anatomy of humor: Segregating cognitive and affective components. *Nature Neuroscience, 4,* 237–238. (p. 55)

Goff, D. C. (1993). Reply to Dr. Armstrong. *Journal of Nervous and Mental Disease, 181,* 604–605. (p. 469)

Goff, D. C., & Simms, C. A. (1993). Has multiple personality disorder remained consistent over time? *Journal of Nervous and Mental Disease, 181,* 595–600. (p. 469)

Goff, L. M., & Roediger, H. L., III. (1998). Imagination inflation for action events: Repeated imaginings lead to illusory recollections. *Memory and Cognition, 26,* 20–33. (p. 282)

Golan, O., Baron-Cohen, S., Chapman, E., & Granader, Y. (2007, May). Facilitating emotional understanding and face processing in young children with autism spectrum conditions, using animations of vehicles with faces. Paper presented at the International Meeting for Autism Research (IMFAR), Seattle, WA. (p. 147)

Gold, M., & Yanof, D. S. (1985). Mothers, daughters, and girlfriends. *Journal of Personality and Social Psychology, 49,* 654–659. (p. 161)

Goldapple, K., Segal, Z., Garson, C., Lau, M., Bieling, P., Kennedy, S., & Mayberg, H. (2004). Modulation of cortical-limbic pathways in major depression. *Archives of General Psychiatry, 61,* 34–41. (p. 515)

Golden, R. N., Gaynes, B. N., Ekstrom, R. D., Hamer, R. M., Jacobsen, F. M., Suppes, T., Wisner, K. L., & Nemeroff, C. B. (2005). The efficacy of light therapy in the treatment of mood disorders: A review and meta-analysis of the evidence. *American Journal of Psychiatry, 162,* 656–662. (p. 509)

Goldfried, M. R. (2001). Integrating gay, lesbian, and bisexual issues into mainstream psychology. *American Psychologist, 56,* 977–988. (p. 474)

Goldfried, M. R., & Padawer, W. (1982). Current status and future directions in psychotherapy. In M. R. Goldfried (Ed.),

Converging themes in psychotherapy: Trends in psychodynamic, humanistic, and behavioral practice. New York: Springer. (p. 510)

Goldfried, M. R., Raue, P. J., & Castonguay, L. G. (1998). The therapeutic focus in significant sessions of master therapists: A comparison of cognitive-behavioral and psychodynamic-interpersonal interventions. *Journal of Consulting and Clinical Psychology, 66,* 803–810. (p. 510)

Golding, J. M. (1996). Sexual assault history and women's reproductive and sexual health. *Psychology of Women Quarterly, 20,* 101–121. (p. 553)

Golding, J. M. (1999). Sexual-assault history and the long-term physical health problems: Evidence from clinical and population epidemiology. *Current Directions in Psychological Science, 8,* 191–194. (p. 464)

Goldstein, A. P., Glick, B., & Gibbs, J. C. (1998). *Aggression replacement training: A comprehensive intervention for aggressive youth* (rev. ed.). Champaign, IL: Research Press. (p. 551)

Goldstein, I. (2000, August). Male sexual circuitry. *Scientific American,* pp. 70–75. (p. 42)

Goldstein, I., Lue, T. F., Padma-Nathan, H., Rosen, R. C., Steers, W. D., & Wicker, P. A. (1998). Oral sildenafil in the treatment of erectile dysfunction. *New England Journal of Medicine, 338,* 1397–1404. (p. 23)

Goleman, D. (2006). *Social intelligence.* New York: Bantam Books. (p. 318)

Gómez, R. L., Bootzin, R. R., & Nadel, L. (2006). Naps promote abstraction in language-learning infants. *Psychological Science, 17,* 670–674. (p. 78)

Gonsalves, B., Reber, P. J., Gitelman, D. R., Parrish, T. B., Mesulam, M-M., & Paller, K. A. (2004). Neural evidence that vivid imagining can lead to false remembering. *Psychological Science, 15,* 655–659. (p. 282)

Goodale, M. A., & Milner, D. A. (2004). *Sight unseen: An exploration of conscious and unconscious vision.* Oxford: Oxford University Press. (p. 67)

Goodale, M. A., & Milner, D. A. (2006). One brain—two visual systems. *The Psychologist, 19,* 660–663. (p. 67)

Goodall, J. (1968). The behaviour of free-living chimpanzees in the Gombe Stream Reserve. *Animal Behaviour Monographs, 1,* 161–311. (p. 119)

Goodall, J. (1986). *The chimpanzees of Gombe: Patterns of behavior.* Cambridge, MA: Harvard University Press. (p. 546)

Goodall, J. (1998). Learning from the chimpanzees: A message humans can understand. *Science, 282,* 2184–2185. (p. 17)

Goodchilds, J. (1987). Quoted by Carol Tavris, Old age is not what it used to be. *The New York Times Magazine: Good Health Magazine,* September 27, pp. 24–25, 91–92. (p. 164)

Goode, E. (1999, April 13). If things taste bad, 'phantoms' may be at work. *New York Times* (www.nytimes.com). (p. 199)

Goodhart, D. E. (1986). The effects of positive and negative thinking on performance in an achievement situation. *Journal of Personality and Social Psychology, 51,* 117–124. (p. 443)

Goodman, G. S. (2006). Children's eyewitness memory: A modern history and contemporary commentary. *Journal of Social Issues, 62,* 811–832. (p. 284)

Goodman, G. S., Ghetti, S., Quas, J. A., Edelstein, R. S., Alexander, K. W., Redlich, A. D., Cordon, I. M., & Jones, D. P. H. (2003). A prospective study of memory for child sexual abuse: New findings relevant to the repressed-memory controversy. *Psychological Science, 14,* 113–118. (p. 286)

Goodstein, L., & Glaberson, W. (2000, April 9). The well-marked roads to homicidal rage. *New York Times* (www.nytimes.com). (p. 445)

Goodwin, F. K., & Morrison, A. R. (1999). Scientists in bunkers: How appeasement of animal rights activism has failed. *Cerebrum, 1*(2), 50–62. (p. 26)

Gopnik, A., & Meltzoff, A. N. (1986). Relations between semantic and cognitive development in the one-word stage: The specificity hypothesis. *Child Development, 57,* 1040–1053. (p. 307)

Goranson, R. E. (1978). *The hindsight effect in problem solving.* Unpublished manuscript, cited by G. Wood (1984), Research methodology: A decision-making perspective. In A. M. Rogers & C. J. Scheirer (Eds.), *The G. Stanley Hall Lecture Series* (Vol. 4). Washington, DC. (p. 11)

Gordon, P. (2004). Numerical cognition without words: Evidence from Amazonia. *Science, 306,* 496–499. (p. 306)

Gore-Felton, C., Koopman, C., Thoresen, C., Arnow, B., Bridges, E., & Spiegel, D. (2000). Psychologists' beliefs and clinical characteristics: Judging the veracity of childhood sexual abuse memories. *Professional Psychology: Research and Practice, 31,* 372–377. (p. 286)

Gortmaker, S. L., Must, A., Perrin, J. M., Sobol, A. M., & Dietz, W. H. (1993). Social and economic consequences of overweight in adolescence and young adulthood. *New England Journal of Medicine, 329,* 1008–1012. (p. 351)

Gosling, S. D., Gladdis, S., & Vazire, S. (2007). Personality impressions based on Facebook profiles. Paper presented to the Society for Personality and Social Psychology meeting. (p. 438)

Gosling, S. D., Ko, S. J., Mannarelli, T., & Morris, M. E. (2002). A room with a cue: Personality judgments based on offices and bedrooms. *Journal of Personality and Social Psychology, 82,* 379–398. (p. 438)

Gosling, S. D., Kwan, V. S. Y., & John, O. P. (2003). A dog's got personality: A cross-species comparative approach to personality judgments in dogs and humans. *Journal of Personality and Social Psychology, 85,* 1161–1169. (p. 433)

Gotlib, I. H., & Hammen, C. L. (1992). *Psychological aspects of depression: Toward a cognitive-interpersonal integration.* New York: Wiley. (p. 479)

Gottesman, I. I. (1991). *Schizophrenia genesis: The origins of madness.* New York: Freeman. (p. 485)

Gottesman, I. I. (2001). Psychopathology through a life span–genetic prism. *American Psychologist, 56,* 867–881. (p. 484)

Gottfredson, L. S. (2002a). Where and why g matters: Not a mystery. *Human Performance, 15,* 25–46. (p. 315)

Gottfredson, L. S. (2002b). g: Highly general and highly practical. In R. J. Sternberg & E. L. Grigorenko (Eds.), *The general factor of intelligence: How general is it?* Mahwah, NJ: Erlbaum. (p. 315)

Gottfredson, L. S. (2003a). Dissecting practical intelligence theory: Its claims and evidence. *Intelligence, 31,* 343–397. (p. 315)

Gottfredson, L. S. (2003b). On Sternberg's "Reply to Gottfredson." *Intelligence, 31,* 415–424. (p. 315)

Gottfried, J. A., O'Doherty, J., & Dolan, R. J. (2003). Encoding predictive reward value in human amygdala and orbitofrontal cortex. *Science, 301,* 1104–1108. (p. 228)

Gould, E. (2007). How widespread is adult neurogenesis in mammals? *Nature Neuroscience, 8,* 481–488. (p. 57)

Gould, S. J. (1981). *The mismeasure of man.* New York: Norton. (p. 319)

Gould, S. J. (1997, June 12). Darwinian fundamentalism. *The New York Review of Books, XLIV*(10), 34–37. (p. 117)

Grabe, S., Ward, L. M., & Hyde, J. S. (2008). The role of the media in body image concerns among women: A meta-analysis of experimental and correlational studies. *Psychological Bulletin, 134,* 460–476. (p. 349)

Grady, C. L., McIntosh, A. R., Horwitz, B., Maisog, J. M., Ungeleider, L. G., Mentis, M. J., Pietrini, P., Schapiro, M. B., & Haxby, J. V. (1995). Age-related reductions in human recognition memory due to impaired encoding. *Science, 269,* 218–221. (p. 277)

Graf, P. (1990). Life-span changes in implicit and explicit memory. *Bulletin of the Psychonomic Society, 28,* 353–358. (p. 167)

Graham, J. E., Christian, L. M., & Kiecolt-Glaser, J. K. (2006). Marriage, health, and immune function. In S. R. H. Beach & others (Eds.), *Relational processes and DSM-V: Neuroscience, assessment, prevention, and treatment.* Washington, DC: American Psychiatric Association. (p. 409)

Gray, P. B., Yang, C-F. J., & Pope, Jr., H. G. (2006). Fathers have lower salivary testosterone levels than unmarried men and married non-fathers in Beijing, China. *Proceedings of the Royal Society, 273,* 333–339. (p. 359)

Gray-Little, B., & Burks, N. (1983). Power and satisfaction in marriage: A review and critique. *Psychological Bulletin, 93,* 513–538. (p. 560)

Green, J. D., Sedikides, C., & Gregg, A. P. (2008). Forgotten but not gone: The recall and recognition of self-threatening memories. *Journal of Experimental Social Psychology, 44,* 547–561. (p. 426)

Green, J. T., & Woodruff-Pak, D. S. (2000). Eyeblink classical conditioning: Hippocampal formation is for neutral stimulus associations as cerebellum is for association-response. *Psychological Bulletin, 126,* 138–158. (p. 272)

Greenberg, J. (2008). Understanding the vital human quest for self-esteem. *Perspectives on Psychological Science, 3,* 48–55. (p. 447)

Greene, R. L. (1987). Effects of maintenance rehearsal on human memory. *Psychological Bulletin, 102,* 403–413. (p. 261)

Greenfeld, L. A. (1998). *Alcohol and crime: An analysis of national data on the prevalence of alcohol involvement in crime.* Washington, DC: Document NCJ–168632, Bureau of Justice Statistics (www.ojp.usdoj.gov/bjs). (p. 549)

Greenwald, A. G. (1992). Subliminal semantic activation and subliminal snake oil. Paper presented to the American Psychological Association Convention, Washington, DC. (pp. 182, 427)

Greenwald, A. G., McGhee, D. E., & Schwartz, J. L. K. (1998). Measuring individual differences in implicit cognition: The implicit association test. *Journal of Personality and Social Psychology, 74,* 1464–1480. (p. 543)

Greenwald, A. G., Oakes, M. A., & Hoffman, H. (2003). Targets of discrimination: Effects of race on responses to weapons holders. *Journal of Experimental Social Psychology, 39,* 399. (p. 543)

Greenwald, A. G., Spangenberg, E. R., Pratkanis, A. R., & Eskenazi, J. (1991). Double-blind tests of subliminal self-help audiotapes. *Psychological Science, 2,* 119–122. (p. 182)

Greenwood, M. R. C. (1989). Sexual dimorphism and obesity. In A. J. Stunkard & A. Baum (Eds.), *Perspectives in behavioral medicine: Eating, sleeping, and sex.* Hillsdale, NJ: Erlbaum. (p. 350)

Greers, A. E. (2004). Speech, language, and reading skills after early cochlear implantation. *Archives of Otolaryngology—Head & Neck Surgery, 130,* 634–638. (p. 304)

Gregg, L., & Tarrier, N. (2007). Virtual reality in mental health: A review of the literature. *Social Psychiatry and Psychiatric Epidemiology, 42,* 343–354. (p. 498)

Gregory, R. L. (1978). *Eye and brain: The psychology of seeing* (3rd ed.). New York: McGraw-Hill. (p. 213)

Gregory, R. L., & Gombrich, E. H. (Eds.). (1973). *Illusion in nature and art.* New York: Charles Scribner's Sons. (p. 217)

Greif, E. B., & Ulman, K. J. (1982). The psychological impact of menarche on early adolescent females: A review of the literature. *Child Development, 53,* 1413–1430. (p. 155)

Greist, J. H., Jefferson, J. W., & Marks, I. M. (1986). *Anxiety and its treatment: Help is available.* Washington, DC: American Psychiatric Press. (p. 462)

Grèzes, J., & Decety, J. (2001). Function anatomy of execution, mental simulation, observation, and verb generation of actions: A meta-analysis. *Human Brain Mapping, 12,* 1–19. (p. 308)

Griffiths, M. (2001). Sex on the Internet: Observations and implications for Internet sex addiction. *Journal of Sex Research, 38,* 333–342. (p. 89)

Grill-Spector, K., & Kanwisher, N. (2005). Visual recognition: As soon as you know it is there, you know what it is. *Psychological Science, 16,* 152–160. (p. 292)

Grilo, C. M., & Pogue-Geile, M. F. (1991). The nature of environmental influences on weight and obesity: A behavior genetic analysis. *Psychological Bulletin, 110,* 520–537. (p. 353)

Grinker, R. R. (2007). *Unstrange minds: Remapping the world of autism.* New York: Basic Books. (p. 146)

Grobstein, C. (1979, June). External human fertilization. *Scientific American,* pp. 57-67. (p. 138)

Groothuis, T. G. G., & Carere, C. (2005). Avian personalities: Characterization and epigenesis. *Neuroscience and Biobehavioral Reviews, 29,* 137–150. (p. 433)

Gross, A. E., & Crofton, C. (1977). What is good is beautiful. *Sociometry, 40,* 85–90. (p. 558)

Gross, M., Nakamura, L., Pascual-Leone, A., & Fregni, F. (2007). Has repetitive transcranial magnetic stimulation (rTMS) treatment for depression improved? A systematic review and meta-analysis comparing the recent vs. the earlier rTMS studies. *Acta Psychiatrica Scandinavica, 116,* 165–173. (p. 519)

Grossberg, S. (1995). The attentive brain. *American Scientist, 83,* 438–449. (p. 216)

Grossman, M., & Wood, W. (1993). Sex differences in intensity of emotional experience: A social role interpretation. *Journal of Personality and Social Psychology, 65,* 1010–1022. (p. 385)

Gruder, C. L. (1977). Choice of comparison persons in evaluating oneself. In J. M. Suls & R. L. Miller (Eds.), *Social comparison processes.* New York: Hemisphere. (p. 396)

Grunebaum, M. F., Ellis, S. P., Li, S., Oquendo, M. A., & Mann, J. J. (2004). Antidepressants and suicide risk in the United States, 1985–1999. *Journal of Clinical Psychiatry, 65,* 1456–1462. (p. 516)

Guerin, B. (1986). Mere presence effects in humans: A review. *Journal of Personality and Social Psychology, 22,* 38–77. (p. 538)

Guerin, B. (2003). Language use as social strategy: A review and an analytic framework for the social sciences. *Review of General Psychology, 7,* 251–298. (p. 302)

Guiso, L., Monte, F., Sapienza, P., & Zingales, L. (2008). Culture, gender, and math. *Science, 320,* 1164–1165. (p. 330)

Gunderson, E. (2001, August 1). MTV is a many splintered thing. *USA Today,* pp. D1, D2. (p. 251)

Gustafson, D., Lissner, L., Bengtsson, C., Björkelund, C., & Skoog, I. (2004). A 24-year follow-up of body mass index and cerebral atrophy. *Neurology, 63,* 1876–1881. (p. 350)

Gustafson, D., Rothenberg, E., Blennow, K., Steen, B., & Skoog, I. (2003). An 18-year follow-up of overweight and risk of Alzheimer disease. *Archives of Internal Medicine, 163,* 1524–1528. (p. 350)

Gustavson, C. R., Garcia, J., Hankins, W. G., & Rusiniak, K. W. (1974). Coyote predation control by aversive conditioning. *Science, 184,* 581–583. (p. 233)

Gustavson, C. R., Kelly, D. J., & Sweeney, M. (1976). Prey-lithium aversions I: Coyotes and wolves. *Behavioral Biology, 17,* 61–72. (p. 233)

Guttmacher Institute. (1994). *Sex and America's teenagers.* New York: Alan Guttmacher Institute. (pp. 162, 362)

Guttmacher Institute. (2000). *Fulfilling the promise: Public policy and U.S. family planning clinics.* New York: Alan Guttmacher Institute. (p. 162)

Haber, R. N. (1970, May). How we remember what we see. *Scientific American,* pp. 104–112. (p. 258)

Haddock, G., & Zanna, M. P. (1994). Preferring "housewives" to "feminists." *Psychology of Women Quarterly, 18,* 25–52. (p. 544)

Haidt, J. (2006). *The happiness hypothesis: Finding modern truth in ancient wisdom.* New York: Basic Books. (p. 157)

Hakuta, K., Bialystok, E., & Wiley, E. (2003). Critical evidence: A test of the critical-period hypothesis for second-language acquisition. *Psychological Science, 14,* 31–38. (p. 305)

Halberstadt, J., O'Shea, R. P., & Forgas, J. (2006). Outgroup fanship in Australia and New Zealand. *Australian Journal of Psychology, 58,* 159–165. (p. 546)

Halberstadt, J. B., Niedenthal, P. M., & Kushner, J. (1995). Resolution of lexical ambiguity by emotional state. *Psychological Science, 6,* 278–281. (p. 217)

Haldeman, D. C. (1994). The practice and ethics of sexual orientation conversion therapy. *Journal of Consulting and Clinical Psychology, 62,* 221–227. (p. 364)

Haldeman, D. C. (2002). Gay rights, patient rights: The implications of sexual orientation conversion therapy. *Professional Psychology: Research and Practice, 33,* 260–264. (p. 364)

Hall, C. S., Dornhoff, W., Blick, K. A., & Weesner, K. E. (1982). The dreams of college men and women in 1950 and 1980: A comparison of dream contents and sex differences. *Sleep, 5,* 188–194. (p. 80)

Hall, C. S., & Lindzey, G. (1978). *Theories of personality* (2nd ed.). New York: Wiley. (p. 428)

Hall, G. S. (1904). *Adolescence: Its psychology and its relations to physiology, anthropology, sex, crime, religion and education* (Vol. I). New York: Appleton-Century-Crofts. (p. 154)

Hall, J. A. (1984). *Nonverbal sex differences: Communication accuracy and expressive style.* Baltimore: Johns Hopkins University Press. (p. 385)

Hall, J. A. (1987). On explaining gender differences: The case of nonverbal communication. In P. Shaver & C. Hendrick (Eds.), *Review of Personality and Social Psychology, 7,* 177–200. (pp. 127, 385)

Hall, J. A. Y., & Kimura, D. (1994). Dermatoglyphic assymetry and sexual orientation in men. *Behavioral Neuroscience, 108,* 1203–1206. (p. 367)

Hall, J. G. (2003). Twinning. *Lancet, 362,* 735–743. (p. 107)

Hall, S. S. (2004, May). The good egg. *Discover,* pp. 30-39. (p. 138)

Hall, W. (2006). The mental health risks of adolescent cannabis use. *PloS Medicine, 3*(2), e39. (p. 96)

Halpern, C. T., Joyner, K., Udry, J. R., & Suchindran, C. (2000). Smart teens don't have sex (or kiss much either). *Journal of Adolescent Health, 26*(3), 213–215. (p. 362)

Halpern, D. F. (2000). *Sex-related ability differences: Changing perspectives, changing minds.* Mahwah, NJ: Erlbaum. (p. 329)

Halpern, D. F. (2005, May 20). Response to Drs. Pinker and Spelke. www.edge.org. (p. 330)

Halpern, D. F., Benbow, C. P., Geary, D. C., Gur, R. C., Hyde, J. S., & Gernsbacher, M. A. (2007). The science of sex differences in science and mathematics. *Psychological Science in the Public Interest, 8,* 1–51. (pp. 328, 329, 330)

Hamann, S., Herman, R. A., Nolan, C. L., & Wallen, K. (2004). Men and women differ in amygdala response to visual sexual stimuli. *Nature Neuroscience, 7,* 411–416. (p. 359)

Hammack, P. L., (2005). The life course development of human sexual orientation: An integrative paradigm. *Human Development, 48,* 267–290. (pp. 363, 365)

Hammersmith, S. K. (1982, August). Sexual preference: An empirical study from the Alfred C. Kinsey Institute for Sex Research. Paper presented at the meeting of the American Psychological Association, Washington, DC. (p. 365)

Hampson, R. (2000, April 10). In the end, people just need more room. *USA Today,* p. 19A. (p. 354)

Hampson, S. E., & Goldberg, L. R. (2006). A first large cohort study of personality trait stability over the years between elementary school and midlife. *Journal of Personality and Social Psychology, 91,* 763–779. (p. 174)

Hancock, K. J., & Rhodes, G. (2008). Contact, configural coding and the other-race effect in face recognition. *British Journal of Psychology, 99,* 45–56. (p. 547)

Hankin, B. L., & Abramson, L. Y. (2001). Development of gender differences in depression: An elaborated cognitive vulnerability-transactional stress theory. women dress to impress. *Hormones and Behavior, 51,* 40–45. (p. 358)

Hasin, D. S., Goodwin, R. D., Stinson, F. S., & Grant, B. F. (2005). Epidemiology of major depressive disorder: Results from the National Epidemiologic Survey on *Psychological Bulletin, 127,* 773–796. (p. 477)

Hansen, C. H., & Hansen, R. D. (1988). Finding the face-in-the-crowd: An anger superiority effect. *Journal of Personality and Social Psychology, 54,* 917–924. (p. 384)

Harbaugh, W. T., Mayr, U., & Burghart, D. R. (2007). Neural responses to taxation and voluntary giving reveal motives for charitable donations. *Science, 316,* 1622–1625. (p. 562)

Harber, K. D. (1998). Feedback to minorities: Evidence of a positive bias. *Journal of Personality and Social Psychology, 74,* 622–628. (p. 543)

Hardin, C., & Banaji, M. R. (1993). The influence of language on thought. *Social Cognition, 11,* 277–308. (p. 306)

Hare, R. D. (1975). Psychophysiological studies of psychopathy. In D. C. Fowles (Ed.), *Clinical applications of psychophysiology.* New York: Columbia University Press. (p. 487)

Harker, L. A., & Keltner, D. (2001). Expressions of positive emotion in women's college yearbook pictures and their relationship to personality and life outcomes across adulthood. *Journal of Personality and Social Psychology, 80,* 112–124. (p. 392)

Harkins, S. G., & Szymanski, K. (1989). Social loafing and group evaluation. *Journal of Personality and Social Psychology, 56,* 934–941. (p. 539)

Harlow, H. F., Harlow, M. K., & Suomi, S. J. (1971). From thought to therapy: Lessons from a primate laboratory. *American Scientist, 59,* 538–549. (p. 149)

Harmon-Jones, E., Abramson, L. Y., Sigelman, J., Bohlig, A., Hogan, M. E., & Harmon-Jones, C. (2002). Proneness to hypomania/mania symptoms or depression symptoms and asymmetrical frontal cortical responses to an anger-evoking event. *Journal of Personality and Social Psychology, 82,* 610–618. (p. 379)

Harper, C., & McLanahan, S. (2004). Father absence and youth incarceration. *Journal of Research on Adolescence, 14,* 369–397. (p. 551)

Harris, A., & Lurigio, A. J. (2007). Mental illness and violence: A brief review of research and assessment strategies. *Aggression and Violent Behavior, 12,* 542–551. (p. 460)

Harris, B. (1979). Whatever happened to Little Albert? *American Psychologist, 34,* 151–160. (p. 235)

Harris, J. A. (1999). Review and methodological considerations in research on testosterone and aggression. *Aggression and Violent Behavior, 4,* 273–291. (p. 549)

Harris, J. R. (1998). *The nurture assumption.* New York: Free Press. (pp. 120, 151)

Harris, J. R. (2000). Beyond the nurture assumption: Testing hypotheses about the child's environment. In J. G. Borkowski & S. L. Ramey (Eds.), *Parenting and the child's world: Influences on academic, intellectual, and social-emotional development.* Washington, DC: APA Books. (p. 120)

Harris, J. R. (2006). *No two are alike: Human nature and human individuality.* New York: Norton. (p. 109)

Harris, J. R. (2007, August 8). Do pals matter more than parents? *The Times* (www.timesonline.co.uk). (p. 120)

Harris, R. J. (1994). The impact of sexually explicit media. In J. Brant & D. Zillmann (Eds.), *Media effects: Advances in theory and research.* Hillsdale, NJ: Erlbaum. (p. 553)

Harrison, Y., & Horne, J. A. (2000). The impact of sleep deprivation on decision making: A review. *Journal of Experimental Psychology: Applied, 6,* 236–249. (p. 76)

Harriston, K. A. (1993, December 24). 1 shakes, 1 snoozes: Both win: 45 million. *Washington Post* release (in *Tacoma News Tribune,* pp. A1, A2). (p. 445)

Hartmann, E. (1981, April). The strangest sleep disorder. *Psychology Today,* pp. 14, 16, 18. (p. 79)

Harvard Mental Health Letter. (2002, February). EMDR (Eye movement and reprocessing). *Harvard Mental Health Letter, 18,* 4–5. (p. 508)

Haselton, M. G., Mortezaie, M., Pillsworth, E. G., Bleske-Rechek, A., & Frederick, D. A. (2006). Ovulatory shifts in human female ornamentation: Near ovulation, women dress to impress. *Archives of General Psychiatry, 62,* 1097–1106. (p. 471)

Haslam, N., & Levy, S. R. (2006). Essentialist beliefs about homosexuality: Structure and implications for prejudice. *Personality and Social Psychology Bulletin, 32,* 471–485. (p. 368)

Haslam, S. A., & Reicher, S. (2007). Beyond the banality of evil: Three dynamics of an interactionist social psychology of tyranny. *Personality and Social Psychology Bulletin, 33,* 615–622. (p. 529)

Hassan, B., & Rahman, Q. (2007). Selective sexual orientation-related differences in object location memory. *Behavioral Neuroscience, 121,* 625–633. (p. 368)

Hatfield, E. (1988). Passionate and companionate love. In R. J. Sternberg & M. L. Barnes (Eds.), *The psychology of love.* New Haven, CT: Yale University Press. (p. 559)

Hatfield, E., & Sprecher, S. (1986). *Mirror, mirror . . . The importance of looks in everyday life.* Albany: State University of New York Press. (p. 557)

Hathaway, S. R. (1960). *An MMPI Handbook* (Vol. 1, Foreword). Minneapolis: University of Minnesota Press (rev. ed., 1972). (p. 433)

Haxby, J. V. (2001, July 7). Quoted by B. Bower, Faces of perception. *Science News,* pp. 10–12. See also J. V. Haxby, M. I. Gobbini, M. L.

Furey, A. Ishai, J. L. Schouten, & P. Pietrini, Distributed and overlapping representations of faces and objects in ventral temporal cortex. *Science, 293,* 2425–2430. (p. 189)

Haynes, J-D., & Rees, G. (2005). Predicting the orientation of invisible stimuli from activity in human primary visual cortex. *Nature Neuroscience, 8,* 686–691. (p. 182)

Haynes, J-D., & Rees, G. (2006). Decoding mental states from brain activity in humans. *Nature Reviews Neuroscience, 7,* 523–534. (p. 182)

Head Start. (2005). Head Start program fact sheet. www.acf.hhs.gov/programs//hsb/research/22005.htm. (p. 327)

Health Canada. (2007). *Canadian addiction survey: Substance use by Canadian youth.* Health Canada Publication 4946 (www.hc-sc.gc.ca). (p. 97)

Hebb, D. O. (1980). *Essay on mind.* Hillsdale, NJ: Erlbaum. (pp. 235, 375)

Hebl, M. R., & Mannix, L. M. (2003). The weight of obesity in evaluating others: A mere proximity effect. *Personality and Social Psychology Bulletin, 29,* 28–38. (p. 351)

Hedges, L. V., & Nowell, A. (1995). Sex differences in mental test scores, variability, and numbers of high-scoring individuals. *Science, 269,* 41–45. (pp. 328, 329)

Hedström, P., Liu, K-Y., & Nordvik, M. K. (2008). Interaction domains and suicides: A population-based panel study of suicides in the Stockholm metropolitan area, 1991–1999. *Social Forces,* in press. (p. 475)

Heider, F. (1958). *The psychology of interpersonal relations.* New York: Wiley. (p. 525)

Heiman, J. R. (1975, April). The physiology of erotica: Women's sexual arousal. *Psychology Today,* pp. 90–94. (p. 359)

Heine, S. J., & Hamamura, T. (2007). In search of East Asian self-enhancement. *Personality and Social Psychology Review, 11,* 4–27. (p. 448)

Heins, M. (2004, December 14). Quoted by B. Kloza, Violent Christmas games. *ScienCentralNews* (www.sciencecentral.com). (p. 552)

Hejmadi, A., Davidson, R. J., & Rozin, P. (2000). Exploring Hindu Indian emotion expressions: Evidence for accurate recognition by Americans and Indians. *Psychological Science, 11,* 183–187. (p. 384)

Helgeson, V. S., Reynolds, K. A., & Tomich, P. L. (2006). A meta-analytic review of benefit finding and growth. *Journal of Consulting and Clinical Psychology, 74,* 797–816. (p. 465)

Heller, W. (1990, May/June). Of one mind: Second thoughts about the brain's dual nature. *The Sciences,* pp. 38–44. (p. 60)

Helmreich, W. B. (1992). *Against all odds: Holocaust survivors and the successful lives they made in America.* New York: Simon & Schuster. (pp. 153, 426)

Helmreich, W. B. (1994). Personal correspondence. Department of Sociology, City University of New York. (p. 426)

Helms, J. E., Jernigan, M., & Mascher, J. (2005). The meaning of race in psychology and how to change it: A methodological perspective. *American Psychologist, 60,* 27–36. (p. 332)

Helmuth, L. (2001). Boosting brain activity from the outside in. *Science, 292,* 1284–1286. (p. 519)

Hembree, R. (1988). Correlates, causes, effects, and treatment of test anxiety. *Review of Educational Research, 58,* 47–77. (p. 378)

Henderson, J. M. (2007). Regarding scenes. *Current Directions in Psychological Science, 16,* 219–222. (p. 183)

Henkel, L. A., Franklin, N., & Johnson, M. K. (2000, March). Cross-modal source monitoring confusions between perceived and imagined events. *Journal of Experimental Psychology: Learning, Memory, & Cognition, 26,* 321–335. (p. 283)

Henley, N. M. (1989). Molehill or mountain? What we know and don't know about sex bias in language. In M. Crawford & M. Gentry (Eds.), *Gender and thought: Psychological perspectives.* New York: Springer-Verlag. (p. 307)

Henninger, P. (1992). Conditional handedness: Handedness changes in multiple personality disordered subject reflect shift in hemispheric dominance. *Consciousness and Cognition, 1,* 265–287. (p. 470)

Herbert, J. D., Lilienfeld, S. O., Lohr, J. M., Montgomery, R. W., O'Donohue, W. T., Rosen, G. M., & Tolin, D. F. (2000). Science and pseudoscience in the development of eye movement desensitization and reprocessing: Implications for clinical psychology. *Clinical Psychology Review, 20,* 945–971. (p. 508)

Herek, G. M. (2006). Legal recognition of same-sex relationships in the United States: A social science perspective. *American Psychologist, 61,* 607–621. (p. 363)

Herman, C. P., & Polivy, J. (1980). Restrained eating. In A. J. Stunkard (Ed.), *Obesity.* Philadelphia: Saunders. (p. 356)

Herman-Giddens, M. E., Wang, L., & Koch, G. (2001). Secondary sexual characteristics in boys: Estimates from the National Health and Nutrition Examination Survey III, 1988–1994. *Archives of Pediatrics and Adolescent Medicine, 155,* 1022–1028. (p. 155)

Hernandez, A. E., & Li, P. (2007). Age of acquisition: Its neural and computational mechanisms. *Psychological Bulletin, 133,* 638–650. (p. 304)

Herrmann, D. (1982). Know thy memory: The use of questionnaires to assess and study memory. *Psychological Bulletin, 92,* 434–452. (p. 287)

Herrmann, E., Call, J., Hernández-Lloreda, M. V., Hare, B., & Tomasello, M. (2007). Humans have evolved specialized skills of social cognition: The cultural intelligence hypothesis. *Science, 317,* 1360–1365. (p. 248)

Herrnstein, R. J., & Loveland, D. H. (1964). Complex visual concept in the pigeon. *Science, 146,* 549–551. (p. 238)

Herrnstein, R. J., & Murray, C. A. (1994). *The bell curve: Intelligence and class structure in American life.* New York: Free Press. (p. 331)

Hershenson, M. (1989). *The moon illusion.* Hillsdale, NJ: Erlbaum. (p. 210)

Hertenstein, M. J., Keltner, D., App, B. Bulleit, B., & Jaskolka, A. (2006). Touch communicates distinct emotions. *Emotion, 6,* 528–533. (p. 150)

Hertenstein, M. J., Verkamp, J. M., Kerestes, A. M., & Holmes, R. M. (2006). The communicative functions of touch in humans, nonhumans primates, and rats: A review and synthesis of the empirical research. *Genetic, Social, and*

General Psychology Monographs, 132, 5–94. (p. 196)

Herz, R. S. (2001). Ah sweet skunk! Why we like or dislike what we smell. *Cerebrum, 3*(4), 31–47. (pp. 203, 204)

Herz, R. S., Beland, S. L., & Hellerstein, M. (2004). Changing odor hedonic perception through emotional associations in humans. *International Journal of Comparative Psychology, 17,* 315–339. (p. 204)

Hess, E. H. (1956, July). Space perception in the chick. *Scientific American,* pp. 71–80. (p. 214)

Hettema, J. M., Neale, M. C., & Kendler, K. S. (2001). A review and meta-analysis of the genetic epidemiology of anxiety disorders. *American Journal of Psychiatry, 158,* 1568–1578. (p. 467)

Hewlett, B. S. (1991). *Intimate fathers: The nature and context of Aka Pygmy.* Ann Arbor: University of Michigan Press. (p. 151)

Hickok, G., Bellugi, U., & Klima, E. S. (2001, June). Sign language in the brain. *Scientific American,* pp. 58–65. (p. 60)

Hilgard, E. R. (1986). *Divided consciousness: Multiple controls in human thought and action.* New York: Wiley. (p. 86)

Hilgard, E. R. (1992). Dissociation and theories of hypnosis. In E. Fromm & M. R. Nash (Eds.), *Contemporary hypnosis research.* New York: Guilford. (p. 86)

Hill, C. E., & Nakayama, E. Y. (2000). Client-centered therapy: Where has it been and where is it going? A comment on Hathaway. *Journal of Clinical Psychology, 56,* 961–875. (p. 496)

Hill, H., & Johnston, A. (2001). Categorizing sex and identity from the biological motion of faces. *Current Biology, 11,* 880–885. (p. 386)

Hines, M. (2004). *Brain gender.* New York: Oxford University Press. (p. 129)

Hingson, R. W., Heeren, T., & Winter, M. R. (2006). Age at drinking onset and alcohol dependence. *Archives of Pediatrics & Adolescent Medicine, 160,* 739–746. (p. 99)

Hintzman, D. L. (1978). *The psychology of learning and memory.* San Francisco: Freeman. (p. 264)

Hinz, L. D., & Williamson, D. A. (1987). Bulimia and depression: A review of the affective variant hypothesis. *Psychological Bulletin, 102,* 150–158. (p. 348)

Hirsch, J. (2003). Obesity: Matter over mind? *Cerebrum, 5*(1), 7–18. (p. 351)

HMHL. (2002, January). Disaster and trauma. *Harvard Mental Health Letter,* pp. 1–5. (p. 400)

HMHL. (2002, August). Smoking and depression. *Harvard Mental Health Letter,* pp. 6–7. (p. 476)

HMHL. (2007, February). Electroconvulsive therapy. *Harvard Mental Health Letter,* pp. 1–4. (p. 517)

Hobson, J. A. (1995, September). Quoted by C. H. Colt, The power of dreams. *Life,* pp. 36–49. (p. 82)

Hobson, J. A. (2003). *Dreaming: An introduction to the science of sleep.* New York: Oxford. (p. 82)

Hobson, J. A. (2004). *13 dreams Freud never had: The new mind science.* New York: Pi Press. (p. 82)

Hodgkinson, V. A., & Weitzman, M. S. (1992). *Giving and volunteering in the United States.* Washington, DC: Independent Sector. (p. 563)

Hoebel, B. G., & Teitelbaum, P. (1966). Effects of forcefeeding and starvation on food intake and body weight in a rat with ventromedial hypothalamic lesions. *Journal of Comparative and Physiological Psychology, 61*, 189–193. (p. 345)

Hoeft, F., Watson, C. L., Kesler, S. R., Bettinger, K. E., & Reiss, A. L. (2008). Gender differences in the mesocorticolimbic system during computer game-play. *Journal of Psychiatric Research, 42*, 253–258. (p. 89)

Hoffman, C., & Hurst, N. (1990). Gender stereotypes: Perception or rationalization? *Journal of Personality and Social Psychology, 58*, 197–208. (p. 545)

Hoffman, D. D. (1998). *Visual intelligence: How we create what we see.* New York: Norton. (p. 190)

Hogan, R. (1998). Reinventing personality. *Journal of Social and Clinical Psychology, 17*, 1–10. (p. 437)

Hoge, C. W., & Castro, C. A. (2006). Post-traumatic stress disorder in UK and U.S. forces deployed to Iraq. *Lancet, 368*, 837. (p. 464)

Hoge, C. W., Castro, C. A., Messer, S. C., McGurk, D., Cotting, D. I., & Koffman, R. L. (2004). Combat duty in Iraq and Afghanistan, mental health problems, and barriers to care. *New England Journal of Medicine, 351*, 13–22. (p. 464)

Hoge, C. W., Terhakopian, A., Castro, C. A., Messer, S. C., & Engel, C. C. (2007). Association of posttraumatic stress disorder with somatic symptoms, health care visits, and absenteeism among Iraq War veterans. *American Journal of Psychiatry, 164*, 150–153. (p. 464)

Hogg, M. A. (1996). Intragroup processes, group structure and social identity. In W. P. Robinson (Ed.), *Social groups and identities: Developing the legacy of Henri Tajfel.* Oxford: Butterworth Heinemann. (p. 546)

Hogg, M. A. (2006). Social identity theory. In P. J. Burke (Ed.), *Contemporary social psychological theories.* Stanford, CA: Stanford University Press. (p. 546)

Hohmann, G. W. (1966). Some effects of spinal cord lesions on experienced emotional feelings. *Psychophysiology, 3*, 143–156. (p. 376)

Hokanson, J. E., & Edelman, R. (1966). Effects of three social responses on vascular processes. *Journal of Personality and Social Psychology, 3*, 442–447. (p. 390)

Holahan, C. K., & Sears, R. R. (1995). *The gifted group in later maturity.* Stanford, CA: Stanford University Press. (p. 322)

Holden, C. (1993). Wake-up call for sleep research. *Science, 259*, 305. (p. 76)

Holden, C. (2007). Mental illness: The next frontier. *Science, 317*, 23. (p. 485)

Holliday, R. E., & Albon, A. J. (2004). Minimizing misinformation effects in young children with cognitive interview mnemonics. *Applied Cognitive Psychology, 18*, 263–281. (p. 284)

Hollis, K. L. (1997). A "new" functional analysis. *American Psychologist, 52*, 956–965. (p. 230)

Hollon, S. D., & 10 others. (2005). Prevention of relapse following cognitive therapy vs. medications in moderate to severe depression. *Archives of General Psychiatry, 62*, 417–422. (p. 506)

Hollon, S. D., Thase, M. E., & Markowitz, J. C. (2002). Treatment and prevention of depression. *Psychological Science in the Public Interest, 3*, 39–77. (p. 515)

Holm-Denoma, J., Joiner, T., Vohs, K., & Heatherton, T. (2008). The "freshman fifteen" (the freshman five actually): Predictors and possible explanations. *Health Psychology, 27*, S3–S9. (p. 354)

Holstege, G., Georgiadis, J. R., Paans, A. M. J., Meiners, L. C., van der Graaf, F. H. C. E., & Reinders, A. A. T. S (2003a). Brain activation during male ejaculation. *Journal of Neuroscience, 23*, 9185–9193. (p. 357)

Holstege, G., Reinders, A. A. T., Paans, A. M. J., Meiners, L. C., Pruim, J., & Georgiadis, J. R. (2003b). *Brain activation during female sexual orgasm.* Program No. 727.7. Washington, DC: Society for Neuroscience. (p. 357)

Holzman, P. S., & Matthysse, S. (1990). The genetics of schizophrenia: A review. *Psychological Science, 1*, 279–286. (p. 183)

Home Office. (2003). *Prevalence of drug use: Key findings from the 2002/2003 British Crime Survey.* London: Research, Development and Statistics Directorate, Home Office. (p. 94)

Homer, B. D., Solomon, T. M., Moeller, R. W., Mascia, A., DeRaleau, L., & Halkitis, P. N. (2008). Methamphetamine abuse and impairment of social functioning: A review of the underlying neurophysiological causes and behavioral implications. *Psychological Bulletin, 134*, 301–310. (p. 92)

Hooper, J., & Teresi, D. (1986). *The three-pound universe.* New York: Macmillan. (p. 49)

Hooykaas, R. (1972). *Religion and the rise of modern science.* Grand Rapids, MI: Eerdmans. (p. 12)

Horn, J. L. (1982). The aging of human abilities. In J. Wolman (Ed.), *Handbook of developmental psychology.* Englewood Cliffs, NJ: Prentice-Hall. (p. 167)

Horner, V., Whiten, A., Flynn, E., & de Waal, F. B. M. (2006). Faithful replication of foraging techniques along cultural transmission chains by chimpanzees and children. *Proceedings of the National Academy of Sciences, 103*, 13878–13883. (p. 310)

Horowitz, T. S., Cade, B. E., Wolfe, J. M., & Czeisler, C. A. (2003). Searching night and day: A dissociation of effects of circadian phase and time awake on visual selective attention and vigilance. *Psychological Science, 14*, 549–557. (p. 76)

Horwood, L. J., & Fergusson, D. M. (1998). Breastfeeding and later cognitive and academic outcomes. *Pediatrics, 101*(1). (p. 18)

House, J. S., Landis, K. R., & Umberson, D. (1988). Social relationships and health. *Science, 241*, 540–545. (p. 410)

Houts, A. C., Berman, J. S., & Abramson, H. (1994). Effectiveness of psychological and pharmacological treatments for nocturnal enuresis. *Journal of Consulting and Clinical Psychology, 62*, 737–745. (p. 497)

Hovatta, I., Tennant, R. S., Helton, R., Marr, R. A., Singer, O., Redwine, J. M., Ellison, J. A., Schadt, E. E., Verma, I. M., Lockhart, D. J., & Barlow, C. (2005). Glyoxalase 1 and glutathione reductase 1 regulate anxiety in mice. *Nature, 438*, 662–666. (p. 467)

Howard Hughes Medication Institute. (2008). The quivering bundles that let us hear. (www.hhmi.org/senses/c120.html). (p. 194)

Howe, M. L. (1997). Children's memory for traumatic experiences. *Learning and Individual Differences, 9*, 153–174. (p. 284)

Howell, R. T., & Howell, C. J. (2008). The relation of economic status to subjective well-being in developing countries: A meta-analysis. *Psychological Bulletin, 134*, 536–560. (p. 394)

Hoyer, G., & Lund, E. (1993). Suicide among women related to number of children in marriage. *Archives of General Psychiatry, 50*, 134–137. (p. 474)

Hu, F. B., Li, T. Y., Colditz, G. A., Willett, W. C., & Manson, J. E. (2003). Television watching and other sedentary behaviors in relation to risk of obesity and type 2 diabetes mellitus in women. *Journal of the American Medical Association, 289*, 1785–1791. (p. 353)

Hu, X-Z., Lipsky, R. H., Zhu, G., Akhtar, L. A., Taubman, J., Greenberg, B. D., Xu, K., Arnold, P. D., Richter, M. A., Kennedy, J. L., Murphy, D. L., & Goldman, D. (2006). Serotonin transporter promoter gain-of-function genotypes are linked to obsessive-compulsive disorder. *American Journal of Human Genetics, 78*, 815–826. (p. 467)

Hubel, D. H. (1979, September). The brain. *Scientific American*, pp. 45–53. (p. 183)

Hubel, D. H., & Wiesel, T. N. (1979, September). Brian mechanisms of vision. *Scientific American*, pp. 150–162. (p. 188)

Hublin, C., Kaprio, J., Partinen, M., Heikkila, K., & Koskenvuo, M. (1997). Prevalence and genetics of sleepwalking—A population-based twin study. *Neurology, 48*, 177–181. (p. 79)

Hublin, C., Kaprio, J., Partinen, M., & Koskenvuo, M. (1998). Sleeptalking in twins: Epidemiology and psychiatric comorbidity. *Behavior Genetics, 28*, 289–298. (p. 79)

Hucker, S. J., & Bain, J. (1990). Androgenic hormones and sexual assault. In W. Marshall, R. Law, & H. Barbaree (Eds.), *The handbook on sexual assault.* New York: Plenum. (p. 359)

Hudson, J. I., Hiripi, E., Pope, H. G., & Kessler, R. C. (2007). The prevalence and correlates of eating disorders in the National Comorbidity Survey Replication. *Biological Psychiatry, 61*, 348–358. (p. 348)

Huey, E. D., Krueger, F., & Grafman, J. (2006). Representations in the human prefrontal cortex. *Current Directions in Psychological Science, 15*, 167–171. (p. 53)

Hugenberg, K., & Bodenhausen, G. V. (2003). Facing prejudice: Implicit prejudice and the perception of facial threat. *Psychological Science, 14*, 640–643. (p. 543)

Hughes, H. C. (1999). *Sensory exotica: A world beyond human experience.* Cambridge, MA: MIT Press. (p. 181)

Hugick, L. (1989, July). Women play the leading role in keeping modern families close. *Gallup Report, No. 286*, p. 27–34. (p. 128)

Huizink, A. C., & Mulder, E. J. (2006). Maternal smoking, drinking or cannabis use during pregnancy and neurobehavioral and cognitive functioning in human offspring. *Neuroscience and Biobehavioral Reviews, 30*, 24–41. (p. 96)

Hulbert, A. (2005, November 20). The prodigy puzzle. *New York Times Magazine* (www.nytimes.com). (p. 322)

Hull, H. R., Morrow, M. L., Dinger, M. K., Han, J. L., & Fields, D. A. (2007, November 20). Characterization of body weight and composition changes during the sophomore year of college. *BMC Women's Health, 7,* 21 (biomed-central.com). (p. 76)

Hull, J. G., & Bond, C. F., Jr. (1986). Social and behavioral consequences of alcohol consumption and expectancy: A meta-analysis. *Psychological Bulletin, 99,* 347–360. (p. 90)

Hull, J. M. (1990). *Touching the rock: An experience of blindness.* New York: Vintage Books. (pp. 274, 557)

Hulme, C., & Tordoff, V. (1989). Working memory development: The effects of speech rate, word length, and acoustic similarity on serial recall. *Journal of Experimental Child Psychology, 47,* 72–87. (p. 266)

Hummer, R. A., Rogers, R. G., Nam, C. B., & Ellison, C. G. (1999). Religious involvement and U.S. adult mortality. *Demography, 36,* 273–285. (p. 414)

Humphrey, S. E., Nahrgang, J. D., & Morgeson, F. P. (2007). Integrating motivational, social, and contextual work design features: A meta-analytic summary and theoretical extension of the work design literature. *Journal of Applied Psychology, 92,* 1332-1356. (p. 442)

Hunsberger, J. G., Newton, S. S., Bennett, A. H., Duman, C. H., Russell, D. S., Salton, S. R., & Duman, R. S. (2007). Antidepressant actions of the exercise-regulated gene VGF. *Nature Medicine, 13,* 1476–1482. (p. 412)

Hunsley, J., & Di Giulio, G. (2002). Dodo bird, phoenix, or urban legend? The question of psychotherapy equivalence. *Scientific Review of Mental Health Practice, 1,* 11–22. (p. 506)

Hunt, C., Slade, T., & Andrews, G. (2004). Generalized anxiety disorder and major depressive disorder comorbidity in the National Survey of Mental Health and Well-Being. *Depression and Anxiety, 20,* 23–31. (p. 462)

Hunt, E., & Carlson, J. (2007). Considerations relating to the study of group differences in intelligence. *Perspectives on Psychological Science, 2,* 194–213. (p. 333)

Hunt, J. M. (1982). Toward equalizing the developmental opportunities of infants and preschool children. *Journal of Social Issues, 38*(4), 163–191. (p. 326)

Hunt, M. (1974). *Sexual behavior in the 1970s.* Chicago: Playboy Press. (p. 360)

Hunt, M. (1990). *The compassionate beast: What science is discovering about the humane side of humankind.* New York: William Morrow. (p. 9)

Hunt, M. (1993). *The story of psychology.* New York: Doubleday. (p. 235)

Hunter, S., & Sundel, M. (Eds.). (1989). *Midlife myths: Issues, findings, and practice implications.* Newbury Park, CA: Sage. (p. 168)

Hurst, M. (2008, April 22). Who gets any sleep these days? Sleep patterns of Canadians. *Canadian Social Trends.* Statistics Canada Catalogue No. 11–008. (p. 75)

Hussein, S. (2002, July 17 and August 28). Speeches to the Iraqi people as reported by various media. (p. 564)

Huston, A. C., Donnerstein, E., Fairchild, H., Feshbach, N. D., Katz, P. A., & Murray, J. P. (1992). *Big world, small screen: The role of television in American society.* Lincoln: University of Nebraska Press. (p. 251)

Hyde, J. (2005). The gender similarities hypothesis. *American Psychologist, 60,* 581–592. (pp. 126, 127)

Hyde, J. S. (1983, November). Bem's gender schema theory. Paper presented at GLCA Women's Studies Conference, Rochester, IN. (p. 281)

Hyde, J. S., Fennema, E., & Lamon, S. J. (1990). Gender differences in mathematics performance: A meta-analysis. *Psychological Bulletin, 107,* 139–155. (p. 329)

Hyde, J. S., Mezulis, A. H., & Abramson, L. Y. (2008). The ABCs of depression: Integrating affective, biological, and cognitive models to explain the emergence of the gender difference in depression. *Psychological Review, 115,* 291–313. (p. 329, 472)

Hyman, R. (1981). Cold reading: How to convince strangers that you know all about them. In K. Frazier (Ed.), *Paranormal borderlands of science.* Buffalo, NY: Prometheus. (p. 434)

Iacoboni, M. (2008). *Mirroring people: The new science of how we connect with others.* New York: Farrar, Straus & Giroux. (pp. 248, 249)

IAP. (2006, June 21). IAP statement on the teaching of evolution. *The Interacademy Panel on International Issues* (www.interacademies.net/iap). (p. 132)

Ickes, W., Snyder, M., & Garcia, S. (1997). Personality influences on the choice of situations. In R. Hogan, J. Johnson, & S. Briggs (Eds.). *Handbook of personality psychology.* San Diego, CA: Academic Press. (p. 439)

Idson, L. C., & Mischel, W. (2001). The personality of familiar and significant people: The lay perceiver as a social-cognitive theorist. *Journal of Personality and Social Psychology, 80,* 585–596. (p. 526)

Ikonomidou, C., Bittigau, P., Ishimaru, M. J., Wozniak, D. F., Koch, C., Genz, K., Price, M. T., Stefovska, V., Hoerster, F., Tenkova, T., Dikranian, K., & Olney, J. W. (2000). Ethanol-induced apoptotic neurodegeneration and fetal alcohol syndrome. *Science, 287,* 1056–1060. (p. 138)

Ilardi, S. S., Karwoski, L., Lehman, K. A., Stites, B. A., & Steidtmann, D. (2007). *We were never designed for this: The depression epidemic and the promise of therapeutic lifestyle change.* Unpublished manuscript, University of Kansas, in press. (pp. 411, 476, 520)

Independent Sector. (2002). *Faith and philanthropy: The connection between charitable giving behavior and giving to religion.* Washington, DC: Author. (p. 563)

Ingham, A. G., Levinger, G., Graves, J., & Peckham, V. (1974). The Ringelmann effect: Studies of group size and group performance. *Journal of Experimental Social Psychology, 10,* 371–384. (p. 538)

Inglehart, R. (1990). *Culture shift in advanced industrial society.* Princeton, NJ: Princeton University Press. (pp. 170, 171, 371, 442)

Inglehart, R. (2008, June 30). Subjective well-being in 97 countries based on reported happiness and life satisfaction, equally weighted. World Values Survey distributed by University of Michigan News Service: umich.edu/news/happy_08/HappyChart.pdf. (p. 394)

Inglehart, R. (2009). Cultural change and democracy in Latin America. In F. Hagopian (Ed.), *Contemporary Catholicism, religious pluralism and democracy in Latin America.* South Bend, IN: Notre Dame University Press, in press. (pp. 394, 442)

Inzlicht, M., & Ben-Zeev, T. (2000). A threatening intellectual environment: Why females are susceptible to experiencing problem-solving deficits in the presence of males. *Psychological Science, 11,* 365–371. (p. 333)

Inzlicht, M., & Gutsell, J. N. (2007). Running on empty: Neural signals for self-control failure. *Psychological Science, 18,* 933–937. (p. 441)

Ipsos. (2006, February 21). Sexual behaviour and lack of knowledge threaten health of Canadian teens. Ipsos Reid (www.ipsos-na.com). (p. 361)

IPU. (2008). Women in national parliaments: Situation as of 30 April 2008. International Parliamentary Union (www.ipu.org). (p. 127)

IPU. (2009). Women in national parliaments: Situation as of 3 May 2009. International Parliamentary Union (www.ipu.org). (p. 127)

Iraq Family Health Survey Study Group. (2008). Violence-related mortality in Iraq from 2002 to 2006. *New England Journal of Medicine, 358,* 484–493. (p. 525)

Ironson, G., Solomon, G. F., Balbin, E. G., O'Cleirigh, C., George, A., Kumar, M., Larson, D., & Woods, T. E. (2002). The Ironson-Woods spiritual/ religiousness index is associated with long survival, health behaviors, less distress, and low cortisol in people with HIV/AIDS. *Annals of Behavioral Medicine, 24,* 34–48. (p. 415)

Irwin, M. R., Cole, J. C., & Nicassio, P. M. (2006). Comparative meta-analysis of behavioral interventions for insomnia and their efficacy in middle-aged adults and in older adults 55+ years of age. *Health Psychology, 25,* 3–14. (p. 78)

Ishida, A., Mutoh, T., Ueyama, T., Brando, H., Masubuchi, S., Nakahara, D., Tsujimoto, G., & Okamura, H. (2005). Light activates the adrenal gland: Timing of gene expression and glucocorticoid release. *Cell Metabolism, 2,* 297–307. (p. 509)

Iso, H., Simoda, S., & Matsuyama, T. (2007). Environmental change during postnatal development alters behaviour. *Behavioural Brain Research, 179,* 90–98. (p. 57)

Ito, T. A., Miller, N., & Pollock, V. E. (1996). Alcohol and aggression: A meta-analysis on the moderating effects of inhibitory cues, triggering events, and self-focused attention. *Psychological Bulletin, 120,* 60–82. (p. 549)

Iversen, L. L. (2000). *The science of marijuana.* New York: Oxford. (p. 96)

Iyengar, S. S., & Lepper, M. R. (2000). When choice is demotivating: Can one desire too much of a good thing? *Journal of Personality and Social Psychology, 79,* 995–1006. (p. 442)

Izard, C. E. (1977). *Human emotions.* New York: Plenum Press. (p. 389)

Jablensky, A. (1999). Schizophrenia: Epidemiology. *Current Opinion in Psychiatry, 12,* 19–28. (p. 483)

Jackson, J. M., & Williams, K. D. (1988). *Social loafing: A review and theoretical analysis.* Unpublished manuscript, Fordham University. (p. 538)

Jackson, J. S., Brown, K. T., Brown, T. N., & Marks, B. (2001). Contemporary immigration policy orientations among dominant-group members in western Europe. *Journal of Social Issues, 57,* 431–456. (p. 544)

Jackson, S. W. (1992). The listening healer in the history of psychological healing. *American Journal Psychiatry, 149,* 1623–1632. (p. 510)

Jacobi, C., Hayward, C., deZwaan, M., Kraemer, H. C., & Agras, W. S. (2004). Coming to terms with risk factors for eating disorders: Application of risk terminology and suggestions for a general taxonomy. *Psychological Bulletin, 130,* 19–65. (p. 348)

Jacobs, B. L. (1987). How hallucinogenic drugs work. *American Scientist, 75,* 386–392. (p. 95)

Jacobs, B. L. (1994). Serotonin, motor activity, and depression-related disorders. *American Scientist, 82,* 456–463. (pp. 412, 476)

Jacobs, B. L. (2004). Depression: The brain finally gets into the act. *Current Directions in Psychological Science, 13,* 103–106. (p. 515)

Jacobs, B., van Praag, H., & Gage, F. H. (2000). Adult brain neurogenesis and psychiatry: A novel theory of depression. *Molecular Psychiatry, 5,* 262–269. (p. 476)

Jacques, C., & Rossion, B. (2006). The speed of individual face categorization. *Psychological Science, 17,* 485–492. (p. 179)

Jacques-Tiura, A. J., Abbey, A., Parkhill, M. R., & Zawacki, T. (2007). Why do some men misperceive women's sexual intentions more frequently than others do? An application of the confluence model. *Personality and Social Psychology Bulletin, 33,* 1467–1480. (p. 527)

James, K. (1986). Priming and social categorizational factors: Impact on awareness of emergency situations. *Personality and Social Psychology Bulletin, 12,* 462–467. (p. 274)

James, W. (1890). *The principles of psychology* (Vol. 2). New York: Holt. (pp. 87, 196, 276, 287, 376, 531)

James, W. (1902; reprinted 1958). *Varieties of religious experience.* New York: Mentor Books. (p. 391)

Jamison, K. R. (1993). *Touched with fire: Manic-depressive illness and the artistic temperament.* New York: Free Press. (p. 472)

Jamison, K. R. (1995). *An unquiet mind.* New York: Knopf. (pp. 472, 516)

Janis, I. L. (1982). *Groupthink: Psychological studies of policy decisions and fiascoes.* Boston: Houghton Mifflin. (p. 540)

Janis, I. L. (1986). Problems of international crisis management in the nuclear age. *Journal of Social Issues, 42*(2), 201–220. (p. 294)

Javitt, D. C., & Coyle, J. T. (2004, January). Decoding schizophrenia. *Scientific American,* pp. 48–55. (p. 483)

Jeffery, R. W., Drewnowski, A., Epstein, L. H., Stunkard, A. J., Wilson, G. T., Wing, R. R., & Hill, D. R. (2000). Long-term maintenance of weight loss: Current status. *Health Psychology, 19,* No. 1 (Supplement), 5–16. (p. 356)

Jenkins, J. G., & Dallenbach, K. M. (1924). Obliviscence during sleep and waking. *American Journal of Psychology, 35,* 605–612. (p. 279)

Jenkins, J. M., & Astington, J. W. (1996). Cognitive factors and family structure associated with theory of mind development in young children. *Developmental Psychology, 32,* 70–78. (p. 145)

Jensen, J. P., & Bergin, A. E. (1988). Mental health values of professional therapists: A national interdisciplinary survey. *Professional Psychology: Research and Practice, 19,* 290–297. (p. 511)

Jessberger, S., Aimone, J. B., & Gage, F. H. (2008). Neurogenesis. In *Learning and memory: A comprehensive reference.* Oxford: Elsevier. (p. 57)

Job, D. E., Whalley, H. C., McIntosh, A. M., Owens, D. G. C., Johnstone, E. C., & Lawrie, S. M. (2006). Grey matter changes can improve the prediction of schizophrenia in subjects at high risk. *BMC Medicine, 4,* 29. (p. 483)

John, O. P., & Srivastava, S. (1999). The Big Five trait taxonomy: History, measurement, and theoretical perspectives. In L. A. Pervin & O. P. John (Eds.), *Handbook of personality: Theory and research.* New York: Guilford. (p. 436)

Johnson, D. L., Wiebe, J. S., Gold, S. M., Andreasen, N. C., Hichwa, R. D., Watkins, G. L., & Ponto, L. L. B. (1999). Cerebral blood flow and personality: A positron emission tomography study. *American Journal of Psychiatry, 156,* 252–257. (p. 433)

Johnson, E. J., & Goldstein, D. (2003). Do defaults save lives? *Science, 302,* 1338–1339. (p. 301)

Johnson, J. A. (2007, June 26). Not so situational. Commentary on the SPSP listserv (spsp-discuss@stolaf.edu). (p. 529)

Johnson, J. G., Cohen, P., Kotler, L., Kasen, S., & Brook, J. S. (2002). Psychiatric disorders associated with risk for the development of eating disorders during adolescence and early adulthood. *Journal of Consulting and Clinical Psychology, 70,* 1119–1128. (p. 348)

Johnson, J. S., & Newport, E. L. (1991). Critical period affects on universal properties of language: The status of subjacency in the acquisition of a second language. *Cognition, 39,* 215–258. (p. 305)

Johnson, L. C. (2001, July 10). The declining terrorist threat. *New York Times* (www.nytimes.com). (p. 299)

Johnson, M. E., & Hauck, C. (1999). Beliefs and opinions about hypnosis held by the general public: A systematic evaluation. *American Journal of Clinical Hypnosis, 42,* 10–20. (p. 85)

Johnson, M. H. (1992). Imprinting and the development of face recognition: From chick to man. *Current Directions in Psychological Science, 1,* 52–55. (p. 150)

Johnson, M. H., & Morton, J. (1991). *Biology and cognitive development: The case of face recognition.* Oxford: Blackwell Publishing. (p. 139)

Johnson, S. K. (2008). *Medically unexplained illness: Gender and biopsychosocial implications.* Washington, DC: American Psychological Association. (p. 468)

Johnson, W., McGue, M., & Krueger, R. F. (2005). Personality stability in late adulthood: A behavioral genetic analysis. *Journal of Personality, 73,* 523–552. (p. 174)

Johnston, L. D., O'Malley, P. M., Bachman, J. G., & Schulenberg, J. E. (2007). *Monitoring the Future: National results on adolescent drug use: Overview of key findings, 2006.* Bethesda, MD: National Institute on Drug Abuse. (p. 99)

Johnston, L. D., O'Malley, P. M., Bachman, J. G., & Schulenberg, J. E. (2008). *Monitoring the Future: National results on adolescent drug use: Overview of key findings, 2007.* Bethesda, MD: National Institute on Drug Abuse. (pp. 94, 97)

Johnston, L. D., O'Malley, P. M., Bachman, J. G., & Schulenberg, J. E. (2009). *Monitoring the Future: National results on adolescent drug use: Overview of key findings, 2008.* Bethesda, MD: National Institute on Drug Abuse. (p. 98)

Joiner, T. (2006). *Why people die by suicide.* Cambridge, MA: Harvard University Press. (p. 475)

Jolly, A. (2007). The social origin of mind. *Science, 317,* 1326. (p. 309)

Jones, A. C., & Gosling, S. D. (2005). Temperament and personality in dogs (*Canis familiaris*): A review and evaluation of past research. *Applied Animal Behaviour Science, 95,* 1–53. (p. 433)

Jones, J. M. (2003, February 12). Fear of terrorism increases amidst latest warning. *Gallup News Service* (www.gallup.com/releases/pr030212.asp). (p. 464)

Jones, J. M. (2007, July 25). Latest Gallup update shows cigarette smoking near historical lows. *Gallup Poll News Service* (poll.gallup.com). (p. 93)

Jones, J. T., Pelham, B. W., Carvallo, M., & Mirenberg, M. C. (2004). How do I love thee? Let me count the Js: Implicit egotism and interpersonal attraction. *Journal of Personality and Social Psychology, 87,* 665–683. (p. 555)

Jones, L. (2000, December). Skeptics New Year quiz. *Skeptical Briefs,* p. 11. (p. 435)

Jones, M. C. (1924). A laboratory study of fear: The case of Peter. *Journal of Genetic Psychology, 31,* 308–315. (p. 498)

Jones, S. S. (2007). Imitation in infancy: The development of mimicry. *Psychological Science, 18,* 593–599. (p. 249)

Jones, S. S., Collins, K., & Hong, H-W. (1991). An audience effect on smile production in 10–month-old infants. *Psychological Science, 2,* 45–49. (p. 387)

Jones, W. H., Carpenter, B. N., & Quintana, D. (1985). Personality and interpersonal predictors of loneliness in two cultures. *Journal of Personality and Social Psychology, 48,* 1503–1511. (p. 26)

Jonides, J., Lewis, R. L., Nee, D. E., Lustig, C. A., Berman, M. G., & Moore, K. S. (2008). The mind and brain of short-term memory. *Annual Review of Psychology, 59,* 193–224. (p. 266)

Joseph, J. (2001). Separated twins and the genetics of personality differences: A critique. *American Journal of Psychology, 114,* 1–30. (p. 109)

Jung-Beeman, M., Bowden, E. M., Haberman, J., Frymiare, J. L., Arambel-Liu, S., Greenblatt, R., Reber, P. J., & Kounios, J. (2004). Neural activity when people solve verbal problems with insight. *PloS Biology 2*(4), e111. (p. 293)

Kagan, J. (1976). Emergent themes in human development. *American Scientist, 64,* 186–196. (p. 152)

Kagan, J. (1984). *The nature of the child.* New York: Basic Books. (p. 149)

Kagan, J. (1995). On attachment. *Harvard Review of Psychiatry, 3,* 104–106. (p. 151)

Kagan, J. (1998). *Three seductive ideas.* Cambridge, MA: Harvard University Press. (p. 174)

ATL
Kagan, J., Arcus, D., Snidman, N., Feng, W. Y., Hendler, J., & Greene, S. (1994). Reactivity in infants: A cross-national comparison. *Developmental Psychology, 30,* 342–345. (p. 111)

Kagan, J., Lapidus, D. R., & Moore, M. (December, 1978). Infant antecedents of cognitive functioning: A longitudinal study. *Child Development, 49*(4), 1005–1023. (p. 174)

Kagan, J., & Snidman, N. (2004). *The long shadow of temperament.* Cambridge, MA: Belknap Press. (p. 111)

Kagan, J., Snidman, N., & Arcus, D. M. (1992). Initial reactions to unfamiliarity. *Current Directions in Psychological Science, 1,* 171–174. (p. 111)

Kahlor, L., & Morrison, D. (2007). Television viewing and rape myth acceptance among college women. *Sex Roles, 56,* 729–739. (p. 553)

Kahneman, D. (1999). Assessments of objective happiness: A bottom-up approach. In D. Kahneman, E. Diener, & N. Schwartz (Eds.), *Understanding well-being: Scientific perspectives on enjoyment and suffering.* New York: Russell Sage Foundation. (p. 200)

Kahneman, D. (2005, January 13). What were they thinking? Q&A with Daniel Kahneman. *Gallup Management Journal* (gmj.gallup.com). (p. 295)

Kahneman, D. (2005, February 10). Are you happy now? *Gallup Management Journal* interview (www.gmj.gallup.com). (p. 393)

Kahneman, D., Fredrickson, B. L., Schreiber, C. A., & Redelmeier, D. A. (1993). When more pain is preferred to less: Adding a better end. *Psychological Science, 4,* 401–405. (p. 200)

Kahneman, D., Krueger, A. B., Schkade, D. A., Schwarz, N., & Stone, A. A. (2004). A survey method for characterizing daily life experience: The day reconstruction method. *Science, 306,* 1776–1780. (p. 392)

Kahneman, D., & Renshon, J. (2007, January/February). Why hawks win. *Foreign Policy* (www.foreignpolicy.com). (p. 448)

Kahneman, D., & Tversky, A. (1972). Subjective probability: A judgment of representativeness. *Cognitive Psychology, 3,* 430–454. (p. 20)

Kail, R. (1991). Developmental change in speed of processing during childhood and adolescence. *Psychological Bulletin, 109,* 490–501. (p. 165)

Kaiser Family Foundation. (2003, October 28). New study finds children age zero to six spend as much time with TV, computers and video games as playing outside. www.kff.org/entmedia/entmedia102803nr.cfm. (p. 18)

Kaiser. (2001). Inside-out: A report on the experiences of lesbians, gays and bisexuals in America and the public's views on issues and policies related to sexual orientation. The Henry J. Kaiser Foundation (www.kff.org). (p. 368)

Kamarck, T., & Jennings, J. R. (1991). Biobehavioral factors in sudden cardiac death. *Psychological Bulletin, 109,* 42–75. (p. 402)

Kamil, A. C., & Cheng, K. (2001). Way-finding and landmarks: The multiple-bearings hypothesis. *Journal of Experimental Biology, 204,* 103–113. (p. 271)

Kaminski, J., Cali, J., & Fischer, J. (2004). Word learning in a domestic dog: Evidence for "fast mapping." *Science, 304,* 1682–1683. (p. 311)

Kanaya, T., Scullin, M. H., & Ceci, S. J. (2003). The Flynn effect and U.S. policies: The impact of rising IQ scores on American society via mental retardation diagnoses. *American Psychologist, 58,* 778–790. (p. 323)

Kandel, D. B., & Raveis, V. H. (1989). Cessation of illicit drug use in young adulthood. *Archives of General Psychiatry, 46,* 109–116. (p. 100)

Kandel, E. R., & Schwartz, J. H. (1982). Molecular biology of learning: Modulation of transmitter release. *Science, 218,* 433–443. (p. 268)

Kaplan, A. (2004). Exploring the gene-environment nexus in anorexia, bulimia. *Psychiatric Times, 21* (www.psychiatrictimes.com/p040801b.html). (p. 348)

Kaplan, H. I., & Saddock, B. J. (Eds.). (1989). *Comprehensive textbook of psychiatry, V.* Baltimore, MD: Williams and Wilkins. (p. 514)

Kaplan, R. M., & Kronick, R. G. (2006). Marital status and longevity in the United States population. *Journal of Epidemiology and Community Health, 60,* 760–765. (p. 410)

Kaprio, J., Koskenvuo, M., & Rita, H. (1987). Mortality after bereavement: A prospective study of 95,647 widowed persons. *American Journal of Public Health, 77,* 283–287. (p. 401)

Kaptchuk, T. J., Stason, W. B., Davis, R. B., Legedza, A. R. T., Schnyer, R. N., Kerr, C. E., Stone, D. A., Nam, B. H., Kirsch, I., & Goldman, R. H. (2006). Sham device v inert pill: Randomised controlled trial of two placebo treatments. *British Medical Journal, 332,* 391–397. (p. 200)

Karacan, I., Aslan, C., & Hirshkowitz, M. (1983). Erectile mechanisms in man. *Science, 220,* 1080–1082. (p. 74)

Karacan, I., Goodenough, D. R., Shapiro, A., & Starker, S. (1966). Erection cycle during sleep in relation to dream anxiety. *Archives of General Psychiatry, 15,* 183–189. (p. 74)

Karau, S. J., & Williams, K. D. (1993). Social loafing: A meta-analytic review and theoretical integration. *Journal of Personality and Social Psychology, 65,* 681–706. (p. 538)

Kark, J. D., Shemi, G., Friedlander, Y., Martin, O., Manor, O., & Blondheim, S. H. (1996). Does religious observance promote health? Mortality in secular vs. religious kibbutzim in Israel. *American Journal of Public Health, 86,* 341–346. (p. 414)

Karni, A., Meyer, G., Rey-Hipolito, C., Jezzard, P., Adams, M. M., Turner, R., & Ungerleider, L. G. (1998). The acquisition of skilled motor performance: Fast and slow experience-driven changes in primary motor cortex. *Proceedings of the National Academy of Sciences, 95,* 861–868. (p. 119)

Karni, A., & Sagi, D. (1994). Dependence on REM sleep for overnight improvement of perceptual skills. *Science, 265,* 679–682. (p. 82)

Karno, M., Golding, J. M., Sorenson, S. B., & Burnam, A. (1988). The epidemiology of obsessive-compulsive disorder in five US communities. *Archives of General Psychiatry, 45,* 1094–1099. (p. 464)

Karremans, J. C., Stroebe, W., & Claus, J. (2006). Beyond Vicary's fantasies: The impact of subliminal priming and brand choice. *Journal of Experimental Social Psychology, 42,* 792–798. (p. 182)

Kasen, S., Chen, H., Sneed, J., Crawford, T., & Cohen, P. (2006). Social role and birth cohort influences on gender-linked personality traits in women: A 20-year longitudinal analysis. *Journal of Personality and Social Psychology, 91,* 944–958. (p. 128)

Kashima, Y., Siegal, M., Tanaka, K., & Kashima, E. S. (1992). Do people believe behaviours are consistent with attitudes? Towards a cultural psychology of attribution processes. *British Journal of Social Psychology, 31,* 111–124. (p. 124)

Kasser, T. (2000). Two versions of the American dream: Which goals and values make for a high quality of life? In E. Diener (Ed.), *Advances in quality of life theory and research.* Dordrecht, Netherlands: Kluwer. (p. 395)

Kasser, T. (2002). *The high price of materialism.* Cambridge, MA: MIT Press. (p. 395)

Kaufman, A. S., Reynolds, C. R., & McLean, J. E. (1989). Age and WAIS-R intelligence in a national sample of adults in the 20- to 74-year age range: A cross-sectional analysis with educational level controlled. *Intelligence, 13,* 235–253. (p. 167)

Kaufman, J., & Zigler, E. (1987). Do abused children become abusive parents? *American Journal of Orthopsychiatry, 57,* 186–192. (p. 153)

Kaufman, J. C., & Baer, J. (2002). I bask in dreams of suicide: Mental illness, poetry, and women. *Review of General Psychology, 6,* 271–286. (p. 472)

Kaufman, L., & Kaufman, J. H. (2000). Explaining the moon illusion. *Proceedings of the National Academy of Sciences, 97,* 500–505. (p. 210)

Kayser, C. (2007, April/May). Listening with your eyes. *Scientific American Mind,* pp. 24–29. (p. 202)

Kazdin, A. E., & Benjet, C. (2003). Spanking children: Evidence and issues. *Current Directions in Psychological Science, 12,* 99–103. (p. 242)

Keesey, R. E., & Corbett, S. W. (1983). Metabolic defense of the body weight set-point. In A. J. Stunkard & E. Stellar (Eds.), *Eating and its disorders.* New York: Raven Press. (p. 346)

Keith, S. W., & 19 others (2006). Putative contributors to the secular increase in obesity: Exploring the roads less traveled. *International Journal of Obesity, 30,* 1585–1594. (p. 353)

Keller, J. (2007, March 9). As football players get bigger, more of them risk a dangerous sleep disorder. *Chronicle of Higher Education,* pp. A43–A44. (p. 79)

Keller, M. B., McCullough, J. P., Klein, D. N., Arnow, B., Dunner, D. L., Gelenberg, A. J., Markowitz, J. C., Nemeroff, C. B., Russell, J. M., Thase, M. E., Trivedi, M. H., & Zajecka J. (2000). A comparison of nefazodone, the cognitive behavioral-analysis system of psychotherapy, and their combination for the treatment of chronic depression. *New England Journal of Medicine, 342,* 1462–1470. (p. 515)

Kellerman, J., Lewis, J., & Laird, J. D. (1989). Looking and loving: The effects of mutual gaze on feelings of romantic love. *Journal of Research in Personality, 23,* 145–161. (p. 383)

Kellermann, A. L. (1997). Comment: Gunsmoke—changing public attitudes toward smoking and firearms. *American Journal of Public Health, 87,* 910–913. (p. 548)

Kellermann, A. L., Rivara, F. P., Rushforth, N. B., Banton, H. G., Feay, D. T., Francisco, J. T., Locci, A. B., Prodzinski, J., Hackman, B. B., & Somes, G. (1993). Gun ownership as a risk factor for homicide in the home. *New England Journal of Medicine, 329,* 1084–1091. (p. 548)

Kellermann, A. L., Somes, G., Rivara, F. P., Lee, R. K., & Banton, J. G. (1998). Injuries and deaths due to firearms in the home. *Journal of Trauma, 45,* 263–267. (p. 548)

Kelley, J., & De Graaf, N. D. (1997). National context, parental socialization, and religious belief: Results from 15 nations. *American Sociological Review, 62,* 639–659. (p. 110)

Kelling, S. T., & Halpern, B. P. (1983). Taste flashes: Reaction times, intensity, and quality. *Science, 219,* 412–414. (p. 202)

Kellner, C. H., & 15 others. (2005). Relief of expressed suicidal intent by ECT: A consortium for research in ECT study. *American Journal of Psychiatry, 162,* 977–982. (p. 517)

Kellner, C. H., & 16 others (2006). Continuation electroconvulsive therapy vs. pharmacotherapy for relapse prevention in major depression: A multisite study from the Consortium for Research in Electroconvulsive Therapy (CORE). *Archives of General Psychiatry, 63,* 1337–1344. (p. 517)

Kelly, A. E. (2000). Helping construct desirable identities: A self-presentational view of psychotherapy. *Psychological Bulletin, 126,* 475–494. (p. 502)

Kelly, D. J., Quinn, P. C., Slater, A. M., Lee, K., Ge, L., & Pascalis, O. (2007). The other-race effect develops during infancy: Evidence of perceptual narrowing. *Psychological Science, 18,* 1084–1089. (p. 547)

Kelly, I. W. (1997). Modern astrology: A critique. *Psychological Reports, 81,* 1035–1066. (p. 434)

Kelly, I. W. (1998). Why astrology doesn't work. *Psychological Reports, 82,* 527–546. (p. 434)

Kelly, T. A. (1990). The role of values in psychotherapy: A critical review of process and outcome effects. *Clinical Psychology Review, 10,* 171–186. (p. 511)

Kempe, R. S., & Kempe, C. C. (1978). *Child abuse.* Cambridge, MA: Harvard University Press. (p. 153)

Kempermann, G., Kuhn, H. G., & Gage, F. H. (May, 1998). Experience-induced neurogenesis in the senescent dentate gyrus. *Journal of Neuroscience, 18*(9), 3206–3212. (p. 166)

Kendall-Tackett, K. A. (Ed.). (2004). *Health consequences of abuse in the family: A clinical guide for evidence-based practice.* Washington, DC: American Psychological Association. (p. 153)

Kendall-Tackett, K. A., Williams, L. M., & Finkelhor, D. (1993). Impact of sexual abuse on children: A review and synthesis of recent empirical studies. *Psychological Bulletin, 113,* 164–180. (pp. 153, 285)

Kendler, K. S. (1997). Social support: A genetic-epidemiologic analysis. *American Journal of Psychiatry, 154,* 1398–1404. (p. 439)

Kendler, K. S. (1998, January). Major depression and the environment: A psychiatric genetic perspective. *Pharmacopsychiatry, 31*(1), 5–9. (p. 473)

Kendler, K. S., Gardner, C. O., & Prescott, C. A. (2006). Toward a comprehensive developmental model for major depression in men. *American Journal of Psychiatry, 163,* 115–124. (p. 473)

Kendler, K. S., Gatz, M., Gardner, C. O., & Pedersen, N. L. (2006). A Swedish national twin study of lifetime major depression. *American Journal of Psychiatry, 163,* 109–114. (p. 475)

Kendler, K. S., Jacobson, K. C., Myers, J., & Prescott, C. A. (2002a). Sex differences in genetic and environmental risk factors for irrational fears and phobias. *Psychological Medicine, 32,* 209–217. (p. 467)

Kendler, K. S., Karkowski, L. M., & Prescott, C. A. (1999). Fears and phobias: Reliability and heritability. *Psychological Medicine, 29,* 539–553. (p. 467)

Kendler, K. S., Myers, J., & Prescott, C. A. (2002b). The etiology of phobias: An evaluation of the stress-diathesis model. *Archives of General Psychiatry, 59,* 242–248. (p. 467)

Kendler, K. S., Neale, M. C., Kessler, R. C., Heath, A. C., & Eaves, L. J. (1992). Generalized anxiety disorder in women: A population-based twin study. *Archives of General Psychiatry, 49,* 267–272. (p. 467)

Kendler, K. S., Neale, M. C., Thornton, L. M., Aggen, S. H., Gilman, S. E., & Kessler, R. C. (2002). Cannabis use in the last year in a U.S. national sample of twin and sibling pairs. *Psychological Medicine, 32,* 551–554. (p. 98)

Kendler, K. S., Thornton, L. M., & Gardner, C. O. (2001). Genetic risk, number of previous depressive episodes, and stressful life events in predicting onset of major depression. *American Journal of Psychiatry, 158,* 582–586. (p. 473)

Kennedy, S., & Over, R. (1990). Psychophysiological assessment of male sexual arousal following spinal cord injury. *Archives of Sexual Behavior, 19,* 15–27. (p. 42)

Kenrick, D. T., & Funder, D. C. (1988). Profiting from controversy: Lessons from the person-situation debate. *American Psychologist, 43,* 23–34. (p. 438)

Kenrick, D. T., & Gutierres, S. E. (1980). Contrast effects and judgments of physical attractiveness: When beauty becomes a social problem. *Journal of Personality and Social Psychology, 38,* 131–140. (p. 360)

Kenrick, D. T., Gutierres, S. E., & Goldberg, L. L. (1989). Influence of popular erotica on judgments of strangers and mates. *Journal of Experimental Social Psychology, 25,* 159–167. (p. 360)

Kenrick, D. T., Nieuweboer, S., & Bunnk, A. P. (in press). Universal mechanisms and cultural diversity: Replacing the blank slate with a coloring book. In M. Schaller, S. Heine, A. Norenzayan, T. Yamagishi, & T. Kameda (Eds.), *Evolution, culture, and the human mind.* Mahwah, NJ: Erlbaum. (pp. 116, 117)

Kensinger, E. A. (2007). Negative emotion enhances memory accuracy: Behavioral and neuroimaging evidence. *Current Directions in Psychological Science, 16,* 213–218. (p. 268)

Keough, K. A., Zimbardo, P. G., & Boyd, J. N. (1999). Who's smoking, drinking, and using drugs? Time perspective as a predictor of substance use. *Basic and Applied Social Psychology, 2,* 149–164. (p. 421)

Kernis, M. H. (2003). Toward a conceptualization of optimal self-esteem. *Psychological Inquiry, 14,* 1–26. (p. 449)

Kerr, N. L., & Bruun, S. E. (1983). Dispensability of member effort and group motivation losses: Free-rider effects. *Journal of Personality and Social Psychology, 44,* 78–94. (p. 539)

Kessler, M., & Albee, G. (1975). Primary prevention. *Annual Review of Psychology, 26,* 557–591. (p. 521)

Kessler, R. C. (2000). Posttraumatic stress disorder: The burden to the individual and to society. *Journal of Clinical Psychiatry, 61*(suppl. 5), 4–12. (p. 464)

Kessler, R. C. (2001). Epidemiology of women and depression. *Journal of Affective Disorders, 74,* 5–1. (p. 477)

Kessler, R. C., Akiskal, H. S., Ames, M., Birnbaum, H., Greenberg, P., Hirschfeld, R. M. A., Jin, R., Merikangas, K. R., Simon, G. E., & Wang, P. S. (2006). Prevalence and effects of mood disorders on work performance in a nationally representative sample of U.S. workers. *American Journal of Psychiatry, 163,* 1561–1568. (p. 472)

Kessler, R. C., Berglund, P., Demler, O., Jin, R., Merikangos, K. R., & Walters, E. E. (2005). Lifetime prevalence and age-of-onset distributions of DSM-IV disorders in the National Comorbidity Survey Replication. *Archives of General Psychiatry, 62,* 593–602. (p. 458, 488)

Kessler, R. C., Foster, C., Joseph, J., Ostrow, D., Wortman, C., Phair, J., & Chmiel, J. (1991). Stressful life events and symptom onset in HIV infection. *American Journal of Psychiatry, 148,* 733–738. (p. 405)

Kessler, R. C., Soukup, J., Davis, R. B., Foster, D. F., Wilkey, S. A., Van Rompay, M. I., & Eisenberg, D. M. (2001). The use of complementary and alternative therapies to treat anxiety and depression in the United States. *American Journal of Psychiatry, 158,* 289–294. (p. 507)

Keynes, M. (1980, December 20/27). Handel's illnesses. *Lancet,* pp. 1354–1355. (p. 472)

Keys, A., Brozek, J., Henschel, A., Mickelsen, O., & Taylor, H. L. (1950). *The biology of human starvation.* Minneapolis: University of Minnesota Press. (p. 343)

Kiecolt-Glaser, J. K., & Glaser, R. (1995). Psychoneuroimmunology and health consequences: Data and shared mechanisms. *Psychosomatic Medicine, 57,* 269–274. (p. 405)

Kiecolt-Glaser, J. K., & Newton, T. L. (2001). Marriage and health: His and hers. *Psychological Bulletin, 127,* 472–503. (p. 410)

Kiecolt-Glaser, J. K., Page, G. G., Marucha, P. T., MacCallum, R. C., & Glaser, R. (1998). Psychological influences on surgical recovery: Perspectives from psychoneuroimmunology. *American Psychologist, 53,* 1209–1218. (p. 404)

Kihlstrom, J. F. (1990). The psychological unconscious. In L. A. Pervin (Ed.), *Handbook of personality: Theory and research.* New York: Guilford Press. (pp. 281, 427)

Kihlstrom, J. F. (1994). The social construction of memory. Paper presented at the American Psychological Society convention. (p. 282)

Kihlstrom, J. F. (1997, November 11). Freud as giant pioneer on whose shoulders we should stand. Social Psychology listserv posting (spsp@stolaf.edu). (p. 428)

Kihlstrom, J. F. (2005). Dissociative disorders. *Annual Review of Clinical Psychology, 1,* 227–253. (p. 470)

Kihlstrom, J. F. (2006). Repression: A unified theory of a will-o'-the-wisp. *Behavioral and Brain Sciences, 29,* 523. (p. 426)

Kihlstrom, J. F., & McConkey, K. M. (1990). William James and hypnosis: A centennial reflection. *Psychological Science, 1,* 174–177. (p. 87)

Killeen, P. R., & Nash, M. R. (2003). The four causes of hypnosis. *Internal Journal of Clinical and Experimental Hypnosis, 51,* 195–231. (p. 87)

Kim, B. S. K., Ng, G. F., & Ahn, A. J. (2005). Effects of client expectation for counseling success, client-counselor worldview match, and client adherence to Asian and European American cultural values on counseling process with Asian Americans. *Journal of Counseling Psychology, 52,* 67–76. (p. 511)

Kim, H., & Markus, H. R. (1999). Deviance or uniqueness, harmony or conformity? A cultural analysis. *Journal of Personality and Social Psychology, 77,* 785–800. (p. 124)

Kimble, G. A. (1956). *Principles of general psychology.* New York: Ronald. (p. 232)

Kimble, G. A. (1981). *Biological and cognitive constraints on learning.* Washington, DC: American Psychological Association. (p. 232)

Kimmel, A. J. (1998). In defense of deception. *American Psychologist, 53,* 803–805. (p. 28)

King, L. A., Hicks, J. A., Krull, J. L., & Del Gaiso, A. K. (2006). Positive affect and the experience of meaning in life. *Journal of Personality and Social Psychology, 90,* 179–196. (p. 392)

King, M., & Bartlett, A. (2006). What same sex civil partnerships may mean for health. *Journal of Epidemiology and Community Health, 60,* 188–191. (p. 363)

King, R. N., & Koehler, D. J. (2000). Illusory correlations in graphological interference. *Journal of Experimental Psychology: Applied, 6,* 336–348. (p. 434)

Kinnier, R. T., & Metha, A. T. (1989). Regrets and priorities at three stages of life. *Counseling and Values, 33,* 182–193. (p. 170)

Kirby, D. (2002). Effective approaches to reducing adolescent unprotected sex, pregnancy, and childbearing. *Journal of Sex Research, 39,* 51–57. (p. 362)

Kirkpatrick, B., Fenton, W. S., Carpenter, W. T., Jr., & Marder, S. R. (2006). The NIMH-MATRICS consensus statement on negative symptoms. *Schizophrenia Bulletin, 32,* 214–219. (p. 482)

Kirkpatrick, L. (1999). Attachment and religious representations and behavior. In J. Cassidy & P. R. Shaver (Eds.), *Handbook of attachment.* New York: Guilford. (p. 150)

Kirmayer, L. J., & Sartorius, N. (2007). Cultural models and somatic syndromes. *Psychosomatic Medicine, 69,* 832–840. (p. 468)

Kirsch, I. (1996). Hypnotic enhancement of cognitive-behavioral weight loss treatments: Another meta-reanalysis. *Journal of Consulting and Clinical Psychology, 64,* 517–519. (p. 85)

Kirsch, I., & Braffman, W. (2001). Imaginative suggestibility and hypnotizability. *Current Directions in Psychological Science, 10,* 57–61. (p. 84)

Kirsch, I., Deacon, B. J., Huedo-Medina, T. B., Scoboria, A., Moore, T. J., & Johnson, B. T. (2008) Initial severity and antidepressant benefits: A meta-analysis of data submitted to the Food and Drug Administration. *Public Library of Science Medicine, 5,* e45. (p. 516)

Kirsch, I., & Lynn, S. J. (1995). The altered state of hypnosis. *American Psychologist, 50,* 846–858. (p. 85)

Kirsch, I., Moore, T. J., Scoboria, A., & Nicholls, S. S. (2002, July 15). New study finds little difference between effects of antidepressants and placebo. *Prevention and Treatment* (journals.apa.org/prevention). (p. 516)

Kirsch, I., & Sapirstein, G. (1998). Listening to Prozac but hearing placebo: A meta-analysis of antidepressant medication. *Prevention and Treatment, 1,* posted June 26 at journals.apa.org/prevention/volume1. (pp. 22, 516)

Kisley, M. A., Wood, S., & Burrows, C. L. (2007). Looking at the sunny side of life: Age-related change in an event-related potential measure of the negativity bias. *Psychological Science, 18,* 838–843. (p. 171)

Kitts, R. L. (2005). Gay adolescents and suicide: Understanding the association. *Adolescence, 40,* 621–628. (p. 363)

Kivimaki, M., Leino-Arjas, P., Luukkonen, R., Rihimaki, H., & Kirjonen, J. (2002). Work stress and risk of cardiovascular mortality: Prospective cohort study of industrial employees. *British Medical Journal, 325,* 857. (p. 408)

Klayman, J., & Ha, Y-W. (1987). Confirmation, disconfirmation, and information in hypothesis testing. *Psychological Review, 94,* 211–228. (p. 293)

Klein, D. N., & 16 others. (2003). Therapeutic alliance in depression treatment: Controlling for prior change and patient characteristics. *Journal of Consulting and Clinical Psychology, 71,* 997–1006. (p. 510)

Klein, E., Kreinin, I., Chistyakov, A., Koren, D., Mecz, L., Marmur, S., Ben-Shachar, D., & Feinsod, M. (1999). Therapeutic efficacy of right prefrontal slow repetitive transcranial magnetic stimulation in major depression. *Archives of General Psychiatry, 56,* 315–320. (p. 518)

Kleinfeld, J. (1998). *The myth that schools short-change girls: Social science in the service of deception.* Washington, DC: Women's Freedom Network. Available from ERIC, Document ED423210, and via www.uaf.edu/northern/schools/myth.html. (p. 330)

Kleinke, C. L. (1986). Gaze and eye contact: A research review. *Psychological Bulletin, 1000,* 78–100. (p. 383)

Kleinmuntz, B., & Szucko, J. J. (1984). A field study of the fallibility of polygraph lie detection. *Nature, 308,* 449–450. (p. 380)

Kleitman, N. (1960, November). Patterns of dreaming. *Scientific American,* pp. 82–88. (p. 72)

Klemm, W. R. (1990). Historical and introductory perspectives on brainstem-mediated behaviors. In W. R. Klemm & R. P. Vertes (Eds.), *Brainstem mechanisms of behavior.* New York: Wiley. (p. 45)

Kline, D., & Schieber, F. (1985). Vision and aging. In J. E. Birren & K. W. Schaie (Eds.), *Handbook of the psychology of aging.* New York: Van Nostrand Reinhold. (p. 164)

Kline, G. H., Stanley, S. M., Markman, J. H., Olmos-Gallo, P. A., St. Peters, M., Whitton, S. W., & Prado, L. M. (2004). Timing is everything: Pre-engagement cohabitation and increased risk for poor marital outcomes. *Journal of Family Psychology, 18,* 311–318. (p. 169)

Klineberg, O. (1938). Emotional expression in Chinese literature. *Journal of Abnormal and Social Psychology, 33,* 517–520. (p. 386)

Klineberg, O. (1984). Public opinion and nuclear war. *American Psychologist, 39,* 1245–1253. (p. 566)

Klinke, R., Kral, A., Heid, S., Tillein, J., & Hartmann, R. (1999). Recruitment of the auditory cortex in congenitally deaf cats by long-term cochlear electrostimulation. *Science, 285,* 1729–1733. (p. 214)

Kluft, R. P. (1991). Multiple personality disorder. In A. Tasman & S. M. Goldfinger (Eds.), *Review of Psychiatry* (Vol. 10). Washington, DC: American Psychiatric Press. (p. 469)

Klump, K. L., & Culbert, K. M. (2007). Molecular genetic studies of eating disorders: Current status and future directions. *Current Directions in Psychological Science, 16,* 37–41. (p. 348)

Knapp, S., & VandeCreek, L. (2000, August). Recovered memories of childhood abuse: Is there an underlying professional consensus? *Professional Psychology: Research and Practice, 31,* 365–371. (p. 286)

Knickmeyer, E. (2001, August 7). In Africa, big is definitely better. *Seattle Times,* p. A7. (p. 348)

Knight, W. (2004, August 2). Animated face helps deaf with phone chat. NewScientist.com. (p. 202)

Knoblich, G., & Oellinger, M. (2006, October/November). The Eureka moment. *Scientific American Mind,* pp. 38–43. (p. 293)

Knutson, K. L., Spiegel, K., Penev, P., & Van Cauter, E. (2007). The metabolic consequences of sleep deprivation. *Sleep Medicine Reviews, 11,* 163–178. (p. 76)

Ko, C-K., Yen, J-Y., Chen, C-C., Chen, S-H., & Yen, C-F. (2005). Proposed diagnostic criteria of Internet addiction for adolescents. *Journal of Nervous and Mental Disease, 193,* 728–733. (p. 89)

Koenig, H. G., & Larson, D. B. (1998). Use of hospital services, religious attendance, and religious affiliation. *Southern Medical Journal, 91,* 925–932. (p. 415)

Koenig, L. B., McGue, M., Krueger, R. F., & Bouchard, T. J., Jr. (2005). Genetic and environmental influences on religiousness: Findings for retrospective and current religiousness ratings. *Journal of Personality, 73,* 471–488. (p. 110)

Koenigs, M., Young, L., Adolphs, R., Tranel, D., Cushman, F., Hauser, M., & Damasio, A. (2007). Damage to the prefrontal cortex increases utilitarian moral judgements. *Nature, 446,* 908–911. (p. 54)

Kohlberg, L. (1981). *The philosophy of moral development: Essays on moral development* (Vol. I). San Francisco: Harper & Row. (p. 158)

Kohlberg, L. (1984). *The psychology of moral development: Essays on moral development* (Vol. II). San Francisco: Harper & Row. (p. 158)

Kohler, I. (1962, May). Experiments with goggles. *Scientific American,* pp. 62–72. (p. 215)

Köhler, W. (1925; reprinted 1957). *The mentality of apes.* London: Pelican. (p. 310)

Kohn, P. M., & Macdonald, J. E. (1992). The survey of recent life experiences: A decontaminated hassles scale for adults. *Journal of Behavioral Medicine, 15,* 221–236. (p. 401)

Kolassa, I-T., & Elbert, T. (2007). Structural and functional neuroplasticity in relation to traumatic stress. *Current Directions in Psychological Science, 16,* 321–325. (p. 467)

Kolata, G. (1986). Youth suicide: New research focuses on a growing social problem. *Science, 233,* 839–841. (p. 474)

Kolata, G. (1987). Metabolic catch-22 of exercise regimens. *Science, 236,* 146–147. (p. 356)

Kolb, B. (1989). Brain development, plasticity, and behavior. *American Psychologist, 44,* 1203–1212. (p. 56)

Kolb, B., & Whishaw, I. Q. (1998). Brain plasticity and behavior. *Annual Review of Psychology, 49,* 43–64. (p. 118)

Kolb, B., & Whishaw, I. Q. (2006). *An introduction to brain and behavior* (2nd ed.). New York: Worth Publishers. (p. 317)

Kolker, K. (2002, December 8). Video violence disturbs some: Others scoff at influence. *Grand Rapids Press,* pp. A1, A12. (p. 552)

Kolodziej, M. E., & Johnson, B. T. (1996). Interpersonal contact and acceptance of persons with psychiatric disorders: A research synthesis. *Journal of Consulting and Clinical Psychology, 64,* 1387–1396. (p. 460)

Koltko-Rivera, M. E. (2006). Rediscovering the later version of Maslow's hierarchy of needs: Self-transcendence and opportunities for theory, research, and unification. *Review of General Psychology, 10,* 302–317. (p. 342)

Kopta, S. M., Lueger, R. J., Saunders, S. M., & Howard, K. I. (1999). Individual psychotherapy outcome and process research: Challenges leading to greater turmoil or a positive transition? *Annual Review of Psychology, 30,* 441–469. (p. 506)

Kosslyn, S. M. (2005). Reflective thinking and mental imagery: A perspective on the development of posttraumatic stress disorder. *Development and Psychopathology, 17,* 851–863. (p. 464)

Kosslyn, S. M., & Koenig, O. (1992). *Wet mind: The new cognitive neuroscience.* New York: Free Press. (p. 40)

Kosslyn, S. M., Thompson, W. L., Costantini-Ferrando, M. F., Alpert, N. M., & Spiegel, D. (2000). Hypnotic visual illusion alters color processing in the brain. *American Journal of Psychiatry, 157,* 1279–1284. (p. 86)

Kotchick, B. A., Shaffer, A., & Forehand, R. (2001). Adolescent sexual risk behavior: A multi-system perspective. *Clinical Psychology Review, 21,* 493–519. (p. 361)

Koten, J. W., Jr., Wood, G., Hagoort, P., Goebel, R., Propping, P., Willmes, K., & Boomsma, D. I. (2009). Genetic contribution to variation in cognitive function: An fMRI study in twins. *Science, 323,* 1737–1740. (p. 325)

Kotkin, M., Daviet, C., & Gurin, J. (1996). The Consumer Reports mental health survey. *American Psychologist, 51,* 1080–1082. (p. 505)

Kraft, R. N. (2002). *Memory perceived: Recalling the Holocaust.* Westport, CT: Praeger. (p. 286)

Kramer, A. F., & Erickson, K. I. (2007). Capitalizing on cortical plasticity: Influence of physical activity on cognition and brain function. *Trends in Cognitive Sciences, 11,* 342–348. (p. 412)

Kranz, F., & Ishai, A. (2006). Face perception is modulated by sexual preference. *Current Biology, 16,* 63–68. (p. 366)

Kraus, N., Malmfors, T., & Slovic, P. (1992). Intuitive toxicology: Expert and lay judgments of chemical risks. *Risk Analysis, 12,* 215–232. (p. 301)

Kraut, R. E., & Johnston, R. E. (1979). Social and emotional messages of smiling: An ethological approach. *Journal of Personality and Social Psychology, 37,* 1539–1553. (p. 387)

KRC Research & Consulting. (2001, August 7). Memory isn't quite what it used to be (survey for General Nutrition Centers). *USA Today,* p. D1. (p. 166)

Krebs, D. L., & Denton, K. (2005). Toward a more pragmatic approach to morality: A critical evaluation of Kohlberg's model. *Psychological Review, 112,* 629–649. (p. 158)

Kring, A. M., & Gordon, A. H. (1998). Sex differences in emotion: Expression, experience, and physiology. *Journal of Personality and Social Psychology, 74,* 686–703. (p. 386)

Kristof, N. D. (2004, July 21). Saying no to killers. *New York Times* (www.nytimes.com). (p. 561)

Kroll, R., Danis, S., Moreau, M., Waldbaum, A., Shifren, J., & Wekselman, K. (2004, October). Testosterone transdermal patch (TPP) significantly improved sexual function in naturally menopausal women in a large Phase III study. Paper presented to the American Society of Reproductive Medicine annual meeting, Philadelphia. (p. 358)

Krosnick, J. A., Betz, A. L., Jussim, L. J., & Lynn, A. R. (1992). Subliminal conditioning of attitudes. *Personality and Social Psychology Bulletin, 18,* 152–162. (p. 182)

Krueger, A. (2007, November/December). What makes a terrorist. *The American* (www.american.com). (p. 550)

Kruger, J., & Dunning, D. (1999). Unskilled and unaware of it: How difficulties in recognizing one's own incompetence lead to inflated self-assessments. *Journal of Personality and Social Psychology, 77,* 1121–1134. (p. 444)

Kruger, J., Epley, N., Parker, J., & Ng, Z-W. (2005). Egocentrism over e-mail: Can we communicate as well as we think? *Journal of Personality and Social Psychology, 89,* 925–936. (pp. 145, 385)

Krupa, D. J., Thompson, J. K., & Thompson, R. F. (1993). Localization of a memory trace in the mammalian brain. *Science, 260,* 989–991. (p. 272)

Krützen, M., Mann, J., Heithaus, M. R., Connor, R. C., Bejder, L., & Sherwin, W. B. (2005). Cultural transmission of tool use in bottlenose dolphins. *Proceedings of the National Academy of Sciences, 102,* 8939–8943. (p. 311)

Kubey, R., & Csikszentmihalyi, M. (2002, February). Television addiction is no mere metaphor. *Scientific American,* pp. 74–80. (p. 251)

Kübler, A., Winter, S., Ludolph, A. C., Hautzinger, M., & Birbaumer, N. (2005). Severity of depressive symptoms and quality of life in patients with amyotrophic lateral sclerosis. *Neurorehabilitation and Neural Repair, 19*(3), 182–193. (p. 393)

Kubzansky, L. D., Sparrow, D., Vokanas, P., & Kawachi, I. (2001). Is the glass half empty or half full? A prospective study of optimism and coronary heart disease in the normative aging study. *Psychosomatic Medicine, 63,* 910–916. (p. 403)

Kuhl, P. K., & Meltzoff, A. N. (1982). The bimodal perception of speech in infancy. *Science, 218,* 1138–1141. (p. 303)

Kuhn, D. (2006). Do cognitive changes accompany developments in the adolescent brain? *Perspectives on Psychological Science, 1,* 59–67. (p. 156)

Kujala, U. M., Kaprio, J., Sarna, S., & Koskenvuo, M. (1998). Relationship of leisure-time physical activity and mortality: The Finnish twin cohort. *Journal of the American Medical Association, 279,* 440–444. (p. 412)

Kulkin, H. S., Chauvin, E. A., & Percle, G. A. (2000). Suicide among gay and lesbian adolescents and young adults: A review of the literature. *Journal of Homosexuality, 40,* 1–29. (p. 364)

Kunkel, D. (2001, February 4). *Sex on TV.* Menlo Park, CA: Henry J. Kaiser Family Foundation (www.kff.org). (p. 361)

Kunkel, D., Cope-Farrar, K., Biely, E., Farinola, W. J. M., & Donnerstein, E. (2001). *Sex on TV (2): A biennial report to the Kaiser Family Foundation.* Menlo Park, CA: Kaiser Family Foundation. (p. 553)

Kuntsche, E., Knibbe, R., Gmel, G., & Engels, R. (2005). Why do young people drink? A review of drinking motives. *Clinical Psychology Review, 25,* 841–861. (p. 99)

Kupper, N., & Denollet, J. (2007). Type D personality as a prognostic factor in heart disease: Assessment and mediating mechanisms. *Journal of Personality Assessment, 89,* 265–276. (p. 402)

Kurdek, L. A. (2005). What do we know about gay and lesbian couples? *Current Directions in Psychological Science, 14,* 251–254. (p. 363)

Kurtz, P. (1983, Spring). Stars, planets, and people. *The Skeptical Inquirer,* pp. 65–68. (p. 435)

Kushner, M. G., Kim, S. W., Conahue, C., Thuras, P., Adson, D., Kotlyar, M., McCabe, J., Peterson, J., & Foa, E. B. (2007). D-cycloserine augmented exposure therapy for obsessive-compulsive disorder. *Biological Psychiatry, 62,* 835–838. (p. 514)

Kutas, M. (1990). Event-related brain potential (ERP) studies of cognition during sleep: Is it more than a dream? In R. R. Bootzin, J. F. Kihlstrom, & D. Schacter (Eds.), *Sleep and cognition.* Washington, DC: American Psychological Association. (p. 70)

L'Engle, M. (1972). *A wind in the door.* Bantam Doubleday Dell Books for Young Readers. (p. 10)

Labouvie-Vief, G., & Schell, D. A. (1982). Learning and memory in later life. In B. B. Wolman (Ed.), *Handbook of developmental psychology.* Englewood Cliffs, NJ: Prentice-Hall. (p. 167)

Lacayo, R. (1995, June 12). Violent reaction. *Time Magazine,* pp. 25–39. (p. 16)

Lacey, H. P., Smith, D. M., & Ubel, P. A. (2006). Hope I die before I get old: Mispredicting happiness across the lifespan. *Journal of Happiness Studies, 7,* 167–182. (p. 170)

Lachman, M. E. (2004). Development in midlife. *Annual Review of Psychology, 55*, 305–331. (p. 168)

Ladd, E. C. (1998, August/September). The tobacco bill and American public opinion. *The Public Perspective*, pp. 5–19. (p. 100)

Ladd, G. T. (1887). *Elements of physiological psychology*. New York: Scribner's. (p. 65)

LaFleur, D. L., Pittenger, C., Kelmendi, B., Gardner, T., Wasylink, S., Malison, R. T., Sanacora, G., Krystal, J. H., & Coric, V. (2006). N-acetylcysteine augmentation in serotonin reuptake inhibitor refractory obsessive-compulsive disorder. *Psychopharmacology, 184*, 254–256. (p. 467)

Laird, J. D. (1974). Self-attribution of emotion: The effects of expressive behavior on the quality of emotional experience. *Journal of Personality and Social Psychology, 29*, 475–486. (p. 388)

Laird, J. D. (1984). The real role of facial response in the experience of emotion: A reply to Tourangeau and Ellsworth, and others. *Journal of Personality and Social Psychology, 47*, 909–917. (p. 388)

Laird, J. D., Cuniff, M., Sheehan, K., Shulman, D., & Strum, G. (1989). Emotion specific effects of facial expressions on memory for life events. *Journal of Social Behavior and Personality, 4*, 87–98. (p. 388)

Lakin, J. L., & Chartrand, T. L. (2003). Using nonconscious behavioral mimicry to create affiliation and rapport. *Psychological Science, 14*, 334–339. (p. 532)

Lalumière, M. L., Blanchard, R., & Zucker, K. J. (2000). Sexual orientation and handedness in men and women: A meta-analysis. *Psychological Bulletin, 126*, 575–592. (p. 367)

Lam, R. W., Levitt, A. J., Levitan, R. D., Enns, M. W., Morehouse, R., Michalak, E. E., & Tam, E. M. (2006). The Can-SAD study: A randomized controlled trial of the effectiveness of light therapy and fluoxetine in patients with winter seasonal affective disorder. *American Journal of Psychiatry, 163*, 805–812. (p. 509)

Lambert, K. (2008, August/September). Depressingly easy. *Scientific American Mind*, pp. 31–37. (p. 411)

Lambert, K. G. (2005). Rising rates of depression in today's society: Consideration of the roles of effort-based rewards and enhanced resilience in day-to-day functioning. *Neuroscience and Biobehavioral Reviews, 30*, 497–510. (p. 411)

Lambert, W. E. (1992). Challenging established views on social issues: The power and limitations of research. *American Psychologist, 47*, 533–542. (p. 307)

Lambert, W. E., Genesee, F., Holobow, N., & Chartrand, L. (1993). Bilingual education for majority English-speaking children. *European Journal of Psychology of Education, 8*, 3–22. (p. 307)

Lambird, K. H., & Mann, T. (2006). When do ego threats lead to self-regulation failure? Negative consequences of defensive high self-esteem. *Personality and Social Psychology Bulletin, 32*, 1177–1187. (p. 449)

Lampinen, J. M. (2002). What exactly is déjà vu? *Scientific American* (scieam.com/askexpert/biology/biology63). (p. 275)

Landau, M. J., Solomon, S., Greenberg, J., Cohen, F., Pyszczynski, T., Arndt, J.,

Miller, C. H., Ogilvie, D. M., & Cook, A. (2004). Deliver us from evil: The effects of mortality salience and reminders of 9/11 on support for President George W. Bush. *Personality and Social Psychology Bulletin, 30*, 1136–1150. (p. 546)

Landauer, T. (2001, September). Quoted by R. Herbert, You must remember this. *APS Observer*, p. 11. (p. 287)

Landauer, T. K., & Whiting, J. W. M. (1979). Correlates and consequences of stress in infancy. In R. Munroe, B. Munroe, & B. Whiting (Eds.), *Handbook of cross-cultural human development*. New York: Garland. (p. 399)

Landry, M. J. (2002). MDMA: A review of epidemiologic data. *Journal of Psychoactive Drugs, 34*, 163–169. (p. 95)

Langer, E. J. (1983). *The psychology of control*. Beverly Hills, CA: Sage. (p. 442)

Langlois, J. H., Kalakanis, L., Rubenstein, A. J., Larson, A., Hallam, M., & Smoot, M. (2000). Maxims or myths of beauty? A meta-analytic and theoretical review. *Psychological Bulletin, 126*, 390–423. (pp. 557, 558)

Langlois, J. H., Roggman, L. A., Casey, R. J., Ritter, J. M., Rieser-Danner, L. A., & Jenkins, V. Y. (1987). Infant preferences for attractive faces: Rudiments of a stereotype? *Developmental Psychology, 23*, 363–369. (p. 557)

Lángström, N., Rahman, Q., Carlström, E., & Lichtenstein, P. (2008). Genetic and environmental effects on same-sex sexual behavior: A population study of twins in Sweden. *Archives of Sexual Behavior, 37*. (p. 366)

Larkin, K., Resko, J. A., Stormshak, F., Stellflug, J. N., & Roselli, C. E. (2002). Neuroanatomical correlates of sex and sexual partner preference in sheep. Paper presented at Society for Neuroscience convention. (p. 366)

Larsen, R. J., & Diener, E. (1987). Affect intensity as an individual difference characteristic: A review. *Journal of Research in Personality, 21*, 1–39. (pp. 111, 383)

Larsen, R. J., Kasimatis, M., & Frey, K. (1992). Facilitating the furrowed brow: An unobtrusive test of the facial feedback hypothesis applied to unpleasant affect. *Cognition and Emotion, 6*, 321–338. (p. 389)

Larsson, H., Tuvblad, C., Rijsdijk, F. V., Andershed, H., Grann, M., & Lichetenstein, P. (2007). A common genetic factor explains the association between psychopathic personality and antisocial behavior. *Psychological Medicine, 37*, 15–26. (p. 487)

Larzelere, R. E. (2000). Child outcomes of nonabusive and customary physical punishment by parents: An updated literature review. *Clinical Child and Family Psychology Review, 3*, 199–221. (p. 242)

Larzelere, R. E., & Kuhn, B. R. (2005). Comparing child outcomes of physical punishment and alternative disciplinary tactics: A meta-analysis. *Clinical Child and Family Psychology Review, 8*, 1–37. (p. 242)

Larzelere, R. E., Kuhn, B. R., & Johnson, B. (2004). The intervention selection bias: An underrecognized confound in intervention research. *Psychological Bulletin, 130*, 289–303. (p. 242)

Lashley, K. S. (1950). In search of the engram. In *Symposium of the Society for Experimental Biology*

(Vol. 4). New York: Cambridge University Press. (p. 267)

Lassiter, G. D., & Irvine, A. A. (1986). Videotaped confessions: The impact of camera point of view on judgments of coercion. *Journal of Personality and Social Psychology, 16*, 268–276. (p. 527)

Latané, B. (1981). The psychology of social impact. *American Psychologist, 36*, 343–356. (p. 538)

Latané, B., & Dabbs, J. M., Jr. (1975). Sex, group size and helping in three cities. *Sociometry, 38*, 180–194. (p. 562)

Laudenslager, M. L., & Reite, M. L. (1984). Losses and separations: Immunological consequences and health implications. *Review of Personality and Social Psychology, 5*, 285–312. (p. 408)

Laumann, E. O., Gagnon, J. H., Michael, R. T., & Michaels, S. (1994). *The social organization of sexuality: Sexual practices in the United States*. Chicago: University of Chicago Press. (pp. 115, 363)

Laws, K. R., & Kokkalis, J. (2007). Ecstasy (MDMA) and memory function: A meta-analytic update. *Human Psychopharmacology: Clinical and Experimental, 22*, 381–388. (p. 95)

Lazaruk, W. (2007). Linguistic, academic, and cognitive benefits of French immersion. *Canadian Modern Language Review, 63*, 605–628. (p. 307)

Lazarus, R. S. (1990). Theory-based stress measurement. *Psychological Inquiry, 1*, 3–13. (p. 401)

Lazarus, R. S. (1991). Progress on a cognitive-motivational-relational theory of emotion. *American Psychologist, 46*, 352–367. (p. 382)

Lazarus, R. S. (1998). Fifty years of the research and theory of R. S. Lazarus: An analysis of historical and perennial issues. Mahwah, NJ: Erlbaum. (pp. 382, 398)

Le Grand, R., Mondloch, C. J., Maurer, D., & Brent, H. P. (2004). Impairment in holistic face processing following early visual deprivation. *Psychological Science, 15*, 762–768. (p. 214)

Lea, S. E. G. (2000). Towards an ethical use of animals. *The Psychologist, 13*, 556–557. (p. 27)

Leach, P. (1993). Should parents hit their children? *The Psychologist: Bulletin of the British Psychological Society, 6*, 216–220. (p. 242)

Leach, P. (1994). *Children first*. New York: Knopf. (p. 242)

Leaper, C., & Ayres, M. M. (2007). A meta-analytic review of gender variations in adults' language use: Talkativeness, affiliative speech, and assertive speech. *Personality and Social Psychology Review, 11*, 328–363. (p. 127)

Leary, M. R. (1999). The social and psychological importance of self-esteem. In R. M. Kowalski & M. R. Leary (Eds.), *The social psychology of emotional and behavioral problems*. Washington, DC: APA Books. (p. 447)

Leary, M. R., Haupt, A. L., Strausser, K. S., & Chokel, J. T. (1998). Calibrating the sociometer: The relationship between interpersonal appraisals and state self-esteem. *Journal of Personality and Social Psychology, 74*, 1290–1299. (p. 370)

Leary, W. E. (1998, September 28). Older people enjoy sex, survey says. *New York Times* (www.nytimes.com). (p. 164)

LeDoux, J. (1996). The emotional brain: The mysterious underpinnings of emotional life. New York: Simon & Schuster. (p. 272)

LeDoux, J. E. (2002). The synaptic self. London: Macmillan. (pp. 119, 381)

LeDoux, J. E., & Armony, J. (1999). Can neurobiology tell us anything about human feelings? In D. Kahneman, E. Diener, & N. Schwartz (Eds.), Well-being: The foundations of hedonic psychology. New York: Sage. (p. 382)

Lefcourt, H. M. (1982). Locus of control: Current trends in theory and research. Hillsdale, NJ: Erlbaum. (p. 441)

Legrand, L. N., Iacono, W. G., & McGue, M. (2005). Predicting addiction. American Scientist, 93, 140–147. (p. 99)

Lehman, A. F., Steinwachs, D. M., Dixon, L. B., Goldman, H. H., Osher, F., Postrado, L., Scott, J. E., Thompson, J. W., Fahey, M., Fischer, P., Kasper, J. A., Lyles, A., Skinner, E. A., Buchanan, R., Carpenter, W. T., Jr., Levine, J., McGlynn, E. A., Rosenheck, R., & Zito, J. (1998). Translating research into practice: The schizophrenic patient outcomes research team (PORT) treatment recommendations. Schizophrenia Bulletin, 24, 1–10. (p. 513)

Lehman, D. R., Wortman, C. B., & Williams, A. F. (1987). Long-term effects of losing a spouse or child in a motor vehicle crash. Journal of Personality and Social Psychology, 52, 218–231. (p. 172)

Leigh, B. C. (1989). In search of the seven dwarves: Issues of measurement and meaning in alcohol expectancy research. Psychological Bulletin, 105, 361–373. (p. 90)

Leitenberg, H., & Henning, K. (1995). Sexual fantasy. Psychological Bulletin, 117, 469–496. (pp. 359, 360)

Lemonick, M. D. (2002, June 3). Lean and hungrier. Time, p. 54. (p. 345)

Lennox, B. R., Bert, S., Park, G., Jones, P. B., & Morris, P. G. (1999). Spatial and temporal mapping of neural activity associated with auditory hallucinations. Lancet, 353, 644. (p. 53)

Lenzenweger, M. F., Dworkin, R. H., & Wethington, E. (1989). Models of positive and negative symptoms in schizophrenia: An empirical evaluation of latent structures. Journal of Abnormal Psychology, 98, 62–70. (p. 513)

Lerner, M. J. (1980). The belief in a just world: A fundamental delusion. New York: Plenum Press. (p. 545)

Leserman, J., Jackson, E. D., Petitto, J. M., Golden, R. N., Silva, S. G., Perkins, D. O., Cai, J., Folds, J. D., & Evans, D. L. (1999). Progression to AIDS: The effects of stress, depressive symptoms, and social support. Psychosomatic Medicine, 61, 397–406. (p. 405)

Lester, W. (2004, May 26). AP polls: Nations value immigrant workers. Associated Press release. (p. 544)

Leucht, S., Barnes, T. R. E., Kissling, W., Engel, R. R., Correll, C., & Kane, J. M. (2003). Relapse prevention in schizophrenia with new-generation antipsychotics: A systematic review and exploratory meta-analysis of randomized, controlled trials. American Journal of Psychiatry, 160, 1209–1222. (p. 514)

LeVay, S. (1991). A difference in hypothalamic structure between heterosexual and homosexual men. Science, 253, 1034–1037. (p. 366)

LeVay, S. (1994, March). Quoted in D. Nimmons, Sex and the brain. Discover, p. 64–71. (p. 366)

Levenson, R. W. (1992). Autonomic nervous system differences among emotions. Psychological Science, 3, 23–27. (p. 379)

Lever, J. (2003, November 11). Personal correspondence reporting data responses volunteered to Elle/MSNBC.com survey of weight perceptions. (p. 349)

Levin, I. P., & Gaeth, G. J. (1988). How consumers are affected by the framing of attribute information before and after consuming the product. Journal of Consumer Research, 15, 374–378. (p. 301)

Levin, R., & Nielsen, T. A. (2007). Disturbed dreaming, posttraumatic stress disorder, and affect distress: A review and neurocognitive model. Psychological Bulletin, 133, 482–528. (p. 81)

Levine, J. A., Eberhardt, N. L., & Jensen, M. D. (1999). Role of nonexercise activity thermogenesis in resistance to fat gain in humans. Science, 283, 212–214. (p. 352)

Levine, J. A., Lanningham-Foster, L. M., McCrady, S. K., Krizan, A. C., Olson, L. R., Kane, P. H., Jensen, M. D., & Clark, M. M. (2005). Interindividual variation in posture allocation: Possible role in human obesity. Science, 307, 584–586. (p. 352)

Levine, R., Sato, S., Hashimoto, T., & Verma, J. (1995). Love and marriage in eleven cultures. Journal of Cross-Cultural Psychology, 26, 554–571. (p. 560)

Levine, R. V., & Norenzayan, A. (1999). The pace of life in 31 countries. Journal of Cross-Cultural Psychology, 30, 178–205. (pp. 17, 122)

Lewandowski, G. W., Jr., Aron, A., & Gee, J. (2007). Personality goes a long way: The malleability of opposite-sex physical attractiveness. Personality Relationships, 14, 571–585. (p. 558)

Lewicki, P., Hill, T., & Czyzewska, M. (1992). Nonconscious acquisition of information. American Psychologist, 47, 796–801. (p. 427)

Lewicki, P., Hill, T., & Czyzewska, M. (1997). Hidden covariation detection: A fundamental and ubiquitous phenomenon. Journal of Experimental Psychology: Learning, Memory, and Cognition, 23, 221–228. (p. 427)

Lewinsohn, P. M., Hoberman, H., Teri, L., & Hautziner, M. (1985). An integrative theory of depression. In S. Reiss & R. Bootzin (Eds.), Theoretical issues in behavior therapy. Orlando, FL: Academic Press. (p. 472)

Lewinsohn, P. M., Petit, J., Joiner, T. E., Jr., & Seeley, J. R. (2003). The symptomatic expression of major depressive disorder in adolescents and young adults. Journal of Abnormal Psychology, 112, 244–252. (p. 472)

Lewinsohn, P. M., Rohde, P., & Seeley, J. R. (1998). Major depressive disorder in older adolescents: Prevalence, risk factors, and clinical implications. Clinical Psychology Review, 18, 765–794. (p. 472)

Lewis, C. S. (1967). Christian reflections. Grand Rapids, MI: Eerdmans. (p. 277)

Lewis, D. O., Pincus, J. H., Bard, B., Richardson, E., Prichep, L. S., Feldman, M., & Yeager, C. (1988). Neuropsychiatric, psychoeducational, and family characteristics of 14 juveniles condemned to death in the United States. American Journal of Psychiatry, 145, 584–589. (p. 153)

Lewis, D. O., Pincus, J. H., Feldman, M., Jackson, L., & Bard, B. (1986). Psychiatric, neurological, and psychoeducational characteristics of 15 death row inmates in the United States. American Journal of Psychiatry, 143, 838–845. (p. 548)

Lewis, D. O., Yeager, C. A., Swica, Y., Pincus, J. H., & Lewis, M. (1997). Objective documentation of child abuse and dissociation in 12 murderers with dissociative identity disorder. American Journal of Psychiatry, 154, 1703–1710. (p. 470)

Lewontin, R. (1976). Race and intelligence. In N. J. Block & G. Dworkin (Eds.), The IQ controversy: Critical readings. New York: Pantheon. (p. 331)

Lewontin, R. (1982). Human diversity. New York: Scientific American Library. (pp. 114, 332)

Li, J. C., Dunning, D., & Malpass, R. L. (1996). Cross-racial identification among European-Americans basketball fandom and the contact hypothesis. Unpublished manuscript, Cornell University. (p. 547)

Li, J., Laursen, T. M., Precht, D. H., Olsen, J., & Mortensen, P. B. (2005). Hospitalization for mental illness among parents after the death of a child. New England Journal of Medicine, 352, 1190–1196. (p. 172)

Licata, A., Taylor, S., Berman, M., & Cranston, J. (1993). Effects of cocaine on human aggression. Pharmacology Biochemistry and Behavior, 45, 549–552. (p. 94)

Lieberman, J. A. (2006). Comparative effectiveness of antipsychotic drugs. Archives of General Psychiatry, 63, 1069–1072. (p. 514)

Lieberman, J. A., & 11 others. (2005). Effectiveness of antipsychotic drugs in patients with chronic schizophrenia. New England Journal of Medicine, 353, 1209–1223. (p. 514)

Lieberman, M. D., Eisenberger, N. L., Crockett, M. J., Tom, S. M., Pfeifer, J. H., & Way, B. M. (2007). Putting feelings into words: Affect labeling disrupts amygdala activity in response to affective stimuli. Psychological Science, 18, 421–428. (p. 410)

Lilienfeld, S. O., & Arkowitz, H. (2007, April/May). Autism: An epidemic. Scientific American Mind, pp. 82–83. (p. 146)

Lilienfeld, S. O., & Arkowitz, H. (2007, December, 2006/January, 2007). Taking a closer look: Can moving your eyes back and forth help to ease anxiety? Scientific American Mind, pp. 80–81. (p. 508)

Lilienfeld, S. O., Lynn, S. J., Kirsch, I., Chaves, J. F., Sarbin, T. R., Ganaway, G. K., & Powell, R. A. (1999). Dissociative identity disorder and the sociocognitive model: Recalling the lessons of the past. Psychological Bulletin, 125, 507–523. (p. 470)

Lilienfeld, S. O., Wood, J. M., & Garb, H. N. (2001, May). What's wrong with this picture? Scientific American, pp. 81–87. (p. 425)

Linde, K., & 10 others. (2005). Acupuncture for patients with migraine: A randomized controlled trial. Journal of the American Medical Association, 293, 2118–2125. (p. 406)

Linder, D. (1982). Social trap analogs: The tragedy of the commons in the laboratory. In V. J. Derlega & J. Grzelak (Eds.), Cooperative and helping behavior: Theories and research. New York: Academic Press. (p. 564)

Lindskold, S. (1978). Trust development, the GRIT proposal, and the effects of conciliatory acts on conflict and cooperation. *Psychological Bulletin, 85,* 772–793. (p. 567)

Lindskold, S., & Han, G. (1988). GRIT as a foundation for integrative bargaining. *Personality and Social Psychology Bulletin, 14,* 335–345. (p. 567)

Linville, P. W., Fischer, G. W., & Fischhoff, B. (1992). AIDS risk perceptions and decision biases. In J. B. Pryor & G. D. Reeder (Eds.), *The social psychology of HIV infection.* Hillsdale, NJ: Erlbaum. (p. 300)

Lippa, R. A. (2002). Gender-related traits of heterosexual and homosexual men and women. *Archives of Sexual Behavior, 31,* 83–98. (p. 365)

Lippa, R. A. (2005). *Gender, nature, and nurture* (2nd ed.). Mahwah, NJ: Erlbaum. (p. 128)

Lippa, R. A. (2005). Sexual orientation and personality. *Annual Review of Sex Research, 16,* 119–153. (p. 363)

Lippa, R. A. (2006). Is high sex drive associated with increased sexual attraction to both sexes? It depends on whether you are male or female. *Psychological Science, 17,* 46–52. (p. 364)

Lippa, R. A. (2006). The gender reality hypothesis. *American Psychologist, 61,* 639–640. (p. 128)

Lippa, R. A. (2007a). The relation between sex drive and sexual attraction to men and women: A cross-national study of heterosexual, bisexual, and homosexual men and women. *Archives of Sexual Behavior, 36,* 209–222. (p. 368)

Lippa, R. A. (2007b). The preferred traits of mates in a cross-national study of heterosexual and homosexual men and women: An examination of biological and cultural influences. *Archives of Sexual Behavior, 36,* 193–208. (pp. 364, 368, 557)

Lippa, R. A. (2008) Sex differences and sexual orientation differences in personality: Findings from the BBC Internet survey. *Archives of Sexual Behavior, Special Issue: Biological research on sex-dimorphic behavior and sexual orientation, 37*(1), 173–187. (pp. 115, 128, 368)

Lippman, J. (1992, October 25). Global village is characterized by a television in every home. *Grand Rapids Press,* p. F9. (p. 251)

Lipps, H. M. (1999). *A new psychology of women: Gender, culture, and ethnicity.* Mountain View, CA: Mayfield Publishing. (p. 544)

Lipsitt, L. P. (2003). Crib death: A biobehavioral phenomenon? *Current Directions in Psychological Science, 12,* 164–170. (p. 141)

Livesley, W. J., & Jang, K. L. (2008). The behavioral genetics of personality disorder. *Annual Review of Clinical Psychology, 4,* 247–274. (p. 487)

Livingstone, M., & Hubel, D. (1988). Segregation of form, color, movement, and depth: Anatomy, physiology, and perception. *Science, 240,* 740–749. (p. 190)

LoBue, V., & DeLoache, J. S. (2008). Detecting the snake in the grass: Attention to fear-relevant stimuli by adults and young children. *Psychological Science, 19,* 284–289. (p. 466)

Loehlin, J. C., Horn, J. M., & Ernst, J. L. (2007). Genetic and environmental influences on adult life outcomes: Evidence from the Texas adoption project. *Behavior Genetics, 37,* 463–476. (p. 110)

Loehlin, J. C., McCrae, R. R., & Costa, P. T., Jr. (1998). Heritabilities of common and measure-specific components of the Big Five personality factors. *Journal of Research in Personality, 32,* 431–453. (p. 436)

Loehlin, J. C., & Nichols, R. C. (1976). *Heredity, environment, and personality.* Austin: University of Texas Press. (p. 107)

Loewenstein, G., & Furstenberg, F. (1991). Is teenage sexual behavior rational? *Journal of Applied Social Psychology, 21,* 957–986. (p. 240)

Loftus, E. (1995, March/April). Remembering dangerously. *Skeptical Inquirer,* pp. 20–29. (p. 426)

Loftus, E. F. (1979). The malleability of human memory. *American Scientist, 67,* 313–320. (p. 282)

Loftus, E. F. (1980). Memory: Surprising new insights into how we remember and why we forget. Reading, MA: Addison-Wesley. (p. 84)

Loftus, E. F. (2001, November). Imagining the past. *The Psychologist, 14,* 584–587. (p. 282)

Loftus, E. F., & Ketcham, K. (1994). *The myth of repressed memory.* New York: St. Martin's Press. (pp. 80, 267)

Loftus, E. F., Levidow, B., & Duensing, S. (1992). Who remembers best? Individual differences in memory for events that occurred in a science museum. *Applied Cognitive Psychology, 6,* 93–107. (p. 282)

Loftus, E. F., & Loftus, G. R. (1980). On the permanence of stored information in the human brain. *American Psychologist, 35,* 409–420. (p. 267)

Loftus, E. F., Milo, E. M., & Paddock, J. R. (1995). The accidental executioner: Why psychotherapy must be informed by science. *The Counseling Psychologist, 23,* 300–309. (p. 285)

Loftus, E. F., & Palmer, J. C. (October, 1974). Reconstruction of automobile destruction: An example of the interaction between language and memory. *Journal of Verbal Learning & Verbal Behavior, 13*(5), 585–589. (p. 282)

Logan, T. K., Walker, R., Cole, J., & Leukefeld, C. (2002). Victimization and substance abuse among women: Contributing factors, interventions, and implications. *Review of General Psychology, 6,* 325–397. (p. 98)

Logue, A. W. (1998a). Laboratory research on self-control: Applications to administration. *Review of General Psychology, 2,* 221–238. (p. 240)

Logue, A. W. (1998b). Self-control. In W. T. O'Donohue (Ed.), *Learning and behavior therapy.* Boston, MA: Allyn & Bacon. (p. 240)

London, P. (1970). The rescuers: Motivational hypotheses about Christians who saved Jews from the Nazis. In J. Macaulay & L. Berkowitz (Eds.), *Altruism and helping behavior.* New York: Academic Press. (p. 251)

Looy, H. (2001). Sex differences: Evolved, constructed, and designed. *Journal of Psychology and Theology, 29,* 301–313. (p. 117)

Lopes, P. N., Brackett, M. A., Nezlek, J. B., Schutz, A., Sellin, II, & Salovey, P. (2004). Emotional intelligence and social interaction. *Personality and Social Psychology Bulletin, 30,* 1018–1034. (p. 318)

Lord, C. G., Lepper, M. R., & Preston, E. (1984). Considering the opposite: A corrective strategy for social judgment. *Journal of*

Personality and Social Psychology, 47, 1231–1247. (p. 297)

Lord, C. G., Ross, L., & Lepper, M. (1979). Biased assimilation and attitude polarization: The effects of prior theories on subsequently considered evidence. *Journal of Personality and Social Psychology, 37,* 2098–2109. (p. 297)

Lorenz, K. (1937). The companion in the bird's world. *Auk, 54,* 245–273. (p. 150)

Los Angeles Times. (1998, 14 March). Daughters give birth on same day. P. A15. (p. 21)

Louie, K., & Wilson, M. A. (2001). Temporally structured replay of awake hippocampal ensemble activity during rapid eye movement sleep. *Neuron, 29,* 145–156. (p. 82)

Lourenco, O., & Machado, A. (1996). In defense of Piaget's theory: A reply to 10 common criticisms. *Psychological Review, 103,* 143–164. (p. 148)

Lovaas, O. I. (1987). Behavioral treatment and normal educational and intellectual functioning in young autistic children. *Journal of Consulting and Clinical Psychology, 55,* 3–9. (p. 500)

Lowry, P. E. (1997). The assessment center process: New directions. *Journal of Social Behavior and Personality, 12,* 53–62. (p. 445)

Lu, Z-L., Su, Y., & Wang, Q. (2008, November). Talking about others facilitates theory of mind in Chinese preschoolers. *Developmental Psychology, 44*(6), 1726–1736. (p. 145)

Lu, Z-L., Williamson, S. J., & Kaufman, L. (1992). Behavioral lifetime of human auditory sensory memory predicted by physiological measures. *Science, 258,* 1668–1670. (p. 266)

Lubinski, D., & Benbow, C. P. (1992). Gender differences in abilities and preferences among the gifted: Implications for the math-science pipeline. *Current Directions in Psychological Science, 1,* 61–66. (p. 328)

Lubinski, D., & Benbow, C. P. (2006). Study of mathematically precocious youth after 35 years: Uncovering antecedents for the development of math-science expertise. *Perspectives on Psychological Science, 1,* 316–345. (p. 322)

Lucas, A., Morley, R., Cole, T. J., Lister, G., & Leeson-Payne, C. (1992). Breast milk and subsequent intelligence quotient in children born preterm. *Lancet, 339,* 261–264. (p. 22)

Lucas, R. E. (2007a). Adaptation and the set-point model of subjective well-being. *Current Directions in Psychological Science, 16,* 75–79. (p. 393)

Lucas, R. E. (2007b). Long-term disability is associated with lasting changes in subjective well-being: Evidence from two nationally representative longitudinal studies. *Journal of Personality and Social Psychology, 92,* 717–730. (p. 393)

Lucas, R. E. (2008). Personality and subjective well-being. In M. Eid & R. Larsen (Eds.), *The science of subjective well-being.* New York: Guilford. (p. 397)

Lucas, R. E., Clark, A. E., Georgellis, Y., & Diener, E. (2003). Re-examining adaptation and the setpoint model of happiness: Reactions to changes in marital status. *Journal of Personality and Social Psychology, 84,* 527–539. (p. 172)

Lucas, R. E., Clark, A. E., Georgellis, Y., & Diener, E. (2004). Unemployment alters the set point for life satisfaction. *Psychological Science, 15,* 8–13. (p. 396)

Lucas, R. E., & Donnellan, M. B. (2007). How stable is happiness? Using the STARTS model to estimate the stability of life satisfaction. *Journal of Research in Personality, 41,* 1091–1098. (p. 397)

Ludwig, A. M. (1995). *The price of greatness: Resolving the creativity and madness controversy.* New York: Guilford Press. (pp. 365, 472)

Luria, A. M. (1968). In L. Solotaroff (Trans.), *The mind of a mnemonist.* New York: Basic Books. (p. 257)

Lustig, C., & Buckner, R. L. (2004). Preserved neural correlates of priming in old age and dementia. *Neuron, 42,* 865–875. (p. 271)

Lutgendorf, S. K., Russell, D., Ullrich, P., Harris, T. B., & Wallace, R. (2004). Religious participation, interleukin-6, and mortality in older adults. *Health Psychology, 23,* 465–475. (p. 415)

Lyall, S. (2005, November 29). What's the buzz? Rowdy teenagers don't want to hear it. *New York Times* (www.nytimes.com). (p. 164)

Lykins, A. D., Meana, M., & Strauss, G. P. (2008). Sex differences in visual attention to erotic and non-erotic stimuli. *Archives of Sexual Behavior, 37,* 219–228. (p. 364)

Lykken, D. T. (1991). Science, lies, and controversy: An epitaph for the polygraph. Invited address upon receipt of the Senior Career Award for Distinguished Contribution to Psychology in the Public Interest, American Psychological Association convention. (p. 380)

Lykken, D. T. (1995). *The antisocial personalities.* Hillsdale, NJ: Erlbaum. (p. 549)

Lykken, D. T. (1999). *Happiness.* New York: Golden Books. (p. 324)

Lykken, D. T. (2001). Happiness—stuck with what you've got? *The Psychologist, 14,* 470–473. (p. 110)

Lykken, D. T., & Tellegen, A. (1996). Happiness is a stochastic phenomenon. *Psychological Science, 7,* 186–189. (p. 397)

Lyman, D. R. (1996). Early identification of chronic offenders: Who is the fledgling psychopath? *Psychological Bulletin, 120,* 209–234. (p. 488)

Lynch, G. (2002). Memory enhancement: The search for mechanism-based drugs. *Nature Neuroscience, 5* (suppl.), 1035–1038. (p. 268)

Lynch, G., & Staubli, U. (1991). Possible contributions of long-term potentiation to the encoding and organization of memory. *Brain Research Reviews, 16,* 204–206. (p. 268)

Lynn, M. (1988). The effects of alcohol consumption on restaurant tipping. *Personality and Social Psychology Bulletin, 14,* 87–91. (p. 90)

Lynn, R. (1991, Fall/Winter). The evolution of racial differences in intelligence. *The Mankind Quarterly, 32,* 99–145. (p. 331)

Lynn, R. (2001). *Eugenics: A reassessment.* Westport, CT: Praeger/Greenwood. (p. 331)

Lynn, S. J., Rhue, J. W., & Weekes, J. R. (1990). Hypnotic involuntariness: A social cognitive analysis. *Psychological Review, 97,* 169–184. (p. 86)

Lynne, S. D., Graber, J. A., Nichols, T. R., Brooks-Gunn, J., & Botvin, G. J. (2007). Links between pubertal timing, peer influences, and externalizing behaviors among urban students followed through middle school. *Journal of Adolescent Health, 40,* 181.e7–181.e13. (p. 156)

Lyons, L. (2002, June 25). Are spiritual teens healthier? *Gallup Tuesday Briefing,* Gallup Organization (www.gallup.com/poll/tb/religValue/20020625b.asp). (p. 414)

Lyons, L. (2003, September 23). Oh, boy: Americans still prefer sons. *Gallup Poll Tuesday Briefing* (www.gallup.com). (p. 544)

Lyons, L. (2004, February 3). Growing up lonely: Examining teen alienation. *Gallup Poll Tuesday Briefing* (www.gallup.com). (p. 160)

Lyons, L. (2005, January 4). Teens stay true to parents' political perspectives. *Gallup Poll News Service* (www.gallup.com). (p. 161)

Lytton, H., & Romney, D. M. (1991). Parents' differential socialization of boys and girls: A meta-analysis. *Psychological Bulletin, 109,* 267–296. (p. 131)

Lyubomirsky, S. (2001). Why are some people happier than others? The role of cognitive and motivational processes in well-being. *American Psychologist, 56,* 239–249. (p. 395)

Lyubomirsky, S., King, L., & Diener, E. (2005). The benefits of frequent positive affect: Does happiness lead to success? *Psychological Bulletin, 131,* 803–855. (p. 392)

Ma, L. (1997, September). On the origin of Darwin's ills. *Discover,* p. 27. (p. 463)

Maas, J. B. (1999). *Power sleep. The revolutionary program that prepares your mind and body for peak performance.* New York: HarperCollins. (pp. 76, 78)

Maass, A., & Russo, A. (2003). Directional bias in the mental representation of spatial events: Nature or culture? *Psychological Science, 14,* 296–301. (p. 306)

Maass, A., D'Ettole, C., & Cadinu, M. (2008). Checkmate? The role of gender stereotypes in the ultimate intellectual sport. *European Journal of Social Psychology, 38,* 231–245. (p. 333)

Maass, A., Karasawa, M., Politi, F., & Suga, S. (2006). Do verbs and adjectives play different roles in different cultures? A cross-linguistic analysis of person representation. *Journal of Personality and Social Psychology, 90,* 734–750. (p. 124)

Macaluso, E., Frith, C. D., & Driver, J. (2000). Modulation of human visual cortex by cross-modal spatial attention. *Science, 289,* 1206–1208. (p. 202)

Maccoby, E. E. (1990). Gender and relationships: A developmental account. *American Psychologist, 45,* 513–520. (p. 128)

Maccoby, E. E. (1995). Divorce and custody: The rights, needs, and obligations of mothers, fathers, and children. *Nebraska Symposium on Motivation, 42,* 135–172. (p. 130)

Maccoby, E. E. (1998). *The paradox of gender.* Cambridge, MA: Harvard University Press. (p. 128)

Maccoby, E. E. (2002). Gender and group process: A developmental perspective. *Current Directions in Psychological Science, 11,* 54–58. (p. 539)

MacDonald, N. (1960). Living with schizophrenia. *Canadian Medical Association Journal, 82,* 218–221. (p. 481)

MacDonald, T. K., & Hynie, M. (2008). Ambivalence and unprotected sex: Failure to predict sexual activity and decreased condom use. *Journal of Applied Social Psychology, 38,* 1092–1107. (p. 361)

MacDonald, T. K., Zanna, M. P., & Fong, G. T. (1995). Decision making in altered states: Effects of alcohol on attitudes toward drinking and driving. *Journal of Personality and Social Psychology, 68,* 973–985. (p. 90)

MacFarlane, A. (1978, February). What a baby knows. *Human Nature,* pp. 74–81. (p. 139)

Macfarlane, J. W. (1964). Perspectives on personality consistency and change from the guidance study. *Vita Humana, 7,* 115–126. (p. 155)

Machin, S., & Pekkarinen, T. (2008). Global sex differences in test score variability. *Science, 322,* 1331–1332. (p. 330)

Maciejewski, P. K., Zhang, B., Block, S. D., & Prigerson, H. G. (2007). An empirical examination of the stage theory of grief. *Journal of the American Medical Association, 297,* 722–723. (p. 172)

Mack, A., & Rock, I. (2000). *Inattentional blindness.* Cambridge, MA: MIT Press. (p. 69)

MacKinnon, D. W., & Hall, W. B. (1972). Intelligence and creativity. In *Proceedings, XVIIth International Congress of Applied Psychology* (Vol. 2). Brussels: Editest. (p. 317)

MacLachlan, M., Desmond, D., & Horgan, O. (2003). Psychological correlates of illusory body experience. *Journal of Rehabilitation Research and Development, 40,* 59–66. (p. 197)

MacNeilage, P. F., & Davis, B. L. (2000). On the origin of internal structure of word forms. *Science, 288,* 527–531. (p. 303)

Maddox, K. B. (2004). Perspectives on racial phenotypicality bias. *Personality and Social Psychology Review, 8,* 383–401. (p. 543)

Madrian, B. C., & Shea, D. F. (2001). The power of suggestion: Inertia in 401(k) participation and savings behavior. *Quarterly Journal of Economics, 116,* 1149–1187. (p. 301)

Maes, H. H. M., Neale, M. C., & Eaves, L. J. (1997). Genetic and environmental factors in relative body weight and human adiposity. *Behavior Genetics, 27,* 325–351. (p. 353)

Maestripieri, D. (2003). Similarities in affiliation and aggression between cross-fostered rhesus macaque females and their biological mothers. *Developmental Psychobiology, 43,* 321–327. (p. 110)

Maestripieri, D. (2005). Early experience affects the intergenerational transmission of infant abuse in rhesus monkeys. *Proceedings of the National Academy of Sciences, 102,* 9726–9729. (p. 152)

Magnusson, D. (1990). Personality research—challenges for the future. *European Journal of Personality, 4,* 1–17. (p. 487)

Magnusson, P. E. E., Rasmussen, F., Lawlor, D. A., Tynelius, P., & Gunnell, D. (2006). Association of body mass index with suicide mortality: A prospective cohort study of more than one million men. *American Journal of Epidemiology, 163,* 1–8. (p. 474)

Maguire, E. A., Spiers, H. J., Good, C. D., Hartley, T., Frackowiak, R. S. J., & Burgess, N. (2003a). Navigation expertise and the human hippocampus: A structural brain imaging analysis. *Hippocampus, 13,* 250–259. (p. 271)

Maguire, E. A., Valentine, E. R., Wilding, J. M., & Kapur, N. (2003b). Routes to remembering: The brains behind superior memory. *Nature Neuroscience, 6*, 90–95. (pp. 263, 271)

Mahncke, H. W., Connor, B. B., Appelman, J., Ahsanuddin, O. N., Hardy, J. L., Wood, R. A., Joyce, N. M., Boniske, T., Atkins, S. M., & Merzenich, M. M. (2006). Memory enhancement in healthy older adults using a brain plasticity-based training program: A randomized control study. *Proceedings of the National Academy of Sciences, 103*, 12523–12528. (p. 167)

Mahowald, M. W., & Ettinger, M. G. (1990). Things that go bump in the night: The parsomias revisited. *Journal of Clinical Neurophysiology, 7*, 119–143. (p. 79)

Maier, S. F., Watkins, L. R., & Fleshner, M. (1994). Psychoneuroimmunology: The interface between behavior, brain, and immunity. *American Psychologist, 49*, 1004–1017. (p. 404)

Major, B., Carrington, P. I., & Carnevale, P. J. D. (1984). Physical attractiveness and self-esteem: Attribution for praise from an other-sex evaluator. *Personality and Social Psychology Bulletin, 10*, 43–50. (p. 557)

Major, B., Schmidlin, A. M., & Williams, L. (1990). Gender patterns in social touch: The impact of setting and age. *Journal of Personality and Social Psychology, 58*, 634–643. (p. 127)

Malamuth, N. M. (1996). Sexually explicit media, gender differences, and evolutionary theory. *Journal of Communication, 46*, 8–31. (p. 551)

Malamuth, N. M., & Check, J. V. P. (1981). The effects of media exposure on acceptance of violence against women: A field experiment. *Journal of Research in Personality, 15*, 436–446. (p. 360)

Malamuth, N. M., Linz, D., Heavey, C. L., Barnes, G., & Acker, M. (1995). Using the confluence model of sexual aggression to predict men's conflict with women: A 10-year follow-up study. *Journal of Personality and Social Psychology, 69*, 353–369. (p. 553)

Malamuth, N. M., Sockloskie, R. J., Koss, M. P., & Tanaka, J. S. (1991). Characteristics of aggressors against women: Testing a model using a national sample of college students. *Journal of Consulting and Clinical Psychology, 59*, 670–681. (p. 553)

Malan, D. H. (1978). The case of the secretary with the violent father. In H. Davanloo (Ed.), *Basic principles and techniques in short-term dynamic psychotherapy.* New York: Spectrum. (p. 495)

Malinosky-Rummell, R., & Hansen, D. J. (1993). Long-term consequences of childhood physical abuse. *Psychological Bulletin, 114*, 68–79. (p. 152)

Malkiel, B. (2004). *A random walk down Wall Street* (8th ed.). New York: Norton. (p. 297)

Malkiel, B. G. (1989). Is the stock market efficient? *Science, 243*, 1313–1318. (p. 20)

Malkiel, B. G. (1995, June). Returns from investing in equity mutual funds 1971 to 1991. *Journal of Finance*, pp. 549–572. (p. 20)

Malle, B. F. (2006). The actor-observer asymmetry in attribution: A (surprising) meta-analysis. *Psychological Bulletin, 132*, 895–919. (p. 526)

Malle, B. F., Knobe, J. M., & Nelson, S. E. (2007). Actor-observer asymmetries in explanations of behavior: New answers to an old question. *Journal of Personality and Social Psychology, 93*, 491–514. (p. 526)

Malmquist, C. P. (1986). Children who witness parental murder: Post-traumatic aspects. *Journal of the American Academy of Child Psychiatry, 25*, 320–325. (p. 426)

Malnic, B., Hirono, J., Sato, T., & Buck, L. B. (1999). Combinatorial receptor codes for odors. *Cell, 96*, 713–723. (p. 203)

Manber, R., Bootzin, R. R., Acebo, C., & Carskadon, M. A. (1996). The effects of regularizing sleep-wake schedules on daytime sleepiness. *Sleep, 19*, 432–441. (p. 78)

Mandel, D. (1983, March 13). One man's holocaust: Part II. The story of David Mandel's journey through hell as told to David Kagan. *Wonderland Magazine (Grand Rapids Press)*, pp. 2–7. (p. 343)

Maner, J. K., DeWall, C. N, Baumeister, R. F., & Schaller, M. (2007). Does social exclusion motivate interpersonal reconnection? Resolving the "porcupine problem." *Journal of Personality and Social Psychology, 92*, 42–55. (p. 371)

Mann, T., Tomiyama, A. J., Westling, E., Lew, A-M., Samuels, B., & Chatman, J. (2007). Medicare's search for effective obesity treatments: Diets are not the answer. *American Psychologist, 62*, 220–233. (p. 355)

Manson, J. E. (2002). Walking compared with vigorous exercise for the prevention of cardiovascular events in women. *New England Journal of Medicine, 347*, 716–725. (p. 412)

Maquet, P. (2001). The role of sleep in learning and memory. *Science, 294*, 1048–1052. (p. 82)

Maquet, P., Peters, J-M., Aerts, J., Delfiore, G., Degueldre, C., Luxen, A., & Franck, G. (1996). Functional neuroanatomy of human rapid-eye-movement sleep and dreaming. *Nature, 383*, 163–166. (p. 82)

Mar, R. A., & Oatley, K. (2008). The function of fiction is the abstraction and simulation of social experience. *Perspectives on Psychological Science, 3*, 173–192. (p. 249)

Marangell, L. B., Martinez, M., Jurdi, R. A., & Zboyan, H. (2007). Neurostimulation therapies in depression: A review of new modalities. *Acta Psychiatrica Scandinavica, 116*, 174–181. (p. 517)

Marcus, B., Machilek, F., & Schütz, A. (2006). Personality in cyberspace: Personal web sites as media for personality expressions and impressions. *Journal of Personality and Social Psychology, 90*, 1014–1031. (p. 438)

Maren, S. (2007). The threatened brain. *Science, 317*, 1043–1044. (p. 467)

Margolis, M. L. (2000). Brahms' lullaby revisited: Did the composer have obstructive sleep apnea? *Chest, 118*, 210–213. (p. 79)

Markowitsch, H. J. (1995). Which brain regions are critically involved in the retrieval of old episodic memory? *Brain Research Reviews, 21*, 117–127. (p. 271)

Markus, G. B. (1986). Stability and change in political attitudes: Observe, recall, and "explain." *Political Behavior, 8*, 21–44. (p. 283)

Markus, H. R., & Kitayama, S. (1991). Culture and the self: Implications for cognition, emotion, and motivation. *Psychological Review, 98*, 224–253. (pp. 124, 306, 390)

Markus, H. R., & Nurius, P. (1986). Possible selves. *American Psychologist, 41*, 954–969. (p. 446)

Markus, H. R., Uchida, Y., Omoregie, H., Townsend, S. S. M., & Kitayama, S. (2006). Going for the gold: Models of agency in Japanese and American contexts. *Psychological Science, 17*, 103–112. (p. 124)

Marley, J., & Bulia, S. (2001). Crimes against people with mental illness: Types, perpetrators and influencing factors. *Social Work, 46*, 115–124. (p. 460)

Marmot, M. G., Bosma, H., Hemingway, H., Brunner, E., & Stansfeld, S. (1997). Contribution of job control and other risk factors to social variations in coronary heart disease incidence. *Lancet, 350*, 235–239. (p. 408)

Marschark, M., Richman, C. L., Yuille, J. C., & Hunt, R. R. (1987). The role of imagery in memory: On shared and distinctive information. *Psychological Bulletin, 102*, 28–41. (p. 263)

Marsh, A. A., Elfenbein, H. A., & Ambady, N. (2003). Nonverbal "accents": Cultural differences in facial expressions of emotion. *Psychological Science, 14*, 373–376. (p. 387)

Marsh, H. W., & Craven, R. G. (2006). Reciprocal effects of self-concept and performance from a multidimensional perspective: Beyond seductive pleasure and unidimensional perspectives. *Perspectives on Psychological Science, 1*, 133–163. (p. 447)

Marsh, H. W., & Parker, J. W. (1984). Determinants of student self-concept: Is it better to be a relatively large fish in a small pond even if you don't learn to swim as well? *Journal of Personality and Social Psychology, 47*, 213–231. (p. 396)

Marshall, M. J. (2002). *Why spanking doesn't work.* Springville, UT: Bonneville Books. (p. 242)

Marshall, R. D., Bryant, R. A., Amsel, L., Suh, E. J., Cook, J. M., & Neria, Y. (2007). The psychology of ongoing threat: Relative risk appraisal, the September 11 attacks, and terrorism-related fears. *American Psychologist, 62*, 304–316. (p. 296)

Marteau, T. M. (1989). Framing of information: Its influences upon decisions of doctors and patients. *British Journal of Social Psychology, 28*, 89–94. (p. 300)

Martin, C. K., Anton, S. D., Walden, H., Arnett, C., Greenway, F. L., & Williamson, D. A. (2007). Slower eating rate reduces the food intake of men, but not women: Implications for behavioural weight control. *Behaviour Research and Therapy, 45*, 2349–2359. (p. 356)

Martin, C. L., & Ruble, D. (2004). Children's search for gender cues. *Current Directions in Psychological Science, 13*, 67–70. (p. 131)

Martin, C. L., Ruble, D. N., & Szkrybalo, J. (2002). Cognitive theories of early gender development. *Psychological Bulletin, 128*, 903–933. (p. 131)

Martin, R. J., White, B. D., & Hulsey, M. G. (1991). The regulation of body weight. *American Scientist, 79*, 528–541. (p. 346)

Martin, R. M., Goodall, S. H., Gunnell, D., & Smith, G. D. (2007). Breast feeding in infancy and social mobility: 60-year follow-up of the Boyd Orr cohort. *Archives of Disease in Childhood, 92*, 317–321. (p. 21)

Martin, S. J., Kelly, I. W., & Saklofske, D. H. (1992). Suicide and lunar cycles: A critical review over 28 years. *Psychological Reports, 71,* 787–795. (p. 488)

Martino, S. C., Collins, R. L., Kanouse, D. E., Elliott, M., & Berry, S. H. (2005). Social cognitive processes mediating the relationship between exposure to television's sexual content and adolescents' sexual behavior. *Journal of Personality and Social Psychology, 89,* 914–924. (p. 361)

Martins, Y., Preti, G., Crabtree, C. R., & Wysocki, C. J. (2005). Preference for human body odors is influenced by gender and sexual orientation. *Psychological Science, 16,* 694–701. (p. 366)

Marx, J. (2007). Evidence linking *DISC1* gene to mental illness builds. *Science, 318,* 1062–1063. (p. 485)

Masicampo, E. J., & Baumeister, R. F. (2008). Toward a physiology of dual-process reasoning and judgment: Lemonade, willpower, and the expensive rule-based analysis. *Psychological Science, 19,* 255–260. (p. 441)

Maslow, A. H. (1970). *Motivation and personality* (2nd ed.). New York: Harper & Row. (pp. 342, 430)

Maslow, A. H. (1971). *The farther reaches of human nature.* New York: Viking Press. (p. 342)

Mason, C., & Kandel, E. R. (1991). Central visual pathways. In E. R. Kandel, J. H. Schwartz, & T. M. Jessell (Eds.), *Principles of neural science* (3rd ed.). New York: Elsevier. (p. 39)

Mason, H. (2003, March 25). Wake up, sleepy teen. *Gallup Poll Tuesday Briefing* (www.gallup.com). (p. 76)

Mason, H. (2003, September 2). Americans, Britons at odds on animal testing. *Gallup Poll News Service* (www.gallup.com). (p. 27)

Mason, H. (2005, January 25). Who dreams, perchance to sleep? *Gallup Poll News Service* (www.gallup.com). (pp. 75, 76)

Mason, H. (2005, February 22). How many teens are on mood medication? *The Gallup Organization* (www.gallup.com). (p. 455)

Mason, R. A., & Just, M. A. (2004). How the brain processes causal inferences in text. *Psychological Science, 15,* 1–7. (p. 60)

Masse, L. C., & Tremblay, R. E. (1997). Behavior of boys in kindergarten and the onset of substance use during adolescence. *Archives of General Psychiatry, 54,* 62–68. (p. 98)

Massimini, M., Ferrarelli, F., Huber, R., Esser, S. K., Singh, H., & Tononi, G. (2005). Breakdown of cortical effective connectivity during sleep. *Science, 309,* 2228–2232. (p. 71)

Mast, M. S., & Hall, J. A. (2006). Women's advantage at remembering others' appearance: A systematic look at the why and when of a gender difference. *Personality and Social Psychology Bulletin, 32,* 353–364. (p. 558)

Masten, A. S. (2001). Ordinary magic: Resilience processes in development. *American Psychologist, 56,* 227–238. (p. 153)

Masters, W. H., & Johnson, V. E. (1966). *Human sexual response.* Boston: Little, Brown. (p. 357)

Mastroianni, G. R. (2002). Milgram and the Holocaust: A reexamination. *Journal of Theoretical and Philosophical Psychology, 22,* 158–173. (p. 536)

Mastroianni, G. R., & Reed, G. (2006). Apples, barrels, and Abu Ghraib. *Sociological Focus, 39,* 239–250. (p. 529)

Masuda, T., & Kitayama, S. (2004). Perceiver-induced constraint and attitude attribution in Japan and the US: A case for the cultural dependence of the correspondence bias. *Journal of Experimental Social Psychology, 40,* 409–416. (p. 526)

Masuda, T., Ellsworth, P. C., Mesquita, B., Leu, J., Tanida, S., & Van de Veerdonk, E. (2008). Placing the face in context: Cultural differences in the perception of facial emotion. *Journal of Personality and Social Psychology, 94,* 365–381. (p. 388)

Mataix-Cols, D., Rosario-Campos, M. C., & Leckman, J. F. (2005). A multidimensional model of obsessive-compulsive disorder. *American Journal of Psychiatry, 162,* 228–238. (p. 467)

Mataix-Cols, D., Wooderson, S., Lawrence, N., Brammer, M. J., Speckens, A., & Phillips, M. L. (2004). Distinct neural correlates of washing, checking, and hoarding symptom dimensions in obsessive-compulsive disorder. *Archives of General Psychiatry, 61,* 564–576. (p. 467)

Mather, M., Canli, T., English, T., Whitfield, S., Wais, P., Ochsner, K., Gabrieli, J. D. E., & Carstensen, L. L. (2004). Amygdala responses to emotionally valenced stimuli in older and younger adults. *Psychological Science, 15,* 259–263. (p. 171)

Matsumoto, D. (1994). *People: Psychology from a cultural perspective.* Pacific Grove, CA: Brooks/Cole. (p. 306)

Matsumoto, D., & Ekman, P. (1989). American-Japanese cultural differences in intensity ratings of facial expressions of emotion. *Motivation and Emotion, 13,* 143–157. (p. 387)

Matsumoto, D., & Willingham, B. (2006). The thrill of victory and the agony of defeat: Spontaneous expressions of medal winners of the 2004 Athens Olympic Games. *Journal of Personality and Social Psychology, 91,* 568–581. (p. 387)

Matsuzawa, T. (2007). Comparative cognitive development. *Developmental Science, 10,* 97–103. (p. 310)

Matthews, R. N., Domjan, M., Ramsey, M., & Crews, D. (2007). Learning effects on sperm competition and reproductive fitness. *Psychological Science, 18,* 758–762. (p. 230)

Maurer, D., & Maurer, C. (1988). *The world of the newborn.* New York: Basic Books. (p. 139)

May, C., & Hasher, L. (1998). Synchrony effects in inhibitory control over thought and action. *Journal of Experimental Psychology: Human Perception and Performance, 24,* 363–380. (p. 71)

May, P. A., & Gossage, J. P. (2001). Estimating the prevalence of fetal alcohol syndrome: A summary. *Alcohol Research and Health, 25,* 159–167. (p. 138)

Mayberg, H. S. (2006). Defining neurocircuits in depression: Strategies toward treatment selection based on neuroimaging phenotypes. *Psychiatric Annals, 36,* 259–268. (p. 518)

Mayberg, H. S. (2007). Defining the neural circuitry of depression: Toward a new nosology with therapeutic implications. *Biological Psychiatry, 61,* 729–730. (p. 518)

Mayberg, H. S., Lozano, A. M., Voon, V., McNeely, H. E., Seminowicz, D., Hamani, C., Schwalb, J. M., & Kennedy, S. H. (2005). Deep brain stimulation for treatment-resistant depression. *Neuron, 45,* 651–660. (p. 518)

Mayberry, R. I., Lock, E., & Kazmi, H. (2002). Linguistic ability and early language exposure. *Nature, 417,* 38. (p. 305)

Mayer, J. D., Salovey, P., & Caruso, D. (2002). *The Mayer-Salovey-Caruso emotional intelligence test (MSCEIT).* Toronto: Multi-Health Systems, Inc. (p. 318)

Mayer, J. D., Salovey, P., & Caruso, D. R. (2008). Emotional intelligence: New ability or eclectic traits? *American Psychologist, 63,* 503–517. (p. 318)

Mays, V. M., Cochran, S. D., & Barnes, N. W. (2007). Race, race-based discrimination, and health outcomes among African Americans. *Annual Review of Psychology, 58,* 201–225. (p. 401)

Mazure, C., Keita, G., & Blehar, M. (2002). *Summit on women and depression: Proceedings and recommendations.* Washington, DC: American Psychological Association (www.apa.org/pi/wpo/women&depression.pdf). (p. 477)

Mazzoni, G., & Memon, A. (2003). Imagination can create false autobiographical memories. *Psychological Science, 14,* 186–188. (p. 282)

Mazzoni, G., & Vannucci, M. (2007). Hindsight bias, the misinformation effect, and false autobiographical memories. *Social Cognition, 25,* 203–220. (p. 283)

Mazzuca, J. (2002, August 20). Teens shrug off movie sex and violence. *Gallup Tuesday Briefing* (www.gallup.com/poll/tb/educayouth/20020820b.asp). (p. 253)

McAneny, L. (1996, September). Large majority think government conceals information about UFO's. *Gallup Poll Monthly,* pp. 23–26. (p. 275)

McBurney, D. H. (1996). *How to think like a psychologist: Critical thinking in psychology.* Upper Saddle River, NJ: Prentice-Hall. (p. 53)

McBurney, D. H., & Collings, V. B. (1984). *Introduction to sensation and perception* (2nd ed.). Englewood Cliffs, NJ: Prentice-Hall. (p. 212)

McBurney, D. H., & Gent, J. F. (1979). On the nature of taste qualities. *Psychological Bulletin, 86,* 151–167. (p. 201)

McCain, N. L., Gray, D. P., Elswick, R. K., Jr., Robins, J. W., Tuck, I., Walter, J. M., Rausch, S. M., & Ketchum, J. M. (2008). A randomized clinical trial of alternative stress management interventions in persons with HIV infection. *Journal of Consulting and Clinical Psychology, 76,* 431–441. (p. 405)

McCann, I. L., & Holmes, D. S. (1984). Influence of aerobic exercise on depression. *Journal of Personality and Social Psychology, 46,* 1142–1147. (p. 411)

McCann, U. D., Eligulashvili, V., & Ricaurte, G. A. (2001). (+-)3,4-Methylenedioxymethamphetamine ('Ecstasy')-induced serotonin neurotoxicity: Clinical studies. *Neuropsychobiology, 42,* 11–16. (p. 95)

McCarthy, P. (1986, July). Scent: The tie that binds? *Psychology Today,* pp. 6, 10. (p. 203)

McCaul, K. D., & Malott, J. M. (1984). Distraction and coping with pain. *Psychological Bulletin, 95,* 516–533. (p. 201)

McCauley, C. R. (2002). Psychological issues in understanding terrorism and the response to terrorism. In C. E. Stout (Ed.), *The psychology of terrorism* (Vol. 3). Westport, CT: Praeger/Greenwood. (p. 540)

McCauley, C. R., & Segal, M. E. (1987). Social psychology of terrorist groups. In C. Hendrick (Ed.), *Group processes and intergroup relations.* Beverly Hills, CA: Sage. (p. 540)

McClearn, G. E., Johansson, B., Berg, S., Pedersen, N. L., Ahern, F., Petrill, S. A., & Plomin, R. (1997). Substantial genetic influence on cognitive abilities in twins 80 or more years old. *Science, 276,* 1560–1563. (p. 326)

McClellan, J. M., Susser, E., & King, M-C. (2007). Schizophrenia: A common disease caused by multiple rare alleles. *British Journal of Psychiatry, 190,* 194–199. (p. 485)

McClendon, B. T., & Prentice-Dunn, S. (2001). Reducing skin cancer risk: An intervention based on protection motivation theory. *Journal of Health Psychology, 6,* 321–328. (p. 527)

McClintock, M. K., & Herdt, G. (1996, December). Rethinking puberty: The development of sexual attraction. *Current Directions in Psychological Science, 5*(6), 178–183. (p. 155)

McClure, E. B. (2000). A meta-analytic review of sex differences in facial expression processing and their development in infants, children, and adolescents. *Psychological Bulletin, 126,* 424–453. (p. 328)

McConkey, K. M. (1995). Hypnosis, memory, and the ethics of uncertainty. *Australian Psychologist, 30,* 1–10. (p. 85)

McConnell, R. A. (1991). National Academy of Sciences opinion on parapsychology. *Journal of the American Society for Psychical Research, 85,* 333–365. (p. 218)

McCool, G. (1999, October 26). Mirror-gazing Venezuelans top of vanity stakes. *Toronto Star* (via web.lexis-nexis.com). (p. 557)

McCormick, C. M., & Witelson, S. F. (1991). A cognitive profile of homosexual men compared to heterosexual men and women. *Psychoneuroendocrinology, 16,* 459–473. (p. 367)

McCrae, R. R., & Costa, P. T., Jr. (1986). Clinical assessment can benefit from recent advances in personality psychology. *American Psychologist, 41,* 1001–1003. (p. 436)

McCrae, R. R., & Costa, P. T., Jr. (1990). *Personality in adulthood.* New York: Guilford. (p. 168)

McCrae, R. R., & Costa, P. T., Jr. (1994). The stability of personality: Observations and evaluations. *Current Directions in Psychological Science, 3,* 173–175. (pp. 174, 437)

McCrae, R. R., Costa, P. T., Jr., de Lirna, M. P., Simoes, A., Ostendorf, F., Angleitner, A., Marusic, I., Bratko, D., Caprara, G. V., Barbaranelli, C., Chae, J-H., & Piedmont, R. L. (1999). Age differences in personality across the adult life span: Parallels in five cultures. *Developmental Psychology, 35,* 466–477. (p. 436)

McCrae, R. R., Costa, P. T., Jr., Ostendorf, F., Angleitner, A., Hrebickova, M., Avia, M. D., Sanz, J., Sanchez-Bernardos, M. L., Kusdil, M. E., Woodfield, R., Saunders, P. R., & Smith, P. B. (2000). Nature over nurture: Temperament, personality, and life span

development. *Journal of Personality and Social Psychology, 78,* 173–186. (p. 111)

McCrae, R. R., Terracciano, A., & Khoury, B. (2007). Dolce far niente: The positive psychology of personality stability and invariance. In A. D. Ong & M. H. Van Dulmen (Eds.), *Oxford handbook of methods in positive psychology.* New York: Oxford University Press. (p. 111)

McCullough, M. E., & Laurenceau, J-P. (2005). Religiousness and the trajectory of self-rated health across adulthood. *Personality and Social Psychology Bulletin, 31,* 560–573. (p. 414)

McCullough, M. E., Hoyt, W. T., Larson, D. B., Koenig, H. G., & Thoresen, C. (2000). Religious involvement and mortality: A meta-analytic review. *Health Psychology, 19,* 211–222. (p. 414)

McDermott, T. (2005). *Perfect soldiers: The 9/11 hijackers: Who they were, why they did it.* New York: HarperCollins. (p. 550)

McEvoy, S. P., Stevenson, M. R., McCartt, A. T., Woodward, M., Hawroth, C., Palamara, P., & Ceracelli, R. (2005). Role of mobile phones in motor vehicle crashes resulting in hospital attendance: A case-crossover study. *British Medical Journal, 33,* 428. (p. 68)

McEvoy, S. P., Stevenson, M. R., & Woodward, M. (2007). The contribution of passengers versus mobile phone use to motor vehicle crashes resulting in hospital attendance by the driver. *Accident Analysis and Prevention, 39,* 1170–1176. (p. 68)

McFadden, D. (2002). Masculinization effects in the auditory system. *Archives of Sexual Behavior, 31,* 99–111. (p. 367)

McFarland, C., & Ross, M. (1987). The relation between current impressions and memories of self and dating partners. *Psychological Bulletin, 13,* 228–238. (p. 283)

McGaugh, J. L. (1994). Quoted by B. Bower, Stress hormones hike emotional memories. *Science News, 146,* 262. (p. 268)

McGaugh, J. L. (2003). *Memory and emotion: The making of lasting memories.* New York: Columbia University Press. (pp. 257, 269)

McGhee, P. E. (June, 1976). Children's appreciation of humor: A test of the cognitive congruency principle. *Child Development, 47*(2), 420–426. (p. 147)

McGrath, J. J., & Welham, J. L. (1999). Season of birth and schizophrenia: A systematic review and meta-analysis of data from the Southern hemisphere. *Schizophrenia Research, 35,* 237–242. (p. 484)

McGrath, J., Welham, J., & Pemberton, M. (1995). Month of birth, hemisphere of birth and schizophrenia. *British Journal of Psychiatry, 167,* 783–785. (p. 484)

McGue, M., & Bouchard, T. J., Jr. (1998). Genetic and environmental influences on human behavioral differences. *Annual Review of Neuroscience, 21,* 1–24. (p. 109)

McGue, M., Bouchard, T. J., Jr., Iacono, W. G., & Lykken, D. T. (1993). Behavioral genetics of cognitive ability: A life-span perspective. In R. Plomin & G. E. McClearn (Eds.), *Nature, nurture and psychology.* Washington, DC: American Psychological Association. (p. 325)

McGuire, M. T., Wing, R. R., Klem, M. L., Lang, W., & Hill, J. O. (1999). What predicts

weight regain in a group of successful weight losers? *Journal of Consulting and Clinical Psychology, 67,* 177–185. (p. 356)

McGurk, H., & MacDonald, J. (1976). Hearing lips and seeing voices. *Nature, 264,* 746–748. (p. 202)

McHugh, P. R. (1995a). Witches, multiple personalities, and other psychiatric artifacts. *Nature Medicine, 1*(2), 110–114. (p. 469)

McHugh, P. R. (1995b). Resolved: Multiple personality disorder is an individually and socially created artifact. *Journal of the American Academy of Child and Adolescent Psychiatry, 34,* 957–959. (p. 470)

McKenna, K. Y. A., & Bargh, J. A. (1998). Coming out in the age of the Internet: Identity "demarginalization" through virtual group participation. *Journal of Personality and Social Psychology, 75,* 681–694. (p. 540, 555)

McKenna, K. Y. A., & Bargh, J. A. (2000). Plan 9 from cyberspace: The implications of the Internet for personality and social psychology. *Personality and Social Psychology Review, 4,* 57–75. (p. 555)

McKenna, K. Y. A., Green, A. S., & Gleason, M. E. J. (2002). What's the big attraction? Relationship formation on the Internet. *Journal of Social Issues, 58,* 9–31. (p. 555)

McLaughlin, C. S., Chen, C., Greenberger, E., & Biermeier, C. (1997). Family, peer, and individual correlates of sexual experience among Caucasian and Asian American late adolescents. *Journal of Personality and Social Psychology: Journal of Research on Adolescence, 7,* 33–53. (p. 361)

McMurray, B. (2007). Defusing the childhood vocabulary explosion. *Science, 317,* 631. (p. 302)

McMurray, C. (2004, January 13). U.S., Canada, Britain: Who's getting in shape? *Gallup Poll Tuesday Briefing* (www.gallup.com). (p. 411)

McMurray, J. (2006, August 28). Cause of deadly Comair crash probed. Associated Press release. (p. 298)

McNally, R. J. (1999). EMDR and Mesmerism: A comparative historical analysis. *Journal of Anxiety Disorders, 13,* 225–236. (p. 509)

McNally, R. J. (2003). *Remembering trauma.* Cambridge, MA: Harvard University Press. (pp. 283, 286, 465)

McNally, R. J. (2007). Betrayal trauma theory: A critical appraisal. *Memory, 15,* 280–294. (p. 286)

McNally, R. J., Bryant, R. A., & Ehlers, A. (2003). Does early psychological intervention promote recovery from posttraumatic stress? *Psychological Science in the Public Interest, 4,* 45–79. (p. 465)

McNeil, B. J., Pauker, S. G., & Tversky, A. (1988). On the framing of medical decisions. In D. E. Bell, H. Raiffa, & A. Tversky (Eds.), *Decision making: Descriptive, normative, and prescriptive interactions.* New York: Cambridge University Press. (p. 300)

McPherson, J. M., Smith-Lovin, L., & Brashears, M. E. (2006). Social isolation in America: Changes in core discussion networks over two decades. *American Sociological Review, 71,* 353–375. (p. 478)

Meador, B. D., & Rogers, C. R. (1984). Person-centered therapy. In R. J. Corsini (Ed.), *Current psychotherapies* (3rd ed.). Itasca, IL: Peacock. (p. 497)

Medical Institute for Sexual Health. (1994, April). Condoms ineffective against human papilloma virus. *Sexual Health Update,* p. 2. (p. 362)

Mednick, S. A., Huttunen, M. O., & Machon, R. A. (1994). Prenatal influenza infections and adult schizophrenia. *Schizophrenia Bulletin, 20,* 263–267. (p. 483)

Mehl, M. R., Gosling, S. D., & Pennebaker, J. W. (2006). Personality in its natural habitat: Manifestations and implicit folk theories of personality in daily life. *Journal of Personality and Social Psychology, 90,* 862–877. (p. 438)

Mehl, M. R., & Pennebaker, J. W. (2003). The sounds of social life: A psychometric analysis of students' daily social environments and natural conversations. *Journal of Personality and Social Psychology, 84,* 857–870. (p. 17)

Mehl, M. R., Vazire, S., Ramirez-Esparza, N., Slatcher, R. B., & Pennebaker, J. W. (2007). Are women really more talkative than men? *Science, 317,* 82. (p. 128)

Mehta, M. R. (2007). Cortico-hippocampal interaction during up-down states and memory consolidation. *Nature Neuroscience, 10,* 13–15. (p. 271)

Meichenbaum, D. (1977). *Cognitive-behavior modification: An integrative approach.* New York: Plenum Press. (p. 502)

Meichenbaum, D. (1985). *Stress inoculation training.* New York: Pergamon. (p. 502)

Meltzoff, A. N. (1988). Infant imitation after a 1-week delay: Long-term memory for novel acts and multiple stimuli. *Developmental Psychology, 24,* 470–476. (p. 249)

Meltzoff, A. N., & Moore, M. K. (1989). Imitation in newborn infants: Exploring the range of gestures imitated and the underlying mechanisms. *Developmental Psychology, 25,* 954–962. (p. 249)

Meltzoff, A. N., & Moore, M. K. (1997). Explaining facial imitation: A theoretical model. *Early Development and Parenting, 6,* 179–192. (p. 249)

Melzack, R. (1990, February). The tragedy of needless pain. *Scientific American,* pp. 27–33. (p. 88)

Melzack, R. (1992, April). Phantom limbs. *Scientific American,* pp. 120–126. (p. 199)

Melzack, R. (1998, February). Quoted in Phantom limbs. *Discover,* p. 20. (p. 199)

Melzack, R. (2005). Evolution of the neuromatrix theory of pain. *Pain Practice, 5,* 85–94. (p. 199)

Melzack, R., & Wall, P. D. (1965). Pain mechanisms: A new theory. *Science, 150,* 971–979. (p. 199)

Melzack, R., & Wall, P. D. (1983). *The challenge of pain.* New York: Basic Books. (p. 199)

Mendle, J., Turkheimer, E., & Emery, R. E. (2007). Detrimental psychological outcomes associated with early pubertal timing in adolescent girls. *Developmental Review, 27,* 151–171. (p. 156)

Mendolia, M., & Kleck, R. E. (1993). Effects of talking about a stressful event on arousal: Does what we talk about make a difference? *Journal of Personality and Social Psychology, 64,* 283–292. (p. 410)

Merari, A. (2002). Explaining suicidal terrorism: Theories versus empirical evidence. Invited address to the American Psychological Association. (p. 540)

Merskey, H. (1992). The manufacture of personalities: The production of multiple personality disorder. *British Journal of Psychiatry, 160,* 327–340. (p. 469)

Merton, R. K. (1938; reprinted 1970). *Science, technology and society in seventeenth-century England.* New York: Fertig. (p. 12)

Merton, R. K., & Kitt, A. S. (1950). Contributions to the theory of reference group behavior. In R. K. Merton & P. F. Lazarsfeld (Eds.), *Continuities in social research: Studies in the scope and method of the American soldier.* Glencoe, IL: Free Press. (p. 395)

Merzenich, M. (2007). Quoted at Posit Science Brain Fitness Program (www.positscience.com). (p. 167)

Messinis, L., Kyprianidou, A., Malefaki, S., & Papathanasopoulos, P. (2006). Neuropsychological deficits in long-term frequent cannabis users. *Neurology, 66,* 737–739. (p. 96)

Mestel, R. (1997, April 26). Get real, Siggi. *New Scientist* (www.newscientist.com/ns/970426/siggi.html). (p. 81)

Meston, C. M., & Buss, D. M. (2007). Why humans have sex. *Archives of Sexual Behavior, 36,* 477–507. (p. 359)

Meston, C. M., & Frohlich, P. F. (2000). The neurobiology of sexual function. *Archives of General Psychiatry, 57,* 1012–1030. (p. 358)

Metcalfe, J. (1986). Premonitions of *insight* predict impending error. *Journal of Experimental Psychology: Learning, Memory, and Cognition, 12,* 623–634. (p. 293)

Metcalfe, J. (1998). Cognitive optimism: Self-deception or memory-based processing heuristics. *Personality and Social Psychology Review, 2,* 100–110. (p. 296)

Meyer-Bahlburg, H. F. L. (1995). Psycho-neuroendocrinology and sexual pleasure: The aspect of sexual orientation. In P. R. Abramson & S. D. Pinkerton (Eds.), *Sexual nature/sexual culture.* Chicago: University of Chicago Press. (p. 367)

Mezulis, A. M., Abramson, L. Y., Hyde, J. S., & Hankin, B. L. (2004). Is there a universal positivity bias in attributions? A meta-analytic review of individual, developmental, and cultural differences in the self-serving attributional bias. *Psychological Bulletin, 130,* 711–747. (p. 447)

Michaels, J. W., Bloomel, J. M., Brocato, R. M., Linkous, R. A., & Rowe, J. S. (1982). Social facilitation and inhibition in a natural setting. *Replications in Social Psychology, 2,* 21–24. (p. 538)

Middlebrooks, J. C., & Green, D. M. (1991). Sound localization by human listeners. *Annual Review of Psychology, 42,* 135–159. (p. 196)

Mikulincer, M., & Shaver, P. R. (2001). Attachment theory and intergroup bias: Evidence that priming the secure base schema attenuates negative reactions to out-groups. *Journal of Personality and Social Psychology, 81,* 97–115. (p. 547)

Milan, R. J., Jr., & Kilmann, P. R. (1987). Interpersonal factors in premarital contraception. *Journal of Sex Research, 23,* 289–321. (p. 361)

Miles, D. R., & Carey, G. (1997). Genetic and environmental architecture of human aggression. *Journal of Personality and Social Psychology, 72,* 207–217. (p. 548)

Milgram, S. (1963). Behavioral study of obedience. *Journal of Abnormal & Social Psychology, 67*(4), 371–378. (p. 534)

Milgram, S. (1974). *Obedience to authority.* New York: Harper & Row. (pp. 534, 535, 537)

Millar, J. K., & 19 others. (2005). DISC1 and PDE4B are interacting genetic factors in schizophrenia that regulate cAMP signaling. *Science, 310,* 1187–1191. (p. 485)

Miller, E. J., & Halberstadt, J. (2005). Media consumption, body image and thin ideals in New Zealand men and women. *New Zealand Journal of Psychology, 34,* 189–195. (p. 349)

Miller, E. J., Smith, J. E., & Trembath, D. L. (2000). The "skinny" on body size requests in personal ads. *Sex Roles, 43,* 129–141. (p. 351)

Miller, G. (2004). Axel, Buck share award for deciphering how the nose knows. *Science, 306,* 207. (p. 203)

Miller, G. (2008). Tackling alcoholism with drugs. *Science, 320,* 168–170. (p. 98)

Miller, G., Tybur, J. M., & Jordan, B. D. (2007). Ovulatory cycle effects on tip earnings by lap dancers: Economic evidence for human estrus? *Evolution and Human Behavior, 28,* 375–381. (p. 358)

Miller, G. A. (1956). The magical number seven, plus or minus two: Some limits on our capacity for processing information. *Psychological Review, 63,* 81–97. (p. 266)

Miller, G. E., & Wrosch, C. (2007). You've gotta know when to fold 'em. *Psychological Science, 18,* 773–777. (p. 401)

Miller, J. G., & Bersoff, D. M. (1995). Development in the context of everyday family relationships: Culture, interpersonal morality and adaptation. In M. Killen & D. Hart (Eds.), *Morality in everyday life: A developmental perspective.* New York: Cambridge University Press. (p. 158)

Miller, K. I., & Monge, P. R. (1986). Participation, satisfaction, and productivity: A meta-analytic review. *Academy of Management Journal, 29,* 727–753. (p. 441)

Miller, L. (2005, January 4). U.S. airlines have 34 deaths in 3 years. *Associated Press.* (p. 298)

Miller, L. K. (1999). The savant syndrome: Intellectual impairment and exceptional skill. *Psychological Bulletin, 125,* 31–46. (p. 314)

Miller, N. E. (1983). Understanding the use of animals in behavioral research: Some critical issues. *Annals of the New York Academy of Sciences, 406,* 113–118. (p. 26)

Miller, N. E. (1995). Clinical-experimental interactions in the development of neuroscience: A primer for nonspecialists and lessons for young scientists. *American Psychologist, 50,* 901–911. (p. 345)

Miller, P. J. O., Aoki, K., Rendell, L. E., & Amano, M. (2008). Stereotypical resting behavior of the sperm whale. *Current Biology, 18,* R21–R23. (p. 70)

Miller, S. D., Blackburn, T., Scholes, G., White, G. L., & Mamalis, N. (1991). Optical differences in multiple personality disorder: A second look. *Journal of Nervous and Mental Disease, 179,* 132–135. (p. 470)

Mills, M., & Melhuish, E. (1974). Recognition of mother's voice in early infancy. *Nature, 252,* 123–124. (p. 139)

Milton, J., & Wiseman, R. (2002). A response to Storm and Ertel (2002). *Journal of Parapsychology, 66,* 183–185. (p. 220)

Mineka, S. (1985). The frightful complexity of the origins of fears. In F. R. Brush & J. B. Overmier (Eds.), *Affect, conditioning and cognition: Essays on the determinants of behavior.* Hillsdale, NJ: Erlbaum. (p. 466)

Mineka, S., & Zinbarg, R. (1996). Conditioning and ethological models of anxiety disorders: Stress-in-dynamic-context anxiety models. In D. Hope (Ed.), *Perspectives on anxiety, panic, and fear* (Nebraska Symposium on Motivation). Lincoln: University of Nebraska Press. (pp. 465, 466)

Mineka, S., & Zinbarg, R. (2006). A contemporary learning theory perspective on the etiology of anxiety disorders: It's not what you thought it was. *American Psychologist, 61,* 10–26. (p. 465)

Miner-Rubino, K., Winter, D. G., & Stewart, A. J. (2004). Gender, social class, and the subjective experience of aging: Self-perceived personality change from early adulthood to late midlife. *Personality and Social Psychology Bulletin, 30,* 1599–1610. (p. 170)

Minsky, M. (1986). *The society of mind.* New York: Simon & Schuster. (p. 66)

Mischel, W. (1968). *Personality and assessment.* New York: Wiley. (p. 437)

Mischel, W. (1981). Current issues and challenges in personality. In L. T. Benjamin, Jr. (Ed.), *The G. Stanley Hall Lecture Series* (Vol. 1). Washington, DC: American Psychological Association. (p. 445)

Mischel, W. (1984). Convergences and challenges in the search for consistency. *American Psychologist, 39,* 351–364. (p. 437)

Mischel, W. (2004). Toward an integrative science of the person. *Annual Review of Psychology, 55,* 1–22. (p. 437)

Mischel, W., Shoda, Y., & Peake, P. K. (1988). The nature of adolescent competencies predicted by preschool delay of gratification. *Journal of Personality and Social Psychology, 54,* 687–696. (p. 158)

Mischel, W., Shoda, Y., & Rodriguez, M. L. (1989). Delay of gratification in children. *Science, 244,* 933–938. (pp. 158, 240)

Miserandino, M. (1991). Memory and the seven dwarfs. *Teaching of Psychology, 18,* 169–171. (p. 273)

Mita, T. H., Dermer, M., & Knight, J. (1977). Reversed facial images and the mere-exposure hypothesis. *Journal of Personality and Social Psychology, 35,* 597–601. (p. 556)

Mitchell, D. B. (2006). Nonconscious priming after 17 years: Invulnerable implicit memory? *Psychological Science, 17,* 925–929. (p. 258)

Mitchell, T. R., Thompson, L., Peterson, E., & Cronk, R. (1997). Temporal adjustments in the evaluation of events: The "rosy view." *Journal of Experimental Social Psychology, 33,* 421–448. (p. 263)

Mitte, K. (2005). Meta-analysis of cognitive-behavioral treatments for generalized anxiety disorder: A comparison with pharmacotherapy. *Psychological Bulletin, 131,* 785–795. (p. 503)

Moffitt, T. E., Caspi, A., Harrington, H., & Milne, B. J. (2002). Males on the life-course-persistent and adolescence-limited antisocial pathways: Follow-up at age 26 years. *Development and Psychopathology, 14,* 179–207. (p. 174)

Moffitt, T. E., Caspi, A., Harrington, H., Milne, B. J., Melchior, M., Goldberg, D., & Poulton, R. (2007a). Generalized anxiety disorder and depression: Childhood risk factors in a birth cohort followed to age 32. *Psychological Medicine, 37,* 441–452. (p. 462)

Moffitt, T. E., Caspi, A., & Rutter, M. (2006). Measured gene-environment interactions in psychopathology: Concepts, research strategies, and implications for research, intervention, and public understanding of genetics. *Perspectives on Psychological Science, 1,* 5–27. (p. 476)

Moffitt, T. E., Harrington, H., Caspi, A., Kim-Cohen, J., Goldberg, D., Gregory, A. M., & Poulton, R. (2007b). Depression and generalized anxiety disorder: Cumulative and sequential comorbidity in a birth cohort followed prospectively to age 32 years. *Archives of General Psychiatry, 64,* 651–660. (p. 462)

Moghaddam, F. M. (2005). The staircase to terrorism: A psychological exploration. *American Psychologist, 60,* 161–169. (p. 540)

Moises, H. W., Zoega, T., & Gottesman, I. I. (2002, July 3). The glial growth factors deficiency and synaptic destabilization hypothesis of schizophrenia. *BMC Psychiatry, 2*(8) (www.biomedcentral.com/1471-244X/2/8). (p. 484)

Mondloch, C. J., Lewis, T. L., Budreau, D. R., Maurer, D., Dannemiller, J. L., Stephens, B. R., & Kleiner-Gathercoal, K. A. (1999). Face perception during early infancy. *Psychological Science, 10,* 419–422. (p. 139)

Money, J. (1987). Sin, sickness, or status? Homosexual gender identity and psychoneuroendocrinology. *American Psychologist, 42,* 384–399. (pp. 365, 367)

Money, J., Berlin, F. S., Falck, A., & Stein, M. (1983). *Antiandrogenic and counseling treatment of sex offenders.* Baltimore: Department of Psychiatry and Behavioral Sciences, The Johns Hopkins University School of Medicine. (p. 359)

Mooallem, J. (2009, February 19). Rescue flight. *New York Times Magazine* (www.nytimes.com). (p. 150)

Moody, R. (1976). *Life after life.* Harrisburg, PA: Stackpole Books. (p. 95)

Mook, D. G. (1983). In defense of external invalidity. *American Psychologist, 38,* 379–387. (p. 25)

Moorcroft, W. H. (2003). *Understanding sleep and dreaming.* New York: Kluwer/Plenum. (pp. 72, 77, 83)

Moore, D. W. (2004, December 17). Sweet dreams go with a good night's sleep. *Gallup News Service* (www.gallup.com). (p. 74)

Moore, D. W. (2005, June 16). Three in four Americans believe in paranormal. *Gallup New Service* (www.gallup.com). (p. 218)

Moore, D. W. (2006, February 6). Britons out-drink Canadians, Americans. *Gallup News Service* (poll.gallup.com). (p. 99)

Moore, D. W. (2006, March 10). Close to 6 in 10 Americans want to lose weight. *Gallup News Service* (poll.gallup.com). (p. 355)

Moore, M. K., & Meltzoff, A. N. (2008). Factors affecting infants' manual search for occluded objects and the genesis of object permanence. *Infant Behavior & Development, 31,* 168–180. (p. 144)

Mor, N., & Winquist, J. (2002). Self-focused attention and negative affect: A meta-analysis. *Psychological Bulletin, 128,* 638–662. (p. 478)

Moreland, R. L., & Beach, S. R. (1992). Exposure effects in the classroom: The development of affinity among students. *Journal of Experimental Social Psychology, 28,* 255–276. (pp. 555, 556)

Morell, V. (1995). Zeroing in on how hormones affect the immune system. *Science, 269,* 773–775. (p. 403)

Morell, V. (2008, March). Minds of their own: Animals are smarter than you think. *National Geographic,* pp. 37–61. (p. 309)

Morelli, G. A., Rogoff, B., Oppenheim, D., & Goldsmith, D. (1992). Cultural variation in infants' sleeping arrangements: Questions of independence. *Developmental Psychology, 26,* 604–613. (p. 125)

Moreno, C., Laje, G., Blanco, C., Jiang, H., Schmidt, A. B., & Olfson, M. (2007). National trends in the outpatient diagnosis and treatment of bipolar disorder in youth. *Archives of General Psychiatry, 64,* 1032–1039. (p. 471)

Morey, R. A., Inan, S., Mitchell, T. V., Perkins, D. O., Lieberman, J. A., & Belger, A. (2005). Imaging frontostriatal function in ultra-high-risk, early, and chronic schizophrenia during executive processing. *Archives of General Psychiatry, 62,* 254–262. (p. 483)

Morgan, A. B., & Lilienfeld, S. O. (2000). A meta-analytic review of the relation between antisocial behavior and neuropsychological measures of executive function. *Clinical Psychology Review, 20,* 113–136. (p. 487)

Morin, R., & Brossard, M. A. (1997, March 4). Communication breakdown on drugs. *Washington Post,* pp. A1, A6. (p. 161)

Morrison, A. R. (2003). The brain on night shift. *Cerebrum, 5*(3), 23–36. (p. 74)

Morrison, C. (2007). *What does contagious yawning tell us about the mind?* Unpublished manuscript, University of Leeds. (p. 532)

Mortensen, E. L., Michaelsen, K. F., Sanders, S. A., & Reinisch, J. M. (2002). The association between duration of breastfeeding and adult intelligence. *Journal of the American Medical Association, 287,* 2365–2371. (p. 21)

Mortensen, P. B. (1999). Effects of family history and place and season of birth on the risk of schizophrenia. *New England Journal of Medicine, 340,* 603–608. (p. 483)

Moscovici, S. (1985). Social influence and conformity. In G. Lindzey & E. Aronson (Eds.), *The handbook of social psychology* (3rd ed). Hillsdale, N.J.: Erlbaum. (p. 541)

Moses, E. B., & Barlow, D. H. (2006). A new unified treatment approach for emotional disorders based on emotion science. *Current Directions in Psychological Science, 15,* 146–150. (p. 503)

Mosher, W. D., Chandra, A., & Jones, J. (2005, September 15). Sexual behavior and selected health measures: Men and women 15–44 years of age, United States, 2002. *Advance Data from Vital and Health Statistics*, No. 362, National Center for Health Statistics, Centers for Disease Control and Prevention, U.S. Department of Health and Human Services. (pp. 363, 364)

Moss, A. J., Allen, K. F., Giovino, G. A., & Mills, S. L. (1992, December 2). Recent trends in adolescent smoking, smoking-update correlates, and expectations about the future. *Advance Data No. 221* (from Vital and Health Statistics of the Centers for Disease Control and Prevention). (p. 92)

Moss, H. A., & Susman, E. J. (1980). Longitudinal study of personality development. In O. G. Brim, Jr., & J. Kagan (Eds.), *Constancy and change in human development*. Cambridge, MA: Harvard University Press. (p. 174)

Motivala, S. J., & Irwin, M. R. (2007). Sleep and immunity: Cytokine pathways linking sleep and health outcomes. *Current Directions in Psychological Science, 16*, 21–25. (p. 76)

Moulton, S. T., & Kosslyn, S. M. (2008). Using neuroimaging to resolve the psi debate. *Journal of Cognitive Neuroscience, 20*, 182–192. (p. 220)

Moyer, K. E. (1983). The physiology of motivation: Aggression as a model. In C. J. Scheier & A. M. Rogers (Eds.), *G. Stanley Hall Lecture Series* (Vol. 3). Washington, DC: American Psychological Association. (p. 548)

Mroczek, D. K. (2001). Age and emotion in adulthood. *Current Directions in Psychological Science, 10*, 87–90. (p. 170)

Mroczek, D. K., & Kolarz, D. M. (1998). The effect of age on positive and negative affect: A developmental perspective on happiness. *Journal of Personality and Social Psychology, 75*, 1333–1349. (p. 168)

Muhlnickel, W. (1998). Reorganization of auditory cortex in tinnitus. *Proceedings of the National Academy of Sciences, 95*, 10340–10343. (p. 53)

Mulcahy, N. J., & Call, J. (2006). Apes save tools for future use. *Science, 312*, 1038–1040. (p. 310)

Muller, J. E., Mittleman, M. A., Maclure, M., Sherwood, J. B., & Tofler, G. H. (1996). Triggering myocardial infarction by sexual activity. *Journal of the American Medical Association, 275*, 1405–1409. (p. 357)

Muller, J. E., & Verier, R. L. (1996). Triggering of sudden death—Lessons from an earthquake. *New England Journal of Medicine, 334*, 461. (p. 401)

Mullin, C. R., & Linz, D. (1995). Desensitization and resensitization to violence against women: Effects of exposure to sexually violent films on judgments of domestic violence victims. *Journal of Personality and Social Psychology, 69*, 449–459. (p. 253)

Mulrow, C. D. (1999, March). Treatment of depression—newer pharmacotherapies, summary. *Evidence Report/Technology Assessment, 7*. Agency for Health Care Policy and Research, Rockville, MD. (http://www.ahrq.gov/ clinic/ deprsumm.htm). (p. 515)

Murphy, G. E., & Wetzel, R. D. (1990). The lifetime risk of suicide in alcoholism. *Archives of General Psychiatry, 47*, 383–392. (p. 474)

Murphy, S. T., Monahan, J. L., & Zajonc, R. B. (1995). Additivity of nonconscious affect: Combined effects of priming and exposure. *Journal of Personality and Social Psychology, 69*, 589–602. (p. 381)

Murray, C. (2006). Changes over time in the Black-White difference on mental tests: Evidence from the children of the 1979 cohort of the National Longitudinal Survey of Youth. *Intelligence, 34*, 527–540. (p. 331)

Murray, C. (2007). The magnitude and components of change in the Black-White IQ difference from 1920 to 1991: A birth cohort analysis of the Woodcock-Johnson standardizations. *Intelligence, 35*, 305–318. (p. 331)

Murray, C. A., & Herrnstein, R. J. (1994, October 31). Race, genes and I.Q.—An apologia. *New Republic*, pp. 27–37. (p. 331)

Murray, C. J., & Lopez, A. D. (Eds.). (1996). *The global burden of disease: A comprehensive assessment of mortality and disability from diseases, injuries, and risk factors in 1990 and projected to 2020.* Cambridge, MA: Harvard University Press. (p. 453)

Murray, H. A., & Wheeler, D. R. (1937). A note on the possible clairvoyance of dreams. *Journal of Psychology, 3*, 309–313. (pp. 15, 219)

Murray, J. P. (2008). Media violence: The effects are both real and strong. *American Behavioral Scientist, 51*, 1212–1230. (p. 251)

Murray, R., Jones, P., O'Callaghan, E., Takei, N., & Sham, P. (1992). Genes, viruses, and neurodevelopmental schizophrenia. *Journal of Psychiatric Research, 26*, 225–235. (p. 483)

Murray, R. M., Morrison, P. D., Henquet, C., & Di Forti, M. (2007). Cannabis, the mind and society: The hash realities. *Nature Reviews: Neuroscience, 8*, 885–895. (p. 96)

Murray, S. L., Rose, P., Bellavia, G. M., Holmes, J. G., & Kusche, A. G. (2002). When rejection stings: How self-esteem constrains relationship-enhancement processes. *Journal of Personality and Social Psychology, 83*, 556–573. (p. 447)

Musick, M. A., Herzog, A. R., & House, J. S. (1999). Volunteering and mortality among older adults: Findings from a national sample. *Journals of Gerontology, 54B*, 173–180. (p. 414)

Mustanski, B. S., & Bailey, J. M. (2003). A therapist's guide to the genetics of human sexual orientation, *Sexual and Relationship Therapy, 18*, 1468–1479. (p. 366)

Mustanski, B. S., Bailey, J. M., & Kaspar, S. (2002). Dermatoglyphics, handedness, sex, and sexual orientation. *Archives of Sexual Behavior, 31*, 113–122. (p. 367)

Myers, D. G. (1993). *The pursuit of happiness*. New York: Harper. (pp. 396, 397)

Myers, D. G. (2000). *The American paradox: Spiritual hunger in an age of plenty.* New Haven, CT: Yale University Press. (p. 396)

Myers, D. G. (2001, December). Do we fear the right things? *American Psychological Society Observer*, p. 3. (p. 298)

Myers, D. G. (2002). *Intuition: Its powers and perils.* New Haven, CT: Yale University Press. (p. 20)

Myers, D. G. (2008). *Social psychology* (9th ed.). New York: McGraw-Hill. (p. 447)

Myers, D. G., & Bishop, G. D. (1970). Discussion effects on racial attitudes. *Science, 169*, 78–779. (p. 540)

Myers, D. G., & Diener, E. (1995). Who is happy? *Psychological Science, 6*, 10–19. (p. 396)

Myers, D. G., & Diener, E. (1996, May). The pursuit of happiness. *Scientific American.* (p. 396)

Myers, D. G., & Scanzoni, L. D. (2005). *What God has joined together?* San Francisco: HarperSanFrancisco. (pp. 169, 364)

Nagourney, A. (2002, September 25). For remarks on Iraq, Gore gets praise and scorn. *New York Times* (www.nytimes.com). (p. 528)

Nairn, R. G. (2007). Media portrayals of mental illness, or is it madness? A review. *Australian Psychologist, 42*, 138–146. (p. 460)

Napolitan, D. A., & Goethals, G. R. (1979). The attribution of friendliness. *Journal of Experimental Social Psychology, 15*, 105–113. (p. 526)

Nasar, J., Hecht, P., & Wener, R. (2008). Mobile telephones, distracted attention, and pedestrian safety. *Accident Analysis and Prevention, 40*, 69–75. (p. 68)

Nash, M. R. (2001, July). The truth and the hype of hypnosis. *Scientific American*, pp. 47–55. (p. 85)

National Academy of Sciences, Institute of Medicine. (1982). *Marijuana and health.* Washington, DC: National Academies Press. (p. 96)

National Academy of Sciences. (1999). *Marijuana and medicine: Assessing the science base* (by J. A. Benson, Jr. & S. J. Watson, Jr.). Washington, DC: National Academies Press. (p. 96)

National Academy of Sciences. (2001). *Exploring the biological contributions to human health: Does sex matter?* Washington, DC: Institute of Medicine, National Academies Press. (p. 129)

National Center for Complementary and Alternative Medicine. (2006). What is complementary and alternative medicine? nccam.nih.gov/ health/whatiscam. (p. 406)

National Center for Health Statistics. (1990). *Health, United States, 1989.* Washington, DC: U.S. Department of Health and Human Services. (p. 165)

National Center for Health Statistics. (2004, December 15). Marital status and health: United States, 1999–2002 (by Charlotte A. Schoenborn). *Advance Data from Vital and Human Statistics, number 351.* Centers for Disease Control and Prevention. (p. 410)

National Institute of Mental Health. (1982). *Television and behavior: Ten years of scientific progress and implications for the eighties.* Washington, DC: U. S. Government Printing Office. (p. 252)

National Institute of Mental Health. (1999). *ADHD: Attention deficit hyperactivity disorder.* Bethesda, MD: National Institute of Health Publication No. 96–3572, 1994, update July 1, 1999. (p. 455)

National Institute of Mental Health. (2003). *Attention deficit hyperactivity disorder.* Bethesda, MD: National Institute of Mental Health. (p. 455)

National Institute of Mental Health. (2008). The numbers count: Mental disorders in America (nimh.nih.gov). (pp. 458, 488, 489)

National Institute on Drug Abuse. (2004). NIDA InfoFacts: Marijuana. www.nida.nih.gov/ Infofax/marijuana.html. (p. 96)

National Institutes of Health. (1998). Clinical guidelines on the identification evaluation and treatment of overweight and obesity in adults. Executive summary, Obesity Education Initiative, National Heart, Lung, and Blood Institute. (p. 355)

National Research Council. (1990). *Human factors research needs for an aging population.* Washington, DC: National Academies Press. effect. (p. 164)

National Safety Council (2008). Transportation mode comparisons, from *Injury Facts* (via correspondence with Kevin T. Fearn, Research & Statistical Services Department). (p. 298)

National Sleep Foundation (2009) *2009 sleep in America poll: Summary of findings.* Washington, DC: National Sleep Foundation (www.sleepfoundation.org). (p. 79)

NCASA (2007). *Wasting the best and the brightest: Substance abuse at America's colleges and universities.* New York: National Center on Addiction and Drug Abuse, Columbia University. (p. 99)

NCHS (2007). *Health, United States, 2007.* Hyattsville, MD: National Center for Health Statistics. (p. 349)

NCTV News. (1987, July-August). More research links harmful effects to non-violent porn, p. 12. (p. 552)

Neese, R. M. (1991, November/December). What good is feeling bad? The evolutionary benefits of psychic pain. *The Sciences*, pp. 30–37. (pp. 198, 233)

Neidorf, S., & Morin, R. (2007, May 23). Four-in-ten Americans have close friends or relatives who are gay. *Pew Research Center Publications* (pewresearch.org). (p. 565)

Neisser, U. (1979). The control of information pickup in selective looking. In A. D. Pick (Ed.), *Perception and its development: A tribute to Eleanor J. Gibson.* Hillsdale, NJ: Erlbaum. (p. 69)

Neisser, U., Boodoo, G., Bouchard, T. J., Jr., Boykin, A. W., Brody, N., Ceci, S. J., Halpern, D. F., Loehlin, J. C., Perloff, R., Sternberg, R. J., & Urbina, S. (1996). Intelligence: Knowns and unknowns. *American Psychologist, 51,* 77–101. (pp. 325, 333)

Neisser, U., Winograd, E., & Weldon, M. S. (1991). Remembering the earthquake: "What I experienced" vs. "How I heard the news." Paper presented to the Psychonomic Society convention. (p. 269)

Neitz, J., Geist, T., & Jacobs, G. H. (1989). Color vision in the dog. *Visual Neuroscience, 3,* 119–125. (p. 191)

Nelson, C. A., III, Zeanah, C. H., Fox, N. A., Marshall, P. J., Smyke, A. T., & Guthrie, D. (2007). Cognitive recovery in socially deprived young children: The Bucharest Early Intervention Project. *Science, 318,* 1937–1940. (p. 326)

Nelson, M. D., Saykin, A. J., Flashman, L. A., & Riordan, H. J. (1998). Hippocampal volume reduction in schizophrenia as assessed by magnetic resonance imaging. *Archives of General Psychiatry, 55,* 433–440. (p. 483)

Nelson, N. (1988). *A meta-analysis of the life-event/health paradigm: The influence of social support.* Unpublished doctoral dissertation, Temple University, Philadelphia. (p. 410)

Nemeth, C. J., & Ormiston, M. (2007). Creative idea generation: Harmony versus stimulation. *European Journal of Social Psychology, 37,* 524–535. (p. 541)

Nesca, M., & Koulack, D. (1994). Recognition memory, sleep and circadian rhythms. *Canadian Journal of Experimental Psychology, 48,* 359–379. (p. 280)

Nestoriuc, Y., Rief, W., & Martin, A. (2008). Meta-analysis of biofeedback for tension-type headache: Efficacy, specificity, and treatment moderators. *Journal of Consulting and Clinical Psychology, 76,* 379–396. (p. 412)

Neumann, R., & Strack, F. (2000). "Mood contagion": The automatic transfer of mood between persons. *Journal of Personality and Social Psychology, 79,* 211–223. (p. 389, 532)

Newberg, A., & D'Aquili, E. (2001). *Why God won't go away: Brain science and the biology of belief.* New York: Simon & Schuster. (p. 413)

Newcomb, M. D., & Harlow, L. L. (1986). Life events and substance use among adolescents: Mediating effects of perceived loss of control and meaninglessness in life. *Journal of Personality and Social Psychology, 51,* 564–577. (p. 98)

Newcombe, N. S., Drummey, A. B., Fox, N. A., Lie, E., & Ottinger-Alberts, W. (2000). Remembering early childhood: How much, how, and why (or why not). *Current Directions in Psychological Science, 9,* 55–58. (p. 142)

Newman, A. J., Bavelier, D., Corina, D., Jezzard, P., & Neville, H. J. (2002). A critical period for right hemisphere recruitment in American Sign Language processing. *Nature Neuroscience, 5,* 76–80. (p. 305)

Newman, L. S., & Baumeister, R. F. (1996). Toward an explanation of the UFO abduction phenomenon: Hypnotic elaboration, extraterrestrial sadomasochism, and spurious memories. *Psychological Inquiry, 7,* 99–126. (p. 85)

Newport, E. L. (1990). Maturational constraints on language learning. *Cognitive Science, 14,* 11–28. (p. 305)

Newport, F. (2001, February). Americans see women as emotional and affectionate, men as more aggressive. *The Gallup Poll Monthly,* pp. 34–38. (p. 385)

Newport, F. (2002, July 29). Bush job approval update. *Gallup News Service* (www.gallup.com/poll/releases/pr020729.asp). (p. 566)

Newport, F. (2007, June 11). Majority of Republicans doubt theory of evolution. *Gallup Poll* (www.galluppoll.com). (p. 133)

Newport, F., Jones, J. M., Saad, L., & Carroll, J. (2007, April 27). Gallup poll review: 10 key points about public opinion on Iraq. *The Gallup Poll* (www.galluppoll.com). (p. 127)

Newport, F., Moore, D. W., Jones, J. M., & Saad, L. (2003, March 21). Special release: American opinion on the war. *Gallup Poll Tuesday Briefing* (www.gallup.com). (p. 530)

Nezlek, J. B. (2001). Daily psychological adjustment and the planfulness of day-to-day behavior. *Journal of Social and Clinical Psychology, 20,* 452–475. (p. 441)

Ng, S. H. (1990). Androcentric coding of *man* and *his* in memory by language users. *Journal of Experimental Social Psychology, 26,* 455–464. (p. 307)

Ng, W. W. H., Sorensen, K. L., & Eby, L. T. (2006). Locus of control at work: A meta-analysis. *Journal of Organizational Behavior, 27,* 1057–1087. (p. 441)

NHTSA. (2000). *Traffic safety facts 1999: Older population.* Washington, DC: National Highway Traffic Safety Administration (National Transportation Library: www.ntl.bts.gov). (p. 165)

NHTSA. (2006, April). The 100-car naturalistic driving study phase II: Results of the 100-car field experiment. Washington, DC: National Highway Traffic Safety Administration (www.nhtsa.gov). (p. 68)

Nickell, J. (1996, May/June). A study of fantasy proneness in the thirteen cases of alleged encounters in John Mack's abduction. *Skeptical Inquirer*, pp. 18–20, 54. (p. 85)

Nicol, S. E., & Gottesman, I. I. (1983). Clues to the genetics and neurobiology of schizophrenia. *American Scientist, 71,* 398–404. (p. 486)

Nicolaus, L. K., Cassel, J. F., Carlson, R. B., & Gustavson, C. R. (1983). Taste-aversion conditioning of crows to control predation on eggs. *Science, 220,* 212–214. (p. 233)

NIDA. (2002). Methamphetamine abuse and addiction. *Research Report Series.* National Institute on Drug Abuse, NIH Publication 02–4210. (p. 91)

NIDA. (2005, May). Methamphetamine. *NIDA Info Facts.* National Institute on Drug Abuse. (p. 91)

Nielsen, K. M., Faergeman, O., Larsen, M. L., & Foldspang, A. (2006). Danish singles have a twofold risk of acute coronary syndrome: Data from a cohort of 138,290 persons. *Journal of Epidemiology and Community Health, 60,* 721–728. (p. 410)

Niemiec, R. (2009, May 26). Personal communication from Education Director, VIA Institute on Character. (p. 459)

Nier, J. A. (2004). Why does the "above average effect" exist? Demonstrating idiosyncratic trait definition. *Teaching of Psychology, 31,* 53–54. (p. 448)

NIH. (2001, July 20). Workshop summary: Scientific evidence on condom effectiveness for sexually transmitted disease (STD) prevention. Bethesda: National Institute of Allergy and Infectious Diseases, National Institutes of Health. (p. 362)

NIH. (2006, December 4). NIDA researchers complete unprecedented scan of human genome that may help unlock the genetic contribution to tobacco addiction. *NIH News,* National Institutes of Health (www.nih.gov). (p. 98)

NIMH. (2002, April 26). U.S. suicide rates by age, gender, and racial group. National Institute of Mental Health (www.nimh.nih.gov/research/suichart.cfm). (p. 474)

NIMH. (2003). *Attention deficit hyperactivity disorder.* Bethesda, MD: National Institute of Mental Health. (p. 455)

Nisbett, R. E., & Cohen, D. (1996). *Culture of honor: The psychology of violence in the South.* Boulder, CO: Westview Press. (p. 551)

Nisbett, R. E., & Ross, L. (1980). *Human inference: Strategies and shortcomings of social judgment.* Englewood Cliffs, NJ: Prentice-Hall. (p. 294)

Nixon, G. M., Thompson, J. M. D., Han, D. Y., Becroft, D. M., Clark, P. M., Robinson, E., Waldie, K. E., Wild, C. J., Black, P. N., & Mitchell, E. A. (2008). Short sleep duration in middle childhood: Risk factors and consequences. *Sleep, 31,* 71–78. (p. 76)

Noel, J. G., Forsyth, D. R., & Kelley, K. N. (1987). Improving the performance of failing students by overcoming their self-serving attributional biases. *Basic and Applied Social Psychology, 8,* 151–162. (p. 442)

Noice, H., & Noice, T. (2006). What studies of actors and acting can tell us about memory and cognitive functioning. *Current Directions in Psychological Science, 15,* 14–18. (p. 263)

Nolen-Hoeksema, S. (2001). Gender differences in depression. *Current Directions in Psychological Science, 10,* 173–176. (p. 477)

Nolen-Hoeksema, S. (2003). *Women who think too much: How to break free of overthinking and reclaim your life.* New York: Holt. (p. 477)

Nolen-Hoeksema, S., & Larson, J. (1999). *Coping with loss.* Mahwah, NJ: Erlbaum. (p. 172)

NORC. (2007). National Opinion Research Center (University of Chicago) General Social Survey data, 1972 through 2004, accessed via sda.berkeley.edu. (p. 371)

Nordgren, L. F., van der Pligt, J., & van Harreveld, F. (2006). Visceral drives in retrospect: Explanations about the inaccessible past. *Psychological Science, 17,* 635–640. (p. 344)

Nordgren, L. F., van der Pligt, J., & van Harreveld, F. (2007). Evaluating Eve: Visceral states influence the evaluation of impulsive behavior. *Journal of Personality and Social Psychology, 93,* 75–84. (p. 344)

Norem, J. K. (2001). *The positive power of negative thinking: Using defensive pessimism to harness anxiety and perform at your peak.* New York: Basic Books. (p. 443)

Norton, K. L., Olds, T. S., Olive, S., & Dank, S. (1996). Ken and Barbie at life size. *Sex Roles, 34,* 287–294. (p. 349)

Norton, P. J., & Price, E. C. (2007). A meta-analytic review of adult cognitive-behavioral treatment outcome across the anxiety disorders. *Journal of Nervous and Mental Disease, 195,* 521–531. (p. 503)

Nowak, R. (1994). Nicotine scrutinized as FDA seeks to regulate cigarettes. *Science, 263,* 1555–1556. (p. 93)

Nowell, A., & Hedges, L. V. (1998). Trends in gender differences in academic achievement from 1960 to 1994: An analysis of differences in mean, variance, and extreme scores. *Sex Roles, 39,* 21–43. (p. 330)

NSF. (2001, October 24). Public bounces back after Sept. 11 attacks, national study shows. *NSF News,* National Science Foundation (www.nsf.gov/od/lpa/news/press/ol/pr0185.htm). (p. 400)

NSF. (2008). *2008 sleep in America poll.* National Sleep Foundation (sleepfoundation.org). (p. 75)

Nurnberger, J. I., Jr., & Bierut, L. J. (2007, April). Seeking the connections: Alcoholism and our genes. *Scientific American,* pp. 46–53. (p. 98)

Nuttin, J. M., Jr. (1987). Affective consequences of mere ownership: The name letter effect in twelve European languages. *European Journal of Social Psychology, 17,* 381–402. (p. 555)

O'Connor, A. (2004, February 6). Study details 30-year increase in calorie consumption. *New York Times* (www.nytimes.com). (p. 354)

O'Connor, A. (2004, May 14). Pressure to go along with abuse is strong, but some soldiers find strength to refuse. *New York Times* (www.nytimes.com). (p. 541)

O'Connor, P., & Brown, G. W. (1984). Supportive relationships: Fact or fancy? *Journal of Social and Personal Relationships, 1,* 159–175. (p. 511)

O'Donnell, L., Stueve, A., O'Donnell, C., Duran, R., San Doval, A., Wilson, R. F., Haber, D., Perry, E., & Pleck, J. H. (2002). Long-term reductions in sexual initiation and sexual activity among urban middle schoolers in the reach for health service learning program. *Journal of Adolescent Health, 31,* 93–100. (p. 362)

O'Keeffe, C., & Wiseman, R. (2005). Testing alleged mediumship: Methods and results. *British Journal of Psychology, 96,* 165–179. (p. 435)

O'Neil, J. (2002, September 3). Vital signs: Behavior: Parent smoking and teenage sex. *New York Times.* (p. 19)

O'Neill, M. J. (1993). The relationship between privacy, control, and stress responses in office workers. Paper presented to the Human Factors and Ergonomics Society convention. (p. 408)

O'Reardon, J. P., & 12 others. (2007). Efficacy and safety of transcranial magnetic stimulation in the acute treatment of major depression: A multisite randomized controlled trial. *Biological Psychiatry, 62,* 1208–1216. (p. 519)

Oaten, M., & Cheng, K. (2006a). Longitudinal gains in self-regulation from regular physical exercise. *British Journal of Health Psychology, 11,* 717–733. (p. 441)

Oaten, M., & Cheng, K. (2006b). Improved self-control: The benefits of a regular program of academic study. *Basic and Applied Social Psychology, 28,* 1–16. (p. 441)

Oberlander, J., & Gill, A. J. (2006). Language with character: A stratified corpus comparison of individual differences in e-mail communication. *Discourse Processes, 42,* 239–270. (p. 438)

Oberman, L. M., & Ramachandran, V. S. (2007). The simulating social mind: The role of the mirror neuron system and simulation in the social and communicative deficits of autism spectrum disorders. *Psychological Bulletin, 133,* 310–327. (p. 147)

Oetting, E. R., & Beauvais, F. (1987). Peer cluster theory, socialization characteristics, and adolescent drug use: A path analysis. *Journal of Counseling Psychology, 34,* 205–213. (p. 99)

Oetting, E. R., & Beauvais, F. (1990). Adolescent drug use: Findings of national and local surveys. *Journal of Social and Personal Relationships, 1,* 159–175. (p. 99)

Oettingen, G., & Mayer, D. (2002). The motivating function of thinking about the future: Expectations versus fantasies. *Journal of Personality and Social Psychology, 83,* 1198–1212. (p. 442)

Oettingen, G., & Seligman, M. E. P. (1990). Pessimism and behavioural signs of depression in East versus West Berlin. *European Journal of Social Psychology, 20,* 207–220. (p. 442)

Offer, D., Ostrov, E., Howard, K. I., & Atkinson, R. (1988). *The teenage world: Adolescents' self-image in ten countries.* New York: Plenum. (p. 161)

Ogden, C. L., Fryar, C. D., Carroll, M. D., & Flegal, K. M. (2004, October 27). Mean body weight, heights, and body mass index, United States 1960–2002. *Advance Data from Vital and Health Statistics,* No. 347. (p. 354)

Öhman, A. (1986). Face the beast and fear the face: Animal and social fears as prototypes for evolutionary analyses of emotion. *Psychophysiology, 23,* 123–145. (p. 466)

Öhman, A., Lundqvist, D., & Esteves, F. (2001). The face in the crowd revisited: A threat advantage with schematic stimuli. *Journal of Personality and Social Psychology, 80,* 381–396. (p. 384)

Oishi, S., Diener, E. F., Lucas, R. E., & Suh, E. M. (1999). Cross-cultural variations in predictors of life satisfaction: Perspectives from needs and values. *Personality and Social Psychology Bulletin, 25,* 980–990. (p. 342)

Olatunji, B. O., Cisler, J. M., & Tolin, D. T. (2007). Quality of life in the anxiety disorders: A meta-analytic review. *Clinical Psychology Review, 27,* 572–581. (p. 461)

Olds, J. (1958). Self-stimulation of the brain. *Science, 127,* 315–324. (p. 48)

Olds, J. (1975). Mapping the mind onto the brain. In F. G. Worden, J. P. Swazey, & G. Adelman (Eds.), *The neurosciences: Paths of discovery.* Cambridge, MA: MIT Press. (p. 48)

Olds, J., & Milner, P. (1954). Positive reinforcement produced by electrical stimulation of the septal area and other regions of rat brain. *Journal of Comparative and Physiological Psychology, 47,* 419–427. (p. 48)

Olff, M., Langeland, W., Draijer, N., & Gersons, B. P. R. (2007). Gender differences in posttraumatic stress disorder. *Psychological Bulletin, 135,* 183–204. (p. 465)

Olfson, M., Gameroff, M. J., Marcus, S. C., & Jensen, P. S. (2003). National trends in the treatment of attention deficit hyperactivity disorder. *American Journal of Psychiatry, 160,* 1071–1077. (p. 455)

Olfson, M., Marcus, S. C., Wan, G. J., & Geissler, E. C. (2004). National trends in the outpatient treatment of anxiety disorders. *Journal of Clinical Psychiatry, 65,* 1166–1173. (p. 514)

Olfson, M., Shaffer, D., Marcus, S. C., & Greenberg, T. (2003). Relationship between antidepressant medication treatment and suicide in adolescents. *Archives of General Psychiatry, 60,* 978–982. (p. 515)

Oliner, S. P., & Oliner, P. M. (1988). *The altruistic personality: Rescuers of Jews in Nazi Europe.* New York: Free Press. (p. 251)

Olshansky, S. J., Passaro, D. J., Hershow, R. C., Layden, J., Carnes, B. A., Brody, J., Hayflick, L., Butler, R. N., Allison, D. B., & Ludwig, D. S. (2005). A potential decline in life expectancy in the United States in the 21st century. *New England Journal of Medicine, 352,* 1138–1145. (p. 350)

Olsson, A., & Phelps, E. A. (2004). Learned fear of "unseen" faces after Pavlovian, observational, and instructed fear. *Psychological Science, 15,* 822–828. (p. 466)

Olweus, D., Mattsson, A., Schalling, D., & Low, H. (1988). Circulating testosterone levels and aggression in adolescent males: A causal analysis. *Psychosomatic Medicine, 50,* 261–272. (p. 549)

Oman, D., Kurata, J. H., Strawbridge, W. J., & Cohen, R. D. (2002). Religious attendance and cause of death over 31 years. *International Journal of Psychiatry in Medicine, 32,* 69–89. (p. 414)

Onishi, N. (2008, June 13). Japan, seeking trim waists, measures millions. *New York Times* (www.nytimes.com). (p. 350)

ORB (2008, January). Update on Iraqi casualty data. *Opinion Research Business* (London) (www.opinion.co.uk). (p. 525)

Oren, D. A., & Terman, M. (1998). Tweaking the human circadian clock with light. *Science, 279,* 333–334. (p. 71)

Orne, M. T., & Evans, F. J. (1965). Social control in the psychological experiment: Antisocial behavior and hypnosis. *Journal of Personality and Social Psychology, 1,* 189–200. (p. 85)

Osborne, C., Manning, W. D., & Smock, P. J. (2007). Married and cohabiting parents' relationship stability: A focus on race and ethnicity. *Journal of Marriage and Family, 69,* 1345–1366. (p. 169)

Osborne, J. W. (1997). Race and academic disidentification. *Journal of Educational Psychology, 89,* 728–735. (p. 334)

Osborne, L. (1999, October 27). A linguistic big bang. *New York Times Magazine* (www.nytimes.com). (p. 304)

Osgood, C. E. (1962). *An alternative to war or surrender.* Urbana: University of Illinois Press. (p. 567)

Osgood, C. E. (1980). GRIT: A strategy for survival in mankind's nuclear age? Paper presented at the Pugwash Conference on New Directions in Disarmament. (p. 567)

OSS Assessment Staff. (1948). *The assessment of men.* New York: Rinehart. (p. 445)

Ost, L. G., & Hugdahl, K. (1981). Acquisition of phobias and anxiety response patterns in clinical patients. *Behaviour Research and Therapy, 16,* 439–447. (p. 466)

Ostfeld, A. M., Kasl, S. V., D'Atri, D. A., & Fitzgerald, E. F. (1987). *Stress, crowding, and blood pressure in prison.* Hillsdale, NJ: Erlbaum. (p. 409)

Oswald, A. J., & Powdthavee, N. (2006). *Does happiness adapt? A longitudinal study of disability with implications for economists and judges* (Discussion Paper No. 2208). Bonn: Institute for the Study of Labor. (p. 393)

Ott, C. H., Lueger, R. J., Kelber, S. T., & Prigerson, H. G. (2007). Spousal bereavement in older adults: Common, resilient, and chronic grief with defining characteristics. *Journal of Nervous and Mental Disease, 195,* 332–341. (p. 172)

Ouellette, J. A., & Wood, W. (1998). Habit and intention in everyday life: The multiple processes by which past behavior predicts future behavior. *Psychological Bulletin, 124,* 54–74. (p. 445)

Overmier, J. B., & Murison, R. (1997). Animal models reveal the "psych" in the psychosomatics of peptic ulcers. *Current Directions in Psychological Science, 6,* 180–184. (p. 408)

Owen, A. M., Coleman, M. R., Boly, M., Davis, M. H., Laureys, S., & Pickard, J. D. (2006). Detecting awareness in the vegetative state. *Science, 313,* 1402. (p. 44)

Oxfam. (2005, March 26). Three months on: New figures show tsunami may have killed up to four times as many women as men. Oxfam Press Release (www.oxfam.org.uk). (p. 130)

Ozer, E. J., Best, S. R., Lipsey, T. L., & Weiss, D. S. (2003). Predictors of posttraumatic stress disorder and symptoms in adults: A meta-analysis. *Psychological Bulletin, 129,* 52–73. (p. 464)

Ozer, E. J., & Weiss, D. S. (2004). Who develops posttraumatic stress disorder. *Current Directions in Psychological Science, 13,* 169–172. (pp. 464, 465)

Özgen, E. (2004). Language, learning, and color perception. *Current Directions in Psychological Science, 13,* 95–98. (pp. 306, 307)

Pacifici, R., Zuccaro, P., Farre, M., Pichini, S., Di Carlo, S., Roset, P. N., Ortuno, J., Pujadus, M., Bacosi, A., Menoyo, E., Segura, J., & de la Torre, R. (2001). Effects of repeated doses of MDMA ("Ecstasy") on cell-mediated immune response in humans. *Life Sciences, 69,* 2931–2941. (p. 95)

Padgett, V. R. (1989). Predicting organizational violence: An application of 11 powerful principles of obedience. Paper presented to the American Psychological Association convention. (p. 536)

Page, S. (1977). Effects of the mental illness label in attempts to obtain accommodation. *Canadian Journal of Behavioral Science, 9,* 84–90. (p. 460)

Page, S. E. (2007). *The difference: How the power of diversity creates better groups, firms, schools, and societies.* Princeton, NJ: Princeton University Press. (p. 541)

Pagnin, D., de Queiroz, V., Pini, S., & Cassano, G. B. (2004). Efficacy of ECT in depression: A meta-analytic review. *Journal of ECT, 20,* 13–20. (p. 517)

Paivio, A. (1986). *Mental representations: A dual coding approach.* New York: Oxford University Press. (p. 263)

Palace, E. M. (1995). Modification of dysfunctional patterns of sexual response through autonomic arousal and false physiological feedback. *Journal of Consulting and Clinical Psychology, 63,* 604–615. (p. 381)

Palladino, J. J., & Carducci, B. J. (1983). "Things that go bump in the night": Students' knowledge of sleep and dreams. Paper presented at the meeting of the Southeastern Psychological Association. (p. 70)

Pallier, C., Colomé, A., & Sebastián-Gallés, N. (2001). The influence of native-language phonology on lexical access: Exemplar-based versus abstract lexical entries. *Psychological Science, 12,* 445–448. (p. 303)

Palmer, S., Schreiber, C., & Box, C. (1991). Remembering the earthquake: "Flashbulb" memory for experienced vs. reported events. Paper presented to the Psychonomic Society convention. (p. 269)

Pandelaere, M., & Dewitte, S. (2006). Is this a question? Not for long. The statement bias. *Journal of Experimental Social Psychology, 42,* 525–531. (p. 284)

Pandey, J., Sinha, Y., Prakash, A., & Tripathi, R. C. (1982). Right-left political ideologies and attribution of the causes of poverty. *European Journal of Social Psychology, 12,* 327–331. (p. 527)

Panksepp, J. (2007). Neurologizing the psychology of affects: How appraisal-based constructivism and basic emotion theory can coexist. *Perspectives on Psychological Science, 2,* 281–295. (p. 379)

Panzarella, C., Alloy, L. B., & Whitehouse, W. G. (2006). Expanded hopelessness theory of depression: On the mechanisms by which social support protects against depression. *Cognitive Theory and Research, 30,* 307–333. (p. 478)

Park, C. L. (2007). Religiousness/spirituality and health: A meaning systems perspective. *Journal of Behavioral Medicine, 30,* 319–328. (p. 414)

Park, D. C., Lautenschlager, G., Hedden, T., Davidson, N. S., Smith, A. D., & Smith, P. K. (2002). Models of visuospatial and verbal memory across the adult life span. *Psychology and Aging, 17,* 299–320. (p. 167)

Park, G., Lubinski, D., & Benbow, C. P. (2007). Contrasting intellectual patterns predict creativity in the arts and sciences. *Psychological Science, 18,* 948–952. (p. 322)

Park, R. L. (1999, July 12). Liars never break a sweat. *New York Times* (www.nytimes.com). (p. 380)

Parker, E. S., Cahill, L., & McGaugh, J. L. (2006). A case of unusual autobiographical remembering. *Neurocase, 12,* 35–49. (p. 276)

Parker, S., Nichter, M., Nichter, M., & Vuckovic, N. (1995). Body image and weight concerns among African American and white adolescent females: Differences that make a difference. *Human Organization, 54,* 103–114. (p. 347)

Passell, P. (1993, March 9). Like a new drug, social programs are put to the test. *New York Times,* pp. C1, C10. (p. 23)

Pastalkova, E., Serrano, P., Pinkhasova, D., Wallace, E., Fenton, A. A., & Sacktor, T. C. (2006). Storage of spatial information by the maintenance mechanism of LTP. *Science, 313,* 1141–1144. (p. 268)

Pate, J. E., Pumariega, A. J., Hester, C., & Garner, D. M. (1992). Cross-cultural patterns in eating disorders: A review. *Journal of the American Academy of Child and Adolescent Psychiatry, 31,* 802–809. (p. 348)

Patel, S. R., Malhotra, A., White, D. P., Gottlieb, D. J., & Hu, F. B. (2006). Association between reduced sleep and weight gain in women. *American Journal of Epidemiology, 164,* 947–954. (p. 76)

Patrick, H., Knee, C. R., Canevello, A., & Lonsbary, C. (2007). The role of need fulfillment in relationship functioning and well-being: A self-determination theory perspective. *Journal of Personality and Social Psychology, 92,* 434–457. (p. 370)

Patten, S. B., Wang, J. L., Williams, J. V. A., Currie, S., Beck, C. A., Maxwell, C. J., & el-Guebaly, N. (2006). Descriptive epidemiology of major depression in Canada. *Canadian Journal of Psychiatry, 51,* 84–90. (p. 471)

Patterson, D. R. (2004). Treating pain with hypnosis. *Current Directions in Psychological Science, 13,* 252–255. (p. 85)

Patterson, F. (1978, October). Conversations with a gorilla. *National Geographic,* pp. 438–465. (p. 311)

Patterson, G. R. (2005). The next generation of PTMO models. *The Behavior Therapist, 28,* 27–33. (p. 242)

Patterson, G. R., Chamberlain, P., & Reid, J. B. (1982). A comparative evaluation of parent training procedures. *Behavior Therapy, 13,* 638–650. (pp. 242, 551)

Patterson, G. R., Reid, J. B., & Dishion, T. J. (1992). *Antisocial boys.* Eugene, OR: Castalia. (p. 551)

Patterson, P. H. (2007). Maternal effects on schizophrenia risk. *Science, 318,* 576–577. (p. 483)

Patterson, R. (1951). *The riddle of Emily Dickinson.* Boston: Houghton Mifflin. (p. 480)

Patton, G. C., Coffey, C., Carlin, J. B., Degenhardt, L., Lynskey, M., & Hall, W. (2002). Cannabis use and mental health of young people: Cohort study. *British Medical Journal, 325,* 1195–1198. (p. 96)

Paulesu, E., Demonet, J-F., Fazio, F., McCrory, E., Chanoine, V., Brunswick, N., Cappa, S. F., Cossu, G., Habib, M., Frith, C. D., & Frith, U. (2001). Dyslexia: Cultural diversity and biological unity. *Science, 291,* 2165–2167. (p. 26)

Paulos, J. A. (1995). *A mathematician reads the newspaper.* New York: Basic Books. (p. 516)

Paus, T., Zijdenbos, A., Worsley, K., Collins, D. L., Blumenthal, J., Giedd, J. N., Rapoport, J. L., & Evans, A. C. (1999). Structural maturation of neural pathways in children and adolescents: In vivo study. *Science, 283,* 1908–1911. (p. 140)

Pavlov, I. (1927). *Conditioned reflexes: An investigation of the physiological activity of the cerebral cortex.* Oxford: Oxford University Press. (p. 228)

Payne, B. K. (2006). Weapon bias: Split-second decisions and unintended stereotyping. *Current Directions in Psychological Science, 15,* 287–291. (p. 543)

Payne, B. K., & Corrigan, E. (2007). Emotional constraints on intentional forgetting. *Journal of Experimental Social Psychology, 43,* 780–786. (p. 281)

Pedersen, N. L., Plomin, R., McClearn, G. E., & Friberg, L. (1988). Neuroticism, extraversion, and related traits in adult twins reared apart and reared together. *Journal of Personality and Social Psychology, 55,* 950–957. (p. 109)

Peeters, A., Barendregt, J. J., Willekens, F., Mackenbach, J. P., & Mamum, A. A. (2003). Obesity in adulthood and its consequences for life expectancy: A life-table analysis. *Annals of Internal Medicine, 138,* 24–32. (p. 350)

Peigneux, P., Laureys, S., Fuchs, S., Collette, F., Perrin, F., Reggers, J., Phillips, C., Degueldre, C., Del Fiore, G., Aerts, J., Luxen, A., & Maquet, P. (2004). Are spatial memories strengthened in the human hippocampus during slow wave sleep? *Neuron, 44,* 535–545. (pp. 77, 271)

Pekkanen, J. (1982, June). Why do we sleep? *Science, 82,* p. 86. (p. 78)

Pelham, B. W. (1993). On the highly positive thoughts of the highly depressed. In R. F. Baumeister (Ed.), *Self-esteem: The puzzle of low self-regard.* New York: Plenum. (p. 447)

Pendick, D. (1994, January/February). The mind of violence. *Brain Work: The Neuroscience Newsletter,* pp. 1–3, 5. (p. 549)

Pennebaker, J. (1990). *Opening up: The healing power of confiding in others.* New York: William Morrow. (p. 426)

Pennebaker, J. W. (2002, January 28). Personal communication. (p. 566)

Pennebaker, J. W., Barger, S. D., & Tiebout, J. (1989). Disclosure of traumas and health among Holocaust survivors. *Psychosomatic Medicine, 51,* 577–589. (p. 410)

Pennebaker, J. W., & O'Heeron, R. C. (1984). Confiding in others and illness rate among spouses of suicide and accidental death victims. *Journal of Abnormal Psychology, 93,* 473–476. (p. 410)

Pennebaker, J. W., & Stone, L. D. (2003). Words of wisdom: Language use over the life span. *Journal of Personality and Social Psychology, 85,* 291–301. (p. 171)

Penny, H., & Haddock, G. (2007). Anti-fat prejudice among children: The "mere proximity" effect in 5–10 year olds. *Journal of Experimental Social Psychology, 43,* 678–683. (p. 351)

Peplau, L. A. (1982). Research on homosexual couples: An overview. *Journal of Homosexuality, 8(2),* 3–8. 229–240. (p. 364)

Peplau, L. A., & Fingerhut, A. W. (2007). The close relationships of lesbians and gay men. *Annual Review of Psychology, 58,* 405–424. (pp. 169, 363)

Peplau, L. A., & Garnets, L. D. (2000). A new paradigm for understanding women's sexuality and sexual orientation. *Journal of Social Issues, 56,* 329–350. (p. 364)

Peppard, P. E., Szklo-Coxe, M., Hia, K. M., & Young, T. (2006). Longitudinal association of sleep-related breathing disorder and depression. *Archives of Internal Medicine, 166,* 1709–1715. (p. 79)

Pepperberg, I. M. (2006). Grey parrot numerical competence: A review. *Animal Cognition, 9,* 377–391. (p. 310)

Pereira, A. C., Huddleston, D. E., Brickman, A. M., Sosunov, A. A., Hen, R., McKhann, G. M., Sloan, R., Gage, F. H., Brown, T. R., & Small, S. A. (2007). An *in vivo* correlate of exercise-induced neurogenesis in the adult dentate gyrus. *Proceedings of the National Academy of Sciences, 104,* 5638–5643. (pp. 57, 166)

Pereira, G. M., & Osburn, H. G. (2007). Effects of participation in decision making on performance and employee attitudes: A quality circles meta-analysis. *Journal of Business Psychology, 22,* 145–153. (p. 166)

Perkins, A., & Fitzgerald, J. A. (1997). Sexual orientation in domestic rams: Some biological and social correlates. In L. Ellis & L. Ebertz (Eds.), *Sexual orientation: Toward biological understanding.* Westport, CT: Praeger Publishers. (p. 365)

Perlmutter, M. (1983). Learning and memory through adulthood. In M. W. Riley, B. B. Hess, & K. Bond (Eds.), *Aging in society: Selected reviews of recent research.* Hillsdale, NJ: Erlbaum. (p. 167)

Perls, T., & Silver, M. H., with Lauerman, J. F. (1999). *Living to 100: Lessons in living to your maximum potential.* Thorndike, ME: Thorndike Press. (p. 404)

Perra, O., Williams, J. H. G., Whiten, A., Fraser, L., Benzie, H., & Perrett, D. I. (2008). Imitation and 'theory of mind' competencies in discrimination of autism from other neurodevelopmental disorders. *Research in Autism Disorders, 2,* 456–468. (p. 147)

Perrett, D. I., Harries, M., Misflin, A. J., & Chitty, A. J. (1988). Three stages in the classification of body movements by visual neurons. In H. B. Barlow, C. Blakemore, & M. Weston Smith (Eds.), *Images and understanding.* Cambridge: Cambridge University Press. (p. 189)

Perrett, D. I., Hietanen, J. K., Oram, M. W., & Benson, P. J. (1992). Organization and functions of cells responsive to faces in the temporal cortex. *Philosophical Transactions of the Royal Society of London: Series B, 335,* 23–30. (p. 189)

Perrett, D. I., Lee, K. J., Penton-Voak, I., Rowland, D., Yoshikawa, S., Burt, D. M., Henzi, S. P., Castles, D. L., & Akamatsu, S. (1998, August). Effects of sexual dimorphism on facial attractiveness. *Nature, 394,* 884–887. (p. 544)

Perrett, D. I., May, K. A., & Yoshikawa, S. (1994). Facial shape and judgments of female attractiveness. *Nature, 368,* 239–242. (p. 189)

Persky, S., & Blascovich, J. (2005). Consequences of playing violent video games in immersive virtual environments. In A. Axelsson & R. Schroeder (Eds.). *Work and play in shared virtual environments.* New York: Springer. (p. 552)

Pert, C. (1986). Quoted in J. Hooper & D. Teresi, *The three-pound universe.* New York: Macmillan. (p. 49)

Pert, C. B., & Snyder, S. H. (1973). Opiate receptor: Demonstration in nervous tissue. *Science, 179,* 1011–1014. (p. 38)

Perugini, E. M., Kirsch, I., Allen, S. T., Coldwell, E., Meredith, J., Montgomery, G. H., & Sheehan, J. (1998). Surreptitious observation of responses to hypnotically suggested hallucinations: A test of the compliance hypothesis. *International Journal of Clinical and Experimental Hypnosis, 46,* 191–203. (p. 86)

Peschel, E. R., & Peschel, R. E. (1987). Medical insights into the castrati in opera. *American Scientist, 75,* 578–583. (p. 359)

Peters, T. J., & Waterman, R. H., Jr. (1982). *In search of excellence: Lessons from America's best-run companies.* New York: Harper & Row. (p. 245)

Peterson, C., & Barrett, L. C. (1987). Explanatory style and academic performance among university freshmen. *Journal of Personality and Social Psychology, 53,* 603–607. (p. 442)

Peterson, C., Peterson, J., & Skevington, S. (1986). Heated argument and adolescent development. *Journal of Social and Personal Relationships, 3,* 229–240. (p. 157)

Peterson, C., & Seligman, M. E. P. (2004). *Character strengths and virtues: A handbook and classification.* New York: Oxford University Press. (p. 458)

Peterson, L. R., & Peterson, M. J. (1959). Short-term retention of individual verbal items. *Journal of Experimental Psychology, 58,* 193–198. (p. 266)

Petitto, L. A., & Marentette, P. F. (1991). Babbling in the manual mode: Evidence for the ontogeny of language. *Science, 251,* 1493–1496. (p. 303)

Petry, N. M., Barry, D., Pietrzak, R. H., & Wagner, J. A. (2008). Overweight and obesity are associated with psychiatric disorders:

Results from the National Epidemiologic Survey on Alcohol and Related Conditions. *Psychosomatic Medicine, 70,* 288–297. (p. 351)

Pettegrew, J. W., Keshavan, M. S., & Minshew, N. J. (1993). 31P nuclear magnetic resonance spectroscopy: Neurodevelopment and schizophrenia. *Schizophrenia Bulletin, 19,* 35–53. (p. 483)

Petticrew, C., Bell, R., & Hunter, D. (2002). Influence of psychological coping on survival and recurrence in people with cancer: Systematic review. *British Medical Journal, 325,* 1066. (p. 405)

Petticrew, M., Fraser, J. M., & Regan, M. F. (1999). Adverse life events and risk of breast cancer: A meta-analysis. *British Journal of Health Psychology, 4,* 1–17. (p. 405)

Pettifor, J. P. (2004). Professional ethics across national boundaries. *European Psychologist, 9,* 264–272. (p. 27)

Pettigrew, T. F. (1998). Reactions toward the new minorities of western Europe. *Annual Review of Sociology, 24,* 77-103. (p. 544)

Pettigrew, T. F. (2006). A two-level approach to anti-immigrant prejudice and discrimination. In R. Mahalingam (Ed.), *Cultural psychology of immigrants.* Mahwah, NJ: Erlbaum. (p. 544)

Pettigrew, T. F., Christ, O., Wagner, U., & Stellmacher, J. (2007). Direct and indirect intergroup contact effects on prejudice: A normative interpretation. *International Journal of Intercultural Relations, 31,* 411–425. (p. 565)

Pettigrew, T. F., & Tropp, L. R. (2006). A meta-analytic test of intergroup contact theory. *Journal of Personality and Social Psychology, 90,* 751–783. (p. 565)

Pew. (2003). *Views of a changing world 2003. The Pew Global Attitudes Project.* Washington, DC: Pew Research Center for the People and the Press (http://people-press.org/reports/pdf/185.pdf). (p. 130)

Pew. (2006, September 21). Publics of Asian powers hold negative views of one another. Pew Global Attitudes Project Report, Pew Research Center (pewresearch.org). (p. 546)

Pew. (2007, January 24). Global warming: A divide on causes and solutions. Pew Research Center for the People and the Press. (p. 296)

Pew Research Center. (2006, November 14). Attitudes toward homosexuality in African countries (pewresearch.org). (p. 363)

Pew Research Center. (2007, July 18). Modern marriage: "I like hugs. I like kisses. But what I really love is help with the dishes." Pew Research Center (www.pewresearch.org). (p. 560)

Pfammatter, M., Junghan, U. M., Brenner, H. D. (2006). Efficacy of psychological therapy in schizophrenia: Conclusions from meta-analyses. *Schizophrenia Bulletin, 32,* S64–S80. (p. 507)

Phelps, J. A., Davis J. O., & Schartz, K. M. (1997). Nature, nurture, and twin research strategies. *Current Directions in Psychological Science, 6,* 117–120. (p. 485)

Philip Morris. (2003). Philip Morris USA youth smoking prevention. Teenage attitudes and behavior study, 2002. In "Raising kids who don't smoke," vol. 1(2). (p. 93)

Philip Morris Companies, Inc. (1999, October 13). Referenced in Myron Levin, Philip Morris'

new campaign echoes medical experts, *Los Angeles Times.* (p. 92)

Phillips, D. P. (1985). Natural experiments on the effects of mass media violence on fatal aggression: Strengths and weaknesses of a new approach. In L. Berkowitz (Ed.), *Advances in experimental social psychology* (Vol. 19). Orlando, FL: Academic Press. (p. 532)

Phillips, D. P., Carstensen, L. L., & Paight, D. J. (1989). Effects of mass media news stories on suicide, with new evidence on the role of story content. In D. R. Pfeffer (Ed.), *Suicide among youth: Perspectives on risk and prevention.* Washington, DC: American Psychiatric Press. (p. 532)

Phillips, J. L. (1969). *Origins of intellect: Piaget's theory.* San Francisco: Freeman. (p. 145)

Piaget, J. (1930). *The child's conception of physical causality.* London: Routledge & Kegan Paul. (p. 143)

Piaget, J. (1932). *The moral judgment of the child.* New York: Harcourt, Brace & World. (p. 158)

Picchioni, M. M., & Murray, R. M. (2007). Schizophrenia. *British Medical Journal, 335,* 91–95. (p. 482)

Pieters, G. L. M., de Bruijn, E. R. A., Maas, Y., Hultijn, W., Vandereycken, W., Peuskens, J., & Sabbe, B. G. (2007). Action monitoring and perfectionism in anorexia nervosa. *Brain and Cognition, 63,* 42–50. (p. 348)

Pike, K. M., & Rodin, J. (1991). Mothers, daughters, and disordered eating. *Journal of Abnormal Psychology, 100,* 198–204. (p. 348)

Piliavin, J. A. (2003). Doing well by doing good: Benefits for the benefactor. In C. L. M. Keyes & J. Haidt (Eds.), *Flourishing: Positive psychology and the life well-lived.* Washington, DC: American Psychological Association. (p. 158)

Pillemer, D. (1998). *Momentous events, vivid memories.* Cambridge, MA: Harvard University Press. (p. 166)

Pillemer, D. B., Ivcevic, Z., Gooze, R. A., & Collins, K. A. (2007). Self-esteem memories: Feeling good about achievement success, feeling bad about relationship distress. *Personality and Social Psychology Bulletin, 33,* 1292–1305. (p. 371)

Pillemer, D. G. (1995). *What is remembered about early childhood events?* Invited paper presentation to the American Psychological Society convention. (p. 141)

Pillsworth, E. G., & Haselton, M. G. (2006). Male sexual attractiveness predicts differential ovulatory shifts in female extra-pair attraction and male mate retention. *Evolution and Human Behavior, 27,* 247–258. (p. 358)

Pillsworth, M. G., & Haselton, M. G., & Buss, D. M. (2004). Ovulatory shifts in female desire. *Journal of Sex Research, 41,* 55–65. (p. 358)

Pinel, J. P. J. (1993). *Biopsychology* (2nd ed). Boston: Allyn & Bacon. (p. 345)

Pingitore, R., Dugoni, B. L., Tindale, R. S., & Spring, B. (1994). Bias against overweight job applicants in a simulated employment interview. *Journal of Applied Psychology, 79,* 909–917. (p. 351)

Pinker, S. (1990, September-October). Quoted by J. de Cuevas, "No, she holded them loosely." *Harvard Magazine,* pp. 60–67. (p. 302)

Pinker, S. (1995). The language instinct. *The General Psychologist, 31,* 63–65. (p. 312)

Pinker, S. (1998). Words and rules. *Lingua, 106,* 219–242. (p. 302)

Pinker, S. (2002, September 9). A biological understanding of human nature: A talk with Steven Pinker. *The Edge Third Culture Mail List* (www.edge.org). (pp. 110, 114)

Pinker, S. (2005, April 22). *The science of gender and science: A conversation with Elizabeth Spelke.* Harvard University (www.edge.org). (p. 330)

Pinker, S. (2007, March 19). A history of violence. *New Republic* (available at www.edge.org). (p. 296)

Pinker, S. (2008). *The sexual paradox: Men, women, and the real gender gap.* New York: Scribner. (p. 128)

Pinstrup-Andersen, P., & Cheng, F. (2007). Still hungry. *Scientific American, 297,* 96–103. (p. 354)

Pipe, M-E. (1996). Children's eyewitness memory. *New Zealand Journal of Psychology, 25,* 36–43. (p. 284)

Pipe, M-E., Lamb, M. E., Orbach, Y., & Esplin, P. W. (2004). Recent research on children's testimony about experienced and witnessed events. *Developmental Review, 24,* 440–468. (p. 285)

Piper, A., Jr. (1998, Winter). Multiple personality disorder: Witchcraft survives in the twentieth century. *Skeptical Inquirer,* pp. 44–50. (p. 469)

Pipher, M. (2002). *The middle of everywhere: The world's refugees come to our town.* New York: Harcourt Brace. (pp. 371, 401)

Pitman, R. K., & Delahanty, D. L. (2005). Conceptually driven pharmacologic approaches to acute trauma. *CNS Spectrums, 10*(2), 99–106. (p. 269)

Pitman, R. K., Sanders, K. M., Zusman, R. M., Healy, A. R., Cheema, F., Lasko, N. B., Cahill, L., & Orr, S. P. (2002). Pilot study of secondary prevention of posttraumatic stress disorder with propranolol. *Biological Psychiatry, 51,* 189–192. (p. 269)

Plassmann, H., O'Doherty, J., Shiv, B., & Rangel, A. (2008). Marketing actions can modulate neural representations of experienced pleasantness. *Proceedings of the National Academy of Sciences, 105,* 1050–1054. (p. 202)

Pliner, P. (1982). The effects of mere exposure on liking for edible substances. *Appetite: Journal for Intake Research, 3,* 283–290. (p. 347)

Pliner, P., Pelchat, M., & Grabski, M. (1993). Reduction of neophobia in humans by exposure to novel foods. *Appetite, 20,* 111–123. (p. 347)

Plöderl, M., & Fartacek, R. (2005). Suicidality and associated risk factors among lesbian, gay, and bisexual compared to heterosexual Austrian adults. *Suicide and Life-Threatening Behavior, 35,* 661–670. (p. 363)

Plomin, R. (1999). Genetics and general cognitive ability. *Nature, 402* (Suppl), C25–C29. (pp. 314, 324)

Plomin, R. (2001). Genetics and behaviour. *The Psychologist, 14,* 134–139. (p. 324)

Plomin, R. (2003). General cognitive ability. In R. Plomin, J. C. DeFries, I. W. Craig, & P. McGuffin (Eds.), *Behavioral genetics in a postgenomic world.* Washington, DC: APA Books. (p. 325)

Plomin, R., & Bergeman, C. S. (1991). The nature of nurture: Genetic influence on "environmental" measures. *Behavioral and Brain Sciences, 14,* 373–427. (p. 112)

Plomin, R., Corley, R., Caspi, A., Fulker, D. W., & DeFries, J. (1998). Adoption results for self-reported personality: Evidence for non-additive genetic effects? *Journal of Personality and Social Psychology, 75,* 211–219. (p. 109)

Plomin, R., & Daniels, D. (1987). Why are children in the same family so different from one another? *Behavioral and Brain Sciences, 10,* 1–60. (p. 120)

Plomin, R., & DeFries, J. C. (1998, May). The genetics of cognitive abilities and disabilities. *Scientific American,* pp. 62–69. (p. 326)

Plomin, R., DeFries, J. C., McClearn, G. E., & Rutter, M. (1997). *Behavioral genetics.* New York: Freeman. (pp. 107, 113, 326, 353, 366, 484)

Plomin, R., & Kovas, Y. (2005). Generalist genes and learning disabilities. *Psychological Bulletin, 131,* 592–617. (p. 325)

Plomin, R., McClearn, G. E., Pedersen, N. L., Nesselroade, J. R., & Bergeman, C. S. (1988). Genetic influence on childhood family environment perceived retrospectively from the last half of the life span. *Developmental Psychology, 24,* 37–45. (p. 112)

Plomin, R., & McGuffin, P. (2003). Psychopathology in the postgenomic era. *Annual Review of Psychology, 54,* 205–228. (p. 476)

Plomin, R., Reiss, D., Hetherington, E. M., & Howe, G. W. (January, 1994). Nature and nurture: Genetic contributions to measures of the family environment. *Developmental Psychology, 30*(1), 32–43. (p. 112)

Plotkin, H. (1994). *Darwin machines and the nature of knowledge.* Cambridge, MA: Harvard University Press. (p. 474)

Plous, S., & Herzog, H. A. (2000). Poll shows researchers favor lab animal protection. *Science, 290,* 711. (p. 27)

Polivy, J., & Herman, C. P. (1985). Dieting and binging: A causal analysis. *American Psychologist, 40,* 193–201. (p. 356)

Polivy, J., & Herman, C. P. (1987). Diagnosis and treatment of normal eating. *Journal of Personality and Social Psychology, 55,* 635–644. (p. 356)

Polivy, J., & Herman, C. P. (2002). Causes of eating disorders. *Annual Review of Psychology, 53,* 187–213. (p. 348)

Pollak, S., Cicchetti, D., & Klorman, R. (1998). Stress, memory, and emotion: Developmental considerations from the study of child maltreatment. *Developmental Psychopathology, 10,* 811–828. (p. 231)

Pollak, S. D., & Kistler, D. J. (2002). Early experience is associated with the development of categorical representations for facial expressions of emotion. *Proceedings of the National Academy of Sciences, 99,* 9072–9076. (p. 384)

Pollak, S. D., & Tolley-Schell, S. A. (2003). Selective attention to facial emotion in physically abused children. *Journal of Abnormal Psychology, 112,* 323–328. (p. 384)

Pollard, R. (1992). 100 years in psychology and deafness: A centennial retrospective. Invited address to the American Psychological Association convention, Washington, DC. (p. 307)

Polusny, M. A., & Follette, V. M. (1995). Long-term correlates of child sexual abuse: Theory and review of the empirical literature. *Applied & Preventive Psychology, 4,* 143–166. (p. 153)

Poole, D. A., & Lindsay, D. S. (1995). Interviewing preschoolers: Effects of nonsuggestive techniques, parental coaching and leading questions on reports of nonexperienced events. *Journal of Experimental Child Psychology, 60,* 129–154. (p. 284)

Poole, D. A., & Lindsay, D. S. (2001). Children's eyewitness reports after exposure to misinformation from parents. *Journal of Experimental Psychology: Applied, 7,* 27–50. (p. 284)

Poole, D. A., & Lindsay, D. S. (2002). Reducing child witnesses' false reports of misinformation from parents. *Journal of Experimental Child Psychology, 81,* 117–140. (p. 284)

Poon, L. W. (1987). Myths and truisms: Beyond extant analyses of speed of behavior and age. Address to the Eastern Psychological Association convention. (p. 165)

Popenoe, D. (1993). The evolution of marriage and the problem of stepfamilies: A biosocial perspective. Paper presented at the National Symposium on Stepfamilies, Pennsylvania State University. (p. 124)

Popenoe, D., & Whitehead, B. D. (2002). *Should we live together?* (2nd ed.). New Brunswick, NJ: The National Marriage Project, Rutgers University. (p. 169)

Popkin, B. M. (2007, September). The world is fat. *Scientific American,* pp. 88–95. (pp. 353, 354)

Poremba, A., & Gabriel, M. (2001). Amygdalar efferents initiate auditory thalamic discriminative training-induced neuronal activity. *Journal of Neuroscience, 21,* 270–278. (p. 48)

Porter, D., & Neuringer, A. (1984). Music discriminations by pigeons. *Journal of Experimental Psychology: Animal Behavior Processes, 10,* 138–148. (p. 238)

Porter, S., Birt, A. R., Yuille, J. C., & Lehman, D. R. (2000, November). Negotiating false memories: Interviewer and rememberer characteristics relate to memory distortion. *Psychological Science, 11,* 507–510. (p. 282)

Porter, S., & Peace, K. A. (2007). The scars of memory: A prospective, longitudinal investigation of the consistency of traumatic and positive emotional memories in adulthood. *Psychological Science, 18,* 435–441. (p. 286)

Porter, S., & ten Brinke, L. (2008). Reading between the lies: Identifying concealed and falsified emotions in universal facial expressions. *Psychological Science, 19,* 508–514. (p. 384)

Posner, M. I., & Carr, T. H. (1992). Lexical access and the brain: Anatomical constraints on cognitive models of word recognition. *American Journal of Psychology, 105,* 1–26. (p. 55)

Posthuma, D., & de Geus, E. J. C. (2006). Progress in the molecular-genetic study of intelligence. *Current Directions in Psychological Science, 15,* 151–155. (p. 325)

Poulton, R., & Milne, B. J. (2002). Low fear in childhood is associated with sporting prowess in adolescence and young adulthood. *Behaviour Research and Therapy, 40,* 1191–1197. (p. 487)

Powell, K. E., Thompson, P. D., Caspersen, C. J., & Kendrick, J. S. (1987). Physical activity and the incidence of coronary heart disease. *Annual Review of Public Health, 8,* 253–287. (p. 412)

Powell, L. H., Schahabi, L., & Thoresen, C. E. (2003). Religion and spirituality: Linkages to physical health. *American Psychologist, 58,* 36–52. (p. 415)

Powell, R. A., & Boer, D. P. (1994). Did Freud mislead patients to confabulate memories of abuse? *Psychological Reports, 74,* 1283–1298. (p. 426)

Powers, M. B., & Emmelkamp, P. M. G. (2008). Virtual reality exposure therapy for anxiety disorders: A meta-analysis. *Journal of Anxiety Disorders, 22,* 561–569. (p. 498)

Pratkanis, A. R., & Greenwald, A. G. (1988). Recent perspectives on unconscious processing: Still no marketing applications. *Psychology and Marketing, 5,* 337–353. (p. 182)

PRB. (2002). *2002 women of our world.* Population Reference Bureau (www.prb.org). (p. 544)

Prentice, D. A., & Miller, D. T. (1993). Pluralistic ignorance and alcohol use on campus: Some consequences of misperceiving the social norm. *Journal of Personality and Social Psychology, 64,* 243–256. (p. 99)

Presley, C. A., Meilman, P. W., & Lyerla, R. (1997). *Alcohol and drugs on American college campuses: Issues of violence and harrassment.* Carbondale: Core Institute, Southern Illinois University. (p. 90)

Pressman, S. D., & Cohen, S. (2005). Does positive affect influence health? *Psychological Bulletin, 131,* 925–971. (p. 392)

Price, G. M., Uauq, R., Breeze, E., Bulpitt, C. J., & Fletcher, A. E. (2006). Weight, shape, and mortality risk in older persons: Elevated waist-hip ratio, not high body mass index, is associated with a greater risk of death. *American Journal of Clinical Nutrition, 84,* 449–460. (p. 350)

Pringle, P. J., Geary, M. P., Rodeck, C. H., Kingdom, J. C., Kayamba-Kay's, S., & Hindmarsh, P. C. (2005). The influence of cigarette smoking on antenatal growth, birth size, and the insulin-like growth factor axis. *Journal of Clinical Endocrinology and Metabolism, 90,* 2556–2562. (p. 138)

Prioleau, L., Murdock, M., & Brody, N. (1983). An analysis of psychotherapy versus placebo studies. *The Behavioral and Brain Sciences, 6,* 275–310. (p. 510)

Pronin, E. (2007). Perception and misperception of bias in human judgment. *Trends in Cognitive Sciences, 11,* 37–43. (p. 448)

Pronin, E., Berger, J., & Molouki, S. (2007). Alone in a crowd of sheep: Asymmetric perceptions of conformity and their roots in an introspection illusion. *Journal of Personality and Social Psychology, 92,* 585–595. (p. 534)

Pronin, E., & Ross, L. (2006). Temporal differences in trait self-ascription: When the self is seen as an other. *Journal of Personality and Social Psychology, 90,* 197–209. (p. 527)

Propper, R. E., Stickgold, R., Keeley, R., & Christman, S. D. (2007). Is television traumatic? Dreams, stress, and media exposure in the aftermath of September 11, 2001. *Psychological Science, 18,* 334–340. (p. 81)

Provine, R. R. (2001). *Laughter: A scientific investigation.* New York: Penguin. (p. 17)

Pryor, J. H., Hurtado, S., Saenz, V. B., Korn, J. S., Santos, J. L., & Korn, W. S. (2006). *The American freshman: National norms for fall 2006*. Los Angeles: UCLA Higher Education Research Institute. (pp. 329, 477)

Pryor, J. H., Hurtado, S., Saenz, V. B., Lindholm, J. A., Korn, W. S., & Mahoney, K. M. (2005). *The American freshman: National norms for fall 2005*. Los Angeles: Higher Education Research Institute, UCLA. (p. 115)

Pryor, J. H., Hurtado, S., Sharkness, J., & Korn, W. S. (2007). *The American freshman: National norms for fall 2007*. Los Angeles: UCLA Higher Education Research Institute. (pp. 128, 370)

Psychologist. (2003, April). Who's the greatest? *The Psychologist, 16*, p. 17. (p. 148)

Puhl, R. M., & Latner, J. D. (2007). Stigma, obesity, and the health of the nation's children. *Psychological Bulletin, 133*, 557–580. (p. 351)

Putnam, F. W. (1991). Recent research on multiple personality disorder. *Psychiatric Clinics of North America, 14*, 489–502. (p. 470)

Putnam, F. W. (1995). Rebuttal of Paul McHugh. *Journal of the American Academy of Child and Adolescent Psychiatry, 34*, 963. (p. 470)

Putnam, R. (2000). *Bowling alone*. New York: Simon and Schuster. (p. 123)

Pyszczynski, T., Hamilton, J. C., Greenberg, J., & Becker, S. E. (1991). Self-awareness and psychological dysfunction. In C. R. Snyder & D. O. Forsyth (Eds.), *Handbook of social and clinical psychology: The health perspective*. New York: Pergamon. (p. 478)

Pyszczynski, T. A., Solomon, S., & Greenberg, J. (2002). *In the wake of 9/11: The psychology of terror*. Washington, DC: American Psychological Association. (p. 546)

Qirko, H. N. (2004). "Fictive kin" and suicide terrorism. *Science, 304*, 49–50. (p. 540)

Quinn, P. C., Bhatt, R. S., Brush, D., Grimes, A., & Sharpnack, H. (2002). Development of form similarity as a Gestalt grouping principle in infancy. *Psychological Science, 13*, 320–328. (p. 206)

Quinn, P. J., Williams, G. M., Najman, J. M., Andersen, M. J., & Bor, W. (2001). The effect of breastfeeding on child development at 5 years: A cohort study. *Journal of Pediatrics & Child Health, 3*, 465–469. (p. 21)

Rahman, Q., & Koerting, J. (2008). Sexual orientation-related differences in allocentric spatial memory tasks. *Hippocampus, 18*, 55–63. (p. 368)

Rahman, Q., & Wilson, G. D. (2003). Born gay? The psychobiology of human sexual orientation. *Personality and Individual Differences, 34*, 1337–1382. (pp. 366, 368)

Rahman, Q., Wilson, G. D., & Abrahams, S. (2003). Biosocial factors, sexual orientation and neurocognitive functioning. *Psychoneuro-endocrinology, 29*, 867–881. (p. 368)

Raine, A. (1999). Murderous minds: Can we see the mark of Cain? *Cerebrum: The Dana Forum on Brain Science 1*(1), 15–29. (pp. 487, 548)

Raine, A. (2005). The interaction of biological and social measures in the explanation of antisocial and violent behavior. In D. M. Stoff & E. J. Susman (Eds.), *Developmental psychobiology of aggression*. New York: Cambridge University Press. (pp. 487, 548)

Raine, A., Lencz, T., Bihrle, S., LaCasse, L., & Colletti, P. (2000). Reduced prefrontal gray matter volume and reduced autonomic activity in antisocial personality disorder. *Archives of General Psychiatry, 57*, 119–127. (p. 487)

Rainville, P., Duncan, G. H., Price, D. D., Carrier, B., & Bushnell, M. C. (1997). Pain affect encoded in human anterior cingulate but not somatosensory cortex. *Science, 277*, 968–971. (p. 87)

Raison, C. L., Klein, H. M., & Steckler, M. (1999). The mood and madness reconsidered. *Journal of Affective Disorders, 53*, 99–106. (p. 488)

Rajendran, G., & Mitchell, P. (2007). Cognitive theories of autism. *Developmental Review, 27*, 224–260. (p. 146)

Ralston, A. (2004). Enough rope. Interview for ABC TV, Australia, by Andrew Denton (www.abc.net.au/enoughrope/stories/s1227885.htm). (p. 339)

Ramachandran, V. S., & Blakeslee, S. (1998). *Phantoms in the brain: Probing the mysteries of the human mind*. New York: Morrow. (pp. 40, 57, 199)

Ramachandran, V. S., & Oberman, L. M. (2006, November). Broken mirrors: A theory of autism. *Scientific American*, pp. 63–69. (pp. 147, 249)

Ramirez-Esparza, N., Gosling, S. D., Benet-Martínez, V., Potter, J. P., & Pennebaker, J. W. (2006). Do bilinguals have two personalities? A special case of cultural frame switching. *Journal of Research in Personality, 40*, 99–120. (p. 306)

Rand, C. S. W., & Macgregor, A. M. C. (1990). Morbidly obese patients' perceptions of social discrimination before and after surgery for obesity. *Southern Medical Journal, 83*, 1390–1395. (p. 351)

Rand, C. S. W., & Macgregor, A. M. C. (1991). Successful weight loss following obesity surgery and perceived liability or morbid obesity. *Internal Journal of Obesity, 15*, 577–579. (p. 351)

Randi, J. (1999, February 4). 2000 club mailing list e-mail letter. (p. 220)

Randi, J. (2008). 'Twas Brillig . . . Last chance to win the million-dollar challenge. *Skeptic, 14*(1), 6. (p. 220)

Rapoport, J. L. (1989, March). The biology of obsessions and compulsions. *Scientific American*, pp. 83–89. (pp. 463, 466)

Räsänen, S., Pakaslahti, A., Syvalahti, E., Jones, P. B., & Isohanni, M. (2000). Sex differences in schizophrenia: A review. *Nordic Journal of Psychiatry, 54*, 37–45. (p. 482)

Ray, J. (2005, April 12). U.S. teens walk away from anger: Boys and girls manage anger differently. *The Gallup Organization* (www.gallup.com). (p. 391)

Ray, O., & Ksir, C. (1990). *Drugs, society, and human behavior* (5th ed.). St. Louis: Times Mirror/Mosby. (p. 94)

Raynor, H. A., & Epstein, L. H. (2001). Dietary variety, energy regulation, and obesity. *Psychological Bulletin, 127*, 325–341. (p. 346)

Reason, J. (1987). The Chernobyl errors. *Bulletin of the British Psychological Society, 40*, 201–206. (p. 540)

Reason, J., & Mycielska, K. (1982). *Absent-minded? The psychology of mental lapses and every-day errors*. Englewood Cliffs, NJ: Prentice-Hall. (p. 216)

Reed, P. (2000). Serial position effects in recognition memory for odors. *Journal of Experimental Psychology: Learning, Memory, and Cognition, 26*, 411–422. (p. 261)

Rees, M. (1999). *Just six numbers: The deep forces that shape the universe*. New York: Basic Books. (p. 133)

Regan, P. C., & Atkins, L. (2007). Sex differences and similarities in frequency and intensity of sexual desire. *Social Behavior and Personality, 34*, 95–102. (p. 115)

Reichenberg, A., Gross, R., Weiser, M., Bresnahan, M., Silverman, J., Harlap, S., Rabinoqitz, J., Shulman, C., Malaspina, D., Lubin, G., Knobler, H Y., Davidson, M., & Susser, E. (2007). Advancing paternal age and autism. *Archives of General Psychiatry, 63*, 1026–1032. (p. 146)

Reichenberg, A., & Harvey, P. D. (2007). Neuropsychological impairments in schizophrenia: Integration of performance-based and brain imaging findings. *Psychological Bulletin, 133*, 833–858. (p. 481)

Reichman, J. (1998). *I'm not in the mood: What every woman should know about improving her libido*. New York: Morrow. (p. 358)

Reifman, A., & Cleveland, H. H. (2007). Shared environment: A quantitative review. Paper presented to the Society for Research in Child Development, Boston, MA. (p. 110)

Reiner, W. G., & Gearhart, J. P. (2004). Discordant sexual identity in some genetic males with cloacal exstrophy assigned to female sex at birth. *New England Journal of Medicine, 350*, 333–341. (p. 129)

Reis, H. T., & Aron, A. (2008). Love: What is it, why does it matter, and how does it operate? *Perspectives on Psychological Science, 3*, 80–86. (p. 560)

Reisenzein, R. (1983). The Schachter theory of emotion: Two decades later. *Psychological Bulletin, 94*, 239–264. (p. 381)

Reiser, M. (1982). *Police psychology*. Los Angeles: LEHI. (p. 218)

Reitzle, M. (2006). The connections between adulthood transitions and the self-perception of being adult in the changing contexts of East and West Germany. *European Psychologist, 11*, 25–38. (p. 162)

Remafedi, G. (1999). Suicide and sexual orientation: Nearing the end of controversy? *Archives of General Psychiatry, 56*, 885–886. (p. 364)

Remley, A. (1988, October). From obedience to independence. *Psychology Today*, pp. 56–59. (p. 125)

Renner, M. J., & Renner, C. H. (1993). Expert and novice intuitive judgments about animal behavior. *Bulletin of the Psychonomic Society, 31*, 551–552. (p. 118)

Renner, M. J., & Rosenzweig, M. R. (1987). *Enriched and impoverished environments: Effects on brain and behavior*. New York: Springer-Verlag. (p. 118)

Renninger, K. A., & Granott, N. (2005). The process of scaffolding in learning and development. *New Ideas in Psychology, 23*(3), 111–114. (p. 148)

Rentfrow, P. J., & Gosling, S. D. (2003). The Do Re Mi's of everyday life: The structure and personality correlates of music preferences. *Journal of Personality and Social Psychology, 84,* 1236–1256. (p. 438)

Rentfrow, P. J., & Gosling, S. D. (2006). Message in a ballad: The role of music preferences in interpersonal perception. *Psychological Science, 17,* 236–242. (p. 438)

Repetti, R. L., Taylor, S. E., & Seeman, T. E. (2002). Risky families: Family social environments and the mental and physical health of offspring. *Psychological Bulletin, 128,* 330–366. (p. 399)

Rescorla, R. A., & Wagner, A. R. (1972). A theory of Pavlovian conditioning: Variations in the effectiveness of reinforcement and nonreinforcement. In A. H. Black & W. F. Perokasy (Eds.), *Classical conditioning II: Current theory.* New York: Appleton-Century-Crofts. (p. 232)

Resnick, M. D., Bearman, P. S., Blum, R. W., Bauman, K. E., Harris, K. M., Jones, J., Tabor, J., Beuhring, T., Sieving, R., Shew, M., Bearinger, L. H., & Udry, J. R. (1997). Protecting adolescents from harm: Findings from the National Longitudinal Study on Adolescent Health. *Journal of the American Medical Association, 278,* 823–832. (p. 19, 161)

Resnick, R. A., O'Regan, J. K., & Clark, J. J. (1997). To see or not to see: The need for attention to perceive changes in scenes. *Psychological Science, 8,* 368–373. (p. 69)

Resnick, S. M. (1992). Positron emission tomography in psychiatric illness. *Current Directions in Psychological Science, 1,* 92–98. (p. 483)

Responsive Community. (1996, Fall). Age vs. weight. Page 83 (reported from a *Wall Street Journal* survey). (p. 355)

Reuters. (2000, July 5). Many teens regret decision to have sex (National Campaign to Prevent Teen Pregnancy survey). www.washingtonpost.com. (p. 361)

Reyna, V. F., & Farley, F. (2006). Risk and rationality in adolescent decision making: Implications for theory, practice, and public policy. *Psychological Science in the Public Interest, 7*(1), 1–44. (p. 156)

Reynolds, A. J., Temple, J. A., Robertson, D. L., & Manri, E. A. (2001). Long-term effects of an early childhood intervention on educational achievement and juvenile arrest. *Journal of the American Medical Association, 285,* 2339–2346. (p. 327)

Rholes, W. S., & Simpson, J. A. (Eds.). (2004). *Adult attachment: Theory, research, and clinical implications.* New York: Guilford. (p. 152)

Rholes, W. S., Simpson, J. A., & Friedman, M. (2006). Avoidant attachment and the experience of parenting. *Personality and Social Psychology Bulletin, 32,* 275–285. (p. 152)

Ribeiro, R., Gervasoni, D., Soares, E. S., Zhou, Y., Lin, S-C., Pantoja, J., Lavine, M., & Nicolelis, M. A. L. (2004). Long-lasting novelty-induced neuronal reverberation during slow-wave sleep in multiple forebrain areas. *PloS Biology, 2*(1), e37 (www.plosbiology.org). (p. 77)

Ricciardelli, L. A., & McCabe, M. P. (2004). A biopsychosocial model of disordered eating and the pursuit of muscularity in adolescent boys. *Psychological Bulletin, 130,* 179–205. (p. 348)

Rice, M. E., & Grusec, J. E. (1975). Saying and doing: Effects on observer performance. *Journal of Personality and Social Psychology, 32,* 584–593. (p. 251)

Richeson, J. A., & Shelton, J. N. (2007). Negotiating interracial interactions. *Current Directions in Psychological Science, 16,* 316–320. (p. 565)

Rieff, P. (1979). *Freud: The mind of a moralist* (3rd ed.). Chicago: University of Chicago Press. (p. 428)

Rieger, G., Chivers, M. L., & Bailey, J. M. (2005). Sexual arousal patterns of bisexual men. *Psychological Science, 16,* 579–584. (p. 363)

Riis, J., Loewenstein, G., Baron, J., Jepson, C., Fagerlin, A., & Ubel, P. A. (2005). Ignorance of hedonic adaptation to hemodialysis: A study using ecological momentary assessment. *Journal of Experimental Psychology: General, 134,* 3–9. (p. 393)

Riley, L. D., & Bowen, C. (2005). The sandwich generation: Challenges and coping strategies of multigenerational families. *The Family Journal, 13,* 52–58. (p. 168)

Rindermann, H. (2007). The *g*-factor of international cognitive ability comparisons: The homogeneity of results in PISA, TIMSS, PIRLS and IQ-tests across nations. *European Journal of Personality, 21,* 667–7006. (p. 315)

Ring, K. (1980). *Life at death: A scientific investigation of the near-death experience.* New York: Coward, McCann & Geoghegan. (p. 95)

Ripple, C. H., & Zigler, E. F. (2003). Research, policy, and the federal role in prevention initiatives for children. *American Psychologist, 58,* 482–490. (p. 327)

Risch, N., Herrell, R., Lehner, T., Liang, K-Y., Eaves, L., Hoh, J., Griem, A., Kovacs, M., Ott, J., & Merkangas, R. (2009). Interaction between the serotonin transporter gene (5-HTTLPR), stressful life events, and risk of depression. *Journal of the American Medical Association, 301,* 2462–2471. (p. 476)

Riskind, J. H., Beck, A. T., Berchick, R. J., Brown, G., & Steer, R. A. (1987). Reliability of DSM-III diagnoses for major depression and generalized anxiety disorder using the structured clinical interview for DSM-III. *Archives of General Psychiatry, 44,* 817–820. (p. 458)

Rizzolatti, G., Fadiga, L., Fogassi, L., & Gallese, V. (2002). From mirror neurons to imitation: Facts and speculations. In A. N. Meltzoff & W. Prinz (Eds.), *The imitative mind: Development, evolution, and brain bases.* Cambridge: Cambridge University Press, 2002. (p. 248)

Rizzolatti, G., Fogassi, L., & Gallese, V. (2006, November). Mirrors in the mind. *Scientific American,* pp. 54–61. (p. 248)

Roberson, D., Davidoff, J., Davies, I. R. L., & Shapiro, L. R. (2004). The development of color categories in two languages: A longitudinal study. *Journal of Experimental Psychology: General, 133,* 554–571. (p. 306)

Roberson, D., Davies, I. R. L., Corbett, G. G., & Vandervyver, M. (2005). Free-sorting of colors across cultures: Are there universal grounds for grouping? *Journal of Cognition and Culture, 5,* 349–386. (p. 306)

Roberts, B. W., Caspi, A., & Moffitt, T. E. (2001). The kids are alright: Growth and stabili-ty in personality development from adolescence to adulthood. *Journal of Personality and Social Psychology, 81,* 670–683. (p. 174)

Roberts, B. W., Caspi, A., & Moffitt, T. E. (2003). Work experiences and personality development in young adulthood. *Journal of Personality and Social Psychology, 84,* 582–593. (p. 174)

Roberts, B. W., & DelVecchio, W. F. (2000). The rank-order consistency of personality traits from childhood to old age: A quantitative review of longitudinal studies. *Psychological Bulletin, 126,* 3–25. (p. 437)

Roberts, B. W., Kuncel, N. R., Shiner, R., Caspi, A., & Goldberg, L. R. (2007). The power of personality: The comparative validity of personality traits, socioeconomic status, and cognitive ability for predicting important life outcomes. *Perspectives on Psychological Science, 2,* 313–345. (p. 437)

Roberts, B. W., & Mroczek, D. (2008). Personality trait change in adulthood. *Current Directions in Psychological Science, 17,* 31–35. (p. 174)

Roberts, B. W., Walton, K. E., & Viechtbauer, W. (2006). Patterns of mean-level change in personality traits across the life course: A meta-analysis of longitudinal studies. *Psychological Bulletin, 132,* 1–25. (p. 174)

Roberts, L. (1988). Beyond Noah's ark: What do we need to know? *Science, 242,* 1247. (p. 409)

Roberts, T-A. (1991). Determinants of gender differences in responsiveness to others' evaluations. *Dissertation Abstracts International, 51*(8–B). (p. 128)

Robins, L., & Regier, D. (Eds.). (1991). *Psychiatric disorders in America.* New York: Free Press. (p. 489)

Robins, L. N., Davis, D. H., & Goodwin, D. W. (1974). Drug use by U.S. Army enlisted men in Vietnam: A follow-up on their return home. *American Journal of Epidemiology, 99,* 235–249. (p. 100)

Robins, R. W., & Trzesniewski, K. H. (2005). Self-esteem development across the lifespan. *Current Directions in Psychological Science, 14*(3), 158–162. (p. 170)

Robins, R. W., Trzesniewski, K. H., Tracy, J. L., Gosling, S. D., & Potter, J. (2002). Global self-esteem across the lifespan. *Psychology and Aging, 17,* 423–434. (p. 160)

Robinson, F. P. (1970). *Effective study.* New York: Harper & Row. (p. 29)

Robinson, J. (2002, October 8). What percentage of the population is gay? *Gallup Tuesday Briefing* (www.gallup.com/poll/tb/religValue/20021008b.asp). (p. 363)

Robinson, J. P., & Martin, S. P. (2007, October). Not so deprived: Sleep in America, 1965–2005. *Public Opinion Pros* (www.publicopinionpros.com). (p. 75)

Robinson, T. E., & Berridge, K. C. (2003). Addiction. *Annual Review of Psychology, 54,* 25–53. (p. 89)

Robinson, T. N. (1999). Reducing children's television viewing to prevent obesity. *Journal of the American Medical Association, 282,* 1561–1567. (p. 356)

Robinson, T. N., Borzekowski, D. L. G., Matheson, D. M., & Kraemer, H. C. (2007).

Effects of fast food branding on children's taste preferences. *Archives of Pediatric and Adolescent Medicine, 161,* 792–797. (p. 216)

Rochat, F. (1993). How did they resist authority? Protecting refugees in Le Chambon during World War II. Paper presented at the American Psychological Association convention. (p. 536)

Rock, I., & Palmer, S. (1990, December). The legacy of Gestalt psychology. *Scientific American,* pp. 84–90. (p. 206)

Rodin, J. (1986). Aging and health: Effects of the sense of control. *Science, 233,* 1271–1276. (pp. 408, 409, 442)

Roediger, H. (2001, September). Quoted by R. Herbert, Doing a number on memory. *APS Observer,* pp. 1, 7–11. (p. 280)

Roediger, H. L., & Karpicke, J. D. (2006). Test-enhanced learning: Taking memory tests improves long-term retention. *Psychological Science, 17,* 249–255. (p. 261)

Roediger, H. L., III, Wheeler, M. A., & Rajaram, S. (1993). Remembering, knowing, and reconstructing the past. In D. L. Medin (Ed.), *The psychology of learning and motivation: Advances in research and theory* (Vol. 30). Orlando, FL: Academic Press. (p. 282)

Roehling, M. V. (1999). Weight-based discrimination in employment: Psychological and legal aspects. *Personnel Psychology, 52,* 969–1016. (p. 351)

Roehling, M. V., Roehling, P. V., & Pichler, S. (2007). The relationship between body weight and perceived weight-related employment discrimination: The role of sex and race. *Journal of Vocational Behavior, 71,* 300–318. (p. 351)

Roenneberg, T., Kuehnle, T., Pramstaller, P. P., Ricken, J., Havel, M., Guth, A., Merrow, M. (2004). A marker for the end of adolescence. *Current Biology, 14,* R1038–R1039. (p. 71)

Roese, N. J., & Summerville, A. (2005). What we regret most . . . and why. *Personality and Social Psychology Bulletin, 31,* 1273-1285. (p. 170)

Roesser, R. (1998). What you should know about hearing conservation. *Better Hearing Institute* (www.betterhearing.org). (p. 195)

Rogers, C. R. (1958). Reinhold Niebuhr's *The self and the dramas of history:* A criticism. *Pastoral Psychology, 9,* 15–17. (p. 447)

Rogers, C. R. (1961). *On becoming a person: A therapist's view of psychotherapy.* Boston: Houghton Mifflin. (p. 496)

Rogers, C. R. (1980). *A way of being.* Boston: Houghton Mifflin. (pp. 430, 496)

Rohan, K. J., Roecklein, K. A., Lindsey, K. T., Johnson, L. G., Lippy, R. D., Lacy, T. J., & Barton, F. B. (2007). A randomized controlled trial of cognitive-behavioral therapy, light therapy, and their combination for seasonal affective disorder. *Journal of Consulting and Clinical Psychology, 75,* 489–500. (p. 509)

Rohan, M. J., & Zanna, M. P. (1996). Value transmission in families. In C. Seligman, J. M. Olson, & M. P. Zanna (Eds.), *The psychology of values: The Ontario Symposium* (Vol. 8). Mahwah, NJ: Erlbaum. (p. 110)

Rohner, R. P. (1986). *The warmth dimension: Foundations of parental acceptance-rejection theory.* Newbury Park, NJ: Sage. (p. 125)

Rohner, R. P., & Veneziano, R. A. (2001). The importance of father love: History and contemporary evidence. *Review of General Psychology, 5,* 382–405. (pp. 152, 154)

Rohrer, D., & Pashler, H. (2007). Increasing retention without increasing study time. *Current Directions in Psychological Science, 16,* 183–186. (p. 261)

Roiser, J. P., Cook, L. J., Cooper, J. D., Rubinsztein, D. C., & Sahakian, B. J. (2005). Association of a functional polymorphism in the serotonin transporter gene with abnormal emotional processing in Ecstasy users. *American Journal of Psychiatry, 162,* 609–612. (p. 95)

Rokach, A., Orzeck, T., Moya, M., & Exposito, F. (2002). Causes of loneliness in North America and Spain. *European Psychologist, 7,* 70–79. (p. 26)

Rosch, E. (1978). Principles of categorization. In E. Rosch & B. L. Lloyd (Eds.), *Cognition and categorization.* Hillsdale, NJ: Erlbaum. (p. 292)

Rose, A. J., & Rudolph, K. D. (2006). A review of sex differences in peer relationship processes: Potential trade-offs for the emotional and behavioral development of girls and boys. *Psychological Bulletin, 132,* 98–131. (p. 128)

Rose, J. S., Chassin, L., Presson, C. C., & Sherman, S. J. (1999). Peer influences on adolescent cigarette smoking: A prospective sibling analysis. *Merrill-Palmer Quarterly, 45,* 62–84. (pp. 92, 120)

Rose, R. J., Kaprio, J., Winter, T., Dick, D. M., Viken, R. J., Pulkkinen, L., & Koskenvuo, M. (2002). Femininity and fertility in sisters with twin brothers: Prenatal androgenization? Cross-sex socialization? *Psychological Science, 13,* 263–266. (p. 365)

Rose, R. J., Viken, R. J., Dick, D. M., Bates, J. E., Pulkkinen, L., & Kaprio, J. (2003). It *does* take a village: Nonfamiliar environments and children's behavior. *Psychological Science, 14,* 273–277. (p. 120)

Rose, S. (1999). Precis of lifelines: Biology, freedom, determinism. *Behavioral and Brain Sciences, 22,* 871–921. (p. 117)

Rose, S., Bisson, J., & Wessely, S. (2003). A systematic review of single-session psychological interventions ('debriefing') following trauma. *Psychotherapy and Psychosomatics, 72,* 176–184. (p. 465)

Roselli, C. E., Larkin, K., Schrunk, J. M., & Stormshak, F. (2004). Sexual partner preference, hypothalamic morphology and aromatase in rams. *Physiology and Behavior, 83,* 233–245. (p. 366)

Roselli, C. E., Resko, J. A., & Stormshak, F. (2002). Hormonal influences on sexual partner preference in rams. *Archives of Sexual Behavior, 31,* 43–49. (p. 366)

Rosenbaum, M. (1986). The repulsion hypothesis: On the nondevelopment of relationships. *Journal of Personality and Social Psychology, 51,* 1156–1166. (p. 559)

Rosenberg, N. A., Pritchard, J. K., Weber, J. L., Cann, H. M., Kidd, K. K., Zhivotosky, L. A., & Feldman, M. W. (2002). Genetic structure of human populations. *Science, 298,* 2381–2385. (p. 114)

Rosenhan, D. L. (1973). On being sane in insane places. *Science, 179,* 250–258. (p. 459)

Rosenthal, R., Hall, J. A., Archer, D., DiMatteo, M. R., & Rogers, P. L. (1979). The PONS test: Measuring sensitivity to nonverbal cues. In S. Weitz (Ed.), *Nonverbal communication* (2nd ed.). New York: Oxford University Press. (pp. 328, 384)

Rosenzweig, M. R. (1984). Experience, memory, and the brain. *American Psychologist, 39,* 365–376. (p. 118)

Roseth, C. J., Johnson, D. W., & Johnson, R. T. (2008). Promoting early adolescents' achievement and peer relationships: The effects of cooperative, competitive, and individualistic goal structures. *Psychological Bulletin, 134,* 223–246. (p. 566)

Ross, J. (2006, December). Sleep on a problem . . . it works like a dream. *The Psychologist, 19,* 738–740. (p. 77)

Ross, M., McFarland, C., & Fletcher, G. J. O. (1981). The effect of attitude on the recall of personal histories. *Journal of Personality and Social Psychology, 40,* 627–634. (p. 281)

Ross, M., Xun, W. Q. E., & Wilson, A. E. (2002). Language and the bicultural self. *Personality and Social Psychology Bulletin, 28,* 1040–1050. (p. 306)

Rossi, P. J. (1968). Adaptation and negative aftereffect to lateral optical displacement in newly hatched chicks. *Science, 160,* 430–432. (p. 214)

Rostosky, S. S., Wilcox, B. L., Wright, M. L. C., & Randall, B. A. (2004). The impact of religiosity on adolescent sexual behavior: A review of the evidence. *Journal of Adolescent Research, 19,* 677–697. (p. 362)

Roth, T., Roehrs, T., Zwyghuizen-Doorenbos, A., Stpeanski, E., & Witting, R. (1988). Sleep and memory. In I. Hindmarch & H. Ott (Eds.), *Benzodiazepine receptor ligans, memory and information processing.* New York: Springer-Verlag. (p. 81)

Rothbart, M. K., Ahadi, S. A., & Evans, D. E. (2000). Temperament and personality: Origins and outcomes. *Journal of Personality and Social Psychology, 78,* 122–135. (p. 111)

Rothbart, M., Fulero, S., Jensen, C., Howard, J., & Birrell, P. (1978). From individual to group impressions: Availability heuristics in stereotype formation. *Journal of Experimental Social Psychology, 14,* 237–255. (p. 547)

Rothbaum, B. O. (2006). Virtual reality exposure therapy. In B. O. Rothbaum (Ed.), *Pathological anxiety: Emotional processing in etiology and treatment.* New York: Guilford. (p. 498)

Rothbaum, F., & Tsang, B. Y-P. (1998). Lovesongs in the United States and China: On the nature of romantic love. *Journal of Cross-Cultural Psychology, 29,* 306–319. (p. 124)

Rothman, A. J., & Salovey, P. (1997). Shaping perceptions to motivate healthy behavior: The role of message framing. *Psychological Bulletin, 121,* 3–19. (p. 300)

Rothstein, W. G. (1980). The significance of occupations in work careers: An empirical and theoretical review. *Journal of Vocational Behavior, 17,* 328–343. (p. 170)

Rotton, J., & Kelly, I. W. (1985). Much ado about the full moon: A metaanalysis of lunar-lunacy research. *Psychological Bulletin, 97,* 286–306. (p. 488)

Rovee-Collier, C. (1989). The joy of kicking: Memories, motives, and mobiles. In P. R.

Solomon, G. R. Goethals, C. M. Kelley, & B. R. Stephens (Eds.), *Memory: Interdisciplinary approaches.* New York: Springer-Verlag. (p. 142)

Rovee-Collier, C. (1993). The capacity for long-term memory in infancy. *Current Directions in Psychological Science, 2,* 130–135. (p. 275)

Rovee-Collier, C. (1997). Dissociations in infant memory: Rethinking the development of implicit and explicit memory. *Psychological Review, 104,* 467–498. (p. 142)

Rovee-Collier, C. (1999). The development of infant memory. *Current Directions in Psychological Science, 8,* 80–85. (p. 142)

Rowe, D. C. (1990). As the twig is bent? The myth of child-rearing influences on personality development. *Journal of Counseling and Development, 68,* 606–611. (p. 110)

Rowe, D. C. (2005). Under the skin: On the impartial treatment of genetic and environmental hypotheses of racial differences. *American Psychologist, 60,* 60–70. (p. 332)

Rowe, D. C., Almeida, D. M., & Jacobson, K. C. (1999). School context and genetic influences on aggression in adolescence. *Psychological Science, 10,* 277–280. (p. 548)

Rowe, D. C., Jacobson, K. C., & Van den Oord, E. J. C. G. (1999). Genetic and environmental influences on vocabulary IQ: Parental education level as moderator. *Child Development, 70*(5), 1151–1162. (p. 327)

Rowe, D. C., Vazsonyi, A. T., & Flannery, D. J. (1994). No more than skin deep: Ethnic and racial similarity in developmental process. *Psychological Review, 101*(3), 396. (p. 125)

Rowe, D. C., Vazsonyi, A. T., & Flannery, D. J. (1995). Ethnic and racial similarity in developmental process: A study of academic achievement. *Psychological Science, 6,* 33–38. (p. 125)

Rozin, P., Dow, S., Mosovitch, M., & Rajaram, S. (1998). What causes humans to begin and end a meal? A role for memory for what has been eaten, as evidenced by a study of multiple meal eating in amnesic patients. *Psychological Science, 9,* 392–396. (p. 346)

Rozin, P., Millman, L., & Nemeroff, C. (1986). Operation of the laws of sympathetic magic in disgust and other domains. *Journal of Personality and Social Psychology, 50,* 703–712. (p. 231)

Ruback, R. B., Carr, T. S., & Hopper, C. H. (1986). Perceived control in prison: Its relation to reported crowding, stress, and symptoms. *Journal of Applied Social Psychology, 16,* 375–386. (p. 442)

Rubenstein, J. S., Meyer, D. E., & Evans, J. E. (2001). Executive control of cognitive processes in task switching. *Journal of Experimental Psychology: Human Perception and Performance, 27,* 763–797. (p. 68)

Rubin, D. C., Rahhal, T. A., & Poon, L. W. (1998). Things learned in early adulthood are remembered best. *Memory and Cognition, 26,* 3–19. (p. 166)

Rubin, J. Z., Pruitt, D. G., & Kim, S. H. (1994). *Social conflict: Escalation, stalemate, and settlement.* New York: McGraw-Hill. (p. 566)

Rubin, L. B. (1985). *Just friends: The role of friendship in our lives.* New York: Harper & Row. (p. 128)

Rubin, Z. (1970). Measurement of romantic love. *Journal of Personality and Social Psychology, 16,* 265–273. (p. 383)

Rubio, G., & López-Ibor, J. J. (2007). Generalized anxiety disorder: A 40-year follow-up study. *Acta Psychiatrica Scandinavica, 115,* 372–379. (p. 462)

Rubonis, A. V., & Bickman, L. (1991). Psychological impairment in the wake of disaster: The disaster-psychopathology relationship. *Psychological Bulletin, 109,* 384–399. (p. 401)

Ruchlis, H. (1990). *Clear thinking: A practical introduction.* Buffalo, NY: Prometheus Books. (p. 293)

Rudman, L. A., & Goodwin, S. A. (2004). Gender differences in automatic in-group bias: Why do women like women more than men like men? *Journal of Personality and Social Psychology, 87,* 494–509. (p. 544)

Ruffin, C. L. (1993). Stress and health—little hassles vs. major life events. *Australian Psychologist, 28,* 201–208. (p. 401)

Rule, B. G., & Ferguson, T. J. (1986). The effects of media violence on attitudes, emotions, and cognitions. *Journal of Social Issues, 42*(3), 29–50. (p. 253)

Rumbaugh, D. M. (1977). *Language learning by a chimpanzee: The Lana project.* New York: Academic Press. (p. 311)

Rumbaugh, D. M., & Savage-Rumbaugh, S. (1978). Chimpanzee language research: Status and potential. *Behavior Research Methods & Instrumentation, 10,* 119–131. (p. 312)

Rumbaugh, D. M., & Savage-Rumbaugh, S. (1994, January/February). Language and apes. *Psychology Teacher Network,* pp. 2–5, 9. (p. 312)

Rumbaugh, D. M., & Washburn, D. A. (2003). *Intelligence of apes and other rational beings.* New Haven, CT: Yale University Press. (p. 313)

Rush, A. J., & 12 others from the STAR*D Study team. (2006). Bupropion-SR, Sertaline, or Venlafaxine-XR after failure of SSRIs for depression. *New England Journal of Medicine, 354,* 1231–1242. (p. 516)

Rushton, J. P. (1975). Generosity in children: Immediate and long-term effects of modeling, preaching, and moral judgment. *Journal of Personality and Social Psychology, 31,* 459–466. (p. 251)

Rushton, J. P., & Jensen, A. R. (2005). Thirty years of research on race differences in cognitive ability. *Psychology, Public Policy, and Law, 11,* 235–294. (p. 331)

Rushton, J. P., & Jensen, A. R. (2006). The totality of available evidence shows the race IQ gap still remains. *Psychological Science, 17,* 921–922. (p. 331)

Russell, B. (1930/1985). *The conquest of happiness.* London: Unwin Paperbacks. (p. 396)

Rusting, C. L., & Nolen-Hoeksema, S. (1998). Regulating responses to anger: Effects of rumination and distraction on angry mood. *Journal of Personality and Social Psychology, 74,* 790–803. (p. 391)

Rutter, M., and the English and Romanian Adoptees (ERA) study team. (1998). Developmental catch-up, and deficit, following adoption after severe global early privation. *Journal of Child Psychology and Psychiatry, 39,* 465–476. (p. 152)

Ruys, K. I., & Stapel, D. A. (2008). The secret life of emotions. *Psychological Science, 19,* 385–391. (p. 381)

Ryan, R. (1999, February 2). Quoted by Alfie Kohn, In pursuit of affluence, at a high price. *New York Times* (www.nytimes.com). (p. 395)

Ryan, R. M., & Deci, E. L. (2004). Avoiding death or engaging life as accounts of meaning and culture: Comment on Pyszczynski et al. (2004). *Psychological Bulletin, 130,* 473–477. (p. 449)

Ryckman, R. M., Robbins, M. A., Kaczor, L. M., & Gold, J. A. (1989). Male and female raters' stereotyping of male and female physiques. *Personality and Social Psychology Bulletin, 15,* 244–251. (p. 350)

Ryder, A. G., Yang, J., Zhu, X., Yao, S., Yi, J., Heine, S. J., & Bagby, R. M. (2008). The cultural shaping of depression: Somatic symptoms in China, psychological symptoms in North America? *Journal of Abnormal Psychology, 117,* 300–313. (p. 468)

Saad, L. (2001, December 17). Americans' mood: Has Sept. 11 made a difference? *Gallup Poll News Service* (www.gallup.com/poll/releases/pr011217.asp). (p. 401)

Saad, L. (2002, November 21). Most smokers wish they could quit. *Gallup News Service* (www.gallup.com). (p. 93)

Sabbagh, M. A., Xu, F., Carlson, S. M., Moses, L. J., & Lee, K. (2006). The development of executive functioning and theory of mind: A comparison of Chinese and U.S. preschoolers. *Psychological Science, 17,* 74–81. (p. 145)

Sabini, J. (1986). Stanley Milgram (1933–1984). *American Psychologist, 41,* 1378–1379. (p. 534)

Sachdev, P., & Sachdev, J. (1997). Sixty years of psychosurgery: Its present status and its future. *Australian and New Zealand Journal of Psychiatry, 31,* 457–464. (p. 519)

Sackett, P. R., Borneman, M. J., & Connelly, B. S. (2008). High-stakes testing in higher education and employment: Appraising the evidence for validity and fairness. *American Psychologist, 63,* 215–227. (p. 333)

Sackett, P. R., Hardison, C. M., & Cullen, M. J. (2004). On interpreting stereotype threat as accounting for African American-White differences on cognitive tests. *American Psychologist, 59,* 7–13. (p. 333)

Sacks, O. (1985). *The man who mistook his wife for a hat.* New York: Summit Books. (pp. 197, 270)

Sadato, N., Pascual-Leone, A., Grafman, J., Ibanez, V., Deiber, M-P., Dold, G., & Hallett, M. (1996). Activation of the primary visual cortex by Braille reading in blind subjects. *Nature, 380,* 526–528. (p. 56)

Sagan, C. (1987, February 1). The fine art of baloney detection. *Parade.* (p. 219)

Sakurai, T., Amemiya, A., Ishii, M., Matsuzaki, I., Chemelli, R. M., Tanaka, H., Williams, S. C., Richardson, J. A., Kozlowski, G. P., Wilson, S., Arch, J. R. S., Buckingham, R. E., Haynes, A. C., Carr, S. A., Annan, R. S., McNulty, D. E., Liu, W-S., Terrett, J. A., Elshourbagy, N. A., Bergsma, D. J., & Yanagisawa, M. (1998). Orexins and orexin receptors: A family of hypothalamic neuropeptides and G protein-coupled receptors that regulate feeding behavior. *Cell, 92,* 573–585. (p. 345)

Salmela-Aro, K., & Nurmi, J-E. (2007). Self-esteem during university studies predicts career characteristics 10 years later. *Journal of Vocational Behavior, 70,* 463–477. (p. 447)

Salmon, P. (2001). Effects of physical exercise on anxiety, depression, and sensitivity to stress: A unifying theory. *Clinical Psychology Review, 21,* 33–61. (pp. 412, 520)

Salovey, P. (1990, January/February). Interview. *American Scientist,* pp. 25–29. (p. 392)

Salthouse, T. (2006). Mental exercise and mental aging: Evaluating the validity of the "use it or lose it" hypothesis. *Perspectives on Psychological Science, 1,* 68–87. (p. 168)

Salthouse, T. (2007). Reply to Schooler: Consistent is not conclusive. *Perspectives on Psychological Science, 2,* 30–32. (p. 168)

Sampson, E. E. (2000). Reinterpreting individualism and collectivism: Their religious roots and monologic versus dialogic person–other relationship. *American Psychologist, 55,* 1425–1432. (p. 123)

Samuels, J., & Nestadt, G. (1997). Epidemiology and genetics of obsessive-compulsive disorder. *International Review of Psychiatry, 9,* 61–71. (p. 464)

Samuels, S., & McCabe, G. (1989). Quoted by P. Diaconis & F. Mosteller, Methods for studying coincidences. *Journal of the American Statistical Association, 84,* 853–861. (p. 21)

Sanders, A. R., & 22 others. (2008). No significant association of 14 candidate genes with schizophrenia in a large European ancestry sample: Implications for psychiatric genetics. *American Journal of Psychiatry, 165,* 497–506. (p. 485)

Sanders, G., Sjodin, M., & de Chastelaine, M. (2002). On the elusive nature of sex differences in cognition hormonal influences contributing to within-sex variation. *Archives of Sexual Behavior, 31,* 145–152. (p. 367)

Sanders, G., & Wright, M. (1997). Sexual orientation differences in cerebral asymmetry and in the performance of sexually dimorphic cognitive and motor tasks. *Archives of Sexual Behavior, 26,* 463–479. (p. 368)

Sandfort, T. G. M., de Graaf, R., Bijl, R., & Schnabel, P. (2001). Same-sex sexual behavior and psychiatric disorders. *Archives of General Psychiatry, 58,* 85–91. (pp. 363, 364)

Sandkühler, S., & Bhattacharya, J. (2008). Deconstructing insight: EEG correlates of insightful problem solving. *PloS ONE, 3,* e1459 (www.plosone.org). (p. 293)

Sandler, W., Meir, I., Padden, C., & Aronoff, M. (2005). The emergence of grammar: Systematic structure in a new language. *Proceedings of the National Academy of Sciences, 102,* 2261–2265. (p. 304)

Sanford, A. J., Fray, N., Stewart, A., & Moxey, L. (2002). Perspective in statements of quantity, with implications for consumer psychology. *Psychological Science, 13,* 130–134. (p. 301)

Sanz, C., Blicher, A., Dalke, K., Gratton-Fabri, L., McClure-Richards, T., & Fouts, R. (1998, Winter-Spring). Enrichment object use: Five chimpanzees' use of temporary and semi-permanent enrichment objects. *Friends of Washoe, 19*(1,2), 9–14. (p. 311)

Sanz, C., Morgan, D., & Gulick, S. (2004). New insights into chimpanzees, tools, and termites from the Congo Basin. *American Naturalist, 164,* 567–581. (p. 310)

Sapadin, L. A. (1988). Friendship and gender: Perspectives of professional men and women. *Journal of Social and Personal Relationships, 5,* 387–403. (p. 128)

Sapolsky, B. S., & Tabarlet, J. O. (1991). Sex in primetime television: 1979 versus 1989. *Journal of Broadcasting and Electronic Media, 35,* 505–516. (pp. 361, 553)

Sapolsky, R. (2003, September). Taming stress. *Scientific American,* pp. 87–95. (p. 473)

Sapolsky, R. (2005). The influence of social hierarchy on primate health. *Science, 308,* 648–652. (pp. 408, 409)

Sato, K. (1987). Distribution of the cost of maintaining common resources. *Journal of Experimental Social Psychology, 23,* 19–31. (p. 564)

Saul, S. (2007, March 15). F.D.A. warns of sleeping pills' strange effects. *New York Times* (www.nytimes.com). (p. 78)

Saulny, S. (2006, June 21). A legacy of the storm: Depression and suicide. *New York Times* (www.nytimes.com). (p. 401)

Savage-Rumbaugh, E. S., Murphy, J., Sevcik, R. A., Brakke, K. E., Williams, S. L., & Rumbaugh, D. M., with commentary by Bates, E. (1993). Language comprehension in ape and child. *Monographs of the Society for Research in Child Development, 58* (no. 233), 1–254. (p. 312)

Savic, I., Berglund, H., & Lindstrom, P. (2005). Brain response to putative pheromones in homosexual men. *Proceedings of the National Academy of Sciences, 102,* 7356–7361. (p. 366)

Savitsky, K., Epley, N., & Gilovich, T. (2001). Do others judge us as harshly as we think? Overestimating the impact of our failures, shortcomings, and mishaps. *Journal of Personality and Social Psychology, 81,* 44–56. (p. 446)

Savitsky, K., & Gilovich, T. (2003). The illusion of transparency and the alleviation of speech anxiety. *Journal of Experimental Social Psychology, 39,* 618–625. (p. 446)

Savoy, C., & Beitel, P. (1996). Mental imagery for basketball. *International Journal of Sport Psychology, 27,* 454–462. (p. 308)

Sawyer, M. G., Arney, F. M., Baghurst, P. A., Clark, J. J., Graetz, B. W., Kosky, R. J., Nurcombe, B., Patton, G. C., Prior, M. R., Raphael, B., Rey, J., Whaites, L. C., & Zubrick, S. R. (2000). *The mental health of young people in Australia.* Canberra: Mental Health and Special Programs Branch, Commonwealth Department of Health and Aged Care. (p. 473)

Scarr, S. (1989). Protecting general intelligence: Constructs and consequences for interventions. In R. J. Linn (Ed.), *Intelligence: Measurement, theory, and public policy.* Champaign: University of Illinois Press. (p. 315)

Scarr, S. (1990). Back cover comments on J. Dunn & R. Plomin (1990), *Separate lives: Why siblings are so different.* New York: Basic Books. (p. 112)

Scarr, S. (1993, May/June). Quoted by *Psychology Today,* Nature's thumbprint: So long, superparents, p. 16. (p. 120)

Schab, F. R. (1991). Odor memory: Taking stock. *Psychological Bulletin, 109,* 242–251. (p. 204)

Schachter, S., & Singer, J. E. (1962). Cognitive, social and physiological determinants of emotional state. *Psychological Review, 69,* 379–399. (pp. 377, 380)

Schacter, D. L. (1992). Understanding implicit memory: A cognitive neuroscience approach. *American Psychologist, 47,* 559–569. (p. 270)

Schacter, D. L. (1996). *Searching for memory: The brain, the mind, and the past.* New York: Basic Books. (pp. 166, 270, 271, 284, 427)

Schafer, G. (2005). Infants can learn decontextualized words before their first birthday. *Child Development, 76,* 87–96. (p. 303)

Schall, T., & Smith, G. (2000, Fall). Career trajectories in baseball. *Chance,* pp. 35–38. (p. 164)

Scheier, M. F., & Carver, C. S. (1992). Effects of optimism on psychological and physical well-being: Theoretical overview and empirical update. *Cognitive Therapy and Research, 16,* 201–228. (p. 409)

Schein, E. H. (1956). The Chinese indoctrination program for prisoners of war: A study of attempted brainwashing. *Psychiatry, 19,* 149–172. (p. 528)

Scherer, K. R., Banse, R., & Wallbott, H. G. (2001). Emotion inferences from vocal expression correlate across languages and cultures. *Journal of Cross-Cultural Psychology, 32,* 76–92. (p. 384)

Schiavi, R. C., & Schreiner-Engel, P. (1988). Nocturnal penile tumescence in healthy aging men. *Journal of Gerontology: Medical Sciences, 43,* M146–M150. (p. 74)

Schilt, T., de Win, M. M. L, Koeter, M., Jager, G., Korf, D. J., van den Brink, W., & Schmand, B. (2007). Cognition in novice Ecstasy users with minimal exposure to other drugs. *Archives of General Psychiatry, 64,* 728–736. (p. 95)

Schimel, J., Arndt, J., Pyszczynski, T., & Greenberg, J. (2001). Being accepted for who we are: Evidence that social validation of the intrinsic self reduces general defensiveness. *Journal of Personality and Social Psychology, 80,* 35–52. (p. 432)

Schimmack, U., & Lucas, R. (2007). Marriage matters: Spousal similarity in life satisfaction. *Schmollers Jahrbuch, 127,* 1–7. (p. 397)

Schimmack, U., Oishi, S., & Diener, E. (2005). Individualism: A valid and important dimension of cultural differences between nations. *Personality and Social Psychology Review, 9,* 17–31. (p. 123)

Schkade, D., Sunstein, C. R., & Hastie, R. (2006). *What happened on deliberation day?* University of Chicago Law and Economics, Olin Working Paper No. 298. (p. 540)

Schlaug, G., Jancke, L., Huang, Y., & Steinmetz, H. (1995). In vivo evidence of structural brain asymmetry in musicians. *Science, 267,* 699–701. (p. 45)

Schmidt, F. L., & Hunter, J. E. (1998). The validity and utility of selection methods in personnel psychology: Practical and theoretical implications of 85 years of research findings. *Psychological Bulletin, 124,* 262–274. (p. 445)

Schmitt, D. P. (2005). Sociosexuality from Argentina to Zimbabwe: A 48-nation study of sex, culture, and strategies of human mating. *Behavioral and Brain Sciences, 28*, 247–311. (p. 116)

Schmitt, D. P. (2007). Sexual strategies across sexual orientations: How personality traits and culture relate to sociosexuality among gays, lesbians, bisexuals, and heterosexuals. *Journal of Psychology and Human Sexuality, 18*, 183–214. (pp. 115, 116)

Schmitt, D. P., & Allik, J. (2005). Simultaneous administration of the Rosenberg Self-esteem Scale in 53 nations: Exploring the universal and culture-specific features of global self-esteem. *Journal of Personality and Social Psychology, 89*, 623–642. (p. 448)

Schmitt, D. P., Allik, J., McCrae, R. R., & Benet-Martínez, V., with many others. (2007). The geographic distribution of Big Five personality traits: Patterns and profiles of human self-description across 56 nations. *Journal of Cross-Cultural Psychology, 38*, 173–212. (p. 436)

Schmitt, D. P., & Pilcher, J. J. (2004). Evaluating evidence of psychological adaptation: How do we know one when we see one? *Psychological Science, 15*, 643–649. (p. 114)

Schnall, E., Wassertheil-Smnoller, S., Swencionis, C., Zemon, V., Tinker, L., O'Sullivan, M. J., Van Horn, L., & Goodwin, M. (2008). The relationship between religion and cardiovascular outcomes and all-cause mortality in the women's health initiative observational study. *Psychology and Health*, in press. (p. 414)

Schnaper, N. (1980). Comments germane to the paper entitled "The reality of death experiences" by Ernst Rodin. *Journal of Nervous and Mental Disease, 168*, 268–270. (p. 95)

Schneider, R. H., Alexander, C. N., Staggers, F., Rainforth, M., Salerno, J. W., Hartz, A., Arndt, S., Barnes, V. A., & Nidich, S. (2005). Long-term effects of stress reduction on mortality in persons > or = 55 years of age with systemic hypertension. *American Journal of Cardiology, 95*, 1060–1064. (p. 413)

Schneider, S. L. (2001). In search of realistic optimism: Meaning, knowledge, and warm fuzziness. *American Psychologist, 56*, 250–263. (p. 443)

Schneiderman, N. (1999). Behavioral medicine and the management of HIV/AIDS. *International Journal of Behavioral Medicine, 6*, 3–12. (p. 405)

Schoenborn, C. A., & Adams, P. F. (2008). Sleep duration as a correlate of smoking, alcohol use, leisure-time physical inactivity, and obesity among adults: United States, 2004–2006. Centers for Disease Control and Prevention (www.cdc.gov/nchs). (p. 76)

Schoeneman, T. J. (1994). Individualism. In V. S. Ramachandran (Ed.), *Encyclopedia of human behavior*. San Diego: Academic Press. (p. 124)

Schofield, J. W. (1986). Black-White contact in desegregated schools. In M. Hewstone & R. Brown (Eds.), *Contact and conflict in intergroup encounters*. Oxford: Basil Blackwell. (p. 565)

Schonfield, D., & Robertson, B. A. (1966). Memory storage and aging. *Canadian Journal of Psychology, 20*, 228–236. (p. 167)

Schooler, J. W., Gerhard, D., & Loftus, E. F. (1986). Qualities of the unreal. *Journal of Experimental Psychology: Learning, Memory, and Cognition, 12*, 171–181. (p. 282)

Schuman, H., & Scott, J. (June, 1989). Generations and collective memories. *American Sociological Review, 54*(3), 359–381. (p. 166)

Schwartz, B. (1984). *Psychology of learning and behavior* (2nd ed.). New York: Norton. (pp. 234, 465)

Schwartz, B. (2000). Self-determination: The tyranny of freedom. *American Psychologist, 55*, 79–88. (p. 442)

Schwartz, B. (2004). *The paradox of choice: Why more is less.* New York: Ecco/HarperCollins. (p. 442)

Schwartz, J., & Estrin, J. (2004, November 7). Living for today, locked in a paralyzed body. *New York Times* (www.nytimes.com). (p. 393)

Schwartz, J. M., Stoessel, P. W., Baxter, L. R., Jr., Martin, K. M., & Phelps, M. E. (1996). Systematic changes in cerebral glucose metabolic rate after successful behavior modification treatment of obsessive-compulsive disorder. *Archives of General Psychiatry, 53*, 109–113. (pp. 503, 519)

Schwartz, S. H., & Rubel, T. (2005). Sex differences in value priorities: Cross-cultural and multimethod studies. *Journal of Personality and Social Psychology, 89*, 1010–1028. (p. 127)

Schwarz, N., Strack, F., Kommer, D., & Wagner, D. (1987). Soccer, rooms, and the quality of your life: Mood effects on judgments of satisfaction with life in general and with specific domains. *European Journal of Social Psychology, 17*, 69–79. (p. 276)

Sclafani, A. (1995). How food preferences are learned: Laboratory animal models. *Proceedings of the Nutrition Society, 54*, 419–427. (p. 347)

Scott, D. J., & others. (2004, November 9). U-M team reports evidence that smoking affects human brain's natural "feel good" chemical system (press release by Kara Gavin). University of Michigan Medical School (www.med.umich.edu). (p. 93)

Scott, D. J., Stohler, C. S., Egnatuk, C. M., Wang, H., Koeppe, R. A., & Zubieta, J-K. (2007). Individual differences in reward responding explain placebo-induced expectations and effects. *Neuron, 55*, 325–336. (p. 200)

Scott, W. A., Scott, R., & McCabe, M. (1991). Family relationships and children's personality: A cross-cultural, cross-source comparison. *British Journal of Social Psychology, 30*, 1–20. (p. 125)

Sdorow, L. M. (2005). The people behind psychology. In B. Perlman, L. McCann, & W. Buskist (Eds.), *Voices of experience: Memorable talks from the National Institute on the Teaching of Psychology*. Washington, DC: American Psychological Society. (p. 425)

Seal, K. H., Bertenthal, D., Miner, C. R., Sen, S., & Marmar, C. (2007). Bringing the war back home: Mental health disorders among 103,788 U.S. veterans returning from Iraq and Afghanistan seen at Department of Veterans Affairs facilities. *Archives of Internal Medicine, 167*, 467–482. (p. 464)

Seamon, J. G., Philbin, M. M., & Harrison, L. G. (2006). Do you remember proposing marriage to the Pepsi machine? False recollections from a campus walk. *Psychonomic Bulletin and Review, 13*, 752–756. (p. 282)

Sebat, J., & 31 others. (2007). Strong association of de novo copy number mutations with autism. *Science, 316*, 445–449. (p. 146)

Sechrest, L., Stickle, T. R., & Stewart, M. (1998). The role of assessment in clinical psychology. In A. Bellack, M. Hersen (series eds.), & C. R. Reynolds (vol. ed.), *Comprehensive clinical psychology: Vol. 4. Assessment*. New York: Pergamon. (p. 425)

Seeman, P., Guan, H-C., & Van Tol, H. H. M. (1993). Dopamine D4 receptors elevated in schizophrenia. *Nature, 365*, 441–445. (p. 483)

Segal, N. L. (1999). *Entwined lives: Twins and what they tell us about human behavior.* New York: Dutton. (p. 109)

Segal, N. L. (2000). Virtual twins: New findings on within-family environmental influences on intelligence. *Journal of Educational Psychology, 92*, 442–448. (p. 109)

Segal, N. L., McGuire, S. A., Havlena, J., Gill, P., & Hershberger, S. L. (2007). Intellectual similarity of virtual twin pairs: Developmental trends. *Personality and Individual Differences, 42*, 1209–1219. (p. 326)

Segall, M. H., Dasen, P. R., Berry, J. W., & Poortinga, Y. H. (1990). *Human behavior in global perspective: An introduction to cross-cultural psychology.* New York: Pergamon. (pp. 115, 130, 148)

Segerstrom, S. C. (2007). Stress, energy, and immunity. *Current Directions in Psychological Science, 16*, 326–330. (p. 398)

Segerstrom, S. C., Taylor, S. E., Kemeny, M. E., & Fahey, J. L. (1998). Optimism is associated with mood, coping, and immune change in response to stress. *Journal of Personality and Social Psychology, 74*, 1646–1655. (p. 409)

Seidler, G. H., & Wagner, F. E. (2006). Comparing the efficacy of EMDR and trauma-focused cognitive-behavioral therapy in the treatment of PTSD: A meta-analytic study. *Psychological Medicine, 36*, 1515–1522. (p. 508)

Seidlitz, L., & Diener, E. (1998). Sex differences in the recall of affective experiences. *Journal of Personality and Social Psychology, 74*, 262–271. (p. 477)

Self, C. E. (1994). *Moral culture and victimization in residence halls.* Unpublished master's thesis. Bowling Green University. (p. 99)

Seligman, M. E. P. (1975). *Helplessness: On depression, development and death.* San Francisco: Freeman. (p. 441)

Seligman, M. E. P. (1991). *Learned optimism.* New York: Knopf. (pp. 65, 441, 478)

Seligman, M. E. P. (1994). *What you can change and what you can't.* New York: Knopf. (pp. 120, 412, 428, 447)

Seligman, M. E. P. (1995). The effectiveness of psychotherapy: The Consumer Reports study. *American Psychologist, 50*, 965–974. (pp. 478, 505, 509)

Seligman, M. E. P. (2002). *Authentic happiness: Using the new positive psychology to realize your potential for lasting fulfillment.* New York: Free Press. (pp. 443, 447, 503)

Seligman, M. E. P. (2004). Eudaemonia, the good life. A talk with Martin Seligman. www.edge.org. (p. 443)

Seligman, M. E. P., Steen, T. A., Park, N., & Peterson, C. (2005). Positive psychology progress: Empirical validation of interventions. *American Psychologist, 60,* 410–421. (pp. 397, 443)

Seligman, M. E. P., & Yellen, A. (1987). What is a dream? *Behavior Research and Therapy, 25,* 1–24. (p. 72)

Sellers, H. (2010). *Face first.* New York: Riverhead Books. (p. 179)

Selye, H. (1936). A syndrome produced by diverse nocuous agents. *Nature, 138,* 32. (p. 399)

Selye, H. (1976). *The stress of life.* New York: McGraw-Hill. (p. 399)

Sen, A. (2003). Missing women—revisited. *British Medical Journal, 327,* 1297–1298. (p. 544)

Senghas, A., & Coppola, M. (2001). Children creating language: How Nicaraguan Sign Language acquired a spatial grammar. *Psychological Science, 12,* 323–328. (p. 304)

Sengupta, S. (2001, October 10). Sept. 11 attack narrows the racial divide. *New York Times* (www.nytimes.com). (p. 566)

Senju, A., Maeda, M., Kikuchi, Y., Hasegawa, T., Tojo, Y., & Osanai, H. (2007). Absence of contagious yawning in children with autism spectrum disorder. *Biology Letters, 3,* 706–708. (pp. 147, 249)

Sensenbrenner, F. J. (2004, March 11). Quoted by C. Hulse, Vote in House offers a shield in obesity suits. *New York Times* (www.nytimes.com). (p. 350)

Service, R. F. (1994). Will a new type of drug make memory-making easier? *Science, 266,* 218–219. (p. 268)

Seto, M. C., & Barbaree, H. E. (1995). The role of alcohol in sexual aggression. *Clinical Psychology Review, 15,* 545–566. (p. 90)

Shadish, W. R., & Baldwin, S. A. (2005). Effects of behavioral marital therapy: A meta-analysis of randomized controlled trials. *Journal of Consulting and Clinical Psychology, 73,* 6–14. (p. 506)

Shadish, W. R., Matt, G. E., Navarro, A. M., & Phillips, G. (2000). The effects of psychological therapies under clinically representative conditions: A meta-analysis. *Psychological Bulletin, 126,* 512–529. (p. 506)

Shafir, E., & LeBoeuf, R. A. (2002). Rationality. *Annual Review of Psychology, 53,* 491–517. (p. 298)

Shanahan, L., McHale, S. M., Osgood, D. W., & Crouter, A. C. (2007). Conflict frequency with mothers and fathers from middle childhood to late adolescence: Within- and between-families comparisons. *Developmental Psychology, 43,* 539–550. (pp. 160, 161)

Shapiro, F. (1989). Efficacy of the eye movement desensitization procedure in the treatment of traumatic memories. *Journal of Traumatic Stress, 2,* 199–223. (p. 508)

Shapiro, F. (1995). *Eye movement desensitization and reprocessing: Basic principles, protocols, and procedures.* New York: Guilford. (p. 508)

Shapiro, F. (1999). Eye movement desensitization and reprocessing (EMDR) and the anxiety disorders: Clinical and research implications of an integrated psychotherapy treatment. *Journal of Anxiety Disorders, 13,* 35–67. (p. 508)

Shapiro, F. (Ed.). (2002). *EMDR as an integrative psychotherapy approach: Experts of diverse orienta-tions explore the paradigm prism.* Washington, DC: APA Books. (p. 508)

Shapiro, F. (2007). EMDR and case conceptualization from an adaptive information processing perspective. In F. Shapiro, F. W. Kaslow, & L. Maxfield (Eds.), *Handbook of EMDR and family therapy processes.* Hoboken, NJ: Wiley. (p. 508)

Sharma, A. R., McGue, M. K., & Benson, P. L. (1998). The psychological adjustment of United States adopted adolescents and their nonadopted siblings. *Child Development, 69,* 791–802. (p. 110)

Shattuck, P. T. (2006). The contribution of diagnostic substitution to the growing administrative prevalence of autism in US special education. *Pediatrics, 117,* 1028–1037. (p. 146)

Shaver, P. R., & Mikulincer, M. (2007). Adult attachment strategies and the regulation of emotion. In J. J. Gross (Ed.), *Handbook of emotion regulation.* New York: Guilford Press. (p. 152)

Shaver, P. R., Morgan, H. J., & Wu, S. (1996). Is love a basic emotion? *Personal Relationships, 3,* 81–96. (p. 389)

Shaw, H. L. (1989–90). Comprehension of the spoken word and ASL translation by chimpanzees (Pan troglodytes). *Friends of Washoe, 9*(1/2), 8–19. (p. 312)

Sheehan, S. (1982). *Is there no place on earth for me?* Boston: Houghton Mifflin. (p. 480)

Sheldon, K. M., Elliot, A. J., Kim, Y., & Kasser, T. (2001). What is satisfying about satisfying events? Testing 10 candidate psychological needs. *Journal of Personality and Social Psychology, 80,* 325–339. (p. 370)

Sheldon, K. M., & Niemiec, C. P. (2006). It's not just the amount that counts: Balanced need satisfaction also affects well-being. *Journal of Personality and Social Psychology, 91,* 331–341. (p. 370)

Sheldon, M. S., Cooper, M. L., Geary, D. C., Hoard, M., & DeSoto, M. C. (2006). Fertility cycle patterns in motives for sexual behavior. *Personality and Social Psychology Bulletin, 32,* 1659–1673. (p. 358)

Shenton, M. E. (1992). Abnormalities of the left temporal lobe and thought disorder in schizophrenia: A quantitative magnetic resonance imaging study. *New England Journal of Medicine, 327,* 604–612. (p. 483)

Shepard, R. N. (1990). *Mind sights.* New York: Freeman. (pp. 28, 216)

Shepherd, C. (1997, April). News of the weird. *Funny Times,* p. 15. (p. 109)

Shepherd, C. (1999, June). News of the weird. *Funny Times,* p. 21. (p. 354)

Sher, L. (2006). Alcohol consumption and suicide. *QJM: An International Journal of Medicine, 99,* 57–61. (p. 474)

Shergill, S. S., Bays, P. M., Frith, C. D., & Wolpert, D. M. (2003). Two eyes for an eye: The neuroscience of force escalation. *Science, 301,* 187. (p. 564)

Sherif, M. (1966). *In common predicament: Social psychology of intergroup conflict and cooperation.* Boston: Houghton Mifflin. (p. 565)

Sherman, P. W., & Flaxman, S. M. (2001). Protecting ourselves from food. *American Scientist, 89,* 142–151. (p. 347)

Sherry, D., & Vaccarino, A. L. (1989). Hippocampus and memory for food caches in black-capped chickadees. *Behavioral Neuroscience, 103,* 308–318. (p. 271)

Shettleworth, S. J. (1973). Food reinforcement and the organization of behavior in golden hamsters. In R. A. Hinde & J. Stevenson-Hinde (Eds.), *Constraints on learning.* London: Academic Press. (p. 244)

Shettleworth, S. J. (1993). Where is the comparison in comparative cognition? Alternative research programs. *Psychological Science, 4,* 179–184. (p. 267)

Shinkareva, S. V., Mason, R. A., Malave, V. L., Wang, W., Mitchell, T. M., & Just, M. A. (2008, January 2). Using fMRI brain activation to identify cognitive states associated with perceptions of tools and dwellings. *PloS One 3*(1), 31394. (p. 66)

Shotland, R. L. (1984, March 12). Quoted in Maureen Dowd, 20 years after the murder of Kitty Genovese, the question remains: Why? *The New York Times,* p. B1. (p. 561)

Showers, C. (1992). The motivational and emotional consequences of considering positive or negative possibilities for an upcoming event. *Journal of Personality and Social Psychology, 63,* 474–484. (p. 443)

Shulman, P. (2000, June). The girl who loved math. *Discover,* pp. 67–70. (p. 329)

Sieff, E. M., Dawes, R. M., & Loewenstein, G. (1999). Anticipated versus actual reaction to HIV test results. *The American Journal of Psychology, 112,* 297–313. (p. 393)

Siegel, J. (2001). The REM sleep-memory consolidation hypothesis. *Science, 294,* 1058–1063. (p. 82)

Siegel, J. M. (2003, November). Why we sleep. *Scientific American,* pp. 92–97. (p. 77)

Siegel, R. K. (1977, October). Hallucinations. *Scientific American,* pp. 132–140. (p. 96)

Siegel, R. K. (1980). The psychology of life after death. *American Psychologist, 35,* 911–931. (p. 96)

Siegel, R. K. (1982, October). Quoted by J. Hooper, Mind tripping. *Omni,* pp. 72–82, 159–160. (p. 95)

Siegel, R. K. (1984, March 15). Personal communication. (p. 95)

Siegel, R. K. (1990). *Intoxication.* New York: Pocket Books. (pp. 89, 94, 96)

Siegel, S. (2005). Drug tolerance, drug addiction, and drug anticipation. *Current Directions in Psychological Science, 14,* 296–300. (pp. 226, 235)

Siegler, R. S., & Ellis, S. (1996). Piaget on childhood. *Psychological Science, 7,* 211–215. (p. 143)

Silbersweig, D. A., Stern, E., Frith, C., Cahill, C., Holmes, A., Grootoonk, S., Seaward, J., McKenna, P., Chua, S. E., Schnorr, L., Jones, T., & Frackowiak, R. S. J. (1995). A functional neuroanatomy of hallucinations in schizophrenia. *Nature, 378,* 176–179. (p. 483)

Silva, A. J., Stevens, C. F., Tonegawa, S., & Wang, Y. (1992). Deficient hippocampal long-term potentiation in alpha-calcium-calmodulin kinase II mutant mice. *Science, 257,* 201–206. (p. 268)

Silva, C. E., & Kirsch, I. (1992). Interpretive sets, expectancy, fantasy proneness, and dissociation as predictors of hypnotic response. *Journal of Personality and Social Psychology, 63,* 847–856. (p. 84)

Silver, M., & Geller, D. (1978). On the irrelevance of evil: The organization and individual action. *Journal of Social Issues, 34,* 125–136. (p. 537)

Silveri, M. M., Rohan, M. L., Pimental, P. J., Gruber, S. A., Rosso, I. M., & Yurgelun-Todd, D. A. (2006). Sex differences in the relationship between white matter microstructure and impulsivity in adolescents. *Magnetic Resonance Imaging, 24,* 833–841. (p. 156)

Silverman, K., Evans, S. M., Strain, E. C., & Griffiths, R. R. (1992). Withdrawal syndrome after the double-blind cessation of caffeine consumption. *New England Journal of Medicine, 327,* 1109–1114. (p. 91)

Simek, T. C., & O'Brien, R. M. (1981). *Total golf: A behavioral approach to lowering your score and getting more out of your game.* Huntington, NY: B-MOD Associates. (p. 245)

Simek, T. C., & O'Brien, R. M. (1988). A chaining-mastery, discrimination training program to teach Little Leaguers to hit a baseball. *Human Performance, 1,* 73–84. (p. 245)

Simon, G. E., & Savarino, J. (2007). Suicide attempts among patients starting depression treatment with medications or psychotherapy. *American Journal of Psychiatry, 164,* 1029–1034. (p. 516)

Simon, G. E., Von Korff, M., Saunders, K., Miglioretti, D. L., Crane, P. K., van Belle, G., & Kessler, R. C. (2006). Association between obesity and psychiatric disorders in the U.S. population. *Archives of General Psychiatry, 63,* 824–830. (p. 351)

Simon, H. (2001, February). Quoted by A. M. Hayashi, When to trust your gut. *Harvard Business Review,* pp. 59–65. (p. 300)

Simons, D. J. (1996). In sight, out of mind: When object representations fail. *Psychological Science, 7,* 301–305. (p. 69)

Simons, D. J., & Ambinder, M. S. (2005). Change blindness: Theory and consequences. *Current Directions in Psychological Science, 14,* 44–48. (p. 69)

Simons, D. J., & Chabris, C. F. (1999). Gorillas in our midst: Sustained inattentional blindness for dynamic events. *Perception, 28,* 1059–1074. (p. 69)

Simonton, D. K. (1988). Age and outstanding achievement: What do we know after a century of research? *Psychological Bulletin, 104,* 251–267. (p. 167)

Simonton, D. K. (1990). Creativity in the later years: Optimistic prospects for achievement. *The Gerontologist, 30,* 626–631. (p. 167)

Simonton, D. K. (1992). The social context of career success and course for 2,026 scientists and inventors. *Personality and Social Psychology Bulletin, 18,* 452–463. (p. 318)

Simonton, D. K. (2000). Creativity: Cognitive, personal, developmental, and social aspects. *American Psychologist, 55,* 151–158. (p. 317)

Simonton, D. K. (2000). Methodological and theoretical orientation and the long-term disciplinary impact of 54 eminent psychologists. *Review of General Psychology, 4,* 13–24. (p. 253)

Sinclair, R. C., Hoffman, C., Mark, M. M., Martin, L. L., & Pickering, T. L. (1994). Construct accessibility and the misattribution of arousal: Schachter and Singer revisited. *Psychological Science, 5,* 15–18. (p. 381)

Singelis, T. M., & Sharkey, W. F. (1995). Culture, self-construal, and embarrassability. *Cross-Cultural Psychology, 26,* 622–644. (p. 124)

Singelis, T. M., Bond, M. H., Sharkey, W. F., & Lai, C. S. Y. (1999). Unpackaging culture's influence on self-esteem and embarrassability: The role of self-construals. *Journal of Cross-Cultural Psychology, 30,* 315–341. (p. 124)

Singer, J. L. (1981). Clinical intervention: New developments in methods and evaluation. In L. T. Benjamin, Jr. (Ed.), *The G. Stanley Hall Lecture Series* (Vol. 1). Washington, DC: American Psychological Association. (p. 506)

Singer, T., Seymour, B., O'Doherty, J., Kaube, H., Dolan, R. J., & Frith, C. (2004). Empathy for pain involves the affective but not sensory components of pain. *Science, 303,* 1157–1162. (pp. 200, 249)

Singh, D. (1993). Adaptive significance of female physical attractiveness: Role of waist-to-hip ratio. *Journal of Personality and Social Psychology, 65,* 293–307. (p. 116)

Singh, D. (1995). Female health, attractiveness, and desirability for relationships: Role of breast asymmetry and waist-to-hip ratio. *Ethology and Sociobiology, 16,* 465–481. (p. 116)

Singh, D., & Randall, P. K. (2007). Beauty is in the eye of the plastic surgeon: Waist-hip ration (WHR) and women's attractiveness. *Personality and Individual Differences, 43,* 329–340. (p. 116)

Singh, S. (1997). *Fermat's enigma: The epic quest to solve the world's greatest mathematical problem.* New York: Bantam Books. (p. 317)

Singh, S., & Riber, K. A. (1997, November). Fermat's last stand. *Scientific American,* pp. 68–73. (p. 318)

Sipski, M. L., & Alexander, C. J. (1999). Sexual response in women with spinal cord injuries: Implications for our understanding of the able bodied. *Journal of Sex and Marital Therapy, 25,* 11–22. (p. 42)

Sireteanu, R. (1999). Switching on the infant brain. *Science, 286,* 59, 61. (p. 214)

Sjöstrum, L. (1980). Fat cells and body weight. In A. J. Stunkard (Ed.), *Obesity.* Philadelphia: Saunders. (p. 351)

Skinner, B. F. (1953). *Science and human behavior.* New York: Macmillan. (p. 240)

Skinner, B. F. (1956). A case history in scientific method. *American Psychologist, 11,* 221–233. (p. 241)

Skinner, B. F. (1957). *Verbal behavior.* Englewood Cliffs, NJ: Prentice-Hall. (p. 304)

Skinner, B. F. (1961, November). Teaching machines. *Scientific American,* pp. 91–102. (p. 240)

Skinner, B. F. (1983, September). Origins of a behaviorist. *Psychology Today,* pp. 22–33. (pp. 244, 478)

Skinner, B. F. (1985). *Cognitive science and behaviorism.* Unpublished manuscript, Harvard University. (p. 304)

Skinner, B. F. (1986). What is wrong with daily life in the Western world? *American Psychologist, 41,* 568–574. (p. 245)

Skinner, B. F. (1988). The school of the future. Address to the American Psychological Association convention. (p. 245)

Skinner, B. F. (1989). Teaching machines. *Science, 243,* 1535. (p. 245)

Skinner, B. F. (1990). Address to the American Psychological Association convention. (p. 243)

Skitka, L. J., Bauman, C. W., & Mullen, E. (2004). Political tolerance and coming to psychological closure following the September 11, 2001, terrorist attacks: An integrative approach. *Personality and Social Psychology Bulletin, 30,* 743–756. (p. 391)

Skoog, G., & Skoog, I. (1999). A 40-year follow-up of patients with obsessive-compulsive disorder. *Archives of General Psychiatry, 56,* 121–127. (p. 464)

Skov, R. B., & Sherman, S. J. (1986). Information-gathering processes: Diagnosticity, hypothesis-confirmatory strategies, and perceived hypothesis confirmation. *Journal of Experimental Social Psychology, 22,* 93–121. (p. 293)

Slater, E., & Meyer, A. (1959). *Confinia psychiatra.* Basel: S. Karger AG. (p. 472)

Slater, L. (2000, November 19). How do you cure a sex addict? *New York Times Magazine* (www.nytimes.com). (p. 515)

Sleep Foundation. (2006). *The ABC's of back-to-school sleep schedules: The consequences of insufficient sleep.* National Sleep Foundation (press release) (www.sleepfoundation.org). (p. 76)

Sloan, R. P. (2005). Field analysis of the literature on religion, spirituality, and health. Columbia University (available at www.metanexus.net/tarp). (p. 414)

Sloan, R. P., & Bagiella, E. (2002). Claims about religious involvement and health outcomes. *Annals of Behavioral Medicine, 24,* 14–21. (p. 414)

Sloan, R. P., Bagiella, E., & Powell, T. (1999). Religion, spirituality, and medicine. *Lancet, 353,* 664–667. (p. 414)

Sloan, R. P., Bagiella, E., VandeCreek, L., & Poulos, P. (2000). Should physicians prescribe religious activities? *New England Journal of Medicine, 342,* 1913–1917. (p. 414)

Slovic, P., Finucane, M., Peters, E., & MacGregor, D. G. (2002). The affect heuristic. In T. Gilovich, D. Griffin, & D. Kahneman (Eds.), *Intuitive judgment: Heuristics and biases.* New York: Cambridge University Press. (p. 92)

Small, M. F. (1997). Making connections. *American Scientist, 85,* 502–504. (p. 125)

Small, M. F. (2002, July). What you can learn from drunk monkeys. *Discover,* pp. 40–45. (p. 98)

Smedley, A., & Smedley, B. D. (2005). Race as biology is fiction, racism as a social problem is real: Anthropological and historical perspectives on the social construction of race. *American Psychologist, 60,* 16–26. (p. 332)

Smelser, N. J., & Mitchell, F. (Eds.). (2002). *Terrorism: Perspectives from the behavioral and social sciences.* Washington, DC: National Research Council, National Academies Press. (p. 547)

Smith, A. (1983). Personal correspondence. (p. 482)

Smith, C. (2006, January 7). Nearly 100, LSD's father ponders his "problem child." *New York Times* (www.nytimes.com). (pp. 95, 402)

Smith, E., & Delargy, M. (2005). Locked-in syndrome. *British Medical Journal, 330,* 406–409. (p. 393)

Smith, J. E., Waldorf, V. A., & Trembath, D. L. (1990). "Single white male looking for thin, very attractive . . ." *Sex Roles, 23,* 675–685. (p. 351)

Smith, M. B. (1978). Psychology and values. *Journal of Social Issues, 34,* 181–199. (p. 431)

Smith, M. L., & Glass, G. V. (1977). Meta-analysis of psychotherapy outcome studies. *American Psychologist, 32,* 752–760. (p. 506)

Smith, M. L., Glass, G. V., & Miller, R. L. (1980). *The benefits of psychotherapy.* Baltimore: Johns Hopkins Press. (p. 506)

Smith, S. M., McIntosh, W. D., & Bazzini, D. G. (1999). Are the beautiful good in Hollywood? An investigation of the beauty-and-goodness stereotype on film. *Basic and Applied Social Psychology, 21,* 69–80. (p. 557)

Smith, T. B., Bartz, J., & Richards, P. S. (2007). Outcomes of religious and spiritual adaptations to psychotherapy: A meta-analytic review. *Psychotherapy Research, 17,* 643–655. (p. 511)

Smith, T. W. (1998, December). *American sexual behavior: Trends, sociodemographic differences, and risk behavior* (National Opinion Research Center GSS Topical Report No. 25). (pp. 361, 362, 363, 364)

Smith, T. W. (2005). *Troubles in America: A study of negative life events across time and sub-groups* (GSS Topical Report No 40., National Opinion Research Center, University of Chicago). (p. 504)

Smolak, L., & Murnen, S. K. (2002). A meta-analytic examination of the relationship between child sexual abuse and eating disorders. *International Journal of Eating Disorders, 31,* 136–150. (p. 348)

Smoreda, Z., & Licoppe, C. (2000). Gender-specific use of the domestic telephone. *Social Psychology Quarterly, 63,* 238–252. (p. 128)

Snedeker, J., Geren, J., & Shafto, C. L. (2007). Starting over: International adoption as a natural experiment in language development. *Psychological Science, 18,* 79–86. (p. 303)

Snodgrass, S. E., Higgins, J. G., & Todisco, L. (1986). The effects of walking behavior on mood. Paper presented at the American Psychological Association convention. (p. 389)

Snyder, M. (1984). When belief creates reality. In L. Berkowitz (Ed.), *Advances in experimental social psychology* (Vol. 18). New York: Academic Press. (p. 459)

Snyder, S. H. (1984). Neurosciences: An integrative discipline. *Science, 225,* 1255–1257. (p. 37)

Snyder, S. H. (1986). *Drugs and the brain.* New York: Scientific American Library. (p. 516)

Social Watch. (2006, March 8). No country in the world treats its women as well as its men (www.socialwatch.org). (p. 130)

Society for Personality Assessment. (2005). The status of the Rorschach in clinical and forensic practice: An official statement by the Board of Trustees of the Society for Personality Assessment. *Journal of Personality Assessment, 85,* 219–237. (p. 425)

Soloman, D. (December 12, 2004). The science of second guessing. *The New York Times Magazine.* (p. 314)

Solomon, D. A., Keitner, G. I., Miller, I. W., Shea, M. T., & Keller, M. B. (1995). Course of illness and maintenance treatments for patients with bipolar disorder. *Journal of Clinical Psychiatry, 56,* 5–13. (p. 516)

Solomon, J. (1996, May 20). Breaking the silence. *Newsweek,* pp. 20–22. (p. 460)

Solomon, M. (1987, December). Standard issue. *Psychology Today,* pp. 30–31. (p. 557)

Sommer, R. (1969). *Personal space.* Englewood Cliffs, NJ: Prentice-Hall. (p. 122)

Søndergård, L., Kvist, K., Andersen, P. K., & Kessing, L. V. (2006). Do antidepressants prevent suicide? *International Clinical Psychopharmacology, 21,* 211–218. (p. 516)

Song, S. (2006, March 27). Mind over medicine. *Time,* p. 47. (p. 86)

Sontag, S. (1978). *Illness as metaphor.* New York: Farrar, Straus, & Giroux. (p. 405)

Sørensen, H. J., Mortensen, E. L., Reinisch, J. M., & Mednick, S. A. (2005). Breastfeeding and risk of schizophrenia in the Copenhagen Perinatal Cohort. *Acta Psychiatrica Scandinavica, 112,* 26–29. (p. 482)

Sørensen, H. J., Mortensen, E. L., Reinisch, J. M., & Mednick, S. A. (2006). Height, weight, and body mass index in early adulthood and risk of schizophrenia. *Acta Psychiatrica Scandinavica, 114,* 49–54. (p. 482)

Sorkhabi, N. (2005). Applicability of Baumrind's parent typology to collective cultures: Analysis of cultural explanations of parent socialization effects. *International Journal of Behavioral Development, 29,* 552–563. (p. 154)

Soussignan, R. (2001). Duchenne smile, emotional experience, and autonomic reactivity: A test of the facial feedback hypothesis. *Emotion, 2,* 52–74. (p. 389)

Sowell, T. (1991, May/June). Cultural diversity: A world view. *American Enterprise,* pp. 44–55. (p. 567)

Spalding, K. L., & 14 others. (2008). Dynamics of fat cell turnover in humans. *Nature, 453,* 783–787. (p. 351)

Spanos, N. P. (1982). A social psychological approach to hypnotic behavior. In G. Weary & H. L. Mirels (Eds.), *Integrations of clinical and social psychology.* New York: Oxford. (p. 85)

Spanos, N. P. (1986). Hypnosis, nonvolitional responding, and multiple personality: A social psychological perspective. *Progress in Experimental Personality Research, 14,* 1–62. (p. 469)

Spanos, N. P. (1991). Hypnosis, hypnotizability, and hypnotherapy. In C. R. Snyder & D. R. Forsyth (Eds.), *Handbook of social and clinical psychology: The health perspective.* New York: Pergamon Press. (p. 85)

Spanos, N. P. (1994). Multiple identity enactments and multiple personality disorder: A sociocognitive perspective. *Psychological Bulletin, 116,* 143–165. (pp. 86, 469)

Spanos, N. P. (1996). *Multiple identities and false memories: A sociocognitive perspective.* Washington, DC: American Psychological Association Books. (pp. 85, 86, 469)

Spanos, N. P., & Coe, W. C. (1992). A social-psychological approach to hypnosis. In E. Fromm &

M. R. Nash (Eds.), *Contemporary hypnosis research.* New York: Guilford. (p. 86)

Spelke, E. (2005). Sex differences in intrinsic aptitude for mathematics and science? A critical review. *American Psychologist, 60,* 950–958. (p. 330)

Spencer, K. M., Nestor, P. G., Perlmutter, R., Niznikiewicz, M. A., Klump, M. C., Frumin, M., Shenton, M. E., & McCarley, R. W. (2004). Neural synchrony indexes disordered perception and cognition in schizophrenia. *Proceedings of the National Academy of Sciences, 101,* 17288–17293. (p. 483)

Spencer, S. J., Steele, C. M., & Quinn, D. M. (1997). *Stereotype threat and women's math performance.* Unpublished manuscript, Hope College. (p. 333)

Sperling, G. (1960). The information available in brief visual presentations. *Psychological Monographs, 74* (Whole No. 498). (p. 265)

Sperry, R. W. (1964). Problems outstanding in the evolution of brain function. James Arthur Lecture, American Museum of Natural History, New York. Cited by R. Ornstein (1977), *The psychology of consciousness* (2nd ed.). New York: Harcourt Brace Jovanovich. (p. 59)

Sperry, R. W. (1985). Changed concepts of brain and consciousness: Some value implications. *Zygon, 20,* 41–57. (p. 190)

Speth, J. G. (2008). *Bridge at the edge of the world: Capitalism, the environment, and crossing from crisis to sustainability.* New Haven, CT: Yale University Press. (p. 394)

Spiegel, D. (2007). The mind prepared: Hypnosis in surgery. *Journal of the National Cancer Institute, 99,* 1280–1281. (p. 86)

Spiegel, D. (2008, January 31). Coming apart: Trauma and the fragmentation of the self. Dana Foundation (www.dana.org). (p. 470)

Spiegel, K., Leproult, R., L'Hermite-Balériaux, M., Copinschi, G., Penev, P. D., & Van Cauter, E. (2004). Leptin levels are dependent on sleep duration: Relationships with sympathovagal balance, carbohydrate regulation, cortisol, and thyrotropin. *Journal of Clinical Endocrinology and Metabolism, 89,* 5762–5771. (p. 76)

Spiegel, K., Leproult, R., & Van Cauter, E. (1999). Impact of sleep debt on metabolic and endocrine function. *Lancet, 354,* 1435–1439. (p. 76)

Spielberger, C., & London, P. (1982). Rage boomerangs. *American Health, 1,* 52–56. (p. 403)

Spitzer, R. L., & Skodol, A. E. (2000). *DSM-IV-TR casebook: A learning companion to the Diagnostic and Statistical Manual of Mental Disorders, Fourth Edition, Text Revision.* Washington, DC: American Psychiatric Publications. (p. 468)

Spitzer, R. L., Skodol, A. E., & Gibbon, M. (1982). Reply. *Archives of General Psychiatry, 39,* 623–624. (p. 474)

Spradley, J. P., & Phillips, M. (1972). Culture and stress: A quantitative analysis. *American Anthropologist, 74,* 518–529. (p. 122)

Sprecher, S. (1989). The importance to males and females of physical attractiveness, earning potential, and expressiveness in initial attraction. *Sex Roles, 21,* 591–607. (p. 557)

Sprecher, S., & Sedikides, C. (1993). Gender differences in perceptions of emotionality: The case of close heterosexual relationships. *Sex Roles, 28,* 511–530. (p. 385)

Spring, B. (2007). Evidence-based practice in clinical psychology: Why it is, why it matters; what you need to know. *Journal of Clinical Psychology, 63,* 611–631. (p. 507)

Spring, B., Pingitore, R., Bourgeois, M., Kessler, K. H., & Bruckner, E. (1992). The effects and non-effects of skipping breakfast: Results of three studies. Paper presented at the American Psychological Association convention. (p. 356)

Squire, L. R. (1992). Memory and the hippocampus: A synthesis from findings with rats, monkeys, and humans. *Psychological Review, 99,* 195–231. (p. 271)

Srivastava, A., Locke, E. A., & Bartol, K. M. (2001). Money and subject well-being: It's not the money, it's the motives. *Journal of Personality and Social Psychology, 80,* 959–971. (p. 395)

Srivastava, S., John, O. P., Gosling, S. D., & Potter, J. (2003). Development of personality in early and middle adulthood: Set like plaster or persistent change? *Journal of Personality & Social Psychology, 84,* 1041–1053. (p. 436)

Srivastava, S., McGonigal, K. M., Richards, J. M., Butler, E. A., & Gross, J. J. (2006). Optimism in close relationships: How seeing things in a positive light makes them so. *Journal of Personality and Social Psychology, 91,* 143–153. (p. 442)

St. Clair, D., Xu, M., Wang, P., Yu, Y., Fang, Y., Zhang, F., Zheng, X., Gu, N., Feng, G., Sham, P., & He, L. (2005). Rates of adult schizophrenia following prenatal exposure to the Chinese famine of 1959–1961. *Journal of the American Medical Association, 294,* 557–562. (p. 483)

Stack, S. (1992). Marriage, family, religion, and suicide. In R. Maris, A. Berman, J. Maltsberger, & R. Yufit (Eds.), *Assessment and prediction of suicide.* New York: Guilford Press. (p. 474)

Stafford, R. S., MacDonald, E. A., & Finkelstein, S. N. (2001). National patterns of medication treatment for depression, 1987 to 2001. *Primary Care Companion Journal of Clinical Psychiatry, 3,* 232–235. (p. 515)

Stager, C. L., & Werker, J. F. (1997). Infants listen for more phonetic detail in speech perception than in word-learning tasks. *Nature, 388,* 381–382. (p. 302)

Stanford University Center for Narcolepsy. (2002). Narcolepsy is a serious medical disorder and a key to understanding other sleep disorders (www.med.stanford.edu/school/Psychiatry/narcolepsy). (p. 79)

Stanley, J. C. (1997). Varieties of intellectual talent. *Journal of Creative Behavior, 31,* 93–119. (p. 322)

Stanovich, K. (1996). *How to think straight about psychology.* New York: HarperCollins. (p. 420)

Stark, R. (2003a). *For the glory of God: How monotheism led to reformations, science, witchhunts, and the end of slavery.* Princeton, NJ: Princeton University Press. (p. 12)

Stark, R. (2003b, October-November). False conflict: Christianity is not only compatible with science—it created it. *American Enterprise,* pp. 27–33. (p. 12)

Stathopoulou, G., Powers, M. B., Berry, A. C., Smiths, J. A. J., & Otto, M. W. (2006). Exercise interventions for mental health: A quantitative and qualitative review. *Clinical Psychology: Science and Practice, 13,* 179–193. (p. 520)

Statistics Canada. (1999). *Statistical report on the health of Canadians.* Prepared by the Federal, Provincial and Territorial Advisory Committee on Population Health for the Meeting of Ministers of Health, Charlottetown, PEI, September 16–17, 1999. (p. 161)

Statistics Canada. (2002). (www.statcan.ca). (p. 122)

Statistics Canada. (2007). Languages in Canada: 2001 Census (www.statcan.ca). (p. 307)

Statistics Canada. (2007). Overweight and obesity, by province and territory, 2003 and 2005 (www.statcan.ca/english/freepub/16–253–XIE/2 006000/ t446_en.htm). (p. 350)

Statistics Canada. (2008). *Victims and persons accused of homicide, by age and sex.* (Table 253–003). (p. 127)

Steel, P., Schmidt, J., & Schultz, J. (2008). Refining the relationship between personality and subject well-being. *Psychological Bulletin, 134,* 138–161. (p. 396)

Steele, C. (1990, May). A conversation with Claude Steele. *APS Observer,* pp. 11–17. (p. 331)

Steele, C. M. (1995, August 31). Black students live down to expectations. *New York Times.* (p. 333)

Steele, C. M. (1997). A threat in the air: How stereotypes shape intellectual identity and performance. *American Psychologist, 52,* 613–629. (p. 333)

Steele, C. M., & Josephs, R. A. (1990). Alcohol myopia: Its prized and dangerous effects. *American Psychologist, 45,* 921–933. (p. 90)

Steele, C. M., Spencer, S. J., & Aronson, J. (2002). Contending with group image: The psychology of stereotype and social identity threat. *Advances in Experimental Social Psychology, 34,* 379–440. (p. 333)

Steinberg, L. (1987, September). Bound to bicker. *Psychology Today,* pp. 36–39. (p. 161)

Steinberg, L. (2007). Risk taking in adolescence: New perspectives from brain and behavioral science. *Current Directions in Psychological Science, 16,* 55–59. (p. 156)

Steinberg, L., & Morris, A. S. (2001). Adolescent development. *Annual Review of Psychology, 52,* 83–110. (pp. 154, 156, 161)

Steinberg, L., & Scott, E. S. (2003). Less guilty by reason of adolescence: Developmental immaturity, diminished responsibility, and the juvenile death penalty. *American Psychologist, 58,* 1009–1018. (p. 157)

Steinberg, N. (1993, February). Astonishing love stories (from an earlier United Press International report). *Games,* p. 47. (p. 556)

Steinhauer, J. (1999, November 29). Number of twins rises: So does parental stress. *New York Times* (www.nytimes.com). (p. 107)

Steinhauer, J., & Holson, L. M. (2008, September 20). As text messages fly, danger lurks. *New York Times* (www.nytimes.com). (p. 161)

Steinmetz, J. E. (1999). The localization of a simple type of learning and memory: The cerebellum and classical eyeblink conditioning. *Contemporary Psychology, 7,* 72–77. (p. 272)

Stengel, E. (1981). Suicide. In *The new Encyclopaedia Britannica, macropaedia* (Vol. 17, pp. 777–782). Chicago: Encyclopaedia Britannica. (p. 474)

Stern, M., & Karraker, K. H. (1989). Sex stereotyping of infants: A review of gender labeling studies. *Sex Roles, 20,* 501–522. (p. 217)

Stern, S. L., Dhanda, R., & Hazuda, H. P. (2001). Hopelessness predicts mortality in older Mexican and European Americans. *Psychosomatic Medicine, 63,* 344–351. (p. 409)

Sternberg, E. M. (2001). *The balance within: The science connecting health and emotions.* New York: Freeman. (p. 403)

Sternberg, E. M. (2006). A compassionate universe? *Science, 311,* 611–612. (p. 318)

Sternberg, R. J. (1985). *Beyond IQ: A triarchic theory of human intelligence.* New York: Cambridge University Press. (p. 316)

Sternberg, R. J. (1988). Applying cognitive theory to the testing and teaching of intelligence. *Applied Cognitive Psychology, 2,* 231–255. (p. 317)

Sternberg, R. J. (1999). The theory of successful intelligence. *Review of General Psychology, 3,* 292–316. (p. 316)

Sternberg, R. J. (2003). Our research program validating the triarchic theory of successful intelligence: Reply to Gottfredson. *Intelligence, 31,* 399–413. (pp. 316, 317)

Sternberg, R. J. (2006). The Rainbow Project: Enhance the SAT through assessments of analytical, practical, and creative skills. *Intelligence, 34,* 321–350. (p. 316)

Sternberg, R. J. (2007, July 6). Finding students who are wise, practical, and creative. *The Chronicle Review* (www.chronicle.com). (p. 316)

Sternberg, R. J., & Kaufman, J. C. (1998). Human abilities. *Annual Review of Psychology, 49,* 479–502. (p. 313)

Sternberg, R. J., & Lubart, T. I. (1991). An investment theory of creativity and its development. *Human Development,* 1–31. (p. 317)

Sternberg, R. J., & Lubart, T. I. (1992). Buy low and sell high: An investment approach to creativity. *Psychological Science, 1,* 1–5. (p. 317)

Sternberg, R. J., & Wagner, R. K. (1993). The g-ocentric view of intelligence and job performance is wrong. *Current Directions in Psychological Science, 2,* 1–5. (p. 316)

Sternberg, R. J., Grigorenko, E. L., & Kidd, K. K. (2005). Intelligence, race, and genetics. *American Psychologist, 60,* 46–59. (p. 332)

Sternberg, R. J., Wagner, R. K., Williams, W. M., & Horvath, J. A. (1995). Testing common sense. *American Psychologist, 50,* 912–927. (p. 316)

Stetter, F., & Kupper, S. (2002). Autogenic training: A meta-analysis of clinical outcome studies. *Applied Psychophysiology and Biofeedback, 27,* 45–98. (p. 412)

Stewart, B. (2002, April 6). Recall of the wild. *New York Times* (www.nytimes.com). (p. 27)

Stice, E. (2002). Risk and maintenance factors for eating pathology: A meta-analytic review. *Psychological Bulletin, 128,* 825–848. (p. 348)

Stice, E., Shaw, H., & Marti, C. N. (2007). A meta-analytic review of eating disorder prevention programs: Encouraging findings. *Annual Review of Clinical Psychology, 3,* 233–257. (p. 349)

Stice, E., Spangler, D., & Agras, W. S. (2001). Exposure to media-portrayed thin-ideal images adversely affects vulnerable girls: A longitudinal experiment. *Journal of Social and Clinical Psychology, 20,* 270–288. (p. 349)

Stickgold, R. (2000, March 7). Quoted by S. Blakeslee, For better learning, researchers endorse "sleep on it" adage. *New York Times,* p. F2. (p. 82)

Stickgold, R., Hobson, J. A., Fosse, R., & Fosse, M. (2001). Sleep, learning, and dreams: Off-line memory processing. *Science, 294,* 1052–1057. (p. 82)

Stickgold, R., Malia, A., Maquire, D., Roddenberry, D., & O'Connor, M. (2000, October 13). Replaying the game: Hypnagogic images in normals and amnesics. *Science, 290,* 350–353. (p. 81)

Stinson, D. A., Logel, C., Zanna, M. P., Holmes, J. G., Cameron, J. J., Wood, J. V., & Spencer, S. J. (2008). The cost of lower self-esteem: Testing a self- and social-bonds model of health. *Journal of Personality and Social Psychology, 94,* 412–428. (p. 411)

Stith, S. M., Rosen, K. H., Middleton, K. A., Busch, A. L., Lunderberg, K., & Carlton, R. P. (2000). The intergenerational transmission of spouse abuse: A meta-analysis. *Journal of Marriage and the Family, 62,* 640–654. (p. 251)

Stockton, M. C., & Murnen, S. K. (1992). Gender and sexual arousal in response to sexual stimuli: A meta-analytic review. Paper presented at the American Psychological Society convention. (p. 359)

Stone, A. A., & Neale, J. M. (1984). Effects of severe daily events on mood. *Journal of Personality and Social Psychology, 46,* 137–144. (p. 393)

Stone, A. A., Schwartz, J. E., Broderick, J. E., & Shiffman, S. S. (2005). Variability of momentary pain predicts recall of weekly pain: A consequences of the peak (or salience) memory heuristic. *Personality and Social Psychology Bulletin, 31,* 1340–1346. (p. 200)

Stone, G. (2006, February 17). Homeless man discovered to be lawyer with amnesia. *ABC News* (abcnews.go.com). (p. 469)

Stone, R. (2005). In the wake: Looking for keys to posttraumatic stress. *Science, 310,* 1605. (p. 464)

Stoolmiller, M. (1999). Implications of the restricted range of family environments for estimates of heritability and nonshared environment in behavior-genetic adoption studies. *Psychological Bulletin, 125,* 392–409. (p. 110)

Stoppard, J. M., & Gruchy, C. D. G. (1993). Gender, context, and expression of positive emotion. *Personality and Social Psychology Bulletin, 19,* 143–150. (p. 385)

Storbeck, J., Robinson, M. D., & McCourt, M. E. (2006). Semantic processing precedes affect retrieval: The neurological case for cognitive primary in visual processing. *Review of General Psychology, 10,* 41–55. (p. 382)

Storm, L. (2000). Research note: Replicable evidence of psi: A revision of Milton's (1999)

meta-analysis of the ganzfeld data bases. *Journal of Parapsychology, 64,* 411–416. (p. 220)

Storm, L. (2003). Remote viewing by committee: RV using a multiple agent/multiple percipient design. *Journal of Parapsychology, 67,* 325–342. (p. 220)

Storms, M. D. (1973). Videotape and the attribution process: Reversing actors' and observers' points of view. *Journal of Personality and Social Psychology, 27,* 165–175. (p. 527)

Storms, M. D. (1981). A theory of erotic orientation development. *Psychological Review, 88,* 340–353. (p. 365)

Storms, M. D. (1983). *Development of sexual orientation.* Washington, DC: Office of Social and Ethical Responsibility, American Psychological Association. (p. 365)

Strack, F., Martin, L., & Stepper, S. (1988). Inhibiting and facilitating conditions of the human smile: A nonobtrusive test of the facial feedback hypothesis. *Journal of Personality and Social Psychology, 54,* 768–777. (p. 389)

Strack, S., & Coyne, J. C. (1983). Social confirmation of dysphoria: Shared and private reactions to depression. *Journal of Personality and Social Behavior, 44,* 798–806. (p. 479)

Strahan, E. J., Spencer, S. J., & Zanna, M. P. (2002). Subliminal priming and persuasion: Striking while the iron is hot. *Journal of Experimental Social Psychology, 38,* 556–568. (p. 182)

Stranahan, A. M., Khalil, D., & Gould, E. (2006). Social isolation delays the positive effects of running on adult neurogenesis. *Nature Neuroscience, 9,* 526–533. (p. 57)

Strand, S., Deary, I. J., & Smith, P. (2006). Sex differences in cognitive abilities test scores: A UK national picture. *British Journal of Educational Psychology, 76,* 463–480. (pp. 328, 330)

Stratton, G. M. (1896). Some preliminary experiments on vision without inversion of the retinal image. *Psychological Review, 3,* 611–617. (p. 214)

Straub, R. O., Seidenberg, M. S., Bever, T. G., & Terrace, H. S. (1979). Serial learning in the pigeon. *Journal of the Experimental Analysis of Behavior, 32,* 137–148. (p. 312)

Straus, M. A., & Gelles, R. J. (1980). *Behind closed doors: Violence in the American family.* New York: Anchor/Doubleday. (p. 242)

Straus, M. A., Sugarman, D. B., & Giles-Sims, J. (1997). Spanking by parents and subsequent antisocial behavior of children. *Archives of Pediatric Adolescent Medicine, 151,* 761–767. (p. 242)

Strawbridge, W. J. (1999). Mortality and religious involvement: A review and critique of the results, the methods, and the measures. Paper presented at a Harvard University conference on religion and health, sponsored by the National Institute for Health Research and the John Templeton Foundation. (p. 414)

Strawbridge, W. J., Cohen, R. D., & Shema, S. J. (1997). Frequent attendance at religious services and mortality over 28 years. *American Journal of Public Health, 87,* 957–961. (p. 414)

Strawbridge, W. J., Shema, S. J., Cohen, R. D., & Kaplan, G. A. (2001). Religious attendance increases survival by improving and maintaining good health behaviors, mental health, and social relationships. *Annals of Behavioral Medicine, 23,* 68–74. (p. 414)

Strayer, D. L., & Drews, F A. (2007). Cell-phone-induced driver distraction. *Current Directions in Psychological Science, 16,* 128–131. (p. 68)

Strayer, D. L., Drews, F. A., & Johnston, W. A. (2003). Cell phone-induced failures of visual attention during simulated driving. *Journal of Experimental Psychology: Applied, 9,* 23–32. (p. 68)

Strayer, D. L., & Johnston, W. A. (2001). Driven to distraction: Dual-task studies of simulated driving and conversing on a cellular telephone. *Psychological Science, 12,* 462–466. (p. 68)

Striegel-Moore, R. M., & Bulik, C. M. (2007). Risk factors for eating disorders. *American Psychologist, 62,* 181–198. (pp. 348, 349)

Striegel-Moore, R. M., Silberstein, L. R., & Rodin, J. (1993). The social self in bulimia nervosa: Public self-consciousness, social anxiety, and perceived fraudulence. *Journal of Abnormal Psychology, 102,* 297–303. (p. 348)

Stroebe, M., Stroebe, W., & Schut, H. (2001). Gender differences in adjustment to bereavement: An empirical and theoretical review. *Review of General Psychology, 5,* 62–83. (p. 172)

Stroebe, M., Stroebe, W., Schut, H., Zech, E., & van den Bout, J. (2002). Does disclosure of emotions facilitate recovery from bereavement? Evidence from two prospective studies. *Journal of Consulting and Clinical Psychology, 70,* 169–178. (p. 172)

Stroebe, W., Schut, H., & Stroebe, M. S. (2005). Grief work, disclosure and counseling: Do they help the bereaved? *Clinical Psychology Review, 25,* 395–414. (p. 172)

Strupp, H. H. (1986). Psychotherapy: Research, practice, and public policy (How to avoid dead ends). *American Psychologist, 41,* 120–130. (p. 510)

Stumpf, H., & Jackson, D. N. (1994). Gender-related differences in cognitive abilities: Evidence from a medical school admissions testing program. *Personality and Individual Differences, 17,* 335–344. (p. 328)

Stunkard, A. J., Harris, J. R., Pedersen, N. L., & McClearn, G. E. (1990). A separated twin study of the body mass index. *New England Journal of Medicine, 322,* 1483–1487. (p. 353)

Subiaul, F., Cantlon, J. F., Holloway, R. L., & Terrace, H. S. (2004). Cognitive imitation in rhesus macaques. *Science, 305,* 407–410. (p. 248)

Subrahmanyam, K., & Greenfield, P. (2008). Online communication and adolescent relationships. *The Future of Children, 18,* 119–146. (p. 161)

Suddath, R. L., Christison, G. W., Torrey, E. F., Casanova, M. F., & Weinberger, D. R. (1990). Anatomical abnormalities in the brains of monozygotic twins discordant for schizophrenia. *New England Journal of Medicine, 322,* 789–794. (p. 485)

Sue, S. (2006). Research to address racial and ethnic disparities in mental health: Some lessons learned. In S. I. Donaldson, D. E. Berger, & K. Pezdek (Eds.), *Applied psychology: New frontiers and rewarding careers.* Mahwah, NJ: Erlbaum. (p. 511)

Suedfeld, P. (1998). Homo invictus: The indomitable species. *Canadian Psychology, 38,* 164–173. (p. 465)

Suedfeld, P. (2000). Reverberations of the Holocaust fifty years later: Psychology's contributions to understanding persecution and genocide. *Canadian Psychology, 41,* 1–9. (p. 465)

Suedfeld, P., & Mocellin, J. S. P. (1987). The "sensed presence" in unusual environments. *Environment and Behavior, 19,* 33–52. (p. 96)

Sugita, Y. (2004). Experience in early infancy is indispensable for color perception. *Current Biology. 14,* 1267–1271. (p. 212)

Suinn, R. M. (1997). Mental practice in sports psychology: Where have we been, where do we go? *Clinical Psychology: Science and Practice, 4,* 189–207. (p. 308)

Sullivan, P. F., Neale, M. C., & Kendler, K. S. (2000). Genetic epidemiology of major depression: Review and meta-analysis. *American Journal of Psychiatry, 157,* 1552–1562. (p. 475)

Suls, J. M., & Tesch, F. (1978). Students' preferences for information about their test performance: A social comparison study. *Journal of Experimental Social Psychology, 8,* 189–197. (p. 396)

Summers, M. (1996, December 9). Mister clean. *People Weekly,* pp. 139–142. (p. 453)

Sunstein, C. R. (2007). On the divergent American reactions to terrorism and climate change. *Columbia Law Review, 107,* 503–557. (p. 296)

Suomi, S. J. (1986). Anxiety-like disorders in young nonhuman primates. In R. Gettleman (Ed.), *Anxiety disorders of childhood.* New York: Guilford Press. (p. 466)

Suppes, P. (1982). Quoted by R. H. Ennis, Children's ability to handle Piaget's propositional logic: A conceptual critique. In S. Modgil & C. Modgil (Eds.), *Jean Piaget: Consensus and controversy.* New York: Praeger. (p. 148)

Surgeon General. (1986). *The surgeon general's workshop on pornography and public health,* June 22–24. Report prepared by E. P. Mulvey & J. L. Haugaard and released by Office of the Surgeon General on August 4, 1986. (p. 553)

Surgeon General. (1999). *Mental health: A report of the surgeon general.* Rockville, MD: U.S. Department of Health and Human Services. (p. 460)

Susser, E., Neugenbauer, R., Hoek, H. W., Brown, A. S., Lin, S., Labovitz, D., & Gorman, J. M. (1996). Schizophrenia after prenatal famine. *Archives of General Psychiatry, 53*(1), 25–31. (p. 483)

Susser, E. S., Herman, D. B., & Aaron, B. (2002, August). Combating the terror of terrorism. *Scientific American,* pp. 70–77. (p. 464)

Sutcliffe, J. S. (2008). Insights into the pathogenesis of autism. *Science, 321,* 208–209. (p. 146)

Sutherland, A. (2006). *Bitten and scratched: Life and lessons at the premier school for exotic animal trainers.* New York: Viking. (p. 246)

Swann, Jr., W. B., Chang-Schneider, C., & McClarty, K. L. (2007). Do people's self-views matter? Self-concept and self-esteem in everyday life. *American Psychologist, 62,* 84–94. (p. 447)

Sweat, J. A., & Durm, M. W. (1993). Psychics: Do police departments really use them? *Skeptical Inquirer, 17,* 148–158. (p. 218)

Swerdlow, N. R., & Koob, G. F. (1987). Dopamine, schizophrenia, mania, and depression: Toward a unified hypothesis of cortico-stiato-pallido-thalamic function (with commentary). *Behavioral and Brain Sciences, 10,* 197–246. (p. 483)

Swim, J. K. (1994). Perceived versus meta-analytic effect sizes: An assessment of the accuracy of gender stereotypes. *Journal of Personality and Social Psychology, 66,* 21–36. (p. 544)

Symbaluk, D. G., Heth, C. D., Cameron, J., & Pierce, W. D. (1997). Social modeling, monetary incentives, and pain endurance: The role of self-efficacy and pain perception. *Personality and Social Psychology Bulletin, 23,* 258–269. (p. 200)

Symond, M. B., Harris, A. W. F., Gordon, E., & Williams, L. M. (2005). "Gamma synchrony" in first-episode schizophrenia: A disorder of temporal connectivity? *American Journal of Psychiatry, 162,* 459–465. (p. 483)

TADS (Treatment for Adolescents with Depression Study Team). (2004). Fluoxetine, cognitive-behavioral therapy, and their combination for adolescents with depression: Treatment for adolescents with depression study (TADS) randomized controlled trial. *Journal of the American Medical Association, 292,* 807–820. (p. 515)

Taha, F. A. (1972). A comparative study of how sighted and blind perceive the manifest content of dreams. *National Review of Social Sciences, 9*(3), 28. (p. 80)

Taheri, S. (2004). The genetics of sleep disorders. *Minerva Medica, 95,* 203–212. (p. 76)

Taheri, S. (2004a, 20 December). Does the lack of sleep make you fat? *University of Bristol Research News* (www.bristol.ac.uk). (p. 353)

Taheri, S., Lin, L., Austin, D., Young, T., & Mignot, E. (2004b). Short sleep duration is associated with reduced leptin, elevated ghrelin, and increased body mass index. *PloS Medicine, 1*(3), e62. (p. 353)

Tajfel, H. (Ed.). (1982). *Social identity and intergroup relations.* New York: Cambridge University Press. (p. 546)

Talarico, J. M., & Rubin, D. C. (2003). Confidence, not consistency, characterizes flashbulb memories. *Psychological Science, 14,* 455–461. (p. 269)

Talarico, J. M., & Rubin, D. C. (2007). Flashbulb memories are special after all: in phenomenology, not accuracy. *Applied Cognitive Psychology, 21,* 557–578. (p. 269)

Talbot, M. (2002, June 2). Hysteria hysteria. *New York Times* (www.nytimes.com). (p. 532)

Tamres, L. K., Janicki, D., & Helgeson, V. S. (2002). Sex differences in coping behavior: A meta-analytic review and an examination of relative coping. *Personality and Social Psychology Review, 6,* 2–30. (p. 128)

Tangney, J. P., Baumeister, R. F., & Boone, A. L. (2004). High self-control predicts good adjustment, less pathology, better grades, and interpersonal success. *Journal of Personality, 72,* 271–324. (p. 441)

Tannen, D. (1990). *You just don't understand: Women and men in conversation.* New York: Morrow. (pp. 26, 128)

Tannenbaum, P. (2002, February). Quoted in R. Kubey & M. Csikszentmihalyi, Television addiction is no mere metaphor. *Scientific American,* pp. 74–80. (p. 184)

Tanner, J. M. (1978). *Fetus into man: Physical growth from conception to maturity.* Cambridge, MA: Harvard University Press. (p. 155)

Tarbert, J. (2004, May 14). Bad apples, bad command, or both? *Dart Center for Journalism and Trauma* (www.dartcenter.org). (p. 530)

Tarmann, A. (2002, May/June). Out of the closet and onto the Census long form. *Population Today, 30,* pp. 1, 6. (p. 363)

Taubes, G. (2001). The soft science of dietary fat. *Science, 291,* 2536–2545. (p. 356)

Taubes, G. (2002, July 7). What if it's all been a big fat lie? *New York Times* (www.nytimes.com). (p. 356)

Tavris, C. (1982, November). Anger defused. *Psychology Today,* pp. 25–35. (p. 391)

Taylor, P. J., Russ-Eft, D. F., & Chan, D. W. L. (2005). A meta-analytic review of behavior modeling training. *Journal of Applied Psychology, 90,* 692–709. (p. 250)

Taylor, S., Kuch, K., Koch, W. J., Crockett, D. J., & Passey, G. (1998). The structure of posttraumatic stress symptoms. *Journal of Abnormal Psychology, 107,* 154–160. (p. 464)

Taylor, S. E. (1989). *Positive illusions.* New York: Basic Books. (p. 297)

Taylor, S. E. (2002). *The tending instinct: How nurturing is essential to who we are and how we live.* New York: Times Books. (p. 128)

Taylor, S. E. (2006). Tend and befriend: Biobehavioral bases of affiliation under stress. *Current Directions in Psychological Science, 15,* 273–277. (p. 399)

Taylor, S. E., Cousino, L. K., Lewis, B. P., Gruenewald, T. L., Gurung, R. A. R., & Updegraff, J. A. (2000). Biobehavioral responses to stress in females: Tend-and-befriend, not fight-or-flight. *Psychological Review, 107,* 411–430. (p. 399)

Taylor, S. E., Pham, L. B., Rivkin, I. D., & Armor, D. A. (1998). Harnessing the imagination: Mental simulation, self-regulation, and coping. *American Psychologist, 53,* 429–439. (p. 308)

Taylor, S. P., & Chermack, S. T. (1993). Alcohol, drugs and human physical aggression. *Journal of Studies on Alcohol,* Supplement No. 11, 78–88. (p. 549)

Tedeschi, R. G., & Calhoun, L. G. (2004). Posttraumatic growth: Conceptual foundations and empirical evidence. *Psychological Inquiry, 15,* 1–18. (p. 465)

Teghtsoonian, R. (1971). On the exponents in Stevens' law and the constant in Ekinan's law. *Psychological Review, 78,* 71–80. (p. 183)

Teicher, M. H. (2002, March). The neurobiology of child abuse. *Scientific American,* pp. 68–75. (p. 153)

Teran-Santos, J., Jimenez-Gomez, A., & Cordero-Guevara, J. (1999). The association between sleep apnea and the risk of traffic accidents. *New England Journal of Medicine, 340,* 847–851. (p. 79)

Terman, J. S., Terman, M., Lo, E-S., & Cooper, T. B. (2001). Circadian time of morning light administration and therapeutic response in winter depression. *Archives of General Psychiatry, 58,* 69–73. (p. 509)

Terman, M., Terman, J. S., & Ross, D. C. (1998). A controlled trial of timed bright light and negative air ionization for treatment of winter depression. *Archives of General Psychiatry, 55,* 875–882. (p. 509)

Terracciano, A., Costa, P. T., Jr., & McCrae, R. R. (2006). Personality plasticity after age 30. *Personality and Social Psychology Bulletin, 32,* 999–1009. (pp. 125, 174)

Terrace, H. S. (1979, November). How Nim Chimpsky changed my mind. *Psychology Today,* pp. 65–76. (p. 312)

Tesser, A., Forehand, R., Brody, G., & Long, N. (1989). Conflict: The role of calm and angry parent-child discussion in adolescent development. *Journal of Social and Clinical Psychology, 8,* 317–330. (p. 161)

Tetlock, P. E. (1988). Monitoring the integrative complexity of American and Soviet policy rhetoric: What can be learned? *Journal of Social Issues, 44,* 101–131. (p. 566)

Thaler, R. H., & Sunstein, C. R. (2008). *Nudge: Improving decisions about health, wealth, and happiness.* New Haven, CT: Yale University Press. (p. 301)

Thatcher, R. W., Walker, R. A., & Giudice, S. (1987). Human cerebral hemispheres develop at different rates and ages. *Science, 236,* 1110–1113. (pp. 140, 174)

Thayer, R. E. (1987). Energy, tiredness, and tension effects of a sugar snack versus moderate exercise. *Journal of Personality and Social Psychology, 52,* 119–125. (p. 411)

Thayer, R. E. (1993). Mood and behavior (smoking and sugar snacking) following moderate exercise: A partial test of self-regulation theory. *Personality and Individual Differences, 14,* 97–104. (p. 411)

Théoret, H., Halligan, H., Kobayashi, M., Fregni, F., Tager-Flusberg, H., & Pascual-Leone, A. (2005). Impaired motor facilitation during action observation in individuals with autism spectrum disorder. *Current Biology, 15,* R84–R85. (p. 147)

Thernstrom, M. (2006, May 14). My pain, my brain. *New York Times* (www.nytimes.com). (p. 200)

Thiel, A., Hadedank, B., Herholz, K., Kessler, J., Winhuisen, L., Haupt, W. F., & Heiss, W-D. (2006). From the left to the right: How the brain compensates progressive loss of language function. *Brain and Language, 98,* 57–65. (p. 57)

Thiele, T. E., Marsh, D. J., Ste. Marie, L., Bernstein, I. L., & Palmiter, R. D. (1998). Ethanol consumption and resistance are inversely related to neuropeptide Y levels. *Nature, 396,* 366–369. (p. 98)

Thomas, A., & Chess, S. (1977). *Temperament and development.* New York: Brunner/Mazel. (p. 111)

Thomas, A., & Chess, S. (1986). The New York Longitudinal Study: From infancy to early adult life. In R. Plomin & J. Dunn (Eds.), *The study of temperament: Changes, continuities, and challenges.* Hillsdale, NJ: Erlbaum. (p. 174)

Thomas, L. (1983). *The youngest science: Notes of a medicine watcher.* New York: Viking Press. (p. 39)

Thomas, L. (1992). *The fragile species.* New York: Scribner's. (pp. 133, 304, 506)

Thompson, C. P., Frieman, J., & Cowan, T. (1993). Rajan's memory. Paper presented to the American Psychological Society convention. (p. 267)

Thompson, J. K., Jarvie, G. J., Lahey, B. B., & Cureton, K. J. (1982). Exercise and obesity: Etiology, physiology, and intervention. *Psychological Bulletin, 91,* 55–79. (p. 356)

Thompson, P. M., Cannon, T. D., Narr, K. L., van Erp, T., Poutanen, V-P., Huttunen, M., Lönnqvist, J., Standerskjöld-Nordenstam, C-G., Kaprio, J., Khaledy, M., Dail, R., Zoumalan, C. I., & Toga, A. W. (2001). Genetic influences on brain structure. *Nature Neuroscience, 4,* 1253–1258. (p. 325)

Thompson, P. M., Giedd, J. N., Woods, R. P., MacDonald, D., Evans, A. C., & Toga, A. W. (2000). Growth patterns in the developing brain detected by using continuum mechanical tensor maps. *Nature, 404,* 190–193. (p. 140)

Thompson, R., Emmorey, K., & Gollan, T. H. (2005). "Tip of the fingers" experiences by Deaf signers. *Psychological Science, 16,* 856–860. (p. 278)

Thomson, R., & Murachver, T. (2001). Predicting gender from electronic discourse. *British Journal of Social Psychology, 40,* 193–208 (and personal correspondence from T. Murachver, May 23, 2002). (p. 128)

Thorndike, A. L., & Hagen, E. P. (1977). *Measurement and evaluation in psychology and education.* New York: Macmillan. (p. 320)

Thorndike, E. L. (1898). Animal intelligence: An experimental study of the associative processes in animals. *Psychological Review Monograph Supplement 2*(4), Whole No. 8). (p. 237)

Thorne, J., with Rothstein, L. (1993). *You are not alone: Words of experience and hope for the journey through depression.* New York: HarperPerennial. (p. 453)

Thornton, B., & Moore, S. (1993). Physical attractiveness contrast effect: Implications for self-esteem and evaluations of the social self. *Personality and Social Psychology Bulletin, 19,* 474–480. (p. 557)

Thornton, G. C., III, & Rupp, D. E. (2005). *Assessment centers in human resource management: Strategies for prediction, diagnosis, and development.* Mahwah, NJ: Erlbaum. (p. 445)

Thorpe, W. H. (1974). *Animal nature and human nature.* London: Methuen. (p. 313)

Tickle, J. J., Hull, J. G., Sargent, J. D., Dalton, M. A., & Heatherton, T. F. (2006). A structural equation model of social influences and exposure to media smoking on adolescent smoking. *Basic and Applied Social Psychology, 28,* 117–129. (p. 92)

Tiedens, L. Z. (2001). Anger and advancement versus sadness and subjugation: The effect of negative emotion expressions on social status conferral. *Journal of Personality and Social Psychology, 80,* 86–94. (p. 391)

Time. (1997, December 22). Greeting card association data, p. 19. (p. 128)

Time/CNN Survey. (1994, December 19). Vox pop: Happy holidays, *Time.* (p. 470)

Timlin, M. T., Pereira, M. A., Story, M., & Neumark-Sztainer, D. (2008). Breakfast eating and weight change in a 5-year prospective analysis of adolescents: Project EAT (Eating Among Teens). *Pediatrics, 121,* e638–e645. (p. 18)

Timmerman, T. A. (2007). "It was a thought pitch": Personal, situational, and target influences on hit-by-pitch events across time. *Journal of Applied Psychology, 92,* 876–884. (p. 549)

Tinbergen, N. (1951). *The study of instinct.* Oxford: Clarendon. (p. 340)

Tirrell, M. E. (1990). Personal communication. (p. 230)

Tolin, D. F., & Foa, E. B. (2006). Sex differences in trauma and posttraumatic stress disorder: A quantitative review of 25 years of research. *Psychological Bulletin, 132,* 959–992. (p. 465)

Tollefson, G. D., Fawcett, J., Winokur, G., Beasley, C. M., et al. (1993). Evaluation of suicidality during pharmacologic treatment of mood and nonmood disorders. *Annals of Clinical Psychiatry, 5*(4), 209–224. (p. 516)

Tollefson, G. D., Rampey, A. H., Beasley, C. M., & Enas, G. G. (1994). Absence of a relationship between adverse events and suicidality during pharmacotherapy for depression. *Journal of Clinical Psychopharmacology, 14,* 163–169. (p. 516)

Tolman, E. C., & Honzik, C. H. (1930). Introduction and removal of reward, and maze performance in rats. *University of California Publications in Psychology, 4,* 257–275. (p. 243)

Tolstoy, L. (1904). *My confessions.* Boston: Dana Estes. (P. 7)

Tondo, L., Jamison, K. R., & Baldessarini, R. J. (1997). Effect of lithium maintenance on suicidal behavior in major mood disorders. In D. M. Stoff & J. J. Mann (Eds.), *The neurobiology of suicide: From the bench to the clinic.* New York: New York Academy of Sciences. (p. 516)

Toni, N., Buchs, P-A., Nikonenko, I., Bron, C. R., & Muller, D. (1999). LTP promotes formation of multiple spine synapses between a single axon terminal and a dendrite. *Nature, 402,* 421–442. (p. 268)

Torrey, E. F. (1986). *Witchdoctors and psychiatrists.* New York: Harper & Row. (p. 510)

Torrey, E. F., & Miller, J. (2002). *The invisible plague: The rise of mental illness from 1750 to the present.* New Brunswick, NJ: Rutgers University Press. (p. 484)

Torrey, E. F., Miller, J., Rawlings, R., & Yolken, R. H. (1997). Seasonality of births in schizophrenia and bipolar disorder: A review of the literature. *Schizophrenia Research, 28,* 1–38. (p. 484)

Towler, G. (1986). From zero to one hundred: Coaction in a natural setting. *Perceptual and Motor Skills, 62,* 377–378. (p. 538)

Tracey, J. L., & Robins, R. W. (2004). Show your pride: Evidence for a discrete emotion expression. *Psychological Science, 15,* 194–197. (p. 389)

Trautwein, U., Lüdtke, O., Köller, O., & Baumert, J. (2006). Self-esteem, academic self-concept, and achievement: How the learning environment moderates the dynamics of self-concept. *Journal of Personality and Social Psychology, 90,* 334–349. (p. 447)

Treffert, D. A., & Christensen, D. D. (2005, December). Inside the mind of a savant. *Scientific American.* (p. 315)

Treffert, D. A., & Wallace, G. L. (2002). Island of genius—The artistic brilliance and dazzling memory that sometimes accompany autism and other disorders hint at how all brains work. *Scientific American, 286,* 76–86. (p. 314)

Treisman, A. (1987). Properties, parts, and objects. In K. R. Boff, L. Kaufman, & J. P. Thomas (Eds.), *Handbook of perception and human performance.* New York: Wiley. (p. 205)

Tremblay, R. E., Pihl, R. O., Vitaro, F., & Dobkin, P. L. (1994). Predicting early onset of male antisocial behavior from preschool behavior. *Archives of General Psychiatry, 51,* 732–739. (p. 487)

Trewin, D. (2001). *Australian social trends 2001.* Canberra: Australian Bureau of Statistics. (p. 130)

Triandis, H. C. (1981). Some dimensions of intercultural variation and their implications for interpersonal behavior. Paper presented at the American Psychological Association convention. (p. 122)

Triandis, H. C. (1994). *Culture and social behavior.* New York: McGraw-Hill. (pp. 124, 551)

Triandis, H. C., Bontempo, R., Villareal, M. J., Asai, M., & Lucca, N. (1988). Individualism and collectivism: Cross-cultural perspectives on self-ingroup relationships. *Journal of Personality and Social Psychology, 54,* 323–338. (p. 124)

Trickett, P. K., & McBride-Chang, C. (1995). The developmental impact of different forms of child abuse and neglect. *Developmental Review, 15,* 311–337. (p. 153)

Trillin, C. (2006, March 27). Alice off the page. *The New Yorker,* p. 44. (p. 430)

Trimble, J. E. (1994). Cultural variations in the use of alcohol and drugs. In W. J. Lonner & R. Malpass (Eds.), *Psychology and culture.* Boston: Allyn & Bacon. (p. 99)

Triplett, N. (1898). The dynamogenic factors in pacemaking and competition. *American Journal of Psychology, 9,* 507–533. (p. 537)

Trolier, T. K., & Hamilton, D. L. (1986). Variables influencing judgments of correlational relations. *Journal of Personality and Social Psychology, 50,* 879–888. (p. 19)

Troller, J. N., Anderson, T. M., Sachdev, P. S., Brodaty, H., & Andrews, G. (2007). Age shall not weary them: Mental health in the middle-aged and the elderly. *Australian and New Zealand Journal of Psychiatry, 41,* 581–589. (p. 171)

Trut, L. N. (1999). Early canid domestication: The farm-fox experiment. *American Scientist, 87,* 160–169. (p. 113)

Tsai, J. L., & Chentsova-Dutton, Y. (2003). Variation among European Americans in emotional facial expression. *Journal of Cross-Cultural Psychology, 34,* 650–657. (p. 388)

Tsai, J. L., Miao, F. F., Seppala, E., Fung, H. H., & Yeung, D. Y. (2007). Influence and adjustment goals: Sources of cultural differences in ideal affect. *Journal of Personality and Social Psychology, 92,* 1102–1117. (p. 388)

Tsang, Y. C. (1938). Hunger motivation in gastrectomized rats. *Journal of Comparative Psychology, 26,* 1–17. (p. 344)

Tsuang, M. T., & Faraone, S. V. (1990). *The genetics of mood disorders.* Baltimore, MD: Johns Hopkins University Press. (p. 475)

Tuber, D. S., Miller, D. D., Caris, K. A., Halter, R., Linden, F., & Hennessy, M. B. (1999). Dogs in animal shelters: Problems, suggestions, and needed expertise. *Psychological Science, 10,* 379–386. (p. 27)

Tuerk, P. W. (2005). Research in the high-stakes era: Achievement, resources, and No Child Left Behind. *Psychological Science, 16,* 419–425. (p. 326)

Tully, T. (2003). Reply: The myth of a myth. *Current Biology, 13,* R426. (p. 228)

Tulving, E. (1996, August 18). Quoted in J. Gatehouse, Technology revealing brain's secrets. *Montreal Gazette,* p. A3. (p. 271)

Turkheimer, E., Haley, A., Waldron, M., D'Onofrio, B., & Gottesman, I. I. (2003). Socioeconomic status modifies heritability of IQ in young children. *Psychological Science, 14,* 623–628. (pp. 326, 327)

Turner, J. C. (1987). *Rediscovering the social group: A self-categorization theory.* New York: Basil Blackwell. (p. 546)

Turner, J. C. (2007) Self-categorization theory. In R. Baumeister & K. Vohs (Eds.), *Encyclopedia of social psychology.* Thousand Oaks, CA: Sage. (p. 546)

Turpin, A. (2005, April 3). The science of psi. *FT Weekend,* pp. W1, W2. (p. 218)

Tutu, D. (1999). *No future without forgiveness.* New York: Doubleday. (p. 370)

Tversky, A. (1985, June). Quoted in K. McKean, Decisions, decisions. *Discover,* pp. 22–31. (p. 295)

Tversky, A., & Kahneman, D. (1974). Judgment under uncertainty: Heuristics and biases. *Science, 185,* 1124–1131. (p. 294)

Twenge, J. (2006). *Generation me.* New York: Free Press. (pp. 448, 467)

Twenge, J. M. (1997). Changes in masculine and feminine traits over time: A meta-analysis. *Sex Roles 36*(5–6), 305–325. (p. 132)

Twenge, J. M., Baumeister, R. F., DeWall, C. N., Ciarocco, N. J., & Bartels, J. M. (2007). Social exclusion decreases prosocial behavior. *Journal of Personality and Social Psychology, 92,* 56–66. (p. 371)

Twenge, J. M., Baumeister, R. F., Tice, D. M., & Stucke, T. S. (2001). If you can't join them, beat them: Effects of social exclusion on aggressive behavior. *Journal of Personality and Social Psychology, 81,* 1058–1069. (pp. 371, 550)

Twenge, J. M., & Campbell, W. K. (2001). Age and birth cohort differences in self-esteem: A cross-temporal meta-analysis. *Personality and Social Psychology Review, 5,* 321–344. (p. 160)

Twenge, J. M., Catanese, K. R., & Baumeister, R. F. (2002). Social exclusion causes self-defeating behavior. *Journal of Personality and Social Psychology, 83,* 606–615. (pp. 371, 550)

Twenge, J. M., Catanese, K. R., & Baumeister, R. F. (2003). Social exclusion and the deconstructed state: Time perception, meaninglessness, lethargy, lack of emotion, and self-awareness. *Journal of Personality and Social Psychology, 85,* 409–423. (p. 550)

Twenge, J. M., Gentile, B., DeWall, C. D., Ma, D., & Lacefield, K. (2008). *A growing disturbance: Increasing psychopathology in young people 1938-2007 in a meta-analysis of the MMPI.*

Unpublished manuscript, San Diego State University. (p. 473)

Twenge, J. M., Konrath, S., Foster, J. D., Campbell, W. K., & Bushman, B. J. (2008). Egos inflating over time: A cross-temporary meta-analysis of the Narcissistic Personality Inventory. *Journal of Personality, 76,* 875–902. (p. 448)

Twenge, J. M., & Nolen-Hoeksema, S. (2002). Age, gender, race, socioeconomic status, and birth cohort differences on the children's depression inventory: A meta-analysis. *Journal of Abnormal Psychology, 111,* 578–588. (p. 160)

Tyler, K. A. (2002). Social and emotional outcomes of childhood sexual abuse: A review of recent research. *Aggression and Violent Behavior, 7,* 567–589. (p. 153)

U. S. Department of State (2004, April). *Patterns of global terrorism 2003: Appendix G.* (www.state.gov). (p. 296)

U. S. Senate Select Committee on Intelligence (2004, July 9). *Report of the U.S. intelligence community's prewar intelligence assessments on Iraq.* www.gpoaccess.gov/serialset/creports/iraq.html. (pp. 15, 293, 540)

Uchino, B. N., Cacioppo, J. T., & Kiecolt-Glaser, J. K. (1996). The relationship between social support and physiological processes: A review with emphasis on underlying mechanisms and implications for health. *Psychological Bulletin, 119,* 488–531. (p. 409)

Uchino, B. N., Uno, D., & Holt-Lunstad, J. (1999). Social support, physiological processes, and health. *Current Directions in Psychological Science, 8,* 145–148. (p. 409)

Uddin, L. Q., Kaplan, J. T., Molnar-Szakacs, I., Zaidel, E., & Iacoboni, M. (2005). Self-face recognition activates a frontoparietal "mirror" network in the right hemisphere: An event-related fMRI study. *NeuroImage, 25,* 926–935. (p. 60)

Uddin, L. Q., Molnar-Szakacs, Il., Zaidel, E., & Iacoboni, M. (2006). rTMS to the right inferior parietal lobule disrupts self-other discrimination. *Social Cognitive Affective Neuroscience, 1,* 65–71. (p. 60)

Udry, J. R. (2000). Biological limits of gender construction. *American Sociological Review, 65,* 443–457. (p. 129)

Uga, V., Lemut, M. C., Zampi, C., Zilli, I., & Salzarulo, P. (2006). Music in dreams. *Consciousness and Cognition, 15,* 351–357. (p. 81)

UK ECT Review Group. (2003). Efficacy and safety of electroconvulsive therapy in depressive disorders: A systematic review and meta-analysis. *Lancet, 361,* 799–808. (p. 517)

Ulrich, R. E. (1991). Animal rights, animal wrongs and the question of balance. *Psychological Science, 2,* 197–201. (p. 26)

UNAIDS. (2005). *AIDS epidemic update, December 2005.* United Nations (www.unaids.org). (p. 405)

UNAIDS. (2008). *Report on the global AIDS epidemic.* United Nations (www.unaids.org). (p. 405)

UNICEF (2006). *The state of the world's children 2007.* New York: UNICEF. (p. 130)

Urbany, J. E., Bearden, W. O., & Weilbaker, D. C. (1988). The effect of plausible and exaggerated reference prices on consumer perceptions and price search. *Journal of Consumer Research, 15,* 95–110. (p. 301)

Urry, H. L., Nitschke, J. B., Dolski, I., Jackson, D. C., Dalton, K. M., Mueller, C. J., Rosenkranz, M. A., Ryff, C. D., Singer, B. H., & Davidson, R. J. (2004). Making a life worth living: Neural correlates of well-being. *Psychological Science, 15,* 367–372. (p. 379)

Ursu, S., Stenger, V. A., Shear, M. K., Jones, M. R., & Carter, C. S. (2003). Overactive action monitoring in obsessive-compulsive disorder: Evidence from functional magnetic resonance imaging. *Psychological Science, 14,* 347–353. (p. 467)

USAID. (2004, January). *The ABCs of HIV prevention.* www.usaid.gov. (p. 405)

Vaidya, J. G., Gray, E. K., Haig, J., & Watson, D. (2002). On the temporal stability of personality: Evidence for differential stability and the role of life experiences. *Journal of Personality and Social Psychology, 83,* 1469–1484. (p. 436)

Vaillant, G. E. (1977). *Adaptation to life.* New York: Little, Brown. (p. 283)

Vaillant, G. E. (2002). *Aging well: Surprising guideposts to a happier life from the landmark Harvard study of adult development.* Boston: Little, Brown. (p. 410)

Valenstein, E. S. (1986). *Great and desperate cures: The rise and decline of psychosurgery.* New York: Basic Books. (p. 519)

Valkenburg, P. M., & Peter, J. (2009). Social consequences of the Internet for adolescents. *Current Directions in Psychological Science, 18,* 1–5. (p. 161)

Van Cauter, E., Holmback, U., Knutson, K., Leproult, R., Miller, A., Nedeltcheva, A., Pannain, S., Penev, P., Tasali, E., & Spiegel, K. (2007). Impact of sleep and sleep loss on neuroendocrine and metabolic function. *Hormone Research, 67(1),* Supp. 1: 2–9. (p. 76)

van den Boom, D. (1990). Preventive intervention and the quality of mother-infant interaction and infant exploration in irritable infants. In W. Koops, H. J. G. Soppe, J. L. van der Linden, P. C. M. Molenaar, & J. J. F. Schroots (Eds.), *Developmental psychology research in The Netherlands.* The Netherlands: Uitgeverij Eburon. Cited by C. Hazan & P. R. Shaver (1994). Deeper into attachment theory. *Psychological Inquiry, 5,* 68–79. (p. 151)

van den Boom, D. C. (1995). Do first-year intervention effects endure? Follow-up during toddlerhood of a sample of Dutch irritable infants. *Child Development, 66,* 1798–1816. (p. 151)

Van Dyke, C., & Byck, R. (1982, March). Cocaine. *Scientific American,* pp. 128–141. (p. 94)

van Engen, M. L., & Willemsen, T. M. (2004). Sex and leadership styles: A meta-analysis of research published in the 1990s. *Psychological Reports, 94,* 3–18. (p. 127)

van Goozen, S. H. M., Fairchild, G., Snoek, H., & Harold, G. T. (2007). The evidence for a neurobiological model of childhood antisocial behavior. *Psychological Bulletin, 133,* 149–182. (p. 487)

van Hemert, D. A., Poortinga, Y. H., & van de Vijver, F. J. R. (2007). Emotion and culture: A meta-analysis. *Cognition and Emotion, 21,* 913–943. (p. 388)

van IJzendoorn, M. H., & Juffer, F. (2005). Adoption is a successful natural intervention enhancing adopted children's IQ and school performance. *Current Directions in Psychological Science, 14,* 326–330. (p. 326)

van IJzendoorn, M. H., & Juffer, F. (2006). The Emanual Miller Memorial Lecture 2006: Adoption as intervention. Meta-analytic evidence for massive catch-up and plasticity in physical, socio-emotional, and cognitive development. *Journal of Child Psychology and Psychiatry, 47,* 1228–1245. (pp. 110, 326)

van IJzendoorn, M. H., & Kroonenberg, P. M. (1988). Cross-cultural patterns of attachment: A meta-analysis of the strange situation. *Child Development, 59,* 147–156. (p. 151)

Van Leeuwen, M. S. (1978). A cross-cultural examination of psychological differentiation in males and females. *International Journal of Psychology, 13,* 87–122. (p. 130)

Van Rooy, D. L., & Viswesvaran, C. (2004). Emotional intelligence: A meta-analytic investigation of predictive validity and nomological net. *Journal of Vocational Behavior, 65,* 71–95. (p. 318)

Van Yperen, N. W., & Buunk, B. P. (1990). A longitudinal study of equity and satisfaction in intimate relationships. *European Journal of Social Psychology, 20,* 287–309. (p. 560)

Van Zeijl, J., Mesman, J., Van IJzendoorn, M. H., Bakermans-Kranenburg, M. J., Juffer, F., Stolk, M. N., Koot, H. M., & Alink, L. R. A. (2006). Attachment-based intervention for enhancing sensitive discipline in mothers of 1- to 3-year-old children at risk for externalizing behavior problems: A randomized controlled trial. *Journal of Consulting and Clinical Psychology, 74,* 994–1005. (p. 151)

Vance, E. B., & Wagner, N. N. (1976). Written descriptions of orgasm: A study of sex differences. *Archives of Sexual Behavior, 5,* 87–98. (p. 357)

Vandenberg, S. G., & Kuse, A. R. (1978). Mental rotations: A group test of three-dimensional spatial visualization. *Perceptual and Motor Skills, 47,* 599–604. (p. 329)

Vanman, E. J., Saltz, J. L., Nathan, L. R., & Warren, J. A. (2004). Racial discrimination by low-prejudiced Whites. *Psychological Science, 15,* 711–714. (p. 543)

Vaughn, K. B., & Lanzetta, J. T. (1981). The effect of modification of expressive displays on vicarious emotional arousal. *Journal of Experimental Social Psychology, 17,* 16–30. (p. 389)

Vazire, S., & Gosling, S. D. (2004). e-Perceptions: Personality impressions based on personal websites. *Journal of Personality and Social Psychology, 87,* 123–132. (p. 438)

Vecera, S. P., Vogel, E. K., & Woodman, G. F. (2002). Lower region: A new cue for figure-ground assignment. *Journal of Experimental Psychology: General, 131,* 194–205. (p. 209)

Vekassy, L. (1977). Dreams of the blind. *Magyar Pszichologiai Szemle, 34,* 478–491. (p. 80)

Verbeek, M. E. M., Drent, P. J., & Wiepkema, P. R. (1994). Consistent individual differences in early exploratory behaviour of male great tits. *Animal Behaviour, 48,* 1113–1121. (p. 433)

Verhaeghen, P., & Salthouse, T. A. (1997). Meta-analyses of age-cognition relations in adulthood: Estimates of linear and nonlinear age effects and structural models. *Psychological Bulletin, 122,* 231–249. (p. 165)

Vertes, R., & Siegel, J. (2005). Time for the sleep community to take a critical look at the purported role of sleep in memory processing. *Sleep, 28,* 1228–1229. (p. 82)

Vigil, J. M., Geary, D. C., & Byrd-Craven, J. (2005). A life history assessment of early childhood sexual abuse in women. *Developmental Psychology, 41,* 553–561. (p. 155)

Vigliocco, G., & Hartsuiker, R. J. (2002). The interplay of meaning, sound, and syntax in sentence production. *Psychological Bulletin, 128,* 442–472. (p. 302)

Vining, E. P. G., Freeman, J. M., Pillas, D. J., Uematsu, S., Carson, B. S., Brandt, J., Boatman, D., Pulsifer, M. B., & Zukerberg, A. (1997). Why would you remove half a brain? The outcome of 58 children after hemispherectomy—The Johns Hopkins Experience: 1968 to 1996. *Pediatrics, 100,* 163–171. (p. 56)

Vita, A. J., Terry, R. B., Hubert, H. B., & Fries, J. F. (1998). Aging, health risks, and cumulative disability. *New England Journal of Medicine, 338,* 1035–1041. (p. 93)

Vitello, P. (2006, June 12). A ring tone meant to fall on deaf ears. *New York Times* (www.nytimes.com). (p. 164)

Vittengl, J. R., Clark, L. A., Dunn, T. W., & Jarrett, R. B. (2007). Reducing relapse and recurrence in unipolar depression: A comparative meta-analysis of cognitive-behavioral therapy's effects. *Journal of Consulting and Clinical Psychology, 75,* 475–488. (p. 515)

Voas, D. (2008, March/April). Ten million marriages: An astrological detective story. *Skeptical Inquirer,* pp. 52–55. (p. 434)

von Hippel, W. (2007). Aging, executive functioning, and social control. *Current Directions in Psychological Science, 16,* 240–244. (p. 166)

von Senden, M. (1932). *The perception of space and shape in the congenitally blind before and after operation.* Glencoe, IL: Free Press. (p. 213)

Voyer, D., Postma, A., Brake, B., & Imperato-McGinley, J. (2007). Gender differences in object location memory: A meta-analysis. *Psychonomic Bulletin & Review, 14,* 23–38. (p. 328)

Vyazovskiy, V. V., Cirelli, C., Pfister-Genskow, M., Faraguna, U., & Tononi, G. (2008). Molecular and electrophysiological evidence for net synaptic potentiation in wake and depression in sleep. *Nature Neuroscience, 11,* 200–208. (p. 77)

Waber, R. L., Shiv, B., Carmon, & Ariely, D. (2008). Commercial features of placebo and therapeutic efficacy. *Journal of the American Medical Association, 299,* 1016–1017. (p. 22)

Wadden, T. A., Vogt, R. A., Foster, G. D., & Anderson, D. A. (1998). Exercise and the maintenance of weight loss: 1-year follow-up of a controlled clinical trial. *Journal of Consulting and Clinical Psychology, 66,* 429–433. (p. 356)

Wade, K. A., Garry, M., Read, J. D., & Lindsay, D. S. (2002). A picture is worth a thousand lies: Using false photographs to create false childhood memories. *Psychonomic Bulletin & Review, 9,* 597–603. (p. 282)

Wade, N. G., Worthington, E. L., Jr., & Vogel, D. L. (2006). Effectiveness of religiously tailored interventions in Christian therapy. *Psychotherapy Research, 17,* 91–105. (p. 511)

Wagner, U., Gais, S., Haider, H., Verleger, R., & Born, J. (2004). Sleep inspires insight. *Nature, 427,* 352–355. (p. 77)

Wagstaff, G. (1982). Attitudes to rape: The "just world" strikes again? *Bulletin of the British Psychological Society, 13,* 275–283. (p. 527)

Wahlberg, D. (2001, October 11). We're more depressed, patriotic, poll finds. *Grand Rapids Press,* p. A15. (p. 400)

Wai, J., Lubinski, D., & Benbow, C. P. (2005). Creativity and occupational accomplishments among intellectually precocious youths: An age 13 to age 33 longitudinal study. *Journal of Educational Psychology, 97,* 484–492. (p. 322)

Wakefield, J. C. (1992). Disorder as a harmful dysfunction: A conceptual critique of DSM-III-R's definition of mental disorder. *Psychological Review, 99,* 232–247. (p. 455)

Wakefield, J. C. (2006). What makes a mental disorder mental? *Philosophy, Psychiatry, and Psychology, 13,* 123–131. (p. 455)

Wakefield, J. C., & Spitzer, R. L. (2002). Lowered estimates—but of what? *Archives of General Psychiatry, 59,* 129–130. (p. 465)

Walker, M. P., & Stickgold, R. (2006). Sleep, memory, and plasticity. *Annual Review of Psychology, 57,* 139–166. (p. 77)

Walker, W. R., Skowronski, J. J., & Thompson, C. P. (2003). Life is pleasant—and memory helps to keep it that way! *Review of General Psychology, 7,* 203–210. (p. 171)

Wall, P. D. (2000). *Pain: The science of suffering.* New York: Columbia University Press. (p. 199)

Wallace, D. S., Paulson, R. M., Lord, C. G., & Bond, C. F., Jr. (2005). Which behaviors do attitudes predict? Meta-analyzing the effects of social pressure and perceived difficulty. *Review of General Psychology, 9(3),* 214–227. (p. 528)

Wallach, M. A., & Wallach, L. (1983). *Psychology's sanction for selfishness: The error of egoism in theory and therapy.* New York: Freeman. (p. 432)

Wallach, M. A., & Wallach, L. (1985, February). How psychology sanctions the cult of the self. *Washington Monthly,* pp. 46–56. (p. 432)

Walsh, T., & 35 others. (2008). Rare structural variants disrupt multiple genes in neurodevelopmental pathways in schizophrenia. *Science, 320,* 539–543. (p. 485)

Walster (Hatfield), E., Aronson, V., Abrahams, D., & Rottman, L. (1966). Importance of physical attractiveness in dating behavior. *Journal of Personality and Social Psychology, 4,* 508–516. (p. 556)

Wampold, B. E. (2001). *The great psychotherapy debate: Models, methods, and findings.* Mahwah, NJ: Erlbaum. (p. 510)

Wampold, B. E. (2007). Psychotherapy: The humanistic (and effective) treatment. *American Psychologist, 62,* 857–873. (p. 510)

Wampold, B. E., Mondin, G. W., Moody, M., & Ahn, H. (1997). The flat earth as a metaphor for the evidence for uniform efficacy of bona fide psychotherapies: Reply to Crits-Christoph (1997) and Howard et al. (1997). *Psychological Bulletin, 122,* 226–230. (p. 506)

Wang, S-H., Baillargeon, R., & Brueckner, L. (2004). Young infants' reasoning about hidden objects: Evidence from violation-of-expectation tasks with test trials only. *Cognition, 93,* 167–198. (p. 144)

Wansink, B., & van Ittersum, K. (2003). Bottoms up! The influence of elongation on pouring and consumption volume. *Journal of Consumer Research, 30,* 455–464. (p. 208)

Wansink, B., & van Ittersum, K. (2005). Shape of glass and amount of alcohol poured: Comparative study of effect of practice and concentration. *British Medical Journal, 331,* 1512–1514. (p. 208)

Ward, A., & Mann, T. (2000). Don't mind if I do: Disinhibited eating under cognitive load. *Journal of Personality and Social Psychology, 78,* 753–763. (p. 356)

Ward, C. (1994). Culture and altered states of consciousness. In W. J. Lonner & R. Malpass (Eds.), *Psychology and culture.* Boston: Allyn & Bacon. (p. 89)

Ward, K. D., Klesges, R. C., & Halpern, M. T. (1997). Predictors of smoking cessation and state-of-the-art smoking interventions. *Journal of Social Issues, 53,* 129–145. (p. 93)

Ward, L. M., & Friedman, K. (2006). Using TV as a guide: Associations between television viewing and adolescents' sexual attitudes and behavior. *Journal of Research on Adolescence, 16,* 133–156. (p. 361)

Wardle, J., Cooke, L. J., Gibson, L., Sapochnik, M., Sheiham, A., & Lawson, M. (2003). Increasing children's acceptance of vegetables: A randomized trial of parent-led exposure. *Appetite, 40,* 155–162, 201)

Wargo, E. (2007, December). Understanding the have-knots. *APS Observer,* pp. 18–21. (p. 412)

Warner, J., McKeown, E., Johnson, K., Ramsay, A., Cort, C., & King, M. (2004). Rates and predictors of mental illness in gay men, lesbians and bisexual men and women. *British Journal of Psychiatry, 185,* 479–485. (p. 364)

Wason, P. C. (1960). On the failure to eliminate hypotheses in a conceptual task. *Quarterly Journal of Experimental Psychology, 12,* 129–140. (p. 293)

Wason, P. C. (1981). The importance of cognitive illusions. *The Behavioral and Brain Sciences, 4,* 356. (p. 293)

Wasserman, E. A. (1993). Comparative cognition: Toward a general understanding of cognition in behavior. *Psychological Science, 4,* 156–161. (p. 238)

Wasserman, E. A. (1995). The conceptual abilities of pigeons. *American Scientist, 83,* 246–255. (p. 310)

Waterman, A. S. (1988). Identity status theory and Erikson's theory: Commonalities and differences. *Developmental Review, 8,* 185–208. (p. 160)

Watkins, E. R. (2008). Constructive and unconstructive repetitive thought. *Psychological Bulletin, 134,* 163–206. (p. 471)

Watson, D. (2000). *Mood and temperament.* New York: Guilford Press. (pp. 392, 411)

Watson, D., Suls, J., & Haig, J. (2002). Global self-esteem in relation to structural models of personality and affectivity. *Journal of Personality and Social Psychology, 83,* 185–197. (p. 447)

Watson, J. B. (1913). Psychology as the behaviorist views it. *Psychological Review, 20,* 158–177. (pp. 227, 235)

Watson, J. B., & Rayner, R. (1920). Conditioned emotional reactions. *Journal of Experimental Psychology, 3,* 1–14. (p. 235)

Watson, R. I., Jr. (1973). Investigation into deindividuation using a cross-cultural survey technique. *Journal of Personality and Social Psychology, 25,* 342–345. (p. 539)

Watson, S. J., Benson, J. A., Jr., & Joy, J. E. (2000). NEWS AND VIEWS—Marijuana and medicine: Assessing the science base: A summary of the 1999 Institute of Medicine report. *Archives of General Psychiatry, 57,* 547–553. (p. 96)

Wayment, H. A., & Peplau, L. A. (1995). Social support and well-being among lesbian and heterosexual women: A structural modeling approach. *Personality and Social Psychology Bulletin, 21,* 1189–1199. (p. 169)

Weaver, J. B., Masland, J. L., & Zillmann, D. (1984). Effect of erotica on young men's aesthetic perception of their female sexual partners. *Perceptual and Motor Skills, 58,* 929–930. (p. 360)

Webb, W. B. (1992). *Sleep: The gentle tyrant.* Bolton, MA: Anker. (pp. 74, 78)

Webb, W. B., & Campbell, S. S. (1983). Relationships in sleep characteristics of identical and fraternal twins. *Archives of General Psychiatry, 40,* 1093–1095. (p. 75)

Webley, K. (2009, June 15). Behind the drop in Chinese adoptions. *Time,* p. 55. (p. 544)

Weinberg, M. S., & Williams, C. (1974). *Male homosexuals: Their problems and adaptations.* New York: Oxford University Press. (p. 364)

Weinberger, D. R. (2001, March 10). A brain too young for good judgment. *New York Times* (www.nytimes.com). (p. 157)

Weinstein, N. D. (1980). Unrealistic optimism about future life events. *Journal of Personality and Social Psychology, 39,* 806–820. (p. 443)

Weinstein, N. D. (1982). Unrealistic optimism about susceptibility to health problems. *Journal of Behavioral Medicine, 5,* 441–460. (p. 443)

Weinstein, N. D. (1996, October 4). 1996 optimistic bias bibliography. (weinstein_c@aesop.rutgers.edu). (p. 443)

Weis, S., & Suß, H-M. (2007). Reviving the search for social intelligence: A multitrait-multimethod study of its structure and construct validity. *Personality and Individual Differences, 42,* 3–14. (p. 318)

Weiskrantz, L. (1986). *Blindsight: A case study and implications.* Oxford: Oxford University Press. (p. 190)

Weiss, A., King, J. E., & Enns, R. M. (2002). Subjective well-being is heritable and genetically correlated with dominance in chimpanzees (Pan troglodytes*). Journal of Personality and Social Psychology, 83,* 1141–1149. (p. 396)

Weiss, A., King, J. E., & Figueredo, A. J. (2000). The heritability of personality factors in chimpanzees (Pan troglodytes). *Behavior Genetics, 30,* 213–221. (p. 396)

Weiss, A., King, J. E., & Perkins, L. (2006). Personality and subjective well-being in orangutans (Pongo pygmaeus and Pongo abelii). *Journal of Personality and Social Psychology, 90,* 501–511. (p. 433)

Weissman, M. M., Bland, R. C., Canino, G. J., Faravelli, C., Greenwald, S., Hwu, H-G., Joyce, P. R., Karam, E. G., Lee, C-K., Lellouch, J., Lepine, J-P., Newman, S. C., Rubio-Stepic, M., Wells, J. E., Wickramaratne, P. J., Wittchen, H-U., & Yeh, E-K. (1996). Cross-national epidemiology of major depression and bipolar disorder. *Journal of the American Medical Association, 276,* 293–299. (p. 473)

Weisz, J. R., Rothbaum, F. M., & Blackburn, T. C. (1984). Standing out and standing in: The psychology of control in America and Japan. *American Psychologist, 39,* 955–969. (p. 124)

Welch, J. M., Lu, J., Rodriquiz, R. M., Trotta, N. C., Peca, J., Ding, J-D., Feliciano, C., Chen, M., Adams, J. P., Luo, J., Dudek, S. M., Weinberg, R. J., Calakos, N., Wetsel, W. C., & Feng, G. (2007). Cortico-striatal synaptic defects and OCD-like behaviours in *Sapap3*-mutant mice. *Nature, 448,* 894–900. (p. 467)

Welch, W. W. (2005, February 28). Trauma of Iraq war haunting thousands returning home. *USA Today* (www.usatoday.com). (p. 464)

Weller, S., & Davis-Beaty, K. (2002). The effectiveness of male condoms in prevention of sexually transmitted diseases (protocol). *Cochrane Database of Systematic Reviews,* Issue 4, Art. No. CD004090. (p. 362)

Wellings, K., Collumbien, M., Slaymaker, E., Singh, S., Hodges, Z., Patel, D., & Bajos, N. (2006). Sexual behaviour in context: A global perspective. *Lancet, 368,* 1706–1728. (p. 361)

Wellman, H. M., & Gelman, S. A. (1992). Cognitive development: Foundational theories of core domains. *Annual Review of Psychology, 43,* 337–375. (p. 144)

Wells, G. L. (1981). Lay analyses of causal forces on behavior. In J. Harvey (Ed.), *Cognition, social behavior and the environment.* Hillsdale, NJ: Erlbaum. (p. 225)

Wender, P. H., Kety, S. S., Rosenthal, D., Schulsinger, F., Ortmann, J., & Lunde, I. (1986). Psychiatric disorders in the biological and adoptive families of adopted individuals with affective disorders. *Archives of General Psychiatry, 43,* 923–929. (p. 475)

Wener, R., Frazier, W., & Farbstein, J. (1987, June). Building better jails. *Psychology Today,* pp. 40–49. (p. 442)

Westen, D. (1996). Is Freud really dead? Teaching psychodynamic theory to introductory psychology. Presentation to the Annual Institute on the Teaching of Psychology, St. Petersburg Beach, FL. (p. 424)

Westen, D. (1998). The scientific legacy of Sigmund Freud: Toward a psychodynamically informed psychological science. *Psychological Bulletin, 124,* 333–371. (p. 426)

Westen, D. (2007). *The political brain: The role of emotion in deciding the fate of the nation.* New York: PublicAffairs. (p. 383)

Westen, D., & Morrison, K. (2001). A multidimensional meta-analysis of treatments for depression, panic, and generalized anxiety disorder: An empirical examination of the status of empirically supported therapies. *Journal of Consulting and Clinical Psychology, 69,* 875–899. (p. 506)

Weuve, J., Kang, J. H., Manson, J. E., Breteler, M. M. B., Ware, J. H., &

Grodstein, F. (2004). Physical activity, including walking, and cognitive function in older women. *Journal of the American Medical Association, 292,* 1454–1460. (p. 166)

Whalen, P. J., Kagan, J., Cook, R. G., Davis, F. C., Kim, H., Polis, S., McLaren, D. G., Somerville, L. H., McLean, A. A., Maxwell, J. S., & Johnstone, T. (2004). Human amygdala responsibility to masked fearful eye whites. *Science, 302,* 2061. (pp. 381, 382)

Whalen, P. J., Shin, L. M., McInerney, S. C., Fisher, H., Wright, C. I., & Rauch, S. L. (2001). A functional MRI study of human amygdala responses to facial expressions of fear versus anger. *Emotion, 1,* 70–83. (p. 379)

Wheeler, B. W., Gunnell, D., Metcalfe, C., Stephens, P., & Martin, R. M. (2008). The population impact on incidence of suicide and non-fatal self harm of regulatory action against the use of selective serotonin reuptake inhibitors in under 18s in the United Kingdom: Ecological study. *British Medical Journal, 336,* 542–545. (p. 516)

Wheelwright, J. (2004, August). Study the clones first. *Discover,* pp. 44–50. (p. 108)

White, G. L., & Kight, T. D. (1984). Misattribution of arousal and attraction: Effects of salience of explanations for arousal. *Journal of Experimental Social Psychology, 20,* 55–64. (p. 559)

White, H. R., Brick, J., & Hansell, S. (1993). A longitudinal investigation of alcohol use and aggression in adolescence. *Journal of Studies on Alcohol,* Supplement No. 11, 62–77. (p. 549)

White, K. M. (1983). Young adults and their parents: Individuation to mutuality. *New Directions for Child Development, 22,* 61–76. (p. 162)

White, L., & Edwards, J. (1990). Emptying the nest and parental well-being: An analysis of national panel data. *American Sociological Review, 55,* 235–242. (p. 170)

White, R. A. (1998). Intuition, heart knowledge, and parapsychology. *Journal of the American Society for Psychical Research, 92,* 158–171. (p. 219)

Whitehead, B. D., & Popenoe, D. (2001). *The state of our unions 2001: The social health of marriage in America.* Rutgers University: The National Marriage Project. (p. 169)

Whiten, A., & Boesch, C. (2001, January). Cultures of chimpanzees. *Scientific American,* pp. 60–67. (p. 310)

Whiten, A., & Byrne, R. W. (1988). Tactical deception in primates. *Behavioral and Brain Sciences, 11,* 233–244, 267–273. (p. 17)

Whiting, B. B., & Edwards, C. P. (1988). *Children of different worlds: The formation of social behavior.* Cambridge, MA: Harvard University Press. (p. 125)

Whitley, B. E., Jr. (1990). The relationships of heterosexuals' attributions for the causes of homosexuality to attitudes toward lesbians and gay men. *Personality and Social Psychology Bulletin, 16,* 369–377. (p. 368)

Whitley, B. E., Jr. (1999). Right-wing authoritarianism, social dominance orientation, and prejudice. *Journal of Personality and Social Psychology, 77,* 126–134. (p. 546)

Whitlock, J. R., Heynen, A. L., Shuler, M. G., & Bear, M. F. (2006). Learning induces long-term potentiation in the hippocampus. *Science, 313,* 1093–1097. (p. 268)

WHO. (1979). *Schizophrenia: An international followup study.* Chicester, England: Wiley. (p. 482)

WHO. (2000). *Effectiveness of male latex condoms in protecting against pregnancy and sexually transmitted infections.* World Health Organization (www.who.int). (p. 362)

WHO. (2002). *The global burden of disease.* Geneva: World Health Organization (www.who.int/msa/mnh/ems/dalys/intro.htm). (p. 471)

WHO. (2003). *The male latex condom: Specification and guidelines for condom procurement.* Department of Reproductive Health and Research, Family and Community Health, World Health Organization. (p. 362)

WHO. (2004). Prevalence, severity, and unmet need for treatment of mental disorders in the World Health Organization World Mental Health Surveys. *Journal of the American Medical Association, 291,* 2581–2590. (p. 478)

WHO. (2008). *Mental health (nearly 1 million annual suicide deaths).* Geneva: World Health Organization (www.who.int/mental_health/en). (p. 474)

WHO. (2008). *Mental health and substance abuse: Facts and figures.* Geneva: World Health Organization (www.who.int). (pp. 88, 453)

WHO. (2008). *Schizophrenia.* Geneva: World Health Organization (www.who.int). (p. 480)

WHO. (2008). *Suicide rates per 100,000 by country, year and sex.* Geneva: World Health Organization (www.who.int). (p. 474)

WHO. (2008). *WHO report on the global tobacco epidemic, 2008.* Geneva: World Health Organization (www.who.int). (p. 92)

WHO. (2009, visited May 25). *Course and outcome of schizophrenia.* World Health Organization (http://www.searo.who.int/en/Section1174/Section1199/Section1567/Section1827_8055.htm). (p. 482)

Whooley, M. A., & Browner, W. S. (1998). Association between depressive symptoms and mortality in older women. *Archives of Internal Medicine, 158,* 2129–2135. (p. 403)

Whorf, B. L. (1956). Science and linguistics. In J. B. Carroll (Ed.), *Language, thought, and reality: Selected writings of Benjamin Lee Whorf.* Cambridge, MA: MIT Press. (p. 306)

Wickelgren, W. A. (1977). *Learning and memory.* Englewood Cliffs, NJ: Prentice-Hall. (p. 263)

Widiger, T. A., & Trull, T. J. (2007). Plate tectonics in the classification of personality disorder: Shifting to a dimensional model. *American Psychologist, 62,* 71–83. (p. 486)

Widom, C. S. (1989a). Does violence beget violence? A critical examination of the literature. *Psychological Bulletin, 106,* 3–28. (p. 153)

Widom, C. S. (1989b). The cycle of violence. *Science, 244,* 160–166. (p. 153)

Wiens, A. N., & Menustik, C. E. (1983). Treatment outcome and patient characteristics in an aversion therapy program for alcoholism. *American Psychologist, 38,* 1089–1096. (p. 499)

Wierson, M., & Forehand, R. (1994). Parent behavioral training for child noncompliance: Rationale, concepts, and effectiveness. *Current Directions in Psychological Science, 3,* 146–149. (p. 246)

Wierzbicki, M. (1993). Psychological adjustment of adoptees: A meta-analysis. *Journal of Clinical Child Psychology, 22,* 447–454. (p. 110)

Wiesel, T. N. (1982). Postnatal development of the visual cortex and the influence of environment. *Nature, 299,* 583–591. (p. 214)

Wigdor, A. K., & Garner, W. R. (1982). *Ability testing: Uses, consequences, and controversies.* Washington, DC: National Academy Press. (p. 333)

Wilcox, A. J., Baird, D. D., Dunson, D. B., McConnaughey, D. R., Kesner, J. S., & Weinberg, C. R. (2004). On the frequency of intercourse around ovulation: Evidence for biological influences. *Human Reproduction, 19,* 1539–1543. (p. 358)

Wilder, D. A. (1981). Perceiving persons as a group: Categorization and intergroup relations. In D. L. Hamilton (Ed.), *Cognitive processes in stereotyping and intergroup behavior.* Hillsdale, NJ: Erlbaum. (p. 546)

Wilford, J. N. (1999, February 9). New findings help balance the cosmological books. *New York Times* (www.nytimes.com). (p. 133)

Williams, C. L., & Berry, J. W. (1991). Primary prevention of acculturative stress among refugees. *American Psychologist, 46,* 632–641. (p. 401)

Williams, H. J., Owen, M. J., & O'Donovan, M. C. (2007). Is COMT a susceptibility gene for schizophrenia? *Schizophrenia Bulletin, 33,* 635–641. (p. 485)

Williams, J. E., & Best, D. L. (1990). *Measuring sex stereotypes: A multination study.* Newbury Park, CA: Sage. (p. 127)

Williams, J. E., Paton, C. C., Siegler, I. C., Eigenbrodt, M. L., Nieto, F. J., & Tyroler, H. A. (2000). Anger proneness predicts coronary heart disease risk: Prospective analysis from the artherosclerosis risk in communities (ARIC) study. *Circulation, 101*(17), 2034–2040. (p. 402)

Williams, J. H. G., Waister, G. D., Gilchrist, A., Perrett, D. I., Murray, A. D., & Whiten, A. (2006). Neural mechanisms of imitation and 'mirror neuron' functioning in autistic spectrum disorder. *Neuropsychogia, 44,* 610–621. (pp. 171, 249)

Williams, K. D. (2007). Ostracism. *Annual Review of Psychology, 58,* 425–452. (pp. 371, 372)

Williams, K. D., & Zadro, L. (2001). Ostracism: On being ignored, excluded and rejected. In M. Leary (Ed.), *Rejection.* New York: Oxford University Press. (p. 371)

Williams, R. (1993). *Anger kills.* New York: Times Books. (p. 402)

Williams, S. L. (1987). Self-efficacy and mastery-oriented treatment for severe phobias. Paper presented to the American Psychological Association convention. (p. 498)

Willis, J., & Todorov, A. (2006). First impressions: Making up your mind after a 100-ms. exposure to a face. *Psychological Science, 17,* 592–598. (p. 384)

Willis, S. L., Tennstedt, S. L., Marsiske, M., Ball, K., Elias, J., Koepke, K. M., Morris, J. N., Rebok, G. W., Unverzagt, F. W., Stoddars, A. M., & Wright, E. (2006). Long-term effects of cognitive training on everyday functional outcomes in older adults. *Journal of the American Medical Association, 296,* 2805–2814. (p. 168)

Willmuth, M. E. (1987). Sexuality after spinal cord injury: A critical review. *Clinical Psychology Review, 7,* 389–412. (p. 360)

Wilson, A. E., & Ross, M. (2001). From chump to champ: People's appraisals of their earlier and present selves. *Journal of Personality and Social Psychology, 80,* 572–584. (p. 449)

Wilson, C. M., & Oswald, A. J. (2002). How does marriage affect physical and psychological health? A survey of the longitudinal evidence. Working paper, University of York and Warwick University. (p. 410)

Wilson, J. Q. (1993). *The moral sense.* New York: Free Press. (p. 158)

Wilson, R. C., Gaft, J. G., Dienst, E. R., Wood, L., & Bavry, J. L. (1975). *College professors and their impact on students.* New York: Wiley. (p. 539)

Wilson, R. S. (1979). Analysis of longitudinal twin data: Basic model and applications to physical growth measures. *Acta Geneticae medicae et Gemellologiae, 28,* 93–105. (p. 141)

Wilson, R. S., & Matheny, A. P., Jr. (1986). Behavior-genetics research in infant temperament: The Louisville twin study. In R. Plomin & J. Dunn (Eds.), *The study of temperament: Changes, continuities, and challenges.* Hillsdale, NJ: Erlbaum. (p. 111)

Wilson, R. S., Beck, T. L., Bienias, J. L., & Bennett, D. A. (2007). Terminal cognitive decline: Accelerated loss of cognition in the last years of life. *Psychosomatic Medicine, 69,* 131–137. (p. 168)

Wilson, T. D. (2002). *Strangers to ourselves: Discovering the adaptive unconscious.* Cambridge, MA: Harvard University Press. (p. 68)

Wilson, T. D. (2006). The power of social psychological interventions. *Science, 313,* 1251–1252. (p. 334)

Wilson, W. A., & Kuhn, C. M. (2005). How addiction hijacks our reward system. *Cerebrum, 7*(2), 53–66. (p. 98)

Windholz, G. (1989, April-June). The discovery of the principles of reinforcement, extinction, generalization, and differentiation of conditional reflexes in Pavlov's laboratories. *Pavlovian Journal of Biological Science, 26,* 64–74. (p. 231)

Windholz, G. (1997). Ivan P. Pavlov: An overview of his life and psychological work. *American Psychologist, 52,* 941–946. (p. 229)

Winner, E. (2000). The origins and ends of giftedness. *American Psychologist, 55,* 159–169. (p. 322)

Wiseman, R., Jeffreys, C., Smith, M., & Nyman, A. (1999). The psychology of the seance. *The Skeptical Inquirer, 23*(2), 30–33. (p. 283)

Wisman, A., & Goldenberg, J. L. (2005). From the grave to the cradle: Evidence that mortality salience engenders a desire for offspring. *Journal of Personality and Social Psychology, 89,* 46–61. (p. 154)

Witelson, S. F., Kigar, D. L., & Harvey, T. (1999). The exceptional brain of Albert Einstein. *Lancet, 353,* 2149–2153. (p. 54)

Witvliet, C. V. O., Ludwig, T., & Vander Laan, K. (2001). Granting forgiveness or harboring grudges: Implications for emotions, physiology, and health. *Psychological Science, 12,* 117–123. (p. 391)

Witvliet, C. V. O., & Vrana, S. R. (1995). Psychophysiological responses as indices of affective dimensions. *Psychophysiology, 32,* 436–443. (p. 379)

Wixted, J. T., & Ebbesen, E. B. (1991). On the form of forgetting. *Psychological Science, 2,* 409–415. (p. 277)

Wolak, J., Mitchell, K., & Finkelhor, D. (2007). Unwanted and wanted exposure to online pornography in a national sample of youth Internet users. *Pediatrics, 119,* 247–257. (p. 551)

Wolfson, A. R., & Carskadon, M. A. (1998). Sleep schedules and daytime functioning in adolescents. *Child Development, 69,* 875–887. (p. 82)

Woll, S. (1986). So many to choose from: Decision strategies in videodating. *Journal of Social and Personal Relationships, 3,* 43–52. (p. 557)

Wolpe, J. (1958). *Psychotherapy by reciprocal inhibition.* Stanford, CA: Stanford University Press. (p. 498)

Wolpe, J., & Plaud, J. J. (1997). Pavlov's contributions to behavior therapy: The obvious and the not so obvious. *American Psychologist, 52,* 966–972. (p. 498)

Wonderlich, S. A., Joiner, T. E., Jr., Keel, P. K., Williamson, D. A., & Crosby, R. D. (2007). Eating disorder diagnoses: Empirical approaches to classification. *American Psychologist, 62,* 167–180. (p. 348)

Wong, D. F., Wagner, H. N., Tune, L. E., Dannals, R. F., et al. (1986). Positron emission tomography reveals elevated D_2 dopamine receptors in drug-naive schizophrenics. *Science, 234,* 1588–1593. (p. 483)

Wong, M. M., & Csikszentmihalyi, M. (1991). Affiliation motivation and daily experience: Some issues on gender differences. *Journal of Personality and Social Psychology, 60,* 154–164. (p. 128)

Wood, J. M. (2003, May 19). Quoted by R. Mestel, Rorschach tested: Blot out the famous method? Some experts say it has no place in psychiatry. *Los Angeles Times* (www.latimes.com). (p. 425)

Wood, J. M. (2006, Spring). The controversy over Exner's Comprehensive System for the Rorschach: The critics speak. *Independent Practitioner* (works.bepress.com/james_wood/7). (p. 425)

Wood, J. M., Bootzin, R. R., Kihlstrom, J. F., & Schacter, D. L. (1992). Implicit and explicit memory for verbal information presented during sleep. *Psychological Science, 3,* 236–239. (p. 280)

Wood, J. M., Nezworski, M. T., Garb, H. N., & Lilienfeld, S. O. (2006). The controversy over the Exner Comprehensive System and the Society for Personality Assessment's white paper on the Rorschach. *Independent Practitioner, 26.* (p. 425)

Wood, J. V., Saltzberg, J. A., & Goldsamt, L. A. (1990a). Does affect induce self-focused attention? *Journal of Personality and Social Psychology, 58,* 899–908. (p. 478)

Wood, J. V., Saltzberg, J. A., Neale, J. M., Stone, A. A., & Rachmiel, T. B. (1990b). Self-focused attention, coping responses, and distressed mood in everyday life. *Journal of Personality and Social Psychology, 58,* 1027–1036. (p. 478)

Wood, W. (1987). Meta-analytic review of sex differences in group performance. *Psychological Bulletin, 102,* 53–71. (p. 127)

Wood, W., & Eagly, A. (2002). A cross-cultural analysis of the behavior of women and men: Implications for the origins of sex differences.

Psychological Bulletin, 128, 699–727. (pp. 117, 127, 129, 132)

Wood, W., & Eagly, A. H. (2007). Social structural origins of sex differences in human mating. In S. W. Gagestad & J. A. Simpson (Eds.), *The evolution of mind: Fundamental questions and controversies.* New York: Guilford Press. (pp. 117, 127, 129)

Wood, W., & Neal, D. T. (2007, October). A new look at habits and the habit-goal interface. *Psychological Review, 114,* 843–863. (p. 226)

Wood, W., Lundgren, S., Ouellette, J. A., Busceme, S., & Blackstone, T. (1994). Minority influence: A meta-analytic review of social influence processes. *Psychological Bulletin, 115,* 323–345. (p. 541)

Woods, N. F., Dery, G. K., & Most, A. (1983). Recollections of menarche, current menstrual attitudes, and premenstrual symptoms. In S. Golub (Ed.), *Menarche: The transition from girl to woman.* Lexington, MA: Lexington Books. (p. 155)

Woodward, B. (2002). *Bush at war.* New York: Simon & Schuster. (p. 10)

Woody, E. Z., & McConkey, K. M. (2003). What we don't know about the brain and hypnosis, but need to: A view from the Buckhorn Inn. *International Journal of Clinical and Experimental Hypnosis, 51,* 309–338. (p. 87)

Woolcock, N. (2004, September 3). Driver thought everyone else was on wrong side. *The Times,* p. 22. (p. 534)

World Federation for Mental Health. (2005). ADHD: The hope behind the hype (www.wfmh.org). (p. 455)

World Health Organization. (2004a). *Prevention of mental disorders: Effective interventions and policy options. Summary report.* Geneva: World Health Organization, Department of Mental Health and Substance Abuse. (p. 488)

World Health Organization. (2004b). Prevalence, severity, and unmet need for treatment of mental disorders in the World Health Organization World Mental Health Surveys. *Journal of the American Medical Association, 291,* 2581–2590. (p. 489)

World Health Organization. (2007). *Obesity and overweight.* (www.who.int/dietphysicalactivity/publications/facts/obesity/en/). (p. 348)

Worobey, J., & Blajda, V. M. (1989). Temperament ratings at 2 weeks, 2 months, and 1 year: Differential stability of activity and emotionality. *Developmental Psychology, 25,* 257–263. (p. 111)

Worthington, E. L., Jr. (1989). Religious faith across the life span: Implications for counseling and research. *The Counseling Psychologist, 17,* 555–612. (p. 157)

Worthington, E. L., Jr., Kurusu, T. A., McCullogh, M. E., & Sandage, S. J. (1996). Empirical research on religion and psychotherapeutic processes and outcomes: A 10-year review and research prospectus. *Psychological Bulletin, 119,* 448–487. (p. 511)

Wortman, C. B., & Silver, R. C. (1989). The myths of coping with loss. *Journal of Consulting and Clinical Psychology, 57,* 349–357. (p. 172)

Wren, C. S. (1999, April 8). Drug survey of children finds middle school a pivotal time. *New York Times* (www.nytimes.com). (p. 99)

Wright, I. C., Rabe-Hesketh, S., Woodruff, P. W. R., David, A. S., Murray, R. M., &

Bullmore, E. T. (2000). Meta-analysis of regional brain volumes in schizophrenia. *American Journal of Psychiatry, 157,* 16–25. (p. 483)

Wright, J. (2006, March 16). *Boomers in the bedroom: Sexual attitudes and behaviours in the boomer generation.* Ipsos Reid survey (www.ipsos-na.com). (p. 164)

Wright, P., Takei, N., Rifkin, L., & Murray, R. M. (1995). Maternal influenza, obstetric complications, and schizophrenia. *American Journal of Psychiatry, 152,* 1714–1720. (p. 483)

Wright, P. H. (1989). Gender differences in adults' same- and cross-gender friendships. In R. G. Adams & R. Blieszner (Eds.), *Older adult friendships: Structure and process.* Newbury Park, CA: Sage. (p. 128)

Wuethrich, B. (2001, March). Features—GETTING STUPID—Surprising new neurological behavioral research reveals that teenagers who drink too much may permanently damage their brains and seriously compromise their ability to learn. *Discover, 56,* 56–64. (p. 90)

Wulsin, L. R., Vaillant, G. E., & Wells, V. E. (1999). A systematic review of the mortality of depression. *Psychosomatic Medicine, 61,* 6–17. (p. 403)

Wyatt, J. K., & Bootzin, R. R. (1994). Cognitive processing and sleep: Implications for enhancing job performance. *Human Performance, 7,* 119–139. (pp. 81, 280)

Wyatt, R. J., Henter, I., & Sherman-Elvy, E. (2001). Tantalizing clues to preventing schizophrenia. *Cerebrum: The Dana Forum on Brain Science, 3,* pp. 15–30. (p. 484)

Wynne, C. (2008). Aping language: A skeptical analysis of the evidence for nonhuman primate language. *Skeptic, 13*(4), 10–13. (p. 312)

Wynne, C. D. L. (2004). *Do animals think?* Princeton, NJ: Princeton University Press. (p. 312)

Xu, Y., & Corkin, S. (2001). H.M. revisits the Tower of Hanoi puzzle. *Neuropsychology, 15,* 69–79. (p. 270)

Yach, D., Struckler, D., & Brownell, K. D. (2006). Epidemiologic and economic consequences of the global epidemics of obesity and diabetes. *Nature Medicine, 12,* 62–66. (p. 350)

Yamagata, S., & 11 others. (2006). Is the genetic structure of human personality universal? A cross-cultural twin study from North America, Europe, and Asia. *Journal of Personality and Social Psychology, 90,* 987–998. (p. 436)

Yang, N., & Linz, D. (1990). Movie ratings and the content of adult videos: The sex-violence ratio. *Journal of Communication, 40*(2), 28–42. (p. 552)

Yang, S., Markoczy, L., & Qi, M. (2006). Unrealistic optimism in consumer credit card adoption. *Journal of Economic Psychology, 28,* 170–185. (p. 444)

Yankelovich Partners. (1995, May/June). Growing old. *American Enterprise,* p. 108. (p. 163)

Yarnell, P. R., & Lynch, S. (1970, April 25). Retrograde memory immediately after concussion. *Lancet,* pp. 863–865. (p. 268)

Yates, A. (1989). Current perspectives on the eating disorders: I. History, psychological and bio-

logical aspects. *Journal of the American Academy of Child and Adolescent Psychiatry, 28,* 813–828. (p. 348)

Yates, A. (1990). Current perspectives on the eating disorders: II. Treatment, outcome, and research directions. *Journal of the American Academy of Child and Adolescent Psychiatry, 29,* 1–9. (p. 348)

Yates, W. R. (2000). Testosterone in psychiatry. *Archives of General Psychiatry, 57,* 155–156. (p. 359)

Ybarra, O. (1999). Misanthropic person memory when the need to self-enhance is absent. *Personality and Social Psychology Bulletin, 25,* 261–269. (p. 447)

Youngentob, S. L., Kent, P. F., Scheehe, P. R., Molina, J. C., Spear, N. E., & Youngentob, L. M. (2007). Experience-induced fetal plasticity: The effect of gestational ethanol exposure on the behavioral and neurophysiologic olfactory response to ethanol odor in early postnatal and adult rats. *Behavioral Neuroscience, 121,* 1293–1305. (p. 138)

Yücel, M., Solowij, N., Respondek, C., Whittle, S., Fornito, A., Pantelis, C., & Lubman, D. I. (2008). Regional brain abnormalities associated with long-term cannabis use. *Archives of General Psychiatry, 65,* 694–701. (p. 96)

Yuki, M., Maddux, W. W., & Masuda. T. (2007). Are the windows to the soul the same in the East and West? Cultural differences in using the eyes and mouth as cues to recognize emotions in Japan and the United States. *Journal of Experimental Social Psychology, 43,* 303–311. (p. 388)

Zabin, L. S., Emerson, M. R., & Rowland, D. L. (2005). Child sexual abuse and early menarche: The direction of their relationship and its implications. *Journal of Adolescent Health, 36,* 393–400. (p. 155)

Zadra, A., Pilon, M., & Montplairsir, J. (2008). Polysomnographic diagnosis of sleepwalking: Effects of sleep deprivation. *Annals of Neurology, 63,* 513–519. (p. 79)

Zagorsky, J. L. (2007). Do you have to be smart to be rich? The impact of IQ on wealth, income and financial distress. *Intelligence, 35,* 489–501. (p. 315)

Zajonc, R. B. (1965). Social facilitation. *Science, 149,* 269–274. (p. 538)

Zajonc, R. B. (1980). Feeling and thinking: Preferences need no inferences. *American Psychologist, 35,* 151–175. (p. 381)

Zajonc, R. B. (1984a). On the primacy of affect. *American Psychologist, 39,* 117–123. (p. 381)

Zajonc, R. B. (1984b, July 22). Quoted by D. Goleman, Rethinking IQ tests and their value. *The New York Times,* p. D22. (p. 319)

Zajonc, R. B. (1998). Emotions. In D. Gilbert, S. T. Fiske, & G. Lindzey (Eds.), *Handbook of social psychology* (4th ed.). New York: McGraw-Hill. (p. 556)

Zajonc, R. B. (2001). Mere exposure: A gateway to the subliminal. *Current Directions in Psychological Science, 10,* 224–228. (p. 555)

Zammit, S., Rasmussen, F., Farahmand, B., Gunnell, D., Lewis, G., Tynelius, P., & Brobert, G. P. (2007). Height and body mass index in young adulthood and risk of schizophrenia: A longitudinal study of 1,347,520

Swedish men. *Acta Psychiatrica Scandinavica, 116*, 378–385. (p. 482)

Zauberman, G., & Lynch, J. G., Jr. (2005). Resource slack and propensity to discount delayed investments of time versus money. *Journal of Experimental Psychology: General, 134*, 23–37. (p. 297)

Zeidner, M. (1990). Perceptions of ethnic group modal intelligence: Reflections of cultural stereotypes or intelligence test scores? *Journal of Cross-Cultural Psychology, 21*, 214–231. (p. 331)

Zeidner, M., Roberts, R. D., & Matthews, G. (2008). The science of emotional intelligence: Current consensus and controversies. *European Psychologist, 13*, 64–78. (p. 318)

Zeineh, M. M., Engel, S. A., Thompson, P. M., & Bookheimer, S. Y. (2003). Dynamics of the hippocampus during encoding and retrieval of face-name pairs. *Science, 299*, 577–580. (p. 271)

Zhang, H., & Xu, Y. (2006). Teaching of psychology to university students in China. *International Journal of Psychology, 41*, 17–23. (p. 5)

Zhang, J. V., Ren, P-G., Avsian-Kretchmer, O., Luo, C-W., Rauch, R., Klein, C., & Hsueh, A. J. W. (2005). Obestatin, a peptide encoded by the ghrelin gene, opposes ghrelin's effect on food intake. *Science, 310*, 996–999. (p. 346)

Zigler, E. F., & Styfco, S. J. (2001). Extended childhood intervention prepared children for school and beyond. *Journal of the American Medical Association, 285*, 2378–2380. (p. 327)

Zilbergeld, B. (1983). *The shrinking of America: Myths of psychological change.* Boston: Little, Brown. (pp. 505, 507)

Zillmann, D. (1986). Effects of prolonged consumption of pornography. Background paper for *The surgeon general's workshop on pornography and public health,* June 22–24. Report prepared by E. P. Mulvey & J. L. Haugaard and released by Office of the Surgeon General on August 4, 1986. (p. 381)

Zillmann, D. (1989). Effects of prolonged consumption of pornography. In D. Zillmann & J. Bryant (Eds.), *Pornography: Research advances and policy considerations.* Hillsdale, NJ: Erlbaum. (pp. 360, 553)

Zillmann, D., & Bryant, J. (1984). Effects of massive exposure to pornography. In N. Malamuth & E. Donnerstein (Eds.), *Pornography and sexual aggression.* Orlando, FL: Academic Press. (p. 553)

Zimbardo, P. G. (1970). The human choice: Individuation, reason, and order versus deindividuation, impulse, and chaos. In W. J. Arnold & D. Levine (Eds.), *Nebraska Symposium on Motivation, 1969.* Lincoln, NE: University of Nebraska Press. (p. 539)

Zimbardo, P. G. (1972, April). Pathology of imprisonment. *Transaction/ Society,* pp. 4–8. (p. 529)

Zimbardo, P. G. (2001, September 16). Fighting terrorism by understanding man's capacity for evil. Op-ed essay distributed by spsp-discuss@stolaf.edu. (p. 547)

Zimbardo, P. G. (2004, May 25). Journalist interview re: Abu Ghraib prison abuses: Eleven answers to eleven questions. Unpublished manuscript, Stanford University. (p. 530)

Zimbardo, P. G. (2005, January 18). You can't be a sweet cucumber in a vinegar barrel. *The Edge* (www.edge.org). (p. 530)

Zimbardo, P. G. (2007, September). Person x situation x system dynamics. *The Observer* (Association for Psychological Science), p. 43. (p. 529)

Zogby, J. (2006, March). Survey of teens and adults about the use of personal electronic devices and head phones. *Zogby International.* (p. 195)

Zornberg, G. L., Buka, S. L., & Tsuang, M. T. (2000). At issue: The problem of obstetrical complications and schizophrenia. *Schizophrenia Bulletin, 26*, 249–256. (p. 483)

Zou, Z., & Buck, L. B. (2006). Combinatorial effects of odorant mixes in olfactory cortex. *Science, 311*, 1477–1481. (p. 204)

Zubieta, J-K., Bueller, J. A., Jackson, L. R., Scott, D. J., Xu, Y., Koeppe, R. A., Nichols, T. E., & Stohler, C. S. (2005). Placebo effects mediated by endogenous opioid activity on µ-opioid receptors. *Journal of Neuroscience, 25*, 7754–7762. (p. 200)

Zubieta, J-K., Heitzeg, M. M., Smith, Y. R., Bueller, J. A., Xu, K., Xu, Y., Koeppe, R. A., Stohler, C. S., & Goldman, D. (2003). COMT val158met genotype affects µ-opioid neurotransmitter responses to a pain stressor. *Science, 299*, 1240–1243. (p. 199)

Zucker, G. S., & Weiner, B. (1993). Conservatism and perceptions of poverty: An attributional analysis. *Journal of Applied Social Psychology, 23*, 925–943. (p. 527)

Zuckerman, M. (1979). *Sensation seeking: Beyond the optimal level of arousal.* Hillsdale, NJ: Erlbaum. (p. 341)

Zvolensky, M. J., & Bernstein, A. (2005). Cigarette smoking and panic psychopathology. *Current Directions in Psychological Science, 14*, 301–305. (p. 462)

A

A. J., 276
Aarts, H., 384
Abramowitz, J. S., 498
Abrams, D. B., 90, 443, 444
Abrams, L., 278
Abrams, M., 213
Abramson, L. Y., 477, 478
Ackerman, D., 37
Adams, E. M., 21
Adams, P. F., 76
Adelmann, P. K., 170
Adelson, R., 269
Ader, R., 235
Adler, A., 369, 424, 429, 439, 450
Agassi, A., 105
Agassi, J., 105
Ai, A. L., 415
Ainsworth, M. D. S., 151
Airan, R. D., 476
Aird, E. G., 169
Åkerstedt, T., 78
Albarracín, D., 527
Albee, G., 521
Albert ("Little"), 4, 235, 236
Albert, B., 361
Albon, A. J., 284
Alcock, J. E., 275
Aldrich, M. S., 79
Aldridge-Morris, R., 469
Aleman, A., 481, 482
Alexander the Great, 396
Alexander, C. J., 42
Alexander, C. N., 413
Allard, F., 264
Allen, J. B., 368
Allen, K., 410
Allen, N. B., 471
Allen, W., 78, 494
Allik, J., 448
Alloy, L. B., 478
Allport, G. W., 15, 432, 433, 439, 446, 545
Altman, L. K., 405
Alwin, D. F., 125
Amabile, T. M., 317, 392, 447
Amato, P. R., 130
Ambady, N., 384, 387, 438
Ambinder, M. S., 69
Amedi, A., 56
Amen, D. G., 548
Ames, A., 211, 380
Ames, M. A., 367
Amsterdam, J. D., 515
Andersen, R. E., 356
Andersen, S. M., 158
Anderson, A. K., 48
Anderson, B. L., 405
Anderson, C. A., 25, 251, 271, 550, 552, 553
Anderson, D. C., 550
Anderson, I. M., 515
Anderson, J. R., 532
Anderson, R. C., 273
Anderson, S., 474
Anderson, S. E., 155
Anderson, S. R., 312
Andrault, I., 349
Andreasen, N. C., 483
Andrew, M., 508
Angell, M., 406
Angelsen, N. K., 21
Angier, N., 357

Annan, K., 567
Antoni, M. H., 405
Antony, M. M., 466
Antrobus, J., 82
Appleton, J., 293
Archer, J., 127
Archer, R., 427
Arenson, K. W., 329
Aries, E., 127
Aristotle, 2, 5, 160, 225, 291, 369, 552, 557
Arkowitz, H., 146, 507, 508
Armel, K. C., 199
Armony, J., 382
Arnett, J. J., 155, 162
Aron, A. P., 559, 560
Aronson, E., 161
Artiga, A. I., 346
Asch, S. E., 533, 534, 537, 568
Aserinsky, A., 72
Aserinsky, E., 72
Ashbery, J., 481
Ashley (Lady), 132
Askay, S. W., 86
Aspy, C. B., 361
Assanand, S., 346
Astin, A. W., 160
Astin, H. A., 160
Astington, J. W., 145
Atkins, L., 115
Atkinson, R. C., 258, 259
Atta, M., 537
Auden, W. H., 370
Austin, E. J., 322
Averill, J. R., 377, 389, 391
Avery, R. D., 331
Ax, A. F., 379
Axel, R., 203
Ayres, M. M., 127
Azar, B., 197

B

Babad, E., 384
Babyak, M., 520
Bach, J. S., 133, 238
Bachman, J., 99
Backman, L., 168
Bacon, F., 293, 296
Badcock, P. B. T., 471
Baddeley, A. D., 259, 260, 261, 274
Baer, J., 472
Bagemihl, B., 365
Baguma, P., 347
Bahrick, H. P., 261, 273, 277, 278
Bailenson, J. N., 556
Bailey, J. M., 115, 363, 366
Bailey, R. E., 244
Baillargeon, R., 144
Bain, J., 359
Baird, G., 146
Baker, E. L., 85
Baker, R. R., 357
Baker, T. B., 239
Bakermans-Kranenburg, M. J., 151
Baldwin, S. A., 506
Bale, C., 360
Ballard, M. E., 552
Balsam, K. F., 169, 363
Banaji, M. R., 306
Bancroft, J., 358
Bandura, A., 249, 250, 253, 439
Barash, D. P., 66
Barbaree, H. E., 90

Barber, C., 515
Barber, T. X., 86
Barbieri, M., 189
Bard, P., 376, 377, 383, 416, 417
Bargh, J. A., 67, 427, 532, 540, 555
Bar-Haim, Y., 466
Barinaga, M. B., 56, 412
Barkley, R. A., 455
Barlow, D. H., 503
Barnes, M. L., 385
Barnett, P. A., 478
Barnier, A. J., 84
Barnum, P. T., 435
Baron, R. A., 245
Baron-Cohen, S., 146, 147
Barrett, L. C., 442
Barrett, L. F., 379, 385
Barrow, J., 61
Barry, D., 26, 92, 164, 196, 349, 434
Bartholow, B. C., 552
Bartlett, A., 363
Bashore, T. R., 165
Baskind, D. E., 499
Bassett, D. R., 353
Bauer, P. J., 141, 272
Baum, A., 405
Baumeister, H., 453, 488
Baumeister, R. F., 85, 115, 121, 162, 297, 364, 369, 371, 427, 441, 447, 448, 449, 560
Baumgardner, A. H., 447
Baumgardner, A. H., 447
Baumrind, D., 154, 242, 368
Bavelier, D., 304
Beach, S. R., 556
Beaman, A. L., 558
Beardsley, L. M., 456
Beatles (group), 11
Beauchamp, G. K., 346
Beauvais, F., 99
Beck, A. T., 474, 501, 502, 522
Becker, D. V., 385, 386
Becker, I. M., 235
Becker, S., 515
Becklen, R., 69
Beckham, D., 47
Becklen, R., 69
Beckman, M., 156
Beecher, H. W., 306
Beeman, M. J., 60
Beilin, H., 148
Beitel, P., 308
Beitman, B. D., 493
Bell, A. P., 365
Bellis, M. A., 357
Bellows, G., 456
Belmaker, R. H., 517, 519
Belot, M., 557
Belsher, G., 473
Belyaev, D., 113
Bem, D. J., 220, 368
Bem, S. L., 131
Benbow, C. P., 322, 328, 329
Benes, F., 44
Benjet, C., 242
Bennett, W. I., 356
Ben-Shakhar, G., 380
Benson, H., 412, 413
Benson, K., 279

Benson, R., 355
Ben-Zeev, T., 333
Berenbaum, S. A., 329
Berenson, A., 514
Berghuis, P., 96
Bergin, 511
Bergin, A. E., 511
Berkel, J., 414
Berkowitz, L., 390, 550
Berman, M., 549
Berndt, T. J., 161
Bernieri, F., 384
Bernstein, A., 462
Berra, Y., 10
Berridge, K. C., 89, 381
Berry, D. S., 231
Berry, J. W., 401
Berscheid, E., 370, 557, 560
Bersoff, D. M., 158
Berti, A., 60
Bertua, C., 315
Best, D. L., 127
Bettencourt, B. A., 127
Beyerstein, B., 434
Beyerstein, D., 434
Bhatt, R. S., 238
Bhattacharya, J., 293
Bialystok, E., 307
Bickman, L., 401
Biederman, I., 341
Bierut, L. J., 98
Biggs, W., 385
bin Laden, O., 218
Binet, A., 318, 319, 320, 321, 324, 334, 336, 433
Birnbaum, G. E., 152
Birnbaum, S. G., 268
Bishop, G. D., 292, 540
Bisson, J., 508
Biswas-Diener, R., 394
Bjork, R. A., 5, 85
Bjorklund, D. F., 148
Black, J., 54
Blackmore, S., 220
Blair, G., 163
Blajda, V. M., 111
Blakemore, S. J., 197
Blakeslee, S., 40, 57, 199, 248
Blanchard, R., 365
Blanchard-Fields, F., 167
Blanchflower, D. G., 171, 401
Blank, H., 10
Blankenburg, F., 182
Blascovich, J., 399, 552
Blass, T., 535
Blatt, S. J., 510
Bliss, C., 139
Block, J., 158
Blocker, A., 198
Bloom, F. E., 38
Bloom, P., 302
Blum, K., 49
Boag, S., 426
Bocklandt, S., 366
Bodamer, M., 312
Bodenhausen, G. V., 543, 566
Bodkin, J. A., 515

Boehm, K. E., 161
Boer, D. P., 426
Boesch, C., 310
Boesch-Achermann, H., 310
Bogaert, A. F., 363, 365
Bogen, J., 57
Boggiano, M. M., 346
Bohman, M., 110
Bohr, N., 10, 131
Bolger, N., 393
Bolt, R., 529
Bolwig, T. G., 517
Bonacci, A. M., 280, 360
Bonanno, G. A., 172, 464, 465
Bond, C. F., Jr., 384
Bond, M. H., 124
Bond, R., 534
Bonnie, K. E., 310
Bono, C., 385
Bono, L., 385
Bookwala, J., 351
Boos, H. B. M., 483
Booth, D. A., 345
Bootzin, R. R., 81, 280
Boring, E. G., 215
Bornstein, B. F., 150
Bornstein, M. H., 125, 304
Bornstein, R. F., 276, 428, 556
Boron, J. B., 167, 168
Boscarino, J., 399
Bosma, H., 408
Bostwick, J. M., 474
Bosworth, R. G., 56
Bothwell, R. K., 547
Bouchard, T. J., Jr., 108, 109, 325, 326
Bouton, M. E., 466
Bowden, E. M., 60
Bowen, C., 168
Bower, B., 214
Bower, G. H., 262, 265, 274, 275
Bower, J. E., 405
Bower, J. M., 46
Bowers, K. S., 84, 85
Bowers, T. G., 506
Bowles, S., 371
Bowman, H., 311
Boyar, J., 351
Boyatzis, C. J., 252
Boynton, R. M., 191
Bradbury, T. N., 527
Braden, J. P., 331
Bradley, D. R., 205
Bradley, R. B., 153
Braffman, W., 84
Braiker, B., 141
Brainerd, C. J., 142
Brandon, S., 286
Brannon, L. A., 362
Branscombe, N. R., 307
Bransford, J. D., 262, 264
Bratslavsky, E., 560
Braun, S., 95, 138
Braunstein, G. D., 358
Bray, D. W., 445
Bray, G. A., 352
Breedlove, S. M., 366
Brehm, J. W., 541
Brehm, S., 541
Breland, K., 244
Breland, M., 244
Breslau, J., 488
Bressan, P., 215
Brewer, C. L., 6, 112
Brewer, M. B., 123

Brewer, W. F., 262
Brewin, C. R., 268, 464
Bricker, J. B., 361
Briers, B., 239
Briñol, P., 392
Brinson, S. L., 553
Brisette, I., 78
Brislin, R. W., 121
Brissette, I., 478
Broca, P., 54, 55, 62
Broch, H., 219
Brock, T. C., 362
Brody, J. E., 76, 88, 155, 354, 464
Brody, N., 93
Brody, S., 369
Bronner, E., 329
Brontë, E., 472
Brookes, K., 455
Brooks, D. J., 411
Brooks, R., 249
Brossard, M. A., 161
Brown, A. S., 275, 280, 484
Brown, E. L., 196
Brown, G. K., 506
Brown, G. W., 511
Brown, J. A., 266
Brown, J. D., 361
Brown, J. L., 326
Brown, R., 306
Brown, S. L., 172
Brown, S. W., 281
Brownell, K. D., 354
Browner, W. S., 403
Browning, C., 536
Browning, R., 562
Brownmiller, S., 360
Bruce, D., 141
Bruck, M., 284
Brumberg, J. J., 348
Bruun, S. E., 539
Bryant, A. N., 160
Bryant, J., 553
Bryant, R. A., 286
Buchan, J., 240
Buchanan, A., 152
Buchanan, T. W., 268
Buck, L. B., 203, 204
Buckley, K. E., 371
Buckner, R. L., 271
Bucy, P. C., 48
Buddha, The, 391
Buehler, R., 297
Bugelski, B. R., 263
Bugental, D. B., 384
Buka, S. L., 483, 484
Bulia, S., 460
Bulik, C. M., 349
Bullough, V., 363
Bunde, J., 403
Buquet, R., 80
Burcusa, S. L., 473
Burger, J. M., 537
Buri, J. R., 154
Burke, D. M., 167
Burkholder, R., 396
Burks, N., 560
Burlingame, G. M., 503
Burman, B., 170
Burnett, N., 264
Burns, B. C., 300
Burris, C. T., 307
Bush, G. H., 427, 566
Bush, G. W., 10, 296, 528, 546, 556, 564, 566

Bushman, B. J., 280, 360, 391, 448, 549, 553
Buss, A. H., 438
Buss, D. M., 111, 116, 359
Busseri, M. A., 363
Buster, J. E., 358
Butcher, L. M., 325
Butler, A. C., 478
Butler, R. A., 341
Butterfield, F., 461
Buunk, B. P., 560
Byck, R., 94
Byne, W., 368
Bynum, R., 198
Byrne, D., 230, 358
Byrne, J., 219
Byrne, R. W., 17, 311

C

Cade, J., 516
Caesar, J., 396
Cahill, L., 129, 269
Cahn, B. R., 413
Cale, E. M., 486
Calhoun, L. G., 465
Calkins, M. W., 2, 3, 9
Call, J., 310
Call, K. T., 361
Callaghan, T., 145
Calle, E. E., 350
Calvo-Merino, B., 308
Cameron, L., 565
Campbell, D. T., 395, 432
Campbell, P. A., 109
Campbell, R., 109
Campbell, S., 215
Campbell, S. S., 75
Campbell, W. K., 160
Camper, J., 90
Camperio-Ciani, A., 366
Campos, J. J., 207
Canli, T., 386, 467
Cannon, W. B., 344, 376, 377, 383, 399, 400, 416, 417
Cantor, N., 318
Caplan, N., 119
Caputo, D., 444
Carducci, B. J., 70, 559
Carere, C., 433
Carey, B., 270, 458, 471
Carey, E., 21
Carey, G., 467, 548
Carey, L., 21
Carli, L., 127
Carlin, G., 94, 275
Carlson, C. L., 455
Carlson, J., 333
Carlson, M., 152, 562
Carlson, S., 434
Carlson, S. M., 307
Carnahan, T., 529
Carnelley, K. B., 172
Carpenter, B., 398
Carpusor, A., 23
Carr, T. H., 55
Carrière, G., 353
Carroll, J. M., 388
Carroll, J. S., 551
Carroll, L., 459
Carron, A. V., 538
Carskadon, M., 76
Carskadon, M. A., 82
Carstensen, L. I., 167, 171

Carter, J., 459
Carter, R., 38, 459
Cartwright, R. D., 74
Caruso, D., 318
Carver, C. S., 409
Casey, B. J., 156
Cash, T. F., 349
Cash, T., 557
Caspi, A., 106, 111, 174, 476, 487
Cassel, L., 465
Cassidy, J., 150
Castillo, R. J., 456
Castonguay, L. G., 493
Catanese, K. R., 115, 550
Cato, 389
Cattell, R. B., 167
Cavalli-Sforza, L., 332
Ceci, S. J., 284, 327
Centerwall, B. S., 252
Cepeda, N. J., 261
Cerella, J., 165
Cervone, D., 69
Chabris, C. F., 69
Chambless, D. L., 508
Chamove, A. S., 251
Chang, E. C., 443
Chang, P. P., 403
Chaplin, W. F., 383
Charles, S. T., 170
Charpak, G., 219
Chartrand, T. L., 67, 532
Chase, W. G., 264
Chaucer, G., 123
Check, J. V. P., 360
Cheek, J. M., 124
Cheit, R. E., 426
Chekhov, A., 472
Chen, E., 408
Chen, X., 76
Chen, Y. R., 123
Cheney, R., 431
Cheng, F., 354
Cheng, K., 271, 441
Cheng, M., 354
Chentsova-Dutton, Y., 388
Chermack, S. T., 549
Chess, S., 111, 151, 174
Chesterfield (Lord), 45, 248
Chesterton, G. K., 126
Chiarello, C., 60
Chiles, J. A., 506
Chisholm, K., 152
Chivers, M. L., 364
Choi, C. Q., 56
Choi, I., 123
Choi, Y., 123
Chomsky, N., 302, 304, 309, 335, 337
Christakis, D. S., 455
Christakis, N. A., 100, 353
Christensen, A., 510
Christensen, D. D., 315
Christie, A., 85
Christina (Grand Duchess of Tuscany), 114
Christmas, L., 109
Christophersen, E. R., 497
Chugani, H. T., 140
Churchill, W., 480
Cialdini, R. B., 529, 547
Ciarrochi, J., 318
Cicero, 332, 557
Cin, S. D., 92
Clack, B., 565

Clancy, S. A., 73, 283
Clark, K. B., 28
Clark, L. A., 486
Clark, M. P., 28
Clark, R., 401
Clarke, P. R. F., 82
Claudius, 516
Clemens, S., 472
Cleveland, H. H., 110
Clinton, H. R., 526, 543
Clinton, W., 356
Clum, G. A., 506
Coan, J. A., 409, 410
Coe, W. C., 86
Coffey, C. E., 476
Cogan, J. C., 347
Cohen, D., 354, 469, 551
Cohen, G. L., 334
Cohen, K. M., 367
Cohen, N., 235
Cohen, S., 78, 404, 409, 410
Colapinto, J., 129
Colarelli, S. M., 114, 127
Colbert, S., 40
Colcombe, S. J., 166
Cole, K. C., 92
Collings, V. B., 212
Collins, D. W., 329
Collins, F., 106, 133
Collins, N. L., 560
Collins, R. L., 18
Collinson, S. L., 483
Collishaw, S., 473
Colombo, J., 150
Comer, R. J., 454
Comfort, A., 164
Comstock, G., 251
Confucius, 26, 111, 297
Connor-Smith, J. K., 408
Conway, M. A., 166
Cooke, L. J., 201
Cooper, H., 396
Cooper, K. J., 253, 532
Cooper, M. L., 91
Coopersmith, S., 154
Copernicus, N., 12, 317
Coppola, M., 304
Corbett, S. W., 346
Coren, S., 75, 76, 77, 78
Corey, D. P., 194
Corina, D. P., 60
Corkin, S., 270
Corp, N., 17
Correll, J., 543
Corrigan, E., 281
Costa, P. T., Jr., 168, 174, 385, 436, 437
Costello, C. G., 473
Costello, E. J., 489
Coughlin, J. F., 166
Courneya, K. S., 538
Courtney, J. G., 405
Covin, R., 503
Cowan, G., 552
Cowan, N., 266
Cowart, B. J., 201, 202
Cox, J. J., 199
Coyle, J. T., 483
Coyne, J. C., 479
Crabbe, J. C., 97
Craik, F. I. M., 261, 262
Crandall, C. S., 348, 350
Craven, R. G., 447
Crawford, M., 330

Crawley, J. N., 146
Crews, F., 428
Crews, F. T., 90
Crick, F., 36, 63
Crocker, J., 449, 547
Croft, R. J., 95
Crofton, C., 558
Cromwell, T., 529
Crook, T. H., 166
Cross, S., 446
Crowell, J. A., 150
Crowley, M., 562
Csikszentmihalyi, M., 128, 160, 251
Culbert, K. M., 348
Cullen, L. T., 555
Cullum, J., 534
Cunningham, M. R., 558
Cunningham, W. A., 543
Curtis, G. C., 463
Curtis, R. C., 559
Czeisler, C. A., 71

D

D'Aquili, E., 413
da Vinci, L., 287, 291, 489
Dabbs, J. M., Jr., 358, 549, 562
Dahmer, J., 461
Dal Martello, M. F., 215
Daley, T. C., 323
Dallenbach, K. M., 279
Damasio, A. R., 318, 377
Damasio, H., 54
Damon, W., 160
Daniels, D., 120
Danner, D. D., 409
Danso, H., 333
Dante, 168
Dapretto, M., 147
Darby, J., 541
Darley, J. M., 561, 562
Darrach, B., 487
Darwin, C., 113, 114, 132, 133, 134, 199, 232, 233, 236, 315, 340, 387, 388, 428, 463
Daskalakis, Z. J., 517
Daum, I., 272
Davey, G. C. L., 466
David (King), 191
Davidoff, J., 306
Davidson, J. R. T., 489
Davidson, R. J., 379, 413, 476, 548
Davies, D. R., 168
Davies, M. F., 435
Davies, P., 134
Davis, B. E., 141
Davis, B. L., 303
Davis, B., 276
Davis, J. O., 485
Davis, M., 514
Davis, S., 358
Davis-Beaty, K., 362
Dawes, R. M., 564
Dawkins, R., 113, 133
de Beauvoir, S., 28
de Boysson-Bardies, B., 303
de Courten-Myers, G. M., 40, 50
de Cuevas, J., 304
de Fermat, P., 316
de Geus, E. J. C., 325
De Graaf, N. D., 110
De Koninck, J., 80
de Montaigne, M., 451
de Montaigne, M. E., 158

De Vogli, R., 410
de Waal, F., 17
de Waal, F. B. M., 130, 135
de Waard, F., 414
Deacon, B. J., 498
Dean, G. A., 434
DeAngelis, T., 507
Deary, I. J., 328, 330, 437, 547
DeBruine, L. M., 556
Decety, J., 308
Deci, E. L., 370, 449
Deeley, Q., 487
Deffenbacher, K., 196
DeFries, J. C., 326, 366
Dehne, K. L., 362
DeLamater, J. D., 164
Delaney, H. D., 511
Delaney, P. F., 267
Delargy, M., 393
Delgado, J. M. R., 51
DeLoache, J. S., 142, 144, 466
DelVecchio, W. F., 437
Dement, W. C., 71, 72, 73, 75, 76, 78, 79, 81, 103
Demir, E., 366
Denes-Raj, V., 300
DeNeve, K. M., 396
Dennett, D. C., 232
Denollet, J., 402
Denton, K., 90, 158
Denton, R., 534
DePaulo, B. M., 384
Depp, J., 93
Der, G., 21
Dermer, M., 396, 559
Deroche-Garmonet, V., 89
DeRubeis, R. J., 506
Descartes, R., 313
DeSteno, D., 275, 391
Dettman, J. R., 114
Deutsch, J. A., 49
DeValois, K. K., 192
DeValois, R. L., 192
Devilly, G. J., 465, 508
Devine, P. G., 556
Devlin, B., 325
Dew, M. A., 76
DeWall, C. N., 441
Dewitte, S., 284
Diaconis, P., 21
Diamond, J., 114
Diamond, L. M., 364
Diamond, M., 368
DiBiasi, P., 109
DiCaprio, L., 528
Dick, D. M., 325, 487
Dickens, C., 16
Dickens, W. T., 331
Dickerson, S. S., 408
Dickinson, E., 454, 480
Dickinson, H. O., 393
Dickson, B. J., 366
Diener, E., 111, 370, 392, 393, 394, 396, 477, 557
Dietz, W. H., Jr., 356
DiFranza, J. R., 92
DiGiulio, G., 506
Dijksterhuis, A., 299, 384
DiLalla, D. L., 109. 475
Dill, K. E., 552
Dillard, A., 282
Dimberg, U., 249, 381, 389
Dinges, N. G., 306
Dion, K. K., 124, 130

Dion, K. L., 124, 130
Dix, D., 343, 373, 493
Dixon, J., 565
Dobbs, D., 518
Dobel, C., 306
Dobkins, K. R., 56
Doherty, E. W., 93
Doherty, W. J., 93
Dohrenwend, B. P., 401, 464, 489
Dolan, C. M., 350
Dolan, R. J., 55
Dolezal, H., 214, 215
Domhoff, G. W., 80, 82, 83
Domjan, M., 230
Donahoe, J. W., 246, 247
Donnellan, M. B., 397, 439
Donnerstein, E., 251, 252, 253
Doolittle, B., 180
Dorner, G., 367
Dostoevsky, E., 472
Doty, R. L., 165
Doucette, M., 76
Dovidio, J. F., 566
Dowd, M., 558
Downing, P. E., 189
Downs, A. C., 155
Doyle, A. C., 216, 267
Doyle, R., 115
Draguns, J. G., 453, 478
Drake, R. A., 379
Drake, T., 225
Drews, F. A., 68
Druckman, D., 85
Duclos, S. E., 388
Duenwald, M., 514
Duffy, M., 530
Duggan, J. P., 345
Dugger, C. W., 299
Dumont, K. A., 153
Dunn, A. L., 520
Dunn, E. W., 562
Dunning, D., 444, 445, 448
Dunson, D. B., 164
Durgin, F. H., 197
Durm, M. W., 218
Dush, C. M. K., 169
Dutton, D. G., 559
Dweck, C. S., 327

E

Eagly, A. H., 117, 127, 129, 132, 544, 557, 562
Eastman, C. L., 71, 509
Eastwick, P. W., 557
Ebbesen, E. B., 277, 390
Ebbinghaus, H., 260, 261, 263, 277, 278, 281, 286
Eberhardt, J. L., 543
Eccles, J. S., 330
Eckensberger, L. H., 158
Eckert, E. D., 467
Edelman, M. W., 533
Edelman, R., 390
Edelman, S., 405
Edison, T. A., 71, 75, 292, 317
Edwards, C. P., 125
Edwards, J., 170
Edwards, K. J., 497
Efron, Z., 112
Ehrmann, M., 449
Eibl-Eibesfeldt, I., 387
Eich, E., 81
Eichmann, A., 537

Einstein, A., 54, 133, 308, 315
Eisenberg, N., 386
Eiser, J. R., 92
Ekman, P., 384, 387
El Greco, 472
Elaad, E., 380
Elbert, T., 118, 467
Elfenbein, H. A., 387
Eliot, C., 30
Eliot, T. S., 291, 315
Elizabeth (Queen), 218
Elkind, D., 157
Ellenbogen, J. M., 77, 78
Elliot, A. J., 234
Ellis, A., 235, 503, 511
Ellis, B. J., 162, 362
Ellis, L., 367
Ellis, S., 143
Emerson, R. W., 453
Emery, G., 218
Emmelkamp, P. M. G., 498
Emmons, R. A., 397
Emmons, S., 453, 481
Empson, J. A. C., 82
Emslie, C., 349
Endler, N. S., 477, 517
Engemann, K. M., 557
Engen, T., 204
Engle, R. W., 259
Epicharmus, 191
Epley, N., 28, 145, 448
Epstein, J., 483
Epstein, L. H., 346
Epstein, S., 438
Erdberg, P., 425
Erdelyi, M. H., 426, 427
Erel, O., 170
Erickson, K. I., 412
Erickson, M. F., 169
Ericsson, K. A., 316, 327
Erikson, E. H., 152, 159, 160, 163,
    169, 173, 174, 176
Erikson, J., 152
Ernsberger, P., 355
Ertmer, D. J., 303
Escobar-Chaves, S. L., 361
Esser, J. K., 540
Esses, V., 333
Esterson, A., 426
Estrin, J., 393
Etkin, A., 467
Ettinger, M. G., 79
Euston, D. R., 271
Evans, F. J., 85
Evans, G. W., 402
Evans, R. I., 92
Ewing, R., 353
Exline, J. J., 441
Exner, J. E., 425
Eysenck, H. J., 412, 506
Eysenck, M. W., 439

F

Faber, N., 317
Fagan, J. F., III, 332
Fairburn, C. G., 348
Fantz, R. L., 139
Farah, M. J., 56
Faraone, S. V., 475
Farina, A., 456, 459
Farley, F., 156
Farley, M., 464
Farley, T., 354

Farooqi, I. S., 346
Farrington, D. P., 486
Fartacek, R., 363
Feder, H. H., 358
Feeney, D. M., 27
Feeney, J. A., 152
Feinberg, I., 279
Feinberg, T. E., 60
Feingold, A., 348, 557, 558
Fellowes, D., 406
Feng, J., 329
Fenton, W. S., 482
Ferguson, C. J., 252
Ferguson, E. D., 369, 424
Ferguson, T. J., 253
Fergusson, D. M., 18, 473
Fernandez, E., 201
Fernández-Dols, J. M., 387
Ferrell, W., 112
Ferris, C. F., 153
Festinger, L., 530
Feynman, R., 317
Fiedler, K., 275
Field, A. P., 465
Field, T., 118
Fincham, F. D., 527
Fingerhut, A. W., 169, 363
Fink, G. R., 271
Finkel, E. J., 557
Fischer, P., 553
Fischhoff, B., 296, 297
Fischtein, D. S., 115
Fisher, H. E., 169, 357
Fisher, H. T., 498
Fisher, K., 130
Fiske, S. T., 530
Fitzgerald, J. A., 365
Fitzgerald, P. B., 517
Flachsbart, C., 408
Flaxman, S. M., 347
Fleming, I., 409
Fleming, J. H., 387
Fletcher, G. J. O., 527
Fletcher, P. C., 427
Flier, J. S., 353
Flood, M., 551
Flora, S. R., 244
Flouri, E., 152
Flynn, J. R., 323, 328, 331
Foa, E. B., 465, 498
Fodor, J. D., 217
Foerster, O., 51
Follette, V. M., 153
Ford, E. S., 412
Ford, H., 426
Foree, D. D., 244
Forehand, R., 246
Forer, B. R., 435
Forgas, J. P., 275
Forhan, S. E., 362
Forman, D. R., 251
Foss, D. J., 427
Foster, R. G., 71
Foulkes, D., 83
Fouts, R. S., 312
Fowler, J. H., 100, 353
Fowler, M. J., 280
Fowler, R. C., 474
Fowles, D. C., 482
Fox, B. H., 405
Fox, E., 384
Fox, J. L., 57
Fox, R., 244
Fozard, J. L., 164

Fracassini, C., 204
Fraley, R. C., 152
Francesconi, M., 557
Frank, J. D., 510, 511
Frank, R., 123
Frank, S. J., 162
Frankel, A., 435
Frankenburg, W., 141
Franklin, B., 78
Franz, E. A., 59
Fraser, S. C., 529
Frasure-Smith, N., 403
Frattaroli, J., 410
Frayling, T. M., 353
Frederick, D. A., 349
Fredrickson, B. L., 263, 349, 392
Freedman, D. J., 310
Freedman, J. L., 252, 529
Freeman, W. J., 193
Frensch, P. A., 427
Freud, S., 2, 3, 4, 9, 81, 82, 83, 101,
    119, 169, 173, 281, 286, 315,
    419, 420, 421, 422, 423, 424,
    426, 427, 428, 429, 431, 432,
    439, 450, 451, 460, 462, 465,
    468, 474, 490, 494, 495, 501, 522
Frey, K., 389
Freyd, J. J., 153, 285
Friedman, K., 361
Friedman, M., 402, 412, 413
Friedrich, O., 454
Friend, T., 313
Friesen, W. V., 387
Frijda, N. H., 395
Frith, C., 146
Frith, U., 146
Fritsch, G., 51
Frohlich, P. F., 358
Fromkin, V., 303
Fry, A. F., 165
Fryar, C., 359
Fuhriman, A., 503
Fuller, M. J., 155
Fuller, T., 389
Funder, D. C., 158, 436, 438, 479
Furnham, A., 328, 347, 527, 544
Furr, R. M., 479
Furstenberg, F., 240

G

Gable, S. L., 170
Gabriel, M., 48
Gabrieli, J. D. E., 271
Gaertner, L., 550
Gaertner, S. L., 566
Gaeth, G. J., 301
Gage, F. H., 57
Gage, P., 53, 54
Gaillot, M. T., 441
Galambos, N. L., 161, 162
Galanter, E., 181
Galati, D., 387
Galea, S., 464, 465
Galinsky, A. D., 145
Galileo, 114, 133, 291
Gallina, A., 20
Gallina, M., 20
Gallup, G. H., 565
Gallup, G., Jr., 251
Galton, F., 137, 177
Gándara, P., 307
Gandhi, I., 565
Gandhi, M., 27, 250, 315, 541

Gandhi, S., 25
Gangestad, S. W., 116
Garb, H. N., 425
Garber, K., 146
Garcia, J., 232, 233, 236, 247
Gardner, B. I., 311
Gardner, H., 120, 314, 315, 316,
    318, 324, 335
Gardner, J., 394
Gardner, M., 285
Gardner, R. A., 311
Gardner, R. M., 350
Garfield, C., 308
Garner, W. R., 333
Garnets, L. D., 364
Garnets, L., 363
Garon, N., 140
Garrett, B. L., 283
Garry, M., 282, 426
Gatchel, R. J., 198
Gates, W., 132, 299, 316, 556
Gauguelin, M., 435
Gawande, A., 200
Gawin, F. H., 94
Gazzaniga, M. S., 57, 58, 59, 60, 89
Gearhart, J. P., 129
Geary, D. C., 116, 329
Geen, R. G., 252, 390
Geen, R. G., 390
Gehring, W. J., 467
Geisler, C., 481
Geldard, F. A., 191
Geller, D., 537
Gelles, R. J., 242
Gelman, D., 387
Gelman, S. A., 144
Genain, H., 485
Genain, I., 485
Genain, M., 485
Genain, N., 485
Genesee, F., 307
Genevro, J. L., 172
Genovese, K., 561, 562
Gent, J. F., 201
Gentile, D. A., 251, 252, 552
George, L. K., 415
George, M. S., 517, 518, 519
Geraerts, E., 286
Gerard, R., 516
Gerbner, G., 97, 299, 554
Gernsbacher, M. A., 146
Gerrard, M., 361
Gershoff, E. T., 242
Geschwind, N., 54
Gest, S. D., 161
Gfeller, J. D., 86
Gibbons, F. X., 396
Gibbons, R. D., 516
Gibbs, J. C., 158
Gibbs, W. W., 51, 350
Gibran, K., 154
Gibson, E. J., 207
Gibson, H. B., 85
Gigerenzer, G., 298
Gilbert, D. T., 11, 170, 233, 282, 291,
    381, 393, 471
Gilbertson, M. W., 465
Giles, D. E., 73
Gill, A. J., 438
Gill, C., 445
Gillaspy, J. A., Jr., 244
Gillham, J. E., 521
Gilligan, C., 128
Gilovich, T. D., 19, 20, 170, 446

Giltay, E. J., 409
Gingerich, O., 133
Glaberson, W., 445
Gladue, B. A., 367
Gladwell, M., 558
Glaser, R., 405
Glasman, L. R., 527
Glass, R. I., 299
Glass, R. M., 517
Gleaves, D. H., 470
Glenn, N. D., 170
Glick, P., 435, 544
Goel, V., 55
Goethals, G. R., 526
Goff, D. C., 469
Goff, L. M., 282
Golan, O., 147
Gold, M., 161
Goldapple, K., 515
Goldberg, L. R., 174
Golden, R. N., 509
Goldenberg, J. L., 154
Goldfried, M. R., 474, 493, 510
Golding, J. M., 464, 553
Goldstein, A. P., 551
Goldstein, D., 301
Goldstein, I., 23, 42
Goleman, D., 318
Gombrich, E. H., 217
Gómez, R. L., 78
Gonsalves, B., 282
Goodale, M. A., 67
Goodall, J., 17, 119, 546
Goodchilds, J., 164
Goode, E., 199
Goodhart, D. E., 443
Goodman, G. S., 284, 286
Goodstein, L., 445
Goodwin, F. K., 26
Goodwin, S. A., 544
Gopnik, A., 307
Goranson, R. E., 11
Gordon, A. H., 386
Gordon, P., 306
Gore, A., 528
Gore-Felton, C., 286
Gortmaker, S. L., 351, 356
Gosling, S. D., 433, 438
Gossage, J. P., 138
Gotlib, I. H., 478, 479
Gottesman, I. I., 484, 485, 486
Gottfredson, L. S., 315
Gottfried, J. A., 228
Gould, E., 57
Gould, S. J., 117, 133, 319
Grabe, S., 349
Grady, C. L., 277
Graf, P., 167
Graf, S., 105
Graham, J. E., 409
Graham, M., 315
Granott, N., 148
Gray, P. B., 359
Gray-Little, B., 560
Green, B. L., 148
Green, D. M., 196
Green, J. D., 426
Green, J. T., 272
Greenberg, J., 447
Greene, R. L., 261
Greenfeld, L. A., 549
Greenfield, P., 161
Greenwald, A. G., 182, 427, 543

Greenwood, M. R. C., 350
Greers, A. E., 304
Gregg, L., 498
Gregory of Nyssa, 472
Gregory of Sinai, 412
Gregory, R. L., 213, 217
Greif, E. B., 155
Greist, J. H., 462
Greitemeyer, T., 553
Grèzes, J., 308
Griffiths, M., 89
Grill-Spector, K., 292
Grilo, C. M., 353
Grinker, R. R., 146
Grobstein, C., 138
Groothuis, T. G. G., 433
Gross, A. E., 558
Gross, M., 519
Grossarth-Maticek, R., 412
Grossberg, S., 216
Grossman, M., 385
Gruchy, C. D. G., 385
Gruder, C. L., 396
Grunebaum, M. F., 516
Grusec, J. E., 251
Guerin, B., 302, 538
Guiso, L., 330
Gunderson, E., 251
Gustafson, D., 350
Gustavson, A. R., 233
Gustavson, C. R., 233
Gutierres, S. E., 360
Gutsell, J. N., 441

H

H. M., 269, 270
H., S., 427
Ha, Y. W., 293
Haber, R. N., 258
Haddock, G., 351, 544
Hagen, E. P., 320
Haidt, J., 157
Hakes, D. T., 427
Hakuta, K., 305
Halberstadt, J. B., 217, 349, 546
Haldane, J. B. S., 184
Haldeman, D. C., 364
Hale, S., 165
Hall, C. S., 80, 428
Hall, G. S., 154
Hall, J. A., 127, 328, 385, 558
Hall, J. A. Y., 367
Hall, J. G., 107
Hall, S. S., 138
Hall, W., 96
Hall, W. B., 317
Halpern, B. P., 202
Halpern, C. T., 362
Halpern, D. F., 328, 329, 330
Hamamura, T., 448
Hamann, S., 359
Hamilton, D. L., 19
Hammack, P. L., 363, 365
Hammen, C. L., 479
Hammersmith, S. K., 365
Hammerstein, O., 388, 558
Hampson, R., 354
Hampson, S. E., 174
Hancock, K. J., 547
Handel, G. F., 472
Hankin, B. L., 477
Hanks, T., 370
Hansen, C. H., 384

Hansen, D. J., 152
Hansen, R. D., 384
Haraguchi, A., 267
Harbaugh, W. T., 562
Harber, K. D., 543
Hardin, C., 306
Hare, R. D., 487
Harjo, J., 307
Harker, L. A., 392
Harkins, S. G., 539
Harlow, H. F., 150
Harlow, L. L., 98
Harlow, M. K., 149, 150
Harlow. H. F., 149
Harmon-Jones, E., 379
Harper, C., 551
Harris, A., 460
Harris, B., 235
Harris, J. A., 549
Harris, J. R., 109, 120, 151
Harris, R. J., 553
Harrison, Y., 76
Harriston, K. A., 445
Harrow, M., 481
Harrower, M., 427
Härter, M., 453, 488
Hartmann, E., 79
Harton, H. C., 534
Hartsuiker, R. J., 302
Harvey, P. D., 481
Haselton, M. G., 358
Hasher, L., 71
Hasin, D. S., 471
Haslam, N., 368
Haslam, S. A., 529
Hassan, B., 368
Hatfield, E., 556, 557, 559, 560
Hathaway, S. R., 433, 434
Hauck, C., 85
Hawking, S., 314, 337
Haxby, J. V., 189
Haynes, J. D., 182
Hebb, D. O., 235, 375
Hebl, M. R., 351
Hedges, L. V., 328, 329, 330
Hedström, P., 475
Heider, F., 525
Heiman, J. R., 359
Heine, S. J., 448
Heins, M., 552
Hejmadi, A., 384
Helgeson, V. S., 465
Heller, W., 60
Helmreich, W. B., 153, 426
Helms, J. E., 332
Helmuth, L., 519
Helson, H., 395
Hembree, R., 378
Hemingway, E., 472
Henderson, J. M., 183
Henkel, L. A., 283
Henley, N. M., 307
Hennessey, B. A., 317
Henning, K., 359, 360
Henninger, P., 470
Henry, P. E., 349
Herbert, J. D., 508
Herdt, G., 155
Herek, G. M., 363
Hering, E., 191, 192, 221
Herman, C. P., 348, 356
Herman-Giddens, M. E., 155
Hernandez, A. E., 304
Herrmann, D., 287

Herrmann, E., 248
Herrnstein, R. J., 238, 331
Hershenson, M., 210
Hertenstein, M. J., 150, 196
Herz, R. S., 203, 204
Herzog, H., A., 27
Hess, E. H., 214
Hettema, J. M., 467
Hewlett, B. S., 151
Hickok, G., 60
Hilgard, E. R., 86, 87
Hill, C. E., 496
Hill, H., 386
Hinckley, J., 461
Hines, M., 129
Hingson, R. W., 99
Hintzman, D. L., 264
Hinz, L. D., 348
Hippocrates, 399
Hirsch, J., 351
Hitzig, E., 51
Hobson, J. A., 82
Hodgkinson, V. A., 563
Hoebel, B. G., 345
Hoeft, F., 89
Hoffman, C., 545
Hoffman, D. D., 190
Hofmann, A., 95
Hogan, R., 437
Hogarth, W., 493
Hoge, C. W., 464
Hogg, M. A., 546
Hohmann, G. W., 376
Hokanson, J. E., 390
Holahan, C. K., 322
Holden, C., 76, 485
Holland, C., 332
Holliday, R. E., 284
Hollis, K. L., 230
Hollon, S. D., 506, 515
Holm-Denoma, J., 354
Holmes, D. S., 411
Holmes, O. W., 9, 298
Holson, L. M., 161
Holstege, G., 357
Holzman, P. S., 183
Homer, 472
Homer, B. D., 92
Honorton, C., 220
Honzik, C. H., 243
Hooper, J., 49
Hooykaas, R., 12
Horace, 389
Horn, J. L., 167
Horne, J. A., 76
Horner, V., 310
Horney, K., 424, 429, 450, 506
Horowitz, T. S., 76
Horwood, L. J., 18
House, J. S., 410
Houts, A. C., 497
Hovatta, I., 467
Howard, D., 33
Howe, M. L., 284
Howell, C. J., 394
Howell, R. T., 394
Hoy, W., 307
Hoyer, G., 474
Hu, F. B., 353
Hu, X. Z., 467
Hubel, D. H., 183, 188, 190
Hublin, C., 79
Huckabee, M., 356
Hucker, S. J., 359

Hudson, J. I., 348
Huey, E. D., 53
Huff, C., 28
Hugdahl, K., 466
Hugenberg, K., 543
Hughes, H. C., 181
Hugick, L., 128
Huizink, A. C., 96
Hulbert, A., 322
Hull, H. R., 76
Hull, J. G., 90
Hull, J. M., 274, 557
Hull, P., 306
Hulme, C., 266
Hume, D., 225, 541
Hummer, R. A., 414
Humphrey, S. E., 442
Hunsberger, J. G., 412
Hunsley, J., 506
Hunt, C., 462
Hunt, E., 333
Hunt, J. M., 326, 327
Hunt, M., 2, 9, 235, 360
Hunter, J., 160
Hunter, J. E., 445
Hunter, S., 168
Hurst, M., 75
Hurst, N., 545
Hussein, S., 530, 547, 564, 567
Huston, A. C., 251
Huxley, T. H., 459
Hyde, J., 126, 127
Hyde, J. S., 281, 329, 472
Hyman, M., 124
Hyman, R., 434, 435
Hynie, M., 361

I

Iacoboni, M., 248, 249
Iacono, W. G., 473
Ickes, W., 439
Idson, L. C., 526
Ikonomidou, C., 138
Ilardi, S. S., 411, 476, 520
Ingham, A. G., 538
Inglehart, R., 170, 171, 371, 394, 442
Ingram, N., 536
Inzlicht, M., 333, 441
Ironson, G., 415
Irvine, A. A., 527
Irwin, M. R., 76, 78
Ishai, A., 366
Ishida, A., 509
Iso, H., 57
Ito, T. A., 549
Iuzzini, J., 550
Iversen, L. L., 96
Iyengar, S. S., 442
Izard, C. E., 387, 389, 390

J

Jablensky, A., 483
Jackson, D. N., 328
Jackson, J. M., 538
Jackson, J. S., 544
Jackson, S. W., 510
Jacobi, C., 348
Jacobs, B. L., 95, 412, 476, 515
Jacobson, N. S., 510
Jacques, C., 179
Jacques-Tiura, A. J., 527
James, K., 274

James, W., 2, 3, 9, 30, 87, 196, 274, 276, 287, 376, 377, 388, 391, 416, 417, 446, 453, 531
Jamison, K. R., 472, 516
Janda, L. H., 557
Jang, K. L., 487
Janis, I. L., 294, 540, 541
Javitt, D. C., 483
Jefferson, T., 430
Jeffery, R. W., 356
Jenkins, J. G., 279
Jenkins, J. M., 145
Jennings, J. R., 402
Jensen, A. R., 331
Jensen, J. P., 511
Jessberger, S., 57
Job, D. E., 483
John Paul II (Pope), 133, 544
John, O. P., 436
Johnson, B. T., 460
Johnson, D. L., 433
Johnson, D. W., 566
Johnson, E. ("Magic"), 444
Johnson, E. J., 301
Johnson, J. A., 529
Johnson, J. G., 348
Johnson, J. S., 305
Johnson, L. B., 296
Johnson, L. C., 299
Johnson, M. E., 85
Johnson, M. H., 139, 150
Johnson, M. K., 262, 264
Johnson, R. T., 566
Johnson, S. K., 468
Johnson, V. E., 357, 358, 369, 372
Johnson, W., 174
Johnston, A., 386
Johnston, L. D., 94, 97, 98, 99
Johnston, R. E., 387
Johnston, W. A., 68
Joiner, T., 475
Jolly, A., 309
Jones, A. C., 433
Jones, J. M., 93, 464
Jones, J. T., 555
Jones, L., 435
Jones, M. C., 498
Jones, S. S., 249, 387
Jones, W. H., 26
Jonides, J., 266
Joseph, J., 109
Josephs, R. A., 90
Joubert, J., 249, 534
Judd, L., 473
Juffer, F., 110
Jung, C., 154, 424, 450
Jung-Beeman, M., 293
Just, M. A., 60
Juvenal, 164

K

Kagan, J., 111, 149, 151, 152, 174, 433
Kahlor, L., 553
Kahneman, D., 20, 200, 263, 294, 295, 392, 393, 395, 448
Kail, R., 165
Kaltman, S., 172
Kamarck, T., 402
Kamil, A. C., 271
Kaminski, J., 311
Kanaya, T., 323
Kandel, D. B., 100

Kandel, E. R., 39, 267, 268
Kant, I., 213
Kanwisher, N., 292
Kaplan, A., 348
Kaplan, H. I., 514
Kaplan, K. J., 481
Kaplan, R. M., 410
Kaprio, J., 401
Kaptchuk, T. J., 200
Karacan, I., 74
Karau, S. J., 538
Kark, J. D., 414
Karni, A., 82, 119
Karno, M., 463, 464
Karpicke, J. D., 261
Karraker, K. H., 217
Karremans, J. C., 182
Karzai, H., 262
Kasen, S., 128
Kashima, Y., 124
Kasimatis, M., 389
Kasindorf, M., 371
Kasser, T., 395
Kassirer, J. P., 406
Kaufman, A. S., 167
Kaufman, J., 153
Kaufman, J. C., 313, 482
Kaufman, J. H., 210
Kaufman, L., 210
Kayser, C., 202
Kazdin, A. E., 242
Keats, J., 133
Keenan, J. P., 60
Keesey, R. E., 346
Keillor, G., 448
Keith, S. W., 353
Kekulé, A., 77
Keller, H., 140
Keller, J., 79
Keller, M. B., 515
Kellerman, J., 383
Kellermann, A. L., 548
Kelley, J., 110
Kelling, S. T., 202
Kellner, C. H., 517
Kelly, A. E., 502
Kelly, D. J., 547
Kelly, I. W., 434, 488
Kelly, T. A., 511
Keltner, D., 392
Kemeny, M. E., 408
Kempe, C. C., 153
Kempe, R. S., 153
Kempermann, G., 166
Kendall-Tackett, K. A., 153, 285
Kendler, K. S., 98, 439, 467, 473, 475
Kennedy, J. F., 519, 540, 541, 567
Kennedy, R., 519
Kennedy, S., 42
Kenrick, D. T., 116, 117, 360, 438
Kensinger, E. A., 268
Keough, K. A., 421
Kern, P., 109
Kernahan, C., 127
Kernis, M. H., 449
Kerr, N. L., 539
Kerry, J., 556
Kessler, M., 521
Kessler, R. C., 405, 458, 464, 472, 477, 488, 507
Ketcham, K., 80, 267
Keyes, E., 161
Keynes, M., 472

Keys, A., 343, 344, 346
Khaliq, A. (Abdur-Rahman), 260
Kidman, A. D., 405
Kiecolt-Glaser, J. K., 404, 405, 410
Kierkegaard, S., 10
Kight, T. D., 559
Kihlstrom, J. F., 87, 281, 282, 318, 426, 427, 428, 470
Kilburn, J., 252
Killeen, P. R., 87
Kilmann, P. R., 361
Kim, B. S., 511
Kim, H., 124
Kimble, G. A., 232
Kimbro, W., 541
Kimmel, A. J., 28
Kimmel, D., 363
Kimura, D., 329, 367
King, L. A., 392
King, M., 363
King, M. L., Jr., 250
King, R. "Suki", 316
King, R. N., 434
Kinkel, K., 461
Kinnier, R. T., 170
Kipling, R., 546
Kirby, D., 362
Kirkpatrick, B., 482
Kirkpatrick, L., 150
Kirmayer, L. J., 468
Kirsch, I., 22, 84, 85, 516
Kisley, M. A., 171
Kistler, D. J., 384
Kitayama, S., 124, 306, 390, 526
Kitt, A. S., 395
Kitts, R. L., 363
Kivimaki, M., 408
Klayman, J., 293
Kleck, R. E., 410
Klein, D. N., 510
Klein, E., 518
Kleinfeld, J., 330
Kleinke, C. L., 383
Kleinmuntz, B., 380
Kleitman, N., 72
Klemm, W. R., 45
Klentz, B., 558
Kline, D., 164
Kline, G. H., 169
Klineberg, O., 386, 566
Klinke, R., 214
Kluft, R. P., 469
Klump, K. L., 348
Klüver, H., 48
Knapp, S., 286
Knickmeyer, E., 348
Knight, W., 202
Knoblich, G., 293
Knutson, K. L., 76
Ko, C. K., 89
Koehler, D. J., 434
Koelling, R. A., 232, 233, 236
Koenig, H. G., 415
Koenig, L. B., 110
Koenig, O., 40
Koenigs, M., 54
Kohlberg, L., 157, 158, 163, 173, 174, 176
Kohler, I., 215
Köhler, W., 310
Kohn, P. M., 401
Kokkalis, J., 95
Kolarz, D. M., 168
Kolassa, I. T., 467

Kolata, G., 356, 474
Kolb, B., 56, 118, 317
Koletsky, R. J., 355
Kolker, K., 552
Kolodziej, M. E., 460
Koltko-Rivera, M. E., 342
Koob, G. F., 483
Kopta, S. M., 506
Kosslyn, S. M., 40, 86, 220, 464
Kotchick, B. A., 361
Koten, J. W., Jr., 325
Kotkin, M., 505
Koulack, D., 280
Kovas, Y., 325
Kozak, M. J., 498
Kraft, R. N., 286
Kramer, A. F., 166, 412
Kranz, F., 366
Kraus, N., 301
Kraut, R. E., 387
Krebs, D. L., 90, 158
Krech, D., 118
Kring, A. M., 386
Kristof, N. D., 561
Kroll, R., 358
Kronick, R. G., 410
Kroonenberg, P. M., 151
Krosnick, J. A., 182
Krueger, A., 550
Krueger, J., 385
Kruger, J., 145, 385, 444
Krull, D. S., 11
Krupa, D. J., 272
Krützen, M., 311
Ksir, C., 94
Kubey, R., 251
Kübler, A., 393
Kubzansky, L. D., 403
Kuester, L. W., 171
Kuhl, P. K., 303
Kuhn, B. R., 242
Kuhn, C. M., 98
Kuhn, D., 156
Kujala, U. M., 412
Kulkin, H. S., 364
Kung, L. C., 308
Kunkel, D., 361, 553
Kuntsche, E., 99
Kupper, N., 402
Kupper, S., 412
Kurdek, L. A., 363
Kurtz, P., 12, 435
Kuse, A. R., 329
Kushner, M. G., 514
Kutas, M., 70

L

L'Engle, M., 10, 334, 472
Labouvie-Vief, G., 167
Lacayo, R., 16
Lacey, H. P., 170
Lachman, M. E., 168
Ladd, E. C., 100
Ladd, G. T., 65
LaFleur, D. L., 467
Laird, J. D., 383, 388
Lakin, J. L., 532
Lalumière, M. L., 367
Lam, R. W., 509
Lambert, K. G., 411
Lambert, W. E., 307
Lambird, K. H., 449
Lampinen, J. M., 275

Landau, M. J., 546
Landauer, T. K., 287, 399
Landry, M. J., 95
Lange, C., 376, 377, 416, 417
Langer, E. J., 442
Langlois, J. H., 557, 558
Lángström, N., 366
Lanzetta, J. T., 389
Larkin, K., 366
Larsen, J., 385
Larsen, R. J., 111, 383, 389
Larson, D. B., 415
Larson, G., 317
Larson, J., 172
Larsson, H., 487
Larzelere, R. E., 242
Lashley, K. S., 267
Lassiter, G. D., 527
Latané, B., 538, 542, 561, 562
Latner, J. D., 351
Laudenslager, M. L., 408
Laumann, E. O., 115, 363
Laws, K. R., 95
Lazaruk, W., 307
Lazarus, R. J., 383
Lazarus, R. S., 382, 383, 398, 401, 416
Le Grand, R., 214
Lea, S. E. G., 27
Leach, P., 242
Leaper, C., 127
Leary, M. R., 369, 370, 371, 447
Leary, W. E., 164
LeBoeuf, R. A., 298
LeDoux, J. E., 47, 119, 272, 381, 382, 383, 416
Lefcourt, H. M., 441
Legrand, L. N., 99
Lehman, A. F., 513
Lehman, D. R., 172
Leigh, B. C., 90
Leitenberg, H., 359, 360
Lemonick, M. D., 345
Lennon, R., 386
Lennox, B. R., 53
Lenzenweger, M. F., 513
Lepper, M. R., 442
Lerner, M. J., 545
Leserman, J., 405
Lesperance, F., 403
Lester, W., 544
Leucht, S., 514
LeVay, S., 366
Levenson, R. W., 379
Lever, J., 349
Levin, I. P., 301
Levin, R., 81
Levine, J. A., 352
Levine, R., 560
Levine, R. V., 17, 122
Levy, S. R., 368
Lewandowski, G. W., Jr., 558
Lewicki, P., 427
Lewinsohn, P. M., 472
Lewis, B., 108
Lewis, C. S., 159, 277, 379, 428
Lewis, D. O., 153, 470, 548
Lewis, J., 108, 383
Lewis, J. A., 108
Lewis, L., 108
Lewontin, R., 114, 331, 332
Li, J. C., 547
Li, J., 172
Li, P., 304

Licata, A., 94
Licoppe, C., 128
Lieberman, J. A., 514
Lieberman, M. D., 410
Lilienfeld, S. O., 146, 425, 470, 486, 487, 507, 508
Lincoln, A., 315, 430, 489
Lindbergh, C., 219
Linde, K., 406
Linder, D., 564
Lindoerfer, J. S., 540
Lindsay, D. S., 284
Lindskold, S., 567
Lindzey, G., 428
Linville, P. W., 300
Linz, D., 253, 552
Lippa, R. A., 115, 128, 363, 364, 365, 368, 557
Lippman, J., 251
Lipps, H. M., 544
Lipsitt, L. P., 141
Livesley, W. J., 487
Livingstone, M., 190
Lobel, A., 559
LoBue, V., 466
Locke, J., 213, 214, 225
Loehlin, J. C., 107, 110, 436
Loewenstein, G., 240
Loftus, E. F., 80, 84, 267, 282, 285, 426
Loftus, G. R., 267
Logan, T. K., 98
Loges, W. E., 23
Logue, A. W., 240
LoLordo, V. M., 244
London, P., 251, 403
Looy, H., 117
Lopes, P. N., 318
Lopez, A. D., 453
López-Ibor, J. J., 462
Lord, C. G., 297
Lorenz, K., 150
Louie, K., 82
Lourenco, O., 148
Lovaas, O. I., 500
Loveland, D. H., 238
Lowry, P. E., 445
Lu, Z. L., 145, 266
Lubart, T. I., 317
Lubinski, D., 322, 328
Lucas, A., 22
Lucas, G., 361
Lucas, H. L., 486, 487
Lucas, R. E., 172, 393, 396, 397
Ludwig, A. M., 365, 472
Lund, E., 474
Lundberg, G., 406
Luria, A. M., 257
Lurigio, A. J., 460
Lustig, C., 271
Lutgendorf, S. K., 415
Lutgendorf, S., 405
Luus, C. A. E., 361
Lyall, S., 164
Lykins, A. D., 364
Lykken, D. T., 110, 324, 380, 396, 397, 549
Lyman, D. R., 488
Lynch, G., 268
Lynch, J. G., Jr., 297
Lynch, S., 268
Lynn, M., 90
Lynn, R., 331
Lynn, S. J., 86

Lynne, S. D., 156
Lyons, L., 160, 161, 414, 544
Lytton, H., 131
Lyubomirsky, S., 392, 395

M

M'Naughten, D., 461
Ma, L., 463
Ma, Y. Y., 277
Maas, J. B., 76, 78
Maass, A., 124, 306, 333
Macaluso, E., 202
Maccoby, E. E., 128, 130, 539
MacDonald, G., 276, 558
MacDonald, J., 202
Macdonald, J. E., 401
MacDonald, N., 481
MacDonald, S. W. S., 168
MacDonald, T. K., 90, 361
MacFarlane, A., 139
Macfarlane, J. W., 155
Macgregor, A. M. C., 351
Machado, A., 148
Machin, S., 330
Maciejewski, P. K., 172
Mack, A., 69
MacKinnon, D. W., 317
MacLachlan, M., 197
MacNeilage, P. F., 303
Maddox, K. B., 543
Madonna, 218
Madrian, B. C., 301
Madsen, T. M., 517
Maes, H. H. M., 353
Maestripieri, D., 110, 152
Magellan, F., 2, 45
Magnusson, D., 487
Magnusson, P. E. E., 474
Magoun, H., 46
Maguire, E. A., 263, 271
Mahadevan, R., 267
Mahncke, H. W., 167
Mahowald, M. W., 79
Maier, S. F., 404
Major, B., 127, 557
Malamuth, N. M., 360, 551, 553
Malan, D. H., 495
Malinosky-Rummell, R., 152
Malkiel, B., 297
Malkiel, B. G., 20
Malle, B. F., 526
Mallory, G., 341
Malmquist, C. P., 426
Malnic, B., 203
Malott, J. M., 201
Manber, R., 78
Mandel, D., 343
Mandel, H., 460
Maner, J. K., 371
Manilow, B., 446
Mann, T., 355, 356, 449
Mannix, L. M., 351
Manson, J. E., 412
Maquet, P., 82
Mar, R. A., 249
Marangell, L. B., 517
Maratos-Flier, E., 353
Marcus, B., 438
Maren, S., 467
Marentette, P. F., 303
Margolis, M. L., 79
Markowitsch, H. J., 271
Markus, G. B., 283

Markus, H. R., 124, 306, 390, 446
Marley, J., 460
Marmot, M. G., 408
Marschark, M., 263
Marsh, A. A., 387
Marsh, H. W., 396, 447
Marshall, M. J., 242
Marshall, R. D., 296
Marta, 189
Marteau, T. M., 300
Martin, C. K., 356
Martin, C. L., 131
Martin, R. J., 346
Martin, R. M., 21
Martin, S., 322
Martin, S. J., 488
Martin, S. P., 75
Martino, S. C., 361
Martins, Y., 366
Marx, J., 485
Masicampo, E. J., 441
Maslow, A. H., 4, 9, 340, 342, 343, 372, 429, 430, 431, 432, 450
Maslow, M. E. P., 447
Mason, C., 39
Mason, H., 27, 75, 76, 455
Mason, R. A., 60
Masse, L. C., 98
Massimini, M., 71
Mast, M. S., 558
Masten, A. S., 153
Masters, C., 555
Masters, W. H., 357, 358, 369, 372
Mastroianni, G. R., 529, 536
Masuda, T., 388, 526
Mataix-Cols, D., 467
Matheny, A. P., Jr., 111
Mather, M., 171
Matsumoto, D., 306, 387
Matsuzawa, T., 310
Matthews, G., 437
Matthews, R. N., 230
Matthyss, S., 183
Maurer, C., 139
Maurer, D., 139
May, C., 71
May, M., 213
May, P. A., 138
May, R., 106
Mayberg, H. S., 517, 518
Mayberry, R. I., 305
Mayer, D., 442
Mayer, J. D., 318
Mays, V. M., 401
Mazella, R., 558
Mazure, C., 477
Mazzella, R., 348
Mazzoni, G., 282, 283
Mazzuca, J., 253
McAneny, L., 275
McArthur, L. Z., 231
McBride-Chang, C., 153
McBurney, D. H., 53, 201, 212
McCabe, G., 21
McCabe, M. P., 348
McCain, J., 283
McCain, N. L., 405
McCann, I. L., 411
McCann, U. D., 95
McCarthy, P., 203
McCarty, O., 447
McCaul, K. D., 201
McCauley, C. R., 540
McClearn, G. E., 326, 366

McClellan, J. M., 485
McClendon, B. T., 527
McClintock, M. K., 155
McClure, E. B., 328
McConkey, K. M., 84, 85, 87
McConnell, R. A., 218
McCool, G., 557
McCormick, C. M., 367
McCrae, R. R., 111, 168, 174, 436, 437
McCullough, M. E., 414
McDermott, T., 550
McEvoy, S. P., 68
McFadden, D., 367
McFarland, C., 283
McFarland, S., 529
McGaugh, J. L., 257, 268, 269
McGhee, P. E., 147
McGlashan, T. H., 482
McGrath, J., 484
McGue, M., 109, 325
McGuffin, P., 476
McGuire, M. T., 356
McGurk, H., 202
McHugh, P. R., 469, 470
McKenna, K. Y. A., 540, 555
McLanahan, S., 551
McLaughlin, C. S., 361
McMurray, B., 302
McMurray, C., 411
McMurray, J., 298
McNally, R. J., 283, 286, 465, 509
McNeil, B. J., 300
McPherson, J. M., 478
Meador, B. D., 497
Mednick, S. A., 483
Medvec, V. H., 170
Mehl, M. R., 17, 128, 438
Mehta, M. R., 271
Meichenbaum, D., 502
Melchior, L. A., 124
Melhuish, E., 139
Meltzoff, A. N., 144, 249, 303, 307
Melville, H., 16, 454, 525
Melzack, R., 88, 199
Memon, A., 282
Menander of Athens, 81, 103
Mendle, J., 156
Mendolia, M., 410
Menustik, C. E., 499
Merari, A., 540
Merskey, H., 469
Merton, R. K., 12, 395
Merzenich, M., 167
Mesmer, F. A., 508, 509
Messinis, L., 96
Mestel, R., 81
Meston, C. M., 358, 359
Metcalfe, J., 293, 296
Metha, A. T., 170
Meyer, A., 472
Meyer-Bahlburg, H. F. L., 367
Mezulis, A. M., 447
Michaels, J. W., 538
Michelangelo, 163
Middlebrooks, J. C., 196
Mikels, J. A., 167, 171
Mikulincer, M., 152, 547
Milan, R. J., Jr., 361
Miles, D. R., 548
Milgram, S., 534, 535, 536, 537, 542, 568
Millar, J. K., 485
Miller, D. T., 99

Miller, E. J., 349, 351
Miller, G., 98, 203, 358
Miller, G. A., 266
Miller, G. E., 401
Miller, J. G., 158
Miller, K., 559
Miller, K. I., 441
Miller, L., 298
Miller, L. C., 560
Miller, L. K., 314
Miller, N. E., 26, 345
Miller, P. J. O., 70
Miller, S. D., 470
Mills, M., 139
Milne, B. J., 487
Milner, B., 270
Milner, D. A., 67
Milner, P., 48, 50
Milton, J., 220
Mineka, S., 465, 466
Miner-Rubino, K., 170
Ming, S. M., 217
Minsky, M., 66
Mischel, W., 158, 240, 437, 438, 445, 526
Miserandino, M., 273
Mita, T. H., 556
Mitchell, D. B., 258
Mitchell, F., 547
Mitchell, P., 146
Mitchell, T. R., 263
Mitte, K., 503
Mocellin, J. S. P., 96
Moffitt, T. E., 174, 462, 476
Moghaddam, F. M., 540
Moises, H. W., 484
Molaison, H., 270
Molyneux, W., 213, 214
Mondloch, C. J., 139
Money, J., 359, 365, 367
Monge, P. R., 441
Moniz, E., 519
Monroe, M., 117, 532, 558
Mooallem, J., 150
Moody, R., 95
Mook, D. G., 25
Moorcroft, W. H., 72, 77, 83
Moore, B., 172
Moore, D. W., 74, 99, 218, 355
Moore, J., 355
Moore, M. K., 144, 249
Moore, S., 557
Mor, N., 478
Moreland, R. L., 555, 556
Morell, V., 309, 403
Morelli, G. A., 125
Moreno, C., 471
Morey, R. A., 483
Morin, R., 161, 565
Morris, A. S., 154, 156, 161
Morris, C., 56
Morris, R., 549
Morrison, A. R., 26, 74
Morrison, C., 532
Morrison, D., 553
Morrison, K., 506
Morrow, D., 262
Morsella, E., 427
Mortensen, E. L., 21
Mortensen, P. B., 483
Morton, J., 139
Moruzzi, G., 46
Moscovici, S., 541

Moses, 12
Moses, E. B., 503
Mosher, W. D., 363, 364
Moss, A. J., 92
Moss, H. A., 174
Mosteller, F., 21
Motivala, S. J., 76
Moullec, C., 150
Moulton, S. T., 220
Mowrer, O. H., 497
Moyer, K. E., 548
Mozart, A., 322, 472
Mroczek, D. K., 168, 170
Muhlnickel, W., 53
Mulcahy, N. J., 310
Mulder, E. J., 96
Muller, J. E., 357, 401
Mullin, C. R., 253
Mulrow, C. D., 515
Murachver, T., 128
Murison, R., 408
Murnen, S. K., 348, 359
Murphy, G. E., 474
Murphy, L. M., 161
Murphy, S. T., 381
Murray, C., 331
Murray, C. A., 331
Murray, C. J., 453
Murray, H. A., 15, 219
Murray, J. P., 251
Murray, R. M., 96, 482
Murray, R., 483
Murray, S. L., 447
Musick, M. A., 414
Mustanski, B. S., 366, 367
Mycielska, K., 216
Myers, C., 280
Myers, D. G., 20, 169, 298, 364, 396, 397, 447, 540
Myers, L. R., 147, 280, 379
Myers, P., 280, 375, 376
Myers, R., 57

N

Nagourney, A., 528
Nairn, R. G., 460
Nakayama, E. Y., 496
Napoleon, 396, 431
Napolitan, D. A., 526
Nasar, J., 68
Nash, M. R., 85, 87
Neal, D. T., 226
Neale, J. M., 393
Neese, R. M., 198, 233
Neidorf, S., 565
Neisser, U., 69, 269, 325, 333
Neitz, J., 191
Nelson, C. A., III, 326
Nelson, M. D., 483
Nelson, N., 410
Nemeth, C. J., 541
Nesca, M., 280
Nestadt, G., 464
Nestle, M., 354
Nestoriuc, Y., 412
Neumann, R., 389, 532
Neuringer, A., 238
Newberg, A., 413
Newcomb, M. D., 98
Newcombe, N. S., 142
Newman, A. J., 305
Newman, L. S., 85
Newport, E. L., 305

Newport, F., 127, 133, 385, 530, 566
Newton, I., 12, 133, 191, 318, 489
Newton, T. L., 410
Nezlek, J. B., 441
Ng, S. H., 307
Ng, W. W. H., 441
Nichols, R. C., 107
Nickell, J., 85
Nicol, S. E., 486
Nicolaus, 233
Niebuhr, R., 443
Nielsen, K. M., 410
Nielsen, T. A., 81
Niemiec, C. P., 370
Niemiec, R., 459
Nier, J. A., 448
Niesta, D., 234
Nisbett, R. E., 294, 551
Nixon, G. M., 76
Nixon, R. M., 386
Noel, J. G., 442
Noice, H., 263
Noice, T., 263
Nolen-Hoeksema, S., 160, 172, 391, 477
Noller, P., 152
Nordgren, L. F., 344
Norem, J. K., 443
Norenzayan, A., 17, 122
Norris, J., 487
Northall, G. F.,, 233
Norton, K. L., 349
Norton, P. J., 503
Nostradamus, 218
Nowak, R., 93
Nowell, A., 328, 329, 330
Nurius, P., 446
Nurmi, J. E., 447
Nurnberger, J. I., Jr., 98
Nuttin, J. M., Jr., 555

O
O'Brien, R. M., 245
O'Connor, A., 354, 541
O'Connor, P., 511
O'Donnell, L., 362
O'Heeron, R. C., 410
O'Keeffe, C., 435
O'Neil, J., 19
O'Neill, E., 286
O'Neill, M. J., 408
O'Reardon, J. P., 519
Oaten, M., 441
Oates, J. C., 276
Oatley, K., 249
Obama, B. H., 151, 526, 531, 541, 567
Oberlander, J., 438
Oberman, L. M., 147, 249
Odbert, H. S., 433
Oellinger, M., 293
Oetting, E. R., 99
Oettingen, G., 442
Offer, D., 161
Ogden, C. L., 354
Öhman, A., 384, 466
Oishi, S., 342, 394
Olatunji, B. O., 461
Olds, J., 48, 49, 50
Olff, M., 465
Olfson, M., 455, 514, 515
Oliner, P. M., 251
Oliner, S. P., 251

Olshansky, S. J., 350
Olsson, A., 466
Olweus, D., 549
Oman, D., 414
Onishi, N., 350
Oppenheimer, J. R., 11
Oren, D. A., 71
Ormiston, M., 541
Orne, M. T., 85
Osborne, C., 169
Osborne, J. W., 334
Osborne, L., 304
Osgood, C. E., 567
Ost, L. G., 466
Ostfeld, A. M., 409
Oswald, A. J., 171, 393, 394, 401, 410
Ott, C. H., 172
Ouellette, J. A., 445
Over, R., 42
Overmier, J. B., 408
Owen, A. M., 44
Owyang, M. T., 557
Ozer, E. J., 464, 465
Özgen, E., 306, 307

P
Pacifici, R., 95
Padawer, W., 510
Padgett, V. R., 536
Page, S., 460
Page, S. E., 541
Pagnin, D., 517
Paivio, A., 263
Palace, E. M., 381
Palladino, J. J., 70
Pallier, C., 303
Palmer, J. C., 282
Palmer, S., 206, 269
Pandelaere, M., 284
Pandey, J., 527
Panksepp, J., 379
Pankratz, V. S., 474
Panksepp, J., 379
Panzarella, C., 478
Park, C. L., 414
Park, D. C., 167
Park, G., 322
Park, L. E., 449
Park, R. L., 380
Parker, E. S., 276
Parker, J. W., 396
Parker, S., 347
Parks, R., 541
Parsons, B., 368
Parsons, L. M., 46
Parva, S., 407
Pascal, 182
Pashler, H., 261
Passell, P., 23
Pastalkova, E., 268
Pasteur, L., 27, 317
Pate, J. E., 348
Patel, S. R., 76
Patrick, H., 370
Patten, S. B., 471
Patterson, D. R., 85, 86
Patterson, F., 311
Patterson, G. R., 242, 551
Patterson, P. H., 483
Patterson, R., 480
Patton, G. C., 96
Paulesu, E., 26
Paulos, J. A., 516

Paus, T., 140
Pavlov, I., 2, 227, 228, 229, 230, 231, 232, 234, 235, 236, 247, 253, 254, 291, 497
Payne, B. K., 281, 543
Peace, K. A., 286
Pedersen, N. L., 109
Peek, K., 315
Peeters, A., 350
Peigneux, P., 77, 271
Pekkanen, J., 78
Pekkarinen, T., 330
Pelham, B. W., 11, 447
Pendick, D., 549
Penfield, W., 51
Pennebaker, J. W., 17, 171, 410, 426, 566
Penny, H., 351
Peplau, L. A., 169, 363, 364
Peppard, P. E., 79
Pepperberg, I. M., 310
Pereira, A. C., 57, 166
Pereira, G. M., 166
Perkins, A., 365
Perlmutter, M., 167
Perls, T., 404
Perra, O., 147
Perrett, D. I., 189, 544
Perry, N., 142
Persky, S., 552
Pert, C. B., 38, 49
Perugini, E. M., 86
Peschel, E. R., 359
Peschel, R. E., 359
Peter, J., 161
Peters, T. J., 245
Peterson, C., 157, 442, 458
Peterson, L. R., 266
Peterson, M. J., 266
Petiot, Dr., 435
Petitto, L. A., 303
Petry, N. M., 351
Pettegrew, J. W., 483
Petticrew, M., 405
Pettifor, J. P., 27
Pettigrew, T. F., 544, 565
Pfammatter, M., 507
Phelps, E. A., 48, 466
Phelps, J. A., 485
Phelps, M. E., 138, 140
Phillips, D. P., 532
Phillips, J. L., 145
Phillips, M., 122
Piaget, J., 2, 9, 142, 143, 144, 145, 147, 148, 149, 157, 158, 163, 173, 174, 175, 176
Picasso, P., 315
Picchioni, M. M., 482
Pierce, P., 199
Piercy, M., 360
Pieters, G. L. M., 348
Pike, K. M., 348
Pilcher, J. J., 114
Piliavin, J. A., 158
Pillemer, D. B., 371
Pillemer, D. G., 141, 166
Pillsworth, E. G., 358
Pillsworth, M. G., 358
Pinel, J. P. J., 345
Pinel, P., 456, 460, 493
Pingitore, R., 351
Pinker, S., 40, 110, 114, 115, 128, 296, 302, 312, 330
Pinstrup-Andersen, P., 354

Pipe, M. E., 284, 285
Piper, A., Jr., 469
Pipher, M., 109, 371, 401
Pirandello, L., 479
Pirsig, R. M., 13
Pitman, R. K., 269
Pitt, B., 273
Plassmann, H., 202
Plato, 5, 97, 103, 428
Plaud, J. J., 498
Pliner, P., 347
Plöderl, M., 363
Plomin, R., 107, 109, 112, 113, 120, 314, 324, 325, 326, 353, 366, 476, 484
Plotkin, H., 474
Plotnik, H., 474
Plous, S., 27
Pogue-Geile, M. F., 353
Polich, J., 413
Polivy, J., 348, 356
Pollak, S. D., 231, 384
Pollard, R., 307
Pollitt, E., 326
Polusny, M. A., 153
Poole, D. A., 284
Poon, L. W., 165
Popenoe, D., 124, 169
Popkin, B. M., 353, 354
Popkin, S. J., 164
Poremba, A., 48
Porter, D., 238
Porter, S., 282, 286, 384
Posluszny, D. M., 405
Posner, M. I., 55
Posthuma, D., 325
Poulton, R., 487
Powdthavee, N., 393
Powell, K. E., 412
Powell, L. H., 415
Powell, R. A., 426
Powers, M. B., 498
Pratkanis, A. R., 182
Premack, D., 145
Prentice, D. A., 99
Prentice-Dunn, S., 527
Presley, C. A., 90
Presley, E., 11, 420
Pressman, S. D., 392
Price, E. C., 503
Price, G. M., 350
Price, J., 276
Pridgen, P. R., 445
Princess Diana (of Wales), 219
Pringle, P. J., 138
Prioleau, L., 510
Pritchard, R. M., 184
Pronin, E., 448, 527, 534
Propper, R. E., 81
Proust, M., 204
Provine, R. R., 17
Pryor, J. H., 115, 128, 329, 370, 477
Puhl, R. M., 351
Putnam, F. W., 469, 470
Putnam, R., 123
Pyszczynski, T. A., 478, 540, 546, 559

Q
Qirko, H. N., 540
Quanty, M. B., 390
Quinn, P. C., 206
Quinn, P. J., 21

R

Rader, D., 486
Rahman, Q., 366, 367, 368
Raine, A., 487, 488, 548
Rainville, P., 87
Raison, C. L., 488
Rajendran, G., 146
Ralston, A., 339, 341, 342
Ramachandran, V. S., 40, 57, 147, 199, 249, 306
Ramirez-Esparza, N., 306
Ramon y Cajal, S., 37
Rand, C. S. W., 351
Randall, P. K., 116
Randi, J., 12, 220
Rapoport, J. L., 463, 466
Räsänen, S., 482
Raveis, V. H., 100
Rawles, R., 544
Rawlings, J., 157
Ray, J., 391
Ray, O., 94
Rayner, R., 4, 235, 236
Raynor, H. A., 346
Reagan, R., 427, 461
Reason, J., 216, 540
Reed, G., 529
Reed, P., 261
Rees, G., 182
Rees, M. (Sir), 133
Regan, P. C., 115
Regier, D., 489
Reichenberg, A., 146, 481
Reicher, S., 529
Reichman, J., 358
Reifman, A., 110
Reiner, W. G., 129
Reis, H. T., 560
Reisenzein, R., 381
Reiser, M., 218
Reite, M. L., 408
Reitzle, M., 162
Remafedi, G., 364
Remley, A., 125
Renner, C. H., 118
Renner, M. J., 118
Renninger, K. A., 148
Renshon, J., 448
Rentfrow, P. J., 438
Repetti, R. L., 399
Rescorla, R. A., 232
Resnick, M. D., 19, 161
Resnick, R. A., 69
Resnick, S. M., 483
Reyna, V. F., 156
Reynolds, A. J., 327
Rhodes, G., 547
Rholes, W. S., 152
Ribeiro, R., 77
Riber, K. A., 318
Ricciardelli, L. A., 348
Rice, M. E., 251
Richardson, K. D., 547
Richeson, J. A., 565
Riedner, G., 362
Rieff, P., 428
Rieger, G., 363
Riis, J., 393
Riley, L. D., 168
Rindermann, H., 315
Ring, K., 95
Ripple, C. H., 327
Risch, N., 476

Riskind, J. H., 458
Ritzler, B., 427
Rizzolatti, G., 248
Roberson, D., 306
Roberts, B. W., 174, 437
Roberts, L., 409
Roberts, T. A., 128
Robertson, B. A., 167
Robins, L., 489
Robins, L. N., 100
Robins, R. W., 160, 170, 389
Robinson, F. P., 29
Robinson, J., 363
Robinson, J. P., 75
Robinson, T. E., 89
Robinson, T. N., 216, 356
Rochat, F., 536
Rock, I., 69, 206
Rockefeller, J. D., Sr., 431
Rodgers, R., 388, 558
Rodin, J., 348, 408, 409, 442
Rodman, R., 303
Rodriguez, A., 395
Roediger, H. L., III, 261, 280, 282
Roehling, M. V., 351
Roenneberg, T., 71
Roese, N. J., 170
Roesser, R., 195
Rogers, C. R., 4, 9, 429, 430, 431, 432, 439, 447, 450, 451, 495, 496, 497, 522
Rohan, K. J., 509
Rohan, M. J., 110
Rohner, R. P., 125, 152, 154
Rohrer, D., 261
Roiser, J. P., 95
Rokach, A., 26
Romney, D. M., 131
Roosevelt, E., 175, 430
Rorschach, H., 424, 425, 429, 439
Rosch, E., 292
Rose, A. J., 128
Rose, J. S., 92, 120
Rose, R. J., 120, 365
Rose, S., 117, 465
Roselli, C. E., 366
Rosenbaum, M., 559
Rosenberg, N. A., 114
Rosengren, K. S., 142
Rosenhan, D. L., 459, 460
Rosenman, R., 402
Rosenthal, R., 328, 384, 438
Rosenzweig, M. R., 118
Roseth, C. J., 566
Ross, J., 77
Ross, L., 294, 527
Ross, M., 281, 283, 306, 449
Rossi, P. J., 214
Rossion, B., 179
Rostosky, S. S., 362
Roth, T., 81
Rothbart, M. K., 110, 111
Rothbart, M., 547
Rothbaum, B. O., 498
Rothbaum, F., 124
Rothman, A. J., 300
Rothstein, W. G., 170
Rotter, J., 440
Rotton, J., 488
Rousseau, J. J., 142
Rovee-Collier, C., 141, 142, 275
Rowe, D. C., 109, 110, 125, 126, 327, 332, 548
Rowling, J. K., 327

Rozin, P., 231, 346
Ruback, R. B., 442
Rubel, T., 127
Rubenstein, J. S., 68
Rubin, D. C., 166, 269
Rubin, J. Z., 566
Rubin, L. B., 128
Rubin, Z., 383
Rubio, G., 462
Ruble, D., 131
Rubonis, A. V., 401
Ruchlis, H., 293
Rudd, K., 262
Rudman, L. A., 544
Rudner, R., 70
Rudolph, K. D., 128
Ruffin, C. L., 401
Ruiz-Belda, M. A., 387
Rule, B. G., 253
Rumbaugh, D. M., 311, 312, 313
Rünger, D., 427
Rupp, D. E., 445
Rush, A. J., 516
Rush, B., 493
Rushton, J. P., 251, 331
Russell, B., 80, 396
Russell, J. A., 388
Russell, P., 273
Russo, A., 306
Rusting, C. L., 391
Rutland, A., 565
Rutter, M., 152, 366
Ruys, K. I., 381
Ryan, R. M., 370, 395, 449
Ryckman, R. M., 350
Ryder, A. G., 468

S

S., 257, 276
Saad, L., 93, 401
Sabbagh, M. A., 145
Sabini, J., 534
Sachdev, J., 519
Sachdev, P., 519
Sachs, J., 299
Sackett, P. R., 333
Sacks, O., 197, 270
Saddock, B. J., 514
Sadi, 199
Sadato, N., 56
Sagan, C., 12, 133, 219
Sagi, D., 82
Sakurai, T., 345
Salmela-Aro, K., 447
Salmon, P., 412, 520
Salovey, P., 300, 318, 392
Salthouse, T. A., 165, 168
Sampson, E. E., 123
Samuels, J., 464
Samuels, S., 21
Sanders, A. R., 485
Sanders, G., 367, 368
Sandfort, T. G. M., 363, 364
Sandkühler, S., 293
Sandler, W., 304
Sanford, A. J., 301
Sanz, C., 310, 311
Sapadin, L. A., 128
Sapirstein, G., 22
Sapolsky, B. S., 361, 553
Sapolsky, R., 408, 409, 473
Sartorius, N., 468
Sartre, J. P., 132

Sato, K., 564
Saul, S., 78
Saulny, S., 401
Saunders, S., 92
Savage-Rumbaugh, E. S., 312
Savarino, J., 516
Savic, I., 366
Savitsky, K., 446
Savoy, C., 308
Sawyer, M. G., 473
Scanzoni, L. D., 169, 364
Scarr, S., 112, 120, 315
Schab, F. R., 204
Schachter, S., 377, 380, 381, 382, 383, 416
Schacter, D. L., 166, 270, 271, 284, 427
Schafer, G., 303
Schall, T., 164
Scheier, M. F., 409
Schein, E. H., 528
Schell, D. A., 167
Scherer, K. R., 384
Schiavi, R. C., 74
Schieber, F., 164
Schilt, T., 95
Schimel, J., 432
Schimmack, U., 123, 397
Schkade, D., 540
Schlaug, G., 45
Schlesinger, A. M., Jr., 540
Schmidt, F. L., 445
Schmitt, D. P., 114, 115, 116, 436, 448
Schnall, E., 414
Schnaper, N., 95
Schneider, R. H., 413
Schneider, S. L., 443
Schneiderman, N., 405
Schoenborn, C. A., 76
Schoeneman, T. J., 124
Schofield, J. W., 565
Schonfield, D., 167
Schooler, J. W., 282
Schreiner-Engel, P., 74
Schugens, M. M., 272
Schuman, H., 166
Schumann, R., 472
Schwartz, B., 234, 442, 465
Schwartz, J., 393
Schwartz, J. H., 268
Schwartz, J. M., 503, 519
Schwartz, S. H., 127
Schwarz, N., 275, 276
Sclafani, A., 347
Scott, B. A., 387
Scott, D. J., 93, 200
Scott, E. S., 157
Scott, J., 166
Scott, W. A., 125
Sdorow, L. M., 425
Seal, K. H., 464
Seamon, J. G., 282
Sears, R. R., 322
Sebat, J., 146
Sechrest, L., 425
Sedgwick, J., 11
Sedikides, C., 385
Seeman, P., 483
Segal, M. E., 540
Segal, N. L., 109,, 326
Segall, M. H., 115, 130, 148
Segerstrom, S. C., 398, 409
Seidler, G. H., 508

Seidlitz, L., 477
Self, C. E., 99
Seligman, M. E. P., 65, 72, 120, 370, 397, 412, 428, 441, 442, 443, 446, 447, 458, 478, 503, 505, 509
Sellers, H., 179, 189
Selye, H., 399, 400, 407, 416
Sen, A., 544
Seneca, 164, 261, 395, 442
Senghas, A., 304
Sengupta, S., 566
Senju, A., 147, 249
Sensenbrenner, F. J., 350
Service, R. F., 268
Seto, M. C., 90
Seuss (Geisel, Theodor Seuss), 212
Shadish, W. R., 506
Shafir, E., 298
Shafto, M. A., 167
Shakespeare, W., 71, 148, 217, 246, 267, 291, 315, 383, 389, 461, 470, 472, 474, 558
Shanahan, L., 160, 161
Shapiro, F., 508
Sharma, A. R., 110
Shattuck, P. T., 146
Shaver, P. R., 150, 152, 389, 547
Shaw, G. B., 560
Shaw, H. L., 312
Shea, D. F., 301
Sheehan, S., 480
Sheldon, K. M., 358, 370
Shenton, M. E., 483
Shepard, R. N., 28, 216
Shepherd, C., 109, 354
Sher, L., 474
Shereshevskii, 257
Shergill, S. S., 564
Sherif, M., 565, 566
Sherman, P. W., 347
Sherman, S. J., 293
Sherrington, C., 37
Sherry, D., 271
Shettleworth, S. J., 244, 267
Shiffrin, R. M., 258, 259
Shinkareva, S. V., 66
Shotland, R. L., 561
Showers, C., 443
Shulman, P., 329
Sieff, E. M., 393
Siegel, J. M., 77, 82
Siegel, R. K., 89, 94, 95, 96
Siegel, S., 226, 235
Siegler, R. S., 143
Sigmund, B. B., 405
Sigvardsson, S., 110
Silbersweig, D. A., 483
Sill, M., 164
Silva, A. J., 268
Silva, C. E., 84
Silver, M., 537
Silver, R. C., 172
Silveri, M. M., 156
Silverman, K., 91
Simek, T. C., 245
Simms, C. A., 469
Simon, G. E., 351, 516
Simon, H. A., 264, 300
Simon, P., 252
Simon, T., 319
Simons, D. J., 69
Simonton, D. K., 167, 253, 317, 318
Simpson, J. A., 116, 152

Sinclair, R. C., 381
Singelis, T. M., 124
Singer, J. E., 377, 380, 381, 382, 383, 416
Singer, J. L., 506
Singer, T., 200, 249
Singh, D., 116
Singh, S., 317, 318
Singleton, C., 461
Sipski, M. L., 42
Sireteanu, R., 214
Sizemore, C., 469
Sjöstrum, L., 351
Skinner, B. F., 4, 236, 237, 238, 239, 240, 241, 243, 244, 245, 247, 253, 254, 304, 309, 335, 337, 429, 478
Skitka, L. J., 391
Skodol, A. E., 468
Skoog, G., 464
Skoog, I., 464
Skov, R. B., 293
Slater, E., 472
Slater, L., 515
Sloan, R. P., 414
Slovic, P., 92
Small, M. F., 98, 125
Smedley, A., 332
Smedley, B. D., 332
Smelser, N. J., 547
Smith, A., 482, 563
Smith, C., 95, 402
Smith, E., 393
Smith, G., 164
Smith, J. E., 351
Smith, M. B., 431
Smith, M. L., 506
Smith, P. B., 534
Smith, S. M., 557
Smith, T. B., 511
Smith, T. W., 361, 362, 363, 364, 504
Smolak, L., 348
Smoreda, Z., 128
Snedeker, J., 303
Snidman, N., 111
Snodgrass, S., 389
Snyder, M., 459
Snyder, S. H., 37, 38, 516
Solomon, D., 314
Solomon, D. A., 516
Solomon, J., 460
Solomon, M., 557
Sommer, R., 122
Søndergård, L., 516
Song, S., 86
Sontag, S., 405
Sørensen, H. J., 482
Sorkhabi, N., 154
Soussignan, R., 389
Sowell, T., 567
Spalding, K. L., 351
Spanos, N. P., 85, 86, 469
Spearman, C., 314, 324, 335
Specht, J. C., 432
Spelke, E., 330
Spencer, K. M., 483
Spencer, S. J., 333
Sperling, G., 265, 266
Sperry, R. W., 57, 58, 59, 190
Speth, J. G., 394
Spiegel, D., 86, 470
Spiegel, K., 76
Spielberger, C., 403

Spinoza, B., 1
Spitzer, R. L., 465, 468, 474
Spooner, W. A., 427
Spradley, J. P., 122
Sprecher, S., 385, 557
Spring, B., 356, 507
Springer, J., 108
Squire, L. R., 271
Srivastava, A., 395
Srivastava, S., 436, 442
St. Augustine, 133
St. Clair, D., 483
St. John, 472
Stack, S., 474
Stafford, R. S., 515
Stager, C. L., 302
Stanley, J. C., 322
Stanovich, K., 420
Stapel, D. A., 381
Stark, R., 12
Stathopoulou, G., 520
Staubli, U., 268
Steel, P., 396
Steele, C. M., 90, 331, 333
Steer, R. A., 474
Steinberg, L., 154, 156, 157, 161
Steinberg, N., 556
Steinhauer, J., 107, 161
Steinmetz, J. E., 272
Stengel, E., 474
Stern, M., 217
Stern, S. L., 409
Stern, W., 319
Sternberg, E. M., 318, 403
Sternberg, R. J., 313, 316, 317, 324, 332, 335, 385
Stetter, F., 412
Stevens, W., 20
Stewart, B., 27
Stewart, J., 433
Stice, E., 348, 349
Stickgold, R., 77, 81, 82
Stinson, D. A., 411
Stith, S. M., 251
Stockton, M. C., 359
Stohr, O., 108, 109
Stone, A. A., 200, 393
Stone, G., 469
Stone, L. D., 171
Stone, R., 464
Stoolmiller, M., 110
Stoppard, J. M., 385
Storbeck, J., 382
Storm, L., 220
Storms, M. D., 365, 527
Strack, F., 389, 532
Strack, S., 479
Strahan, E. J., 182
Stranahan, A. M., 57
Strand, S., 328, 330
Stratton, G. M., 214, 215
Straub, R. O., 30, 312
Straus, M. A., 242
Stravinsky, I., 238, 315
Strawbridge, W. J., 414
Strayer, D. L., 68
Striegel-Moore, R. M., 348, 349
Stroebe, M., 172
Stroebe, W., 172
Strupp, H. H., 510
Stumpf, H., 328
Stunkard, A. J., 353
Styfco, S. J., 327
Subiaul, F., 248

Subrahmanyam, K., 161
Suddath, R. L., 485
Sue, S., 511
Suedfeld, P., 96, 465
Sugita, Y., 212
Suinn, R. M., 308
Sullivan, A., 140
Sullivan, P. F., 475
Suls, J. M., 396, 403
Summers, M., 453
Summerville, A., 170
Sundel, M., 168
Sunstein, C. R., 296, 301
Suomi, S. J., 466
Suppes, P., 148
Susman, E. J., 174
Süß, H. M., 318
Susser, E., 483
Susser, E. S., 464
Sutcliffe, J. S., 146
Sutherland, A., 246
Sutton, D., 541
Swann, W. B., Jr., 447
Sweat, J. A., 218
Swerdlow, N. R., 483
Swim, J. K., 544
Symbaluk, D. G., 200
Symond, M. B., 483
Szucko, J. J., 380
Szymanski, K., 539

T

Tabarlet, J. O., 361, 553
Taha, F. A., 80
Taheri, S., 76, 353
Tajfel, H., 546
Takahashi, N., 124
Talarico, J. M., 269
Talbot, M., 532
Tamres, L. K., 128
Tangney, J. P., 441
Tannen, D., 26, 128
Tannenbaum, P., 184
Tanner, J. M., 155
Tarbert, J., 530
Tarmann, A., 363
Tarrier, N., 498
Taubes, G., 356
Tavris, C., 391, 425
Taylor, P. J., 250
Taylor, S., 464
Taylor, S. E., 128, 297, 308, 399
Taylor, S. P., 549
Tedeschi, R. G., 465
Teghtsoonian, R., 183
Teicher, M. H., 153
Teitelbaum, P., 345
Tellegen, A., 396, 397
ten Brinke, L., 384
Tennyson, A., 128
Teran-Santos, J., 79
Teresi, D., 49
Terman, J. S., 509
Terman, L. M., 318, 319, 322, 336
Terman, M., 71, 509
Terracciano, A., 125, 174
Terrace, H. S., 15, 312
Tertullian, 547
Tesch, F., 396
Tesser, A., 161
Tetlock, P. E., 566
Thaler, R. H., 301
Thatcher, R. W., 140, 174

Thayer, R. E., 411
Théoret, H., 147
Thernstrom, M., 200
Thiel, A., 57
Thiele, T. E., 98
Thomas, A., 111, 151, 174
Thomas, L., 39, 133, 304, 506
Thomas, S. L., 252
Thompson, C. P., 267
Thompson, D., 284
Thompson, J. K., 356
Thompson, P. M., 140, 325
Thompson, R., 278
Thomson, R., 128
Thorndike, A. L., 236, 247, 320, 324
Thorndike, E. L., 237, 318, 254
Thorne, J., 453
Thornton, B., 557
Thornton, G. C., III, 445
Thorpe, W. H., 313
Tice, D. M., 162, 550
Tickle, J. J., 92
Tiedens, L. Z., 391
Tiger, L., 244
Tillmann, H. C., 369
Timlin, M. T., 18
Timmerman, T. A., 549
Tinbergen, N., 340
Tirrell, M. E., 230, 231
Tockerman, Y. R., 350
Todorov, A., 384
Tolin, D. F., 465
Tolkien, J. R. R., 419
Tollefson, G. D., 516
Tolley-Schell, S. A., 384
Tolman, E. C., 243
Tolstoy, L., 7, 169, 471, 489
Tondo, L., 516
Toni, N., 268
Toole, E., 486, 487
Tordoff, V., 266
Torrey, E. F., 483, 484, 510
Towler, G., 538
Townshend, P., 170, 177
Tracey, J. L., 389
Traub, J., 168
Trautwein, U., 447
Treffert, D. A., 314, 315
Treisman, A., 205
Tremblay, R. E., 98, 487
Trewin, D., 130
Triandis, H. C., 122, 124, 551
Trickett, P. K., 153
Trillin, A., 430
Trillin, C., 430
Trimble, J. E., 99
Triplett, N., 537, 538
Trolier, T. K., 19
Troller, J. N., 171
Tropp, L. R., 565
Trull, T. J., 486
Truman, H. S., 541
Trump, D., 445
Trut, L., 113
Trzesniewski, K. H., 170
Tsai, J. L., 388
Tsang, B. Y. P., 124
Tsang, Y. C., 344
Tschaikovsky, P. I., 308
Tsuang, M. T., 475
Tuber, D. S., 27
Tuerk, P. W., 326
Tully, T., 228

Tulving, E., 271
Turk, D. C., 201
Turkheimer, E., 326, 327
Turner, J. C., 546
Turpin, A., 218
Tutu, D., 370
Tversky, A., 20, 294, 295
Twain, M., 16, 92, 244, 283, 327, 447, 472, 501
Twenge, J. M., 132, 160, 371, 448, 467, 473, 550
Tyler, K. A., 153

U

Uchino, B. N., 409
Uddin, L. Q., 60
Udry, J. R., 129
Uga, V., 81
Ulman, K. J., 155
Ulmer, D., 402, 413
Ulrich, R. E., 26
Urbany, J. E., 301
Urry, H. L., 379
Ursu, S., 467
Uttal, D. H., 142

V

Vaccarino, A. L., 271
Vaidya, J. G., 436
Vaillant, G. E., 283, 370, 410
Valenstein, E. S., 519
Valkenburg, P. M., 161
Vallone, R. E., 11
Van Cauter, E., 76
van den Boom, D., 151
Van Dyke, C., 94
van Engen, M. L., 127
van Goozen, S. H. M., 487
van Hemert, D. A., 388
van IJzendoorn, M. H., 110, 151, 326
van Ittersum, K., 208
Van Leeuwen, M. S., 130
Van Rooy, D. L., 318
Van Yperen, N. W., 560
Van Zeijl, J., 151
Vance, E. B., 357
VandeCreek, L., 286
Vandenberg, S. G., 329
Vanman, E. J., 543
Vannucci, M., 283
Vaughn, K. B., 389
Vazire, S., 438
Vecera, S. P., 209
Vegas, R., 246, 247
Vekassy, L., 80
Veneziano, R. A., 152, 154
Verbeek, M. E. M., 433
Verhaeghen, P., 165
Verier, R. L., 401
Vertes, R., 82
Vessel, E. A., 341
Vigil, J. M., 155
Vigliocco, G., 302
Vining, E. P. G., 56
Virgil, 21, 378, 389
Viswesvaran, C., 318
Vita, A. J., 93
Vitello, P., 164
Vittengl, J. R., 515
Voas, D., 434
Vogel, P., 57

Vohs, K. D., 115
Von Ebner-Eschenbach, M., 167
von Helmholtz, H., 191, 192, 221
von Hippel, W., 166
von Senden, M., 213
Voyer, D., 328
Vrana, S. R., 379
Vyazovskiy, V. V., 77
Vygotsky, L., 148, 175

W

Waber, R. L., 22
Wadden, T. A., 356
Wade, K. A., 282
Wade, N. G., 511
Wager, T. D., 467
Wagner, A. R., 232
Wagner, F. E., 508
Wagner, N. N., 357
Wagner, R. J., 316
Wagner, U., 77
Wagstaff, G., 527
Wahlberg, D., 400
Wai, J., 322
Wakefield, J. C., 455, 465
Walk, R. D., 207
Walker, M. P., 77
Walker, W. R., 171
Wall, P. D., 199
Wallace, D. S., 528
Wallace, G. L., 314
Wallach, L., 432
Wallach, M. A., 432
Waller, J., 537
Walsh, T., 485
Walster (Hatfield), E., 556
Wampold, B. E., 506, 510
Wang, S. H., 144
Wansink, B., 208
Ward, A., 356
Ward, C., 89
Ward, K. D., 93
Ward, L. M., 361
Wardle, J., 201
Wargo, E., 412
Warner, J., 364
Warren, R., 216
Washburn, A. L., 344
Washburn, D. A., 313
Washburn, M. F., 2, 3
Wason, P. C., 293
Wasserman, E. A., 238, 310
Waterman, A. S., 160
Waterman, I., 197
Waterman, R. H., Jr., 245
Waters, E., 150
Watkins, E. R., 471
Watkins, M. J., 261, 262
Watson, D., 392, 411, 447
Watson, J. B., 4, 9, 227, 228, 232, 235, 236, 247, 253
Watson, R. I., Jr., 539
Watson, S. J., 96
Watson, T., 245
Wayment, H. A., 169
Weaver, J. B., 360
Webb, W. B., 74, 75, 78
Weber, E., 182, 183, 184, 222
Webley, K., 544
Wechsler, D., 320, 321, 324, 333, 336
Weil, A., 406
Weinberg, M. S., 364

Weinberger, D. R., 157
Weiner, B., 527
Weinstein, N. D., 443
Weis, S., 318
Weiskrantz, L., 190
Weiss, A., 396, 433
Weiss, D. S., 464, 465
Weissman, M. M., 473
Weisz, J. R., 124
Weitzman, M. S., 563
Welch, J. M., 467
Welch, W. W., 464
Weller, S., 362
Wellings, K., 361
Wellman, H. M., 144
Wells, G. L., 225
Wender, P. H., 475
Wener, R., 442
Werker, J. F., 302
Wernicke, C., 54, 55, 56, 62
West, R. L., 166
Westen, D., 383, 424, 426, 506
Wetzel, R. D., 474
Weuve, J., 166
Whalen, P. J., 379, 381, 382
Wheeler, B. W., 516
Wheeler, D. R., 15, 219
Whishaw, I. Q., 118, 317
White, G. L., 559
White, H. R., 549
White, K. M., 162
White, L., 170
White, R. A., 219
Whitehead, B. D., 169
Whiten, A., 17, 310
Whiting, B. B., 125
Whiting, J. W. M., 399
Whitley, B. E., Jr., 368, 546
Whitlock, J. R., 268
Whitman, C., 379
Whitman, W., 472
Whooley, M. A., 403
Whorf, B. L., 306, 309, 335
Wickelgren, W. A., 263
Widiger, T. A., 486
Widom, C. S., 153
Wiens, A. N., 499
Wierson, M., 246
Wierzbicki, M., 110
Wiesel, T. N., 188, 214
Wiest, J. R., 552
Wigdor, A. K., 333
Wilcox, A. J., 358
Wilde, O., 448
Wilder, D. A., 546
Wiles, A., 317, 318
Wilford, J. N., 133
Wilkens, C., 561
Willemsen, T. M., 127
Williams, C., 364
Williams, C. "Andy", 371
Williams, C. L., 401
Williams, H. J., 485
Williams, J. E., 127, 402
Williams, J. H. G., 171, 249
Williams, K. D., 371, 372, 538
Williams, R., 402
Williams, S., 110
Williams, S. L., 498
Williams, V., 110
Williams, W. M., 327
Williamson, D. A., 348
Willingham, B., 387

Willis, J., 384
Willis, S. L., 168
Willmuth, M. E., 360
Wilson, A. E., 306, 449, 523
Wilson, C. M., 410
Wilson, G. D., 366, 367, 368
Wilson, G. T., 90
Wilson, J. Q., 158
Wilson, M. A., 82
Wilson, R. C., 539
Wilson, R. S., 111, 141, 168
Wilson, T. D., 68, 233, 334
Wilson, W. A., 98
Wiltshire, S., 314
Windholz, G., 229, 231
Winfrey, O., 132, 273
Winkielman, P., 381
Winner, E., 322
Winquist, J., 478
Wiseman, R., 219, 220, 283, 435
Wisman, A., 154
Witelson, S. F., 54, 367
Wittgenstein, L., 133
Witvliet, C. V. O., 379, 391
Wixted, J. T., 277
Wojtowicz, J. M., 515
Wolak, J., 551
Wolfson, A. R., 82
Woll, S., 557
Wolpe, J., 498

Wolpert, E. A., 81
Wonderlich, S. A., 348
Wong, D. F., 483
Wong, M. M., 128
Wood, J. M., 280, 425
Wood, J. V., 478
Wood, M., 329
Wood, W., 117, 127, 129, 132, 226, 385, 445, 541
Woodruff, G., 145
Woodruff-Pak, D. S., 272
Woods, N. F., 155
Woods, T., 76, 332
Woodward, B., 10
Woodward, L. G., 473
Woody, E. Z., 87
Woodyard, D., 238
Woolcock, N., 534
Woolf, V., 472
Worobey, J., 111
Worthington, E. L., Jr., 157, 511
Wortman, C. B., 172
Wren, C. S., 99
Wright, I. C., 483
Wright, J., 164
Wright, M., 368
Wright, P., 483
Wright, P. H., 128
Wrosch, C., 401
Wuethrich, B., 90

Wulsin, L. R., 403
Wundt, W., 2, 3, 9, 31
Wyatt, J. K., 81, 280
Wyatt, R. J., 484
Wynne, C. D., 312

X

Xu, Y., 5, 270
Xun, W. Q. E., 306

Y

Yach, D., 350
Yamagata, S., 436
Yang, N., 552
Yang, S., 444
Yano, S., 322
Yanof, D. S., 161
Yarnell, P. R., 268
Yates, A., 348, 461
Yates, W. R., 359
Ybarra, O., 447
Yellen, A., 72
Young, T., 191, 192, 221
Youngentob, S. L., 138
Youngman, H., 81
Yücel, M., 96
Yufe, J., 108, 109
Yuki, M., 388

Z

Zabin, L. S., 155
Zadra, A., 79
Zadro, L., 371
Zagorsky, J. L., 315
Zajonc, R. B., 319, 381, 382, 383, 416, 538, 555, 556
Zammit, S., 482
Zanna, M. P., 110, 544
Zauberman, G., 297
Zeidner, M., 318, 331
Zeineh, M. M., 271
Zeno, 496
Zhang, H., 5
Zhang, J. V., 346
Zigler, E. F., 153, 327
Zilbergeld, B., 505, 507
Zillmann, D., 360, 381, 553
Zillmer, E., 427
Zimbardo, P. G., 529, 530, 539, 547
Zinbarg, R., 465, 466
Zogby, J., 195
Zornberg, G. L., 483
Zou, Z., 204
Zubieta, J. K., 199, 200
Zucker, G. S., 527
Zucker, K. J., 363
Zuckerman, M., 341
Zvolensky, M. J., 462

A

Absolute thresholds, 181
Abu Ghraib Prison, 530
Abuse, repressed or constructed memories of, 285–286
Academic self-concept, 447
Acceptance
  in client-centered therapy, 496
  in Rogers' person-centered perspective, 430
Accidents
  selective attention and, 68
  sleep deprivation and, 76
Accommodation
  in Piaget's theory, 143
  visual, 186
Acetylcholine (ACh), 38
Achievement motivation, B-7
Acquisition, in classical conditioning, 230–231
Action(s)
  attitudes and, 527–531
  inappropriate, in schizophrenia, 481
Action potentials, 36
Activation-synthesis theory of sleep, 82–83
Active listening, in client-centered therapy, 496
Activity level, obesity and, 353
Adaptation
  in evolutionary psychology, 113
  perceptual, 214–215
  sensory, 183–184
Adaptation-level phenomenon, 395
Addiction, 88–89
ADHD (attention-deficit hyperactivity disorder), 455
Adolescence, 154–161
  cognitive development in, 157–158
  physical development in, 155–157
  sexuality in, 361–362
  social development in, 159–161
Adoption studies, of intelligence, 325–326
Adrenal glands, 43
Adrenaline, 43
Adulthood, 163–173
  ages and stages of, 168–169
  cognitive development in, 166–168
  commitments in, 169–170
  death and dying and, 172–173
  emerging, 162
  physical development in, 163–166
  social development in, 168–173
Aerobic exercise, stress management and, 411–412
Aggression, 548–554
  biology of, 548–549
  biopsychosocial approach to, 554
  gender and, 127
  observational learning and, 551–554
  psychological factors in, 549–550
  social-cultural factors in, 550–551
Aging, biopsychosocial influences on, 171
Agonist molecules, 39
Agoraphobia, 463
Agreeableness, 436
AIDS, stress and, 404–405
Alarm reaction, 400
Alcohol use, 89–91, 97
  aggression and, 549
  during pregnancy, 138
  teen pregnancy and, 361
Algorithms, 292
All-or-none response, 36
Alpha waves, 72
Alternative therapies, 507–509
Altruism, 561–563
  bystander intervention and, 561–562

Alzheimer's disease, 268
Ames illusion, 211
Amnesia, 269–271. *See also* Forgetting
  infantile, 141, 272
  source, 283–284
Amphetamines, 91–92
Amplitude, of sound waves, 193
Amygdala, 48
Anal stage, 422
Analytical intelligence, 316
Anger, 389–391
  heart and, 402–403
Angular gyrus, 54
Animals
  as research subjects, 26–27
  same-sex attraction in, 365
  thinking and language in, 309–313
Anorexia nervosa, 348
Antagonist molecules, 39
Anterior cingulate cortex, 467
Antianxiety drugs, 514
Antidepressant drugs, 415–516, 514–516
Antipsychotic drugs, 513–514
Antisocial observational learning, 251–253
Antisocial personality disorders, 486–488
Anvil (bone), 194
Anxiety
  free-floating, 462
  stranger, 149
Anxiety disorders, 461–467
  antianxiety drugs and, 514
  biological perspective on, 466–467
  generalized anxiety disorder, 461, 462
  learning perspective on, 465–466
  obsessive-compulsive disorder, 461, 463–464
  panic disorder, 461, 462
  phobias, 461, 462–463
  post-traumatic stress disorder, 461, 464–465
Aphasia, 54
Applied research, 8
Arousal, optimum, 341
Assimilation, in Piaget's theory, 143
Association, language development and, 304
Association areas, 53–54
Associative learning, 226–227. *See also* Classical conditioning; Operant conditioning
Astrologers, 434–435
Attachment, 149–153
  adult relationships and, 152
  deprivation of, 152–153
  differences in, 151–153
  origins of, 149–150
Attention, selective, 68–70, 87, 481
Attention-deficit hyperactivity disorder (ADHD), 455
Attitudes
  actions and, 527–531
  cognitive dissonance and, 530–531
  role-playing and, 529
  scientific, 11–13
Attraction, 555–560
  physical attractiveness and, 556–558
  proximity and, 555–556
  reward theory of, 559
  romantic love and, 559–560
  similarity and, 558–559
Attractiveness, physical, attraction and, 556–558
Attributional style, 442–444
Attribution theory, 525–527
Atypical antipsychotics, 514
Audition. *See also* Hearing
  definition of, 193
Auditory cortex, 194
Auditory nerve, 194

Authoritarian parents, 153
Authoritative parents, 153–154
Autism, 146–147
Automatic prejudice, 543
Automatic processing, 260
Autonomic nervous system, 40
  emotions and, 378–379
  shyness and, 433
Autonomy vs. shame and doubt stage, 159
Availability heuristic, 295–296
Aversive conditioning, 499–500
Aversive events, aggression and, 549–550
Axons, 35

B

Babbling stage, 303
Bachelor's degree, for careers in psychology, C-1—C-3
Back-to-sleep position, 141
Barbiturates, 91
Basal metabolic rate, 346
Basic research, 8
Basic trust, 152
Basilar membrane, 194
Behavior, reciprocal determinism and, 439–440
Behavioral neuroscientists, 35
Behavioral perspective, 6, 7
Behavior control, 237
Behavior feedback phenomenon, 389
Behavior geneticists, 35
Behavior genetics, 105–112
  gene-environment interactions and, 111–112
  genes and, 106
  temperament and personality and, 110–111
  twin and adoption studies of, 106–110
Behavior genetics perspective, 6, 7
Behaviorism, 227
Behaviorists, 4
Behavior modeling, 248, 250. *See also* Observational learning
Behavior modification, 500
Behavior rating scales, for performance appraisal, B-6
Behavior therapies, 497–500, 504
  classical conditioning techniques in, 497–500
  operant conditioning techniques in, 500
Belief(s)
  catastrophizing, cognitive therapy for, 501–502
  prejudice and, 542
Belief perseverance, 297
Belonging, need for, 369–372
  pain of ostracism and, 371–372
  survival and, 369–370
  sustaining relationships and, 370–371
Bias
  confirmation, 293–294
  hindsight, 10–11
  ingroup, 546
  in intelligence testing, 333–334
  self-serving, 447–448
Big Five factors, 436
Bilingual advantage, 307
Binge-eating disorder, 348
Binocular cues, 207–208
Biochemical influences, on aggression, 549

Biological influences, 35–62. *See also* Biopsychosocial approach; *specific influences*
  on aggression, 548–549
  brain and. *See* Brain
  on drug use, 97–98
  endocrine system and, 42–43
  nervous system and, 39–42
  neural communication and, 35–39
  on pain, 198–199
  on sexual behavior, 357–359
  on sexual orientation, 366–368
  on taste preferences, 346
Biological perspective
  on anxiety disorders, 466–467
  on mood disorders, 474–476
Biological predispositions
  classical conditioning and, 232–234
  operant conditioning and, 243–244
Biological psychologists, 8
Biological psychology, 35
Biological rhythms, sleep and, 70–74
Biomedical therapies, 493, 512–520
  brain stimulation, 516–519
  drug therapies, 513–516
  psychosurgery, 519
  therapeutic life-style change, 519–520
Biopsychologists, 35
Biopsychosocial approach, 6. *See also* Biological influences; Psychological influences; Social-cultural influences
  to aggression, 554
  to aging, 171
  to depression, 476, 477
  to development, 132
  to emotion, 388
  to learning, 233–234
  to pain, 200
  to perception, 217
  to personality, 441
  to psychological disorders, 456, 457
  to sexual motivation, 359, 360
  to stress, 407
Bipolar cells, 186–187
Bipolar disorder, 471–472
Birth order, sexual orientation and, 365
Bitter taste, 201
Blindness
  change, 69
  inattentional, 69
Blindsight, 190
Blind spot, 187
B lymphocytes, 403
Body chemistry, hunger and, 344
Body contact, attachment and, 149–150
Bottom-up processing, 80, 180
Brain, 44–61
  aggression and, 548–549
  alcohol and, 90
  anxiety and, 467
  cerebral cortex of. *See* Cerebral cortex
  consciousness and, 66–70
  deep brain stimulation and, 517–518
  in depression, 476
  development of, experience and, 118–119
  dual processing and, 66–67
  emotions and, 379
  extraversion and, 433
  gender differences in, 129
  hemispheres of. *See* Cerebral hemispheres
  hunger and, 344–346
  information storage in, 267–272
  lesioning, 44
  lower-level structures of, 44–49
  memory storage in, 258, 267–272

  mirror neurons in, 147, 248–249
  neural networks of, 40
  plasticity of, 56–57
  schizophrenia and, 482–484
  selective attention and, 68–70
  sexual orientation and, 366
  split-brain studies of, 57–60
  study of, 44, 45
  two-track mind and. *See* Two-track brain
Brainstem, 44–46
Brain stimulation, 516–519
Breathing reflex, 139
Brightness constancy, 212
Broca's area, 54–55
Bulimia nervosa, 348
Bystander effect, 561–562

C

Caffeine, 92, 97
Callings, B–1
CAM (complementary and alternative medicine), 406
Cancer, stress and, 405, 407
Cannabinoid receptors, 96
Cannon-Bard theory of emotion, 376, 377
Careers, B–1
Careers in psychology, C–1—C–10
  bachelor's degree and, C–1—C–3
  postgraduate degrees and, C–3—C–4, C–9—C–10
  subfields of psychology and, C–4—C–9
Caring, psychotherapy and, 510–511
Case studies, 15–16
Catastrophes, 400–401
Catastrophizing beliefs, cognitive therapy for, 501–502
Catatonia, 481
Catatonic schizophrenia, 482
Categorization, prejudice and, 547
Catharsis, 390
Catharsis hypothesis, 552
Causation, correlation and, 18–19
Cell body, of neurons, 35
Central nervous system (CNS), 39, 40–42. *See also* Brain
Central route persuasion, 528
Central tendency measures, A–1—A–2
Cerebellum, 46–47
  memory and, 272
Cerebral cortex, 50–57
  association areas of, 53–54
  language and, 54–56
  motor functions of, 51
  sensory functions of, 51–53
  structure of, 50, 51
Cerebral hemispheres, 47
  right-left differences in intact brain and, 60–61
  split-brain studies of, 57–60
Chameleon effect, 532
Change blindness, 69
Charisma, B–11
Checklists, for performance appraisal, B–6
Child-rearing. *See also* Parenting
  culture and, 125
  gender and, 131
Children
  brain development of, 140
  cognitive development of, 144–148
  eyewitness recall of, 284–285
  families and, 169–170
  memory in, 142
  motor development of, 141
  social development of, 153–154

Chromosomes, 106
Chunking, 264
Circadian rhythm, 71
Clairvoyance, 218
Classical conditioning, 226–235
  acquisition in, 230–231
  applications of, 235
  behavior therapies using, 497–500
  biological predispositions and, 232–234
  cognitive processes in, 232
  discrimination in, 232
  extinction in, 231
  of fear, 465–466
  generalization in, 231
  higher-order, 230–231
  operant conditioning contrasted with, 246–247
  Pavlov's experiments on, 228–232, 234–235
  spontaneous recovery in, 231
Client-centered therapy, 496, 504
Clinical neuropsychologists, C–8
Clinical psychologists, 8, 512, C–5
Clinical social workers, 512
Closure, form perception and, 206
CNS (central nervous system), 39, 40–42. *See also* Brain
Cocaine, 94, 97
Cochlea, 194
Cocktail party effect, 68
Cognition. *See also* Language; Memory; Social-cognitive perspective; Thinking
  classical conditioning and, 232
  definition of, 142, 291
  emotions and, 379–383
  operant conditioning and, 243
  prejudice and, 547
  reciprocal determinism and, 439–440
Cognitive-behavioral therapy, 503, 504
Cognitive development
  in adolescence, 157–158
  in adulthood, 166–168
  dreams and, 83
  during infancy and childhood, 142–148
  Piaget's stages of, 143–148
Cognitive dissonance theory, 530–531
Cognitive maps, 243
Cognitive neuroscience, 4, 66
Cognitive perspective, 6, 7
Cognitive psychologists, 8, C–5
Cognitive revolution, 501
Cognitive therapies
  of Beck, for depression, 501–503
  cognitive-behavioral, 503, 504
Cold, receptors for, 197
Collective unconscious, 424
Collectivism, 123–124
Color constancy, 212
Color vision, 191–192
Command-and-control management, B–12
Commitments, in adulthood, 169
Common sense, 10
Communication
  conflict resolution and, 566
  facilitated, 507
  neural, 35–39. *See also* Neurotransmitters
Community psychologists, C–5—C–6
Companionate love, 560
Complementary and alternative medicine (CAM), 406
Concept(s), 291–292
  animal thinking and, 310
Conception, 137
Conciliation, conflict resolution and, 566–567
Concrete operational stage, 143, 146–148
Conditioned reinforcers, 239

Conditioned response (CR), 229
Conditioned stimulus (CS), 229
Conditioning. *See also* Classical conditioning;
    Operant conditioning
    higher-order, 230–231
Cones, 186, 188
Confirmation bias, 293–294
Conflict, 563–567
    enemy perceptions and, 564–565
    peacemaking and, 565–567
    social traps and, 563–564
Conformity, 532–534, 537
Connectedness, form perception and, 206
Connectionism, 258
Conscience, 421–422
Conscientiousness, 436
Consciousness, 65–102
    brain and, 66–70
    definition of, 65
    divided, hypnosis as, 86–87
    dreams and, 80–83
    drugs and, 88–100
    hypnosis and, 84–87
    sleep and. *See* Sleep
Conscious processing, serial, 67
Conservation, in preoperational stage, 144
Constructed memories of abuse, 285–286
Contact, conflict resolution and, 565
Content validity, 322
Context
    perceptual set and, 216–217
    retrieval and, 274–275
    social. *See* Social-cognitive perspective
Continuity, form perception and, 206
Continuity/stages issue, 137, 173–174
Continuous reinforcement, 240
Control
    external locus of, 441
    internal locus of, 441
    perceived, 408–409
    personal, 441–444, 541
    social, 541
Control group, 22
Conventional morality, 158
Conversion disorder, 468
Cooperation, 565–566
Coping, with stress, 408–410
Cornea, 186
Coronary heart disease, stress and, 402–403
Corpus callosum, 57, 58
Correlation, 18–21, A–4—A–6
    causation and, 18–19
    illusory, 19–20, A–5—A–6
    negative, 18
    perceived order in random events and, 20–21
    positive, 18, 19–20
    reliability and, 321
Correlation coefficients, A–4—A–5
Counseling psychologists, 8, C–6—C–7
Counselors, 512
Counterconditioning, 498
CR (conditioned response), 229
Crack cocaine, 94
Creative intelligence, 316
Creative thinking, sleep and, 77–78
Creativity, intelligence and, 316–318
Crisis debriefing, 507
Critical periods, 150
    language development and, 304–305
    for sensory and perceptual development, 214
Critical thinking, 13, 30
Cross-sectional studies, A–7
Crystallized intelligence, 167
CS (conditioned stimulus), 229

Culture, 121–126. *See also* Social-cultural influences
    behavior and, 25–26
    child-rearing and, 125
    definition of, 121
    developmental similarities across groups and,
        125–126
    nonverbal communication and, 386–388
    physical attractiveness and, 557
    psychotherapy and, 511
    self and, 123–124
    on taste preferences, 346–347
    variation across cultures and, 122
    variation over time and, 123
Curiosity, scientific, 11
Curious skepticism, 12

D

Daily hassles, 401
Death and dying, 172–173
    suicide and, 474–475
    terminal decline and, 168
Declarative memory, 269–272
Decline effect, A–6
Deep brain stimulation, 517–518
Defense mechanisms, 423
Defensive self-esteem, 449
Deindividuation, 537, 539
Déjà vu, 275
Delayed reinforcers, 239–240
Delay of gratification, 158
Delta-9-tetrahydrocannabinol (THC), 96
Delta waves, 73
Delusions, 480
Dendrites, 35
Denial, 423
Deoxyribonucleic acid (DNA), 106
Dependence, on psychoactive drugs, 88
Dependent variable, 23–24
Depression. *See also* Mood disorders
    antidepressant drugs for, 415–516
    Beck's therapy for, 501–503
    biopsychosocial approach to, 476, 477
    brain in, 476
    causes of, 472–480
    deep brain stimulation for, 517–518
    electroconvulsive therapy for, 516–517
    heart and, 403
    magnetic stimulation for, 518–519
    major depressive disorder, 470–471
    suicide and, 474–475
    vicious cycle of, 478–480
Depth cues, 207
Depth perception, 207–209
Descriptive research, 15–18
    case study method for, 15–16
    naturalistic observation for, 17–18
    survey method for, 16
Descriptive statistics, A–1—A–6
    central tendency measures, A–1—A–2
    correlation, A–4—A–6
    measures of variation, A–3—A–4
Desensitization, violence-viewing effect and, 253
Development, biopsychosocial approach to, 132
Developmental psychologists, 8, C–7
Developmental psychology, 137–177
    major issues in, 137. *See also* Continuity/stages
        issue; Nature-nurture issue; Stability/change
        issue
*Diagnostic and Statistical Manual of Mental
    Disorders* (DSM-IV-TR), 457–458
DID (dissociative identity disorder), 469–470
Difference thresholds, 182–183

Difficult babies, 110
Discrimination
    prejudice and, 542
    between stimuli, in classical conditioning, 232
Discriminative stimulus, 238
Disease. *See* Illness
Disinhibition, alcohol and, 90
Disorganized schizophrenia, 482
Displacement, 423
Dispositional attributions, 526
Dissociation, hypnosis and, 86–87
Dissociative disorders, 468–470
Dissociative identity disorder (DID), 469–470
Distributed study time, 261, 287
Distributions
    normal curve, 321, A–3—A–4
    skewed, A–2
Division of labor, 121
Dizygotic twins, 107
DNA (deoxyribonucleic acid), 106
Doctoral degrees, for careers in psychology, C–4,
    C–5
Dopamine, 38
    in schizophrenia, 483
Double-blind procedure, 22–23, 513
Down syndrome, 322
Dreams, 80–83
    content of, 80–81, 421
    functions of, 81–83
Drive-reduction theory, 340–341
Drugs, psychoactive. *See* Psychoactive drugs
Drug therapies, 513–516
Dual processing, 66–67. *See also* Two-track brain

E

Ear, 193–195
Eardrum, 193–194
Early adulthood, 163
Early experience, intelligence and, 326
Easy babies, 110
Eating disorders, 348–349
Echoic memory, 266
Eclectic approach, 493
Ecstasy (drug), 95, 97
ECT (electroconvulsive therapy), 516–517
Education
    for careers in psychology, C–1—C–4,
        C–9—C–10
    intelligence and, 327
    operant conditioning and, 245
Educational psychologists, C–7
EEG (electroencephalogram), 45
Effect size, A–8
Effortful processing, 260–262
Ego, 421
Egocentrism, in preoperational stage, 145
Ejaculation, premature, 358
Electra complex, 422
Electroconvulsive therapy (ECT), 516–517
Electroencephalogram (EEG), 45
Electromagnetic energy, 185
Embryo, 138
EMDR (eye movement desensitization and repro-
    cessing), 508–509
Emerging adulthood, 162
Emotion(s), 375–398
    autonomic nervous system and, 378–379
    biopsychosocial approach to, 388
    brain and, 379, 381–383
    Cannon-Bard theory of, 376, 377
    culture and, 386–388
    definition of, 376
    detecting, 328–329, 383–385

Emotion(s) (continued)
embodied, 378–383
experienced, 389–397
expressed, 383–389
facial expressions and, 388–389
gender and, 328–329, 385–386
inappropriate, in schizophrenia, 481
James-Lange theory of, 376–377
memory and, 275–276
nonverbal behavior and, 385–386
prejudice and, 546–547
stress and. See Stress
two-factor theory of, 377
Emotional intelligence, 318
Emotion focused coping, 408
Empathy, 158, 386
in client-centered therapy, 496
psychotherapy and, 510–511
in Rogers' person-centered perspective, 430
Empirical approach, 12
Empirically derived tests, 434
Employee engagement, B–8—B–9
Employee satisfaction, B–7—B–8
Encoding, 258, 259–265
failure of, 277
levels of processing and, 259–262
of meaning, 262–263
organizing information for, 264–265
visual, 263
Endocrine system, 42–43
Endorphins, 38, 91, 199
Enemy perceptions, 564–565
Energy therapies, 507
Environment
definition of, 105
gene interaction with, 111–112
Environmental influences
creativity and, 318
on intelligence, 325–327
on obesity, 353–354
reciprocal determinism and, 439–440
Environmental relatives, genetic relatives versus, 109–110
Epinephrine, 43
Equity, 560
Erectile disorder, 74, 358
Erogenous zones, 422
Erotic plasticity, 364
ESP (extrasensory perception), 218–220
Estrogens, sexual behavior and, 358, 359
Ethics
of animal research, 26–27
of human research, 27–28
Ethnicity
intelligence test scores and, 331–332
prejudice and. See Prejudice
Evaluating psychotherapies, 504–512
alternative therapies and, 507–509
commonalities among psychotherapies and, 509–511
culture and values and, 511
effectiveness and, 505–507
Evidence-based practice, 507
Evolutionary perspective, 6, 7
Evolutionary psychology, 113–117
current status of, 114–115
genetic legacy and, 114
human sexuality and, 115–117
instincts and, 340
natural selection and adaptation and, 113
Excitatory signals, 36
Excitement phase of sexual response cycle, 357
Exercise
aerobic, stress management and, 411–412

health and, 412
mood and, 411–412
Exhaustion phase of general adaptation syndrome, 400
Expectancy effects, of alcohol, 90–91
Expectations, intelligence testing and, 333–334
Experience
brain development and, 118–119
early, intelligence and, 326
peers and, 120–121
prior, happiness and, 395
Experiment(s), 21–24
animals as subjects of, 26–27
application to daily life, 25
humans as subjects of, 27–28
independent and dependent variables and, 23–24
random assignment and, 22–23
Experimental group, 22–23
Experimental psychologists, C–7
Expertise, creativity and, 317
Explanatory style, 477–478
Explicit memory, 269–272
Exposure therapies, 498
External locus of control, 441
External stimuli, sexual behavior and, 359–360
Extinction, in classical conditioning, 231
Extrasensory perception (ESP), 218–220
Extraversion, 436
brain and, 433
Eye, 186–188
Eye movement desensitization and reprocessing (EMDR), 508–509
Eyewitness recall, of children, 284–285

F

Face-to-face therapy, 495
Facial expressions, 388–389
Facial feedback effect, 388–389
Facilitated communication, 507
Factor analysis, 314, 433
False consensus effect, 427
Familiarity, attachment and, 150
Family therapy, 503–504
FAS (fetal alcohol syndrome), 138
Fat cells, 351
Fathers. See also Parent(s); Parenting
presence of, sexual restraint in adolescence and, 362
Fear
conditioning of, 235, 465–466
objects of, 298–299
Feature detectors, 188–189
Feel-good, do-good phenomenon, 392
Fermat's last theorem, 316–317
Fetal alcohol syndrome (FAS), 138
Fetus, 138
Fight or flight response, 399, 550
Figure-ground relationship, 205
Fissures, of cortex, 50
Fixation, 294, 422
Fixed-interval schedules, 240–241
Fixed-ratio schedules, 240, 241
Flashbulb memories, 269
Flat affect, in schizophrenia, 481
Flow, B–1
Fluid intelligence, 167
Flynn effect, 323
fMRI (functional magnetic resonance imaging), 45
Foot-in-the-door phenomenon, 528–529
Forensic psychologists, C–7—C–8
Forgetting, 276–281. See also Amnesia
encoding failure and, 277

retrieval failure and, 278–281
storage decay and, 277–278
Formal operational stage, 143, 148, 157
Form perception, 205–206
Fovea, 188
Framing, 300–301
Fraternal birth-order effect, 365
Fraternal twins, 107
Free association, 420, 494
Free-floating anxiety, 462
Free radicals, 77–78
Frequency, of sound waves, 193
Frontal lobes, 50
Frustration-aggression principle, 549–550
Functional magnetic resonance imaging (fMRI), 45
Fundamental attribution error, 526

G

g (general intelligence), 314
Ganglion cells, 187
GAS (general adaptation syndrome), 399–400
Gate-control theory, 199
Gays, 363. See also Sexual orientation
Gender, 126–131
aggression and, 127
behavior and, 26
brain and, 129
child-rearing and, 131
emotion and, 328–329, 385–386
intelligence test scores and, 328–330
nature-nurture issue and, 129–131
nonverbal communication and, 385–386
sexuality and, 115
sex versus, 126
similarities and differences and, 126–128
social connectedness and, 128
social power and, 127
Gender identity, 131, 422
Gender roles, 130
Gender schemas, 131, 143
Gender typing, 131
Gene(s), 106. See also Genetic influences
expressed, 106
interactions with environment, 111–112
self-regulating nature of, 111
General adaptation syndrome (GAS), 399–400
General intelligence (g), 314
Generalization, in classical conditioning, 231
Generalized anxiety disorder, 461, 462
General self-concept, 447
Generation Me, 448
Generativity vs. stagnation stage, 159
Genetic influences
on aggression, 548
on anxiety, 466–467
on intelligence, 324–325
on mood disorders, 474–475
on obesity, 353
in schizophrenia, 484–485
sexual orientation and, 366
Genetic relatives, environmental relatives versus, 109–110
Genital stage, 422
Genuineness
in client-centered therapy, 496
in Rogers' person-centered perspective, 430
Gestalt, 205
Ghrelin, 345
Giftedness, 322
Glucose, hunger and, 344
Goal setting, leadership and, B–10—B–11
Graduated and Reciprocated Initiatives in Tension-Reduction (GRIT), 567

Graduate study, for careers in psychology, C-3—C-4, C-9—C-10
Graphic rating scales, for performance appraisal, B-6
Gratification, delay of, 158
Gray matter, 129
Great person theory of leadership, B-11
GRIT (Graduated and Reciprocated Initiatives in Tension-Reduction), 567
Group influence, 537-541
    deindividuation and, 537
    group polarization and, 539-541
    groupthink and, 540-541
    power of individuals and, 541
    social facilitation and, 537-538
    social loafing and, 538-539
Grouping, form perception and, 205-206
Group polarization, 539-541
Group pressure, conformity and, 533-534
Group therapy, 503
Groupthink, 540-541
Growth, sleep and, 78
Guide to psychotherapists, for consumers, 512
Guilt, teen pregnancy and, 361
Guilty knowledge test, 380

H

Habituation, 360
Hair cells, 194, 195
Hallucinations, 73
    in schizophrenia, 481
Hallucinogens, 95-96
Hammer (bone), 194
Happiness, 391-397
    adaptation-level phenomenon and, 395
    increasing, 397
    others' attainments and, 395-396
    predictors of, 396-397
Health. See also Illness
    in adulthood, 165-166
    exercise and, 412
    mental. See Psychological disorders
    spirituality and, 413-415
Health promotion, 408-415
    coping with stress and, 408-410
    stress management and, 411-415
Health psychologists, C-8
Hearing, 193-196
    ear and, 193-195
    loudness perception and, 195
    sound location and, 196
    sound waves and, 193
    tinnitus and, 199
Heart, stress and, 402-403
Helping behavior, 562-563
Helplessness, learned, 441-442, 477
Heritability
    of intelligence, 327-328
    of personality traits, 436
Heterosexual orientation, 363. See also Sexual orientation
Heuristics, 292, 294-296
Hierarchies
    of needs, 342
    organizing information into, 264-265
Higher-order conditioning, 230-231
Hindsight bias, 10-11
Hippocampus, 47
    memory and, 271
    stress and, 476
Hollow face illusion, 67
Homeostasis, 341
Homosexual orientation, 363. See also Sexual orientation

Hope, psychotherapy and, 510
Horizontal-vertical illusion, 208
Hormones, 42-43
    aggression and, 549
    prenatal, sexual orientation and, 367-368
    response to stress and, 399
    sexual behavior and, 358-359
    stress, memory and, 268-269
Hue, 185
Human factors psychology, B-2, B-12—B-14
Humanistic perspective, 429-432
    evaluation of, 431-432
    of Maslow, 429-430
    of Rogers, 430-431
    self and, 431
Humanistic psychology, 4
Humanistic therapies, 495-497
Human research subjects, 27-28
Humility, 12
Hunger, 343-356
    obesity and weight control and, 347-356
    physiology of, 344-346
    psychology of, 346-347
Hypnagogic sensations, 73
Hypnosis, 84-87
    definition of, 84
    as divided consciousness, 86-87
    inducement to act against one's will and, 85
    for pain relief, 85-86
    recall of forgotten events and, 84-85
    as social phenomenon, 86
    susceptibility to, 84
    therapeutic use of, 85
Hypnotherapists, 85
Hypnotic induction, 84
Hypochondriasis, 468
Hypothalamus, 48-49
    hunger and, 345
Hypotheses, 14

I

ICD-10 (International Classification of Diseases), 457
Iconic memory, 266
Id, 421
Identical twins, 106-107
Identification, 422
Identity
    gender, 131, 422
    social, 159-160
Ignorance, teen pregnancy and, 361
I-knew-it-all-along phenomenon, 10-11
Illness
    psychophysiological, 403
    stress and, 398-401
    susceptibility to, stress and, 403-404
Illusory correlation, A-5—A-6
Image(s), thinking in, 307-309
Imagery, 263
Imagination, creativity and, 317
Imagination effect, 282-283
Imagined stimuli, sexual behavior and, 360
Imitation
    language development and, 304
    violence-viewing effect and, 252-253
Immediate reinforcers, 239
Immune system, stress and, 403-404
Implementation intentions, B-10—B-11
Implicit learning, 427
Implicit memory, 269-272
Impotence, 74, 358
Imprinting, 150
Inattention, selective, 69-70

Inattentional blindness, 69
Incentives, 341
Independent variable, 23-24
Individualism, 123, 124, 158
    humanistic perspective and, 432
Industrial-organizational (I/O) psychologists, 8, C-8
Industrial-organizational (I/O) psychology, B-2—B-15
    human factors psychology, B-2, B-12—B-14
    organizational psychology, B-2, B-7—B-12
    personnel psychology, B-2, B-3—B6
Industry vs. inferiority stage, 159
Infant(s)
    brain development of, 140
    cognitive development of, 142-144
    memory in, 141-142
    motor development of, 141
    social development of, 149-153
    stranger anxiety in, 149
Infantile amnesia, 141, 272
Inferential statistics, A-6—A-8
Inferiority complex, 424
Influence. See Group influence; Social influence
Informational social influence, 534
Information processing
    automatic, 260
    bottom-up, 180
    dreams as, 82, 83
    dual, 66-67. See also Two-track brain
    effortful, 260-262
    top-down, 180
    visual, 188-191
Information-processing models, of memory, 258-259
Ingroup, 545-546
Ingroup bias, 546
Inhibitory signals, 36
Initiative vs. guilt stage, 159
Inner ear, 194
Innovation, preservation of, 121
Insanity defense, 461
Insecure attachment, 151
Insight, 293
    animal thinking and, 310
Insight therapies, 495
Insomnia, 78
Instincts, 340
Insulin, 344
Integrity vs. despair stage, 159
Intellectual disability, 322-323
Intelligence, 313-334
    aging and, 167-168
    analytical, 316
    assessment of. See Intelligence tests
    creative, 316
    creativity and, 316-318
    crystallized, 167
    definition of, 313-318
    emotional, 318
    environmental influences on, 325-327
    ethnicity and, 331-332
    extremes of, 322-323
    fluid, 167
    gender and, 328-330
    general (g), 314
    genetic influences on, 324-325
    heritability of, 327-328
    multiple, 314-316
    practical, 316
    sexual restraint in adolescence and, 362
Intelligence quotient (IQ), 319-320
Intelligence tests, 319-323
    bias and, 333-334

Intelligence tests (continued)
  construction of, 320–323
  Flynn effect and, 323
  group differences in scores on, 328–334
  origins of, 319–320
  reliability of, 321
  standardization of, 321
  validity of, 322–323
Intensity, of light, 185–186
Interaction
  of genes and environment, 111–112. See also
    Environmental influences; Genetic influences;
    Nature-nurture issue
  sensory, 202
Interference, 279–280
Intermittent reinforcement, 240
Internal locus of control, 441
Interneurons, 39
Interposition, as depth cue, 209
Interpretation, in psychoanalysis, 494
Interview(s), B–4—B–5
  interviewer illusion and, B–4—B–5
  predicting performance using, B–4
  structured, B–5
  unstructured, B–5
Interviewer illusion, B–4—B–5
Intimacy, 160
  in adulthood, 169
Intimacy vs. role confusion stage, 159
Intrinsic motivation, creativity and, 317–318
Intuition, 10–11, 298–300
I/O. See Industrial-organizational entries
IQ (intelligence quotient), 319–320
Iris, 186

J

James-Lange theory of emotion, 376–377
Jobs, B–1. See also Career entries; Industrial-
  organizational (I/O) psychology
Joint-vision process, B–12
Just noticeable difference (jnd), 182–183
Just-world phenomenon, 545

K

Kinesthesis, 197
Knowledge work, B–2

L

Labeling, of psychological disorders, 459–461
Labor, division of, 121
Language, 302–313
  animal thinking and, 309–313
  brain and, 54–56
  definition of, 302
  development of, 302–305
  influence on thinking, 306–307
  productive, development of, 303
  receptive, development of, 302–303
  thinking in images and, 307–309
Language acquisition device, 304
Late adulthood, 163
  physical changes in, 164
Latency, 422
Latent content, 81–82, 421
Latent learning, 243
Lateral hypothalamus, hunger and, 345
Law of effect, 237
Leadership, B–9—B–12
  choosing appropriate style of, B–11—B–12
  goal setting for, B–10—B–11
  harnessing job-relevant skills and, B–9—B–10

Learned helplessness, 441–442, 477
Learning, 225–255. See also Education
  associative, 226–227. See also Classical condi-
    tioning; Operant conditioning
  biopsychosocial approach to, 233–234
  definition of, 225
  implicit, 427
  latent, 243
  observational. See Observational learning
  rehearsal and, 260–261
Learning perspective, on anxiety disorders, 465–466
Lens (of eye), 186
Leptin, 346
Lesbians, 363. See also Sexual orientation
Lesioning, of brain, 44
Levels of analysis, 6–7. See also Biopsychosocial
  approach
Levels of processing, encoding and, 259–262
Lie detection, 380
Life changes, significant, 401
Life events, stressful, 400–401
Life span, well-being cross, 170–171
Life-span perspective, 154
Light and shadow, as depth cue, 209
Light energy, 185–186
Light exposure therapy, 509
Lightness constancy, 212
Limbic system, 47–49
Linear perspective, as depth cue, 209
Linguistic determinism, 306
Listening, active, in client-centered therapy, 496
Lithium, 516
Lobes, of cortex, 50
Lobotomy, 519
Longitudinal studies, A–7
Long-term memory, 258, 267
Long-term potentiation (LTP), 268
Loudness, 193
  perception of, 195
Love
  in adulthood, 169–170
  romantic, 559–560
LSD (lysergic acid diethylamide), 95–96
LTP (long-term potentiation), 268
Lymphocytes, 403

M

Macrophages, 403
Magnetic resonance imaging (MRI), 45
Magnetic stimulation, 518–519
Mainstreaming, 323
Major depressive disorder, 470–471
Mania, 471
Manifest content, 81, 421
Marijuana, 96, 97
Marriage, 169
Masking stimuli, 182
Massed practice, 261, 287
Mass media, teen pregnancy and, 361
Master's degree, for careers in psychology, C–4
Math ability, gender and, 329
Mating preferences, natural selection and,
  116–117
Maturation, 140
  infant memory and, 141–142
MDMA (methylenedioxymethamphetamine), 95,
  97
Mean, A–1—A–2
  regression toward, A–6
Meaning, encoding, 262–263
Meaningfulness, aging and, 167
Median, A–1—A–2
Medical model, of psychological disorders, 456

Meditation, stress management and, 412–413
Medulla, 45
Melatonin, 71
Memory, 257–289
  of abuse, repressed or constructed, 285–286
  aging and, 166–167
  alcohol and, 90
  construction of, 281–286
  definition of, 257
  dreams and, 82
  echoic, 266
  encoding and, 258, 259–265
  explicit (declarative), 269–272
  flashbulb, 269
  forgetting and, 276–281
  hypnosis and, 84–85
  iconic, 266
  imagination effect and, 282–283
  implicit (nondeclarative), 269–272
  improving, 287
  during infancy and childhood, 141–142
  information-processing models of, 258–259
  long-term, 258, 267
  misinformation effect and, 282
  moods and, 275–276
  nonverbal, gender and, 328
  of pain, 199–200
  retrieval and, 258, 273–276
  sensory, 258, 265–266
  sleep and, 77–78
  state-dependent, 275
  storage in brain, 258, 267–272
  stress hormones and, 268–269
  three-stage processing model of, 258, 259
  working/short-term, 258, 259, 266
Memory construction, 281–286
Memory traces, 267
Menarche, 155
Menopause, 164
Mental age, 319
Mental health. See Psychological disorders
Mental retardation, 322–323
Mental set, 294
Mere exposure effect, 150, 556
Metabolism, obesity and, 352–353
Methamphetamine, 91–92, 97
Methylenedioxymethamphetamine (MDMA), 95,
  97
Middle adulthood, 163
  physical changes in, 164
Middle ear, 194
Mild cognitive impairment, 268
Mind
  theory of, 145–147, 249
  two-track. See Two-track brain
  unconscious. See Unconscious
Minnesota Multiphasic Personality Inventory
  (MMPI), 433–435
Mirror-image perceptions, 564–565
Mirror neurons, 147, 248–249
Misattribution, source, 283–284
Misinformation effect, 282
MMPI (Minnesota Multiphasic Personality
  Inventory), 433–435
Mnemonics, 263
Mode, A–1—A–2
Modeling, 248, 250. See also Observational learning
Monocular cues, 208, 209
Monozygotic twins, 106–107
Mood(s)
  changing levels of, 392–393
  exercise and, 411–412
  memories and, 275–276
Mood-congruent memories, 275–276

Mood disorders
  biological perspective on, 474–476
  biopsychosocial perspective on, 476–477
  bipolar disorder, 471–472
  causes of, 472–480
  drug therapy for, 516
  major depressive disorder, 470–471
  social-cognitive perspective on, 476–480
Mood-stabilizing drugs, 516
Moon illusion, 210–211
Moral development, 157–158
Moral reasoning, 158
Mothers. *See* Parent(s); Parenting; Pregnancy
Motivation, 339–372
  achievement, B–7
  drives and incentives and, 340–341
  hierarchy of needs and, 342
  hunger and, 343–356
  instincts and, 340
  intrinsic, creativity and, 317–318
  need to belong and, 369–372
  optimum arousal and, 341
  sexual, 357–369
  in workplace. *See* Organizational psychology;
    Personnel psychology
Motor cortex, 51
Motor development, during infancy and childhood, 141
Motor neurons, 39
MRI (magnetic resonance imaging), 45
Multiple intelligences, 314–316
Mutations, 113
Myelin sheath, 35

N

Narcissism, 448
Narcolepsy, 78–79
Naturalistic observation, 17–18
Natural killer cells, 403
Natural selection, 113
  anxiety and, 466
  mating preferences and, 116–117
Nature-nurture issue, 5, 129–134, 137. *See also*
  Behavior genetics; Culture; Environmental
  influences; Evolutionary psychology; Gender;
  Genetic influences; Parent(s); Peers
  gender and, 129–131
  interaction of genes and environment and,
    111–112
  puberty and, 156
Near-death experiences, 95–96
Needs, hierarchy of, 342
Negative reinforcement, 239
Negative symptoms, of schizophrenia, 482
Neo-Freudian perspective, 423–424
Neophobia, 347
Nerves, 39
Nervous system, 39–42
  autonomic, 40
  central, 39, 40–42. *See also* Brain
  parasympathetic, 40
  peripheral, 39–40
  somatic, 39–40
  sympathetic, 40
Neural communication, 35–39
  neurons and, 35–37
  neurotransmitters and, 37, 38–39
Neural influences, on aggression, 548–549
Neural networks, 40
Neural pathways
  dreams and, 82, 83
  pruning process and, 118
Neural processing, alcohol and, 90

Neurogenesis, 57
Neurons, 35–37
  communication by, 36–37. *See also*
    Neurotransmitters
  interneurons, 39
  mirror, 147, 248–249
  motor, 39
  sensory, 39
Neuropsychologists, 35, C–8
Neuroscience perspective, 6, 7
Neuroticism, 436
Neurotransmitters, 37, 38–39
  mood disorders and, 476
  in schizophrenia, 483
Neutral stimulus (NS), 228, 229
Newborns, 139
New Lanark Mills, B–8
Nicotine, 92–93, 97
Night terrors, 79
Nociceptors, 198
Nondeclarative memory, 269–272
Nondirective therapy, 496
Nonverbal communication, 383–389
  culture and, 386–388
  detecting emotion and, 383–385
  facial expressions and, 388–389
  gender and, 385–386
Norepinephrine (noradrenaline), 38, 43, 476
Normal curve, 321, A–3—A–4
Normative social influence, 534
  informational, 534
NS (neutral stimulus), 228, 229
Numerical ability, of animals, 310

O

Obedience, 534–537
Obesity, 347–356
  environmental influences on, 353–354
  physiology of, 351–353
  sleep deprivation and, 76
  social effects of, 350–351
  weight loss and, 354–356
Obestatin, 345–346
Object permanence, 144
Observation, naturalistic, 17–18
Observational learning, 227, 248–253
  of aggression, 551–554
  antisocial, 251–253
  anxiety and, 466
  applications of, 250–253
  Bandura's experiments on, 249–250
  mirror neurons and, 248–249
  prosocial, 250–251
Obsessive-compulsive disorder (OCD), 461,
  463–464
Occam's razor, 133
Occipital lobes, 50
OCD (obsessive-compulsive disorder), 461,
  463–464
Oedipus complex, 422
Olfaction, 202–204
One-word stage, 303
Online matchmaking, 555
Openness, 436
Operant behavior, 236
Operant chambers, 237
Operant conditioning, 226–227, 236–247
  applications of, 244–246
  behavior therapies using, 500
  biological predispositions and, 243–244
  classical conditioning contrasted with, 246–247
  cognition and, 243
  language development and, 304

  punishment and, 241–243
  reinforcement schedules and, 240–241
  reinforcers and, 238–240
  shaping behavior and, 237–238
  Skinner's experiments in, 236–243, 244
Operational definitions, 15
Opiates, 91
Opponent-process theory, 192
Optic nerve, 187
Optimism
  attribution and, 442–444
  health and, 409
Oral stage, 422
Order, perceived in random events, 20–21
Organization
  concepts and, 292
  of information, for encoding, 264–265
Organizational psychology, B–2, B–7—B–12
  employee satisfaction and engagement and,
    B–7—B–9
  managing and, B–9—B–12
Orgasm, 357
Orgasmic dysfunction, 358
Ostracism, 371–372
Other-race effect, 547
Outcome research, on psychotherapies, 505–506
Outer ear, 193–194
Outgroup, 546
Outsourcing, B–2
Oval window, 194
Overconfidence, 11, 296–297
Overlearning, 30, 261
Oxytocin, 399

P

Pain, 198–201
  biological influences on, 198–199
  biopsychosocial approach to, 200
  controlling, 200–201
  hypnosis for relief of, 85–86
  psychological influences on, 199–200
  receptors for, 197
  social-cultural influences on, 200
Palm readers, 434–435
Panic disorder, 461, 462
Paradoxical sleep, 74
Parallel processing, 190–191
  unconscious, 67
Paranoid schizophrenia, 482
Parapsychology, 218
Parasympathetic nervous system, 40
  emotions and, 378–379
Parent(s)
  adolescents and, 160–161
  early experiences and, 118–120
  infant attachment and, 149–153
Parenting. *See also* Child-rearing
  operant conditioning and, 245–246
  parenting styles and, 153–154
Parietal lobes, 50
Partial reinforcement, 240
Passionate love, 559–560
Passwords, retrieving, 280
Peacemaking, 565–567
Peak experiences, 430
Peers
  in adolescence, 161
  experience and, 120–121
Perception(s), 179
  biopsychosocial approach to, 217
  definition of, 80
  depth, 207–209
  disturbed, in schizophrenia, 481

Perception(s) *(continued)*
  of facial expressions, 388–389
  form, 205–206
  of others, conflict and, 564–565
  perceptual constancy and, 210–212
Perceptual adaptation, 214–215
Perceptual constancy, 210–212
Perceptual interpretation, 213–220
  extrasensory perception and, 218–220
  perceptual adaptation and, 214–215
  perceptual set and, 215–217
  sensory deprivation and, 213–214
Perceptual organization, 205–212
  depth perception and, 207–209
  form perception and, 205–206
  perceptual constancy and, 210–212
Perceptual set, 215–217
Performance appraisal, B–5—B–6
Peripheral nervous system (PNS), 39–40
Peripheral route persuasion, 528
Permissive parents, 153
Personal control, 441–444, 541
Personality, 419–451
  biopsychosocial approach to, 441
  definition of, 419
  development of, 422
  humanistic perspective on, 429–432
  psychoanalytic perspective on, 420–428
  self and, 446–449
  social-cognitive perspective on, 439–445
  structure of, 421–422
  temperament and, 110–111
  trait perspective on, 432–438
  Types A and B, 402
Personality disorders, antisocial, 486–488
Personality inventories, 433–435
Personal space, 122
Person-centered perspective, 430–431
Personnel psychology, B–2, B–3—B6
  discovering strengths and, B–3
  interviews and, B–4—B–5
  performance appraisal and, B–5—B–6
Personnel selection, B–3—B–5
  interviews for, B–4—B–5
Person-situation controversy, 437–438
Persuasion, central and peripheral route, 528
Pessimism
  attribution and, 442–444
  heart and, 403
Pets, coping with stress and, 410
PET (positron-emission tomography) scans, 45
Phallic stage, 422
Phantom limb sensations, 199
Phobias, 461, 462–463
  agoraphobia, 463
  social, 462
  specific, 462
Physical aggression, gender and, 127
Physical attractiveness, attraction and, 556–558
Physical changes, in adulthood, 163–166
Physical dependence, on psychoactive drugs, 88
Physical development
  in adolescence, 155–157
  in adulthood, 163–166
  in infancy and childhood, 140–141
Physiological psychologists, 35
Pitch, 193
Pituitary gland, 43
PK (psychokinesis), 218
Placebo effect, 22–23, 406, 513
Placenta, 138
Plasticity
  of brain, 56–57
  erotic, 364

Plateau phase of sexual response cycle, 357
Pleasure principle, 421
PNS (peripheral nervous system), 39–40
Polygraphs, 380
Ponzo illusion, 210, 211
Pop-out, 70
Population, 16
Positive psychology, 443
Positive reinforcement, 239
Positive symptoms, of schizophrenia, 482
Positive transfer, 280
Positron-emission tomography (PET) scans, 45
Postconventional morality, 158
Postgraduate degrees
  for careers in psychology, C–3—C–4, C–9—C–10
  preparing for, C–9—C–10
Posthypnotic suggestions, 85
Post-traumatic growth, 465
Post-traumatic stress disorder (PTSD), 461,
    464–465
Postural sway, 84
Power, of individuals, 541
Practical intelligence, 316
Precognition, 218
Preconscious area, 420
Preconventional morality, 158
Predictive validity, 323
Pregnancy, 138
  in adolescence, 361
  maternal virus during, schizophrenia and,
    483–484
Prejudice, 542–547
  automatic, 543
  cognitive roots of, 547
  definition of, 542
  degree of, 542, 544
  emotional roots of, 546–547
  social roots of, 545–546
Premature ejaculation, 358
Prenatal development, 138
Preoperational stage, 143, 144–145
Preservation of innovation, 121
Pressure sense, 197
Primacy effect, 261
Primary reinforcers, 239
Primary sex characteristics, 155
Priming, 67, 182, 274
Proactive interference, 279, 280
Problem-focused coping, 408
Problem solving, 292–294
Productive language, development of, 303
Progressive relaxation, 498
Projection, 423
Projective tests, 424–426
Prosocial behavior, 250–251
Prosocial observational learning, 250–251
Prosopagnosia, 179
Prosthetics, 51
Protective effects, of sleep, 77–78
Protein molecules, 106
Prototypes, 292
Proximity
  and attraction, 555–556
  form perception and, 206
Pruning process, 118
Psychiatric social workers, 512
Psychiatrists, 8, 512
Psychoactive drugs, 88–100
  addiction to, 88–89
  dependence on, 88
  influences on use of, 97–100
  tolerance to, 88
  withdrawal from, 88
Psychoanalysis, 420–421, 494–495

Psychoanalytic perspective, 420–428
  evaluation of, 426–428
  Freudian, 420–423, 426–428
  neo-Freudian, 423–424
  projective tests and, 424–426
  psychodynamic, 424
  unconscious and, 420–423
Psychodynamic perspective, 6, 7
Psychodynamic theory, 424
Psychodynamic therapy, 495, 504
Psychokinesis (PK), 218
Psychological contracts, B–2
Psychological dependence, on psychoactive
    drugs, 88
Psychological disorders, 453–491
  anxiety disorders, 461–467
  attention-deficit hyperactivity disorder, 455
  biopsychosocial approach to, 456–457, 457
  classification of, 457–459
  definition of, 454–455
  dissociative disorders, 468–470
  labeling of, 459–461
  medical model of, 456
  mood disorders, 470–480
  personality disorders, 486–488
  prevention of, 520–521
  rates of, 488–489
  schizophrenia, 480–486
  somatoform disorders, 468
Psychological influences. *See also* Biopsychosocial
    approach; *specific influences*
  on aggression, 549–550
  on drug use, 98–99
  on pain, 199–200
  on schizophrenia, 486
  on sexual behavior, 359–360
Psychology
  contemporary, 5–9
  definition of, 4
  frequently asked questions about, 25–28
  globalization of, 5
  levels of analysis of. *See* levels of analysis
  questions of, 5
  reasons to study, 1, 9–13
  roots of, 2–4
  as science, 4
  studying, 29–30
  subfields of, 7–9
  value judgments in, 28
Psychometric psychologists, C–8
Psychopathy, 486
Psychopharmacology, 513–516
Psychophysics, 181
Psychophysiological illnesses, 403
Psychosexual stages, 422
Psychosocial stages, 159–160
Psychosurgery, 519
Psychotherapists, consumer's guide to, 512
Psychotherapy(ies), 493–504
  behavior therapies, 497–500
  cognitive therapies, 501–503
  evaluation of. *See* Evaluating psychotherapies
  group and family therapies, 503–504
  humanistic, 495–497
  integration of, 493
  psychoanalysis, 494–495
  psychodynamic, 495, 504
  therapists providing, 512
Psychotic disorders, 480. *See also* Schizophrenia
  antipsychotic drugs for, 513–514
PTSD (post-traumatic stress disorder), 461,
    464–465
Puberty, 155
Punishers, 241

Punishment, 241–243
Pupil (of eye), 186
PYY, 346

Q

Quantitative psychologists, C–8

R

Random assignment, 22–23
Random events, perceived order in, 20–21
Randomized clinical trials, 506
Random samples, 16
Range, A–3
Rationalization, 423
Reaction formation, 423
Reality principle, 421
Reasoning
  development of, 157
  moral, 158
  statistical. See Statistics
Rebirthing therapies, 507
Recall, 273
  eyewitness, of children, 284–285
  hypnosis and, 84–85
Recency effect, 261
Receptive language, development of, 302–303
Reciprocal determinism, 439–440
Reciprocity norm, 563
Recognition, 273
  aging and, 167
Recovered-memory therapies, 507
Recuperation, sleep and, 77–78
Reflexes, 41
  in newborn, 139
Refractory period, 357–358
Regression toward the mean, A–6
Rehabilitation psychologists, C–8
Rehearsal, 258, 260–261, 308–309
Reinforcement
  anxiety and, 466
  continuous, 240
  language development and, 304
  negative, 239
  partial (intermittent), 240
  positive, 239
Reinforcement schedules, 240–241
Reinforcers, 238–240
  conditioned (secondary), 239
  delayed, 239–240
  immediate, 239
  primary, 239
Relational aggression, gender and, 127
Relative deprivation
  aggression and, 551
  happiness and, 395–396
Relative height, as depth cue, 209
Relative luminance, 212
Relative motion, as depth cue, 209
Relative size, as depth cue, 209
Relaxation
  progressive, 498
  stress management and, 412, 413
Relearning, 273
Reliability
  of intelligence tests, 321
  of projective tests, 425
Religious engagement, sexual restraint in adoles-
    cence and, 362
REM rebound, 83
REM sleep, 72, 73–74, 80–81, 82–83
Repetitive transcranial magnetic stimulation
    (rTMS), 518–519

Replication, 15
Representativeness heuristic, 294–295
Repression, 281, 420, 423, 426–427
  of memories of abuse, 285–286
Research
  animals as subjects for, 26–27
  applied, 8
  basic, 8
  descriptive, 15–18
  experimental, 21–24
  human subjects for, 27–28
  outcome, on psychotherapies, 505–506
  scientific attitude and, 11–13
  scientific method and, 14–15
  statistics and, A–1—A–9
Residual schizophrenia, 482
Resistance, in psychoanalysis, 494
Resistance phase of general adaptation syndrome,
    400
Resolution phase of sexual response cycle,
    357–358
Respondent behavior, 236
Responses
  conditioned, 229
  unconditioned, 228, 229
Reticular formation, 46
Retina, 186–188
Retinal disparity, 207–208
Retrieval, 258, 273–276
  failure of, 278–281
  of passwords, 280
Retrieval cues, 273–276
Retroactive interference, 279–280
Reuptake, 37
Reward centers, 48–49
Reward deficiency syndrome, 49
Reward theory of attraction, 559
Rites of passage, 162
Rods, 186, 188
Role(s), 130, 529
  gender, 130
Role-playing, attitudes and, 529
Romantic love, 559–560
Rorschach inkblot test, 425
rTMS (repetitive transcranial magnetic stimula-
    tion), 518–519
Rubber-hand illusion, 197

S

Salty taste, 201–202
Sampling, random, 16
Savant syndrome, 314–315
Scapegoat theory of prejudice, 547
Scatterplots, A–4, A–5
Schedules of reinforcement, 240–241
Schemas, 131
  gender, 131, 143
  perceptual set and, 216
Schizophrenia, 480–486
  acute (reactive), 482
  causes of, 482–486
  chronic (process), 482
  onset and development of, 481–482
  symptoms of, 480–481
  types of, 482
School psychologists, C–8
Scientific attitude, 11–13
Scientific method, 14–15
SCN (suprachiasmatic nucleus), 71
Secondary reinforcers, 239
Secondary sex characteristics, 155
Second-order conditioning, 231
Secure attachment, 151

Secure self-esteem, 449
Selection effect, 112
Selective attention, 68–70
  disorganized thinking and, 481
  hypnotic pain relief and, 87
Selective inattention, 69–70
Selective serotonin reuptake inhibitors (SSRIs), 515
Self, 446–449
  culture and, 123–124
Self-actualization, 429–430
Self-awareness, alcohol and, 90
Self-concept
  academic, 447
  general, 447
  humanistic perspective on, 431
Self-control, alcohol and, 90
Self-disclosure, 560
Self-esteem, 446–449
  benefits of, 447
  defensive, 449
  secure, 449
  self-serving bias and, 447–448
Self-serving bias, 447–448
Self-transcendence, 429
Semicircular canals, 197
Sensation, 179, 180–184
  definition of, 80
  gender and, 328
  sensory adaptation and, 183–184
  thresholds and, 181–183
Sensorimotor stage, 143, 144
Sensory abilities, in adulthood, 164–165
Sensory adaptation, 183–184
Sensory cortex, 51–53
Sensory interaction, 202
Sensory memory, 258, 265–266
Sensory neurons, 39
Separated twins, 108–109
Serial conscious processing, 67
Serial position effect, 261, 262
Serotonin, 38, 268
  mood disorders and, 476
Service learning, sexual restraint in adolescence
    and, 362
Set point, 346, 352–353
Settling point, 346
Sex, gender versus, 126
Sex chromosomes, 129
Sexual behavior, 357–369
  in adolescence, 361–362
  alcohol and, 91
  external stimuli and, 359–360
  hormones and, 358–359
  imagined stimuli and, 360
  sexual orientation and, 363–368
  sexual response cycle and, 357–358
  values and, 368–369
Sexual disorders, 358
Sexuality
  evolutionary explanation of, 115–117
  gender differences in, 115
  natural selection and mating preferences and,
    116–117
Sexually transmitted infections (STIs), in adoles-
    cence, 362
Sexual motivation, biopsychosocial approach to,
    359, 360
Sexual orientation, 363–368
  in animals, 365
  brain and, 366
  genes and, 366
  origins of, 364–368
  prenatal hormones and, 367–368
  statistics on, 363–364

Sexual response cycle, 357–358
Shape constancy, 210
Shaping, 237–238
Short-term memory, 258, 259
Similarity
    and attraction, 558–559
    form perception and, 206
Situational attributions, 526
Size constancy, 210–211
Size-distance relationship, 210–211
Skepticism, curious, 12
Skewed distributions, A–2
Skinner box, 237
Sleep, 70–80
    biological rhythms and, 70–74
    disorders of, 78–79
    dreams and, 80–83
    functions of, 75–78
    loss of, 75–76, 77
    paradoxical, 74
    REM, 72, 73–74, 80–81, 82–83
    stages of, 71–73
    theories of, 77–78
Sleep apnea, 79
Sleep loss, obesity and, 353
Sleep spindles, 73
Sleeptalking, 79
Sleepwalking, 79
Slow-to-warm-up infants, 111
Smell sense, 202–204
Social bonds. See Attachment; Belonging,
    need for
Social clock, 168–169
Social-cognitive perspective, 439–445
    assessing behavior in situations and, 445
    evaluation of, 445
    on mood disorders, 476–480
    personal control and, 441–444
    reciprocal influences and, 439–440
Social connectedness, gender and, 128
Social control, 541
Social-cultural influences. See also Biopsychosocial
    approach; Culture; specific influences
    on aggression, 550–551
    on drug use, 99–100
    on pain, 200
Social-cultural perspective, 6, 7
Social development
    in adolescence, 159–161
    in adulthood, 168–173
    during infancy and childhood, 149–154
Social exchange theory, 562–563
Social facilitation, 537–538
Social factors, in prejudice, 545–546
Social identity, 159–160
Social inequalities, prejudice and, 545
Social influence, 531–541
    conformity and obedience and, 532–537
    group influence and, 537–541
    hypnosis and, 86
    informational, 534
    normative, 534
    on obesity, 353
Social leadership, B–11
Social learning theory, gender typing and, 131
Social loafing, 538–539
Social phobias, 462
Social power, gender and, 127
Social psychologists, 8, C–9
Social psychology, 525–569
    attitudes and actions and, 527–531
    attribution theory and, 525–527
    social influences and. See Social influence
    social relations and. See Social relations

Social relations, 542–567
    aggression and, 548–554
    altruism and, 561–563
    attraction and, 555–560
    conflict and peacemaking and, 563–567
    prejudice and, 542–547
Social relationships, obesity and, 350–351
Social-responsibility norm, 563
Social support, coping with stress and, 409–410
Social traps, 563–564
Sociopathy, 486
Somatic nervous system, 39–40
Somatoform disorders, 468
Sound waves, 193
Source amnesia (source misattribution),
    283–284
Sour taste, 201
Spacing effect, 261
Spatial ability, gender and, 329
Specific phobias, 462
Speech, telegraphic, 303
Spelling, gender and, 328
Spermarche, 155
Spillover effect, 379–381
Spinal cord, 41–42
Spirituality, health and, 413–415
Split-brain studies, 57–60
Split-half reliability, 321
Spontaneous recovery, in classical conditioning,
    231
Spontaneous remission, 406
Sport psychologists, C–9
Sports, operant conditioning and, 245
Spotlight effect, 446
SQ3R method, 29–30
SSRIs (selective serotonin reuptake inhibitors),
    515
Stability, of personality traits, 436
Stability/change issue, 137, 174–175
Standard deviation, A–3—A–4
Standardization, of intelligence tests, 321
Stanford-Binet test, 319
Stanford Hypnotic Susceptibility Scale, 84
State-dependent memory, 275
Statistical significance, A–7—A–8
Statistics, A–1—A–9
    descriptive, A–1—A–6
    inferential, A–6—A–8
Stereotypes, 542
Stereotype threat, 333
Stimulants, 91–95
Stimulus(i)
    conditioned, 229
    discriminative, 238
    external, sexual behavior and, 359–360
    imagined, sexual behavior and, 360
    masking, 182
    neutral, 228, 229
    subliminal, 181–182
    unconditioned, 228, 229
Stimulus generalization, anxiety and, 466
Stirrup (bone), 194
STIs (sexually transmitted infections), in adoles-
    cence, 362
Storage, 258, 265–272
    decay of, 277–278
    sensory memory and, 265–266
Stranger anxiety, 149
Strange situation, 151
Stress, 398–407
    biopsychosocial approach to, 407
    brain and, 476
    coping with, 408–410
    definition of, 398

    events provoking stress responses and,
        400–401
    heart and, 402–403
    illness and, 398–401
    management of, 411–415
    post-traumatic stress disorder and, 461,
        464–465
    responses to, 399–400
    susceptibility to disease and, 403–407
Stress hormones, memory and, 268–269
Stress inoculation training, 502–503
Stressors, 398
Stress reactions, 398
Structured interviews, B–5
Study tips, 29–30, 287
Subgoals, B–10—B–11
Subjective well-being, 392
Subliminal stimulation, 181–182
Successive approximations, 237
Suicide, 474–475
Supercell clusters, 188
Superego, 421–422
Superordinate goals, 565–566
Suprachiasmatic nucleus (SCN), 71
Surveys, 16
Survival, social bonds and, 369–370
Swallowing reflex, 139
Sweet taste, 201–202
Sympathetic nervous system, 40
    emotions and, 378
Synapses, 37
    information storage and, 267–268
Synaptic gaps (synaptic clefts), 37
Systematic desensitization, 498

T

Taijin-kyofusho, 456
Tardive dyskinesia, 514
Task leadership, B–11
Taste preferences, 346–347
Taste sense, 201–202
Teen pregnancy, 361
Telegraphic speech, 303
Telepathy, 218
Television, observational learning and, 251–252
Temperament
    attachment and, 151
    personality and, 110–111
    sexual orientation and, 368
Temporal lobes, 50
Tend-and-befriend response, 399
10-year rule, B–7
Teratogens, 138
Terminal decline, 168
Test(s)
    empirically derived, 434
    guilty knowledge, 380
    intelligence. See Intelligence tests
    personality inventories, 433–435
    projective, 424–426
Testing effect, 261
Testosterone, 129
    sexual behavior and, 358–359
Test-retest reliability, 321
Test taking tips, 30
Thalamus, 46
THC (delta-9-tetrahydrocannabinol), 96
Theories, 14–15
Theory of mind, 145–147, 249
Therapeutic alliance, 510
Therapeutic life-style change, 519–520
Therapy(ies), 493–523
    biomedical. See Biomedical therapies

eclectic approach to, 493
history of, 493
preventive, 520–521
psychological. *See* Psychotherapy(ies)
Thinking, 291–301. *See also* Cognition; Reasoning
in animals, 309–313
belief perseverance and, 297
concepts and, 291–292
critical, 13, 30
disorganized, in schizophrenia, 480–481
framing and, 300–301
heuristics and, 292, 294–296
influence of language on, 306–307
intuition and, 298–300
overconfidence and, 296–297
problem solving and, 292–294
social, 525–531
Thirst, 339, 342
Three-color (trichromatic) theory, 191
360-degree feedback, B–6
Three-stage processing model of memory, 258, 259
Thresholds, 36, 181–183
absolute, 181
difference, 182–183
subliminal stimulation and, 181–182
Tinnitus, 199
T lymphocytes, 403
Token economies, 500
Tolerance, to psychoactive drugs, 88
Tonguing reflex, 139
Top-down processing, 80, 180
Touch sense, 196–197
Traits, 432–438
assessment of, 433–435
astrology and, 434–435
Big Five factors, 436
person-situation controversy and, 437–438
Tranquilizers, 91
Transfer, positive, 280
Transference, in psychoanalysis, 494
Transformational leadership, B–11
Trichromatic (three-color) theory, 191
Trust
basic, 152
psychotherapy and, 510
Trust vs. mistrust stage, 159
Tutored human enrichment, 326
Twins
fraternal (dizygotic), 107
identical (monozygotic), 106–107
separated, 108–109
virtual, 109

Twin studies, 106–110
Two-factor theory of emotion, 377
Two-track brain
emotion and, 381–383
hypnosis and, 86–87
vision and, 67
Two-word stage, 303
Types A and B personalities, 402

U

Umami, 201
Unconditional positive regard, 430
in client-centered therapy, 496
Unconditioned response (UR), 228, 229
Unconditioned stimulus (US), 228, 229
Unconscious
collective, 424
contemporary view of, 426, 427
projective tests and, 424–426
psychoanalytic perspective on, 420–423
Unconscious parallel processing, 67
Universal grammar, 304
Unstructured interviews, B–5
UR (unconditioned response), 228, 229
US (unconditioned stimulus), 228, 229

V

Validity
of intelligence tests, 322–323
of projective tests, 425
Value(s)
psychotherapy and, 511
sexual behavior and, 368–369
Value judgments, 28
Values in Action Classification of Strengths, 459
Variable(s), independent and dependent, 23–24
Variable-interval schedules, 241
Variable-ratio schedules, 240, 241
Variation, measures of, A–3—A–4
Ventromedial hypothalamus, hunger and, 345
Venturesome personality, creativity and, 317
Verbal ability, gender and, 328
Vestibular sacs, 197
Vestibular sense, 197
Video games, aggression and, 552
Violence-viewing effect, 251–253
Viral infections, during pregnancy, schizophrenia and, 483–484
Virtual reality exposure therapy, 498
Virtual twins, 109

Vision, 185–192
color, 191–192
eye and, 186–188
information processing and, 188–191
light energy and, 185–186
restored, 213–214
two-track mind and, 67
Visual action track, 67
Visual cliff, 207
Visual encoding, 263
Visual perception track, 67
Vivid cases, prejudice and, 547
Voice effect, B–12

W

WAIS (Wechsler Adult Intelligence Scale), 320
Warmth, receptors for, 197
Wavelength, of light, 185
Wealth, well-being and, 393–395
Weber's law, 183
Wechsler Adult Intelligence Scale (WAIS), 320
Wechsler Intelligence Scale for Children (WISC), 320
Weight loss, 354–356
Well-being
subjective, 392
wealth and, 393–395
Wernicke's area, 54
White matter, 129
WISC (Wechsler Intelligence Scale for Children), 320
Wish fulfillment, dreams and, 81–82, 83
Withdrawal, from psychoactive drugs, 88
Wording, of surveys, 16
Work, 170. *See also* Career *entries;* Industrial-organizational (I/O) psychology; Jobs
Working/short-term memory, 258, 259, 266
Workplace, operant conditioning and, 245

X

X chromosome, 129

Y

Y chromosome, 129
Young-Helmholtz trichromatic (three-color) theory, 191

Z

Zygotes, 138